★ 2001 ★
PEOPLE
ENTERTAINMENT
ALMANAC

★ 2001 ★ PEOPLE ENTERTAINMENT ALMANAC

CREATED AND PRODUCED BY
CADER BOOKS • NEW YORK

YEAR-IN-REVIEW

ROYALS

SCREEN

TUBE

SONG

PAGES

STAGE

20th-CENTURY TIMELINE

PEOPLE EXTRAS

CELEB REGISTER

Cader Books
38 E. 29 Street
New York, NY 10016
www.caderbooks.com
For news and updates, send your e-mail and street address to
people@caderbooks.com

First Edition

1 3 5 7 9 10 8 6 4 2

Printed in the United States of America

CONTENTS

TUBE   147

SONG   201

PAGES 277

STAGE 325

TIMELINE 349

PEOPLE EXTRAS 381

THE PEOPLE REGISTER 403

PHOTO CREDITS

STAFF

Editor in Chief
Michael Cader

Senior Editor
Steve Baumgartner

Editor
Amy Woodbury

Design
Charles Kreloff, Stephen Hughes

Photo Research
Joan Meisel

Consulting Editor
Seth Godin

PEOPLE WEEKLY
Carol Wallace, Managing Editor
Nora P. McAniff, President
Robert D. Jurgrau, Group Business Manager
Eric Levin, Supervising Editor

PEOPLE Contributors
Jane Bealer, Robert Britton, Richard Burgheim, Betsy Castillo, Sal
Covarrubias, Steven Dougherty, Nancy Eils, Margery Frohlinger, Murray Goldwaser, Suzy Im, Jamie Katz, Terry Kelleher, Amy Linden,
Michael A. Lipton, Denise Lynch, Evie McKenna, Samantha Miller, Florence Nishida, James Oberman, Stan Olson, Susan Radlauer, Leah
Rozen, Randy Vest, Anthony White, Céline Wojtala

ACKNOWLEDGMENTS

Many people and organizations have generously lent their time, resources, and expertise to help make this project possible. Special thanks go to: Academy of Recording Arts and Sciences; Bill Adams, Walden Book Company, Inc.; Frank Alkyer, *Down Beat;* Jennifer Allen, PMK; Simon Applebaum, Cablevision; Bridget Aschenberg, ICM; Alan Axelrod; Robert Azcuy, Itsy Bitsy Productions; Michael Barson, Putnam; Anita Bedra, Reprise Records; Michelle Bega, Rogers & Cowan, Inc.; Jennifer Belodeau, Barnes & Noble; Andi Berger, PMK; Cindi Berger; Marion Billings, M/S Billings Publicity, Ltd.; Helen Blake, National Infomercial Marketing Association; Jeff Blitz, Writers Guild of America, west; Judy Boals, Berman, Boals & Flynn; Matthew Bradley, Viking; Sandy Bresler, Bresler, Kelly, and Associates; Gerry Byrne, *Variety;* Brad Cafarelli, Bragman, Nyman, Cafarelli; Fr. John Catoir, Christophers; Center for the Book, Library of Congress; Center for Media and Public Affairs; Vicki Charles, Loud Records; Marylou Chlipala, Carnegie Mellon School of Drama; Bob Christie, National Academy of Television Arts and Sciences; Robert C. Christopher, The Pulitzer Prizes; Steve Clar; Rosie Cobbe, Fraser & Dunlop; Camille Cline; Dan Cohen, Caroline Records; Sam Cohn; Ace Collins; Sarah Cooper, O. W. Toad Ltd.; Don Corathers, *Dramatics* magazine; Angela Corio, Recording Industry Association of America; Marie Costanza, NYU/Tisch Musical Theater Dept.; Kendal Culp, Random House; Louise Danton, National Academy of Television Arts and Sciences; Leslie Dart, PMK; Gary N. DaSilva; Jennifer DeGuzman, MTV; Paul Dergarabedian, Exhibitor Relations; Steve Devick, Platinum Records; Mark Dillion, Capitol Records; Joan Dim, NYU, Tisch School of the Arts; Heather Dinwiddie, American Symphony Orchestra League; Dramatists Guild; Steve Dworman, *Infomercial Marketing Report;* Marilyn Egol, RCA Victor; Allen Eichhorn; Ed Enright, *Down Beat;* Kenneth Ewing; Charmaine Ferenczi, The Tantleff Office; Ophir Finkelthal, Virgin Records; Karen Forester, Country Music Association; Diane Fortiay, Island Records; Susan Geller, Susan Geller & Associates; Heather Gifford, National Academy of Recording Artists; Debbie Gilwood; Michelle Gluckman, American Society of Magazine Editors; Bob Gregg, Paramount; Amanda Grossman, Capitol Records; Tracey Guest, Dutton Signet; Ned Hammad, *Pulse!;* Cynthia Harris, Little, Brown; Heidi, Def Jam Records; Tom Hill, Nick at Nite; Patricia Hodges, Time Warner; Hollywood Chamber of Commerce; Hollywood Foreign Press Association; Dave Howard, Hofflund/Pollone Agency; Jane Huebsch, American Symphony Orchestra League; Patrick Ingram, Bantam; Gary Ink, *Publishers Weekly;* M. Jackson, AUDELCO; A. J. Jacobs; Elizabeth Jarret; Kristin Joerg, Bantam Books; Steve Jukes, Judy Daish Associates; Susan S. Kaplan, *Billboard;* Joyce Ketay, Joyce Ketay Agency; Amanda Kimmel, Dell; John Kings, Texas Center for Writers; Pat Kingsley; Leonard Klady, *Vari-* ety; Judy Krug, American Library Association; Amy Leavell, Capricorn Records; Marleah Leslie; Ruth Levine, Penguin; Stacey Levitt, Rachel McCallister & Associates; Ed Limato, ICM; Elizabeth Maas, The League of American Theatres and Producers; Tracy Mann, Righteous Babe Recordings; Joe Marich; Howard Marcantel, National Academy of Cable Programming; Nicole Marti, Viking Books; Jaye Maynard, NYU; Angela Medina, Juilliard School of Drama; Gilbert Medina, William Morris Agency; Lisa Meredith, National Cable Forum; Suzanne Mikesell, *Pulse!;* Jason Mitchell, Chronicle; T. J. Mitchell, Hofflund/Pollone Agency; Jessica Morell; Jamie Morris, *Soap Opera Digest;* Nara Nahm, Pantheon; Vincent Nasso, Nielsen Media Research; The National Book Foundation; Karen Kriendler Nelson, Richard Tucker Foundation; Patricia Nicolescu, Quigley Publishing Co., Inc.; Shannon O'Boyle, *Advertising Age;* David O'Connor; Catherine Olim, PMK; Bob Palmer; Charlotte Parker, Parker Public Relations; Gilbert Parker, William Morris; Karen Pascho; Jeffrey Pasternak, Simon & Schuster; Liz Perl, Berkley; Craig Phillips, 20th Century Fox International; Aaron Pinkham; Eileen Potrock, Itsy Bitsy Productions; Ronnie Pugh, Country Music Hall of Fame; Myra Quinn, Peter Brown Agency; Joe Regal, Irene Reichbach, Harcourt-Brace; Russell & Volkening; Tom Reidy, Tuneful Productions; Jonathan S. Renes, DMB&B; Sandy Rice, PMK; Rock and Roll Hall of Fame; Sandee Richardson, *Steve Dworman's Infomercial Marketing Report;* Richard Rodzinski, Van Cliburn Competition; Bradley Roberts, *Pollstar;* Cynthia Robinson, American Library Association's Office for Intellectual Freedom; Bradley J. Rogers, *Pollstar;* Ami Roosevelt; Rachel Rosenberg, Northwestern University School of Speech; Howard Rosenstone, Rosenstone/ Wender; Sheryl Rothmuller, NBC Entertainment Press and Publicity; Lucy Sabini, RCA; Heidi Schaeffer, ICM; Bill Schelble; Ken Schneider, Knopf; Mitch Schneider, Warner Brothers Records; Rachel Schnoll, Viking; Elaine Schock, RCA Records; Nancy Seltzer, Nancy Seltzer & Associates, Inc.; Greg Sharko, ATP Media Relations; John Sheehan, Center for Media and Public Affairs; Paul Shefrin, The Shefrin Company; Barry Sherman, University of Georgia; Jane Sindell, CAA; Smithsonian Institution, Division of Community Life; Robert Stein, United Talent Agency; Carol Stone, PMK; Laine Sutton, *Jeopardy!;* Jack Tantleff, The Tantleff Office; Jonathan Taylor, *Variety;* Prof. Mark Tucker, Columbia University; Terry Tuma, Yale School of Drama; Georgina Warwick, *Jeopardy!;* Rebecca Watson, Broadway Books; Kate Weaver, Avon Books; Sarah Webster, O. W. Toad Ltd.; Murray Weissman, Weissman Angellotti; Windi Wentworth, PBS; Moira Whalon; *Whitaker's Almanac;* Heather Willis, *Pulse!;* Patricia Willis, Beinecke Library, Yale University; Staci Wolfe; Lea Yardum, Weissman/Delson Communications.

THE YEAR IN REVIEW

JANUARY

Fears about the end of the world are quelled when the year 2000 arrives with a lot of fanfare and little fright. An estimated 175 million tune into ABC's around-the-clock coverage, while over at NBC, **Katie Couric** is heard saying, "This is really boring.... Boring is good in these circumstances." In Las Vegas, **Barbra Streisand** plays to a sell-out crowd, and starts the year off right with a record-setting gross for a single U.S. concert, taking in $14.7 million (beating the record set by the Three Tenors).

The state of Maryland is persuaded to save the **200-year-old Griggs house**, located in Baltimore County, which was used in the *Blair Witch Project*'s climactic ending, just before the house itself is due for a climactic meeting with a wrecking ball. The building was previously historically insignificant.

Jamal "Shyne" Barrow, 21, a protégé of **Sean "Puffy" Combs**, 30, is indicted for attempted murder and three lesser charges in connection with a December shooting at Club NY in New York City in which three people were injured. Combs is charged with two counts of criminal possession of a weapon, while girlfriend Jennifer Lopez, 29, who was also present, is not charged. After the gunfire, Combs fled the scene in a Lincoln Navigator with Lopez. Also indicted is Comb's bodyguard, Anthony Jones. A trial is due in late 2000 or early 2001.

The following month,

Combs and Jones are indicted on additional charges of bribing a witness. They are accused of offering Combs's driver, Wardel Fenderson, $50,000 in cash and a diamond ring to say he owned a gun police found as Combs sped away from the Times Square nightclub.

Time Warner, the world's largest media and entertainment company (and the parent of PEOPLE), and **America Online**, the world's largest provider of Internet access, announce that they will merge in an all-stock deal valued at $350 billion. AOL's chairman and chief executive, Steve

Revelers welcome in the millennium in New York City's Times Square.

Case, is expected to be chairman of the merged company, which will be called AOL Time Warner. Time Warner's chairman and chief executive, Gerald Levin, will be CEO.

Michael Jordan is coming back to basketball, only this time in the front office. The former Chicago Bulls superstar reaches an agreement with the Washington Wizards that gives Jordan, 36, control of the team's basketball operations—including making trades, drafting players, and signing free agents. The hiring of Jordan is viewed as a move to bring attention and respect to the franchise. Jordan, who left basketball prior to the start of the 1999 lockout-shortened season after leading the Bulls to their sixth championship in eight years, has been biding his time playing golf, appearing in commercials, even starring in some movies.

In June, Jordan launches his own record label, and proclaims his discovery Jill Scott as "the next Erykah Badu."

David Letterman, 52, undergoes quintuple heart bypass surgery. "They also installed an E-Z pass," he jokes afterward. While he recovers, pals such as Regis Philbin, Paul Shaffer, and Charles Grodin tape interviews with stars like Julia Roberts, Jerry Seinfeld, Bruce Willis, Danny DeVito, Bill Cosby, Steve Martin, and Sarah Jessica Parker that are shown along with memorable

past interviews the stars did with Letterman. When Letterman returns to the show in Feburary, he draws his biggest ratings in six years. He reassures fans, "I'm on CBS. I ain't dead."

In a stunning announcement, *Spin City* star **Michael J. Fox** says he is leaving the popular, four-year-old ABC sitcom at the end of the current season. "I feel that right now my time and energy would be better spent with my family and working toward a cure for Parkinson's disease. This does not mean I am retiring from acting, producing or directing," Fox, 38, says in a statement, "only that I want to relieve the strain of producing and performing a weekly network series." In May the actor launches the Michael J. Fox Foundation for Parkinson's Research. "Our goal is obsolescence," he declares. In July, Fox sells a memoir of his battle with the disease to Hyperion Books for between $3 and $4 million. Charlie Sheen signs on for the starring role in the show, and production is relocated to Los Angeles for the fall season.

Marc Brown, creator of the Arthur the aardvark children's book series, is retiring after 25 years, so he can return to his first love: painting. His books spawned a PBS cartoon series (which will continue) and a touring stage company featuring fel-

low characters Binky Barnes (a bulldog) and D.W. (Arthur's kid sister).

It's over between **Arnold Schwarzenegger** and Planet Hollywood, just as the chain emerges from bankruptcy court. The action star says he is terminating his five-year contract with the financially troubled theme-restaurant chain. "It was lots of fun and very challenging to come up with and develop the celebrity restaurant concept on an international level," says Schwarzenegger, 52, who has sold his interest in the Orlando-based company. "Of course, I am disappointed that the company did not continue with the success I had expected and hoped for."

FEBRUARY

It's announced that actor **Gene Wilder** is being treated for lymphoma, first diagnosed last year, at Sloan-Kettering Cancer Center in New York City. Wilder, 64, lost his wife Gilda Radner to ovarian cancer in 1989. Following the death of Radner, Wilder opened Gilda's Club in Manhattan, which supports cancer patients and their families.

The daughter of Hollywood's original "Scream King," **Boris Karloff**, is suing Universal Studios for $10 million over the use of her father's name and image. Sarah Karloff alleges that the studio is using the image of the late movie star (the talkies' first Frankenstein) and not paying royalties to her, the actor's sole heir, as per the terms of a 1996 deal she struck with Universal. Boris Karloff died in 1969. Sarah's lawsuit claims that the studio told interested

parties that Boris's likeness was unavailable and instead offered a slightly different one to avoid paying royalties. "It's like they advertise a Buick with all the amenities, then they give them a knock-off that is so similar consumers may not be able to tell the difference," Sarah's attorney says.

Barbie, 40, is getting a millennium makeover. Among the improvements: a belly button, which will replace the current unsightly seam at her waist. "Jewel Girl," as the new model Barbie will be called, is due out in August and will be the first Barbie to be made with a midsection material that allows much more human, natural movement.

It's announced that the London-based insurance underwriters Goshawk Syndicate, the firm that insures ABC's ratings sensation **Who Wants to Be a Millionaire**, is suing to get out of its contract (the court papers were filed in Britain in January). It claims the questions on the ABC quiz show are too easy, which puts the insurer at risk of shelling out too much prize money. ABC says the network is planning no changes to the show. According to one interpretation of the lawsuit, Goshawk is essentially asking *Millionaire* to ask harder questions and pick dumber contestants.

In May, the show is sued for $2 million by Mensa member and computer programmer Robert Gelbman,

The ever-so-briefly happy couple pose beatifically on Who Wants to Marry a Multi-Millionaire?

who appeared on *Millionaire* in August, 1999. He claims a $32,000 question about the order of the signs of the Zodiac was ambiguously worded. "The problem is that the question doesn't specify whether it's based on the Zodiac cycle or the calendar year," Gelbman says.

Millionaire makes news again when **Rosie O'Donnell** serves as a "phone friend," helping contestant Jerry Halpin, with his $32,000 question: "What title was taken away from Diana when she divorced Prince Charles?" Halpin and Rosie correctly concur that it was "Her Royal Highness." (Rosie had told Halpin that if he were wrong, she'd pay him the money out of guilt.)

Kermit, Miss Piggy, and the rest of the **Jim Henson Muppet gang** will take up residence at Charlie Chaplin's old Hollywood studios in April, following the Henson Company's purchase of the five-acre site for $12.5 million. How perfect that Piggy will live where *The Great Dictator* was produced.

Rick Rockwell, 42, a real estate investor and motivational speaker who lives near San Diego, meets and marries Darva Conger, 34, an emergency-room nurse, after a two-hour prime-time competition on Fox's *Who Wants to Marry a Multi-Millionaire?* The Fox special is a surprise ratings hit, but the backlash begins almost immediately.

Reports quickly surface that a restraining order was issued against Rockwell in 1991 following accusations by fiancée Debbie Goyne that he hit and threatened to kill her. Other reports question the millionaire's true worth and it comes to light that Rockwell is a former B-movie actor and comic. Another restraining order against Rockwell is also discovered, this one from 1982, filed by his former roomate, Mark Brandon, who claimed that Rockwell verbally threatened him and physically attacked him.

The marriage lasts about as long as the honeymoon provided by the show. Describing himself as a "romantic" who still believes in the institution of marriage, Rockwell indicates that he and Conger slept in separate rooms for all but one night of their Caribbean trip and there was no sex involved. Afterwards they retreat to their separate homes.

In March Conger files annulment papers in which she calls the marriage a "mutual mistake...entered into solely for an entertainment purpose." She says that the union was never consummated and that Fox failed to inform her that Rockwell "had a history of problems with his prior girlfriends and was the subject of at least one restraining order for threatening and dangerous behavior." While she isn't keeping her husband, Conger will hold onto the Isuzu

Trooper and the $35,000 diamond ring she won on the show. As Rockwell returns to his stand-up comedy career, Conger is fired from her nursing job. Later in the year she appears on the cover of *Playboy* (and inside in a pictorial) for unreported terms. "*Playboy* stepped in and helped me out when I had no other avenues open to me and really saved my bacon," she tells a press conference.

Kathie Lee Gifford, 46, announces that she will not return to her syndicated morning show with Regis Philbin once her contract expires in July.

Carlos Santana wins Grammys in every category for which he is nominated, including the night's top honors: album of the year (*Supernatural*), record of the year (for his single with singer Rob Thomas, "Smooth"), and song of the year ("Smooth" again). In all, Santana himself collects eight awards, matching Michael Jackson's 1983 record for the most Grammys won in a single year. (The song of the year trophy went to the songwriters of "Smooth," Itaal Shur and Rob Thomas.) Santana, 52, tells reporters backstage he is proud "to be able to demonstrate to the people that deepness and class can be as profitable as shallowness and crass." Still, the No. 1 topic on early a.m. TV and radio shows the next day

Carlos Santana celebrates his record-tying Grammy haul.

is presenter **Jennifer Lopez**'s dress. Or lack of it. Lopez's outfit, a green and yellow silk chiffon Donatella Versace scarf dress, was cut all the way down to her navel, then split apart again and fell to the floor. (Only a brooch kept the actress-singer from full exposure.)

Charles Schulz, 77, dies in his sleep after a battle with colon cancer. The following day, the last original *Peanuts* comic strip runs in Sunday newspapers.

Cats, the longest-running production in Broadway his-

tory, announces that it will meow its last "Memory" on June 25 (later extended to September 10). The plotless musical extravaganza, which set T. S. Eliot poems to Andrew Lloyd Webber music, plays 7,485 performances over 18 years.

Halle Berry, 33, driving a rented Chevy Blazer, allegedly runs a red light, strikes another vehicle, and then flees the scene of the accident. The actress cuts her forehead and requires 22 stitches, while the other driver, Heta Raythatha, 27, is treated for a broken wrist.

Raythatha subsequently sues Berry for negligence, claiming that she is permanently disabled from back injuries and is suffering emotional distress.

In April, Berry is charged with leaving the scene of an accident, and is subsequently sentenced to three years probation, a fine of $13,500, and 200 hours of community service, after pleading no contest. Berry tells the court she has no memory of the crash and "would never leave someone injured, even if it were an accident that I weren't involved in."

MARCH

Bodyguard **Trevor Rees-Jones**, the sole survivor of the August 1997 car crash that killed Princess Diana and two others, admits he still feels haunted by the fact that the Princess died "on my shift" and claims that he would have gladly traded his life for hers. Rees-Jones's comments come as he publishes his new book, *The Bodyguard's Story*. Rees-Jones, a former paratrooper who was injured in the crash, tells PEOPLE: "A couple of times I felt if I had died, instead of them, it would have been much easier both for me personally and for everybody else."

The book also details the nature of the Diana-Dodi relationship. Rees-Jones disputes Mohamed Al Fayed's claim that his son and Diana picked out an engagement ring in Monte Carlo. He also says in the book that Al Fayed's aides arranged for him to speak to a London tabloid, so Rees-Jones could say he'd heard Diana crying out for Dodi after the crash. In the book he now admits that he only recalled hearing the word "Dodi" later in a dream.

This year's **Oscars** are plagued by snafus: first eight bags of more than 4,000 ballots are mysteriously lost and have to be remailed. Then 54 unengraved golden statuettes are stolen from a loading dock of the Railway Express shipping company near Los Angeles. Fifty-two of the statuettes are later discovered near a grocery store dumpster by Willie Fulgear, 61, who salvages items for a living. Lawrence Ledent, 38, an employee of Railway Express, is charged with the theft (he later pleads no contest to the charges). Dock worker Anthony Hart is later

indicted as well.

Fulgear receives a $50,000 reward from the shipper and a seat at the Oscar ceremony. "If anybody says honesty don't pay, send them to me," he declares.

John and **Patsy Ramsey** tell Barbara Walters on *20/20* and her nearly 20 million viewers that they would be willing to submit to lie-detector tests. (Patsy Ramsey also notes that the findings of such tests have never been considered as admissible evidence in a court of law.) The couple appear in connection with the publication of their new book, *The Death of Innocence*, about the still-unsolved 1996 murder of their 6-year-old daughter JonBenet. The parents have remained under a cloud of suspicion by the public and law authorities ever since news of the brutal killing first broke. After a 13-month investigation, a grand jury was unable to file any charges in the case.

Eventually, the Ramseys do submit to a lie-detector test—but one administered by an independent panel hired by them, rather than by law-enforcement officials. The findings of the test, which Boulder police say they will not accept, show that the Ramseys are innocent in the unresolved Christmas 1996 murder of their 6-year-old daughter, JonBenet.

Nationally syndicated radio show host **Dr. Laura**

Schlessinger, 53, encounters a firestorm of protest over comments she made on the air that characterized homosexuality as deviant behavior and a biological error. Though she apologizes— "Regrettably, some of the words I've used have hurt some people, and I am sorry for that. Words that I have used in a clinical context have been perceived as judgment"—opponents are far from satisfied.

Several hundred demonstrators gather outside the Paramount Pictures gates, and the Gay and Lesbian Alliance Against Defamation leader Joan Garry declares "they bought a battle with the gay community." The group calls for sponsors and viewers to boycott Dr. Laura's planned TV show. Proctor & Gamble, the first major advertiser for the television show, eventually bows to the pressure, yanking its ads from both the talk radio show and the upcoming syndicated TV program. In further repercussions, Xerox and the online branch of Toys 'R Us, also withdraw their advertising, as other major companies like AT&T and American Express announce that they won't place ads on the television show. The Canadian Broadcast Standards Council rules that Schlessinger's "unremittingly heavy-handed and unambiguously negative characterization" of gays is in violation of Canadian industry codes on human rights.

Cybill Shepherd, 50, tells all in her memoir, *Cybill Disobedience*. Among the revelations are tales of her trysts with Elvis Presley, Don Johnson, Bruce Willis, and two Hollywood stuntmen (with whom she romped simultaneously). Cybill elaborates on having "fun in Elvis's bed—his kisses were so slow and deliberate, his skin so smooth." It ended, she says, once he gave her pills—which she flushed down the toilet. The biggest disclosure is that she and her *Moonlighting* costar Bruce Willis—who battled off the screen—initially got friendly at her house in a Laz-Z-Boy lounger shortly after they first met on the set. Her liaison with Don Johnson, while they were making *The Long Hot Summer* for TV, was "fast, furious…[and] over in five minutes."

Dan Marino, the most prolific passer in National Football League history, announces his retirement after 17 years with the Miami Dolphins. "I can say I have been blessed with a career greater than I could imagine," the quarterback, 38, says at a highly emotional news conference. Marino cited health and family reasons for his departure. His only regret: never winning a Super Bowl. Even so, as he retires, Marino is widely considered the greatest quarterback never to win an NFL championship.

In June, San Francisco 49er **Steve Young**, 38, another one of the all-time great quarterbacks, hangs up his helmet. He says that repeated concussions have made the game too dangerous for him to play.

Stephen King's latest novella, *Riding the Bullet*—available only on the Internet—proves so popular that several online booksellers can't meet the astounding initial demand to download digital copies. The e-book racks up 400,000 orders during its first 24 hours for sale. "I'm stunned," says Jack Romanos, CEO of King's publisher, Simon & Schuster. King, 52, clearly raises the profile of electronic books dramatically, and the repercussions continue to be felt during the year. The King story sells more cyberspace copies than any of his bestselling novels did on their first day. Romanos compares the breakthrough to the revolution with paperback books more than 30 years ago. Critics point out, however, that because of disappointed readers who couldn't download the story, no one should use the word "revolution" just yet.

King advances the e-publishing agenda even further in July, when he leaves Simon & Schuster behind and publishes a serialized version of *The Plant*, a story originally written in 1984, directly from his own Web site.

MTV actor-comedian **Tom Green**, 28, discloses that he has testicular cancer, considered to be one of the most curable cancers in young men. He undergoes surgery for the removal of lymph nodes and is expected to recover fully. Green films an MTV special about his illness and treatment.

Jaws author **Peter Benchley** recants. More than a

Diana Ross is all smiles when announcing her summer tour with two replacement Supremes.

quarter century since he published his runaway 1974 bestseller (which, in turn, became Steven Spielberg's first box-office smash in 1975), Benchley is now saying that if he had it all to do over again, no way would he make his shark a villain.

Kathleen Turner has British theatergoers' knickers in a twist. The actress, 45, appears stark naked in the new stage version of *The Graduate*, based on the 1967 movie that made a star of Dustin Hoffman. Turner plays Mrs. Robinson, who seduces recent college grad Benjamin Braddock, played onstage by Matthew Rhys. The theater production features Turner's Robinson stepping out of the bathroom wearing only a towel—which she then drops to the floor. For the rest of the scene, Turner is starkers. In the movie, Mrs. Robinson only removed a stocking. Jerry Hall steps into the role later in the year, and vows to perform it the same way.

Diana Ross and the Supremes are getting back together for a summer tour, but without any original Supremes. Ross is to be backed Scherrie Payne and Lynda Laurence, who both briefly sang with the group after Ross had left it, rather than founding member Mary Wilson and Cindy Birdsong. In July, the tour is cancelled after reportedly playing to half-empty halls.

Antiques Roadshow appraisers Russ Pritchard and George Juno are removed from the high-rated PBS program after reports surface—later confirmed by the show's producers, Boston station WGBH—that the men staged an on-air appraisal of a rare Confederate sword during the show's debut season in 1997. Juno, who owns an Allentown, Pa., antiques business, denies any wrongdoing. "There were no fake interviews. It was pressure put on the station by our competitors in an attempt to get us off the show."

APRIL

Leonardo DiCaprio isn't exactly Barbara Walters—and ABC wants to make that clear. The star interviews President Clinton about the environment for a TV special that ABC airs to mark this year's Earth Day. But journalists at ABC are critical at being usurped by a movie actor. ABC News boss David

Westin says that DiCaprio was filmed touring the White House—and that it was Clinton who suggested the Q&A. In an e-mail to ABC News staffers, Westin said, "We did not send [DiCaprio] to interview the President. No one is that stupid." But White House deputy press secretary Jake Siewert says that ABC made the interview request in February and stated it was "Leonardo DiCaprio that would ask the questions." After all the pre-show controversy, the program itself, designed to attract younger viewers, draws poor ratings.

Six years in the making, the surviving Beatles announce plans to publish a 360-page *Beatles Anthology* this fall. It is an attempt by **Paul McCartney, George Harrison** and **Ringo Starr** to set the record straight about themselves and the late John Lennon, McCartney's spokesman Geoff Baker reports. "It goes across the board," Baker says of the lavishly illustrated volume. "It is about the Beatles as a band, the music, but it deals with everything else—the tours, the drugs, the disputes." Among the revelations in the book: It wasn't McCartney—as has been long believed—who caused the band to break up 30 years ago, but it was Lennon who was the first to leave. The book also says that four years ago, the three Beatles said no to a $175 million offer to tour America, Germany, and Japan.

Wall Street money manager **Dana Giacchetto**, 37—whose clients include Ben Stiller, Gwyneth Paltrow, Courteney Cox Arquette, Matt Damon and the rock band Phish—is charged with allegedly misappropriating $9 million from his celebrity clients and is released on a $1 million bond. He is jailed shortly thereafter, his bail revoked, after being caught with 80 airline tickets (to such destinations as Rome, Singapore and Tokyo), $4,000 in small bills, and an altered passport. Giacchetto said he was on his way to Rome to propose marriage to his girlfriend. Giacchetto is then indicted on five counts of securities fraud and other offenses in U.S. District Court.

Sportscaster and former Olympic swimmer **Donna deVarona**, 52, is asking for $5 million in an age and sex discrimination lawsuit she files in a New York City federal court against ABC Sports. She alleges that she was sacked two years ago (after more than 30 years with the network) because ABC felt she no longer appealed to men between ages 18 and 39. ABC Sports contends that deVarona's suit has no merit.

Heavy metal rock band **Metallica** files suit to ban **Napster**, the company responsible for software that allows the swapping of copyrighted songs for free on the Internet, from allowing the distribution of its songs. Soon thereafter, Rapper **Dr. Dre** files his own copyright lawsuit against the Web firm. "I don't like people stealing my music," Dre says. "Napster has built a business based on large-scale piracy."

In July, in a separate action from music industry powers, a federal judge issues a preliminary injunction requiring Napster to stop allowing the exchange of copyrighted music. A stay is granted while the fight ensues.

MAY

Jerry Seinfeld appears on a U.S. postage stamp. The TV series *Seinfeld* is but one of 15 stamps depicting '90s pop culture issued by the U.S. Postal Service as part of its "Celebrate the Century" series. Other stamps depict such landmarks as the movies *Titanic* and *Jurassic Park*, cell phones, the World Wide Web, and sports utility vehicles. Selections were made by public balloting.

The distinguished voice of actor **Patrick Stewart**—still best known as Capt. Jean-Luc Picard on TV's *Star Trek: The Next Generation*—rises in anger to bite the hand that feeds him. The accomplished actor, appearing on Broadway in *The Ride Down Mt. Morgan* by Arthur Miller, denounces his producers (including the powerful Shubert Organziation) from the stage, saying that they aren't promoting the show. Actors Equity subsequently rules against Stewart, 59. Essentially, the actors union tells Stewart not to argue with the landlord. He must make a public apology to the Shuberts.

Disney, which owns ABC, and **Time Warner Cable** (Time Warner is the parent of PEOPLE) fail to come to terms over transmission of the network's signal. As a result, some 3.5 million Time Warner Cable customers across the country—including key markets in New York, Texas, North Carolina, California, Ohio, and Pennsylvania—lose their ability to watch ABC. At issue is money and Disney's desire that Time Warner carry additional Disney channels on its systems. The timing, coming at the beginning of May sweeps, prevents some viewers from seeing such highly touted shows as ABC's celebrity version of *Who*

Wants to Be a Millionaire. After significant outcry, Time Warner calls a truce and ABC's signal returns within a day and a half.

Rosie O'Donnell and **Drew Carey** are the big winners in those celebrity editions of *Millionaire*, raising $500,000 each for charity. Both celebrities decided not to have a go at the $1 million top prize, viewing it as too big a gamble for the causes which would be helped by their winnings. "I don't think I could risk it," Rosie said on the air, "because that's too much money."

Former child star **Gary Coleman** announces that he intends to seek a California senate seat. The 4' 8" ex-star of *Diff'rent Strokes*, 32, says he has yet to decide upon his party affiliation, but "I'm such a radical…I might have to run independent." Coleman, who once filed for bankruptcy but now says he's financially stable, has worked as a security agent.

Clive Davis, the music honcho who helped launch the careers of Billy Joel, Bruce Springsteen, and Whitney Houston, among others, and who recently coproduced Carlos Santana's comeback CD *Supernatural*, is out as head of Arista Records, which he founded 25 years ago. For the past six months Davis has been locked in a power struggle with the label's German parent company, Bertelsmann, which has a mandatory retirement age of 60. Davis, who is 66, departs July 1. His replacement is Grammy-winning producer Antonio "L.A." Reid, who's been running LaFace Records for Arista for the past 11 years with Kenneth "Babyface" Edmonds.

Then in August, Davis reunites with BMG as 50/50 partners in J Records, reportedly financed for $150 million.

A London spokesperson announces that **Elizabeth Hurley**, 34, and her live-in boyfriend of 13 years, **Hugh Grant**, 39, have agreed to "temporarily split up." It's described as "a mutual and amicable decision."

Jennifer Aniston, Courteney Cox Arquette, Lisa Kudrow, Matt LeBlanc, Matthew Perry, and **David Schwimmer** clinch a deal in the final stages of negotiations in which they agree to return en masse for $20 million a year each for the next two years at least. Besides getting a bigger chunk of the lucrative syndication rights of the show, the actors will see their salaries mushroom to $750,000 per episode. The previous season—the sitcom's sixth—they were collecting a reported $125,000 each per show.

This rock star is once again calling himself Prince.

Teen country superstar **LeAnn Rimes** files a lawsuit against her father and former comanager, claiming the two are responsible for the spending more than $7 million of her earnings. In papers filed in Dallas County Court, Rimes, 17, accuses Wilbur C. Rimes and Lyle Walker of taking money from LeAnn Rimes Entertainment Inc. for personal use. Rimes and her mother, Betty, are suing for unspecified damages. (Rimes's parents divorced last year.) The lawyer for her father calls the accusations "completely false" while a representative for Walker claims that his client is actually owed money.

The **Artist Formerly Known as Prince** announces that forevermore he would like to be known as

Prince. "On December 31 1999, my publishing contract with Warner-Chappell expired, thus emancipating the name I was given before birth—Prince—from all long-term restrictive documents," the Minneapolis rocker (who was born Prince Rogers Nelson) tells a press conference. "I will now go back to using my name instead of the symbol I adopted to free myself from all undesirable relationships."

Dana Carvey testifies in San Francisco Superior Court in his lawsuit against Elias Hanna, the San Francisco surgeon who performed bypass heart surgery on him in 1998. The former *Saturday Night Live* star, 44, is suing the surgeon for operating on the wrong artery during the surgery. "I remember just lying in my bed just sobbing," Carvey, who had gone under the knife to clear a blocked artery, says in court. "I can't believe they connected it to the wrong artery." He subsequently required another angioplasty surgery to clear the blocked artery. The suit is settled for $7.5 million for the economic losses claimed, and Carvey says the proceeds will be divided among charities, including those involved in heart research. "This lawsuit, from the beginning, was about accountability and doing everything I could to make sure that it wouldn't happen to someone else," said Carvey.

Dorothy's ruby slippers have a new home, and it's not in Kansas. For $666,000, Los Angeles collector Dave Elkouby, 36, purchases the glittery red shoes worn by Judy Garland in the 1939 classic *The Wizard of Oz* at a mega-auction of Hollywood memorabilia at New York's Christie's East. Other items in the sale included *Oz* costar Bert Lahr's Cowardly Lion pawlike shoe ($25,850), the 1937 Phantom III Rolls-Royce from the James Bond flick *Goldfinger* ($402,000), and Christopher Reeve's Superman man costume ($56,400).

JUNE

Rapper **Eminem**'s *The Marshall Mathers LP*—his second CD—sells 1.76 million copies its first week out, making it the fastest-selling rap album ever, and the biggest first-week of sales ever for a solo act, toppling a record set only the previous week by the

release of Britney Spears' new album. Later in the month, the singer is charged with two felony weapons charges in Warren, Mich., stemming from a skirmish in the parking lot of the Hot Rocks Cafe in suburban Detroit. He allegedly pulled an unloaded gun on a man who tried to kiss his wife, Kimberly Mathers. The man subsequently files a civil suit over the incident.

Shortly thereafter, in a separate incident, Eminem, is charged with felony possession of a concealed weapon and misdemeanor brandishing of a firearm after scuffling with Douglas Dail, a member of rival group Insane Clown Posse. And in July, Eminem's wife Kim Mathers, 25, attempts suicide at the couple's suburban Detroit home.

Actor **Patrick Swayze**, 47, escapes injury but is forced to make an emergency landing of the twin-engine Cessna 414A plane he is flying outside of Phoenix. He lands on a street and loses a section of the plane's wing after hitting a streetlight. Allegations surface that Swayze may have been drinking, but Federal investigators conclude that a broken clamp on a pressure hose probably caused depressurization of the cabin of Swayze's plane.

Harrison Ford, 57, makes his own emergency landing at an airport in Lincoln, Neb. later in the month after his six-passenger Beach encounters wind shear. No one is injured in the incident.

Survivor debuts on CBS, and by the middle of the month the reality-based show is drawing nearly 3 million more viewers than Regis Philbin's hit quiz show *Who Wants to Be a Millionaire*. *Survivor* pits 16 castaways on a tropical Malaysian island in a contest of endurance and group dynamics. The eventual winner will get to take home $1 million and once again enjoy the luxury of indoor plumbing.

Bob Hope undergoes emergency surgery to stop some gastrointestinal bleeding. The legendary entertainer, who recently turned 97, recovers quickly and returns home a day earlier than expected.

'N Sync serenades 300 guests at 12-year-old Rachel Colburn's bat mitzvah in suburban Washington, D.C. They sing for 40 minutes, then hang around to sign autographs. Rachel's dad, AOL executive David Colburn, claims to have a relationship with 'N Sync. *The Washington Post* suggests that his paying the group a $250,000 performance fee didn't hurt, either.

Universal Pictures files a $5 million lawsuit against **Mike Myers**, claiming he's breached his contract on the film, *Dieter*, based on a German Expressionist film buff

Tiger Woods celebrates the first of three remarkable major tournament victories during the year as he claims the U.S. Open crown.

character he created for *Saturday Night Live*. Though Myers wrote the script, he feels it is not ready to be filmed. He was to have been paid upwards of $20 million for doing the project.

The actor files his own countersuit against Universal, alleging fraud, assault, and invasion of privacy, saying that the film company tried to "bully" him into doing the movie. The following month, coproducer Imagine Entertainment files its own $30 million suit against Myers. A three-way settlment is reached in August on undisclosed terms, and the parties agree to work together on a new film.

Radio host **Don Imus**, 59, suffers five broken ribs, a collapsed lung, a broken collar bone, and a separated shoulder after being thrown 10 feet up in the air off a horse on his New Mexico ranch.

Tiger Woods, 24, wins the 100th U.S. Open golf championship at Pebble Beach, Calif. by a record 15 strokes, and becomes the the youngest player ever to win all four of golf's major tournaments. His overall score of 272 ties the record for the Open (also held by Jack Nicklaus and Lee Janzen), and he is the first player ever to finish at 12 under par. Woods continues his record-setting dominance of the game through the summer, taking the British Open in a record 19-under par. Then in August Woods takes the PGA Championship in a dramatic playoff, becoming the first player to win three straight majors since Ben Hogan in 1953. He's also the first golfer to win back-to-back PGA titles since Denny Shute repeated in 1937.

After eight months of drama and legal wrangling, the U.S. Supreme Court refuses to intervene in the international custody case and **Elian Gonzalez**, 6, returns home to Cuba with his father Juan Miguel, where he receives a hero's welcome. President Clinton says justice has been done. Cuban President Fidel Castro makes good on his promise not to attend the homecoming.

JULY

Nine people are killed, and many others crushed or trampled, in a stampede by fans rushing the stage at an outdoor **Pearl Jam** concert in Copenhagen, Denmark. Danish radio reports that mem-

bers of the music group begged the crowd to move back, but their appeals went unheeded. The concert, part of a four-day event for which 10,000 tickets were sold, was stopped when the tragedy occurred. The band goes into seclusion, canceling the rest of their European tour, and calls for Danish officials to step up their investigation of how the incident occurred. Children and adults alike line up nationwide for a mid-

night release of **J. K. Rowling's** *Harry Potter and the Goblet of Fire*. By all accounts the book sells a substantial portion of its record first printing of 4 million copies in the first few days, sending U.S. publisher Scholastic back to press for another 3 million copies. Rowling, 35, continues to be entangled in a legal dispute with writer Nancy K. Stouffer of Camp Hill, Penn., over ownership and creation of the

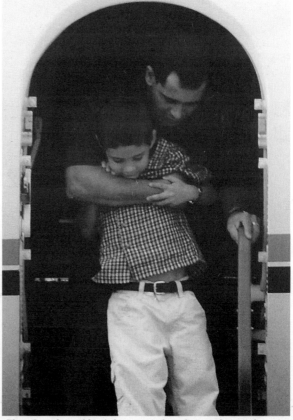

Elian Gonzalez and his father emerge from their airplane as they return to Cuba.

term "muggles" and other elements of the Potter series.

Tina Turner, 60, announces before 75,000 fans in Zurich, Switzerland that she will retire at the end of her current world concert tour. "I've been performing for 44 years. I really should hang up my dancing shoes." Her final concert is scheduled to take place in San Francisco in November.

The British Academy of Film and Television Arts (BAFTA) announces that it will hand out its annual awards on February 25 next year, one month ahead of the Oscars. In previous years BAFTA has followed the Oscars, and many of the winners have been the same.

Pete Sampras, 28, wins a record-breaking 13th Grand Slam tennis championship, taking the Wimbledon title in a four-set victory over Australia's Patrick Rafter, 6-7 (10), 7-6 (5), 6-4, 6-2.

Hours after an episode of the *The Jerry Springer Show* ("Secret Mistresses Confronted") airs in which Ralf Panitz and his wife, Eleanor Panitz, accuse his former wife on air of stalking them, 52-year-old Nancy Campbell-Panitz is found beaten to death in Sarasota, Fla. Ralf, 40, is arrested and held without bail on a second-degree murder charge, and Eleanor, 35, is held, and later released on bail, as a material witness.

Judge Ruben Castillo of the U.S. District Court in Chicago rules on behalf of photographers Stephen Green and Paul Natkin, in their suit against **Oprah Winfrey**, accusing her of unfair use of some 11 copyrighted photos—without permission—in her bestselling 1996 book, *Make the Connection: Ten Steps to a Better Body and Better Life*. From 1986 to 1992, Green and Natkin had shot thousands of behind-the-scenes pictures of Oprah and her TV guests. In August, Winfrey settles with the two photographers. The talk show queen will apparently pay the lensmen an undisclosed amount.

Brad Pitt, 36, and **Jennifer Aniston**, 31, wed in a lavish affair carrying a price tag said to be $1 million. The celebration includes a fireworks display that culminates in a heart-shaped display over the Pacific. The 200 guests under a huge white tent erected on the ocean-bluff estate of TV producer Marcy Carsey include Cameron Diaz and most of Aniston's *Friends*— Lisa Kudrow, David Schwimmer, Matthew Perry, and Courteney Cox Arquette with husband David Arquette— along with Pitt's *Fight Club* costar, Edward Norton and his date, Salma Hayek, as well as David Spade, Jon Lovitz, and Kathy Najimy.

Lance Armstrong—the superman who overcame testicular cancer that had

spread to his lungs and brain and then battled to win the 1999 Tour de France— repeats his Tour triumph. Armstrong, 28, wins cycling's top race, beating second-place German finisher Jan Ullrich by a solid 6 minutes, 2 seconds. Despite the cheers and accolades, a victorious Armstrong still insists, "I'm not a superstar. I'm a regular guy."

AUGUST

Comedian **Dennis Miller** debuts as the newest member of ABC's *Monday Night Football* broadcast team, to ratings 28 percent below the those of the preseason opener a year ago.

Ex-Beatles member **Paul McCartney**, the highest-profile Beatle around, announces that he plans to release a new dance track that will feature outtakes from original recording sessions that the Fab Four made in clubs between 1965 and

1969. The 3½-minute cut, "Free Now," is a collaboration with Welsh band Super Furry Animals and will be on the new CD *The Liverpool Sound Collage*. "It's a new little piece of the Beatles," McCartney tells reporters.

Hollywood's most famous lesbian couple, comedian **Ellen DeGeneres**, 42, and actor **Anne Heche**, 31, announce that they are breaking up. "Unfortunately, we have decided to end our relationship. It is an amicable parting, and we greatly value the 3½ years we have spent together." No further explanation is given for the split and not even close associates seem able to provide a reason. In the odd aftermath, a very thirsty Heche shows up on the doorstep of Araceli Campiz in sunny Fresno, Calif. Campiz recounts, "She wanted to watch a movie, but the VCR was broken." Heche seemed not to be drunk, drugged, ill—but unready to leave any time soon. So Campiz called the sheriff's department, which dispatched deputies, who were told by Heche that she was "God, and was going to take everyone back to heaven…in a spaceship." They took her to a hospital. The next morning, a composed Heche, accompanied by her manager, returned to pick up the SUV she'd left on the road, had a tow truck fill up the gas tank, and drove off, thus ending her odd odyssey.

Richard Hatch, 39, dubbed the "naked fat guy," takes home the $1 million prize on CBS's *Survivor* in the two-hour finale of the top-rated summer series. Runner-up Kelly Wiglesworth, 23, walks away with $100,000. But it will probably be Susan Hawk's embittered speech before the final two contestants that will linger longest in viewers' memories. She tells Kelly: "You're two-faced and manipulative, which is why you'll fail in life…. If I ever pass you on the street and you were lying there dying of thirst, I wouldn't give you a drink of water. I'd let the vultures take you and do what they will to you with no regrets." Nearly 52 million viewers tune in, making it the second most-watched TV show of the year, behind the Super Bowl.

SEPTEMBER

NBC agrees to pay *Survivor* **producer Mark Burnett** more than $35 million for his next reality project, which will put an American contestant into space. The show, titled *Destination Mir*, is expected to debut in fall 2001.

The inaugural **Latin Grammy Awards** are handed out in Los Angeles in forty different categories—and **Carlos Santana**, the big winner at February's Grammys, claims three more trophies.

Barbara Walters, 68, signs a new five-year contract with ABC for a reported $12 million a year—a record for a news personality.

Barbra Streisand holds her final farewell performances at New York City's Madison Square Garden. The tickets, which sold out immediately, are priced from $125 to $2,500. She closes the last concert with her trademark, "People."

TRIBUTES

BARBARA CARTLAND

For seven decades, English author Barbara Cartland charmed readers by conjuring up a fanciful version of her own primly mannered youth: the genteel dances and elegant ball gowns, pure damsels and wealthy suitors, and no sex—please!—until the man slips a wedding ring on his lady's finger. Lovemaking was "like going to the lavatory," she said. "You never spoke about it."

Before the 98-year-old Cartland died in her sleep at her 400-acre estate in Hertfordshire, England, she had spun a remarkable 723 novels of old-fashioned courtship, from *The Devil in Love* to *The Goddess and the Gaiety Girl.* Sales reached 1 billion copies around the globe. Cartland, whom Queen Elizabeth made a Dame in 1991, played the role to the hilt with her big hair, jewels, white fox furs, and her trademark pink chiffon. The color, she said, "helps you to be clever."

Born near Birmingham to army major Bertram and Polly Cartland, she and brothers Ronald and Anthony led a pampered life. After completing high school and finishing school, Cartland wrote newspaper gossip columns and published her first novel, *Jigsaw,* at 24. (By the '60s she was the premier romance novelist in the world.) She married wealthy Scotsman Alexander McCorquodale in 1927—and had a daughter, Raine, now 70—before a wrenching divorce six years later. In 1936 she wed her ex's cousin Hugh McCorquodale—a blissful union that produced two sons and lasted until his death in 1963. Sons Ian, 62, and Glen, 60, ran the business and researched her books.

Cartland hobnobbed with high-profile friends such as Sir Winston Churchill and Lord Mountbatten. She was also step-grandmother to Princess Diana (Raine married Di's father in 1976), whose fantasies of Prince Charming were stoked by the books she read as a youth, some of them Cartland's. Because "Prince Charles did not match these heroes," the writer said, "the marriage began to crumble." Cartland's own romantic dreams, son Ian recalls fondly, had a happier denouement. "She found real love with my father," he says. "That was her ideal."

DOUGLAS FAIRBANKS JR.

"I never tried to compete with him," Douglas Fairbanks Jr. said last year of his swashbuckling movie star father. "To start with, he was the most physically agile person I knew. He could climb anything." The younger Fairbanks, who died in Manhattan of Parkinson's disease at 90, made his own remarkable climb, appearing in nearly 80 films, including *The Prisoner of Zenda* (1937) and *Gunga Din* (1939). "He had an enormous, blazing smile," says actor Christopher Lee of his friend's appeal onscreen and off. "It wasn't put on. It was totally natural."

Women noticed. He married rising starlet Joan Crawford in 1929 (they divorced four years later) and had an affair with Marlene Dietrich. Using his celebrity clout, he became a U.S. goodwill ambassador before going to war. As a naval officer from 1941 to 1946, Fairbanks was highly decorated for, among other exploits, leading a British flotilla in the North Atlantic. Says his friend historian Arthur Schlesinger Jr.: "He stood for gallantry in a notably ungallant time." Fairbanks served under Adm. Lord Louis Mountbatten, who introduced him to his nephew Prince Philip and the future Queen Elizabeth. They would become guests at the London home Fairbanks shared with his wife, Mary Lee Hartford, and their three daughters.

After Mary Lee's death in 1988, Fairbanks married former QVC contractor Vera Shelton in 1991. He served on boards from the Motion Picture Academy to the

Council on Foreign Relations but never lost his love for the greasepaint. After seeing 1993's *Jurassic Park*, he sent Steven Spielberg a fan letter. "He wrote back and said, 'When I got your letter I was so excited, I put it up on my wall,'" recalled Fairbanks last year. "So I wrote back: 'I just put your letter up on my wall!'"

JOHN GIELGUD

"Theatricality," Sir John Gielgud once said, "was the first, and abiding, thing about the theater I loved: costumes, scenery, magic." Designers and stagehands may have supplied the first two, but over the course of a 79-year career in theater, TV and more than 75 films, Gielgud always provided the magic. The regal actor, who died at age 96 at his home in Buckinghamshire, England, "was undoubtedly the greatest theatrical figure of our time," says actor-director Richard Attenborough. Though his credits ranged from Shakespeare to *Caligula*, Gielgud won his Oscar for a droll turn as Dudley Moore's tart-tongued valet in 1981's *Arthur*, a film he initially rejected as "smutty [and] common."

Gielgud sought the spotlight only onstage, keeping private his 40-year relationship with Martin Hensler, who died last year. And despite the voice Sir Alec Guinness called "a silver trumpet muffled in silk," he

was anything but an authority figure among friends, who adored his many faux pas ("Gielgoofs"). Exhibit A: He once asked Elizabeth Taylor, "Didn't poor Richard [Burton] marry some terrible film star?"

The London-born son of a stockbroker, Sir John—he was knighted in 1953—never retired, appearing in 1998's *Elizabeth*. Until his final days, says his niece Maina Gielgud, "It was always, 'I wish I had more work.' That was his life."

ALEC GUINNESS

The Force was always with him. For 60 years, Sir Alec Guinness mesemerized audiences with an elastic face and understated elegance. He played it both straight and slapstick, won two Oscars, and sailed on his own smooth sea. "He wore his Obi-Wan Kenobi robe as if it were a tuxedo," recalls his *Star Wars* costar Carrie Fisher. "While the rest of us were sitting on the set, it was as if he were sitting on the deck of a yacht." The 86-year-old's long and placid voyage came to an end in the cancer ward of King Edward VII Hospital in Midhurst, West Sussex, England, not far the country home in Hampshire he shared with Merula, 86, his wife of 62 years and an artist.

The child of poverty and loneliness, Guinness was an elusive presence. "I can walk through a crowd at the stage door, who are presumably

waiting to see me," he told Britain's *Daily Telegraph* in 1993, "and nobody will notice me at all." Though extremely shy, he nurtured his comrades. "We all felt we knew him in a way," say *Star Wars* pal Mark Hamill. Recalls costar Harrison Ford: "He helped me find a place to live and made sure I knew where to eat. It was a prince of the theater being very generous to an apprentice."

Guinness was active until the end. He starred in a BBC TV family comedy in 1996 and published his third book of memoirs in 1999. And yet for all his celebrity, his calling was always clear. Once asked how he would like his obituary to read, Guinness replied, "If my ghost could hover outside some London underground station on a foggy November night just as the crowds were pouring down, I'd like to see the newspaper poster: ACTOR DIES."

DOUG HENNING

As the first magician to wear tie-dyed outfits and sport a look more hippie than Houdini, Doug Henning rarely lived his life as a conformist. Indeed, even in death he bucked the odds. Diagnosed with liver cancer on September 26, 1999, Henning received only one chemotherapy treatment before swearing off it for good, no doubt alarming his doctors at L.A.'s Cedars-Sinai hospital. "[The chemo caused] such a terrible reaction because his body was so sensitive and pure, being a lifelong organic-foods vegetarian, that it really almost killed him," recalls his wife, Debby Henning, 45. So in October 1999 her husband returned to the couple's Spanish-stucco rental home in Beverly Hills where, on his own, he went off the IV fluids and fasted for nine days. According to Debby, at the end of that period the swelling in his side had gone down. "Dougie roused himself," she recalls, "and said, 'I think I'm better.' He felt he had revived himself." Henning then began eating again, and his spirits soared. "Nature gave him a little more time," says Debby, "but in the end it took its course."

By his death at 52, Henning was a recognized pioneer in his art. Beginning in 1974, the shaggy-haired illusionist brought magic to the masses, appearing on Broadway, television, and in Las Vegas, where he got the lion's share of the glory long before Siegfried & Roy. "He gave magic shows a different look," observed Penn Jillete of the popular magic act Penn & Teller. "Henning came on with this style that matched the '70s, doing tricks for modern audiences. That opened it up to all the zillions of magic specials that have been on TV since." Henning began his wizardry as a boy in Winnipeg, Man. The son of Clarke, a pilot, and Shirley, a homemaker

(both now deceased), he witnessed a magician levitate a girl on television when he was 6. Impressed, he asked his mother for a magic kit and by 14 was earning $15 a week levitating his sister at parties. In 1970, Henning graduated from Ontario's McMaster University, where he studied psychology while moonlighting as a magician.

Committed to his craft, Henning put together a show in Toronto called *Spellbound* that wowed audiences and attracted American producers. In 1974 he appeared on Broadway in *The Magic Show*, which ran for several years, making Henning a star.

He added TV to his repertoire, appearing annually for eight years. His 1975 NBC special, which he insisted run live and without commercials, garnered an astonishing 50 million viewers.

In 1981, after a brief marriage to self-help author Barbara De Angelis, Henning met artist Debby Douillard at a transcendental meditation school in Fairfield, Iowa. They married by the end of the year, and she helped design sets for his shows. The couple, who never had children, was inseparable after that, traveling the world, including a 1986 trip to India, where they studied with Maharishi Mahesh Yogi. That same year Henning sold his illusions to David Copperfield and other magicians and devoted himself to the TM movement full time. He even helped design a theme

park, Veda Land, a $1.5 billion venture in Niagara Falls, Ont., that would feature spiritually themed rides such as the Magic Flying Chariot Ride, where parkgoers would travel through the molecular structure of a rose. After years of planning his colleagues still hope Veda Land will open by 2005. Not completing the park was a disappointment, but his wife says Henning himself was a happy man. "He left life very fulfilled." Debbie says.

HEDY LAMARR

Hedy Lamarr was not a diva; she just played one in the movies. She was billed as "the most beautiful woman in the world" as she vamped her way from 1938's *Algiers* to 1949's *Samson and Delilah*, yet her son Anthony Loder, 52, says that when he was a child, "the only reason I knew she was famous was once a police officer pulled us over, and instead of giving her a ticket, he recognized her and told her to take us out for ice cream."

Glamor queen was just a line on her résumé to Lamarr, who died in her sleep in an Orlando suburb at age 85. Denise Loder-DeLuca, 54, Lamarr's other child by the third of her six husbands, actor John Loder (Lamarr and second husband Gene Markey also adopted a son, James, now 60 and a retired cop), says she talked to her mother often, and "she sounded like she was 38. She was totally hip and chic."

Born in Vienna, Lamarr first made a splash at age 19 by skinny-dipping in the racy 1933 Czech film *Ecstasy*. She set sail for America in 1937, and her ship came in even before her ship came in—MGM mogul Louis B. Mayer signed her on the liner en route to New York City.

If Lamarr looked bored onscreen, it's because she was. "Any girl can be glamorous," she once said. "All you have to do is stand still and look stupid." This was an actor for whom playing stupid was a stretch: In 1940 she invented an antijamming technique for radio signals that was largely ignored then but was employed by the U.S. military during the Cuban missile crisis and is still in use today. "If you have a cell phone, you are using her technology," says Anthony.

In later years, Lamarr stayed feisty by suing everyone from the authors of her ghostwritten autobiography (the suit was dismissed) to Mel Brooks, who mocked her name in *Blazing Saddles* (they settled out of court). She was also arrested twice, but not convicted, for shoplifting. Perhaps it was absentmindedness; in one case she had checks totaling $14,000 in her purse. "Nobody," says Loder, "could tell her what to do."

TOM LANDRY

Once, a woman in pink leotards put a silly hat on Tom Landry. It was the stern and stoic football coach's birthday, and his Dallas Cowboy players had sent him a singing telegram. Then they watched, holding their breath, to see how he'd react. "She made him sing and tap-dance with her," says former Cowboy Charlie Waters. "And he did."

A tap-dancing Tom Landry is hardly the image most people had of the buttoned-down coach, who died of leukemia, at 75, leaving his wife, Alicia, and two grown children. An innovative strategist who won 270 games and two Super Bowls in 29 years with the Cowboys, Landry was impassive on the sidelines beneath his trademark fedora. But off the field he was beloved by his men. Says former Cowboy quarterback Danny White: "He cared about the players far more than the wins and losses."

Landry hailed from tiny Mission, Texas, and flew a B-17 into combat in World War II, volunteering even after his older brother Robert was killed. A star defensive back for the New York Giants during the '50s, he was hired to coach a start-up team in Dallas in 1960 and, in time, turned the hapless franchise into an NFL powerhouse. "He was like a father you wanted to please," says former Cowboy Drew Pearson. "He'd give you this

subtle look and it was worth a thousand words."

Fired in 1989, Landry, a born-again Christian, bade his players a tearful farewell and was active in his church for the next 10 years. Diagnosed with leukemia in 1999, he never lost the self-deprecating humor that so many hadn't known he possessed. Once, in 1983, he was praised for surviving as a coach for so long. "Look at it another way," said Landry. "I've been at this job for 23 years and never had a promotion."

MARY JENKINS LANGSTON

Salad was never Mary Jenkins Langston's strong point. But at Graceland, where she worked for 26 years, including 11 as Elvis Presley's cook, there never was much call for lettuce. Whenever the King craved down-home comfort food, though, Langston, 78, who died in Memphis after two strokes, was the person he called. And he called her all the time.

Elvis, Langston said in 1996, "loved my homemade vegetable beef soup with corn bread." And he loved her famous fried peanut butter and banana sandwiches, her hamburger steaks, her breakfasts (scrambled eggs, pork sausage patties, biscuits dripping with butter), and her hot dogs with sauerkraut, inhaled three at a time. Fish wasn't allowed in the door. "He didn't like chicken much either," she said, "and he didn't like turkey. Once he ate collard greens, corn bread, and buttermilk for two weeks."

At home, Langston adhered to pretty much the same nutritional philosophy. "They had peanut butter and banana sandwiches at Graceland," says Langston's nephew Fate "Shorty" Mosely, 56, whom she raised. "And we'd have them too, and they were good." Elvis gave Langston a three-bedroom house and frequently tucked $100 bills in her pocket. He also gave her three Cadillacs. "He was just a sweet person," said Langston, whose husband, George, died in 1997. "I don't know why he ate so much. It might have been loneliness."

LARRY LINVILLE

While *M*A*S*H* established Alan Alda as Hollywood's Mr. Nice Guy, costar Larry Linville came to be recognized worldwide as a sniveling, snitching loser. Linville, of course, was duly grateful. Had he not been cast as Maj. Frank Burns in the milestone CBS sitcom (1972–83), "I wouldn't have been a star," the actor once said. "Where the hell would I be?"

Actually, the sky might once have been the limit for the 60-year-old actor, who had lung cancer and died of pneumonia in Manhattan.

Raised in Sacramento, Calif., he studied aeronautical engineering at the University of Colorado in the late '50s, then switched to London's Royal Academy of Dramatic Arts and never stopped learning. "He knew the intricacies of the pyramids," says friend Gary Burghoff, who played *M*A*S*H*'s Radar O'Reilly, "and how to build an airplane. If ever there was a Renaissance man, it was Larry."

And if ever there was a weasel, it was Frank Burns. Inspired, Linville said, by "every idiot I've ever known," Frank became the bane of the 4077th Army surgical unit. Linville left the show in 1977 after five seasons, saying he was "sated" with the character nicknamed Ferret Face. A few failed sitcoms later, he described the decision, without regret, as "my own choice to be stupid and…jump off cliffs."

Married five times, he produced a daughter, Kelly, now 30 and a photo technician in L.A. (His widow, Deborah Guyden, works for a Manhattan bank.) After *M*A*S*H*, he plunged into regional theater. Despite having lost one lung to cancer—a disease he handled "courageously," says his daughter—Linville tap-danced last year in his musical-comedy debut in Millburn, N.J. "I wish his life had been less colorful, with a few less cigarettes and alcohol," says series creator

Larry Gelbart. "He lived large, but I wish he'd lived long, too."

JEAN MACARTHUR

As Japanese bombs shook Gen. Douglas MacArthur's underground command center on the Philippine island of Corregidor in December 1941, his wife, Jean, never gave a thought to escaping to safety with their 3-year-old son, Arthur. "We have drunk from the same cup," she said at the time. "We three shall stay together." Three months later, on President Roosevelt's orders, MacArthur (who would soon become commander of the Allied forces in the Pacific) and his family finally fled in a PT boat, just ahead of the advancing enemy.

Once the very symbol of the loyal military spouse, Jean MacArthur, who died at the age of 101, became in later years a beloved member of high society.

Ensconced on the 32nd floor of New York City's elite Waldorf Towers apartments after the general's death in 1964, she was feted by the likes of the late publisher Malcolm Forbes, who threw her a 90th-birthday party attended by Frank Sinatra, Barbara Walters, and other luminaries. It was not uncommon even for presidents as disparate as Ronald Reagan and Bill Clinton to seek her friendship. Yet for all the plaudits she received—including the

Medal of Freedom, the nation's highest award for civilian patriotic service— the vivacious widow typically responded with a self-effacing, "People are so good to me."

A symbol of white-gloved propriety and World War II–vintage patriotic devotion, Jean MacArthur was attended at her final bedside, in New York City's Lenox Hill Hospital, by her only child, Arthur, 61, an extremely private Manhattanite who years ago distanced himself from his mother and strong-willed father.

Born in Nashville in 1898 to a banker and his wife, Jean Marie Faircloth seemed destined to marry a soldier. After her parents divorced when she was 8, she and her two brothers were raised in the home of their maternal grandfather, Capt. Richard Beard, a Confederate veteran who venerated military service.

After graduating from Soule College in Murfreesboro, Tenn., Jean set out to see the world. It was on a 1935 trip to Asia that she met divorcé Douglas MacArthur at a shipboard party. Though 18 years her senior, the smitten officer sent her flowers the next day, and "that," she was fond of saying, "was that." The couple married in 1937, and Arthur was born the next year.

Just before her husband's death, Jean helped to establish the Norfolk-based General Douglas MacArthur Foundation, which memorializes his career and fosters military leadership, and later the Jean MacArthur Research Center, which houses the general's archives. Befriending notables including Prince Albert of Monaco, columnist James Brady, and then–U.S. Ambassador to the United Nations George Bush, she enjoyed such passions as baseball, opera, and lunches with the famous, delighting guests with her charm, wit, and sense of adventure. "When I went to one of Malcolm Forbes's hot-air balloon expeditions in 1989 in France, she was in the house party along with people like Walter Cronkite and the King of Romania," recalls columnist Liz Smith. "I didn't like ballooning, and I would go out every morning and say, 'Oh, God, I don't think so.' And then I see Mrs. MacArthur being helped into the balloon by Malcolm. There won't be any more grand old ladies like her."

NANCY MARCHAND

In January 2000, as the *Sopranos* gang celebrated their four-trophy win backstage at the Golden Globes in L.A., the mafia saga's capo, James Gandolfini, wanted to share his joy with costar Nancy Marchand, who'd earned a supporting-actress award. But Marchand, suffering from lung cancer, remained at her home on the East Coast. "He called on his cell phone," says David Proval, who played Soprano family nemesis Richie Aprile in the second season of HBO's Mob hit. "And you know what she said? 'Yeah, yeah, all right. Terrific. I'm going to sleep. I'll speak to you tomorrow.' And she hung up on him!" In the words of Dominic Chianese (Tony Soprano's Uncle Junior), "She wasn't into small talk."

Marchand, who died at home, the day before her 72nd birthday, always exuded that purse-lipped power. Stern-browed and reedy—her lifelong nickname was "Nun"—she could take control of any scene, whether as Mrs. Pynchon, the aristocratic newspaper publisher on CBS's *Lou Grant* (1977–82), or Livia, *The Sopranos'* murderous matriarch. Off-camera, too, she made her presence felt. "Even when she was smoking a mile a minute or cursing like a stevedore, she did it with elegance," says *Grant* star Ed Asner. Yet arriving on the set, "she dressed like a bag lady," says friend Robert Walden, who played reporter Joe Rossi. "She had this big cloth shopping bag she could've sold as a workout tool—it was that heavy."

Somehow the actor known for portraying patrician ladies (like Harrison Ford's mother in 1995's remake of *Sabrina*) reached in and pulled out Livia, the put-upon yet diabolically crafty mother of Tony Soprano (Gandolfini). "She would never say, 'This is the best ole I ever had,'" recalls series creator and executive producer David Chase. "But I know she enjoyed doing it. A couple of times she'd say, 'That woman is a hoot.'"

But Livia was more than a juicy role—she was a lifeline. Marchand had been fighting lung cancer and pulmonary disease for several years when she auditioned for *The Sopranos* in 1997. "We knew she had some physical problems," says Chase. "But hiring her was not a mercy mission. She was just so good. Any minute with her, we would have taken." Marchand was just as grateful. "The show kept her going," says Aida Turturro, who plays black sheep daughter Janice.

Although Marchand often needed to breathe from an oxygen tank between takes, "she was pretty stoic," recalls Chianese. But she deteriorated after her husband of 47 years, Paul Sparer, 75, died in 1999, soon after being diagnosed with cancer himself. "More than anything else I think she had a broken heart after my father died," says daughter Katie C. Sparer Bowe, 44, an actor and mother of three.

Marchand grew up, more Pynchon than Soprano, in a suburb of Buffalo. She was the daughter of a dentist, Raymond, and a pianist, Marjorie. "We had only the royal WASPs on my side of the track," Marchand told *The Washington Post* in 1979. After studying drama

at Pittsburgh's Carnegie Institute of Technology (now Carnegie-Mellon University), she married Sparer. For the next two decades she juggled acting with raising Katie; David, now 47, a lawyer; and Rachel, 39, an opera singer. "Plenty of times we had the Coney Island special," says Katie. "Hot dogs and beans."

Marchand steadily built up solid credentials on stage and television (she was Rod Steiger's wallflower girlfriend in the original 1953 *Marty*), but she didn't become a recognizable star and four-time Emmy winner until she was cast as *Lou Grant*'s Mrs. Pynchon in 1977. After that came film work (*The Bostonians, Regarding Henry*) and *The Sopranos*. Whatever the part, "I loooove to act," she once said.

The Sopranos had to go on without the actor Turturro calls "our mom, our leader." Said producer Chase: "Nancy was a white Anglo-Saxon Protestant from Buffalo, and she was in with a bunch of very voluble Italians. But she was very much a part of the family. It's going to be really sad without her."

WALTER MATTHAU

As a 31-year-old novice director, Charlie Matthau was plenty nervous when he arrived on the set of 1995's *The Grass Harp*. Doubly so: He was directing a legendary actor. Times three: The actor was his father, Walter. Charlie gingerly approached his

star to whisper some directions in his ear. "The whole crew was watching us," Charlie recalls, "And he yelled in this really loud voice, 'Bulls—! I'm not doing that!' Then we all started laughing. That was kind of his way of breaking the ice."

Now Hollywood will have to find someone else to take over as gruff Daddy. Matthau, 79, died of a heart attack in Santa Monica. His death hit his 10-time costar in high jinks, Jack Lemmon, hard. "I have lost someone I've loved as a brother, as my closest friend and a remarkable human being," Lemmon, 75, said. "We have also lost one of the best damn actors we'll ever see."

Matthau was buried, according to Jewish law, the following day at Pierce Brothers Westwood Village Memorial Park in Los Angeles, where the interred include Marilyn Monroe and Dean Martin. Lemmon, Carol Burnett, and Matthau's children (the others, by his late first wife, Grace, are Jenny, 43, a cooking teacher, and David, 46, a radio news broadcaster) were among the 50 guests who saw the actor laid to rest, as he wished, in a plain pine casket.

Born Walter Matuschanskayasky in 1920, Matthau was raised by his Lithuanian seamstress mother, Rose, in Manhattan's mostly Jewish Lower East Side. His Russian father, Milton, an electrician turned process server, deserted the family when Walter was a toddler. "He never had a father, really," says Charlie. "I think he saw his own father, like, twice in his own life. So he was determined to be the father that he never had."

Young Walter was a self-starter, running a card game on the roof of his building at age 6 and hanging around the neighborhood's Yiddish theaters selling snacks. He got his first break at age 11, getting a part in a play called *The Dishwasher.* "I was shaped by the whole experience of the Depression," he told *The San Francisco Examiner* in a rare serious moment in 1996. "The humiliation of the competition in the theater, the humiliation of poverty."

He spent three years as a U.S. Army Air Corps radio operator and cryptographer in England in World War II. Glenda Jackson, his costar in 1978's *House Calls* and 1980's *Hopscotch* and now a member of the British Parliament, recalls Matthau telling her that "he visited Cambridge, and he asked a don [professor] directions to somewhere. The man said, 'I'm going that way. If you follow me I'll take you there.' Walter, being Walter, was attempting to make conversation. At which point the don turned around and said, 'I said I would take you where you wished to go, I did not say I would enter into

conversation with you.' He loved that."

Returning to the States, Matthau studied acting on the G.I. Bill at New York's New School for Social Research. By 1948 he was working regularly on Broadway. But with a face seemingly designed by a cartoonist—all jowls and eyelids topped off by a nose on loan from W. C. Fields—he was consigned to jouneyman work on stage and in films such as 1957's *A Face in the Crowd.* "I could play the guy next door," he told *Interview* in 1994. "I *am* the guy next door." He didn't break out as a leading man until he played an Oscar and won another. He perfected the cantankerous slob Oscar Madison to Art Carney's Felix Unger in the 1965 Broadway production of *The Odd Couple,* and followed it as the cantankerous shyster Whiplash Willie Gingrich to Jack Lemmon's hapless TV cameraman in 1966's *The Fortune Cookie,* for which he won Best Supporting Actor honors. That teaming with Lemmon—chopped liver and white bread—was so delicious that, for the 1968 film of *The Odd Couple,* Lemmon took the role Carney had created. The result was a smash, the fifth highest-grossing film of the year. They would keep working together through 1998's *The Odd Couple II,* their comedy tics aging like fine wine. "The main thing I like about Jack," Matthau

told PEOPLE in 1998, "is that he bathes every day, so I don't have to worry about being assaulted odoriferously."

In real life, though, the pair confessed they had never exchanged a cross word. Ann-Margret, costar of both 1993's *Grumpy Old Men* and its 1995 sequel, says, "Walter used to whisper to me, 'You know, when you talk to Jack today, please try to cheer him up, because he's not feeling well.' It was so cute. Because whenever there was something wrong with Walter, Jack would come up to me and whisper, 'You know, Walter is not feeling good today. Could you cheer him up?' It was such a sweet thing. They loved each other so much."

In fact, Matthau had little in common with his crusty screen alter egos—he was a Mozart lover who once guest-conducted the Los Angeles Mozart Orchestra and was, he told *The Odd Couple's* author, Neil Simon, a natural to play fussy Felix Unger. But like Oscar Madison, he did cop to a lifelong love of the ponies. "He was a compulsive gambler," says Tony Curtis, a friend since the pair studied acting together in the late 1940s. "He was diabolical. He knew how to handicap every horse. He knew everything about gambling except how to win. He was always broke."

So broke, in fact, that in

he '50s, Matthau owed bookies several hundred thousand dollars. Luck finally shone for him at two-or-one odds. He got a part in Broadway's *Will Success Spoil Rock Hunter?* and fell in love with cast member Carol Marcus, the former bride of *The Human Comedy* author William Saroyan. At the time, Matthau was married to Grace Johnson, whom he had wed in 1948. Matthau and Johnson divorced in 1958 and he married Carol the following year. "From beginning to end, this was a great love affair," says Gloria Vanderbilt. Carol said in 1992, "My favorite thing in the world is to sleep with him and wake up and see those sparkling eyes looking at me."

And he knew how to keep those around him in stitches. "We couldn't wait for him to come into the makeup trailer in the morning," Carol Burnett remembers. "He would just regale us with very raunchy jokes and then turn right around and put a CD of his favorite opera on and start singing!" One time, Burnett recalls, the pair were on a plane together when they saw Jackie Onassis on board. "And I leaned over to Walter and said, 'Aaaah, if this plane goes down I get third billing.' And he said, "Yes, and she gets second.'"

That keen sense of humor carried him through countless health crises: In 1966,

Matthau suffered a heart attack, which caused him to quit smoking, and a decade later he underwent a quadruple bypass operation. He beat cancer three different times. All of which made Charlie decide he had better write his father a detailed note in a Father's Day card last year. "You are a giant," the card read. "The most loyal and patient husband, and as a father, a volcanic and infinite explosion of unconditional love, universal wisdom and a supernova of everything that is right and good in this world. Apart from that, however, I'm not very pleased with you!" The child-hating grouch of *The Bad News Bears* and *Dennis the Menace* "broke down all of a sudden and cried," says Charlie. "And then he never mentioned it again."

JOHN CARDINAL O'CONNOR

O'Connor, who died at age 80 after an eight-month battle with cancer, never shied from controversy during his 16-year tenure as archbishop of New York, most notably in his unwavering defense of church teaching on such charged issues as abortion and homosexuality. But to his legions of fans, both Catholic and not, he was a beacon of moral authority as well as a prince of the church. As William Cardinal Baum, an American repre-

sentative of the Vatican, put it during the three-hour funeral mass, O'Connor "served the rich, the poor, the powerful, the powerless."

A Philadelphia native who left high school at 16 to begin preparing for the priesthood, O'Connor started his career as a parish priest and a teacher in a Catholic high school, then served 27 years as a military chaplain. He was bishop of Scranton, Pa., and relatively unknown in the church hierarchy when Pope John Paul II tapped him to head the archdiocese of New York in 1984. O'Connor relished the power of his big-city pulpit, threatening Catholic politicians with excommunication for favoring a woman's right to abortion.

But he was not just a hard-shell church conservative. He was equally adamant in his support of trade unions, homeless people and the disabled, especially children. During the height of the AIDS crisis in New York City, O'Connor made unannounced late-night visits to Manhattan's St. Clare's Hospital, where he had established a ward for treating people with AIDS. "He said he talked with the patients and bathed them, took their bedpans, washed their hair," says former mayor Ed Koch, a close friend of O'Connor's despite their many differences of opinion over politics. "He was emotionally moved by their plight."

As the cardinal lost strength after undergoing surgery to remove a brain tumor last August, he spent more time at his simply decorated four-story townhouse behind St. Patrick's Cathedral, where, a chronic insomniac, he had passed many nights reading history and theology. "He died very, very peacefully," says Bishop James McHugh of Rockville Center, N.Y., one of a dozen friends and family members who were at O'Connor's bedside when the end came. "He signaled to everyone that he was in the hands of God and whenever God was ready, he was ready to go."

TITO PUENTE

For Tito Puente, being alive meant being onstage. Even recently, when his heart began to fail, the percussionist kept his band on the road, playing with symphony orchestras in Dallas, Toledo and Puerto Rico. "I have not taken a vacation in my whole life," said Puente, 77, who died after open heart surgery. "I never had the time."

But the man musicians called El Rey (The King) could certainly keep time. A master of the timbales—the high-pitched drums that help give Latin music its distinctive snap—Puente brought his trademark gusto and flair to up to 300 shows a year, smiling, shouting, and rock-

ing like the dancer he had once hoped to be. He released nearly 120 albums of his fiery Latin jazz tunes. "His music made people wild," recalls Rita Moreno, a longtime friend.

The first of three children born to Puerto Rican parents in New York, Puente grew up in Spanish Harlem. And though he dropped out of high school to play with a Latin band, Puente eventually earned a spot at the prestigious Juilliard School, where he studied music theory. Forming the Tito Puente Orchestra in the late '40s, the bandleader launched his distinctive form of Latin jazz and mambo onto the pop charts, where it continues to power the hits of Ricky Martin, Gloria Estefan, and Marc Anthony.

A multiple Grammy winner who has performed for presidents, Puente—who had three children from two marriages—played himself in the 1992 film *The Mambo Kings*. "I'm a showman," he once said. "I'm giving the people good vibes."

CHARLES SCHULZ

Like his immortal alter ego Charlie Brown, Charles "Sparky" Schulz never stopped trying to kick the football. So it wasn't enough for the 77-year-old *Peanuts* cartoonist, weakened by chemotherapy to treat his colon cancer, to merely go skating with his daughter Jill Transki and her 1-year-old,

Kylie, at the Snoopy-themed Redwood Empire Ice Arena in Santa Rosa, Calif.

The following day, Schulz, a passionate sports fan, watched the Buick Invitational golf tournament on TV with a few friends before spending the afternoon at Jill's, where he played with his granddaughter and watched a hockey game with son Monte, 48. When Schulz's wife, Jeannie, 60, called to say she was back from running errands, he asked Jill for a ride home. In the car he told her he "was just not feeling right" and later complained of chest pains. Alarmed, Jill summoned Monte, but after a doctor paid a house call to check Schulz's blood pressure and pulse, they left around 9 p.m. "I went over to Dad and said I loved him, like I always do," she recalls. "And he said, 'I don't think I'm going to make it.' He'd said this before, so we didn't take it too seriously. But something told me it was different this time."

Less than an hour later, Schulz died peacefully in his sleep—the very night before the last original *Peanuts* comic strip was to run in the Sunday papers. The timing was "prophetic and magical," says close friend and fellow cartoonist Lynn Johnston, 52, the creator of *For Better or for Worse*. "He made one last deadline. There's romance in that."

And as some 355 million daily readers in 75 countries

read Schulz's goodbye panel that morning—a "Dear Friends" letter—there was plenty of grief, none of it good, over the mirthful moralist who had brightened the world for nearly half a century with hapless Charlie Brown, tart-tongued Lucy, sage Linus, and the rest of the lovable *Peanuts* gang.

The tremendous outpouring of affection unleashed in December 1999 by his disclosure of his illness and retirement took Schulz by surprise. "He was overwhelmed," says friend and cartoonist Kevin Fagan (*Drabble*). "He couldn't believe how much he had touched people's lives." As creator of the most widely syndicated comic strip in history, Schulz added "security blanket" to the popular lexicon; his quote "Happiness is a warm puppy" is in *Bartlett's*; and Snoopy, perhaps his most enduring icon, was stenciled on the helmets of American soldiers in Vietnam.

Sensitive, introspective and even insecure, Schulz also broke ground by depicting love, hope, pain, and loss—with laugh-out-loud humor mixed with compassion. "There used to be so many taboo things in cartoons, and he blasted that to smithereens by discussing literature, philosophy, psychiatry, and all that," says Rheta Grimsley Johnson, author of the 1989 biography *Good Grief: The Story of Charles M. Schulz*. "But in a larger sense he showed there was a market for innocence.

People may by seduced by glitter, sophomoric stunts and shock radio, but deep down we all yearn for something simple and profound that will endure. He gave it to us."

The wit and wisdom in *Peanuts* was forged from a lifetime of slights, hurts, and hard lessons. "He used the strip as therapy," says comic-strip artist Chris Browne (*Hagar the Horrible*). "He reached into the muck of his own soul and came up with diamonds."

The only child of Carl, a barber, and his wife, Dena, in St. Paul, Charles Monroe Schulz was a shy, skinny teenager with a bad complexion who flunked algebra, physics, English, and Latin. He learned his art through a correspondence course, only to see his drawings rejected for his high school senior yearbook. "I was a bland, stupid-looking kid who started off badly and failed everything," Schulz once said.

Drafted into the army at 21, he entered boot camp just before his mother died following an excruciating bout with cancer; the loss and loneliness, he said, scarred him for life. Serving as an infantryman in France and Germany, Schulz became a good, if sentimental, soldier. He once refused to toss a grenade into an enemy artillery bunker because he saw a little black mutt run into it. "He told me, 'Well, I can't kill a dog. So I

just put the grenade away and left,' " recalls Amy Lago, his longtime editor at United Media.

But it was after World War II that Schulz suffered the unkindest cut. Working as an art instructor at the Minneapolis correspondence school in which he had once enrolled from afar, he fell hard for Donna Johnson, an auburn beauty in accounting. Schulz proposed after a long courtship, and when Johnson said no (only to marry fireman Allan Wold), the rejection sent him reeling. "It is a blow to everything that you are. Your appearance. Your personality," he told Rheta Grimsley Johnson. He never quite got over it. Years later, when Schulz, who married Joyce Halverson in 1949, saw Donna walking down the street, the pain was so deep, he said, "it was like not a day had passed." About a week before Schulz died, the two spoke again, according to Wold's daughter.

Schulz, of course, would immortalize Johnson as Charlie Brown's unrequited love (the Little Red-Haired Girl) in *Peanuts*. Begun in 1950, the strip soon made Schulz a wealthy man. An admitted workaholic, he was also a doting father to the five kids he had with Halverson.

By 1969 the family had settled in Santa Rosa, where Schulz built the Redwood arena. It was there, after his 23-year marriage ended, that he met Jeannie Forsyth, a gregarious divorcée and mother of two daughters, whom he married in 1974. Every day for years, Schulz would drive his maroon Mercedes (license plate WDSTK1, for Woodstock) to the Redwood rink's Warm Puppy coffee shop, where he sat at the same table, ate the same breakfast (coffee and an English muffin with jelly), then walked the same path to his stone-and-redwood studio at One Snoopy Place.

Schulz once said that "a cartoonist is someone who has to draw the same thing every day without repeating himself"—and he made the job look deceptively simple. He did all the artwork and lettering himself, with no assistants to darken blacks or erase pencil marks. Says longtime friend Mell Lazarus, 72, the creator of *Momma* and *Miss Peach:* "He once asked me, 'Why should I hire someone to do my letters? Does Arnold Palmer hire someone to chip the green for him?'" Even when Schulz began suffering tremors in his drawing hand following heart surgery in 1981, he persevered.

Still, he got writer's block—and wasn't above commiserating with junior colleagues. "Sometimes he would call and say, 'I can't think of any ideas,'" says cartoonist Cathy Guisewite, 49 (*Cathy*). "It meant that even the greatest of greats runs out of ideas and has to face the same blank page as I do. I found that to be the most encouraging and sup-

portive thing he could say."

A strict Christian and lifelong teetotaler, Schulz was prone to melancholy and to panic attacks (he once said he felt like a dog frantically chasing the family car thinking "he is being left alone forever"). But he could also be peevish, crabby, and brutally candid. Cartoonist Mort Walker (*Beetle Bailey*) will never forget the time Schulz responded to a suggestion Walker made at a cartoonists' convention by saying, "That's the stupidest thing I've ever heard!" Later, says Walker, Schulz came over to him. " 'I'm sorry,' he said. 'That was *Lucy* speaking.'"

Schulz, who had been feeling unwell for weeks before undergoing the emergency abdominal surgery that revealed his cancer in late 1999, found his illness unbearable. A series of minor strokes had affected his speech and vision. "He told me he was thinking faster than he could get it out," says daughter Meredith Hodges, 50, a horse and mule trainer in Loveland, Colo. (and the inspiration, Schulz once said, for the ornery Lucy). "He cried some too—he was feeling the pain of knowing he had cancer and was going to die."

As his depression worsened, Schulz fought back. "He was out and about, trying to play golf and things," says Monte, a writer who had hoped to finish his second novel before his father's passing. Schulz had planned

on flying to New York in his Cessna (with son Craig, 47, piloting) to receive a Lifetime Achievement Award from the National Cartoonists Society in May. But it was not to be. "He didn't want to feel bad all the time, and he just decided to let go," says Monte. "His characters died, and he went with them."

In Schulz's hometown the St. Paul College of Visual Arts created a scholarship for fledgling cartoonists in his honor, and to mark *Peanuts'* 50th anniversary in October 2000, Santa Rosa dedicated a four-foot-high bronze sculpture of Charlie Brown with Snoopy. "Some residents wanted to name a street after him, but Sparky was a very private person," says Santa Rosa Mayor Janet Condren. "He didn't want to be in the spotlight."

It's doubtful that the accolades would have gone to Schulz's head. "All his life he just wanted to be witty and carefree like Snoopy, but despite all the success he still felt like Charlie Brown," says Amy Lago. "He had more layers than a vidalia onion," concludes Johnson. "You can't be that kind of genius and just be simple." His children, however, have memories as sharp and clear as the lines Schulz once drew. "He was the only person I ever met who never said a swear word to anybody—for him, cursing was 'Good grief!' and 'Augh!' " says Craig. "If I had to sum up my feelings about Dad it would be this: He was the finest example of a human being I ever met."

ROGER VADIM

How to explain the peculiar charms of Roger Vadim, the French director who seduced such world-renowned beauties as Brigitte Bardot, Jane Fonda, and Catherine Deneuve—and helped to make them stars? Ann Biderman, a screenwriter who was his girlfriend in 1984, argued back then that Vadim was more soothing than sizzling. "People expect him to be a sex maniac with horns," she told PEOPLE, "but he is truly the most relaxed person I've ever known." With typical *sangfroid*, Vadim once wrote about snoozing in the same bed with Bardot and Ursula Andress. But, defends director Alexander Whitelaw, "he didn't say it boastfully."

Few men could boast such conquests as Vadim, who died of cancer at age 72 in a Paris hospital with his fifth wife, actress Marie-Christine Barrault, 55, at his bedside. Fonda, Deneuve, and his four children (Nathalie, 42, with Danish actress Annette Stroyberg; Christian, 36, with Deneuve; Vanessa, 31, with Fonda; and son Vania, about 25, with steel heiress Catherine Schneider) had visited before the end. "I was much more upset and moved than I thought I would be," Fonda, 62, who was married

to Vadim from 1965 to 1973, said two days later. Bardot, 65, his wife from 1952 to 1957, called Vadim "seduction itself" and said she still loved him "completely," although she has married three times since. "They were only husbands," she told France's *Nice-Matin*.

Born in Paris in 1928, Vadim (his middle name), the son of Russian-born French diplomat Igor Plemiannikov and his wife, Marie-Antoinette, grew up fast: he was 9 and his sister, Helene, now a film editor, was 8 when their father died of a heart attack. "I aged more in that instant than I have ever aged since," he wrote in his autobiography. As a teenager living near the Alps, Vadim helped the French Resistance by guiding refugees on skis over the mountains to Switzerland. "When Paris was liberated, I was hungry for everything—experience, sex, art, friendship, freedom and craziness," Vadim told PEOPLE in 1984.

Working as an assistant to director Marc Allégret in Paris, Vadim in 1949 spotted 14-year-old brunette Brigitte Bardot modeling in *Elle* magazine and arranged a screen test. They became lovers when she was 15 and he 21, but her parents attempted to end the relationship until Bardot tried to kill herself. When she turned 18, Vadim married her and began reporting for *Paris Match*, which assigned him to the 1953 Cannes Film

Festival. There he paraded the little-known Bardot, whom he had talked into going blonde, for the paparazzi. Leaving journalism to return to film, he whipped up a scandal when he made Bardot the lead in his first film, *And God Created Woman* (1956). It showed no frontal nudity but was banned by the Catholic Church because of the heroine's loose morals. "The film was awful!" admits biographer Jeffrey Robinson. "But he had a vision. There was always the appreciation of the beautiful women—and the eroticism." When Bardot dumped Vadim for her costar, Jean-Louis Trintignant, the director shrugged it off. "You don't have the right to be happy in love if you're jealous," he once said.

Vadim married 20ish actress Stroyberg, lived with (but didn't marry) 17-year-old Catherine Deneuve, and wed Fonda, whom he started seeing when she was 24; he put all three in sexy movies (most notably Fonda's campy 1968 sci-fi flick *Barbarella*). After his divorce from Fonda, Vadim married Schneider in 1975 before wedding Barrault, who was a grown-up 43 when they fell in love in 1987. "It took him 60 years to get to that point," Robinson says. "He told me, 'I saved the best for last.'" Daniel Toscan du Plantier—Barrault's ex-husband but also a friend of Vadim's—calls him "a happy man. He was someone in whom there was so much satisfaction to the end of his life. The films merely reflected his happiness."

JIM VARNEY

In November 1999, Jim Varney—better known as Ernest, the wide-mouthed, redneck goofball he played in nine movies and some 4,000 TV ads—was the center of attention at the L.A. premiere of *Toy Story 2*. The actor, who played the voice of Slinky Dog in the animated films, had been battling lung and brain cancer since 1998; now, with his strength back after radiation therapy, "he was able to walk down the carpet," says ex-wife Janie. "He was really proud of that." Many of the movie's stars, including Tom Hanks, came over to wish him well. As he waited for the film to start, he turned to his friend, attorney Bill "Hoot" Gibson, and smiled. "Hoot," he said, "it's been a great adventure."

The adventure ended when Varney, 50, finally succumbed at his home in White House, Tenn., about 30 miles from Nashville. All along he had insisted that his illness enlightened him. "You don't really appreciate life," he told PEOPLE last year, "until you look death in the eyes."

Varney began acting at age 8 in his native Lexington, Ky., doing stand-up before inventing Ernest for a 1980 raceway park ad. Colleagues viewed the history-and-Shakespeare buff with near awe. "This guy could do a Hamlet soliloquy and be the dumbest redneck in the same breath," says Gil Templeton, a writer on many Ernest films. Twice married and divorced, he struggled for years with depression and alcohol abuse but managed, with the help of medication, to overcome both. In the end he had few regrets: If he could live his life over, he said in 1999, "I wouldn't change much. I'd be right where I am."

LORETTA YOUNG

The image seems indelible: Loretta Young, elegantly coiffed and dressed, sweeping down a spiral staircase to introduce each episode of her weekly 1953–61 TV show. "The funny thing is that most people don't even remember my show, just the entrance," Young said in a 1989 interview. "And the entrance they're thinking of is a fallacy. It just didn't happen that way."

Young actually entered through a set of double doors, but the mistake is understandable; the actor, who died of ovarian cancer at age 87, always seemed the kind of star who would make the grandest of grand entrances. Between 1928 and 1953 she appeared in some 90 feature films, winning an Oscar for *The Farmer's Daughter* in 1948, and then switched to TV, earning three Emmys for NBC's *The Loretta Young Show*. "What I learned from Loretta was if you wanted to be in this business, it had to be class and dignity at all times," says Norman Brokaw, chairman of William Morris and her agent for 50 years. "She always dressed, even if she was just going to the market."

Born in Salt Lake City, Young made her movie debut at age 4 as a fairy in the silent *The Primrose Ring*. Her first leading role was in *Laugh, Clown, Laugh*, opposite Lon Chaney, when she was just 15.

Despite her famous rectitude—she attended Mass daily and fined actors who cursed on her set—the thrice-married Young had a high-profile fling with Spencer Tracy. And Judy Lewis, 64, her adopted daughter—she has two sons, Christopher, 56, and Peter, 55, from her seond marriage, to producer Thomas Lewis—claimed to be the result of a romance between Young and Clark Gable.

After a second TV show ended in 1963, Young devoted her formidable energies to various Catholic charities in Phoenix and L.A., taking only occasional roles. In 1989 she appeared in a made-for-TV movie titled *Lady in a Corner* but scoffed when asked about doing another TV series. "I would end up doing bits," she said. "I have never played bits. I don't want to start now."

★

Oklahoma Rep. **Carl Albert**, 91, who rose from a humble background in the Sooner state hamlet of Bug Tussle to become Speaker of the U.S. House from 1971 to 1976, in McAlester, Okla.

Tennis ace **Bunny Austin**, who was one of the game's highest-ranked players in the 1930s but is best remembered for helping to introduce shorts as the sport's uniform for men (replacing heavy white flannel trousers), in Coulsdon, England. He was 94.

Gorilla Willie B., 41, whose isolation for 27 years in Zoo Atlanta drew public outrage in the '80s, of heart failure.

Cartoon artist **Carl Barks**, who drew Donald Duck for more than 40 years and created the ducat-delirious Scrooge McDuck, in Grants Pass, Ore. He was 99.

Bart the Bear, 23, a 1,580-lb. grizzly whose roles with Brad Pitt in *Legends of the Fall,* Daryl Hannah in *The Clan of the Cave Bear,* and Anthony Hopkins in *The Edge* made him the Ursa Major of Hollywood stars, died "peacefully, surrounded by his family and friends at his home in Utah," according to one of his trainers, Lynne Seus. Bart, whose greatest acting part was that of the leading bear in 1989's *The Bear,* had been battling cancer.

Actor and director **Paul Bartel**, 61, whose best-known work was the 1982 black comedy *Eating Raoul,* of an apparent heart attack in New York City, shortly after he was diagnosed with liver cancer.

Helen Beardsley, 70, whose true-life tale of raising a brood of 20 kids became the bestselling 1964 book *Who Gets the Drumstick?* (and the basis of the 1968 hit film *Yours, Mine and Ours*, in which Lucille Ball played the author), of complications from Parkinson's disease in Healdsburg, Calif.

Saxophonist and singer **Tex Beneke**, 86, whose dulcet Dixie voice is heard on the Glenn Miller Orchestra hits "Chattanooga Choo Choo" and "I Got a Gal in Kalamazoo," in Costa Mesa, Calif.

The body of **Selina Bishop**, the 22-year-old daughter of blues guitarist Elvin Bishop ("Fooled Around and Fell in Love"), was discovered dismembered in a duffel bag near Antioch, Calif. The bodies of an elderly couple, also dismembered, were found as well.

Copper-haired tennis titan **Don Budge**, 84, who in 1938 became the first player to win the Grand Slam (taking the top honor at Wimbledon and in the championships of Australia, France, and the United States), in Scranton, Pa., following injuries sustained in an auto accident.

28 Days star Sandra Bullock's mother, German-born opera singer **Helga Bullock**, 63, after a lengthy illness, at her home in Arlington, Va.

Food writer **Craig Claiborne**, 79, who grew up on butter beans, corn bread, and catfish in the Mississippi Delta and became an international arbiter of haute cuisine, in Manhattan. The first man to be named culinary editor of *The New York Times*, Claiborne had more than a dozen cookbooks to his credit. He touched off a flurry of angry letters to the editor in 1975 when he wrote a front-page story about a 31-course meal he and fellow scribe Pierre Franey shared in a Paris restaurant for $4,000.

LIFE photographer **Ed Clark**, at 88, in Sarasota, Fla. His most memorable shot was perhaps that of the tear-streaked face of Navy accordionist Graham Jackson as he played after the death of Franklin Roosevelt in 1945.

Canadian actor **John Colicos**, 71, a talented Shakespearean player (at 22, he was the youngest ever to play King Lear at London's Old Vic Theatre) who was better known for his role on the '70s sci-fi TV show *Battlestar Galactica*, in Toronto.

Unguent idea man **Ivan DeBlois Combe**, 88, who

helped concoct the over-the-counter acne ointment Clearasil in the early 1950s, in Greenwich, Conn. As chairman of a company bearing his name, he made a fortune developing and marketing products like Lanacane, Vagisil, and Odor-Eaters to remedy some of life's more indelicate disorders.

British author and physician **Alex Comfort**, 80, who wrote 1972's *The Joy of Sex*, in Banbury, England. The illustrated erotic manual, subtitled *A Gourmet Guide to Lovemaking*, is still in print, having sold more than 12 million copies.

George Crowley, 80, whose work on electrically heated flying suits for World War II pilots led to a patent for the first thermostatically controlled electric blanket, of pneumonia, in Pinehurst, N.C. He still slept under one of his creations. "He loved them," his wife told *The New York Times*. "We have one on our king-size bed right now."

Former *New York Times* managing editor **Clifton Daniel**, 87, who married President Truman's daughter Margaret in 1956, in Manhattan of complications from a stroke and heart disease.

Toonsmith **Marc Davis**, 86, one of Disney's "nine old men," a core group of early animators that Walt wryly likened to the United States Supreme Court, in Los Ange-

les. Known at the studio as the "ladies man," he earned the title for masterminding the designs of heroines and villainesses like Cinderella and Cruella de Vil. After leaving animation in 1961, he had a hand in designing rides for the Disney parks.

Col. Thomas W. Ferebee, 81, who on Aug. 6, 1945, pushed the lever that dropped an atomic bomb on Hiroshima, in Windermere, Fla. Ferebee took a nap as his bomber Enola Gay made its way back to an air base. He said he had never had any guilt about being the first man to deploy a nuclear weapon. "I'm convinced that the bombing saved many lives," he said.

Adman **Robert Gage**, 78, who directed some of TV's best-loved commercials (including the one for Life cereal featuring Mikey and those for Cracker Jack starring actor Jack Gilford), of a staph infection in New York City.

Italian actor **Vittorio Gassman**, 77, who starred in the 1974 Italian version of *Scent of a Woman* and was married to actress Shelley Winters (his second of four wives) from 1952 to 1954, of a heart attack in Rome.

Maestro of the morbid **Edward Gorey**, 75, whose inky illustrations and wickedly witty poetry and prose filled more than 100 books

(including the classics *The Gashlycrumb Tinies and The Doubtful Guest*), in Hyannis, Mass., following a heart attack. Gorey's drawings were animated for the opening titles of the PBS *Mystery!* series.

British actor **Charles Gray**, 71, whose portrayal of the villain Ernst Stavro Blofeld in the 1971 James Bond film *Diamonds Are Forever* inspired the satirical Dr. Evil character in Mike Myers's Austin Powers movies, of undisclosed causes, in London. He also played the narrator in *The Rocky Horror Picture Show*.

Scottish composer **Iain Hamilton**, 78, who wrote four symphonies but is best known for turning Tolstoy's *Anna Karenina* into an opera, of undisclosed causes in London.

Original shock rocker **Screamin' Jay Hawkins**, 70—whose five-decade career often found him rising from a flaming, zebra-skinned coffin to howl his 1956 masterpiece "I Put a Spell on You"—of complications following intestinal surgery in Paris.

General Mills executive **John Holahan**, 83, who in 1963 came up with the marshmallow bits that led to his creation of Lucky Charms cereal, as a result of a traffic accident in Orono, Minn.

Patient impatiens grower **Claude Hope,** 93, who, through years of hybridizing, saw a previously unruly posy from Latin America take root as the No. 1 bedding plant in the U.S., at his Costa Rican farm in Dulce Nombre de Jesús.

Starlet-turned-shutterbug **Jean Howard,** 89, whose photographs of such stars as Vivien Leigh and Humphrey Bogart appeared in her popular 1989 coffee-table book, *Jean Howard's Hollywood: A Photo Memoir* (with James Watters), at her home in Beverly Hills.

Songbird **Doris Coley Kenner Jackson,** 58, who sang with the girl group the Shirelles (and sang the lead on their 1959 hit "Dedicated to the One I Love"), of breast cancer in Sacramento.

Sam Jaffe, 98, who as a top Hollywood agent in the '30s and '40s represented Golden Age greats like Humphrey Bogart and Lauren Bacall, in Los Angeles.

Eva Jagger, 87, the mother of rocker Mick Jagger, of a heart condition in London. Mrs. Jagger was last seen in public with her famous son in March, when she accompanied him to the opening of an arts center named in his honor at his alma mater Dartford Grammar in Kent.

After almost a year and a half battling lung cancer,

talk show host **Judy Jarvis,** 54, whose Connecticut-based syndicated radio show was cohosted with her son Jason—making them the only such duo in that medium—in Hartford, Conn.

Character actor **Arnold H. Johnson,** 78, who had the role of George Hutton on TV's *Sanford and Son,* of kidney failure, in L.A.

Actor **Todd Karns,** 79, who played Harry Bailey in *It's a Wonderful Life* (and memorably delivered the toast at its end: "To my big brother George, the richest man in town!"), of lung cancer in Ajijic, Mexico.

Hairstylist **Michael Kazan,** 92, who coiffed models and bigwigs like Greta Garbo and Natalie Wood and helped make the bouffant, the French twist and the pageboy top dos of the '50s and '60s, in New York City.

Russian-born actor **Lila Kedrova,** who won a Best Supporting Actress Oscar for playing a dying prostitute in 1964's *Zorba the Greek* and picked up a Tony in 1984 for the same role in the Broadway musical version of the film, of undisclosed causes in Sault Sainte Marie, Ont. She was believed to be 82.

Terpsichorean **Fred Kelly,** 83, whose dancing was considered as accomplished as that of his movie-star brother Gene Kelly but who opted

for a career as a producer, director, choreographer, and dance instructor, of cancer, in Tucson. As the proprietor of a dance studio in New Jersey, Fred taught some moves to a young John Travolta.

Medley-maker and performer **Pee Wee King,** 86, who was born Julius Frank Anthony Kuczynski and wrote or cowrote more than 400 country tunes, including the 1950 Patti Page hit "Tennessee Waltz" (which eventually became that state's official song), in Louisville, Ky.

TV sidekick **Durward Kirby,** 88, known for his comedic characters on *The Garry Moore Show* and for cohosting *Candid Camera,* with Allen Funt, from 1961 to 1966, of congestive heart failure, in Fort Myers, Fla.

Musician **Michael Koda,** 51, who formed the rock group Brownsville Station and wrote its 1973 hit "Smokin' in the Boys' Room," of complications from kidney dialysis in Chelsea, Mich.

Indianapolis Colts running back **Fred Lane,** 24, was fatally shot by his wife, Deidra, during a marital dispute at their home in Charlotte, N.C.

Horseman **Lucien Laurin,** 88, who trained 1973 Triple Crown winner Secretariat, regarded by many as the greatest thoroughbred that ever raced, in Miami.

Joyce Leviton, 76, who served as PEOPLE's Atlanta Bureau Chief from 1974 to 1994, of cancer in Atlanta.

Swedish neurosurgeon **Petter Lindstrom**, 93, who was married to Oscar-winning actress Ingrid Bergman for 10 years until she left him—amid scandal—for Italian director Roberto Rossellini in the late '40s, in Sonoma, Calif. He was the father of TV film critic Pia Lindstrom.

Tony Maffatone, 56, a former Navy SEAL who is credited with inspiring Sylvester Stallone's Rambo character, in a scuba-diving accident off New York's Fire Island.

Alice Sheets Marriott, 92, who, with her late husband J. Willard, opened a nine-stool root beer stand in 1927 and built it into a vast hotel and hospitality chain, in Washington, D.C.

Satirist **Don Martin**, 68, who drew a bead on society's foibles and deflated them in countless *MAD* magazine cartoons, of esophageal cancer, in Miami. Renowned for his onomatopoeic coinages (*ga-shpluct* accompanied a drawing of a boot trudging through mud; a wet mackerel ricocheting off a man's face produced *spladap*), Martin at one point in his life came up with SHTOINK for a vanity license plate.

Character actor **Helen Martin**, who played nosy neighbor Pearl Shay on the NBC sitcom 227 from 1985 to 1990, of a heart attack, in L.A.

Character actor **John Milford,** who appeared in hundreds of TV and movie productions and also used his training as a civil engineer to help create the design for the bronze stars that grace Hollywood's Walk of Fame, of complications from melanoma in L.A.

Quarterback **Bill Munson**, 58, who during his 16 years in the NFL played for the Detroit Lions, L.A. Rams, and Buffalo Bills, among other teams, drowned in the swimming pool at his home in Lodi, Calif.

Tip-top tapper **Harold Nicholas**, 79, the younger member of the dancing Nicholas Brothers who appeared in more than 50 musical films, of heart failure in New York City. His surviving brother Fayard is 82.

Henry J. Nicols, 26, hemophiliac Boy Scout who contracted HIV from a blood transfusion in 1984 and, as an Eagle Scout, launched an AIDS education crusade that drew worldwide attention, in Cooperstown, N.Y., from injuries sustained in a car crash.

Composer **Jack Nitzsche**, 63, who won an Oscar for the theme to 1982's *An Officer and a Gentleman*, of cardiac

arrest in Hollywood.

Author **Patrick O'Brian**, 85, whose exquisite 20-novel Aubrey-Maturin series, set during the Napoleonic era, looked at love, sex, death, manners, seafaring, passion, music, language, food, botany and, above all, the nature of friendship, in Dublin. Initially dismissed by many as a crafter of "mere" historical fiction, O'Brian later found himself compared to the writer he most admired: Jane Austen.

Rock and roller **Dave Peverett**, 56, lead singer of the 1970s group Foghat ("Slow Ride"), of complications from kidney cancer, in Orlando.

Stock car pioneer **Lee Petty**, 86—patriarch of the racing dynasty that includes his son Richard Petty, 62, the Winston Cup legend; grandson Kyle, 39; and great-grandson Adam, 19, who made his debut at the Winston Cup this month—at Moses Cone Hospital in Greensboro, N.C., weeks after undergoing surgery for a stomach aneurysm.

Actor **Justin Pierce**, 25, who played a nihilistic, drug-using teen in the 1995 film *Kids,* was found dead in a Las Vegas hotel room. He had apparently hanged himself.

Onetime cleaning lady **Annie Oneta Plummer**, 63, who since 1992 made it her mission to provide a dictionary to every third-grade student in Savannah, of breast cancer. Known as the Dictionary Lady, she saw to the distribution of more than 20,000 of the reference books and inspired like movements in other communities.

French-born flutist **Jean-Pierre Rampal**, 78, who piped tunes from Bach to Bacharach on his 18-karat-gold flute and became the world's most popular performer on that instrument, in Paris.

Tatiana Riabouchinska, a Moscow-born ballet star of the '30s and '40s whose demi-pliés and grands jetés were captured on film by Disney animators and reinterpreted by a graceful hippopotamus in the 1940 classic *Fantasia*, in L.A. She was 84.

Hockey high scorer **Maurice Richard**, 78, who went by the nickname the Rocket and was arguably his game's greatest player, in Montreal. He had been suffering from stomach cancer and Parkinson's disease.

Disco diva **Vicki Sue Robinson**, 45, whose "Turn the Beat Around" has been a dance-floor standard since 1976, of cancer in Wilton, Conn.

Raphael de Rothschild, 23, a scion of the French billionaire banking family, of an apparent heroin overdose on a New York City sidewalk. **Robert Runcie**, 78, the former archbishop of Canterbury who united Prince Charles and Diana Spencer in marriage, of prostate cancer in Hertfordshire, England. In time, Lord Runcie condemned the 1981 royal union as "arranged" and accused Diana of being an "actress" and "a schemer."

Basketball guard **Malik Sealy**, 30, who played for the Minnesota Timberwolves, in a car crash near Minneapolis.

Versatile actor **Max Showalter**, 83, whose many film and theater roles included starring with Marilyn Monroe in 1953's *Niagara* and with Betty Grable in Broadway's *Hello, Dolly!*, of cancer in Middletown, Conn.

Former Treasury Secretary and energy czar **William Simon**, 72, who was best known for managing the oil crisis in the 1970s and as a philanthropist who gave away a third of his $350 million fortune to various charities, of complications from pulmonary fibrosis, in Santa Barbara, Calif.

Guitarist **Jerome Smith**, 47, who was a founding member of the 1970s disco group KC and the Sunshine Band, in Palm Beach Gardens, Fla., when the asphalt roller he was operating accidentally turned over and crushed him. He was employed by a local draining and paving outfit.

Actor **Craig Stevens**, 81, who gave up his dentistry studies to pursue a Hollywood career and from 1958 to 1961 played the title role of the jazz-loving private eye in TV's *Peter Gunn*, in L.A.

Chart-topping pop singer **William Oliver Swofford**, who went by the monomoniker Oliver and had back-to-back hits in 1969 with "Good Morning Starshine" (from the musical *Hair*) and "Jean" (from *The Prime of Miss Jean Brodie*), in Shreveport, La., of lymphoma.

R&B performer **Johnnie Taylor**, 62, who had the chart-toppers "Who's Making Love" in 1968 and "Disco Lady" in 1976, of a heart attack in Dallas.

Following a cardiorespiratory arrest, the Kansas City Chiefs' **Derrick Thomas**, 33, a nine-time Pro Bowl linebacker, at the Miami hospital where he was recovering from a car crash that had left him paralyzed from the chest down.

Rose Marie Thomas, 86, the widow of comedian Danny Thomas and the mother of actor Marlo Thomas, in Beverly Hills. She was the head of fundraising for St. Jude's Children's Research Hospital in Memphis.

Claire Trevor, 90, the sultry-voiced actor best known for her Academy Award–winning turn as a hard-drinking torch singer in 1948's *Key Largo*, of respiratory ailments at a hospital near her home in Newport Beach, Calif. Trevor, who starred alongside such legends as John Wayne (*Stagecoach*) and Humphrey Bogart (*Dead End*), appeared in more than 60 films.

Philanthropist **Mary MacLeod Trump,** 88, the Scottish-born mother of Donald Trump, in New Hyde Park, N.Y.

Inventor **Edward Craven Walker,** 82, whose bright idea back in 1963 was to bottle a mixture of substances resembling oil and water, place it atop a hot lightbulb and market the result as the lava lamp, of cancer in Hampshire, England. The lava lamp rode the wave of '60s psychedelia, but Walker once remarked, "If you buy my lamp, you won't need drugs."

Home builder **James Walter**, 77, whose prefab, finish-it-yourself shell-frame haciendas once sold for as little as $1,195 and made the billion-dollar Jim Walter business synonymous with affordable housing, of complications from lung cancer, in Tampa.

Playful suit **Russell L. Wenkstern**, 87, who was once the chief executive of Tonka Toys and helped develop the yellow Mighty Dump truck, one of the company's perennial bestsellers, in Minnesota.

Rock and roller **Douglas Allen Woody**, 44, a longtime bass player for the Allman Brothers Band, was found dead in a New York City motel room.

Musician **Paul Young**, 53, who, as one of the two lead singers in the British group Mike + the Mechanics, was the voice heard in their 1985 hit "All I Need Is a Miracle," of a heart attack in Manchester, England.

Retired Adm. **Elmo Zumwalt Jr.**, 79, whose order to spary the defoliant Agent Orange in Vietnam may have caused the cancer death of his namesake son in 1988, in Durham, N.C.

MARRIAGES

Cowboys quarterback **Troy Aikman**, 33, exchanged vows with his team's former PR staffer Rhonda Worthey, 31.

Actor **Ellen Barkin**, 46, and billionaire Revlon chief **Ron Perelman**, in a traditional Jewish ceremony in New York City. It was Barkin's second marriage and Perelman's fourth.

Actor **Candice Bergen**, 54, and real estate magnate **Marshall Rose,** 63. Both bride and groom had lost their previous spouses to disease when mutual friend Don Hewitt, executive producer of *60 Minutes,* fixed them up.

TV honcho **Steven Bochco,** 56, married Dayna Kalins, 51, president of his production company, in L.A.

Comedian **David Brenner**, 55, and his girlfriend of eight years, Elizabeth Slater, mid-30s, in Las Vegas during his live HBO special. The couple have two young sons.

Country crooner **Gary Chapman**, 42, who split from singer Amy Grant in 1999 after 16½ years, married Jennifer Pittman, 31, a former animal trainer, at Chapman's farm in Williamson County, Tenn. His dog, Simon, acted as ring bearer.

28-year-old tennis player **Mary Joe Fernandez** and IMG agent Anthony Godsick, 29. Among the nearly 400 guests were tennis greats Billie Jean King and Monica Seles, a bridesmaid.

Former House Speaker **Newt Gingrich,** 57, and his paramour of the past seven years, former congressional aide Callista Bisek, 34, exchanged wedding vows before 150 guests at a hotel in Alexandria, Va. It was his third marriage and her first.

Christian pop superstar **Amy Grant**, 39, and country-music crooner **Vince Gill**, 42, near Nashville. It was the second marriage for both of them.

Three years after they escaped their native Cuba together in a boat, New York Yankees pitching phenom **Orlando "El Duque" Hernandez**, 31, and dance teacher Noris Bosch, 22, on Valentine's Day at St. Catherine's of Sienna Church in Miami.

Film-production assistant **Karis Jagger**, 29, firstborn daughter of Mick Jagger, and **Jonathan Watson**, 33, in San Francisco. Among the guests were Mick, Karis's mother, actor and author Marsha Hunt, 53, and model Jerry Hall, 44, whose annulment from the Rolling Stone was finalized nearly a year prior.

Actor **David Keith**, 45, who had a part in the hit submarine saga *U-571*, and Nancy Clark, 28, a publicist, in Knoxville, Tenn., both for the first time.

In a small private ceremony in New Orleans, **Emeril Lagasse**, 40, the Bam! Man of cable's Food Network, and Alden Lovelace, 33, a real estate broker. The next afternoon, some 500 guests feasted at a fais-do-do held at one of the chef's local eateries.

In New York City, film and TV critic **Pia Lindstrom**, 61, and lawyer Jack Adler. The ceremony was held at the home of Lindstrom's half-sister, actress Isabella Rossellini. Their mother was Ingrid Bergman.

Ex-morning person **Joan Lunden**, 49, and her steady sweetie of the past three years, Jeff Konigsberg, who runs summer camps for kids. It was the first marriage for him, the second for Lunden, who divorced eight years ago.

Singer and guitarist **Dave Matthews**, 33, who fronts the rock band bearing his name, married his longtime love, Ashley Harper, 27, at the Matthews family farm outside Charlottesville, Va. After a nine-day honeymoon, the groom resumed his concert schedule, the bride her medical studies in Seattle.

Amy Hart Redford, 29, an actress and the younger of actor Robert Redford's two daughters, and **Mark Mann**, a photographer in his early 30s, in Utah.

Genial string-bean actor **Judge Reinhold**, 42, and model Amy Miller, 30, in her hometown of Scott, Ark. It was his second marriage, her first. The groom first got a gander at his future bride last April at church in Malibu. "After I saw her, I couldn't tell you one single word the pastor said that day," he said.

Backstreet Boy **Kevin Richardson**, 28, and actor Kristin Willits, 29. The longtime couple met in 1993, when both were employed at the Disney-MGM Studios theme park: She was dancing in *Beauty and the Beast* while he portrayed a Teenage Mutant Ninja Turtle.

Actor **Christian Slater**, 30, and former TV producer Ryan Haddon, 29. Haddon was escorted down the aisle by her maternal grandfather to the strains of Wagner's "Bridal Chorus"; Slater carried the couple's 10-month-old son, Jaden, down the aisle to the *Star Wars* theme.

X-Men's **Patrick Stewart**, 60, more famous as Capt. Jean-Luc Picard on *Star Trek: The Next Generation*, exchanged aye, ayes with his longtime ladylove **Wendy Neuss**, 45, a TV and film producer, in Beverly Hills.

American Beauty actor **Mena Suvari**, 21, and Robert Brinkmann, 38, a cinematographer.

Actor **Lesley Ann Warren**, 53, and her longtime swain Ron Taft, 52, an entertainment executive, in the Beverly Hills restaurant where they'd had their first date in July 1991. "I never felt more beautiful," says Warren (it was her second marriage). "Everyone was crying."

Scott Weiland, 32, the lead singer for the Stone Temple Pilots, and model Mary Forsberg, 25, in L.A. It was his second marriage, her first.

Miramax Films cochairman **Robert Weinstein**, 45, and **Annie Clayton**, 31, a former assistant editor at HarperCollins, in New York City.

Singer **Carnie Wilson**, 32, the daughter of Beach Boy Brian Wilson, and rock and roller **Rob Bonfiglio**, 32, in L.A. Attending the ceremony were members of Carnie's now disbanded trio Wilson Phillips—her sister Wendy Wilson and actress Chynna Phillips.

Kristi Yamaguchi, 29, Olympic figure skating gold medalist, and Florida Panthers hockey player **Bret Hedican**, 29, in Hawaii.

PARTINGS

Citing irreconcilable differences, *Family Ties* matriarch **Meredith Baxter**, 52, filed to end her 4½-year marriage to screenwriter Michael Blodgett, 60, in L.A.

In L.A., **Gary Busey**, 56, filed for divorce from his wife of nearly four years, actor Tiani Warden Busey, 32, citing irreconcilable differences.

In Nevada, **Darva Conger**, 34, filed for an annulment. In court papers she said she and her husband, Rick Rockwell, 42, made a "mutual mistake" when they wed on TV's *Who Wants to Marry a Multi-Millionaire?*

Former House Speaker **Newt Gingrich**, 56, and his second wife, Marianne, 48, finalized their divorce. Since filing for divorce from his wife of 18 years last July, Gingrich has acknowledged his relationship with a 34-year-old clerk for the House Agriculture Committee, Callista Bisek, dating back to 1993.

Melanie Gulzar, 24, better known by the names Scary Spice and Mel B, and her husband of 16 months, Jimmy Gulzar, 32, a dancer. "Everyone knows they haven't been getting on," said Scary's grandmother Mary Dixon to a British newspaper. The couple have an 11-month-old daughter, Phoenix Chi.

Designer **Tommy Hilfiger**, 49, whose once thriving brand-name business has fallen on hard times, announced that he is splitting from his wife of 20 years, Susie Hilfiger, 41. The couple have four children.

English actor **Patsy Kensit** (*Lethal Weapon 2*), 32, announced in London that she has separated from her husband, Oasis singer **Liam Gallagher**, 27. The pair reportedly separated once before—17 months after their April 1997 marriage. The couple's son, Lennon, named after Gallagher's Beatles hero, was born last September.

After 30 years of marriage and three children, singer **Patti LaBelle**, 55, and her manager husband, L. Armstead Edwards, announced that they were splitting up.

Singer **Annie Lennox**, 45, and her husband of 12 years, Uri Fruchtmann, 47, a film producer, have separated. The couple have two children—Lola, 9, and Tali, 7.

Citing irreconcilable differences, former *One Day at a Time* star **Mackenzie Phillips**, 40, filed for divorce from her husband of three years, Michael Barakan, 45, a musician, in L.A. The couple have agreed to share custody of their son, Shane Adams Barakan, 13.

In L.A. actor **Sheryl Lee Ralph**, 44, who plays Brandy's stepmother on the UPN sitcom *Moesha*, filed for divorce from her husband of nine years, Eric Maurice, 39. Ralph cited irreconcilable differences and is seeking joint custody of the couple's two kids, Etiene, 8, and Ivy-Victoria, 5.

Nearly six years after their White House wedding (the first such ceremony there since Tricia Nixon's in 1971), the mar-

riage of **Tony Rodham**, 45, the brother of First Lady Hillary Rodham Clinton, and **Nicole Boxer Rodham**, 32, the daughter of California Sen. Barbara Boxer, is on the rocks. Nicole filed for divorce, stating in court papers that she and her husband had been separated for 10 months. Tony contested the action.

Actor **Meg Ryan**, 38, and fellow actor **Dennis Quaid**, 46, announced that they were separating after nine years of marriage. The official statement called the decision "mutual and amicable."

Married…with Children actor **Katey Sagal**, 46, filed for divorce from her husband of almost seven years, musician Jack White, 46, in L.A. The couple have two children, Sarah, 6, and Jackson, 4.

Actor **Kiefer Sutherland**, 33, filed for divorce from former model Kelly Winn, 38, his wife of three years. Sutherland cited irreconcilable differences.

The wife of comic actor **Damon Wayans** (*Mo' Money, Blankman*), 40, filed for divorce in Los Angeles. Lisa Wayans, 37, cited irreconcilable differences and is seeking joint custody of the four children born to the couple during their 16-year marriage.

The husband of *Laugh-In*'s funny lady **Joanne Worley**, 60, filed for divorce in Los Angeles superior court. Actor Richard Perry, 66, her husband of 25 years, cited irreconcilable differences.

51

BIRTHS

CNN correspondent **Christiane Amanpour**, 42, and her husband of 19 months, **James Rubin**, 40, chief spokesman for Secretary of State Madeleine Albright, welcomed their first child, Darius John (8 lbs. 6 oz.), in Washington, D.C.

Five-time Olympic gold medalist **Bonnie Blair**, 36, now a corporate spokeswoman and motivational speaker, and her husband, four-time Olympic speed-skating medalist **David Cruikshank**, 31, had a second child, daughter **Blair Cruikshank** (8 lbs. 12 oz.), in Milwaukee. Son Grant is 2.

Actor **Albert Brooks**, 52, and his wife, Kimberly, 34, founder of shoppingtheworld.com, had their second child, daughter Claire Elizabeth (7 lbs. 8 oz.), in L.A. Son Jacob Eli is 18 months old.

Actor **Jon Cryer** (*Pretty in Pink*), 35, and his wife, actor **Sarah Trigger** (*Grand Canyon*), 32, had their first child, **Charlie Austin** (7 lbs. 10 oz.), in L.A.

Actor **Ellen Dolan**, 44, who plays Margo Hughes on the daytime soap opera *As the World Turns*, gave birth to her first child, daughter Angela Emmett (8 lbs. 6 oz.), in New York City. Daddy is businessman Doug Jeffrey, 50ish.

A new daughter has 80-year-old actor **James Doohan**, who played *Star Trek*'s Scotty, absolutely beaming. His wife, Wende, 43, gave birth to Sarah (7 lbs. 13 oz.) in Kirkland, Wash. The couple have two grown sons—Eric, 23, and Thomas, 21.

With fiancé **Michael Douglas**, 55, by her side, actor **Catherine Zeta-Jones**, 30, gave birth in Los Angeles to a 7 lb. 7 oz., 21½-inch son, **Dylan Michael Douglas.**

TV actor **Erik Estrada**, 50, and his third wife, Nanette, 40, an entertainment production coordinator, welcomed a daughter, Francesca Natalia (7 lbs. 6 oz.), in Burbank. Estrada, whose long-running motorcycle melodrama *CHiPs* was pulled to the side of the road in 1983, has two sons, ages 12 and 13, from his second marriage.

In London, Oasis musician **Noel Gallagher** and his wife, Meg Matthews, both in their early 30s, greeted their first child, daughter Anais (7 lbs. 2 oz.), named after the racy novelist Anaïs Nin.

In New York, PEOPLE's Sexiest Man Alive **Richard Gere**, 50, became a first-time father when longtime girlfriend **Carey Lowell** (*Law and Order*), 39, delivered Homer James Jigme Gere (8 lbs. 12 oz.). The Gere-Lowell home also includes her 9-year-old daughter Hannah.

Retired hockey hero **Wayne Gretzky**, 39, and his wife, actor **Janet Jones** (*The Flamingo Kid*), also 39, welcomed their fourth child, **Tristan Wayne Gretzky** (7 lbs. 8 oz.), in L.A. Tristan joins brothers Ty and Trevor, who are 10 and 7, respectively. Big sis Paulina is 11.

Metallica lead singer and guitarist **James Hetfield**, 36, and his wife Francesca, 30, a part-

time water-aerobics instructor, had son Castor Virgil (9 lbs. 6 oz.) in San Francisco. Big sis Cali is 2.

Model **Iman**, 45, gave birth to a girl, 7 lb. 4 oz. Alexandria Zahra Jones, in New York City. Husband, **David Bowie**, (whose original surname was Jones), 53, was there to cut the umbilical cord. She has a daughter, 22, and he has a son, 29, from prior marriages.

Actor **Melina Kanakaredes**, 33, who plays Dr. Sydney Hansen on NBC's *Providence*, and her husband of almost eight years, **Peter Constantinides**, 34, a chef, greeted their first child, a daughter (7 lbs. 12 oz.), in L.A.

As the World Turns actor **Lesli Kay**, 34, and her former costar **Keith Coulouris**, 32, welcomed son Jackson William Coulouris (7 lbs. 3 oz.) in New York City.

Actor **Elizabeth Keifer**, 37, who plays redhead Blake Marler on the daytime soap opera *Guiding Light*, and her husband, Bobby Convertino, 44, a construction manager, welcomed son Keifer Jack (9 lbs.) in Morristown, N.J. Married three years, the couple have a daughter, Isabella Grace, who turned 2 this year.

CNN talk show host **Larry King**, 66, and his sixth wife, **Shawn**, 40, welcomed second son **Cannon Edward** (7 lbs. 2 oz.) in L.A. Big brother Chance is almost 15 months old.

Actor and martial-arts master **Jet Li**, 37, and his wife, **Nina**, 38, welcomed daughter **Jane** (6 lbs. 13 oz.) in L.A.

Oscar-nominated actor **William H. Macy** (*Fargo*), 50, and his wife, actor **Felicity Huffman** (*Sports Night*), 37, had their first child, daughter Sofia Grace Macy (7 lbs. 14 oz.), in L.A.

Five days shy of her 42nd birthday and three weeks ahead of her due date, **Madonna** gave birth to Rocco Ritchie, 5 lbs. 9 oz., in L.A. with father **Guy Ritchie**, 31, standing by. Madonna's daughter by Carlos Leon, Lourdes ("Lola"), is 3.

In London, British actor **Samantha Morton**, 22, nominated for an Oscar for her role as a mute laundress in *Sweet and Lowdown*, gave birth to 9 lb. 4 oz. daughter Esmé. Dad is British actor **Charlie Creed-Miles** (*The Fifth Element*), 27.

Former Clinton White House press secretary **Dee Dee Myers**, 38, gave birth to her first child, Katharine (5 lbs. 11 oz.), in Los Angeles. Dad Todd Purdum, 40, is a journalist.

Jimmy Osmond, 36, youngest of the singing Osmond Brothers, and his wife, Michelle, 32, welcomed son Arthur Wyatt (8 lbs. 7 oz.) in Branson, Mo. The couple have two other children, Sophia, 5, and Zachary, 2.

As the World Turns star **Michael Park**, 31, and his wife, Laurie, 30, a music therapist, celebrated the birth of their second child, Kathleen Rose (7 lbs.), in New York City.

Actors **Chynna Phillips**, 32, and **Billy Baldwin**, 37, who married in 1995, welcomed their first child, daughter Jameson Leon Baldwin (7 lbs. 2 oz.), in New York City.

In Houston, 1984 Olympic gold medal gymnast and author **Mary Lou Retton**, 32, and her husband, Shannon Kelley, 34, a financial analyst, bounced their third daughter, Skyla Brae Kelley (6 lbs. 1 oz.). Daughters Shayla Rae and McKenna Lane are 5 and 3, respectively.

Rap music mogul **Russell Simmons**, 42, and his wife, Kimora Lee, 24, greeted daughter Ming Lee Evelyn Simmons (6 lbs. 15 oz.) in New York City. She's the couple's first child.

Sharon Stone, 42, and her husband, *San Francisco Examiner* executive editor **Phil Bronstein**, 49, adopted a baby boy named Roan Joseph.

Fall Guy gal **Heather Thomas**, 42, delivered her first baby, daughter India Rose (8 lbs. 12 oz.). The actor, who costarred on the popular TV series with Lee Majors from 1981 to '86 and has since worked as a screenwriter, is married to Skip Brittenham, 58, an entertainment attorney. Thomas is stepmother to his two daughters, ages 18 and 21.

Actor **Kristin Scott Thomas** (*The English Patient*), 40, and her husband, François Olivennes, 41, a doctor and fertility specialist, welcomed their third child, George (approximately 8 lbs.), in Paris. The couple have two other children, Hannah, 12, and Joseph, 9.

Actor **John Travolta**, 46, and his wife of eight and a half years, actor **Kelly Preston**, 37, welcomed new daughter Ella Bleu (9 lbs.) in L.A. Son Jett, named in honor of Travolta's love of aviation, is 8.

Actor **Frederique Van Der Wal**, 32, and boyfriend Nicholas Klein, 43, welcomed daughter Scyler Pim (7 lbs. 5 oz.) in New York City.

In New York City, monomonikered megamodel and actor **Vendela**, 33, and her husband, Norwegian businessman **Olaf Thommessen**, 34, welcomed their second child, a 7 lb. 4 oz. daughter, Hanna. Daughter Julia is 2.

Singer, actor and ex-Miss America **Vanessa L. Williams**, 37, and her husband, L.A. Laker **Rick Fox**, 30, had their first chid, **Sasha Gabriella Fox** (7 lbs. 13 oz.), in New York City. Williams has three children from her first marriage; Fox, one child from a previous relationship.

Happy, Texas actor **Steve Zahn**, 32, and wife **Robyn Peterman**, 34, an actor (*Sour Grapes*) and the daughter of catalog clothier J. Peterman of *Seinfeld* fame, welcomed their first child, 8 lb. 2 oz. Henry James, in New York City.

ROYALS

THE ONCE MERRY MEN AND WOMEN OF WINDSOR

"I want to be as famous as the queen of England," the ambitious young Andy Warhol proclaimed back in the 1950s. He might as well have said that he wanted to be as famous as the Atlantic Ocean. The current British royal family has something that vast and immemorial about it. In the three centuries of its reign, other crowned families of Europe have been executed or packed off. But the Windsors still occupy the throne—and the public eye—as implacable and seemingly enduring as the planet Jupiter.

It hasn't been easy. The Windsors are expected to behave like the Cleavers even when they're feeling like the Simpsons. Being famous is more than their fate; in a sense it's their job. As the real decision-making power of the monarchy has dwindled, the public symbolism has become more important. On more than one occasion in the past, however, Britons have seemed ready to rid themselves of a dynasty that could look costly, shiftless, and Teutonic. The lessons of the past are not lost on the Windsors, who take their family history not just as a source of pride but also as a series of warnings to the present. Like her father, George VI, Elizabeth II has been a model of dignity and decorum. But a stroll among her ancestors in

the National Portrait Gallery is enough to remind her of any number of hot-blooded blue bloods in her line.

Where does the Windsor saga begin? Actually, with the German Hanoverian kings. The royals like to consider Queen Victoria their matriarch because, while she was from the House of Hanover herself, her marriage to Prince Albert of Saxe-Coburg-Gotha established the present branch of the family tree. So emphasizing Albert's line allows the Windsors to distance themselves from Victoria's Hanoverian predecessors. Starting with **George I**, who was imported to England from Germany in 1714, the five increasingly preposterous rulers had made the British people rue almost the very idea of royalty.

After monarchs who alternated between extravagant skirt-chasing and outright incompetence, **Victoria** acceded to the crown in 1837, the niece of the last Hanoverian king, William IV. Immediately she made it her business to undo their legacy. She brought the monarchy a bit of wholesome romance through a devoted marriage to her German husband, **Prince Albert**. Indeed the transformation of the royal reputation may be Albert's achievement even more than Victoria's. With the middle classes taking

power from the spoiled and lazy aristocrats, Albert gave them a royal family that the common man could both look up to and identify with: wreathed in pomp and ceremony but frugal, sober, dutiful, and monogamous.

Though Victoria's name has come to stand for prudishness, it was as much Albert who brought the moralizing strain to their marriage. As a young woman, the Queen didn't blush to size him up bluntly in her diary. ("Such a pretty mouth," she noted. "A beautiful figure, broad in the shoulders, and a fine waist.") But Albert worried that their children would take after his wayward parents, who had divorced in a tangle of adulteries. Above all he vowed that Edward, heir to the throne, would be raised in an atmosphere of hard schooling and abstinence. Naturally, Edward grew up to be dim, jolly, and goatish.

Upon Albert's death in 1861, Victoria, just 42 years old, plunged down a black hole of widowhood. Albert's bedroom was kept as it was on the day of his death, even to the extent of having fresh bedclothes laid out every night. She eventually roused herself sufficiently to regain the public's affection and lived long enough to see her nine children and forty grandchildren married into most of the royal families of

Europe. On her deathbed she was supported by her grandson Kaiser Wilhelm of Germany, who 13 years later would lead his nation into war against hers.

When Victoria died in 1901, after the longest reign in her nation's history, her reputation for rectitude had become so stultifying that her womanizing heir, son **Edward VII**, found himself lionized for the same habits that had caused so much trouble for so many Hanoverian kings. Throughout his life the insatiable Edward conducted a series of lengthy affairs with some of the most celebrated beauties of the day, including the actresses Lillie Langtry and Sarah Bernhardt. With prosperity at home and a vast empire abroad, the public was willing to overlook the moral lapses of a robust and even randy monarch. After nine popular years on the throne he was followed by **George V**, prim, exacting, and a stickler for impeccable dress. George led the country through World War I when he changed the family name from the Germanic Saxe-Coburg-Gotha to Windsor. He also encouraged closer ties between the royals and the people by allowing the Windsors to marry British nobles and commoners. Indeed among the first to benefit from this new trend was the present Queen Mother, a noblewoman who married George's son Albert, the future George VI.

George VI became the monarch, however, only after his elder brother abdicated. Crowned **Edward VIII** in 1936, the young man was already intent upon marriage to Wallis Warfield Simpson, a divorced American married to a British businessman. But the government would hear nothing of it and presented Edward with a choice—the lady or the land—hoping that he would choose the former and in the process remove a king who showed signs of Nazi sympathies. After a reign of almost a year, he resigned, and bearing the newly invented title of Duke of Windsor, he left England for the Conti-

nent and Wallis Simpson. They would return home only for rare visits—and, decades later, to be buried.

England was shaken—indeed on the night of Edward's abdication the sentries around Buckingham Palace were issued live ammunition for the first time in modern history. The public's reaction may have been overestimated, but when Edward's younger brother, Albert, now **George VI**, came to the throne in December 1936, all of Britain was poised for the worst.

For that matter, so was Albert. He had never expected to be king (formal speaking engagements left

The Queen Mother celebrates her landmark one hundredth birthday.

FOLLOW THE ROYAL LINE

The Windsors are but the latest of many families to rule the kingdom. Here is the complete lineage for Britain's crown according to *Whitaker's Almanac*, listed by year of accession.

Saxons and Danes

Egbert	827
Ethelwulf	839
Ethelbald	858
Ethelbert	858
Ethelred	866
Alfred the Great	871
Edward the Elder	899
Athelstan	925
Edmund	940
Edred	946
Edwy	955
Edgar	959
Edward the Martyr	975
Ethelred II	978
Edmund Ironside	1016
Canute the Dane	1017
Harold I	1035
Hardicanute	1040
Edward the Confessor	1042
Harold II	1066

The House of Normandy

William I	1066
William II	1087
Henry I	1100
Stephen	1135

The House of Plantagenet

Henry II	1154
Richard I	1189
John	1199
Henry III	1216
Edward I	1272
Edward II	1307
Edward III	1327
Richard II	1377

The House of Lancaster

Henry IV	1399
Henry V	1413
Henry VI	1422

The House of York

Edward IV	1461
Edward V	1483
Richard II	1483

The House of Tudor

Henry VII	1485
Henry VIII	1509
Edward VI	1547
Jane	1553
Mary I	1553
Elizabeth I	1558

The House of Stuart

James I (VI of Scotland)	1603
Charles I	1625

[Commonwealth declared, 1649]

The House of Stuart (restored)

Charles II	1660
James II	1685
(VII of Scotland)	
William II and Mary II	1689
Anne	1702

The House of Hanover

George I	1714
George II	1727
George III	1760
George IV	1820
William IV	1830
Victoria	1837

The House of Saxe-Coburg

Edward VII	1901

The House of Windsor

George V	1910
Edward VIII	1936
George VI	1936
Elizabeth II	1952

him shaken and depressed), and when he learned he was suddenly to take the throne, he went to his mother, Queen Mary, and wept for an hour. No wonder it was rumored that George VI was too frail to survive the coronation ceremony.

But his very narrowness and humility turned out to be qualities that were once again in favor among the British people. George VI and his wife, the current **Queen Mother**, Elizabeth, provided Britain with a center of gravity during the grim days of World War II, remaining in Buckingham Palace even when London was being fractured by German bombs and refusing to send Princesses Elizabeth and Margaret out of the country. No wonder Adolf Hitler called her "the most dangerous woman in Europe." King George's family represented what the English wanted during these terrible years: a conscientious and principled king, a winning queen, and two likable young princesses, Elizabeth and Margaret.

Still thriving at 100 and recovered from replacement of her left hip two years ago, the Queen Mother has become a beloved national institution. The oldest living British royal ever, having surpassed Queen Victoria's granddaughter Princess Alice, her landmark birthday was the lead occasion for a "decades birthday" thrown by Queen Elizabeth. The black-tie ball, attended by 900 people, also commemorated other notable royal birthdays: Princess Margaret's seventieth, Princess Anne's fiftieth, and Prince Andrew's fortieth.

Adored for her approachability and cheerful mien, the QM was described by photographer Cecil Beaton as "the great mother figure and nanny of us all." A red-hot number in the '20s, she still likes "drinky-poos" (gin and tonic) before dinner, but she has never forgiven President Jimmy Carter for his shameful breach of etiquette: he kissed her on the lips.

London merchants have long been said to quake when they see her coming. It's not her taste in tulle, it's that she reportedly rarely pays her accounts. And she's still keen as a tack. Says one old friend about her wicked wit: "She doesn't take prisoners."

Born Lady Elizabeth Bowes-Lyon, the serenely beautiful young woman was the Diana of her day. But fearing life in the royal fishbowl, she twice rejected marriage proposals from the painfully shy, stammering Prince Albert, who called her "the most wonderful person in the world."

It is amazing that this five-foot-tall aristocrat, the last Empress of India and the honorary colonel of 18 regiments, who has probably never cooked a meal or made a bed, is considered "everybody's mum." But the festivities surrounding her ninetieth birthday in 1990 confirmed the devotion she has long inspired.

When King George, a heavy smoker, died of lung cancer in 1952 at the age of 57, his daughter **Elizabeth II** took up the scepter knowing that her main job would be to preserve the gains her parents had made. Admittedly, Elizabeth, a constitutional monarch who reigns but does not rule. Yet no one trifles with the 74-year-old woman known at Buckingham Palace as The Boss. Part of her power is ex officio: It is bad form to contradict Her Most Excellent Majesty, Elizabeth the Second, by the Grace of God, of the United Kingdom of Great Britain and Northern Ireland and of Her other Realms and Territories, Queen, Head of the Commonwealth, Defender of the Faith. It is also hard to disagree with someone whom *Fortune* magazine reckons as the world's richest woman (though her Web site maintains that "the Queen's wealth has often been greatly exaggerated").

But much of Elizabeth's authority arises from the immovable force of her character. This is the monarch who at 27 overrode the objections of advisers and ordered her coronation to be televised because, she said, "I have to be seen to be believed." And who continued to appear in public and ride in open cars after her husband's favorite uncle,

Lord Mountbatten, was assassinated by an IRA bomb in 1979. And who in 1982 coolly kept a disturbed intruder talking on the edge of her bed until she could summon help.

She grew up during the London blitz and matured in the ensuing period of auster-ity. The world's wealthiest woman still wanders around Buckingham Palace turning off lights. The heat is kept low and there are no objec-tions; there never are. And when one of her favorite dogs killed a hare, the Queen carefully picked it up and presented it to the kitchen staff. "We can eat this," she announced.

When Elizabeth II rings, a staff of 300 jumps. When she is in London, the prime minister calls on her every Tuesday to brief her on gov-ernment matters. Though not a quick study, Elizabeth is as-siduous, has a phenomenal

THE VULGAR SUBJECT OF MONEY

Loaded as they are, the Windsors prefer not to tarnish themselves so with money. They never carry cash, not a penny. And it's not because they carry American Express, instead. Elizabeth's famous pocketbook is a stage prop. It sometimes contains only mints for her horses. Other-wise, the Windsors come in contact with currency the way other people encounter God—mostly on Sundays. Before church, Charles is reportedly provided with a £5 note for the collection plate; he likes to have it sprayed and ironed by his valet, then neatly creased and left for him beneath his clove box. (You know, the box that holds your before-dinner clove. You probably have one around some-where.)

The Windsor wealth is complicated. A considerable portion is their own, acquired by them or their ancestors with personal funds. That would include San-dringham and Balmoral, two of the royal country estates, which they own the way the Cartwrights owned the Ponderosa. Both were purchased during Queen Vic-toria's reign. But the greater part of the wealth that surrounds them is held in trust for the nation. That means the Windsors can wear it, sit on it, eat off it, and go lightheartedly skipping down its glinting corridors. They just can't sew any name tags on it or cart it off to Christie's for auction.

If Britain should ever decide to get rid of the royal family, though, it would be a messy divorce. There's some confusion about which of their property belongs to the state and which is their own. In par-ticular, who rightly possesses the lavish gifts from foreign potentates? Like the 2,000-year-old necklace from Egypt's for-mer King Farouk?

And some of the royals' riches actually do benefit the public. It seems that Wind-sor Castle, their weekend residence, where construction began in the eleventh century, may be perched atop oil deposits worth an estimated $1 billion. Queen Elizabeth II has given a white-gloved thumbs-up for exploratory drilling on a site somewhere between the royal house-hold golf course and the royal household cricket ground. Any revenue generated will go directly to the Treasury.

By anyone's count, though, the total number is a whopper. *Fortune* magazine has calculated that the Queen is one of the richest people in the world. Recent accounts have reckoned her fortune at anywhere from $450 million to $16 billion (often depending upon whether one includes the property held in trust for the nation). Charles, meanwhile, was believed to be worth about $400 million as of 1991, which would still place him among Britain's 40 wealthiest people. To para-phrase Mel Brooks: It is good to be Queen.

memory, and often embarrasses ministers by knowing more about issues than they do.

Elizabeth's hold on her subjects begins with her family. When as a 13-year-old she met a dashing cadet, she instantly decided that he was Midshipman Right. Five years later she had not changed her mind, and so in 1947 she married **Prince Philip** of Greece, a great-great-grandchild of Queen Victoria. Queen Elizabeth and Prince Philip celebrated their golden wedding anniversary this year, reminding the world that marital happiness can indeed flourish in a royal family. The two attended a service of thanksgiving at Westminster Abbey, where they were married, and later celebrated the occasion with a garden party at Buckingham Palace. Four thousand couples also marking their fiftieth anniversary were invited to share in the revelry.

Although Elizabeth has inevitably dominated her husband in the public realm, in the world of the Windsor family the Duke of Edinburgh has had authority over educating the children: first Prince Charles and Princess Anne, later Princes Andrew and Edward. But Elizabeth's will is what holds the family and the royal public image together.

Her own image is not universally admired, at least from a fashion point of view. Dressing in a style that can be characterized as pseudo-frumpy, the queen stays out of the tabloids and gets her work done. While her hair is done every Monday at four p.m. by Charles Martyn, her hairdresser for the last two decades, she reads state papers and seldom glances in the mirror. Not everyone is happy about her diffidence. "I sometimes wish she had been a bit more of a clothes person," wistfully admits her couturier of four decades, Sir Hard Amies. "She doesn't care, basically. She listens to our advice, then goes off and wears shabby shoes because they're comfortable." But in fact Elizabeth does care about her appearance. Her outfits—the boxy, brightly colored clothes, clunky handbags, unfashionable reading glasses—are chosen with great deliberation to be unthreatening to women, unobtrusive to men, and easily seen by the crowds that line her path. If she were chic, she would be French, but this queen is British to her bones. That means a love of silver service and afternoon tea, bland food, sweetish wine, jigsaw puzzles, Dick Francis mysteries, and, most of all, tramps in the country amid her Thoroughbreds and her dogs. The Queen herself feeds her six corgis and two dorgis (a mix of dachshund and corgi), cutting up their meat and mixing it with biscuits in their separate bowls set out every afternoon by a footman.

No one takes better care of business than Her Majesty, who has long since realized that her maritally vexed offspring have created a throne-threatening PR problem for the House of Windsor. At the close of 1992, in a now-famous speech, she noted, "It has turned out to be an *annus horribilis*." If not the language of the common man, it was certainly a sentiment commonly understood. And things got even more horrible a few days after that speech. On the Queen's forty-fifth wedding anniversary, a fire gutted a corner of Windsor Castle, causing damages of up to $60 million. As a debate brewed over who should bear the cost of repairs, Elizabeth, with her unerring sense for image damage control, proclaimed that she would give up a centuries-old royal perk by commencing to pay income tax on her private fortune, as well as pony up $8.5 million toward refurbishing the castle. In 1996 she went one step further, opening 19 state rooms in Buckingham Palace to public tours (leaving 631 rooms still off-limits) while she and the family were taking their annual summer retreat to Balmoral.

Perhaps to counteract an image of the royals as freeloaders, the Queen set up a secret committee in 1996 to consider several astonishing reforms to the monarchy. The most startling change is already in effect. The "Family Firm" pays their own way with the $90 million earned annually from their estates, rather than collecting $12.75 million per year from taxpayers as they did in the past. The Queen tightened the belt even further last year, cutting $8 million in costs for travel and the upkeep of the Windsor's eight palaces, as part of continuing efforts to make the monarchy less expensive, more open, and more modern. Other proposals include streamlining the royal family to include only the monarch, the consort, and the children; lifting the 295-year-old ban on royals marrying Catholics; and severing the formal links with the Church of England. Many of these progressive suggestions need Parliament's stamp of approval, however, and British politicians' reluctance to tamper with tradition means that the Queen's proposals may remain just that for some time to come. And, on her own initiative, the Queen pronounced an end to compulsory bowing and curtsying (though they're still appreciated).

Despite her attempts to set things straight with the monarchy, Elizabeth has often been unpopular. In response to public outcry, she appeared on live television in an unprecedented effort to share her family's grief over the death of Princess Diana. And within eight months the Queen could be found on her first official foray ever to a pub (during a tour of Devon) and riding in a taxi (another first, to promote environmentally friendly liquefied petroleum fuel). Last year she started a Web site, which received over 12.5 million visits in its first two months, and she now has a highly-paid communications director on her staff.

Though her popularity with the people took a hit when Diana died, Elizabeth's resolve rarely wavers, and she is always fully aware of her royal responsibilities. As former prime minister Margaret Thatcher said in a televised program screened on the Queen's seventieth birthday, "She is the most conscientious lady. Whatever duty requires, she will do and will go on doing for the rest of her days." The Queen's biographer Ben Pimlott notes, "The monarchy provides the social glue that binds people together." And as the headlines of the past year show, even if they no longer rule the waves, the royals still serve a purpose, and "people remain enormously interested in all things royal."

THE SON ALSO RISES: THE YOUNG WINDSORS

When **Charles, the Prince of Wales**, walked beside his two sons; his father, Duke of Edinburgh; and his former brother-in-law, Charles, Earl Spencer; behind Princess Diana's cortege, savvy observers noticed something extraordinary: The future King of England, usually a pillar of protocol, had parted with tradition by wearing a blue Savile Row suit to the funeral. It was neither a symbol of disrespect nor a fickle fashion statement. Rather, says royal author Brian Hoey, "It was Diana's favorite blue suit, and she helped him choose it. She preferred him in blue [rather] than black or gray. It was a lovely, silent compliment to her."

The windsurfing-parachuting-scuba-diving Action Prince of the 1970s and the oratorical Philosopher Prince of the 1980s had morphed from the Self-absorbed Prince of the early 1990s. Finally, perhaps, Charles might be finding his true colors. His comportment in the aftermath of Diana's death—tearfully receiving the coffin in France, tenderly consoling his sons, distraughtly walking alone in the misty Scottish highlands outside Balmoral—went a long way toward softening his image as the poster boy for royal stoics, and he is now becoming less formal with his public as well.

Routinely derided as both parent and public figure, he has never quite managed to capture the public's heart, though polls have shown him to be Charles is more popular now than he was before Diana's death. "Charles was eclipsed by Diana's dazzle," says Peter Archer, the royals correspondent for the British Press Association. "Now people are taking notice [of him again]."

It's also possible—even likely—that Diana's death has changed him. We've now seen Charles as a doting father, devoted to helping his sons bear the loss of their mother. He may never match Diana in public displays of affection, but at least there have been some, which has been notable. Charles does have much in common with his sons: Both boys are avid huntsmen who love the country life Charles favors, and they are now showing interest in the artistic pursuits that delight their dad. For his part, Charles has indulged in kid-friendly outings, something we never used to see.

The prince has also taken steps to make a place for longtime love Camilla Parker Bowles in his family life. In early 1999 the two made their first public appearance as a couple, exiting the Ritz Hotel after attending a party for Camilla's sister Annabel Elliott's birthday before a crowd of hundreds of photog-

raphers. The next day approving commentary on the milestone dominated Britain's news, and the pair made two more public appearances over the next eight days. Now, though, spottings of the two are less notable occasions.

Getting Britons to *support* the union is another matter, though. Polls show the public still strongly opposed to any formal union. The Queen had not formally met Camilla until a brief encounter earlier in the year, but she was not invited to the "decade birthdays" celebration thrown at Windsor Castle in July (though her ex-husband, Andrew Parker Bowles, the Queen Mother's godson, was in attendance).

Charles will likely continue to take his cue from his mother, as he has for years. From his early childhood at Buckingham Palace, the Queen's eldest son learned that duty always came before pleasure. Until he was 32 years old he lived at home with his parents. Then he found a lovely bride and promptly fulfilled his duty to beget heirs.

Now all he can do is wait for his mother to pass him the scepter. And some newspaper articles have depicted his relations with "Mummy" as chronically strained. Meanwhile, Elizabeth is ticking away better than Big Ben, and Charles could end up like his great-great-grandfather King Edward VII, who held the title of Prince of Wales for almost 60 years before his mother, Queen Victoria, passed away.

So much of Charles's behavior, however, is a matter of upbringing and thankless experience. Just weeks after entering the world as heir to the throne in 1948, he was left in the care of nannies while his parents performed their endless royal duties. "There's a famous old photo," says royal author Anthony Holden, "of the Queen arriving home on a train after a coronation tour and greeting her mother and sister [Princess Margaret] with a kiss, then greeting Charles, who was about 4 years old, with a handshake and straightening his collar. That tells the whole story."

In 1971, a year after graduating from Trinity College in Cambridge, the prince enlisted in the Royal Navy, where he served for five years flying helicopters and serving on frigates. Already, at a polo match in the early '70s, he had met Camilla Shand, whose great-grandmother Alice Keppel, had had an affair with Edward VII. Though they hit it off immediately, Camilla, reportedly having no interest in marrying Charles and becoming a public figure, wed cavalry officer Andrew Parker Bowles in 1973.

During the subsequent years, Charles has contributed eloquently and

provocatively to the public discourse on the preservation of architecture, the environment, and the language. In 1997 he even fulfilled the grand though slightly depressing role of handing over Hong Kong and its 6.5 million imperial subjects to the Chinese government. That June the prince joined Chinese president Jiang Zemin at a transition ceremony that marked a symbolic sunset over the British empire.

Preparing to ascend to the throne, however, wasn't enough to keep together his marriage with **Lady Diana Spencer**. In his diaries of 1986 and 1987, as reported in *The Prince of Wales*, an authorized biography by Jonathan Dimbleby, he wrote, "How awful incompatibility is…I never thought it would end up like this. How could I have got it all so wrong?"

As the world celebrated that fairy-tale marriage—seen by millions worldwide on July 29, 1981—the seeds of its failure began to become apparent. While the couple was touring Portugal in February 1987, photographers started to notice the first signs of marital strain—topped off by the pair taking separate suites at a palace in Lisbon.

Royal watchers maintain Prince Philip had urged his son to marry a quiet girl and produce an heir. Charles, though less cynical, certainly married a girl—and, at 20, 12 years his junior, that's what she was—for whom he

was ill-suited. In December 1992 the Prince and Princess of Wales announced an official separation that finally ended the long charade of their once idealized marriage.

Shortly thereafter, the last hope of a happy ending quickly faded. A racy taped phone chat between Prince Charles and his then confidante and current love interest, Camilla Parker Bowles, was published worldwide. Charles revealed, among other steamy things, his surprising desire to live inside her "trousers or something." He purportedly declared his love for her and gushed, "In the next life, I should like to come back as your knickers."

Then came new revelations of a sexually charged phone conversation in which Diana discussed with *her* confidant, James Gilbey, her fear of getting pregnant. So in December 1993, when the tearful princess announced that she was greatly curtailing her public life, it appeared that the Palace had finally succeeded in reining her in.

"The dream is over. The people's darling will never become queen," proclaimed columnist John Casey in the *Evening Standard*.

In 1994, the second year of their official separation, the union of the prince and princess seemed to unspool with a special savagery and at indecent length in every possible medium. Worse, Charles and the House of Windsor itself seemed to lose in the process the public sympathy they so desperately tried to engender. The fire was fueled by the principals themselves, cooperating with unseemly disclosures and partisan biographies about lovers old and new, alienation of feelings, eating disorders, and suicide attempts. Caught in this murderous crossfire, Charles and Diana found themselves the villains of a klieg-lit reality that had finally, and sadly, overtaken the soft-focus fairy tale. In August of 1996, after much wrangling on both sides, the fairy tale legally ended in divorce.

Struggling to overcome his image as the diffident twit who allowed his marriage to founder, the prince rolled up his sleeves and wrestled with the demon of publicity. Charles maintained that he remained faithful to Diana "until it became clear that the marriage had irretrievably broken down." (But another '94 tome, *Camilla: The King's Mistress,* claims that Charles spent the night before his wedding with Parker Bowles.)

In January 1995, Camilla and her husband, Andrew, abandoned the charade that their union was intact, ending their 21-year marriage. Palace insiders were convinced that Charles's startling confessions and Camilla's split were part of an elaborate long-range plan designed to bring their 25-year relationship out of the shadows—and set the stage for another royal marriage.

Prince William in his final days at Eton.

Before Diana's death, Queen Elizabeth herself demanded that the prince scrap his dream of marrying Parker Bowles, warning him that it could cost him the throne. And in the aftermath of her tragic accident, it appeared highly unlikely that he could marry Camilla in the foreseeable future without deeply offending public opinion.

But now Diana's longtime rival is using the front door again. You've got to hand it to her: Over the past six years, Parker Bowles has been condemned, resurrected, and buried again. Yet she has come through it all with her humor and patience intact.

While marriage is still highly uncertain, Charles's place as future sovereign appears far more secure. "Absolutely, he will be king if he outlives his mother," says Hoey. "There's no question of William bypassing him. William wouldn't want it, the Queen wouldn't want it, and I don't think the country would want it. It's his destiny."

Diana had begun with one overriding duty—to produce an heir, preferably male.

And she was fortunate enough within two years of her marriage to produce two towheads (known as the heir and the spare), to whom she referred proudly, proprietarily, as "my boys." Demonstrative where Charles was reserved, preferring fun to formality, she gave **Prince William**, 18, and **Prince Harry**, 16, a sense of childhood that no Windsor would have or could have. By all accounts, William, who lives with the burden of being Charles's heir, felt the pain of his parents breakup, and his mother's death, most acutely. "William already hates press photographers," says Judy Wade, a royals reporter. "This will deepen any anger he has." Harry has seemed positively ebullient on public outings.

William, the boy who seems destined to be king, is leaving childhood behind. A rambunctious toddler who grew into a reserved primary-schooler, he has been learning to cope with the peculiar demands of royal life. He must prepare for a role that will become more public over time, and one that will expose his every misstep. Upon the urging of his grandfather, Wills entered Eton, one of England's most exclusive public (meaning "private") schools, the first heir to the British throne to do so. The school has been educational home to many British luminaries since 1440, including Gladstone, Pitt the Elder, and 18 other prime ministers.

In his final year he was both a prefect and captain of the swim team. Having graduated recently, he is now enjoying his "gap year," the find-yourself pre-college break that is de rigueur for upper-class Brits. Next year he'll start college at St. Andrews University in Scotland. Brother Harry remains at Eton.

Taller than his father at 6' 1½", William has grown into a thoughtful young man with a strong sense of duty and little of the Windsors' emotional detachment. "When you discover you can give joy to people…there is nothing quite like it," Diana once told *The New Yorker*. "William has begun to understand that, too. And I am hoping it will grow in him." Though William could, as one royal watcher suggested half-seriously years ago, "decide to go backpacking in Nepal and not come back," that doesn't seem likely. After all, he is—and always will be—his mother's son. "He knows how much Diana would want him to do the job he was born to do," says Lord Jeffrey Archer, a close friend of Diana's. "He will be conscious of that and, in her memory, do it even better."

Now William's grief is giving way to good times. An excellent student (he won Eton's Sword of Honour, given to the best all-around cadet), he also clocked the school's best times since 1987 in the 50- and 100-meter junior freestyle swims. As avid a country sportsman

as his father, he'll be "shooting anything that moves, fishing in the icy River Dee, having what passes for a picnic with footmen serving him," says Brian Hoey.

Now that the fair-haired prince has turned 18, he is bidding farewell to his cosseted boyhood. Though convention dictates that he be addressed as "Your Royal Highness," he has insisted that all continue calling him plain William for the moment. He can also expect heightened intrusions into his privacy by the world's rough-and-tumble tabloids, which until now have observed a hands-off policy toward the future king. Despite his dislike of media attention, William did agree to mark his recent coming-of-age by releasing written answers to questions submitted by a press representative.

He likes action movies, casual clothes, and dancing. He also shares the royals' love of horses and has said previously that he loves to read, particularly action-adventure fiction and nonfiction.

But much as he tries, this is no average kid, from his mom's sapphire eyes and his striking physique to the constant companionship of bodyguards. "William's shoes are always so shiny, his trousers well-pressed," marvels an Eton bookshop owner. "He looks different from the others." Royals author Judy Wade says, "He has replaced his mother as the royal star" and he's not sure he likes it.

"William has a hard time with public exposure, let alone being a teenager's pinup," she notes.

William is clearly being schooled in the ways of a future monarch. He regularly visited his grandmother at Windsor Castle, across the Thames from Eton. "The Queen is determined there will be no mistakes with his upbringing or career development," says Hoey. "He's the hope for the future."

Diana, of course, dreamed of nothing less for her son. "She always used to say she wanted William to be happy, and it's quite clear she wanted him to be king," says Archer.

Diana and Charles were not the only royals having trouble making peace with the idea of separate households. Hitched for 16 years, Charles's younger sister, **Princess Anne**, and Captain Mark Phillips were initially drawn together by their passion for horses (both are extraordinary equestrians: Phillips coached America's Olympic team in 1996). But Anne's interests were much broader—she is president of the Save the Children Fund and was even nominated for the Nobel Peace Prize a few years back. Last year she was the royal family's busiest member, clocking 679 official engagements. Says Anne of her work, "You have to decide at the end of the day if you can live with yourself."

You also have to decide if you can live with your husband, and the affirmative

answer increasingly came into doubt. The couple finally separated in 1989, and after divorcing, Anne married long-time love Timothy Laurence, five years her junior, in 1992. As close to her mother as any of her siblings, Anne staged her second wedding as an intimate family affair, attended by only a handful of relatives, including her two children with Phillips, **Peter** and **Zara**. A university student, Peter currently serves as a sporty, down-to-earth role model for William, while his bubbly sister "loves to tease William and make him blush, which he does easily," says Hoey. "She has a wonderful ability to deflate egos."

Anne's second brother, rowdy **Prince Andrew, Duke of York**, has had his fair share of marital bad luck as well. After a plucky performance in the Falklands conflict, helicopter pilot Andy seemed interested mainly in oat-sowing and club-crawling with a string of steamy ladies, culminating with former soft-porn star Koo Stark. What well-bred English girl would marry Andrew and put up with him?

And so, when the prince's roving eye fell upon Sarah Ferguson in 1985, the nation breathed a collective sigh of relief. A strapping, worldly wench who loved a good time, Fergie seemed perfectly suited to her happy-go-lucky hubby. But while **Sarah, Duchess of York**,

produced two lovely daughters, **Princesses Beatrice** and **Eugenie**, she also committed gaffe after gaffe. If the Yorks often struck the public as a pair of heedless hedonists, at least they originally seemed besotted with each other. But Fergie's erratic behavior quickly brought that into doubt as well. After a series of romantic trysts and crass missteps on her part, the duchess was formally separated from the duke in 1992. Later that year London tabs were abrim with graphic photos of Fergie on the Riviera cavorting topless with her American-born "financial adviser," John Bryan, who was shown smooching the bare instep of her foot while her young daughters looked on. She later confessed that the publication of those photos had been her "most humiliating experience."

Fergie was left scrambling to settle debts reaching more than $6 million by selling off the rights to her children's cartoon character, Budgie the Helicopter, opening a cable television channel, hosting a documentary in the Australian outback, and launching her own perfume.

No stranger to the ups and downs of yo-yo diets, Fergie is well qualified for her current $1.7 million-a-year stint as a Weight Watchers spokeswoman, sharing such confessions as: "My problem, you see, is the bum. My daughters say, 'Give us your wiggle, Mummy.'"

A ROYAL CALENDAR

A listing of birthdays and other special royal milestones. (Source: *Whitaker's Almanac*)

Lady Wessex (Sophie)	January 20, 1965
Prince Andrew	February 19, 1960
Prince Edward	March 10, 1964
Princess Eugenie	March 23, 1990
Queen Elizabeth	April 21, 1926
The Queen's coronation	June 2, 1953
Prince Philip	June 10, 1921
Prince William	June 21, 1982
Queen Mother	August 4, 1900
Princess Beatrice	August 8, 1988
Princess Anne	August 15, 1950
Princess Margaret	August 21, 1930
Prince Henry	September 15, 1984
Duchess of York (Sarah)	October 15, 1959
Prince Charles	November 14, 1948
The Queen's wedding	November 20, 1947

As she admitted on the *Oprah Winfrey Show*, "I was never cut out for royalty." But she is cut out for celebrity. Her newest role is a stint as a London-based correspondent for the *Today* show in the U.S.

In 1996 the Yorks finally decided to split officially, contending that, unlike the Waleses, their decision was "theirs alone," and not precipitated by a letter from the Queen. According to court insiders, however, Andrew and Fergie are still the closest of friends. They lived on separate floors of Andrew's mansion, Sunninghill, for years and even now that Fergie lives in nearby Birch Hall (which the Queen helped purchase), "We have breakfast, lunch, tea, and dinner together," Fergie told *Hello!*, calling her ex "a great man."

Prince Edward, Elizabeth's youngest, had his turn in the headlines last year, as he wed Sophie Rhys-Jones in a ceremony that seemed designed to prove the royals aren't so different from the rest of us.

Instead of a fairy-tale confection, Sophie looked tanned and slim (she had reportedly lost some 10 pounds) and wore a sleek, sophisticated coat dress in ivory silk inlaid with 325,000 beads by designer Samantha Shaw, along with a black-and-white pearl necklace designed by her fiancé. Of the 560 guests, most were friends and relatives of the couple, not other crowned heads or dignitaries.

Newly titled the Earl and Countess of Wessex by the Queen, the couple took only an abbreviated honeymoon. As a pal of Edward's noted, "They're busy people."

Which is what those who know them believe will help make this a lasting union. Though she bears a passing resemblance to the late Diana, Sophie Wessex, as she is known professionally, has continued her PR work. "The royal family [is] doing an exceptional job in the public role," she told the BBC. "I don't see a massive need for me to do the same thing."

An unsurprising characterization from the woman who married the first child of a reigning monarch to—*gulp*—take a real job. Initially employed as a gofer with Andrew Lloyd Webber's Really Useful Theatre Company and eventually rising to overseas manager of *Cats* and *Starlight Express*, Edward left Webber's company and now is joint managing director of a television production company, Ardent Productions. His company produced a game show featuring off-color jokes about his mother, and he lobbied to market the television rights to his wedding but was turned down by the Queen. Currently, he is producing a TV movie about the Queen Mother for NBC. Loyal to his dreams as well as the British ideal of monarchy, the Queen's youngest child is, ran one editorial, "on the way to becoming the first really modern royal."

Edward's fascination with the theater is hardly unusual among the Windsors. Indeed, if the family reigned in Beverly Hills instead of Westminster, the Queen's younger sister, **Princess Margaret**, would be the family's Elizabeth Taylor. She has been onstage since age six, when she had a walk-on part in her father's coronation. With her theatrical props—a tortoiseshell cigarette holder, a tumbler of Famous Grouse whiskey, and a circle of intimates in the arts—the princess has played varied roles: tragic lover, wife, mother, divorcée, and regal grand dame. She emanates star quality, complete with romantic intrigues, erratic public behavior, mysterious health problems, and Sunset Boulevard brass. "I can't imagine anything more wonderful," she once said, "than being who I am."

Precocious and irrepressible as a child, the violet-eyed and theatrical Margaret wrapped George VI around her finger. Other men proved harder to keep. As a teenager she fell hard for a dashing fighter pilot, Peter Townsend, 16 years her senior, but finally passed him up at 22 when her union with the divorced Townsend was declared acceptable only if she would give up her claim to the throne and her royal income and if she would spend five years abroad.

Several years later Margaret walked the aisle with photographer Antony Armstrong-Jones (who became **Lord Snowdon** after the wedding). She produced two children with the artistic commoner: **David (Viscount Linley)** and **Lady Sarah Armstrong-Jones**. But their 18-year marriage was not a picture-book affair. Initially rejecting separation as too scandalous, both partners discreetly sizzled with old and new flames until the tabs ran pictures of Margaret and her lover Roddy Llewellyn, a gardener and wannabe pop singer 17 years her junior. An uncontested divorce was granted in 1978.

But Margaret's son, David, did his part to show the happy side of royal life—his marriage in 1993 to Serena Stanhope, a blue blood with cover-girl looks, was a windfall for the monarchy, and their lavish nuptials at St. Margaret's Church were billed as the Wedding of the Year, drawing 650 guests.

Though Margaret suffered a mild stroke last year at a party in Barbados, she does not appear to show any lasting effects—she was in a wheelchair at Edward's wedding, but that was because she had scalded her feet in the bathtub.

As comfortable as the lives of the Windsors seem, ultimately being royal carries with it an incalculable personal price tag. Family members live with constant world scrutiny. And it is an irony of their station that even though they live their whole lives in public, they can barely speak their minds there. But the true value of the royal family lies in the realm of patriotic lumps in the throat. They have, at least until now, given Britain a symbol of nationhood.

SUCCESSION: THE BUCK HOUSE BULLPEN

Under rules codified in the eighteenth century, rightful candidates to the British crown move up inexorably except for two disqualifiers: They cannot be Catholic (or marry into that faith) or be born out of wedlock. Unlike some European monarchies, which abide by the centuries-old Salic law—the exclusion of women from succession—the Court of St. James owes its vitality in great part to females. Victoria and the current queen, for instance, are two of history's longest-reigning sovereigns. This is not to say that Britain's accession rules are not sexist: A monarch is succeeded by his or her eldest son, then by that son's sons in descending order of age, and only then by that son's daughters. The line starts again with the monarch's next youngest son, and so on, ending with the sovereign's daughters and their children. After the offspring are accounted for, the sovereign's brothers come next, followed finally by sisters. From there the line marches through uncles, aunts, and full courts of cousins, including two newborn members of the clan.

Here are the top 25 in the royal bullpen:

1. HRH The Prince of Wales, 52
   (Prince Charles)
2. HRH Prince William of Wales, 18
   (son of Prince Charles)
3. HRH Prince Henry of Wales, 16
   (second son of Prince Charles)
4. HRH The Duke of York (Prince Andrew), 40
   (second son of Queen Elizabeth)
5. HRH Princess Beatrice of York, 12
   (daughter of Prince Andrew)
6. HRH Princess Eugenie of York, 10
   (second daughter of Prince Andrew)
7. HRH Prince Edward, 36
   (third son of Queen Elizabeth)
8. HRH The Princess Royal (Princess Anne), 50
   (daughter of Queen Elizabeth)
9. Peter Phillips, 23
   (the highest-ranking commoner, son of Princess Anne)
10. Zara Phillips, 19
    (daughter of Princess Anne)
11. HRH Princess Margaret, Countess of Snowdon, 70
    (sister of Queen Elizabeth)
12. Viscount Linley (David), 39
    (son of Princess Margaret)
13. Charles Patrick Inigo Armstrong–Jones, 1
    (son of Viscount Linley)
14. Lady Sarah Chatto, 36
    (daughter of Princess Margaret)
15. Samuel David Benedict Chatto, 4
    (son of Lady Sarah Chatto)
16. Arthur David Nathaniel Chatto, 1
    (son of Lady Sarah Chatto)
17. HRH The Duke of Gloucester, 56
    (grandson of King George V, Queen Elizabeth's cousin)
18. The Earl of Ulster (Alexander), 26
    (son of the Duke of Gloucester)
19. Lady Davina Windsor, 23
    (daughter of the Duke of Gloucester)
20. Lady Rose Windsor, 20
    (second daughter of the Duke of Gloucester)
21. HRH The Duke of Kent (Edward), 65
    (cousin to both Queen Elizabeth and Prince Philip and son of George, Duke of Kent, younger brother of Kings Edward VII and George VI)
22. Edward Windsor, Baron Downpatrick, 12
    (son of the Duke of Kent's eldest son, the Earl of St. Andrews, who was dropped from the line when he married a Catholic)
23. Lady Marina Windsor, 8
    (daughter of the Earl of St. Andrews)
24. Lady Amelia Windsor, 5
    (second daughter of the Earl of St. Andrews)
25. Lord Nicholas Windsor, 30
    (second son of the Duke of Kent)

ROYAL HOUSES AROUND THE WORLD

Though they rarely get the tabloid treatment of their British counterparts, less conspicuous royals do reign throughout the world. Here's an international round-up of the places where the crown still glitters.

BELGIUM

Current monarch: King Albert II (crowned 1993)

King Albert II, prince of Liège, was born on June 6, 1934. He is the son of King Leopold III and Queen Astrid, born princess of Sweden, and the brother of the late King Baudouin of Belgium.

The Royal Family:

King Albert II was married to Paola Ruffo di Calabria, the daughter of a princely Italian family, in 1959. The king and queen have three children: Prince Philippe (b. 1960), Princess Astrid (b. 1962), who is now married to the Archduke Lorenz of East Austria, and Prince Laurent (b. 1963). The royal palace is in Brussels.

DENMARK

Current monarch: Queen Margrethe II (crowned 1972)

Margrethe Alexandrine Thorhildur Ingrid, the eldest daughter of King Frederik IX and Queen Ingrid of Denmark, was born on April 16, 1940.

The Royal Family:

Margrethe married French diplomat Henri-Marie-Jean-André, count de Laborde de Monpezat, in 1967 (he changed his name to Prince Henrik upon marriage). The queen and consort have two sons, Prince Frederik (b. 1968) and Prince Joachim (b. 1969; married in 1995 to Princess Alexandra). Crown Prince Frederik, as the official heir to the Danish throne, will eventually become King Frederik X. Besides the official residence in Copenhagen, the family also has a small mansion in southern France at Cahors, the home district of Prince Henrik.

JAPAN

Current monarch: Emperor Akihito (crowned 1989)

Born on December 23, 1933, Emperor Akihito is the eldest son of the late Emperor Hirohito (posthumously known as Emperor Showa) and Empress Nagako.

The Royal Family:

Emperor Akihito married Michiko Shoda in 1959. She is the eldest daughter of the Shoda family, a prominent name in Japanese industrial and academic circles. The emperor and empress live in the imperial palace in Tokyo, and they have three children: Crown Prince Naruhito (b. 1960; married in 1993 to Crown Princess Masako amid much public attention), Prince Akishino (b. 1965; married in 1990 to Princess Kiko), and Princess Sayako (b. 1969).

LIECHTENSTEIN

Current monarch: Prince Hans Adam II (crowned 1989)

His Serene Highness Prince Hans Adam II is the eldest son of the late Prince Franz Josef II of Liechtenstein and Countess Gina von Wilczek. He was born on February 14, 1945.

The Princial Family:

Hans Adam II married Countess Marie Kinsky von Wchinitz and Tettau of Prague in 1967. The couple has four children: Crown Prince Alois (b. 1968; married to Duchess Sophie of Bavaria in 1993; son Joseph Wenzel Maximilian Maria b. 1995; daughter Marie Caroline Immaculata b. 1996), Prince Maximilian (b. 1969), Prince Constantin (b. 1972), and Princess Tatjana (b. 1973). The royal family resides in the Vaduz Castle.

LUXEMBOURG

Current monarch: Grand Duke Jean (crowned 1964)

Grand Duke Jean was born on January 5, 1921. He is the eldest son of the late Grand Duchess Charlotte and Prince Felix of Luxembourg, prince of Bourbon Parma.

The Royal Family:

Grand Duke Jean was married to Princess Joséphine-Charlotte of Belgium in 1953. She is the daughter of Prince Leopold of Belgium and Princess Astrid of Sweden, and the sister of the late King Baudouin of Belgium. The royal couple resides in the Castle of Colmar-Berg in Luxembourg, and they have five children: Princess Marie-Astrid (b. 1954), Prince Henri (b. 1955; the hereditary grand duke of Luxembourg), Prince Jean and his twin sister Princess Margaretha (b. 1957), and Prince Guillaume (b. 1963).

MONACO

Current monarch: Prince Rainier III (crowned 1949)

The Sovereign Prince of Monaco and head of the House of Grimaldi, Prince Rainier III, was born on May 31, 1923. He is the grandson of the late Prince Louis II of Monaco and the son of Princess Charlotte and Prince Pierre, count of Polignac.

The Royal Family:

Prince Rainier III married American actress Grace Kelly (1929–1982) in 1956. She was the daughter of John B. and Margaret Kelly of Philadelphia. The couple had three children: Princess Caroline (b. 1957), married to Prince Ernst August of Hanover; Crown Prince Albert (b. 1958); and Princess Stephanie (b. 1965; married in 1995 to her French-born former bodyguard Daniel Ducruet, 32; now divorced). The Princely Palace is located on the Rock of Monaco, and the family owns a private residence in Paris.

THE NETHERLANDS

Current monarch: Queen Beatrix (crowned 1980)

Beatrix Wilhemina Armgard was born on January 31, 1938, the first child of Queen Juliana and Prince Bernhard of the Netherlands.

The Royal Family:

Queen Beatrix was married to a German diplomat, Claus van Amsberg, prince of the Netherlands, in 1966, and the royal couple now resides in the Huis ten Bosch Palace in the Hague. The queen and prince have three sons: Prince Willem-Alexander Claus Georg Ferdinand (b. 1967), Prince Johan Friso Bernhard Christiaan David (b. 1968), and Prince Constantijn Christof Frederik Aschwin (b. 1969).

NORWAY

Current monarch: King Harald (crowned 1991)

Born on February 21, 1937, King Harald is the firstborn son of the late King Olav V and Princess Märtha.

The Royal Family:

The announcement that King Harald was to marry commoner Sonja Haraldsen in 1968 triggered much debate about the future of the Norwegian monarchy. Since their marriage, however, Queen Sonja has been accepted by the public. The king and queen, who reside in the royal palace in Oslo, have a daughter, Princess Märtha Louise (b. 1971), and a son, Crown Prince Haakon (b. 1973).

SPAIN

Current monarch: King Juan Carlos (crowned 1975)

Juan Carlos de Borbón y Borbón was born on January 5, 1938. He is the first son of Don Juan de Borbón y Battenberg and Doña María de las Mercedes de Borbón y Orleans, and the grandson of King Alfonso XIII and Queen Victoria Eugenia, who was herself the granddaughter of Queen Victoria of England.

The Royal Family:

King Juan Carlos married Princess Sofía, the daughter of King Paul I and Queen Fredericka of Greece, in 1962. The king and queen have three children: Princess Elena (b. 1963), Princess Cristina (b. 1965), and Crown Prince Felipe (b. 1968). Princess Elena, second in line for the throne, married banker Jaime de Marichalar, 31, in March 1995. It was Spain's first royal wedding since 1906. The Palacio de La Zarzuela, the family's official residence, is situated five kilometers outside of Madrid. Their summer residence, the Palace of Marivent, is in the city of Palma de Mallorca on the island of Mallorca.

SWEDEN

Current monarch: Carl XVI Gustaf (crowned 1973)

Carl XVI Gustaf was born on April 30, 1946, the youngest child and only son of hereditary Prince Gustaf Adolf of Sweden and Princess Sibylla of Sachsen-Coburg-Gotha.

The Royal Family:

Carl XVI Gustaf married commoner Silvia Renate Sommerlath, daughter of Walther and Alice Sommerlath of the Federal Republic of Germany, in 1976. The king and queen have three children: Princess Victoria (b. 1977), Prince Carl Philip (b. 1979), and Princess Madeleine (b. 1982). In 1980 the Swedish act of succession was changed to allow females the same rights of succession as males; the crown passes to the eldest child regardless of sex. Thus, eldest daughter Victoria has been named the crown princess and successor to Carl XVI Gustaf. The family lived in the royal palace in Stockholm until 1981, when they moved to Drottningholm Palace on the outskirts of the city.

SCREEN

PICKS & PANS 2000

Leo hit *The Beach,* Mel was both *Patriot* and *Chicken,* and Sandra spent *28 Days* in rehab. Here's the year in film as seen by PEOPLE critic Leah Rozen and, where noted, senior writer Tom Gliatto [TG]. Asterisks mark their top choices.

THE ADVENTURES OF ROCKY AND BULLWINKLE
Robert De Niro, Jason Alexander, Rene Russo, Piper Perabo, Randy Quaid
Miscalculated would be a polite word for this tedious adaptation. (PG)

ALICE AND MARTIN
Juliet Binoche, Alexis Loret
This painful family drama lumbers on and on. [TG] (R)

ALL I WANNA DO
Gaby Hoffmann, Kirsten Dunst, Rachael Leigh Cook, Heather Matarazzo
A group of smart, rebellious adolescent girls protest when their snooty boarding school threatens to go coed. A boisterously amusing coming-of-age tale set just before the dawn of '60s feminism. (PG-13)

* ALMOST FAMOUS
Billy Crudup, Kate Hudson, Frances McDormand, Jason Lee, Patrick Fugit, Philip Seymour Hoffman
Writer-director Cameron Crowe (*Jerry Maguire*), has turned (and slightly fictionalized) his own story about coming of age at the end of the Age of Aquarius as a teen journalist on the road reporting for *Rolling Stone* into the best, most appealing movie of his already noteworthy career (his output includes *Say Anything* and *Singles*). (R)

AMERICAN PIMP
Documentary
Provocative documentary by brothers Albert and Allen Hughes (*Dead Presidents*) allows chest-thumping pimps to brag about being alternative businessmen. (Not rated)

AMERICAN PSYCHO
Christian Bale, Chloë Sevigny
It is thanks entirely to director-coscripter Mary Harron that the sicko novel turns into a satire on narcissism and consumerism run amok in the '80s. Her take keeps *Psycho* almost amusing for its first third—then it thins out badly. (R)

THE ART OF WAR
Wesley Snipes, Anne Archer, Donald Sutherland
This inept and interminable action flick makes those ho-hum Steven Seagal and Jean-Claude Van Damme movies look like Oscar contenders. Maybe it's time for Snipes, who squanders his talent here, to forget about saving the world with this action-hero thing. (R)

AUTUMN IN NEW YORK
Richard Gere, Winona Ryder
They don't make 'em like they used to, and this romantic tearjerker proves that maybe it's time to stop trying. (PG-13)

BATTLEFIELD EARTH
John Travolta, Barry Pepper
Incoherent, ugly, and pointless. (PG-13)

THE BEACH
Leonardo DiCaprio, Virginie Ledoyen
A footloose American discovers a tropical Eden, occupied by a motley international community of dropouts. *The Beach* has no feel whatever for creating characters, and it never establishes an identity of its own. (R)

BEYOND THE MAT
Mick "Mankind" Foley
This affectionate if bloody documentary looks at the grandly masochistic careers and unspectacular domestic lives of pro wrestlers. (R)

THE BIG KAHUNA
Kevin Spacey, Danny DeVito, Peter Facinelli
Three salesmen, holed up in a hospitality suite in a hotel in Wichita, Kans., wait to sweet-talk prospective customers (big kahunas) into industrial lubricants. Despite showy performances, this talky drama about lives and lies never transcends its static, stage-bound roots. (R)

BIG MOMMA'S HOUSE
Martin Lawrence
The star comic in a dress. No more, no less. (PG-13)

THE BIG TEASE
Craig Ferguson, Frances Fisher, Mary McCormack
A mildly amusing mockumentary about the misadventures that beset a Scottish hairdresser when he travels from Glasgow to Los Angeles for a prestigious styling competition. (R)

BLESS THE CHILD
Kim Basinger, Jimmy Smits, Christina Ricci, Rufus Sewell
A young saint in the making is kidnapped and threatened with death by a Satanic cult. The thrills are cheap and unearned. (R)

*BOILER ROOM
Giovanni Ribisi, Vin Diesel, Ben Affleck, Ron Rifkin, Nia Long, Nicky Katt
A timely, compelling drama about young would-be financial whizzes who toil at a crooked brokerage firm. (R)

BOSSA NOVA
Amy Irving
Delectable if lightweight romantic farce about an American widow in Rio de Janeiro and her various friends and would-be lovers. (R)

BOYS AND GIRLS
Freddie Prinze Jr., Claire Forlani
Only in movieland could two such attractive young people be so oblivious to the frantic signals of their hormones. [TG] (PG-13)

BRING IT ON
Kirsten Dunst, Jesse Bradford
There's much to cheer for in this sassy teen comedy about a princess of pep who learns there's more to life than waving pom-poms. (PG-13)

BUT I'M A CHEERLEADER
Natasha Lyonne, Clea DuVall, Cathy Moriarty, RuPaul Charles
A high school student is packed off to a prisonlike coed camp dedicated to turning teen sissies into he-men and suspected lesbians into perfect housewives. *Cheerleader* often leans too hard on stereotypes, but offers nervy, on-target performances. (R)

BUTTERFLY
Fernando Fernán Gómez, Manuel Lozano
Yet another foreign film about friendship between a child and an oldster. Here, a boy and his teacher bond on the eve of the Spanish Civil War. Sweet but small. (R)

CECIL B. DEMENTED
Melanie Griffith, Stephen Dorff
A slightly over-the-hill Hollywood actress is kidnapped to

star in an underground movie. Loud, ugly, and nearly always unfunny. [TG] (R)

THE CELL
Jennifer Lopez, Vince Vaughn, Vincent D'Onofrio
A psychiatrist mentally tiptoes into the mind of a killer. Sleek images, awful drama. (R)

CENTER STAGE
Amanda Schull, Zoe Saldana, Susan May Pratt, Ethan Stiefel, Sascha Radetsky, Peter Gallagher
Hackneyed backstage drama about a trio of baby ballerinas competing to rise en pointe in New York City. (PG-13)

*CHICKEN RUN
Animated, with the voices of Mel Gibson, Julia Sawalha, Jane Horrocks, Miranda Richardson
A flock of birds yearns to fly the coop at Tweedy's Chicken Farm. *Run* is visually inventive, and its characters are plump with personality. Im-peck-able fun. (G)

CHUCK & BUCK
Mike White, Chris Weitz
Stalking his boyhood pal, an oddball 27-year-old wants the two to resume where they left off, including experimenting with sex. Weirdly watchable. (R)

THE CLOSER YOU GET
Ian Hart, Niamh Cusack
In a declining Irish town, the menfolk decide that the female pickings are both numerically slender and insufficiently sexy, so they place a personals ad in the *Miami Herald*, inviting American bachelorettes to a St. Martha's Day dance. *Closer* is more wee-cutesy than charming, although it does emit a faint romantic glow. [TG] (PG-13)

COMMITTED
Heather Graham, Casey Affleck, Luke Wilson
When her husband unexpectedly moves out of their Manhattan pad, Graham's character sets out

after him, even though she has no idea where he might have gone; her luminous performance keeps the viewer hanging on through this genial though rambling romantic drama. (R)

COTTON MARY
Madhur Jaffrey
The latest period piece by the Merchant-Ivory team is set in newly independent India in 1954, where an Anglo-Indian nurse blatantly insinuates herself into the lives of her English employers. (R)

COYOTE UGLY
Piper Perabo
A girl singer-songwriter works at a Manhattan watering hole where the scantily clad female bartenders dance on the counter. With a premise like that, what do you expect? (PG-13)

THE CREW
Richard Dreyfuss, Burt Reynolds, Seymour Cassel, Dan Hedaya
When this quartet of retired mobsters finds itself facing eviction from a Miami residential hotel that's about to be gentrified, they fake a murder to scare off potential new tenants. Complications—way too many and too few of them funny—ensue. (PG-13)

CROUPIER
Clive Owen
Intriguing British thriller about a struggling British novelist who gets a job as a croupier in a shady London casino and discovers that real life trumps fiction. (Not rated)

THE CUP
Orgyen Tobgyal, Janyang Lodro
This charming wisp of a comedy shows how residents of a remote Tibetan monastery go loopy over soccer during the 1998 World Cup. (G)

DINOSAUR
Animated
Visually impressive but dramatically uninspired tale of exodus. Not for nothing does the movie carry a PG rating; parents should think twice before carting along anyone still too young to spell Tyrannosaurus rex. (PG)

DISNEY'S THE KID
Bruce Willis, Spencer Breslin
A high-powered image consultant comes face-to-face with his 7-year-old self. A surprisingly sweet, at times touching, comic fantasy. (PG)

DOWN TO YOU
Freddie Prinze Jr., Julia Stiles
Freddie Prinze Jr., soulful-eyed, puppyish and earnest, stars with Julia Stiles in a by-the-numbers tale of first love at college. It's so high school. (PG-13)

DROWNING MONA
Bette Midler, Danny DeVito, Jamie Lee Curtis, Neve Campbell, Casey Affleck, William Fichtner
This labored comedy sinks from the start. A harridan's Yugo plunges into a lake, and the investigating sheriff soon discovers everyone in town had reason to wish Mona gone. (PG-13)

EAST IS EAST
Om Puri, Linda Bassett
In this high-spirited comedy drama, seven Anglo-Pakistani siblings figure out their place in '70s England. Puri and Bassett give especially fine performances as the strict Pakistani father and the soft-touch British mum. (R)

EAST-WEST
Sandrine Bonnaire, Catherine Deneuve
With WWII over, a Russian doctor living in France heeds Stalin's call urging all true patriots to return and rebuild the motherland—right before the Iron Curtain clangs down, trapping him and his family in a life of privation and suspicion. An unsatisfying, strangely conflicted epic. [TG] (PG-13)

8½ WOMEN
John Standing, Matthew Delamere, Vivian Wu, Toni Collette
A financier, rich and recently widowed, transforms his stately country home into a seraglio for mistresses. Director Peter Greenaway has a perverse genius for making naked flesh look as unappealing as wood pulp, and the women here are quarrelsome, demented, and overpowering. One peculiar film. [TG] (R)

ERIN BROCKOVICH
Julia Roberts, Albert Finney, Aaron Eckhart, Marg Helgenberger
A feisty, twice-divorced mother with only a high school diploma finds documents that eventually lead to evidence of water contamination. Splendid and inspiring—thanks to sharp direction and a powerhouse star performance. (R)

EYE OF THE BEHOLDER
Ashley Judd, Ewan McGregor
Femme fatale Ashley Judd stabs her victim and sobs, "Merry Christmas, Daddy!" She's a mess. So is this thriller. (R)

THE EYES OF TAMMY FAYE
Documentary
A daffy, very forgiving portrait of former televangelist Tammy Faye Bakker. (PG-13)

FANTASIA/2000
Animated
2000 is rarely adventurous enough to seem like more than a do-gooder's attempt at shoving classical music down kids' throats by wrapping it in cartoons. (G)

THE FILTH AND THE FURY
John Lydon
Were the Sex Pistols, England's notorious 1970s punk band, heirs to such cheeky music-hall performers as Benny Hill? That's the sole interesting conceit in this annoyingly glib documentary. (R)

FINAL DESTINATION
Devon Sawa, Ali Larter
Classmates who fleed a jet before it exploded begin meeting grisly ends. *Destination* isn't clever enough—nor is its mostly teenage cast skilled enough—to make viewers care whether the characters live or die. (R)

*THE FIVE SENSES
Mary-Louise Parker, Gabrielle Rose, Daniel MacIvor, Philippe Volter
Five residents of an apartment building desperately try to make a connection with another human being. Praiseworthy but slow. (R)

THE FLINTSTONES IN VIVA ROCK VEGAS
Mark Addy, Stephen Baldwin, Kristen Johnston, Jane Krakowski
More enjoyably relaxed and more kid-oriented than its predecessor, *The Flintstones* (1994). Not great, but by no means extinct. [TG] (PG)

*FREQUENCY
Dennis Quaid, Jim Caviezel, Andre Braugher, Elizabeth Mitchell
A rewardingly tricky supernatural drama in which an adult son is able to yak to his long-dead father via an old ham radio. Directed with verve, *Frequency* boasts an ingenious script, plenty of heart and solid, affecting performances. (PG-13)

GIRL ON THE BRIDGE
Vanessa Paradis, Daniel Auteuil
For most women, when a man starts throwing knives at you, it's time to scram. But not for the heroine of this exceedingly slight dramatic fable.(R)

*GLADIATOR
Russell Crowe, Joaquin Phoenix, Connie Nielsen, Richard Harris, Oliver Reed
Too preposterous to be mistaken for a great movie—but its pull is

potent, thanks to the razzle-dazzle fight scenes and a magnetic performance by Crowe, who shows just the right combination of heart and brawn. (R)

GONE IN 60 SECONDS
Nicolas Cage, Angelina Jolie
And forgotten even faster. After six years of clean living, a car thief gets dragged back into hot-wiring when his younger brother crosses a crime boss. A loud, essentially silly picture featuring good actors in dumb parts. (PG-13)

GOSSIP
James Marsden, Lena Headey
Vile trifle about chic college kids who let a rumor get way out of control. (R)

GROOVE
Hamish Linklater, Lola Glaudini
An agreeable trifle of a movie, about one of those underground parties where teens and young adults, fueled by the feel-good drug Ecstasy, stay up all night dancing to techno music. Energetically directed and nonjudgmentally written. (R)

HAMLET
Ethan Hawke, Diane Venora, Kyle MacLachlan, Julia Stiles, Bill Murray, Liev Schreiber
Director-adapter Michael Almereyda's film presents Hamlet as a video artist hell-bent on solving the murder of his business-mogul father, who headed the mighty Denmark Corporation. The happy surprise is how well the hypermodern concept works, making you rethink and rehear the play. (R)

HANGING UP
Meg Ryan, Diane Keaton, Lisa Kudrow, Walter Matthau, Adam Arkin
This comedy-drama about three sisters and their relationships with each other and their dying father could, and should, be affecting. But the movie settles

again and again for cuteness. (PG-13)

HELD UP
Jamie Foxx
Foxx is taken hostage during a convenience-store stickup out in the middle of nowhere. Junk food without even the benefit of artificial flavoring. (PG-13)

HERE ON EARTH
Leelee Sobieski, Chris Klein
The filmmakers responsible for this turgid, shameless *Love Story* steal owe a major apology—in writing—to any non-adolescent cursed to sit through it. (PG-13)

HIGH FIDELITY
John Cusack, Iben Hjejle, Jack Black, Todd Louiso, Lisa Bonet
A hip, knowing romantic comedy about how certain young men put off growing up until they are finally too miserable to postpone it any longer. (R)

HIGHLANDER: ENDGAME
Christopher Lambert, Adrian Paul
The heroes of the *Highlander* movies may be immortal, but let's hope they won't be swinging their swords into perpetuity. This inane third sequel to 1986's *Highlander* again improbably stars that most stolid of Frenchmen, Lambert, as Connor MacLeod, a Scotsman who has been fighting off foes who would behead him (the only way to kill an immortal) since the 1500s. (R)

HOLLOW MAN
Kevin Bacon, Elisabeth Shue, Josh Brolin
An invisible man is mentally not all there. Viewers may feel the same about the movie; the surprises end early. [TG] (R)

L'HUMANITÉ
Emmanuel Schotté, Séverine Caneele
While investigating the rape and murder of a girl, a police detec-

tive becomes increasingly obsessed with his voluptuous neighbor and her loutish boyfriend. Glacially paced but weirdly compelling. (Not rated)

HUMAN TRAFFIC
John Simm, Lorraine Pilkington
This comedy about club kids drugging the weekend away in Cardiff, Wales, overdoses on cuteness. [TG] (R)

I DREAMED OF AFRICA
Kim Basinger, Vincent Perez
An upper-class, divorced heroine heads from Venice to Africa with her new husband and young son to start a fresh life in beautiful, remote Kenya. Plenty hap-

---

2000'S TOP TEN GROSSERS

This year moviegoers chose to accept *M:I-2*, giving Tom Cruise his biggest hit to date. He wasn't alone—George Clooney, Russell Crowe, and Martin Lawrence did their best box office ever, too. On the other hand, *Scary Movie*'s success wasn't due to its stars; its massive gross came from grossing out the masses. Here are 2000's top smashes, as of Sept. 10. (Source: *Variety*)

1. Mission: Impossible 2
2. Gladiator
3. The Perfect Storm
4. X-Men
5. Scary Movie
6. What Lies Beneath
7. Dinosaur
8. Erin Brockovich
9. Nutty Professor II: The Klumps
10. Big Momma's House

pens, but *Africa*'s plodding pacing and minimalist approach results in a seemingly endless ramble. (PG-13)

ISN'T SHE GREAT
Bette Midler, Nathan Lane, Stockard Channing
Depicting Jacqueline Susann as a lovable monster who would stop at nothing to get worldwide fame, *Great* alternates between scorn and overripe bathos. A bad movie made by good people. (R)

JESUS' SON
Billy Crudup
A drug-abusing loser crawls through one misery after another before reaching an oasis of peace. Somber yet moving, it's like *Drugstore Cowboy*, only the high feels unexpectedly religious. (R)

*JOE GOULD'S SECRET
Ian Holm, Stanley Tucci, Hope Davis
A disturbing drama about the years a writer at *The New Yorker* spent chronicling a brilliant, eccentric, drunken derelict. *Secret*—by turns affecting, baffling and diffuse—is about how, even if life has no final answers, one has to keep asking questions. (R)

KEEPING THE FAITH
Edward Norton, Ben Stiller, Jenna Elfman
A pleasant but slack comedy about a priest, a rabbi, and the school-days friend they both fall for. Norton and Stiller have nicely contrasting comedy styles, but neither has much oomph as a romantic lead. [TG] (PG-13)

THE LAST SEPTEMBER
Dame Maggie Smith, Michael Gambon, Fiona Shaw
It's 1920 and the Anglo-Irish aristocracy in Ireland fails to grasp how profoundly independence will change their world.

Despite a strong cast, this period drama seems slight. (R)

LOSER
Jason Biggs, Mena Suvari
This obvious romantic comedy in college flunks out. (PG-13)

*LOVE AND BASKETBALL
Omar Epps, Sanaa Lathan, Alfre Woodard, Debbi Morgan
In tracking the athletic and romantic progress of both its ball-playing heroine and the cute boy next door, *Love & Basketball* briskly and with humor covers much ground about sports and competitiveness, mothers and daughters, and fathers and sons. Swish! (PG-13)

LOVE & SEX
Famke Janssen, Jon Favreau
Janssen's appealing performance is the main reason to seek out this overly cute sitcom. (Not rated)

LOVE'S LABOUR'S LOST
Kenneth Branagh, Natascha McElhone, Alicia Silverstone, Matthew Lillard, Nathan Lane, Alessandro Nivola
A misguided musical adaptation of Shakespeare's slight-on-plot comedy. The over-the-top production numbers are ungainly, and no one croons with distinction. (PG)

ME, MYSELF & IRENE
Jim Carrey, Renee Zellweger
Carrey's split personalities battle for dominance while trying to save Zellweger from thugs. Not altogether satisfying, but writer-directors Peter and Bobby Farrelly are the most original comic minds in Hollywood today. [TG] (R)

ME MYSELF I
Rachel Griffiths, David Roberts, Sandy Winton
A single, successful magazine writer wonders what would have happened if she had accepted a marriage proposal 13 years ear-

lier from her then-beau, an architect. After being hit by a car, she magically gets to find out. Sprightly and amusing. (R)

MIFUNE
Anders W. Berthelsen, Jesper Asholt, Iben Hjejle
A darkly amusing comedy about a Copenhagen yuppie who returns to his family's rural farm to take care of his slow-witted brother and falls in love with a hooker turned housekeeper. The movie has an edgy, freewheeling feel; there's a spontaneity that might be missing if scenes were perfectly lit or fancily shot. (R)

MISSION: IMPOSSIBLE 2
Tom Cruise, Thandie Newton, Ving Rhames, Dougray Scott
A slick, facile piece of moviemaking boasting as much actual soul as a stale soda cracker. Woozily ridiculous, but director John Woo brings his usual visual dazzle to the action scenes. (PG-13)

MISSION TO MARS
Gary Sinise, Tim Robbins, Don Cheadle, Connie Nielsen, Jerry O'Connell
A dull, lead-footed bit of sci-fi blather that will thrill special effects-starved 12-year-olds but leave anyone older yawning. (PG)

MY DOG SKIP
Kevin Bacon, Frankie Muniz
One doesn't have to love dogs to be won over by this sweet, nostalgic family film in which a terrier's love and loyalty help transform a shy, friendless boy into an outgoing, self-confident youth. (PG)

THE NEXT BEST THING
Madonna, Rupert Everett, Benjamin Bratt, Illeana Douglas
A straight woman and a happily homosexual man have a baby. Despite its up-to-date gay twist, *Next* is a decidedly old-fashioned weepie—and irredeemably sappy. (PG-13)

NEXT FRIDAY
Ice Cube
Rapper Ice Cube wrote and stars in a dumb comedy about a homeboy's misadventures in the suburbs. Drug, sex, and potty jokes abound. (R)

THE NINTH GATE
Johnny Depp, Frank Langella, Lena Olin, Emmanuelle Seigner
A rare-books dealer is hired to compare the three remaining copies of a tome that supposedly contains the secret to conjuring the devil. *Ninth* starts off decently but winds up spectacularly silly. (R)

NOT ONE LESS
Wei Minzhi
A 13-year-old substitute teacher in rural China heads to the city to track down a missing student. Director Zhang Yimou artfully depicts a China tourists rarely see. (G)

*NURSE BETTY
Renee Zellweger, Morgan Freeman, Chris Rock, Greg Kinnear
This idiosyncratic dark comedy about a likable young woman who becomes convinced that she is a character on a soap opera is full of surprises, impeccable acting, and smart writing. Zellweger gives an extraordinary, multilayered performance that suggests Doris Day at her most resilient. Freeman adds tragic grandeur and Rock contributes comic zing. (R)

NUTTY PROFESSOR II: THE KLUMPS
Eddie Murphy, Janet Jackson
This patchy, relentlessly vulgar sequel can use all the Murphy it can get. (PG-13)

THE ORIGINAL KINGS OF COMEDY
Steve Harvey, D.L. Hughley, Cedric the Entertainer, Bernie Mac
A funny documentary that captures the four comics' touring show, much of it revolving around racial differences. (R)

PASSION OF MIND
Demi Moore, Stellan Skarsgard, William Fichtner, Sinead Cusack
A sluggish psychological drama in which Moore's character carries on two vastly different lives simultaneously. (PG-13)

THE PATRIOT
Mel Gibson, Heath Ledger, Joely Richardson, Jason Isaacs
During its first half, the rousing *Patriot* shows the causes and costs behind the birth of the nation. Things then turn clichéd and obvious, but Gibson and the well-staged, bloodily realistic battle scenes keep one's interest from flagging. (R)

THE PERFECT STORM
George Clooney, Mark Wahlberg, Mary Elizabeth Mastrantonio, Diane Lane
The movie's tempest scenes are spectacular. But when everyone's dry, the movie's all wet. (PG-13)

*PITCH BLACK
Vin Diesel, Radha Mitchell, Cole Hauser
When a planet's three suns set, a nasty murderer's polished eyeballs enable him to steer refugees clear of flying creatures intent on eating humans. A brawny, stylish sci-fi saga. (R)

1999'S OVERSEAS MONEYMAKERS

American comedies don't always thrive on foreign soil: *Austin* had less power abroad, and *Big Daddy* wasn't. But romantic comedies seem to translate fine: *You've Got Mail, Runaway Bride, Shakespeare in Love,* and *Notting Hill* all outgrossed their American runs overseas. Score one for the universal language of love. Meanwhile, two foreign-language productions penetrated the traditionally Hollywood-heavy list: Italy's *Life Is Beautiful* and *Asterix & Obelix,* the live-action version of the beloved French comic strip. (Source: *Variety*)

Rank	Title	Gross (in millions)
1.	Star Wars: Episode I—The Phantom Menace	490
2.	The Matrix	285
3.	The Mummy	258
4.	Notting Hill	247
5.	Tarzan	221
6.	Shakespeare in Love	189
7.	The Sixth Sense	177
8.	A Bug's Life	170
9.	Runaway Bride	156
10.	The World Is Not Enough	136
11.	You've Got Mail	126
12.	Entrapment	124
13.	Enemy of the State	114
14.	Asterix & Obelix	110
15.	Eyes Wide Shut	105
16.	Austin Powers: The Spy Who Shagged Me (tie)	104
16.	Wild Wild West (tie)	104
18.	Life Is Beautiful	93
19.	Meet Joe Black	88
20.	The Haunting	86

POKÉMON: THE MOVIE 2000
Animated
Three mythical birds escape from island aviaries and ruin the weather. Ash, a human trainer of the magical Pokémon menagerie, must capture the birds to save the world. Arduous, slow, and repetitive. (G)

PRICE OF GLORY
Jimmy Smits
Stuck on the canvas. Earnest but clichéd boxing drama stars Smits as a dad who pushes his sons into pugilistic careers. (PG-13)

READY TO RUMBLE
David Arquette, Scott Caan, Oliver Platt, Joe Pantoliano, Rose McGowan
Wrestling fans Arquette and Caan travel to Atlanta to persuade their favorite grappler to return to the ring. If you check your brain at the door, there are some chuckles to be had. (PG-13)

REINDEER GAMES
Ben Affleck, Charlize Theron, Gary Sinise
An ex-con is coerced into helping to rob a casino. Sacrificing logic to excessive cleverness, *Games*'s plot ends up with too many holes to count. (R)

THE REPLACEMENTS
Keanu Reeves, Gene Hackman
As fake as artificial turf. The plot is predictable, the romance tepid, and character development is minimal. (PG-13)

RESTLESS
Catherine Kellner, David Wu
A diverting romantic comedy about young Americans on the loose in Beijing, Predictable stories, interesting backgrounds. (Not rated)

RETURN TO ME
David Duchovny, Minnie Driver, Bonnie Hunt, Jim Belushi, Carroll O'Connor
A widower falls in love with a waitress, not realizing that the transplanted ticker thumping in her chest previously belonged to his late beloved wife. This congenial romantic comedy really shouldn't work, but darned if it doesn't. (PG)

THE ROAD TO EL DORADO
Animated, with voices by Kevin Kline, Kenneth Branagh, Rosie Perez
Dorado is entertaining enough and will divert youthful viewers, but as feature-length 'toons go, it lacks the psychological depth of *The Lion King*, the romantic sweep of *Beauty and the Beast*, or the flat-out laughs of the *Toy Story* series. (PG)

ROAD TRIP
Breckin Meyer, Amy Smart, Tom Green
Road Trip aspires to be this summer's *American Pie*. It features the same gross-out sensibility and the same underlying affection for its main characters, a quartet of dorky male college students. High art this ain't. (R)

ROMEO MUST DIE
Jet Li, Aaliyah, Delroy Lindo, Isaiah Washington, Russell Wong
This limb-crushing thriller proves yet again just how infinitely adaptable Shakespeare can be, even when none of his actual text is used. Long on graceful and graphic action, short on poetry. (R)

RULES OF ENGAGEMENT
Tommy Lee Jones, Samuel L. Jackson, Guy Pearce, Anne Archer, Ben Kingsley
Out to explore the uncertainties of pulling triggers, this military drama ends up pulling its punches. Jones and Jackson have a fine time playing off each other, but *Rules* stacks the deck too heavily in favor of Jackson's character. (R)

RUNNING FREE
Chase Moore, Jan Decleir
This children's film, sentimentally appealing and beautifully photographed, briskly follows a horse from enslaved birth to adult triumph. (G)

*SAVING GRACE
Brenda Blethyn, Craig Fergusin
A proper upper-class matron resorts to growing marijuana as a way of digging herself out of debt. Blethyn's affecting, ruefully honest performance provides a special grace. (R)

SCARY MOVIE
Shawn Wayans, Marlon Wayans, Cheri Oteri, Anna Faris, Jon Abrahams
A steady barrage of gags about sex, flatulence, sex organs, and other topics that adolescents and young adults find hoot-worthy. (R)

SCREAM 3
Neve Campbell, Courteney Cox Arquette, David Arquette, Parker Posey
The emphasis on knowing, self-referential gags makes for a better movie, but enough already. (R)

SCREWED
Norm Macdonald
The title tells all. You will be exactly that if you sit through this mirthless misfire of a comedy about a botched kidnapping. Stick to TV, Norm. (PG-13)

SHAFT
Samuel L. Jackson, Vanessa Williams
Genial, action-packed junk food. The plot is little more than an excuse for Jackson to model Armani's leather line for men, utter hip patter, and play with guns. Right on! (R)

SHANGHAI NOON
Jackie Chan, Owen Wilson, Lucy Liu
A member of the Chinese Imperial Guard teams up with a swaggering would-be outlaw to rescue a kidnapped princess in

Nevada. A highly affable action comedy. (PG-13)

THE SKULLS
Joshua Jackson
Bone-headed thriller. Ivy League senior is recruited to join a prestigious secret society and discovers—the horror, the horror—that it's evil. (PG-13)

SMALL TIME CROOKS
Woody Allen, Tracey Ullman, Hugh Grant
A Kramdenesque couple starts a cookie business as a front for a crime scheme. Allen's satire on the nouveau riche is more cheerfully droll than many of his recent entries. (PG)

SNOW DAY
Chevy Chase
Dumb comedy for kids advocates mob action as its pipsqueak heroes plot to sabotage the town's only snowplow. Why? They want a second day off from school. (PG)

SOLOMON & GAENOR
Ioan Gruffudd, Nia Roberts
Think of this as *Romeo and Juliet* set in Wales in 1911. Starcrossed Solomon (Gruffudd) is Jewish and Gaenor is Christian. Extravagantly romantic, but well acted and beautifully shot. (R)

SPACE COWBOYS
Clint Eastwood, Tommy Lee Jones, James Garner, Donald Sutherland, Courtney B. Vance, Loren Dean
Has there ever been a leisurely, touching space epic—let alone one with senior-citizen heroes? Now there is. [TG] (PG-13)

STEAL THIS MOVIE
Vincent D'Onofrio, Janeane Garofalo, Jeanne Tripplehorn
The career of the '60s preeminent radical, Abbie Hoffman, is badly dramatized. [TG] (R)

SUNSHINE
Ralph Fiennes, Jennifer Ehle, Rosemary Harris, Rachel Weisz
As two world wars, the Holocaust, and communist purges beset Hungary, the men from three generations of a Jewish family make ever greater compromises, trying to fit into a culture that will always view them as outsiders. Fiennes plays all three men; the movie often plays like a soap opera. (R)

SUPERNOVA
Angela Bassett, James Spader, Lou Diamond Phillips, Robin Tunney
A medical rescue spaceship answers a distress signal and comes to the aid of a mysterious stranger; several others on board soon meet nasty endings. All of this plays out even more boringly than it reads. (PG-13)

THE TAO OF STEVE
Donal Logue, Greer Goodman
An unlikely babe magnet finally learns to say what he means and mean what he says. A refreshingly quirky romantic comedy. (R)

THOMAS AND THE MAGIC RAILROAD
Alec Baldwin, Peter Fonda
A painfully simple tale about a little toy steam engine that could, *Thomas* will bore silly anyone above the age of 5. (G)

TIME CODE
Saffron Burrows, Salma Hayek, Stellan Skarsgard, Jeanne Tripplehorn
Director Mike Figgis shot this movie in one day with four digital video cameras, each recording a separate plot thread. Then he divided the screen image into quadrants, and we watch four stories unfolding simultaneously. *Code* is actually fun, largely because of its satirical soap-opera setting: an L.A. film production company full of colossal egos in empty heads. (R)

TITAN A.E.
Animated, with the voices of Matt Damon, Drew Barrymore, Bill Pullman
Way-cool-looking, but looks aren't everything. Story and characters also count, and in those areas *Titan* is little more than *Flash Gordon* with attitude and a rock soundtrack. (PG)

TRIXIE
Emily Watson, Nick Nolte, Dermot Mulroney, Nathan Lane, Brittany Murphy, Lesley Ann Warren
A none-too-bright private detective stumbles on a murder and zeroes in on her chief suspect, a philandering state senator. Pretty much a mess, the oddball *Trixie* will strike most viewers as annoying and inordinately pleased with itself. (R)

TURN IT UP
Pras, Ja Rule, Vondie Curtis Hall
This feeble gangsta drama features the Fugees' Pras as a would-be rapper who moonlights as muscle for a drug dealer and cavalierly shoots dead a half-dozen rival hoods. (R)

*28 DAYS
Sandra Bullock, Viggo Mortensen, Dominic West, Elizabeth Perkins
Under court order, a goodtime girl enters rehab. Without minimizing the devastation wrought by drinking and drugging and the painful tolls on the road to sobriety, *28 Days* manages to find plenty of humor in its heroine's struggle to admit that she has a problem and in her subsequent battle to clean up. (PG-13)

U-571
Matthew McConaughey, Bill Paxton, Harvey Keitel, Jon Bon Jovi
This submarine drama is rugged, fast-paced and tells a nifty story, but its main characters never come across as more than types

and its crew members barely register. (PG-13)

UP AT THE VILLA

Kristin Scott Thomas, Sean Penn, Anne Bancroft, Jeremy Davies
A vapid romantic drama set in Italy in 1938 in which a miscast Penn has to saunter around in a tux and project an air of suave insouciance; he and Scott Thomas generate as much heat as you'd get rubbing ice cubes. (PG-13)

THE VIRGIN SUICIDES

Kirsten Dunst, Kathleen Turner
When five beautifully listless girls begin to overexcite the local boys, their mother decrees they can no longer leave the house, and they commit suicide. A dreamy, slightly silly, alluring ode to the adolescent feminine mystique. [TG] (R)

WAKING THE DEAD

Billy Crudup, Jennifer Connelly
A young congressional candidate keeps glimpsing his girlfriend, who supposedly died in an explosion a decade earlier. Is she real or merely a vision he

has summoned in his moment of need? By the time the wan *Waking the Dead* finally gets around to fuzzily answering that question, most viewers will have given up on the film itself. (R)

THE WAY OF THE GUN

Ryan Phillippe, Benicio Del Toro, Juliette Lewis, Taye Diggs, James Caan
This talky, twisty, and triggerhappy crime drama in which everyone has an ulterior motive follows career thugs Parker (Phillippe) and Longbaugh (Del Toro) (the last

WORKING TITLES

Would *The Black Hills Project* have caused the same Internet groundswell of interest as *The Blair Witch Project*? Here's a variety of releases that shed their original names on their way to release.

What was once...	Eventually became...	What was once...	Eventually became...
Against All Enemies	The Siege	The Kiss	Living Out Loud
Austinpussy	Austin Powers: The Spy Who Shagged Me	The League	Any Given Sunday
		The Loners	Easy Rider
Billy the Third	Tommy Boy	Made Men	GoodFellas
Black and White	Trading Places	The Magic Hour	Twilight
The Black Hills Project	The Blair Witch Project	Most Valuable Pooch	Air Bud
Blue Vision	In Dreams	My Posse Don't Do Homework	Dangerous Minds
Bookworm	The Edge		
The Boys in the Bank	Dog Day Afternoon	Navy Cross	G.I. Jane
A Boy's Life	E. T., the Extra-Terrestrial	Old Friends	As Good As It Gets
		Paris Match	French Kiss
Called Home	Witness	Parker	Payback
Captain Starshine	Galaxy Quest	The Party	Can't Hardly Wait
Cheer Fever	Bring It On	People Like Us	Philadelphia
The Colony	Double Team	Prison Rodeo	Stir Crazy
Coma Guy	While You Were Sleeping	The Quest	Coming to America
		The Rainbow Warrior	On Deadly Ground
Daddy's Home	Look Who's Talking	The Rest of Daniel	Forever Young
Extremely Violent	Last Action Hero	Rocket Boys	October Sky
Father Goose	Fly Away Home	Scary Movie	Scream
Finished with Engines	No Way Out	Ship of Fools	The Impostors
The Flood	Hard Rain	Simon Says	Die Hard with a Vengeance
Force Majeure	Return to Paradise		
The Forlorn	Addicted to Love	Simple Simon	Mercury Rising
Goodnight Moon	Stepmom	The Soldier's Wife	The Crying Game
Guy Gets Kid	Big Daddy	Teeny-Weenies	Honey, I Shrunk the Kids
Hot and Cold	Weekend at Bernie's		
An Indian in the City	Jungle 2 Jungle	Ten Soldiers	Red Dawn
I Was a Teenage Teenager	Clueless	3000	Pretty Woman

names of outlaws Butch Cassidy and the Sundance Kid). Director-writer Christopher McQuarrie's first effort seems more an exercise in style, but it's still showy and smart enough to mark him as a filmmaker with a future. (R)

WHAT LIES BENEATH
Harrison Ford, Michelle Pfeiffer
Elegantly shot and teased along by small, sly touches of humor, *Beneath* aspires to sophisticated psycho-horror. It eventually skitters off into slick formula, yet remains a cut above most ghost stories. [TG] (PG-13)

WHAT PLANET ARE YOU FROM?
Garry Shandling, Annette Bening, John Goodman, Greg Kinnear
As a first step in his planet's plan to conquer Earth, an alien must impregnate a woman—and soon discovers it takes a whole lot more than murmuring "uh-huh" to keep Earth women happy. A sweetly goofy comedy. (R)

WHERE THE HEART IS
Natalie Portman, Ashley Judd, Stockard Channing, James Frain
On her way to California, a spunky 17-year-old is left barefoot and pregnant—literally—at a Wal-Mart in rural Oklahoma by her beau. She secretly sets up house in the store, has her baby

there, and is soon befriended by excessively colorful locals. Tepidly directed, *Heart* dithers on and on to no great effect. (PG-13)

WHERE THE MONEY IS
Paul Newman, Linda Fiorentino, Dermot Mulroney
Essentially a TV movie blessed with dream casting, this crime caper owes what modest charm it has primarily to Newman. (PG-13)

WHIPPED
Amanda Peet, Brian Van Holt
This smug, charmless sex comedy about three on-the-make bachelors who all fall for Peet's beguiling, adorable free spirit should do much to advance the cause of celibacy. (R)

THE WHOLE NINE YARDS
Bruce Willis, Matthew Perry, Rosanna Arquette, Amanda Peet
When a gangland hit man moves in next door and befriends his dentist neighbor, the dentist is drawn into a complicated revenge scheme. Laughs are meagerly doled out in this strained black comedy. (R)

THE WISDOM OF CROCODILES
Jude Law
Law is a kind of vampire—or, at least, a man whose biological abnormality requires occasional infusions of blood via another

person's jugular. There's a lot of nonsense in the story, but Law is excellent. (R)

*WONDER BOYS
Michael Douglas, Tobey Maguire, Frances McDormand, Robert Downey Jr., Katie Holmes
An English professor's wife has just left him, his married lover (McDormand) has announced she is pregnant with his baby, and his editor (Downey) has arrived from Manhattan expecting to see a completed manuscript. An appealingly shaggy, largely unpredictable comedy.

X-MEN
Hugh Jackman, Patrick Stewart, Famke Janssen, Halle Berry, Ian McKellen, Anna Paquin
At what point did comic-book superheroes become psychologically tortured and prone to philosophical posturing? They have the right, but that doesn't help the action sequences. [TG] (PG-13)

THE TOP 100 BOX-OFFICE FILMS OF ALL TIME

This list ranks the largest money-making movies of all time based on domestic (U.S. and Canada) box-office receipts. Figures are accurate through September 10, 2000; summer blockbusters are still earning. (Source: *Variety*)

Rank	Film (year of release)	B.O. Gross	Rank	Film (year of release)	B.O. Gross
1.	Titanic (1997)	$600,788,188	50.	Air Force One (1997)	172,888,056
2.	Star Wars (1977)	460,998,007	51.	Rain Man (1988)	172,825,435
3.	Star Wars: Episode I—The Phantom	430,984,033	52.	Apollo 13 (1995)	172,070,496
	Menace (1999)		53.	The Matrix (1999)	171,479,930
4.	E.T., the Extra-Terrestrial (1982)	399,804,539	54.	Tarzan (1999)	171,010,381
5.	Jurassic Park (1993)	357,067,947	55.	Three Men and a Baby (1987)	167,780,960
6.	Forrest Gump (1994)	329,693,974	56.	Robin Hood: Prince of Thieves (1991)	165,493,908
7.	The Lion King (1994)	312,855,561	57.	The Exorcist (1973)	165,000,000
8.	Return of the Jedi (1983)	309,205,079	58.	Big Daddy (1999)	163,479,795
9.	Independence Day (1996)	306,169,268	59.	Batman Returns (1992)	162,831,698
10.	The Sixth Sense (1999)	293,488,346	60.	A Bug's Life (1998)	162,798,565
11.	The Empire Strikes Back (1980)	290,271,960	61.	The Waterboy (1998)	161,487,252
12.	Home Alone (1990)	285,761,243	62.	The Sound of Music (1965)	160,476,331
13.	Jaws (1975)	260,000,000	63.	The Firm (1993)	158,340,292
14.	Batman (1989)	251,188,924	64.	Fatal Attraction (1987)	156,645,693
15.	Men in Black (1997)	250,016,330	65.	The Sting (1972)	156,000,000
16.	Raiders of the Lost Ark (1981)	242,374,454	66.	Close Encounters of the Third Kind (1977)	155,691,323
17.	Twister (1996)	241,721,524	67.	The Mummy (1999)	155,385,488
18.	Ghostbusters (1984)	238,600,000	68.	Who Framed Roger Rabbit (1988)	154,112,492
19.	Beverly Hills Cop (1984)	234,760,478	69.	X-Men (2000)	154,032,233
20.	Toy Story 2 (1999)	245,628,367	70.	Jerry Maguire (1996)	153,962,592
21.	The Lost World: Jurassic Park (1997)	229,086,123	71.	Beverly Hills Cop II (1987)	153,665,036
22.	Mrs. Doubtfire (1993)	219,195,051	72.	Gremlins (1984)	153,083,102
23.	Ghost (1990)	217,631,306	73.	Runaway Bride (1999)	152,257,409
24.	Aladdin (1992)	217,350,219	74.	Rambo: First Blood Part II (1985)	150,415,432
25.	Saving Private Ryan (1998)	216,335,085	75.	Scary Movie (2000)	149,642,372
26.	Mission: Impossible 2 (2000)	214,343,454	76.	As Good As It Gets (1997)	148,266,088
27.	Back to the Future (1985)	208,242,016	77.	Lethal Weapon 2 (1989)	147,253,986
28.	Austin Powers:		78.	True Lies (1994)	146,282,411
	The Spy Who Shagged Me (1999)	206,040,086	79.	Beauty and the Beast (1991)	145,863,363
29.	Terminator 2: Judgment Day (1991)	204,843,345	80.	The Santa Clause (1994)	144,833,357
30.	Armageddon (1998)	201,578,182	81.	Lethal Weapon 3 (1992)	144,731,527
31.	Gone With the Wind (1939)	198,648,910	82.	Dr. Dolittle (1998)	144,156,609
32.	Indiana Jones and the Last Crusade (1989)	197,171,806	83.	Rush Hour (1998)	144,061,225
33.	Toy Story (1995)	191,796,233	84.	101 Dalmatians (1961)	143,992,148
34.	Dances with Wolves (1990)	184,208,848	85.	What Lies Beneath (2000)	142,381,640
35.	Batman Forever (1995)	184,031,112	85.	The Jungle Book (1967)	141,843,612
36.	Gladiator (2000)	184,229,225	86.	National Lampoon's Animal House (1978)	141,600,000
37.	The Fugitive (1993)	183,875,760	87.	Pocahontas (1995)	141,579,773
38.	Grease (1978)	181,513,510	88.	A Few Good Men (1992)	141,340,178
39.	Liar Liar (1997)	181,410,615	89.	The Blair Witch Project (1999)	140,539,099
40.	Mission: Impossible (1996)	180,981,866	90.	Deep Impact (1998)	140,464,664
41.	Indiana Jones and		91.	Look Who's Talking (1989)	140,088,813
	the Temple of Doom (1984)	179,870,271	92.	The Rocky Horror Picture Show (1975)	139,876,417
42.	The Perfect Storm (2000)	178,684,608	93.	Sister Act (1992)	139,605,150
43.	Pretty Woman (1990)	178,406,268	94.	Saturday Night Fever (1977)	139,486,124
44.	Tootsie (1982)	177,200,000	95.	Stuart Little (1999)	139,268,434
45.	Top Gun (1986)	176,781,728	96.	Platoon (1986)	138,530,565
46.	There's Something About Mary (1998)	176,483,808	97.	Good Will Hunting (1997)	138,433,435
47.	Snow White and the Seven Dwarfs (1937)	175,263,233	98.	Ransom (1996)	136,492,681
48.	"Crocodile" Dundee (1986)	174,803,506	99.	Godzilla (1998)	136,314,294
49.	Home Alone 2: Lost in New York (1992)	173,585,516	100.	101 Dalmatians (1996)	136,182,161

THE TOP 100 BOX-OFFICE FILMS OF 1999

Sequels ruled the roost in 1999. *The Phantom Menace* outgrossed all but the first *Star Wars* entries, while Austin, Buzz, and Woody were even bigger the second time out. But you had to have a *Sixth Sense* to predict *everyone* would want to see dead people. (Grosses are for U.S. and Canada box office, and are limited to the calendar year; starred films earned additional income in 1998.) (Source: *Variety*)

Rank	Film	B.O. Gross	Rank	Film	B.O. Gross
1.	Star Wars: Episode I—The Phantom Menace	430,443,350	51.	Any Given Sunday	45,752,119
2.	The Sixth Sense	276,386,495	52.	House on Haunted Hill	40,489,824
3.	Toy Story 2	208,851,257	53.	The Talented Mr. Ripley	39,771,649
4.	Austin Powers: The Spy Who Shagged Me	205,444,716	54.	Bicentennial Man	39,610,696
5.	The Matrix	171,479,930	55.	Cruel Intentions	38,267,302
6.	Tarzan	170,904,824	56.	10 Things I Hate About You	38,178,166
7.	Big Daddy	163,479,795	57.	My Favorite Martian	36,850,101
8.	The Mummy	155,385,488	58.	8MM	36,610,578
9.	Runaway Bride	152,054,428	59.	Fight Club	36,351,732
10.	The Blair Witch Project	140,539,099	60.	The Thin Red Line*	35,755,689
11.	The World Is Not Enough	117,877,025	61.	A Bug's Life*	35,209,001
12.	Notting Hill	116,089,678	62.	For Love of the Game	35,188,641
13.	Double Jeopardy	114,032,117	63.	Instinct	34,105,207
14.	Wild Wild West	113,805,681	64.	Mickey Blue Eyes	33,864,342
15.	Analyze This	106,885,658	65.	The Best Man	33,581,815
16.	The General's Daughter	102,705,852	66.	The 13th Warrior	32,698,900
17.	American Pie	101,800,949	67.	October Sky	32,683,932
18.	Inspector Gadget	97,403,112	68.	Lake Placid	31,770,423
19.	Shakespeare In Love*	94,078,225	69.	Random Hearts	31,020,443
20.	Sleepy Hollow	92,839,722	70.	Mighty Joe Young*	30,603,681
21.	The Haunting	91,240,529	71.	Superstar	30,150,814
22.	Patch Adams*	88,575,238	72.	Mystery Men	29,762,011
23.	Entrapment	87,704,396	73.	Dogma	28,983,260
24.	Pokémon: The First Movie	84,091,099	74.	The Out of Towners	28,544,120
25.	Payback	81,526,121	75.	The Other Sister	27,807,627
26.	Stuart Little	79,403,127	76.	Galaxy Quest	27,311,918
27.	The Green Mile	76,682,014	77.	Baby Geniuses	27,151,490
28.	Deep Blue Sea	73,648,228	78.	The Story of Us	27,100,031
29.	American Beauty	71,017,815	79.	Blast from the Past	26,613,620
30.	The Thomas Crown Affair	69,282,369	80.	The Insider	26,135,523
31.	Blue Streak	67,760,741	81.	Saving Private Ryan*	25,529,826
32.	Bowfinger	66,458,770	82.	The Wood	25,059,642
33.	Life	64,062,587	83.	Anna and the King	24,732,782
34.	The Bone Collector	63,739,165	84.	Arlington Road	24,711,498
35.	She's All That	63,465,522	85.	T-Rex: Back to the Cretaceous*	24,604,821
36.	End of Days	63,181,290	86.	Man on the Moon	24,550,700
37.	Three Kings	59,223,104	87.	Mysteries of Egypt*	23,670,867
38.	A Civil Action*	56,554,385	88.	The Iron Giant	23,159,305
39.	Stepmom*	55,702,051	89.	EDtv	22,508,680
40.	Eyes Wide Shut	55,691,208	90.	At First Sight	22,365,133
41.	Never Been Kissed	55,474,756	91.	The Faculty*	21,874,186
42.	Forces of Nature	52,957,800	92.	The Bachelor	21,266,456
43.	Varsity Blues	52,894,169	93.	Stir of Echoes	21,133,087
44.	Message in a Bottle	52,880,016	94.	Enemy of the State*	19,521,933
45.	You've Got Mail	52,059,121	95.	Waking Ned Devine*	19,456,791
46.	South Park: Bigger, Longer, and Uncut	52,037,603	96.	Doug's 1st Movie	19,440,449
47.	Stigmata	50,014,865	97.	Summer of Sam	19,288,130
48.	Life Is Beautiful*	47,457,371	98.	An Ideal Husband	18,542,974
49.	Deuce Bigalow: Male Gigolo	46,538,329	99.	Everest*	18,468,249
50.	The Prince of Egypt*	46,306,557	100.	Being John Malkovich	18,243,969

THE AMERICAN FILM INSTITUTE'S TOP 100

To celebrate 100 years of movie making (1896–1996), more than 1,500 ballots were sent to leaders in the industry (and a few outsiders, including President and Mrs. Clinton) to rank the top American films. Controversial outcome? You bet. See how your favorites match up with their list. Those in bold are also among PEOPLE's movie critic Leah Rozen's list of the best (see page 93).

1. **Citizen Kane** (1941)
2. **Casablanca** (1942)
3. **The Godfather** (1972)
4. **Gone With the Wind** (1939)
5. Lawrence of Arabia (1962)
6. **The Wizard of Oz** (1939)
7. **The Graduate** (1967)
8. On the Waterfront (1954)
9. **Schindler's List** (1993)
10. **Singin' in the Rain** (1952)
11. It's a Wonderful Life (1946)
12. **Sunset Boulevard** (1950)
13. The Bridge on the River Kwai (1957)
14. **Some Like It Hot** (1959)
15. Star Wars (1977)
16. **All About Eve** (1950)
17. **The African Queen** (1951)
18. **Psycho** (1960)
19. **Chinatown** (1974)
20. One Flew Over the Cuckoo's Nest (1975)
21. **The Grapes of Wrath** (1940)
22. **2001: A Space Odyssey** (1968)
23. **The Maltese Falcon** (1941)
24. **Raging Bull** (1980)
25. **E.T., the Extra-Terrestrial** (1982)
26. **Dr. Strangelove** (1964)
27. Bonnie and Clyde (1967)
28. Apocalypse Now (1979)
29. Mr. Smith Goes to Washington (1939)
30. The Treasure of Sierra Madre (1948)
31. Annie Hall (1977)
32. The Godfather Part II (1974)
33. **High Noon** (1952)
34. To Kill a Mockingbird (1962)
35. **It Happened One Night** (1934)
36. Midnight Cowboy (1969)
37. **The Best Years of Our Lives** (1946)
38. **Double Indemnity** (1944)
39. Doctor Zhivago (1965)
40. North by Northwest (1959)
41. West Side Story (1961)
42. **Rear Window** (1954)
43. King Kong (1933)
44. **The Birth of a Nation** (1915)
45. A Streetcar Named Desire (1951)
46. A Clockwork Orange (1971)
47. Taxi Driver (1976)
48. **Jaws** (1975)
49. **Snow White and the Seven Dwarfs** (1937)
50. **Butch Cassidy and the Sundance Kid** (1969)
51. The Philadelphia Story (1940)
52. From Here to Eternity (1953)
53. Amadeus (1984)
54. All Quiet on the Western Front (1930)
55. **The Sound of Music** (1965)
56. M*A*S*H (1970)
57. The Third Man (1949)
58. Fantasia (1940)
59. **Rebel Without a Cause** (1955)
60. Raiders of the Lost Ark (1981)
61. Vertigo (1958)
62. Tootsie (1982)
63. Stagecoach (1939)
64. Close Encounters of the Third Kind (1977)
65. The Silence of the Lambs (1991)
66. **Network** (1976)
67. **The Manchurian Candidate** (1962)
68. An American in Paris (1951)
69. **Shane** (1953)
70. The French Connection (1971)
71. Forrest Gump (1994)
72. Ben-Hur (1959)
73. Wuthering Heights (1939)
74. **The Gold Rush** (1925)
75. Dances with Wolves (1990)
76. City Lights (1931)
77. **American Graffiti** (1973)
78. Rocky (1976)
79. The Deer Hunter (1978)
80. **The Wild Bunch** (1969)
81. Modern Times (1936)
82. Giant (1956)
83. Platoon (1986)
84. Fargo (1996)
85. Duck Soup (1933)
86. Mutiny on the Bounty (1935)
87. **Frankenstein** (1931)
88. Easy Rider (1969)
89. Patton (1970)
90. The Jazz Singer (1927)
91. My Fair Lady (1964)
92. A Place in the Sun (1951)
93. The Apartment (1960)
94. GoodFellas (1990)
95. **Pulp Fiction** (1994)
96. **The Searchers** (1956)
97. **Bringing Up Baby** (1938)
98. **Unforgiven** (1992)
99. Guess Who's Coming to Dinner (1967)
100. Yankee Doodle Dandy (1942)

THE AMERICAN FILM INSTITUTE'S TOP 100 COMEDIES

Following up on their Top 100 list (see previous page), the American Film Institute celebrated the new millennium by listing the twentieth century's top comedies. Once again, film fans found omitted favorites to be no laughing matter; the AFI's Web site reported the voting public's favorite to be the unlisted *Porky's*. As before, the bolded films below are also among PEOPLE's movie critic Leah Rozen's list of the best (see page 93).

1. **Some Like It Hot** (1959)
2. Tootsie (1982)
3. **Dr. Strangelove or: How I Learned to Stop Worrying and Love the Bomb** (1964)
4. Annie Hall (1977)
5. Duck Soup (1933)
6. Blazing Saddles (1974)
7. M*A*S*H (1970)
8. **It Happened One Night** (1934)
9. **The Graduate** (1967)
10. Airplane! (1980)
11. The Producers (1968)
12. **A Night at the Opera** (1935)
13. Young Frankenstein (1974)
14. **Bringing Up Baby** (1938)
15. The Philadelphia Story (1940)
16. **Singin' in the Rain** (1952)
17. The Odd Couple (1968)
18. **The General** (1927)
19. **His Girl Friday** (1940)
20. The Apartment (1960)
21. A Fish Called Wanda (1988)
22. Adam's Rib (1949)
23. When Harry Met Sally (1989)
24. Born Yesterday (1950)
25. **The Gold Rush** (1925)
26. Being There (1979)
27. There's Something About Mary (1998)
28. Ghostbusters (1984)
29. **This Is Spinal Tap** (1984)
30. Arsenic and Old Lace (1944)
31. Raising Arizona (1987)
32. The Thin Man (1934)
33. Modern Times (1936)
34. Groundhog Day (1993)
35. Harvey (1950)
36. National Lampoon's Animal House (1978)
37. The Great Dictator (1940)
38. City Lights (1931)
39. Sullivan's Travels (1941)
40. It's a Mad, Mad, Mad, Mad World (1963)
41. Moonstruck (1987)
42. Big (1988)
43. **American Graffiti** (1973)
44. My Man Godfrey (1936)
45. Harold and Maude (1972)
46. Manhattan (1979)
47. Shampoo (1975)
48. A Shot in the Dark (1964)
49. To Be or Not to Be (1942)
50. Cat Ballou (1965)
51. The Seven Year Itch (1955)
52. Ninotchka (1939)
53. Arthur (1981)
54. The Miracle of Morgan's Creek (1944)
55. **The Lady Eve** (1941)
56. Abbott and Costello Meet Frankenstein (1948)
57. Diner (1982)
58. It's a Gift (1934)
59. A Day at the Races (1937)
60. Topper (1937)
61. What's Up, Doc? (1972)
62. Sherlock, Jr. (1924)
63. Beverly Hills Cop (1984)
64. Broadcast News (1987)
65. Horse Feathers (1932)
66. Take the Money and Run (1969)
67. Mrs. Doubtfire (1993)
68. The Awful Truth (1937)
69. Bananas (1971)
70. Mr. Deeds Goes to Town (1936)
71. Caddyshack (1980)
72. Mr. Blandings Builds His Dream House (1948)
73. Monkey Business (1931)
74. 9 to 5 (1980)
75. She Done Him Wrong (1933)
76. Victor/Victoria (1982)
77. The Palm Beach Story (1942)
78. Road to Morocco (1942)
79. The Freshman (1925)
80. Sleeper (1973)
81. The Navigator (1924)
82. Private Benjamin (1980)
83. Father of the Bride (1950)
84. Lost in America (1985)
85. Dinner at Eight (1933)
86. City Slickers (1991)
87. Fast Times at Ridgemont High (1982)
88. Beetlejuice (1988)
89. The Jerk (1979)
90. Woman of the Year (1942)
91. The Heartbreak Kid (1972)
92. Ball of Fire (1941)
93. Fargo (1996)
94. Auntie Mame (1958)
95. Silver Streak (1976)
96. Sons of the Desert (1933)
97. **Bull Durham** (1988)
98. The Court Jester (1956)
99. The Nutty Professor (1963)
100. Good Morning, Vietnam (1987)

HOLLYWOOD'S FOOTPRINTS OF FAME

The first footprints at Grauman's Chinese Theater, as it was originally called, were made by Norma Talmadge in 1927 when, legend holds, she accidentally stepped in wet concrete outside the building. Since then over 190 stars have been immortalized, along with their hands and feet—and sometimes noses (Jimmy Durante), fists (John Wayne), and legs (Betty Grable). This year, influential ex-Warner Bros. executives Terry Semel and Robert Daly received the honor usually reserved for on-screen legends. The full Forecourt of the Stars at Mann's includes:

Abbott & Costello
Don Ameche
Julie Andrews
Edward Arnold
Fred Astaire
Gene Autry
John Barrymore
Freddie Bartholomew
Anne Baxter
Warren Beatty
Wallace Beery
Jack Benny
Edgar Bergen
Joan Blondell
Humphrey Bogart
Charles Boyer
Joe E. Brown
Yul Brynner
George Burns
Cantinflas
Eddie Cantor
Jim Carrey
Jackie Chan
Maurice Chevalier
Sean Connery
Gary Cooper
Jackie Cooper
Jeanne Crain
Joan Crawford
Bing Crosby
Tom Cruise
Robert Daly
Bebe Daniels
Linda Darnell
Marion Davies
Bette Davis
Doris Day
Olivia de Havilland
Cecil B. DeMille
The Dionne Quintuplets
Kirk Douglas
Michael Douglas
Marie Dressler
Donald Duck
Irene Dunne
Jimmie Durante
Deanna Durbin
Clint Eastwood
Nelson Eddy
Douglas Fairbanks
Alice Faye

Rhonda Fleming
Henry Fonda
Joan Fontaine
Harrison Ford
Clark Gable
Ava Gardner
Judy Garland
Greer Garson
Janet Gaynor
Richard Gere
Mel Gibson
Danny Glover
Whoopi Goldberg
Betty Grable
Cary Grant
Johnny Grant
Rosa Grauman (founder Sid
    Grauman's mother)
Sid Grauman
Tom Hanks
Ann Harding
Jean Harlow
Rex Harrison
William S. Hart
Susan Hayward
Rita Hayworth
Van Heflin
Sonja Henie
Jean Hersholt
William F. "Bill" Hertz
Charlton Heston
Bob Hope
Ron Howard
Rock Hudson
George Jessel
Van Johnson
Al Jolson
Danny Kaye
Michael Keaton
Gene Kelly
Deborah Kerr
Alan Ladd
Dorothy Lamour
Charles Laughton
Jack Lemmon
Mervyn LeRoy
Harold Lloyd
Sophia Loren
Myrna Loy
George Lucas
William Lundigan

Jeanette MacDonald
Ali MacGraw
Shirley MacLaine
Victor McLaglen
Steve McQueen
Fredric March
Dean Martin
Tony Martin
The Marx Brothers
James Mason
Marcello Mastroianni
Walter Matthau
Lauritz Melchior
Ray Milland
Hayley Mills
Carmen Miranda
Tom Mix
Marilyn Monroe
Colleen Moore
Eddie Murphy
George Murphy
Hildegarde Neff
Pola Negri
Paul Newman
Jack Nicholson
Jack Oakie
Margaret O'Brien
Donald O'Connor
Al Pacino
Louella Parsons
Gregory Peck
Mary Pickford
Ezio Pinza
Sidney Poitier
Dick Powell
Eleanor Powell
William Powell
Tyrone Power
Anthony Quinn
George Raft
Burt Reynolds
Debbie Reynolds
The Ritz Brothers
Edward G. Robinson
May Robson
Ginger Rogers
Roy Rogers
Mickey Rooney
Jane Russell
Rosalind Russell
Susan Sarandon

Arnold Schwarzenegger
Steven Seagal
Peter Sellers
Terry Semel
Norma Shearer
Jean Simmons
Frank Sinatra
Red Skelton
Steven Spielberg
Sylvester Stallone
Barbara Stanwyck
Star Trek crew (William
    Shatner, Leonard Nimoy,
    DeForest Kelley, James
    Doohan, Michelle Nichols,
    George Takei, Walter Koenig)
Star Wars characters
George Stevens
Jimmy Stewart
Meryl Streep
Gloria Swanson
Constance Talmadge
Norma Talmadge
Elizabeth Taylor
Robert Taylor
Shirley Temple
Danny Thomas
Gene Tierney
John Travolta
Lana Turner
Rudy Vallee
Dick Van Dyke
W. S. Van Dyke
Raoul Walsh
Denzel Washington
John Wayne
Clifton Webb
Oskar Werner
Richard Widmark
Esther Williams
Robin Williams
Bruce Willis
Jane Withers
Natalie Wood
Joanne Woodward
Monty Woolley
Jane Wyman
Diana Wynyard
Loretta Young
Robert Zemeckis
Adolph Zukor

THE BIGGEST HITS, YEAR BY YEAR

The following are the top five movies of the year based on data from *Variety*, beginning with 1939, when a Hollywood legend, *Gone With the Wind*, hit the theaters. Dollar figures listed are rentals (the amount of money collected by the studio), rather than box-office grosses, a relatively new method of measuring a film's box-office strength. (Figures for 1941 films, with the exception of *Sergeant York*, are rough estimates.)

1939

1. *Gone With the Wind*	$77,641,106
2. *The Wizard of Oz*	4,544,851
3. *The Hunchback of Notre Dame* (tie)	1,500,000
3. *Jesse James* (tie)	1,500,000
3. *Mr. Smith Goes to Washington* (tie)	1,500,000

1940

1. *Fantasia*	$41,660,000
2. *Pinocchio*	40,442,000
3. *Boom Town*	4,586,415
4. *Rebecca* (tie)	1,500,000
4. *Santa Fe Trail* (tie)	1,500,000

1941

1. *Sergeant York*	$6,135,707
2. *Dive Bomber* (tie)	1,500,000
2. *Honky Tonk* (tie)	1,500,000
2. *The Philadelphia Story* (tie)	1,500,000
2. *A Yank in the R.A.F.* (tie)	1,500,000

1942

1. *Bambi*	$47,265,000
2. *Mrs. Miniver*	5,390,009
3. *Yankee Doodle Dandy*	4,719,681
4. *Random Harvest*	4,665,501
5. *Casablanca*	4,145,178

1943

1. *This Is the Army*	$8,301,000
2. *For Whom the Bell Tolls*	7,100,000
3. *The Outlaw*	5,075,000
4. *The Song of Bernadette*	5,000,000
5. *Stage Door Canteen*	4,339,532

1944

1. *Going My Way*	$6,500.000
2. *Meet Me in St. Louis*	5,132,202
3. *Since You Went Away*	4,924,756
4. *30 Seconds over Tokyo*	4,471,080
5. *White Cliffs of Dover*	4,045,250

1945

1. *The Bells of St. Mary's*	$8,000,000
2. *Leave Her to Heaven*	5,500,000
3. *Spellbound*	4,970,583
4. *Anchors Aweigh*	4,778,679
5. *The Valley of Decision*	4,566,374

1946

1. *Song of the South*	$29,228,717
2. *The Best Years of Our Lives* (tie)	11,300,000
2. *Duel in the Sun* (tie)	11,300,000
4. *The Jolson Story*	7,600,000
5. *Blue Skies*	5,700,000

1947

1. *Welcome Stranger*	$6,100,000
2. *The Egg and I*	5,500,000
3. *Unconquered*	5,250,000
4. *Life with Father*	5,057,000
5. *Forever Amber*	5,000,000

1948

1. *The Red Shoes*	$5,000,000
2. *Red River*	4,506,825
3. *The Paleface*	4,500,000
4. *The Three Musketeers*	4,306,876
5. *Johnny Belinda*	4,266,000

1949

1. *Samson and Delilah*	$11,500,000
2. *Battleground*	5,051,143
3. *Jolson Sings Again* (tie)	5,000,000
3. *The Sands of Iwo Jima* (tie)	5,000,000
5. *I Was a Male War Bride*	4,100,000

1950

1. *Cinderella*	$41,087,000
2. *King Solomon's Mines*	5,586,000
3. *Annie Get Your Gun*	4,919,394
4. *Cheaper by the Dozen*	4,425,000
5. *Father of the Bride*	4,054,405

1951

1. *Quo Vadis?*	$11,901,662
2. *Alice in Wonderland*	7,196,000
3. *Show Boat*	5,533,000
4. *David and Bathsheba*	4,720,000
5. *The Great Caruso*	4,531,000

1952

1. *This Is Cinerama*	$15,400,000
2. *The Greatest Show on Earth*	14,000,000
3. *The Snows of Kilimanjaro*	6,500,000
4. *Ivanhoe*	6,258,000
5. *Hans Christian Andersen*	6,000,000

1953

1. *Peter Pan*	$37,584,000
2. *The Robe*	17,500,000
3. *From Here to Eternity*	12,200,000
4. *Shane*	9,000,000
5. *How To Marry a Millionaire*	7,300,000

1954

1. *White Christmas*	$12,000,000
2. *20,000 Leagues Under the Sea*	11,267,000
3. *Rear Window*	9,812,271
4. *The Caine Mutiny*	8,700,000
5. *The Glenn Miller Story*	7,590,994

1955

1. *Lady and the Tramp*	$40,249,000
2. *Cinerama Holiday*	12,000,000
3. *Mister Roberts*	8,500,000
4. *Battle Cry*	8,100,000
5. *Oklahoma!*	7,100,000

1956

1. *The Ten Commandments*	$43,000,000
2. *Around the World in 80 Days*	23,120,000
3. *Giant*	14,000,000
4. *Seven Wonders of the World*	12,500,000
5. *The King and I*	8,500,000

1957

1. *The Bridge on the River Kwai*	$17,195,000
2. *Peyton Place*	11,500,000
3. *Sayonara*	10,500,000
4. *Old Yeller*	10,050,000
5. *Raintree County*	5,962,839

1958

1. *South Pacific*	$17,500,000
2. *Auntie Mame*	9,300,000
3. *Cat on a Hot Tin Roof*	8,785,162
4. *No Time for Sergeants*	7,500,000
5. *Gigi*	7,321.423

1959

1. *Ben-Hur*	$36,992,088
2. *Sleeping Beauty*	21,998,000
3. *The Shaggy Dog*	12,317,000
4. *Operation Petticoat*	9,321,555
5. *Darby O'Gill and the Little People*	8,336,000

1960

1. *Swiss Family Robinson*	$20,178,000
2. *Psycho*	11,200,000
3. *Spartacus*	10,300,454
4. *Exodus*	8,331,582
5. *The Alamo*	7,918,776

1961

1. *101 Dalmatians*	$68,648,000
2. *West Side Story*	19,645,570
3. *The Guns of Navarone*	13,000,000
4. *El Cid*	12,000,000
5. *The Absent-Minded Professor*	11,426,000

1962

1. *How the West Was Won*	$20,932,883
2. *Lawrence of Arabia*	20,310,000
3. *The Longest Day*	17,600,000
4. *In Search of the Castaways*	9,975,000
5. *The Music Man*	8,100,000

1963

1. *Cleopatra*	$26,000,000
2. *It's a Mad, Mad, Mad, Mad World*	20,849,786
3. *Tom Jones*	16,925,988
4. *Irma La Douce*	11,921,784
5. *The Sword in the Stone*	10,475,000

1964

1. *Mary Poppins*	$45,000,000
2. *Goldfinger*	22,997,706
3. *The Carpetbaggers*	15,500,000
4. *My Fair Lady*	12,000,000
5. *From Russia with Love*	9,924,279

1965

1. *The Sound of Music*	$79,975,000
2. *Doctor Zhivago*	47,116,811
3. *Thunderball*	28,621,434
4. *Those Magnificent Men in Their Flying Machines*	14,000,000
5. *That Darn Cat*	12,628,000

1966

1. *Hawaii*	$15,553,018
2. *The Bible*	15,000,000
3. *Who's Afraid of Virginia Woolf?*	14,500,000
4. *A Man for All Seasons*	12,750,000
5. *Lt. Robin Crusoe, USN*	10,164,000

1967

1. *The Jungle Book*	$60,964,000
2. *The Graduate*	44,090,729
3. *Guess Who's Coming to Dinner*	25,500,000
4. *Bonnie and Clyde*	22,800,000
5. *The Dirty Dozen*	20,403,826

1968

1. *Funny Girl*	$26,325,000
2. *2001: A Space Odyssey*	25,521,917
3. *The Odd Couple*	20,000,000
4. *Bullitt*	19,000,000
5. *Romeo and Juliet*	17,473,000

1969

1. Butch Cassidy and the Sundance Kid	$46,039,000
2. The Love Bug	23,150,000
3. Midnight Cowboy	20,499,282
4. Easy Rider	19,100,000
5. Hello, Dolly!	15,200,000

1970

1. Love Story	$50,000,000
2. Airport	45,220,118
3. M*A*S*H	36,720,000
4. Patton	28,100,000
5. The Aristocats	26,462,000

1971

1. Fiddler on the Roof	$38,251,196
2. Billy Jack	32,500,000
3. The French Connection	26,315,000
4. Summer of '42	20,500,000
5. Diamonds Are Forever	19,726,829

1972

1. The Godfather	$86,691,000
2. The Poseidon Adventure	42,000,000
3. What's Up Doc?	28,000,000
4. Deliverance	22,600,000
5. Jeremiah Johnson	21,900,000

1973

1. The Exorcist	$89,000,000
2. The Sting	78,212,000
3. American Graffiti	55,128,175
4. Papillon	22,500,000
5. The Way We Were	22,457,000

1974

1. The Towering Inferno	$52,000,000
2. Blazing Saddles	47,800,000
3. Young Frankenstein	38,823,000
4. Earthquake	35,849,994
5. The Trial of Billy Jack	31,100,000

1975

1. Jaws	$129,549,325
2. One Flew over the Cuckoo's Nest	59,939,701
3. The Rocky Horror Picture Show	49,782,690
4. Shampoo	23,822,000
5. Dog Day Afternoon	22,500,000

1976

1. Rocky	$56,524,972
2. A Star Is Born	37,100,000
3. King Kong	36,915,000
4. Silver Streak	30,018,000
5. All the President's Men	30,000,000

1977

1. Star Wars	$270,918,000
2. Close Encounters of the Third Kind	82,750,000
3. Saturday Night Fever	74,100,000
4. Smokey and the Bandit	58,949,939
5. The Goodbye Girl	41,839,170

1978

1. Grease	$96,300,000
2. Superman	82,800,000
3. National Lampoon's Animal House	70,826,000
4. Every Which Way but Loose	51,900,000
5. Jaws 2	50,431,964

1979

1. Kramer vs. Kramer	$59,986,335
2. Star Trek: The Motion Picture	56,000,000
3. The Jerk	42,989,656
4. Rocky II	42,169,387
5. Alien	40,300,000

1980

1. The Empire Strikes Back	$173,814,000
2. 9 to 5	59,100,000
3. Stir Crazy	58,364,420
4. Airplane!	40,610,000
5. Any Which Way You Can	40,500,000

1981

1. Raiders of the Lost Ark	$115,598,000
2. Superman II	65,100,000
3. On Golden Pond	61,174,744
4. Arthur	42,000,000
5. Stripes	40,886,589

1982

1. E.T., the Extra-Terrestrial	$228,168,939
2. Tootsie	96,292,736
3. Rocky III	66,262,796
4. An Officer and a Gentleman	55,223,000
5. Porky's	54,000,000

1983

1. Return of the Jedi	$191,648,000
2. Terms of Endearment	50,250,000
3. Trading Places	40,600,000
4. WarGames	38,519,833
5. Superman III	37,200,000

1984

1. Ghostbusters	$130,211,324
2. Indiana Jones and the Temple of Doom	109,000,000
3. Beverly Hills Cop	108,000,000
4. Gremlins	79,500,000
5. The Karate Kid	43,432,881

1985

1. *Back to the Future*	$104,408,738
2. *Rambo: First Blood Part II*	78,919,250
3. *Rocky IV*	76,023,246
4. *The Color Purple*	47,900,000
5. *Out of Africa*	43,103,469

1986

1. *Top Gun*	$79,400,000
2. *"Crocodile" Dundee*	70,227,000
3. *Platoon*	69,742,143
4. *The Karate Kid, Part II*	58,362,026
5. *Star Trek IV: The Voyage Home*	56,820,071

1987

1. *Three Men and a Baby*	$81,313,000
2. *Beverly Hills Cop II*	80,857,776
3. *Fatal Attraction*	70,000,000
4. *Good Morning, Vietnam*	58,103,000
5. *The Untouchables*	36,866,530

1988

1. *Rain Man*	$86,813,000
2. *Who Framed Roger Rabbit*	81,244,000
3. *Coming to America*	65,000,000
4. *"Crocodile" Dundee II*	57,300,000
5. *Twins*	57,715,127

1989

1. *Batman*	$150,500,000
2. *Indiana Jones and the Last Crusade*	115,500,000
3. *Lethal Weapon 2*	79,500,000
4. *Back to the Future Part II*	72,319,630
5. *Honey, I Shrunk the Kids*	72,007,000

1990

1. *Home Alone*	$140,099,000
2. *Ghost*	98,200,000
3. *Pretty Woman*	81,905,530
4. *Dances with Wolves*	81,537,971
5. *Teenage Mutant Ninja Turtles*	67,650,000

1991

1. *Terminator 2: Judgment Day*	$112,500,000
2. *Robin Hood: Prince of Thieves*	86,000,000
3. *Beauty and the Beast*	69,415,000
4. *Hook*	65,000,000
5. *City Slickers*	60,750,000

1992

1. *Aladdin*	$111,740,683
2. *Home Alone 2: Lost in New York*	103,377,614
3. *Batman Returns*	100,100,000
4. *Lethal Weapon 3*	80,000,000
5. *A Few Good Men*	71,000,000

1993

1. *Jurassic Park*	$212,953,437
2. *Mrs. Doubtfire*	111,000,000
3. *The Fugitive*	97,000,000
4. *The Firm*	77,047,044
5. *Sleepless in Seattle*	64,930,137

1994

1. *The Lion King*	$173,057,366
2. *Forrest Gump*	156,000,000
3. *True Lies*	80,000,000
4. *The Santa Clause*	74,348,689
5. *The Flintstones*	70,753,383

1995

1. *Batman Forever*	$105,100,000
2. *Toy Story*	103,200,000
3. *Apollo 13*	92,642,370
4. *Pocahontas*	67,848,010
5. *Casper*	49,160,810

1996

1. *Independence Day*	$177,190,000
2. *Twister*	133,464,330
3. *Mission: Impossible*	93,067,933
4. *Jerry Maguire*	74,937,042
5. *The Rock*	70,600,000

1997

1. *The Lost World: Jurassic Park*	$130,086,760
2. *Men in Black*	114,110,497
3. *Liar Liar*	95,931,900
4. *Air Force One*	77,734,801
5. *Batman & Robin*	58,492,667

1998

1. *Titanic*	$324,425,520
2. *Armageddon*	104,806,521
3. *Saving Private Ryan*	89,619,599
4. *There's Something About Mary*	74,537,493
5. *Godzilla*	70,850,116

THE 100 BEST MOVIES OF ALL TIME

They are the celluloid touchstones of our inner life, the enduring echoes of various generations, and the most bittersweet of social commentaries played out 10 yards high. PEOPLE's movie critic Leah Rozen has selected 100 of the greatest, an assignment as agonizing as having to pick the 10 greatest home runs ever hit in baseball.

ADAM'S RIB (1949)
Katharine Hepburn and Spencer Tracy as married attorneys on opposite sides of an attempted murder case. The smartest and funniest of their five pairings.

THE ADVENTURES OF ROBIN HOOD (1938)
There have been other Robin Hoods, including Kevin Costner and Sean Connery, but never one as appealingly roguish as Errol Flynn. A rousing adventure.

THE AFRICAN QUEEN (1951)
In a splendidly comic and sweet romance, the mismatched Humphrey Bogart and Katharine Hepburn take a slow love boat up the river in steamy Africa.

ALL ABOUT EVE (1950)
Smart and tart. Director-writer Joseph Mankiewicz's acerbic masterpiece about theater folk, with Bette Davis at her caustic best.

AMERICAN GRAFFITI (1973)
In George Lucas's influential hit film, a group of California teenagers, including Ron Howard and Richard Dreyfuss, spend one long night in 1962 cruising in cars and goofing off.

BACK STREET (1941)
A vintage weepie about a woman who gives up everything for love. This second of three filmed versions of Fannie Hurst's potboiler shines brightly thanks to the incomparable Margaret Sullavan and Charles Boyer.

BADLANDS (1973)
Martin Sheen and Sissy Spacek play a young couple who go on an aimless killing spree in a chilling cult film by director Terence Malick.

BEAUTY AND THE BEAST (1946)
French surrealist Jean Cocteau's sophisticated version of the classic fairy tale *La Belle et la bete* is for grown-up romantics. Then again, the 1991 Disney version, a musical, is pretty swell too.

BELLE DE JOUR (1967)
Director Luis Buñuel's deliciously creepy movie about a bourgeois Paris housewife, a radiant Catherine Deneuve, who spends her days working in a brothel. Or does she?

THE BEST YEARS OF OUR LIVES (1946)
A moving drama about the domestic and occupational difficulties facing three returning World War II vets, with Fredric March, Dana Andrews, and Harold Russell, a real vet who had lost both arms in the war.

THE BICYCLE THIEF (1948)
Director Vittorio de Sica's heartbreaking drama, a linchpin of Italian neo-realism, about a workman who loses everything when his bicycle is stolen.

THE BIRTH OF A NATION (1915)
The first blockbuster. Although parts now seem irredeemably racist, director D. W. Griffith's epic Civil War drama is still a sight to behold.

BLADE RUNNER (1982)
The future as you don't want it to be. Gruff guy Harrison Ford stars in director Ridley Scott's greatlooking sci-fi drama.

BRINGING UP BABY (1938)
A ditzy Katharine Hepburn sets her sights on zoology professor Cary Grant in a delightful screwball comedy. And love that tiger.

BULL DURHAM (1988)
A great romance movie disguised as a baseball picture. Susan Sarandon gets to choose between minor leaguers Kevin Costner and Tim Robbins, both of whom pitch woo her way.

BUTCH CASSIDY AND THE SUNDANCE KID (1969)
In one of the all-time cool buddy movies, Paul Newman and Robert Redford display big star charisma and charm as gallivanting outlaws.

CAGED (1949)
If you see just one women-inprison film, make it this one. Eleanor Parker stars as the good girl gone wrong.

CASABLANCA (1942)
A kiss is still a kiss, but the ones here have real staying power. This is Hollywood movie-making at its most stylishly satisfying, with Humphrey Bogart and Ingrid Bergman.

CHINATOWN (1974)
Jack Nicholson's nose gets sliced and lots of other nasty things happen in director Roman Polanski's jaundiced thriller set in '30s Los Angeles.

CITIZEN KANE (1941)
The granddaddy of all biopics, though innovative director-star Orson Welles had to change the name from William Randolph Hearst to Charles Foster Kane. A must-see for anyone interested in movies.

THE CROWD (1928)
This silent movie, directed by King Vidor, movingly depicts the everyday life of a young whitecollar worker and his wife in New

York City. It shows just how fluid and powerful the images in silent film had become right before sound took over.

DAVID COPPERFIELD (1934)
A perfect film adaptation of Charles Dickens's novel about the adventures of an orphaned youth. W. C. Fields is a hoot as Mr. Micawber.

DAY FOR NIGHT (1973)
French director François Truffaut's valentine to movie-making contains sly references and in-jokes to many of his earlier films. With Jacqueline Bisset and Jean-Pierre Léaud.

DEAD MAN WALKING (1995)
No matter where you stand on the death penalty, this powerful drama scores in telling the story of a nun (Susan Sarandon) who guides a murderer (Sean Penn) to contrition before his execution. Tim Robbins directed.

DO THE RIGHT THING (1989)
Director Spike Lee's street-smart drama about one very hot summer day in a tense Brooklyn neighborhood has plenty to say about race relations and the need for more and better communication.

DOUBLE INDEMNITY (1944)
Barbara Stanwyck, at her bad-girl best, sweet-talks Fred MacMurray into helping her kill her husband. Billy Wilder directed.

DR. STRANGELOVE... (1962)
A savagely funny black comedy, though it's a tad dated now, about the nuclear bomb and world politics. Stanley Kubrick directed and Peter Sellers and George C. Scott star.

THE EMPIRE STRIKES BACK (1980)
The best of the *Star Wars* trilogy. Stars Harrison Ford, Carrie Fisher, and Mark Hamill.

E.T., THE EXTRA-TERRESTRIAL (1982)
It may be simple-minded and sentimental, but who can resist this sweet tale of the friendship between a suburban youth and an alien marooned on Earth?

FRANKENSTEIN (1931)
Still the eeriest, and most humane, version of Mary Wollstonecraft Shelley's classic monster tale. With Boris Karloff as the big guy.

THE GENERAL (1926)
Buster Keaton, one of the comic glories of the silent era, piles on brilliant sight gag after sight gag in this Civil War comedy.

THE GODFATHER (1972)
A family drama about the troubled and violent Corleone clan. Director Francis Ford Coppola, with the help of Marlon Brando, James Caan, and a very young Al Pacino, made the ultimate gangster film.

THE GOLD RUSH (1925)
Charlie Chaplin's little tramp seeks his fortune in the Yukon. Watch for the justly famous shoe-eating scene in which Chaplin twirls shoelaces with a fork as if eating spaghetti.

GONE WITH THE WIND (1939)
This Civil War–era drama is big and long and we wouldn't change a minute of it. Except maybe the ending. But, tomorrow's another day, and maybe Rhett will come back then. With Clark Gable and Vivien Leigh.

THE GRADUATE (1968)
In a wonderfully wry comedy, Dustin Hoffman passes his first summer after college floating in his parents' pool and having a desultory affair with Anne Bancroft. Nearly 30 years later, this one still seems fresh.

THE GRAPES OF WRATH (1940)
Director John Ford's masterful adaptation of John Steinbeck's bleak novel about depression-era Oklahomans who head off for what they hope will be a better life in California. With Henry Fonda and Jane Darwell.

A HARD DAY'S NIGHT (1964)
The swinging '60s encapsulated, minus the politics. This first Beatles film is flat-out zany fun.

HIGH NOON (1952)
The Western pared to its bone. With Gary Cooper as the principled lawman who has to go it alone against the bad guys.

HIS GIRL FRIDAY (1940)
Speed is of the essence in this newspaper comedy, with Rosalind Russell and Cary Grant competing to see who can insult the other faster.

HOLIDAY INN (1942)
When Bing Crosby starts singing "White Christmas," you just know it's going to snow in time. Crosby and Fred Astaire costar in this chipper musical as the owners of a hotel where they put on shows with holiday themes.

HUD (1963)
Paul Newman as one of the screen's first anti-heroes, an amoral cowboy who brings no good to all whom he touches. With Melvyn Douglas and Patricia Neal.

INVASION OF THE BODY SNATCHERS (1955)
Low-budget, paranoid '50s sci-fi allegory about aliens taking over residents of a small town. The '78 remake can't hold a pod to it.

IT HAPPENED ONE NIGHT (1934)
Screwball comedy meets road picture in director Frank Capra's jaunty film about a runaway heiress who spars and sparks with a newspaperman. With Claudette Colbert and Clark Gable.

JAWS (1975)
Jumbo shark on the loose. Director Steven Spielberg scored his first blockbuster with this bloody thriller. Dig John Williams's carnivorous score.

THE LADY EVE (1941)
Wickedly entertaining comedy by director Preston Sturges about a con woman (Barbara Stanwyck) who hustles a youthful million-aire (Henry Fonda), only to realize almost too late that she's actually in love with the big lug.

THE LAST METRO (1980)
A moving drama about a French theatrical troupe in occupied Paris during World War II. François Truffaut directed, and Catherine Deneuve and Gérard Depardieu star.

LONE STAR (1996)
Director John Sayles's sweeping drama about fathers and sons, the past catching up to us, and cultural diversity, all crammed into the lives of folks in one small Texas border town.

LONG DAY'S JOURNEY INTO NIGHT (1962)
Playwright Eugene O'Neill's autobiographical masterpiece, brought to the screen with all the hurt showing. Katharine Hepburn digs deep as the morphine-addicted mother. Also stars Ralph Richardson and Jason Robards.

LONGTIME COMPANION (1990)
An AIDS drama about a tight-knit group of male friends in New York City in the 1980s which poignantly depicts just how devastating the disease is to both those who have it and those they leave behind.

MCCABE AND MRS. MILLER (1971)
Director Robert Altman's lyrically haunting look at how the West was wasted, with Warren Beatty as a gunfighter who sets up a brothel and Julie Christie as his opium-addicted madam.

THE MALTESE FALCON (1941)
Love that black bird. With Humphrey Bogart as private eye Sam Spade, who takes no guff from anyone, including conniving Mary Astor.

THE MANCHURIAN CANDIDATE (1962)
A sharp-witted political thriller, from which one suspects Oliver Stone learned much of what he knows. With Frank Sinatra, Laurence Harvey, and Angela Lansbury.

MEAN STREETS (1973)
Loyalty among thieves only goes so far, as a group of boyhood friends in Little Italy discover upon growing up. Martin Scors-ese's breakthrough film, with Robert De Niro and Harvey Keitel.

MILDRED PIERCE (1945)
The ultimate Joan Crawford movie. She plays a suburban divorcée who makes a fortune as a hard-working restaurateur, only to see her spoiled daughter steal her beau.

NETWORK (1976)
Biliousness raised to high art. Paddy Chayefsky's sharp satire about the influence of the media. With Peter Finch, William Holden, and Faye Dunaway.

A NIGHT AT THE OPERA (1935)
The Marx Brothers reek loony havoc when—and before and after—the fat lady sings. Also stars Margaret Dumont, the matronly butt of so many of Groucho's jokes.

NIGHTS OF CABIRIA (1957)
Italian director Federico Fellini, in directing wife Giuletta Masina in her greatest role as a hard-luck prostitute in Rome, made a near-perfect film that will have you laughing one minute, near tears the next. The musical *Sweet Charity* is based on *Cabiria*.

NOTORIOUS (1946)
Alfred Hitchcock at his perversely romantic best. Sexy and scary, with American agent Cary Grant sending lady love Ingrid Bergman to wed a covert Nazi.

PERSONA (1966)
The personalities of two women, a nurse and the mentally ill patient she is caring for, begin to overlap and mesh in Swedish filmmaker Ingmar Bergman's brooding, disturbing drama. With Liv Ullmann and Bibi Andersson.

PICNIC AT HANGING ROCK (1975)
Spooky goings-on at a girls' school in turn-of-the-century Australia when several of the students mysteriously vanish, seemingly into thin air, while at a picnic. Peter Weir directed.

PLACES IN THE HEART (1984)
A lovely movie about human frailty and redemption from director Robert Benton. Sally Field stars as a newly widowed Texas farm woman who perseveres despite hard times.

THE PLAYER (1992)
Director Robert Altman zings Hollywood in a biting satire about a studio executive who gets away with murder. Tim Robbins has the lead, but masses of other big names show up for cameos.

PSYCHO (1960)
Janet Leigh, get away from that shower. Hitchcock's scalding shocker stars Tony Perkins as a twisted hotel keeper who doesn't like his guests to check out.

PULP FICTION (1994)
Violent, amusing, and cleverly structured, director Quentin Tarantino's movie is vastly more entertaining than the horde of imitations it has spawned. With John Travolta, Bruce Willis, and Samuel L. Jackson.

THE PURPLE ROSE OF CAIRO (1984)
When the hero (Jeff Daniels) of a '30s movie steps out of the screen to begin making time with one of his biggest fans (Mia Farrow), the line between real life during the depression and movie fantasy becomes all too clear in Woody Allen's comic masterpiece.

QUEEN CHRISTINA (1937)
Greta Garbo is at her most androgynously alluring in a romanticized Hollywood biopic about a 17th-century Swedish queen. Check out Garbo's enigmatic expression in the famous final shot.

THE QUIET MAN (1952)
John Wayne and director John Ford left the Wild West behind for the greener fields of Ireland, with splendid results. In this boisterous, appealing love story, Wayne plays an American boxer who woos Irish lass Maureen O'Hara.

RAGING BULL (1980)
Director Martin Scorsese's penetrating look at the troubled life of pugilist Jake La Motta boasts one of Robert De Niro's finest performances.

RASHOMON (1950)
Truth proves elusive as four people involved each give differing accounts of a rape-murder in Japanese director Akira Kurosawa's brilliant drama.

REAR WINDOW (1954)
James Stewart and a sexy Grace Kelly star in Alfred Hitchcock's sophisticated thriller about an invalided photographer who spots a murder across his apartment courtyard.

REBEL WITHOUT A CAUSE (1955)
Alienated teens reign supreme as James Dean—who died before the movie was released—and Natalie Wood express the suffering of their generation.

ROMAN HOLIDAY (1953)
A charming romp with Audrey Hepburn at her most appealingly gamine as a princess who ditches her royal duties and takes up with Gregory Peck, an American newspaperman.

SAVING PRIVATE RYAN (1998)
War is hell, and never more so than in director Steven Spielberg's monumental film about a group of American soldiers who land in France on D-Day. Tom Hanks's final command, "Earn this," haunts us still.

SCHINDLER'S LIST (1983)
Director Steven Spielberg's powerful retelling of the story of businessman Oskar Schindler, who saved hundreds of Jews from the Nazi gas chambers during World War II. With Liam Neeson as Schindler and Ben Kingsley as his Jewish factory foreman.

THE SEARCHERS (1956)
In a multilayered Western by director John Ford, John Wayne spends years searching for his niece, Natalie Wood, after she is captured by Native Americans. One of the most influential films ever made.

SHANE (1953)
A retired gunfighter rides into town and helps out a homesteading couple and their young son. Sounds simple, but it's anything but. With Alan Ladd, Jean Arthur, and Brandon de Wilde.

THE SHOP AROUND THE CORNER (1940)
The famed "Lubitsch Touch," so named for the sophisticated comedy work of director Ernst Lubitsch, shines bright in a charming romance about two bickering shop clerks. With Jimmy Stewart and the matchless Margaret Sullavan.

SHOWBOAT (1936)
This classic musical about life aboard a Mississippi riverboat features dandy Jerome Kern tunes and a glimpse of why Paul Robeson and Helen Morgan were such electrifying performers in their day.

SINGIN' IN THE RAIN (1952)
A musical about Hollywood's awkward transition from silents to talkies, this one can't be beat, especially for Gene Kelly's singing and dancing of the damp title number.

SNOW WHITE AND THE SEVEN DWARFS (1937)
Walt Disney's first feature-length animated feature still shimmers brightly, though Snow White's brusque farewell to the dwarfs at the movie's end seems a mite ungrateful.

SOME LIKE IT HOT (1959)
The funniest movie ever made about cross-dressing. Tony Curtis and Jack Lemmon star as musicians who, after witnessing a mob hit, go undercover with an all-girl band, whose members include Marilyn Monroe. Billy Wilder directed.

THE SOUND OF MUSIC (1965)
Sure, it's sugary, but any time Julie Andrews is on screen in this Rogers and Hammerstein musical about the would-be nun who comes to stay with the Von Trapp family, all is gloriously forgiven.

SULLIVAN'S TRAVELS (1941)
A Hollywood director (Joel McCrea) rediscovers the meaning of life while traveling across America in director Preston Sturges's quick-witted comedy.

SUNSET BOULEVARD (1950)
The original. In director Billy Wilder's savage look at the underbelly of Hollywood, silent star Gloria Swanson made her big comeback playing, appropriately enough, a silent star hoping to make a comeback.

SWEET SMELL OF SUCCESS (1957)
Everyone's corrupt or corruptible in this atmospheric melodrama about nasty dealings between a Broadway press agent (Tony Curtis) and a powerful Manhattan newspaper columnist (Burt Lancaster).

TARZAN AND HIS MATE (1934)
The second of the Johnny

Weismuller films about Edgar Rice Borroughs' ape man, and the best of the series. Maureen O'Sullivan, dressed in next to nothing, makes a perky Jane.

THE TERMINATOR (1984)
Pure nihilistic fun, this sci-fi action thriller deservedly made muscleman Arnold Schwarzenegger, who plays a singularly focused android, into a big star.

THELMA AND LOUISE (1991)
Two good girls go wrong. A feminist firecracker of a movie, with strong performances by Susan Sarandon and Geena Davis. And check out the truly buff Brad Pitt.

THIS IS SPINAL TAP (1984)
This is a blast. Turn your amps up to 11 as you chuckle your way through this comic moc-umentary about a heavy metal rock group and its hangers-on. Rob Reiner directed.

TITANIC (1997)
For sheer scope and size, you gotta love it. Director James Cameron made going to the movies seem like something special again. This water-logged drama turned Leonardo DiCaprio into a household name—at least in households containing teenage girls.

TO HAVE AND HAVE NOT (1944)
Romantic sparks fly in Humphrey Bogart and Lauren Bacall's first pairing, a World War II drama that borrows more than a little from *Casablanca* but boasts a comic zing all its own.

TOP HAT (1935)
Fred Astaire and Ginger Rogers dance (and sing) "Cheek to Cheek" and other great Irving Berlin tunes in their most glorious teaming. Keep an eye peeled for a young Lucille Ball in the flower shop.

2001: A SPACE ODYSSEY (1968)
Director Stanley Kubrick's

TOP FILM SOUNDTRACKS
We love to go to the movies, but a good soundtrack means we can take them home with us, too. And fans do, as this list indicates. (Source: RIAA)

Soundtrack	Sales (in millions)
The Bodyguard	17
Saturday Night Fever	15
Purple Rain	13
Forrest Gump	12
Dirty Dancing	11
Titanic	11
The Lion King	10
Top Gun	9
Footloose	8
Grease	8
Waiting to Exhale	7
The Big Chill	6
Flashdance	6
Pure Country	6
City of Angels	5
The Jazz Singer	5
Space Jam	5
Evita	5

hauntingly beautiful and enormously influential science fiction thriller. And watch out for HAL.

UNFORGIVEN (1992)
Clint Eastwood directed and stars in a mature, meditative Western about an ex–hired gun turned farmer who goes on one last killing spree.

WHITE HEAT (1949)
Jimmy Cagney at his sinister best as a gangster who can't cut his ties to his mother's apron strings. Great ending.

WHO FRAMED ROGER RABBIT (1988)
It's 'toon time as animated characters and actors interact to solve a crime in a technological bit of trickery that shows just how far animation has come since the days of Gertie the Dinosaur. 'Toon or no 'toon, Jessica Rabbit (voiced by Kathleen Turner) is vavavoom.

THE WILD BUNCH (1969)
Director Sam Peckinpah's violent tale of revenge shakes the good

ol' Western by its spurs. With William Holden, Ernest Borgnine, and Robert Ryan.

WITNESS (1985)
Cultures clash as a big-city detective (Harrison Ford) hides out among the Amish in order to protect a young Amish boy who has witnessed a murder.

THE WIZARD OF OZ (1939)
Is once a year often enough? This entertaining children's musical—assuming that the kids are old enough to sit through the flying monkeys—features stellar performances by Judy Garland, Bert Lahr, Ray Bolger, and Jack Haley.

WRITTEN ON THE WIND (1956)
So bad it's good. A steamy melodrama about a very messed-up family, directed by Douglas Sirk, the master of glossy high camp, and starring Rock Hudson, Lauren Bacall, and Dorothy Malone.

THE BRIGHTEST STARS, BY YEAR

In today's high-pressure movie business, the most valuable commodity is a star who shines so bright that he or she can "open" a movie—filling seats on the basis of pure popularity regardless of the allure of the story line. Every year since 1933, Quigley Publishing has polled more than 500 moviehouse owners nationwide to determine which stars they regarded as the surest-fire box-office draw.

1933
1. Marie Dressler
2. Will Rogers
3. Janet Gaynor
4. Eddie Cantor
5. Wallace Beery
6. Jean Harlow
7. Clark Gable
8. Mae West
9. Norma Shearer
10. Joan Crawford

1934
1. Will Rogers
2. Clark Gable
3. Janet Gaynor
4. Wallace Beery
5. Mae West
6. Joan Crawford
7. Bing Crosby
8. Shirley Temple
9. Marie Dressler
10. Norma Shearer

1935
1. Shirley Temple
2. Will Rogers
3. Clark Gable
4. Fred Astaire & Ginger Rogers
5. Joan Crawford
6. Claudette Colbert
7. Dick Powell
8. Wallace Beery
9. Joe E. Brown
10. James Cagney

1936
1. Shirley Temple
2. Clark Gable
3. Fred Astaire and Ginger Rogers
4. Robert Taylor
5. Joe E. Brown
6. Dick Powell
7. Joan Crawford
8. Claudette Colbert
9. Jeanette MacDonald
10. Gary Cooper

1937
1. Shirley Temple
2. Clark Gable
3. Robert Taylor
4. Bing Crosby
5. William Powell
6. Jane Withers
7. Fred Astaire & Ginger Rogers
8. Sonja Henie
9. Gary Cooper
10. Myrna Loy

1938
1. Shirley Temple
2. Clark Gable
3. Sonja Henie
4. Mickey Rooney
5. Spencer Tracy
6. Robert Taylor
7. Myrna Loy
8. Jane Withers
9. Alice Faye
10. Tyrone Power

1939
1. Mickey Rooney
2. Tyrone Power
3. Spencer Tracy
4. Clark Gable
5. Shirley Temple
6. Bette Davis
7. Alice Faye
8. Errol Flynn
9. James Cagney
10. Sonja Henie

1940
1. Mickey Rooney
2. Spencer Tracy
3. Clark Gable
4. Gene Autry
5. Tyrone Power
6. James Cagney
7. Bing Crosby
8. Wallace Beery
9. Bette Davis
10. Judy Garland

1941
1. Mickey Rooney
2. Clark Gable
3. Abbott & Costello
4. Bob Hope
5. Spencer Tracy
6. Gene Autry
7. Gary Cooper
8. Bette Davis
9. James Cagney
10. Spencer Tracy

1942
1. Abbott & Costello
2. Clark Gable
3. Gary Cooper
4. Mickey Rooney
5. Bob Hope
6. James Cagney
7. Gene Autry
8. Betty Grable
9. Greer Garson
10. Spencer Tracy

1943
1. Betty Grable
2. Bob Hope
3. Abbott & Costello
4. Bing Crosby
5. Gary Cooper
6. Greer Garson
7. Humphrey Bogart
8. James Cagney
9. Mickey Rooney
10. Clark Gable

1944
1. Bing Crosby
2. Gary Cooper
3. Bob Hope
4. Betty Grable
5. Spencer Tracy
6. Greer Garson
7. Humphrey Bogart
8. Abbott & Costello
9. Cary Grant
10. Bette Davis

1945
1. Bing Crosby
2. Van Johnson
3. Greer Garson
4. Betty Grable
5. Spencer Tracy
6. Humphrey Bogart (tie)
6. Gary Cooper (tie)
8. Bob Hope
9. Judy Garland
10. Margaret O'Brien

1946
1. Bing Crosby
2. Ingrid Bergman
3. Van Johnson
4. Gary Cooper
5. Bob Hope
6. Humphrey Bogart
7. Greer Garson
8. Margaret O'Brien
9. Betty Grable
10. Roy Rogers

1947
1. Bing Crosby
2. Betty Grable
3. Ingrid Bergman
4. Gary Cooper
5. Humphrey Bogart
6. Bob Hope
7. Clark Gable
8. Gregory Peck
9. Claudette Colbert
10. Alan Ladd

1948
1. Bing Crosby
2. Betty Grable
3. Abbott & Costello
4. Gary Cooper
5. Bob Hope
6. Humphrey Bogart
7. Clark Gable
8. Cary Grant
9. Spencer Tracy
10. Ingrid Bergman

1949

1. Bob Hope
2. Bing Crosby
3. Abbott & Costello
4. John Wayne
5. Gary Cooper
6. Cary Grant
7. Betty Grable
8. Esther Williams
9. Humphrey Bogart
10. Clark Gable

1950

1. John Wayne
2. Bob Hope
3. Bing Crosby
4. Betty Grable
5. James Stewart
6. Abbott & Costello
7. Clifton Webb
8. Esther Williams
9. Spencer Tracy
10. Randolph Scott

1951

1. John Wayne
2. Dean Martin & Jerry Lewis
3. Betty Grable
4. Abbott & Costello
5. Bing Crosby
6. Bob Hope
7. Randolph Scott
8. Gary Cooper
9. Doris Day
10. Spencer Tracy

1952

1. Dean Martin & Jerry Lewis
2. Gary Cooper
3. John Wayne
4. Bing Crosby
5. Bob Hope
6. James Stewart
7. Doris Day
8. Gregory Peck
9. Susan Hayward
10. Randolph Scott

1953

1. Gary Cooper
2. Dean Martin & Jerry Lewis
3. John Wayne
4. Alan Ladd
5. Bing Crosby
6. Marilyn Monroe
7. James Stewart

8. Bob Hope
9. Susan Hayward
10. Randolph Scott

1954

1. John Wayne
2. Dean Martin & Jerry Lewis
3. Gary Cooper
4. James Stewart
5. Marilyn Monroe
6. Alan Ladd
7. William Holden
8. Bing Crosby
9. Jane Wyman
10. Marlon Brando

1955

1. James Stewart
2. Grace Kelly
3. John Wayne
4. William Holden
5. Gary Cooper
6. Marlon Brando
7. Dean Martin & Jerry Lewis
8. Humphrey Bogart
9. June Allyson
10. Clark Gable

1956

1. William Holden
2. John Wayne
3. James Stewart
4. Burt Lancaster
5. Glenn Ford
6. Dean Martin & Jerry Lewis
7. Gary Cooper
8. Marilyn Monroe
9. Kim Novak
10. Frank Sinatra

1957

1. Rock Hudson
2. John Wayne
3. Pat Boone
4. Elvis Presley
5. Frank Sinatra
6. Gary Cooper
7. William Holden
8. James Stewart
9. Jerry Lewis
10. Yul Brynner

1958

1. Glenn Ford
2. Elizabeth Taylor
3. Jerry Lewis
4. Marlon Brando
5. Rock Hudson
6. William Holden
7. Brigitte Bardot
8. Yul Brynner
9. James Stewart
10. Frank Sinatra

1959

1. Rock Hudson
2. Cary Grant
3. James Stewart
4. Doris Day
5. Debbie Reynolds
6. Glenn Ford
7. Frank Sinatra
8. John Wayne
9. Jerry Lewis
10. Susan Hayward

1960

1. Doris Day
2. Rock Hudson
3. Cary Grant
4. Elizabeth Taylor
5. Debbie Reynolds
6. Tony Curtis
7. Sandra Dee
8. Frank Sinatra
9. Jack Lemmon
10. John Wayne

1961

1. Elizabeth Taylor
2. Rock Hudson
3. Doris Day
4. John Wayne
5. Cary Grant
6. Sandra Dee
7. Jerry Lewis
8. William Holden
9. Tony Curtis
10. Elvis Presley

1962

1. Doris Day
2. Rock Hudson
3. Cary Grant
4. John Wayne
5. Elvis Presley
6. Elizabeth Taylor
7. Jerry Lewis
8. Frank Sinatra
9. Sandra Dee
10. Burt Lancaster

1963

1. Doris Day
2. John Wayne
3. Rock Hudson
4. Jack Lemmon
5. Cary Grant
6. Elizabeth Taylor
7. Elvis Presley
8. Sandra Dee
9. Paul Newman
10. Jerry Lewis

1964

1. Doris Day
2. Jack Lemmon
3. Rock Hudson
4. John Wayne
5. Cary Grant
6. Elvis Presley
7. Shirley MacLaine
8. Ann-Margret
9. Paul Newman
10. Jerry Lewis

1965

1. Sean Connery
2. John Wayne
3. Doris Day
4. Julie Andrews
5. Jack Lemmon
6. Elvis Presley
7. Cary Grant
8. James Stewart
9. Elizabeth Taylor
10. Richard Burton

1966

1. Julie Andrews
2. Sean Connery
3. Elizabeth Taylor
4. Jack Lemmon
5. Richard Burton
6. Cary Grant
7. John Wayne
8. Doris Day
9. Paul Newman
10. Elvis Presley

1967

1. Julie Andrews
2. Lee Marvin
3. Paul Newman
4. Dean Martin
5. Sean Connery
6. Elizabeth Taylor
7. Sidney Poitier
8. John Wayne
9. Richard Burton
10. Steve McQueen

1968
1. Sidney Poitier
2. Paul Newman
3. Julie Andrews
4. John Wayne
5. Clint Eastwood
6. Dean Martin
7. Steve McQueen
8. Jack Lemmon
9. Lee Marvin
10. Elizabeth Taylor

1969
1. Paul Newman
2. John Wayne
3. Steve McQueen
4. Dustin Hoffman
5. Clint Eastwood
6. Sidney Poitier
7. Lee Marvin
8. Jack Lemmon
9. Katharine Hepburn
10. Barbra Streisand

1970
1. Paul Newman
2. Clint Eastwood
3. Steve McQueen
4. John Wayne
5. Elliott Gould
6. Dustin Hoffman
7. Lee Marvin
8. Jack Lemmon
9. Barbra Streisand
10. Walter Matthau

1971
1. John Wayne
2. Clint Eastwood
3. Paul Newman
4. Steve McQueen
5. George C. Scott
6. Dustin Hoffman
7. Walter Matthau
8. Ali MacGraw
9. Sean Connery
10. Lee Marvin

1972
1. Clint Eastwood
2. George C. Scott
3. Gene Hackman
4. John Wayne
5. Barbra Streisand
6. Marlon Brando
7. Paul Newman
8. Steve McQueen
9. Dustin Hoffman
10. Goldie Hawn

1973
1. Clint Eastwood
2. Ryan O'Neal
3. Steve McQueen
4. Burt Reynolds
5. Robert Redford
6. Barbra Streisand
7. Paul Newman
8. Charles Bronson
9. John Wayne
10. Marlon Brando

1974
1. Robert Redford
2. Clint Eastwood
3. Paul Newman
4. Barbra Streisand
5. Steve McQueen
6. Burt Reynolds
7. Charles Bronson
8. Jack Nicholson
9. Al Pacino
10. John Wayne

1975
1. Robert Redford
2. Barbra Streisand
3. Al Pacino
4. Charles Bronson
5. Paul Newman
6. Clint Eastwood
7. Burt Reynolds
8. Woody Allen
9. Steve McQueen
10. Gene Hackman

1976
1. Robert Redford
2. Jack Nicholson
3. Dustin Hoffman
4. Clint Eastwood
5. Mel Brooks
6. Burt Reynolds
7. Al Pacino
8. Tatum O'Neal
9. Woody Allen
10. Charles Bronson

1977
1. Sylvester Stallone
2. Barbra Streisand
3. Clint Eastwood
4. Burt Reynolds
5. Robert Redford
6. Woody Allen
7. Mel Brooks
8. Al Pacino
9. Diane Keaton
10. Robert De Niro

1978
1. Burt Reynolds
2. John Travolta
3. Richard Dreyfuss
4. Warren Beatty
5. Clint Eastwood
6. Woody Allen
7. Diane Keaton
8. Jane Fonda
9. Peter Sellers
10. Barbra Streisand

1979
1. Burt Reynolds
2. Clint Eastwood
3. Jane Fonda
4. Woody Allen
5. Barbra Streisand
6. Sylvester Stallone
7. John Travolta
8. Jill Clayburgh
9. Roger Moore
10. Mel Brooks

1980
1. Burt Reynolds
2. Robert Redford
3. Clint Eastwood
4. Jane Fonda
5. Dustin Hoffman
6. John Travolta
7. Sally Field
8. Sissy Spacek
9. Barbra Streisand
10. Steve Martin

1981
1. Burt Reynolds
2. Clint Eastwood
3. Dudley Moore
4. Dolly Parton
5. Jane Fonda
6. Harrison Ford
7. Alan Alda
8. Bo Derek
9. Goldie Hawn
10. Bill Murray

1982
1. Burt Reynolds
2. Clint Eastwood
3. Sylvester Stallone
4. Dudley Moore
5. Richard Pryor
6. Dolly Parton
7. Jane Fonda
8. Richard Gere
9. Paul Newman
10. Harrison Ford

1983
1. Clint Eastwood
2. Eddie Murphy
3. Sylvester Stallone
4. Burt Reynolds
5. John Travolta
6. Dustin Hoffman
7. Harrison Ford
8. Richard Gere
9. Chevy Chase
10. Tom Cruise

1984
1. Clint Eastwood
2. Bill Murray
3. Harrison Ford
4. Eddie Murphy
5. Sally Field
6. Burt Reynolds
7. Robert Redford
8. Prince
9. Dan Aykroyd
10. Meryl Streep

1985
1. Sylvester Stallone
2. Eddie Murphy
3. Clint Eastwood
4. Michael J. Fox
5. Chevy Chase
6. Arnold Schwarzenegger
7. Chuck Norris
8. Harrison Ford
9. Michael Douglas
10. Meryl Streep

1986
1. Tom Cruise
2. Eddie Murphy
3. Paul Hogan
4. Rodney Dangerfield
5. Bette Midler
6. Sylvester Stallone
7. Clint Eastwood
8. Whoopi Goldberg
9. Kathleen Turner
10. Paul Newman

1987
1. Eddie Murphy
2. Michael Douglas
3. Michael J. Fox
4. Arnold Schwarzenegger
5. Paul Hogan
6. Tom Cruise
7. Glenn Close
8. Sylvester Stallone

9. Cher
10. Mel Gibson

1988

1. Tom Cruise
2. Eddie Murphy
3. Tom Hanks
4. Arnold Schwarzenegger
5. Paul Hogan
6. Danny DeVito
7. Bette Midler
8. Robin Williams
9. Tom Selleck
10. Dustin Hoffman

1989

1. Jack Nicholson
2. Tom Cruise
3. Robin Williams
4. Michael Douglas
5. Tom Hanks
6. Michael J. Fox
7. Eddie Murphy
8. Mel Gibson
9. Sean Connery
10. Kathleen Turner

1990

1. Arnold Schwarzenegger
2. Julia Roberts
3. Bruce Willis
4. Tom Cruise
5. Mel Gibson
6. Kevin Costner
7. Patrick Swayze
8. Sean Connery

9. Harrison Ford
10. Richard Gere

1991

1. Kevin Costner
2. Arnold Schwarzenegger
3. Robin Williams
4. Julia Roberts
5. Macaulay Culkin
6. Jodie Foster
7. Billy Crystal
8. Dustin Hoffman
9. Robert De Niro
10. Mel Gibson

1992

1. Tom Cruise
2. Mel Gibson
3. Kevin Costner
4. Jack Nicholson
5. Macaulay Culkin
6. Whoopi Goldberg
7. Michael Douglas
8. Clint Eastwood
9. Steven Seagal
10. Robin Williams

1993

1. Clint Eastwood
2. Tom Cruise
3. Robin Williams
4. Kevin Costner
5. Harrison Ford
6. Julia Roberts
7. Tom Hanks
8. Mel Gibson
9. Whoopi Goldberg

10. Sylvester Stallone

1994

1. Tom Hanks
2. Jim Carrey
3. Arnold Schwarzenegger
4. Tom Cruise
5. Harrison Ford
6. Tim Allen
7. Mel Gibson
8. Jodie Foster
9. Michael Douglas
10. Tommy Lee Jones

1995

1. Tom Hanks
2. Jim Carrey
3. Brad Pitt
4. Harrison Ford
5. Robin Williams
6. Sandra Bullock
7. Mel Gibson
8. Demi Moore
9. John Travolta
10. Kevin Costner (tie)
10. Michael Douglas (tie)

1996

1. Tom Cruise (tie)
1. Mel Gibson (tie)
3. John Travolta
4. Arnold Schwarzenegger
5. Sandra Bullock
6. Robin Williams
7. Sean Connery
8. Harrison Ford

9. Kevin Costner
10. Michelle Pfeiffer

1997

1. Harrison Ford
2. Julia Roberts
3. Leonardo DiCaprio
4. Will Smith
5. Tom Cruise
6. Jack Nicholson
7. Jim Carrey
8. John Travolta
9. Robin Williams
10. Tommy Lee Jones

1998

1. Tom Hanks
2. Jim Carrey
3. Leonardo DiCaprio
4. Robin Williams
5. Meg Ryan
6. Mel Gibson
7. Adam Sandler
8. Eddie Murphy
9. Cameron Diaz
10. Julia Roberts

1999

1. Julia Roberts
2. Tom Hanks
3. Adam Sandler
4. Bruce Willis
5. Mike Myers
6. Tom Cruise
7. Will Smith
8. Mel Gibson
9. Meg Ryan
10. Sandra Bullock

THE ALL-TIME LEADING MEN AND WOMEN

Awarding points on a descending scale of 10, PEOPLE has analyzed Quigley Publishing's yearly film stars rankings to determine the most popular screen actors of all time.

Rank	Actor	Score	Rank	Actor	Score	Rank	Actor	Score
1.	John Wayne	172	18.	Harrison Ford (tie)	55	34.	John Travolta	37
2.	Clint Eastwood	165	18.	Robert Redford (tie)	55	35.	Sean Connery	36
3.	Bing Crosby	111	20.	Arnold Schwarzenegger	53	36.	Julie Andrews	35
4.	Gary Cooper	102	21.	Sylvester Stallone	50	37.	Humphrey Bogart (tie)	34
5.	Clark Gable	91	22.	Shirley Temple (tie)	49	37.	Gary Cooper (tie)	34
6.	Burt Reynolds	90	22.	Mel Gibson (tie)	49	37.	Jack Nicholson (tie)	34
7.	Bob Hope	84	24.	Barbra Streisand (tie)	48	40.	Kevin Costner (tie)	33
8.	Paul Newman	76	24.	Spencer Tracy (tie)	48	40.	William Holden (tie)	33
9.	Tom Cruise	73	24.	Robin Williams (tie)	48	42.	Jim Carrey	31
10.	Doris Day	72	27.	Steve McQueen	47	43.	Elvis Presley	29
11.	Rock Hudson	69	28.	Dean Martin		44.	Jane Fonda (tie)	28
12.	Betty Grable	66		& Jerry Lewis (tie)	46	44.	Will Rogers (tie)	28
13.	Cary Grant	62	28.	Mickey Rooney (tie)	46	46.	Michael Douglas	25
14.	Eddie Murphy	60	30.	Elizabeth Taylor	44	47.	Garson Greer	24
15.	Abbott & Costello (tie)	57	31.	Dustin Hoffman	42	48.	Woody Allen (tie)	22
15.	Tom Hanks (tie)	57	32.	Julia Roberts	41	48.	Jerry Lewis (tie)	22
17.	James Stewart	56	33.	Jack Lemmon	40	50.	Glenn Ford	21

SUPERSTAR FILMOGRAPHIES

The filmographies for some of Hollywood's most important, most popular people list only full-length feature films to which these actors and directors contributed significantly. Included are some early works released directly onto video years after completion.

WOODY ALLEN
Director/screenwriter/actor

What's New, Pussycat? (screenwriter/actor, 1965)

What's Up, Tiger Lily? (director/screenwriter/actor, 1966)

Casino Royale (co-screenwriter/actor, 1967)

Take the Money and Run (director/co-screenwriter/actor, 1969)

Bananas (director/screenwriter/actor, 1971)

Play It Again, Sam (screenwriter/actor, 1972)

*Everything You Always Wanted To Know About Sex** (*but were afraid to ask) (director/co-screenwriter/actor, 1972)

Sleeper (director/screenwriter/actor, 1973)

Love and Death (director/screenwriter/actor, 1975)

The Front (actor, 1976)

Annie Hall (director/co-screenwriter/actor, 1977; Academy Awards for best picture, best director, best original screenplay)

Interiors (director/screenwriter/ actor, 1978)

Manhattan (director/co-screenwriter/actor, 1979)

Stardust Memories (director/screenwriter/actor, 1980)

A Midsummer Night's Sex Comedy (director/screenwriter/actor, 1982)

Zelig (director/screenwriter/actor, 1983)

Broadway Danny Rose (director/screenwriter/actor, 1984)

The Purple Rose of Cairo (director/screenwriter, 1985)

Hannah and Her Sisters (director/screenwriter/actor, 1986; Academy Award for best original screenplay)

Radio Days (director/screenwriter/actor, 1987)

King Lear (actor, 1987)

September (director/screenwriter, 1987)

Another Woman (director/screenwriter, 1988)

"Oedipus Wrecks," in *New York Stories* (director/co-screenwriter/actor, 1989)

Crimes and Misdemeanors (director/screenwriter/actor, 1989)

Alice (director/screenwriter, 1990)

Scenes from a Mall (actor, 1991)

Shadows and Fog (director/screenwriter/actor, 1992)

Husbands and Wives (director/screenwriter/actor, 1992)

Manhattan Murder Mystery (director/screenwriter/actor, 1993)

Bullets over Broadway (director/co-screenwriter, 1994)

Mighty Aphrodite (director/screenwriter/actor, 1995)

Everyone Says I Love You (director/screenwriter/actor, 1996)

Deconstructing Harry (director/screenwriter/actor, 1997)

Wild Man Blues (documentary subject, 1998)

The Impostors (actor, 1998)

Antz (cartoon voice, 1998)

Celebrity (director/screenwriter/actor, 1998)

Sweet and Lowdown (director/screenwriter/actor, 1999)

Small Time Crooks (director/screenwriter/actor, 2000)

KEVIN BACON
Actor

National Lampoon's Animal House (1978)

Friday the 13th (1980)

Only When I Laugh (1981)

Forty Deuces (1982)

Diner (1982)

Enormous Changes at the Last Minute (1983)

Footloose (1984)

Quicksilver (1986)

White Water Summer (a.k.a. *Rites of Summer*, 1987)

End of the Line (1987)

Planes, Trains & Automobiles (1987)

She's Having a Baby (1988)

Criminal Law (1989)

The Big Picture (1989)

Tremors (1990)

Flatliners (1990)

Queens Logic (1991)

Pyrates (1991)

He Said, She Said (1991)

JFK (1991)

A Few Good Men (1992)

The River Wild (1994)

The Air Up There (1994)

Balto (cartoon voice, 1995)

Murder in the First (1995)

Apollo 13 (1995)

Sleepers (1996)

Losing Chase (1996)

Picture Perfect (1997)

Telling Lies in America (1997)

Digging to China (1998)

Wild Things (1998)

Stir of Echoes (1999)

My Dog Skip (2000)

Hollow Man (2000)

SANDRA BULLOCK
Actor

Who Shot Patakango? (1990)

Religion, Inc. (1990—videotape)

When the Party's Over (1992)

Who Do I Gotta Kill? (1992)

Love Potion No. 9 (1992)

The Vanishing (1993)

Fire on the Amazon (1992—videotape)

Demolition Man (1993)

The Thing Called Love (1993)

Wrestling Ernest Hemingway (1993)

Speed (1994)

While You Were Sleeping (1995)

The Net (1995)

Two If by Sea (1996)

A Time To Kill (1996)

In Love and War (1997)

Speed 2: Cruise Control (1997)

Hope Floats (1998)

Prince of Egypt (cartoon voice, 1998)

Practical Magic (1998)

Forces of Nature (1999)

Gun Shy (actor/producer, 2000)

28 Days (2000)

Miss Congeniality (2000)

NICOLAS CAGE
Actor

Fast Times at Ridgemont High (1982)

Valley Girl (1983)

Rumble Fish (1983)

Racing with the Moon (1984)

The Cotton Club (1984)

Birdy (1984)

The Boy in Blue (1986)

Peggy Sue Got Married (1986)

Raising Arizona (1987)

Moonstruck (1987)

Vampire's Kiss (1989)

Wild at Heart (1990)

Time to Kill (1990—videotape)

Fire Birds (1990)

Zandalee (1991)

Honeymoon in Vegas (1992)

Red Rock West (1992)

Amos and Andrew (1993)

Deadfall (1993)

Guarding Tess (1994)

It Could Happen to You (1994)

Trapped in Paradise (1994)

Kiss of Death (1995)

Leaving Las Vegas (1995; Academy Award for best actor)

The Rock (1996)

Con Air (1997)

Face/Off (1997)

City of Angels (1998)

Snake Eyes (1998)

8mm (1999)

Bringing Out the Dead (1999)

Gone in Sixty Seconds (2000)

Family Man (2000)

JIM CARREY
Actor

Finders Keepers (1984)

Once Bitten (1985)

Peggy Sue Got Married (1986)

The Dead Pool (1988)

Pink Cadillac (1989)

Earth Girls Are Easy (1989)

High Strung (1994—videotape)

Ace Ventura: Pet Detective (1994)

The Mask (1994)

Dumb & Dumber (1994)

Batman Forever (1995)

Ace Ventura: When Nature Calls (1995)

The Cable Guy (1996)

Liar Liar (1997)

The Truman Show (1998)

Simon Birch (1998)

Man on the Moon (1999)

Me, Myself & Irene (2000)

How the Grinch Stole Christmas (2000)

GLENN CLOSE
Actor

The World According to Garp (1982)

The Big Chill (1983)

The Stone Boy (1984)

Greystoke: The Legend of

Tarzan, Lord of the Apes (voice, 1984)

The Natural (1984)

Jagged Edge (1985)

Maxie (1985)

Fatal Attraction (1987)

Dangerous Liaisons (1988)

Light Years (cartoon voice, 1988)

Immediate Family (1989)

Hamlet (1990)

Reversal of Fortune (1990)

Meeting Venus (1991)

The Paper (1994)

The House of the Spirits (1994)

Mary Reilly (1996)

101 Dalmatians (1996)

Mars Attacks! (1996)

Paradise Road (1997)

Air Force One (1997)

In & Out (1997)

Cookie's Fortune (1999)

Tarzan (cartoon voice, 1999)

102 Dalmatians (2000)

SEAN CONNERY
Actor

No Road Back (1956)

Action of the Tiger (1957)

Another Time, Another Place (1958)

Hell Drivers (1957)

Time Lock (1957)

A Night to Remember (1958)

Tarzan's Greatest Adventure (1959)

Darby O'Gill and the Little People (1959)

On the Fiddle (1961)

The Frightened City (1961)

The Longest Day (1962)

Dr. No (1962)

From Russia with Love (1963)

Goldfinger (1964)

Woman of Straw (1964)

Marnie (1964)

Thunderball (1965)

The Hill (1965)

A Fine Madness (1966)

You Only Live Twice (1967)

Shalako (1968)

Bowler and Bonnet (1969, director)

The Molly Maguires (1970)

The Red Tent (1971)

The Anderson Tapes (1971)

Diamonds Are Forever (1971)

The Offence (or Something like the Truth, 1973)

Zardoz (1974)

Murder on the Orient Express (1974)

Ransom (1974)

The Wind and the Lion (1975)

The Man Who Would Be King (1975)

The Terrorists (1975)

Robin and Marian (1976)

The Next Man (1976)

A Bridge Too Far (1977)

The Great Train Robbery (1979)

Meteor (1979)

Cuba (1979)

Outland (1981)

Time Bandits (1981)

Wrong Is Right (1981)

G'ole (1982)

Five Days One Summer (1982)

Never Say Never Again (1983)

Sword of the Valiant (1984)

Highlander (1985)

The Name of the Rose (1986)

The Untouchables (1987; Academy Award for best supporting actor)

The Presidio (1988)

Memories of Me (1988)

Indiana Jones and the Last Crusade (1989)

Family Business (1989)

The Hunt for Red October (1990)

The Russia House (1990)

Highlander II: The Quickening (1991)

Robin Hood: Prince of Thieves (1991)

Medicine Man (1992)

Rising Sun (1993)

A Good Man in Africa (1994)

Just Cause (1995)

First Knight (1995)

Dragonheart (voice, 1996)

The Rock (1996)

The Avengers (1998)

Playing by Heart (1998)

Entrapment (1999)

Finding Forrester (2000)

KEVIN COSTNER
Actor/director/producer

Shadows Run Black (1981)

Night Shift (1982)

Stacy's Knights (1982)

The Big Chill (played corpse, all other scenes edited out, 1983)

The Gunrunner (1983)

Table for Five (1983)

Testament (1983)

American Flyers (1985)

Fandango (1985)

Silverado (1985)

Sizzle Beach, U.S.A. (1986)

No Way Out (1987)

The Untouchables (1987)

Bull Durham (1988)

Chasing Dreams (1989)

Field of Dreams (1989)

Dances with Wolves (actor/director/producer, 1990; Academy Awards for best picture, best director)

Revenge (1990)

Robin Hood: Prince of Thieves (1991)

JFK (1991)

The Bodyguard (actor/producer, 1992)

A Perfect World (1993)

Wyatt Earp (actor/producer, 1994)

Rapa Nui (co-producer, 1994)

The War (1994)

Waterworld (actor/producer, 1995)

Tin Cup (1996)

The Postman (actor/director/co-producer, 1997)

Message in a Bottle (1999)

For Love of the Game (1999)

Thirteen Days (2000)

TOM CRUISE
Actor

Endless Love (1981)
Taps (1981)
Losin' It (1983)
The Outsiders (1983)
Risky Business (1983)
All the Right Moves (1983)
Legend (1986)
Top Gun (1986)
The Color of Money (1986)
Cocktail (1988)
Rain Man (1988)
Born on the Fourth of July (1989)
Days of Thunder (1990)
Far and Away (1992)
A Few Good Men (1992)
The Firm (1993)
Interview with the Vampire (1994)
Mission: Impossible (actor/co-producer, 1996)
Jerry Maguire (1996)
Eyes Wide Shut (1999)
Magnolia (1999)
Mission: Impossible 2 (2000)

CLINT EASTWOOD
Actor/director/producer

Francis in the Navy (1955)
Lady Godiva (1955)
Never Say Goodbye (actor,1955)
Revenge of the Creature (1955)
Tarantula (1955)
The Traveling Saleslady (1956)
Star in the Dust (1956)
Escapade in Japan (1957)
Ambush at Cimarron Pass (1958)
Lafayette Escadrille (1958)
A Fistful of Dollars (1964)
For a Few Dollars More (1965)
The Good, the Bad, and the Ugly (1966)
Coogan's Bluff (1968)
Hang 'Em High (1968)
The Witches (1968)
Where Eagles Dare (1968)

Paint Your Wagon (1969)
Kelly's Heroes (1970)
Two Mules for Sister Sara (1970)
The Beguiled (1971)
Dirty Harry (1971)
Play Misty For Me (actor/director, 1971)
Joe Kidd (1972)
Breezy (1973)
High Plains Drifter (actor/director, 1973)
Magnum Force (1973)
Thunderbolt and Lightfoot (1974)
The Eiger Sanction (actor/director, 1974)
The Outlaw Josey Wales (actor/director, 1975)
The Enforcer (1976)
The Gauntlet (actor/director, 1977)
Every Which Way but Loose (1978)
Escape from Alcatraz (1979)
Any Which Way You Can (1980)
Bronco Billy (actor/director, 1980)
Firefox (actor/director/producer, 1982)
Honkytonk Man (actor/director/producer, 1982)
Sudden Impact (actor/director/producer, 1983)
City Heat (1984)
Tightrope (actor/producer, 1984)
Pale Rider (actor/director/producer, 1985)
Heartbreak Ridge (actor/director/producer, 1986)
Bird (director/producer, 1988)
The Dead Pool (actor/producer, 1988)
Pink Cadillac (1989)
The Rookie (actor/director, 1990)
White Hunter, Black Heart (actor/director/producer, 1990)
Unforgiven (actor/director/producer, 1992; Academy Awards for

best director and best film)
In the Line of Fire (actor/producer, 1993)
A Perfect World (actor/director, 1993)
The Bridges of Madison County (actor/director, 1995)
Absolute Power (actor/director, 1997)
Midnight in the Garden of Good and Evil (director/co-producer, 1997)
True Crime (actor/director, 1999)
Space Cowboys (actor/director/co-producer, 2000)

HARRISON FORD
Actor

Dead Heat on a Merry-Go-Round (1966)
Luv (1967)
A Time for Killing (1967)
Journey to Shiloh (1968)
Getting Straight (1970)
American Graffiti (1973)
The Conversation (1974)
Heroes (1977)
Force 10 from Navarone (1978)
Star Wars (1977)
The Frisco Kid (1979)
Apocalypse Now (1979)
Hanover Street (1979)
The Empire Strikes Back (1980)
Raiders of the Lost Ark (1981)
Blade Runner (1982)
Return of the Jedi (1983)
Indiana Jones and the Temple of Doom (1984)
Witness (1985)
The Mosquito Coast (1986)
Frantic (1988)
Working Girl (1988)
Indiana Jones and the Last Crusade (1989)
Presumed Innocent (1990)
Regarding Henry (1991)
Patriot Games (1992)
The Fugitive (1993)
Clear and Present Danger (1994)
Sabrina (1995)

The Devil's Own (1997)
Air Force One (1997)
Six Days, Seven Nights (1998)
Random Hearts (1999)
What Lies Beneath (2000)

JODIE FOSTER
Actor/director

Napoleon and Samantha (1972)
Kansas City Bomber (1972)
Tom Sawyer (1973)
One Little Indian (1973)
Alice Doesn't Live Here Anymore (1974)
Echoes of a Summer (1976)
Bugsy Malone (1976)
Taxi Driver (1976)
The Little Girl Who Lives Down the Lane (1976)
Freaky Friday (1977)
Candleshoe (1977)
Moi, fleur bleue (1977)
Il Casotto (1977)
Carny (1980)
Foxes (1980)
O'Hara's Wife (1982)
Les Sang des autres (The Blood of Others) (1984)
The Hotel New Hampshire (1984)
Mesmerized (actor/co-producer, 1986)
Siesta (1987)
Five Corners (1988)
The Accused (1988; Academy Award for best actress)
Stealing Home (1988)
Backtrack (1989)
The Silence of the Lambs (1991; Academy Award for best actress)
Little Man Tate (actor/director, 1991)
Shadows and Fog (1992)
Sommersby (1993)
Maverick (1994)
Nell (1994)
Home for the Holidays (director, 1995)
Contact (1997)
Anna and the King (1999)

MEL GIBSON
Actor/director

Summer City (1977)
Tim (1979)
Mad Max (1979)
Attack Force Z (1981)
Gallipoli (1981)
The Road Warrior (1981)
The Year of Living Danger-ously (1982)
The Bounty (1984)
Mrs. Soffel (1984)
The River (1984)
Mad Max Beyond Thunder-dome (1985)
Lethal Weapon (1987)
Tequila Sunrise (1988)
Lethal Weapon 2 (1989)
Air America (1990)
Bird on a Wire (1990)
Hamlet (1990)
Forever Young (1992)
Lethal Weapon 3 (1992)
The Man Without a Face (actor/director, 1993)
Maverick (1994)
Braveheart (actor/director/producer, 1995; Academy Awards for best director and best picture)
Pocahontas (cartoon voice, 1995)
Ransom (1996)
Conspiracy Theory (1997)
Lethal Weapon 4 (1998)
Payback (1999)
Chicken Run (cartoon voice, 2000)
The Patriot (2000)
What Women Want (2000)

WHOOPI GOLDBERG
Actor

The Color Purple (1985)
Jumpin' Jack Flash (1986)
Burglar (1987)
Fatal Beauty (1987)
Clara's Heart (1988)
The Telephone (1988)
Beverly Hills Brats (1989)
Homer and Eddie (1989)
Ghost (1990; Academy Award for best supporting actress)
The Long Walk Home (1990)
Soapdish (1991)
The Player (1992)
Sarafina! (1992)
Sister Act (1992)
Made in America (1993)
Sister Act 2: Back in the Habit (1993)
Corrina, Corrina (1994)
The Lion King (cartoon voice, 1994)
The Pagemaster (cartoon voice, 1994)
The Little Rascals (1994)
Star Trek: Generations (1994)
Boys on the Side (1995)
Moonlight & Valentino (1995)
Theodore Rex (1996, video)
Eddie (1996)
Bogus (1996)
The Associate (1996)
In & Out (1997)
An Alan Smithee Film: Burn Hollywood Burn (1998)
How Stella Got Her Groove Back (1998)
The Rugrats Movie (cartoon voice, 1998)
The Deep End of the Ocean (1999)
Get Bruce (1999)
Girl, Interrupted (1999)
The Adventures of Rocky and Bullwinkle (2000)
Monkeybone (2000)

TOM HANKS
Actor

He Knows You're Alone (1980)
Splash (1984)
Bachelor Party (1984)
The Man with One Red Shoe (1985)
Volunteers (1985)
The Money Pit (1986)
Nothing in Common (1986)
Every Time We Say Goodbye (1986)
Dragnet (1987)
Big (1988)
Punchline (1988)
The Burbs (1989)
Turner and Hooch (1989)
Joe Versus the Volcano (1990)
The Bonfire of the Vanities (1990)
Radio Flyer (1992)
A League of Their Own (1992)
Sleepless in Seattle (1993)
Philadelphia (1993; Academy Award for best actor)
Forrest Gump (1994; Academy Award for best actor)
Apollo 13 (1995)
Toy Story (cartoon voice, 1995)
That Thing You Do! (writer/director/actor, 1996)
Saving Private Ryan (1998)
You've Got Mail (1998)
Toy Story 2 (cartoon voice, 1999)
The Green Mile (1999)
Cast Away (2000)

ANTHONY HOPKINS
Actor

The Lion in Winter (1968)
Hamlet (1969)
The Looking Glass War (1970)
When Eight Bells Toll (1971)
Young Winston (1972)
A Doll's House (1973)
The Girl From Petrovka (1974)
Juggernaut (1974)
All Creatures Great and Small (1975)
Audrey Rose (1977)
A Bridge Too Far (1977)
International Velvet (1978)
Magic (1978)
A Change of Seasons (1980)
The Elephant Man (1980)
The Bounty (1984)
The Good Father (1986)
84 Charing Cross Road (1987)
The Dawning (1988)
A Chorus of Disapproval (1987)
Desperate Hours (1990)
The Silence of the Lambs (1991; Academy Award for best actor)
Freejack (1992)
Howards End (1992)
The Efficiency Expert (1992)
Bram Stoker's Dracula (1992)
Chaplin (1992)
The Remains of the Day (1993)
Shadowlands (1993)
The Trial (1993)
The Road to Wellville (1994)
Legends of the Fall (1994)
The Innocent (1995)
Nixon (1995)
August (actor/director, 1996)
Surviving Picasso (1996)
The Edge (1997)
Amistad (1997)
The Mask of Zorro (1998)
Meet Joe Black (1998)
Instinct (1999)
Titus (1999)
Mission: Impossible 2 (2000)
How the Grinch Stole Christ-mas (2000)

HELEN HUNT
Actor

Rollercoaster (1977)
Girls Just Want to Have Fun (1985)
Trancers (a.k.a. Future Cop) (1985)
Peggy Sue Got Married (1986)
Project X (1987)
Stealing Home (1988)
Miles from Home (1988)
Next of Kin (1989)
The Waterdance (1992)
Only You (1992)
Bob Roberts (1992)
Mr. Saturday Night (1992)
Kiss of Death (1995)
Twister (1996)
As Good As It Gets (1997; Academy Award for best actress)
Pay It Forward (2000)
What Women Want (2000)
Cast Away (2000)
Dr. T and the Women (2000)

NICOLE KIDMAN
Actor

Bush Christmas (1983)
BMX Bandits (1983)

Archer's Adventure (1985)

The Wacky World of Wills and Burke (1985)

Windrider (1986)

Nightmaster (1987)

The Bit Part (1987)

Emerald City (1988)

Dead Calm (1989)

Days of Thunder (1990)

Flirting (1991)

Billy Bathgate (1991)

Far and Away (1992)

My Life (1993)

Malice (1993)

To Die For (1994)

Batman Forever (1995)

The Portrait of a Lady (1996)

The Peacemaker (1997)

Practical Magic (1998)

Eyes Wide Shut (1999)

Moulin Rouge (2000)

SPIKE LEE
Director/producer/screenwriter/actor

She's Gotta Have It (director/producer/screenwriter/actor, 1986)

School Daze (director/producer/screenwriter/actor, 1988)

Do the Right Thing (director/producer/screenwriter/actor, 1989)

Mo' Better Blues (director/producer/screenwriter/actor, 1990)

Lonely in America, (actor, 1990)

Jungle Fever (director/producer/screenwriter/actor, 1991)

Malcolm X (director/producer/co-screenwriter/actor, 1992)

Crooklyn (director/producer/co-screenwriter/actor, 1994)

Clockers (director/co-producer/co-screenwriter, 1995)

Girl 6 (director/producer, 1996)

Get On The Bus (director/producer, 1996)

When We Were Kings (interviewee, 1996)

4 Little Girls (director/producer, 1997)

He Got Game (director/producer/screenwriter, 1998)

Summer of Sam (director/co-producer/co-screenwriter, 1999)

The Original Kings of Comedy (director/co-producer, 2000)

Bamboozled (director/co-producer/writer, 2000)

DEMI MOORE
Actor/Producer

Choices (1981)

Parasite (1982)

Young Doctors in Love (1982)

Blame It on Rio (1984)

No Small Affair (1984)

St. Elmo's Fire (1985)

About Last Night (1986)

One Crazy Summer (1986)

Wisdom (1986)

The Seventh Sign (1988)

We're No Angels (1989)

Ghost (1990)

Mortal Thoughts (actor/co-producer, 1991)

Nothing but Trouble (1991)

The Butcher's Wife (1991)

A Few Good Men (1992)

Indecent Proposal (1993)

Disclosure (1994)

The Scarlet Letter (1995)

Now and Then (1995)

The Juror (1996)

The Hunchback of Notre Dame (cartoon voice, 1996)

Striptease (1996)

Beavis and Butt-Head Do America (cartoon voice, 1996)

Austin Powers: International Man of Mystery (co-producer, 1997)

G.I. Jane (1997)

Deconstructing Harry (1997)

Passion of Mind (2000)

JACK NICHOLSON
Actor/producer/screenwriter/director

Cry Baby Killer (1958)

Studs Lonigan (1960)

Too Soon to Love (1960)

The Wild Ride (1960)

Little Shop of Horrors (1961)

The Broken Land (1962)

The Raven (1963)

The Terror (1963)

Thunder Island (screenwriter, 1963)

Ensign Pulver (1964)

Back Door to Hell (1964)

The Fortune (1965)

Flight to Fury (actor/screenwriter, 1966)

Ride in the Whirlwind (actor/producer/screenwriter, 1966)

Hell's Angels on Wheels (1966)

The Shooting (actor/producer, 1967)

The Trip (screenwriter, 1967)

St. Valentine's Day Massacre (1967)

Head (actor/producer/screenwriter, 1968)

Psych-Out (1968)

Easy Rider (1969)

Five Easy Pieces (1970)

On a Clear Day You Can See Forever (1970)

Rebel Rousers (1970)

Carnal Knowledge (1971)

Drive, He Said (director/producer/screenwriter, 1971)

A Safe Place (1971)

The King of Marvin Gardens (1972)

The Last Detail (1973)

Chinatown (1974)

The Fortune (1975)

One Flew over the Cuckoo's Nest (1975; Academy Award for best actor)

The Passenger (1975)

Tommy (1975)

The Last Tycoon (1976)

The Missouri Breaks (1976)

Goin' South (actor/director, 1978)

The Shining (1980)

The Border (1981)

The Postman Always Rings Twice (1981)

Reds (1981)

Terms of Endearment (1983; Academy Award for best supporting actor)

Prizzi's Honor (1985)

Heartburn (1986)

Broadcast News (1987)

Ironweed (1987)

The Witches of Eastwick (1987)

Batman (1989)

The Two Jakes (actor/director, 1990)

Man Trouble (1992)

A Few Good Men (1992)

Hoffa (1992)

Wolf (1994)

The Crossing Guard (1995)

Mars Attacks! (1996)

The Evening Star (1996)

Blood and Wine (1997)

As Good As It Gets (1997; Academy Award for best actor)

GWYNETH PALTROW
Actor

Shout (1991)

Hook (1991)

Flesh and Bone (1993)

Malice (1993)

Mrs. Parker and the Vicious Circle (1994)

Seven (1995)

Moonlight and Valentino (1995)

Jefferson in Paris (1995)

The Pallbearer (1996)

Emma (1996)

Hard Eight (1997)

A Perfect Murder (1997)

Sliding Doors (1998)

Hush (1998)

Great Expectations (1998)

Shakespeare in Love (1998; Academy Award for best actress)

The Talented Mr. Ripley (1999)

Duets (2000)

Bounce (2000)

MICHELLE PFEIFFER
Actor

The Hollywood Knights (1980)
Falling in Love Again (1980)
Charlie Chan and the Curse of the Dragon Queen (1981)
Grease 2 (1982)
Scarface (1983)
Into the Night (1985)
Ladyhawke (1985)
Sweet Liberty (1986)
Amazon Women on the Moon (1987)
The Witches of Eastwick (1987)
Dangerous Liaisons (1988)
Married to the Mob (1988)
Tequila Sunrise (1988)
The Fabulous Baker Boys (1989)
The Russia House (1990)
Frankie and Johnny (1991)
Batman Returns (1992)
Love Field (1992)
The Age of Innocence (1993)
Wolf (1994)
Dangerous Minds (1995)
Up Close and Personal (1996)
To Gillian on Her 37th Birthday (1996)
One Fine Day (1996)
A Thousand Acres (1997)
Prince of Egypt (cartoon voice, 1998)
William Shakespeare's A Midsummer Night's Dream (1999)
The Deep End of the Ocean (1999)
The Story of Us (1999)
What Lies Beneath (2000)

BRAD PITT
Actor

Cutting Class (1989)
Happy Together (1989)
Across the Tracks (1991)
Thelma & Louise (1991)
Johnny Suede (1991)
Cool World (1992)
A River Runs Through It (1992)
True Romance (1993)

Kalifornia (1993)
The Favor (1994)
Interview with the Vampire (1994)
Legends of the Fall (1994)
Seven (1995)
Twelve Monkeys (1995)
Sleepers (1996)
The Devil's Own (1997)
Seven Years in Tibet (1997)
Meet Joe Black (1998)
Fight Club (1999)

JULIA ROBERTS
Actor

Satisfaction (1988)
Mystic Pizza (1988)
Blood Red (1989)
Steel Magnolias (1989)
Pretty Woman (1990)
Flatliners (1990)
Sleeping with the Enemy (1991)
Dying Young (1991)
Hook (1991)
The Player (1992)
The Pelican Brief (1993)
I Love Trouble (1994)
Ready to Wear (1994)
Something to Talk About (1995)
Mary Reilly (1996)
Everyone Says I Love You (1996)
My Best Friend's Wedding (1997)
Conspiracy Theory (1997)
Stepmom (1998)
Notting Hill (1999)
Runaway Bride (1999)
Erin Brockovich (2000)

MEG RYAN
Actor

Rich and Famous (1981)
Amityville 3-D (1983)
Armed and Dangerous (1986)
Top Gun (1986)
Innerspace (1987)
Promised Land (1987)
D.O.A. (1988)
The Presidio (1988)

When Harry Met Sally... (1989)
Joe Versus the Volcano (1990)
The Doors (1991)
Prelude to a Kiss (1992)
Sleepless in Seattle (1993)
Flesh and Bone (1993)
When a Man Loves a Woman (1994)
I.Q. (1994)
French Kiss (actor/co-producer, 1995)
Restoration (1995)
Courage Under Fire (1996)
Addicted to Love (1997)
Anastasia (cartoon voice, 1997)
City of Angels (1998)
Hurlyburly (1998)
You've Got Mail (1998)
Hanging Up (2000)
Proof of Life (2000)

WINONA RYDER
Actor

Lucas (1986)
Square Dance (1987)
Beetlejuice (1988)
1969 (1988)
Heathers (1989)
Great Balls of Fire! (1989)
Welcome Home, Roxy Carmichael (1990)
Mermaids (1990)
Edward Scissorhands (1990)
Night on Earth (1991)
Bram Stoker's Dracula (1992)
The Age of Innocence (1993)
Reality Bites (1994)
The House of the Spirits (1994)
Little Women (1994)
How to Make an American Quilt (1995)
Boys (1996)
Looking for Richard (1996)
The Crucible (1996)
Alien Resurrection (1997)
Celebrity (1998)
August in New York (2000)
Lost Souls (2000)

SUSAN SARANDON
Actor

Joe (1970)
Lady Liberty (a.k.a. Mortadella) (1972)
Lovin' Molly (1974)
The Front Page (1974)
The Rocky Horror Picture Show (1975)
The Great Waldo Pepper (1975)
Dragonfly (1976)
The Great Smokey Roadblock (actor/co-producer, 1976)
Checkered Flag or Crash (1977)
The Other Side of Midnight (1977)
Pretty Baby (1978)
King of the Gypsies (1978)
Something Short of Paradise (1979)
Loving Couples (1980)
Atlantic City (1981)
Tempest (1982)
The Hunger (1983)
The Buddy System (1984)
Compromising Positions (1985)
The Witches of Eastwick (1987)
Bull Durham (1988)
Sweet Hearts Dance (1988)
The January Man (1989)
A Dry White Season (1989)
White Palace (1990)
Thelma & Louise (1991)
Bob Roberts (1992)
Light Sleeper (1992)
Lorenzo's Oil (1992)
The Client (1994)
Safe Passage (1994)
Little Women (1994)
Dead Man Walking (1995)
James and the Giant Peach (cartoon voice, 1996)
Twilight (1998)
Stepmom (1998)
Anywhere But Here (1999)
Cradle Will Rock (1999)
Joe Gould's Secret (2000)
Rugrats in Paris (cartoon voice, 2000)

ARNOLD SCHWARZENEGGER
Actor

Hercules in New York (1974)
Stay Hungry (1976)
Pumping Iron (1977)
The Villain (1979)
Conan the Barbarian (1982)
Conan the Destroyer (1984)
The Terminator (1984)
Commando (1985)
Red Sonja (1985)
Raw Deal (1986)
Predator (1987)
The Running Man (1987)
Red Heat (1988)
Twins (1988)
Total Recall (1989)
Kindergarten Cop (1990)
Terminator 2: Judgment Day (1991)
Last Action Hero (1993)
True Lies (1994)
Junior (1994)
Eraser (1996)
Jingle All the Way (1996)
Batman & Robin (1997)
End of Days (1999)
The 6th Day (2000)

MARTIN SCORSESE
Director/producer/screen-writer

Who's That Knocking at My Door? (director/screenwriter/actor, 1969)
Street Scenes 1970 (director/actor, 1970)
Boxcar Bertha (director, 1972)
Mean Streets (director/screenwriter, 1973)
Alice Doesn't Live Here Anymore (director, 1974)
Taxi Driver (director, 1976)
New York, New York (director, 1977)
American Boy: A Profile of Steven Prince (director, 1978)
The Last Waltz (director/actor, 1978)
Raging Bull (director/actor, 1980)

The King of Comedy (director/actor, 1983)
After Hours (director, 1985)
The Color of Money (director, 1986)
The Last Temptation of Christ (director, 1988)
"Life Lessons" in New York Stories (director, 1989)
GoodFellas (director/co-screenwriter, 1990)
Made in Milan (director, 1990)
The Grifters (producer, 1990)
Cape Fear (director, 1991)
The Age of Innocence (director/co-screenwriter, 1993)
Clockers (co-producer, 1995)
Casino (director/co-screenwriter, 1995)
Kundun (director, 1997)
Bringing Out the Dead (director, 1999)

STEVEN SPIELBERG
Director/producer/screen-writer

Duel (director, telefilm, 1971; U.S. theatrical release, 1984)
The Sugarland Express (director/co-screenwriter, 1974)
Jaws (director, 1975)
Close Encounters of the Third Kind (director/screenwriter, 1977)
1941 (director, 1979)
Raiders of the Lost Ark (director, 1981)
E.T., the Extra-Terrestrial (director/co-producer, 1982)
Poltergeist (co-producer/co-screenwriter, 1982)
"Kick the Can," in Twilight Zone—The Movie (director/co-producer, 1983)
Indiana Jones and the Temple of Doom (director, 1984)
The Color Purple (director/co-producer, 1985)
Empire of the Sun (director/co-producer, 1987)
Always (director/co-producer, 1989)
Indiana Jones and the Last Crusade (director, 1989)
Hook (director, 1991)

An American Tail II: Fievel Goes West (co-producer, 1991)
Jurassic Park (director, 1993)
Schindler's List (director/producer, 1993; Academy Awards for best director, best picture)
The Lost World: Jurassic Park (director, 1997)
Amistad (director/co-producer, 1997)
Saving Private Ryan (director/co-producer, 1998; Academy Award for best director)

SYLVESTER STALLONE
Actor/director/screenwriter

A Party at Kitty and Stud's (reissued as The Italian Stallion) (1970)
Bananas (1971)
The Lords of Flatbush (actor/co-screenwriter, 1974)
Capone (1975)
Death Race 2000 (1975)
Farewell, My Lovely (1975)
No Place to Hide (1975)
The Prisoner of Second Avenue (1975)
Cannonball (1976)
Rocky (actor/screenwriter/fight choreographer, 1976)
F.I.S.T. (actor/co-screenwriter, 1978)
Paradise Alley (actor/director/screenwriter, 1978)
Rocky II (actor/director/screenwriter/fight choreographer, 1979)
Victory (1981)
Nighthawks (1981)
First Blood (actor/co-screenwriter, 1982)
Rocky III (actor/director/screenwriter/fight choreographer, 1982)
Staying Alive (director/co-producer/co-screenwriter, 1983)
Rhinestone (actor/co-screenwriter, 1984)
Rambo: First Blood, Part II (actor/co-screenwriter, 1985)

Rocky IV (actor/director/screenwriter, 1985)
Cobra (actor/screenwriter, 1986)
Over the Top (actor/co-screenwriter, 1987)
Rambo III (actor/co-screenwriter, 1988)
Lock Up (1989)
Tango and Cash (1989)
Rocky V (actor/screenwriter, 1990)
Oscar (1991)
Stop! or My Mom Will Shoot (1992)
Cliffhanger (actor/co-screenwriter, 1993)
Demolition Man (1993)
The Specialist (1994)
Judge Dredd (1995)
Assassins (1995)
Daylight (1996)
Cop Land (1997)
An Alan Smithee Film: Burn Hollywood Burn (1998)
Antz (cartoon voice, 1998)
Get Carter (2000)

SHARON STONE
Actor

Stardust Memories (1980)
Deadly Blessing (1981)
Bolero (1981)
Irreconcilable Differences (1984)
King Solomon's Mines (1985)
Allan Quartermain and the Lost City of Gold (1987)
Action Jackson (1988)
Above the Law (1988)
Personal Choice (a.k.a. Beyond the Stars) (1989)
Blood and Sand (1989)
Total Recall (1990)
He Said, She Said (1991)
Scissors (1991)
Year of the Gun (1991)
Basic Instinct (1992)
Where Sleeping Dogs Lie (1992)
Diary of a Hitman (1992)
Sliver (1993)
Intersection (1994)

The Specialist (1994)
The Quick and the Dead (1995)
Casino (1995)
Diabolique (1996)
Last Dance (1996)
Sphere (1998)
Antz (cartoon voice, 1998)
The Mighty (1998)
The Muse (1999)
Simpatico (1999)

MERYL STREEP
Actor

Julia (1977)
The Deer Hunter (1978)
Manhattan (1979)
The Seduction of Joe Tynan (1979)
Kramer vs. Kramer (1979; Academy Award for best supporting actress)
The French Lieutenant's Woman (1981)
Sophie's Choice (1982; Academy Award for best actress)
Still of the Night (1982)
Silkwood (1983)
Falling in Love (1984)
Plenty (1985)
Out of Africa (1985)
Heartburn (1986)
Ironweed (1987)
A Cry in the Dark (1988)
She-Devil (1989)
Postcards from the Edge (1990)
Defending Your Life (1991)
Death Becomes Her (1992)
The House of the Spirits (1994)
The River Wild (1994)
The Bridges of Madison County (1995)
Before and After (1996)
Marvin's Room (1996)
One True Thing (1998)
Antz (cartoon voice, 1998)
Dancing with Lughnasa (1998)
Music of the Heart (1999)

EMMA THOMPSON
Actor/screenwriter

Henry V (1989)
The Tall Guy (1989)
Impromptu (1990)
Dead Again (1991)
Howard's End (1992)
Peter's Friends (1992)
Much Ado About Nothing (1993)
The Remains of the Day (1993)
In the Name of the Father (1993)
Junior (1994)
Carrington (1995)
Sense and Sensibility (actor/screenwriter, 1995; Academy Award for best adapted screenplay)
The Winter Guest (1997)
Primary Colors (1998)

JOHN TRAVOLTA
Actor

The Devil's Rain (1975)
Carrie (1976)
Saturday Night Fever (1977)
Grease (1978)
Moment by Moment (1978)
Urban Cowboy (1980)
Blow Out (1981)
Staying Alive (1983)
Two of a Kind (1983)
Perfect (1985)
The Experts (1989)
Look Who's Talking (1989)
Look Who's Talking Too (1990)
Shout (1991)
Eyes of an Angel (1991)
Look Who's Talking Now (1993)
Pulp Fiction (1994)
Get Shorty (1995)
White Man's Burden (1995)
Broken Arrow (1996)
Phenomenon (1996)
Michael (1996)
Face/Off (1997)
She's So Lovely (1997)
Mad City (1997)
Primary Colors (1998)
A Civil Action (1998)

The Thin Red Line (1998)
The General's Daughter (1999)
Battlefield Earth (2000)
Lucky Numbers (2000)

DENZEL WASHINGTON
Actor

Carbon Copy (1981)
A Soldier's Story (1984)
Power (1986)
Cry Freedom (1987)
Glory (1989; Academy Award for best supporting actor)
For Queen and Country (1989)
Reunion (1989)
The Mighty Quinn (1989)
Mo' Better Blues (1990)
Heart Condition (1990)
Ricochet (1991)
Mississippi Masala (1991)
Malcolm X (1992)
Much Ado About Nothing (1993)
The Pelican Brief (1993)
Philadelphia (1993)
Crimson Tide (1995)
Virtuosity (1995)
Devil in a Blue Dress (1995)
Courage Under Fire (1996)
The Preacher's Wife (1996)
Fallen (1998)
He Got Game (1998)
The Siege (1998)
The Bone Collector (1999)
The Hurricane (1999)
Remember the Titans (2000)

ROBIN WILLIAMS
Actor

Can I Do It...Til I Need Glasses? (1977)
Popeye (1980)
The World According to Garp (1982)
The Survivors (1983)
Moscow on the Hudson (1984)
Seize the Day (1986)
The Best of Times (1986)
Club Paradise (1986)
Good Morning, Vietnam (1987)
The Adventures of Baron Munchausen (1989)

Dead Poets Society (1989)
Cadillac Man (1990)
Awakenings (1990)
Dead Again (1991)
Shakes the Clown (1991)
Hook (1991)
The Fisher King (1991)
FernGully: The Last Rainforest (cartoon voice, 1992)
Aladdin (cartoon voice, 1992)
Toys (1992)
Mrs. Doubtfire (1993)
Being Human (1994)
Nine Months (1994)
To Wong Foo, Thanks for Everything, Julie Newmar (1994)
Jumanji (1995)
The Birdcage (1996)
Jack (1996)
The Secret Agent (1996)
Hamlet (1996)
Fathers' Day (1997)
Flubber (1997)
Good Will Hunting (1997; Academy Award for best supporting actor)
Deconstructing Harry (1997)
What Dreams May Come (1998)
Jakob the Liar (1999)
Get Bruce (1999)
Bicentennial Man (1999)

THE TOP VIDEOS, YEAR BY YEAR

Billboard magazine has been tracking video sales since 1980 and rentals since 1982. First we bought Jane Fonda workout tapes, then cartoon classics. Now *Austin Powers* sequel has provided another shagadelic video performance, but Tae-Bo has inherited Jane's legacy, and the boy bands are selling through.

1980

Sales
1. The Godfather
2. Saturday Night Fever
3. Superman
4. M*A*S*H
5. The Godfather, Part II
6. Blazing Saddles
7. 10
8. Grease
9. The Sound of Music
10. Halloween

1981

Sales
1. Airplane!
2. Caddyshack
3. 9 to 5
4. Superman
5. Alien
6. Star Trek
7. Fame
8. Ordinary People
9. The Elephant Man
10. Popeye

1982

Sales
1. Clash of the Titans
2. An American Werewolf in London
3. Atlantic City
4. Stir Crazy
5. The Jazz Singer
6. The Blue Lagoon
7. Kramer vs. Kramer
8. Casablanca
9. Raging Bull
10. Jane Fonda's Workout

Rentals
1. Clash of the Titans
2. An American Werewolf in London
3. Arthur
4. Star Wars
5. Fort Apache, the Bronx
6. For Your Eyes Only
7. On Golden Pond
8. Stripes
9. The Cannonball Run
10. Superman II

1983

Sales
1. Jane Fonda's Workout
2. Star Trek II: The Wrath of Khan
3. An Officer and a Gentleman
4. The Compleat Beatles
5. Rocky III
6. Playboy Vol. I
7. Poltergeist
8. Star Wars
9. Blade Runner
10. The Road Warrior

Rentals
1. An Officer and a Gentleman
2. Star Trek II: The Wrath of Khan
3. The Road Warrior
4. Rocky III
5. Poltergeist
6. First Blood
7. Das Boot
8. Night Shift
9. Blade Runner
10. Sophie's Choice

1984

Sales
1. Jane Fonda's Workout
2. Raiders of the Lost Ark
3. Making Michael Jackson's "Thriller"
4. Flashdance
5. Duran Duran
6. Risky Business
7. 48 Hrs.
8. Do It Debbie's Way
9. Trading Places
10. The Jane Fonda Workout Challenge

Rentals
1. Raiders of the Lost Ark
2. Risky Business
3. Flashdance
4. 48 Hrs.
5. Tootsie
6. Mr. Mom
7. Sudden Impact
8. Trading Places
9. Blue Thunder
10. Making Michael Jackson's "Thriller"

1985

Sales
1. Jane Fonda's Workout
2. Jane Fonda's Prime Time Workout
3. Making Michael Jackson's "Thriller"
4. Purple Rain
5. Gone with the Wind
6. The Jane Fonda Workout Challenge
7. Raiders of the Lost Ark
8. Raquel, Total Beauty and Fitness
9. We Are the World—The Video Event
10. Wham! The Video

Rentals
1. The Karate Kid
2. The Terminator
3. Police Academy
4. Romancing the Stone
5. Revenge of the Nerds
6. The Natural
7. Starman
8. The Empire Strikes Back
9. Bachelor Party
10. Splash

1986

Sales
1. Jane Fonda's New Workout
2. Jane Fonda's Workout
3. Pinocchio
4. Beverly Hills Cop
5. The Sound of Music
6. Jane Fonda's Prime Time Workout
7. Casablanca
8. Gone With the Wind
9. The Wizard of Oz
10. The Best of John Belushi

Rentals
1. Back to the Future
2. Beverly Hills Cop
3. Prizzi's Honor
4. Witness
5. Ghostbusters
6. Rambo: First Blood Part II
7. Return of the Jedi
8. Cocoon

9. Mask
10. Gremlins

1987

Sales
1. Jane Fonda's Low Impact Aerobic Workout
2. Jane Fonda's New Workout
3. Sleeping Beauty
4. Top Gun
5. Callanetics
6. The Sound of Music
7. Kathy Smith's Body Basics
8. Indiana Jones and the Temple of Doom
9. Star Trek III: The Search for Spock
10. Star Trek II: The Wrath of Khan

Rentals
1. Short Circuit
2. Top Gun
3. Back to School
4. Indiana Jones and the Temple of Doom
5. Down and Out in Beverly Hills
6. The Color of Money
7. Ferris Bueller's Day Off
8. Stand By Me
9. Ruthless People
10. Aliens

1988

Sales
1. Lady and the Tramp
2. Callanetics
3. Jane Fonda's Low Impact Aerobic Workout
4. Star Trek IV: The Voyage Home
5. Start Up with Jane Fonda
6. An American Tail
7. Jane Fonda's New Workout
8. Pink Floyd: The Wall
9. Dirty Dancing
10. Sleeping Beauty

Rentals
1. Dirty Dancing
2. Lethal Weapon
3. Fatal Attraction

4. *The Untouchables*
5. *The Witches of Eastwick*
6. *No Way Out*
7. *Outrageous Fortune*
8. *Robocop*
9. *Stakeout*
10. *Tin Men*

1989

Sales

1. *Cinderella*
2. *E.T., the Extra-Terrestrial*
3. *Jane Fonda's Complete Workout*
4. *Moonwalker*
5. *Callanetics*
6. *Dirty Dancing*
7. *The Wizard of Oz: The 50th Anniversary Edition*
8. *Lethal Weapon*
9. *U2 Rattle and Hum*
10. *Pink Floyd: The Delicate Sound of Thunder*

Rentals

1. *Big*
2. *Die Hard*
3. *A Fish Called Wanda*
4. *Three Men and a Baby*
5. *Beetlejuice*
6. *Coming to America*
7. *Cocktail*
8. *Twins*
9. *Bull Durham*
10. *"Crocodile" Dundee II*

1990

Sales

1. *Bambi*
2. *New Kids on the Block: Hangin' Tough Live*
3. *The Little Mermaid*
4. *Lethal Weapon 2*
5. *The Wizard of Oz: The 50th Anniversary Edition*
6. *Batman*
7. *Honey, I Shrunk the Kids*
8. *The Land Before Time*
9. *Who Framed Roger Rabbit*
10. *Teenage Mutant Ninja Turtles: Cowabunga, Shredhead*

Rentals

1. *Look Who's Talking*
2. *When Harry Met Sally*
3. *Parenthood*
4. *K-9*
5. *Dead Poets Society*
6. *Steel Magnolias*

7. *Sea of Love*
8. *Turner & Hooch*
9. *Black Rain*
10. *Internal Affairs*

1991

Sales

1. *Pretty Woman*
2. *The Little Mermaid*
3. *Peter Pan*
4. *The Jungle Book*
5. *The Three Tenors in Concert*
6. *Richard Simmons: Sweatin' to the Oldies*
7. *Teenage Mutant Ninja Turtles: The Movie*
8. *The Terminator*
9. *Ducktales: The Movie*
10. *Total Recall*

Rentals

1. *Ghost*
2. *Pretty Woman*
3. *GoodFellas*
4. *Bird on a Wire*
5. *Flatliners*
6. *The Hunt for Red October*
7. *Kindergarten Cop*
8. *Total Recall*
9. *Sleeping with the Enemy*
10. *Another 48 Hrs.*

1992

Sales

1. *Fantasia*
2. *101 Dalmations*
3. *The Jungle Book*
4. *Robin Hood: Prince of Thieves*
5. *Cherfitness: A New Attitude*
6. *Fievel Goes West*
7. *1992 Playboy Video Playmate Calendar*
8. *Home Alone*
9. *The Rescuers Down Under*
10. *Playboy: Sexy Lingerie IV*

Rentals

1. *Thelma and Louise*
2. *The Silence of the Lambs*
3. *The Fisher King*
4. *City Slickers*
5. *Backdraft*
6. *Cape Fear*
7. *The Hand That Rocks the Cradle*
8. *Father of the Bride*
9. *Deceived*
10. *What About Bob?*

1993

Sales

1. *Beauty and the Beast*
2. *Pinocchio*
3. *101 Dalmatians*
4. *Playboy Celebrity Centerfold: Jessica Hahn*
5. *Sister Act*
6. *Playboy Playmate of the Year 1993: Anna Nicole Smith*
7. *Cindy Crawford/Shape Your Body Workout*
8. *Home Alone 2: Lost in New York*
9. *Disney's Sing Along Songs: Friend Like Me*
10. *Beethoven*

Rentals

1. *Sister Act*
2. *Patriot Games*
3. *Under Siege*
4. *A League of Their Own*
5. *A Few Good Men*
6. *Scent of a Woman*
7. *Unforgiven*
8. *Sneakers*
9. *Passenger 57*
10. *The Bodyguard*

1994

Sales

1. *Aladdin*
2. *Playboy Celebrity Centerfold: Dian Parkinson*
3. *Yanni: Live at the Acropolis*
4. *Free Willy*
5. *Mrs. Doubtfire*
6. *The Fugitive*
7. *The Return of Jafar*
8. *The Fox and the Hound*
9. *Ace Ventura: Pet Detective*
10. *Beauty and the Beast*

Rentals

1. *Sleepless in Seattle*
2. *Philadelphia*
3. *In the Line of Fire*
4. *The Pelican Brief*
5. *The Fugitive*
6. *The Firm*
7. *Carlito's Way*
8. *Sliver*
9. *Ace Ventura: Pet Detective*
10. *Mrs. Doubtfire*

1995

Sales

1. *The Lion King*
2. *Forrest Gump*
3. *Speed*
4. *Jurassic Park*
5. *The Mask*
6. *Playboy: The Best of Pamela Anderson*
7. *Snow White and the Seven Dwarfs*
8. *The Crow*
9. *Pink Floyd: Pulse*
10. *Yanni: Live at the Acropolis*

Rentals

1. *The Shawshank Redemption*
2. *True Lies*
3. *Disclosure*
4. *Speed*
5. *The Client*
6. *Clear and Present Danger*
7. *When a Man Loves a Woman*
8. *Dumb and Dumber*
9. *Just Cause*
10. *Outbreak*

1996

Sales

1. *Babe*
2. *Apollo 13*
3. *Pulp Fiction*
4. *Playboy: The Best of Jenny McCarthy*
5. *The Aristocats*
6. *Batman Forever*
7. *Jumanji*
8. *Pocahontas*
9. *Cinderella*
10. *Heavy Metal*

Rentals

1. *Braveheart*
2. *The Usual Suspects*
3. *Seven*
4. *Heat*
5. *Twelve Monkeys*
6. *Get Shorty*
7. *Crimson Tide*
8. *Casino*
9. *Executive Decision*
10. *The Net*

1997

Sales

1. *Riverdance—The Show*
2. *Lord of the Dance*
3. *Independence Day*
4. *Jerry Maguire*
5. *101 Dalmatians*
6. *Space Jam*
7. *Toy Story*
8. *Bambi*
9. *Star Wars Trilogy—Special Edition*
10. *The Hunchback of Notre Dame*

Rentals

1. *Fargo*
2. *Scream*
3. *Donnie Brasco*
4. *Sling Blade*
5. *Absolute Power*
6. *The First Wives Club*
7. *Sleepers*
8. *Phenomenon*
9. *Ransom*
10. *Jerry Maguire*

1998

Sales

1. *Austin Powers: International Man of Mystery*
2. *Hercules*
3. *As Good As It Gets*
4. *Men in Black*
5. *Spice World*
6. *The Little Mermaid: The Special Edition*
7. *My Best Friend's Wedding*
8. *Grease: 20th Anniversary Edition*
9. *Air Force One*
10. *Titanic*

Rentals

1. *L.A. Confidential*
2. *Face/Off*
3. *As Good As It Gets*
4. *Good Will Hunting*
5. *Devil's Advocate*
6. *Boogie Nights*
7. *The Full Monty*
8. *The Game*
9. *Wag the Dog*
10. *Austin Powers: International Man of Mystery*

1999

Sales

1. *Austin Powers: International Man of Mystery*
2. *Tae-Bo Workout*
3. *Armageddon*
4. *A Bug's Life*
5. *Blade*
6. *Mulan*
7. *The Wedding Singer*
8. *'N the Mix with 'N Sync*
9. *You've Got Mail*
10. *Backstreet Boys: Home-coming—Live in Orlando*
11. *Lion King II: Simba's Pride*
12. *There's Something About Mary*
13. *Ever After: A Cinderella Story*
14. *Antz*
15. *Dr. Dolittle*
16. *Titanic*
17. *Rush Hour*
18. *Babe: Pig in the City*
19. *Small Soldiers*
20. *Playboy's Celebrities*

Rentals

1. *Enemy of the State*
2. *There's Something About Mary*
3. *The Truman Show*
4. *Elizabeth*
5. *Ronin*
6. *Armageddon*
7. *Saving Private Ryan*
8. *The Siege*
9. *Payback*
10. *American History X*
11. *A Civil Action* (tie)
11. *The Negotiator* (tie)
13. *Analyze This*
14. *Stepmom*
15. *The Waterboy*
16. *Pleasantville*
17. *8MM*
18. *You've Got Mail*
19. *Meet Joe Black*
20. *Rush Hour*

OSCAR—DECADE BY DECADE

For 72 years Oscar has been handed out—now he's at an age for savoring life's achievements. "He rattles," says Olivia de Havilland, holding her 1949 Oscar to the phone receiver and shaking him to illustrate. Ernest Borgnine, a 1955 winner, complains that his Oscar "flakes." Jack Lemmon, who took his *Mr. Roberts* Oscar home in 1956, says the statue rusted: "I had to send him back to the Academy to be redipped." But, ah, how nice to have the old guy around.

Sure, like any sexagenarian, Oscar has taken his lumps. He's been called "a cruel joke" (Marion Davies), "a heartbreaker" (Orson Welles), and "something to be feared" (George C. Scott). But don't count him out. Oscar's imprimatur can add $25 million or more to a winning film's gross, double an actor's salary, and at least triple the size of his ego.

What a shock, then, to learn that Oscar started life as a patsy. In 1927, MGM kingpin Louis B. Mayer and 35 cronies decided to form an Academy of Motion Picture Arts and Sciences. Forget the high-toned blather of the first charter seeking "the improvement and advancement of the…profession." What Mayer really wanted was to stop the advance of film unions. An Academy would keep labor disputes in

the hands of the studios. As a carrot to actors, writers, directors, and technicians, Mayer formed a committee to find "some little way" of rewarding merit in film.

While Mayer finagled, MGM art director Cedric Gibbons doodled a sketch of a naked man with a sword, standing on a reel of film. Today Oscar is a thirteen-and-a-half inch, eight-and-a-half pound trophy cast in a metal alloy, then plated in turn with copper, nickel, silver, and finally gold. At Oscar's debut in 1929, some laughed. Screenwriter Frances (*The Champ*) Marion believed Hollywood had found its ideal symbol, "an athletic body…with half his head, that part which held his brains, completely sliced off."

But, hey, Oscar didn't need brains. The studio bosses controlled the nominations and virtually hand-picked the winners. It took years for Oscar to clean house—the Academy did not even start using sealed envelopes until 1941. Since then the Academy, which has grown from a scant 36 members in 1927 to the 4,523 voting members of today, has tried to discourage machinations, especially ad campaigns, to influence voting. It hasn't succeeded, of course. But Oscar, by dint of sheer perseverance, has become, in the words of 1957 winner

Alec (*The Bridge on the River Kwai*) Guinness, "the most highly prized [award] of all." At this point, the grandstanding and costuming have become as much a reason for tuning in the Oscars as finding out the winners. "Well, hell—let's face it," says Katharine Hepburn, recipient of a record four Oscars for acting, "It's our track meet. It's painful but it's thrilling."

THE FIRST DECADE

1927–1936

Oscar threw his first party in 1929. The press stayed away. A black-tie crowd clapped politely as all 12 awards were distributed in under five minutes. The three Best Actor nominees didn't bother to show up. Janet Gaynor, first Best Actress winner, gamely tried to act thrilled. "Had I known what it would come to mean in the next few years," she said later, "I'm sure I'd have been overwhelmed." It was the first and last Oscar bust. The Depression and the sound era soon made movies into the ideal escapism, and Oscar's touch came to mean box-office gold. Some aspired to win. Others conspired. As ever in Hollywood, greed, jealousy, and raw ambition added up to a helluva show.

The first Best Actor winner, Emil Jannings, had scooted

home to Germany before collecting his Oscar scroll. His later Nazi propaganda films—done, he said, under duress—made him a favorite with Hitler. Marlene Dietrich disputed the Führer on the talents of her *Blue Angel* costar: "He was a terrible ham."

★

First ceremony: Hollywood's elite jammed the Roosevelt Hotel to hear Al Jolson put down the Oscar as a "paperweight." Jolie's film, *The Jazz Singer*—an early talkie—had been disqualified; only silent films were eligible. The Academy was suspicious of new trends. Some things never change.

★

The WWI air extravaganza *Wings*, starring Buddy Rogers, Clara Bow, and Richard Arlen, was the first Best Picture winner. With tinted color in the battle scenes and noise machines in the theaters to simulate plane crashes, here was a primitive *Top Gun* that showed the Academy's early fondness for spectacle.

★

In 1930, Norma Shearer, winner for *The Divorcée*, posed for a photograph with Oscar two days *before* the ceremony. "She sleeps with the boss," sniped Joan Crawford. Rumor had it that MGM's Irving Thalberg pressured employees to vote for his wife.

★

Oscar's first tie: Fredric March (*Dr. Jekyll and Mr. Hyde*) and Wallace Beery

(*The Champ*) shared the 1931 gold. Both had recentlyadopted children. "Odd,"
said March, "that Wally and I were given awards for best male performance."

★

Clark Gable and Claudette Colbert both took Oscars for Frank Capra's 1934 comedy, *It Happened One Night*, as did Capra and the film—the only clean sweep in Academy history until *One Flew over the Cuckoo's Nest* duplicated the feat in 1975. No one expected it. Everybody still thinks Gable won for *Gone With the Wind*.

★

The Academy invented a new category, Best Song, prompted by Fred Astaire & Ginger Rogers's dancing and singing of "The Continental" in 1934's *The Gay Divorcee*.

★

Bette Davis collected an award for 1935's *Dangerous*, and gave the statue its name. Reflecting that the trophy "resembled the backside" of her first husband, bandleader Harmon Oscar Nelson Jr., she dubbed her prize Oscar. The moniker stuck.

THE SECOND DECADE

1937–1946

The Oscar ceremony was establishment now, broadcast on radio. In 1939 Gone with the Wind *became the most popular and profitable film ever. But this was also a time of war, as reflected in movies*

from Mrs. Miniver *to* The Best Years of Our Lives. *Winston Churchill hailed* Miniver *as "propaganda worth a hundred battleships." As a wartime cost-cutting measure, the Academy ended its elaborate banquets and took the show inside a theater, where food and drink could no longer distract from the ego battles.*

Walt Disney is given a special honorary award for 1938's *Snow White and the Seven Dwarfs*, featuring one large Oscar and seven tiny ones.

★

Gone With the Wind, then the costliest movie in history ($3,957,000) wins eight Oscars, a record not broken until 1958's *Gigi*. Leigh was the triumphant victor, Gable the disgruntled loser. "This was my last chance," he groaned. He was right.

Hattie McDaniel, Miss Scarlett's maid, was the first black actor to win an Oscar. Hattie sobbed on accepting her plaque (supporting players didn't receive full statues until 1943).

★

Playing George M. Cohan in 1942, James Cagney—America's favorite tough guy—became the first actor to win an Oscar for a musical. "Don't forget," said Jimmy in his acceptance speech, "it was a pretty good part."

★

Bogie told Ingrid Bergman in *Casablanca* that their wartime love story "didn't amount to a hill of beans in this crazy world." Except for winning the Best Picture Oscar of 1943 and the hearts of all romantics.

★

Barry Fitzgerald's role as a twinkly old priest in 1944's *Going My Way* made him a popular winner. But at home a few days later, he forgot that wartime Oscars were made of plaster instead of bronze and decapitated his prize with a golf club.

★

The Lost Weekend, the Best Picture of 1945, offered an unsparing portrait of an alcoholic, by Ray Milland. "I gave it everything I had," said the actor. He must have. Accepting the Oscar, a speechless Milland simply bowed and departed.

THE THIRD DECADE

1947–1956

No sooner had the war ended over there than the Academy embarked on its own war at home. The enemy? Television. The little black box was emptying movie theaters at an alarming rate. The studios retaliated at first with sex, violence and Cinemascope, then gave in. So did Oscar. The Academy Awards were telecast for the first time in 1953. Variety's headline heralded a new era: "1ST MAJOR PIX— TV WEDDING BIG CLICK."

Many years prior, actor Walter Huston said he asked his son, John, "If you ever become a writer or director, please find a good part for your old man." John complied with *The Treasure of the Sierra Madre* and won 1948 Oscars for them both.

★

Joseph Mankiewicz's crackerjack 1950 comedy *All About Eve* still holds the record—14 nominations. Though *Eve* won six Oscars, including Best Picture, costars Bette Davis and Anne Baxter both lost to *Born Yesterday's* Judy Holliday.

★

Vivien Leigh copped her second Best Actress Oscar in 1951 for *A Streetcar Named Desire*. When the award was announced in Hollywood, Leigh was in New York starring in *Antony and Cleopatra* with then-husband Laurence Olivier.

★

In Hollywood, Donald O'Connor watched Shirley Booth's reaction in New York on being named 1952's Best Actress for *Come Back, Little Sheba*. Meanwhile, the largest single audience (about 80 million) in TV's five-year history saw the first Oscarcast.

★

Having fought to play Maggio in 1953's *From Here to Eternity*, Frank Sinatra triumphed. Said the Best Supporting Actor, "I ducked the party and took a walk. Just me and Oscar." The salty version of James Jones's Army-barracks novel won a whopping eight Oscars, including Best Picture. And Deborah Kerr's sexy roll on the sand with Burt Lancaster cracked her saintly image.

★

A year before her royal wedding in 1956, *The Country Girl's* Grace Kelly scored an upset victory over Judy Garland in *A Star is Born*. Kelly confided: "I wanted to win so badly, I was afraid that I would stand up no matter which name was read out."

★

First-time film producer Michael Todd nabbed the 1956 Best Picture Oscar with his star-studded *Around the World in 80 Days*. "Imagine this—and being married to Liz, too," he enthused.

THE FOURTH DECADE

1957–1966

The times they were a-changing. Drugs, hippies, the youth movement, civil rights demonstrations, the Kennedy assassination: Many films dealt with these social and political upheavals. But you couldn't tell by Oscar. Relevant was out; big was in. The Academy awarded either historical epics (Ben-Hur, The Bridge on the River Kwai, Lawrence of Arabia, A Man for All Seasons) or blockbuster musicals (Gigi, West Side Story, My Fair Lady, The Sound of Music). The most controversial move on the Academy's part was to issue a formal slap to those who tried to "buy" Oscar nominations by purchasing self-congratulatory ads in the trade papers. Few paid heed.

Joanne Woodward, the new Mrs. Paul Newman, collected her 1957 Oscar for *The Three Faces of Eve* in a $100 dress she made herself. Joan Crawford claimed Hollywood glamour "had been set back twenty years." When Paul finally won his Oscar, twenty-nine years later, clothes weren't a problem. He didn't show up at all.

★

In 1959, Best Picture *Ben-Hur* took a record eleven Oscars, including Best Actor for Charlton Heston, who got the part after Burt Lancaster dropped out. "It was hard work," said Chuck, who drove a mean chariot. But some questioned his talents. "That Heston," said actor Aldo Ray, "what a hamola."

★

Denounced in Congress in 1950 for her adulterous affair with Roberto Rossellini, Ingrid Bergman ended her decade-long Hollywood exile by presenting a 1959 Best Picture Oscar to *Gigi* producer Arthur Freed. She said her recipe for happiness was "good health and a poor memory."

★

Sporting a tracheotomy scar from a near-fatal bout of pneumonia, Liz Taylor scored a sympathy Oscar for 1960's *Butterfield 8.* In 1966 Liz won Oscar No. 2 for *Who's Afraid of Virginia Woolf?*, but railed at the Academy when fifth husband Richard Burton failed to win too.

★

"I'd like to think it will help," said Sidney Poitier after Anne Bancroft opened the envelope and, for 1963's *Lilies of the Field*, he became the first black Best Actor winner. "But I don't believe my Oscar will be a magic wand that will wipe away the restrictions on job opportunities for Negro actors."

★

Sisters and Best Actress nominees Lynn and Vanessa Redgrave, cited respectively for 1966's *Georgy Girl* and *Morgan!*, were only the second sister nominees in Oscar history. And they came from a notable British acting family to boot. Maybe so. But Liz Taylor still whupped them both.

THE FIFTH DECADE

1967–1976

Oscar neared its half-century mark in a reactionary mood. Breakthrough films such as Bonnie and Clyde, The Graduate, *and* Easy Rider *ended up losers. In 1968, the year of* 2001: A Space Odyssey, Oliver! *won the Best Picture prize. Yikes. No wonder a streaker felt the need to defame one of the decade's Academy telecasts. Then, a rebel cry was heard in filmland. Newcomers Dustin Hoffman and Jon Voight dared to duke it out with the Duke, John Wayne, for the statue. They failed, but their X-rated* Midnight Cowboy *took the Best Picture prize in 1969. Jane Fonda raised hackles with her Vietnam views and won anyway. The warring factions of the Academy were creating sparks.*

For the second time in Oscar history, a tie was declared. *Funny Girl*'s Barbra Streisand and *The Lion in Winter*'s Katharine Hepburn received the same number of votes from the 1968 Academy's 3,030 members. Designer Edith Head was "shocked," not by the tie but by Streisand's tacky peeka-boo pantsuit.

★

John Wayne had to let it all hang out in 1969 as bloated, one-eyed Rooster Cogburn to finally collect his first Oscar at 62 after 250 movies. "Wow," drawled the Duke, "if I had known, I would have put that eye patch on 35 years earlier."

★

Deriding the Oscars as a "meat parade," George C. Scott declined his nomination as 1970's Best Actor. "My God!" exclaimed Goldie Hawn as she opened the envelope and read the winner's name, "It's George C. Scott."

★

When Marlon Brando was voted 1972's Best Actor, he sent Apache Sacheen Littlefeather to reject the Oscar for all the Native Americans Hollywood had demeaned. "Childish," scowled Charlton Heston. "Wonderful," gushed Jane Fonda.

★

Would-be comic Robert Opel snuck backstage at the 1974

Oscars ceremony, flustering emcee David Niven as the cameras cut away to spare home viewers the streaker's shortcomings. The hit of a dull show, Opel was found murdered five years later in his San Francisco sex shop.

★

Struggling actor Sylvester Stallone took half a week to write a script for himself about an underdog fighter. He lost the Best Actor Oscar, but the sleeper film won the title as Best Picture of 1976. "*Rocky* will be remembered," said Sly with typical modesty.

THE SIXTH DECADE

1977–1986

Oscar had a goal now. Ignoring the films of George Lucas and Steven Spielberg became a full-time job. The Hardy Boys of the zap-happy set combined their youthful fantasies with dazzling special effects to create eight of the top 10 box office hits of all time (E.T., Star Wars, Return of the Jedi, The Empire Strikes Back, Jaws, Raiders of the Lost Ark, Indiana Jones, and Back to the Future). Not a Best Picture winner in the bunch. The Academy, doing penance for scorning Vietnam in the previous decade, anointed politically themed films from The Deer Hunter to Platoon. A vote for Gandhi, the movie, was a vote for Gandhi, the man. Oscar, typically late, began sporting a social conscience.

Accepting her Best Supporting Actress Oscar for 1976's *Julia*, Vanessa Redgrave dismissed as "Zionist hoodlums" those who showed up to protest her politics. The audience booed, Vanessa had to dine later with her two bodyguards, and a confused Jack Nicholson cracked, "What are these Zionists? I've been skiing."

★

"It's simply terrific. This is something," sputtered Diane Keaton after accepting the 1977 Best Actress prize for *Annie Hall* from first winner Janet Gaynor. Her co-star and former boyfriend Woody Allen stayed home and shrugged off the Academy as meaningless: "I just don't think they know what they're doing."

★

Robert Redford and Warren Beatty have never won Oscars for their acting. That might make sense. Instead, each (Redford for 1980's *Ordinary People* and Beatty for 1981's *Reds*) took the prize as Best Director—a pinnacle Hitchcock, Bergman, Fellini, and Welles never reached. Go figure.

★

Jane Fonda rushed from the 1982 Academy Awards show to present her ailing father and *On Golden Pond* costar, Henry, with the long-overdue first Oscar of his 47-year career. "Hell, if I hadn't won, I wouldn't be able to walk with my head up anymore," Fonda said to his wife, Shirlee. He died five months later.

★

Gidget gets respect: For 1984's *Places in the Heart*, Sally Field won a second Oscar and spoke the words that will haunt her forever: "You like me! You like me!"

★

Perennial also-ran Paul Newman won for reprising his 1961 *Hustler* role in 1986's *The Color of Money*. "After losing six times, I felt it cruel and unusual punishment to attend," said the no-show.

★

Writer-director Oliver Stone took the 1986 Best Picture Oscar for *Platoon*, based on his wartime experiences in Vietnam—a film almost no studio wanted to make.

★

In 1987 Marlee Matlin of *Children of a Lesser God* became the first hearing-impaired Best Actress winner. "After I'm alone I'm going to scream," she said.

THE SEVENTH DECADE

1987–1996

Oscar continues his old traditions by heaping awards on elder statesmen—from Clint Eastwood, Paul Newman, and Sean Connery to Jack Palance, Jessica Tandy, and Martin Landau—who should have been recognized long before. Best Director continues to be a fickle category—how could Oscar recognize Apollo 13 *for seemingly everything except Ron Howard's direction? But the drought finally ends for tra-*

IN THE NAME OF PRODUCTION

More and more celebrity actors are starting their own production companies. But how did they get such funny names? Here's a list of some luminary-owned companies and the inspiration behind their appellations.

Actor	Production Company	Where the Name Came From
Tim Allen	Boxing Cats Prods.	A memorable image from one of Mr. Allen's dreams
Antonio Banderas	Green Moon LLC	Federico García Lorca's poetry attributes Andalusians dark skin not to the sun but to the light of the green moon
Kevin Costner	TIG Productions	The nickname of his grandmother
Clint Eastwood	Malpaso Productions	A creek in Carmel, Calif., and a Spanish expression meaning "dangerous step," which critics mistakenly assumed he made in forming the company
Jodie Foster	Egg Pictures	The egg as a symbol of protection
Tom Hanks	Clavius Base	The otherworldly planet in Stanley Kubrick's *2001: A Space Odyssey*
Dustin Hoffman	Punch Productions	After the Punchinello character in *Punch and Judy* shows
Elizabeth Hurley and Hugh Grant	Simian Productions	Inspired by Ms. Hurley's affection for and preservation efforts toward chimps
Meg Ryan	Prufrock Pictures	Alluding to one of her favorite poems, T. S. Eliot's "Love Song of J. Alfred Prufrock"
Wesley Snipes	Amen Ra Films	Has been roughly translated to "an unseen source of all creation"; also a reference to the Egyptian sun god, and reportedly an acronym for "Africans Minds Engaged 'N Royal Affairs"
Denzel Washington	Mundy Lane Entertainment	The street he grew up on in Mount Vernon, New York
Sigourney Weaver	Goatcay Prods.	The name of a favorite island retreat

ditional punching bag Steven Spielberg. *Of course it took the culturally significant* Schindler's List *to get the Oscar monkey off of Spielberg's back (after three previous Best Director nominations), rather than his second-highest grossing movie of all time,* Jurassic Park—*making it clear that he was chosen as best director, not most successful. In 1995,* Forrest Gump *bucks the conventional wisdom that box-office favorites don't play well in Academy-land, becoming the highest-grossing picture ever to claim the Best Picture Award.*

In 1988, a barely dressed, slightly tattooed Cher wins Best Actress and announces, "I don't think that this means I am somebody, but I guess I'm on my way."

★

The telecast hits new lows in production values in 1989, with the dreadful Snow White musical opening giving Oscar a black eye.

★

Whoopi Goldberg becomes only the second African-American woman to claim an acting award, as Best Supporting Actress for her role in 1990's *Ghost*.

★

Jack Palance shows he's no old-timer by performing one-handed push-ups by way of accepting his Best Supporting Actor statuette for *City Slickers*. And he provides Oscar host Billy Crystal with a year's worth of material.

★

Lizzy Gardiner, the winner for best costume design on *Priscilla, Queen of the Desert*, makes a memorable imprint on the 1995 ceremonies in her dress fashioned from American Express gold cards.

★

Jessica Lange is 1995's Best Actress for a 1991 performance: Trapped for years by Orion Pictures' financial woes, her *Blue Sky* languished on a bank vault's floor.

★

In 1996, actors get tougher to categorize. Mel Gibson wins trophies for producing and directing—but not acting in—*Braveheart*. Similarly, first-time scripter Emma Thompson takes Best Adapted Screenplay honors for her *Sense and Sensibility*.

★

As Decade Seven closes, the academy's love for independent film burns brighter than ever. *The English Patient*'s sweep makes it an all-time champ; trophies not taken by the big-studio rejects go to the off-Hollywood likes of *Fargo*, *Sling Blade*, and *Shine*. Were it not for Cuba Gooding Jr.'s *Jerry Maguire* win, no major Oscar would have stayed in Tinseltown.

THE EIGHTH DECADE

1997 and counting

It's too early to note trends for Decade Eight—especially considering how quickly the Academy's tastes turn—but at least the signs are getting clearer. Titanic's *record-tying cruise aside, small films continue to lead the charge, and the big studios' fretting becomes louder. For 1998,* Shakespeare in Love *claims a striking 13 nominations and 7 statuettes, overtaking the early front-runner and box-office leader,* Saving Private Ryan. *Even though Spielberg is recognized for his directing talents for only the second time, it still looks as if he is passed over again. As the promotional drumbeats of Miramax and others become louder, it's unclear how much longer Oscar will shine on the culturally accomplished over box-office favorites.*

At the 70th Academy Awards, Oscar offers a "family portrait," filling the stage with past acting honorees. Though the segment's appeal was tested by appearing over three hours into the ceremony, star power works its

magic, with particularly strong applause for Gregory Peck and Shirley Temple Black.

★

Oscar moves to Sunday night for the first time in its history in 1999, and the telecast is marked as the longest ever. The surest sign of life comes from two-time winner Italian actor/director/writer Roberto Benigni, who literally jumps for joy on his way to the podium and exclaims, "I want to kiss everybody because you are the measure of joy." And he means it.

★

Driving Miss Daisy producers Richard and Lili Fini Zanuck take charge of the 2000 ceremony and promise sweeping changes: Kiss those dance sequences goodbye! Yet the "streamlined" show still runs nearly four hours—and Robin Williams's musical performance of "Blame Canada" from *South Park: Bigger, Longer and Uncut* is hailed as a standout moment. Meanwhile, five trophies go to *American Beauty*, which becomes the first Best Picture from DreamWorks SKG.

FILM AWARDS

NATIONAL SOCIETY OF FILM CRITICS
Annual Award for Best Film

1966	Blow-Up
1967	Persona
1968	Shame
1969	Z
1970	M*A*S*H
1971	Claire's Knee
1972	The Discreet Charm of the Bourgeoisie
1973	Day for Night
1974	Scenes from a Marriage
1975	Nashville
1976	All The President's Men
1977	Annie Hall
1978	Get Out Your Handkerchiefs
1979	Breaking Away
1980	Melvin and Howard
1981	Atlantic City
1982	Tootsie
1983	Night of the Shooting Stars
1984	Stranger Than Paradise
1985	Ran
1986	Blue Velvet
1987	The Dead
1988	The Unbearable Lightness of Being
1989	Drugstore Cowboy
1990	GoodFellas
1991	Life Is Sweet
1992	Unforgiven
1993	Schindler's List
1994	Pulp Fiction
1995	Babe
1996	Breaking the Waves
1997	L.A. Confidential
1998	Out of Sight
1999	Topsy-Turvy
	Being John Malkovich

SUNDANCE FILM FESTIVAL
GRAND JURY PRIZE

1978	Girlfriends
1979	Spirit in the Wind
1981	Heartland
	Gal Young Un

Dramatic

1982	Street Music
1983	Purple Haze
1984	Old Enough
1985	Blood Simple
1986	Smooth Talk
1987	Waiting for the Moon
	Trouble with Dick
1988	Heat and Sunlight
1989	True Love

1990	Chameleon Street
1991	Poison
1992	In the Soup
1993	Ruby in Paradise
	Public Access
1994	What Happened Was . . .
1995	The Brothers McMullen
1996	Welcome to the Dollhouse
1997	Sunday
1998	Slam
1999	Three Seasons
2000	Girlfight
	You Can Count on Me

FILMMAKERS TROPHY
Dramatic

1989	Powwow Highway
1990	House Party
1991	Privilege
1992	Zebrahead
1993	Fly By Night
1994	Clerks
1995	Angela
1996	Girls Town
1997	In the Company of Men
1998	Smoke Signals
1999	Tumbleweeds
2000	Girlfight

AUDIENCE AWARD
Dramatic

1989	sex, lies and videotape
1990	Longtime Companion
1991	One Cup of Coffee (released as "Pastime")
1992	The Waterdance
1993	El Mariachi
1994	Spanking the Monkey
1995	Picture Bride
1996	Care of the Spitfire Grill (released as "The Spitfire Grill")
1997	Hurricane (released as "Hurricane Streets") love jones
1998	Smoke Signals
1999	Three Seasons
2000	Two Family House

CANNES FILM FESTIVAL
Palme d'Or for Best Film

1946	La Bataille du rail (France)
1947	Antoine et Antoinette (France)
1948	No festival
1949	The Third Man (G.B.)
1950	No festival
1951	Miracle in Milan (Italy)
	Miss Julie (Sweden)

1952	Othello (Morocco)
	Two Cents Worth of Hope (Italy)
1953	Wages of Fear (France)
1954	Gate of Hell (Japan)
1955	Marty (U.S.)
1956	World of Silence (France)
1957	Friendly Persuasion (U.S.)
1958	The Cranes are Flying (U.S.S.R.)
1959	Black Orpheus (France)
1960	La Dolce Vita (Italy)
1961	Viridiana (Spain)
	Une Aussi longue absence (France)
1962	The Given Word (Brazil)
1963	The Leopard (Italy)
1964	The Umbrellas of Cherbourg (France)
1965	The Knack (G.B.)
1966	A Man and a Woman (France)
	Signore e Signori (Italy)
1967	Blow-Up (G.B.)
1968	Festival disrupted; no awards
1969	If... (G.B.)
1970	M*A*S*H (U.S.)
1971	The Go-Between (G.B.)
1972	The Working Class Goes to Paradise (Italy)
	The Mattei Affair (Italy)
1973	Scarecrow (U.S.)
	The Hireling (G.B.)
1974	The Conversation (U.S.)
1975	Chronicle of the Burning Years (Algeria)
1976	Taxi Driver (U.S.)
1977	Padre Padrone (Italy)
1978	L'Albero Degli Zoccoli (Italy)
1979	The Tin Drum (Germany)
	Apocalypse Now (U.S.)
1980	All That Jazz (U.S.)
	Kagemusha (Japan)
1981	Man of Iron (Poland)
1982	Missing (U.S.)
	Yol (Turkey)
1983	The Ballad of Narayama (Japan)
1984	Paris, Texas (Germany)
1985	When Father Was Away On Business (Yugoslavia)
1986	The Mission (G.B.)
1987	Under the Sun of Satan (France)
1988	Pelle the Conqueror (Denmark)
1989	sex, lies and videotape (U.S.)
1990	Wild at Heart (U.S.)
1991	Barton Fink (U.S.)
1992	The Best Intentions (Denmark)
1993	The Piano (New Zealand)
	Farewell My Concubine (Hong Kong)
1994	Pulp Fiction (U.S.)
1995	Underground (Bosnia)

1996	Secrets and Lies (G.B.)
1997	The Taste of Cherry (Iran)
	The Eel (Japan)
1998	Eternity and a Day (Greece-Italy-France)
1999	Rosetta (Belgium)
2000	Dancer in the Dark (Denmark)

VENICE FILM FESTIVAL

Golden Lion [for Best Film or Best Foreign Film]

1932	No official award
1933	No festival
1934	Man of Aran (G.B.)
1935	Anna Karenina (U.S.)
1936	Der Kaiser von Kalifornien (Germany)
1937	Un Carnet debal (France)
1938	Olympia (Germany)
1939	No award given
1940	Der Postmeister (Germany)
1941	Ohm Kruger (Germany)
1942	Der grosse König (Germany)
1943	No festival
1944	No festival
1945	No festival
1946	The Southerner (U.S.)
1947	Sirena (Czechoslovakia)
1948	Hamlet (G.B.)
1949	Manon (France)
1950	Justice is Done (France)
1951	Rashomon (Japan)
1952	Forbidden Games (France)
1953	No award given
1954	Romeo and Juliet (Italy/G.B.)
1955	Ordet (Denmark)
1956	No award given
1957	Aparajito (India)
1958	Muhomatsu no Issho (Japan)
1959	Il Generale della Rovere (Italy)
1960	Le Passage du Rhin (France)
1961	Last Year at Marienbad (France)
1962	Childhood of Ivan (U.S.S.R.)
1963	Le Mani sulla città (Italy)
1964	Red Desert (Italy)
1965	Of a Thousand Delights (Italy)
1966	Battle of Algiers (Italy)
1967	Belle de Jour (France)
1968	Die Aristen in der Zirkuskuppel (Germany)

Jury and award system discontinued 1969–79

1980	Gloria (U.S.)
	Atlantic City (France/Canada)
1981	Die Bleierne Zeit (Germany)
1982	The State of Things (Germany)
1983	Prénom Carmen (France/Switzerland)
1984	Year of the Quiet Sun (Poland)
1985	Sans toit ni loi (Vagabonde) (France)

1986	Le Rayon vert (France)
1987	Au revoir, les enfants (France)
1988	The Legend of the Holy Drinker (Italy)
1989	A City of Sadness (Taiwan)
1990	Rosencrantz and Guildenstern Are Dead (G.B.)
1991	Urga (U.S.S.R./France)
1992	The Story of Qiu Ju (China)
1993	Blue (France)
	Short Cuts (U.S.)
1994	Before the Rain (Macedonia)
	Vive L'Amour (Taiwan)
1995	Cyclo (France-Vietnam)
1996	Michael Collins (Great Britain-U.S.)
1997	Hana-bi (Fireworks) (Japan)
1998	The Way We Laughed (Italy)
1999	Not One Less (China)

BERLIN FILM FESTIVAL AWARD

Golden Bear Award for Best Film

1953	The Wages of Fear (France)
1954	Hobson's Choice (G.B.)
1955	The Rats (Germany)
1956	Invitation to the Dance (G.B.)
1957	Twelve Angry Men (U.S.)
1958	The End of the Day (Sweden)
1959	The Cousins (France)
1960	Lazarillo de Tormes (Spain)
1961	La Notte (Italy)
1962	A Kind of Loving (G.B.)
1963	Oath of Obedience (Germany)
	The Devil (Italy)
1964	Dry Summer (Turkey)
1965	Alphaville (France)
1966	Cul-de-Sac (G.B.)
1967	Le Depart (Belgium)
1968	Ole Dole Duff (Sweden)
1969	Early Years (Yugoslavia)
1970	No award
1971	The Garden of the Finzi-Continis (Italy)
1972	The Canterbury Tales (Italy)
1973	Distant Thunder (India)
1974	The Apprenticeship of Duddy Kravitz (Canada)
1975	Orkobefogadas (Hungary)
1976	Buffalo Bill and the Indians (U.S.) [award declined]
1977	The Ascent (U.S.S.R.)
1978	The Trouts (Spain)
	The Words of Max (Spain)
1979	David (Germany)
1980	Heartland (U.S.)
	Palermo Oder Wolfsburg (Germany)
1981	Di Presa Di Presa (Spain)
1982	Die Sehnsucht der Veronica Voss (Germany)
1983	Ascendancy (G.B.)

	The Beehive (Spain)
1984	Love Streams (U.S.)
1985	Wetherby (G.B.)
	Die Frau und der Fremde (Germany)
1986	Stammhein (Germany)
1987	The Theme (U.S.S.R.)
1988	Red Sorghum (China)
1989	Rain Man (U.S.)
1990	Music Box (U.S.)
	Larks on a String (Czechoslovakia)
1991	House of Smiles (Italy)
1992	Grand Canyon (U.S.)
1993	The Woman from the Lake of Scented Souls (China)
	The Wedding Banquet (Taiwan/U.S.)
1994	In the Name of the Father (UK/Ireland)
1995	Live Bait (France)
1996	Sense and Sensibility (G.B.)
1997	The People vs. Larry Flynt (U.S.)
1998	Central Station (Brazil)
1999	The Thin Red Line (U.S.)
2000	Magnolia (U.S.)

INDEPENDENT SPIRIT AWARDS

These prizes are considered the Oscars of the independent film world.

Best Feature

1986	After Hours
1987	Platoon
1988	River's Edge
1989	Stand and Deliver
1990	sex, lies and videotape
1991	The Grifters
1992	Rambling Rose
1993	The Player
1994	Short Cuts
1995	Pulp Fiction
1996	Leaving Las Vegas
1997	Fargo
1998	The Apostle
1999	Election

Best First Feature

1987	Spike Lee, director
She's Gotta Have It
1988	Emile Ardolino, director
Dirty Dancing
1989	Donald Petrie, director
Mystic Pizza
1990	Michael Lehmann, director
Heathers
1991	Whit Stillman, producer/director
Metropolitan
1992	Matty Rich, director
Straight Out of Brooklyn
1993	Neal Jimenez and Michael

Steinberg, directors
The Waterdance

1994 Robert Rodriguez, director
El Mariachi

1995 David O. Russell, director
Spanking the Monkey

1996 Edward Burns, director
The Brothers McMullen

1997 Billy Bob Thornton, director
Sling Blade

1998 Kasi Lemmons, director
Eve's Bayou

1999 Spike Jonze, director
Being John Malkovich
Daniel Myrick & Eduardo
Sanchez, directors
The Blair Witch Project

Best Director

1986 Martin Scorsese
After Hours

1987 Oliver Stone
Platoon

1988 John Huston
The Dead

1989 Ramon Menendez
Stand and Deliver

1990 Steven Soderbergh
sex, lies and videotape

1991 Charles Burnett
To Sleep with Anger

1992 Martha Coolidge
Rambling Rose

1993 Carl Franklin
One False Move

1994 Robert Altman
Short Cuts

1995 Quentin Tarantino
Pulp Fiction

1996 Mike Figgis
Leaving Las Vegas

1997 Joel Coen
Fargo

1998 Robert Duvall
The Apostle

1999 Alexander Payne
Election

Best Screenplay

1986 Horton Foote
The Trip to Bountiful

1987 Oliver Stone
Platoon

1988 Neal Jimenez
River's Edge

1989 Ramon Menendez and Tom
Musca
Stand and Deliver

1990 Gus Van Sant Jr. and Daniel Yost
Drugstore Cowboy

1991 Charles Burnett
To Sleep with Anger

1992 Gus Van Sant Jr.
My Own Private Idaho

1993 Neal Jimenez
The Waterdance

1994 Robert Altman and Frank
Barhydt
Short Cuts

1995 David O. Russell
Spanking the Monkey

1996 Christopher McQuarrie
The Usual Suspects

1997 Joel Coen and Ethan Coen
Fargo

1998 Kevin Smith
Chasing Amy

1999 Alexander Payne & Jim Taylor
Election

Best Cinematographer

1986 Toyomichi Kurita
Trouble In Mind

1987 Bob Richardson
Platoon

1988 Haskell Wexler
Matewan

1989 Sven Nykvist
*The Unbearable Lightness of
Being*

1990 Robert Yeoman
Drugstore Cowboy

1991 Fred Elmes
Wild at Heart

1992 Walt Lloyd
Kafka

1993 Frederick Elmes
Night on Earth

1994 Lisa Rinzler
Menace II Society

1995 John Thomas
Barcelona

1996 Declan Quinn
Leaving Las Vegas

1997 Roger Deakins
Fargo

1998 Declan Quinn
Kama Sutra

1999 Lisa Rinzler
Three Seasons

Best Actor

1986 M. Emmet Walsh
Blood Simple

1987 James Woods
Salvador

1988 Dennis Quaid
The Big Easy

1989 Edward James Olmos
Stand and Deliver

1990 Matt Dillon
Drugstore Cowboy

1991 Danny Glover
To Sleep with Anger

1992 River Phoenix
My Own Private Idaho

1993 Harvey Keitel
Bad Lieutenant

1994 Jeff Bridges
American Heart

1995 Samuel L. Jackson
Pulp Fiction

1996 Sean Penn
Dead Man Walking

1997 William H. Macy
Fargo

1998 Robert Duvall
The Apostle

1999 Richard Farnsworth
The Straight Story

Best Actress

1986 Geraldine Page
The Trip to Bountiful

1987 Isabella Rossellini
Blue Velvet

1988 Sally Kirkland
Anna

1989 Jodie Foster
Five Corners

1990 Andie MacDowell
sex, lies, and videotape

1991 Anjelica Huston
The Grifters

1992 Judy Davis
Impromptu

1993 Fairuza Balk
Gas, Food, Lodging

1994 Ashley Judd
Ruby in Paradise

1995 Linda Fiorentino
The Last Seduction

1996 Elisabeth Shue
Leaving Las Vegas

1997 Frances McDormand
Fargo

1998 Julie Christie
Afterglow

1999 Hilary Swank
Boys Don't Cry

Best Supporting Actor

1988 Morgan Freeman
Street Smart

1989 Lou Diamond Phillips
Stand and Deliver

1990 Max Perlich
Drugstore Cowboy

1991 Bruce Davison
Longtime Companion

1992 David Strathairn
City of Hope

1993 Steve Buscemi
Reservoir Dogs

1994 Christopher Lloyd
Twenty Bucks

1995	Chazz Palmintieri
	Bullets over Broadway
1996	Benicio Del Toro
	The Usual Suspects
1997	Benecio Del Toro
	Basquiat
1998	Jason Lee
	Chasing Amy
1999	Steve Zahn
	Happy, Texas

Best Supporting Actress

1988	Anjelica Huston
	The Dead
1989	Rosanna De Soto
	Stand and Deliver
1990	Laura San Giacomo
	sex, lies and videotape
1991	Sheryl Lee Ralph
	To Sleep with Anger
1992	Diane Ladd
	Rambling Rose
1993	Alfre Woodard
	Passion Fish
1994	Lili Taylor
	Household Saints
1995	Dianne Wiest
	Bullets over Broadway
1996	Mare Winningham
	Georgia
1997	Elizabeth Pena
	Lone Star
1998	Debbi Morgan
	Eve's Bayou
1999	Chloë Sevigny
	Boys Don't Cry

Best Foreign Film

1986	Kiss of the Spider Woman
1987	A Room with a View
1988	My Life as a Dog
1989	Wings of Desire
1990	My Left Foot
1991	Sweetie
1992	An Angel at My Table
1993	The Crying Game
1994	The Piano
1995	Red
1996	Before the Rain
1997	Secrets and Lies
1998	The Sweet Hereafter
1999	Run Lola Run

MTV MOVIE AWARDS

Best Movie

1992	Terminator 2: Judgment Day
1993	A Few Good Men
1994	Menace II Society
1995	Pulp Fiction
1996	Seven
1997	Scream

1998	Titanic
1999	There's Something About Mary
2000	The Matrix

Best Male Performance

1992	Arnold Schwarzenegger
	Terminator 2: Judgment Day
1993	Denzel Washington
	Malcolm X
1994	Tom Hanks
	Philadelphia
1995	Brad Pitt
	Interview with the Vampire
1996	Jim Carrey
	Ace Ventura: When Nature Calls
1997	Tom Cruise
	Jerry Maguire
1998	Leonardo DiCaprio
	Titanic
1999	Jim Carrey
	The Truman Show
2000	Keanu Reeves
	The Matrix

Best Female Performance

1992	Linda Hamilton
	Terminator 2: Judgment Day
1993	Sharon Stone
	Basic Instinct
1994	Janet Jackson
	Poetic Justice
1995	Sandra Bullock
	Speed
1996	Alicia Silverstone
	Clueless
1997	Claire Danes
	William Shakespeare's Romeo and Juliet
1998	Neve Campbell
	Scream 2
1999	Cameron Diaz
	There's Something About Mary
2000	Sarah Michelle Gellar
	Cruel Intentions

Breakthrough Performance

1992	Edward Furlong
	Terminator 2: Judgment Day
1993	Marisa Tomei
	My Cousin Vinny
1994	Alicia Silverstone
	The Crush
1995	Kirsten Dunst
	Interview with the Vampire
1996	George Clooney
	From Dusk Till Dawn
1997	Matthey McConaughey
	A Time To Kill
1998	Heather Graham
	Boogie Nights
1999	James Van Der Beek
	Varsity Blues

	Katie Holmes
	Disturbing Behavior
2000	Haley Joel Osment
	The Sixth Sense
	Julia Stiles
	10 Things I Hate About You

Best Comedic Performance

1992	Billy Crystal
	City Slickers
1993	Robin Williams
	Aladdin
1994	Robin Williams
	Mrs. Doubtfire
1995	Jim Carrey
	Dumb and Dumber
1996	Jim Carrey
	Ace Ventura: When Nature Calls
1997	Jim Carrey
	The Cable Guy
1998	Jim Carrey
	Liar, Liar
1999	no award
2000	Adam Sandler
	Big Daddy

Best Villain

1992	Rebecca DeMornay
	The Hand That Rocks the Cradle
1993	Jennifer Jason Leigh
	Single White Female
1994	Alicia Silverstone
	The Crush
1995	Dennis Hopper
	Speed
1996	Kevin Spacey
	Seven
1997	Jim Carrey
	The Cable Guy
1998	Mike Myers
	Austin Powers: International Man of Mystery
1999	Matt Dillon
	There's Something About Mary
	Stephen Dorff
	Blade
2000	Mike Myers
	Austin Powers: The Spy Who Shagged Me

Best On-Screen Duo

1992	Mike Myers and Dana Carvey
	Wayne's World
1993	Mel Gibson and Danny Glover
	Lethal Weapon 3
1994	Harrison Ford and Tommy Lee Jones
	The Fugitive
1995	Keanu Reeves and Sandra Bullock
	Speed
1996	Chris Farley and David Spade

Tommy Boy

1997	Sean Connery and Nicolas Cage *The Rock*
1998	John Travolta and Nicolas Cage *Face/Off*
1999	Jackie Chan and Chris Tucker *Rush Hour*
2000	Mike Myers and Verne Troyer, *Austin Powers: The Spy Who* *Shagged Me*

Best Song

1992	Bryan Adams "(Everything I Do) I Do It For You" *(Robin Hood: Prince of Thieves)*
1993	Whitney Houston "I Will Always Love You" *(The Bodyguard)*
1994	Michael Jackson "Will You Be There" *(Free Willy)*
1995	Stone Temple Pilots "Big Empty" *(The Crow)*
1996	Brandy "Sittin' up in My Room" *(Waiting to Exhale)*
1997	Bush "Machinehead" *(Fear)*
1998	Will Smith "Men in Black" *(Men in Black)*
1999	Aerosmith "I Don't Want to Miss a Thing" *(Armageddon)*
2000	"Uncle F**ka" *(South Park: Bigger, Longer, and Uncut)*

Best Kiss

1992	Macaulay Culkin and Anna Chlumsky *My Girl*
1993	Marisa Tomei and Christian Slater *Untamed Heart*
1994	Woody Harrelson and Demi Moore *Indecent Proposal*
1995	Jim Carrey and Lauren Holly *Dumb and Dumber*
1996	Natasha Henstridge and Anthony Guidere *Species*
1997	Will Smith and Vivica A. Fox *Independence Day*
1998	Adam Sandler and Drew Barrymore *The Wedding Singer*
1999	Gwyneth Paltrow and Joseph Fiennes *Shakespeare In Love*
2000	Selma Blair and Sarah Michelle Gellar *Cruel Intentions*

Best Action Sequence

1992	Terminator 2: Judgment Day
1993	Lethal Weapon 3
1994	The Fugitive
1995	Speed
1996	Braveheart
1997	Twister
1998	Face/Off
1999	Armageddon
2000	Star Wars: Episode 1—The Phantom Menace

Best Fight

1996	Adam Sandler and Bob Barker *Happy Gilmore*
1997	Fairuza Balk and Robin Tunney *The Craft*
1998	Will Smith and Cockroach *Men in Black*
1999	Ben Stiller and Puffy the Dog *There's Something About Mary*
2000	Spike Jonze *Being John Malkovich*

DIRECTOR'S GUILD AWARDS

1948–49	*A Letter to Three Wives* Joseph Mankiewicz
1949–50	*All the King's Men* Robert Rossen
1950–51	*All About Eve* Joseph Mankiewicz
1951	*A Place in the Sun* George Stevens
1952	*The Quiet Man* John Ford
1953	*From Here to Eternity* Fred Zinnemann
1954	*On the Waterfront* Elia Kazan
1955	*Marty* Delbert Mann
1956	*Giant* George Stevens
1957	*Bridge on the River Kwai* David Lean
1958	*Gigi* Vincente Minnelli
1959	*Ben-Hur* William Wyler
1960	*The Apartment* Billy Wilder
1961	*West Side Story* Robert Wise and Jerome Robbins
1962	*Lawrence of Arabia* David Lean
1963	*Tom Jones* Tony Richardson
1964	*My Fair Lady* George Cukor
1965	*The Sound of Music* Robert Wise
1966	*A Man for All Seasons* Fred Zinnemann

1967	*The Graduate* Mike Nichols
1968	*The Lion in Winter* Anthony Harvey
1969	*Midnight Cowboy* John Schlesinger
1970	*Patton* Franklin J. Schaffner
1971	*The French Connection* William Friedkin
1972	*The Godfather* Francis Ford Coppola
1973	*The Sting* George Roy Hill
1974	*The Godfather Part II* Francis Ford Coppola
1975	*One Flew over the* *Cuckoo's Nest* Milos Forman
1976	*Rocky* John G. Avildsen
1977	*Annie Hall* Woody Allen
1978	*The Deer Hunter* Michael Cimino
1979	*Kramer vs. Kramer* Robert Benton
1980	*Ordinary People* Robert Redford
1981	*Reds* Warren Beatty
1982	*Gandhi* Richard Attenborough
1983	*Terms of Endearment* James L. Brooks
1984	*Amadeus* Milos Forman
1985	*The Color Purple* Steven Spielberg
1986	*Platoon* Oliver Stone
1987	*The Last Emperor* Bernardo Bertolucci
1988	*Rain Man* Barry Levinson
1989	*Born on the Fourth of July* Oliver Stone
1990	*Dances with Wolves* Kevin Costner
1991	*The Silence of the Lambs* Jonathan Demme
1992	*Unforgiven* Clint Eastwood
1993	*Schindler's List* Steven Spielberg
1994	*Forrest Gump* Robert Zemeckis
1995	*Apollo 13* Ron Howard
1996	*The English Patient* Anthony Minghella
1997	*Titanic* James Cameron
1998	*Saving Private Ryan* Steven Spielberg
1999	*American Beauty* Sam Mendes

THE ACADEMY AWARDS

	1927–28	1928–29	1929–30
Picture	Wings	Broadway Melody	All Quiet on the Western Front
Actor	Emil Jannings, The Last Command; The Way of All Flesh	Warner Baxter, In Old Arizona	George Arliss, Disraeli
Actress	Janet Gaynor, Seventh Heaven; Street Angel; Sunrise	Mary Pickford, Coquette	Norma Shearer, The Divorcée
Director	Frank Borzage, Seventh Heaven; Lewis Milestone, Two Arabian Knights	Frank Lloyd, The Divine Lady; Weary River; Drag	Lewis Milestone, All Quiet on the Western Front
Adapted Screenplay	Benjamin Glazer, Seventh Heaven	—	—
Original Story	Ben Hecht, Underworld	Hans Kraly, The Patriot	Frances Marion, The Big House
Cinematography	Sunrise	White Shadows in the South Seas	With Byrd at the South Pole
Interior Decoration	The Dove and The Tempest	The Bridge of San Luis Rey	King of Jazz
Sound	—	—	The Big House

OSCAR RECORDS

Most awards in any category: Walt Disney, 27 regular and six special

Most honored films: *Ben-Hur* in 1959 and *Titanic* in 1997, with 11 each, and *West Side Story* in 1961, with 10

Most nominated films: *All About Eve* and *Titanic*, with 14 each, and *Gone With the Wind, From Here to Eternity, Mary Poppins, Who's Afraid of Virginia Woolf?, Forrest Gump,* and *Shakespeare in Love,* with 13 each

Most nominated films to receive no awards: *The Turning Point* and *The Color Purple,* with 11 each

Most Best Actor awards: Spencer Tracy, Fredric March, Gary Cooper, Marlon Brando, Dustin Hoffman, Tom Hanks, and Jack Nicholson, with two each

Most Best Director awards: John Ford with four, for *The Informer, The Grapes of Wrath, How Green Was My Valley,* and *The Quiet Man*

Most Best Actress awards: Katharine Hepburn with four, for *Morning Glory, Guess Who's Coming to Dinner, The Lion in Winter,* and *On Golden Pond*

Best Actress awards for debut performances: Shirley Booth for *Come Back, Little Sheba,* Barbra Streisand for *Funny Girl,* and Marlee Matlin for *Children of a Lesser God*

First African-American Oscar winner: Hattie McDaniel, Best Supporting Actress, in *Gone With the Wind*

	1930–31	1931–32	1932–33
Picture	Cimarron	Grand Hotel	Cavalcade
Actor	Lionel Barrymore, A Free Soul	Wallace Beery, The Champ; Fredric March, Dr. Jekyll and Mr. Hyde	Charles Laughton, The Private Life of Henry VIII
Actress	Marie Dressler, Min and Bill	Helen Hayes, The Sin of Madelon Claudet	Katharine Hepburn, Morning Glory
Supporting Actor	—	—	—
Supporting Actress	—	—	—
Director	Norman Taurog, Skippy	Frank Borzage, Bad Girl	Frank Lloyd, Cavalcade
Adapted Screenplay/ Screenplay	Howard Estabrook, Cimarron	Edwin Burke, Bad Girl	Victor Heerman and Sarah Y. Mason, Little Women
Original Story	John Monk Saunders, The Dawn Patrol	Francis Marion, The Champ	Robert Lord, One Way Passage
Song	—	—	—
Score	—	—	—
Cinematography	Tabu	Shanghai Express	A Farewell to Arms
Interior Decoration	Cimarron	Transatlantic	Cavalcade
Film Editing	—	—	—
Sound	Paramount Studio Sound Department	Paramount Studio Sound Department	A Farewell to Arms
Short Films	—	Flower and Trees (Cartoons); The Music Box (Comedy); Wrestling Swordfish (Novelty)	The Three Little Pigs (Cartoons); So This Is Harris (Comedy); Krakatoa (Novelty)

POPULAR AND PRAISED

Few films claim the hearts of both the moviegoing public and the majority of the Academy of Motion Picture Arts and Sciences. In fact, only 10 of the top 100 moneymakers of all time have won best-picture Oscars. Those films are listed below, ranked in order of amount grossed. (Source: Variety)

1.	Titanic	1997
2.	Forrest Gump	1994
3.	Gone With the Wind	1939
4.	Dances with Wolves	1990
5.	Rain Man	1988
6.	The Sound of Music	1965
7.	The Sting	1973
8.	Platoon	1986
9.	The Godfather	1972
10.	The Silence of the Lambs	1991

1934 | 1935 | 1936 | 1937

1934	1935	1936	1937
It Happened One Night	*Mutiny on the Bounty*	*The Great Ziegfeld*	*The Life of Emile Zola*
Clark Gable, *It Happened One Night*	Victor McLaglen, *The Informer*	Paul Muni, *The Story of Louis Pasteur*	Spencer Tracy, *Captains Courageous*
Claudette Colbert, *It Happened One Night*	Bette Davis, *Dangerous*	Luise Rainer, *The Great Ziegfeld*	Luise Rainer, *The Good Earth*
—	—	Walter Brennan, *Come and Get It*	Joseph Schildkraut, *The Life of Emile Zola*
—	—	Gale Sondergaard, *Anthony Adverse*	Alice Brady, *In Old Chicago*
Frank Capra, *It Happened One Night*	John Ford, *The Informer*	Frank Capra, *Mr. Deeds Goes to Town*	Leo McCarey, *The Awful Truth*
Robert Riskin, *It Happened One Night*	Dudley Nichols, *The Informer*	Pierre Collings and Sheridan Gibney, *The Story of Louis Pasteur*	Heinz Herald, Geza Herczeg, and Norman Reilly Raine, *The Life of Emile Zola*
Arthur Caesar, *Manhattan Melodrama*	Ben Hecht and Charles MacArthur, *The Scoundrel*	Pierre Collings and Sheridan Gibney, *The Story of Louis Pasteur*	William A. Wellman and Robert Carson, *A Star is Born*
"The Continental" *(The Gay Divorcée)*	"Lullaby of Broadway" *(Gold Diggers of 1935)*	"The Way You Look Tonight" *(Swing Time)*	"Sweet Leilani" *(Waikiki Wedding)*
One Night of Love	*The Informer*	*Anthony Adverse*	*100 Men and a Girl*
Cleopatra	*A Midsummer Night's Dream*	*Anthony Adverse*	*The Good Earth*
The Merry Widow	*The Dark Angel*	*Dodsworth*	*Lost Horizon*
Eskimo	*A Midsummer Night's Dream*	*Anthony Adverse*	*Lost Horizon*
One Night of Love	*Naughty Marietta*	*San Francisco*	*The Hurricane*
The Tortoise and the Hare (Cartoons); *La Cucaracha* (Comedy); *City of Wax* (Novelty)	*Three Orphan Kittens* (Cartoons); *How To Sleep* (Comedy); *Wings over Mt. Everest* (Novelty)	*Country Cousin* (Cartoons); *Bored of Education* (One-Reel); *The Public Pays* (Two-Reel); *Give Me Liberty* (Color)	*The Old Mill* (Cartoons); *Private Life of the Gannetts* (One-Reel); *Torture Money* (Two-Reel); *Penny Wisdom* (Color)

DISNEY'S WINNING TUNES

Disney has dominated the Oscar Best Song category in recent years, winning eight times in the last 11 years. In total, the studio has won 11 times in this category; Paramount still leads with 16 wins.

Song	Film	Year
"When You Wish Upon a Star"	*Pinocchio*	1940
"Zip-a-Dee-Doo-Dah"	*Song of the South*	1947
"Chim Chim Cher-ee"	*Mary Poppins*	1964
"Under the Sea"	*The Little Mermaid*	1989
"Sooner or Later"	*Dick Tracy*	1990
"Beauty and the Beast"	*Beauty and the Beast*	1991
"A Whole New World"	*Aladdin*	1992
"Can You Feel the Love Tonight"	*The Lion King*	1994
"Colors of the Wind"	*Pocahontas*	1995
"You Must Love Me"	*Evita*	1996
"You'll Be in My Heart"	*Tarzan*	1999

	1938	1939	1940
Picture	*You Can't Take It with You*	*Gone With the Wind*	*Rebecca*
Actor	Spencer Tracy, *Boys Town*	Robert Donat, *Goodbye, Mr. Chips*	James Stewart, *The Philadelphia Story*
Actress	Bette Davis, *Jezebel*	Vivien Leigh, *Gone With the Wind*	Ginger Rogers, *Kitty Foyle*
Supporting Actor	Walter Brennan, *Kentucky*	Thomas Mitchell, *Stagecoach*	Walter Brennan, *The Westerner*
Supporting Actress	Fay Bainter, *Jezebel*	Hattie McDaniel, *Gone With the Wind*	Jane Darwell, *The Grapes of Wrath*
Director	Frank Capra, *You Can't Take It with You*	Victor Fleming, *Gone With the Wind*	John Ford, *The Grapes of Wrath*
Screenplay	Ian Dalrymple, Cecil Lewis, and W. P. Lipscomb, *Pygmalion*	Sidney Howard, *Gone With the Wind*	Donald Ogden Stewart, *The Philadelphia Story*
Original Screenplay/ Original Story	Eleanore Griffin and Dore Schary, *Boys Town*	Lewis R. Foster, *Mr. Smith Goes to Washington*	Preston Sturges, *The Great McGinty*; Benjamin Glazer and John S. Toldy, *Arise, My Love*
Song	"Thanks for the Memory" *(Big Broadcast of 1938)*	"Over the Rainbow" *(The Wizard of Oz)*	"When You Wish upon a Star" *(Pinocchio)*
Score/Original Score	*Alexander's Ragtime Band; The Adventures of Robin Hood*	*Stagecoach; The Wizard of Oz*	*Tin Pan Alley; Pinocchio*
Cinematography	*The Great Waltz*	*Wuthering Heights* (B&W); *Gone With the Wind* (Color)	*Rebecca* (B&W); *The Thief of Bagdad* (Color)
Interior Decoration	*The Adventures of Robin Hood*	*Gone With the Wind*	*Pride and Prejudice* (B&W); *The Thief of Bagdad* (Color)
Film Editing	*The Adventures of Robin Hood*	*Gone With the Wind*	*North West Mounted Police*
Sound	*The Cowboy and the Lady*	*When Tomorrow Comes*	*Strike Up the Band*
Special Effects	—	*The Rains Came*	*The Thief of Bagdad*
Short Films	*Ferdinand the Bull* (Cartoons); *That Mothers Might Live* (One-Reel); *Declaration of Independence* (Two-Reel)	*The Ugly Duckling* (Cartoons); *Busy Little Bears* (One-Reel); *Sons of Liberty* (Two-Reel)	*Milky Way* (Cartoons); *Quicker 'N a Wink* (One-Reel); *Teddy, the Rough Rider* (Two-Reel)
Documentaries	—	—	—

66 Is it just me, or has it been a millennium since I last hosted the show? 99

—Billy Crystal, host, 1999

1941	1942	1943	1944
How Green Was My Valley	Mrs. Miniver	Casablanca	Going My Way
Gary Cooper, Sergeant York	James Cagney, Yankee Doodle Dandy	Paul Lukas, Watch on the Rhine	Bing Crosby, Going My Way
Joan Fontaine, Suspicion	Greer Garson, Mrs. Miniver	Jennifer Jones, The Song of Bernadette	Ingrid Bergman, Gaslight
Donald Crisp, How Green Was My Valley	Van Heflin, Johnny Eager	Charles Coburn, The More the Merrier	Barry Fitzgerald, Going My Way
Mary Astor, The Great Lie	Teresa Wright, Mrs. Miniver	Katina Paxinou, For Whom the Bell Tolls	Ethel Barrymore, None but the Lonely Heart
John Ford, How Green Was My Valley	William Wyler, Mrs. Miniver	Michael Curtiz, Casablanca	Leo McCarey, Going My Way
Sidney Buchman and Seton I. Miller, Here Comes Mr. Jordan	George Froeschel, James Hilton, Claudine West, and Arthur Wimperis, Mrs. Miniver	Julius J. Epstein, Philip G. Epstein, and Howard Koch, Casablanca	Frank Butler and Frank Cavett, Going My Way
Harry Segall, Here Comes Mr. Jordan; Herman J. Mankiewicz and Orson Welles, Citizen Kane	Michael Kanin and Ring Lardner Jr., Woman of the Year; Emeric Pressburger, The Invaders	Norman Krasna, Princess O'Rourke; William Saroyan, The Human Comedy	Lamar Trotti, Wilson; Leo McCarey, Going My Way
"The Last Time I Saw Paris" (Lady Be Good)	"White Christmas" (Holiday Inn)	"You'll Never Know" (Hello, Frisco, Hello)	"Swinging on a Star" (Going My Way)
All That Money Can Buy (Dramatic); Dumbo (Musical)	Now, Voyager (Dramatic or Comedy); Yankee Doodle Dandy (Musical)	The Song of Bernadette (Dramatic or Comedy); This Is the Army (Musical)	Since You Went Away (Dramatic or Comedy); Cover Girl (Musical)
How Green Was My Valley (B&W); Blood and Sand (Color)	Mrs. Miniver (B&W); The Black Swan (Color)	The Song of Bernadette (B&W); The Phantom of the Opera (Color)	Laura (B&W); Wilson (Color)
How Green Was My Valley (B&W); Blossoms in the Dust (Color)	This Above All (B&W); My Gal Sal (Color)	The Song of Bernadette (B&W); The Phantom of the Opera (Color)	Gaslight (B&W); Wilson (Color)
Sergeant York	The Pride of the Yankees	Air Force	Wilson
That Hamilton Woman	Yankee Doodle Dandy	This Land Is Mine	Wilson
I Wanted Wings	Reap the Wild Wind	Crash Dive	Thirty Seconds over Tokyo
Lend a Paw (Cartoons); Of Pups and Puzzles (One-Reel); Main Street on the March (Two-Reel)	Der Fuehrer's Face (Cartoons); Speaking of Animals and Their Families (One-Reel); Beyond the Line of Duty (Two-Reel)	Yankee Doodle Mouse (Cartoons); Amphibious Fighters (One-Reel); Heavenly Music (Two-Reel)	Mouse Trouble (Cartoons); Who's Who in Animal Land (One-Reel); I Won't Play (Two-Reel)
Churchill's Island	Battle of Midway; Kokoda Front Line; Moscow Strikes Back; Prelude to War	December 7th (Short); Desert Victory (Feature)	With the Marines at Tarawa (Short); The Fighting Lady (Feature)

	1945	**1946**	**1947**
Picture	*The Lost Weekend*	*The Best Years of Our Lives*	*Gentleman's Agreement*
Actor	Ray Milland, *The Lost Weekend*	Fredric March, *The Best Years of Our Lives*	Ronald Colman, *A Double Life*
Actress	Joan Crawford, *Mildred Pierce*	Olivia de Havilland, *To Each His Own*	Loretta Young, *The Farmer's Daughter*
Supporting Actor	James Dunn, *A Tree Grows in Brooklyn*	Harold Russell, *The Best Years of Our Lives*	Edmund Gwenn, *Miracle on 34th Street*
Supporting Actress	Anne Revere, *National Velvet*	Anne Baxter, *The Razor's Edge*	Celeste Holm, *Gentleman's Agreement*
Director	Billy Wilder, *The Lost Weekend*	William Wyler, *The Best Years of Our Lives*	Elia Kazan, *Gentleman's Agreement*
Screenplay	Charles Brackett and Billy Wilder, *The Lost Weekend*	Robert E. Sherwood, *The Best Years of Our Lives*	George Seaton, *Miracle on 34th Street*
Original Screenplay/ Original Story	Richard Schweizer, *Marie-Louise;* Charles G. Booth, *The House on 92nd Street*	Muriel and Sydney Box, *The Seventh Veil;* Clemence Dane, *Vacation from Marriage*	Sidney Sheldon, *The Bachelor and the Bobby-Soxer;* Valentine Davies, *Miracle on 34th Street*
Song	"It Might As Well Be Spring" *(State Fair)*	"On the Atchison, Topeka and Santa Fe" *(The Harvey Girls)*	"Zip-A-Dee-Doo-Dah" *(Song of the South)*
Score—Dramatic or Comedy/ Musical	*Spellbound; Anchors Aweigh*	*The Best Years of Our Lives; The Jolson Story*	*A Double Life; Mother Wore Tights*
Cinematography	*The Picture of Dorian Gray* (B&W); *Leave Her to Heaven* (Color)	*Anna and the King of Siam* (B&W); *The Yearling* (Color)	*Great Expectations* (B&W); *Black Narcissus* (Color)
Costume Design	—	—	—
Interior Decoration, through 1946; Art Direction—Set Decoration, from 1947	*Blood on the Sun* (B&W); *Frenchman's Creek* (Color)	*Anna and the King of Siam* (B&W); *The Yearling* (Color)	*Great Expectations* (B&W); *Black Narcissus* (Color)
Film Editing	*National Velvet*	*The Best Years of Our Lives*	*Body and Soul*
Sound	*The Bells of St. Mary's*	*The Jolson Story*	*The Bishop's Wife*
Special Effects	*Wonder Man*	*Blithe Spirit*	*Green Dolphin Street*
Short Films	*Quiet Please* (Cartoons); *Stairway to Light* (One-Reel); *Star in the Night* (Two-Reel)	*The Cat Concerto* (Cartoons); *Facing Your Danger* (One-Reel); *A Boy and His Dog* (Two-Reel)	*Tweetie Pie* (Cartoons); *Goodbye Miss Turlock* (One-Reel); *Climbing the Matterhorn* (Two-Reel)
Documentaries	*Hitler Lives?* (Short); *The True Glory* (Feature)	*Seeds of Destiny* (Short)	*First Steps* (Short); *Design for Death* (Feature)

> 66 Since my acceptance speech last year, they asked me to stay the hell off the furniture. 99
>
> —Roberto Benigni, Best Actor, 1998

1948	1949	1950	1951
Hamlet	*All the King's Men*	*All About Eve*	*An American in Paris*
Laurence Olivier, *Hamlet*	Broderick Crawford, *All the King's Men*	José Ferrer, *Cyrano de Bergerac*	Humphrey Bogart, *The African Queen*
Jane Wyman, *Johnny Belinda*	Olivia de Havilland, *The Heiress*	Judy Holliday, *Born Yesterday*	Vivien Leigh, *A Streetcar Named Desire*
Walter Huston, *The Treasure of the Sierra Madre*	Dean Jagger, *Twelve O'Clock High*	George Sanders, *All About Eve*	Karl Malden, *A Streetcar Named Desire*
Claire Trevor, *Key Largo*	Mercedes McCambridge, *All the King's Men*	Josephine Hull, *Harvey*	Kim Hunter, *A Streetcar Named Desire*
John Huston, *The Treasure of the Sierra Madre*	Joseph L. Mankiewicz, *A Letter to Three Wives*	Joseph L. Mankiewicz, *All About Eve*	George Stevens, *A Place in the Sun*
John Huston, *The Treasure of the Sierra Madre*	Joseph L. Mankiewicz, *A Letter to Three Wives*	Joseph L. Mankiewicz, *All About Eve*	Michael Wilson and Harry Brown, *A Place in the Sun*
Richard Schweizer and David Wechsler, *The Search*	Douglas Morrow, *The Stratton Story* (Motion Picture Story); Robert Pirosh, *Battleground* (Story and Screenplay)	Edna & Edward Anhalt, *Panic in the Streets* (Motion Picture Story); Charles Brackett, Billy Wilder, and D.M. Marshman Jr., *Sunset Boulevard* (Story and Screenplay)	Paul Dehn and James Bernard, *Seven Days to Noon* (Motion Picture Story); Alan Jay Lerner, *An American in Paris* (Story and Screenplay)
"Buttons and Bows" *(The Paleface)*	"Baby, It's Cold Outside" *(Neptune's Daughter)*	"Mona Lisa" *(Captain Carey, USA)*	"In the Cool, Cool, Cool of the Evening" *(Here Comes the Groom)*
The Red Shoes; Easter Parade	*The Heiress; On the Town*	*Sunset Boulevard; Annie Get Your Gun*	*A Place in the Sun; An American in Paris*
The Naked City (B&W); *Joan of Arc* (Color)	*Battleground* (B&W); *She Wore a Yellow Ribbon* (Color)	*The Third Man* (B&W); *King Solomon's Mines* (Color)	*A Place in the Sun* (B&W); *An American in Paris* (Color)
Hamlet (B&W); *Joan of Arc* (Color)	*The Heiress* (B&W); *Adventures of Don Juan* (Color)	*All About Eve* (B&W); *Samson and Delilah* (Color)	*A Place in the Sun* (B&W); *An American in Paris* (Color)
Hamlet (B&W); *The Red Shoes* (Color)	*The Heiress* (B&W); *Little Women* (Color)	*Sunset Boulevard* (B&W); *Samson and Delilah* (Color)	*A Streetcar Named Desire* (B&W); *An American in Paris* (Color)
The Naked City	*Champion*	*King Solomon's Mines*	*A Place in the Sun*
The Snake Pit	*Twelve O'Clock High*	*All About Eve*	*The Great Caruso*
Portrait of Jennie	*Mighty Joe Young*	*Destination Moon*	*When Worlds Collide*
The Little Orphan (Cartoons); *Symphony of a City* (One-Reel); *Seal Island* (Two-Reel)	*For Scent-imental Reasons* (Cartoons); *Aquatic House Party* (One-Reel); *Van Gogh* (Two-Reel)	*Gerald McBoing-Boing* (Cartoons); *Grandad of Races* (One-Reel); *In Beaver Valley* (Two-Reel)	*Two Mouseketeers* (Cartoons); *World of Kids* (One-Reel); *Nature's Half Acre* (Two-Reel)
Toward Independence (Short); *The Secret Land* (Feature)	*A Chance To Live* and *So Much for So Little* (Short); *Daybreak in Udi* (Feature)	*Why Korea?* (Short); *The Titan: Story of Michelangelo* (Feature)	*Benjy* (Short); *Kon-Tiki* (Feature)

66 The whole thing is like a dream. I don't remember it at all. 99

—Gwyneth Paltrow, Best Actress, 1998

	1952	1953	1954
Picture	*The Greatest Show on Earth*	*From Here to Eternity*	*On the Waterfront*
Actor	Gary Cooper, *High Noon*	William Holden, *Stalag 17*	Marlon Brando, *On the Waterfront*
Actress	Shirley Booth, *Come Back, Little Sheba*	Audrey Hepburn, *Roman Holiday*	Grace Kelly, *The Country Girl*
Supporting Actor	Anthony Quinn, *Viva Zapata!*	Frank Sinatra, *From Here to Eternity*	Edmond O'Brien, *The Barefoot Contessa*
Supporting Actress	Gloria Grahame, *The Bad and the Beautiful*	Donna Reed, *From Here to Eternity*	Eva Marie Saint, *On the Waterfront*
Director	John Ford, *The Quiet Man*	Fred Zinnemann, *From Here to Eternity*	Elia Kazan, *On the Waterfront*
Screenplay	Charles Schnee, *The Bad and the Beautiful*	Daniel Taradash, *From Here to Eternity*	George Seaton, *The Country Girl*
Story/Story and Screenplay	Frederic M. Frank, Theodore St. John, and Frank Cavett, *The Greatest Show on Earth*; T.E.B. Clarke, *The Lavender Hill Mob*	Ian McLellan Hunter, *Roman Holiday*; Charles Brackett, Walter Reisch, and Richard Breen, *Titanic*	Philip Yordan, *Broken Lance*; Budd Schulberg, *On the Waterfront*
Song	"High Noon (Do Not Forsake Me, Oh My Darlin')" *(High Noon)*	"Secret Love" *(Calamity Jane)*	"Three Coins in the Fountain" *(Three Coins in the Fountain)*
Score—Dramatic or Comedy/Musical	*High Noon*; *With a Song in My Heart*	*Lili*; *Call Me Madam*	*The High and the Mighty*; *Seven Brides for Seven Brothers*
Cinematography	*The Bad and the Beautiful* (B&W); *The Quiet Man* (Color)	*From Here to Eternity* (B&W); *Shane* (Color)	*On the Waterfront* (B&W); *Three Coins in the Fountain* (Color)
Costume Design	*The Bad and the Beautiful* (B&W); *Moulin Rouge* (Color)	*Roman Holiday* (B&W); *The Robe* (Color)	*Sabrina* (B&W); *Gate of Hell* (Color)
Art Direction—Set Decoration	*The Bad and the Beautiful* (B&W); *Moulin Rouge* (Color)	*Julius Caesar* (B&W); *The Robe* (Color)	*On the Waterfront* (B&W); *20,000 Leagues Under the Sea* (Color)
Film Editing	*High Noon*	*From Here to Eternity*	*On the Waterfront*
Foreign Language Film	—	—	—
Sound	*Breaking the Sound Barrier*	*From Here to Eternity*	*The Glenn Miller Story*
Special Effects	*Plymouth Adventure*	*The War of the Worlds*	*20,000 Leagues Under the Sea*
Short Films	*Johann Mouse* (Cartoons); *Light in the Window* (One-Reel); *Water Birds* (Two-Reel)	*Toot, Whistle, Plunk and Boom* (Cartoons); *The Merry Wives of Windsor Overture* (One-Reel); *Bear Country* (Two-Reel)	*When Magoo Flew* (Cartoons); *This Mechanical Age* (One-Reel); *A Time Out of War* (Two-Reel)
Documentaries	*Neighbours* (Short); *The Sea Around Us* (Feature)	*The Alaskan Eskimo* (Short); *The Living Desert* (Feature)	*Thursday's Children* (Short); *The Vanishing Prairie* (Feature)

1955	1956	1957	1958
Marty	*Around the World in 80 Days*	*The Bridge on the River Kwai*	*Gigi*
Ernest Borgnine, *Marty*	Yul Brynner, *The King and I*	Alec Guinness, *The Bridge on the River Kwai*	David Niven, *Separate Tables*
Anna Magnani, *The Rose Tattoo*	Ingrid Bergman, *Anastasia*	Joanne Woodward, *The Three Faces of Eve*	Susan Hayward, *I Want to Live!*
Jack Lemmon, *Mister Roberts*	Anthony Quinn, *Lust for Life*	Red Buttons, *Sayonara*	Burl Ives, *The Big Country*
Jo Van Fleet, *East of Eden*	Dorothy Malone, *Written on the Wind*	Miyoshi Umeki, *Sayonara*	Wendy Hiller, *Separate Tables*
Delbert Mann, *Marty*	George Stevens, *Giant*	David Lean, *The Bridge on the River Kwai*	Vincente Minnelli, *Gigi*
Paddy Chayefsky, *Marty*	James Poe, John Farrow, and S.J. Perelman, *Around the World in 80 Days* (Adapted)	Pierre Boulle, *The Bridge on the River Kwai* (Adapted)	Alan Jay Lerner, *Gigi* (Adapted)
Daniel Fuchs, *Love Me or Leave Me*; William Ludwig and Sonya Levien, *Interrupted Melody*	Dalton Trumbo (aka Robert Rich), *The Brave One*; Albert Lamorisse, *The Red Balloon* (Original)	George Wells, *Designing Woman*	Nathan E. Douglas and Harold Jacob Smith, *The Defiant Ones*
"Love is a Many-Splendored Thing" *(Love Is a Many-Splendored Thing)*	"Whatever Will Be, Will Be (Que Será, Será)" *(The Man Who Knew Too Much)*	"All the Way" *(The Joker Is Wild)*	"Gigi" *(Gigi)*
Love is a Many-Splendored Thing; Oklahoma!	*Around the World in 80 Days; The King and I*	*The Bridge on the River Kwai*	*The Old Man and the Sea; Gigi*
The Rose Tattoo (B&W); *To Catch a Thief* (Color)	*Somebody up There Likes Me* (B&W); *Around the World in 80 Days* (Color)	*The Bridge on the River Kwai*	*The Defiant Ones* (B&W); *Gigi* (Color)
I'll Cry Tomorrow (B&W); *Love Is a Many-Splendored Thing* (Color)	*The Solid Gold Cadillac* (B&W); *The King and I* (Color)	*Les Girls*	*Gigi*
The Rose Tattoo (B&W); *Picnic* (Color)	*Somebody up There Likes Me* (B&W); *The King and I* (Color)	*Sayonara*	*Gigi*
Picnic	*Around the World in 80 Days*	*The Bridge on the River Kwai*	*Gigi*
—	*La Strada* (Italy)	*The Nights of Cabiria* (Italy)	*My Uncle* (France)
Oklahoma!	*The King and I*	*Sayonara*	*South Pacific*
The Bridges at Toko-Ri	*The Ten Commandments*	*The Enemy Below*	*tom thumb*
Speedy Gonzales (Cartoon); *Survival City* (One-Reel); *The Face of Lincoln* (Two-Reel)	*Mister Magoo's Puddle Jumper* (Cartoons); *Crashing the Water Barrier* (One-Reel); *The Bespoke Overcoat* (Two-Reel)	*Birds Anonymous* (Cartoons); *The Wetback Hound* (Live Action)	*Knighty Knight Bugs* (Cartoons); *Grand Canyon* (Live Action)
Men Against the Arctic (Short); *Helen Keller in Her Story* (Feature)	*The True Story of the Civil War* (Short); *The Silent World* (Feature)	*Albert Schweitzer* (Feature)	*AMA Girls* (Short); *White Wilderness* (Feature)

	1959	**1960**	**1961**
Picture	*Ben-Hur*	*The Apartment*	*West Side Story*
Actor	Charlton Heston, *Ben-Hur*	Burt Lancaster, *Elmer Gantry*	Maximilian Schell, *Judgment at Nuremburg*
Actress	Simone Signoret, *Room at the Top*	Elizabeth Taylor, *Butterfield 8*	Sophia Loren, *Two Women*
Supporting Actor	Hugh Griffith, *Ben-Hur*	Peter Ustinov, *Spartacus*	George Chakiris, *West Side Story*
Supporting Actress	Shelley Winters, *The Diary of Anne Frank*	Shirley Jones, *Elmer Gantry*	Rita Moreno, *West Side Story*
Director	William Wyler, *Ben-Hur*	Billy Wilder, *The Apartment*	Robert Wise and Jerome Robbins, *West Side Story*
Adapted Screenplay	Neil Paterson, *Room at the Top*	Richard Brooks, *Elmer Gantry*	Abby Mann, *Judgment at Nuremberg*
Story and Screenplay	Russell Rouse and Clarence Greene, story; Stanley Shapiro and Maurice Richlin, screenplay, *Pillow Talk*	Billy Wilder and I.A.L. Diamond, *The Apartment*	William Inge, *Splendor in the Grass*
Song	"High Hopes" *(A Hole in the Head)*	"Never on Sunday" *(Never on Sunday)*	"Moon River" *(Breakfast at Tiffany's)*
Score	*Ben-Hur* (Dramatic or Comedy); *Porgy and Bess* (Musical)	*Exodus* (Dramatic or Comedy); *Song Without End (The Story of Franz Liszt)* (Musical)	*Breakfast at Tiffany's* (Dramatic or Comedy); *West Side Story* (Musical)
Cinematography	*The Diary of Anne Frank* (B&W); *Ben-Hur* (Color)	*Sons and Lovers* (B&W); *Spartacus* (Color)	*The Hustler* (B&W); *West Side Story* (Color)
Costume Design	*Some Like It Hot* (B&W); *Ben-Hur* (Color)	*The Facts of Life* (B&W); *Spartacus* (Color)	*La Dolce Vita* (B&W); *West Side Story* (Color)
Art Direction—Set Decoration	*The Diary of Anne Frank* (B&W); *Ben-Hur* (Color)	*The Apartment* (B&W); *Spartacus* (Color)	*The Hustler* (B&W); *West Side Story* (Color)
Film Editing	*Ben-Hur*	*The Apartment*	*West Side Story*
Foreign Language Film	*Black Orpheus* (France)	*The Virgin Spring* (Sweden)	*Through a Glass Darkly* (Sweden)
Sound	*Ben-Hur*	*The Alamo*	*West Side Story*
Sound Effects (Editing)	—	—	—
Visual Effects	—	—	—
Special Effects	*Ben-Hur*	*The Time Machine*	*The Guns of Navarone*
Short Films	*Moonbird* (Cartoons); *The Golden Fish* (Live Action)	*Munro* (Cartoons); *Day of the Painter* (Live Action)	*Ersatz (The Substitute)* (Cartoons); *Seawards the Great Ships* (Live Action)
Documentaries	*Glass* (Short); *Serengeti Shall Not Die* (Feature)	*Giuseppina* (Short); *The Horse with the Flying Tail* (Feature)	*Project Hope* (Short); *Le Ciel et la boue (Sky Above and Mud Beneath)* (Feature)

1962	1963	1964	1965
Lawrence of Arabia	Tom Jones	My Fair Lady	The Sound of Music
Gregory Peck, *To Kill a Mockingbird*	Sidney Poitier, *Lilies of the Field*	Rex Harrison, *My Fair Lady*	Lee Marvin, *Cat Ballou*
Anne Bancroft, *The Miracle Worker*	Patricia Neal, *Hud*	Julie Andrews, *Mary Poppins*	Julie Christie, *Darling*
Ed Begley, *Sweet Bird of Youth*	Melvyn Douglas, *Hud*	Peter Ustinov, *Topkapi*	Martin Balsam, *A Thousand Clowns*
Patty Duke, *The Miracle Worker*	Margaret Rutherford, *The V.I.P.s*	Lila Kedrova, *Zorba the Greek*	Shelley Winters, *A Patch of Blue*
David Lean, *Lawrence of Arabia*	Tony Richardson, *Tom Jones*	George Cukor, *My Fair Lady*	Robert Wise, *The Sound of Music*
Horton Foote, *To Kill a Mockingbird*	John Osborne, *Tom Jones*	Edward Anhalt, *Beckett*	Robert Bolt, *Doctor Zhivago*
Ennio de Concini, Alfredo Giannetti, and Pietro Germi, *Divorce—Italian Style*	James R. Webb, *How the West Was Won*	S. H. Barnett, story; Peter Stone and Frank Tarloff, screenplay, *Father Goose*	Frederic Raphael, *Darling*
"Days of Wine and Roses" *(Days of Wine and Roses)*	"Call Me Irresponsible" *(Papa's Delicate Condition)*	"Chim Chim Cher-ee" *(Mary Poppins)*	"The Shadow of Your Smile" *(The Sandpiper)*
Lawrence of Arabia (Original); The Music Man (Adaptation)	Tom Jones (Original); Irma La Douce (Adaptation)	Mary Poppins (Original); My Fair Lady (Adaptation)	Doctor Zhivago (Original); The Sound of Music (Adaptation)
The Longest Day (B&W); Lawrence of Arabia (Color)	Hud (B&W); Cleopatra (Color)	Zorba the Greek (B&W); My Fair Lady (Color)	Ship of Fools (B&W); Doctor Zhivago (Color)
Whatever Happened to Baby Jane? (B&W); The Wonderful World of the Brothers Grimm (Color)	8½ (B&W); Cleopatra (Color)	The Night of the Iguana (B&W); My Fair Lady (Color)	Darling (B&W); Doctor Zhivago (Color)
To Kill a Mockingbird (B&W); Lawrence of Arabia (Color)	America America (B&W); Cleopatra (Color)	Zorba the Greek (B&W); My Fair Lady (Color)	Ship of Fools (B&W); Doctor Zhivago (Color)
Lawrence of Arabia	How the West Was Won	Mary Poppins	The Sound of Music
Sundays and Cybèle (France)	8½ (Italy)	Yesterday, Today and Tomorrow (Italy)	The Shop on Main Street (Czechoslovakia)
Lawrence of Arabia	How the West Was Won	My Fair Lady	The Sound of Music
—	It's a Mad, Mad, Mad, Mad World	Goldfinger	The Great Race
—	Cleopatra	Mary Poppins	Thunderball
The Longest Day	—	—	—
The Hole (Cartoons); Heureux Anniversaire (Live Action)	The Critic (Cartoons); An Occurrence at Owl Creek Bridge (Live Action)	The Pink Phink (Cartoons); Casals Conducts: 1964 (Live Action)	The Dot and the Line (Cartoons); The Chicken (Le Poulet) (Live Action)
Dylan Thomas (Short); Black Fox (Feature)	Chagall (Short); Robert Frost: A Lover's Quarrel with the World (Feature)	Nine from Little Rock (Short); Jacques-Yves Cousteau's World Without Sun (Feature)	To Be Alive! (Short); The Eleanor Roosevelt Story (Feature)

	1966	1967	1968
Picture	*A Man for All Seasons*	*In the Heat of the Night*	*Oliver!*
Actor	Paul Scofield, *A Man for All Seasons*	Rod Steiger, *In the Heat of the Night*	Cliff Robertson, *Charly*
Actress	Elizabeth Taylor, *Who's Afraid of Virginia Woolf?*	Katharine Hepburn, *Guess Who's Coming to Dinner*	Katharine Hepburn, *The Lion in Winter*; Barbra Streisand, *Funny Girl*
Supporting Actor	Walter Matthau, *The Fortune Cookie*	George Kennedy, *Cool Hand Luke*	Jack Albertson, *The Subject Was Roses*
Supporting Actress	Sandy Dennis, *Who's Afraid of Virginia Woolf?*	Estelle Parsons, *Bonnie and Clyde*	Ruth Gordon, *Rosemary's Baby*
Director	Fred Zinnemann, *A Man for All Seasons*	Mike Nichols, *The Graduate*	Carol Reed, *Oliver!*
Adapted Screenplay	Robert Bolt, *A Man for All Seasons*	Stirling Silliphant, *In the Heat of the Night*	James Goldman, *The Lion in Winter*
Story and Screenplay	Claude Lelouch, story; Pierre Uytterhoeven and Claude Lelouch, screenplay, *A Man and a Woman*	William Rose, *Guess Who's Coming to Dinner?*	Mel Brooks, *The Producers*
Song	"Born Free" *(Born Free)*	"Talk to the Animals" *(Doctor Dolittle)*	"The Windmills of Your Mind" *(The Thomas Crown Affair)*
Score	*Born Free* (Original); *A Funny Thing Happened on the Way to the Forum* (Adaptation)	*Thoroughly Modern Millie* (Original); *Camelot* (Adaptation)	*The Lion in Winter* (Nonmusical); *Oliver!* (Musical)
Cinematography	*Who's Afraid of Virginia Woolf?* (B&W); *A Man for All Seasons*	*Bonnie and Clyde*	*Romeo and Juliet*
Costume Design	*Who's Afraid of Virginia Woolf?* (B&W); *A Man for All Seasons* (Color)	*Camelot*	*Romeo and Juliet*
Art Direction—Set Decoration	*Who's Afraid of Virginia Woolf?* (B&W); *Fantastic Voyage* (Color)	*Camelot*	*Oliver!*
Film Editing	*Grand Prix*	*In the Heat of the Night*	*Bullitt*
Foreign Language Film	*A Man and a Woman* (France)	*Closely Watched Trains* (Czechoslovakia)	*War and Peace* (U.S.S.R.)
Sound	*Grand Prix*	*In the Heat of the Night*	*Oliver!*
Sound Effects (Editing)	*Grand Prix*	*The Dirty Dozen*	—
Visual Effects	*Fantastic Voyage*	*Doctor Dolittle*	*2001: A Space Odyssey*
Short Films	*Herb Alpert and the Tijuana Brass Double Feature* (Cartoons); *Wild Wings* (Live Action)	*The Box* (Cartoons); *A Place to Stand* (Live Action)	*Winnie the Pooh and the Blustery Day* (Cartoons); *Robert Kennedy Remembered* (Live Action)
Documentaries	*A Year Toward Tomorrow* (Short); *The War Game* (Feature)	*The Redwoods* (Short); *The Anderson Platoon* (Feature)	*Why Man Creates* (Short); *Journey into Self* (Feature)

1969	**1970**	**1971**	**1972**
Midnight Cowboy	Patton	The French Connection	The Godfather
John Wayne, True Grit	George C. Scott, Patton	Gene Hackman, The French Connection	Marlon Brando, The Godfather
Maggie Smith, The Prime of Miss Jean Brodie	Glenda Jackson, Women in Love	Jane Fonda, Klute	Liza Minnelli, Cabaret
Gig Young, They Shoot Horses, Don't They?	John Mills, Ryan's Daughter	Ben Johnson, The Last Picture Show	Joel Grey, Cabaret
Goldie Hawn, Cactus Flower	Helen Hayes, Airport	Cloris Leachman, The Last Picture Show	Eileen Heckart, Butterflies Are Free
John Schlesinger, Midnight Cowboy	Franklin J. Schaffner, Patton	William Friedkin, The French Connection	Bob Fosse, Cabaret
Waldo Salt, Midnight Cowboy	Ring Lardner Jr., M*A*S*H	Ernest Tidyman, The French Connection	Mario Puzo and Francis Ford Coppola, The Godfather
William Goldman, Butch Cassidy and the Sundance Kid	Francis Ford Coppola and Edmund H. North, Patton	Paddy Chayefsky, The Hospital	Jeremy Larner, The Candidate
"Raindrops Keep Fallin' on My Head" (Butch Cassidy and the Sundance Kid)	"For All We Know" (Lovers and Other Strangers)	"Theme from Shaft" (Shaft)	"The Morning After" (The Poseidon Adventure)
Butch Cassidy and the Sundance Kid (Nonmusical); Hello Dolly! (Musical)	Love Story (Original Score); Let It Be (Original Song Score)	Summer of '42 (Dramatic); Fiddler on the Roof (Adapted)	Limelight (Dramatic); Cabaret (Adapted)
Butch Cassidy and the Sundance Kid	Ryan's Daughter	Fiddler on the Roof	Cabaret
Anne of the Thousand Days	Cromwell	Nicholas and Alexandra	Travels with My Aunt
Hello Dolly!	Patton	Nicholas and Alexandra	Cabaret
Z	Patton	The French Connection	Cabaret
Z (Algeria)	Investigation of a Citizen Above Suspicion (Italy)	The Garden of the Finzi-Continis (Italy)	The Discreet Charm of the Bourgeoisie (France)
Hello Dolly!	Patton	Fiddler on the Roof	Cabaret
—	—	—	—
Marooned	Tora! Tora! Tora!	Bedknobs and Broomsticks	—
It's Tough to Be a Bird (Cartoons); The Magic Machines (Live Action)	Is It Always Right To Be Right? (Cartoons); The Resurrection of Broncho Billy (Live Action)	The Crunch Bird (Animated); Sentinels of Silence (Live Action)	A Christmas Carol (Animated); Norman Rockwell's World...An American Dream (Live Action)
Czechoslovakia 1968 (Short); Arthur Rubinstein—The Love of Life (Feature)	Interviews with My Lai Veterans (Short); Woodstock (Feature)	Sentinels of Silence (Short); The Hellstrom Chronicle (Feature)	This Tiny World (Short); Marjoe (Feature)

	1973	1974	1975
Picture	*The Sting*	*The Godfather Part II*	*One Flew over the Cuckoo's Nest*
Actor	Jack Lemmon, *Save the Tiger*	Art Carney, *Harry and Tonto*	Jack Nicholson, *One Flew over the Cuckoo's Nest*
Actress	Glenda Jackson, *A Touch of Class*	Ellen Burstyn, *Alice Doesn't Live Here Anymore*	Louise Fletcher, *One Flew over the Cuckoo's Nest*
Supporting Actor	John Houseman, *The Paper Chase*	Robert De Niro, *The Godfather Part II*	George Burns, *The Sunshine Boys*
Supporting Actress	Tatum O'Neal, *Paper Moon*	Ingrid Bergman, *Murder on the Orient Express*	Lee Grant, *Shampoo*
Director	George Roy Hill, *The Sting*	Francis Ford Coppola, *The Godfather Part II*	Milos Forman, *One Flew over the Cuckoo's Nest*
Adapted Screenplay	William Peter Blatty, *The Exorcist*	Francis Ford Coppola and Mario Puzo, *The Godfather Part II*	Lawrence Hauben and Bo Goldman, *One Flew over the Cuckoo's Nest*
Original Screenplay	David S. Ward, *The Sting*	Robert Towne, *Chinatown*	Frank Pierson, *Dog Day Afternoon*
Song	"The Way We Were" *(The Way We Were)*	"We May Never Love Like This Again" *(The Towering Inferno)*	"I'm Easy" *(Nashville)*
Score	*The Way We Were* (Original); *The Sting* (Adaptation)	*The Godfather Part II* (Original); *The Great Gatsby* (Adaptation)	*Jaws* (Original); *Barry Lyndon* (Adaptation)
Cinematography	*Cries and Whispers*	*The Towering Inferno*	*Barry Lyndon*
Costume Design	*The Sting*	*The Great Gatsby*	*Barry Lyndon*
Art Direction—Set Decoration	*The Sting*	*The Godfather Part II*	*Barry Lyndon*
Film Editing	*The Sting*	*The Towering Inferno*	*Jaws*
Foreign Language Film	*Day for Night* (France)	*Amarcord* (Italy)	*Dersu Uzala* (U.S.S.R.)
Sound	*The Exorcist*	*Earthquake*	*Jaws*
Visual Effects	—	—	—
Short Films	*Frank Film* (Animated); *The Bolero* (Live Action)	*Closed Mondays* (Animated); *One-Eyed Men Are Kings* (Live Action)	*Great* (Animated); *Angel and Big Joe* (Live Action)
Documentaries	*Princeton: A Search for Answers* (Short); *The Great American Cowboy* (Feature)	*Don't* (Short); *Hearts and Minds* (Feature)	*The End of the Game* (Short); *The Man Who Skied down Everest* (Feature)

> 66 The Oscars made my pits wet. 99
>
> —Kevin Costner, 1989

1976	1977	1978	1979
Rocky	*Annie Hall*	*The Deer Hunter*	*Kramer vs. Kramer*
Peter Finch, *Network*	Richard Dreyfuss, *The Goodbye Girl*	Jon Voight, *Coming Home*	Dustin Hoffman, *Kramer vs. Kramer*
Faye Dunaway, *Network*	Diane Keaton, *Annie Hall*	Jane Fonda, *Coming Home*	Sally Field, *Norma Rae*
Jason Robards, *All the President's Men*	Jason Robards, *Julia*	Christopher Walken, *The Deer Hunter*	Melvyn Douglas, *Being There*
Beatrice Straight, *Network*	Vanessa Redgrave, *Julia*	Maggie Smith, *California Suite*	Meryl Streep, *Kramer vs. Kramer*
John G. Avildsen, *Rocky*	Woody Allen, *Annie Hall*	Michael Cimino, *The Deer Hunter*	Robert Benton, *Kramer vs. Kramer*
William Goldman, *All the President's Men*	Alvin Sargent, *Julia*	Oliver Stone, *Midnight Express*	Robert Benton, *Kramer vs. Kramer*
Paddy Chayefsky, *Network*	Woody Allen and Marshall Brickman, *Annie Hall*	Nancy Dowd, story; Waldo Salt and Robert C. Jones, screenplay, *Coming Home*	Steve Tesich, *Breaking Away*
"Evergreen" *(A Star Is Born)*	"You Light Up My Life" *(You Light Up My Life)*	"Last Dance" *(Thank God It's Friday)*	"It Goes Like It Goes" *(Norma Rae)*
The Omen (Original); *Bound for Glory* (Adaptation)	*Star Wars* (Original); *A Little Night Music* (Adaptation)	*Midnight Express* (Original); *The Buddy Holly Story* (Adaptation)	*A Little Romance* (Original); *All That Jazz* (Adaptation)
Bound for Glory	*Close Encounters of the Third Kind*	*Days of Heaven*	*Apocalypse Now*
Fellini's Casanova	*Star Wars*	*Death on the Nile*	*All That Jazz*
All the President's Men	*Star Wars*	*Heaven Can Wait*	*All That Jazz*
Rocky	*Star Wars*	*The Deer Hunter*	*All That Jazz*
Black and White in Color (Ivory Coast)	*Madame Rosa* (France)	*Get Out Your Handkerchiefs* (France)	*The Tin Drum* (Federal Republic of Germany)
All the President's Men	*Star Wars*	*The Deer Hunter*	*Apocalypse Now*
—	*Star Wars*	—	*Alien*
Leisure (Animated); *In the Region of Ice* (Live Action)	*Sand Castle* (Animated); *I'll Find a Way* (Live Action)	*Special Delivery* (Animated); *Teenage Father* (Live Action)	*Every Child* (Animated); *Board and Care* (Live Action)
Number Our Days (Short); *Harlan County, U.S.A.* (Feature)	*Gravity Is My Enemy* (Short); *Who Are the DeBolts? And Where Did They Get Nineteen Kids?* (Feature)	*The Flight of the Gossamer Condor* (Short); *Scared Straight!* (Feature)	*Paul Robeson: Tribute to an Artist* (Short); *Best Boy* (Feature)

66 I'm survivor. That's why they gave it me. I'm still here.99
—Michael Caine, Best Supporting Actor, 1999

	1980	1981	1982
Picture	*Ordinary People*	*Chariots of Fire*	*Gandhi*
Actor	Robert De Niro, *Raging Bull*	Henry Fonda, *On Golden Pond*	Ben Kingsley, *Gandhi*
Actress	Sissy Spacek, *Coal Miner's Daughter*	Katharine Hepburn, *On Golden Pond*	Meryl Streep, *Sophie's Choice*
Supporting Actor	Timothy Hutton, *Ordinary People*	John Gielgud, *Arthur*	Louis Gossett Jr., *An Officer and a Gentleman*
Supporting Actress	Mary Steenburgen, *Melvin and Howard*	Maureen Stapleton, *Reds*	Jessica Lange, *Tootsie*
Director	Robert Redford, *Ordinary People*	Warren Beatty, *Reds*	Richard Attenborough, *Gandhi*
Adapted Screenplay	Alvin Sargent, *Ordinary People*	Ernest Thompson, *On Golden Pond*	Costa-Gavras and Donald Stewart, *Missing*
Original Screenplay	Bo Goldman, *Melvin and Howard*	Colin Welland, *Chariots of Fire*	John Briley, *Gandhi*
Song	"Fame" *(Fame)*	"Arthur's Theme (Best That You Can Do)" *(Arthur)*	"Up Where We Belong" *(An Officer and a Gentleman)*
Original Score	*Fame*	*Chariots of Fire*	*E.T., the Extra-Terrestrial; Victor/Victoria* (Song Score/Adaptation)
Cinematography	*Tess*	*Reds*	*Gandhi*
Costume Design	*Tess*	*Chariots of Fire*	*Gandhi*
Art Direction—Set Decoration	*Tess*	*Raiders of the Lost Ark*	*Gandhi*
Film Editing	*Raging Bull*	*Raiders of the Lost Ark*	*Gandhi*
Foreign Language Film	*Moscow Does Not Believe in Tears* (U.S.S.R.)	*Mephisto* (Hungary)	*Volver A Empezar (To Begin Again)* (Spain)
Sound	*The Empire Strikes Back*	*Raiders of the Lost Ark*	*Gandhi*
Sound Effects (Editing)	—	—	*E.T., the Extra-Terrestrial*
Makeup	—	*An American Werewolf in London*	*Quest for Fire*
Visual Effects	—	*Raiders of the Lost Ark*	*E.T., the Extra-Terrestrial*
Short Films	*The Fly* (Animated); *The Dollar Bottom* (Live Action)	*Crac* (Animated); *Violet* (Live Action)	*Tango* (Animated); *A Shocking Accident* (Live Action)
Documentaries	*Karl Hess: Toward Liberty* (Short); *From Mao to Mozart: Isaac Stern in China* (Feature)	*Genocide* (Short); *Close Harmony* (Feature)	*If You Love This Planet* (Short); *Just Another Missing Kid* (Feature)

1983	1984	1985	1986
Terms of Endearment	Amadeus	Out of Africa	Platoon
Robert Duvall, Tender Mercies	F. Murray Abraham, Amadeus	William Hurt, Kiss of the Spider Woman	Paul Newman, The Color of Money
Shirley MacLaine, Terms of Endearment	Sally Field, Places in the Heart	Geraldine Page, The Trip to Bountiful	Marlee Matlin, Children of a Lesser God
Jack Nicholson, Terms of Endearment	Haing S. Ngor, The Killing Fields	Don Ameche, Cocoon	Michael Caine, Hannah and Her Sisters
Linda Hunt, The Year of Living Dangerously	Peggy Ashcroft, A Passage to India	Anjelica Huston, Prizzi's Honor	Dianne Wiest, Hannah and Her Sisters
James L. Brooks, Terms of Endearment	Milos Forman, Amadeus	Sydney Pollack, Out of Africa	Oliver Stone, Platoon
James L. Brooks, Terms of Endearment	Peter Shaffer, Amadeus	Kurt Luedtke, Out of Africa	Ruth Prawer Jhabvala, A Room with a View
Horton Foote, Tender Mercies	Robert Benton, Places in the Heart	William Kelley, Pamela Wallace, and Earl W. Wallace, Witness	Woody Allen, Hannah and Her Sisters
"Flashdance...What a Feeling" (Flashdance)	"I Just Called To Say I Love You" (The Woman in Red)	"Say You, Say Me" (White Nights)	"Take My Breath Away" (Top Gun)
The Right Stuff; Yentl (Song Score/Adaptation)	A Passage to India; Purple Rain (Song Score)	Out of Africa	'Round Midnight
Fanny & Alexander	The Killing Fields	Out of Africa	The Mission
Fanny & Alexander	Amadeus	Ran	A Room with a View
Fanny & Alexander	Amadeus	Out of Africa	A Room with a View
The Right Stuff	The Killing Fields	Witness	Platoon
Fanny & Alexander (Sweden)	Dangerous Moves (Switzerland)	The Official Story (Argentina)	The Assault (The Netherlands)
The Right Stuff	Amadeus	Out of Africa	Platoon
The Right Stuff	—	Back to the Future	Aliens
—	Amadeus	Mask	The Fly
Return of the Jedi	Indiana Jones and the Temple of Doom	Cocoon	Aliens
Sundae in New York (Animated); Boys and Girls (Live Action)	Charade (Animated); Up (Live Action)	Anna & Bella (Animated); Molly's Pilgrim (Live Action)	A Greek Tragedy (Animated); Precious Images (Live Action)
Flamenco at 5:15 (Short); He Makes Me Feel Like Dancin' (Feature)	The Stone Carvers (Short); The Times of Harvey Milk (Feature)	Witness to War: Dr. Charlie Clements (Short); Broken Rainbow (Feature)	Women—For America, for the World (Short); Artie Shaw: Time Is All You've Got and Down and out in America (Feature)

	1987	**1988**	**1989**
Picture	*The Last Emperor*	*Rain Man*	*Driving Miss Daisy*
Actor	Michael Douglas, *Wall Street*	Dustin Hoffman, *Rain Man*	Daniel Day-Lewis, *My Left Foot*
Actress	Cher, *Moonstruck*	Jodie Foster, *The Accused*	Jessica Tandy, *Driving Miss Daisy*
Supporting Actor	Sean Connery, *The Untouchables*	Kevin Kline, *A Fish Called Wanda*	Denzel Washington, *Glory*
Supporting Actress	Olympia Dukakis, *Moonstruck*	Geena Davis, *The Accidental Tourist*	Brenda Fricker, *My Left Foot*
Director	Bernardo Bertolucci, *The Last Emperor*	Barry Levinson, *Rain Man*	Oliver Stone, *Born on the Fourth of July*
Adapted Screenplay	Mark Peploe and Bernardo Bertolucci, *The Last Emperor*	Christopher Hampton, *Dangerous Liaisons*	Tom Schulman, *Dead Poets Society*
Original Screenplay	John Patrick Shanley, *Moonstruck*	Ronald Bass and Barry Morrow, *Rain Man*	Alfred Uhry, *Driving Miss Daisy*
Song	"(I've Had) The Time of My Life" *(Dirty Dancing)*	"Let the River Run" *(Working Girl)*	"Under the Sea" *(The Little Mermaid)*
Original Score	*The Last Emperor*	*The Milagro Beanfield War*	*The Little Mermaid*
Cinematography	*The Last Emperor*	*Mississippi Burning*	*Glory*
Costume Design	*The Last Emperor*	*Dangerous Liaisons*	*Henry V*
Art Direction—Set Decoration	*The Last Emperor*	*Dangerous Liaisons*	*Batman*
Film Editing	*The Last Emperor*	*Who Framed Roger Rabbit*	*Born on the Fourth of July*
Foreign Language Film	*Babette's Feast* (Denmark)	*Pelle the Conqueror* (Denmark)	*Cinema Paradiso* (Italy)
Sound	*The Last Emperor*	*Bird*	*Glory*
Sound Effects (Editing)	—	*Who Framed Roger Rabbit*	*Indiana Jones and the Last Crusade*
Makeup	*Harry and the Hendersons*	*Beetlejuice*	*Driving Miss Daisy*
Visual Effects	*Innerspace*	*Who Framed Roger Rabbit*	*The Abyss*
Short Films	*The Man Who Planted Trees* (Animated); *Ray's Male Heterosexual Dance Hall* (Live Action)	*Tin Toy* (Animated); *The Appointments of Dennis Jennings* (Live Action)	*Balance* (Animated); *Work Experience* (Live Action)
Documentaries	*Young at Heart* (Short); *The Ten-Year Lunch: The Wit and the Legend of the Algonquin Round Table* (Feature)	*You Don't Have To Die* (Short); *Hotel Terminus: The Life and Times of Klaus Barbie* (Feature)	*The Johnstown Flood* (Short); *Common Threads: Stories from the Quilt* (Feature)

> 66 I would have voted for Warren Beatty for president for one big reason. Vice President Jack Nicholson. 99
> —Billy Crystal, host, 1999

1990	1991	1992	1993
Dances with Wolves	*The Silence of the Lambs*	*Unforgiven*	*Schindler's List*
Jeremy Irons, *Reversal of Fortune*	Anthony Hopkins, *The Silence of the Lambs*	Al Pacino, *Scent of a Woman*	Tom Hanks, *Philadelphia*
Kathy Bates, *Misery*	Jodie Foster, *The Silence of the Lambs*	Emma Thompson, *Howards End*	Holly Hunter, *The Piano*
Joe Pesci, *GoodFellas*	Jack Palance, *City Slickers*	Gene Hackman, *Unforgiven*	Tommy Lee Jones, *The Fugitive*
Whoopi Goldberg, *Ghost*	Mercedes Ruehl, *The Fisher King*	Marisa Tomei, *My Cousin Vinny*	Anna Paquin, *The Piano*
Kevin Costner, *Dances with Wolves*	Jonathan Demme, *The Silence of the Lambs*	Clint Eastwood, *Unforgiven*	Steven Spielberg, *Schindler's List*
Michael Blake, *Dances with Wolves*	Ted Tally, *The Silence of the Lambs*	Ruth Prawer Jhabvala, *Howards End*	Steven Zaillian, *Schindler's List*
Bruce Joel Rubin, *Ghost*	Callie Khouri, *Thelma & Louise*	Neil Jordan, *The Crying Game*	Jane Campion, *The Piano*
"Sooner or Later (I Always Get My Man)" *(Dick Tracy)*	"Beauty and the Beast" *(Beauty and the Beast)*	"A Whole New World" *(Aladdin)*	"Streets of Philadelphia" *(Philadelphia)*
Dances with Wolves	*Beauty and the Beast*	*Aladdin*	*Schindler's List*
Dances with Wolves	*JFK*	*A River Runs Through It*	*Schindler's List*
Cyrano de Bergerac	*Bugsy*	*Bram Stoker's Dracula*	*The Age of Innocence*
Dick Tracy	*Bugsy*	*Howards End*	*Schindler's List*
Dances with Wolves	*JFK*	*Unforgiven*	*Schindler's List*
Journey of Hope (Switzerland)	*Mediterraneo* (Italy)	*Indochine* (France)	*Belle Epoque* (Spain)
Dances with Wolves	*Terminator 2: Judgment Day*	*The Last of the Mohicans*	*Jurassic Park*
The Hunt for Red October	*Terminator 2: Judgment Day*	*Bram Stoker's Dracula*	*Jurassic Park*
Dick Tracy	*Terminator 2: Judgment Day*	*Bram Stoker's Dracula*	*Mrs. Doubtfire*
Total Recall	*Terminator 2: Judgment Day*	*Death Becomes Her*	*Jurassic Park*
Creature Comforts (Animated); *The Lunch Date* (Live Action)	*Manipulation* (Animated); *Session Man* (Live Action)	*Mona Lisa Descending a Staircase* (Animated); *Omnibus* (Live Action)	*The Wrong Trousers* (Animated); *Black Rider* (Live Action)
Days of Waiting (Short); *American Dream* (Feature)	*Deadly Deception: General Electric, Nuclear Weapons and Our Environment* (Short); *In the Shadow of the Stars* (Feature)	*Educating Peter* (Short); *The Panama Deception* (Feature)	*Defending Our Lives* (Short); *I Am a Promise: The Children of Stanton Elementary School* (Feature)

> 66 The Academy asks that your speech be no longer than the movie itself. 99
>
> —Danny Kaye, 1951

	1994	1995	1996
Picture	Forrest Gump	Braveheart	The English Patient
Actor	Tom Hanks, Forrest Gump	Nicolas Cage, Leaving Las Vegas	Geoffrey Rush, Shine
Actress	Jessica Lange, Blue Sky	Susan Sarandon, Dead Man Walking	Frances McDormand, Fargo
Supporting Actor	Martin Landau, Ed Wood	Kevin Spacey, The Usual Suspects	Cuba Gooding Jr., Jerry Maguire
Supporting Actress	Dianne Wiest, Bullets over Broadway	Mira Sorvino, Mighty Aphrodite	Juliette Binoche, The English Patient
Director	Robert Zemeckis, Forrest Gump	Mel Gibson, Braveheart	Anthony Minghella, The English Patient
Adapted Screenplay	Eric Roth, Forrest Gump	Emma Thompson, Sense and Sensibility	Billy Bob Thornton, Sling Blade
Original Screenplay	Roger Avary and Quentin Tarantino, Pulp Fiction	Christopher McQuarrie, The Usual Suspects	Ethan Coen & Joel Coen, Fargo
Best Song	"Can You Feel the Love Tonight" (The Lion King)	"Colors of the Wind" (Pocahontas)	"You Must Love Me" (Evita)
Original Score	The Lion King	The Postman (Il Postino)	Emma (Musical or Comedy); The English Patient (Drama)
Cinematography	Legends of the Fall	Braveheart	The English Patient
Costume Design	The Adventures of Priscilla, Queen of the Desert	Restoration	The English Patient
Art Direction—Set Decoration	The Madness of King George	Restoration	The English Patient
Film Editing	Forrest Gump	Apollo 13	The English Patient
Foreign Language Film	Burnt by the Sun	Antonia's Line	Kolya
Sound	Speed	Apollo 13	The English Patient
Sound Effects (Editing)	Speed	Braveheart	The Ghost and the Darkness
Makeup	Ed Wood	Braveheart	The Nutty Professor
Visual Effects	Forrest Gump	Babe	Independence Day
Short Films	Bob's Birthday (Animated); Franz Kafka's It's a Wonderful Life and Trevor (Live Action)	A Close Shave (Animated); Lieberman in Love (Live Action)	Quest (Animated); Dear Diary (Live Action)
Documentaries	A Time for Justice (Short); Maya Lin: A Strong Clear Vision (Feature)	One Survivor Remembers (Short); Anne Frank Remembered (Feature)	Breathing Lessons: The Life and Work of Mark O'Brien (Short); When We Were Kings (Feature)

1997	1998	1999
Titanic	*Shakespeare in Love*	*American Beauty*
Jack Nicholson, *As Good As It Gets*	Roberto Benigni, *Life Is Beautiful*	Kevin Spacey, *American Beauty*
Helen Hunt, *As Good As It Gets*	Gwyneth Paltrow, *Shakespeare in Love*	Hilary Swank, *Boys Don't Cry*
Robin Williams, *Good Will Hunting*	James Coburn, *Affliction*	Michael Caine, *The Cider House Rules*
Kim Basinger, *L.A. Confidential*	Judi Dench, *Shakespeare in Love*	Angelina Jolie, *Girl, Interrupted*
James Cameron, *Titanic*	Steven Spielberg, *Saving Private Ryan*	Sam Mendes, *American Beauty*
Brian Helgeland and Curtis Hanson, *L.A. Confidential*	Bill Condon, *Gods and Monsters*	Alan Ball, *American Beauty*
Ben Affleck and Matt Damon, *Good Will Hunting*	Marc Norman and Tom Stoppard, *Shakespeare in Love*	John Irving, *The Cider House Rules*
"My Heart Will Go On" *(Titanic)*	"When You Believe" *(Prince of Egypt)*	"You'll Be in My Heart," *(Tarzan)*
The Full Monty (Musical or Comedy); *Titanic* (Drama)	*Shakespeare in Love* (Musical or Comedy); *Life Is Beautiful* (Drama)	John Corigliano, *The Red Violin*
Titanic	*Saving Private Ryan*	*American Beauty*
Titanic	*Shakespeare in Love*	*Topsy-Turvy*
Titanic	*Shakespeare in Love*	*Sleepy Hollow*
Titanic	*Saving Private Ryan*	*The Matrix*
Character	*Life Is Beautiful*	*All About My Mother*
Titanic	*Saving Private Ryan*	*The Matrix*
Titanic	*Saving Private Ryan*	*The Matrix*
Men in Black	*Elizabeth*	*Topsy-Turvy*
Titanic	*What Dreams May Come*	*The Matrix*
Geri's Game (Animated); *Visas and Virtue* (Live Action)	*Bunny* (Animated); *Election Night (Valgaften)* (Live Action)	*The Old Man and the Sea* (Animated); *My Mother Dreams the Satan's Disciples in New York* (Live Action)
A Story of Healing (Short); *The Long Way Home* (Feature)	*The Personals: Improvisations on Romance in the Golden Years* (Short); *The Last Days* (Feature)	*King Gimp* (Short); *One Day in September* (Feature)

PICKS & PANS 1999–2000

What won't the networks do? Now that paycable premieres some of TV's best dramas, the broadcast webs are rewriting their rules for keeping viewers happy. This season, that meant reality shows, game shows, multiple episodes per week, and half the *Ally*. PEOPLE's Terry Kelleher appraises the new and revisits some old favorites.

ACTION
FOX

Extremely edgy Hollywood humor that tends toward the outrageous even when the characters don't talk dirty. Pretty bleepin' funny.

ALLY
FOX

The half-hour version of the hit. Sometimes a single plot fills the slot neatly; other episodes seem as if an announcer forgot to say, "We now join *Ally McBeal*, already in progress."

ALLY MCBEAL
FOX

Ally McBeal continues to amuse, surprise and, yes, titillate. But you get the feeling that creator David E. Kelley is overdosing the characters on his brand of aphrodisiac.

AMERICAN HIGH
FOX

Filmmaker R. J. Cutler followed a group of Highland Park students through the academic year. His footage, supplemented by the subjects' video diaries, tells achingly real stories of desperate teenage love, emerging sexual identity, athletic pressure, and parental confusion.

ANGEL
The WB

Sexy, conscience-plagued vampire (and Buffy the Vampire Slayer's ex) turns knight errant of the underside. The pilot has that *Buffy* blend of chills and humor.

ARLI$$
HBO

To put this in the appropriate jock-world parlance, *Arli$$* is like a high draft choice who becomes an established starter but never fulfills his superstar potential.

BABY BLUES
The WB

This animated family comedy, based on the syndicated comic strip, puts a few surprisingly funny twists on ordinary domestic complaints and situations.

BATTERY PARK
NBC

Fairly promising sitcom featuring eccentric cops—although its creators had better flesh out the female regulars.

THE BEAT
UPN

This police pastiche isn't breaking new ground, but *The Beat* patrols its turf with style and a welcome touch of humor.

BIG BROTHER
CBS

A "reality" series in which 10 strangers occupy a two-bedroom house rigged with cameras and microphones to record their every move and utterance, however aimless or banal. Evict them all!

BRUTALLY NORMAL
The WB

Another high school series. If you like *Popular* (see below), here's the shorter, funnier version.

CITY OF ANGELS
CBS

A struggling inner-city hospital. The nine-person ensemble (with seven actors of color) makes *City of Angels* worth nurturing. But here's a plea to executive producer Steven Bochco: Be quirky later. Get real first.

CLEOPATRA 2525
Syndicated

A stripper who went into a coma during cosmetic breast surgery in 2001 wakes up in the middle of a 26th-century war. Halfway entertaining nonsense.

CLERKS
ABC

The 1994 movie was distinguished by deadpan, foulmouthed humor and a decidedly downscale look. So why raise the characters from drudgery to "comic-book-hero status"? Why on a broadcast network? And why as a celebrity spoof-fest? Bad idea.

COLD FEET
NBC

Three young Seattle couples in plots from sitcom-standard to out of left field. Inconsistent—but on occasion, truth and comedy converge.

*THE CORNER
HBO

This miniseries immerses you in the lives of drug addicts and dealers in a poor Baltimore neighborhood—and it says: Do not turn away, these are human beings. Daring, very potent television.

D.C.
The WB

It's tempting to dismiss this drama series—about five recent college graduates sharing a house and striving for success in Washington—as *West Wing Lite* or *MTV D.C.* Fortunately, Gabriel Olds gives an intelligent performance as a Capitol Hill aide trying to balance idealism and ambition.

FALCONE
CBS

A mafia soldier is really an undercover FBI agent. Though lacking the black comedy of *The Sopranos*, this may be the grittiest Mob drama since CBS's '80s classic *Wiseguy*.

*FREAKS AND GEEKS
NBC

Intelligent sophomore Lindsay finds herself gravitating toward her school's antiestablishment "freaks," while sweet, undersize brother Sam pals with a couple of "geeks." The young actors are natural and convincing, and the high school characters manage to be funny without too much *Dawson's Creek* glibness.

GOD, THE DEVIL, AND BOB
NBC

The Almighty and Lucifer strike a deal that makes a shiftless, porn-watching autoworker responsible for proving humans as redeemable. Not divine, but blessed with a sense of humor.

GRAPEVINE
CBS

A reworking of the short-lived 1992 sitcom about sexually active Miami singles. Though it has some assets, the in-jokes and constant comments to the camera are too gimmicky for words.

GREED
FOX

A *Who Wants to Be a Millionaire* copy, with five-person "teams"

encouraged to knock off their mates. That, friends, is a capital sin.

HARSH REALM
FOX

Another dark, paranoid drama from Chris Carter, creator of *The X-Files* and *Millennium*, this one in a virtual-reality war game. Capably acted, artfully creepy, and no fun.

HOLLYWOOD OFF-RAMP
E!

The Twilight Zone goes to Tinseltown in this anthology series. Handicapped by a lack of atmosphere (it's filmed in Vancouver) and an obviously limited budget, *Hollywood Off-Ramp* manages to take us on a fairly intriguing ride.

THE INVISIBLE MAN
SCI FI Channel

Forced to play guinea pig in a secret government program, a career thief is equipped with a synthetic gland enabling invisibility—the better to sneak among villains and thwart them. Side effect: he must be injected with a "counteragent" every several days, or his eyes turn horror-movie red and he behaves like a kill-crazed beast. A surprisingly fresh take.

JACK & JILL
The WB

Two cute twentysomething neighbors waste a lot of time denying their feelings for each other. By and large, this comedy has nothing to say that it couldn't get across better in half the time.

JACK OF ALL TRADES
Syndicated

A cocky secret agent swashbuckles for President Thomas Jefferson. Jack tries to cross the old *Wild Wild West* with a Mel Brooks romp—and such silliness never hurt anyone.

JUDGING AMY
CBS

A lawyer and single parent quits New York City, accepts a family-court judgeship in her native Hartford, Conn., and moves in with her mother, a semiretired social worker inclined to meddle and argue. The jury's out.

JUST SHOOT ME
NBC

This sitcom set at fictional *Blush* magazine is not a model of consistency, but it sometimes manages episodes worthy of a time capsule.

LADIES MAN
CBS

A father of three is outargued by the females in his house, poor guy. The comedy tends to be forced and obvious.

LATELINE
Showtime

The promising but vanishing sitcom about a *Nightline*-type news program is back—again. Is this *Lateline*'s chance to overcome inconsistency and also fulfill its huge creative potential?

THE LIST
VH1

Celebrities argue for their top-three favorites in various pop-music categories. A fun mix of camaraderie and one-upmanship.

LOVE & MONEY
CBS

An heiress takes up with an unsuitably working-class hunk. Apart from David Ogden Stiers and Swoosie Kurtz as snooty-parent stereotypes, there's not a lot to love.

MAKING THE BAND
ABC

A strangely watchable reality series: Which five would-be pop idols (out of seven finalists) will be chosen to make up the new "boy band" O-Town?

*MALCOLM IN THE MIDDLE
FOX

A reluctant boy genius has a life of continual embarrassment. *Malcolm* scores high in comic aptitude.

THE MARTIN SHORT SHOW
Syndicated

With an accent on comedy, Short's talk-variety venture is proving to be—as Short's pointy-haired Ed Grimley character might put it—fairly decent, I must say.

M.Y.O.B.
NBC

The latest in a line of series featuring a jaded, media-savvy teen who talks directly to the audience. Too tube-conscious.

MYSTERIOUS WAYS
NBC

A little *X-Files*, a little *Touched by an Angel*. Average drama.

NOW AND AGAIN
CBS

An insurance executive's brain is placed in a sleek, superstrong body built for secret agent dirty work. Sure, it's derivative; it's also stylish, clever, and unpredictable.

NYPD BLUE
ABC

NYPD Blue's trademarks are still in evidence: the layered characterizations; the slangy, pungent dialogue; the black humor that usually makes you laugh in spite of yourself.

ODD MAN OUT
ABC

A 15-year-old boy feels like a discrimination victim in a house dominated by females—a family that lives for the battle-of-the-sexes banter of today. Not for mature audiences.

OH BABY
Lifetime

After you've had a child through artificial insemination, what do you do for an encore? This sitcom is still funnier than average, though single parenthood seems routine compared with the pregnancy.

OPPOSITE SEX
FOX

In this middling "lighthearted drama," 15-year-old Jed is enrolled at a previously all-girl private academy with only two other male students. *Opposite Sex* seems undecided whether to get sensitive or to let the hormones rage.

THE OTHERS
NBC

A small group of New England residents facilitate and interpret communications between live human beings and, for want of a better term, ghosts. One big plus is that *The Others* seems more concerned with touching us than scaring us.

THE PARKERS
UPN

Kim Parker is now a first-year student at the local junior college. And so is Kim's mother, the irrepressible Nikki. This *Moesha* spin-off is awfully broad, but it gets by.

POPULAR
The WB

Two cliques at a suburban high school: the "popular" group (attractive) vs. the nonconformists (also attractive). With its gimmicky camera work and flights of surrealism, *Popular* tries too hard to be hip.

RESURRECTION BLVD.
Showtime

Stern patriarch Roberto Santiago—a man of the ring—grooms middle son Carlos to be a boxing champion. But when a street punk puts Carlos out of commission, Roberto's premed-student son Alex decides to quit school and pick up the boxing mantle. The cast is strong; with less-clichéd scripts, *Resurrection Blvd.* could rise up swinging.

ROSWELL
The WB

Teen shows are the rage; it's handy to combine elements of *X-Files* and *Buffy;* and, hey, logic is irrelevant. That said, this teen alien drama has appeal.

SAMMY
NBC

This lackluster animated series centers on a TV actor (voiced by, and drawn to resemble, cocreator David Spade) and the sponging, randy dad who invades his Hollywood life after a long absence.

SECRET AGENT MAN
UPN

You can find amusing ideas in this spy spoof. But the lead is wooden, the sexual-tension lacks wit and sizzle, and the show is often overly pleased with its own irony.

SEX AND THE CITY
HBO

Columnist Carrie and her circle of singles still want men but find them wanting. *Sex* is showing more creative staying power than expected, despite a tendency to dive too low in the taste department.

SNOOPS
ABC

David E. Kelley, the creator of *Ally McBeal*, *The Practice*, and *Chicago Hope*, has finally spread himself too thin: it's hard to imagine a flimsier enterprise than this new detective series.

*THE SOPRANOS
HBO

Justly extolled for its brilliant blend of compelling drama and mordant humor, TV's top

"family" drama shows no
signs of slippage.

SOUL FOOD
Showtime

Soul Food retains the messy,
large-hearted spirit of the 1997
movie. This multigenerational
African-American comedy-
drama is inconsistent, but it
whets the appetite.

*SPONGEBOB SQUAREPANTS
Nickelodeon

The life of an irrationally
exuberant sea sponge. This
Saturday-morning comic delight
is well worth diving for.

SPY GROOVE
MTV

This animated series is hip but
easy to skip: the spy-spoof game
is pretty much played out.

STARK RAVING MAD
NBC

Raving turns on the personality
clash between eccentric,
temperamental horror novelist
Ian Stark (Tony Shalhoub from
Wings) and Henry McNeely
(Neil Patrick Harris, 10 years
after the debut of *Doogie Howser,
M.D.*), the jumpy, phobic editor
assigned to keep Ian on the ball.
A talented cast, but little to rave
about.

STRIP MALL
Comedy Central

Wallowing in sex and reveling in
tackiness—or vice versa—this
comedy serial loves being low-
brow. I admit laughing when
Tammi got turned on by a hot
Chihuahua, but I wouldn't come
to *Strip Mall* for quality goods.

STRONG MEDICINE
Lifetime

An ambitious research-oriented
physician and a fiery working-
class healer struggling to keep
open a women's free clinic must
learn to work together.

TALK TO ME
ABC

Kyra Sedgwick as a female
Howard Stern. Given nothing
clever to say, Sedgwick over-
compensates with an extra-
punchy delivery, and *Talk to Me*
only grows more desperate.

THEN CAME YOU
ABC

Sitcom about two lovers: 33-
year-old woman, 22-year-old
man. The premiere gave hope
for funny answers about whether
great sex and growing affection
can outweigh disparities in age
and income . . . but the other
episodes were farcical letdowns.

*THIRD WATCH
NBC

Chaotic, compelling drama
about New York City cops,
paramedics and firefighters; may
be overcrowded with well-acted
characters.

TIME OF YOUR LIFE
FOX

Party of Five's Sarah (Jennifer
Love Hewitt) is a naif in New
York. Weep profusely, smile
winningly: that's Sarah's
pattern, and Hewitt fans figure
to be there for her.

TITUS
FOX

Autobiographical stand-up
Christopher Titus looks into
the camera and complains
continually about the malign
influence of his alcoholic, overbearing, oft-divorced father. If
this sounds more painful than
funny, you've hit on the show's
main problem.

TURN BEN STEIN ON
Comedy Central

Know-it-all Stein's not on the
money yet—he needs to rein
himself in or go with one guest.
Still, it would be a loss to the
talk-show medium if Stein failed
in his latest venture.

THE VIEW
ABC

The View would benefit from,
say, a 10-percent reduction in
fawning over guests. What else
needs changing? Not much. The
format still clicks almost every
time the women sit down with
their coffee mugs to gab about
the hot hopics of the day. There's
an air of candor that can't be
faked.

THE WAR NEXT DOOR
USA

Original enough to be a summer
bright spot. An ex-CIA agent's
old nemesis moves in next door
to continue their "eternal dance
of death."

WASTELAND
ABC

Attractive, acutely self-aware
twentysomethings. You'll wish
they'd quit overanalyzing their
feelings and make some new
acquaintances.

*THE WEST WING
NBC

A crackling drama series that
focuses on the tireless loyalists
who serve the chief executive;
the sterling cast talks the
Washington talk without the
vagueness and oversimplifica-
tion so often heard when TV
drama ventures into politics.

WINNING LINES
CBS

Billed as "the biggest game
show ever to hit prime time,"
Lines is a confusing *Millionaire*
imitation that doesn't pay off.

WONDERLAND
ABC

Mental illness in the raw—set in
the psychiatric department of a
New York City hospital. Tough to
watch, but worth it.

YOUNG AMERICANS
The WB

Plausibility is not a priority for
this teen drama.

THE MOST POPULAR SHOWS ON TV

The following chart shows America's TV favorites every year beginning in 1949.
(Sources: *Variety* and, after 1949–50, Nielsen Media Research)

1949–50

1.	The Texaco Star Theater	NBC
2.	Toast of the Town (Ed Sullivan)	CBS
3.	Arthur Godfrey's Talent Scouts	CBS
4.	Fireball Fun for All	NBC
5.	Philco Television Playhouse	NBC
6.	Fireside Theatre	NBC
7.	The Goldbergs	CBS
8.	Suspense	CBS
9.	The Ford Television Theater	CBS
10.	Cavalcade of Stars	DUMONT

1950–51

1.	The Texaco Star Theater	NBC
2.	Fireside Theatre	NBC
3.	Your Show of Shows	NBC
4.	Philco Television Playhouse	NBC
5.	The Colgate Comedy Hour	NBC
6.	Gillette Cavalcade of Sports	NBC
7.	Arthur Godfrey's Talent Scouts	CBS
8.	Mama	CBS
9.	Robert Montgomery Presents	NBC
10.	Martin Kane, Private Eye	NBC
11.	Man Against Crime	CBS
12.	Somerset Maugham Theatre	NBC
13.	Kraft Television Theatre	NBC
14.	Toast of the Town (Ed Sullivan)	CBS
15.	The Aldrich Family	NBC
16.	You Bet Your Life	NBC
17.	Armstrong Circle Theater (tie)	NBC
17.	Big Town (tie)	CBS
17.	Lights Out (tie)	NBC
20.	The Alan Young Show	CBS

1951–52

1.	Arthur Godfrey's Talent Scouts	CBS
2.	The Texaco Star Theater	NBC
3.	I Love Lucy	CBS
4.	The Red Skelton Show	NBC
5.	The Colgate Comedy Hour	NBC
6.	Fireside Theatre	NBC
7.	The Jack Benny Program	CBS
8.	Your Show of Shows	NBC
9.	You Bet Your Life	NBC
10.	Arthur Godfrey and His Friends	CBS
11.	Mama	CBS
12.	Philco Television Playhouse	NBC
13.	Amos 'n' Andy	CBS
14.	Big Town	CBS
15.	Pabst Blue Ribbon Bouts	CBS
16.	Gillette Cavalcade of Sports	NBC
17.	The Alan Young Show	CBS
18.	All-Star Revue (tie)	NBC
18.	Dragnet (tie)	NBC
20.	Kraft Television Theatre	NBC

1952–53

1.	I Love Lucy	CBS
2.	Arthur Godfrey's Talent Scouts	CBS
3.	Arthur Godfrey and His Friends	CBS
4.	Dragnet	NBC
5.	The Texaco Star Theater	NBC
6.	The Buick Circus Hour	NBC
7.	The Colgate Comedy Hour	NBC
8.	Gangbusters	NBC
9.	You Bet Your Life	NBC
10.	Fireside Theatre	NBC
11.	The Red Buttons Show	CBS
12.	The Jack Benny Program	CBS
13.	Life with Luigi	CBS
14.	Pabst Blue Ribbon Bouts	CBS
15.	Goodyear Television Playhouse	NBC
16.	The Life of Riley	NBC
17.	Mama	CBS
18.	Your Show of Shows	NBC
19.	What's My Line?	CBS
20.	Strike It Rich	CBS

1953–54

1.	I Love Lucy	CBS
2.	Dragnet	NBC
3.	Arthur Godfrey's Talent Scouts (tie)	CBS
3.	You Bet Your Life (tie)	NBC
5.	The Bob Hope Show	NBC
6.	The Buick-Berle Show	NBC
7.	Arthur Godfrey and His Friends	CBS
8.	The Ford Television Theater	NBC
9.	The Jackie Gleason Show	CBS
10.	Fireside Theatre	NBC
11.	The Colgate Comedy Hour (tie)	NBC
11.	This Is Your Life (tie)	NBC
13.	The Red Buttons Show	CBS
14.	The Life of Riley	NBC
15.	Our Miss Brooks	CBS
16.	Treasury Men in Action	NBC
17.	All-Star Revue (Martha Raye)	NBC
18.	The Jack Benny Program	CBS
19.	Gillette Cavalcade of Sports	NBC
20.	Philco Television Playhouse	NBC

1954–55

1.	I Love Lucy	CBS
2.	The Jackie Gleason Show	CBS
3.	Dragnet	NBC
4.	You Bet Your Life	NBC
5.	Toast of the Town (Ed Sullivan)	CBS
6.	Disneyland	ABC
7.	The Bob Hope Show	NBC
8.	The Jack Benny Program	CBS
9.	The Martha Raye Show	NBC
10.	The George Gobel Show	NBC
11.	The Ford Television Theater	NBC
12.	December Bride	CBS
13.	The Buick-Berle Show	NBC
14.	This Is Your Life	NBC
15.	I've Got a Secret	CBS
16.	Two for the Money	CBS
17.	Your Hit Parade	NBC
18.	The Millionaire	CBS
19.	General Electric Theater	CBS
20.	Arthur Godfrey's Talent Scouts	CBS

1955–56

1. The $64,000 Question — CBS
2. I Love Lucy — CBS
3. The Ed Sullivan Show — CBS
4. Disneyland — ABC
5. The Jack Benny Program — CBS
6. December Bride — CBS
7. You Bet Your Life — NBC
8. Dragnet — NBC
9. I've Got a Secret — CBS
10. General Electric Theater — CBS
11. Private Secretary (tie) — CBS
11. The Ford Television Theater (tie) — NBC
13. The Red Skelton Show — CBS
14. The George Gobel Show — NBC
15. The $64,000 Challenge — CBS
16. Arthur Godfrey's Talent Scouts — CBS
17. The Lineup — CBS
18. Shower of Stars — CBS
19. The Perry Como Show — NBC
20. The Honeymooners — CBS

1956–57

1. I Love Lucy — CBS
2. The Ed Sullivan Show — CBS
3. General Electric Theater — CBS
4. The $64,000 Question — CBS
5. December Bride — CBS
6. Alfred Hitchcock Presents — CBS
7. I've Got a Secret (tie) — CBS
7. Gunsmoke (tie) — CBS
9. The Perry Como Show — NBC
10. The Jack Benny Program — CBS
11. Dragnet — NBC
12. Arthur Godfrey's Talent Scouts — CBS
13. The Millionaire (tie) — CBS
13. Disneyland (tie) — ABC
15. Shower of Stars — CBS
16. The Lineup — CBS
17. The Red Skelton Show — CBS
18. You Bet Your Life — NBC
19. The Life and Legend of Wyatt Earp — ABC
20. Private Secretary — CBS

1957–58

1. Gunsmoke — CBS
2. The Danny Thomas Show — CBS
3. Tales of Wells Fargo — NBC
4. Have Gun, Will Travel — CBS
5. I've Got a Secret — CBS
6. The Life and Legend of Wyatt Earp — ABC
7. General Electric Theater — CBS
8. The Restless Gun — NBC
9. December Bride — CBS
10. You Bet Your Life — NBC
11. Alfred Hitchcock Presents (tie) — CBS
11. Cheyenne (tie) — ABC
13. The Tennessee Ernie Ford Show — NBC
14. The Red Skelton Show — CBS
15. Wagon Train (tie) — NBC
15. Sugarfoot (tie) — ABC
15. Father Knows Best (tie) — CBS
18. Twenty-One — NBC
19. The Ed Sullivan Show — CBS
20. The Jack Benny Program — CBS

1958–59

1. Gunsmoke — CBS
2. Wagon Train — NBC
3. Have Gun, Will Travel — CBS
4. The Rifleman — ABC
5. The Danny Thomas Show — CBS
6. Maverick — ABC
7. Tales of Wells Fargo — NBC
8. The Real McCoys — ABC
9. I've Got a Secret — CBS
10. Wyatt Earp — ABC
11. The Price Is Right — NBC
12. The Red Skelton Show — CBS
13. Zane Grey Theater (tie) — CBS
13. Father Knows Best (tie) — CBS
15. The Texan — CBS
16. Wanted: Dead or Alive (tie) — CBS
16. Peter Gunn (tie) — NBC
18. Cheyenne — ABC
19. Perry Mason — CBS
20. The Tennessee Ernie Ford Show — NBC

1959–60

1. Gunsmoke — CBS
2. Wagon Train — NBC
3. Have Gun, Will Travel — CBS
4. The Danny Thomas Show — CBS
5. The Red Skelton Show — CBS
6. Father Knows Best (tie) — CBS
6. 77 Sunset Strip (tie) — ABC
8. The Price Is Right — NBC
9. Wanted: Dead or Alive — CBS
10. Perry Mason — CBS
11. The Real McCoys — ABC
12. The Ed Sullivan Show — CBS
13. The Bing Crosby Show — ABC
14. The Rifleman — ABC
15. The Tennessee Ernie Ford Show — NBC
16. The Lawman — ABC
17. Dennis the Menace — CBS
18. Cheyenne — ABC
19. Rawhide — CBS
20. Maverick — ABC

1960–61

1. Gunsmoke — CBS
2. Wagon Train — NBC
3. Have Gun, Will Travel — CBS
4. The Andy Griffith Show — CBS
5. The Real McCoys — ABC
6. Rawhide — CBS
7. Candid Camera — CBS
8. The Untouchables (tie) — ABC
8. The Price Is Right (tie) — NBC
10. The Jack Benny Program — CBS
11. Dennis the Menace — CBS
12. The Danny Thomas Show — CBS
13. My Three Sons (tie) — ABC
13. 77 Sunset Strip (tie) — ABC
15. The Ed Sullivan Show — CBS
16. Perry Mason — CBS
17. Bonanza — NBC
18. The Flintstones — ABC
19. The Red Skelton Show — CBS
20. Alfred Hitchcock Presents — CBS

1961–62

1.	Wagon Train	NBC
2.	Bonanza	NBC
3.	Gunsmoke	CBS
4.	Hazel	NBC
5.	Perry Mason	CBS
6.	The Red Skelton Show	CBS
7.	The Andy Griffith Show	CBS
8.	The Danny Thomas Show	CBS
9.	Dr. Kildare	NBC
10.	Candid Camera	CBS
11.	My Three Sons	ABC
12.	The Garry Moore Show	CBS
13.	Rawhide	CBS
14.	The Real McCoys	ABC
15.	Lassie	CBS
16.	Sing Along with Mitch	NBC
17.	Dennis the Menace (tie)	CBS
17.	Marshal Dillon (tie) (Gunsmoke reruns)	CBS
19.	Ben Casey	ABC
20.	The Ed Sullivan Show	CBS

1962–63

1.	The Beverly Hillbillies	CBS
2.	Candid Camera (tie)	CBS
2.	The Red Skelton Show (tie)	CBS
4.	Bonanza (tie)	NBC
4.	The Lucy Show (tie)	CBS
6.	The Andy Griffith Show	CBS
7.	Ben Casey (tie)	ABC
7.	The Danny Thomas Show (tie)	CBS
9.	The Dick Van Dyke Show	CBS
10.	Gunsmoke	CBS
11.	Dr. Kildare (tie)	NBC
11.	The Jack Benny Program (tie)	CBS
13.	What's My Line?	CBS
14.	The Ed Sullivan Show	CBS
15.	Hazel	NBC
16.	I've Got a Secret	CBS
17.	The Jackie Gleason Show	CBS
18.	The Defenders	CBS
19.	The Garry Moore Show (tie)	CBS
19.	To Tell the Truth (tie)	CBS

1963–64

1.	The Beverly Hillbillies	CBS
2.	Bonanza	NBC
3.	The Dick Van Dyke Show	CBS
4.	Petticoat Junction	CBS
5.	The Andy Griffith Show	CBS
6.	The Lucy Show	CBS
7.	Candid Camera	CBS
8.	The Ed Sullivan Show	CBS
9.	The Danny Thomas Show	CBS
10.	My Favorite Martian	CBS
11.	The Red Skelton Show	CBS
12.	I've Got a Secret (tie)	CBS
12.	Lassie (tie)	CBS
12.	The Jack Benny Program (tie)	CBS
15.	The Jackie Gleason Show	CBS
16.	The Donna Reed Show	ABC
17.	The Virginian	NBC
18.	The Patty Duke Show	ABC
19.	Dr. Kildare	NBC
20.	Gunsmoke	CBS

1964–65

1.	Bonanza	NBC
2.	Bewitched	ABC
3.	Gomer Pyle, U.S.M.C.	CBS
4.	The Andy Griffith Show	CBS
5.	The Fugitive	ABC
6.	The Red Skelton Hour	CBS
7.	The Dick Van Dyke Show	CBS
8.	The Lucy Show	CBS
9.	Peyton Place (II)	ABC
10.	Combat	ABC
11.	Walt Disney's Wonderful World of Color	NBC
12.	The Beverly Hillbillies	CBS
13.	My Three Sons	ABC
14.	Branded	NBC
15.	Petticoat Junction (tie)	CBS
15.	The Ed Sullivan Show (tie)	CBS
17.	Lassie	CBS
18.	The Munsters (tie)	CBS
18.	Gilligan's Island (tie)	CBS
20.	Peyton Place (V)	ABC

1965–66

1.	Bonanza	NBC
2.	Gomer Pyle, U.S.M.C.	CBS
3.	The Lucy Show	CBS
4.	The Red Skelton Hour	CBS
5.	Batman (II)	ABC
6.	The Andy Griffith Show	CBS
7.	Bewitched (tie)	ABC
7.	The Beverly Hillbillies (tie)	CBS
9.	Hogan's Heroes	CBS
10.	Batman (I)	ABC
11.	Green Acres	CBS
12.	Get Smart	NBC
13.	The Man from U.N.C.L.E.	NBC
14.	Daktari	CBS
15.	My Three Sons	CBS
16.	The Dick Van Dyke Show	CBS
17.	Walt Disney's Wonderful World of Color (tie)	NBC
17.	The Ed Sullivan Show (tie)	CBS
19.	The Lawrence Welk Show (tie)	ABC
19.	I've Got a Secret (tie)	CBS

1966–67

1.	Bonanza	NBC
2.	The Red Skelton Hour	CBS
3.	The Andy Griffith Show	CBS
4.	The Lucy Show	CBS
5.	The Jackie Gleason Show	CBS
6.	Green Acres	CBS
7.	Daktari (tie)	CBS
7.	Bewitched (tie)	ABC
7.	The Beverly Hillbillies (tie)	CBS
10.	Gomer Pyle, U.S.M.C. (tie)	CBS
10.	The Virginian (tie)	NBC
10.	The Lawrence Welk Show (tie)	ABC
10.	The Ed Sullivan Show (tie)	CBS
14.	The Dean Martin Show (tie)	CBS
14.	Family Affair (tie)	CBS
16.	Smothers Brothers Comedy Hour	CBS
17.	The CBS Friday Night Movie (tie)	CBS
17.	Hogan's Heroes (tie)	CBS
19.	Walt Disney's Wonderful World of Color	NBC
20.	Saturday Night at the Movies	NBC

1967–68

1.	The Andy Griffith Show	CBS
2.	The Lucy Show	CBS
3.	Gomer Pyle, U.S.M.C.	CBS
4.	Gunsmoke (tie)	CBS
4.	Family Affair (tie)	CBS
4.	Bonanza (tie)	NBC
7.	The Red Skelton Hour	CBS
8.	The Dean Martin Show	NBC
9.	The Jackie Gleason Show	CBS
10.	Saturday Night at the Movies	NBC
11.	Bewitched	ABC
12.	The Beverly Hillbillies	CBS
13.	The Ed Sullivan Show	CBS
14.	The Virginian	NBC
15.	The CBS Friday Night Movie (tie)	CBS
15.	Green Acres (tie)	CBS
17.	The Lawrence Welk Show	ABC
18.	Smothers Brothers Comedy Hour	CBS
19.	Gentle Ben	CBS
20.	Tuesday Night at the Movies	NBC

1968–69

1.	Rowan and Martin's Laugh-In	NBC
2.	Gomer Pyle, U.S.M.C.	CBS
3.	Bonanza	NBC
4.	Mayberry R.F.D.	CBS
5.	Family Affair	CBS
6.	Gunsmoke	CBS
7.	Julia	NBC
8.	The Dean Martin Show	NBC
9.	Here's Lucy	CBS
10.	The Beverly Hillbillies	CBS
11.	Mission: Impossible (tie)	CBS
11.	Bewitched (tie)	ABC
11.	The Red Skelton Hour (tie)	CBS
14.	My Three Sons	CBS
15.	The Glen Campbell Goodtime Hour	CBS
16.	Ironside	NBC
17.	The Virginian	NBC
18.	The F.B.I.	ABC
19.	Green Acres	CBS
20.	Dragnet	NBC

1969–70

1.	Rowan and Martin's Laugh-In	NBC
2.	Gunsmoke	CBS
3.	Bonanza	NBC
4.	Mayberry R.F.D.	CBS
5.	Family Affair	CBS
6.	Here's Lucy	CBS
7.	The Red Skelton Hour	CBS
8.	Marcus Welby, M.D.	ABC
9.	The Wonderful World of Disney	NBC
10.	The Doris Day Show	CBS
11.	The Bill Cosby Show	NBC
12.	The Jim Nabors Hour	CBS
13.	The Carol Burnett Show	CBS
14.	The Dean Martin Show	NBC
15.	My Three Sons (tie)	CBS
15.	Ironside (tie)	NBC
15.	The Johnny Cash Show (tie)	ABC
18.	The Beverly Hillbillies	CBS
19.	Hawaii Five-O	CBS
20.	Glen Campbell Goodtime Hour	CBS

1970–71

1.	Marcus Welby, M.D.	ABC
2.	The Flip Wilson Show	NBC
3.	Here's Lucy	CBS
4.	Ironside	NBC
5.	Gunsmoke	CBS
6.	The ABC Movie of the Week	ABC
7.	Hawaii Five-O	CBS
8.	Medical Center	CBS
9.	Bonanza	NBC
10.	The F.B.I.	ABC
11.	The Mod Squad	ABC
12.	Adam-12	NBC
13.	Rowan and Martin's Laugh-In (tie)	NBC
13.	The Wonderful World of Disney (tie)	NBC
15.	Mayberry R.F.D.	CBS
16.	Hee Haw	CBS
17.	Mannix	CBS
18.	The Men from Shiloh	NBC
19.	My Three Sons	CBS
20.	The Doris Day Show	CBS

1971–72

1.	All in the Family	CBS
2.	The Flip Wilson Show	NBC
3.	Marcus Welby, M.D.	ABC
4.	Gunsmoke	CBS
5.	The ABC Movie of the Week	ABC
6.	Sanford and Son	NBC
7.	Mannix	CBS
8.	Funny Face (tie)	CBS
8.	Adam-12 (tie)	NBC
10.	The Mary Tyler Moore Show	CBS
11.	Here's Lucy	CBS
12.	Hawaii Five-O	CBS
13.	Medical Center	CBS
14.	The NBC Mystery Movie	NBC
15.	Ironside	NBC
16.	The Partridge Family	ABC
17.	The F.B.I.	ABC
18.	The New Dick Van Dyke Show	CBS
19.	The Wonderful World of Disney	NBC
20.	Bonanza	NBC

1972–73

1.	All in the Family	CBS
2.	Sanford and Son	NBC
3.	Hawaii Five-O	CBS
4.	Maude	CBS
5.	Bridget Loves Bernie (tie)	CBS
5.	The NBC Sunday Mystery Movie (tie)	NBC
7.	The Mary Tyler Moore Show (tie)	CBS
7.	Gunsmoke (tie)	CBS
9.	The Wonderful World of Disney	NBC
10.	Ironside	NBC
11.	Adam-12	NBC
12.	The Flip Wilson Show	NBC
13.	Marcus Welby, M.D.	ABC
14.	Cannon	CBS
15.	Here's Lucy	CBS
16.	The Bob Newhart Show	CBS
17.	ABC Tuesday Movie of the Week	ABC
18.	NFL Monday Night Football	ABC
19.	The Partridge Family (tie)	ABC
19.	The Waltons (tie)	CBS

1973–74

1.	All in the Family	CBS
2.	The Waltons	CBS
3.	Sanford and Son	NBC
4.	M*A*S*H	CBS
5.	Hawaii Five-0	CBS
6.	Maude	CBS
7.	Kojak (tie)	CBS
7.	The Sonny and Cher Comedy Hour (tie)	CBS
9.	The Mary Tyler Moore Show (tie)	CBS
9.	Cannon (tie)	CBS
11.	The Six Million Dollar Man	ABC
12.	The Bob Newhart Show (tie)	CBS
12.	The Wonderful World of Disney (tie)	NBC
14.	The NBC Sunday Mystery Movie	NBC
15.	Gunsmoke	CBS
16.	Happy Days	ABC
17.	Good Times (tie)	CBS
17.	Barnaby Jones (tie)	CBS
19.	NFL Monday Night Football (tie)	ABC
19.	The CBS Friday Night Movie (tie)	CBS

1974–75

1.	All in the Family	CBS
2.	Sanford and Son	NBC
3.	Chico and the Man	NBC
4.	The Jeffersons	CBS
5.	M*A*S*H	CBS
6.	Rhoda	CBS
7.	Good Times	CBS
8.	The Waltons	CBS
9.	Maude	CBS
10.	Hawaii Five-0	CBS
11.	The Mary Tyler Moore Show	CBS
12.	The Rockford Files	NBC
13.	Little House on the Prairie	NBC
14.	Kojak	CBS
15.	Police Woman	NBC
16.	S.W.A.T.	ABC
17.	The Bob Newhart Show	CBS
18.	The Wonderful World of Disney (tie)	NBC
18.	The Rookies (tie)	ABC
20.	Mannix	CBS

1975–76

1.	All in the Family	CBS
2.	Rich Man, Poor Man	ABC
3.	Laverne and Shirley	ABC
4.	Maude	CBS
5.	The Bionic Woman	ABC
6.	Phyllis	CBS
7.	Sanford and Son (tie)	NBC
7.	Rhoda (tie)	CBS
9.	The Six Million Dollar Man	ABC
10.	The ABC Monday Night Movie	ABC
11.	Happy Days	ABC
12.	One Day at a Time	CBS
13.	The ABC Sunday Night Movie	ABC
14.	The Waltons (tie)	CBS
14.	M*A*S*H (tie)	CBS
16.	Starsky and Hutch (tie)	ABC
16.	Good Heavens (tie)	ABC
18.	Welcome Back, Kotter	ABC
19.	The Mary Tyler Moore Show	CBS
20.	Kojak	CBS

1976–77

1.	Happy Days	ABC
2.	Laverne and Shirley	ABC
3.	The ABC Monday Night Movie	ABC
4.	M*A*S*H	CBS
5.	Charlie's Angels	ABC
6.	The Big Event	NBC
7.	The Six Million Dollar Man	ABC
8.	The ABC Sunday Night Movie (tie)	ABC
8.	Baretta (tie)	ABC
8.	One Day at a Time (tie)	CBS
11.	Three's Company	ABC
12.	All in the Family	CBS
13.	Welcome Back, Kotter	ABC
14.	The Bionic Woman	ABC
15.	The Waltons (tie)	CBS
15.	Little House on the Prairie (tie)	NBC
17.	Barney Miller	ABC
18.	60 Minutes (tie)	CBS
18.	Hawaii Five-0 (tie)	CBS
20.	NBC Monday Night at the Movies	NBC

1977–78

1.	Laverne and Shirley	ABC
2.	Happy Days	ABC
3.	Three's Company	ABC
4.	Charlie's Angels (tie)	ABC
4.	All in the Family (tie)	CBS
4.	60 Minutes (tie)	CBS
7.	Little House on the Prairie	NBC
8.	M*A*S*H (tie)	CBS
8.	Alice (tie)	CBS
10.	One Day at a Time	CBS
11.	How the West Was Won	ABC
12.	Eight Is Enough	ABC
13.	Soap	ABC
14.	The Love Boat	ABC
15.	NBC Monday Night Movie	NBC
16.	NFL Monday Night Football	ABC
17.	Barney Miller (tie)	ABC
17.	Fantasy Island (tie)	ABC
19.	The Amazing Spider-Man (tie)	CBS
19.	Project U.F.O. (tie)	NBC

1978–79

1.	Laverne and Shirley	ABC
2.	Three's Company	ABC
3.	Mork & Mindy	ABC
4.	Happy Days (tie)	ABC
4.	The Ropers (tie)	ABC
6.	What's Happening!! (tie)	ABC
6.	Alice (8:30) (tie)	CBS
8.	M*A*S*H	CBS
9.	One Day at a Time (Monday)	CBS
10.	Taxi	ABC
11.	60 Minutes (tie)	CBS
11.	Charlie's Angels (tie)	ABC
13.	Angie	ABC
14.	Alice (9:30)	CBS
15.	All in the Family	CBS
16.	WKRP in Cincinnati (tie)	CBS
17.	Soap (tie)	ABC
18.	Eight Is Enough	ABC
19.	All in the Family	CBS
20.	Barney Miller (tie)	ABC
20.	CBS Sunday Night Movie (tie)	CBS

1979–80

1.	60 Minutes	CBS
2.	Three's Company	ABC
3.	That's Incredible	ABC
4.	M*A*S*H	CBS
5.	Alice	CBS
6.	Dallas	CBS
7.	Flo	CBS
8.	The Jeffersons	CBS
9.	The Dukes of Hazzard	CBS
10.	One Day at a Time	CBS
11.	WKRP in Cincinnati	CBS
12.	Goodtime Girls	ABC
13.	Archie Bunker's Place	CBS
14.	Taxi	ABC
15.	Eight Is Enough	ABC
16.	Little House on the Prairie	NBC
17.	House Calls	CBS
18.	Real People	NBC
19.	CHiPs	NBC
20.	Happy Days	ABC

1980–81

1.	Dallas	CBS
2.	60 Minutes	CBS
3.	The Dukes of Hazzard	CBS
4.	Private Benjamin	CBS
5.	M*A*S*H	CBS
6.	The Love Boat	ABC
7.	The NBC Tuesday Night Movie	NBC
8.	House Calls	CBS
9.	The Jeffersons (tie)	CBS
9.	Little House on the Prairie (tie)	NBC
11.	The Two of Us	CBS
12.	Alice	CBS
13.	Real People (tie)	NBC
13.	Three's Company (tie)	ABC
15.	The NBC Movie of the Week (tie)	NBC
15.	One Day at a Time (tie)	CBS
17.	Too Close for Comfort (tie)	ABC
17.	Magnum, P.I. (tie)	CBS
19.	Diff'rent Strokes (tie)	NBC
19.	NFL Monday Night Football (tie)	ABC

1981–82

1.	Dallas (9:00)	CBS
2.	Dallas (10:00)	CBS
3.	60 Minutes	CBS
4.	Three's Company (tie)	ABC
4.	CBS NFL Football Post 2 (tie)	CBS
6.	The Jeffersons	CBS
7.	Joanie Loves Chachi	ABC
8.	The Dukes of Hazzard (9:00)	CBS
9.	Alice (tie)	CBS
9.	The Dukes of Hazzard (8:00) (tie)	CBS
11.	The ABC Monday Night Movie (tie)	ABC
11.	Too Close for Comfort (tie)	ABC
13.	M*A*S*H	CBS
14.	One Day at a Time	CBS
15.	NFL Monday Night Football	ABC
16.	Falcon Crest	CBS
17.	Archie Bunker's Place (tie)	CBS
17.	The Love Boat (tie)	ABC
19.	Hart to Hart	ABC
20.	Trapper John, M.D.	CBS

1982–83

1.	60 Minutes	CBS
2.	Dallas	CBS
3.	M*A*S*H (tie)	CBS
4.	Magnum, P.I. (tie)	CBS
5.	Dynasty	ABC
6.	Three's Company	ABC
7.	Simon & Simon	CBS
8.	Falcon Crest	CBS
9.	NFL Monday Night Football	ABC
10.	The Love Boat	ABC
11.	One Day at a Time (Sunday)	CBS
12.	Newhart (Monday)	CBS
13.	The Jeffersons (tie)	CBS
13.	The A Team (tie)	NBC
15.	The Fall Guy (9:00)	ABC
16.	Newhart (Sunday, 9:30)	CBS
17.	The Mississippi	CBS
18.	9 to 5	ABC
19.	The Fall Guy	ABC
20.	The ABC Monday Night Movie	ABC

1983–84

1.	Dallas	CBS
2.	Dynasty	ABC
3.	The A Team	NBC
4.	60 Minutes	CBS
5.	Simon & Simon	CBS
6.	Magnum, P.I.	CBS
7.	Falcon Crest	CBS
8.	Kate & Allie	CBS
9.	Hotel	ABC
10.	Cagney & Lacey	CBS
11.	Knots Landing	CBS
12.	The ABC Sunday Night Movie (tie)	ABC
12.	The ABC Monday Night Movie (tie)	ABC
14.	TV's Bloopers & Practical Jokes	NBC
15.	AfterMASH	CBS
16.	The Fall Guy	ABC
17.	The Four Seasons	CBS
18.	The Love Boat	ABC
19.	Riptide	NBC
20.	The Jeffersons	CBS

1984–85

1.	Dynasty	ABC
2.	Dallas	CBS
3.	The Cosby Show	NBC
4.	60 Minutes	CBS
5.	Family Ties	NBC
6.	The A Team (tie)	NBC
6.	Simon & Simon (tie)	CBS
8.	Knots Landing	CBS
9.	Murder, She Wrote	CBS
10.	Falcon Crest (tie)	CBS
10.	Crazy Like a Fox (tie)	CBS
12.	Hotel	ABC
13.	Cheers	NBC
14.	Riptide (tie)	NBC
14.	Who's the Boss? (tie)	ABC
16.	Magnum, P.I.	CBS
17.	Hail to the Chief	ABC
18.	Newhart	CBS
19.	Kate & Allie	CBS
20.	The NBC Monday Night Movie	NBC

1985–86

1.	The Cosby Show	NBC
2.	Family Ties	NBC
3.	Murder, She Wrote	CBS
4.	60 Minutes	CBS
5.	Cheers	NBC
6.	Dallas (tie)	CBS
6.	Dynasty (tie)	ABC
6.	The Golden Girls (tie)	NBC
9.	Miami Vice	NBC
10.	Who's the Boss?	ABC
11.	Perfect Strangers	ABC
12.	Night Court	NBC
13.	The CBS Sunday Night Movie	CBS
14.	Highway to Heaven (tie)	NBC
14.	Kate & Allie (tie)	CBS
16.	NFL Monday Night Football	ABC
17.	Newhart	CBS
18.	Knots Landing (tie)	CBS
18.	Growing Pains (tie)	ABC
20.	227	NBC

1986–87

1.	The Cosby Show	NBC
2.	Family Ties	NBC
3.	Cheers	NBC
4.	Murder, She Wrote	CBS
5.	Night Court	NBC
6.	The Golden Girls	NBC
7.	60 Minutes	CBS
8.	Growing Pains	ABC
9.	Moonlighting	ABC
10.	Who's the Boss?	ABC
11.	Dallas	CBS
12.	Nothing in Common	NBC
13.	Newhart	CBS
14.	Amen	NBC
15.	227	NBC
16.	Matlock (tie)	NBC
16.	CBS Sunday Night Movie (tie)	CBS
16.	NBC Monday Night Movie (tie)	NBC
19.	NFL Monday Night Football (tie)	ABC
19.	Kate & Allie (tie)	CBS

1987–88

1.	The Cosby Show	NBC
2.	A Different World	NBC
3.	Cheers	NBC
4.	Growing Pains (Tuesday)	ABC
5.	Night Court	NBC
6.	The Golden Girls	NBC
7.	Who's the Boss?	ABC
8.	60 Minutes	CBS
9.	Murder, She Wrote	CBS
10.	The Wonder Years	ABC
11.	Alf	NBC
12.	Moonlighting (tie)	ABC
12.	L.A. Law (tie)	NBC
14.	NFL Monday Night Football	ABC
15.	Matlock (tie)	NBC
15.	Growing Pains (Wednesday) (tie)	ABC
17.	Amen	NBC
18.	Family Ties	NBC
19.	Hunter	NBC
20.	The CBS Sunday Night Movie	CBS

1988–89

1.	Roseanne (9:00) (tie)	ABC
1.	The Cosby Show (tie)	NBC
3.	Roseanne (8:30) (tie)	ABC
3.	A Different World (tie)	NBC
5.	Cheers	NBC
6.	60 Minutes	CBS
7.	The Golden Girls	NBC
8.	Who's the Boss?	ABC
9.	The Wonder Years	ABC
10.	Murder, She Wrote	CBS
11.	Empty Nest	NBC
12.	Anything but Love	ABC
13.	Dear John	NBC
14.	Growing Pains	ABC
15.	Alf (tie)	NBC
15.	L.A. Law (tie)	NBC
17.	Matlock	NBC
18.	Unsolved Mysteries (tie)	NBC
18.	Hunter (tie)	NBC
20.	In the Heat of the Night	NBC

1989–90

1.	Roseanne	ABC
2.	The Cosby Show	NBC
3.	Cheers	NBC
4.	A Different World	NBC
5.	America's Funniest Home Videos	ABC
6.	The Golden Girls	NBC
7.	60 Minutes	CBS
8.	The Wonder Years	ABC
9.	Empty Nest	NBC
10.	Chicken Soup	ABC
11.	NFL Monday Night Football	ABC
12.	Unsolved Mysteries	NBC
13.	Who's the Boss?	ABC
14.	L.A. Law (tie)	NBC
14.	Murder, She Wrote (tie)	CBS
16.	Grand	NBC
17.	In the Heat of the Night	NBC
18.	Dear John	NBC
19.	Coach	ABC
20.	Matlock	NBC

1990–91

1.	Cheers	NBC
2.	60 Minutes	CBS
3.	Roseanne	ABC
4.	A Different World	NBC
5.	The Cosby Show	NBC
6.	NFL Monday Night Football	ABC
7.	America's Funniest Home Videos	ABC
8.	Murphy Brown	CBS
9.	America's Funniest People (tie)	ABC
9.	Designing Women (tie)	CBS
9.	Empty Nest (tie)	NBC
12.	Golden Girls	NBC
13.	Murder, She Wrote	CBS
14.	Unsolved Mysteries	NBC
15.	Full House	ABC
16.	Family Matters	ABC
17.	Coach (tie)	ABC
17.	Matlock (tie)	NBC
19.	In the Heat of the Night	NBC
20.	Major Dad	CBS

1991–92

1.	60 Minutes	CBS
2.	Roseanne	ABC
3.	Murphy Brown	CBS
4.	Cheers	NBC
5.	Home Improvement	ABC
6.	Designing Women	CBS
7.	Coach	ABC
8.	Full House	ABC
9.	Murder, She Wrote (tie)	CBS
9.	Unsolved Mysteries (tie)	NBC
11.	Major Dad (tie)	CBS
11.	NFL Monday Night Football (tie)	ABC
13.	Room For Two	ABC
14.	The CBS Sunday Night Movie	CBS
15.	Evening Shade	CBS
16.	Northern Exposure	CBS
17.	A Different World	NBC
18.	The Cosby Show	NBC
19.	Wings	NBC
20.	America's Funniest Home Videos (tie)	ABC
20.	Fresh Prince of Bel Air (tie)	NBC

1992–93

1.	60 Minutes	CBS
2.	Roseanne	ABC
3.	Home Improvement	ABC
4.	Murphy Brown	CBS
5.	Murder, She Wrote	CBS
6.	Coach	ABC
7.	NFL Monday Night Football	ABC
8.	The CBS Sunday Night Movie (tie)	CBS
8.	Cheers (tie)	NBC
10.	Full House	ABC
11.	Northern Exposure	CBS
12.	Rescue: 911	CBS
13.	20/20	ABC
14.	The CBS Tuesday Night Movie (tie)	CBS
14.	Love & War (tie)	CBS
16.	Fresh Prince of Bel Air (tie)	NBC
16.	Hangin' with Mr. Cooper (tie)	ABC
16.	The Jackie Thomas Show (tie)	ABC
19.	Evening Shade	CBS
20.	Hearts Afire (tie)	CBS
20.	Unsolved Mysteries (tie)	NBC

1993–94

1.	Home Improvement	ABC
2.	60 Minutes	CBS
3.	Seinfeld	NBC
4.	Roseanne	ABC
5.	Grace Under Fire	ABC
6.	These Friends of Mine	ABC
7.	Frasier	NBC
8.	Coach (tie)	ABC
8.	NFL Monday Night Football (tie)	ABC
10.	Murder, She Wrote	CBS
11.	Murphy Brown	CBS
12.	Thunder Alley	ABC
13.	The CBS Sunday Night Movie	CBS
14.	20/20	ABC
15.	Love & War	CBS
16.	Primetime Live (tie)	ABC
16.	Wings (tie)	NBC
18.	NYPD Blue	ABC
19.	Homicide: Life on the Street	NBC
20.	Northern Exposure	CBS

1994–95

1.	Seinfeld	NBC
2.	ER	NBC
3.	Home Improvement	ABC
4.	Grace Under Fire	ABC
5.	NFL Monday Night Football	ABC
6.	60 Minutes	CBS
7.	NYPD Blue	ABC
8.	Friends	NBC
9.	Roseanne (tie)	ABC
9.	Murder, She Wrote (tie)	CBS
11.	Mad About You	NBC
12.	Madman of the People	NBC
13.	Ellen	ABC
14.	Hope & Gloria	NBC
15.	Frasier	NBC
16.	Murphy Brown	CBS
17.	20/20	ABC
18.	CBS Sunday Movie	CBS
19.	NBC Monday Night Movies	NBC
20.	Dave's World	CBS

1995–96

1.	ER	NBC
2.	Seinfeld	NBC
3.	Friends	NBC
4.	Caroline in the City	NBC
5.	NFL Monday Night Football	ABC
6.	The Single Guy	NBC
7.	Home Improvement	ABC
8.	Boston Common	NBC
9.	60 Minutes	CBS
10.	NYPD Blue	ABC
11.	Frasier (tie)	NBC
11.	20/20 (tie)	ABC
13.	Grace Under Fire	ABC
14.	Coach (tie)	ABC
14.	NBC Monday Night Movies (tie)	NBC
16.	Roseanne	ABC
17.	The Nanny	CBS
18.	Murphy Brown (tie)	CBS
18.	Primetime Live (tie)	ABC
18.	Walker, Texas Ranger (tie)	CBS

1996–97

1.	ER	NBC
2.	Seinfeld	NBC
3.	Suddenly Susan	NBC
4.	Friends (tie)	NBC
4.	The Naked Truth (tie)	NBC
6.	Fired Up	NBC
7.	NFL Monday Night Football	ABC
8.	The Single Guy	NBC
9.	Home Improvement	ABC
10.	Touched by an Angel	CBS
11.	60 Minutes	CBS
12.	20/20	ABC
13.	NYPD Blue	ABC
14.	CBS Sunday Movie	CBS
15.	Primetime Live	ABC
16.	Frasier	NBC
17.	Spin City	ABC
18.	NBC Sunday Night Movie (tie)	NBC
18.	The Drew Carey Show (tie)	ABC
20.	The X-Files	FOX

1997–98

1.	Seinfeld	NBC
2.	ER	NBC
3.	Veronica's Closet	NBC
4.	Friends	NBC
5.	NFL Monday Night Football	ABC
6.	Touched by an Angel	CBS
7.	60 Minutes	CBS
8.	Union Square	NBC
9.	CBS Sunday Movie	CBS
10.	Frasier (tie)	NBC
10.	Home Improvement (tie)	ABC
10.	Just Shoot Me (tie)	NBC
13.	Dateline NBC–Tuesday	NBC
14.	NFL Monday Showcase	ABC
15.	Dateline NBC–Monday	NBC
16.	The Drew Carey Show (tie)	ABC
16.	Fox NFL Sunday Post-Game Show (tie)	FOX
18.	20/20	ABC
19.	NYPD Blue (tie)	ABC
19.	Primetime Live (tie)	ABC
19.	The X-Files (tie)	FOX

1998–1999

1.	ER	NBC
2.	Friends	NBC
3.	Frasier	NBC
4.	NFL Monday Night Football	ABC
5.	Jesse (tie)	NBC
5.	Veronica's Closet (tie)	NBC
7.	60 Minutes	CBS
8.	Touched by an Angel	CBS
9.	CBS Sunday Movie	CBS
10.	20/20–Wednesday	ABC
11.	Home Improvement	ABC
12.	Everybody Loves Raymond	CBS
13.	NYPD Blue	ABC
14.	Law and Order	NBC
15.	The Drew Carey Show (tie)	ABC
15.	20/20–Friday (tie)	ABC
17.	Jag (tie)	CBS
17.	NFL Monday Night Showcase (tie)	ABC
17.	Providence (tie)	NBC
17.	Dateline Friday (tie)	NBC

1999–2000

1.	Who Wants to Be a Millionaire–Tuesday	ABC
2.	Who Wants to Be a Millionaire–Thursday	ABC
3.	Who Wants to Be a Millionaire–Sunday	ABC
4.	E.R.	NBC
5.	Friends	NBC
6.	NFL Monday Night Football	ABC
7.	Frasier	NBC
8.	Frasier (9:30)	NBC
9.	60 Minutes	CBS
10.	The Practice	ABC
11.	Touched by an Angel	CBS
12.	Law and Order	NBC
13.	Everybody Loves Raymond (tie)	CBS
13.	NFL Monday Showcase (tie)	ABC
15.	Jesse	NBC
16.	CBS Sunday Movie (tie)	CBS
16.	Daddio (tie)	NBC
18.	NYPD Blue (tie)	ABC
18.	Stark Raving Mad (tie)	NBC
20.	Dharma and Greg	ABC

1999-2000 SPECIAL RATINGS

The following are Nielsen ratings for a variety of special categories for the most recent season. (Source: Nielsen Media Research)

SYNDICATED TALK SHOWS
1. The Oprah Winfrey Show, KingWorld
2. Jerry Springer, Studios USA
3. The Rosie O'Donnell Show, Warner Bros.
4. Live with Regis and Kathie Lee, Buena Vista
5. Maury, Studios USA
6. The Montel Williams Show, Paramount
7. Sally Jessy Raphael, Studios USA
8. Ricki Lake, Columbia Tristar
9. The Jenny Jones Show, Warner Bros.
10. Donny & Marie, Columbia Tristar

SOAPS
1. The Young and the Restless, CBS
2. The Bold and the Beautiful, CBS
3. General Hospital, ABC (tie)
3. Days of Our Lives, NBC (tie)
5. All My Children, ABC
6. As the World Turns, CBS
7. One Life to Live, ABC
8. Guiding Light, CBS
9. Port Charles, ABC
10. Passions, NBC

SYNDICATED QUIZ AND GAME SHOWS
1. Wheel of Fortune, KingWorld
2. Jeopardy!, KingWorld
3. Wheel of Fortune (weekend), KingWorld
4. Hollywood Squares, KingWorld
5. Family Feud, Pearson Television
6. Match Game, Pearson Television
7. Newlywed Game/Dating Game Hour, Columbia Tristar

SATURDAY MORNING CHILDREN'S PROGRAMS
1. Pokémon, The WB (10:00-10:30 a.m.)
2. Pokémon, The WB (8:30-9 a.m.)
3. Disney's 1 Saturday Morning, ABC (9:30-10:00 a.m.)
4. Pokémon, The WB (10:30-11:00 a.m.)
5. Hang Time, NBC
6. Men in Black, The WB (10:30-11:00 a.m.)
7. Disney's 1 Saturday Morning, ABC (10:00-10:30 a.m.)
8. City Guys, NBC
9. Saved by the Bell, NBC
10. Disney's 1 Saturday Morning, ABC (9:00-9:30 a.m.)

THE TOP 50 TELEVISION SHOWS

These single broadcasts drew the largest percentages of the viewing public. Disappointed *Seinfeld* fans can take heart that while its finale attracted only about 41% of TV homes to place 64th, its audience of 40.5 million viewers makes it the 12th-most-watched broadcast in history. (Source: Nielsen Media Research)

Rank	Program	Date
1.	M*A*S*H	February 28, 1983
2.	Dallas ("Who Shot J.R.?")	November 21, 1980
3.	Roots, Part 8 (conclusion)	January 30, 1977
4.	Super Bowl XVI	January 24, 1982
5.	Super Bowl XVII	January 30, 1983
6.	Winter Olympics	February 23, 1994
7.	Super Bowl XX	January 26, 1986
8.	Gone With the Wind, Part 1	November 7, 1976
9.	Gone With the Wind, Part 2	November 8, 1976
10.	Super Bowl XII	January 15, 1978
11.	Super Bowl XIII	January 21, 1979
12.	Bob Hope Christmas Show	January 15, 1970
13.	Super Bowl XVIII (tie)	January 22, 1984
13.	Super Bowl XIX (tie)	January 20, 1985
15.	Super Bowl XIV	January 20, 1980
16.	Super Bowl XXX	January 28, 1996
17.	ABC Theater ("The Day After")	November 20, 1983
18.	Roots, Part 6 (tie)	January 28, 1977
18.	The Fugitive (tie)	August 29, 1967
20.	Super Bowl XXI	January 25, 1987
21.	Roots, Part 5	January 27, 1977
22.	Super Bowl XXVIII (tie)	January 30, 1994
22.	Cheers (tie)	May 20, 1993
24.	The Ed Sullivan Show (TV debut of The Beatles)	February 9, 1964
25.	Super Bowl XXVII	January 31, 1993

Rank	Program	Date
26.	Bob Hope Christmas Show	January 14, 1971
27.	Roots, Part 3	January 25, 1977
28.	Super Bowl XXXII	January 23, 1998
29.	Super Bowl XI (tie)	January 9, 1977
29.	Super Bowl XV (tie)	January 25, 1981
31.	Super Bowl VI	January 16, 1972
32.	Winter Olympics (tie)	February 25, 1994
33.	Roots, Part 2 (tie)	January 24, 1977
34.	The Beverly Hillbillies	January 8, 1964
35.	Roots, Part 4 (tie)	January 26, 1977
35.	The Ed Sullivan Show (with The Beatles) (tie)	February 16, 1964
37.	Super Bowl XXIII	January 22, 1989
38.	The 43rd Academy Awards	April 7, 1970
39.	Super Bowl XXXI	January 26, 1997
40.	The Thorn Birds, Part 3	March 29, 1983
41.	The Thorn Birds, Part 4	March 30, 1983
42.	NFC championship game	January 10, 1982
43.	The Beverly Hillbillies	January 15, 1964
44.	Super Bowl VII	January 14, 1973
45.	Thorn Birds, Part 2	March 28, 1983
46.	Super Bowl IX (tie)	January 12, 1975
46.	The Beverly Hillbillies (tie)	February 26, 1964
48.	Super Bowl X (tie)	January 18, 1976
48.	Airport (tie)	November 11, 1973
48.	Love Story (tie)	October 1, 1972
48.	Cinderella (tie)	February 22, 1965

MOST-WATCHED MOVIES ON TELEVISION

This list includes network prime-time feature films, both those made for theaters and those (including miniseries) made specifically for TV (*). Although *The Wizard of Oz*'s best showing misses our list at No. 34, many years of high ratings have made it, overall, the most popular movie ever shown on TV. (Source: Nielsen Media Research)

Rank	Movie	Air Date
1.	Roots, Part 8*	January 30, 1977
2.	Gone With the Wind, Part 1	November 7, 1976
3.	Gone With the Wind, Part 2	November 8, 1976
4.	The Day After*	November 20, 1983
5.	Roots, Part 6*	January 28, 1977
6.	Roots, Part 5*	January 27, 1977
7.	Roots, Part 3*	January 25, 1977
8.	Roots, Part 2*	January 24, 1977
9.	Roots, Part 4*	January 26, 1977
10.	The Thorn Birds, Part 3*	March 29, 1983
11.	The Thorn Birds, Part 4*	March 30, 1983
12.	The Thorn Birds, Part 2*	March 28, 1983
13.	Love Story (tie)	October 1, 1972
13.	Airport (tie)	November 11, 1973
13.	Roots, Part 7* (tie)	January 29, 1977

Rank	Movie	Air Date
16.	The Winds of War, Part 7*	February 13, 1983
17.	Roots, Part 1*	January 23, 1977
18.	The Winds of War, Part 2*	February 7, 1983
19.	The Thorn Birds, Part 1*	March 27, 1983
20.	The Godfather, Part 2	November 18, 1974
21.	Jaws	November 4, 1979
22.	The Poseidon Adventure	October 27, 1974
23.	The Birds (tie)	January 16, 1968
23.	True Grit (tie)	November 12, 1972
25.	Patton	November 19, 1972
26.	The Bridge on the River Kwai	September 25, 1966
27.	Jeremiah Johnson (tie)	January 18, 1976
27.	Helter Skelter, Part 2 (tie)*	April 2, 1976
29.	Rocky (tie)	February 4, 1979
29.	Ben-Hur (tie)	February 14, 1971

PEOPLE'S FAVORITE 50 TV STARS

The most popular TV personalities are not necessarily the most influential, but rather the sort of folks you'd like to know in real life. This year PEOPLE's Michael A. Lipton rethinks and freshens his list of tube all-stars:

TIM ALLEN
It's so nice to have a klutz around the house, but nobody could screw up as hilariously or nail the punchlines as deftly as Allen, *Home Improvement*'s hammer-handed dufus dad.

JAMES ARNESS
With his weatherbeaten face, loping gait, and laconic delivery, he stood alone as TV's last—and best—Western hero.

BEA ARTHUR
The first sitcom feminist: her foghorn voice, bristly authority, and, er, Maude-lin wit reduced mere men to spineless jellyfish.

LUCILLE BALL
Those lips (pouting ruefully), those eyes (pop-eyed with surprise), that voice ("Rick-kyyyy!") always delivered 24-karat comedy.

JACK BENNY
Well! He got more laughs with That Look than Uncle Miltie ever did in a dress or Benny's old crony Burns did waving his cigar.

RAYMOND BURR
With his imposing baritone and X-ray eyes that penetrated the most ingenious alibis, Burr's Perry Mason never rested his defense till the guilty party (never, of course, his poor, framed client) confessed on the stand.

JOHNNY CARSON
Silver-haired, silver-tongued paterfamilias to Jay and Dave, this wise old night owl could give a hoot about returning to the throne he held for four glorious decades.

RICHARD CHAMBERLAIN
Let's see: '60s dreamboat Dr. Kildare leaves TV to Hamlet it up on the British stage, then triumphantly returns as the King of the Miniseries. There's gotta be a movie of the week here...

GEORGE CLOONEY
A Kildare for the '90s—and *ER*'s first breakout star—Clooney, more magnetic than an MRI scan, set pulses fluttering with just a cocked head, a raised brow, and a sly grin.

KATIE COURIC
She's your tomboyish kid sister all grown up, and while there's a mule-like kick to her interviews, her big heart and feisty twinkle keep her warm.

WALTER CRONKITE
America's most trusted anchor earned the nickname "Old Ironpants" through his marathon coverage of conventions, assassinations, and resignations, but it was his gosh-darn, oh-boyish enthusiasm that made him the man to watch reporting the moon shots.

PHIL DONAHUE
"Caller, are you there?" Earnest, excitable, daring, and dashing (literally, into the audience), the snow-thatched maestro of daytime talk left no taboo unturned, no trauma untreated.

DAVID DUCHOVNY
A minimalist actor with sad, basset eyes and a sly-like-a-fox humor, he is the exemplar of '90s cool and cynicism.

PETER FALK
As the raincoat-rumpled detective with the frog-horn voice, Falk brought an ironic sense of mischief to his role as a regular guy besting the arrogant elites.

MICHAEL J. FOX
From *Family Ties* to *Spin City*, TV's most endearing comic actor made us love him even more for his valiant real-life battle with Parkinson's disease.

DENNIS FRANZ
The blustery, beer-bellied blue-collar joe as macho sex symbol. You got a problem with dat?

JAMES GANDOLFINI
In New Jersey mob family boss (and suburban family guy) Tony Soprano, Gandolfini essays TV's most complex characterization: the warm-hearted, cold-blooded monster you root for.

JAMES GARNER
Despite a body wracked by wear and tear, and a face etched with wisdom and woe, Garner remains TV's most credible—and comedic—action star.

JACKIE GLEASON
How sweet it was to see The Great One storm, scheme, and suffer as Ralph Kramden, the Willy Loman of bus drivers.

KELSEY GRAMMER
Portraying TV's favorite shrink, the pompous yet endearing Dr. Frasier Crane, in two hit series (*Cheers* and *Frasier*), Grammer has managed to balance his character's comic bluster with a wry, deadpan wit.

LARRY HAGMAN
So gleefully villainous, he made the viewer his grinning accomplice. We were completely in thrall of devilish J.R., TV's most hissable, kissable antihero.

ALFRED HITCHCOCK
TV transformed the film name into a household face—an eru-

dite gargoyle whose drollery and drop-dead delivery made for a murderously marvelous one-man-show-within-the-show.

DAVID JANSSEN

A haggard, haunted underdog whose raspy voice and soulful brow served him brilliantly, whether playing fugitives or feds.

MICHAEL LANDON

From Little Joe Cartwright to big man on the prairie to angelic emissary, Landon made sentimentality a virtue, wrung drama out of decency, and rang true.

ANGELA LANSBURY

How did Cabot Cove manage to rack up the nation's highest murder rate? Ask this nebbishy doyenne of TV crimesolvers.

LASSIE

The wonder dog of our childhoods.

JAY LENO

The hardest-working man in showbiz sweated bullets to show us he is as good as—or, as his ratings would indicate, better than—Letterman.

GROUCHO MARX

An icon of '30s movie comedy, Groucho reinvented himself in the '50s as *You Bet Your Life*'s acerbic and irreverent emcee.

ELIZABETH MONTGOMERY

Sure, she bewitched us with that wiggly nose, but beyond the levity (and levitation), a serious TV-movie actress was in the wings.

MARY TYLER MOORE

She can still turn the world on with her smile. Yet for most of us, she'll always remain winsome single girl Mary Richards, her cap forever aloft, frozen in time.

LEONARD NIMOY

Who says a pointy-eared intellectual can't be a sex symbol? Star Trekkers melded their minds with Spock's and became one with the sci-fi universe.

ROSIE O'DONNELL

Okay, so she's no Oprah. But with her showbiz connections, breezy banter, and self-effacing, seat-of-the-pants wit, O'Donnell revitalized daytime talk.

JERRY ORBACH

As cynical yet shrewd Det. Lennie Briscoe, the flatfoot heart and soul of *Law & Order*, he gives this rapid-paced, city-slick crime drama the jagged edge of realism.

SARAH JESSICA PARKER

As Carrie, the spunkiest of *Sex & the City*'s man-hungry vixens, she turns Manhattan hanky-panky into a wholesome, athletic, even adventurous experience. She's never funnier than in post-coital recaps with her equally randy girlfriends.

REGIS PHILBIN

Morning TV's twinkle-eyed curmudgeon Reege blossomed into an evening superstar as the jocular host of the megahit *Who Wants to Be a Millionaire*. (Final answer: You bet your life Regis now is one, many times over.)

GILDA RADNER

The madcap heart and soul of the original *Saturday Night Live*.

DONNA REED

A suburban TV mom for the ages —smart, beautiful, and sunny.

MICHAEL RICHARDS

A maniac for all seasons: All he had to do to get laughs was walk/stagger/glide/boogie/tumble through Seinfeld's door.

THE ROCK

Can you smell what he's cooking? This cocky pro wrestler is a TV superhero for the new millennium.

FRED ROGERS

It really was a beautiful day in the neighborhood when this genial, sweet, protective grown-up first sat down 30 years ago, laced up his sneakers, and

became every kid's best friend.

ROY ROGERS

The quintessential TV cowboy, tall in the saddle, handy with a six-shooter, yet for the most part, just plain Trigger-happy.

FRED SAVAGE

The joys and agonies of adolescence were wonderfully expressed in Savage's tender, perpetually wide-eyed visage.

TOM SELLECK

TV's merriest manchild, he spent his Magnum opus living out every guy's fantasies—and has a bright new career in sitcoms.

PHIL SILVERS

Ten-HUT! His Sgt. Bilko was a fast-squawking, never-balking con artist supreme who tweaked authority and energized '50s TV.

HOMER SIMPSON

Slobbus americanus, he eclipses his bratty son Bart, and has even been known to dispense pearls of Homer-spun wisdom.

SUZANNE SOMERS

A sitcom sexpot turned infomericial empress—no ifs, ands, or buttmasters about it.

DICK VAN DYKE

Limber-limbed, rubber-faced, G-rated precursor to Jim Carrey, he could trip the light fantastic (even while tripping over an ottoman).

VANNA WHITE

She turns letters—and heads— with a sensual body language all her own.

OPRAH WINFREY

So empathetic is this talk-show tsarina with her guests—and so upfront about herself it's scary— that she could be having a ball one day, and bawling the next.

HENRY WINKLER

Aaaaaaay! This retro '70s-cum-'50s sitcom star exuded the cool we all wished we'd had in our not-so-happy high school days.

PEOPLE'S 50 FORMATIVE SHOWS

The mark of all memorable series is their profound, or at least pervasive, impact on pop culture. No sooner are they on the air—like 1998's *The Sopranos*—than it's impossible to remember how we got along without them. Here are PEOPLE's shows of shows.

THE ADVENTURES OF SUPERMAN

More than 40 years later, this show starring George Reeves as the Man of Steel is still the only good superhero series TV has ever produced.

ALL IN THE FAMILY

At the heart of this epochal sitcom were the corrosive working-class prejudices of Archie Bunker, a Northern redneck. His political arguments make *Crossfire* seem tame.

AN AMERICAN FAMILY

In their time (the 1970s), the exhibitionistic Loud family opened themselves up to freak-show derision. But they paved the way for the current rage of reality-based shows and all those voyeuristic video-clip shows.

THE ANDY GRIFFITH SHOW

The precursor of the so-called rusticoms of the '60s, this quiet masterpiece had heart, humor, wisdom, and—often over-looked—an outstanding cast..

BONANZA

The Cartwrights, a larger-than-life clan, made the Ponderosa worth visiting every week.

THE BULLWINKLE SHOW

Jay Ward's kaleidoscopic, pun-crammed cartoon about a dense moose and a plucky flying squirrel delighted kids of all ages.

BURNS AND ALLEN

This iconoclastic '50s show glee-fully disregarded TV tradition, including the observance of "the fourth wall." Their comic chemistry has never been duplicated.

CANDID CAMERA

"When you least expect it / You're elected / You're the star today." Alan Funt milked hilarious results from simply filming people in situations when they thought no one was watching.

CHARLIE'S ANGELS

A brilliant TV concept: staff a standard detective show with a gorgeous trio (Farrah Fawcett, Kate Jackson, and Jaclyn Smith) in sausage-skin clothing. Producer Aaron Spelling's first megahit was also his finest hour.

CHEERS

The pluperfect pinnacle of the sitcom genre.

THE COSBY SHOW

Witty, warm, and winning, the domestic experiences of the Huxtables touted family values without sermonizing.

DATELINE

A corporate bean-counter's delight, *Dateline* proves—up to four times a week!— that a steady mix of hard-edged investigative reporting and heart-tugging human interest stories can replace more expensive and riskier sitcoms and dramas.

THE DICK VAN DYKE SHOW

For the first half of the '60s, the only place on the planet funnier than the Petrie household was Rob's office at the apocryphal *Alan Brady Show*.

DRAGNET

The show's deliberately laconic style ("Just the facts, ma'am") only underscored the gritty power of its tales of cops and miscreants.

GUNSMOKE

TV's archetypal and longest-running Western.

HILL STREET BLUES

Creator Steven Bochco spiced up his precinct house gumbo with a rich mix of characters, multi-tiered narratives, wry humor and a dash of fatalism.

THE HONEYMOONERS

The antics of a bus driver and a sewer worker in a Brooklyn tenement yielded a priceless vein of American humor. Jackie Gleason and Art Carney were sublime.

JEOPARDY!

The thinking person's game show.

L.A. LAW

A powerhouse legal drama complex, unpredictable, imaginative, and always rewarding.

THE LARRY SANDERS SHOW

This sardonic backstage tour of a talk show was TV's funniest satire, perhaps because we loved to see the medium mock itself.

LEAVE IT TO BEAVER

Took the familiar family sitcom formula of the '50s and gave it a devious adolescent twist. Show stealer: Eddie Haskell.

THE MARY TYLER MOORE SHOW

A magical confluence of concept, cast, and material made this the high-water mark of '70s television.

M*A*S*H

Hands-down, the most successful series ever spun off from a feature film.

MASTERPIECE THEATRE

From *I, Claudius* to *Upstairs, Downstairs* to *The Jewel in the Crown*, this drama anthology series remains the crown jewel in PBS's lineup.

MIAMI VICE

Against a gaudy SoFlo backdrop of neon and pastels, cute cops chase after well-armed cocaine cowboys in flashy sport scars and cigarette boats. The only reason TV has ever furnished to stay home on Friday nights.

MISSION: IMPOSSIBLE

Your mission, should you decide to accept it, is to name a better adventure series than this taut, gripping espionage exercise.

NIGHTLINE

A provident opportunity to hash out the day's big news event.

THE ODD COUPLE

Opposites amuse, but never so much as in this impeccably cast, tone-perfect comedy about a pair of mismatched, middle-aged, Manhattan neo-bachelors.

THE ROCKFORD FILES

The couch potato's choice: a sly, undemanding, endlessly entertaining delight.

ROSEANNE

An adventurous, abrasive, authentic, and always amusing examination of the struggles of a working-class family.

ROUTE 66

The first dramatic series to be shot entirely on location, this '60s cross-country odyssey of two footloose do-gooders in a Corvette put prime time on the road to more sophisticated adult fare.

ROWAN AND MARTIN'S LAUGH-IN

With zany banter, double entendres, and go-go dancers (including Goldie Hawn), this late-'60s comedy cavalcade nudged TV into the age of hipsters.

ST. ELSEWHERE

Piquant and volatile, this Jack-in-the-box drama about a lesser Boston hospital ran from intense tragedy to bawdy comedy.

SATURDAY NIGHT LIVE

In a quarter-century of wildly uneven skits and ensembles, this comedy factory has churned out an endless line of comic stars.

SEINFELD

An hermetic, exquisitely maintained comedy of contemporary urban manners and mores.

SESAME STREET

This jauntily educational PBS series for pre-schoolers is culturally diverse, inventive and altogether admirable.

77 SUNSET STRIP

The most influential of the Sputnik-era private eye series was this ultra-cool conceit which starred Efrem Zimbalist Jr. and Roger Smith as a pair of suave, college-educated judo experts.

THE SIMPSONS

You'd need a shelf full of books like this *Almanac* and a crack research staff to run down all the pop culture references in a single episode of this puckish cartoon about the post-nuclear family.

60 MINUTES

The ultimate news magazine.

THE SOPRANOS

Only on cable could you get away with this profane, violent, sexy, and satiric profile of an angst-ridden, shrink-wrapped New Jersey Mafia family man—and his dysfunctional domestic clan.

STAR TREK

This notorious cult favorite was little-honored during its original '60s run but became a rerun staple and has launched a thriving industry of spin-offs.

SURVIVOR

Not since *Gilligan's Island* have such contentious castaways been thrown together—except that cranky Rudy, salty Susan, tricky Richard and company were all real contestants in the first run of a groundbreaking game show that

may signal the end of primetime as we know it.

THIRTYSOMETHING

Though dismissed by cynics as yuppie whining, this was in fact a drama of rare pathos, complexity, and insight.

TODAY

The oldest, and in our book, the best of the matinal infotainment bandwagons.

THE TONIGHT SHOW

It's a tradition as comfortable as flannel pajamas: awaiting the sandman while watching Johnny's (and now Jay's) guests play musical chairs.

THE TWILIGHT ZONE

This spine-tingling supernatural anthology was penetrating, often profound, but above all, singularly spooky.

WALT DISNEY PRESENTS

Over four decades, under a variety of banners and working alternately for each of the three major networks, the Disney studio consistently turned out the tube's finest, most indelible family fare.

WILL & GRACE

The interplay between the neurotic title characters and their uninhibited sidekicks is so deft, it almost doesn't matter that this is network TV's first gay-themed hit sitcom. Almost.

THE X-FILES

"The truth is out there." Really out there. But week after week, this suspenseful series transforms paranormal and outright bizarre concepts into gripping, credible drama.

YOUR SHOW OF SHOWS

The apex of the variety show, this '50s favorite thrived on the versatile comedic talents of Sid Caesar and Imogene Coca and a stable of writers, including Mel Brooks, Larry Gelbart, Neil Simon, and Woody Allen.

SOME OF THE GOOD DIE YOUNG

Everyone remembers the long-running hits, but what about the quality shows that disappeared before they were old enough to walk? Of the countless shows that died after one season or less, here are 30 that PEOPLE critic Terry Kelleher misses the most.

THE ASSOCIATES
ABC, 1979
Effervescent sitcom set at a law firm. An early showcase for a major talent named Martin Short.

BEACON HILL
CBS, 1975
Derided as an expensive American imitation of *Upstairs, Downstairs,* this drama never got a chance to prove its worth.

THE BEN STILLER SHOW
FOX, 1992–93
Before he got hot on the big screen, Stiller starred in a hip half-hour sketch series with rock-bottom ratings.

THE BOB NEWHART SHOW
NBC, 1961–62
Not Newhart's first sitcom—or his second, third, or fourth. We're talking about his very first series, an acclaimed comedy-variety show that lasted just one season.

BUFFALO BILL
NBC, 1983–84
Dabney Coleman was an egotistical local TV personality in this unusually pungent sitcom. Geena Davis and Max Wright stood out in a strong supporting cast.

CALL TO GLORY
ABC, 1984–85
Craig T. Nelson starred as an Air Force officer and family man caught up in the historic events of the 1960s. Soared briefly but failed to maintain altitude.

CALUCCI'S DEPARTMENT
CBS, 1973
We still have a soft spot for this forgotten sitcom starring James Coco as the head of a New York City unemployment office. Sadly, the show got fired.

EAST SIDE, WEST SIDE
CBS, 1963–64
George C. Scott played a social worker (who later became a congressional aide) in a serious-minded drama that didn't shy away from controversial subjects.

EZ STREETS
CBS, 1996–97
Not your standard cops and crooks show, but rather a moody drama of moral ambiguity in a decaying city. In other words, it had "low ratings" written all over it.

THE FAMOUS TEDDY Z
CBS, 1989–90
Smart sitcom set at a Hollywood talent agency featured Alex Rocco's fabulous characterization of super-pushy Al Floss.

FOR THE PEOPLE
CBS, 1965
William Shatner, before *Star Trek,* starred in this classy drama about a New York City prosecutor. This line on his resume almost makes up for *T. J. Hooker.*

FRANK'S PLACE
CBS, 1987–88
Tim Reid played a New Orleans restaurateur in a low-key comedy with some serious moments and no annoying laugh track. Too few viewers sampled this delectation.

GUN
ABC, 1997
Top-notch, Robert Altman–produced anthology that followed a gun from owner to owner. Shot blanks in the ratings.

HE & SHE
CBS, 1967–68
Real-life husband and wife Richard Benjamin and Paula Prentiss were the nominal stars, but Jack Cassidy stole the show as a vain actor with a superhero complex.

THE LAW AND MR. JONES
ABC, 1960–61
Not a Hall of Fame show, really, but James Whitmore may have been the most likable lawyer in TV history.

LIFELINE
NBC, 1978
Documentary series with a strong, simple concept: Follow one doctor each week. Twenty years later, in the age of "reality" shows, it might have been a hit.

MAX HEADROOM
ABC, 1987
Heady combination of sci-fi and TV satire. Not a smash, but quite a conversation piece.

MIDDLE AGES
CBS, 1992
Peter Riegert headed a fine ensemble cast in this short-lived drama about a group of guys on the cusp of 40.

MY WORLD AND WELCOME TO IT
NBC, 1969–70
A James Thurber–like cartoonist (William Windom) had Walter Mittyish dreams depicted through animation. Maybe it was too imaginative for a mass audience.

NICHOLS
NBC, 1971–72
James Garner took a laudable gamble with this offbeat Western about a reluctant sheriff trying to keep order without carrying a gun.

THE NIGHT STALKER
ABC, 1974–75
Humor and horror combined, with Darren McGavin as a rough-around-the-edges reporter covering vampires, werewolves, and other undesirables.

NOTHING SACRED
ABC, 1997–98
An unorthodox Catholic priest (Kevin Anderson) in a poor urban parish. A good idea bravely executed. No wonder it was canceled.

POLICE SQUAD!
ABC, 1982
Yes, those successful *Naked Gun* movies with Leslie Nielsen were based on a zany comedy series that ABC axed after a handful of episodes. One of the all-time least brilliant network decisions.

PROFIT
FOX, 1996
Daring drama about a frighteningly enterprising young man (Adrian Pasdar) clawing his way toward the top of the corporate ladder.

THE RICHARD BOONE SHOW
NBC, 1963–64
Fresh from *Have Gun Will Travel*, Boone starred in an anthology series with a regular repertory company (including Harry Morgan and Robert Blake). Will someone please resurrect this concept?

SHANNON'S DEAL
NBC, 1990 and 1991
Filmmaker John Sayles created this well-crafted series about a flawed lawyer (Jamey Sheridan).

SKAG
NBC, 1980
Gutsy drama starred Karl Malden as an old-fashioned blue-collar breadwinner trying to adjust to new realities.

SQUARE PEGS
CBS, 1982–83
Enjoyably quirky sitcom about two misfit high school girls, one of whom was the delightful Sarah Jessica Parker.

TRIALS OF O'BRIEN
CBS, 1965–66
The pre-Columbo Peter Falk was a defense lawyer with a disordered personal life in this drama with a light touch. Saturday-night viewers preferred Lawrence Welk. Go figure.

A YEAR IN THE LIFE
NBC, 1987–88
Intelligent extended-family drama with the reliable Richard Kiley in the patriarch's role.

TRIVIAL TRIUMPHS

The answer: See below. The question? Who are *Celebrity Jeopardy!*'s all-time highest earners? These totals reflect the winnings donated to each celeb's charity or charities of choice. (P.S. Andy Richter won the 1999 tourney.) (Source: *Jeopardy!*)

Jerry Orbach	$34,000	Laura Innes	$24,400
Charles Shaughnessy	$31,800	Sam Waterston	$23,800
Andy Richter	$29,400	Jeff Greenfield	$23,000
Norman Schwarzkopf	$28,000	Peter Krause	$22,000
Jon Stewart	$28,000	Wallace Langham	$21,800
Kareem Abdul-Jabbar	$27,000	Gil Bellows	$21,200
Mark McEwen	$26,700	Michael McKean	$20,400
Bob Costas	$25,000	Robin Quivers	$19,500
Cheech Marin	$25,000	Jodi Applegate	$19,401
Thomas Gibson	$24,400	Jim Lampley	$19,200

HOW TO GET TICKETS TO TELEVISION SHOWS

Say what you want about television, but at least it's free (more or less). Not only that, but you can also obtain free tickets to see talk shows, game shows, and situation comedies, most of which tape in New York, Chicago, or Los Angeles. Here's how.

NEW YORK

THE DAILY SHOW

Call (212) 586-2477 or send a post-card with your name, address, phone number, and the number of tickets desired to *The Daily Show*, 513 West 54th St., New York, NY 10019. *The Daily Show* generally tapes in the evening, Monday through Thursday. You may request up to four tickets; a ticket does not guarantee admission. Any extra seats for the following week's tapings are made available on Fridays, 11:30 a.m. to 1:00 p.m., at the phone number above. You must be 18 or older to attend.

EMERIL LIVE

The Food Network conducts a ticket lottery, and sign-ups occur once or twice a year. Entry dates are posted on www.foodtv.com before each lottery period begins. To sign up, you may send an e-mail through The Food Network's Web site, www.foodtv.com Winners are picked in groups throughout the year and are informed by phone 15 to 30 days before the taping date. Food Network does not accept phone calls regarding ticket requests or the ticket lottery.

LATE NIGHT WITH CONAN O'BRIEN

Mail one postcard per show with your name, address, phone number, pre-ferred show date (optional), and number of tickets desired (max of five) to *Late Night* Tickets, c/o NBC, 30 Rockefeller Plaza, New York, NY 10112. Tickets are also available by phone request. Call (212) 664-3057 for more information. The waiting list is about four to six weeks, and the ticket office will try to accommodate specific requests. A limited number of day-of-

taping general admission and standby tickets are available Tuesday through Friday at 9:00 a.m. on the 49th Street side of the building (same address as above). Standbys are distributed one per person on a first-come–first-served basis and, like called-in tickets, do not guarantee admission. Minimum age is 16. Call (212) 664-3057 for details or (212) 664-3056 for an updated show schedule.

THE LATE SHOW WITH DAVID LETTERMAN

To request two tickets, send one (and only one) postcard with your name, address, and daytime and evening phone numbers to *Late Show* Tickets, The Ed Sullivan Theater, 1697 Broadway, New York, NY 10019. Waiting time may be in excess of nine months, and specific dates generally cannot be accommodated. Tapings are Monday through Thursday. When a reservation is cancelled within eight weeks of its show date, that seat is reassigned through *The Late Show*'s online area at www.cbs.com. The site has also run special, Web-only ticket contests. Finally, standby tickets are available on the day of the show by calling (212) 247-6497 at 11:00 a.m. The ticket recipient must have ID to match the name given when calling in. It is advised that you dress warmly as the studio is kept cold. Minimum age is 18. For more information, call (212) 975-5300, or visit www.cbs.com.

LIVE WITH REGIS

Send a postcard with your name, address, phone number, and the desired number of tickets (limit of four per request) to *Live* Tickets, Ansonia Station, P.O. Box 777, New York, NY 10023-0777. There may be a wait (up to several months) for tickets. On show days, standby numbers may be requested at 8:00 a.m. on West 67th Street and Columbus Avenue. Receiving a number does not

guarantee admission. Standbys will be seated on a first-come–first-served basis after ticketholders have been seated. Minimum age is 10. Ticket holders may be required to show ID before entering the studio, and it is suggested that you dress warmly to attend the taping, as the studio is kept cold. For more ticket and taping information, call (212) 456-3537.

THE MAURY SHOW

For ticket information and taping schedules, call the ticket line, (212) 547-8400, and leave a message, recording your name, address, and phone number. A representative will contact you. Tickets can also be reserved by postcard. Write to: *The Maury Show*, 15 Penn Plaza, New York, NY 10001. Standby tickets are available starting at 9:15 a.m. on the day of the taping at Hotel Pennsylvania, Grand Ballroom, 15 Penn Plaza, New York. To reserve by e-mail, visit: www.studiosusa.com/maury. Minimum age is 16.

THE MONTEL WILLIAMS SHOW

To request reservations up to three weeks in advance of the show date, call the ticket line at (212) 989-8101 and leave a message, recording your full name and day and evening phone numbers. Call no later than the day before the show date. To reserve via e-mail, contact tickets@montelshow.com. Whether you request tickets by phone or e-mail, a representative must speak with you to confirm dates and times of taping, which vary from show to show. To confirm reservations, call (212) 830-0364. For air date information only, call (212) 830-0300. The studio is located at 433 West 53rd St., New York, NY 10019. There is a minimum age of 17 and a dressy-casual dress code; no white shirts, black shirts, hats, sunglasses, or scarves on the head are permitted. The studio is kept cool, so dress accordingly.

QUEEN LATIFAH

Send a self-addressed, stamped envelope to Ticket Requests, P.O. Box 2656, G.P.O., New York, NY 10199. Requests may also be faxed to (917) 661-4306, or phoned in to (877) 485-7144. Web requests for the following season are taken through April at www.latifahshow.warnerbros.com/cmp/tickets.html.

RICKI LAKE

Send a postcard with your address and number of tickets (maximum of four) desired to *The Ricki Lake Show*, Ticket Office, 226 W. 26th St., 4th Fl., New York, NY 10001. To request tickets online, e-mail: tickets@ricki.com. All tickets are distributed on a first-come–first-served basis two to three weeks before the show and do not guarantee admission. Standby tickets are available at the studio (above address) one hour before taping. Minimum age is 18. For more information, call (212) 352-3322.

THE ROSIE O'DONNELL SHOW

Requests (maximum of two tickets) are accepted only during March, April, May, and June preceding the season. Send one (and only one) postcard to NBC Tickets, c/o *The Rosie O'Donnell Show*, 30 Rockefeller Plaza, New York, NY 10112. There is a twelve-month wait for tickets, and representatives cannot honor requests for specific dates. Standby tickets are available on the day of the show at the NBC Page Desk on the West 49th Street side of the studio lobby, opposite the Rockefeller Center Garage. These tickets are distributed at 8:00 a.m. but do not guarantee admission. Call (212) 664-4000 for information. Minimum age is five years old.

SALLY JESSY RAPHAEL

Send a postcard with your address and the date and number of tickets desired to *Sally Jessy Raphael* Tickets, 15 Penn Plaza, Office 2, New York, NY 10001. Tickets may also be ordered by phoning (212) 244-3595, or by logging on to www.sallyjr.com; all ticket requests must be confirmed by the show via phone or e-mail. For the truly last-minute spectator, seating at 15 Penn Plaza is often available on taping days (selected Mondays, Tuesdays, and Wednesdays); arrive by 9:15 a.m. Please be 18 or older.

SATURDAY NIGHT LIVE

To obtain tickets for next season, send one postcard with your name and address to NBC Tickets, *Saturday Night Live*, 30 Rockefeller Plaza, New York, NY 10112. NBC accepts postcards during the month of August only, and these requests will be entered into a lottery drawing. If you are selected, you will be notified by mail one to two weeks in advance that you have received two tickets to either the dress rehearsal or the live broadcast. *SNL* tapes from September to May only. It is not possible to request specific dates, but standby tickets are available on the Saturdays of original shows at 9:15 a.m.; line up at the NBC Studios' page desk in the lobby of 30 Rockefeller Plaza. Standbys are given on a first-come–first-served basis, and only one per person; they do not guarantee admission. Minimum age is 16. For more information, call (212) 664-4000. Phone reservations are not available.

THE VIEW

Tickets may be ordered by sending name, address, daytime phone, and desired date to Tickets, *The View*, 320 West 66th St., New York, NY 10023. Web users can submit requests at: abc.go.com/theview. Tickets will arrive four to six months after the request has been received. Because ticket distribution may be in excess of studio capacity, seating for ticket holders is on a first-come–first-served basis; arrive no later than 10:00 a.m. To try for last-minute seating, arrive at 320 West 66th St. before 10:00 a.m. to put

your name on the day's standby list. Minimum age is 18.

CHICAGO

THE JENNY JONES SHOW

For tickets, call (312) 836-9485 at least three weeks in advance. When calling, you must have a local Chicago phone number where you will be staying. The show is taped on Tuesday, Thursday, and Friday, at 9:45 a.m. and 1:45 p.m. If you do not have tickets, you may arrive at the studio at 9:00 a.m. on the day of taping for possible seating. The studio is located at the NBC Tower, 454 North Columbus Dr., Chicago, IL 60611. Minimum age is 18.

JERRY SPRINGER

Write to *The Jerry Springer Show* (Tickets), 454 N. Columbus Dr., 2nd Fl., Chicago, IL 60611, with your name, address, local phone number, number of tickets, and date desired, or call (312) 321-5365. Requests should be made at least one month in advance. Tickets are generally mailed out one to three weeks before the taping, and there is a minimum age of 10 required to attend. Audience members may not wear shorts and must present proper ID before entering the studio.

OPRAH

Tickets are not available by mail, but reservations to appear in the studio audience can be made by calling (312) 591-9222. These lines are often busy as soon as the caller line opens at 9:00 a.m. Central Time. Reservations are taken no more than 30 days in advance of the show. Audience members must be 18 years old or over with a photo ID. Children 16 and 17 may attend only if accompanied by a parent with birth certificate identification.

LOS ANGELES

THE LATE LATE SHOW WITH CRAIG KILBORN

Call On-Camera Audiences at (213) 833-6469 or write to them at *The Late Late Show with Craig Kilborn*, c/o On-Camera Audiences, 224 East Olive Ave., #205, Burbank, CA 91502.Tapings are Monday through Friday afternoons at CBS Television City in Los Angeles; plan to arrive by 4:30 and for the show to finish by 7:00.

POLITICALLY INCORRECT WITH BILL MAHER

Call the ticket line at (323) 575-4321 to make a reservation, or e-mail a ticket request at http://abc.go.com/pi/ns/pi_tickets.html. Tickets are available up to one month in advance. All reservations, which you must have before coming to the studio, are taken on a first-come–first-served basis. If you do not receive a confirmation call, you do not have a reservation. The studio is located at CBS Television City, 7800 Beverly Blvd., Los Angeles, CA, at the corner of Beverly and Fairfax. Arrival time is 4:00 on Monday, Tuesday, and Thursday. The studio is kept cold, so dress accordingly. Minimum age is 18.

THE TONIGHT SHOW WITH JAY LENO

Send a self-addressed, stamped envelope with the date of the show you would like to see and the number of tickets desired (maximum of four) to NBC Tickets, 3000 W. Alameda Ave., Burbank, CA 91523. Please include three alternate show dates; the more "lead time" you give, the better the chances the program can fulfill your first request. Tickets will be mailed two to three weeks before the show. On the day of tapings, tickets are available at the Burbank ticket counter off the California Street side of the studio facility. Hours are 8:00 a.m. to 5:00 p.m., Monday through Friday, but arrive early as tickets are distributed on a first-come–first-served basis and do

not guarantee admission. The minimum age to attend is 16 and photo ID is required. For recorded ticket information, taping schedules, group bookings, and directions to the Burbank, CA, studios, call NBC Studios at (818) 840-3537.

FRASIER, MOESHA, *AND MORE*

Paramount Guest Relations handles the reservations for shows such as *Frasier, Moesha, Two Guys and a Girl*, and *Dharma & Greg*. You may request tickets by calling Paramount Guest Relations at (323) 956-1777 between 9:00 a.m. and 6:00 p.m., Monday through Friday. Reservations become available five working days before each scheduled show and are taken on a first-come–first-served basis while the supply lasts. A limited number of standby tickets are available by phone but do not guarantee admission. Production schedules vary from week to week. For recorded ticket and taping information, call the Paramount Guest Relations line at (323) 956-5575.

FRIENDS *AND OTHER SERIES*

Audiences Unlimited distributes limited numbers of tickets for many of the situation comedies shot before live audiences in the Los Angeles area. They have tickets for favorites such as *Friends, Everybody Loves Raymond*, and *The Drew Carey Show*, as well as award shows, new programs like *Geena*, and programs on Nickelodeon.

For schedule information, studio locations, age restrictions, a list of shows with available tickets, and to order tickets up to 60 days in advance, call (818) 753-3470. A one-month advance show taping-filming schedule is available by calling (818) 753-3470, ext. 802, or by sending a self-addressed, stamped envelope to Audiences Unlimited, 100 Universal City Plaza, Building 153, Universal City, CA 91608. Tickets are available by mail from the same address.

Tickets may be requested on line at www.tvtickets.com up to 30 days before the show date. Your computer will print out your tickets, which will

only be activated after you leave a voice-mail at (818) 753-3470 with the name of the show, show date and time, the number of tickets, and your name.

If you are visiting Universal Studios Hollywood, you may stop by the TV ticket booth located in the Entertainment Center to get tickets for selected shows filming that week.

Tickets to some shows, such as *Friends*, are only available by mail order, and there is typically a four- to six-month wait. Tickets are limited for all shows, so include alternate choices. There is a six-ticket maximum per request.

HOW TO GET ON AUDIENCE-PARTICIPATION SHOWS

We all play along with the game shows when we watch at home, but only a few of us make it on to the air to play the games for real. Here are the wheres and hows on becoming a contestant on some of the leading shows.

JEOPARDY!

Every year, over 15,000 trivia buffs apply for some 400 contestant slots. All contestants must first pass a 50-question test. Los Angeles test dates are available from the *Jeopardy!* contestant line, (310) 244-5367, Monday through Friday, from 10:00 to 4:00. The test dates are scheduled intermittently throughout the year, so call two to three weeks prior to being in the Los Angeles area to schedule an appointment. For information about out-of-town and tournament contestant searches, watch your local *Jeopardy!* station for announcements, or keep an eye on: www.spe.sony.com/tv/shows/jeopardy. Successful test-takers are invited to play a mock version of the game. If that goes well, they may be called to be scheduled as

contestants, from one month to one year after the tryout.

To participate in the studio audience, send a self-addressed stamped envelope to *Jeopardy!* Tickets, P.O. Box 3763, Hollywood, CA 90028, or call 800-482-9840. *Jeopardy!* is generally taped Tuesdays and Wednesdays, with five shows each day.

MTV SHOWS

MTV airs several shows with audience participants, contestants, and dancers, among them *Total Request Live, Say What? Karaoke,* and the annual spring break and summertime specials. Many of these shows require auditions and/or advance reservations. MTV sets up individual audience participation hot lines for each show that will be taped. Hotline numbers are

broadcast on MTV and on local radio stations approximately one month to two weeks before each event. Information and phone numbers for individual shows are available on the MTV Web site (www.mtv.com). Shows involving extensive participation, such as *Real World* and *Road Rules,* generally require a five-minute audition video and often hold open casting calls around the country. Check the Web site at www.bunim-murray.com for further details. For more MTV casting information, call the Viewer Service Hotline at (212) 258-8700.

THE PRICE IS RIGHT

Since all of the contestants on *The Price Is Right* are selected from the audience, call the 24-hour ticket hotline number at

HI, MOM!

Once *Today* unveiled their streetside windows in 1994, visiting fans looked in while friends at home looked on. Now ever-more New York City shows air with an eye to outside crowds. Turn up at one of these programs to make a stand for your favorite stars.

Today airs weekday mornings from 7 a.m. to 9 a.m. Fans gather at West 49th Street and Rockefeller Plaza (between Fifth Avenue and Avenue of the Americas).

Good Morning, America, also airing from 7 a.m. to 9 a.m., adds to the crowd to West 44th Street and Broadway. Watchers begin arriving at 6:30; some are admitted into the studio.

The Early Show has the 7 a.m. to 9 a.m. slot on CBS. Best spot for a cameo is at Trump International Plaza, Fifth Avenue and 59th Street.

MTV's *Total Request Live*, at 1515 Broadway on West 44th Street, attracts standby hopefuls at 2:30. Many who don't get in congregate outside the second-story glass-walled studio—just watch that Times Square traffic!

(323) 575-2449 for the most up-to-date taping schedule and ticket information, or (323) 575-2458 for information about individual tickets. Tickets can be requested by sending a note specifying your preferred date and number of tickets (the maximum is ten) and a self-addressed, stamped envelope to *The Price Is Right*, 7800 Beverly Blvd., Los Angeles, CA 90036. Allow four to six weeks for a response. Tickets are also available from the ticket window at the above address starting one week prior to the date of taping up to the day before taping. The office is open from 9:00 to 5:00 on business days, except Mondays through Thursdays of taping, when it is open from 7:30 a.m. to 5:00 p.m. No tickets are available on the day of taping, but you may request a "Nonticket slip," which, like priority and standby tickets, does not guarantee admission. Priority numbers are distributed starting at 7:30 a.m. Admission to the studio is on a first-come–first-served basis for ticket holders. *The Price Is Right* is usually taped on Mondays at 1:15 and 4:30 and on Tuesdays, Wednesdays, and Thursdays at 2:30. Ticket holders are processed several hours before each taping begins for name-tag distribution, interviews, and admission to the studio. Minimum age is 18. Photo ID and a document with your Social Security number are required at the taping.

WHEEL OF FORTUNE

Los Angeles residents should send postcards including name, address, and phone number to *Wheel of Fortune*, 10202 W. Washington Blvd., Culver City, CA 90232. Candidates whose postcards are randomly selected will be given auditions, which involve a fill-in-the-blank test and a mock game. These auditions are held sporadically throughout the year. Non-Angelenos should watch for *Wheel*'s nationwide contestant searches, which are announced on your local *Wheel* station. The most up-to-date information on auditions is available by calling (213) 520-5555, Monday through Friday, from 10:00 a.m. to 6:00 p.m., Pacific Standard Time. For information on attending the show as an audience member, call (800) 482-9840.

WHO WANTS TO BE A MILLIONAIRE

To be in the audience, send a postcard to *Who Wants to Be a Millionaire*, Columbia University Station, P.O. Box 250225, New York, NY 10025. Up to four tickets per household are available on a first-come–first-served basis. Audience members must be at least 18 years old. To find contestants, *Millionaire* periodically opens phone lines which administer a timed test. Testing dates are announced during *Millionaire* broadcasts and on the show's area at ABC's Web site (abc.go.com/prime-time/millionaire). Callers will specify the show date for which they intend to qualify. Those who answer all three multipart questions correctly are eligible for the drawing for their specified show date; from each date's eligible group, forty become randomly chosen semifinalists. Semifinalists later compete in another timed phone test. The perfect scorers on this second test are entered in another random drawing, resulting in ten finalists for each show date. These finalists will appear on the program. Applicants may only take the phone test once a day, and no one under 18 may compete on the program. Further rules and regulations can be found on *Millionaire*'s Web site.

STARS WITH SOAPY ROOTS

Ricky Martin, Usher, and Sarah Michelle Gellar are just a few of the many who were big on daytime before they became bigtime. Test your soap-opera memory against our list.

Actor	Character	Soap
Richard Dean Anderson	Dr. Jeff Webber	General Hospital
Armand Assante	Dr. Mike Powers	The Doctors
Kevin Bacon	Tim Werner	Guiding Light
Alec Baldwin	Billy Allison Aldrich	The Doctors
Bonnie Bedelia	Sandy Porter	Love of Life
Tom Berenger	Timmy Siegel	One Life to Live
Corbin Bernsen	Kenny Graham	Ryan's Hope
Yasmine Bleeth	Ryan Fenelli	Ryan's Hope
Carol Burnett	Verla Grubbs	All My Children
Ellen Burstyn	Dr. Kate Bartok	The Doctors
Kate Capshaw	Jinx Avery Mallory	The Edge of Night
Tia Carrere	Jade Soong	General Hospital
Dixie Carter	Olivia Brandeis "Brandy" Henderson	The Edge of Night
Nell Carter	Ethel Green	Ryan's Hope
Gabrielle Carteris	Tracy Julian	Another World
Shaun Cassidy	Dusty Walker	General Hospital
Lacey Chabert	Bianca Montgomery	All My Children
Jill Clayburgh	Grace Bolton	Search for Tomorrow
Dabney Coleman	Dr. Tracy Brown	Bright Promise
Courteney Cox	Bunny	As the World Turns
Ted Danson	Tim Conway	Somerset
Olympia Dukakis	Barbara Moreno	Search for Tomorrow
Morgan Fairchild	Jennifer Phillips	Search for Tomorrow
Laurence Fishburne	Joshua West	One Life to Live
Faith Ford	Julia Shearer	Another World
Vivica A. Fox	Dr. Stephanie Simmons	The Young and the Restless
Morgan Freeman	Roy Bingham	Another World
Sarah Michelle Gellar	Kendall Hart	All My Children
Thomas Gibson	Samuel R. "Sam" Fowler	Another World
Kelsey Grammer	Dr. Canard	Another World
Charles Grodin	Matt Crane	The Young Marrieds
Larry Hagman	Ed Gibson	The Edge of Night
Mark Hamill	Kent Murray	General Hospital
David Hasselhoff	Bill "Snapper" Foster	The Young and the Restless
Anne Heche	Marley Hudson	Another World
Lauren Holly	Julie Chandler	All My Children
Kate Jackson	Daphne Harridge	Dark Shadows
James Earl Jones	Dr. Jim Frazier	Guiding Light

Actor	Character	Soap
Tommy Lee Jones	Dr. Mark Toland	One Life to Live
Raul Julia	Miguel Garcia	Love of Life
Kevin Kline	Woody Reed	Search for Tomorrow
Don Knotts	Wilbur Peabody	Search for Tomorrow
Téa Leoni	Lisa Di Napoli	Santa Barbara
Judith Light	Karen Martin	One Life to Live
Hal Linden	Larry Carter	Search for Tomorrow
Ray Liotta	Joey Perini	Another World
Ricky Martin	Miguel Morez	General Hospital
Marsha Mason	Judith Cole	Love of Life
Demi Moore	Jackie Templeton	General Hospital
Kate Mulgrew	Mary Ryan Fenelli	Ryan's Hope
Luke Perry	Ned Bates	Loving
Regis Philbin	Malachy Malone	Ryan's Hope
Phylicia Rashad	Courtney Wright	One Life to Live
Christopher Reeve	Benno ("Beanie" or "Ben") Harper	Love of Life
Ving Rhames	Czaja Carnek	Another World
Eric Roberts	Ted Bancroft	Another World
Meg Ryan	Betsy Stewart	As the World Turns
Pat Sajak	Kevin Hathaway	Days of Our Lives
Susan Sarandon	Sarah	Search for Tomorrow
Kyra Sedgwick	Julia Shearer	Another World
Tom Selleck	Jed Andrews	The Young and the Restless
Christian Slater	D. J. LaSalle	Ryan's Hope
Rick Springfield	Dr. Noah Drake	General Hospital
John Stamos	Blackie Parrish	General Hospital
Marisa Tomei	Marcy Thompson	As the World Turns
Janine Turner	Laura Templeton	General Hospital
Kathleen Turner	Nola Dancy Aldrich	The Doctors
Cicely Tyson	Martha Frazier	Guiding Light
Blair Underwood	Bobby Blue	One Life to Live
Usher	Raymond	The Bold and the Beautiful
Jack Wagner	Frisco Jones	General Hospital
Christopher Walken	Michael Bauer	Guiding Light
Sigourney Weaver	Avis Ryan	Somerset
Billy Dee Williams	Dr. Jim Frazier	Guiding Light
JoBeth Williams	Brandy Sheloo	Guiding Light
Robin Wright	Kelly Capwell	Santa Barbara

THE EMMY AWARDS

As the television industry has developed over the years, so has the business of television awards—so much so that the Emmys are now presented in two separate ceremonies to accommodate the growth of categories. The following presents a wide selection of winners in major areas throughout Emmy's history.

	1949	1950
Actor	—	Alan Young
Actress	—	Gertrude Berg
Drama	—	*Pulitzer Prize Playhouse*, ABC
Variety Program	—	*The Alan Young Show*, CBS
Game Show	—	*Truth or Consequences*, CBS
Children's Show	*Time for Beany*, KTLA	*Time for Beany*, KTLA

	1951	1952	1953
Actor	Sid Caesar	Thomas Mitchell	Donald O'Connor, *Colgate Comedy Hour*, NBC
Actress	Imogene Coca	Helen Hayes	Eve Arden, *Our Miss Brooks*, CBS
Drama	*Studio One*, CBS	*Robert Montgomery Presents*, NBC	*U.S. Steel Hour*, ABC
Mystery, Action, or Adventure	—	*Dragnet*, NBC	*Dragnet*, NBC
Comedy	*Red Skelton Show*, NBC	*I Love Lucy*, CBS	*I Love Lucy*, CBS
Comedian	Red Skelton, NBC	Lucille Ball, CBS; Jimmy Durante, NBC	—
Variety Program	*Your Show of Shows*, NBC	*Your Show of Shows*, NBC	*Omnibus*, CBS
Game Show	—	*What's My Line?*, CBS	*This is Your Life*, NBC; *What's My Line?*, CBS
Children's Program	—	*Time for Beany*, KTLA	*Kukla, Fran & Ollie*, NBC

	1954	1955	1956
Actor	Danny Thomas, *Make Room for Daddy*, ABC	Phil Silvers, *The Phil Silvers Show*, CBS	Robert Moss, *Father Knows Best*, NBC
Actress	Loretta Young, *The Loretta Young Show*, NBC	Lucille Ball, *I Love Lucy*, CBS	Loretta Young, *The Loretta Young Show*, NBC
Drama	*U.S. Steel Hour*, ABC	*Producers' Showcase*, NBC	*Playhouse 90*, CBS
Mystery, Action, or Adventure	*Dragnet*, NBC	*Disneyland*, ABC	—
Comedy	*Make Room for Daddy*, ABC	*The Phil Silvers Show*, CBS	—
Comedian	—	Phil Silvers, CBS; Nanette Fabray, NBC	Sid Caesar, *Caesar's Hour*, NBC; Nanette Fabray, *Caesar's Hour*, NBC
Variety Series	*Disneyland*, ABC	*The Ed Sullivan Show*, CBS	—
Game Show	*This Is Your Life*, NBC	*The $64,000 Question*, CBS	—
Children's Program	*Lassie*, CBS	*Lassie*, CBS	—

	1957	**1958–59**	**1959–60**
Drama	*Gunsmoke*, CBS	*The Alcoa Hour/Goodyear Playhouse*, NBC; *Playhouse 90*, CBS	*Playhouse 90*, CBS
Actor—Series	—	Raymond Burr, *Perry Mason*, CBS (Drama)	Robert Stack, *The Untouchables*, ABC
Actress—Series	—	Loretta Young, *The Loretta Young Show*, NBC (Drama)	Jane Wyatt, *Father Knows Best*, CBS
Supporting Actor—Series	—	Dennis Weaver, *Gunsmoke*, CBS	—
Supporting Actress—Drama Series	—	Barbara Hale, *Perry Mason*, CBS	—
Director—Drama	—	George Schaefer, *Little Moon of Aloban*, NBC; Jack Smight, *Eddie*, NBC	Robert Mulligan, *The Moon and Sixpence*, NBC
Writer—Drama	—	James Costigan, *Little Moon of Alban*, NBC; Alfred Brenner and Ken Hughes, *Eddie*, NBC	Rod Serling, *The Twilight Zone*, CBS
Comedy	*The Phil Silvers Show*, CBS	*The Jack Benny Show*, CBS	*Art Carney Special*, NBC
Actor—Comedy Series	Robert Young, *Father Knows Best*, NBC	Jack Benny, *The Jack Benny Show*, CBS	Dick Van Dyke, *The Dick Van Dyke Show*, CBS
Actress—Comedy Series	Jane Wyatt, *Father Knows Best*, NBC	Jane Wyatt, *Father Knows Best*, CBS & NBC	Jane Wyatt, *Father Knows Best*, CBS
Supporting Actor—Comedy Series	Carl Reiner, *Caesar's Hour*, NBC	Tom Poston, *The Steve Allen Show*, NBC	—
Supporting Actress—Comedy Series	Ann B. Davis, *The Bob Cummings Show*, CBS and NBC	Ann B. Davis, *The Bob Cummings Show*, NBC	—
Director—Comedy/Comedy Series	—	Peter Tewksbury, *Father Knows Best*, CBS	Ralph Levy and Bud Yorkin, *The Jack Benny Hour Specials*, CBS
Writer—Comedy/Comedy Series	Nat Hiken, Billy Friedberg, Phil Sharp, Terry Ryan, Coleman Jacoby, Arnold Rosen, Sidney Zelinko, A.J. Russell, and Tony Webster, *The Phil Silvers Show*, CBS	Sam Perrin, George Balzer, Hal Goldman, and Al Gordon, *The Jack Benny Show*, CBS	Sam Perrin, George Balzer, Hal Goldman, and Al Gordon, *The Jack Benny Show*, CBS
Variety Program	*The Dinah Shore Chevy Show*, NBC	*The Dinah Shore Chevy Show*, NBC	*The Fabulous Fifties*, CBS
Game Show	—	*What's My Line?*, CBS	—
Children's Program	—	—	*Huckleberry Hound*, SYN

	1960–61	1961–62	1962–63
Actor	Raymond Burr, *Perry Mason*, CBS	E.G. Marshall, *The Defenders*, CBS	E.G. Marshall, *The Defenders*, CBS
Actress	Barbara Stanwyck, *The Barbara Stanwyck Show*, NBC	Shirley Booth, *Hazel*, NBC	Shirley Booth, *Hazel*, NBC
Drama	*Macbeth*, NBC	*The Defenders*, CBS	*The Defenders*, CBS
Director—Drama	George Schaefer, *Macbeth*, NBC	Franklin Schaffner, *The Defenders*, CBS	Stuart Rosenberg, *The Defenders*, CBS
Writer—Drama	Rod Serling, *The Twilight Zone*, CBS	Reginald Rose, *The Defenders*, CBS	Robert Thorn, Reginald Rose, *The Defenders*, CBS
Comedy	*The Jack Benny Show*, CBS	*The Bob Newhart Show*, NBC	*The Dick Van Dyke Show*, CBS
Director—Comedy	Sheldon Leonard, *The Danny Thomas Show*, CBS	Nat Hiken, *Car 54, Where Are You?*, NBC	John Rich, *The Dick Van Dyke Show*, CBS
Writer—Comedy	Sherwood Schwartz, Dave O'Brien, Al Schwartz, Martin Ragaway, and Red Skelton, *The Red Skelton Show*, CBS	Carl Reiner, *The Dick Van Dyke Show*, CBS	Carl Reiner, *The Dick Van Dyke Show*, CBS
Variety Program	*Astaire Time*, NBC	*The Garry Moore Show*, CBS	*The Andy Williams Show*, NBC
Individual Performance—Variety or Music Program/Series	Fred Astaire, *Astaire Time*, NBC	Carol Burnett, *The Garry Moore Show*, CBS	Carol Burnett, *Julie and Carol at Carnegie Hall*, CBS; *Carol and Company*, CBS
Panel, Quiz or Audience Participation	—	—	*College Bowl*, CBS
Children's Program	*Young People's Concert: Aaron Copland's Birthday Party*, CBS	*New York Philharmonic Young People's Concerts with Leonard Bernstein*, CBS	*Walt Disney's Wonderful World of Color*, NBC

THE RATINGS CONNECTION

Having the No. 1 rated show for a season doesn't necessarily guarantee Emmy success…or does it? Here is a list of the No. 1 shows that have also won the top honors—along with those that have achieved the dubious distinction of winning the ratings race but losing the Emmy battle.

EMMY WINNERS
Texaco Star Theatre
I Love Lucy
The $64,000 Question
Gunsmoke
Rowan and Martin's Laugh-In
All in the Family
60 Minutes
The Cosby Show
Cheers
Seinfeld
ER

EMMY LOSERS
Arthur Godfrey's Talent Scouts
Wagon Train
The Beverly Hillbillies
Bonanza
The Andy Griffith Show
Marcus Welby, M.D.
Happy Days
Laverne and Shirley
Three's Company
Dallas
Dynasty
Roseanne
Home Improvement

	1963–64	**1964–65**	**1965–66**
Drama	*The Defenders*, CBS	In 1964–65 the entire award system was changed for one year, and there were no awards given in individual categories that in any way match the categories from other years.	*The Fugitive*, ABC
Actor—Drama Series	Jack Klugman, *The Defenders*, CBS		Bill Cosby, *I Spy*, NBC
Actress—Drama Series	Shelley Winters, *Two Is The Number*, NBC		Barbara Stanwyck, *The Big Valley*, ABC
Supporting Actor—Drama Series	Albert Parker, *One Day In The Life of Ivan Denisovich*, NBC	—	James Daly, *Eagle in a Cage*, NBC
Supporting Actress—Drama Series	Ruth White, *Little Moon of Alban*, NBC	—	Lee Grant, *Peyton Place*, ABC
Writer—Drama	Ernest Kinay, *The Defenders*, CBS	—	Sydney Pollack, *The Game*, NBC
Director—Drama	Tom Gries, *East Side/West Side*, CBS	—	Millard Lampell, *Eagle in a Cage*, NBC
Comedy	*The Dick Van Dyke Show*, CBS	—	*The Dick Van Dyke Show*, CBS
Actor—Comedy Series	Dick Van Dyke, *The Dick Van Dyke Show*, CBS	—	Dick Van Dyke, *The Dick Van Dyke Show*, CBS
Actress—Comedy Series	Mary Tyler Moore, *The Dick Van Dyke Show*, CBS	—	Mary Tyler Moore, *The Dick Van Dyke Show*, CBS
Supporting Actor—Comedy Series	—	—	Don Knotts, *The Andy Griffith Show*, CBS
Supp. Actress—Comedy Series	—	—	Alice Pearce, *Bewitched*, ABC
Director—Comedy	Jerry Paris, *The Dick Van Dyke Show*, CBS	—	William Asher, *Bewitched*, ABC
Writer—Comedy	Carl Reiner, Sam Denoff, and Bill Penky, *The Dick Van Dyke Show*, CBS	—	Bill Persky, Sam Denoff, *The Dick Van Dyke Show*, CBS
Variety Program	*The Danny Kaye Show*, CBS	—	*The Andy Williams Show*, NBC
Director—Variety or Music	Robert Scheerer, *The Danny Kaye Show*, CBS	—	Alan Handley, *The Julie Andrews Show*, NBC
Writer—Variety	—	—	Al Gordon, Hal Goldman, and Sheldon Keller, *An Evening with Carol Channing*, CBS
Children's Program	*Discovery '63-'64*, ABC	—	*A Charlie Brown Christmas*, CBS

WINNING TEAMS

Looking for a rare wedding gift? Consider his-and-hers Emmies: Only seven married couples have ever sported matching trophies. One duo, *St. Elsewhere*'s Daniels and Bartlett, won for playing a husband and wife onscreen.

Hume Cronyn & Jessica Tandy
William Daniels & Bonnie Bartlett
Danny DeVito & Rhea Perlman
Phil Donahue & Marlo Thomas
Alfred Lunt & Lynn Fontanne
George C. Scott & Colleen Dewhurst
Christine Lahti & Thomas Schlamme

	1966–67	1967–68	1968–69
Drama Series	*Mission: Impossible,* CBS	*Mission: Impossible,* CBS	*NET Playhouse,* NET
Actor—Drama Series	Bill Cosby, *I Spy,* NBC	Bill Cosby, *I Spy,* NBC	Carl Betz, *Judd, for the Defense,* ABC
Actress—Drama Series	Barbara Bain, *Mission: Impossible,* CBS	Barbara Bain, *Mission: Impossible,* CBS	Barbara Bain, *Mission: Impossible,* CBS
Supporting Actor—Drama	Eli Wallach, *The Poppy Is Also a Flower,* ABC	Milburn Stone, *Gunsmoke,* CBS	—
Supporting Actress—Drama	Agnes Moorehead, *The Wild, Wild West,* CBS	Barbara Anderson, *Ironside,* NBC	Susan Saint James, *The Name of the Game,* NBC
Director—Drama	Alex Segal, *Death of a Salesman,* CBS	Paul Bogart, *Dear Friends,* CBS	David Green, *The People Next Door,* CBS
Writer—Drama	Bruce Geller, *Mission: Impossible,* CBS	Loring Mandel, *Do Not Go Gentle into That Good Night,* CBS	J. P. Miller, *The People Next Door,* CBS
Comedy	*The Monkees,* NBC	*Get Smart,* NBC	*Get Smart,* NBC
Actor—Comedy Series	Don Adams, *Get Smart,* NBC	Don Adams, *Get Smart,* NBC	Don Adams, *Get Smart,* NBC
Actress—Comedy Series	Lucille Ball, *The Lucy Show,* CBS	Lucille Ball, *The Lucy Show,* CBS	Hope Lange, *The Ghost and Mrs. Muir,* NBC
Supporting Actor—Comedy Series	Don Knotts, *The Andy Griffith Show,* CBS	Werner Klemperer, *Hogan's Heroes,* CBS	Werner Klemperer, *Hogan's Heroes,* CBS
Supporting Actress—Comedy Series	Frances Bavier, *The Andy Griffith Show,* CBS	Marion Lorne, *Bewitched,* ABC	—
Director—Comedy/Comedy Series	James Frawley, *The Monkees,* NBC	Bruce Bilson, *Get Smart,* NBC	—
Writer—Comedy/Comedy Series	Buck Henry and Leonard Stern, *Get Smart,* NBC	Allan Burns and Chris Hayward, *He and She,* CBS	Alan Blye, Bob Einstein, Murray Roman, Carl Gottlieb, Jerry Music, Steve Martin, Cecil Tuck, Paul Wayne, Cy Howard, and Mason Williams, *The Smothers Brothers Comedy Hour,* CBS
Variety Program	*The Andy Williams Show,* NBC	*Rowan and Martin's Laugh-In,* NBC	*Rowan and Martin's Laugh-In,* NBC
Director—Variety or Music	Fielder Cook, *Brigadoon,* ABC	Jack Haley, Jr., *Movin' with Nancy,* NBC	—
Writer—Variety or Music	Mel Brooks, Sam Denoff, Bill Persky, Carl Reiner, and Mel Tolkin, *The Sid Caesar, Imogene Coca, Carl Reiner, Howard Morris Special,* CBS	Chris Beard, Phil Hahn, Jack Hanrahan, Coslough Johnson, Paul Keyes, Marc London, Allan Manings, David Panich, Hugh Wedlock, and Digby Wolfe, *Rowan and Martin's Laugh-In,* NBC	—
Children's Program	*Jack and the Beanstalk,* NBC	—	—

	1969–70	1970–71	1971–72
Drama	Marcus Welby, M.D., ABC	The Bold Ones: The Senator, NBC	Elizabeth R, PBS
Actor—Drama Series	Robert Young, Marcus Welby, M.D., ABC	Hal Holbrook, The Bold Ones: The Senator, NBC	Peter Falk, Columbo, NBC
Actress—Drama Series	Susan Hampshire, The Forsyte Saga, NET	Susan Hampshire, The First Churchills, PBS	Glenda Jackson, Elizabeth R., PBS
Supporting Actor—Drama Series	James Brolin, Marcus Welby, M.D., ABC	David Burns, The Price, NBC	Jack Warden, Brian's Song, ABC
Supporting Actress—Drama Series	Gail Fisher, Mannix, CBS	Margaret Leighton, Hamlet, NBC	Jenny Agutter, The Snow Goose, NBC
Director—Drama Series	—	Daryl Duke, The Bold Ones: The Senator, NBC	Alexander Singer, The Bold Ones: The Lawyers, NBC
Writer—Drama	Richard Levinson and William Link, My Sweet Charlie, NBC	Joel Oliansky, The Bold Ones: The Senator, NBC	Richard L. Levinson and William Link, Columbo, NBC
Comedy	My World and Welcome to It, NBC	All in the Family, CBS	All in the Family, CBS
Actor—Comedy Series	William Windom, My World and Welcome to It, NBC	Jack Klugman, The Odd Couple, ABC	Carroll O'Connor, All in the Family, CBS
Actress—Comedy Series	Hope Lange, The Ghost and Mrs. Muir, ABC	Jean Stapleton, All in the Family, CBS	Jean Stapleton, All in the Family, CBS
Supporting Actor—Comedy Series	Michael Constantine, Room 222, ABC	Edward Asner, The Mary Tyler Moore Show, CBS	Edward Asner, The Mary Tyler Moore Show, CBS
Supporting Actress—Comedy Series	Karen Valentine, Room 222, ABC	Valerie Harper, The Mary Tyler Moore Show, CBS	Valerie Harper, The Mary Tyler Moore Show, CBS; Sally Struthers, All in the Family, CBS
Director—Comedy Series	—	Jay Sandrich, The Mary Tyler Moore Show, CBS	John Rich, All in the Family, CBS
Writer—Comedy Series	—	James L. Brooks and Allan Burns, The Mary Tyler Moore Show, CBS	Burt Styler, All in the Family, CBS
Drama/Comedy Special	—	—	Brian's Song, ABC
Variety or Music Series	The David Frost Show, SYN	The David Frost Show, SYN (Talk); The Flip Wilson Show, NBC (Music)	The Dick Cavett Show, ABC (Talk), The Carol Burnett Show, CBS (Music)
Director—Variety or Music	—	Mark Warren, Rowan and Martin's Laugh-In, NBC	Art Fisher, The Sonny & Cher Comedy Hour, CBS
Writer—Variety or Music	—	Herbert Baker, Hal Goodman, Larry Klein, Bob Weiskopf, Bob Schiller, Norman Steinberg, and Flip Wilson, The Flip Wilson Show, NBC	Don Hinkley, Stan Hart, Larry Siegel, Woody Kling, Roger Beatty, Art Baer, Ben Joelson, Stan Burns, Mike Marmer, and Arnie Rosen, The Carol Burnett Show, CBS
Daytime Drama Series	—	—	The Doctors, NBC
Children's Program	Sesame Street, NET	Sesame Street, PBS	Sesame Street, PBS

	1972–73	1973–74	1974–75
Drama	*The Waltons*, CBS	*Upstairs, Downstairs*, PBS	*Upstairs, Downstairs*, PBS
Actor—Drama Series	Richard Thomas, *The Waltons*, CBS	Telly Savalas, *Kojak*, CBS	Robert Blake, *Baretta*, ABC
Actress—Drama Series	Michael Learned, *The Waltons*, CBS	Michael Learned, *The Waltons*, CBS	Jean Marsh, *Upstairs, Downstairs*, PBS
Supporting Actor—Drama/Drama Series	Scott Jacoby, *That Certain Summer*, ABC	Michael Moriarty, *The Glass Menagerie*, ABC	Will Geer, *The Waltons*, CBS
Supporting Actress—Drama/Drama Series	Ellen Corby, *The Waltons*, CBS	Joanna Miles, *The Glass Menagerie*, ABC	Ellen Corby, *The Waltons*, CBS
Director—Drama	Joseph Sargent, *The Marcus Nelson Murders*, CBS	John Korty, *The Autobiography of Miss Jane Pittman*, CBS	George Cukor, *Love Among the Ruins*, ABC
Director—Drama Series	Jerry Thorpe, *Kung Fu*, ABC	Robert Butler, *The Blue Knight*, NBC	Bill Bain, *Upstairs, Downstairs*, PBS
Writer—Drama Series	John McGreevey, *The Waltons*, CBS	Joanna Lee, *The Waltons*, CBS	Howard Fast, *Benjamin Franklin*, CBS
Comedy	*All in the Family*, CBS	*M*A*S*H*, CBS	*The Mary Tyler Moore Show*, CBS
Actor—Comedy Series	Jack Klugman, *The Odd Couple*, ABC	Alan Alda, *M*A*S*H*, CBS	Tony Randall, *The Odd Couple*, ABC
Actress—Comedy Series	Mary Tyler Moore, *The Mary Tyler Moore Show*, CBS	Mary Tyler Moore, *The Mary Tyler Moore Show*, CBS	Valerie Harper, *Rhoda*, CBS
Supporting Actor—Comedy Series	Ted Knight, *The Mary Tyler Moore Show*, CBS	Rob Reiner, *All in the Family*, CBS	Ed Asner, *The Mary Tyler Moore Show*, CBS
Supporting Actress—Comedy Series	Valerie Harper, *The Mary Tyler Moore Show*, CBS	Cloris Leachman, *The Mary Tyler Moore Show*, CBS	Betty White, *The Mary Tyler Moore Show*, CBS
Director—Comedy Series	Jay Sandrich, *The Mary Tyler Moore Show*, CBS	Jackie Cooper, *M*A*S*H*, CBS	Gene Reynolds, *M*A*S*H*, CBS
Writer—Comedy Series	Michael Ross, Bernie West, and Lee Kalcheim, *All in the Family*, CBS	Treva Silverman, *The Mary Tyler Moore Show*, CBS	Ed. Weinberger and Stan Daniels, *The Mary Tyler Moore Show*, CBS
Drama/Comedy Special	*A War of Children*, CBS	*The Autobiography of Miss Jane Pittman*, CBS	
Variety Series	*The Julie Andrews Hour*, ABC	*The Carol Burnett Show*, CBS	*The Carol Burnett Show*, CBS
Director—Variety or Music	Bill Davis, *The Julie Andrews Hour*, ABC	Dave Powers, *The Carol Burnett Show*, CBS	Dave Powers, *The Carol Burnett Show*, CBS

	1972–73	**1973–74**	**1974–75**
Writer—Variety or Music Series	Stan Hart, Larry Siegel, Gail Parent, Woody Kling, Roger Beatty, Tom Patchett, Jay Tarses, Robert Hilliard, Arnie Kogen, Bill Angelos, and Buz Kohan, *The Carol Burnett Show*, CBS	Ed Simmons, Gary Belkin, Roger Beatty, Arnie Kogen, Bill Richmond, Gene Perret, Rudy De Luca, Barry Levinson, Dick Clair, Jenna McMahon, and Barry Harman, *The Carol Burnett Show*, CBS	Ed Simmons, Gary Belkin, Roger Beatty, Arnie Kogen, Bill Richmond, Gene Perret, Rudy De Luca, Barry Levinson, Dick Clair, and Jenna McMahon, *The Carol Burnett Show*, CBS
Variety, Music, or Comedy Special	*Singer Presents Liza with a "Z,"* CBS	*Lily Tomlin*, CBS	*An Evening with John Denver*, ABC
Miniseries/Limited Series	*Tom Brown's Schooldays*, PBS	*Columbo*, NBC	*Benjamin Franklin*, CBS
Actor—Miniseries/Limited Series	Anthony Murphy, *Tom Brown's Schooldays*, PBS	William Holden, *The Blue Knight*, NBC	Peter Falk, *Columbo*, NBC
Actress—Miniseries/Limited Series	Susan Hampshire, *Vanity Fair*, PBS	Mildred Natwick, *The Snoop Sisters*, NBC	Jessica Walter, *Amy Prentiss*, NBC
Daytime Drama Series	*The Edge of Night*, CBS	*The Doctors*, NBC	*The Young and the Restless*, CBS
Actor—Daytime Drama Series	—	Macdonald Carey, *Days of Our Lives*, NBC	Macdonald Carey, *Days of Our Lives*, NBC
Actress—Daytime Drama Series	—	Elizabeth Hubbard, *The Doctors*, NBC	Susan Flannery, *Days of Our Lives*, NBC
Host—Game Show	—	Peter Marshall, *The Hollywood Squares*, NBC	Peter Marshall, *The Hollywood Squares*, NBC
Host—Talk or Service	—	Dinah Shore, *Dinah's Place*, NBC	Barbara Walters, *Today*, NBC
Game Show	—	*Password*, ABC	*Hollywood Squares*, NBC
Talk, Service or Variety Series	—	*The Merv Griffin Show*, SYN	*Dinah!*, SYN
Children's Special	—	*Marlo Thomas and Friends in Free To Be...You and Me*, ABC	*Yes, Virginia, There Is a Santa Claus*, ABC
Children's Entertainment Series	—	*Zoom*, PBS	*Star Trek*, NBC

	1975–76	**1976–77**	**1977–78**
Drama	*Police Story*, NBC	*Upstairs, Downstairs*, PBS	*The Rockford Files*, NBC
Actor—Drama Series	Peter Falk, *Columbo*, NBC	James Garner, *The Rockford Files*, NBC	Edward Asner, *Lou Grant*, CBS
Actress—Drama Series	Michael Learned, *The Waltons*, CBS	Lindsay Wagner, *The Bionic Woman*, ABC	Sada Thompson, *Family*, ABC
Supporting Actor—Drama Series	Anthony Zerbe, *Harry-O*, ABC	Gary Frank, *Family*, ABC	Robert Vaughn, *Washington: Behind Closed Doors*, ABC
Supp. Actress—Drama Series	Ellen Corby, *The Waltons*, CBS	Kristy McNichol, *Family*, ABC	Nancy Marchand, *Lou Grant*, CBS
Director—Drama Series	David Greene, *Rich Man, Poor Man*, ABC	David Greene, *Roots*, ABC	Marvin J. Chomsky, *Holocaust*, NBC
Writer—Drama Series	Sherman Yellen, *The Adams Chronicles*, PBS	Ernest Kinoy and William Blinn, *Roots*, ABC	Gerald Green, *Holocaust*, NBC
Comedy	*The Mary Tyler Moore Show*, CBS	*The Mary Tyler Moore Show*, CBS	*All in the Family*, CBS
Actor—Comedy Series	Jack Albertson, *Chico and the Man*, NBC	Carroll O'Connor, *All in the Family*, CBS	Carroll O'Connor, *All in the Family*, CBS
Actress—Comedy Series	Mary Tyler Moore, *The Mary Tyler Moore Show*, CBS	Beatrice Arthur, *Maude*, CBS	Jean Stapleton, *All in the Family*, CBS

	1975–76	**1976–77**	**1977–78**
Supporting Actor—Comedy Series	Ted Knight, *The Mary Tyler Moore Show*, CBS	Gary Burghoff, *M*A*S*H*, CBS	Rob Reiner, *All in the Family*, CBS
Supporting Actress—Comedy Series	Betty White, *The Mary Tyler Moore Show*, CBS	Mary Kay Place, *Mary Hartman, Mary Hartman*, SYN	Julie Kavner, *Rhoda*, CBS
Director—Comedy/ Comedy Series	Gene Reynolds, *M*A*S*H*, CBS	Alan Alda, *M*A*S*H*, CBS	Paul Bogart, *All in the Family*, CBS
Writer— Comedy Series	David Lloyd, *The Mary Tyler Moore Show*, CBS	Allan Burns, James L. Brooks, Ed. Weinberger, Stan Daniels, David Lloyd, and Bob Ellison, *The Mary Tyler Moore Show*, CBS	Bob Weiskopf and Bob Schiller (Teleplay); Barry Harman and Harve Brosten (Story), *All in the Family*, CBS
Drama/Comedy Special	*Eleanor and Franklin*, ABC	*Eleanor and Franklin: The White House Years*, ABC	ABC
Variety Series	*NBC's Saturday Night*, NBC	*Van Dyke and Company*, NBC	*The Muppet Show*, SYN
Limited Series	*Upstairs, Downstairs*, PBS	*Roots*, ABC	*Holocaust*, NBC
Actor— Limited Series	Hal Holbrook, *Sandburg's Lincoln*, NBC	Christopher Plummer, *The Moneychangers*, NBC	Michael Moriarty, *Holocaust*, NBC
Actress— Limited Series	Rosemary Harris, *Notorious Women*, PBS	Patty Duke Astin, *Captains and the Kings*, NBC	Meryl Streep, *Holocaust*, NBC
Daytime Drama Series	*Another World*, NBC	*Ryan's Hope*, ABC	*Days of Our Lives*, NBC
Actor—Daytime Drama Series	Larry Haines, *Search for Tomorrow*, CBS	Val Dufour, *Search for Tomorrow*, CBS	James Pritchett, *The Doctors*, NBC
Actress—Daytime Drama Series	Helen Gallagher, *Ryan's Hope*, ABC	Helen Gallagher, *Ryan's Hope*, ABC	Laurie Heinemann, *Another World*, NBC
Host—Game Show	Allen Ludden, *Password*, ABC	Bert Convy, *Tattletales*, CBS	Richard Dawson, *Family Feud*, ABC
Host—Talk or Service Series	Dinah Shore, *Dinah!*, SYN	Phil Donahue, *Donahue*, SYN	Phil Donahue, *Donahue*, SYN
Game Show	*The $20,000 Pyramid*, ABC	*Family Feud*, ABC	*The Hollywood Squares*, NBC
Talk, Service or Variety Series	*Dinah!*, SYN	*The Merv Griffin Show*, SYN	*Donahue*, SYN
Children's Entertainment Series	*Big Blue Marble*, SYN	*Zoom*, PBS	*Captain Kangaroo*, CBS

	1978–79	1979–80	1980–81
Drama	*Lou Grant*, CBS	*Lou Grant*, CBS	*Hill Street Blues*, NBC
Actor—Drama Series	Ron Leibman, *Kaz*, CBS	Ed Asner, *Lou Grant*, CBS	Daniel J. Travanti, *Hill Street Blues*, NBC
Actress—Drama Series	Mariette Hartley, *The Incredible Hulk*, CBS	Barbara Bel Geddes, *Dallas*, CBS	Barbara Babcock, *Hill Street Blues*, NBC
Supporting Actor—Drama Series	Stuart Margolin, *The Rockford Files*, NBC	Stuart Margolin, *The Rockford Files*, NBC	Michael Conrad, *Hill Street Blues*, NBC
Supporting Actress—Drama Series	Kristy McNichol, *Family*, ABC	Nancy Marchand, *Lou Grant*, CBS	Nancy Marchand, *Lou Grant*, CBS
Director—Drama Series	Jackie Cooper, *The White Shadow*, CBS	Roger Young, *Lou Grant*, CBS	Robert Butler, *Hill Street Blues*, NBC
Writer—Drama Series	Michele Gallery, *Lou Grant*, CBS	Seth Freeman, *Lou Grant*, CBS	Michael Kozoll and Steven Bochco, *Hill Street Blues*, NBC
Comedy	*Taxi*, ABC	*Taxi*, ABC	*Taxi*, ABC
Actor—Comedy Series	Carroll O'Connor, *All in the Family*, CBS	Richard Mulligan, *Soap*, ABC	Judd Hirsch, *Taxi*, ABC
Actress—Comedy Series	Ruth Gordon, *Taxi*, ABC	Cathryn Damon, *Soap*, ABC	Isabel Sanford, *The Jeffersons*, CBS
Supporting Actor—Comedy Series	Robert Guillaume, *Soap*, ABC	Harry Morgan, *M*A*S*H*, CBS	Danny De Vito, *Taxi*, ABC
Supporting Actress—Comedy Series	Sally Struthers, *All in the Family*, CBS	Loretta Swit, *M*A*S*H*, CBS	Eileen Brennan, *Private Benjamin*, CBS
Director—Comedy Series	Noam Pitlik, *Barney Miller*, ABC	James Burrows, *Taxi*, ABC	James Burrows, *Taxi*, ABC
Writer—Comedy Series	Alan Alda, *M*A*S*H*, CBS	Bob Colleary, *Barney Miller*, ABC	Michael Leeson, *Taxi*, ABC
Drama/Comedy Special	*Friendly Fire*, ABC	*The Miracle Worker*, NBC	*Playing for Time*, CBS
Variety Program	*Steve & Eydie Celebrate Irving Berlin*, NBC	*Baryshnikov on Broadway*, ABC	*Lily: Sold Out*, CBS
Director—Variety or Music	—	Dwight Hemion, *Baryshnikov on Broadway*, ABC	Don Mischer, *The Kennedy Center Honors: A National Celebration of the Performing Arts*, CBS

	1978–79	1979–80	1980–81
Writer—Variety or Music	—	Buz Kohan, *Shirley MacLaine... Every Little Movement*, CBS	Jerry Juhl, David Odell, Chris Langham, *The Muppet Show*, SYN
Limited Series	*Roots: The Next Generations*, ABC	*Edward & Mrs. Simpson*, SYN	*Shogun*, NBC
Actor—Limited Series	Peter Strauss, *The Jericho Mile*, ABC	Powers Boothe, *Guyana Tragedy: The Story of Jim Jones*, CBS	Anthony Hopkins, *The Bunker*, CBS
Actress—Limited Series	Bette Davis, *Strangers: The Story of a Mother and Daughter*, CBS	Patty Duke Astin, *The Miracle Worker*, NBC	Vanessa Redgrave, *Playing for Time*, CBS
Supporting Actor—Limited Series or Special	Marlon Brando, *Roots: The Next Generations*, ABC	George Grizzard, *The Oldest Living Graduate*, NBC	David Warner, *Masada*, ABC
Supporting Actress—Limited Series or Special	Esther Rolle, *Summer of My German Soldier*, NBC	Mare Winningham, *Amber Waves*, ABC	Jane Alexander, *Playing for Time*, CBS
Director—Limited Series or Special	David Greene, *Friendly Fire*, ABC	Marvin J. Chomsky, *Attica*, ABC	James Goldstone, *Kent State*, NBC
Writer—Limited Series or Special	Patrick Nolan and Michael Mann, *The Jericho Mile*, ABC	David Chase, *Off the Minnesota Strip*, ABC	Arthur Miller, *Playing for Time*, CBS
Daytime Drama Series	*Ryan's Hope*, ABC	*Guiding Light*, CBS	*General Hospital*, ABC
Actor—Daytime Drama Series	Al Freeman, Jr., *One Life to Live*, ABC	Douglass Watson, *Another World*, NBC	Douglass Watson, *Another World*, NBC
Actress—Daytime Drama Series	Irene Dailey, *Another World*, NBC	Judith Light, *One Life to Live*, ABC	Judith Light, *One Life to Live*, ABC
Supporting Actor—Daytime Drama Series	Peter Hansen, *General Hospital*, ABC	Warren Burton, *All My Children*, ABC	Larry Haines, *Search for Tomorrow*, CBS
Supporting Actress—Daytime Drama Series	Suzanne Rogers, *Days of Our Lives*, NBC	Francesca James, *All My Children*, ABC	Jane Elliot, *General Hospital*, ABC
Host—Game Show	Dick Clark, *The $20,000 Pyramid*, ABC	Peter Marshall, *The Hollywood Squares*, NBC	Peter Marshall, *The Hollywood Squares*, NBC
Host—Talk or Service	Phil Donahue, *Donahue*, SYN	Phil Donahue, *Donahue*, SYN	Hugh Downs, *Over Easy*, PBS
Game Show	*The Hollywood Squares*, NBC	*The Hollywood Squares*, NBC; *The $20,000 Pyramid*, ABC	*The $20,000 Pyramid*, ABC
Talk, Service or Variety Series	*Donahue*, SYN	*Donahue*, SYN	*Donahue*, SYN
Children's Special	*Christmas Eve on Sesame Street*, PBS	—	*Donahue and Kids*, NBC
Children's Entertainment Series	*Kids Are People Too*, ABC	*Hot Hero Sandwich*, NBC	*Captain Kangaroo*, CBS

	1981–82	1982–83	1983–84
Drama	*Hill Street Blues,* NBC	*Hill Street Blues,* NBC	*Hill Street Blues,* NBC
Actor—Drama Series	Daniel J. Travanti, *Hill Street Blues,* NBC	Ed Flanders, *St. Elsewhere,* NBC	Tom Selleck, *Magnum, P.I.,* CBS
Actress—Drama Series	Michael Learned, *Nurse,* CBS	Tyne Daly, *Cagney & Lacey,* CBS	Tyne Daly, *Cagney & Lacey,* CBS
Supporting Actor—Drama Series	Michael Conrad, *Hill Street Blues,* NBC	James Coco, *St. Elsewhere,* NBC	Bruce Weitz, *Hill Street Blues,* NBC
Supporting Actress—Drama Series	Nancy Marchand, *Lou Grant,* CBS	Doris Roberts, *St. Elsewhere,* NBC	Alfre Woodard, *Hill Street Blues,* NBC
Director—Drama Series	Harry Harris, *Fame,* NBC	Jeff Bleckner, *Hill Street Blues,* NBC	Corey Allen, *Hill Street Blues,* NBC
Writer—Drama Series	Steven Bochco, Anthony Yerkovich, Jeffrey Lewis and Michael Wagner (Teleplay); Michael Kozoll, and Steven Bochco (Story), *Hill Street Blues,* NBC	David Milch, *Hill Street Blues,* NBC	John Ford Noonan (Teleplay); John Masius and Tom Fontana (Story), *St. Elsewhere,* NBC
Comedy	*Barney Miller,* ABC	*Cheers,* NBC	*Cheers,* NBC
Actor—Comedy Series	Alan Alda, *M*A*S*H,* CBS	Judd Hirsch, *Taxi,* NBC	John Ritter, *Three's Company,* ABC
Actress—Comedy Series	Carol Kane, *Taxi,* ABC	Shelley Long, *Cheers,* NBC	Jane Curtin, *Kate & Allie,* CBS
Supporting Actor—Comedy Series	Christopher Lloyd, *Taxi,* ABC	Christopher Lloyd, *Taxi,* NBC	Pat Harrington, Jr., *One Day at a Time,* CBS
Supp. Actress—Comedy Series	Loretta Swit, *M*A*S*H,* CBS	Carol Kane, *Taxi,* NBC	Rhea Perlman, *Cheers,* NBC
Director—Comedy Series	Alan Rafkin, *One Day at a Time,* CBS	James Burrows, *Cheers,* NBC	Bill Persky, *Kate & Allie,* CBS
Writer—Comedy Series	Ken Estin, *Taxi,* ABC	Glen Charles, Les Charles, *Cheers,* NBC	David Angel, *Cheers,* NBC
Drama/Comedy Special	*A Woman Called Golda,* SYN	*Special Bulletin,* NBC	*Something About Amelia,* ABC
Variety, Music, or Comedy Program	*Night of 100 Stars,* ABC	*Motown 25: Yesterday, Today, Forever,* NBC	*The 6th Annual Kennedy Center Honors: A Celebration of the Performing Arts,* CBS
Individual Performance—Variety or Music Program	—	Leontyne Price, *Live From Lincoln Center: Leontyne Price, Zubin Mehta, and the New York Philharmonic,* PBS	Cloris Leachman, *Screen Actors Guild 50th Anniversary Celebration,* CBS
Director—Variety or Music	Dwight Hemion, *Goldie and Kids Listen to Us,* ABC	Dwight Hemion, *Sheena Easton Act I,* NBC	Dwight Hemion, *Here's Television Entertainment,* NBC
Writer—Variety or Music	John Candy, Joe Flaherty, Eugene Levy, Andrea Martin, Rick Moranis, Catherine O'Hara, Dave Thomas, Dick Blasucci, Paul Flaherty, Bob Dolman, John McAndrew, Doug Steckler, M. Bert Rich, Jeffrey Barron, Michael Short, Chris Cluess, Stuart Kreisman, and Brian McConnachie, *SCTV Comedy Network,* NBC	John Candy, Joe Flaherty, Eugene Levy, Andrea Martin, Martin Short, Dick Blasucci, Paul Flaherty, John McAndrew, Doug Steckler, Bob Dolman, Michael Short, and Mary Charlotte Wilcox, *SCTV Network,* NBC	Steve O'Donnell, Gerard Mulligan, Sanford Frank, Joseph E. Toplyn, Christopher Elliott, Matt Wickline, Jeff Martin, Ted Greenberg, David Yazbek, Merrill Markoe, and David Letterman, *Late Night with David Letterman,* NBC

	1981–82	1982–83	1983–84
Limited Series	Marco Polo, NBC	Nicholas Nickleby, SYN	Concealed Enemies, PBS
Actor—Limited Series or Special	Mickey Rooney, Bill, CBS	Tommy Lee Jones, The Executioner's Song, NBC	Laurence Olivier, King Lear, SYN
Actress—Limited Series or Special	Ingrid Bergman, A Woman Called Golda, SYN	Barbara Stanwyck, The Thorn Birds, ABC	Jane Fonda, The Dollmaker, ABC
Supporting Actor—Limited Series or Special	Laurence Olivier, Brideshead Revisited, PBS	Richard Kiley, The Thorn Birds, ABC	Art Carney, Terrible Joe Moran, CBS
Supporting Actress—Limited Series or Special	Penny Fuller, Elephant Man, ABC	Jean Simmons, The Thorn Birds, ABC	Roxana Zal, Something About Amelia, ABC
Director—Limited Series or Special	Marvin J. Chomsky, Inside the Third Reich, ABC	John Erman, Who Will Love My Children?, ABC	Jeff Bleckner, Concealed Enemies, PBS
Writer—Limited Series or Special	Corey Blechman (Teleplay); Barry Morrow (Story), Bill, CBS	Marshall Herskovitz (Teleplay); Edward Zwick, Marshall Herskovitz (Story), Special Bulletin, NBC	William Hanley, Something About Amelia, ABC
Daytime Drama Series	Guiding Light, CBS	The Young & The Restless, CBS	General Hospital, ABC
Actor—Daytime Drama Series	Anthony Geary, General Hospital, ABC	Robert S. Woods, One Life to Live, ABC	Larry Bryggman, As the World Turns, CBS
Actress—Daytime Drama Series	Robin Strasser, One Life To Live, ABC	Dorothy Lyman, All My Children, ABC	Erika Slezak, One Life To Live, ABC
Supporting Actor—Daytime Drama Series	David Lewis, General Hospital, ABC	Darnell Williams, All My Children, ABC	Justin Deas, As the World Turns, CBS
Supporting Actress—Daytime Drama Series	Dorothy Lyman, All My Children, ABC	Louise Shaffer, Ryan's Hope, ABC	Judi Evans, The Guiding Light, CBS
Host—Game Show	Bob Barker, The Price Is Right, CBS	Betty White, Just Men!, NBC	Bob Barker, The Price Is Right, CBS
Host—Talk or Service	Phil Donahue, Donahue, SYN	Phil Donahue, Donahue, SYN	Gary Collins, Hour Magazine, SYN
Game Show	Password Plus, NBC	The New $25,000 Pyramid, CBS	The $25,000 Pyramid, CBS
Talk or Service Series	The Richard Simmons Show, SYN	This Old House, PBS	Woman to Woman, SYN
Children's Special	The Wave, ABC	Big Bird in China, NBC	He Makes Me Feel Like Dancin', NBC
Children's Series	Captain Kangaroo, CBS	Smurfs, NBC	Captain Kangaroo, CBS

	1984–85	**1985–86**	**1986–87**
Drama	*Cagney and Lacey,* CBS	*Cagney & Lacey,* CBS	*L. A. Law,* NBC
Actor—Drama Series	William Daniels, *St. Elsewhere,* NBC	William Daniels, *St. Elsewhere,* NBC	Bruce Willis, *Moonlighting,* ABC
Actress—Drama Series	Tyne Daly, *Cagney & Lacey,* CBS	Sharon Gless, *Cagney & Lacey,* CBS	Sharon Gless, *Cagney & Lacey,* CBS
Supporting Actor—Drama Series	Edward James Olmos, *Miami Vice,* NBC	John Karlen, *Cagney & Lacey,* CBS	John Hillerman, *Magnum, P.I.,* CBS
Supporting Actress—Drama Series	Betty Thomas, *Hill Street Blues,* NBC	Bonnie Bartlett, *St. Elsewhere,* NBC	Bonnie Bartlett, *St. Elsewhere,* NBC
Director—Drama Series	Karen Arthur, *Cagney & Lacey,* CBS	Georg Stanford Brown, *Cagney & Lacey,* CBS	Gregory Hoblit, *L.A. Law,* NBC
Writer—Drama Series	Patricia M. Green, *Cagney & Lacey,* CBS	Tom Fontana, John Tinker, and John Masius, *St. Elsewhere,* NBC	Steven Bochco, Terry Louise Fisher, *L.A. Law,* NBC
Comedy	*The Cosby Show,* NBC	*The Golden Girls,* NBC	*The Golden Girls,* NBC
Actor—Comedy Series	Robert Guillaume, *Benson,* ABC	Michael J. Fox, *Family Ties,* NBC	Michael J. Fox, *Family Ties,* NBC
Actress—Comedy Series	Jane Curtin, *Kate & Allie,* CBS	Betty White, *The Golden Girls,* NBC	Rue McClanahan, *The Golden Girls,* NBC
Supporting Actor—Comedy Series	John Larroquette, *Night Court,* NBC	John Larroquette, *Night Court,* NBC	John Larroquette, *Night Court,* NBC
Supporting Actress—Comedy Series	Rhea Perlman, *Cheers,* NBC	Rhea Perlman, *Cheers,* NBC	Jackée Harry, *227,* NBC
Director—Comedy Series	Jay Sandrich, *The Cosby Show,* NBC	Jay Sandrich, *The Cosby Show,* NBC	Terry Hughes, *The Golden Girls,* NBC
Writer—Comedy Series	Ed. Weinberger, Michael Leeson, *The Cosby Show,* NBC	Barry Fanaro and Mort Nathan, *The Golden Girls,* NBC	Gary David Goldberg, Alan Uger, *Family Ties,* NBC
Drama/Comedy Special	*Do You Remember Love,* CBS	*Love Is Never Silent,* NBC	*Promise,* CBS
Variety, Music, or Comedy Program	*Motown Returns to the Apollo,* NBC	*The Kennedy Center Honors: A Celebration of the Performing Arts,* CBS	*The 1987 Tony Awards,* CBS
Individual Performance—Variety or Music Program	George Hearn, *Sweeney Todd,* PBS	Whitney Houston, *The 28th Annual Grammy Awards,* CBS	Robin Williams, *A Carol Burnett Special: Carol, Carl, Whoopi & Robin,* ABC
Director—Variety or Music	Terry Hughes, *Sweeney Todd,* PBS	Waris Hussein, *Copacabana,* CBS	Don Mischer, *The Kennedy Center Honors: A Celebration of the Performing Arts,* CBS
Writer—Variety or Music	Gerard Mulligan, Sandy Frank, Joe Toplyn, Chris Elliott, Matt Wickline, Jeff Martin, Eddie Gorodetsky, Randy Cohen, Larry Jacobson, Kevin Curran, Fred Graver, Merrill Markoe, and David Letterman, *Late Night with David Letterman,* NBC	David Letterman, Steve O'Donnell, Sandy Frank, Joe Toplyn, Chris Elliott, Matt Wickline, Jeff Martin, Gerard Mulligan, Randy Cohen, Larry Jacobson, Kevin Curran, Fred Graver, and Merrill Markoe, *Late Night with David Letterman,* NBC	Steve O'Donnell, Sandy Frank, Joe Toplyn, Chris Elliott, Matt Wickline, Jeff Martin, Gerard Mulligan, Randy Cohen, Larry Jacobson, Kevin Curran, Fred Graver, Adam Resnick, and David Letterman, *Late Night with David Letterman,* NBC

	1984–85	1985–86	1986–87
Miniseries	*The Jewel in the Crown*, PBS	*Peter the Great*, NBC	*A Year in the Life*, NBC
Actor—Miniseries	Richard Crenna, *The Rape of Richard Beck*, ABC	Dustin Hoffman, *Death of a Salesman*, CBS	James Woods, *Promise*, CBS
Actress—Miniseries	Joanne Woodward, *Do You Remember Love*, CBS	Marlo Thomas, *Nobody's Child*, CBS	Gena Rowlands, *The Betty Ford Story*, ABC
Supporting Actor—Miniseries or Special	Karl Malden, *Fatal Vision*, NBC	John Malkovich, *Death of a Salesman*, CBS	Dabney Coleman, *Sworn to Silence*, ABC
Supporting Actress—Miniseries/ Limited Series or Special	Kim Stanley, *Cat on a Hot Tin Roof*, PBS	Colleen Dewhurst, *Between Two Women*, ABC	Piper Laurie, *Promise*, CBS
Director—Miniseries or Special	Lamont Johnson, *Wallenberg: A Hero's Story*, NBC	Joseph Sargent, *Love Is Never Silent*, NBC	Glenn Jordan, *Promise*, CBS
Writer—Miniseries or Special	Vickie Patik, *Do You Remember Love*, CBS	Ron Cowen and Daniel Lipman (Teleplay); Sherman Yellen (Story), *An Early Frost*, NBC	Richard Friedenberg (Teleplay); Kenneth Blackwell, Tennyson Flowers, and Richard Friedenberg (Story), *Promise*, CBS
Daytime Drama Series	*The Young and the Restless*, CBS	*The Young and the Restless*, CBS	*As the World Turns*, CBS
Actor—Daytime Drama Series	Darnell Williams, *All My Children*, ABC	David Canary, *All My Children*, ABC	Larry Bryggman, *As the World Turns*, CBS
Actress—Daytime Drama Series	Kim Zimmer, *Guiding Light*, CBS	Erika Slezak, *One Life To Live*, ABC	Kim Zimmer, *Guiding Light*, CBS
Supporting Actor—Daytime Drama Series	Larry Gates, *Guiding Light*, CBS	John Wesley Shipp, *As the World Turns*, CBS	Gregg Marx, *As the World Turns*, CBS
Supporting Actress—Daytime Drama Series	Beth Maitland, *The Young and the Restless*, CBS	Leann Hunley, *Days of Our Lives*, NBC	Kathleen Noone, *All My Children*, ABC
Ingenue— Daytime Drama Series	Tracey E. Bregman, *The Young and the Restless*, CBS	Ellen Wheeler, *Another World*, NBC	Martha Byrne, *As the World Turns*, CBS
Younger Leading Man— Daytime Drama Series	Brian Bloom, *As the World Turns*, CBS	Michael E. Knight, *All My Children*, ABC	Michael E. Knight, *All My Children*, ABC
Host—Game Show	Dick Clark, *The $25,000 Pyramid*, CBS	Dick Clark, *The $25,000 Pyramid*, CBS	Bob Barker, *The Price Is Right*, CBS
Host—Talk or Service	Phil Donahue, *Donahue*, SYN	Phil Donahue, *Donahue*, SYN	Oprah Winfrey, *The Oprah Winfrey Show*, SYN
Game Show	*The $25,000 Pyramid*, CBS	*The $25,000 Pyramid*, CBS	*The $25,000 Pyramid*, CBS
Talk, Service or Variety Series	*Donahue*, SYN	*Donahue*, SYN	*The Oprah Winfrey Show*, SYN
Children's Special	*Displaced Person*, PBS	*Anne of Green Gables*, PBS	*Jim Henson's The Storyteller: Hans My Hedgehog*, NBC
Children's Series	*Sesame Street*, PBS	*Sesame Street*, PBS	*Sesame Street*, PBS

	1987–88	1988–89	1989–90
Drama	*thirtysomething*, ABC	*L.A. Law*, NBC	*L.A. Law*, NBC
Actor—Drama Series	Richard Kiley, *A Year in the Life*, NBC	Carroll O'Connor, *In the Heat of the Night*, NBC	Peter Falk, *Columbo*, ABC
Actress—Drama Series	Tyne Daly, *Cagney & Lacey*, CBS	Dana Delany, *China Beach*, ABC	Patricia Wettig, *thirtysomething*, ABC
Supporting Actor—Drama Series	Larry Drake, *L.A. Law*, NBC	Larry Drake, *L.A. Law*, NBC	Jimmy Smits, *L.A. Law*, NBC
Supporting Actress—Drama Series	Patricia Wettig, *thirtysomething*, ABC	Melanie Mayron, *thirtysomething*, ABC	Marg Helgenberger, *China Beach*, ABC
Director—Drama Series	Mark Tinker, *St. Elsewhere*, NBC	Robert Altman, *Tanner '88*, HBO	Thomas Carter, *Equal Justice*, ABC; Scott Winant, *thirtysomething*, ABC
Writer—Drama Series	Paul Haggis, Marshall Herskovitz, *thirtysomething*, ABC	Joseph Dougherty, *thirtysomething*, ABC	David E. Kelley, *L.A. Law*, NBC
Comedy	*The Wonder Years*, ABC	*Cheers*, NBC	*Murphy Brown*, CBS
Actor—Comedy Series	Michael J. Fox, *Family Ties*, NBC	Richard Mulligan, *Empty Nest*, NBC	Ted Danson, *Cheers*, NBC
Actress—Comedy Series	Beatrice Arthur, *The Golden Girls*, NBC	Candice Bergen, *Murphy Brown*, CBS	Candice Bergen, *Murphy Brown*, CBS
Supporting Actor—Comedy Series	John Larroquette, *Night Court*, NBC	Woody Harrelson, *Cheers*, NBC	Alex Rocco, *The Famous Teddy Z*, CBS
Supporting Actress—Comedy Series	Estelle Getty, *The Golden Girls*, NBC	Rhea Perlman, *Cheers*, NBC	Bebe Neuwirth, *Cheers*, NBC
Director—Comedy Series	Gregory Hoblit, *Hooperman*, ABC	Peter Baldwin, *The Wonder Years*, ABC	Michael Dinner, *The Wonder Years*, ABC
Writer—Comedy Series	Hugh Wilson, *Frank's Place*, CBS	Diane English, *Murphy Brown*, CBS	Bob Brush, *The Wonder Years*, ABC
Drama/Comedy Special	*Inherit the Wind*, NBC	*Day One*, CBS	*Caroline?*, CBS; *The Incident*,
Variety, Music, or Comedy Program	*Irving Berlin's 100th Birthday Celebration*, CBS	*The Tracey Ullman Show*, FOX	*In Living Color*, FOX
Individual Performance—Variety or Music Program	Robin Williams, *ABC Presents a Royal Gala*, ABC	Linda Ronstadt, *Canciones de Mi Padre*, PBS	Tracey Ullman, *The Best of the Tracey Ullman Show*, FOX
Director—Variety or Music	Patricia Birch and Humphrey Burton, *Celebrating Gershwin*, PBS	Jim Henson, *The Jim Henson Hour*, NBC	Dwight Hemion, *The Kennedy Center Honors: A Celebration of the Performing Arts*, CBS

	1987–88	1988–89	1989–90
Writer—Variety or Music	Jackie Mason, *Jackie Mason on Broadway*, HBO	James Downey, head writer; John Bowman, A. Whitney Brown, Gregory Daniels, Tom Davis, Al Franken, Shannon Gaughan, Jack Handey, Phil Hartman, Lorne Michaels, Mike Myers, Conan O'Brien, Bob Odenkirk, Herb Sargent, Tom Schiller, Robert Smigel, Bonnie Turner, Terry Turner, and Christine Zander, writers; George Meyer, additional sketches, *Saturday Night Live*, NBC	Billy Crystal, *Billy Crystal: Midnight Train to Moscow*, HBO; James L. Brooks, Heide Perlman, Sam Simon, Jerry Belson, Marc Flanagan, Dinah Kirgo, Jay Kogen, Wallace Wolodarsky, Ian Praiser, Marilyn Suzanne Miller, and Tracey Ullman, *The Tracey Ullman Show*, FOX
Miniseries	*The Murder of Mary Phagan*, NBC	*War and Remembrance*, ABC	*Drug Wars: The Camarena Story*, NBC
Actor—Miniseries or Special	Jason Robards, *Inherit the Wind*, NBC	James Woods, *My Name is Bill W.*, ABC	Hume Cronyn, *Age-Old Friends*, HBO
Actress—Miniseries or Special	Jessica Tandy, *Foxfire*, CBS	Holly Hunter, *Roe vs. Wade*, NBC	Barbara Hershey, *A Killing in a Small Town*, CBS
Supporting Actor—Miniseries or Special	John Shea, *Baby M*, ABC	Derek Jacobi, *The Tenth Man*, CBS	Vincent Gardenia, *Age-Old Friends*, HBO
Supporting Actress—Miniseries or Special	Jane Seymour, *Onassis: The Richest Man in the World*, ABC	Colleen Dewhurst, *Those She Left Behind*, NBC	Eva Marie Saint, *People Like Us*, NBC
Director—Miniseries or Special	Lamont Johnson, *Gore Vidal's Lincoln*, NBC	Simon Wincer, *Lonesome Dove*, CBS	Joseph Sargent, *Caroline?*, CBS
Writer—Miniseries or Special	William Hanley, *The Attic: The Hiding of Anne Frank*, CBS	Abby Mann, Robin Vote, and Ron Hutchison, *Murderers Among Us: The Simon Wiesenthal Story*, HBO	Terrence McNally, *Andre's Mother*, PBS
Daytime Drama Series	*Santa Barbara*, NBC	*Santa Barbara*, NBC	*Santa Barbara*, NBC
Actor—Daytime Drama Series	David Canary, *All My Children*, ABC	David Canary, *All My Children*, ABC	A Martinez, *Santa Barbara*, NBC
Actress—Daytime Drama Series	Helen Gallagher, *Ryan's Hope*, ABC	Marcy Walker, *Santa Barbara*, NBC	Kim Zimmer, *Guiding Light*, CBS
Supp. Actor—Daytime Drama	Justin Deas, *Santa Barbara*, NBC	Justin Deas, *Santa Barbara*, NBC	Henry Darrow, *Santa Barbara*, NBC
Supporting Actress—Daytime Drama Series	Ellen Wheeler, *All My Children*, ABC	Debbi Morgan, *All My Children*, ABC; Nancy Lee Grahn, *Santa Barbara*, NBC	Julia Barr, *All My Children*, ABC
Ingenue—Daytime Drama Series	Julianne Moore, *As the World Turns*, CBS	Kimberly McCullough, *General Hospital*, ABC	Cady McClain, *All My Children*, ABC
Younger Leading Man—Daytime Drama Series	Billy Warlock, *Days of Our Lives*, NBC	Justin Gocke, *Santa Barbara*, NBC	Andrew Kavovit, *As the World Turns*, CBS
Host—Game Show	Bob Barker, *The Price Is Right*, CBS	Alex Trebek, *Jeopardy!*, SYN	Alex Trebek, *Jeopardy!*, SYN; Bob Barker, *The Price Is Right*, CBS
Host—Talk or Service Show	Phil Donahue, *Donahue*, SYN	Sally Jessy Raphael, *Sally Jessy Raphael*, SYN	Joan Rivers, *The Joan Rivers Show*, SYN
Game Show	*The Price Is Right*, CBS	*The $25,000 Pyramid*, CBS	*Jeopardy!*, SYN
Talk, Service, or Variety Series	*The Oprah Winfrey Show*, SYN	*The Oprah Winfrey Show*, SYN	*Sally Jessy Raphael*, SYN
Children's Special	*The Secret Garden*, CBS	*Free To Be…A Family*, ABC	*A Mother's Courage: The Mary Thomas Story*, NBC
Children's Series	*Sesame Street*, PBS	*Newton's Apple*, PBS	*Reading Rainbow*, PBS

	1990–91	1991–92	1992–93
Drama	*L.A. Law,* NBC	*Northern Exposure,* CBS	*Picket Fences,* CBS
Actor—Drama Series	James Earl Jones, *Gabriel's Fire,* ABC	Christopher Lloyd, *Avonlea,* DIS	Tom Skerritt, *Picket Fences,* CBS
Actress—Drama Series	Patricia Wettig, *thirtysomething,* ABC	Dana Delany, *China Beach,* ABC	Kathy Baker, *Picket Fences,* CBS
Supporting Actor—Drama Series	Timothy Busfield, *thirtysomething,* ABC	Richard Dysart, *L.A. Law,* NBC	Chad Lowe, *Life Goes On,* ABC
Supporting Actress—Drama Series	Madge Sinclair, *Gabriel's Fire,* ABC	Valerie Mahaffey, *Northern Exposure,* CBS	Mary Alice, *I'll Fly Away,* NBC
Director—Drama Series	Thomas Carter, *Equal Justice,* ABC	Eric Laneuville, *I'll Fly Away,* NBC	Barry Levinson, *Homicide—Life on the Street,* NBC
Writer—Drama Series	David E. Kelley, *L.A. Law,* NBC	Andrew Schneider and Diane Frolov, *Northern Exposure,* CBS	Tom Fontana, *Homicide—Life on the Street,* NBC
Comedy	*Cheers,* NBC	*Murphy Brown,* CBS	*Seinfeld,* NBC
Actor—Comedy Series	Burt Reynolds, *Evening Shade,* CBS	Craig T. Nelson, *Coach,* ABC	Ted Danson, *Cheers,* NBC
Actress—Comedy Series	Kirstie Alley, *Cheers,* NBC	Candice Bergen, *Murphy Brown,* CBS	Roseanne Arnold, *Roseanne,* ABC
Supporting Actor—Comedy Series	Jonathan Winters, *Davis Rules,* ABC	Michael Jeter, *Evening Shade,* CBS	Michael Richards, *Seinfeld,* NBC
Supp. Actress—Comedy Series	Bebe Neuwirth, *Cheers,* NBC	Laurie Metcalf, *Roseanne,* ABC	Laurie Metcalf, *Roseanne,* ABC
Director—Comedy Series	James Burrows, *Cheers,* NBC	Barnet Kellman, *Murphy Brown,* CBS	Betty Thomas, *Dream On,* HBO
Writer—Comedy Series	Gary Dontzig and Steven Peterman, *Murphy Brown,* CBS	Elaine Pope and Larry Charles, *Seinfeld,* NBC	Larry David, *Seinfeld,* NBC
Variety, Music, or Comedy Program	*The 63rd Annual Academy Awards,* ABC	*The Tonight Show Starring Johnny Carson,* NBC	*Saturday Night Live,* NBC
Individual Performance—Variety or Music Program	Billy Crystal, *The 63rd Annual Academy Awards,* ABC	Bette Midler, *The Tonight Show Starring Johnny Carson,* NBC	Dana Carvey, *Saturday Night Live,* NBC
Director—Variety or Music	Hal Gurnee, *Late Night with David Letterman,* NBC	Patricia Birch, *Unforgettable with Love: Natalie Cole Sings the Songs of Nat King Cole,* PBS	Walter C. Miller, *The 1992 Tony Awards,* CBS
Writer—Variety or Music	Hal Kanter and Buz Kohan, writers; Billy Crystal, David Steinberg, Bruce Vilanch, and Robert Wuhl (Special Material), *The 63rd Annual Academy Awards,* ABC	Hal Kanter and Buz Kohan, writers); Billy Crystal, Marc Shaiman, David Steinberg, Robert Wuhl, and Bruce Vilanch, special material, *The 64rd Annual Academy Awards,* ABC	Judd Apatow, Robert Cohen, David Cross, Brent Forrester, Jeff Kahn, Bruce Kirschbaum, Bob Odenkirk, Sultan Pepper, Dino Stamatopoulos, and Ben Stiller, *The Ben Stiller Show,* FOX
Made for Television Movie	—	*Miss Rose White:* Hallmark Hall of Fame, NBC	*Barbarians at the Gate,* HBO; *Stalin,* HBO
Miniseries	*Separate but Equal,* ABC	*A Woman Named Jackie,* NBC	*Prime Suspect 2,* PBS

	1990–91	1991–92	1992–93
Actor—Miniseries or Special	John Gielgud, *Summer's Lease*, PBS	Beau Bridges, *Without Warning: The James Brady Story*, HBO	Robert Morse, *Tru*, PBS
Actress—Miniseries or Special	Lynn Whitfield, *The Josephine Baker Story*, HBO	Gena Rowlands, *Face of a Stranger*, CBS	Holly Hunter, *The Positively True Adventures of the Alleged Texas Cheerleader-Murdering Mom*, HBO
Supporting Actor—Miniseries or Special	James Earl Jones, *Heat Wave*, TNT	Hume Cronyn, *Neil Simon's Broadway Bound*, ABC	Beau Bridges, *The Positively True Adventures of the Alleged Texas Cheerleader-Murdering Mom*, HBO
Supporting Actress—Miniseries or Special	Ruby Dee, *Decoration Day*, NBC	Amanda Plummer, *Miss Rose White*, NBC	Mary Tyler Moore, *Stolen Babies*, LIF
Director—Miniseries or Special	Brian Gibson, *The Josephine Baker Story*, HBO	Daniel Petrie, *Mark Twain and Me*, DIS	James Sadwith, *Sinatra*, CBS
Writer—Miniseries or Special	Andrew Davies, *House of Cards*, PBS	John Falsey and Joshua Brand, *I'll Fly Away*, NBC	Jane Anderson, *The Positively True Adventures of the Alleged Texas Cheerleader-Murdering Mom*, HBO
Daytime Drama Series	*As the World Turns*, CBS	*All My Children*, ABC	*The Young and the Restless*, CBS
Actor—Daytime Drama Series	Peter Bergman, *The Young and the Restless*, CBS	Peter Bergman, *The Young and the Restless*, CBS	David Canary, *All My Children*, ABC
Actress—Daytime Drama Series	Finola Hughes, *General Hospital*, ABC	Erika Slezak, *One Life to Live*, ABC	Linda Dano, *Another World*, NBC
Supporting Actor—Daytime Drama Series	Bernie Barrow, *Loving*, ABC	Thom Christopher, *One Life to Live*, ABC	Gerald Anthony, *General Hospital*, ABC
Supporting Actress—Daytime Drama Series	Jess Walton, *The Young and the Restless*, CBS	Maeve Kinkead, *Guiding Light*, CBS	Ellen Parker, *Guiding Light*, CBS
Younger Actress—Daytime Drama Series	Anne Heche, *Another World*, NBC	Tricia Cast, *The Young and the Restless*, CBS	Heather Tom, *The Young and the Restless*, CBS
Younger Leading Man—Daytime Drama Series	Rick Hearst, *Guiding Light*, CBS	Kristoff St. John, *The Young and the Restless*, CBS	Monti Sharp, *Guiding Light*, CBS
Host—Game Show	Bob Barker, *The Price Is Right*, CBS	Bob Barker, *The Price Is Right*, CBS	Pat Sajak, *Wheel of Fortune*, SYN
Host—Talk or Service Show	Oprah Winfrey, *The Oprah Winfrey Show*, SYN	Oprah Winfrey, *The Oprah Winfrey Show*, SYN	Oprah Winfrey, *The Oprah Winfrey Show*, SYN
Game Show	*Jeopardy!*, SYN	*Jeopardy!*, SYN	*Jeopardy!*, SYN
Talk, Service, or Variety Series	*The Oprah Winfrey Show*, SYN	*The Oprah Winfrey Show*, SYN	*Good Morning America*, ABC
Children's Special	*You Can't Grow Home Again: A 3-2-1 Contact Extra*, PBS	*Mark Twain and Me*, DIS	*Shades of a Single Protein*, ABC
Children's Series	*Sesame Street*, PBS	*Sesame Street*, PBS	*Reading Rainbow*, PBS; *Tiny Toon Adventures*, SYN (Animated)

	1993–94	1994–95	1995–96
Drama	*Picket Fences*, CBS	*NYPD Blue*, ABC	*ER*, NBC
Actor—Drama Series	Dennis Franz, *NYPD Blue*, ABC	Mandy Patinkin, *Chicago Hope*, CBS	Dennis Franz, *NYPD Blue*, ABC
Actress—Drama Series	Sela Ward, *Sisters*, NBC	Kathy Baker, *Picket Fences*, CBS	Kathy Baker, *Picket Fences*, CBS
Supporting Actor— Drama Series	Fyvush Finkel, *Picket Fences*, CBS	Ray Walston, *Picket Fences*, CBS	Ray Walston, *Picket Fences*, CBS
Supporting Actress— Drama Series	Leigh Taylor-Young, *Picket Fences*, CBS	Julianna Margulies, *ER*, NBC	Tyne Daly, *Christy*, CBS
Director—Drama Series	Daniel Sackheim, *NYPD Blue*, ABC	Mimi Leder, *ER*, NBC	Jeremy Kagan, *Chicago Hope*, CBS
Writer—Drama Series	Ann Biderman, *NYPD Blue*, ABC	Michael Crichton, *ER*, NBC	Darin Morgan, *The X-Files*, Fox
Comedy	*Frasier*, NBC	*Frasier*, NBC	*Frasier*, NBC
Actor—Comedy Series	Kelsey Grammer, *Frasier*, NBC	Kelsey Grammer, *Frasier*, NBC	John Lithgow, *3rd Rock from the Sun*, NBC
Actress—Comedy Series	Candice Bergen, *Murphy Brown*, CBS	Candice Bergen, *Murphy Brown*, CBS	Helen Hunt, *Mad About You*, NBC
Supporting Actor— Comedy Series	Michael Richards, *Seinfeld*, NBC	David Hyde Pierce, *Frasier*, NBC	Rip Torn, *The Larry Sanders Show*, HBO
Supp. Actress—Comedy Series	Laurie Metcalf, *Roseanne*, ABC	Christine Baranski, *Cybill*, CBS	Julia Louis-Dreyfuss, *Seinfeld*, NBC
Director—Comedy Series	James Burrows, *Frasier*, NBC	David Lee, *Frasier*, NBC	Michael Lembeck, *Friends*, NBC
Writer—Comedy Series	David Angel, Peter Casey, and David Lee, *Frasier*, NBC	Chuck Ranberg, Anne Flett-Giordano, *Frasier*, NBC	Joe Keenan, Christopher Lloyd, Rob Greenberg, Jack Burditt, Chuck Ranberg, Anne Flett-Giordano, Linda Morris, and Vic Rauseo, *Frasier*, NBC
Variety, Music, or Comedy Program	*Late Show With David Letterman*, CBS	*The Tonight Show with Jay Leno*, NBC	*Dennis Miller Live*, HBO
Individual Performance— Variety or Music Program	Tracey Ullman, *Tracey Ullman Takes On New York*, HBO	Barbra Streisand, *Barbra Streisand: The Concert*, HBO	Tony Bennett, *Tony Bennett Live by Request: A Valentine Special*, A&E
Director—Variety or Music	Walter C. Miller, *The Tony Awards*, CBS	Jeff Margolis, *The 67th Annual Academy Awards*, ABC	Louis J. Horvitz, *The Kennedy Center Honors*, CBS
Writer—Variety or Music	Jeff Cesario, Mike Dugan, Eddie Feldmann, Gregory Greenberg, Dennis Miller, Kevin Rooney, *Dennis Miller Live*, HBO	Jeff Cesario, Ed Driscoll, David Feldmann, Eddie Feldmann, Gregory Greenberg, Dennis Miller, Kevin Rooney, *Dennis Miller Live*, HBO	Eddie Feldmann, David Feldmann, Mike Gandolfini, Tom Hertz, Leah Krinsky, Dennis Miller, Rick Overton, *Dennis Miller Live*, HBO
Made for Television Movie	*And the Band Played On*, HBO	*Indictment: The McMartin Trial*, HBO	*Truman*, HBO
Miniseries	*Mystery: Prime Suspect 3*, PBS	*Joseph*, TNT	*Gulliver's Travels*, NBC

	1993–94	**1994–95**	**1995–96**
Actor—Miniseries or Special	Hume Cronyn, *Hallmark Hall of Fame: To Dance With the White Dog*, CBS	Raul Julia, *The Burning Season*, HBO	Alan Rickman, *Rasputin*, HBO
Actress—Miniseries or Special	Kirstie Alley, *David's Mother*, CBS	Glenn Close, *Serving in Silence: The Margarethe Cammermeyer Story*, NBC	Helen Mirren, *Prime Suspect: Scent of Darkness*, PBS
Supporting Actor—Miniseries or Special	Michael Goorjian, *David's Mother*, CBS	Donald Sutherland, *Citizen X*, HBO	Tom Hulce, *The Heidi Chronicles*, TNT
Supporting Actress—Miniseries or Special	Cicely Tyson, *Oldest Living Confederate Widow Tells All*, CBS	Judy Davis, *Serving in Silence: The Margarethe Cammemeyer Story*, NBC	Greta Scacchi, *Rasputin*, HBO
Director—Miniseries or Special	John Frankenheimer, *Against the Wall*, HBO	John Frankenheimer, *The Burning Season*, HBO	John Frankenheimer, *Andersonville*, TNT
Writer—Miniseries or Special	Bob Randall, *David's Mother*, CBS	Alison Cross, *Serving in Silence: The Margarethe Cammermeyer Story*, NBC	Simon Moore, *Gulliver's Travels*, NBC
Daytime Drama Series	*All My Children*, ABC	*General Hospital*, ABC	*General Hospital*, ABC
Actor—Daytime Drama Series	Michael Zaslow, *Guiding Light*, CBS	Justin Deas, *Guiding Light*, CBS	Charles Keating, *Another World*, NBC
Actress—Daytime Drama Series	Hillary B. Smith, *One Life to Live*, ABC	Erika Slezak, *One Life to Live*, ABC	Erika Slezak, *One Life to Live*, ABC
Supporting Actor—Daytime Drama Series	Justin Deas, *Guiding Light*, CBS	Jerry Ver Dorn, *Guiding Light*, CBS	Jerry Ver Dorn, *Guiding Light*, CBS
Supporting Actress—Daytime Drama Series	Susan Haskell, *One Life to Live*, ABC	Rena Sofer, *General Hospital*, ABC	Anna Holbrook, *Another World*, NBC
Younger Actress—Daytime Drama Series	Melissa Hayden, *Guiding Light*, CBS	Sarah Michelle Gellar, *All My Children*, ABC	Kimberly McCullough, *General Hospital*, ABC
Younger Leading Man—Daytime Drama Series	Roger Howarth, *One Life to Live*, ABC	Jonathan Jackson, *General Hospital*, ABC	Kevin Mambo, *Guiding Light*, CBS
Host—Talk or Service Show	Oprah Winfrey, *The Oprah Winfrey Show*, SYN	Oprah Winfrey, *The Oprah Winfrey Show*, SYN	Montel Williams, *The Montel Williams Show*, SYN
Game Show	*Jeopardy!*, SYN	*Jeopardy!*, SYN	*The Price Is Right*, CBS
Talk, Service, or Variety Series	*The Oprah Winfrey Show*, SYN-	*The Oprah Winfrey Show*, SYN	*The Oprah Winfrey Show*, SYN
Children's Special	*Dead Drunk: The Kevin Tunell Story*, HBO	*A Child Betrayed: The Calvin Mire Story*, HBO	*Stand Up*, CBS
Children's Series	*Sesame Street*, PBS; *Rugrats*, Nick (Animated)	*Nick News*, Nickelodeon; *Where on Earth is Carmen San Diego?*, Fox (Animated)	*Sesame Street*, PBS; *Animaniacs*, WB (Animated)

	1996–97	1997–98	1998–99
Drama	*Law & Order,* NBC	*The Practice,* ABC	*The Practice,* ABC
Actor—Drama Series	Dennis Franz, *NYPD Blue,* ABC	Andre Braugher, *Homicide: Life on the Street,* NBC	Dennis Franz, *NYPD Blue,* ABC
Actress—Drama Series	Gillian Anderson, *The X-Files,* Fox	Christine Lahti, *Chicago Hope,* CBS	Edie Falco, *The Sopranos,* HBO
Supporting Actor— Drama Series	Hector Elizondo, *Chicago Hope,* CBS	Gordon Clapp, *NYPD Blue,* ABC	Michael Badalucco, *The Practice,* ABC
Supporting Actress— Drama Series	Kim Delaney, *NYPD Blue,* ABC	Camryn Manheim, *The Practice,* ABC	Holland Taylor, *The Practice,* ABC
Director—Drama Series	Mark Tinker, *NYPD Blue,* ABC	Mark Tinker, *Brooklyn South,* CBS and Paris Barclay, *NYPD Blue,* ABC	Paris Barclay, *NYPD Blue,* ABC
Writer—Drama Series	David Milch, Stephen Gaghan, Michael R. Perry, *NYPD Blue,* ABC	Bill Clark, Nicholas Wooton, David Milch, *NYPD Blue,* ABC	James Manos, Jr., David Chase, *The Sopranos,* HBO
Comedy	*Frasier,* NBC	*Frasier,* NBC	*Ally McBeal,* FOX
Actor—Comedy Series	John Lithgow, *3rd Rock from the Sun,* NBC	Kelsey Grammer, *Frasier,* NBC	John Lithgow, *3rd Rock from the Sun,* NBC,
Actress—Comedy Series	Helen Hunt, *Mad About You,* NBC	Helen Hunt, *Mad About You,* NBC	Helen Hunt, *Mad About You,* NBC
Supporting Actor— Comedy Series	Michael Richards, *Seinfeld,* NBC	David Hyde Pierce, *Frasier,* NBC	David Hyde Pierce, *Frasier,* NBC
Supporting Actress— Comedy Series	Kristen Johnston, *3rd Rock from the Sun,* NBC	Lisa Kudrow, *Friends,* NBC	Kristen Johnston, *3rd Rock from the Sun,* NBC
Director—Comedy Series	David Lee, *Frasier,* NBC	Todd Holland, *The Larry Sanders Show,* HBO	Thomas Schlamme, *Will & Grace,* NBC
Writer—Comedy Series	Ellen DeGeneres, Mark Driscoll, Dava Savel, Tracy Newman, and Jonathan Stark, *Ellen,* ABC	Peter Tolan, Garry Shandling, *The Larry Sanders Show,* HBO	Jay Kogen, *Frasier,* NBC
Variety, Music, or Comedy Program	*Tracey Takes On...,* HBO (series) *Chris Rock: Bring the Pain,* HBO (special)	*Late Show with David Letterman,* CBS (series); *The 1997 Tony Awards* (special)	*Late Show With David Letterman,* CBS (series); *1998 Tony Awards,* CBS (special)
Individual Performance— Variety or Music Program	Bette Midler, *Bette Midler: Diva Las Vegas,* HBO	Billy Crystal, *The 70th Annual Academy Awards,* ABC	*John Leguizamo's Freak,* HBO,
Director—Variety or Music	Don Mischer, *Centennial Olympic Games, Opening Ceremonies,* NBC	Louis J. Horvitz, *The 70th Annual Academy Awards,* ABC	Paul Miller, *1998 Tony Awards,* CBS,
Writer—Variety or Music	Chris Rock, *Chris Rock: Bring the Pain,* HBO	Eddie Feldmann, Dennis Miller, David Feldman, Leah Krinsky, Jim Hanna, David Weiss, and Jose Arroyo, *Dennis Miller Live,* HBO	Tom Agna, Vernon Chatman, Louis CK, Lance Crouther, Gregory Greenberg, Ali LeRoi, Steve O'Donnell, Chris Rock, Frank Sebastiano, Chuck Sklar, Jeff Stilson, Wanda Sykes-Hall, Mike Upchurch, *The Chris Rock Show,* HBO
Made for Television Movie	*Miss Evers' Boys,* HBO	*Don King: Only in America,* HBO	*A Lesson Before Dying,* HBO
Miniseries	*Prime Suspect 5: Errors of Judgment,* PBS	*From the Earth to the Moon,* HBO	*Horatio Hornblower,* A&E

	1996–97	1997–98	1998–99
Actor—Miniseries or Special	Armand Assante, *Gotti*, HBO	Gary Sinise, *George Wallace*, TNT	Stanley Tucci, *Winchell*, HBO
Actress—Miniseries or Special	Alfre Woodard, *Miss Evers' Boys*, HBO	Ellen Barkin, *Before Women Had Wings*, ABC	Helen Mirren, *The Passion Of Ayn Rand*, SHO
Supporting Actor—Miniseries or Special	Beau Bridges, *The Second Civil War*, HBO	George C. Scott, *12 Angry Men*, SHO	Peter O'Toole, *Joan Of Arc*, CBS,
Supporting Actress—Miniseries or Special	Diana Rigg, *Rebecca*, PBS	Mare Winningham, *George Wallace*, TNT	Anne Bancroft, *Deep In My Heart*, CBS
Director—Miniseries or Special	Andrei Konchalovsky, *The Odyssey, Parts I and II*, NBC	John Frankenheimer, *George Wallace*, TNT	Allan Arkush, *The Temptations*, NBC
Writer—Miniseries or Special	Horton Foote, *William Faulkner's Old Man*, CBS	Kario Salem, *Don King: Only in America*, HBO	Ann Peacock, *A Lesson Before Dying*, HBO
Daytime Drama Series	*General Hospital*, ABC	*All My Children*, ABC	*General Hospital*, ABC
Actor—Daytime Drama Series	Justin Deas, *Guiding Light*, CBS	Eric Braeden, *The Young and the Restless*, CBS	Anthony Geary, *General Hospital*, ABC
Actress—Daytime Drama Series	Jess Walton, *The Young and the Restless*, CBS	Cynthia Watros, *Guiding Light*	Susan Lucci, *All My Children*, ABC
Supporting Actor—Daytime Drama Series	Ian Buchanan, *The Bold and the Beautiful*, CBS	Steve Burton, *General Hospital*, ABC	Stuart Damon, *General Hospital*, ABC
Supporting Actress—Daytime Drama Series	Michelle Stafford, *The Young and the Restless*, CBS	Julia Barr, *All My Children*, ABC	Sharon Case, *The Young and the Restless*, CBS
Younger Actress—Daytime Drama Series	Sarah Brown, *General Hospital*, ABC	Sarah Brown, *General Hospital*, ABC	Heather Tom, *The Young and the Restless*, CBS
Younger Leading Man—Daytime Drama Series	Kevin Mambo, *Guiding Light*, CBS	Jonathan Jackson, *General Hospital*, ABC	Jonathan Jackson, *General Hospital*, ABC
Talk Show Host	Rosie O'Donnell, *The Rosie O'Donnell Show*, SYN	Rosie O'Donnell, *The Rosie O'Donnell Show*, SYN; and Oprah Winfrey, *The Oprah Winfrey Show*, SYN (tie)	Rosie O'Donnell, *The Rosie O'Donnell Show*, SYN
Game Show	*The Price Is Right*, CBS	*Jeopardy!*, SYN	*Win Ben Stein's Money*, COM
Talk Show	*The Oprah Winfrey Show*, SYN	*The Rosie O'Donnell Show*, SYN	*The Rosie O'Donnell Show*, SYN
Children's Series	*Reading Rainbow*, PBS; *Animaniacs*, WB (Animated)	*Sesame Street*, PBS	*Sesame Street*, PBS (pre-school); *Disney Presents "Bill Nye The Science Guy,"* SYN

1999–2000

Drama	*The West Wing*, NBC
Actor—Drama Series	James Gandolfini, *The Sopranos* HBO
Actress—Drama Series	Sela Ward, *Once and Again*, ABC
Supporting Actor—Drama Series	Richard Schiff, *The West Wing*, NBC
Supporting Actress—Drama Series	Allison Janney, *The West Wing*, NBC
Director—Drama Series	Thomas Schlamme, *The West Wing*, NBC
Writer—Drama Series	Aaron Sorkin, Rick Cleveland, *The West Wing*, NBC
Comedy	*Will & Grace*, NBC
Actor—Comedy Series	Michael J. Fox, *Spin City*, ABC
Actress—Comedy Series	Patricia Heaton, *Everybody Loves Raymond*, CBS
Supporting Actor—Comedy Series	Sean Hayes, *Will & Grace*, NBC
Supporting Actress—Comedy Series	Megan Mullally, *Will & Grace*, NBC
Director—Comedy Series	Todd Holland, *Malcolm in the Middle*, FOX
Writer—Comedy Series	Linwood Boomer, *Malcolm in the Middle*, FOX
Variety, Music, or Comedy Program	*Late Show with David Letterman*, CBS (series); *Saturday Night Live: The 25th Anniversary Special*, NBC (special)
Individual Performance—Variety or Music Program	Eddie Izzard, *Eddie Izzard: Dressed to Kill*, HBO
Director—Variety or Music	Louis J. Horvitz, *72nd Annual Academy Awards*, ABC
Writer—Variety or Music	Eddie Izzard, *Eddie Izzard: Dressed to Kill*, HBO
Made for Television Movie	*Oprah Winfrey Presents: Tuesdays with Morrie*, ABC
Miniseries	*The Corner*, HBO

1999–2000

Actor—Miniseries or Movie	Jack Lemmon, *Oprah Winfrey Presents: Tuesdays with Morrie*, ABC
Actress—Miniseries or Movie	Halle Berry, *Introducing Dorothy Dandridge*, HBO
Supporting Actor—Miniseries or Movie	Hank Azaria, *Oprah Winfrey Presents: Tuesdays with Morrie*, ABC
Supporting Actress—Miniseries or Movie	Vanessa Redgrave, *If These Walls Could Talk 2*, HBO
Director—Miniseries or Movie	Charles S. Dutton, *The Corner*, HBO
Writer—Miniseries or Movie	David Simon, David Mills, *The Corner*, HBO
Daytime Drama Series	*General Hospital*, ABC
Actor—Daytime Drama Series	Anthony Geary, *General Hospital*, ABC
Actress—Daytime Drama Series	Susan Flannery, *The Bold and the Beautiful*, CBS
Supporting Actor—Daytime Drama Series	Shemar Moore, *The Young and the Restless*, CBS
Supporting Actress—Daytime Drama Series	Sarah Brown, *General Hospital*, ABC
Younger Actress—Daytime Drama Series	Camryn Grimes, *The Young and the Restless*, CBS
Younger Leading Man—Daytime Drama Series	David Tom, *The Young and the Restless*, CBS
Talk Show Host	Rosie O'Donnell, *The Rosie O'Donnell Show*, SYN
Game Show	*Who Wants to Be a Millionaire*, ABC
Talk Show	*The Rosie O'Donnell Show*, SYN
Children's Series	*Pinky, Elmira and the Brain*, WB (animated); *Disney Presents: Bill Nye The Science Guy*, SYN

PICKS & PANS 2000

As Napster and MP3 rock the record labels' world (though the labels refused to roll over), fans who still listen to disks had plenty of more melodious sounds to choose from. Herewith the PEOPLE playlist. Asterisks denote our reviewers' "pick of the week" selections during the year.

STIFF UPPER LIP
AC/DC

Lip features the no-frills, blues-based muscle music that has always been AC/DC's forté, but this time around the guys sound a bit weary.

TWENTIETH CENTURY
Alabama

Don't expect anything revolutionary. Here Alabama gives more of the same, and their fans will thank them for it.

ROYAL
The Amazing Crowns

Loud, raucous rockabilly performed at punk speed by Yanks who studied at the amps of the Clash, with shouted choruses patterned after English football chants.

AMBER
Amber

It doesn't take an Einstein to get Amber's relatively simple message: "It can't just be intellectual/ The way I feel is sexual." Unfortunately, her CD's unyielding, water-torture-like dancebeats provide listeners with all they need to resist her seductions.

*SHOKI SHOKI
Femi Anikulapo-Kuti

Like his late father Fela, Femi marries the muscular grooves of James Brown–style funk to the substantial beats of African music. His sturdy, multilayered songs are shorter and more pop-like than Fela's; he also plays saxophone and addresses weighty topics while still getting his groove on.

*ALONE WITH EVERYBODY
Richard Ashcroft

Compelling romantic laments that brim with bruised soul. With lush, soaring melodies and propulsive guitars set against string and horn arrangements held in tight rhythmic rein, *Alone* percolates and seethes with muted emotion.

THE ROAD THAT LED ME TO YOU
Baillie and the Boys

One of the most consistently entertaining acts in country pop.

SOONER OR LATER
BBMak

This trio of British lads all possess lead-vocal voices, and when their choirboy harmonies soar and entwine, the throbbing hearts of teenage girls are turned to porridge. The BBs also have impressive songwriting skills, too.

ABSOLUTE BENSON
George Benson

Absolute proof that the versatile guitarist is a master stylist. Silky and satisfying.

YEEEAH BABY
Big Pun

He died too young, but Latino rapper Big Pun displays giant-size talent on his last CD.

TROUBLE IN THE LAND
Black 47

These Manhattan Irish-pub rockers are back, intertwining Celtic music (provided by tin whistles and uilleann pipes) with a pounding punk-rock guitar attack.

WANDERING MOON
Terence Blanchard

This quietly dazzling "cool" jazz album evokes the breezy cool and virtues sprung from restraint: the joy is in the tease.

CRUSH
Bon Jovi

No one makes clichéd lyrics, nasally vocals, and predictable arena-rock riffs sound so good.

TIME TO DISCOVER
Robert Bradley's Blackwater Surprise

And a most pleasant *Surprise* it is. Growly soul man Bradley gives the blues a fresh and funky urban twist. Detroit smart-mouth rapper Kid Rock guests on two hot tracks.

MERMAID AVENUE: VOLUME II
Billy Bragg & Wilco

The agit-pop Brit and the roots-rocking band reteam with music composed to lyrics written (but never performed) by the late Woody Guthrie. An American beauty.

THE HEAT
Toni Braxton

Braxton's moody alto is best served by lush ballads and more dramatic midtempo songs. Unfortunately much of the material on *The Heat* never rises to the heights of previous hits like "Breathe Again" and "Love Shoulda Brought You Home."

COAST TO COAST
BR5-49

There isn't much on country radio these days that matches the greasy, down-home flavor of "Tell Me Mama" and "Better than This," so put on your Stetson and your string tie and get out those dancin' shoes.

BE HERE SOON
Jeff Bridges
Bridges—yes, that Jeff Bridges—probably should keep his day job, but he is an enjoyable singer who displays the same affability and naturalness that make him such a terrific actor.

IF YOU COULD SEE ME NOW
Julie Budd
The most entertaining aspect of this album of Streisand Lite is the imaginative choice of material: Ellington, Sondheim, and Michael Jackson are included.

20 GREATEST HITS
Glen Campbell
Despite overblown productions aimed at pop radio, Campbell always packed hurtin' in his vocals like a true blue Nashville cat.

I WAS BORN TO LOVE YOU
Eric Carmen
Fans of the immensely talented, classically trained composer of "Go All the Way," "All by Myself," and "Hungry Eyes" will be saddened to find that Carmen has gone Vegas with a vengeance. Schlocking.

*FURNACE ROOM LULLABY
Neko Case & Her Boyfriends
Case has the kind of teary twang and throaty sass that is shared by country's true greats, and *Furnace Room Lullaby* has an unadorned, swinging-doors-and-a-barstool feel, as if it were cut in the wee hours at Tootsie's Orchid Lounge after a show at the Opry.

LOVE GOD MURDER
Johnny Cash
"These songs are just for listening and singing," Cash writes in notes for *Murder*, one of three CDs in this inventive, thematically organized retrospective. "Don't go out and do it."

EQUALLY CURSED AND BLESSED
Catatonia
Some of the uptempo tunes here are catchy despite self-consciously clever or nonsensical lyrics; slower tunes meant to captivate with their dreaminess merely grate. Overall, annoying.

THIS PRETTY PLANET
Tom Chapin
Chapin has become a uniquely appealing singer of children's songs—funny, thoughtful, and warm without ever patronizing his young audience.

TELLING STORIES
Tracy Chapman
Chapman lets her lovely contralto rise and fall in cadences that vary little from track to track; she creates an atmosphere so stately and hushed you wish she would scream and maybe even smash a few antiques.

CHIC
Chic Live at the Budokan
Nile Rodgers and Bernard Edwards's funk supergroup performed this final concert with guests Sister Sledge, Slash, and Steve Winwood in April 1996, shortly before bassist Edwards's death.

WYSIWYG
Chumbawamba
Underlying the percolating rhythms, tough-to-resist sing-along choruses, appealing lead vocals and amusing sound effects are subversive messages that rail against greed and the consumer culture or warn listeners not to become computer zombies. Ax grinding has never sounded this good.

BRUTAL PLANET
Alice Cooper
"It's such a brutal planet/ It's such an ugly world," the original shock rocker snarls. School's out forever, as Alice famously said, but he's still teaching the kids to leaven the metal with harmony, hooks, and humor.

MURDER ON MUSIC ROW
Larry Cordle and Lonesome Standard Time
Most of this album is sprightly bluegrass material picked and sung by Nashville veteran Cordle and his nimble-fingered band. But the album's highlight is the title song, in which Cordle mourns that "drums and rock and roll guitars" have killed good ol' country music.

NUMBER 447
Marshall Crenshaw
To little fanfare (and minuscule sales) rock's now middle-aged boy wonder released this eclectic CD of terrific tunes. It well deserves 2000 plays.

AFTERGLOW
Crowded House
Aussie pop maestro Neil Finn has culled the Crowded House archives for a baker's dozen of unreleased tracks and B-sides. Typically flavorful songcraft, piping hot.

BLOODFLOWERS
The Cure
Robert Smith, the floppy-haired maestro of mope, keeps the quality of his lush, dark, guitar-in-a-bathroom sound uniformly high.

*VOODOO
D'Angelo
Reforging a vibe that embraces jazz, blues, and West African rhythms, neo-soul man D'Angelo channels the sounds and styles of his forebears.

ROAD DOGS
The Charlie Daniels Band
With this package of chug-along, on-the-road songs full of self-indulgent solos, mush-mouthed vocals and tunes as long as a symphony, the Daniels Band can sound like a countrified version of the Grateful Dead.

LIVE ON BREEZE HILL
Rick Danko Band
Just months before his December 1999 death, Danko sounded as soulful and plaintive as ever as he revisited the Band's shuffling classics—sadly, for the last time.

WHITE PONY
Deftones
On their third album, this quintet of very loud Sacramento rockers mixes heavy metal with the angry fury of punk. Once, it would have been called grunge. But by any name, it's still a headbanger's delight.

A SECRET HISTORY
The Divine Comedy
Proclaimed a pop genius in the U.K., head Comedian Neil Hannon deserves the appellation more than his U.S. anonymity. Each of these 17 humor- and melody-filled tracks displays his brilliant gifts as lyricist, vocalist and composer.

FREEDOM IS . . .
The John Doe Thing
The rhythm guitarist of the great L.A. cowboy punk band X is back. Here, his ex-X mate Exene Cervenka contributes a guest vocal.

HAPPY ENDING
Dogstar
Keanu Reeves is savvy enough to let his talented bandmates take most of the spotlight while he anchors the band's rhythmic attack with rock-steady bass—which is all that Dogstar's simple power pop requires.

DUKE ELEGANT
Dr. John
New Orleans R&B veteran Mac "Dr. John" Rebennack recasts Duke Ellington's satin-smooth jazz as sweaty, rhythm-and-blues workouts. The result? Elegant funk.

POP TRASH
Duran Duran
For these seasoned vets, art and pop go hand in hand. Exuberant, guitar-injected rave-ups and dreamy, atmospheric soundscapes that are smartly done, radio-savvy and thoroughly enjoyable.

TRANSCENDENTAL BLUES
Steve Earle
What makes Earle such a magnificent songwriter—and *Blues* one of the great country albums of this year—is how the darkness in his soul ignites such soaring, lovely songs.

DAISIES OF THE GALAXY
Eels
Lurking beneath delicately orchestrated horn and string parts and easy-shuffle tempos are the raw feelings of frustration, anger, and longing. Yet at their best, the Eels recall good-timey '60s groups—only the sentiments are serious.

*I'M DIGGIN' IT
Alecia Elliott
Here's one pre-voting-age singer whose voice turns more heads than her wardrobe. Country prodigy Elliott displays a seasoned vocalist's ability to shift tempos and moods.

THE MENACE
Elastica
Elastica may remind you of Chrissie Hynde or Blondie, but there are plenty of original touches. Snarly fun.

THE MARSHALL MATHERS LP
Eminem
Eminem's potent rhymes and unique perspective are the keys to his success. Proof of his talent—if not his taste—is amply displayed on this bestselling and very, very vulgar CD.

MASTERPIECE THEATRE
En Vogue
The self-proclaimed "Funky Divas" now sound more like divas in a funk.

SONGS FROM AN AMERICAN MOVIE, VOL. ONE: LEARNING HOW TO SMILE
Everclear
A pleasing throwback to the more melodic pop of that the late '60s and '70s.

LARA FABIAN
Lara Fabian
Fabian should mute her overwrought singing—but the major weakness of this album is the banality of its songs.

VAGABOND WAYS
Marianne Faithfull
With her cigarettes-and-whiskey alto and her been-there, done-that-twice persona, Marianne Faithfull, 53, packs all the tools a modern-day torch singer might need. Beautiful and nuanced.

THE CHARMER IS LOUIS FARRAKHAN
Louis Farrakhan
Back in the early '50s, the controversial Nation of Islam minister was a young Boston violinist-singer, joining in the short-lived calypso craze as "The Charmer." An inoffensive—but not exactly charming—curio.

THE MAN IN A JUPITER HAT
Lee Feldman
New York City–raised, conservatory-trained, Fats Waller–inspired piano man Feldman offers wry toasts to a few favorite things such as "Eastern Europe," "Monkeys" and "Drunken Melodies."

SAY IT IS SO
Tim Finn
The New Zealand popsmith (late of Crowded House) recorded this far-from-country CD in Nashville, filling it with hooks and lyric quirks: "She was a shiver looking for a spine."

OUTBOUND
Béla Fleck & the Flecktones
Call it jazzgrass. Banjo plucker extraordinaire Fleck leads her band through a rousing, mostly instrumental song cycle with vocal interludes provided by Shawn Colvin and Jon Anderson.

THE PIZZA TAPES
Jerry Garcia, David Grisman, Tony Rice
The late Grateful Dead–head picks and sings in his high, lonesome wail as he and pals revisit such folk and country oldies as "Long Black Veil."

JUDY GARLAND AT CARNEGIE HALL
Judy Garland
Rock Hudson, Henry Fonda, Richard Burton, and Julie Andrews were among the witnesses when Garland's star was reborn at this historic concert on April 23, 1961.

HEART & SOUL
Crystal Gayle
This winning tribute to the quirky, melody-rich tunes of the great songwriter Hoagy Carmichael proves that the terrific Gayle is as comfortable with pop songs as she is with country music—maybe even more so.

BORN FOR YOU
Kathie Lee Gifford
Kathie Lee drops her coquettish TV schtick and proves herself an adept, even understated vocalist on this cycle of show tunes and pop standards about love's ebb and flow; there's real emotion amid the schmaltzy arrangements.

LET'S MAKE SURE WE KISS GOODBYE

LET'S MAKE SURE WE KISS GOODBYE
Vince Gill
In his consistent musicality, earthiness and astute sense of rhythm, Gill is sounding more and more like Elvis. Constantly topping himself can't be easy, but Gill just gets better and better.

DIZZY IN SOUTH AMERICA
Dizzy Gillespie
Recorded on a 1956 U.S. State Department tour (with Quincy Jones along to arrange), bebop's king pays tribute on "I'm Confessin' " to the trumpeter whose crown he usurped: Louis Armstrong.

ONE ENDLESS NIGHT
Jimmie Dale Gilmore
Gilmore has a voice like a creaking saddle and combines an unapologetic, down-home corniness with subtle irony; his album is full of musical highlights.

TONIGHT AND THE REST OF MY LIFE
Nina Gordon
With melodic hooks and delightfully grand statements, the ex–Veruca Salter fearlessly goes solo.

GUNS N' ROSES LIVE ERA '87–'93
Guns N' Roses
Axl Rose, Slash, and the boys mixed heavy metal, punk, and crowd-pleasing power-pop hooks into an ear-blistering sonic blast. Rose may have been a jerk, but as this CD attests, he and his band could rock.

THIS TIME AROUND
Hanson
The power-rock is generic—think '70s-era Frampton without the vocal phaser—but it's also propulsive and fun and brimming with harmonies.

RHYTHM IN MY SHOES
Jessica Harper
Parents who like to sing to, or with, their children should enjoy this sweet-natured, sprightly album. Harper sings in an ingratiatingly relaxed, swingy style, and her songs have a casual charm.

BEAUTIFUL CREATURE
Juliana Hatfield
A perfectly pleasant collection of folkish pop gems one wishes had more noisy spunk.

INSIDE JOB
Don Henley
Henley vents bile on the usual shadowy cast of suspects: politicians, corporate bigwigs, and (especially) anyone who has ever said anything unkind about Don Henley. Unfortunately, these sleek, R&B-inflected pop tunes sound as soulless as the demons he complains about.

MICHAEL HUTCHENCE
Michael Hutchence
It is difficult to interpret this lackluster collection as the profound statement the late INXS rocker clearly intended it to be. Predictable, and lacking genuine emotion.

GOD & THE FBI
Janis Ian
Nothing in Ian's past output foreshadows this thoroughly delightful, varied, and witty song cycle.

CIRCLE
Indigenous
This Canadian group of Native American blues-rockers is led by vocalist and guitarist Mato Nanji, who plays as if channeling the late native Texan Stevie Ray Vaughan.

TOMORROW TODAY
Al Jarreau
The versatile Jarreau's mellow R&B may not be everyone's cup of chamomile—yet the man is a pop treasure too often overlooked.

SMILE
The Jayhawks
Smile's high points tend to be quieter acoustic moments, but the addition of synthesized keyboards and drums lends a satisfyingly twitchy, 21st-century sound. And if the CD's dark, cryptic pop tunes could use a dose of refreshing directness, leader Gary Louris has crafted several songs worth smiling over.

VOLUME 3: THE LIFE AND TIMES OF S. CARTER
Jay-Z
With inventive imagery and a solid, no-nonsense style, Jay-Z (né Shawn Carter) repeats his allegiance to the streets; his ways with rap make it well worth hearing again.

THE ECLEFTIC
Wyclef Jean
One of the rare artists who appeals to hip-hop's sometimes clashing factions, Jean leaps gracefully from ska to rock to R&B to reggae. Intelligence permeates this strong, complex collection.

2000 YEARS—THE MILLENNIUM CONCERT
Billy Joel
Joel's anthems for Everyman do have their appeal, and the Piano Man pulls out all the stops here for his admirers.

ELTON JOHN'S THE ROAD TO EL DORADO
Elton John
John's heroic vocal style nicely fits the epic, alternating big production ballads with propulsive rockers that keep things lively.

CLAIRVOYANCE
Johnny Society
Living up to a name that's tops in pop, the New York City trio enlists knowing song craft and rare instrumentation (accordion, harpsichord).

REUNION LIVE
The Judds
This emotion-dripping concert seems to have been more memorable for its sentiment than for its music. Die-hard fans probably have all these songs on various albums in their collections; the unconverted would be better off starting with a greatest-hits package, in which the music is less diluted by hoopla.

*KINA
Kina
Singer-songwriter Kina blends classic soul stylings with elements of rock, folk, and blues. With range and expression like this, you can expect Kina to be around for a good long while.

RIDING WITH THE KING
B.B. King & Eric Clapton
King makes the blues a thing of joy, never a downer. Luckily, the lesson seems to have rubbed off on Clapton.

THE KINLEYS II
The Kinleys
The 29-year-old twins percolate along through a lively, varied, brightly melodic collection.

LAY IT DOWN
Jennifer Knapp
If Amy Grant were possessed of some funk, she might sound like Knapp, an uncommonly literate songwriter and uniquely expressive Christian-blues rock singer.

INVINCIBLE SUMMER
k.d. lang
In her new hometown of Los Angeles, the expressive lang takes the local influences—Bacharach, the Beach Boys, techno—and melds them into her own kind of majestic pop. An album to fall in love with—and to.

LESSONS LEARNED
Tracy Lawrence
There are few better country singers than Lawrence, capable of shifting smoothly from contagiously energetic to impressively thoughtful.

JUST NO OTHER WAY
CoCo Lee
A Mariah Carey soundalike whose Euro-disco-style tracks can cause headaches or the grinding of teeth.

THE REMAINS OF TOM LEHRER
Tom Lehrer
Whether the Ivy League math instructor turned satirist had the funniest classroom or the brainiest stage act, no one knows. This witty three-CD box set revisits Lehrer between 1953 and 1999.

PUNISHING KISS
Ute Lemper
German-born chanteuse Lemper shelves her 1930s-era Berlin cabaret act for a contemporary repertoire—by composers as various as Elvis Costello, Tom Waits, and Philip Glass—and shines brilliantly.

G
Gerald Levert
Levert's wounded-Romeo formula wears a bit thin. Luckily the power and emotion of his lived-in baritone saves *G* from being formulaic.

THE NOTORIOUS K.I.M.
Lil' Kim
Kim and her producers can't seem to decide if she should tone down her bad-girl act in favor of a more radio-friendly pop sound or go for the more rugged lyrics that made her debut outrageous and fun.

MORE SONGS FROM POOH CORNER
Kenny Loggins
Loggins displays his usual amiable touch with children's music.

STRONG HEART
Patty Loveless
The bluesy country rocker's best-rounded album, demonstraing the full spectrum of her talent.

THE HOTEL CHILD
Ingrid Lucia and the Flying Neutrinos
The daughter of an itinerant musician and an artist, swing-band vocalist Lucia sings of growing up in flops that were a long way from Eloise's Plaza but no less charming.

LUCY PEARL
Lucy Pearl
The songs on this R&B super-group's debut have a breezy, soulful lilt, and the interplay of male and female voices is delicious. Yet some of the tracks don't amount to much more than extended riffs or elaborate vamps; there is a sense of incompleteness.

I AM
Shelby Lynne
Once a Nashville wunderkind, Lynne seems to be striving for an edgier urban sound that has little, if anything, to do with country music; here, her big voice is wrenched out of shape by overdramatics. A misconceived crossover.

THEN AND NOW
Lynyrd Skynyrd
The unapologetic redneck rockers reprise "Free Bird," "Sweet Home Alabama," and the rest, with Johnny Van Zant taking late bro Ronnie's vocals.

APPALACHIAN JOURNEY
Yo-Yo Ma, Edgar Meyer, Mark O'Connor
James Taylor and Alison Krauss join these cross-pollinating classical and country performers as they search for the holy, haunted heart of American music.

HOMELAND
Miriam Makeba
Before they called it "World Music," there was Makeba, South Africa's own queen of soul. Back in her Homeland after years of exile, she updates her 1967 U.S. pop hit with "Pata Pata 2000."

MAGNOLIA
Aimee Mann
While the soundtrack also includes a handful of songs by others, the star is the intense, brooding Mann; this exposure should help her attain a level of success more commensurate with her considerable talent.

LIVE AT THE VILLAGE VANGUARD
Wynton Marsalis Septet
Eight-and-a-half hours of astonishingly consistent and creative jazz performances.

MAD SEASON
Matchbox Twenty
Mostly splendid pop. Few singers can make a romance gone bad sound so good as Rob Thomas does.

THE INNOCENT YEARS
Kathy Mattea
In places, this country album sounds positively ruminative and New Agey. Slightly sobersided, still enjoyable.

WORKING CLASSICAL
Paul McCartney
Sir Paul kicks out the jams with the London Symphony Orchestra and the Loma Mar Quartet performing his love songs for his late wife, Linda, as lovely orchestral pieces.

DONNIE MCCLURKIN: LIVE IN LONDON AND MORE . . .
Donnie McClurkin
Resisting pop's rich temptations, Detroit soul stirrer McClurkin—whose "I Am" is featured on one of the *Prince of Egypt* soundtracks—sings truly inspired gospel.

BLUE OBSESSION
Michael McDonald
Entire songs can pass without old McDonald unearthing a single non-cliché image. But this blue-eyed balladeer could sing the tally of Census 2000 and make it sound good.

ART OF THE TRIO 4: BACK AT THE VANGUARD
Brad Mehldau
The hot young pianist brings subtle, intelligent craftsmanship to live renderings of instrumental jazz standards and originals.

BURN
Jo Dee Messina
Mae West meets Janis Joplin. Messina is a country artist whose rough-hewn charm is ingratiatingly unaffected.

A MAP OF THE WORLD
Pat Metheny
The genre-jumping guitarist fills this soundtrack album with a mesmerizing stew of jazz, classical, folk, and rock instrumentals.

MINNELLI ON MINNELLI
Liza Minnelli
Liza's tribute to her film director father, Vincente. Avoiding the show-stopping sentimentality she is known for, Liza is in strong voice here—though the show's director, lyricist Fred Ebb, doesn't always rein in his old pal.

BOTH SIDES NOW
Joni Mitchell

Fans are in for a shock: Joni sings 10 tunes from an earlier pop era (as well as two originals) as torch songs, in a husky, smoke-cured alto; in places the sly singer sounds more like the kind of ermine-and-pearls lounge crooners her parents might have swooned for.

NEVER NEVER LAND
Jane Monheit

Few musical efforts are more engaging than a pop standard sung by an intelligent singer backed by imaginative instrumentalists. 22-year-old Monheit—who may remind you of Carly Simon or Rosemary Clooney—is especially alluring.

SO REAL
Mandy Moore

Moore skips along the same sultry but virginal girl-on-the-verge path cleared by Britney Spears. Yet like her idol Madonna, Moore relies on chutzpah to overcome the limitations of a voice that can sound as flimsy as the pop she produces.

THE NIGHT
Morphine

The avant-garde pop trio augment their signature bass-saxophone-drums lineup with organ, strings, guitar, and piano. Jazz-kissed grooves, dance-party songs, bass-driven funk workouts, and eerily lush sonic experiments.

THE SKIFFLE SESSIONS: LIVE IN BELFAST
Van Morrison, Lonnie Donegan, Chris Barber

Donegan created a sensation in 1956 with his tinny hybrid of Appalachian jug-band music, Dixieland, and early rock performed on washboard and broom-handle bass. With Morrison's weighty vocals providing a nice counterpoint, this collaboration is a Belfast blast.

NEW TATTOO
Mötley Crüe

The hoariest of hair bands push the envelope of inanity.

SHADES OF PURPLE
M2M

These complex and truly talented preteen popsters sparkle with the same kind of milky freshness that once rocketed the Spice Girls to stardom.

*FEAR OF FLYING
Mya

With her breathy vocals and street attitude, Mya breathes life and sass into a genre too long held hostage by formula. An unexpected treat in R&B.

WELCOME II NEXTASY
Next

This Minneapolis vocal trio still displays a sexy confidence. What they lack is consistently strong material.

*THE MADDING CROWD
Nine Days

This band boasts two highly talented singer-songwriter-guitarists. With a literate muse and an added layer of sound provided by Hammond organ, Nine Days' pop is absolutely fabulous.

*RETURN OF SATURN
No Doubt

Gwen Stefani introspects to a backbeat, and *Return* brims with No Doubt's peppy new-wave sound.

BORN AGAIN
The Notorious B.I.G.

Sean "Puffy" Combs and a parade of big name rappers build tracks around the late hip-hop great's works in progress—which might or might not have one day become actual songs. A somewhat exploitative and opportunistic album.

*NO STRINGS ATTACHED
'N Sync

Noisy and playful, *No Strings Attached* is good escapist fun, though it lacks a purpose beyond making hordes of screaming girls very happy. There are worse fates.

STANDING ON THE SHOULDER OF GIANTS
Oasis

Oasis continues to construct bright-as-a-penny hooks on songs that are more emotionally charged than ever; a moody, dark and exhilirating celebration of rock and roll.

*FAITH AND COURAGE
Sinéad O'Connor

O'Connor is still capable of creating some of the best music in pop. Assisted by an array of gifted producers, she sings with passion and purpose in these songs about love and spiritual searching.

FROM THERE TO HERE
John Oszajca

Conjuring 1970s-era pop, rock and funk styles, Oszajca eschews the earnestness of that era on this appealing solo debut.

LIVE AT THE GREEK
Jimmy Page & the Black Crowes
These two discs pair Led Zeppelin's guitar avatar with the Crowes' Chris Robinson, who pays devout homage to Led Zep vocalist Robert Plant. **LOVE IN STEREO**

Rahsaan Patterson
With R&B ranging from the understated to the sly and funky, Patterson makes traditional sentiments about love sound sultry and refreshing; here's hoping this powerful performer gains the stardom that has eluded him.

BINAURAL
Pearl Jam
Originators of the Seattle sound go back to basics. Pearl Jam's extended guitar jams and plodding earnestness sound a trifle quaint, but rock bands willing to put it on the line without relying on studio gimmickry or a flip attitude are in short supply.

MP4 (DAYS SINCE A LOST TIME ACCIDENT)
Michael Penn
Catchy melodies that convey complex moods and messages; Penn's soaring harmonies, time signature changes and studio sleights of hand are worthy of the Beatles.

FRANKLY A CAPPELLA: THE PERSUASIONS SING ZAPPA
The Persuasions
Bizarre bedfellows: six middle-aged gentlemen famous for their earnest a cappella vocalizing perform titles by the late avant-garde composer and social satirist. Vocal beauty with bite.

FARMHOUSE
Phish
A collection of well-built, infectious songs that—though they lend themselves to extended improvising—also stand on their own as melodic country-pop tunes.

CAN'T TAKE ME HOME
Pink
The most shocking thing about Pink is her talent. A triple-threat singer-songwriter-heartthrob, this R&B composer sets herself further apart with a confident and understated vocal style.

KISSES IN THE RAIN
John Pizzarelli
Armed with selections from the Great American Songbook (Gershwin, Johnny Mercer, Jimmy Van Heusen, et al) as well as some tasty originals, this spontaneous, sophisticated trio isn't afraid to tinker with the pop standards they hold dear.

THE BEST OF P.M. DAWN
P.M. Dawn
These two New Jersey rappers wrap their rhymes in lovely melodies and high, soaring harmonies

*HE TOUCHED ME
Elvis Presley
On this revelatory CD, Elvis celebrates the gospel music that influenced him as much as did the black R&B upon which his rock kingdom was built.

*MIRROR MIRROR
Kelly Price
With a womanly, from-the-gut voice taking soul from the church and sass from the streets, Price injects feeling and an overriding warmth into what in lesser hands could have been just another bunch of songs about another cheating man. Using humor and a knowing eye to examine infidelity, this singer-songwriter makes her play for the big time.

RADIGAN
Terry Radigan
A successful songwriter making her first venture into solo singing, Radigan is a delicate-going-on-punctilious performer

who can sound like a combination of fey pop-jazz and country, to good effect.

COUNTING SHEEP
Collin Raye
Honky-tonkin' Raye generates ideal playfulness on this appealing children's album.

*BEYOND
Joshua Redman
Beyond showcases Redman's extraordinary sax appeal and impressive but still-maturing talent as a composer and arranger.

SHADES OF BLUE
Francine Reed
With a husky, worldly, and resonant voice, Reed essays standards, rockabilly, gospel, blues and R&B, all infused with her brand of earthy soul.

ECSTASY
Lou Reed
Let us now praise the 58-year-old singer-songwriter for his loud guitars and tender moments: *Ecstasy* is a fine example of an increasingly rare breed, the adult rock and roll record.

*IN THE MOMENT
Dianne Reeves
On this intoxicating live album, Reeves packs loads of oaken-timbred feeling into pop and jazz standards and some sturdy, classically constructed originals.

ANARCHY
Busta Rhymes
Known for his rapid-fire, reggae-influenced delivery and an outrageous, though good-humored, image, Rhymes here reins in his persona in favor of a more direct style.

¡MUY DIVERTIDO!
Marc Ribot y los Cubanos Postizos
Incorporating tasty guitar licks and inventive arrangements, Ribot and crew pay homage to Cuban music with their tongues firmly in cheek and their amps

turned all the way up. Playful, freewheeling, and intoxicating.

THE RUX REVUE
Carl Hancock Rux
Merging poetry, hip-hop, and ambient beats with old-time R&B, this debut album is hypnotic, intense and thought-provoking.

*FROM THE BOTTOM TO THE TOP
Sammie
13-year-old Sammie is already hearing buzz comparing him to two other singers whose pipes seemed far too supple and expressive for their pint sizes—Michael Jackson and Little Stevie Wonder.

AFFIRMATION
Savage Garden
Savage Garden stand apart from the prepackaged R&B teen bands crowd by the mere fact that they write and perform their own material—smart pop songs that actually appeal to grown-ups.

BETTER PART OF ME
Jon Secada
After an opening jolt of Ricky Martinesque fun, this Latin popster's latest is mostly decaf.

THE BEDROOM TAPES
Carly Simon
Dramatic, comic, sweet, and acidic by turns, *Bedroom* is a boffo one-woman performance.

SWEET KISSES
Jessica Simpson
Teen yearnings set to a watery R&B beat.

FORTRESS
Sister Hazel
With a bluesy, folk-rock beat, this Gainesville, Fla., quintet is led by singer-lyricist Ken Block, who sounds like a cross between the Counting Crows' Adam Duritz and power pop rocker Matthew Sweet.

MACHINA/THE MACHINES OF GOD
Smashing Pumpkins
Amidst a swirl of punishingly loud electric guitars and stuttering drumbeats, this grunge act miraculously delivers the most melodic and gorgeously wrought album in its 11-year history.

GUNG HO
Patti Smith
Smith infuses this CD with the freewheeling spirit of her earlier poetic punk; mint Patti.

*HAPPY TO BE HERE
Todd Snider
A throwback to the days when young folkies sang with a twang in their voice, Snider is a singer-songwriter who accompanies himself on guitar and blues harp. He's got an acute sense of humor and lament, but it's his vivid songwriting that makes this Nashville cat one to watch.

*PINK PEARL
Jill Sobule
An entertaining collection of 12 deceptively upbeat tracks, slipping smoothly from country to bossa nova. Often described as Jewel with a sense of humor, Sobule is a peerlessly perky satirist.

NYC GHOSTS & FLOWERS
Sonic Youth
Thurston Moore, Kim Gordon and mates release another wildly noncommercial yet compelling experiment in rock-poetry fusion.

OOPS! . . . I DID IT AGAIN
Britney Spears
A pure pop, guilty pleasure: catchy, deceptively simple melodies within songs that sound like equal parts R&B, new wave and ABBA.

DOMINO
Squeeze
Still hook-sharp tunesmiths without honor or airplay on either side of the Atlantic, Brit new wave vets Glenn Tilbrook and Chris Difford are back with another dozen melodic, offbeat pop beauties.

EIGHTEEN DOWN
Michael Stanley
The king of Cleveland rock returns with 10 new tracks of his muscular midwestern soul (plus three rockin' covers).

*TWO AGAINST NATURE
Steely Dan
Steely Dan returns with nine tracks full of melody, wit, pathos, and other hard-to-find pop attributes. With wryly observant yet cryptic lyrics, juiced-up jazz-rock arrangements and appealing high-register vocals, Steely Dan sounds unlike anything else.

SHADES
Nina Storey
12 gospel-style rock and jazz-grooved songs. At times, Storey gets a bit carried away, filling her wordy songs with Mariah-like melismas and stretching vowels into long ululations that sound like so much caterwauling; she is at her best when she shows restraint.

SUPERGRASS
Supergrass
The band's latest songs are multi-tilayered and well-crafted.

ROYAL BLUE
Koko Taylor
Belting the blues Chicago-style, Koko is joined by royals old (B.B. King) and young (Kenny Wayne Shepherd, Keb' Mo') on her first CD in seven years.

A STONE'S THROW
Mick Taylor
The onetime Rolling Stone whose expressive guitar helped make LPs like *Let It Bleed* classic, Taylor proves he can sing the blues (not bad) as well as play (great).

SWINGIN' AT THE BLUE MOON BAR & GRILL
Steve March Tormé
Mel Tormé's final recording, a lovely duet with his son, is included on the younger Fog's debut album.

LIFEHOUSE ELEMENTS
Pete Townshend
When he wasn't composing sublime three-minute symphonies, inventing the rock opera, or wowing worshipful fans with his windmill guitar-playing, Townshend also found time to fashion a masterful sci-fi musical epic that bears a striking resemblance to *The Matrix*. Here, on synthesizer, he creates baroque majesty.

THE MAN WHO
Travis
A gorgeous swirl of choirboy harmonies and tenderly strummed guitars harking back to the innocent-sounding late-1960s style made popular by Harry Nilsson; irony-free tales of longing that swoop and soar romantically.

TRUE LOVE
True Love
This trio of Hoboken, N.J., powerpop cats has joined a Web collective of hip indie bands (www.cropduster.com) to market this CD of short, sharp, neo-new-wave gems.

TWENTY FOUR SEVEN
Tina Turner
At 60, Turner remains true to herself—energetic and unfailingly Tina. Timeless numbers from a tireless pro.

URBAN KNIGHTS III
Urban Knights
Sixties jazz-pop pioneer Ramsey Lewis ("The In Crowd") contributes keyboards on 10 of these 12 tracks by the latest group of hot, young Chicago musicians he has assembled for this urbane joust.

FRIED GREEN TOMATOES
Ricky Van Shelton
Always calm and confident, this Nashville reliable sounds more in control than ever. Nice work.

BIG LEAGUE ROCKS
Various Artists
Pop songs performed by current and former ballplayers. Sweet swings, but no homers.

CARAVANA CUBANA: LATE NIGHT SESSIONS
Various Artists
An all-star jam of Cuban (and yanqui) greats proves the Buena Vista Social Club is not an exclusive franchise.

FIRE AND SKILL: THE SONGS OF THE JAM
Various Artists
Liam and Noel Gallagher (of Oasis), the Beastie Boys, and Garbage are among the disciples paying tribute to the great British new wave band.

THE I-10 CHRONICLES
Various Artists
Willie Nelson, Adam Duritz, and Eliades Ochoa are among the contributors celebrating the interstate as a musical bridge stretching from Texas to California.

THE MILLION DOLLAR HOTEL
Various Artists
Until U2 returns with a new album this fall, fans must make do with the three new songs (plus three by Bono) on this soundtrack.

SHERYL CROW AND FRIENDS LIVE FROM CENTRAL PARK
Various Artists
The best moments belong to the stellar company she keeps; Crow gets "Happy" with Keith Richards, Eric Clapton, Sarah McLachlan, Stevie Nicks, and the Dixie Chicks.

TWENTIETH CENTURY BLUES— THE SONGS OF NOEL COWARD
Various Artists
Pet Shop Boy wonder Neil Tennant taps Sting, Robbie Williams, and other hip cads to croon Coward.

2GETHER
Various Artists
A boy band formed for a made-for-MTV movie, 2Gether (with Kevin Farley, brother of Chris) contributes the edifying "Say It (Don't Spray It)."

VH1 STORYTELLERS
Various Artists
On this charity benefit album, an impressive cast of stars—including David Bowie and the Eurythmics—re-create old hits in the intimate setting of VH1's popular *Storytellers* series.

WONDER BOYS
Various Artists
Even mixed in among terrific tracks by his '60s peers (including Neil Young, Leonard Cohen, and John Lennon), Bob Dylan's standout new tune is the one that makes this soundtrack a keeper.

BLUES AT SUNRISE
Stevie Ray Vaughan and Double Trouble
More than 70 minutes of soulful slow blues from Vaughan (who died in 1990) burnish this CD, which features late-night jams with Albert King, Johnny Copeland, and other great bluesmen.

FREAK MAGNET
Violent Femmes
Neither a femme nor prone to violence, band auteur Gordon Gano is an endearingly quirky songwriter (best known as composer of 1983's "Blister in the Sun") and perpetual adolescent whose voice is still cracking after all these years.

FAITH IN YOU
Steve Wariner
Long a musician's musician and Nashville favorite, Wariner be discovered by new throngs of fans with this exceptionally imaginative, entertaining album.

LIVE AT MARTYRS'
Chris Whitley
The blues poet and guitar maestro gives minimalist, jazz-flavored treatments to blues, folk, and rock tunes—all thickly atmospheric and bristling with sharp imagery and surprising vocal twists.

*THE BBC SESSIONS
The Who
On these 25 tracks recorded for broadcast between 1965 and 1973, The Who's radio performances are no less explosive than their riotous live concerts.

REEL LIFE VOL. 1, MUSIC FROM HOLLYWOOD: A COLLECTION OF WILD COLONIALS FILM MUSIC
Wild Colonials
Indie film gems warbled by the L.A. alternative rocker Angela McCluskey (with Cyndi Lauper and Dr. John).

RISIN' OUTLAW
Hank Williams III
While he'll have to write and record a few hundred more terrific country tunes to approach his grandfather's genius, he's off to a great start with this debut album.

PERMANENTLY
Mark Wills
Comfy country, delivered with a practiced, heartfelt ease.

HILLBILLY HOMEBOY
Tim Wilson
The raucous *Hillbilly* mixes music and comedy, deftly sending up such much-battered Southern institutions as fireworks stands and stock-car racing with music that's more than competent.

I HOPE YOU DANCE
Lee Ann Womack
With its rueful tone, evocative songs and emotion-drenched, sweet-voiced vocals, this could have been mistaken for a Dolly Parton album. Instead, it's erstwhile Texas firebrand Womack with a winning new sound.

HARD RAIN DON'T LAST
Darryl Worley
With a smoke-cured voice and an easy, back-porch-swing delivery, Worley's white-lightning-pure country sounds as lived-in as an old denim shirt.

NEW DAY DAWNING
Wynonna
Yet another country stalwart turns city slick; Wynonna even sounds a little like Cher. A halfway-decent pop album with a predominantly R&B feel.

*REAL LIVE WOMAN
Trisha Yearwood
With every album, Yearwood sounds smarter and deeper. More musical. Better. This, her ninth album, is a thorough pleasure.

DWIGHTYOAKAMACOUSTIC.NET
Dwight Yoakam
Don't be fooled by the cybertitle. The only thing high-tech about this lovely collection of 25 voice and guitar gems is the microphone.

AND THEN NOTHING TURNED ITSELF INSIDE-OUT
Yo La Tengo
The noisy Hoboken, N.J., group (with husband-wife team Ira Kaplan and Georgia Hubley) turns down the volume to get meditative.

SILVER & GOLD
Neil Young
Like your favorite flannel shirt, Neil Young improves with wear and tear; like that same old shirt, he's a bit threadbare in spots. Young's engaging new album is reminiscent—for better and for worse—of his melodic but slightly bland folk-rock classic *Harvest*.

LIFE'LL KILL YA
Warren Zevon
There is something redemptive about the veteran L.A. singer-songwriter's grumpy, mordant view of the world. He may not be able to hit the high notes, but his songs are clever, burnished gems.

ROCK AND ROLL HALL OF FAME

The Rock and Roll Hall of Fame in Cleveland continues to select the greatest rock and roll musicians for inclusion. A nominee must have released a record at least 25 years prior to induction. Early Influences honors the formative figures in rock.

1986

Chuck Berry
James Brown
Ray Charles
Sam Cooke
Fats Domino
The Everly Brothers
Buddy Holly
Jerry Lee Lewis
Elvis Presley
Little Richard

Early Influences
Robert Johnson
Jimmie Rodgers
Jimmy Yancey

Nonperformers
Alan Freed
Sam Phillips

Lifetime Achievement
John Hammond

1987

The Coasters
Eddie Cochran
Bo Diddley
Aretha Franklin
Marvin Gaye
Bill Haley
B. B. King
Clyde McPhatter
Ricky Nelson
Roy Orbison
Carl Perkins
Smokey Robinson
Big Joe Turner
Muddy Waters
Jackie Wilson

Early Influences
Louis Jordan
T-Bone Walker
Hank Williams

Nonperformers
Leonard Chess
Ahmet Ertegun
Jerry Leiber and Mike Stoller
Jerry Wexler

1988

The Beach Boys
The Beatles
The Drifters
Bob Dylan
The Supremes

Early Influences
Woody Guthrie
Leadbelly
Les Paul

Nonperformer
Berry Gordy Jr.

1989

Dion
Otis Redding
The Rolling Stones
The Temptations
Stevie Wonder

Early Influences
The Ink Spots
Bessie Smith
The Soul Stirrers

Nonperformer
Phil Spector

1990

Hank Ballard
Bobby Darin
The Four Seasons
The Four Tops
The Kinks
The Platters
Simon and Garfunkel
The Who

Early Influences
Louis Armstrong
Charlie Christian
Ma Rainey

Nonperformers
Lamont Dozier
Gerry Goffin and Carole King
Brian Holland and Eddie
   Holland

1991

LaVern Baker
The Byrds
John Lee Hooker
The Impressions
Wilson Pickett
Jimmy Reed
Ike and Tina Turner

Early Influence
Howlin' Wolf

Nonperformers
Dave Bartholomew
Ralph Bass

Lifetime Achievement
Nesuhi Ertegun

1992

Bobby "Blue" Bland
Booker T. and the MG's
Johnny Cash
Jimi Hendrix Experience
The Isley Brothers
Sam and Dave
The Yardbirds

Early Influences
Elmore James
Professor Longhair

Nonperformers
Leo Fender
Doc Pomus
Bill Graham

1993

Ruth Brown
Cream
Creedence Clearwater Revival
The Doors
Etta James
Frankie Lymon and the Teenagers
Van Morrison
Sly and the Family Stone

Early Influence
Dinah Washington

Nonperformers
Dick Clark
Milt Gabler

1994

The Animals
The Band
Duane Eddy
Grateful Dead
Elton John
John Lennon
Bob Marley
Rod Stewart

Early Influence
Willie Dixon

Nonperformer
Johnny Otis

1995

The Allman Brothers Band
Al Green
Janis Joplin
Led Zeppelin
The Vandellas
Neil Young
Frank Zappa

Early Influence
The Orioles

Nonperformer
Paul Ackerman

1996

David Bowie
Gladys Knight and the Pips
Jefferson Airplane
Little Willie John
Pink Floyd
The Shirelles
The Velvet Underground

Early Influence

Pete Seeger

Nonperformer
Tom Donahue

1997

Joni Mitchell
Buffalo Springfield
The Young Rascals
Parliament/Funkadelic
The Jackson Five
The Bee Gees
Crosby, Stills and Nash

Early Influences
Bill Monroe
Mahalia Jackson

Nonperformer
Syd Nathan

1998

The Eagles
Fleetwood Mac
The Mamas and the Papas
Lloyd Price
Santana
Gene Vincent

Early Influence
J. R. Morton

Nonperformer
Allen Toussaint

1999

Billy Joel
Paul McCartney
Curtis Mayfield
Del Shannon
Dusty Springfield
Bruce Springsteen
The Staple Singers

Early Influences
Charles Brown
Bob Willis and His Texas Playboys

Nonperformer
George Martin

2000

Eric Clapton
Earth, Wind & Fire
The Lovin' Spoonful
The Moonglows
Bonnie Raitt
James Taylor

Early Influences
Nat "King" Cole
Billie Holiday

Nonperformer
Clive Davis

JAZZ HALL OF FAME

Down Beat magazine, America's leading jazz publication, conducts an annual poll of both readers and critics to determine the greatest luminaries of the jazz world. The honorees:

	Readers poll	Critics poll			Readers poll	Critics poll
1952	Louis Armstrong	—		1975	Cannonball Adderley	Cecil Taylor
1953	Glenn Miller	—		1976	Woody Herman	King Oliver
1954	Stan Kenton	—		1977	Paul Desmond	Benny Carter
1955	Charlie Parker	—		1978	Joe Venuti	Rahsaan Roland Kirk
1956	Duke Ellington	—		1979	Ella Fitzgerald	Lennie Tristano
1957	Benny Goodman	—		1980	Dexter Gordon	Max Roach
1958	Count Basie	—		1981	Art Blakey	Bill Evans
1959	Lester Young	—		1982	Art Pepper	Fats Navarro
1960	Dizzy Gillespie	—		1983	Stephane Grappelli	Albert Ayler
1961	Billie Holiday	Coleman Hawkins		1984	Oscar Peterson	Sun Ra
1962	Miles Davis	Bix Beiderbecke		1985	Sarah Vaughan	Zoot Sims
1963	Thelonious Monk	Jelly Roll Morton		1986	Stan Getz	Gil Evans
1964	Eric Dolphy	Art Tatum		1987	Lionel Hampton	Johnny Dodds, Thad Jones,
1965	John Coltrane	Earl Hines				Teddy Wilson
1966	Bud Powell	Charlie Christian		1988	Jaco Pastorius	Kenny Clarke
1967	Billy Strayhorn	Bessie Smith		1989	Woody Shaw	Chet Baker
1968	Wes Montgomery	Sidney Bechet,		1990	Red Rodney	Mary Lou Williams
		Fats Waller		1991	Lee Morgan	John Carter
1969	Ornette Coleman	Pee Wee Russell,		1992	Maynard Ferguson	James P. Johnson
		Jack Teagarden		1993	Gerry Mulligan	Edward Blackwell
1970	Jimi Hendrix	Johnny Hodges		1994	Dave Brubeck	Frank Zappa
1971	Charles Mingus	Roy Eldridge,		1995	J. J. Johnson	Julius Hemphill
		Django Reinhardt		1996	Horace Silver	Artie Shaw
1972	Gene Krupa	Clifford Brown		1997	Nat King Cole	Tony Williams
1973	Sonny Rollins	Fletcher Henderson		1998	Frank Sinatra	Elvin Jones
1974	Buddy Rich	Ben Webster		1999		Betty Carter

COUNTRY MUSIC HALL OF FAME

Located in Nashville along with everything else in country music, the Country Music Hall of Fame inducts its honorees each autumn. The enshrined elite:

1962 Roy Acuff
1963 (elections held but no one candidate received enough votes)
1964 Tex Ritter
1965 Ernest Tubb
1966 James R. Denny, George D. Hay, Uncle Dave Macon, Eddy Arnold
1967 Red Foley, J. L. Frank, Jim Reeves, Stephen H. Sholes
1968 Bob Wills
1969 Gene Autry
1970 Original Carter Family (A. P. Carter, Maybelle Carter, Sara Carter), Bill Monroe
1971 Arthur Edward Satherley
1972 Jimmie Davis
1973 Patsy Cline, Chet Atkins
1974 Owen Bradley, Frank "Pee Wee" King

1975 Minnie Pearl
1976 Paul Cohen, Kitty Wells
1977 Merle Travis
1978 Grandpa Jones
1979 Hubert Long, Hank Snow
1980 Connie B. Gay, Original Sons of the Pioneers, Johnny Cash
1981 Vernon Dalhart, Grant Turner
1982 Lefty Frizzell, Marty Robbins, Roy Horton
1983 Little Jimmy Dickens
1984 Ralph Peer, Floyd Tillman
1985 Lester Flatt and Earl Scruggs
1986 Wesley Rose, The Duke of Paducah
1987 Rod Brasfield
1988 Roy Rogers, Loretta Lynn
1989 Jack Stapp, Hank Thompson, Cliffie Stone

1990 Tennessee Ernie Ford
1991 Boudleaux and Felice Bryant
1992 George Jones, Frances Preston
1993 Willie Nelson
1994 Merle Haggard
1995 Roger Miller and Jo Walker-Meador
1996 Patsy Montana, Buck Owens, Ray Price
1997 Harlan Howard, Brenda Lee, Cindy Walker
1998 George Morgan, Elvis Presley, Tammy Wynette, E. W. "Bud" Wendell
1999 Dolly Parton, Johnny Bond, Conway Twitty
2000 Charlie Prodd, Faron Young

TOP CONCERT APPEARANCES

The following survey lists the most successful North American individual concert appearances, based on box-office grosses, for 1999 and for all time. A concert appearance is defined here as all performances in a visit to a single town. (Source: Pollstar)

1999

1.	Woodstock 99 (Dave Matthews Band/Metallica/ Rage Against the Machine/ Red Hot Chili Peppers/KORN)	Rome, New York
2.	Bruce Springsteen & the E Street Band	East Rutherford, New Jersey
3.	Bruce Springsteen & the E Street Band	Philadelphia, Pennsylvania
4.	3 Tenors (Jose Carreras/ Placido Domingo/ Luciano Pavorotti)	Detroit, Michigan
5.	Bruce Springsteen & the E Street Band	Boston, Massachusetts
6.	Dave Matthews Band/ Santana/the Roots	Philadelphia, Pennsylvania
7.	The Rolling Stones/Goo Goo Dolls/Jonny Lang	Chicago, Illinois
8.	The Rolling Stones/Goo Goo Dolls	Boston, Massachusetts
9.	The Rolling Stones/ the Corrs	Philadelphia, Pennsylvania
10.	Bruce Springsteen & the E Street Band	Los Angeles, California
11.	The Rolling Stones/ Brian Adams	Anaheim, California
12.	The Rolling Stones/ the Corrs	Washington, DC
13.	The Rolling Stones/ Sugar Ray	San Jose, California
14.	Phish	Volney, New York
15.	Bruce Springsteen & the E Street Band	Chicago, Illinois
16.	Dave Matthews Band/ Santana/the Roots	East Rutherford, New Jersey
17.	Dave Matthews Band/ Santana/the Roots	Foxboro, Massachusetts
18.	Bruce Springsteen & the E Street Band	Washington, DC
19.	The Rolling Stones/Goo Goo Dolls	Hartford, Connecticut
20.	Bruce Springsteen & the E Street Band	Oakland, California

ALL TIME

1.	Woodstock 99	Rome, New York, 1999
2.	Bruce Springstein & the E Street Band	East Rutherford, New Jersey, 1999
3.	Barbra Streisand	New York City, 1994
4.	Elton John/Billy Joel	East Rutherford, New Jersey, 1994
5.	Barbra Streisand	Las Vegas, 1993
6.	3 Tenors (Jose Carreras/ Placido Domingo/ Luciano Pavarotti)	East Rutherford, New Jersey, 1996
7.	Barbra Streisand	Anaheim, California, 1994
8.	The Rolling Stones	Mexico City, 1995
9.	The Rolling Stones/ Living Colour/ Mar & Magette/ Dou Dov n' Diaye Rose	New York City, 1989
10.	Bette Midler	New York City, 1993
11.	The Rolling Stones/ Pearl Jam	Oakland, California, 1997
12.	The Rolling Stones	East Rutherford, New Jersey, 1994
13.	The Rolling Stones/ Seal	Oakland, California, 1994
14.	The Rolling Stones/ Guns N' Roses/ Living Colour	Los Angeles, 1989
15.	Madonna	Mexico City, 1993
16.	Paul Simon/Simon & Garfunkel	New York City, 1993
17.	3 Tenors (Jose Carreras/ Placido Domingo/ Luciano Pavarotti)	Toronto, Ontario, Canada, 1997
18.	Barbra Streisand	Auburn Hills, Michigan, 1994
19.	Bruce Springsteen & the E Street Band	Philadelphia, 1999 Pennsylvania
20.	Elton John/Billy Joel	Philadelphia, 1994 Pennsylvania

TOP CONCERT TOURS

These are the most successful North American tours of all time, along with year-by-year leaders since 1988. The rankings are based on grosses rather than attendance. (Source: Pollstar)

ALL TIME

Rank	Artist	Year of tour
1.	The Rolling Stones	1994
2.	Pink Floyd	1994
3.	The Rolling Stones	1989
4.	The Rolling Stones	1997
5.	U2	1997
6.	The Eagles	1994
7.	New Kids on the Block	1990
8.	U2	1992
9.	The Rolling Stones	1999
10.	The Eagles	1995
11.	Bruce Springsteen & the E St. Band	1999
12.	Barbara Streisand	1994
13.	Grateful Dead	1994
14.	'N Sync	1999
15.	Dave Matthews Band	1999
16.	Elton John/Billy Joel	1994
17.	Elton John	1998
18.	Grateful Dead	1993
19.	KISS	1996
20.	Boyz II Men	1995

1988

Rank	Artist	Cities/Shows
1.	Pink Floyd	23/35
2.	Van Halen's "Monsters of Rock"	23/26
3.	Def Leppard	94/112
4.	Grateful Dead	33/80
5.	Aerosmith	96/105
6.	Michael Jackson	19/54
7.	AC/DC	105/110
8.	Rod Stewart	82/88
9.	Rat Pack/Ultimate Event	23/41
10.	George Michael	32/46
11.	Whitesnake	83/84
12.	Bruce Springsteen & the E Street Band	21/43
13.	Robert Plant	88/92
14.	Luther Vandross/Anita Baker	26/42
15.	INXS	75/81

1989

Rank	Artist	Cities/Shows
1.	The Rolling Stones	33/60
2.	The Who	27/39
3.	Bon Jovi	129/143
4.	Grateful Dead	33/73
5.	New Kids on the Block	112/143
6.	Neil Diamond	29/69
7.	Metallica	134/140
8.	Elton John	32/47
9.	Rod Stewart	61/71
10.	Beach Boys/Chicago	57/59
11.	Poison	82/83
12.	R.E.M.	84/87
13.	Cinderella	135/136
14.	Barry Manilow	44/123
15.	George Strait	90/104

1990

Rank	Artist	Cities/Shows
1.	New Kids on the Block	122/152
2.	Billy Joel	53/95
3.	Paul McCartney	21/32
4.	Grateful Dead	27/63
5.	Janet Jackson	62/89
6.	Aerosmith	92/101
7.	M. C. Hammer	132/138
8.	Mötley Crüe	103/108
9.	Phil Collins	27/56
10.	Eric Clapton	48/57
11.	David Bowie	41/51
12.	Madonna	12/32
13.	KISS	121/121
14.	Rush	56/63
15.	Depeche Mode	32/33

1991

Rank	Artist	Cities/Shows
1.	Grateful Dead	27/76
2.	ZZ Top	85/106
3.	The Judds	116/126
4.	Rod Stewart	47/59
5.	Paul Simon	72/76
6.	Guns N' Roses	30/43
7.	Bell Biv Devoe/Johnny Gill/Keith Sweat	66/72
8.	Michael Bolton	70/103
9.	Garth Brooks	94/111
10.	Clint Black	92/100
11.	AC/DC	57/60
12.	Sting	64/81
13.	Luther Vandross	50/60
14.	Scorpions	90/93
15.	Van Halen	42/46

1992

Rank	Artist	Cities/Shows
1.	U2	61/73
2.	Grateful Dead	23/55
3.	Guns N' Roses/Metallica	25/25
4.	Neil Diamond	26/69
5.	Bruce Springsteen	36/59
6.	Genesis	24/28
7.	Elton John	32/49
8.	Metallica	87/102
9.	Eric Clapton	30/37
10.	Hammer	123/130
11.	Bryan Adams	92/94
12.	Jimmy Buffett	43/64
13.	Lollapalooza II	29/35
14.	Garth Brooks	78/79
15.	Reba McEntire	102/111

1993

Rank	Artist	Cities/Shows
1.	Grateful Dead	29/81
2.	Rod Stewart	54/68
3.	Neil Diamond	43/75
4.	Paul McCartney	23/23
5.	Bette Midler	29/71
6.	Billy Joel	22/39
7.	Garth Brooks	29/54
8.	Jimmy Buffett	32/52
9.	Reba McEntire	97/105
10.	Kenny G	82/97
11.	"Lollapalooza III"	29/34
12.	Aerosmith	61/66
13.	Clint Black/Wynonna	70/73
14.	Van Halen	32/40
15.	Alan Jackson	98/105

1994

Rank	Artist	Cities/Shows
1.	The Rolling Stones	43/60
2.	Pink Floyd	39/59
3.	The Eagles	32/54
4.	Barbra Streisand	6/22
5.	Grateful Dead	29/84
6.	Elton John/Billy Joel	14/21
7.	Aerosmith	71/76
8.	Lollapalooza IV	33/43
9.	Phil Collins	41/59
10.	Reba McEntire	96/102
11.	Bette Midler	44/54
12.	Billy Joel	40/49
13.	Michael Bolton	84/93
14.	Metallica	49/50
15.	ZZ Top	93/96

1995

Rank	Artist	Cities/Shows
1.	The Eagles	46/58
2.	Boyz II Men	133/134
3.	R.E.M.	63/81
4.	Grateful Dead	20/45
5.	Jimmy Page/Robert Plant	56/68
6.	Van Halen	85/94
7.	Tom Petty and the Heartbreakers	80/89
8.	Reba McEntire	91/101
9.	Elton John	27/41
10.	Elton John/Billy Joel	10/12
11.	Alan Jackson	95/97
12.	Jimmy Buffett	37/52
13.	Yanni	50/59
14.	Vince Gill	82/90
15.	Phish	67/79

1996

Rank	Artist	Cities/Shows
1.	KISS	75/92
2.	Garth Brooks	41/121
3.	Neil Diamond	49/72
4.	Rod Stewart	62/65
5.	Bob Seger	57/64
6.	Jimmy Buffett	28/44
7.	Reba McEntire	83/86
8.	Alanis Morissette	88/98
9.	Hootie & The Blowfish	73/80
10.	Ozzy Osbourne	100/100
11.	AC/DC	74/81
12.	Dave Matthews Band	78/81
13.	George Strait	53/58
14.	Sting	51/56
15.	The Smashing Pumpkins	68/79

1997

Rank	Artist	Cities/Shows
1.	The Rolling Stones	26/33
2.	U2	37/46
3.	Fleetwood Mac	40/44
4.	Metallica	65/77
5.	Brooks & Dunn/ Reba McEntire	66/69
6.	Garth Brooks	28/110
7.	Tina Turner	56/70
8.	The Artist Formerly Known As Prince	71/73
9.	Jimmy Buffett	31/44
10.	Aerosmith	60/63
11.	Phish	34/45
12.	Phil Collins	32/35
13.	Alan Jackson	66/67
14.	ZZ Top	93/94
15.	Bush	69/69

1998

Rank	Artist	Cities/Shows
1.	Elton John	52/63
2.	Dave Matthews Band	76/85
3.	Celine Dion	31/43
4.	Yanni	82/93
5.	Garth Brooks	27/99
6.	Eric Clapton	42/45
7.	Shania Twain	87/92
8.	Janet Jackson	56/60
9.	George Strait Country Music Festival	18/18
10.	The Rolling Stones	13/20
11.	Jimmy Buffett	32/44
12.	Lillith Fair	46/56
13.	Billy Joel	15/38
14.	Aerosmith	67/70
15.	Page/Plant	50/52

1999

Rank	Artist	Cities/Shows
1.	The Rolling Stones	26/34
2.	Bruce Springsteen and the E Street Band	18/54
3.	'N Sync	108/121
4.	Dave Matthews Band	47/62
5.	Shania Twain	60/62
6.	Cher	52/57
7.	Backstreet Boys	40/56
8.	Elton John	55/58
9.	George Strait Country Music Festival	17/17
10.	Bette Midler	33/34
11.	Bob Dylan/Paul Simon	40/46
12.	Phish	46/59
13.	Celine Dion	26/31
14.	Tom Petty and the Heartbreakers	53/67
15.	Jimmy Buffett	27/36

BILLBOARD'S TOP 10 SINGLES

Believe this: even with Ricky Martin shaking his thing, female vocalists young and old ruled the top of the charts in 1999. (Source: *Billboard*)

1946

1. "Prisoner of Love," Perry Como
2. "To Each His Own," Eddy Howard
3. "The Gypsy," Ink Spots
4. "Five Minutes More," Frank Sinatra
5. "Rumors Are Flying," Frankie Carle
6. "Oh! What It Seemed To Be," Frankie Carle
7. "Personality," Johnny Mercer & The Pied Pipers
8. "South America, Take It Away," Bing Crosby & The Andrews Sisters
9. "The Gypsy," Dinah Shore
10. "Oh! What It Seemed To Be," Frank Sinatra

1947

1. "Near You," Francis Craig
2. "Peg O' My Heart," Harmonicats
3. "Heartaches," Ted Weems
4. "Linda," Ray Noble Orchestra & Buddy Clark (tie)
5. "Smoke, Smoke, Smoke (That Cigarette)," Tex Williams (tie)
6. "I Wish I Didn't Love You So," Vaughn Monroe
7. "Peg O' My Heart," Three Suns
8. "Anniversary Song," Al Jolson
9. "Near You," Larry Green Orchestra
10. "That's My Desire," Sammy Kaye

1948

1. "Twelfth Street Rag," Pee Wee Hunt
2. "Mañana (Is Good Enough for Me)," Peggy Lee
3. "Now Is the Hour," Bing Crosby
4. "A Tree in the Meadow," Margaret Whiting
5. "My Happiness," Jon & Sandra Steele
6. "You Can't Be True, Dear," Ken Griffin & Jerry Wayne
7. "Little White Lies," Dick Haymes
8. "You Call Everybody Darlin'," Al Trace
9. "My Happiness," Pied Pipers
10. "I'm Looking Over a Four Leaf Clover," Art Mooney

1949

1. "Riders in the Sky," Vaughn Monroe Orchestra
2. "That Lucky Old Sun," Frankie Laine

3. "You're Breaking My Heart," Vic Damone
4. "Some Enchanted Evening," Perry Como
5. "Slipping Around," Jimmy Wakely & Margaret Whiting
6. "I Can Dream, Can't I?" Andrews Sisters & Gordon Jenkins
7. "Cruising Down the River," Russ Morgan Orchestra
8. "A Little Bird Told Me," Evelyn Knight & The Stardusters
9. "Mule Train," Frankie Laine
10. "Jealous Heart," Al Morgan

1950

1. "Goodnight Irene," Gordon Jenkins & The Weavers
2. "Mona Lisa," Nat King Cole
3. "Third Man Theme," Anton Karas
4. "Sam's Song," Gary & Bing Crosby
5. "Simple Melody," Gary & Bing Crosby
6. "Music, Music, Music," Teresa Brewer
7. "Third Man Theme," Guy Lombardo
8. "Chattanoogie Shoe Shine Boy," Red Foley
9. "Harbor Lights," Sammy Kaye
10. "It Isn't Fair," Sammy Kaye & Don Cornell

1951

1. "Too Young," Nat King Cole
2. "Because of You," Tony Bennett
3. "How High the Moon," Les Paul & Mary Ford
4. "Come On-A My House," Rosemary Clooney
5. "Be My Love," Mario Lanza
6. "On Top of Old Smoky," Weavers
7. "Cold, Cold Heart," Tony Bennett
8. "If," Perry Como
9. "Loveliest Night of the Year," Mario Lanza
10. "Tennessee Waltz," Patti Page

1952

1. "Blue Tango," Leroy Anderson
2. "Wheel of Fortune," Kay Starr
3. "Cry," Johnnie Ray
4. "You Belong to Me," Jo Stafford
5. "Auf Wiederseh'n, Sweetheart," Vera Lynn

6. "I Went to Your Wedding," Patti Page
7. "Half as Much," Rosemary Clooney
8. "Wish You Were Here," Eddie Fisher & Hugo Winterhalter
9. "Here in My Heart," Al Martino
10. "Delicado," Percy Faith

1953

1. "Song From Moulin Rouge," Percy Faith
2. "Vaya con Dios," Les Paul & Mary Ford
3. "Doggie in the Window," Patti Page
4. "I'm Walking Behind You," Eddie Fisher
5. "You, You, You," Ames Brothers
6. "Till I Waltz Again with You," Teresa Brewer
7. "April in Portugal," Les Baxter
8. "No Other Love," Perry Como
9. "Don't Let the Stars Get in Your Eyes," Perry Como
10. "I Believe," Frankie Laine

1954

1. "Little Things Mean a Lot," Kitty Kallen
2. "Wanted," Perry Como
3. "Hey, There," Rosemary Clooney
4. "Sh-Boom," Crew Cuts
5. "Make Love to Me," Jo Stafford
6. "Oh! My Pa-Pa," Eddie Fisher
7. "I Get So Lonely," Four Knights
8. "Three Coins in the Fountain," Four Aces
9. "Secret Love," Doris Day
10. "Hernando's Highway," Archie Bleyer

1955

1. "Cherry Pink and Apple Blossom White," Perez Prado
2. "Rock Around the Clock," Bill Haley & His Comets
3. "The Yellow Rose of Texas," Mitch Miller
4. "Autumn Leaves," Roger Williams
5. "Unchained Melody," Les Baxter
6. "The Ballad of Davy Crockett," Bill Hayes
7. "Love Is a Many-Splendored Thing," Four Aces

8. "Sincerely," McGuire Sisters
9. "Ain't That a Shame," Pat Boone
10. "Dance with Me Henry," Georgia Gibbs

1956

1. "Heartbreak Hotel," Elvis Presley
2. "Don't Be Cruel," Elvis Presley
3. "Lisbon Antigua," Nelson Riddle
4. "My Prayer," Platters
5. "The Wayward Wind," Gogi Grant
6. "Hound Dog," Elvis Presley
7. "The Poor People of Paris," Les Baxter
8. "Whatever Will Be Will Be (Que Sera Sera)," Doris Day
9. "Memories Are Made of This," Dean Martin
10. "Rock and Roll Waltz," Kay Starr

1957

1. "All Shook Up," Elvis Presley
2. "Love Letters in the Sand," Pat Boone
3. "Little Darlin'," Diamonds
4. "Young Love," Tab Hunter
5. "So Rare," Jimmy Dorsey
6. "Don't Forbid Me," Pat Boone
7. "Singing the Blues," Guy Mitchell
8. "Young Love," Sonny James
9. "Too Much," Elvis Presley
10. "Round and Round," Perry Como

1958

1. "Volare (Nel Blu Dipinto Di Blu)," Domenico Modugno
2. "All I Have To Do Is Dream"/ "Claudette," Everly Brothers
3. "Don't"/"I Beg of You," Elvis Presley
4. "Witch Doctor," David Seville
5. "Patricia," Perez Prado
6. "Sail Along Silvery Moon"/ "Raunchy," Billy Vaughn
7. "Catch a Falling Star"/"Magic Moments," Perry Como
8. "Tequila," Champs
9. "It's All in the Game," Tommy Edwards
10. "Return to Me," Dean Martin

1959

1. "The Battle of New Orleans," Johnny Horton
2. "Mack the Knife," Bobby Darin
3. "Personality," Lloyd Price
4. "Venus," Frankie Avalon
5. "Lonely Boy," Paul Anka
6. "Dream Lover," Bobby Darin

7. "The Three Bells," Browns
8. "Come Softly to Me," Fleetwoods
9. "Kansas City," Wilbert Harrison
10. "Mr. Blue," Fleetwoods

1960

1. "Theme from *A Summer Place*," Percy Faith
2. "He'll Have To Go," Jim Reeves
3. "Cathy's Clown," Everly Brothers
4. "Running Bear," Johnny Preston
5. "Teen Angel," Mark Dinning
6. "It's Now or Never," Elvis Presley
7. "Handy Man," Jimmy Jones
8. "I'm Sorry," Brenda Lee
9. "Stuck on You," Elvis Presley
10. "The Twist," Chubby Checker

1961

1. "Tossin' and Turnin'," Bobby Lewis
2. "I Fall to Pieces," Patsy Cline
3. "Michael," Highwaymen
4. "Cryin'," Roy Orbison
5. "Runaway," Del Shannon
6. "My True Story," Jive Five
7. "Pony Time," Chubby Checker
8. "Wheels," String-a-Longs
9. "Raindrops," Dee Clark
10. "Wooden Heart (Muss I Denn)," Joe Dowell

1962

1. "Stranger on the Shore," Mr. Acker Bilk
2. "I Can't Stop Loving You," Ray Charles
3. "Mashed Potato Time," Dee Dee Sharp
4. "Roses Are Red," Bobby Vinton
5. "The Stripper," David Rose
6. "Johnny Angel," Shelley Fabares
7. "Loco-motion," Little Eva
8. "Let Me In," Sensations
9. "The Twist," Chubby Checker
10. "Soldier Boy," Shirelles

1963

1. "Sugar Shack," Jimmy Gilmer & The Fireballs
2. "Surfin' USA," Beach Boys
3. "The End of the World," Skeeter Davis
4. "Rhythm of the Rain," Cascades
5. "He's So Fine," Chiffons
6. "Blue Velvet," Bobby Vinton
7. "Hey Paula," Paul & Paula
8. "Fingertips II," Little Stevie Wonder

9. "Washington Square," Village Stompers
10. "It's All Right," Impressions

1964

1. "I Want To Hold Your Hand," Beatles
2. "She Loves You," Beatles
3. "Hello, Dolly!" Louis Armstrong
4. "Oh, Pretty Woman," Roy Orbison
5. "I Get Around," Beach Boys
6. "Everybody Loves Somebody," Dean Martin
7. "My Guy," Mary Wells
8. "We'll Sing in the Sunshine," Gale Garnett
9. "Last Kiss," J. Frank Wilson & The Cavaliers
10. "Where Did Our Love Go," Supremes

1965

1. "Wooly Bully," Sam the Sham & The Pharaohs
2. "I Can't Help Myself," Four Tops
3. "(I Can't Get No) Satisfaction," Rolling Stones
4. "You Were on My Mind," We Five
5. "You've Lost That Lovin' Feelin'," Righteous Brothers
6. "Downtown," Petula Clark
7. "Help!," Beatles
8. "Can't You Hear My Heartbeat," Herman's Hermits
9. "Crying in the Chapel," Elvis Presley
10. "My Girl," Temptations

1966

1. "The Ballad of the Green Berets," S/Sgt. Barry Sadler
2. "Cherish," Association
3. "(You're My) Soul and Inspiration," Righteous Brothers
4. "Reach Out I'll Be There," Four Tops
5. "96 Tears," ? & the Mysterians
6. "Last Train to Clarksville," Monkees
7. "Monday, Monday," Mamas & the Papas
8. "You Can't Hurry Love," Supremes
9. "Poor Side of Town," Johnny Rivers
10. "California Dreamin'," Mamas & the Papas

1967

1. "To Sir with Love," Lulu
2. "The Letter," Box Tops
3. "Ode to Billie Joe," Bobby Gentry
4. "Windy," Association
5. "I'm a Believer," Monkees
6. "Light My Fire," Doors

7. "Somethin' Stupid," Nancy Sinatra & Frank Sinatra
8. "Happy Together," Turtles
9. "Groovin'," Young Rascals
10. "Can't Take My Eyes Off You," Frankie Valli

1968

1. "Hey Jude," Beatles
2. "Love Is Blue (L'Amour Est Blue)," Paul Mauriat
3. "Honey," Bobby Goldsboro
4. "(Sittin' on) The Dock of the Bay," Otis Redding
5. "People Got To Be Free," Rascals
6. "Sunshine of Your Love," Cream
7. "This Guy's in Love with You," Herb Alpert
8. "The Good, the Bad and the Ugly," Hugo Montenegro
9. "Mrs. Robinson," Simon & Garfunkel
10. "Tighten Up," Archie Bell & The Drells

1969

1. "Sugar, Sugar," Archies
2. "Aquarius/Let the Sunshine In," Fifth Dimension
3. "I Can't Get Next to You," Temptations
4. "Honky Tonk Women," Rolling Stones
5. "Everyday People," Sly & the Family Stone
6. "Dizzy," Tommy Roe
7. "Hot Fun in the Summertime," Sly & the Family Stone
8. "I'll Never Fall in Love Again," Tom Jones
9. "Build Me Up Buttercup," Foundations
10. "Crimson and Clover," Tommy James & The Shondells

1970

1. "Bridge over Troubled Water," Simon & Garfunkel
2. "(They Long To Be) Close to You," Carpenters
3. "American Woman"/"No Sugar Tonight," Guess Who
4. "Raindrops Keep Fallin' on My Head," B. J. Thomas
5. "War," Edwin Starr
6. "Ain't No Mountain High Enough," Diana Ross
7. "I'll Be There," Jackson 5
8. "Get Ready," Rare Earth
9. "Let It Be," Beatles
10. "Band of Gold," Freda Payne

1971

1. "Joy to the World," Three Dog Night
2. "Maggie May"/"Reason To Believe," Rod Stewart
3. "It's Too Late"/"I Feel the Earth Move," Carole King
4. "One Bad Apple," Osmonds
5. "How Can You Mend a Broken Heart," Bee Gees
6. "Indian Reservation," Raiders
7. "Go Away Little Girl," Donny Osmond
8. "Take Me Home, Country Roads," John Denver with Fat City
9. "Just My Imagination (Running Away with Me)," Temptations
10. "Knock Three Times," Dawn

1972

1. "The First Time Ever I Saw Your Face," Roberta Flack
2. "Alone Again (Naturally)," Gilbert O'Sullivan
3. "American Pie," Don McLean
4. "Without You," Nilsson
5. "Candy Man," Sammy Davis Jr.
6. "I Gotcha," Joe Tex
7. "Lean on Me," Bill Withers
8. "Baby Don't Get Hooked on Me," Mac Davis
9. "Brand New Key," Melanie
10. "Daddy Don't You Walk So Fast," Wayne Newton

1973

1. "Tie a Yellow Ribbon 'Round the Ole Oak Tree," Tony Orlando & Dawn
2. "Bad, Bad Leroy Brown," Jim Croce
3. "Killing Me Softly with His Song," Roberta Flack
4. "Let's Get It On," Marvin Gaye
5. "My Love," Paul McCartney & Wings
6. "Why Me," Kris Kristofferson
7. "Crocodile Rock," Elton John
8. "Will It Go Round in Circles," Billy Preston
9. "You're So Vain," Carly Simon
10. "Touch Me in the Morning," Diana Ross

1974

1. "The Way We Were," Barbra Streisand
2. "Seasons in the Sun," Terry Jacks
3. "Love's Theme," Love Unlimited Orchestra
4. "Come and Get Your Love," Redbone
5. "Dancing Machine," Jackson 5
6. "The Loco-motion," Grand Funk Railroad
7. "TSOP," MFSB

8. "The Streak," Ray Stevens
9. "Bennie and the Jets," Elton John
10. "One Hell of a Woman," Mac Davis

1975

1. "Love Will Keep Us Together," Captain & Tennille
2. "Rhinestone Cowboy," Glen Campbell
3. "Philadelphia Freedom," Elton John
4. "Before the Next Teardrop Falls," Freddy Fender
5. "My Eyes Adored You," Frankie Valli
6. "Shining Star," Earth, Wind & Fire
7. "Fame," David Bowie
8. "Laughter in the Rain," Neil Sedaka
9. "One of These Nights," Eagles
10. "Thank God I'm a Country Boy," John Denver

1976

1. "Silly Love Songs," Wings
2. "Don't Go Breaking My Heart," Elton John & Kiki Dee
3. "Disco Lady," Johnnie Taylor
4. "December, 1963 (Oh, What a Night)," Four Seasons
5. "Play That Funky Music," Wild Cherry
6. "Kiss and Say Goodbye," Manhattans
7. "Love Machine, Pt. 1," Miracles
8. "50 Ways To Leave Your Lover," Paul Simon
9. "Love Is Alive," Gary Wright
10. "A Fifth of Beethoven," Walter Murphy & The Big Apple Band

1977

1. "Tonight's the Night (Gonna Be Alright)," Rod Stewart
2. "I Just Want To Be Your Everything," Andy Gibb
3. "Best of My Love," Emotions
4. "Love Theme from *A Star Is Born* (Evergreen)" Barbra Streisand
5. "Angel in Your Arms," Hot
6. "I Like Dreamin'," Kenny Nolan
7. "Don't Leave Me This Way," Thelma Houston
8. "(Your Love Has Lifted Me) Higher and Higher," Rita Coolidge
9. "Undercover Angel," Alan O'Day
10. "Torn Between Two Lovers," Mary MacGregor

1978

1. "Shadow Dancing," Andy Gibb
2. "Night Fever," Bee Gees
3. "You Light Up My Life," Debby Boone
4. "Stayin' Alive," Bee Gees
5. "Kiss You All Over," Exile

6. "How Deep Is Your Love," Bee Gees
7. "Baby Come Back," Player
8. "Love Is Thicker Than Water," Andy Gibb
9. "Boogie Oogie Oogie," A Taste of Honey
10. "Three Times a Lady," Commodores

1979

1. "My Sharona," Knack
2. "Bad Girls," Donna Summer
3. "Le Freak," Chic
4. "Do Ya Think I'm Sexy," Rod Stewart
5. "Reunited," Peaches & Herb
6. "I Will Survive," Gloria Gaynor
7. "Hot Stuff," Donna Summer
8. "Y.M.C.A.," Village People
9. "Ring My Bell," Anita Ward
10. "Sad Eyes," Robert John

1980

1. "Call Me," Blondie
2. "Another Brick in the Wall," Pink Floyd
3. "Magic," Olivia Newton-John
4. "Rock with You," Michael Jackson
5. "Do That to Me One More Time," Captain & Tennille
6. "Crazy Little Thing Called Love," Queen
7. "Coming Up," Paul McCartney
8. "Funkytown," Lipps, Inc.
9. "It's Still Rock and Roll to Me," Billy Joel
10. "The Rose," Bette Midler

1981

1. "Bette Davis Eyes," Kim Carnes
2. "Endless Love," Diana Ross & Lionel Richie
3. "Lady," Kenny Rogers
4. "(Just Like) Starting Over," John Lennon
5. "Jessie's Girl," Rick Springfield
6. "Celebration," Kool & the Gang
7. "Kiss on My List," Daryl Hall & John Oates
8. "I Love a Rainy Night," Eddie Rabbitt
9. "9 to 5," Dolly Parton
10. "Keep On Loving You," REO Speedwagon

1982

1. "Physical," Olivia Newton-John
2. "Eye of the Tiger," Survivor
3. "I Love Rock 'n' Roll," Joan Jett & the Blackhearts
4. "Ebony and Ivory," Paul McCartney & Stevie Wonder

5. "Centerfold," The J. Geils Band
6. "Don't You Want Me," Human League
7. "Jack and Diane," John Cougar
8. "Hurts So Good," John Cougar
9. "Abracadabra," Steve Miller Band
10. "Hard To Say I'm Sorry," Chicago

1983

1. "Every Breath You Take," The Police
2. "Billie Jean," Michael Jackson
3. "Flashdance...What a Feeling," Irene Cara
4. "Down Under," Men at Work
5. "Beat It," Michael Jackson
6. "Total Eclipse of the Heart," Bonnie Tyler
7. "Maneater," Daryl Hall & John Oates
8. "Baby Come to Me," Patti Austin with James Ingram
9. "Maniac," Michael Sembello
10. "Sweet Dreams (Are Made of This)," Eurythmics

1984

1. "When Doves Cry," Prince
2. "What's Love Got To Do with It," Tina Turner
3. "Say Say Say," Paul McCartney & Michael Jackson
4. "Footloose," Kenny Loggins
5. "Against All Odds (Take a Look at Me Now)," Phil Collins
6. "Jump," Van Halen
7. "Hello," Lionel Richie
8. "Owner of a Lonely Heart," Yes
9. "Ghostbusters," Ray Parker Jr.
10. "Karma Chameleon," Culture Club

1985

1. "Careless Whisper," Wham! featuring George Michael
2. "Like a Virgin," Madonna
3. "Wake Me Up Before You Go-Go," Wham!
4. "I Want To Know What Love Is," Foreigner
5. "I Feel for You," Chaka Khan
6. "Out of Touch," Daryl Hall & John Oates
7. "Everybody Wants To Rule the World," Tears for Fears
8. "Money for Nothing," Dire Straits
9. "Crazy for You," Madonna
10. "Take on Me," a-ha

1986

1. "That's What Friends Are For," Dionne & Friends
2. "Say You, Say Me," Lionel Richie

3. "I Miss You," Klymaxx
4. "On My Own," Patti LaBelle & Michael McDonald
5. "Broken Wings," Mr. Mister
6. "How Will I Know," Whitney Houston
7. "Party All the Time," Eddie Murphy
8. "Burning Heart," Survivor
9. "Kyrie," Mr. Mister
10. "Addicted to Love," Robert Palmer

1987

1. "Walk Like an Egyptian," Bangles
2. "Alone," Heart
3. "Shake You Down," Gregory Abbott
4. "I Wanna Dance with Somebody (Who Loves Me)," Whitney Houston
5. "Nothing's Gonna Stop Us Now," Starship
6. "C'est La Vie," Robbie Nevil
7. "Here I Go Again," Whitesnake
8. "The Way It Is," Bruce Hornsby & the Range
9. "Shakedown," Bob Seger
10. "Livin' On a Prayer," Bon Jovi

1988

1. "Faith," George Michael
2. "Need You Tonight," INXS
3. "Got My Mind Set on You," George Harrison
4. "Never Gonna Give You Up," Rick Astley
5. "Sweet Child o' Mine," Guns N' Roses
6. "So Emotional," Whitney Houston
7. "Heaven Is a Place on Earth," Belinda Carlisle
8. "Could've Been," Tiffany
9 "Hands to Heaven," Breathe
10. "Roll with It," Steve Winwood

1989

1. "Look Away," Chicago
2. "My Prerogative," Bobby Brown
3. "Every Rose Has Its Thorn," Poison
4. "Straight Up," Paula Abdul
5. "Miss You Much," Janet Jackson
6. "Cold Hearted," Paula Abdul
7. "Wind Beneath My Wings," Bette Midler
8. "Girl You Know It's True," Milli Vanilli
9. "Baby, I Love Your Way/Freebird Medley," Will to Power
10. "Giving You the Best That I Got," Anita Baker

1990

1. "Hold On," Wilson Phillips
2. "It Must Have Been Love," Roxette
3. "Nothing Compares 2 U," Sinéad O'Connor

4. "Poison," Bell Biv Devoe
5. "Vogue," Madonna
6. "Vision of Love," Mariah Carey
7. "Another Day in Paradise," Phil Collins
8. "Hold On," En Vogue
9. "Cradle of Love," Billy Idol
10. "Blaze of Glory," Jon Bon Jovi

1991

1. "(Everything I Do) I Do It for You," Bryan Adams
2. "I Wanna Sex You Up," Color Me Badd
3. "Gonna Make You Sweat," C+C Music Factory
4. "Rush Rush," Paula Abdul
5. "One More Try," Timmy T.
6. "Unbelievable," EMF
7. "More Than Words," Extreme
8. "I Like the Way (The Kissing Game)," Hi-Five
9. "The First Time," Surface
10. "Baby Baby," Amy Grant

1992

1. "End of the Road," Boyz II Men
2. "Baby Got Back," Sir Mix-A-Lot
3. "Jump," Kris Kross
4. "Save the Best for Last," Vanessa Williams
5. "Baby-Baby-Baby," TLC
6. "Tears in Heaven," Eric Clapton
7. "My Lovin' (You're Never Gonna Get It)," En Vogue
8. "Under the Bridge," Red Hot Chili Peppers
9. "All 4 Love," Color Me Badd
10. "Just Another Day," Jon Secada

1993

1. "I Will Always Love You," Whitney Houston
2. "Whoomp! (There It Is)," Tag Team
3. "Can't Help Falling in Love," UB40
4. "That's the Way Love Goes," Janet Jackson
5. "Freak Me," Silk
6. "Weak," SWV
7. "If I Ever Fall in Love," Shai
8. "Dreamlover," Mariah Carey

9. "Rump Shaker," Wreckx-N-Effect
10. "Informer," Snow

1994

1. "The Sign," Ace of Base
2. "I Swear," All-4-One
3. "I'll Make Love to You," Boyz II Men
4. "The Power of Love," Celine Dion
5. "Hero," Mariah Carey
6. "Stay (I Missed You)," Lisa Loeb & Nine Stories
7. "Breathe Again," Toni Braxton
8. "All for Love," Bryan Adams/Rod Stewart/Sting
9. "All That She Wants," Ace of Base
10. "Don't Turn Around," Ace of Base

1995

1. "Gangsta's Paradise," Coolio featuring L.V.
2. "Waterfalls," TLC
3. "Creep," TLC
4. "Kiss from a Rose," Seal
5. "On Bended Knee," Boyz II Men
6. "Another Night," Real McCoy
7. "Fantasy," Mariah Carey
8. "Take A Bow," Madonna
9. "Don't Take It Personal (Just One of Dem Days)," Monica
10. "This Is How We Do It," Montell Jordan

1996

1. "Macarena (Bayside Boys Mix)," Los Del Rio
2. "One Sweet Day," Mariah Carey & Boyz II Men
3. "Because You Loved Me," Celine Dion
4. "Nobody Knows," The Tony Rich Project
5. "Always Be My Baby," Mariah Carey
6. "Give Me One Reason," Tracy Chapman
7. "Tha Crossroads," Bone Thugs-N-Harmony
8. "I Love You Always Forever," Donna Lewis
9. "You're Makin' Me High/Let It Flow," Toni Braxton
10. "Twisted," Keith Sweat

1997

1. "Candle in the Wind 1997"/"Something About the Way You Look Tonight," Elton John
2. "You Were Meant for Me"/"Foolish Games," Jewel
3. "I'll Be Missing You," Puff Daddy & Faith Evans (Featuring 112)
4. "Un-Break My Heart," Toni Braxton
5. "Can't Nobody Hold Me Down," Puff Daddy (featuring Mase)
6. "I Believe I Can Fly," R. Kelly
7. "Don't Let Go (Love)," En Vogue
8. "Return of the Mack," Mark Morrison
9. "How Do I Live," LeAnn Rimes
10. "Wannabe," Spice Girls

1998

1. "The Boy Is Mine," Brandy & Monica
2. "Too Close," Next
3. "You're Still the One," Shania Twain
4. "Candle in the Wind 1997"/"Some thing About the Way You Look Tonight," Elton John
5. "Been Around the World," Puff Daddy & The Family
6. "How Do I Live," LeAnn Rimes
7. "Nice & Slow," Usher
8. "No, No, No," Destiny's Child
9. "My Way," Usher
10. "My All," Mariah Carey

1999

1. "Believe," Cher
2. "No Scrubs," TLC
3. "Angel of Mind," Monica
4. "Heartbreak Hotel," Whitney Houston featuring Faith Evans and Kelly Price
5. "...Baby One More Time," Britney Spears
6. "Kiss Me," Sixpence None the Richer
7. "Genie in a Bottle," Christina Aguilera
8. "Every Morning," Sugar Ray
9. "Nobody's Supposed to Be Here," Deborah Cox
10. "Livin' La Vida Loca," Ricky Martin

BILLBOARD'S TOP 10 ALBUMS

The Backstreet Boys sang us into the *Millennium*, with rivals 'N Sync hot on their heels. Still, the Top 10 had plenty of room for country, metal, and soul (but no scrubs). (Source: *Billboard*)

1957

1. *My Fair Lady*, original cast
2. *Hymns*, Tennessee Ernie Ford
3. *Oklahoma!*, soundtrack
4. *Around the World in 80 Days*, soundtrack
5. *The King and I*, soundtrack
6. *Calypso*, Harry Belafonte
7. *Love Is the Thing*, Nat King Cole
8. *The Eddy Duchin Story*, soundtrack
9. *Songs of the Fabulous Fifties*, Roger Williams
10. *Film Encores*, Mantovani

1958

1. *My Fair Lady*, original cast
2. *The Music Man*, original cast
3. *Johnny's Greatest Hits*, Johnny Mathis
4. *South Pacific*, soundtrack
5. *Come Fly with Me*, Frank Sinatra
6. *Around the World in 80 Days*, soundtrack
7. *Warm*, Johnny Mathis
8. *South Pacific*, original cast
9. *Ricky*, Ricky Nelson
10. *The King and I*, soundtrack

1959

1. *Music from "Peter Gunn,"* Henry Mancini
2. *Gigi*, soundtrack
3. *South Pacific*, soundtrack
4. *From the Hungry i*, Kingston Trio
5. *The Kingston Trio at Large*, Kingston Trio
6. *Sing Along with Mitch*, Mitch Miller
7. *Inside Shelley Berman*, Shelley Berman
8. *Exotica, Vol. 1*, Martin Denny
9. *My Fair Lady*, original cast
10. *Flower Drum Song*, original cast

1960

1. *The Sound of Music*, original cast
2. *Inside Shelley Berman*, Shelley Berman
3. *The Button-Down Mind of Bob Newhart*, Bob Newhart
4. *Sixty Years of Music America Loves Best, Vol. I*, various artists
5. *Here We Go Again*, Kingston Trio
6. *Sold Out*, Kingston Trio
7. *Heavenly*, Johnny Mathis
8. *South Pacific*, soundtrack
9. *Faithfully*, Johnny Mathis
10. *Outside Shelley Berman*, Shelley Berman

1961

1. *Camelot*, original cast
2. *Great Motion Picture Themes*, various artists
3. *Never on Sunday*, soundtrack
4. *The Sound of Music*, original cast
5. *Exodus*, soundtrack
6. *Knockers Up*, Rusty Warren
7. *G.I. Blues*, Elvis Presley/soundtrack
8. *Sing Along with Mitch*, Mitch Miller
9. *Calcutta*, Lawrence Welk
10. *Tonight in Person*, Limeliters

1962

1. *West Side Story*, soundtrack
2. *Breakfast at Tiffany's*, Henry Mancini
3. *Blue Hawaii*, Elvis Presley/soundtrack
4. *West Side Story*, original cast
5. *The Sound of Music*, original cast
6. *Time Out*, Dave Brubeck
7. *Camelot*, original cast
8. *Your Twist Party*, Chubby Checker
9. *Knockers Up*, Rusty Warren
10. *Judy at Carnegie Hall*, Judy Garland

1963

1. *West Side Story*, soundtrack
2. *Peter, Paul and Mary*, Peter, Paul and Mary
3. *Moving*, Peter, Paul and Mary
4. *Joan Baez in Concert*, Joan Baez
5. *I Left My Heart in San Francisco*, Tony Bennett
6. *Moon River and Other Great Movie Themes*, Andy Williams
7. *Lawrence of Arabia*, soundtrack
8. *Days of Wine and Roses*, Andy Williams
9. *Oliver*, original cast
10. *Modern Sounds in Country and Western Music, Vol. 2*, Ray Charles

1964

1. *Hello, Dolly!*, original cast
2. *In the Wind*, Peter, Paul and Mary
3. *Honey in the Horn*, Al Hirt
4. *The Barbra Streisand Album*, Barbra Streisand
5. *West Side Story*, soundtrack
6. *Peter, Paul and Mary*, Peter, Paul & Mary
7. *The Second Barbra Streisand Album*, Barbra Streisand
8. *Meet the Beatles*, Beatles
9. *The Third Barbra Streisand Album*, Barbra Streisand
10. *Moon River and Other Great Movie Themes*, Andy Williams

1965

1. *Mary Poppins*, soundtrack
2. *Beatles '65*, Beatles
3. *The Sound of Music*, soundtrack
4. *My Fair Lady*, soundtrack
5. *Fiddler on the Roof*, original cast
6. *Goldfinger*, soundtrack
7. *Hello, Dolly!*, original cast
8. *Dear Heart*, Andy Williams
9. *Introducing Herman's Hermits*, Herman's Hermits
10. *Beatles VI*, Beatles

1966

1. *Whipped Cream and Other Delights*, Herb Alpert & the Tijuana Brass
2. *The Sound of Music*, soundtrack
3. *Going Places*, Herb Alpert & the Tijuana Brass
4. *Rubber Soul*, Beatles
5. *What Now My Love*, Herb Alpert & the Tijuana Brass
6. *If You Can Believe Your Eyes and Ears*, Mamas & the Papas
7. *Dr. Zhivago*, soundtrack
8. *Revolver*, Beatles
9. *Color Me Barbra*, Barbra Streisand
10. *Ballad of the Green Berets*, S/Sgt. Barry Sadler

1967

1. *More of the Monkees*, Monkees
2. *The Monkees*, Monkees
3. *Dr. Zhivago*, soundtrack
4. *The Sound of Music*, soundtrack
5. *The Temptations' Greatest Hits*, Temptations
6. *A Man and a Woman*, soundtrack
7. *S.R.O.*, Herb Alpert & the Tijuana Brass

8. *Whipped Cream and Other Delights,* Herb Alpert & the Tijuana Brass
9. *Going Places,* Herb Alpert & the Tijuana Brass
10. *Sgt. Pepper's Lonely Hearts Club Band,* Beatles

1968

1. *Are You Experienced?,* Jimi Hendrix Experience
2. *The Graduate,* Simon & Garfunkel/soundtrack
3. *Disraeli Gears,* Cream
4. *Magical Mystery Tour,* Beatles/soundtrack
5. *Diana Ross and the Supremes' Greatest Hits,* Diana Ross & The Supremes
6. *Sgt. Pepper's Lonely Hearts Club Band,* Beatles
7. *The Doors,* The Doors
8. *Parsley, Sage, Rosemary and Thyme,* Simon & Garfunkel
9. *Vanilla Fudge,* Vanilla Fudge
10. *Blooming Hits,* Paul Mauriat & His Orchestra

1969

1. *In-a-Gadda-Da-Vida,* Iron Butterfly
2. *Hair,* original cast
3. *Blood, Sweat and Tears,* Blood, Sweat and Tears
4. *Bayou Country,* Creedence Clearwater Revival
5. *Led Zeppelin,* Led Zeppelin
6. *Johnny Cash at Folsom Prison,* Johnny Cash
7. *Funny Girl,* soundtrack
8. *The Beatles (The White Album),* Beatles
9. *Donovan's Greatest Hits,* Donovan
10. *The Association's Greatest Hits,* Association

1970

1. *Bridge over Troubled Water,* Simon & Garfunkel
2. *Led Zeppelin II,* Led Zeppelin
3. *Chicago,* Chicago
4. *Abbey Road,* Beatles
5. *Santana,* Santana
6. *Get Ready,* Rare Earth
7. *Easy Rider,* soundtrack
8. *Butch Cassidy and the Sundance Kid,* soundtrack
9. *Joe Cocker!,* Joe Cocker
10. *Three Dog Night Was Captured Live at the Forum,* Three Dog Night

1971

1. *Jesus Christ Superstar,* various artists
2. *Tapestry,* Carole King
3. *Close to You,* Carpenters
4. *Pearl,* Janis Joplin
5. *Abraxas,* Santana
6. *The Partridge Family Album,* Partridge Family
7. *Sweet Baby James,* James Taylor
8. *Tea for the Tillerman,* Cat Stevens
9. *Greatest Hits,* Sly & the Family Stone
10. *Chicago III,* Chicago

1972

1. *Harvest,* Neil Young
2. *Tapestry,* Carole King
3. *American Pie,* Don McLean
4. *Teaser and the Firecat,* Cat Stevens
5. *Hot Rocks, 1964–71,* Rolling Stones
6. *Killer,* Alice Cooper
7. *First Take,* Roberta Flack
8. *America,* America
9. *Music,* Carole King
10. *Madman Across the Water,* Elton John

1973

1. *The World Is a Ghetto,* War
2. *Summer Breeze,* Seals & Crofts
3. *Talking Book,* Stevie Wonder
4. *No Secrets,* Carly Simon
5. *Lady Sings the Blues,* Diana Ross
6. *They Only Come Out at Night,* Edgar Winter Group
7. *I Am Woman,* Helen Reddy
8. *Don't Shoot Me, I'm Only the Piano Player,* Elton John
9. *I'm Still in Love with You,* Al Green
10. *Seventh Sojourn,* Moody Blues

1974

1. *Goodbye Yellow Brick Road,* Elton John
2. *John Denver's Greatest Hits,* John Denver
3. *Band on the Run,* Paul McCartney & Wings
4. *Innervisions,* Stevie Wonder
5. *You Don't Mess Around with Jim,* Jim Croce
6. *American Graffiti,* soundtrack
7. *Imagination,* Gladys Knight & The Pips
8. *Behind Closed Doors,* Charlie Rich
9. *The Sting,* soundtrack
10. *Tres Hombres,* ZZ Top

1975

1. *Elton John—Greatest Hits,* Elton John
2. *John Denver's Greatest Hits,* John Denver
3. *That's the Way of the World,* Earth, Wind & Fire
4. *Back Home Again,* John Denver
5. *Phoebe Snow,* Phoebe Snow
6. *Heart Like a Wheel,* Linda Ronstadt
7. *Captain Fantastic and the Brown Dirt Cowboy,* Elton John
8. *An Evening with John Denver,* John Denver
9. *AWB,* Average White Band
10. *On the Border,* Eagles

1976

1. *Frampton Comes Alive,* Peter Frampton
2. *Fleetwood Mac,* Fleetwood Mac
3. *Wings at the Speed of Sound,* Wings
4. *Greatest Hits, 1971–1975,* Eagles
5. *Chicago IX—Chicago's Greatest Hits,* Chicago
6. *The Dream Weaver,* Gary Wright
7. *Desire,* Bob Dylan
8. *A Night at the Opera,* Queen
9. *History—America's Greatest Hits,* America
10. *Gratitude,* Earth, Wind & Fire

1977

1. *Rumours,* Fleetwood Mac
2. *Songs in the Key of Life,* Stevie Wonder
3. *A Star Is Born,* Barbra Streisand/Kris Kristofferson/soundtrack
4. *Hotel California,* Eagles
5. *Boston,* Boston
6. *A New World Record,* Electric Light Orchestra
7. *Part 3,* K.C. & the Sunshine Band
8. *Silk Degrees,* Boz Scaggs
9. *Night Moves,* Bob Seger & the Silver Bullet Band
10. *Fleetwood Mac,* Fleetwood Mac

1978

1. *Saturday Night Fever,* Bee Gees/various artists/soundtrack
2. *Grease,* John Travolta/Olivia Newton-John/soundtrack
3. *Rumours,* Fleetwood Mac
4. *The Stranger,* Billy Joel
5. *Aja,* Steely Dan
6. *Feels So Good,* Chuck Mangione
7. *The Grand Illusion,* Styx
8. *Simple Dreams,* Linda Ronstadt
9. *Point of Know Return,* Kansas
10. *Slowhand,* Eric Clapton

1979

1. *52nd Street*, Billy Joel
2. *Spirits Having Flown*, Bee Gees
3. *Minute by Minute*, Doobie Brothers
4. *The Cars*, The Cars
5. *Breakfast in America*, Supertramp
6. *Live and More*, Donna Summer
7. *Pieces of Eight*, Styx
8. *Bad Girls*, Donna Summer
9. *Parallel Lines*, Blondie
10. *Blondes Have More Fun*, Rod Stewart

1980

1. *The Wall*, Pink Floyd
2. *The Long Run*, Eagles
3. *Off the Wall*, Michael Jackson
4. *Glass Houses*, Billy Joel
5. *Damn the Torpedoes*, Tom Petty & the Heartbreakers
6. *Against the Wind*, Bob Seger & the Silver Bullet Band
7. *In the Heat of the Night*, Pat Benatar
8. *Eat to the Beat*, Blondie
9. *In Through the Out Door*, Led Zeppelin
10. *Kenny*, Kenny Rogers

1981

1. *Hi Infidelity*, REO Speedwagon
2. *Double Fantasy*, John Lennon & Yoko Ono
3. *Greatest Hits*, Kenny Rogers
4. *Christopher Cross*, Christopher Cross
5. *Crimes of Passion*, Pat Benatar
6. *Paradise Theatre*, Styx
7. *Back in Black*, AC/DC
8. *Voices*, Daryl Hall & John Oates
9. *Zenyatta Mondatta*, The Police
10. *The River*, Bruce Springsteen

1982

1. *Asia*, Asia
2. *Beauty and the Beat*, The Go-Go's
3. *4*, Foreigner
4. *American Fool*, John Cougar
5. *Freeze-Frame*, The J. Geils Band
6. *Escape*, Journey
7. *Get Lucky*, Loverboy
8. *Bella Donna*, Stevie Nicks
9. *Chariots of Fire*, Vangelis/soundtrack
10. *Ghost in the Machine*, The Police

1983

1. *Thriller*, Michael Jackson
2. *Business as Usual*, Men at Work
3. *Synchronicity*, The Police
4. *H2O*, Daryl Hall & John Oates
5. *1999*, Prince
6. *Lionel Richie*, Lionel Richie

7. *Jane Fonda's Workout Record*, Jane Fonda
8. *Pyromania*, Def Leppard
9. *Kissing To Be Clever*, Culture Club
10. *Olivia's Greatest Hits, Vol. 2*, Olivia Newton-John

1984

1. *Thriller*, Michael Jackson
2. *Sports*, Huey Lewis & the News
3. *Can't Slow Down*, Lionel Richie
4. *An Innocent Man*, Billy Joel
5. *Colour by Numbers*, Culture Club
6. *1984*, Van Halen
7. *Eliminator*, ZZ Top
8. *Synchronicity*, The Police
9. *Footloose*, soundtrack
10. *Seven and the Ragged Tiger*, Duran Duran

1985

1. *Born in the U.S.A.*, Bruce Springsteen
2. *Reckless*, Bryan Adams
3. *Like a Virgin*, Madonna
4. *Make It Big*, Wham!
5. *Private Dancer*, Tina Turner
6. *No Jacket Required*, Phil Collins
7. *Beverly Hills Cop*, soundtrack
8. *Suddenly*, Billy Ocean
9. *Purple Rain*, Prince & the Revolution
10. *Songs from the Big Chair*, Tears for Fears

1986

1. *Whitney Houston*, Whitney Houston
2. *Heart*, Heart
3. *Scarecrow*, John Cougar Mellencamp
4. *Afterburner*, ZZ Top
5. *Brothers in Arms*, Dire Straits
6. *Control*, Janet Jackson
7. *Welcome to the Real World*, Mr. Mister
8. *Promise*, Sade
9. *No Jacket Required*, Phil Collins
10. *Primitive Love*, Miami Sound Machine

1987

1. *Slippery When Wet*, Bon Jovi
2. *Graceland*, Paul Simon
3. *Licensed to Ill*, Beastie Boys
4. *The Way It Is*, Bruce Hornsby & the Range
5. *Control*, Janet Jackson
6. *The Joshua Tree*, U2
7. *Fore!*, Huey Lewis & the News
8. *Night Songs*, Cinderella
9. *Rapture*, Anita Baker
10. *Invisible Touch*, Genesis

1988

1. *Faith*, George Michael
2. *Dirty Dancing*, soundtrack
3. *Hysteria*, Def Leppard
4. *Kick*, INXS
5. *Bad*, Michael Jackson
6. *Appetite for Destruction*, Guns N' Roses
7. *Out of the Blue*, Debbie Gibson
8. *Richard Marx*, Richard Marx
9. *Tiffany*, Tiffany
10. *Permanent Vacation*, Aerosmith

1989

1. *Don't Be Cruel*, Bobby Brown
2. *Hangin' Tough*, New Kids on the Block
3. *Forever Your Girl*, Paula Abdul
4. *New Jersey*, Bon Jovi
5. *Appetite for Destruction*, Guns N' Roses
6. *The Raw & the Cooked*, Fine Young Cannibals
7. *GNR Lies*, Guns N' Roses
8. *Traveling Wilburys*, Traveling Wilburys
9. *Hysteria*, Def Leppard
10. *Girl You Know It's True*, Milli Vanilli

1990

1. *Janet Jackson's Rhythm Nation 1814*, Janet Jackson
2. *...But Seriously*, Phil Collins
3. *Soul Provider*, Michael Bolton
4. *Pump*, Aerosmith
5. *Please Hammer Don't Hurt 'Em*, M.C. Hammer
6. *Forever Your Girl*, Paula Abdul
7. *Dr. Feelgood*, Mötley Crüe
8. *The End of the Innocence*, Don Henley
9. *Cosmic Thing*, The B-52's
10. *Storm Front*, Billy Joel

1991

1. *Mariah Carey*, Mariah Carey
2. *No Fences*, Garth Brooks
3. *Shake Your Money Maker*, The Black Crowes
4. *Gonna Make You Sweat*, C+C Music Factory
5. *Wilson Phillips*, Wilson Phillips
6. *To the Extreme*, Vanilla Ice
7. *Please Hammer Don't Hurt 'Em*, M.C. Hammer
8. *The Immaculate Collection*, Madonna
9. *Empire*, Queensryche
10. *I'm Your Baby Tonight*, Whitney Houston

1992

1. *Ropin' the Wind*, Garth Brooks
2. *Dangerous*, Michael Jackson

3. *Nevermind*, Nirvana
4. *Some Gave All*, Billy Ray Cyrus
5. *Achtung Baby*, U2
6. *No Fences*, Garth Brooks
7. *Metallica*, Metallica
8. *Time, Love, & Tenderness*, Michael Bolton
9. *Too Legit To Quit*, Hammer
10. *Totally Krossed Out*, Kris Kross

1993

1. *The Bodyguard*, soundtrack
2. *Breathless*, Kenny G
3. *Unplugged*, Eric Clapton
4. *janet.*, Janet Jackson
5. *Some Gave All*, Billy Ray Cyrus
6. *The Chronic*, Dr. Dre
7. *Pocket Full of Kryptonite*, Spin Doctors
8. *Ten*, Pearl Jam
9. *The Chase*, Garth Brooks
10. *Core*, Stone Temple Pilots

1994

1. *The Sign*, Ace of Base
2. *Music Box*, Mariah Carey
3. *Doggystyle*, Snoop Doggy Dogg
4. *The Lion King*, soundtrack
5. *August & Everything After*, Counting Crows
6. *VS.*, Pearl Jam
7. *Toni Braxton*, Toni Braxton
8. *janet.*, Janet Jackson
9. *Bat out of Hell II: Back into Hell*, Meat Loaf
10. *The One Thing*, Michael Bolton

1995

1. *Cracked Rear View*, Hootie & The Blowfish
2. *The Hits*, Garth Brooks
3. *II*, Boyz II Men
4. *Hell Freezes Over*, Eagles
5. *Crazysexycool*, TLC
6. *Vitalogy*, Pearl Jam
7. *Dookie*, Green Day
8. *Throwing Copper*, Live
9. *Miracles: The Holiday Album*, Kenny G
10. *The Lion King* soundtrack

1996

1. *Jagged Little Pill*, Alanis Morissette
2. *Daydream*, Mariah Carey
3. *Falling into You*, Celine Dion
4. *Waiting to Exhale*, soundtrack
5. *The Score*, Fugees
6. *The Woman in Me*, Shania Twain
7. *Fresh Horses*, Garth Brooks
8. *Anthology 1*, The Beatles
9. *Cracked Rear View*, Hootie & The Blowfish
10. *Mellon Collie and the Infinite Sadness*, The Smashing Pumpkins

1997

1. *Spice*, Spice Girls
2. *Tragic Kingdom*, No Doubt
3. *Falling into You*, Celine Dion
4. *Space Jam*, soundtrack
5. *Pieces of You*, Jewel
6. *Blue*, LeAnn Rimes
7. *Bringing Down the Horse*, The Wallflowers
8. *Life After Death*, The Notorious B.I.G.
9. *Secrets*, Toni Braxton
10. *No Way Out*, Puff Daddy & The Family

1998

1. *Titanic*, soundtrack
2. *Let's Talk About Love*, Celine Dion
3. *Sevens*, Garth Brooks
4. *Backstreet Boys*, Backstreet Boys
5. *Come On Over*, Shania Twain
6. *Yourself or Someone Like You*, Matchbox 20
7. *City of Angels*, soundtrack
8. *Big Willie Style*, Will Smith
9. *Savage Garden*, Savage Garden
10. *Spiceworld*, Spice Girls

1999

1. *Millennium*, Backstreet Boys
2. *...Baby One More Time*, Britney Spears
3. *Come On Over*, Shania Twain
4. **NSync*, 'N Sync
5. *Ricky Martin*, Ricky Martin
6. *Double Live*, Garth Brooks
7. *Americana*, The Offspring
8. *Wide Open Spaces*, Dixie Chicks
9. *Significant Other*, Limp Bizkit
10. *Fanmail*, TLC

THE BESTSELLING ALBUMS OF ALL TIME

The Recording Industry Association of America tracks monthly album sales and awards gold and platinum certification based on the sale of 500,000 units for gold, one million units for platinum, and two million units or more for multiplatinum. Here are the albums that top the lists, organized by category, as of September 2000.

ROCK/POP

26 million
Eagles, *Their Greatest Hits, 1971–1975*, 1977

25 million
Michael Jackson, *Thriller*, 1982

23 million
Pink Floyd, *The Wall*, 1979

22 million
Led Zeppelin, *Led Zeppelin IV*, 1971

21 million
Billy Joel, *Greatest Hits, Volumes I & II*, 1985

18 million
The Beatles, *The Beatles*, 1968
Fleetwood Mac, *Rumours*, 1977

17 million
Whitney Houston/various artists, *The Bodyguard* soundtrack, 1992

16 million
AC/DC, *Back in Black*, 1980
Boston, *Boston*, 1976
Hootie & The Blowfish, *Cracked Rear View*, 1994
Alanis Morissette, *Jagged Little Pill*, 1995

15 million
The Beatles, *1967–1970*, 1993
Bee Gees/various artists, *Saturday Night Fever* soundtrack, 1977
Eagles, *Hotel California*, 1976
Guns N' Roses, *Appetite for Destruction*, 1987
Led Zeppelin, *Physical Graffiti*, 1975
Elton John, *Greatest Hits*, 1974
Pink Floyd, *The Dark Side of the Moon*, 1973
Bruce Springsteen, *Born in the U.S.A.*, 1984

14 million
The Beatles, *1962–1966*, 1993

13 million
Backstreet Boys, *Backstreet Boys*, 1997
Whitney Houston, *Whitney Houston*, 1985
Meat Loaf, *Bat out of Hell*, 1977
Prince and the Revolution, *Purple Rain*, 1984
Santana, *Supernatural*, 1999
Bruce Springsteen, *Bruce Springsteen & the E Street Band Live, 1975–1985*, 1986

12 million
Backstreet Boys, *Millennium*, 1999
Bon Jovi, *Slippery When Wet*, 1986
Boyz II Men, *II*, 1994
Def Leppard, *Hysteria*, 1987
Led Zeppelin, *Led Zeppelin II*, 1969
Metallica, *Metallica*, 1991
Britney Spears, *...Baby One More Time*, 1999
various artists, *Forrest Gump* soundtrack, 1994

11 million
The Beatles, *Sgt. Pepper's Lonely Hearts Club Band*, 1967
The Beatles, *Abbey Road*, 1969
Jewel, *Pieces of You*, 1995
Led Zeppelin, *Houses of the Holy*, 1973
Matchbox 20, *Yourself or Someone Like You*, 1996
James Taylor, *Greatest Hits*, 1976
Pearl Jam, *Ten*, 1991
TLC, *CrazySexyCool*, 1994
various artists, *Dirty Dancing* soundtrack, 1987

10 million
Mariah Carey, *Music Box*, 1993
Mariah Carey, *Daydream*, 1995
Eric Clapton, *Unplugged*, 1992

Phil Collins, *No Jacket Required*, 1985
Celine Dion, *Falling into You*, 1996
Celine Dion, *Let's Talk About Love*, 1997
Doobie Brothers, *Best of the Doobies*, 1976
Green Day, *Dookie*, 1994
Journey, *Journey's Greatest Hits*, 1988
Carole King, *Tapestry*, 1971
Madonna, *Like a Virgin*, 1984
Bob Marley and the Wailers, *Legend*, 1984
George Michael, *Faith*, 1987
Nirvana, *Nevermind*, 1991
'N Sync, **NSYNC*, 1998
No Doubt, *Tragic Kingdom*, 1995
Lionel Richie, *Can't Slow Down*, 1984
Simon and Garfunkel, *Greatest Hits*, 1972
U2, *The Joshua Tree*, 1987
Van Halen, *Van Halen*, 1978
Van Halen, *1984*, 1984
various artists, *The Lion King* soundtrack, 1994
ZZ Top, *Eliminator*, 1983

9 million
Ace of Base, *The Sign*, 1993
Aerosmith, *Greatest Hits*, 1980
Boyz II Men, *Cooleyhighharmony*, 1991
Mariah Carey, *Mariah Carey*, 1991
Def Leppard, *Pyromania*, 1983
Dire Straits, *Brothers in Arms*, 1985
Eagles, *Eagles Greatest Hits Volume II*, 1982
Whitney Houston, *Whitney*, 1987
Billy Joel, *The Stranger*, 1977
Journey, *Escape*, 1981
Madonna, *The Immaculate Collection*, 1990
R.E.O. Speedwagon, *Hi-Infidelity*, 1982
various artists, *The Great Band Era*, 1965

various artists, *Top Gun* soundtrack, 1986

8 million

The Beatles, *The Beatles Anthology Volume 1,* 1995

Michael Bolton, *Time, Love and Tenderness,* 1991

Toni Braxton, *Toni Braxton,* 1993

Fleetwood Mac, *Greatest Hits,* 1988

Michael Jackson, *Bad,* 1987

Led Zeppelin, *Led Zeppelin I,* 1969

New Kids on the Block, *Hangin' Tough,* 1988

Olivia Newton-John/John Travolta, *Grease* soundtrack, 1972

Tom Petty and the Heartbreakers, *Greatest Hits,* 1993

Smashing Pumpkins, *Mellon Collie and the Infinite Sadness,* 1996

Steve Miller Band, *Greatest Hits 1974–1978,* 1978

U2, *Achtung Baby,* 1991

various artists, *Footloose* soundtrack, 1984

Whitesnake, *Whitesnake,* 1987

COUNTRY

17 million
Shania Twain, *Come On Over,* 1997

16 million
Garth Brooks, *No Fences,* 1990

14 million
Garth Brooks, *Ropin' the Wind,* 1991

13 million
Garth Brooks, *Double Live,* 1998

12 million
Kenny Rogers, *Greatest Hits,* 1980

11 million
Shania Twain, *The Woman in Me,* 1995

10 million
Garth Brooks, *The Hits,* 1994
Dixie Chicks, *Wide Open Spaces,* 1998

9 million
Garth Brooks, *Garth Brooks,* 1989
Patsy Cline, *Greatest Hits,* 1967

Billy Ray Cyrus, *Some Gave All,* 1992

8 million
Garth Brooks, *The Chase,* 1991
Garth Brooks, *In Pieces,* 1993

6 million
Garth Brooks, *Fresh Horses,* 1995
Garth Brooks, *Sevens,* 1997
Dixie Chicks, *Fly,* 1999
Alan Jackson, *A Lot About Livin' (And a Little About Love),* 1992
LeAnn Rimes, *Blue,* 1996
George Strait, *Pure Country* soundtrack, 1992

5 million
Alabama, *Alabama's Greatest Hits,* 1986
Alabama, *Mountain Music,* 1982
Brooks & Dunn, *Brand New Man,* 1991
Reba McEntire, *Greatest Hits, Vol. 2,* 1993
Vince Gill, *I Still Believe in You,* 1992
Tim McGraw, *Not a Moment Too Soon,* 1994
Bonnie Raitt, *Luck of the Draw,* 1991
Kenny Rogers, *The Gambler,* 1978
George Strait, *Strait out of the Box,* 1995
Randy Travis, *Always and Forever,* 1987
Wynonna, *Wynonna,* 1992

4 million
Alabama, *Feels So Right,* 1981
Alabama, *Roll On,* 1984
Brooks & Dunn, *Hard Workin' Man,* 1993
Deana Carter, *Did I Shave My Legs For This?,* 1996
Vince Gill, *When Love Finds You,* 1994
Faith Hill, *Faith,* 1998
Alan Jackson, *Don't Rock the Jukebox,* 1991
Alan Jackson, *Who I Am,* 1994
Alan Jackson, *Greatest Hits Collection,* 1995
Waylon Jennings, *Greatest Hits,* 1979
Tim McGraw, *Everywhere,* 1997

Reba McEntire, *For My Broken Heart,* 1991
John Michael Montgomery, *Kickin' It Up,* 1994
Anne Murray, *Greatest Hits,* 1980
Willie Nelson, *Willie and Family Live,* 1978
Willie Nelson, *Always on My Mind,* 1982
Willie Nelson, *Stardust,* 1990
Bonnie Raitt, *Nick of Time,* 1989
LeAnn Rimes, *You Light Up My Life–Inspirational Songs,* 1997
Kenny Rogers, *Ten Years of Gold,* 1978
Kenny Rogers, *20 Greatest Hits,* 1983
Shania Twain, *Come On Over,* 1997
Hank Williams, Jr., *Greatest Hits,* 1982
various artists, *Take Me Home Country Roads,* 1973

3 million
Alabama, *The Closer You Get,* 1983
Alabama, *For the Record—41 Number One Hits,* 1998
Clint Black, *Killin' Time,* 1989
Clint Black, *Put Yourself in My Shoes,* 1990
Garth Brooks, *Beyond the Season,* 1992
Garth Brooks, *The Garth Brooks Collection,* 1994
Charlie Daniels Band, *Million Mile Reflections,* 1978
Faith Hill, *It Matters to Me,* 1995
Faith Hill, *Breathe,* 1999
Alan Jackson, *Greatest Hits Collection,* 1995
Reba McEntire, *Greatest Hits,* 1987
Reba McEntire, *Rumor Has It,* 1990
Reba McEntire, *It's Your Call,* 1992
Reba McEntire, *Read My Mind,* 1994
Tim McGraw, *A Place in the Sun,* 1999
John Michael Montgomery, *John Michael Montgomery,* 1995
John Michael Montgomery, *Life's a Dance,* 1992

Kenny Rogers, *Kenny,* 1979
The Statler Brothers, *Best of The Statler Brothers,* 1975
George Strait, *Blue Clear Sky,* 1996
George Strait, *Carryin' Your Love With Me,* 1997
Randy Travis, *Storms of Life,* 1992
Travis Tritt, *It's All About To Change,* 1991
Dwight Yoakam, *This Time,* 1994

JAZZ

12 million
Kenny G, *Breathless,* 1992

8 million
Kenny G, *Miracles,* 1994

5 million
Kenny G, *Duotones,* 1986

4 million
Kenny G, *Silhouette,* 1988

3 million
George Benson, *Breezin',* 1984
Kenny G, *Kenny G Live,* 1989
Kenny G, *The Moment,* 1996

2 million
Kenny G, *Greatest Hits,* 1997
Miles Davis, *Kind of Blue,* 1959

Platinum
George Benson, *Give Me the Night,* 1980
George Benson, *In Flight,* 1977
George Benson, *Weekend in L.A.,* 1978
Kenny G, *Gravity,* 1985
Herbie Hancock, *Future Shock,* 1983
Bob James/David Sanborn, *Double Vision,* 1991
Al Jarreau, *Breakin' Away,* 1982
Chuck Mangione, *Feels So Good,* 1977
Spyro Gyra, *Morning Dance,* 1979

RAP

10 million
M.C. Hammer, *Please Hammer Don't Hurt 'Em,* 1990
Notorious B.I.G., *Life After Death,* 1997

9 million
Kid Rock, *Devil Without a Cause,* 1998
Will Smith, *Big Willie Style,* 1997
2Pac, *All Eyez On Me,* 1996

8 million
Beastie Boys, *Licensed To Ill,* 1986

7 million
Lauryn Hill, *The Miseducation of Lauryn Hill,* 1998
Puff Daddy and The Family, *No Way Out,* 1997
Vanilla Ice, *To the Extreme,* 1990

6 million
Fugees, *The Score,* 1996
TLC, *Fanmail,* 1999

5 million
Salt-N-Pepa, *Very Necessary,* 1993
2Pac, *Greatest Hits,* 1998

4 million
Arrested Development, *3 Years, 5 Months and 2 Days in the Life of…,* 1992
Bone Thugs-N-Harmony, *E. 1999 Eternal,* 1995
Bone Thugs-N-Harmony, *The Art of War,* 1997
Dr. Dre, *Dr. Dre 2001,* 1999
Fugees, *The Score,* 1996
Jay-Z, *Hard Knock Life, Volume 2,* 1998
Kris Kross, *Totally Krossed Out,* 1992
Makaveli, *Don Killuminati: The 7 Day Theory,* 1996
Mase, *Harlem World,* 1997
Master P, *MP Da Last Don,* 1998
Notorious B.I.G., *Ready to Die,* 1994
Snoop Doggy Dogg, *Doggystyle,* 1993
2Pac, *R U Still Down? (Remember Me),* 1997
Wu-Tang Clan, *Wu-Tang Forever,* 1997

3 million
Beastie Boys, *III Communication,* 1994
Beastie Boys, *Hello Nasty,* 1998
D.J. Jazzy Jeff and The Fresh Prince, *He's the D.J., I'm the Rapper,* 1988
DMX, *It's Dark and Hell is Hot,* 1997

DMX, *…And Then There Was X,* 1999
Dr. Dre, *The Chronic,* 1992
Eminem, *Slim Shady,* 1999
Warren G., *Regulate…G Funk Era,* 1994
Hammer, *Too Legit to Quit,* 1992
Juvenile, *400 Degreez,* 1998
Run-D.M.C., *Raising Hell,* 1986

CLASSICAL

11 million
Titanic soundtrack, 1997

3 million
Andrea Bocelli, *Romanza,* 1997

2 million
Benedictine Monks of Santo Domingo de Silos, *Chant,* 1994
Carreras, Domingo, Pavarotti, *The Three Tenors in Concert,* 1990

1 Million
Back to Titanic soundtrack, 1998
Andrea Bocelli, *Sacred Arias,* 1999
Andrea Bocelli, *Sogno,* 1999
Wendy Carlos, *Switched on Bach,* 1986
Carreras, Domingo, Pavarotti with Mehta, *The Three Tenors in Concert 1994,* 1994
Luciano Pavarotti, *O Holy Night,* London, 1985
Royal Philharmonic Orchestra, *Hooked on Classics,* 1982
Piotr Tchaikovsky performed by Van Cliburn with the RCA Symphony Orchestra/Kirill Kondrashin, *Piano Concerto No. 1 in B-flat Minor, Op. 23,* 1982
Various artists, *250 Years of Great Music—Bach to Bernstein,* 1992

THE ROCK OF AGES: PEOPLE'S FAVORITE 50

Steve Dougherty has been PEOPLE's chief music writer since 1985. Here is his completely subjective list of the 50 albums he'd stock in his personal jukebox.

ATLANTIC R&B 1947–1974 (1991)
Various artists
Before they named it Rock, it was spelled R&B. A chest of pop's buried treasures.

AT THE FILMORE EAST (1979)
The Allman Brothers Band
Soulful sibs Duane and Gregg Allman unveil their new invention, Southern Rock, before a crowd of appreciative Yankees in a watershed New York City live show.

THE BAND (1969)
The Band
Rock 'n' roll's Great American Novel came with a backbeat and Robbie Robertson's story songs, as told by Richard Manuel, Levon Helm, and Rick Danko.

THE BEATLES (1968)
The Beatles
From the classic rock of the opening track to the electronica precursor "Revolution No. 9," the legendary White Album plays like a modern pop history lesson taught by four Fab profs.

ODELAY (1996)
Beck
An album from pop's beat-crazy, wordy rapping kid, Beck Hansen

(no relation to the Oklahoma teen trio), that shows off his heightened senses of rhythm and humor.

CHUCK BERRY'S GOLDEN HITS (1967)
Chuck Berry
The brown-eyed handsome man told Tchaikovsky the news: There is indeed such a thing as a three-minute masterpiece.

MERMAID AVENUE (1998)
Billy Bragg & Wilco
Brit singer Bragg and the country punks of Wilco give a posthumous present to folk icon Woodie Guthrie: a sparkling pop album of the troubadour's wondrous, and previously unsung, songs.

THE RISE AND FALL OF ZIGGY STARDUST AND THE SPIDERS FROM MARS (1972)
David Bowie
Music had never glittered quite like this before and glam rock never sounded so good again.

20 ALL-TIME GREATEST HITS! (1991)
James Brown
You'll feel good! But then, you knew that you would.

LONDON CALLING (1979)
The Clash
They pronounced rock dead,

then celebrated its resurrection on this, a double album without a lame cut in the lot.

MY AIM IS TRUE (1977)
Elvis Costello
He looked punk, acted mean, sounded nasty, and hit right on target in his album debut.

LAYLA AND OTHER ASSORTED LOVE SONGS (1970)
Derek and the Dominoes
Eric Clapton and Duane Allman. 'Nuff said.

THE CHRONIC (1992)
Dr. Dre (with Snoop Doggy Dogg)
Hip-hop's auteur and his pet rapper share their bemused family values.

BRINGING IT ALL BACK HOME (1965), **HIGHWAY 61 REVISITED** (1965), **TIME OUT OF MIND** (1997)
Bob Dylan
For all who question the lasting fuss over the rheumy rock laureate, three masterworks.

I NEVER LOVED A MAN (THE WAY I LOVE YOU) (1967)
Aretha Franklin
They invented soul so she could be queen.

Beck, *Odelay*

Nirvana, *Nevermind*

U2, *Achtung Baby*

WHAT'S GOING ON (1971)
Marvin Gaye
Motown's sex star made hearts and minds quicken with this ambitious song cycle.

ARE YOU EXPERIENCED? (1967)
Jimi Hendrix Experience
That voice. Those songs. That guitar. We're still asking, "Where did this guy come from?"

ARTHUR (DECLINE AND FALL OF THE BRITISH EMPIRE) (1969), **MUSWELL HILLBILLIES** (1971)
The Kinks
Tommy without the pretensions: these are two of plaintive mod genius Ray Davies's brilliantly realized theme albums.

ORIGINAL GOLDEN HITS, VOLS. 1 AND 2 (1969)
Jerry Lee Lewis
Killer tracks from The Killer: All is forgiven.

GROOVIEST 17 ORIGINAL HITS (1959)
Little Richard
"Good Golly Miss Molly," "Tutti Fruiti," "Lucille," "Long Tall Sally," "Rip It Up." Macon, Ga.'s absolutely fabulous former dishwasher screamed 'em all to life at New Orleans's Specialty Records studio.

COURT AND SPARK (1974)
Joni Mitchell
The ultimate chick singer whips one on the boys.

MOBY GRAPE (1967)
Moby Grape
San Francisco's one-masterpiece wonder squeezed all their juice into this ignored collection.

AMERICAN BEAUTY (1970)
The Grateful Dead
Haight-Ashbury's free-form improvisational space cowboys shelve the jams and craft an aptly titled musical masterpiece.

THE BEST OF VAN MORRISON (1990)
Van Morrison
Romance for the soul.

NEVERMIND (1991)
Nirvana
Full of as much old-fashioned tube amplifier feedback as neo-

---

THE 10 MOST OVERRATED ALBUMS

For those contrarians who would rather smash discs than play them, here is a flip-side list of legendary nonlegends in the annals of rock.

SLIPPERY WHEN WET (1986)
Bon Jovi
Hair metal pin-up star Jon Bon Jovi's was the pretty face that helped sell many millions of copies of a mediocre album filled with lyric clichés and generic power chords.

4 WAY STREET (1971)
Crosby, Stills, Nash and Young
They could have used a stop sign.

THE DOORS (1967)
The Doors
As an icon, Jim Morrison can't be beat; but his great looks, leather pants, and lucrative afterlife make people forget he was a mediocre singer and pretentious poet masquerading as a rock star.

USE YOUR ILLUSION I & II (1991)
Guns N' Roses
Out the year punk pretender Axl Rose was rendered irrelevant by the real thing (Kurt Cobain), these two simultaneously released, gibberishly titled albums smelled like a teen record buyer rip-off.

UNTITLED (1971)
Led Zeppelin
The album that gave us "Stairway to Heaven" and other artifacts of arena-ready blowhard rock.

(WHAT'S THE STORY) MORNING GLORY? (1995)
Oasis
They like to compare themselves to the Beatles and Stones but prove with this album's lame lyrics and hand-me-down sound to be in the same league with neither.

ELVIS (TV SPECIAL) (1968)
Elvis Presley
The gig that was trumpeted as his

return to '50s form. Leatherclad in Vegas a year after the Summer of Love, The King was already out of touch with current culture and his music.

THE DREAM OF THE BLUE TURTLES (1985)
Sting
The Police man lured listeners with his pop status, then stung them with stingy jazz.

TOMMY (1969)
The Who
Maybe if Pete had left it to critics to call his own composition "A Rock Opera," it wouldn't make us want to gag.

MODERN R&B
Soulful self-expression is the creed of the great R&B singers of yore. Today's poor imitators, from Mariah Carey to the Backstreet Boys, caterwaul trite lyrics over clichéd arrangements to achieve the appearance, but not the true grit, of emotion. Call it artificial soul.

punk martyr Kurt Cobain's fabled rage, this is a call to get with it for all classic rock-fixated geezers who insist that the music ain't what it used to be.

TEAR THE ROOF OFF (1993)
Parliament Funkadelic
So they did, and something memorable was born.

THE SUN SESSIONS (1987),
ELVIS' GOLDEN RECORDS, VOL. 1 (1958)
Elvis Presley
Rock and roll at its best.

1999 (1982)
Prince
From when he had a name and all the critics loved him in New York, and everywhere else.

MURMUR (1983)
R.E.M.
The debut album that brought "Radio Free Europe" to the promised land. What's it about? Who knows? Who cares?

HISTORY OF OTIS REDDING (1968)
Otis Redding
The greatest soul ever told.

TIM (1985)
The Replacements
Put "Swingin' Party" on replay, never let it stop.

BEGGAR'S BANQUET (1968),
STICKY FINGERS (1971),
THE SINGLES COLLECTION (1989)
The Rolling Stones
The first two are mid-career classics. In the last, an obscure collection of mostly mono, many never released in the U.S. singles, finds the Stones paying tribute to their black American heroes.

NEVER MIND THE BOLLOCKS, HERE'S THE SEX PISTOLS (1977)
Sex Pistols
Unlistenable then, unbeatable now, it mocks, it taunts, it screams, and you can dance to it!

BACK TO MONO (1991)
Phil Spector
Actually four CDs, offering

unforgettable visits by (mostly) girl groups to the little man's Great Wall of Sound.

BORN TO RUN (1975)
Bruce Springsteen
The Boss as rock and roll trades-man, redefining the exuberant yearning to get out on the high-way with a guitar strapped 'cross his back.

STORYTELLER (Boxed Set, 1992)
Rod Stewart
Remember that before he turned out the lights and cuddled up to the Manilow inside him, Rod the mod was an underrated lyricist who rivaled Van Morrison in the U.K. soul crooner department.

HITSVILLE USA: THE MOTOWN SINGLES COLLECTION (1992)
The Supremes, The Four Tops, Smokey Robinson and The Miracles, The Jackson Five, The Temptations, et al.
The soundtrack of the '60s, cour-tesy of Detroit's big wheel, Berry Gordy. (And it's got Mary Wells and Marvin Gaye, too.)

TALKING HEADS 77 (1977)
Talking Heads
Leading the punk revolt from these shores, art school misfit David Byrne makes his bow as one of rock's strangest, and most talented, characters.

ACHTUNG BABY (1991)
U2
The Dubliners finally drop the earnest façade, as well as the endlessly repeated rhythm guitar riff that launched them and deliver a sonic treat recorded in the cold war capital of Berlin.

MEATY BEATY BIG AND BOUNCY (1971)
The Who
Known for their big productions, including the overrated *Tommy* and underrated *Quadrophenia*, the London mods rocked Top 40 radio with these high explosives.

SUMMER TEETH (1999)
Wilco
Pop go the country rockers and craft an edgy masterpiece.

CAR WHEELS ON A GRAVEL ROAD (1998)
Lucinda Williams
The Lake Charles, Louisiana, native takes listeners on a musi-cally and emotionally rich jour-ney through the scarred by-ways of her heartland.

AFTER THE GOLD RUSH (1970)
Neil Young
One nugget from four brilliant decades of work by the once and current rocker.

HIP-HOP RULES

Hip-hop has become such a dominant cultural and com-mercial force that even main-stream superstars have gotten jiggy with this once under-ground music. To wit:

CARLOS SANTANA Yes, he's a genius and a legend, but it was "Maria Maria," penned by Wyclef Jean that brought Carlos to the kids.

BRITNEY SPEARS/'N SYNC They (thankfully) don't rap, but these teen acts have a lot of hip-hop and R&B in their sound.

BRUCE SPRINGSTEEN The rhythm track pushing "Streets of Philadel-phia" is pure hip-hop.

MADONNA An old Public Enemy beat (borrowed from James Brown) serves as the melody line for her hit "Justify My Love."

KORN/KID ROCK/LIMP BIZKIT/POD/PAPA ROACH ET AL This whole new breed of rap-meets-rock wouldn't exist without Run-DMC's "Rock Box" or "King of Rock" back in the mid-'80s.

AEROSMITH These veteran rockers were washed up and strung out until Run-DMC re-did "Walk This Way" with them in 1986.

BECK Sampling music from a variety of sources and making it your own? Hmmm, sounds like you know what.

RAP: ESSENTIAL LISTENING

From its early days in New York City to its dominance worldwide, hip-hop has become a force of nature and culture. Rap started out as a singles phenomenon and morphed into albums by the mid '80s, and certain of those albums are required listening for every fan or wannabe. Here is an admittedly subjective (and short) must-have list of rap and R&B compiled by PEOPLE reviewer Amy Linden.

THE CHRONIC (1993)
Dr. Dre
He introduced what he called The Era of G Funk with a funkadelic feel that made Compton, Calif., the center of rap and Dre a star producer.

RUN-DMC (1983)
Run-DMC
This groundbreaking group and smart record revolutionized the style (from flamboyant outfits to jeans and untied Adidas) and esthetic of rap (adding rock guitars and serious lyrics).

THE LOW END THEORY (1991)
A Tribe Called Quest
With this, its second CD, a truly visionary act made the rap-jazz connection clear and funky.

IT TAKES A NATION OF MILLIONS TO HOLD US BACK (1988)
Public Enemy
Agitprop meets sonic boom to create a CD that still reverberates.

PAID IN FULL (1986)
Eric B. and Rakim
DJ Eric B. brought the soul beats, and rapper Rakim showed why he has few peers.

DE LA SOUL IS DEAD (1991)
De La Soul
After introducing their light-hearted and whimsical style in "D.A.I.S.Y. Age," De La Soul added darkness and menace on this brilliant second album.

AMERIKKA'S MOST WANTED (1990)
Ice Cube
Cube's first solo trip was a synthesis of the rap styles of the musically esoteric East coast and the gang-fixated West coast.

READY TO DIE (1994)
The Notorious B.I.G.
A thug poet with a playa's leer, Biggie established himself as one of the greats right from this explosive debut.

PAUL'S BOUTIQUE (1989)
Beastie Boys
Adding live instrumentation to the cut-and-paste, they took sampling to dizzying and influential heights.

THE MARSHALL MATHERS LP (2000)
Eminem
Love him or hate him, this Dre protégé sold a staggering 1.75 million copies his first week and proved himself the Kurt Cobain of hip-hop, an in-your-face spokesman for disenfranchised white youth.

VOL. 2...HARD KNOCK LIFE (1998)
Jay-Z
One of the top lyricists of the '90s, Jigga broke into the mainstream with some sampling help from, of all sources, the *Annie* orphans of Broadway.

STRAIGHT OUTTA COMPTON (1989)
N.W.A.
This was the introduction of Eazy-E, Dre, and Ice Cube, not to mention the soundtrack to the subsequent L.A. riots.

GREAT ADVENTURES OF SLICK RICK (1988)
Slick Rick
He's one of rap's most beloved characters as well as its best storyteller.

CRIMINAL MINDED (1986)
Boogie Down Productions
KRS-One and the late Scott LaRock delivered a tough, literate record that was a precursor of "gangsta rap."

MAMA SAID KNOCK YOU OUT (1990)
LL Cool J
A star at 16, then washed up, LL unleashed this comeback at 21 and reaffirmed his status as rap's most poetic sex symbol.

ENTER THE WU-TANG: 36 CHAMBERS (1993)
Wu-Tang Clan
This was the introduction to the world of future solo stars Method Man, Ghostface Killah, Raekwon, and ODB aided by RZA's baroque production.

BLACKOUT! (1999)
Method Man/Redman
Two of the best team up for a smoked-out paean to the pleasures of performing stoned.

STRAIGHT OUT THE JUNGLE (1998)
Jungle Brothers
Mixing afrocentricity and house, the JBs introduced the Native Tongues movement, a hippyesque call for a return to simpler values and nonmaterialism.

HARDCORE (1996)
Lil' Kim
Kim's full-frontal wordplay, as raunchy as it gets, changed the rules for female rappers.

FULL CLIP (1999)
Gang Starr
Underrated and underground, DJs Primer and Guru married jazz and soul to produce streettough, rugged rhymes.

THE 50 BEST COUNTRY ALBUMS

PEOPLE's Randy Vest touts this country-album starter set, with additional tips of the Stetson to Webb Pierce, Ernest Tubb, Kitty Wells, Bob Wills, and many others.

THE BEST OF EDDY ARNOLD (1967)
Eddy Arnold
The Tennessee Plowboy shows his smoother side on these (mostly) '60s tracks.

THINKIN' PROBLEM (1994)
David Ball
Among a sea of hat acts, Ball's topper stands out in the crowd, thanks to this twangy tour de force.

KILLIN' TIME (1989)
Clint Black
An incredible, play-it-over-and-over-again debut that garnered Black five No. 1 singles.

NO FENCES (1990)
Garth Brooks
Pure, heartfelt songs recorded just before Garth became GARTH.

HIGH AND DRY (1991)
Marty Brown
Of all the pretenders to Hank's throne, Brown is the real deal.

COME ON COME ON (1992)
Mary Chapin Carpenter
A blissful fusion of country, folk, and rock from the "hometown girl."

I FELL IN LOVE (1990)
Carlene Carter
After years of dabbling in rock, June Carter and Carl Smith's little girl finds her roots in country.

JOHNNY CASH AT FOLSOM PRISON (1968)
Johnny Cash
Cash's live performance for a throng of inmates remains a milestone. "Folsom Prison Blues" can still evoke chills.

KING'S RECORD SHOP (1987)
Rosanne Cash
Produced by then hubby Rodney Crowell, this Grammy-winning album is right on the money.

THE PATSY CLINE STORY (1963)
Patsy Cline
Sublime sounds from country's high priestess of female vocalists.

DIAMONDS AND DIRT (1988)
Rodney Crowell
Singer-songwriter Crowell hit a home run with this critically lauded and commercially successful release.

GUITAR TOWN (1986)
Steve Earle
Rough-housin' Earle found himself a spot on country's crowded map with this inspired outing.

THE BEST OF LEFTY FRIZZELL (1991)
Lefty Frizzell
His style influenced everyone from Willie to Merle to George Jones. Here's the evidence.

WHEN I CALL YOUR NAME (1989)
Vince Gill
The sweetest pipes this side of heaven, caressing material that's just as heavenly.

CHISELED IN STONE (1987)
Vern Gosdin
A hard-edged voice that's packed with pathos.

TRIO (1987)
Emmylou Harris, Dolly Parton, Linda Ronstadt
Three distinct song stylists in a perfect, harmonious blend.

DOWN EVERY ROAD 1962–1994 (1996)
Merle Haggard
A four-disc anthology shows why the Hag is one of country's enduring legends.

HIGHWAYMAN (1985)
The Highwaymen (Johnny Cash, Waylon Jennings, Kris Kristofferson, Willie Nelson)
An inspired collaboration between some of country's elder statesmen.

ROCKIN' IN THE COUNTRY: THE BEST OF WANDA JACKSON (1990)
Wanda Jackson
From rockabilly to Nash-pop, Jackson growls and purrs up a storm.

SHE THINKS I STILL CARE: THE GEORGE JONES COLLECTION (1997)
George Jones
A two-disc set chronicling Jones's often overlooked years with the United Artists label in the '60s.

THE JUDDS (WYNONNA & NAOMI) (1984)
The Judds
Wynonna and her mater never sounded quite as honest or engaging after this memorable debut.

PICKIN' ON NASHVILLE (1989)
Kentucky Headhunters
Raucous rock from the Bluegrass State's (and Arkansas') impish, redneck sons.

SHADOWLAND (1988)
k.d. lang
Lang teams up with legendary producer Owen Bradley to create studio magic.

ANTHOLOGY 1956–80 (1991)
Brenda Lee
The songs are mostly pop, but the pipes are pure country all the way.

20 GREATEST HITS (1987)
Loretta Lynn
From givin' a carousin' hubby what-for to wardin' off a would-be man-stealer, the coal miner's daughter is a tough lady to top.

GOLDEN HITS (1965)
Roger Miller
The King of the Road's loopy takes on booze, buffalo, and Britain.

COUNTRY MUSIC HALL OF FAME (1991)
Bill Monroe
The father of bluegrass and his mandolin. Need we say more?

LEAVE THE LIGHT ON (1989)
Lorrie Morgan
George Morgan's daughter takes center stage and stakes a claim on country's landscape.

WHY LADY WHY (1983)
Gary Morris
A voice of operatic strength surrounding some mighty sturdy songs.

JUST LIKE OLD TIMES (1992)
Heather Myles
A rousing, Bakersfield-influenced sleeper by a dynamic singer.

RED HEADED STRANGER (1975)
Willie Nelson
Bare-bones country by the genre's celebrated redneck outlaw.

WILL THE CIRCLE BE UNBROKEN (1972)
The Nitty Gritty Dirt Band
An historic summit with the likes of Roy Acuff and Mother Maybelle Carter.

THE NEW NASHVILLE CATS (1991)
Mark O'Connor
The country fiddler/classical composer is joined by some 50 heavyweight pickers on this Grammy-winning set.

'80S LADIES (1987)
K. T. Oslin
Sassy and bittersweet songs truthfully sung by a seasoned survivor.

THE BUCK OWENS COLLECTION, 1959–1990 (1992)
Buck Owens
Three CDs worth of classic tunes from the king of the Bakersfield sound and his stalwart Buckaroos.

THE COMPLETE '50S MASTERS (1992)
Elvis Presley
The King's earliest sides (8 CDs!) before Hollywood and mediocrity beckoned.

THE ESSENTIAL RAY PRICE, 1951–62 (1991)
Ray Price
Raw performances from the man once known as the "Cherokee Cowboy" who later found success crooning pop-styled ballads.

FOUR WALLS: THE LEGEND BEGINS (1991)
Jim Reeves
An early, mostly harder-edged Reeves, already showing signs of that vocal "touch of velvet."

THE ESSENTIAL MARTY ROBBINS, 1951–82 (1991)
Marty Robbins
The King of the Balladeers lends his distinct tenor to storytelling songs and country-pop.

WHAT A WOMAN WANTS TO HEAR (1991)
Dawn Sears
Shamefully overlooked powerhouse vocalist whose followup, *Nothin' but Good*, was equally as memorable.

THE ESSENTIAL CONNIE SMITH (1996)
Connie Smith
One of country's greatest female singers of the '60s, '70s, or for that matter, any decade.

STRAIT OUT OF THE BOX (1995)
George Strait
From a winning 16-year career, here are the cream of the crop.

STORMS OF LIFE (1986)
Randy Travis
With this debut album, Travis helped to restore country music's heart and soul. He's never equalled it.

THE VERY BEST OF CONWAY TWITTY (1978)
Conway Twitty
Once called "the best friend a song ever had," Twitty put his own indelible stamp on the country genre.

KEVIN WELCH (1990)
Kevin Welch
Call it alterna-country. This singer-songwriter from Oklahoma brings a poet's sensibility to his work.

THE ESSENTIAL DOTTIE WEST (1996)
Dottie West
West's husky vocals were never better than on these defining 1960s and '70s tracks.

I WONDER DO YOU THINK OF ME (1989)
Keith Whitley
The title cut alone by the late, lamented Whitley will break your heart.

40 GREATEST HITS (1978)
Hank Williams
The Daddy...the King... the Master.

ANNIVERSARY: TWENTY YEARS OF HITS (1987)
Tammy Wynette
Wynette conveys more pain in "Til I Get it Right" than most artists can in their entire repertoire.

GUITARS, CADILLACS, ETC., ETC. (1986)
Dwight Yoakam
California honky-tonk collides with Nashville tradition. A rouser of a debut.

JAZZ: ESSENTIAL LISTENING

Not encyclopedic or definitive, this is simply a list of 50 marvelous jazz albums. The recordings here date from the '20s to the '90s, and they cover a range of styles. Any jazz purist, or for that matter, impurist, will find sins of omission and commission on this list. All we—the jazz jury at PEOPLE—can say is that these albums have enriched our lives immeasurably and given us an almost embarrassing amount of pleasure. To us, these recordings are the easiest sort of listening, full of wit, passion, invention, and beauty.

Cannonball Adderly	*Live at the Jazz Workshop* (1959); reissued as *The Cannonball Adderley Quintet in San Francisco*
Louis Armstrong	*Hot Fives and Sevens,* Vol. II or III (1926–27)
Chet Baker	*My Funny Valentine* (1954)
Count Basie	*The Original American Decca Recordings* (1937–39)
Bix and Tram Beiderbecke	*The Bix Beiderbecke Story,* Vol. II (1927–28)
Art Blakey & The Jazz Messengers	*Moanin'* (1958)
Clifford Brown and Max Roach	*Clifford Brown and Max Roach* (1954–55)
Betty Carter	*Betty Carter* (1966)
Ray Charles	*The Birth of Soul: The Complete Atlantic Rhythm & Blues Recordings 1952–1959* (1991)
Nat King Cole	*Nat King Cole* (1992)
Ornette Coleman	*The Shape of Jazz to Come* (1959–60)
Ornette Coleman	*Free Jazz* (1960)
John Coltrane	*Coltrane* (1957)
John Coltrane	*A Love Supreme* (1964)
Miles Davis	*Birth of the Cool* (1957)
Miles Davis	*Milestones* (1958)
Miles Davis	*Kind of Blue* (1959)
Miles Davis	*Miles Smiles* (1966)
Miles Davis and Gil Evans	*Porgy and Bess* (1958)
Eric Dolphy	*Out to Lunch* (1964)
Duke Ellington	*The Blanton-Webster Band* (1940-42)
Duke Ellington & The Jungle Band	*Rockin' in Rhythm,* Vol. III (1929–31)
Bill Evans	*The Village Vanguard Sessions* (1961)
Art Farmer	*Something to Live For* (1987)
Ella Fitzgerald	*The Gershwin Songbook* (1959)
Ella Fitzgerald	*The Intimate Ella* (1960)
Tommy Flanagan	*Ballads and Blues* (1979)
Bill Frisell	*This Land* (1994)
Errol Garner	*Concert by the Sea* (1956/1987)
Stan Getz/Joao Gilberto	*Getz/Gilberto* (1964)
Benny Goodman	*Carnegie Hall Concert* (1938)
Charlie Haden Quartet West	*Haunted Heart* (1992)
Lionel Hampton	*The Complete Lionel Hampton* (1937–41)
Herbie Hancock	*Maiden Voyage* (1965)
Coleman Hawkins	*Body and Soul: The Complete Coleman Hawkins,* Vol. I (1929–40)
Fletcher Henderson and Don Redman	*Developing an American Orchestra, 1923–1937* (1923–37)
Billie Holiday	*The Quintessential Billie Holiday,* Vol. III, IV, or V (1937–39)
James P. Johnson	*Snowy Morning Blues* (1930, 1944)
Abbey Lincoln	*The World Is Falling Down* (1990)
Charles Mingus	*Mingus Ah Um* (1960)
Charles Mingus	*The Black Saint and the Sinner Lady* (1963)

Modern Jazz Quartet (1956/1987)	*The Complete Last Concert*	Bud Powell	*The Amazing Bud Powell*, Vol. I (1949–51)
Thelonious Monk	*The Unique Thelonious Monk* (1956)	Bud Powell	*The Genius of Bud Powell* (1951)
Thelonious Monk	*Alone in San Francisco* (1959)	Sonny Rollins	*Saxophone Colossus* (1956)
		John Scofield	*Time on My Hands* (1989)
Thelonious Monk	*Monk's Dream* (1962)	Art Tatum	*The Tatum Solo*
Gerry Mulligan	*What Is There to Say?* (1958–59)		*Masterpieces*, Vol. III (1953–55)
Oliver Nelson	*Blues and the Abstract Truth* (1961)	Cecil Taylor	*Unit Structures* (1966)
King Oliver	*King Oliver's Jazz Band 1923* (1923)	Sarah Vaughan and Clifford Brown	*Sarah Vaughan with Clifford Brown* (1954)
Charlie Parker	*The Charlie Parker Story* (1945)	Fats Waller	*The Joint Is Jumpin'* (1929–43)
Charlie Parker (with Dizzy Gillespie, Max Roach, Bud Powell, and Charles Mingus)	*The Greatest Jazz Concert Ever* (1953)	Lester Young	*The Complete Lester Young* (1943–44)

JAZZ TODAY

A new generation of stars is emerging in jazz. Steeped in tradition, technically prodigious, often daring, and always fired by the energy and passion of youth, they are a formidable lot, as varied in style as they are united in their allegiance to the verities of swing, the blues, and improvisation. Here are some standout albums by the the new school.

Geri Allen, *Twenty One* (1994) (piano)

James Carter, *The Real Quietstorm* (1995) (saxophone/flute/clarinet)

Paquito D'Rivera, *Come on Home* (1995)

Marty Ehrlich, *Can You Hear a Motion?* (1994) (various instruments)

Kenny Garrett, *Triology* (1995) (alto sax)

Javon Jackson, *For One Who Knows* (1995) (saxophone)

Hank Jones and Charlie Haden, *Steal Away: Spirituals, Hymns, and Folk Songs* (1995) (piano; bass)

Leroy Jones, *Mo' Cream from the Crop* (1994) (trumpet)

Abbey Lincoln, *Who Used to Dance* (1997)

Joe Lovano, *Celebrating Sinatra* (1997)

Wynton Marsalis, *Live at the Village Vanguard* (1999)

Abbey Lincoln, *A Turtle's Dream* (1994) (vocals)

Marcus Printup, *Song for the Beautiful Woman* (1995) (trumpet)

Joshua Redman, *Wish* (1993)

Eric Reed, *The Swing and I* (1995) (piano)

Poncho Sanchez, *Conga Blue* (1996)

Jacky Terrasson, *Jacky Terrasson* (1995) (piano)

Steve Turre, *Rhythm Within* (1995) (trombone)

Cassandra Wilson, *Blue Skies* (1988) (vocals)

50 GREAT CLASSICAL RECORDINGS

We can't really presume to pick a classical library for all tastes, but PEOPLE's editors will hazard this tendentious consensus of outstanding recordings.

Johann Sebastian Bach	*Brandenburg Concertos*, Munich Bach Orchestra/Karl Richter
Johann Sebastian Bach	*The Well-Tempered Clavier*, BWV 846-893, Davitt Moroney
Samuel Barber	*Adagio for Strings*, Saint Louis Symphony Orchestra/Leonard Slatkin
Béla Bartók	*String Quartets Nos. 1–6*, Emerson Quartet
Ludwig van Beethoven	*Symphonies Nos. 1–9, Complete Cycles*, Berlin Philharmonic/Herbert von Karajan
Ludwig van Beethoven	*Piano Sonata in C Minor, Op. 13, "Pathétique,"* Wilhelm Kempff
Ludwig van Beethoven	*Piano Sonata in C-sharp Minor, Op. 27, No. 2, "Moonlight,"* Wilhelm Kempff
Hector Berlioz	*Symphonie fantastique*, French National Radio Orchestra/Sir Thomas Beecham
Leonard Bernstein	*Chichester Psalms*, John Paul Bogart; Camerata Singers, New York Philharmonic/Leonard Bernstein
Georges Bizet	*Carmen*, Agnes Baltsa, José Carreras; Chorus of the Paris Opéra, Berlin Philharmonic/Herbert von Karajan
Johannes Brahms	*Violin Concerto in D, Op. 77*, Itzhak Perlman; Chicago Symphony Orchestra/Carlo Maria Giulini
Benjamin Britten	*War Requiem, Op. 66*, Lorna Haywood, Anthony Rolfe Johnson, Benjamin Luxon; Atlanta Boy Choir, Atlanta Symphony Orchestra & Chorus/Robert Shaw
Frédéric Chopin	*26 Preludes*, Dmitri Alexeev
Aaron Copland	*Appalachian Spring*, New York Philharmonic/Leonard Bernstein
Claude Debussy	*Images*, Claudio Arrau
Antonín Dvořák	*Symphony No. 9 in E Minor, Op. 95, "From the New World,"* London Symphony Orchestra/István Kertész
César Franck	*Symphony in D Minor*, Berlin Radio Symphony Orchestra/Vladimir Ashkenazy
George Gershwin	*Rhapsody in Blue*, Columbia Symphony Orchestra, New York Philharmonic/Leonard Bernstein
George Gershwin	*Porgy and Bess,* Willard White, Leona Mitchell; Cleveland Orchestra & Chorus/Lorin Maazel
George Frideric Handel	*Messiah*, Heather Harper, Helen Watts, John Wakefield, John Shirley-Quirk; London Symphony Orchestra & Choir/Sir Colin Davis
Joseph Haydn	*Symphonies Nos. 93-104, "London,"* Royal Concertgebouw Orchestra/Sir Colin Davis
Joseph Haydn	*String Quartets, Op. 76, "Erdödy,"* Takács Quartet
Charles Ives	*Three Places in New England*, Boston Symphony Orchestra/Michael Tilson Thomas
Franz Liszt	*Les Préludes*, Philadelphia Orchestra/Riccardo Muti
Gustav Mahler	*Symphony No. 9 in D*, Vienna Philharmonic/Bruno Walter
Felix Mendelssohn	*Violin Concerto in E Minor, Op. 64,* Kyung Wha Chung; Montreal Symphony Orchestra/ Charles Dutoit

Wolfgang Amadeus Mozart	*Symphony No. 41 in C, K. 551, "Jupiter,"* Columbia Symphony Orchestra/Bruno Walter
Wolfgang Amadeus Mozart	*A Little Night Music, K. 525,* Prague Chamber Orchestra/Sir Charles Mackerras
Wolfgang Amadeus Mozart	*The Marriage of Figaro,* Samuel Ramey, Lucia Popp; London Opera Chorus, London Philharmonic Orchestra/Sir George Solti
Wolfgang Amadeus Mozart	*Don Giovanni,* Eberhard Wächter, Joan Sutherland, Elisabeth Schwarzkopf; Philharmonia Orchestra & Chorus/Carlo Maria Giulini
Modest Mussorgsky	*Pictures at an Exhibition,* Montreal Symphony Orchestra/Charles Dutoit
Giacomo Puccini	*La Bohème,* Mirella Freni, Luciano Pavarotti; Chorus of the Deutsche Oper Berlin, Berlin Philharmonic/Herbert von Karajan
Sergei Prokofiev	*Symphony No. 1 in D, Op. 25, "Classical,"* Berlin Philharmonic/Herbert von Karajan
Sergei Rachmaninoff	*Piano Concerto No. 2 in C Minor, Op. 18,* Vladimir Ashkenazy; London Symphony Orchestra/André Previn
Nikolai Rimsky-Korsakov	*Scheherazade, Op. 35,* Royal Concertgebouw Orchestra/Kirill Kondrashin
Gioacchino Rossini	*The Barber of Seville,* Leo Nucci, William Matteuzzi, Cecilia Bartoli; Chorus & Orchestra of the Teatro Comunale di Bologna/Giuseppe Patanè
Camille Saint-Saëns	*The Carnival of the Animals,* Montreal Symphony Orchestra, London Sinfonietta/ Charles Dutoit
Domenico Scarlatti	*Keyboard Sonatas,* Vladimir Horowitz
Arnold Schoenberg	*Verklärte Nacht (Transfigured Night), Op. 4,* Jiri Najnar, Vaclav Bernasek; Talich Quartet
Franz Schubert	*Die Schöne Müllerin, D. 795; Winterreise, D. 911,* Dietrich Fischer-Dieskau, Gerald Moore
Robert Schumann	*Op. 19, "Carnaval: Pretty Scenes on Four Notes,"* Artur Rubinstein
Dmitri Shostakovich	*Symphony No. 5 in D Minor, Op. 47,* Royal Concertgebouw Orchestra/Bernard Haitink
Jean Sibelius	*Symphony No. 5 in E-flat, Op. 82,* Boston Symphony Orchestra/Sir Colin Davis
Igor Stravinsky	*The Rite of Spring,* New York Philharmonic, Cleveland Orchestra/Pierre Boulez
Piotr Ilyich Tchaikovsky	*Symphony No. 6 in B Minor, Op. 74, "Pathétique,"* Leningrad Philharmonic/Evgeny Mravinsky
Piotr Ilyich Tchaikovsky	*Piano Concerto No. 1 in B-flat Minor, Op. 23,* Van Cliburn; RCA Symphony Orchestra/Kirill Kondrashin
Giuseppe Verdi	*Requiem,* Elisabeth Schwarzkopf, Christa Ludwig, Nicolai Gedda, Nicolai Ghiaurov; Philharmonia Orchestra & Chorus/Carlo Maria Giulini
Giuseppe Verdi	*La Traviata,* Joan Sutherland, Luciano Pavarotti; London Opera Chorus, National Philharmonic Orchestra/Richard Bonynge
Antonio Vivaldi	*Concertos for Violin, Strings, and Continuo, Op. 8, Nos. 1–4, "The Four Seasons,"* Alan Loveday; Academy of St. Martin-in-the-Fields/Sir Neville Marriner
Richard Wagner	*The Ring of the Nibelung,* Birgit Nilsson, Wolfgang Windgassen; Chorus & Orchestra of the Bayreuth Festival/Karl Böhm

CLIFFS' CLUES TO OPERA PLOTS

Opera is drama expressed musically, verbally, and visually—the ultimate experience for ears, eyes, and emotions. If you're intimidated by the prospect of sitting through three or more hours of heightened drama in a foreign language, but are intrigued by the passionate, mysterious world of divas and Don Juans, start here, with our summaries of 10 classics. (Dates given indicate the first staged production.)

THE BARBER OF SEVILLE (1782)

Composed by Gioacchino Rossini, text by Sterbini. Based on the novel by Beaumarchais. Set in Seville, Spain, in the 17th century.

Count Almaviva, a Grandee of Spain, loves Rosina, the young ward and bride-to-be of Dr. Bartolo. With the help of Figaro, the town barber and busybody, the Count enters his rival's home disguised as a drunken soldier, then as a music teacher. Having gained access to Rosina, he easily persuades her to take his hand. Almaviva then convinces a notary, procured by Bartolo for his own marriage to Rosina, to marry him to Rosina in Bartolo's absence.

LA BOHÈME (1896)

Composed by Giacomo Puccini, text by Luigi Illica and Giuseppe Giacosa. Based on the novel Scènes de la vie de Bohème by Henri Murger. Set in Paris, France, in the 17th century.

Rodolfo, a poet, lives in the Latin Quarter of Paris with his dear friends—a painter, a philosopher, and a musician—who defy their hunger with cheerfulness and pranks. The quartet of friends is so poor that they resort to burning Rodolfo's poetry to keep warm. But Rodolfo's heart is soon warmed by the frail and consumptive Mimi, who knocks on his door one night, her candle extinguished by a winter draft. The two fall in love, but Mimi grows weaker and weaker. Eventually, her sickness and Rodolfo's overprotectiveness drive the two apart. Mimi's last request is to return to Rodolfo's attic room, where they first met, and where she will die in his arms.

DON CARLOS (1867)

Composed by Giuseppe Verdi, text by G. Méry and C. du Locle. Based on the play by Friedrich von Schiller. Set in France and Spain, during the Spanish Inquisition.

Don Carlos, infante of Spain, is torn between a futile love for Queen Elizabeth, his stepmother, to whom he was once engaged, and a fierce desire to bring freedom to Flanders, a Protestant country under Spanish (Catholic) domain. The queen's attendant, who is deeply in love with Carlos, tells the king, untruthfully, that Carlos and Elizabeth have been unfaithful to him. Carlos is sent to death, ostensibly for demanding to be let go to Flanders. Elizabeth remains at her husband's side, and Carlos escapes his death in the last moments of the opera, saved by the King's father, who takes Carlos into the cloister.

DON GIOVANNI (1787)

Composed by Wolfgang Amadeus Mozart, text by Lorenzo da Ponte. Based on the text Il Convitato by Giovanni Bertati. Set in Seville at the end of the 18th century.

The insatiable lover, Don Juan, jaunts from lass to lass, breaking hearts and wreaking havoc before he is finally dragged into Hell by the statue of the Commendatore who he killed in a duel after attempting to seduce his daughter, Doña Anna.

ELEKTRA (1909)

Composed by Richard Strauss, text by Hugo von Hofmannsthal. Adapted from the play by Sophocles. Set in ancient Mycenae.

Her soul withered by grief, Elektra is bent on avenging the seven-year-old murder of her father, Agamemnon, at the hands of her mother, Klytämnestra, and her mother's lover, Aegisth. Elektra persuades her brother Orest to murder Klytämnestra and Aegisth. The murders send Elektra into a dance of joy that becomes a frenzied dance of death, ending in the explosion of her heart.

LUCIA DI LAMMERMOOR (1835)

Composed by Gaetano Donizetti, text by Salvatore Cammarano. Based on the novel The Bride of Lammermoor by Sir Walter Scott. Set in Scotland in 1700.

Her mother's death is slowly but inexorably driving the tragic Lucia to madness. She loves Edgardo, but their promised union is sabotaged by her brother, who forces her to marry Arturo, a wealthy man she does not love. Tormented by visions of ghosts and spirits and devastated over the loss of Edgardo, Lucia murders her groom on their wedding night, then experiences a series of hallucinations before collapsing and dying of a broken heart.

RIGOLETTO (1851)

Composed by Giuseppe Verdi, text by Francesco Maria Piave. Based on Victor Hugo's Le Roi s'amuse. *Set Mantua, Italy, in the 16th century.*

Rigoletto, a court jester, intends to have the Duke of Mantua murdered for seducing his daughter, Gilda, but brings about the murder of the girl, instead.

The first of a "romantic trilogy," *Rigoletto* is followed by *Il Trovotore* and *La Traviata.*

TOSCA (1900)

Composed by Giacomo Puccini, text by Giuseppe Giacosa and Luigi Illica. Based on the play La Tosca *by Victorien Sardou. Set in Rome, in 1800.*

Floria Tosca, a prima donna, is passionately pursued by the evil Scarpia, chief of the Roman police. Yet Tosca loves Cavaradossi, a painter and a liberal patriot. She attempts to save her lover from execution when he is accused of aiding a fugitive, by pretending to yield to Scarpia's wishes, then killing him. But her actions unwittingly help to destroy her true love, Cavaradossi.

LA TRAVIATA (1853)

Composed by Giuseppe Verdi, text by Francesco Maria Piave. Based on Alexandre Dumas's play La Tame aux Camélias. *Set in Paris and vicinity in 1850.*

Violetta, a courtesan, renounces her life of pleasure in order to be with her gentlemanly lover, Alfredo. But Alfredo's father persuades Violetta that she is a blight on his family and that she must leave Alfredo for the good of his career. She returns to her former protector, with whom Alfredo fights a duel. Alfredo is subsequently forced to flee the country, and will return only to find Violetta dying of consumption.

TRISTAN AND ISOLDE (1865)

Composed and written by Richard Wagner. Set in a ship at sea, in England, and in Ireland, in a legendary time.

Tristan is dispatched to Ireland by his uncle, King Marke, to win him Isolde's hand. Yet Tristan and Isolde have long loved one another, each believing their love to be unrequited. On board the vessel that brings them to Cornwall, they drink what they believe to be a death potion, but is in fact a love potion. King Marke later discovers them in a midnight embrace. Tristan, wounded by one of the king's knights, flees to France. Isolde follows, finds him dying, and she too dies by his side.

THE WORLD'S LARGEST OPERA HOUSES

These houses showcase the world's best singers and stand as monuments to the grandeur of opera.

Opera House	Location	Total Capacity
The Metropolitan Opera	New York, NY	4,065
Cincinnati Opera	Cincinnati, OH	3,630
Lyric Opera of Chicago	Chicago, IL	3,563
San Francisco Opera	San Francisco, CA	3,476
The Dallas Opera	Dallas, TX	3,420

THE GRAMMY AWARDS

Even more so than most award-giving bodies, the National Academy of Recording Arts and Sciences has switched, added, deleted, and renamed its various award categories on a regular basis. The following chart gathers the majority of continuing categories that honor mainstream musical achievement. This means you won't find the awards for polka or jacket liner notes, but you will find years of musical greats (and electorate gaffes) in an easy-to-follow format.

	1958	1959	1960
Record of the Year	Domenico Modugno, "Nel Blu Dipinto Di Blu (Volare)"	Bobby Darin, "Mack the Knife"	Percy Faith, "Theme from *A Summer Place*"
Album of the Year	Henry Mancini, *The Music from Peter Gunn*	Frank Sinatra, *Come Dance with Me*	Bob Newhart, *Button Down Mind*
Song of the Year	Domenico Modugno, "Nel Blu Dipinto Di Blu (Volare)"	Jimmy Driftwood, "The Battle of New Orleans"	Ernest Gold, "Theme from *Exodus*"
Pop Vocal, Female	Ella Fitzgerald, *Ella Fitzgerald Sings the Irving Berlin Song Book*	Ella Fitzgerald, "But Not for Me"	Ella Fitzgerald, *Mack the Knife, Ella in Berlin*
Pop Vocal, Male	Perry Como, "Catch a Falling Star"	Frank Sinatra, *Come Dance with Me*	Ray Charles, *Genius of Ray Charles*
New Artist	—	Bobby Darin	Bob Newhart
Pop Vocal, Duo or Group with Vocal	Louis Prima and Keely Smith, "That Old Black Magic"	Mormon Tabernacle Choir, "Battle Hymn of the Republic"	Eydie Gormé and Steve Lawrence, "We Got Us"
Rhythm and Blues Song	Champs, "Tequila"	Dinah Washington, "What a Diff'rence a Day Makes"	Ray Charles, "Let the Good Times Roll"
Jazz, Soloist	—	Ella Fitzgerald, *Ella Swings Lightly*	—
Jazz, Group	Count Basie, *Basie*	Jonah Jones, *I Dig Chicks*	André Previn, *West Side Story*
Jazz, Big Band/ Large Ensemble Performance	—	—	Henry Mancini, *The Blues and the Beat*
Folk Recording	—	Kingston Trio, *The Kingston Trio at Large*	Harry Belafonte, *Swing Dat Hammer*
Cast Show Album	*The Music Man*	*Porgy and Bess*	*The Sound of Music*
Comedy Recording (Spoken Word/Musical)	David Seville, "The Chipmunk Song"	Shelley Berman, *Inside Shelley Berman;* Homer & Jethro, *The Battle of Kookamonga*	Bob Newhart, *Button Down Mind Strikes Back;* Paul Weston and Jo Stafford, *Jonathan and Darlene Edwards in Paris*
Classical Orchestral Performance	Felix Slatkin, Hollywood Bowl Symphony, *Gaîeté Parisienne*	Charles Munch, conductor, Boston Symphony, *Debussy: Images for Orchestra*	Fritz Reiner, conductor, Chicago Symphony, *Bartók: Music for Strings, Percussion and Celeste*
Opera Recording	Roger Wagner Chorale, *Virtuoso*	Erich Leinsdorf, conductor, Vienna Philharmonic, *Mozart: The Marriage of Figaro*	Erich Leinsdorf, conductor, Rome Opera House Chorus and Orchestra, *Puccini: Turandot* (Solos: Tebaldi, Nilsson, Bjoerling, Tozzi)
Chamber Music Performance	Hollywood String Quartet, *Beethoven: Quartet 130*	Artur Rubinstein, *Beethoven: Sonata No. 21 in C, Op. 53; "Waldstein" Sonata No. 18 in E Flat, Op. 53, No. 3*	Laurindo Almeida, *Conversations with the Guitar*

	1961	1962	1963
Record of the Year	Henry Mancini, "Moon River"	Tony Bennett, "I Left My Heart in San Francisco"	Henry Mancini, "The Days of Wine and Roses"
Album of the Year	Judy Garland, *Judy at Carnegie Hall*	Vaughn Meader, *The First Family*	Barbra Streisand, *The Barbra Streisand Album*
Song of the Year	Henry Mancini and Johnny Mercer, "Moon River"	Leslie Bricusse and Anthony Newley, "What Kind of Fool Am I"	Johnny Mercer and Henry Mancini, "The Days of Wine and Roses"
(Pop) Vocal, Female	Judy Garland, *Judy at Carnegie Hall*	Ella Fitzgerald, *Ella Swings Brightly with Nelson Riddle*	Barbra Streisand, *The Barbra Streisand Album*
(Pop) Vocal, Male	Jack Jones, "Lollipops and Roses"	Tony Bennett, "I Left My Heart in San Francisco"	Jack Jones, "Wives and Lovers"
New Artist	Peter Nero	Robert Goulet	Swingle Singers
Pop Vocal, Duo or Group with Vocal	Lambert, Hendricks & Ross, *High Flying*	Peter, Paul & Mary, "If I Had a Hammer"	Peter, Paul & Mary, "Blowin' in the Wind"
Rhythm and Blues Song	Ray Charles, "Hit the Road, Jack"	Ray Charles, "I Can't Stop Loving You"	Ray Charles, "Busted"
Jazz, Soloist/Small Group	André Previn, *André Previn Plays Harold Arlen*	Stan Getz, *Desafinado*	Bill Evans, *Conversations with Myself*
Jazz, Big Band/Large Ensemble Performance	Stan Kenton, *West Side Story*	Stan Kenton, *Adventures in Jazz*	Woody Herman Band, *Encore: Woody Herman, 1963*
Contemporary Folk	Belafonte Folk Singers, *Belafonte Folk Singers at Home and Abroad*	Peter, Paul & Mary, "If I Had a Hammer"	Peter, Paul & Mary, "Blowin' in the Wind"
Cast Show Album	*How To Succeed in Business Without Really Trying*	*No Strings*	*She Loves Me*
Comedy Recording	Mike Nichols and Elaine May, *An Evening with Mike Nichols and Elaine May*	Vaughn Meader, *The First Family*	Allen Sherman, *Hello Mudduh, Hello Faddah*
Classical Album	Igor Stravinsky, conductor, Columbia Symphony, *Stravinsky Conducts, 1960: Le Sacre du Printemps; Petruchka*	Vladimir Horowitz, *Columbia Records Presents Vladimir Horowitz*	Benjamin Britten, conductor, London Symphony Orchestra and Chorus, *Britten: War Requiem*
Classical Orchestral Performance	Charles Munch, conductor, Boston Symphony, *Ravel: Daphnis et Chloe*	Igor Stravinsky, conductor, Columbia Symphony, *Stravinsky: The Firebird Ballet*	Erich Leinsdorf, conductor, Boston Symphony, *Bartók: Concerto for Orchestra*
Opera Recording	Gabriele Santini, conductor, Rome Opera Chorus and Orchestra, *Puccini: Madama Butterfly*	Georg Solti, conductor, Rome Opera House Orchestra and Chorus (Solos: Price, Vickers, Gorr, Merrill, Tozzi), *Verdi: Aïda*	Erich Leinsdorf, conductor, RCA Italiana Orchestra and Chorus (Solos: Price, Tucker, Elias), *Puccini: Madama Butterfly*
Chamber Music Performance	Jascha Heifetz, Gregor Piatigorsky, William Primrose, *Beethoven: Serenade, Op. 8; Kodaly: Duo for Violin & Cello, Op. 7*	Jascha Heifetz, Gregor Piatigorsky, William Primrose, *The Heifetz-Piatigorsky Concerts with Primrose, Pennario and Guests*	Julian Bream Consort, *An Evening of Elizabethan Music*

	1964	1965	1966
Record of the Year	Stan Getz and Astrud Gilberto, "The Girl from Ipanema"	Herb Alpert & The Tijuana Brass, "A Taste of Honey"	Frank Sinatra, "Strangers in the Night"
Album of the Year	Stan Getz and Joao Gilberto, *Getz/Gilberto*	Frank Sinatra, *September of My Years*	Frank Sinatra, *Sinatra: A Man & His Music*
Song of the Year	Jerry Herman, "Hello, Dolly!"	Paul Francis Webster and Johnny Mandel, "The Shadow of Your Smile (Love Theme from *The Sandpiper*)"	John Lennon and Paul McCartney, "Michelle"
Pop Vocal, Female	Barbra Streisand, "People"	Barbra Streisand, *My Name Is Barbra*	Eydie Gorme, "If He Walked into My Life"
Pop Vocal, Male	Louis Armstrong, "Hello, Dolly!"	Frank Sinatra, "It Was a Very Good Year"	Frank Sinatra, "Strangers in the Night"
Rock Vocal Female, Male	Petula Clark, "Downtown"	Petula Clark, "I Know a Place"; Roger Miller, "King of the Road"	Paul McCartney, "Eleanor Rigby"
New Artist	The Beatles	Tom Jones	—
Pop Vocal, Duo or Group	The Beatles, *A Hard Day's Night*	Anita Kerr Quartet, *We Dig Mancini*	Anita Kerr Quartet, "A Man and a Woman"
Rock Performance, Duo or Group with Vocal	—	Statler Brothers, "Flowers on the Wall"	The Mamas & The Papas, "Monday, Monday"
Rhythm and Blues Song	Nancy Wilson, "How Glad I Am"	James Brown, "Papa's Got a Brand New Bag"	Ray Charles, "Crying Time"
R&B Vocal	—	—	Ray Charles, "Crying Time"
R&B Duo or Group with Vocal	—	—	Ramsey Lewis, "Hold It Right There"
Country Song	Roger Miller, "Dang Me"	Roger Miller, "King of the Road"	Bill Sherrill and Glenn Sutton, "Almost Persuaded"
Country Vocal, Female	Dottie West, "Here Comes My Baby"	Jody Miller, "Queen of the House"	Jeannie Seely, "Don't Touch Me"
Country Vocal, Male	Roger Miller, "Dang Me"	Roger Miller, "King of the Road"	David Houston, "Almost Persuaded"
Jazz, Group	Stan Getz, *Getz/Gilberto*	Ramsey Lewis Trio, *The "In" Crowd*	Wes Montgomery, *Goin' Out of My Head*
Jazz, Big Band/ Large Ensemble Performance	Laurindo Almeida, *Guitar from Ipanema*	Duke Ellington Orchestra, *Ellington '66*	—
Gospel Performance, Duo, Group, Choir or Chorus	—	George Beverly Shea and Anita Ker Quartet, *Southland Favorites*	Porter Wagoner & the Blackwood Bros., *Grand Old Gospel*
Folk Recording	Gale Garnett, *We'll Sing in the Sunshine*	Harry Belafonte, Miriam Makeba, *An Evening with Belafonte/Makeba*	Cortelia Clark, *Blues in the Street*
Cast Show Album	*Funny Girl*	*On a Clear Day You Can See Forever*	*Mame*
Comedy Recording	Bill Cosby, *I Started Out as a Child*	Bill Cosby, *Why Is There Air?*	Bill Cosby, *Wonderfulness*

1964   1965   1966

	1964	1965	1966
Classical Album	Leonard Bernstein, conductor, New York Philharmonic, *Bernstein: Symphony No. 3*	Vladimir Horowitz, *Horowitz at Carnegie Hall: An Historic Return*	Morton Gould conductor, Chicago Symphony, *Ives: Symphony No. 1 in D Minor*
Classical Orchestral Performance	Erich Leinsdorf, conductor, Boston Symphony, *Mahler: Symphony No. 5 in C Sharp Minor*; Berg: *Wozzeck Excerpts*	Leopold Stokowski, conductor, American Symphony, *Ives: Symphony No. 4*	Erich Leinsdorf, conductor, Boston Symphony, *Mahler: Symphony No. 6 in A Minor*
Opera Recording	Herbert von Karajan, conductor, Vienna Philharmonic and Chorus (Solos: Price, Corelli, Merrill, Freni), *Bizet: Carmen*	Karl Bohm, conductor, Orchestra of German Opera, Berlin, (Solos: Fischer-Dieskau, Lear, Wunderlich), *Berg: Wozzeck*	Georg Solti, conductor, Vienna Philharmonic (Solos: Nilsson, Crespin, Ludwig, King, Hotter), *Wagner: Die Walküre*
Chamber Music Performance	Jascha Heifetz, Gregor Piatigorsky (Jacob Lateiner, piano), *Beethoven: Trio No. 1 in E Flat, Op. 1, No. 1*	Juilliard String Quartet, *Bartók: The Six String Quartets*	Boston Symphony Chamber Players, *Boston Symphony Chamber Players*

1967   1968   1969

	1967	1968	1969
Record of the Year	5th Dimension, "Up, Up and Away"	Simon & Garfunkel, "Mrs. Robinson"	5th Dimension, "Aquarius/Let the Sunshine In"
Album of the Year	The Beatles, *Sgt. Pepper's Lonely Hearts Club Band*	Glen Campbell, *By the Time I Get to Phoenix*	Blood, Sweat & Tears, *Blood, Sweat & Tears*
Song of the Year	Jim Webb, "Up, Up and Away"	Bobby Russell, "Little Green Apples"	Joe South, "Games People Play"
Pop Vocal, Female	Bobbie Gentry, "Ode to Billie Joe"	Dionne Warwick, "Do You Know the Way To San Jose"	Peggy Lee, "Is That All There Is"
Pop Vocal, Male	Glen Campbell, "By the Time I Get to Phoenix"	José Feliciano, "Light My Fire"	Harry Nilsson, "Everybody's Talkin'"
New Artist	Bobbie Gentry	José Feliciano	Crosby, Stills & Nash
Pop Vocal	5th Dimension, "Up, Up and Away"	Simon & Garfunkel, "Mrs. Robinson"	5th Dimension, "Aquarius/Let the Sunshine In"
Rock Performance, Duo or Group	5th Dimension, "Up, Up and Away"	—	—
Rhythm and Blues Song	Aretha Franklin, "Respect"	Otis Redding and Steve Cropper, "(Sittin' On) the Dock of the Bay"	Richard Spencer, "Color Him Father"
R&B Vocal, Female	Aretha Franklin, "Respect"	Aretha Franklin, "Chain of Fools"	Aretha Franklin, "Share Your Love With Me"
R&B Vocal, Male	Lou Rawls, "Dead End Street"	Otis Redding, "(Sittin' On) the Dock of the Bay"	Joe Simon, "The Chokin' Kind"

	1967	**1968**	**1969**
R&B Duo or Group with Vocal	Sam & Dave, "Soul Man"	The Temptations, "Cloud Nine"	The Isley Brothers, "It's Your Thing"
Country Song	John Hartford, "Gentle on My Mind"	Bobby Russell, "Little Green Apples"	Shel Silverstein, "A Boy Named Sue"
Country Vocal, Female	Tammy Wynette, "I Don't Wanna Play House"	Jeannie C. Riley, "Harper Valley P.T.A."	Tammy Wynette, "Stand By Your Man"
Country Vocal, Male	Glen Campbell, "Gentle on My Mind"	Johnny Cash, "Folsom Prison Blues"	Johnny Cash, "A Boy Named Sue"
Country Performance, Duo or Group with Vocal	Johnny Cash and June Carter, "Jackson"	Flatt & Scruggs, "Foggy Mountain Breakdown"	Waylon Jennings & The Kimberlys, "MacArthur Park"
Jazz, Group	Cannonball Adderley Quintet, *Mercy, Mercy, Mercy*	Bill Evans Trio, *Bill Evans at the Montreux Jazz Festival*	Wes Montgomery, *Willow Weep For Me*
Jazz, Big Band/ Large Ensemble Performance	Duke Ellington, *Far East Suite*	Duke Ellington, *And His Mother Called Him Bill*	Quincy Jones, "Walking in Space"
Gospel Performance, Duo, Group, Choir or Chorus	Porter Wagoner & The Blackwood Bros. Quartet, *More Grand Old Gospel*	Happy Goodman Family, *The Happy Gospel of the Happy Goodmans*	Porter Wagoner & the Blackwood Bros., *In Gospel Country*
Folk Recording	John Hartford, "Gentle on My Mind"	Judy Collins, "Both Sides Now"	Joni Mitchell, *Clouds*
Cast Show Album	*Cabaret*	*Hair*	*Promises, Promises*
Comedy Recording	Bill Cosby, *Revenge*	Bill Cosby, *To Russell, My Brother, Whom I Slept With*	Bill Cosby, *The Best of Bill Cosby*
Classical Album	Pierre Boulez, conductor, Orchestra and Chorus of Paris National Opera (Solos: Berry, Strauss, Uhl, Doench), *Berg: Wozzeck;* Leonard Berstein, conductor, London Symphony, *Mahler: Symphony No. 8 in E Flat Major ("Symphony of a Thousand")*	—	Walter Carlos, *Switched-On Bach*
Classical Orchestral Performance	Igor Stravinsky, conductor, Columbia Symphony, *Stravinsky: Firebird & Petrouchka Suites*	Pierre Boulez, conductor, New Philharmonic Orchestra, *Boulez Conducts Debussy*	Pierre Boulez, conductor, Cleveland Orchestra, *Boulez Conducts Debussy, Vol. 2: "Images Pour Orchestre"*
Opera Recording	Pierre Boulez, conductor, Orchestra and Chorus of Paris National Opera (Solos: Berry, Strauss, Uhl, Doench), *Berg: Wozzeck*	Erich Leinsdorf, conductor, New Philharmonic Orchestra and Ambrosian Opera Chorus (Soloists: Price, Troyanos, Raskin, Milnes, Shirley, Flagello), *Mozart: Cosi fan tutte*	Herbert von Karajan, conductor, Berlin Philharmonic (Soloists: Thomas, Stewart, Stolze, Dernesch, Keleman, Dominguez, Gayer, Ridderbusch), *Wagner: Siegfried*
Chamber Music Performance	Ravi Shankar and Yehudi Menuhin, *West Meets East*	E. Power Biggs with Edward Tarr Brass Ensemble and Gabrieli Consort, Vittorio Negri, conductor, *Gabrieli: Canzoni for Brass, Winds, Strings & Organ*	The Philadelphia, Cleveland, and Chicago Brass Ensembles, *Gabrieli: Antiphonal Music of Gabrieli (Canzoni for Brass Choirs)*

	1970	1971	1972
Record of the Year	Simon & Garfunkel, "Bridge Over Troubled Water"	Carole King, "It's Too Late"	Roberta Flack, "The First Time Ever I Saw Your Face"
Album of the Year	Simon & Garfunkel, *Bridge Over Troubled Water*	Carole King, *Tapestry*	George Harrison and Friends (Ravi Shankar, Bob Dylan, Leon Russell, Ringo Starr, Billy Preston, Eric Clapton, Klaus Voorman, others), *The Concert for Bangladesh*
Song of the Year	Paul Simon, "Bridge Over Troubled Water"	Carole King, "You've Got a Friend"	Ewan MacColl, "The First Time Ever I Saw Your Face"
Pop Vocal, Female	Dionne Warwick, "I'll Never Fall In Love Again"	Carole King, "Tapestry"	Helen Reddy, "I Am Woman"
Pop Vocal, Male	Ray Stevens, "Everything Is Beautiful"	James Taylor, "You've Got a Friend"	Nilsson, "Without You"
New Artist	The Carpenters	Carly Simon	America
Pop Vocal, Duo or Group with Vocal	Carpenters, "Close to You"	Carpenters, *Carpenters*	Roberta Flack and Donny Hathaway, "Where Is the Love"
Rhythm and Blues Song	Ronald Dunbar, General Johnson, "Patches"	Bill Withers, "Ain't No Sunshine"	Barrett Strong and Norman Whitfield, "Papa Was a Rolling Stone"
R&B Vocal, Female	Aretha Franklin, "Don't Play That Song"	Aretha Franklin, "Bridge Over Troubled Water"	Aretha Franklin, "Young, Gifted & Black"
R&B Vocal, Male	B.B. King, "The Thrill Is Gone"	Lou Rawls, "A Natural Man"	Billy Paul, "Me and Mrs. Jones"
R&B Duo or Group with Vocal	The Delfonics, "Didn't I (Blow Your Mind This Time)"	Ike and Tina Turner, "Proud Mary"	The Temptations, "Papa Was a Rolling Stone"
Country Song	Marty Robbins, "My Woman, My Woman, My Wife"	Kris Kristofferson, "Help Me Make It Through the Night"	Ben Peters, "Kiss an Angel Good Mornin' "
Country Vocal, Female	Lynn Anderson, "Rose Garden"	Sammi Smith, "Help Me Make It Through the Night"	Donna Fargo, "Happiest Girl in the Whole U.S.A."
Country Vocal, Male	Ray Price, "For the Good Times"	Jerry Reed, "When You're Hot, You're Hot"	Charley Pride, *Charley Pride Sings Heart Songs*
Country Performance, Duo or Group with Vocal	Johnny Cash and June Carpenter, "If I Were a Carpenter"	Conway Twitty and Loretta Lynn, "After the Fire Is Gone"	The Statler Brothers, "Class of '57"
Traditional Blues Recording	T-Bone Walker, "Good Feelin' "	Muddy Waters, *They Call Me Muddy Waters*	Muddy Waters, *The London Muddy Waters Session*
Jazz, Soloist	—	Bill Evans, *The Bill Evans Album*	Gary Burton, *Alone at Last*
Jazz, Group	Bill Evans, *Alone*	Bill Evans Trio, *The Bill Evans Album*	Freddie Hubbard, *First Light*
Jazz, Big Band/ Large Ensemble Performance	Miles Davis, *Bitches Brew*	Duke Ellington, *New Orleans Suite*	Duke Ellington, *Togo Brava Suite*
Gospel Performance, Duo, Group, Choir or Chorus	Oak Ridge Boys, "Talk About the Good Times"	Charley Pride, "Let Me Live"	Blackwood Brothers, *L-O-V-E*
Cast Show Album	*Company*	*Godspell*	*Don't Bother Me, I Can't Cope*
Comedy Recording	Flip Wilson, *The Devil Made Me Buy This Dress*	Lily Tomlin, *This Is a Recording*	George Carlin, *FM & AM*

	1970	**1971**	**1972**
Classical Album	Colin Davis, conductor, Royal Opera House Orchestra and Chorus (Solos: Vickers, Veasey Lindholm), *Berlioz: Les Troyens*, Philips	Vladimir Horowitz, *Horowitz Plays Rachmaninoff*	Georg Solti, conductor, Chicago Symphony, Vienna Boys Choir, Vienna State Opera Chorus, Vienna Singverein Chorus and soloists, *Mahler: Symphony No. 8 in E Flat Major (Symphony of a Thousand)*
Classical Orchestral Performance	Pierre Boulez, conductor, Cleveland Orchestra, *Stravinsky: Le Sacre du printemps*	Carlo Maria Giulini, conductor, Chicago Symphony, *Mahler: Symphony No. 1 in D Major*	Georg Solti, conductor, Chicago Symphony, *Mahler: Symphony No. 7 in E Minor*
Opera Recording	Colin Davis, conductor, Royal Opera House Orchestra and Chorus (Solos: Vickers, Veasey, Lindholm), *Berlioz: Les Troyens*	Erich Leinsdorf, conductor, London Symphony and John Alldis Choir (Solos: Price, Domingo, Milnes, Bumbry, Raimondi), *Verdi: Aïda*	Colin Davis, conductor, BBC Symphony/Chorus of Covent Garden (Solos: Gedda, Eda-Pierre, Soyer, Berbie), *Berlioz: Benvenuto Cellini*
Chamber Music Performance	Eugene Istomin, Isaac Stern, Leonard Rose, *Beethoven: The Complete Piano Trios*	Juilliard Quartet, *Debussy: Quartet in G Minor/Ravel: Quartet in F Major*	Julian Bream and John Williams, *Julian & John*

	1973	**1974**	**1975**
Record of the Year	Roberta Flack, "Killing Me Softly with His Song"	Olivia Newton-John, "I Honestly Love You"	Captain & Tennille, "Love Will Keep Us Together"
Album of the Year	Stevie Wonder, *Innervisions*	Stevie Wonder, *Fulfillingness' First Finale*	Paul Simon, *Still Crazy After All These Years*
Song of the Year	Norman Gimbel and Charles Fox, "Killing Me Softly with His Song"	Marilyn and Alan Bergman, Marvin Hamlisch, "The Way We Were"	Stephen Sondheim, "Send In the Clowns"
Pop Vocal, Female	Roberta Flack, "Killing Me Softly with His Song"	Olivia Newton-John, "I Honestly Love You"	Janis Ian, "At Seventeen"
Pop Vocal, Male	Stevie Wonder, "You Are the Sunshine of My Life"	Stevie Wonder, *Fulfillingness' First Finale*	Paul Simon, *Still Crazy After All These Years*
New Artist	Bette Midler	Marvin Hamlisch	Natalie Cole
Pop Vocal, Duo or Group with Vocal	Gladys Knight & The Pips, "Neither One of Us (Wants To Be the First To Say Goodbye)"	Paul McCartney & Wings, "Band on the Run"	Eagles, "Lyin' Eyes"
Rhythm and Blues Song	Stevie Wonder, "Superstition"	Stevie Wonder, "Living for the City"	H. W. Casey, Richard Finch, Willie Clarke, and Betty Wright, "Where Is the Love"
R&B Vocal, Female	Aretha Franklin, "Master of Eyes"	Aretha Franklin, "Ain't Nothing Like the Real Thing"	Natalie Cole, "This Will Be"
R&B Vocal, Male	Stevie Wonder, "Superstition"	Stevie Wonder, "Boogie On Reggae Woman"	Ray Charles, "Living for the City"

	1973	**1974**	**1975**
R&B Duo or Group with Vocal	Gladys Knight & The Pips, "Midnight Train to Georgia"	Rufus, "Tell Me Something Good"	Earth, Wind & Fire, "Shining Star"
Country Song	Kenny O'Dell, "Behind Closed Doors"	Norris Wilson and Bill Sherrill, "A Very Special Love Song"	Chips Moman and Larry Butler, "(Hey Won't You Play) Another Somebody Done Somebody Wrong Song"
Country Vocal, Female	Olivia Newton-John, "Let Me Be There "	Anne Murray, "Love Song"	Linda Ronstadt, "I Can't Help It (If I'm Still in Love with You)"
Country Vocal, Male	Charlie Rich, "Behind Closed Doors"	Ronnie Milsap, "Please Don't Tell Me How the Story Ends"	Willie Nelson, "Blue Eyes Crying in the Rain"
Country Performance, Duo or Group with Vocal	Kris Kristofferson and Rita Coolidge, "From the Bottle to the Bottom"	The Pointer Sisters, "Fairytale"	Kris Kristofferson and Rita Coolidge, "Lover Please"
Traditional Blues Recording	Doc Watson, *Then and Now*	Doc and Merle Watson, *Two Days in November*	Muddy Waters, *The Muddy Waters Woodstock Album*
Jazz, Soloist	Art Tatum, *God Is in the House*	Charlie Parker, *First Recordings!*	Dizzy Gillespie, *Oscar Peterson and Dizzy Gillespie*
Jazz, Group	Supersax, *Supersax Plays Bird*	Oscar Peterson, Joe Pass, and Niels Pedersen, *The Trio*	Return to Forever featuring Chick Corea, *No Mystery*
Jazz, Big Band/ Large Ensemble Performance	Woody Herman, *Giant Steps*	Woody Herman, *Thundering Herd*	Phil Woods with Michel Legrand & His Orchestra, *Images*
Cast Show Album	*A Little Night Music*	*Raisin*	*The Wiz*
Comedy Recording	Cheech & Chong, *Los Cochinos*	Richard Pryor, *That Nigger's Crazy*	Richard Pryor, *Is It Something I Said?*
Classical Album	Pierre Boulez, conductor, New York Philharmonic, *Bartók: Concerto for Orchestra*	Georg Solti, conductor, Chicago Symphony, *Berlioz: Symphonie Fantastique*	Georg Solti, conductor, Chicago Symphony, *Beethoven: Symphonies (9) Complete*
Classical Orchestral Performance	Pierre Boulez, conductor, New York Philharmonic, *Bartók: Concerto for Orchestra*	Georg Solti, conductor, Chicago Symphony, *Berlioz: Symphonie Fantastique*	Pierre Boulez, conductor, New York Philharmonic, *Ravel: Daphnis et Chloë*
Opera Recording	Leonard Bernstein, conductor, Metropolitan Opera Orchestra and Manhattan Opera Chorus (Solos: Horne, McCracken, Maliponte, Krause), *Bizet: Carmen*	Georg Solti, conductor, London Philharmonic (Soloists: Caballé, Domingo, Milnes, Blegen, Raimondi), *Puccini: La Bohème*	Colin Davis, conductor, Royal Opera House, Covent Garden (Solos: Caballé, Baker, Gedda, Ganzarolli, Van Allen, Cotrubas), *Mozart: Cosi fan tutte*
Chamber Music Performance	Gunther Schuller and New England Ragtime Ensemble, *Joplin: The Red Back Book*	Artur Rubinstein, Henryk Szeryng, and Pierre Fournier, *Brahms: Trios (complete)/ Schumann: Trio No. 1 in D Minor*	Artur Rubinstein, Henryk Szeryng, and Pierre Fournier, *Shubert: Trios Nos. 1 in B Flat Major Op. 99 & 2 in E Flat Major Op. 100*

	1976	**1977**	**1978**
Record of the Year	George Benson, "This Masquerade"	Eagles, "Hotel California"	Billy Joel, "Just the Way You Are"
Album of the Year	Stevie Wonder, *Songs in the Key of Life*	Fleetwood Mac, *Rumours*	The Bee Gees and others, *Saturday Night Fever*
Song of the Year	Bruce Johnston, "I Write the Songs"	Joe Brooks, "You Light Up My Life"; Barbra Streisand, "Love Theme from *A Star Is Born* (Evergreen)"	Billy Joel, "Just the Way You Are"
(Pop) Vocal, Female	Linda Ronstadt, *Hasten Down the Wind*	Barbra Streisand, "Love Theme from *A Star Is Born* (Evergreen)"	Anne Murray, "You Needed Me"
(Pop) Vocal, Male	Stevie Wonder, *Songs in the Key of Life*	James Taylor, "Handy Man"	Barry Manilow, "Copacabana (At the Copa)"
New Artist	Starland Vocal Band	Debby Boone	A Taste of Honey
Pop Vocal, Duo or Group with Vocal	Chicago, "If You Leave Me Now"	The Bee Gees, "How Deep Is Your Love"	The Bee Gees, *Saturday Night Fever*
Rhythm and Blues Song	Boz Scaggs and David Paich, "Lowdown"	Leo Sayer and Vini Poncia, "You Make Me Feel Like Dancing"	Paul Jabara, "Last Dance"
R&B Vocal, Female	Natalie Cole, "Sophisticated Lady (She's a Different Lady)"	Thelma Houston, "Don't Leave Me This Way"	Donna Summer, "Last Dance"
R&B Vocal, Male	Stevie Wonder, "I Wish"	Lou Rawls, *Unmistakably Lou*	George Benson, "On Broadway"
R&B Duo or Group with Vocal	Marilyn McCoo and Billy Davis, Jr., "You Don't Have To Be a Star (To Be in My Show)"	Emotions, "Best of My Love"	Earth, Wind & Fire, "All 'n All"
Country Song	Larry Gatlin, "Broken Lady"	Richard Leigh, "Don't It Make My Brown Eyes Blue"	Don Schlitz, "The Gambler"
Country Vocal, Female	Emmylou Harris, *Elite Hotel*	Crystal Gayle, "Don't It Make My Brown Eyes Blue"	Dolly Parton, *Here You Come Again*
Country Vocal, Male	Ronnie Milsap, "(I'm a) Stand by My Woman Man"	Kenny Rogers, "Lucille"	Willie Nelson, "Georgia on My Mind"
Country Performance, Duo or Group with Vocal	Amazing Rhythm Aces, "The End Is Not in Sight (The Cowboy Tune)"	The Kendalls, "Heaven's Just a Sin Away"	Waylon Jennings and Willie Nelson, "Mamas Don't Let Your Babies Grow Up To Be Cowboys"
Ethnic or Traditional Recording	John Hartford, *Mark Twang*	Muddy Waters, *Hard Again*	Muddy Waters, *I'm Ready*
Jazz, Soloist	Count Basie, *Basie & Zoot*	Oscar Peterson, *The Giants*	Oscar Peterson, *Montreux '77, Oscar Peterson Jam*
Jazz, Group	Chick Corea, *The Leprechaun*	Phil Woods, *The Phil Woods Six—Live from the Showboat*	Chick Corea, *Friends*
Jazz, Big Band/ Large Ensemble Performance	Duke Ellington, *The Ellington Suites*	Count Basie & His Orchestra, *Prime Time*	Thad Jones and Mel Lewis, *Live in Munich*
Cast Show Album	*Bubbling Brown Sugar*	*Annie*	*Ain't Misbehavin'*
Comedy Recording	Richard Pryor, *Bicentennial Nigger*	Steve Martin, *Let's Get Small*	Steve Martin, *A Wild and Crazy Guy*
Classical Album	Artur Rubinstein with Daniel Barenboim, conductor, London Philharmonic, *Beethoven: The Five Piano Concertos*	Leonard Bernstein, Vladimir Horowitz, Isaac Stern, Mstislav Rostropovich, Dietrich Fischer-Dieskau, Yehudi Menuhin, Lyndon Woodside, *Concert of the Century* (recorded live at Carnegie Hall May 18, 1976)	Itzhak Perlman with Carlo Maria Giulini, conductor, Chicago Symphony, *Brahms: Concerto for Violin in D Major*

	1976	1977	1978
Classical Orchestral Performance	Georg Solti, conductor, Chicago Symphony, *Strauss: Also Sprach Zarathustra*	Carlo Maria Giulini, conductor, Chicago Symphony, *Mahler: Symphony No. 9 in D Major*	Herbert von Karajan, conductor, Berlin Philharmonic, *Beethoven: Symphonies (9) Complete*
Opera Recording	Lorin Maazel conductor, Cleveland Orchestra and Chorus (Solos: Mitchell, White), *Gershwin: Porgy & Bess*	John De Main, conductor, Houston Grand Opera Production (Solos: Albert, Dale, Smith, Shakesnider, Lane, Brice, Smalls), *Gershwin: Porgy & Bess*	Julius Rudel, conductor, New York City Opera Orchestra and Chorus (Solos: Sills, Titus), *Lehar: The Merry Widow*
Chamber Music Performance	David Munrow, conductor, The Early Music Consort of London, *The Art of Courtly Love*	Juilliard Quartet, *Schöenberg: Quartets for Strings*	Itzhak Perlman and Vladimir Ashkenazy, *Beethoven: Sonatas for Violin and Piano*

GRAMMY AWARD RECORDS

In 1957, the newly formed National Academy of Recording Arts & Sciences first conceived of a peer award to recognize outstanding achievement in the recording field. The Grammys, named after the gramophone statuette, have since expanded from 28 categories to 98. The following artists have all set records in the annals of Grammy history:

Youngest "Album of the Year" winner:
Alanis Morissette, age 21, when *Jagged Little Pill* was named 1995's best LP

Winningest winner:
Georg Solti, the conductor of the Chicago Symphony, has won 31 awards

Winningest female:
Aretha Franklin, with 15 awards (and an uninterrupted winning streak from 1967 to 1974)

Most awards in a single year:
Michael Jackson in 1983, with seven for Album of the Year, *Thriller*; and one for *E.T., the Extra-Terrestrial* as Best Recording for Children; and Carlos Santana in 1999, with eight for Album of the Year, *Supernatural*

Most country awards:
Chet Atkins and Vince Gill with 14

Most jazz awards:
Ella Fitzgerald with 13

Most comedy awards:
Bill Cosby with 9

Most opera awards:
Leontyne Price with 13

	1979	1980	1981
Record of the Year	The Doobie Brothers, "What a Fool Believes"	Christopher Cross, "Sailing"	Kim Carnes, "Bette Davis Eyes"
Album of the Year	Billy Joel, *52nd Street*	Christopher Cross, *Christopher Cross*	John Lennon and Yoko Ono, *Double Fantasy*
Song of the Year	Kenny Loggins and Michael McDonald, "What a Fool Believes"	Christopher Cross, "Sailing"	Donna Weiss and Jackie DeShannon, "Bette Davis Eyes"
Pop Vocal, Female	Dionne Warwick, "I'll Never Love This Way Again"	Bette Midler, "The Rose"	Lena Horne, *Lena Horne: The Lady and Her Music Live on Broadway*
Pop Vocal, Male	Billy Joel, *52nd Street*	Kenny Loggins, "This Is It"	Al Jarreau, *Breakin' Away*
Rock Vocal, Female	Donna Summer, "Hot Stuff"	Pat Benatar, *Crimes of Passion*	Pat Benatar, "Fire and Ice"
Rock Vocal, Male	Bob Dylan, "Gotta Serve Somebody"	Billy Joel, *Glass Houses*	Rick Springfield, "Jessie's Girl"
New Artist	Rickie Lee Jones	Christopher Cross	Sheena Easton
Pop Vocal, Duo or Group with Vocal	The Doobie Brothers, *Minute by Minute*	Barbra Streisand and Barry Gibb, "Guilty"	The Manhattan Transfer, "Boy from New York City"
Rock Performance, Duo or Group with Vocal	The Eagles, "Heartache Tonight"	Bob Seger & the Silver Bullet Band, *Against the Wind*	The Police, "Don't Stand So Close to Me"
Rhythm and Blues Song	David Foster, Jay Graydon, and Bill Champlin, "After the Love Has Gone"	Reggie Lucas and James Mtume, "Never Knew Love Like This Before"	Bill Withers, William Salter, and Ralph MacDonald, "Just the Two of Us"
R&B Vocal, Female	Dionne Warwick, "Déjà Vu"	Stephanie Mills, "Never Knew Love Like This Before"	Aretha Franklin, "Hold On, I'm Comin' "
R&B Vocal, Male	Michael Jackson, "Don't Stop 'Til You Get Enough"	George Benson, *Give Me the Night*	James Ingram, "One Hundred Ways"
R&B Duo or Group with Vocal	Earth, Wind & Fire, "After the Love Has Gone"	Manhattans, "Shining Star"	Quincy Jones, *The Dude*
Country Song	Bob Morrison and Debbie Hupp, "You Decorated My Life"	Willie Nelson, "On the Road Again"	Dolly Parton, "9 to 5"
Country Vocal, Female	Emmylou Harris, *Blue Kentucky Girl*	Anne Murray, "Could I Have This Dance"	Dolly Parton, "9 to 5"
Country Vocal, Male	Kenny Rogers, "The Gambler"	George Jones, "He Stopped Loving Her Today"	Ronnie Milsap, "(There's) No Gettin' Over Me"
Country Performance, Duo or Group with Vocal	Charlie Daniels Band, "The Devil Went Down to Georgia"	Roy Orbison and Emmylou Harris, "That Lovin' You Feelin' Again"	Oak Ridge Boys, "Elvira"
Ethnic or Traditional Recording	Muddy Waters, *Muddy "Mississippi" Waters Live*	Dr. Isaiah Ross, Maxwell Street Jimmy, Big Joe William, Son House, Rev. Robert Wilkins, Little Brother Montgomery, and Sunnyland Slim, *Rare Blues*	B. B. King, *There Must Be a Better World Somewhere*
Jazz Vocal, Female	Ella Fitzgerald, *Fine and Mellow*	Ella Fitzgerald, *A Perfect Match/Ella & Basie*	Ella Fitzgerald, *Digital III at Montreux*
Jazz Vocal, Male	—	George Benson, "Moody's Mood"	Al Jarreau, "Blue Rondo à la Turk"
Jazz, Soloist	Oscar Peterson, *Jousts*	Bill Evans, *I Will Say Goodbye*	John Coltrane, *Bye, Bye Blackbird*

	1979	1980	1981
Jazz, Group	Gary Burton and Chick Corea, *Duet*	Bill Evans, *We Will Meet Again*	Chick Corea and Gary Burton, *Chick Corea and Gary Burton in Concert, Zurich, October 28, 1979*
Jazz, Big Band/ Large Ensemble Performance	Duke Ellington, *At Fargo, 1940 Live*	Count Basie and Orchestra, *On the Road*	Gerry Mulligan & His Orchestra, *Walk on the Water*
Jazz Fusion Performance, Vocal or Instrumental	Weather Report, *8:30*	Manhattan Transfer, "Birdland"	Grover Washington Jr., *Winelight*
Cast Show Album	*Sweeney Todd*	*Evita*	*Lena Horne: The Lady and Her Music Live on Broadway*
Comedy Recording	Robin Williams, *Reality...What a Concept*	Rodney Dangerfield, *No Respect*	Richard Pryor, *Rev. Du Rite*
Classical Album	Georg Solti, conductor, Chicago Symphony Orchestra, *Brahms: Symphonies (4) Complete*	Pierre Boulez, conductor, Orchestre d l'Opera de Paris (Solos: Stratas, Minton, Mazura, Toni Blankenheim), *Berg: Lulu*	Georg Solti, conductor, Chicago Symphony Orchestra and Chorus (Solos: Buchanan, Zakai), *Mahler: Symphony No. 2 in C Minor*
Classical Orchestral Performance	Georg Solti, conductor, Chicago Symphony, *Brahms: Symphonies (4) Complete*	Georg Solti, conductor, Chicago Symphony, *Bruckner: Symphony No. 6 in A Major*	Georg Solti, conductor, Chicago Symphony, *Mahler: Symphony No. 2 in C Minor*
Opera Recording	Colin Davis, conductor, Orchestra and Chorus of the Royal Opera House, Covent Garden (Solos: Vickers, Harper, Summers), *Britten: Peter Grimes*	Pierre Boulez, conductor, Orchestre d l'Opera de Paris (Solos: Stratas, Minton, Mazura, Blankenheim), *Berg: Lulu*	Charles Mackerras, conductor, Vienna Philharmonic (Solos: Zahradnicek, Zitek, Zidek), *Janacek: From the House of the Dead*
Chamber Music Performance	Dennis Russel Davies, conductor, St. Paul Chamber Orchestra, *Copland: Appalachian Spring*	Itzhak Perlman and Pinchas Zukerman, *Music for Two Violins (Moszkowski: Suite for Two Violins/Shostakovich: Duets/ Prokofiev: Sonata for Two Violins)*	Itzhak Perlman, Lynn Harrell, and Vladimir Ashkenazy, *Tchaikovsky: Piano Trio in A Minor*

FAMOUS LOSERS

In 200 Cher broke the Grammy jinx, but it's hard to believe that the following artists have never won a Grammy in a competitive category, although many have been nominated. Asterisks indicate that the performers have, however, belatedly received the NARAS Lifetime Achievement Award.

AC/DC	The Doors	Queen
Beach Boys	The Drifters	Cat Stevens
Chuck Berry*	The Four Tops	Diana Ross
Jackson Browne	Peter Frampton	Lawrence Welk
The Byrds	Benny Goodman*	Kitty Wells*
Patsy Cline*	Grateful Dead	The Who
Sam Cooke*	The Jackson 5	Hank Williams, Sr.*
Creedence Clearwater Revival	Janis Joplin	Neil Young
Cream	Led Zeppelin	
Bing Crosby*	Little Richard*	
Fats Domino*	Pretenders	

	1982	1983	1984
Record of the Year	Toto, "Rosanna"	Michael Jackson, "Beat It"	Tina Turner, "What's Love Got To Do with It"
Album of the Year	Toto, *Toto IV*	Michael Jackson, *Thriller*	Lionel Richie, *Can't Slow Down*
Song of the Year	Johnny Christopher, Mark James, and Wayne Thompson, "Always on My Mind"	Sting, "Every Breath You Take"	Graham Lyle and Terry Britten, "What's Love Got To Do with It"
Pop Vocal, Female	Melissa Manchester, "You Should Hear How She Talks About You"	Irene Cara, "Flashdance...What a Feeling"	Tina Turner, "What's Love got To Do with It"
Pop Vocal, Male	Lionel Richie, "Truly"	Michael Jackson, *Thriller*	Phil Collins, "Against All Odds (Take a Look at Me Now)"
Rock Vocal, Female	Pat Benatar, "Shadows of the Night"	Pat Benatar, "Love Is a Battlefield"	Tina Turner, "Better Be Good to Me"
Rock Vocal, Male	John Cougar, "Hurts So Good"	Michael Jackson, "Beat It"	Bruce Springsteen, "Dancing in the Dark"
New Artist	Men at Work	Culture Club	Cyndi Lauper
Pop Vocal, Duo or Group with Vocal	Joe Cocker and Jennifer Warnes, "Up Where We Belong"	The Police, "Every Breath You Take"	Pointer Sisters, "Jump (For My Love)"
Rock Performance, Duo or Group with Vocal	Survivor, "Eye of the Tiger"	The Police, *Synchronicity*	Prince and the Revolution, *Purple Rain*
Rhythm and Blues Song	Jay Graydon, Steve Lukather, and Bill Champlin, "Turn Your Love Around"	Michael Jackson, "Billie Jean"	Prince, "I Feel for You"
R&B Vocal, Female	Jennifer Holliday, "And I Am Telling You I'm Not Going"	Chaka Khan, *Chaka Khan*	Chaka Khan, "I Feel for You"
R&B Vocal, Male	Marvin Gaye, "Sexual Healing"	Michael Jackson, "Billie Jean"	Billy Ocean, "Caribbean Queen (No More Love on the Run)"
R&B Duo or Group with Vocal	Dazz Band, "Let It Whip"; Earth, Wind & Fire, "Wanna Be With You"	Rufus & Chaka Khan, "Ain't Nobody"	James Ingram and Michael McDonald, "Yah Mo B There"
Country Song	Johnny Christopher, Wayne Thompson, and Mark James, "Always on My Mind"	Mike Reed, "Stranger in My House"	Steve Goodman, "City of New Orleans"
Country Vocal, Female	Juice Newton, "Break It To Me Gently"	Anne Murray, "A Little Good News"	Emmylou Harris, "In My Dreams"
Country Vocal, Male	Willie Nelson, "Always on My Mind"	Lee Greenwood, "I.O.U."	Merle Haggard, "That's the Way Love Goes"
Country Performance, Group	Alabama, *Mountain Music*	Alabama, *The Closer You Get*	The Judds, "Mama He's Crazy"
Traditional Blues Recording	Clarence "Gatemouth" Brown, *Alright Again*	B. B. King, *Blues 'n' Jazz*	John Hammond, Stevie Ray Vaughan & Double Trouble, Sugar Blue, Koko Taylor & The Blues Machine, Luther "Guitar Junior" Johnson, and J. B. Hutto & The New Hawks, *Blues Explosion*
Reggae Recording	—	—	Black Uhuru, *Anthem*
Jazz Vocal, Female	Sarah Vaughan, *Gershwin Live!*	Ella Fitzgerald, *The Best Is Yet to Come*	—
Jazz Vocal, Male	Mel Torme, *An Evening with George Shearing and Mel Torme*	Mel Torme, *Top Drawer*	Joe Williams, *Nothin' but the Blues*
Jazz, Soloist	Miles Davis, *We Want Miles*	Wynton Marsalis, *Think of One*	Wynton Marsalis, *Hot House Flowers*

	1982	1983	1984
Jazz, Group	Phil Woods Quartet, *"More" Live*	The Phil Woods Quartet, *At the Vanguard*	Art Blakey & The Jazz Messengers, *New York Scene*
Jazz, Big Band/ Large Ensemble Performance	Count Basie & His Orchestra, *Warm Breeze*	Rob McConnell and The Boss Brass, *All in Good Time*	Count Basie & His Orchestra, *88 Basie Street*
Jazz Fusion Performance	Pat Metheny Group, *Offramp*	Pat Metheny Group, *Travels*	Pat Metheny Group, *First Circle*
Gospel Performance, Female	—	Amy Grant, "Ageless Medley"	Amy Grant, "Angels"
Gospel Performance, Male	—	Russ Taff, *Walls of Glass*	Michael W. Smith, *Michael W. Smith 2*
Gospel Performance, Duo, Group, Choir or Chorus	—	Sandi Patti and Larnelle Harris, "More Than Wonderful"	Debby Boone and Phil Driscoll, "Keep the Flame Burning"
Ethnic or Traditional Folk Recording	Queen Ida, *Queen Ida and the Bon Temps Zydeco Band on Tour*	Clifton Chenier & His Red Hot Louisiana Band, *I'm Here*	Elizabeth Cotten, *Elizabeth Cotten Live!*
Cast Show Album	*Dreamgirls*	*Cats (Complete Original Broadway Cast Recording)*	*Sunday in the Park with George*
Comedy Recording	Richard Pryor, *Live on the Sunset Strip*	Eddie Murphy, *Eddie Murphy: Comedian*	"Weird Al" Yankovic, "Eat It"
Classical Album	Glenn Gould, *Bach: The Goldberg Variations*	Georg Solti, conductor, Chicago Symphony, *Mahler: Symphony No. 9 in D Major*	Neville Marriner, conductor, Academy of St. Martin-in-the-Fields/Ambrosian Opera Chorus/Choristers of Westminster Abbey, *Amadeus (Original Soundtrack)*
Classical Orchestral Performance	James Levine, conductor, Chicago Symphony, *Mahler: Symphony No. 7 in E Minor (Song of the Night)*	Georg Solti, conductor, Chicago Symphony, *Mahler: Symphony No. 9 in D Major*	Leonard Slatkin, conductor, St. Louis Symphony, *Prokofiev: Symphony No. 5 in B Flat, Op. 100*
Opera Recording	Pierre Boulez, conductor, Bayreuth Festival Orchestra (Solos: Jones, Altmeyer, Wenkel, Hofmann, Jung, Jerusalem, Zednik, McIntyre, Salminen, Becht), *Wagner: Der Ring des Nibelungen*	James Levine, conductor, The Metropolitan Opera Orchestra and Chorus (Solos: Stratas, Domingo, MacNeill), *Verdi: La Traviata*	Lorin Maazel, conductor, Orchestre National de France/Choeurs et Maitrise de Radio France (Solos: Johnson, Esham, Domingo, Raimondi), *Bizet: Carmen*
Chamber Music Performance	Richard Stoltzman and Richard Goode, *Brahms: The Sonatas for Clarinet & Piano, Op. 120*	Mstislav Rostropovich and Rudolph Serkin, *Brahms: Sonata for Cello & Piano in E Minor, Op. 38 & Sonata in F Major, Op. 99*	Juilliard String Quartet, *Beethoven: The Late String Quartets*

	1985	1986	1987
Record of the Year	USA for Africa, "We Are the World"	Steve Winwood, "Higher Love"	Paul Simon, "Graceland"
Album of the Year	Phil Collins, *No Jacket Required*	Paul Simon, *Graceland*	U2, *The Joshua Tree*
Song of the Year	Michael Jackson and Lionel Richie, "We Are the World"	Burt Bacharach and Carole Bayer Sager, "That's What Friends Are For"	James Horner, Barry Mann, and Cynthia Weil, "Somewhere Out There"
Pop Vocal, Female	Whitney Houston, "Saving All My Love for You"	Barbra Streisand, *The Broadway Album*	Whitney Houston, "I Wanna Dance with Somebody (Who Loves Me)"
Pop Vocal, Male	Phil Collins, *No Jacket Required*	Steve Winwood, "Higher Love"	Sting, *Bring on the Night*
Rock Vocal, Female	Tina Turner, "One of the Living"	Tina Turner, "Back Where You Started"	—
Rock Vocal, Male	Don Henley, "The Boys of Summer"	Robert Palmer, "Addicted to Love"	Bruce Springsteen, *Tunnel of Love*
New Artist	Sade	Bruce Hornsby and the Range	Jody Watley
Pop Vocal, Duo or Group with Vocal	USA for Africa, "We Are the World"	Dionne Warwick & Friends featuring Elton John, Gladys Knight, and Stevie Wonder, "That's What Friends Are For"	Bill Medley and Jennifer Warnes, "(I've Had) The Time of My Life"
Rock Performance, Group	Dire Straits, "Money for Nothing"	Eurythmics, "Missionary Man"	U2, *The Joshua Tree*
New Age Recording	—	Andreas Vollenweider, *Down to the Moon*	Yusef Lateef, *Yusef Lateef's Little Symphony*
Rhythm and Blues Song	Narada Michael Walden and Jeffrey Cohen, "Freeway of Love"	Anita Baker, Louis A. Johnson, Gary Bias, "Sweet Love"	Bill Withers, "Lean on Me"
R&B Vocal, Female	Aretha Franklin, "Freeway of Love"	Anita Baker, *Rapture*	Aretha Franklin, *Aretha*
R&B Vocal, Male	Stevie Wonder, *In Square Circle*	James Brown, "Living in America"	Smokey Robinson, "Just To See Her"
R&B Duo or Group with Vocal	Commodores, "Nightshift"	Prince & The Revolution, "Kiss"	Aretha Franklin and George Michael, "I Knew You Were Waiting (For Me)"
Country Song	Jimmy L. Webb, "Highwayman"	Jamie O'Hara, "Grandpa (Tell Me 'Bout the Good Old Days)"	Paul Overstreet and Don Schlitz, *Forever and Ever, Amen*
Country Vocal, Female	Rosanne Cash, "I Don't Know Why You Don't Want Me"	Reba McEntire, "Whoever's in New England"	K. T. Oslin, "80's Ladies"
Country Vocal, Male	Ronnie Milsap, "Lost in the Fifties Tonight (In the Still of the Night)"	Ronnie Milsap, *Lost in the Fifties Tonight*	Randy Travis, *Always & Forever*
Country Performance, Duo or Group with Vocal	The Judds, *Why Not Me*	The Judds, "Grandpa (Tell Me 'Bout the Good Old Days)"	Dolly Parton, Linda Ronstadt, and Emmylou Harris, *Trio*
Country Vocal, Collaboration	—	—	Ronnie Milsap and Kenny Rogers, "Make No Mistake, She's Mine"
Traditional Blues Recording	B. B. King, "My Guitar Sings the Blues"	Albert Collins, Robert Cray, and Johnny Copeland, *Showdown*	Professor Longhair, *Houseparty New Orleans Style*
Contemporary Blues	—	—	Robert Cray Band, *Strong Persuader*

	1985	1986	1987
Reggae Recording	Jimmy Cliff, *Cliff Hanger*	Steel Pulse, *Babylon the Bandit*	Peter Tosh, *No Nuclear War*
Jazz Vocal, Female	Cleo Laine, *Cleo at Carnegie, the 10th Anniversary Concert*	Diane Schuur, *Timeless*	Diane Schuur, *Diane Schuur & The Count Basie Orchestra*
Jazz Vocal, Male	Jon Hendricks and Bobby McFerrin, "Another Night in Tunisia"	Bobby McFerrin, " 'Round Midnight"	Bobby McFerrin, "What Is This Thing Called Love"
Jazz, Soloist	Wynton Marsalis, *Black Codes from the Underground*	Miles Davis, *Tutu*	Dexter Gordon, *The Other Side of 'Round Midnight*
Jazz, Group	Wynton Marsalis Group, *Black Codes from the Underground*	Wynton Marsalis, *J Mood*	Wynton Marsalis, *Marsalis Standard Time, Volume I*
Jazz, Big Band/ Large Ensemble Performance	John Barry and Bob Wilber, *The Cotton Club*	The Tonight Show Band with Doc Severinsen, *The Tonight Show Band with Doc Severinsen*	The Duke Ellington Orchestra, conducted by Mercer Ellington, *Digital Duke*
Jazz Fusion Performance, Vocal or Instrumental	David Sanborn, *Straight to the Heart*	Bob James and David Sanborn, *Double Vision*	Pat Metheny Group, *Still Life (Talking)*
Gospel Performance, Female	Amy Grant, *Unguarded*	Sandi Patti, *Morning Like This*	Deniece Williams, "I Believe in You"
Gospel Performance, Male	Larnelle Harris, "How Excellent Is Thy Name"	Philip Bailey, *Triumph*	Larnelle Harris, *The Father Hath Provided*
Gospel Performance, Duo, Group, Choir or Chorus	Larnelle Harris and Sandi Patti, "I've Just Seen Jesus"	Sandi Patti & Deniece Williams, "They Say"	Mylon LeFevre & Broken Heart, *Crack the Sky*
Traditional Folk Recording	Rockin' Sidney, "My Toot Toot"	Doc Watson, *Riding the Midnight Train*	Ladysmith Black Mambazo, *Shaka Zulu*
Contemporary Folk Recording	—	Arlo Guthrie, John Hartford, Richie Havens, Bonnie Koloc, Nitty Gritty Dirt Band, John Prine and others, *Tribute to Steve Goodman*	Steve Goodman, *Unfinished Business*
Cast Show Album	*West Side Story*	*Follies in Concert*	*Les Misérables*
Comedy Recording	Whoopi Goldberg, *Whoopi Goldberg*	Bill Cosby, *Those of You With or Without Children, You'll Understand*	Robin Williams, *A Night at the Met*
Classical Album	Robert Shaw, conductor, Atlanta Symphony Orchestra and Chorus, (Solo: Aler) *Berlioz: Requiem*	Vladimir Horowitz, *Horowitz: The Studio Recordings, New York 1985*	Vladimir Horowitz, *Horowitz in Moscow*
Classical Orchestral Performance	Robert Shaw, conductor, Atlanta Symphony Orchestra, *Fauré: Pelléas et Mélisande*	Georg Solti, conductor, Chicago Symphony Orchestra, *Liszt: A Faust Symphony*	Georg Solti, conductor, Chicago Symphony Orchestra, *Beethoven: Symphony No. 9 in D Minor*
Opera Recording	Georg Solti, conductor, Chicago Symphony Orchestra and Chorus (Solos: Mazura, Langridge), *Schoenberg: Moses und Aaron*	John Mauceri, conductor, New York City Opera Chorus and Orchestra (Solos: Mills, Clement, Eisler, Lankston, Castle, Reeve, Harrold, Billings), *Bernstein: Candide*	James Levine, conductor, Vienna Philharmonic (Solos: Tomowa-Sintow, Battle, Baltsa, Lakes, Prey), *R. Strauss: Ariadne auf Naxos*
Chamber Music Performance	Emanuel Ax and Yo-Yo Ma, *Brahms: Cello and Piano Sonatas in E Major & F Major*	Yo-Yo Ma and Emanuel Ax, *Beethoven: Cello & Piano Sonata No. 4 in C and Variations*	Itzhak Perlman, Lynn Harrell, and Vladimir Ashkenazy, *Beethoven: The Complete Piano Trios*

	1988	1989	1990
Record of the Year	Bobby McFerrin, "Don't Worry, Be Happy"	Bette Midler, "Wind Beneath My Wings"	Phil Collins, "Another Day in Paradise"
Album of the Year	George Michael, *Faith*	Bonnie Raitt, *Nick of Time*	Quincy Jones, *Back on the Block*
Song of the Year	Bobby McFerrin, "Don't Worry, Be Happy"	Larry Henley and Jeff Silbar, "Wind Beneath My Wings"	Julie Gold, "From a Distance"
Pop Vocal, Female	Tracy Chapman, "Fast Car"	Bonnie Raitt, "Nick of Time"	Mariah Carey, "Vision of Love"
Pop Vocal, Male	Bobby McFerrin, "Don't Worry, Be Happy"	Michael Bolton, "How Am I Supposed to Live Without You"	Roy Orbison, "Oh, Pretty Woman"
Rock Vocal, Female	Tina Turner, *Tina Live in Europe*	Bonnie Raitt, *Nick of Time*	Alannah Myles, "Black Velvet"
Rock Vocal, Male	Robert Palmer, "Simply Irresistible"	Don Henley, *The End of the Innocence*	Eric Clapton, "Bad Love"
New Artist	Tracy Chapman	No award (Milli Vanilli)	Mariah Carey
Pop Vocal, Duo or Group with Vocal	The Manhattan Transfer, *Brasil*	Linda Ronstadt and Aaron Neville, "Don't Know Much"	Linda Ronstadt with Aaron Neville, "All My Life"
Rock Performance, Duo or Group with Vocal	U2, "Desire"	Traveling Wilburys, *Traveling Wilburys, Volume I*	Aerosmith, "Janie's Got a Gun"
New Age Recording	Shadowfax, *Folksongs for a Nuclear Village*	Peter Gabriel, *Passion (Music from The Last Temptation of Christ)*	Mark Isham, *Mark Isham*
Hard Rock	Jethro Tull, *Crest of a Knave*	Living Colour, "Cult of Personality"	Living Colour, *Time's Up*
Metal	—	Metallica, "One"	Metallica, "Stone Cold Crazy"
Alternative	—	—	Sinéad O'Connor, *I Do Not Want What I Haven't Got*
Rap Performance, Solo	D.J. Jazzy Jeff & The Fresh Prince, "Parents Just Don't Understand"	Young MC, "Bust a Move"	M.C. Hammer, "U Can't Touch This"
Rap Performance by a Duo or Group	—	—	Ice-T, Melle Mel, Big Daddy Kane, Kool Moe Dee, and Quincy Jones III, "Back on the Block"
Rhythm and Blues Song	Anita Baker, Skip Scarborough, and Randy Holland, "Giving You the Best That I Got"	Kenny Gamble and Leon Huff, "If You Don't Know Me By Now"	Rick James, Alonzo Mille, and M.C. Hammer, "U Can't Touch This"
R&B Vocal, Female	Anita Baker, "Giving You the Best That I Got"	Anita Baker, *Giving You the Best That I Got*	Anita Baker, *Compositions*
R&B Vocal, Male	Terence Trent D'Arby, *Introducing the Hardline According to Terence Trent D'Arby*	Bobby Brown, "Every Little Step"	Luther Vandross, "Here and Now"
R&B Duo or Group with Vocal	Gladys Knight & The Pips, "Love Overboard"	Soul II Soul featuring Caron Wheeler, "Back to Life"	Ray Charles and Chaka Khan, "I'll Be Good to You"
Country Song	K. T. Oslin, "Hold Me"	Rodney Crowell, "After All This Time"	Jon Vezner and Don Henry, "Where've You Been"

	1988	**1989**	**1990**
Country Vocal, Female	K. T. Oslin, "Hold Me"	k.d. lang, *Absolute Torch and Twang*	Kathy Mattea, "Where've You Been"
Country Vocal, Male	Randy Travis, *Old 8 x 10*	Lyle Lovett, *Lyle Lovett and His Large Band*	Vince Gill, "When I Call Your Name"
Country Performance, Duo or Group with Vocal	The Judds, "Give a Little Love"	The Nitty-Gritty Dirt Band, *Will the Circle Be Unbroken, Volume 2*	The Kentucky Headhunters, *Pickin' on Nashville*
Country Vocal, Collaboration	Roy Orbison and k.d. lang, "Crying"	Hank Williams Jr. and Hank Williams Sr., "There's a Tear in My Beer"	Chet Atkins and Mark Knopfler, "Poor Boy Blues"
Traditional Blues Recording	Willie Dixon, *Hidden Charms*	John Lee Hooker and Bonnie Raitt, "I'm in the Mood"	B.B. King, *Live at San Quentin*
Contemporary Blues	The Robert Cray Band, "Don't Be Afraid of the Dark"	Stevie Ray Vaughan & Double Trouble, *In Step*	The Vaughan Brothers, *Family Style*
Reggae Recording	Ziggy Marley & The Melody Makers, *Conscious Party*	Ziggy Marley & The Melody Makers, *One Bright Day*	Bunny Wailer, *Time Will Tell—A Tribute to Bob Marley*
Jazz Vocal, Female	Betty Carter, *Look What I Got!*	Ruth Brown, *Blues on Broadway*	Ella Fitzgerald, *All That Jazz*
Jazz Vocal, Male	Bobby McFerrin, "Brothers"	Harry Connick Jr., *When Harry Met Sally...*	Harry Connick Jr., *We Are in Love*
Jazz, Soloist	Michael Brecker, *Don't Try This at Home*	Miles Davis, *Aura*	Oscar Peterson, *The Legendary Oscar Peterson Trio Live at the Blue Note*
Jazz, Group	McCoy Tyner, Pharoah Sanders, David Murray, Cecil McBee, and Roy Haynes, *Blues for Coltrane: A Tribute to John Coltrane*	Chick Corea Akoustic Band, *Chick Corea Akoustic Band*	Oscar Peterson Trio, *The Legendary Oscar Peterson Trio Live at the Blue Note*
Jazz, Big Band/ Large Ensemble Performance	Gil Evans & The Monday Night Orchestra, *Bud & Bird*	Miles Davis, *Aura*	George Benson featuring the Count Basie Orchestra; Frank Foster, conductor, "Basie's Bag"
Jazz Fusion Performance, Vocal or Instrumental	Yellowjackets, *Politics*	Pat Metheny Group, *Letter from Home*	Quincy Jones, "Birdland"
Gospel Performance, Female	Amy Grant, *Lead Me On*	CeCe Winans, "Don't Cry"	—
Gospel Performance, Male	Larnelle Harris, *Christmas*	BeBe Winans, "Meantime"	—
Gospel Performance, Duo, Group, Choir or Chorus	The Winans, *The Winans Live at Carnegie Hall*	Take 6, "The Savior Is Waiting"	Rev. James Cleveland, *Having Church*
Traditional Folk Recording	Various artists, *Folkways: A Vision Shared—A Tribute to Woody Guthrie and Leadbelly*	Bulgarian State Female Vocal Choir, *Le Mystère des voix bulgares, Vol. II*	Doc Watson, *On Praying Ground*
Contemporary Folk Recording	Tracy Chapman, *Tracy Chapman*	Indigo Girls, *Indigo Girls*	Shawn Colvin, *Steady On*
Cast Show Album	*Into the Woods*	*Jerome Robbins' Broadway*	*Les Misérables, The Complete Symphonic Recording*

	1988	1989	1990
Comedy Recording	Robin Williams, *Good Morning, Vietnam*	"Professor" Peter Schickele, *P.D.Q. Bach: 1712 Overture and Other Musical Assaults*	"Professor" Peter Schickele, *P.D.Q. Bach: Oedipus Tex & Other Choral Calamities*
Classical Album	Robert Shaw, conductor, Atlanta Symphony Orchestra and Chorus, *Verdi: Requiem and Operatic Choruses*	Emerson String Quartet, *Bartók: 6 String Quartets*	Leonard Bernstein, conductor, New York Philharmonic, *Ives: Symphony No. 2 (and Three Short Works)*
Classical Orchestral Performance	Robert Shaw, conductor, Atlanta Symphony Orchestra, *Rorem: String Symphony;* Louis Lane, conductor, Atlanta Symphony Orchestra, *Sunday Morning* and *Eagles*	Leonard Bernstein, conductor, New York Philharmonic, *Mahler: Sym. No. 3 in D Min.*	Leonard Bernstein, conductor, Chicago Symphony, *Shostakovich: Symphonies No. 1, Op. 10, and No. 7, Op. 60*
Opera Recording	Georg Solti, conductor, Vienna State Opera Choir & Vienna Philharmonic (Solos: Domingo, Norman, Randova, Nimsgern, Sotin, Fischer-Dieskau), *Wagner: Lohengrin*	James Levine, conductor, Metropolitan Opera Orchestra (Solos: Lakes, Moll, Morris, Norman, Behrens, Ludwig), *Wagner: Die Walküre*	James Levine, conductor, Metropolitan Opera Orchestra (Solos: Morris, Ludwig, Jerusalem, Wlaschiha, Moll, Zednik, Rootering), *Wagner: Das Rheingold*
Chamber Music Performance	Murray Perahia and Sir Georg Solti, pianos, with David Corkhill and Evelyn Glennie, percussion, *Bartók: Sonata for Two Pianos and Percussion; Brahms: Variations on a Theme by Joseph Haydn for Two Pianos*	Emerson String Quartet, *Bartók: 6 String Quartets*	Itzhak Perlman, violin; Daniel Barenboim, piano, *Brahms: The Three Violin Sonatas*

GRAMMY CHAMPS

Sir Georg Solti still reigns supreme as the National Academy of Recording Arts and Sciences' most honored musician, though Chick Corea and Emmylou Harris did join the leader's board.

Sir Georg Solti	31	James Mallinson	12
Quincy Jones	26	Paul McCartney	
Vladimir Horowitz	25	(including The Beatles and Wings)	13
Pierre Boulez	23	Pat Metheny (including Pat Metheny Group)	13
Stevie Wonder	21	Leontyne Price	13
Henry Mancini	20	Ray Charles	12
Leonard Bernstein	17	Thomas Z. Shepard	12
John T. Williams	17	Duke Ellington	11
Aretha Franklin	15	Roger Miller	11
Itzhak Perlman	15	Chick Corea	10
Paul Simon (including Simon & Garfunkel)	15	Kenneth "Babyface" Edmonds	10
Chet Atkins	14	Emmylou Harris	10
Eric Clapton	14	Linda Ronstadt	10
David Foster	14	George Harrison	
Vince Gill	14	(including The Beatles	
Robert Shaw (including Robert Shaw Chorale)	14	and Travelling Wilburys)	10
Sting (including The Police)	14	Bobby McFerrin	10
Ella Fitzgerald	13	Alan Menken	10
Michael Jackson	13	Artur Rubinstein	10
Yo-Yo Ma	13	Robert Woods	10

	1991	1992	1993
Record of the Year	Natalie Cole (with Nat "King" Cole), "Unforgettable"	Eric Clapton, "Tears in Heaven"	Whitney Houston, "I Will Always Love You"
Album of the Year	Natalie Cole, *Unforgettable*	Eric Clapton, *Unplugged*	Whitney Houston and others, *The Bodyguard—Original Soundtrack*
Song of the Year	Irving Gordon, "Unforgettable"	Eric Clapton and Will Jennings, "Tears in Heaven"	Alan Menken and Tim Rice, "A Whole New World"
Pop Vocal, Female	Bonnie Raitt, "Something to Talk About"	k.d. lang, "Constant Craving"	Whitney Houston, "I Will Always Love You"
Pop Vocal, Male	Michael Bolton, "When a Man Loves a Woman"	Eric Clapton, "Tears in Heaven"	Sting, "If I Ever Lose My Faith In You"
Rock Vocal, Female	Bonnie Raitt, *Luck of the Draw*	Melissa Etheridge, "Ain't It Heavy"	—
Rock Vocal, Male	—	Eric Clapton, *Tears in Heaven*	—
Rock Song/ Rock Vocal Performance, Solo	Sting, "Soul Cages"	Eric Clapton and Jim Gordon, "Layla"	Meat Loaf, "I'd Do Anything for Love (But I Won't Do That)"
New Artist	Mark Cohn	Arrested Development	Toni Braxton
Pop Vocal, Duo or Group with Vocal	R.E.M., "Losing My Religion"	Celine Dion and Peabo Bryson, "Beauty and the Beast"	Peabo Bryson and Regina Belle, "A Whole New World"
Rock Performance, Duo or Group with Vocal	Bonnie Raitt and Delbert McClinton, "Good Man, Good Woman"	U2, *Achtung Baby*	Aerosmith, "Living on the Edge"
New Age Recording	Mannheim Steamroller, *Fresh Aire 7*	Enya, *Sheperd Moons*	Paul Winter Consort, *Spanish Angel*
Hard Rock	Van Halen, *For Unlawful Carnal Knowledge*	Red Hot Chili Peppers, "Give It Away"	Stone Temple Pilots, "Plush"
Metal	Metallica, *Metallica*	Nine Inch Nails, "Wish"	Ozzy Ozbourne, "I Don't Want To Change the World"
Alternative	R.E.M., *Out of Time*	Tom Waits, *Bone Machine*	U2, *Zooropa*
Rap Performance, Solo	L.L. Cool J, "Mama Said Knock You Out"	Sir Mix-A-Lot, "Baby Got Back"	Dr. Dre, "Let Me Ride"
Rap Performance by a Duo or Group	D.J. Jazzy Jeff & The Fresh Prince, "Summertime"	Arrested Development, "Tennessee"	Digable Planets, "Rebirth of Slick (Cool Like Dat)"
Rhythm and Blues Song	Luther Vandross, Marcus Miller, and Teddy Vann, "Power of Love/Love Power"	L.A. Reid, Babyface, and Daryl Simmons, "End of the Road"	Janet Jackson, James Harris III, and Terry Lewis, "That's the Way Love Goes"
R&B Vocal, Female	Patti LaBelle, *Burnin'*; Lisa Fischer; "How Can I Ease the Pain"	Chaka Khan, *The Woman I Am*	Toni Braxton, "Another Sad Love Song"
R&B Vocal, Male	Luther Vandross, *Power of Love*	Al Jarreau, *Heaven and Earth*	Ray Charles, "A Song For You"
R&B Duo or Group with Vocal	Boyz II Men, *Cooleyhighharmony*	Boyz II Men, "End of the Road"	Sade, "No Ordinary Love"
Country Song	Naomi Judd, John Jarvis, and Paul Overstreet, "Love Can Build a Bridge"	Vince Gill and John Barlow Jarvis, "I Still Believe in You"	Lucinda Williams, "Passionate Kisses"
Country Vocal, Female	Mary-Chapin Carpenter, "Down at the Twist and Shout"	Mary-Chapin Carpenter, "I Feel Lucky"	Mary-Chapin Carpenter, "Passionate Kisses"
Country Vocal, Male	Garth Brooks, *Ropin' the Wind*	Vince Gill, *I Still Believe in You*	Dwight Yoakam, "Ain't That Lonely Yet"

	1991	1992	1993
Country Performance, Duo or Group with Vocal	The Judds, "Love Can Build a Bridge"	Emmylou Harris & The Nash Ramblers, *Emmylou Harris & The Nash Ramblers at the Ryman*	Brooks & Dunn, "Hard Workin' Man"
Country Vocal, Collaboration	Steve Wariner, Ricky Skaggs, and Vince Gill, "Restless"	Travis Tritt and Marty Stuart, "The Whiskey Ain't Workin' "	Reba McEntire and Linda Davis, "Does He Love You"
Traditional Blues Recording	B. B. King, *Live at the Apollo*	Dr. John, *Goin' Back to New Orleans*	B.B. King, *Blues Summit*
Contemporary Blues	Buddy Guy, *Damn Right, I've Got the Blues*	Stevie Ray Vaughan & Double Trouble, *The Sky Is Crying*	Buddy Guy, *Feels Like Rain*
Reggae Recording	Shabba Ranks, *As Raw as Ever*	Shabba Ranks, *X-tra Naked*	Inner Circle, *Bad Boys*
Jazz, Soloist	Stan Getz, "I Remember You"	Joe Henderson, "Lush Life"	Joe Henderson, "Miles Ahead"
Jazz, Group	Oscar Peterson Trio, *Saturday Night at the Blue Note*	Branford Marsalis, *I Heard You Twice the First Time*	Joe Henderson, *So Near, So Far (Musings for Miles)*
Jazz, Big Band/ Large Ensemble Performance	Dizzy Gillespie & The United Nation Orchestra, *Live at the Royal Festival Hall*	McCoy Tyner Big Band, *The Turning Point*	Miles Davis and Quincy Jones, *Miles and Quincy Live at Montreaux*
Jazz Fusion Performance	—	Pat Metheny, *Secret Story*	—
Gospel Performance, Duo, Group, Choir or Chorus	Sounds of Blackness, *The Evolution of Gospel*	Music & Arts Seminar Mass Choir; Edwin Hawkins, choir director, *Edwin Hawkins Music & Arts Seminar Mass Choir: Recorded Live in Los Angeles*	Brooklyn Tabernacle Choir; Carol Cymbala, choir director, *Live...We Come Rejoicing*
Traditional Folk Recording	Ken Burns and John Colby, *The Civil War*	The Chieftains, *Another Country*	The Chieftains, *The Celtic Harp*
Contemporary Folk Recording	John Prine, *The Missing Years*	The Chieftains, *An Irish Evening Live at the Grand Opera House, Belfast*	Nanci Griffith, *Other Voices/Other Rooms*
Cast Show Album	*The Will Rogers Follies*	*Guys and Dolls*	*The Who's Tommy*
Comedy Recording	"Professor" Peter Schickele, *P.D.Q. Bach: WTWP Classical Talkity-Talk Radio*	"Professor" Peter Schickele, *P.D.Q. Bach: Music for an Awful Lot of Winds & Percussion*	George Carlin, *Jammin' in New York*
Classical Album	Leonard Bernstein, conductor, London Symphony Orchestra (Solos: Hadley, Anderson, Ludwig, Green, Gedda, Jones), *Bernstein: Candide*	Leonard Bernstein, conductor, Berlin Philharmonic Orchestra, *Mahler: Symphony No. 9*	Pierre Boulez, conductor, Chicago Symphony Orchestra and Chorus; John Alen John Tomlinson, baritone, *Bartók: The Wooden Prince & C*
Classical Orchestral Performance	Daniel Barenboim, conductor, Chicago Symphony Orchestra, *Corigliano: Symphony No. 1*	Leonard Bernstein, conductor, Berlin Philharmonic Orchestra, *Mahler: Symphony No. 9*	Pierre Boulez, conductor, Chicago Symphony, *Bartók: The Wooden Prince*
Opera Recording	James Levine, conductor, Metropolitan Opera Orchestra and Chorus (Solos: Behrens, Studer, Schwarz, Goldberg, Weikl, Wlaschiha, Salminen), *Wagner: Götterdämmerung*	Georg Solti conductor, Vienna Philharmonic (Solos: Domingo, Varady, Van Dam, Behrens, Runkel, Jo), *R. Strauss: Die Frau Ohne Schatten*	John Nelson, conductor, English Chamber Orchestra and Ambrosian Opera Chorus (Solos: Battle, Horne, Ramey, Aler, McNair, Chance, Mackie, Doss); *Handel: Semele*
Chamber Music Performance	Isaac Stern and Jamie Laredo, violins; Yo-Yo Ma, cello; Emanuel Ax, piano, *Brahms: Piano Quartets*	Yo-Yo Ma, cello; Emanuel Ax, piano, *Brahms: Sonatas for Cello & Piano*	Anne-Sophie Mutter, violin, and James Levine, conductor, Chicago Symphony, *Berg: Violoin Concerto/Rihm: Time Chant*

262

	1994	1995	1996
Record of the Year	Sheryl Crow, "All I Wanna Do"	Seal, "Kiss From a Rose"	Eric Clapton, "Change the World"
Album of the Year	Tony Bennett, *MTV Unplugged*	Alanis Morissette, *Jagged Little Pill*	Celine Dion, *Falling Into You*
Song of the Year	Bruce Springsteen, "Streets of Philadelphia"	Seal, "Kiss From a Rose"	Gordon Kennedy, Wayne Kirk-patrick & Tommy Sims, "Change the World"
Pop Vocal, Female	Sheryl Crow, "All I Wanna Do"	Annie Lennox, "No More 'I Love You's' "	Toni Braxton, "Un-Break My Heart"
Pop Vocal, Male	Elton John, "Can You Feel the Love Tonight"	Seal, "Kiss From a Rose"	Eric Clapton, "Change the World"
Rock Vocal, Female	Melissa Etheridge, "Come to My Window"	Alanis Morissette, "You Oughta Know"	Sheryl Crow, "If It Makes You Happy"
Rock Vocal, Male	Bruce Springsteen, "Streets of Philadelphia"	Tom Petty, "You Don't Know How It Feels"	Beck, "Where It's At"
Rock Song/ Rock Vocal Performance, Solo	Bruce Springsteen, "Streets of Philadelphia"	Glen Ballard and Alanis Moris-sette, "You Oughta Know"	Tracy Chapman, "Give Me One Reason"
New Artist	Sheryl Crow	Hootie & The Blowfish	LeAnn Rimes
Pop Vocal, Duo or Group with Vocal	All-4-One, "I Swear"	Hootie & The Blowfish, "Let Her Cry"	The Beatles, "Free As a Bird"
Rock Performance, Duo or Group with Vocal	Aerosmith, "Crazy"	Blues Traveler, "Run-Around"	Dave Matthews Band, "So Much To Say"
New Age Recording	Paul Winter, "Prayer for the Wild Thing"	George Winston, *Forest*	Enya, *The Memory of Trees*
Hard Rock	Soundgarden, "Black Hole Sun"	Pearl Jam, "Spin the Black Circle"	The Smashing Pumpkins, "Bul-let with Butterfly Wings"
Metal	Soundgarden, "Spoonman"	Nine Inch Nails, "Happiness in Slavery"	Rage Against the Machine, "Tire Me"
Alternative	Green Day, *Dookie*	Nirvana, *MTV Unplugged in New York*	Beck, *Odelay*
Rap Performance, Solo	Queen Latifah, "U.N.I.T.Y."	Coolio, "Gangsta's Paradise"	L.L. Cool J, "Hey Lover"
Rap Performance by a Duo or Group	Salt-N-Pepa, "None of Your Business"	Method Man Featuring Mary J. Blige, "I'll Be There for You"/ "You're All I Need to Get By"	Bone Thugs-N-Harmony, "Tha Crossroads"
Rhythm and Blues Song	Babyface, "I'll Make Love to You"	Stevie Wonder, "For Your Love"	Babyface, "Exhale (Shoop Shoop)"
R&B Vocal, Female	Toni Braxton, "Breathe Again"	Anita Baker, "I Apologize"	Toni Braxton, "You're Makin' Me High"
R&B Vocal, Male	Babyface, "When Can I See You"	Stevie Wonder, "For Your Love"	Luther Vandross, "Your Secret Love"
R&B Duo or Group with Vocal	Boyz II Men, "I'll Make Love to You"	TLC, "Creep"	The Fugees, "Killing Me Softly"
Country Song	Gary Baker and Frank J. Myers, "I Swear"	Vince Gill, "Go Rest High on That Mountain"	Bill Mack, "Blue"
Country Vocal, Female	Mary Chapin Carpenter, "Shut Up and Kiss Me"	Alison Krauss, "Baby, Now That I've Found You"	LeAnn Rimes, "Blue"
Country Vocal, Male	Vince Gill, "When Love Finds You"	Vince Gill, "Go Rest High on That Mountain"	Vince Gill, "Worlds Apart"

	1994	1995	1996
Country Performance, Duo or Group with Vocal	Asleep at the Wheel with Lyle Lovett, "Blues for Dixie"	The Mavericks, "Here Comes the Rain"	Brooks & Dunn, "My Maria"
Country Vocal, Collaboration	Aaron Neville and Trisha Yearwood, "I Fall to Pieces"	Shenandoah & Alison Krauss, "Somewhere in the Vicinity of the Heart"	Vince Gill featuring Alison Krauss & Union Station, "High Lonesome Sound"
Traditional Blues Recording	Eric Clapton, *From the Cradle*	John Lee Hooker, *Chill Out*	James Cotton, *Deep in the Blues*
Contemporary Blues	Pops Staples, *Father Father*	Buddy Guy, *Slippin' In*	Keb' Mo', *Just Like You*
Reggae Recording	Bunny Wailer, *Crucial! Roots Classics*	Shaggy, *Boombastic*	Bunny Wailer, *Hall of Fame—A Tribute to Bob Marley's 50th Anniversary*
Jazz, Soloist	Benny Carter, "Prelude to a Kiss"	Lena Horne, *An Evening With Lena Horne* (vocals); Michael Brecker, *Impressions* (instrumental)	Cassandra Wilson, *New Moon Daughter* (vocals); Michael Brecker, "Cabin Fever" (instrumental)
Jazz, Group/ Jazz, Instrumental Performance, Individual or Group	Ron Carter, Herbie Hancock, Wallace Roney, Wayne Shorter & Tony Williams, *A Tribute to Miles*	McCoy Tyner Trio Featuring Michael Brecker, *Infinity*	Michael Brecker, *Tales from the Hudson*
Jazz, Big Band/ Large Ensemble Performance	McCoy Tyner Big Band, *Journey*	GRP All-Star Big Band & Tom Scott, "All Blues"	Count Basie Orchestra (with The New York Voices), *Live at Manchester Craftsmen's Guild*
Contemporary Jazz Performance	—	Pat Metheny Group, *We Live Here*	Wayne Shorter, *High Life*
Gospel Performance, Duo, Group, Choir or Chorus	The Thompson Community Singers, Rev. Milton Brunson, choir director, *Through God's Eyes* and The Love Fellowship Crusade Choir, Hezekiah Walker, choir director, *Live in Atlanta at Morehouse College* (tie)	The Brooklyn Tabernacle Choir, *Praise Him...Live!*	Shirley Caesar's Outreach Convention Choir, *Just a Word*
Traditional Folk Recording	Bob Dylan, *World Gone Wrong*	Ramblin' Jack Elliott, *South Coast*	Pete Seeger, *Pete*
Contemporary Folk Recording	Johnny Cash, *American Recordings*	Emmylou Harris, *Wrecking Ball*	Bruce Springsteen, *The Ghost of Tom Joad*
Cast Show Album	*Passion*	*Smokey Joe's Cafe—The Songs of Leiber and Stoller*	*Riverdance*
Comedy Recording	Sam Kinison, *Live From Hell*	Jonathan Winters, *Crank Calls*	Al Franken, *Rush Limbaugh Is a Big Fat Idiot*
Classical Album	Pierre Boulez, conductor, Chicago Symphony Orchestra, *Bartok: Concerto for Orch.; Four Orchestral Pieces, Op. 12*	Pierre Boulez, conductor, Cleveland Orchestra and Chorus, *Debussy: La Mer; Nocturnes; Jeux, etc.*	Leonard Slatkin, conductor, various Artists, *Corigliano: Of Rage and Remembrance*
Classical Orchestral Performance	Pierre Boulez, conductor, Chicago Symphony Orchestra, *Bartok: Concerto for Orch.; Four Orchestral Pieces, Op. 12*	Pierre Boulez, conductor, Cleveland Orchestra and Chorus, *Debussy: La Mer; Nocturnes; Jeux, etc.*	Michael Tilson Thomas, conductor, San Francisco Symphony, *Prokofiev: Romeo and Juliet (Scenes from the Ballet)*
Opera Recording	Kent Nagano, conductor, Orchestra and Chorus of Opera de Lyon (Solos: Cheryl Struder, Jerry Hadley, Samuel Ramey, Kenn Chester), *Floyd: Susannah*	Charles Dutoit, conductor, Montreal Symphony Orchestra & Chorus, *Berlioz: Les Troyens*	Richard Hickox, conductor, Opera London, London Symphony Chorus, City of London Sinfonia (Solos: Philip Langridge, Alan Opie, Janice Watson), *Britten: Peter Grimes*
Chamber Music Performance	Daniel Barenboim, piano; Dale Clevenger, horn; Larry Combs, clarinet (Chicago Symphony), Daniele Damiano, bassoon; Hansjorg Schellenberger, oboe (Berlin Philharmonic), *Beethoven/Mozart: Quintets*	Emanuel Ax, piano; Yo-Yo Ma, cello; Richard Stoltzman, clarinet, *Brahms/Beethoven/ Mozart: Clarinet Trios*	Cleveland Quartet, *Corigliano: String Quartet*

	1997	1998	1999
Record of the Year	Shawn Colvin, "Sunny Came Home"	Celine Dion, "My Heart Will Go On"	Santana, "Smooth"
Album of the Year	Bob Dylan, *Time Out of Mind*	Lauryn Hill, *The Miseducation Of Lauryn Hill*	Santana, *Supernatural*
Song of the Year	Shawn Colvin, "Sunny Came Home"	James Horner and Will Jennings, "My Heart Will Go On"	Itaal Shur and Rob Thomas, "Smooth"
Pop Vocal, Female	Sarah McLachlan, "Building a Mystery"	Celine Dion, "My Heart Will Go On"	Sarah McLachlan, "I Will Remember You"
Pop Vocal, Male	Elton John, "Candle in the Wind 1997"	Eric Clapton, "My Father's Eyes"	Sting, "Brand New Day"
Rock Vocal, Female	Fiona Apple, "Criminal"	Alanis Morissette, "Uninvited"	Sheryl Crow, "Sweet Child O' Mine"
Rock Vocal, Male	Bob Dylan, "Cold Irons Bound"	Lenny Kravitz, "Fly Away"	Lenny Kravitz, "American Woman"
Rock Song	Jakob Dylan, "One Headlight"	Alanis Morissette, "Uninvited"	Flea, "Scar Tissue"
New Artist	Paula Cole	Lauryn Hill	Christina Aguilera
Pop Performance, Duo or Group with Vocal	Jamiroquai, "Virtual Insanity"	The Brian Setzer Orchestra, "Jump Jive An' Wail"	Santana, "Maria Maria"
Rock Performance, Duo or Group with Vocal	The Wallflowers, "One Headlight"	Aerosmith, "Pink"	Santana, featuring Everlast, "Put Your Lights On"
New Age Album	Michael Hedges, *Oracle*	Clannad, *Landmarks*	Paul Winter and Friends, *Celtic Solstice*
Hard Rock Performance	The Smashing Pumpkins, "The End Is the Beginning Is the End"	Jimmy Page and Robert Plant, "Most High"	Metallica, "Whiskey in the Jar"
Metal Performance	Tool, *Aenema*	Metallica, "Better Than You"	Black Sabbath, "Iron Man"
Alternative Performance	Radiohead, *OK Computer*	Beastie Boys, *Hello Nasty*	Beck, *Mutations*
Rap Performance, Solo	Will Smith, "Men in Black"	Will Smith, "Gettin' Jiggy Wit It"	Eminem, "My Name Is"
Rap Performance by a Duo or Group	Puff Daddy & Faith Evans featuring 112, "I'll Be Missing You"	Beastie Boys, "Intergalactic"	The Roots & Erykah Badu, "You Got Me"
R&B Song	R. Kelly, "I Believe I Can Fly"	Lauryn Hill, "Doo Wop (That Thing)"	TLC, "No Scrubs"
R&B Vocal, Female	Erykah Badu, "On & On"	Lauryn Hill, "Doo Wop (That Thing)"	Whitney Houston, "It's Not Right But It's Okay"
R&B Vocal, Male	R. Kelly, "I Believe I Can Fly"	Stevie Wonder, "St. Louis Blues"	Barry White, "Staying Power"
R&B Performance, Duo or Group with Vocal	Blackstreet, "No Diggity"	Brandy and Monica, "The Boy Is Mine"	TLC, "No Scrubs"
Country Song	Bob Carlisle & Randy Thomas, "Butterfly Kisses"	Robert John "Mutt" Lange and Shania Twain, "You're Still the One "	Robert John "Mutt" Lange and Shania Twain, "Come on Over"
Country Vocal, Female	Trisha Yearwood, "How Do I Live"	Shania Twain, "You're Still the One"	Shania Twain, "Man! I Feel Like a Woman"
Country Vocal, Male	Vince Gill, "Pretty Little Adriana"	Vince Gill, "If You Ever Have Forever in Mind"	George Jones, "Choices"
Country Performance, Duo or Group with Vocal	Allison Krauss & Union Station, "Looking in the Eyes of Love"	Dixie Chicks, "There's Your Trouble"	Dixie Chicks, "Ready to Run"

	1997	1998	1999
Country Vocal, Collaboration	Trisha Yearwood & Garth Brooks, "In Another's Eyes"	Clint Black, Joe Diffie, Merle Haggard, Emmylou Harris, Alison Krauss, Patty Loveless, Earl Scruggs, Ricky Skaggs, Marty Stuart, Pam Tillis, Randy Travis, Travis Tritt, and Dwight Yoakam, *Same Old Train*	Emmylou Harris, Linda Ronstadt, and Dolly Parton, *After the Gold Rush*
Traditional Blues Album	John Lee Hooker, *Don't Look Back*	Otis Rush, *Any Place I'm Going*	B.B. King, *Blues on the Bayou*
Contemporary Blues Album	Taj Mahal, *Senor Blues*	Keb' Mo', *Slow Down*	Robert Cray Band, *Take Your Shoes Off*
Reggae Album	Ziggy Marley & The Melody Makers, *Fallen Is Babylon*	Sly and Robbie, *Friends*	Burning Spear, *Calling Rastafari*
Jazz, Soloist	Dee Dee Bridgewater, *Dear Ella* (vocals); Doc Cheatham & Nicholas Payton, "Stardust" (instrumental)	Shirley Horn, *I Remember Miles* (vocals); Chick Corea and Gary Burton, "Rhumbata" (instrumental)	Diana Krall, *When I Look in Your Eyes* (vocals); Wayne Shorter, "In Walked Wayne" (instrumental)
Jazz, Instrumental Performance, Individual or Group	Charlie Haden & Pat Metheny, *Beyond the Missouri Sky*	Herbie Hancock, *Gershwin's World*	Gary Burton, Chick Corea, Pat Metheny, Roy Haynes, and Dave Holland, *Like Minds*
Jazz, Large Ensemble Performance	Joe Henderson Big Band, *Joe Henderson Big Band*	Count Basie Orchestra; Grover Mitchell, Director, *Count Plays Duke*	The Bob Florence Limited Edition, *Serendipity 18*
Contemporary Jazz Performance	Randy Brecker, *Into the Sun*	Pat Metheny Group, *Imaginary Day*	David Sanborn, *Inside*
Gospel Album	dc Talk, *Welcome to the Freak Show: dc Talk* (rock); Jars of Clay, *Much Afraid* (pop/contemp.); The Fairfield Four, *I Couldn't Hear Nobody Pray* (trad. soul); Take 6, *Brothers* (contemp. soul); God's Property, *God's Property from Kirk Franlin's Nu Nation* (choir/chorus)	Ashley Cleveland, *You Are There* (rock); Deniece Williams, *This Is My Song* (pop/contemp); Cissy Houston, *He Leadeth Me* (trad. soul); Kirk Franklin, *The Nu Nation Project* (contemp. soul); The Associates; O'Landa Draper, Choir Director, *Reflections* (choir/chorus)	Rebecca St. James, *Pray* (rock); Steven Curtis Chapman, *Speechless* (pop/contemp.); Shirley Caesar, *Christmas with Shirley Caesar* (trad. soul); Yolanda Adams, *Mountain High...Valley Low* (contemp. soul); Brooklyn Tabernacle Choir, *High and Lifted Up* (choir/chorus)
Traditional Folk Album	BeauSoleil, *L'Amour ou La Folie*	The Chieftains with Various Artists, *Long Journey Home*	June Carter Cash, *Press On*
Contemporary Folk Album	Bob Dylan, *Time Out of Mind*	Lucinda Williams, *Car Wheels on a Gravel Road*	Tom Waits, *Mule Variations*
Cast Show Album	*Chicago: The Musical*	*The Lion King*	*Annie Get Your Gun*
Comedy Album	Chris Rock, *Roll with the New*	Mel Brooks & Carl Reiner, *The 2000 Year Old Man in the Year 2000*	Chris Rock, *Bigger and Blacker*
Classical Album	Yo-Yo Ma, violincello; David Zinman, conductor, Philadelphia Orchestra, *Premieres—Cello Concertos (Works of Danielpour, Kirchner, Rouse)*	Robert Shaw, conductor, Atlanta Sym. Orch. Cho.; Atlanta Sym. Orch., *Barber: Prayers of Kierkegaard/Vaughan Williams: Dona Nobis Pacem/Bartok: Cantata Profana*	Michael Tilson Thomas, conductor, San Francisco Sym. Orch., *Stravinsky: Firebird; The Rite of Spring; Persephone*
Classical Orchestral Performance	Pierre Boulez, conductor, The Cleveland Orchestra, The Cleveland Orchestra Chorus, *Berlioz: Symphonie Fantastique; Tristia*	Pierre Boulez, conductor, Chicago Sym. Orch, *Mahler: Sym. No. 9*	Michael Tilson Thomas, conductor, San Francisco Sym. Orch., *Stravinsky: Firebird; The Rite of Spring; Persephone*
Opera Recording	Sir Georg Solti, conductor; Ben Heppner, Herbert Lippert, Karita Mattila, Alan Opie, Rene Pape, Iris Vermillion, Chicago Symphony Chorus, Chicago Symphony Orchestra, *Wagner: Die Meistersinger Von Nurnberg*	Pierre Boulez, conductor; Jessye Norman; Laszlo Polgar; Chicago Symphony Orchestra, *Bartók: Bluebeard's Castle*	John Eliot Gardiner, conductor; Ian Bostridge; Bryn Terfel; Anne Sofie von Otter; Deborah York; London Symphony Orchestra *Stravinsky: The Rake's Progress*
Chamber Music Performance	Emerson String Quartet, *Beethoven: The String Quartets*	André Previn, piano; Gil Shaham, violin, *American Scenes*	Anne Sophie Mutter, violin; Lambert Orkis, piano; *Beethoven: The Violin Sonatas*

ALL THE REST

Ninety-eight categories strong (and that's not even counting the 40 new Latin Grammys), here are all the other Grammy winners from 1999.

Best Pop Collaboration with Vocals: "Smooth," Santana featuring Rob Thomas

Best Pop Instrumental Performance: "El Farol," Santana

Best Dance Recording: "Believe," Cher

Best Pop Album: *Ray of Light,* Madonna

Best Traditional Pop Vocal Performance: *Bennett Sings Ellington—Hot & Cool,* Tony Bennett

Best Rock Instrumental Performance: "The Calling" Santana featuring Eric Clapton

Best Rock Album: *Supernatural,* Santana

Best R&B Album: *Fanmail,* TLC

Best Traditional R&B Vocal Performance: *Staying Power,* Barry White

Best Rap Album: *The Slim Shady LP,* Eminem

Best Country Instrumental Performance: "Bob's Breakdowns," Asleep at the Wheel featuring Tommy Allsup, Floyd Domino, Larry Franklin, Vince Gill, and Steve Wariner

Best Country Album: *Fly,* Dixie Chicks

Best Bluegrass Album: *Ancient Tones,* Ricky Skaggs and Kentucky Thunder

Best Latin Jazz Performance: *Latin Soul,* Poncho Sanchez

Best Latin Pop Performance: *Tiempos,* Ruben Blades

Best Latin Rock/Alternative Performance: *Resurrection,* Chris Perez Band

Best Tropical Latin Performance: *Mambo Birdland,* Tito Puente

Best Mexican-American Music Performance: *100 Anos De Mariachi,* Placido Domingo

Best Tejano Music Performance: *Por Eso Te Amo,* Los Palominos

Best World Music Album: *Livro,* Caetano Veloso

Best Polka Album: *Polkasonic,* Brave Combo

Best Musical Album for Children: *The Adventures of Elmo in Grouchland,* Various Artists

Best Spoken Word Album for Children: *Listen to the Storyteller,* Wynton Marsalis, Graham Greene, and Kate Winslet

Best Spoken Word Album: *The Autobiography of Martin Luther King, Jr.,* LeVar Burton

Best Instrumental Composition: "Joyful Noise Suite,"

Best Instrumental Composition Written for a Motion Picture or for Television: *A Bug's Life,* Randy Newman

Best Song Written for a Motion Picture or for Television: "Beautiful Stranger" (from *Austin Powers: The Spy Who Shagged Me*), Madonna and William Orbit, songwriters

Best Instrumental Arrangement: "Chelsea Bridge," Don Sebesky, arranger (Don Sebesky)

Best Instrumental Arrangement Accompanying Vocal(s): "Lonely Town," Alan Broadbent, arranger (Haden Quartet West featuring Shirley Horn)

Best Recording Package: *Ride With Bob,* Ray Benson, Sally Carns and Buddy Jackson, art directors (*Asleep at the Wheel*)

Best Boxed Recording Package: *Mile Davis—The Complete Bitches Brew Sessions,* Ron Jaramillo and Arnold Levine, art directors

Best Album Notes: *John Coltrane—The Classic Quartet—Complete Impulse! Studio Recordings*

Best Historical Album: *The Duke Ellington Centennial Edition—The Complete RCA Victor Recordings*

Best Engineered Album, Non-Classical: *When I Look In Your Eyes*

Producer of the Year, Non-Classical: Walter Afanasieff

Remixer of the Year, Non-Classical: Club 69 (Peter Rauhofer)

Best Engineered Album, Classical: *Stravinsky: Firebird; The Rite Of Spring; Persephone*

Producer of the Year, Classical: Adam Abeshouse

Best Choral Performance: *Brittin: War Requiem*

Best Instrumental Soloist(s) Performance (with Orchestra): "Prokofiev: Piano Cons. Nos. 1&3/Bartok: Piano Con. No. 3," Martha Argerich, piano; Charles Dutoit, conductor (Orch. Sym. de Montreal)

Best Instrumental Soloist Performance (without Orchestra): *Shostakovich: 24 Preludes & Fugues, Op. 87,* Vladimir Ashkenazy, piano

Best Small Ensemble Performance (with or without Conductor): *Colors of Love* (works of Thomas, Stucky, Tavener, Rands, etc.), Chanticleer

Best Classical Vocal Performance: *Mahler: Des Knaben Wunderhorn,* Thomas Quasthoff, baritone; Anne Sofie von Otter, mezzo soprano

Best Classical Contemporary Composition: "Boulez: Repons" Pierre Boulez, composer (Vincent Bauer, vibraphone; Florent Boffard, piano; Pierre Boulez, conductor; Frederique Cambreling, harp; Michel Cerutti, cimbalom; Daniel Ciampolini, xylophone and glockenspiel; Ens. InterContemporain; Andrew Gerzso, electroacoustic realization; Dimitri Vassilakis, piano)

Best Classical Crossover Album: *Schickele: Hornsmoke* (Piano Con. No. 2 in F Maj. "Ole"; Brass Calendar; Hornsmoke—A Horse Opera.), The Chestnut Brass Co.; Peter Schickele, piano and narrator

Best Short Form Music Video: *Freak on a Leash,* Korn

Best Long Form Music Video: *Band of Gypsys—Live at Fillmore East,* Jimi Hendrix

MTV VIDEO MUSIC AWARDS

BEST VIDEO OF THE YEAR

1984	The Cars	You Might Think
1985	Don Henley	The Boys of Summer
1986	Dire Straits	Money for Nothing
1987	Peter Gabriel	Sledgehammer
1988	INXS	Need You Tonight/Mediate
1989	Neil Young	This Note's for You
1990	Sinead O'Connor	Nothing Compares 2 U
1991	R.E.M.	Losing My Religion
1992	Van Halen	Right Now
1993	Pearl Jam	Jeremy
1994	Aerosmith	Cryin'
1995	TLC	Waterfalls
1996	The Smashing Pumpkins	Tonight, Tonight
1997	Jamiroquai	Virtual Insanity
1998	Madonna	Ray of Light
1999	Lauryn Hill	Doo Wop (That Thing)
2000	Eminem	The Real Slim Shady

BEST MALE VIDEO

1984	David Bowie	China Girl
1985	Bruce Springsteen	I'm on Fire
1986	Robert Palmer	Addicted to Love
1987	Peter Gabriel	Sledgehammer
1988	Prince	U Got the Look
1989	Elvis Costello	Veronica
1990	Don Henley	The End of the Innocence
1991	Chris Isaak	Wicked Game (Concept)
1992	Eric Clapton	Tears in Heaven (Performance)
1993	Lenny Kravitz	Are You Gonna Go My Way
1994	Tom Petty and the Heartbreakers	Mary Jane's Last Dance
1995	Tom Petty and the Heartbreakers	You Don't Know How It Feels
1996	Beck	Where It's At
1997	Beck	The Devil's Haircut
1998	Will Smith	Just the Two of Us
1999	Will Smith	Miami
2000	Eminem	The Real Slim Shady

BEST FEMALE VIDEO

1984	Cyndi Lauper	Girls Just Want To Have Fun
1985	Tina Turner	What's Love Got To Do with It
1986	Whitney Houston	How Will I Know
1987	Madonna	Papa Don't Preach
1988	Suzanne Vega	Luka
1989	Paula Abdul	Straight Up
1990	Sinead O'Connor	Nothing Compares 2 U
1991	Janet Jackson	Love Will Never Do Without You
1992	Annie Lennox	Why
1993	k.d. lang	Constant Craving
1994	Janet Jackson	If
1995	Madonna	Take a Bow
1996	Alanis Morissette	Ironic
1997	Jewel	You Were Meant for Me
1998	Madonna	Ray of Light
1999	Lauryn Hill	Doo Wop (That Thing)
2000	Aaliyah	Try Again

BEST CONCEPT VIDEO

1984	Herbie Hancock	Rockit
1985	Glenn Frey	Smuggler's Blues
1986	a-ha	Take On Me
1987	Peter Gabriel/ Stephen Johnson	Sledgehammer
1988	Pink Floyd	Learning to Fly

BEST GROUP VIDEO

1984	ZZ Top	Legs
1985	USA for Africa	We Are the World
1986	Dire Straits	Money for Nothing
1987	Talking Heads	Wild Wild Life
1988	INXS	Need You Tonight/Mediate
1989	Living Colour	Cult of Personality
1990	The B-52's	Love Shack
1991	R.E.M.	Losing My Religion
1992	U2	Even Better Than the Real Thing
1993	Pearl Jam	Jeremy
1994	Aerosmith	Cryin'
1995	TLC	Waterfalls
1996	Foo Fighters	Big Me
1997	No Doubt	Don't Speak
1998	Backstreet Boys	Everybody (Backstreet's Back)
1999	TLC	No Scrubs
2000	Blink-182	All the Small Things

BEST NEW ARTIST IN A VIDEO

1984	Eurythmics	Sweet Dreams (Are Made of This)
1985	'Til Tuesday	Voices Carry
1986	a-ha	Take On Me
1987	Crowded House	Don't Dream It's Over
1988	Guns N' Roses	Welcome to the Jungle
1989	Living Colour	Cult of Personality
1990	Michael Penn	No Myth
1991	Jesus Jones	Right Here, Right Now
1992	Nirvana	Smells Like Teen Spirit
1993	Stone Temple Pilots	Plush
1994	Counting Crows	Mr. Jones
1995	Hootie & The Blowfish	Hold My Hand
1996	Alanis Morissette	Ironic
1997	Fiona Apple	Sleep to Dream
1998	Natalie Imbruglia	Torn
1999	Eminem	My Name Is
2000	Macy Gray	I Try

BEST RAP VIDEO

1989	D.J. Jazzy Jeff & The Fresh Prince	Parents Just Don't Understand
1990	M.C. Hammer	U Can't Touch This
1991	L.L. Cool J	Mama Said Knock You Out
1992	Arrested Development	Tennessee
1993	Arrested Development	People Everyday
1994	Snoop Doggy Dogg	Doggy Dogg World

1995	Dr. Dre	Keep Their Heads Ringin'
1996	Coolio featuring LV	Gangsta's Paradise
1997	The Notorious B.I.G.	Hypnotize
1998	Will Smith	Gettin' Jiggy Wit It
1999	Jay-Z featuring Ja Rule/Amil-lion	Can I Get a...
2000	Dr. Dre featuring Eminem	Forgot About Dre

BEST DANCE VIDEO

1989	Paula Abdul	Straight Up
1990	M.C. Hammer	U Can't Touch This
1991	C+C Music Factory	Gonna Make You Sweat (Everybody Dance Now)
1992	Prince & the New Power Generation	Cream
1993	En Vogue	Free Your Mind
1994	Salt-N-Pepa w/ En Vogue	Whatta Man
1995	Michael and Janet Jackson	Scream
1996	Coolio	1, 2, 3, 4 (Sumpin' New)
1997	Spice Girls	Wannabe
1998	Prodigy	Smack My Bitch Up
1999	Ricky Martin	Livin' la Vida Loca
2000	Jennifer Lopez	Waiting for Tonight

BEST METAL/HARD ROCK VIDEO

1989	Guns N' Roses	Sweet Child o' Mine
1990	Aerosmith	Janie's Got a Gun
1991	Aerosmith	The Other Side
1992	Metallica	Enter Sandman
1993	Pearl Jam	Jeremy
1994	Soundgarden	Black Hole Sun
1995	White Zombie	More Human Than Human
1996	Metallica	Until It Sleeps
1997	Aerosmith	Falling in Love (Is Hard on the Knees)
1998	Aerosmith	Pink
1999	Korn	Freak on a Leash
2000	Limp Bizkit	Break Stuff

BEST R&B VIDEO

1993	En Vogue	Free Your Mind
1994	Salt-N-Pepa w/ En Vogue	Whatta Man
1995	TLC	Waterfalls
1996	The Fugees	Killing Me Softly
1997	Puff Daddy and the Family	I'll Be Missing You
1998	Wyclef Jean featuring Refugee Allstars	Gone 'Till November
1999	Lauryn Hill	Doo Wop (That Thing)
2000	Destiny's Child	Say My Name

BEST POP VIDEO

| 1999 | Ricky Martin | Livin' la Vida Loca |
| 2000 | 'N Sync | Bye, Bye, Bye |

BEST VIDEO FROM A FILM

1987	Talking Heads	Wild Wild Life [True Stories]
1988	Los Lobos	La Bamba [La Bamba]
1989	U2 with B.B. King	When Love Comes to Town [U2 Rattle and Hum]
1990	Billy Idol	Cradle of Love [The Adventures of Ford Fairlaine]
1991	Chris Isaak	Wicked Game [Wild at Heart]
1992	Queen	Bohemian Rhapsody [Wayne's World]
1993	Alice in Chains	Would? [Singles]
1994	Bruce Springsteen	Streets of Philadelphia [Philadelphia]
1995	Seal	Kiss from a Rose [Batman Forever]
1996	Coolio	Gangsta's Paradise [Dangerous Minds]
1997	Will Smith	Men in Black [Men in Black]
1998	Aerosmith	I Don't Want to Miss a Thing [Armageddon]
1999	Madonna	Beautiful Stranger [Austin Powers: The Spy Who Shagged Me]
2000	Aaliyah	Try Again [Romeo Must Die]

BEST CHOREOGRAPHY IN A VIDEO

1994	Salt-N-Pepa w/ En Vogue	Whatta Man
1995	Michael and Janet Jackson	Scream
1996	Bjork	It's Oh So Quiet
1997	Beck	The New Pollution
1998	Madonna	Ray of Light
1999	Fatboy Slim	Praise You
2000	'N Sync	Bye Bye Bye

BEST ALTERNATIVE VIDEO

1991	Jane's Addiction	Been Caught Stealing
1992	Nirvana	Smells Like Teen Spirit
1993	Nirvana	In Bloom (Version 1—Dresses)
1994	Nirvana	Heart-Shaped Box
1995	Weezer	Buddy Holly
1996	The Smashing Pumpkins	1979
1997	Sublime	What I Got
1998	Green Day	Time of Your Life (Good Riddance)

BEST SPECIAL EFFECTS IN A VIDEO

1984	Herbie Hancock	Rockit
1985	Tom Petty & the Heartbreakers	Don't Come Around Here No More
1986	a-ha	Take On Me
1987	Peter Gabriel	Sledgehammer
1988	Squeeze	Hourglass
1989	Michael Jackson	Leave Me Alone
1990	Tears For Fears	Sowing the Seeds of Love
1991	Faith No More	Falling to Pieces
1992	U2	Even Better Than the Real Thing
1993	Peter Gabriel	Steam
1994	Peter Gabriel	Kiss That Frog
1995	The Rolling Stones	Love Is Strong
1996	The Smashing Pumpkins	Tonight, Tonight
1997	Jamiroquai	Virtual Insanity
1998	Madonna	Frozen

| 1999 | Garbage | Special |
| 2000 | Bjork | All Is Full of Love |

BEST DIRECTION IN A VIDEO

1984	ZZ Top	Sharp Dressed Man
1985	Don Henley	The Boys of Summer
1986	a-ha	Take On Me
1987	Peter Gabriel	Sledgehammer
1988	George Michael	Father Figure
1989	Madonna	Express Yourself
1990	Madonna	Vogue
1991	R.E.M.	Losing My Religion
1992	Van Halen	Right Now
1993	Pearl Jam	Jeremy
1994	R.E.M.	Everybody Hurts
1995	Weezer	Buddy Holly
1996	The Smashing Pumpkins	Tonight, Tonight
1997	Beck	The New Pollution
1998	Madonna	Ray of Light
1999	Fatboy Slim	Praise You
2000	Red Hot Chili Peppers	Californication

BREAKTHROUGH VIDEO

1988	INXS	Need You Tonight/Mediate
1989	Art of Noise, featuring Tom Jones	Kiss
1990	Tears for Fears;	Sowing the Seeds of Love
1991	R.E.M.	Losing My Religion
1992	Red Hot Chili Peppers	Give It Away
1993	Los Lobos	Kiko & The Lavender Moon
1994	R.E.M.	Everybody Hurts
1995	Weezer	Buddy Holly
1996	The Smashing Pumpkins	Tonight, Tonight
1997	Jamiroquai	Virtual Insanity
1998	Prodigy	Smack My Bitch Up
1999	Fatboy Slim	Praise You
2000	Bjork	All Is Full of Love

VIDEO VANGUARD AWARD

1984	The Beatles, David Bowie, Richard Lester
1985	David Byrne, Kevin Godley and Lol Creme, Russell Mulcahy
1986	Madonna and Zbigniew Rybeznski
1987	Julien Temple and Peter Gabriel
1988	Michael Jackson
1989	George Michael
1990	Janet Jackson
1991	(see below)
1992	(see below)
1993	no award given
1994	Tom Petty
1995	R.E.M.
1996	no award given
1997	Mark Romanek, L.L. Cool J
1998	The Beastie Boys

MICHAEL JACKSON VIDEO VANGUARD AWARD

| 1991 | Bon Jovi, Wayne Isham |
| 1992 | Guns N' Roses |

VIEWER'S CHOICE AWARD

1984	Michael Jackson	Thriller
1985	USA for Africa	We Are the World
1986	a-ha	Take On Me
1987	U2	With or Without You
1988	INXS	Need You Tonight/Mediate
1989	Madonna	Like a Prayer
1990	Aerosmith	Janie's Got a Gun
1994	Aerosmith	Cryin'
1995	TLC	Waterfalls
1996	Bush	Glycerine
1997	Prodigy	Breathe
1998	Puff Daddy & The Family featuring The Lox, Lil' Kim, The Notorious B.I.G., and fuzzbubble	It's All About the Benjamins (Rock Remix)
1999	Backstreet Boys	I Want It That Way
2000	'N Sync	Bye, Bye, Bye

THE COUNTRY MUSIC ASSOCIATION AWARDS

	1967	1968	1969
Entertainer	Eddy Arnold	Glen Campbell	Johnny Cash
Song	Dallas Frazier, "There Goes My Everything"	Bobby Russell, "Honey"	Bob Ferguson, "Carroll County Accident"
Female Vocalist	Loretta Lynn	Tammy Wynette	Tammy Wynette
Male Vocalist	Jack Greene	Glen Campbell	Johnny Cash
Album	Jack Greene, *There Goes My Everything*	Johnny Cash, *Johnny Cash at Folsom Prison*	Johnny Cash, *Johnny Cash at San Quentin Prison*
Single	Jack Greene, "There Goes My Everything"	Jeannie C. Riley, "Harper Valley P.T.A."	Johnny Cash, "A Boy Named Sue"
Vocal Group	The Stoneman Family	Porter Wagoner and Dolly Parton	Johnny Cash and June Carter
Musician	Chet Atkins	Chet Atkins	Chet Atkins

	1970	1971	1972
Entertainer	Merle Haggard	Charley Pride	Loretta Lynn
Song	Kris Kristofferson, "Sunday Morning Coming Down"	Freddie Hart, "Easy Loving"	Freddie Hart, "Easy Loving"
Female Vocalist	Tammy Wynette	Lynn Anderson	Loretta Lynn
Male Vocalist	Merle Haggard	Charley Pride	Charley Pride
Album	Merle Haggard, *Okie from Muskogee*	Ray Price, *I Won't Mention It Again*	Merle Haggard, *Let Me Tell You About a Song*
Single	Merle Haggard, "Okie From Muskogee"	Sammi Smith, "Help Me Make It Through the Night"	Donna Fargo, "The Happiest Girl in the Whole U.S.A."
Vocal Group	The Glaser Brother	The Osborne Brothers	The Statler Brothers
Vocal Duo	Porter Wagoner and Dolly Parton	Porter Wagoner and Dolly Parton	Conway Twitty and Loretta Lynn
Musician	Jerry Reed	Jerry Reed	Charlie McCoy

	1973	1974	1975
Entertainer	Roy Clark	Charlie Rich	John Denver
Song	Kenny O'Dell, "Behind Closed Doors"	Don Wayne, "Country Bumpkin"	John Denver, "Back Home Again"
Female Vocalist	Loretta Lynn	Olivia Newton-John	Dolly Parton
Male Vocalist	Charlie Rich	Ronnie Milsap	Waylon Jennings
Album	Charlie Rich, *Behind Closed Doors*	Charlie Rich, *A Very Special Love Song*	Ronnie Milsap, *A Legend in My Time*
Single	Charlie Rich, "Behind Closed Doors"	Cal Smith, "Country Bumpkin"	Freddy Fender, "Before the Next Teardrop Falls"
Vocal Group	The Statler Brothers	The Statler Brothers	The Statler Brothers
Vocal Duo	Conway Twitty and Loretta Lynn	Conway Twitty and Loretta Lynn	Conway Twitty and Loretta Lynn
Musician	Charlie McCoy	Don Rich	Johnny Gimble

	1976	1977	1978
Entertainer	Mel Tillis	Ronnie Milsap	Dolly Parton
Song	Larry Weiss, "Rhinestone Cowboy"	Roger Bowling & Hal Bynum, "Lucille"	Richard Leigh, "Don't It Make My Brown Eyes Blue"
Female Vocalist	Dolly Parton	Crystal Gayle	Crystal Gayle
Male Vocalist	Ronnie Milsap	Ronnie Milsap	Don Williams
Album	Waylon Jennings, Willie Nelson, Tompall Glaser, Jessi Colter, *Wanted—The Outlaws*	Ronnie Milsap, *Ronnie Milsap Live*	Ronnie Milsap, *It Was Almost Like a Song*
Single	Waylon Jennings & Willie Nelson, "Good Hearted Woman"	Kenny Rogers, "Lucille"	The Kendalls, "Heaven's Just a Sin Away"
Vocal Group	The Statler Brothers	The Statler Brothers	The Oak Ridge Boys
Vocal Duo	Waylon Jennings & Willie Nelson	Jim Ed Brown & Helen Cornelius	Kenny Rogers and Dottie West
Musician	Hargus "Pig" Robbins	Roy Clark	Roy Clark

	1979	1980	1981
Entertainer	Willie Nelson	Barbara Mandrell	Barbara Mandrell
Song	Don Schlitz, "The Gambler"	Bobby Braddock & Curly Putman, "He Stopped Loving Her Today"	Bobby Braddock & Curly Putman, "He Stopped Loving Her Today"
Female Vocalist	Barbara Mandrell	Emmylou Harris	Barbara Mandrell
Male Vocalist	Kenny Rogers	George Jones	George Jones
Album	Kenny Rogers, *The Gambler*	Original Motion Picture Soundtrack, *Coal Miner's Daughter*	Don Williams, *I Believe in You*
Single	Charlie Daniels Band, "The Devil Went Down to Georgia"	George Jones, "He Stopped Loving Her Today"	Oak Ridge Boys, "Elvira"
Vocal Group	The Statler Brothers	The Statler Brothers	Alabama
Horizon Award	—	—	Terri Gibbs
Vocal Duo	Kenny Rogers and Dottie West	Moe Bandy and Joe Stampley	David Frizzell and Shelly West
Musician	Charlie Daniels	Roy Clark	Chet Atkins

	1982	1983	1984
Entertainer	Alabama	Alabama	Alabama
Song	Johnny Christopher, Wayne Carson, Mark James, "Always On My Mind"	Johnny Christopher, Wayne Carson, Mark James, "Always On My Mind"	Larry Henley, Jeff Silbar, "Wind Beneath My Wings"
Female Vocalist	Janie Fricke	Janie Fricke	Reba McEntire
Male Vocalist	Ricky Skaggs	Lee Greenwood	Lee Greenwood
Album	Willie Nelson, *Always on My Mind*	Alabama, *The Closer You Get*	Anne Murray, *A Little Good News*
Single	Willie Nelson, "Always on My Mind"	John Anderson, "Swingin' "	Anne Murray, "A Little Good News"
Vocal Group	Alabama	Alabama	The Statler Brothers
Horizon Award	Ricky Skaggs	John Anderson	The Judds
Vocal Duo	David Frizzell and Shelly West	Merle Haggard and Willie Nelson	Willie Nelson & Julio Iglesias
Musician	Chet Atkins	Chet Atkins	Chet Atkins

	1985	1986	1987
Entertainer	Ricky Skaggs	Reba McEntire	Hank Williams Jr.
Song	Lee Greenwood, "God Bless the USA"	Paul Overstreet, Don Schlitz, "On the Other Hand"	Paul Overstreet, Don Schlitz, "Forever and Ever, Amen"
Female Vocalist	Reba McEntire	Reba McEntire	Reba McEntire
Male Vocalist	George Strait	George Strait	Randy Travis
Album	George Strait, *Does Fort Worth Ever Cross Your Mind*	Ronnie Milsap, *Lost in the Fifties Tonight*	Randy Travis, *Always and Forever*
Single	The Judds, "Why Not Me"	Dan Seals, "Bop"	Randy Travis, "Forever and Ever, Amen"
Vocal Group	The Judds	The Judds	The Judds
Horizon Award	Sawyer Brown	Randy Travis	Holly Dunn
Vocal Duo	Anne Murray and Dave Loggins	Dan Seals and Marie Osmond	Ricky Skaggs and Sharon White
Musician	Chet Atkins	Johnny Gimble	Johnny Gimble
Music Video	Hank Williams Jr., *All My Rowdy Friends Are Comin' Over Tonight*	George Jones, *Who's Gonna Fill Their Shoes*	Hank Williams Jr., *My Name Is Bocephus*

	1988	1989	1990
Entertainer	Hank Williams Jr.	George Strait	George Strait
Song	K.T. Oslin, "80's Ladies"	Max D. Barnes, Vern Gosdin, "Chiseled in Stone"	Jon Vezner, Don Henry, "Where've You Been"
Female Vocalist	K.T. Oslin	Kathy Mattea	Kathy Mattea
Male Vocalist	Randy Travis	Ricky Van Shelton	Clint Black
Album	Hank Williams Jr., *Born to Boogie*	Nitty Gritty Dirt Band, *Will the Circle Be Unbroken, Vol. II*	Kentucky HeadHunters, *Pickin' on Nashville*
Single	Kathy Mattea, "Eighteen Wheels and a Dozen Roses"	Keith Whitley, "I'm No Stranger to the Rain"	Vince Gill, "When I Call Your Name"
Vocal Group	Highway 101	Highway 101	Kentucky HeadHunters
Vocal Event	Dolly Parton, Emmylou Harris, Linda Ronstadt, *Trio*	Hank Williams Jr., Hank Williams Sr.	Lorrie Morgan, Keith Whitley
Horizon Award	Ricky Van Shelton	Clint Black	Garth Brooks
Vocal Duo	The Judds	The Judds	The Judds
Musician	Chet Atkins	Johnny Gimble	Johnny Gimble
Music Video	—	Hank Williams Jr., Hank Williams Sr., *There's a Tear in My Beer*	Garth Brooks, *The Dance*

	1991	1992	1993
Entertainer	Garth Brooks	Garth Brooks	Vince Gill
Song	Vince Gill, Tim DuBois, "When I Call Your Name"	Vince Gill, Max D. Barnes, "Look at Us"	Vince Gill, John Barlow Jarvis, "I Still Believe in You"
Female Vocalist	Tanya Tucker	Mary-Chapin Carpenter	Mary-Chapin Carpenter
Male Vocalist	Vince Gill	Vince Gill	Vince Gill
Album	Garth Brooks, *No Fences*	Garth Brooks, *Ropin' the Wind*	Vince Gill, *I Still Believe in You*
Single	Garth Brooks, "Friends in Low Places"	Billy Ray Cyrus, "Achy Breaky Heart"	Alan Jackson, "Chattahoochee"
Vocal Group	Kentucky HeadHunters	Diamond Rio	Diamond Rio
Vocal Event	Mark O'Connor & The New Nashville Cats (featuring Vince Gill, Ricky Skaggs, and Steve Wariner)	Marty Stuart, Travis Tritt	George Jones with Vince Gill, Mark Chesnutt, Garth Brooks, Travis Tritt, Joe Diffie, Alan Jackson, Pam Tillis, T. Graham Brown, Patty Loveless, Clint Black, *I Don't Need Your Rockin' Chair*
Horizon Award	Travis Tritt	Suzy Bogguss	Mark Chesnutt
Vocal Duo	The Judds	Brooks & Dunn	Brooks & Dunn
Musician	Mark O'Connor	Mark O'Connor	Mark O'Connor
Music Video	Garth Brooks, *The Thunder Rolls*	Alan Jackson, *Midnight in Montgomery*	Alan Jackson, *Chattahoochee*

	1994	1995	1996
Entertainer	Vince Gill	Alan Jackson	Brooks & Dunn
Song	Alan Jackson, Jim McBride, "Chattahoochee"	Gretchen Peters, "Independence Day"	Vince Gill, "Go Rest High on That Mountain"
Female Vocalist	Pam Tillis	Alison Krauss	Patty Loveless
Male Vocalist	Vince Gill	Vince Gill	George Strait
Album	*Common Thread: The Songs of the Eagles*	Patty Loveless, *When Fallen Angels Fly*	George Strait, *Blue Clear Sky*
Single	John Michael Montgomery, "I Swear"	Alison Krauss and the Union Station, "When You Say Nothing at All"	George Strait, "Check Yes or No"
Vocal Group	Diamond Rio	The Mavericks	The Mavericks
Vocal Event	Reba McEntire with Linda Davis, "Does He Love You"	Shenandoah with Alison Krauss, "Somewhere in the Vicinity of the Heart"	Dolly Parton with Vince Gill, "I Will Always Love You"
Horizon Award	John Michael Montgomery	Alison Krauss	Bryan White
Vocal Duo	Brooks & Dunn	Brooks & Dunn	Brooks & Dunn
Musician	Mark O'Connor	Mark O'Connor	Mark O'Connor
Music Video	Martina McBride, *Independence Day*	The Tractors, *Baby Likes to Rock It*	Junior Brown, *My Wife Thinks You're Dead*

	1997	1998	1999
Entertainer	Garth Brooks	Garth Brooks	Shania Twain
Song	Matraca Berg, Gary Harrison, "Strawberry Wine"	Billy Kirsch, Steve Wariner, "Holes in the Floor of Heaven"	Annie Roboff, Robin Lerner, Beth Nielsen Chapman, "This Kiss"
Female Vocalist	Trisha Yearwood	Trisha Yearwood	Martina McBride
Male Vocalist	George Strait	George Strait	Tim McGraw
Album	George Strait, *Carrying Your Love With Me*	Tim McGraw, *Everywhere*	Tim McGraw, *A Place in the Sun*
Single	Deana Carter, "Strawberry Wine"	"Holes in the Floor of Heaven," Steve Wariner	"Wide Open Spaces," Dixie Chicks
Vocal Group	Diamond Rio	Dixie Chicks	Dixie Chicks
Vocal Event	Tim McGraw with Faith Hill, "It's Your Love"	Patty Loveless with George Jones, "You Don't Seem to Miss Me"	Vince Gill and Patty Loveless, "My Kind of Woman/My Kind of Man"
Horizon Award	LeAnn Rimes	Dixie Chicks	Jo Dee Messina
Vocal Duo	Brooks & Dunn	Brooks & Dunn	Brooks & Dunn
Musician	Brent Mason	Brent Mason	Randy Scruggs
Music Video	Kathy Mattea, *455 Rocket*	Faith Hill, *This Kiss*	Dixie Chicks, "Wide Open Spaces"

	2000
Entertainer	Dixie Chicks
Song	Lee Ann Womack with Sons of the Desert, "I Hope You Dance"
Female Vocalist	Faith Hill
Male Vocalist	Tim McGraw
Album	Dixie Chicks, *Fly*
Single	Lee Ann Womack with the Sons of the Desert, "I Hope You Dance"
Group	Dixie Chicks
Vocal Event	George Strait and Alan Jackson, "Murder on Music Row"
Horizon Award	Brad Paisley
Duo	Montgomery Gentry
Musician	Hargus "Pig" Robbins
Music Video	Dixie Chicks, *Goodbye Earl*

PICKS & PANS 2000

We were wild about Harry Potter's return, less so about Bridget Jones's. Stephen King went online, while Jackie O. stayed in our hearts. From poetry to politics, here's PEOPLE's year in books, featuring our critics' top choices as noted by asterisks.

FICTION AND POETRY

DESPAIR
André Alexis

A fine-tuned sense of dread links these eight stories by highly regarded newcomer André Alexis. Who knew Canada was a northern *Twilight Zone?*

IN THE NAME OF SALOMÉ
Julia Alvarez

This enchanting novel contrasts the lives of a famous poet and her daughter, who is a mousy closet lesbian.

A RECIPE FOR BEES
Gail Anderson-Dargatz

Fans of Anderson-Dargatz's popular *The Cure for Death by Lightning* may be charmed by her heroine's plucky resilience and folksy wisdom. But *Recipe*'s sketchy characterizations, contrived plot turns and careless writing will convince most readers that *Bees* is, ultimately, a real drone.

DEEP SOUTH
Nevada Barr

Rugged sleuth Anna Pigeon becomes the first woman district ranger at a Mississippi base of Natchez Trace Parkway in this intricate murder tale.

JANE AUSTEN'S CHARLOTTE
Completed by Julia Barrett

When Jane Austen died, she left behind an unfinished novel called *Sanditon*. The celebrated author now must suffer the misfortune of having the work completed (with the title *Charlotte*) by UCLA literature teacher Barrett. A surprisingly charmless tale.

TRANS-SISTER RADIO
Chris Bohjalian

A divorced teacher has fallen hard for her handsome film professor. Problem is, he's a transsexual who has decided to become a woman. *Radio* too often reads like an affable mini-treatise.

WHERE YOU BELONG
Barbara Taylor Bradford

This is a grittier work than Bradford's usual high-society romances, though it lacks their charm and is marred by some seriously banal passages. Still, her many fans will enjoy the surefire formula of tears and pain and love triumphant.

UNDUE INFLUENCE
Anita Brookner

A pretty London bookseller clings to routine, permitting herself one indulgence: flirting with a handsome but married customer. Although the book offers the redeeming pleasures of Brookner's spot-on social observation, the result feels skimpy, like trying to make a meal of tea sandwiches.

QUICKENING
Laura Catherine Brown

Brown explores a young woman's emotional upheavals with sincerity and grace. And yet, this otherwise impressive debut lacks tear-inducing power.

OUTFOXED
Rita Mae Brown

A skulk of foxes turn detective to help investigate the murder of an aging member of the Jefferson Hunt Club. Despite some slapdash writing here and there, this sly whodunit is sufficiently compelling to carry readers through to a surprise finish.

PAWING THROUGH THE PAST
Rita Mae Brown

In cahoots with her tiger cat Sneaky Pie Brown (who gets half credit), the author pens her eighth feline-flavored mystery, this one set at a high school reunion.

STANDOFF
Sandra Brown

Is it good luck for a reporter to have a dream story fall into her lap? Tiel McCoy, heroine of this thriller by the author of *The Alibi*, isn't so sure anymore.

PURPLE CANE ROAD
James Lee Burke

With his 11th Dave Robicheaux mystery, Burke moves far beyond the confines of the crime genre: his magnolia-soaked prose and hallucinogenic tales address a wider world of conscience and consequence.

MEN IN THE OFF HOURS
Anne Carson

Carson, a classics professor, enjoys a growing reputation as a cutting-edge verse experimentalist. Her poems are as beguiling as their off-beat titles, such as "Irony Is Not Enough: Essay on My Life as Catherine Deneuve."

ROUND ROBIN
Jennifer Chiaverini

A sequel to last year's cult bestseller *The Quilter's Apprentice*, this novel reintroduces Sarah McClure, whose life was sew perfect at the end of the last installment—and now is anything but.

GIRL WITH A PEARL EARRING
Tracy Chevalier
The painting of the same title by Vermeer, one of his most famous, provides the inspiration for a beguiling novel that purports to tell the girl's story.

DISGRACE
J.M. Coetzee
Disgrace explores a fallen professor's struggle to reform his life and find honor in a post-apartheid society amid violent change. Winner of the 1999 Booker Prize, this is a gripping tale told with spare prose, steely intelligence and a remarkable degree of tenderness.

LETHAL SEDUCTION
Jackie Collins
The latest bawdy, boisterous lustfest by Collins. Far-fetched and foolish, but fun.

*VOID MOON
Michael Connelly
A reformed pro gambler is determined to go straight—until a compelling reason convinces her to try for one final score. With its razor-sharp suspense, crackling dialogue and raffish cast, Void Moon definitely hits the jackpot.

PLACES IN THE DARK
Thomas H. Cook
Two brothers become involved with the same treacherous temptress in a yarn set on the Maine coastline in the '30s. One brother doesn't live to tell the tale.

RIPTIDE
Catherine Coulter
The heroine of this thriller—on the run from both the law and a stalker—finds a comfy New England manor house to be a nest of treachery.

Douglas Coupland

MISS WYOMING
Douglas Coupland
A hospitalized Hollywood producer has a vision—then discovers that what he experienced was an image, absorbed from a bedside TV during his delirium, of one Susan Colgate—teen beauty queen turned sitcom star turned has-been. Wyoming is a sardonically funny riff on American culture.

RIPTIDE
Catherine Coulter
The heroine of this thriller—on the run from both the law and a stalker—finds a comfy New England manor house to be a nest of treachery.

CROSS DRESSING
Bill Fitzhugh
To avoid insurance fraud charges, a scuzzy ad exec dons clerical attire and assumes his late brother's identity. This wild plot is populated by characters as flat as flounder.

DEMOLITION ANGEL
Robert Crais
A scarred demolitions expert returns to duty when a lunatic starts targeting bomb-squad technicians. Gripping, well-plotted, and explosive.

ATLANTIS FOUND
Clive Cussler
Cussler creates characters with all the depth of a cardboard cutout, plots that creak with predictability and dialogue as sticky as Mississippi mud. Still, we can't put down a Cussler opus. Why? They're fun.

WATERLOO SUNSET
Ray Davies
Former Kinks frontman Davies wrote these interconnected, downbeat but intelligent short stories about an aging British rocker.

THE EMPTY CHAIR
Jeffery Deaver
Stinging suspense starring paraplegic forensic specialist Lincoln Rhyme, memorably played by Denzel Washington in The Bone Collector.

***THE LION'S GAME
Nelson DeMille
A surprisingly complex terrorist vows vengeance against the U.S.; stopping him falls to wisecracking former NYPD homicide detective John Corey. A tense pageturner with a bulletproof plot.

TEA
Stacey D'Erasmo
Tea's shattered heroine comes off as frustratingly shallow as she latches onto one person and then another. Still, her story is compelling enough that we can't help but drink it all in.

CITY OF GOD
E.L. Doctorow
Readers who rise to this inventive, challenging novel about

spirituality and survival will be rewarded.

JIM THE BOY
Tony Earley

Using words like "daggummit," the author, a North Carolina native, gives heaps of Dixie detail to this coming-of-age novel set in the Tar Heel State.

THE DANISH GIRL
David Ebershoff

A fictional account of the marriage of Gerda Wegener and her husband, Einar, a Danish painter who in 1931 became the first person to undergo a sex-change operation.

EATING THE CHESHIRE CAT
Helen Ellis

Ellis's freshman effort is all too sophomoric: a coming-of-age novel filled with gorgons, grotesques, and other repellent freaks.

THEN, SUDDENLY
Lynn Emanuel

In Emanuel's darkly romantic poems, the road to self-knowledge is littered with discarded masks: "I am a woman, one minute, then I am a man,/ I am a carnival of Lynn Emanuels:/ Lynn in the red dress; Lynn sulking . . ./ . . .when what I would really love to be is/ Gertrude Stein spying on Sharon Stone."

BIG CITY EYES
Delia Ephron

Finding a knife hidden in her teenage son's underwear drawer, a divorcee trades New York for clean country living, but the new home turns out to be at least as dangerous as any urban landscape. *Eyes* is a wry, wacky page-turner.

HOT SIX
Janet Evanovich

A Trenton bounty hunter helps a mysterious (and darn sexy) colleague. An engaging mix of slap-

stick, steam, and suspense.

BRIDGET JONES: THE EDGE OF REASON
Helen Fielding

Bridget and Darcy's on-again, off-again romance forms the premise of this sequel, but most of the book is taken up by tedious Lucy Ricardo–like pratfalls. Disappointing.

REMEMBERING BLUE
Connie May Flower

Widowed in her 20s, Mattie Fiona Blue grapples with accepting the death of her young husband, gradually learning to take strength from her memories.

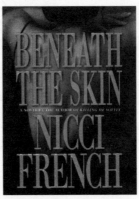

BENEATH THE SKIN
Nicci French

Three women, related only by their petite figures, are forced to confront an ardent admirer's voracious threats. Suspenseful from the start and ending with a brilliant twist, *Beneath* is a tale of sheer terror.

HEARTBREAKER
Julie Garwood

Painfully trite romance.

YOUNG WIVES
Olivia Goldsmith

Call it *First Wives—The Prequel.* Three youthful brides band together to find themselves, their dignity and a little bit of justice

along the way. Wickedly funny female bonding.

SUPERSTAR
Victoria Gotti

Two switched-at-birth babies cross paths. Cheesy character development and heavy-handed prose make this *Star* flame out early.

THE SECOND SILENCE
Eileen Goudge

A once-meek housewife plays detective against her husband. *Silence* reads like a teen mystery played out on Melrose Place.

TIME TO SAY GOOD-BYE
Judith Gould

A young victim of terminal brain cancer locates a young woman with whom she hopes her husband will fall in love. Light and trashy beach reading that also tugs seriously at your heart.

JEMIMA J
Jane Green

An overweight Londoner with a doctored photo enters an online romance with a California fitness guru; now all she has to do is starve off 100 lbs. before meeting him. Entertaining, sweet, and tasty.

THE BRETHREN
John Grisham

A small-time lawyer gets trapped in a sinister conspiracy that spins far beyond his control. What's missing are Grisham's other trademarks: flawed but likable heroes, plot twists grounded firmly in the law and, most important, intelligent writing.

MORE THAN YOU KNOW
Beth Gutcheon

Star-crossed lovers, a haunted house and a murder mystery to solve—what more do you need in a page-turner? A spooky saga with delusions of grandeur.

*AFTERBURN
Colin Harrison

A multimillionaire CEO discovers that his daughter and only surviving offspring is infertile. He surreptitiously advertises for a stranger to bear and rear another child for him—and finds a brainy Barnard dropout just sprung from prison after serving four years of a larceny-related sentence. A stunning, and at times savage, thriller.

IN SEARCH OF AN IMPOTENT MAN
Gaby Hauptmann

Fed up with sex-obsessed men, a gorgeous 35-year-old decides to take out a personal ad for an impotent lover, then falls in love and changes her mind about being "oppressed by an erect penis." A dumb, tedious, flaccid book.

*ALL THE LUCKY ONES ARE DEAD
Gar Anthony Haywood

A private eye in the 'hood investigates whether a late gangsta rapper really did commit suicide. The funky atmosphere, fresh dialogue, and boldly-drawn characters leave little doubt as to why this African-American series is fast becoming a hardboiled classic.

THE VISION OF EMMA BLAU
Ursula Hegi

In 1894, an immigrant builds a business in New Hampshire, and gradually suffers the loss of all he had struggled so fiercely to create. Sounds grim, but it actually makes for a fascinating read.

PORTRAIT OF AN ARTIST, AS AN OLD MAN
Joseph Heller

The final novel by the late *Catch-22* author is, as it happens, about an eminent writer writing his last novel. Great humor abounds.

SICK PUPPY
Carl Hiaasen

A lovably demented ecoterrorist decides to teach some manners to a litterbug. When the bug fails to get the message, things get deliciously out of hand. Hiaasen excels at turning social commentary into savage fun.

THE BEACH CLUB
Elin Hilderbrand

A surprisingly touching summer frolic, centering around a Nantucket hotel. Hilderbrand has a gift for drawing realistic characters, emotional dilemmas, and resolutions.

HUNTING BADGER
Tony Hillerman

In their much-anticipated reunion, Sgt. Jim Chee and Lt. Joe Leaphorn pursue copkillers across the Navajo reservation.

RIVER KING
Alice Hoffman

A burned-out cop sets out to find the truth behind a misfit student's drowning. Hoffman once again demonstrates her passion for the world's walking wounded along with a penchant for the supernatural.

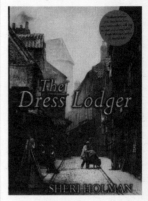

*THE DRESS LODGER
Sheri Holman

In 1831 England, a 15-year-old prostitute must fend off a grave-robbing surgeon who views her baby, born with a rare physical defect, as a science project. A dazzling narrative that pulses with irony, ribald humor, and heartbreaking tragedy.

MR. PERFECT
Linda Howard

After her risqué girl talk gets leaked to the press, Jaine Bright is pursued by the national press—and one particularly offended killer—so she takes refuge with her hunky cop neighbor. Sexy fun.

LOSING JULIA
Jonathan Hull

Well-intentioned but slack novel of an old soldier's fascination with past combat experiences and an intense, doomed affair.

PAY IT FORWARD
Catherine Ryan Hyde
An altruistic novel about a 12-year-old boy who does a good deed for three people, then asks that they each do a good deed for three more. Lo and behold, a movement is born.

THE SEARCH
Iris Johansen
Johansen, who has helped expand the romantic-thriller genre, here explains everything from mud slides to canine training in language so leaden that reading *The Search* is like picking through earthquake rubble: hard work with mostly disappointing results.

*LE MARIAGE
Diane Johnson
Stolen property, lost innocence, Parisian culture clashes, adultery and murder—such is the bewitching brew of Johnson's latest funny and disarming social comedy. Johnson manages to combine Alison Lurie's finely tuned sense of irony and satire with Jane Austen's keen eye for courtship rituals and social nuance.

MOTHER MADE A MAN OUT OF ME
Karen Karbo
Two Oregon women exchange wry observations on the foibles of pregnancy and birth in a comic work of fiction.

STALKER
Faye Kellerman
A likable LAPD rookie—the daughter of Kellerman's earlier creation, Lt. Peter Decker— makes a less-than-arresting debut.

MONSTER
Jonathan Kellerman
Dr. Alex Delaware investigates the slaying of a maximum-security asylum's doctor. Kellerman is in peak form, subtly raising questions about our treatment of the mentally ill, but never interfering with this surprising and complex story of festering evil.

NIGHT WORK
Laurie R. King
In the latest by the Edgar Award–winning author, detective Kate Martinelli investigates a series of brutal murders—and the puzzlement of why all the victims have had candy placed on them.

RIDING THE BULLET
Stephen King
College boy Alan Parker is hitching a ride home to see his stricken mother when he winds up on the exit to uh-oh land with a guy who "was more than dead; he was crazy." King's storytelling craft is undiminished.

PURE POETRY
Binnie Kirshenbaum
In this humorous yet tender novel, the author charts the romances of a neurotic poet whose life comes to a crisis point on her 38th birthday.

THE RUNNING MATE
Joe Klein
A fictional U.S. Senator and Vietnam veteran and his swimsuit designer girlfriend, who still lives with her bisexual ex-husband. Supposedly an implicit attack on the American political system, *Mate* degenerates into sappy romance—and the prose is as lame as the plot.

TEST PATTERN
Marjorie Klein
The year is 1954, and the television is black-and-white. In a fable worthy of *The Twilight Zone*, young Cassie Palmer is able to see snippets of the future in her family's new Magnavox.

NEW ADDRESSES
Kenneth Koch
Each of the 50 poems in this collection takes up an aspect of the distinguished poet's past. Full of comic energy tinged with pathos, this is Koch's best work in a decade.

FALSE MEMORY
Dean Koontz
Dean Koontz reworks the vein of *The Manchurian Candidate* and *The Stepford Wives* in a masterful thriller that explores the horror-filled world of mind control.

SOFT FOCUS
Jayne Ann Krentz
Beautiful, strong-willed heroine meets dashing, powerful hero. They bicker, they banter, they fall madly in love—but Krentz's latest also has a healthy dose of suspense stirred into the suds. No *Big Sleep*, but no snoozer either.

CHAOS THEORY
Gary Krist
In this all-too-real Washington, D.C., thriller, two good kids make a mistake that leads to bloodshed, terror, and a cover-up that consumes public officials.

24 HOURS
Greg Lies
A psycho zeroes in on a picture-perfect Southern family and ensnares them in a diabolocal

extortion scheme. Worth a look.

A CONSPIRACY OF PAPER
David Liss
This historical thriller—set amid the financial markets of early 18th-century London and packed with period detail—will likely appeal to fans of *The Alienist*.

*THE FUNDAMENTALS OF PLAY
Caitlin Macy
Fitzgerald and Hemingway's spirits are evoked by this insightful first novel about new Ivy League grads in early-'90s Manhattan.

*THE TINY ONE
Eliza Minot
In believably childlike prose, *The Tiny One* recounts 8-year-old Via Revere's attempt to come to terms with the car crash that kills her beloved "Mum." Compelling and haunting.

TULIP FEVER
Deborah Moggach
Now that the tulip blossoms have faded for another year, pick this novel to learn how they came to be prized by 17th-century Dutch flower merchants.

GAP CREEK
Robert Morgan
Likely to appeal to fans of Charles Frazier's *Cold Mountain*, this gritty novel tells of a young couple's hardscrabble life in late 19th-century Appalachia.

PLAYING BOTTICELLI
Liza Nelson
A single mom with a hippie past is shaken when she sees an FBI wanted poster for the father of her 15-year-old.

BLONDE
Joyce Carol Oates
Part biography, part voyeuristic fiction, this alluring *Blonde* reconstructs the "snarled, dreamlike, riddlesome" 36 years of Marilyn Monroe's life in a series of fast-paced, convincingly imagined scenarios from a Marilyn's-eye view. Oates's empathetic approach works.

WILD DECEMBERS
Edna O'Brien
There are few writers today who can capture the beauty and harshness of Irish rural life—and at the same time plumb the nether regions of the human heart—quite the way O'Brien can.

BACK ROADS
Tawni O'Dell
O'Dell's debut novel (an Oprah's Book Club choice) follows young Harley Altmyer's struggle with the sins of his parents (one dead, the other in jail) and the demons they left behind.

THE PATIENT
Michael Palmer
ARTIE—Assisted Robotic Tissue Incision and Extraction—is the name given the robot surgeon and star of the ninth medical thriller by Palmer, a real-life M.D.

PLAYING AWAY
Adele Parks
A woman who has it all falls for an oversexed rogue who reminds her of what it's like to party hardy. The heroine is at best unsympathetic and at worst irritatingly stupid.

CARP FISHING ON VALIUM
Graham Parker
The acclaimed singer and songwriter has put out a collection of short stories, some dealing with the rock and roll biz.

*HUGGER MUGGER
Robert B. Parker
Someone is shooting racehorses down Georgia way; time for Spenser to pack up his wisecracks and flex his pummeling muscles. The plot of this hoof-dunit canters along in a nicely old-fashioned way, but Spenser's shadings are fully Y2K-compliant.

BLOOD MONEY
Thomas Perry
The Edgar Award–winning author has his Native American heroine Jane Whitefield trying to steal from the Mafia in order to give to the poor.

*PLAIN TRUTH
Jodi Picoult
An urbane lawyer must navigate clannish conformity and her own preconceptions to determine if and why an obedient Amish teen killed her newborn boy. Absorbing and multidimensional.

WINTER SOLSTICE
Rosamunde Pilcher
Lost souls spend Christmas in a dilapidated estate house in Scotland and help each other back to life. *Solstice* is an occasion to celebrate.

AFTER THE FIRE
Belva Plain
In the 18th novel by the best-selling author, a seemingly picture-perfect family disintegrates and a cheating husband chooses an ignoble tool—the couple's children—to blackmail his wife.

A SLOW BURNING
Stanley Pottinger
Using his background in civil rights work at the Justice Department, the *Fourth Procedure* author fashions a thriller with characters motivated by racism.

DEADLY DECISIONS
Kathy Reichs
Reichs's strong suit once again is her expertise as a real-life forensic specialist. One wishes she had devoted the same attention to the plot.

FOLLOW THE STARS HOME
Luanne Rice
Abandoned by her husband and raising her severely handicapped 12-year-old daughter,

Dianne is too wounded to notice a kindly pediatrician's devotion. A sugary, addictive romance novel.

THE HOUSEGUEST
Agnes Rossi

The guest of the title is a recent widower who comes to America from Ireland with the help of a benefactor and then—the nerve!—takes up with his patron's wife.

THE HUMAN STAIN / PHILIP ROTH

THE HUMAN STAIN
Philip Roth

A college dean who has passed as white (and Jewish) is accused of racism and hounded to resign; meanwhile, he carries on an affair with an illiterate cleaning lady who is being stalked by her Vietnam vet ex-husband. *Stain* is overdrawn and overambitious but never dull.

*HARRY POTTER AND THE GOBLET OF FIRE
J. K. Rowling

Harry faces his greatest challenges so far—and this time, Rowling forgoes the tedious exposition. The best of the series.

ALL WE KNOW OF LOVE
Katie Schneider

Instructed by a vision, a woman pursues her dream of becoming a painter in Florence. In its insights on love, loss, and long-ing, *All We Know* is both haunting and wise.

MOMENT OF TRUTH
Lisa Scottoline

A hard-boiled murder novel that too often lapses into sappy, bodice-ripper prose—and the characters need more realism to make them matter.

THE DARK HOUSE
John Sedgwick

A voyeur who follows random people accidentally stumbles upon a nasty secret about his own kinfolk. Creepy and worthwhile.

FORTUNE'S ROCKS
Anita Shreve

A turn-of-the-century affair between a precocious 15-year-old girl and a married doctor nearly three times her age. So indulgently paced and lavishly detailed that readers may grow impatient—but when Shreve turns to practical, emotional, and moral consequences, *Rocks* achieves a riveting force.

NORA, NORA
Anne Rivers Siddons

In the segregated South of the '60s, a motherless 12-year-old tomboy gets womanly guidance from her 29-year-old hellcat cousin. The cozy *Nora* paints a too-simple picture of the civil rights movement, focusing instead on coming-of-age.

SPECIAL CIRCUMSTANCES
Sheldon Siegel

This sophomoric exercise in lawyer-bashing revolves around the trial of a defense attorney who stands accused of murdering two partners in a posh, profitable San Francisco firm teeming with ruthless, greedy, and unprincipled megalomaniacs. Indefensibly lame.

*HORSE HEAVEN
Jane Smiley

In this wise, spirited novel, the Pulitzer Prize–winning Smiley plumbs the wondrously strange world of horse racing as she chronicles two years on the circuit from Hollywood Park to Saratoga to Paris—but it is the characters of the magnificent thoroughbreds she describes most movingly.

IN AMERICA / a novel / SUSAN SONTAG

IN AMERICA
Susan Sontag

A famed Polish actress in 1876 leads a group of her compatriots to a utopian commune in California.

THE HOUSE ON HOPE STREET
Danielle Steel

This simple story of a courageous woman weathering the worst of life's storms is hard to put down.

IRRESISTIBLE FORCES
Danielle Steel

Torn apart by dueling ambitions, the high-powered couple at the center of Steel's latest romance try to redeem their love.

THE WEDDING
Danielle Steel
The doyenne of modern romance takes us to Hollywood, where a typical family (a producer, a writer, a model, a lawyer, and a doctor) prepare for a wedding... and remember how to love.

WORLD OF PIES
Karen Stolz
A slim, charming novel about small-town youth in the elsewhere turbulent late '60s and '70s.

CHANG AND ENG
Darin Strauss
A haunting fictionalized account of the conjoined twins from whom the now debased term "Siamese twins" derives.

THE FIRST PAPER GIRL IN RED OAK, IOWA
Elizabeth Stuckey-French
The Florida-based author shows a flair for off-the-wall detail in a short-story collection peopled with motley Midwesterners.

LIFE ISN'T ALL HA HA HEE HEE
Meera Syal
This incisive comic novel deftly captures the growing pains of second-generation Indian women who "meet the world head on, head on" in their careers but "bow down gratefully [and] cling to compromise" with their men.

*BIG STONE GAP
Adriana Trigiani
35-year-old pharmacist and self-proclaimed town spinster Ave Maria Mulligan laments her single status to her best pal (sexy Bookmobile librarian Iva Lou Wade) even as she spurns the attentions of hunky coal miner Jack MacChesney and band director Theodore Tipton. Delightfully quirky.

GERTRUDE AND CLAUDIUS
John Updike
In this ingenious prequel to *Hamlet*, Updike dazzles, telling a simple love story and offering brilliantly nuanced portraits of two characters Shakespeare merely sketched.

MORTAL SINS
Penn Williamson
Steamy suspense in the Big Sleazy, skillfully unfurled for maximum chills. Plenty of spicy love scenes, intriguing subplots, and Jazz Age atmosphere.

GIANT STEPS
edited by Kevin Young
An impressive anthology of new African-American poetry; among its poets to watch are Natasha Trethewey (who depicts herself as Ophelia in one poem and Lana Turner in another), Harryette Mullen ("what you can do / is what women do / I know you know / what I mean, don't you") and Young himself, who riffs on Charlie Chan, Langston Hughes, and the late painter Jean-Michel Basquiat.

DATING BIG BIRD
Laura Zigman
Freaked by the ticking of her biological clocks, an unmarried thirtysomething begins researching her options. Starts and ends engagingly, but sags along the way.

NONFICTION

THE MOST BEAUTIFUL WOMAN IN THE WORLD: THE OBSESSIONS, PASSIONS AND COURAGE OF ELIZABETH TAYLOR
Ellis Amburn
What can be said about 68-year-old Elizabeth Taylor that hasn't been said before? Not much, which is precisely what this unauthorized bio delivers. Liz deserves better.

IT'S NOT ABOUT THE BIKE: MY JOURNEY BACK TO LIFE
Lance Armstrong
The author came back from testicular cancer to win the rugged Tour de France bicycle race; his emotion-drenched memoir should be especially useful as an example to cancer patients.

YUKON ALONE: THE WORLD'S TOUGHEST ADVENTURE RACE
John Balzar
A fascinating, brutally honest look at the culture surrounding a treacherous journey inspired by Klondike gold prospectors of the 1890s.

WEDDING BELL BLUES: 100 YEARS OF OUR GREAT ROMANCE WITH MARRIAGE
Michael Barson and Steven Heller
An amusing and gorgeously illustrated study of marriage tips from books and movies.

FROM DAWN TO DECADENCE
Jacques Barzun
Written in delightfully clear, accessible language, this is an engaging and provocative account of 500 years of Western culture, by a masterly historian.

COLTER: THE TRUE STORY OF THE BEST DOG I EVER HAD
Rick Bass
This fetching tale chronicles the life of the author's German shorthaired pointer.

WHAT TO WEAR
Kimberly Bonnell
Illustrations by Eliza Gran
Three cheers for this wonderfully sensible little primer for fashion-impaired women, with witty and practical tips for every situation.

WHERE DID I GO RIGHT?
Bernie Brillstein with David Rensin
With his Santa Claus looks and a Catskills-size heart hiding killer instincts, Bernie Brillstein recounts tales humorous and tragic from his five decades as a

showbiz agent, manager, and producer.

ROSA PARKS
Douglas Brinkley
The defiant act of a not-so-demure seamstress—refusing to give up her bus seat for a white man in 1955—is at the heart of this thorough and exemplary biography.

I'M WILD AGAIN: SNIPPETS FROM MY LIFE AND A FEW BRAZEN THOUGHTS
Helen Gurley Brown
The former *Cosmopolitan* magazine helmer drops names, bares breasts, and serves up lots of clichéd advice in her readers in this frisky, off-the-cuff memoir.

IN A SUNBURNED COUNTRY
Bill Bryson
An Australian travelogue. Too many pages are spent regurgitating history and recounting forays into obscure museums, and too few are devoted to experiences with local culture and weird tourist attractions.

BURT LANCASTER: AN AMERICAN LIFE
Kate Buford
A short and pudgy New York City slum kid turns into an acrobat, then a meat-cooler inspector, and finally a movie star. An absorbing, definitive bio.

FOREVER LIESL: A MEMOIR OF THE SOUND OF MUSIC
Charmian Carr with Jean A. S. Strauss
A sweetly sentimental, PG-rated look back at the filming of the Rodgers and Hammerstein classic.

STICKIN'
James Carville
Insulted that some people regard fealty as "weakness of mind or character," the political strategist and die-hard Clinton apologist argues *The Case for Loyalty*, the subtitle of his new book.

APRONS: ICONS OF THE AMERICAN HOME
Joyce Cheney
In this photo-packed album, Cheney traces trends in the styles of aprons as women's roles in American society changed.

FIRST LOVES
edited by Carmela Ciuraru
Notable poets talk about their favorites. Billy Collins chooses a John Donne poem; Eleanor Wilner salutes Lorenz Hart's lyrics for "The Lady Is a Tramp." Read the commentary, then the poem, and see if it hasn't become more accessible.

*GET HAPPY: THE LIFE OF JUDY GARLAND
by Gerald Clarke
Clarke's masterly biography draws on extensive interviews and Garland's unpublished memoirs to recount a life as woeful as Job's—yet one can't look away.

HOW TO MANAGE YOUR MOTHER
Alyce Faye Cleese and Brian Bates
A psychotherapist and an academic serve up strategies to cope with the full spectrum of problem moms.

EDWARD M. KENNEDY: A BIOGRAPHY
Adam Clymer
A readable and worthy account of the flawed and fascinating senator.

AS NATURE MADE HIM: THE BOY WHO WAS RAISED AS A GIRL
John Colapinto
A baby boy suffers a botched circumcision and his young parents are persuaded to raise him as a girl. The gut-wrenching, absorbing account shows us how psychology's theories *du jour* can be painfully, dreadfully wrong.

AS NATURE MADE HIM
THE BOY WHO WAS RAISED AS A GIRL

JOHN COLAPINTO

THE BLONDE: A CELEBRATION OF THE GOLDEN ERA FROM HARLOW TO MONROE
Barnaby Conrad III
This frothy coffee-table volume strains too hard to be serious. Skip the text and go directly to the pictures.

TAMMY WYNETTE: A DAUGHTER RECALLS HER MOTHER'S TRAGIC LIFE AND DEATH
Jackie Daly
A beautifully written memoir of the beloved country music star.

THE WORLD OF GARDEN DESIGN
by Susan Dooley with the editors of Garden Design magazine
This handsome volume takes a tour of five global gardening styles—those of Italy, Britain, France, Japan, and the tropics—as interpreted in the United States.

BEAUTIFUL AMERICAN ROSE GARDENS
by Mary Tonetti Dorra; photographs by Richard Felber
Two dozen gardeners show us how their favorite roses adapt to climate and setting.

I MAY NOT GET THERE WITH YOU
Michael Eric Dyson
The author, a professor at DePaul University, argues that the legacy of civil rights leader Martin Luther King Jr. has been distorted and exploited—even by his family.

*A HEARTBREAKING WORK OF STAGGERING GENIUS
Dave Eggers
When both his parents die of cancer, a senior in college must juggle responsibility for his 8-year-old brother with his own appetites for fame and romance. Eggers' bag of tricks can seem a tad too self-conscious, but his memoir almost lives up to its title.

AMERICAN RHAPSODY
Joe Eszterhas
The Starr Report, on acid; at once fascinating, shocking, repellent, and pointlessly repetitive.

DOES THIS MAKE ME LOOK FAT?: THE DEFINITIVE RULES FOR DRESSING THIN FOR EVERY HEIGHT, SIZE, AND SHAPE
Leah Feldon
Solid advice on looking anything but.

LINDA MCCARTNEY: A PORTRAIT
Danny Fields
A close friend of his subject's from 1966 until her death in 1998, the biographer, an ex-music manager, offers an insider's look at one of rock music's most enduring marriages.

*GEORGIANA, DUCHESS OF DEVONSHIRE
Amanda Foreman
This meticulously researched biography of Princess Diana's great-great-great-great-aunt reads like a racy historical novel, providing a unique look at a fascinating woman.

STAR STYLE AT THE ACADEMY AWARDS
Patty Fox
Frothy fun about Oscar frocks.

ON THE REZ
Ian Frazier
In this nonfiction work, the author of the bestselling book *Great Plains* recounts experiences with the Oglala Sioux on the rez—slang for reservation.

JOHN GLENN: A MEMOIR
John Glenn with Nick Taylor
The former astronaut and senator recounts his many achievements, including his triumphant return to outer space in 1998.

MY GENERATION
Michael Gross
Can one writer make sense of "fifty years of sex, drugs, rock, revolution, glamour, greed, valor, faith, and silicon chips," in a single (albeit hefty) book? Gross's reach here exceeds his grasp.

PERENNIALS
Linden Hawthorne
Cataloged here are 1,000 flowers for all seasons, with information on when and where they do best.

LOVE ALWAYS, PATSY
Cindy Hazen and Mike Freeman
A remarkable record of Patsy Cline's rise to fame, culled from letters she wrote to teenager Treva Miller, who organized and ran a Cline fan club.

RIVER-HORSE: A VOYAGE ACROSS AMERICA
William Least Heat-Moon
For his latest travelogue, Heat-Moon maps out a 5,000-mile boat journey. Heat-Moon's passion for the nation's geography, history and the preservation of its rivers is infectious—and lucky for us it is, because four months on the water can have its slow stretches, as does this book.

HOW TO OVERTHROW THE GOVERNMENT
Arianna Huffington
If only this earnest manifesto didn't read like the work of a college student who pulled an all-nighter to meet a term-paper deadline.

ANGEL PAWPRINTS: REFLECTIONS ON LOVING AND LOSING A CANINE COMPANION
Edited by Laurel E. Hunt
A book of writings about the death of animals. While a fair number of the included poems, essays, and illustrations are mawkish, others comfort, enlighten and even amuse.

SHRUB: THE SHORT BUT HAPPY POLITICAL LIFE OF GEORGE W. BUSH
Molly Ivins and Lou Dubose
This may well be the Most Boring Political Book Not Actually Written by a Politician.

COUNTRY GARDENING
Theodore James Jr.; photographs by Harry Haralambou
The appealing little Edens in this book are accompanied by design principles, plus starting and maintenance tips.

GARY COOPER OFF CAMERA
Maria Cooper Janis
This intimate photo collection by the screen legend's adoring daughter portrays the actor as far different from the laconic defender of virtue he mastered onscreen.

THE ESSENTIAL LEWIS AND CLARK
edited by Landon Y. Jones
The West's explorers recorded their perilous journey in more than 900,000 words, pared down here by Jones (PEOPLE's former managing editor) into 203 riveting, readable pages.

TOPIARY AND THE ART OF TRAINING PLANTS
David Joyce
For those tempted to turn greenery into living sculpture, pruning poo-bah Joyce offers concise directions for creating basic geometric patterns or elaborate ivy ponies, chickens and bunnies.

MARIAN ANDERSON: A SINGER'S JOURNEY
Allan Keiler
This serious, engaging authorized biography carefully documents the pioneering diva's musical evolution and civic triumphs.

MY GARDEN BOOK
Jamaica Kincaid
A collection of essays about wisteria, useless horticultural tools, highhanded seed sellers, etc.; sprinkled throughout are intriguing autobiographical tidbits about the author.

SEX AND SHOPPING
Judith Krantz
Krantz's lively "story of a nice Jewish girl who had some amazing fun and went interestingly askew" is, until petering out near the end, a joy ride.

AN AMERICAN ALBUM
edited by Lewis H. Lapham and Ellen Rosenbush
From Mark Twain to Alice Walker: 150 years of gems from *Harper's* magazine.

TRUMPET BLUES: THE LIFE OF HARRY JAMES
Peter J. Levinson
Sex, alcohol, and big-band swing: this absorbing biography enhances James' reputation as a musician but makes no attempt to whitewash his less-than-engaging persona.

THE CAMINO
Shirley MacLaine
The otherworldly entertainer details her 500-mile pilgrimage along Spain's Santiago de Compostela Camino. By turns fearful, vain, and hostile, MacLaine makes her eccentricity endearing, even if you scoff at how the spirit moves her.

*LIPSHTICK
Gwen Macsai
This hilarious selection of autobiographical essays serves up plenty of irreverent advice, but Macsai sprinkles her sass with such genuine sweetness that her words become as comforting as a post-breakup bowl of ice cream.

THE KEYS TO THE KINGDOM: HOW MICHAEL EISNER LOST HIS GRIP
Kim Masters
A thoroughly reported and often unflattering portrait of the Disney czar. Much is fascinating, but what will keep readers turning the pages is all the juicy movie-star gossip.

THE UNRULY LIFE OF WOODY ALLEN
Marion Meade
It's all here in this critical biography: reminiscences from Brooklyn boyhood pals, the catalog of neuroses, the ins and outs of filmmaking, Mia and, oh yes, Soon-Yi.

SANDCASTLES
Patti Mitchell and the Leap Foundation
Astonishing, if transient, art that can be created by almost anyone with the patience, the tools (pail, shovel, watering can), and access to a nice, sandy beach.

MY CAT SPIT MCGEE
Willie Morris
With lithe artistry and heaps of humorous Dixie detail, Morris chronicles his conversion from die-hard "dog man" to a blubbering middle-aged mass of affection seduced by a newborn kitten.

THE CIRCUS FIRE
Stewart O'Nan
This compelling account of 7,000 people trying to escape a burning tent during a 1944 circus is a gripping portrayal of selfless bravery and mindless panic.

MY LITTLE RED WAGON: RADIO FLYER MEMORIES
Robert Pasin and Paul Pasin
To celebrate the 80th anniversary of this classic toy, the authors gathered stories and photographs from three generations of satisfied Flyer customers. Their testimonials add up to a nostalgia-fringed tribute to childhood itself.

FAMILY GARDEN
Lucy Peel
This practical guide has advice on planning outdoor spaces for the entire family, where little ones can play safely and learn to appreciate nature's beauty and unhurried pace.

WHIPLASH! AMERICA'S MOST FRIVOLOUS LAWSUITS
James L. Percelay
Actual lawsuits that are sure to amuse, interspersed with lawyer jokes.

IN THE HEART OF THE SEA: THE TRAGEDY OF THE WHALESHIP ESSEX
Nathaniel Philbrick
The true tale that inspired *Moby Dick*. A sperm whale rams a ship's wooden hull, leaving the crew to fight for life in small, leaky boats.

. . . AND NEVER LET HER GO: THOMAS CAPANO, THE DEADLY SEDUCER
Ann Rule
Truly creepy true crime story about prominent Wilmington, Del., lawyer Thomas Capano, who had charm, looks and money—and who killed his young mistress.

ACTUAL INNOCENCE
Barry Scheck, Peter Neufeld, and Jim Dwyer
Two prominent defense lawyers—and a Pulitzer Prize–winning journalist—find the justice system guilty of railroading innocents onto death row.

SWING IT! THE ANDREWS SISTERS STORY
John Sforza
The Andrew Sisters dominated pop music in the '40s, thriving on stage and radio as well as on records; Sforza presents a colorful and flattering (though not sycophantic) portrait of this vital part of American popular culture.

HILLARY'S CHOICE
Gail Sheehy
Drawing on interviews with hundreds of subjects, Sheehy breaks new ground in addressing the big question: Do the Clintons love one another—or is it just a political partnership?

CONNECTING: THE ENDURING POWER OF FEMALE FRIENDSHIP
Sandy Sheehy
This comprehensive study draws on interviews with more than 200 women and girls from coast to coast.

KEEP IT SIMPLE, STUPID: YOU'RE SMARTER THAN YOU LOOK
Judge Judy Sheindlin
This collection of obvious guidelines seems little more than a chance for Sheindlin to cash in on her TV fame.

CYBILL DISOBEDIENCE
Cybill Shepherd
Mixing irreverence with self-reflection, Shepherd delivers not only one of the most hilarious kiss-and-tell memoirs to come out of Hollywood in years but also a moving account of her journey of self-discovery.

TEN THINGS
Maria Shriver
Among the things the NBC newswoman says she wishes she'd known before going out into the real world are: No. 5, Be Willing to Fail; and No. 8, Marriage Is a Hell of a Lot of Work.

JACKIE: HER LIFE IN PICTURES
James Spada
Jackiephiles, rejoice! Further evidence that there will be no letup in efforts to examine every aspect of her beguiling life.

JACQUELINE BOUVIER KENNEDY ONASSIS: A LIFE
Donald Spoto
Spoto relies heavily on copious press coverage of his subject, and is not averse to speculation when information simply does not exist. Jackie O, so-so.

DRIVING OVER LEMONS
Chris Stewart
In this zesty book, subtitled *An Optimist in Andalucía*, the British author describes making a life and a home for his family in sunny southern Spain.

JACKIE, ETHEL, JOAN: WOMEN OF CAMELOT
J. Randy Taraborrelli
This sympathetic book about Kennedy wives reads like *Valley of the Dolls* goes to Washington. Booze, pills, bitchy rivalries—it's all here in this bloated but fun read.

A VAST CONSPIRACY
Jeffrey Toobin
It seems unlikely that any writer could make the Clinton-Lewinsky sex scandal fresh and entertaining, but that's just what Toobin has accomplished.

INVENTING AL GORE: A BIOGRAPHY
Bill Turque
An uneven but well-researched biography of the would-be president.

TAKE THE CANNOLI
Sarah Vowell
Wise, witty, and refreshingly warm-hearted, Vowell's essays on American history, pop culture, and her own family reveal the bonds holding together a great, if occasionally weird, nation.

DOGS WITH JOBS
Merrily Weisbord and Kim Kachanoff
Weisbord and Kachanoff traveled the world to find dogs with work ethics—or at least serious jobs—and not just in traditional canine occupations like sheepherding.

FICTION AND NONFICTION BESTSELLERS

Publishers Weekly began charting the nation's top-selling hardcover fiction in 1895. The first nonfiction lists were published regularly beginning in 1917, and during World War I the trade magazine even tracked the most popular war books. (The Winston Churchill on the fiction lists, by the way, was an American novelist who died in 1947; his British statesman namesake was, of course, a bestselling and Nobel Prize–winning writer of nonfiction.) These rankings are not based on net sales figures but rather on publishers' reports of copies shipped and billed.

1900

Fiction
1. *To Have and To Hold*, Mary Johnston
2. *Red Pottage*, Mary Cholmondeley
3. *Unleavened Bread*, Robert Grant
4. *The Reign of Law*, James Lane Allen
5. *Eben Holden*, Irving Bacheller
6. *Janice Meredith*, Paul Leicester Ford
7. *The Redemption of David Corson*, Charles Frederic Goss
8. *Richard Carvel*, Winston Churchill
9. *When Knighthood Was in Flower*, Charles Major
10. *Alice of Old Vincennes*, Maurice Thompson

1901

Fiction
1. *The Crisis*, Winston Churchill
2. *Alice of Old Vincennes*, Maurice Thompson
3. *The Helmet of Navarre*, Bertha Runkle
4. *The Right of Way*, Gilbert Parker
5. *Eben Holden*, Irving Bacheller
6. *The Visits of Elizabeth*, Elinor Glyn
7. *The Puppet Crown*, Harold MacGrath
8. *Richard Yea-and-Nay*, Maurice Hewlett
9. *Graustark*, George Barr McCutcheon
10. *D'ri and I*, Irving Bacheller

1902

Fiction
1. *The Virginian*, Owen Wister
2. *Mrs. Wiggs of the Cabbage Patch*, Alice Caldwell Hegan
3. *Dorothy Vernon of Haddon Hall*, Charles Major
4. *The Mississippi Bubble*, Emerson Hough
5. *Audrey*, Mary Johnston
6. *The Right of Way*, Gilbert Parker
7. *The Hound of the Baskervilles*, A. Conan Doyle
8. *The Two Vanrevels*, Booth Tarkington
9. *The Blue Flower*, Henry van Dyke
10. *Sir Richard Calmady*, Lucas Malet

1903

Fiction
1. *Lady Rose's Daughter*, Mary Augusta Ward
2. *Gordon Keith*, Thomas Nelson Page
3. *The Pit*, Frank Norris
4. *Lovey Mary*, Alice Hegan Rice
5. *The Virginian*, Owen Wister
6. *Mrs. Wiggs of the Cabbage Patch*, Alice Hegan Rice
7. *The Mettle of the Pasture*, James Lane Allen
8. *Letters of a Self-Made Merchant to His Son*, George Horace Lorimer
9. *The One Woman*, Thomas Dixon Jr.
10. *The Little Shepherd of Kingdom Come*, John Fox Jr.

1904

Fiction
1. *The Crossing*, Winston Churchill
2. *The Deliverance*, Ellen Glasgow
3. *The Masquerader*, anonymous (Katherine Cecil Thurston)
4. *In the Bishop's Carriage*, Miriam Michelson
5. *Sir Mortimer*, Mary Johnston
6. *Beverly of Graustark*, George Barr McCutcheon
7. *The Little Shepherd of Kingdom Come*, John Fox Jr.
8. *Rebecca of Sunnybrook Farm*, Kate Douglas Wiggin
9. *My Friend Prospero*, Henry Harland
10. *The Silent Places*, Stewart Edward White

1905

Fiction
1. *The Marriage of William Ashe*, Mary Augusta Ward
2. *Sandy*, Alice Hegan Rice
3. *The Garden of Allah*, Robert Hichens
4. *The Clansman*, Thomas Dixon Jr.
5. *Nedra*, George Barr McCutcheon
6. *The Gambler*, Katherine Cecil Thurston
7. *The Masquerader*, anonymous (Katherine Cecil Thurston)
8. *The House of Mirth*, Edith Wharton
9. *The Princess Passes*, C. N. and A. M. Williamson
10. *Rose o' the River*, Kate Douglas Wiggin

1906

Fiction
1. *Coniston*, Winston Churchill
2. *Lady Baltimore*, Owen Wister
3. *The Fighting Chance*, Robert W. Chambers
4. *The House of a Thousand Candles*, Meredith Nicholson
5. *Jane Cable*, George Barr McCutcheon
6. *The Jungle*, Upton Sinclair
7. *The Awakening of Helena Ritchie*, Margaret Deland
8. *The Spoilers*, Rex Beach
9. *The House of Mirth*, Edith Wharton
10. *The Wheel of Life*, Ellen Glasgow

1907

Fiction
1. *The Lady of the Decoration*, Frances Little
2. *The Weavers*, Gilbert Parker
3. *The Port of Missing Men*, Meredith Nicholson
4. *The Shuttle*, Frances Hodgson Burnett
5. *The Brass Bowl*, Louis J. Vance
6. *Satan Sanderson*, Hallie Erminie Rives
7. *The Daughter of Anderson Crow*, George Barr McCutcheon
8. *The Younger Set*, Robert W. Chambers
9. *The Doctor*, Ralph Connor
10. *Half a Rogue*, Harold MacGrath

1908

Fiction
1. *Mr. Crewe's Career*, Winston Churchill
2. *The Barrier*, Rex Beach
3. *The Trail of the Lonesome Pine*, John Fox Jr.
4. *The Lure of the Mask*, Harold MacGrath

5. *The Shuttle*, Frances Hodgson Burnett
6. *Peter*, F. Hopkinson Smith
7. *Lewis Rand*, Mary Johnston
8. *The Black Bag*, Louis J. Vance
9. *The Man from Brodney's*, George Barr McCutcheon
10. *The Weavers*, Gilbert Parker

1909

Fiction
1. *The Inner Shrine*, anonymous (Basil King)
2. *Katrine*, Elinor Macartney Lane
3. *The Silver Horde*, Rex Beach
4. *The Man in Lower Ten*, Mary Roberts Rinehart
5. *The Trail of the Lonesome Pine*, John Fox Jr.
6. *Truxton King*, George Barr McCutcheon
7. *54–40 or Fight*, Emerson Hough
8. *The Goose Girl*, Harold MacGrath
9. *Peter*, F. Hopkinson Smith
10. *Septimus*, William J. Locke

1910

Fiction
1. *The Rosary*, Florence Barclay
2. *A Modern Chronicle*, Winston Churchill
3. *The Wild Olive*, anonymous (Basil King)
4. *Max*, Katherine Cecil Thurston
5. *The Kingdom of Slender Swords*, Hallie Erminie Rives
6. *Simon the Jester*, William J. Locke
7. *Lord Loveland Discovers America*, C. N. and A. M. Williamson
8. *The Window at the White Cat*, Mary Roberts Rinehart
9. *Molly Make-Believe*, Eleanor Abbott
10. *When a Man Marries*, Mary Roberts Rinehart

1911

Fiction
1. *The Broad Highway*, Jeffrey Farnol
2. *The Prodigal Judge*, Vaughan Kester
3. *The Winning of Barbara Worth*, Harold Bell Wright
4. *Queed*, Henry Sydnor Harrison
5. *The Harvester*, Gene Stratton Porter
6. *The Iron Woman*, Margaret Deland
7. *The Long Roll*, Mary Johnston
8. *Molly Make-Believe*, Eleanor Abbott
9. *The Rosary*, Florence Barclay
10. *The Common Law*, Robert W. Chambers

1912

Fiction
1. *The Harvester*, Gene Stratton Porter
2. *The Street Called Straight*, Basil King
3. *Their Yesterdays*, Harold Bell Wright
4. *The Melting of Molly*, Maria Thompson Daviess
5. *A Hoosier Chronicle*, Meredith Nicholson
6. *The Winning of Barbara Worth*, Harold Bell Wright
7. *The Just and the Unjust*, Vaughan Kester
8. *The Net*, Rex Beach
9. *Tante*, Anne Douglas Sedgwick
10. *Fran*, J. Breckenridge Ellis

Nonfiction
1. *The Promised Land*, Mary Antin
2. *The Montessori Method*, Maria Montessori

3. *South America*, James Bryce
4. *A New Conscience and an Ancient Evil*, Jane Addams
5. *Three Plays*, Eugène Brieux
6. *Your United States*, Arnold Bennett
7. *Creative Evolution*, Henri Bergson
8. *How to Live on Twenty-four Hours a Day*, Arnold Bennett
9. *Woman and Labor*, Olive Schreiner
10. *Mark Twain*, Albert Bigelow Paine

1913

Fiction
1. *The Inside of the Cup*, Winston Churchill
2. *V.V.'s Eyes*, Henry Sydnor Harrison
3. *Laddie*, Gene Stratton Porter
4. *The Judgment House*, Sir Gilbert Parker
5. *Heart of the Hills*, John Fox Jr.

MOST CHALLENGED (NOT BANNED) BOOKS

Books enrich our lives, but to a certain vocal part of the population they can enrage as well. While the intention of those challenging these books *was* to ban them, most of the books stayed on the shelves because of the efforts of librarians, teachers, parents, and students. Here are the most challenged books in school libraries and curriculums, in the last year, according to the American Library Association's Office for Intellectual Freedom (Jan. 1–Dec. 31, 1999) and between 1982 and 1996 according to People for the American Way.

1982–96
1. *Of Mice and Men*, John Steinbeck
2. *The Catcher in the Rye*, J. D. Salinger
3. *The Chocolate War*, Robert Cormier
4. *I Know Why the Caged Bird Sings*, Maya Angelou
5. *Scary Stories to Tell in the Dark*, Alvin Schwartz
6. *The Adventures of Huckleberry Finn*, Mark Twain
7. *More Scary Stories to Tell in the Dark*, Alvin Schwartz
8. *Go Ask Alice*, anonymous
9. *Bridge to Terabithia*, Katherine Paterson
10. *The Witches*, Roald Dahl

1999
1. The *Harry Potter* series, J. K. Rowling
2. The *Alice* series, Phyllis Reynolds Naylor
3. *The Chocolate War*, Robert Cormier
4. *Blubber*, Judy Blume
5. *Fallen Angels*, Walter Dean Myers
6. *Of Mice and Men*, John Steinbeck
7. *I Know Why the Caged Bird Sings*, Maya Angelou
8. *The Handmaid's Tale*, Margaret Atwood
9. *The Color Purple*, Alice Walker
10. *Snow Falling on Cedars*, David Guterson

6. *The Amateur Gentleman*, Jeffrey Farnol
7. *The Woman Thou Gavest Me*, Hall Caine
8. *Pollyanna*, Eleanor H. Porter
9. *The Valiants of Virginia*, Hallie Erminie Rives
10. *T. Tembarom*, Frances Hodgson Burnett

Nonfiction

1. *Crowds*, Gerald Stanley Lee
2. *Germany and the Germans*, Price Collier
3. *Zone Policeman 88*, Harry A. Franck
4. *The New Freedom*, Woodrow Wilson
5. *South America*, James Bryce
6. *Your United States*, Arnold Bennett
7. *The Promised Land*, Mary Antin
8. *Auction Bridge To-Day*, Milton C. Work
9. *Three Plays*, Eugène Brieux
10. *Psychology and Industrial Efficiency*, Hugo Munsterberg

1914

Fiction

1. *The Eyes of the World*, Harold Bell Wright
2. *Pollyanna*, Eleanor H. Porter
3. *The Inside of the Cup*, Winston Churchill
4. *The Salamander*, Owen Johnson
5. *The Fortunate Youth*, William J. Locke
6. *T. Tembarom*, Frances Hodgson Burnett
7. *Penrod*, Booth Tarkington
8. *Diane of the Green Van*, Leona Dalrymple
9. *The Devil's Garden*, W. B. Maxwell
10. *The Prince of Graustark*, George Barr McCutcheon

1915

Fiction

1. *The Turmoil*, Booth Tarkington
2. *A Far Country*, Winston Churchill
3. *Michael O'Halloran*, Gene Stratton Porter
4. *Pollyanna Grows Up*, Eleanor H. Porter
5. *K*, Mary Roberts Rinehart
6. *Jaffery*, William J. Locke
7. *Felix O'Day*, F. Hopkinson Smith
8. *The Harbor*, Ernest Poole
9. *The Lone Star Ranger*, Zane Grey
10. *Angela's Business*, Henry Sydnor Harrison

1916

Fiction

1. *Seventeen*, Booth Tarkington
2. *When a Man's a Man*, Harold Bell Wright

3. *Just David*, Eleanor H. Porter
4. *Mr. Britling Sees It Through*, H. G. Wells
5. *Life and Gabriella*, Ellen Glasgow
6. *The Real Adventure*, Henry Kitchell Webster
7. *Bars of Iron*, Ethel M. Dell
8. *Nan of Music Mountain*, Frank H. Spearman
9. *Dear Enemy*, Jean Webster
10. *The Heart of Rachael*, Kathleen Norris

1917

Fiction

1. *Mr. Britling Sees It Through*, H. G. Wells
2. *The Light in the Clearing*, Irving Bacheller
3. *The Red Planet*, William J. Locke
4. *The Road to Understanding*, Eleanor H. Porter
5. *Wildfire*, Zane Grey
6. *Christine*, Alice Cholmondeley
7. *In the Wilderness*, Robert S. Hichens
8. *His Family*, Ernest Poole
9. *The Definite Object*, Jeffrey Farnol
10. *The Hundredth Chance*, Ethel M. Dell

General Nonfiction

1. *Rhymes of a Red Cross Man*, Robert W. Service
2. *The Plattsburg Manual*, O. O. Ellis and E. B. Garey
3. *Raymond*, Sir Oliver Lodge
4. *Poems of Alan Seeger*, Alan Seeger
5. *God the Invisible King*, H. G. Wells
6. *Laugh and Live*, Douglas Fairbanks
7. *Better Meals for Less Money*, Mary Green

War Books

1. *The First Hundred Thousand*, Ian Hay
2. *My Home in the Field of Honor*, Frances W. Huard
3. *A Student in Arms*, Donald Hankey
4. *Over the Top*, Arthur Guy Empey
5. *Carry On*, Coningsby Dawson
6. *Getting Together*, Ian Hay
7. *My Second Year of the War*, Frederick Palmer
8. *The Land of Deepening Shadow*, D. Thomas Curtin
9. *Italy, France and Britain at War*, H. G. Wells
10. *The Worn Doorstep*, Margaret Sherwood

1918

Fiction

1. *The U. P. Trail*, Zane Grey

2. *The Tree of Heaven*, May Sinclair
3. *The Amazing Interlude*, Mary Roberts Rinehart
4. *Dere Mable*, Edward Streeter
5. *Oh, Money! Money!*, Eleanor H. Porter
6. *Greatheart*, Ethel M. Dell
7. *The Major*, Ralph Connor
8. *The Pawns Count*, E. Phillips Oppenheim
9. *A Daughter of the Land*, Gene Stratton Porter
10. *Sonia*, Stephen McKenna

General Nonfiction

1. *Rhymes of a Red Cross Man*, Robert W. Service
2. *Treasury of War Poetry*, G. H. Clark
3. *With the Colors*, Everard J. Appleton
4. *Recollections*, Viscount Morley
5. *Laugh and Live*, Douglas Fairbanks
6. *Mark Twain's Letters*, Albert Bigelow Paine, editor
7. *Adventures and Letters of Richard Harding Davis*, Richard Harding Davis
8. *Over Here*, Edgar Guest
9. *Diplomatic Days*, Edith O'Shaughnessy
10. *Poems of Alan Seeger*, Alan Seeger

War Books

1. *My Four Years in Germany*, James W. Gerard
2. *The Glory of the Trenches*, Coningsby Dawson
3. *Over the Top*, Arthur Guy Empey
4. *A Minstrel in France*, Harry Lauder
5. *Private Peat*, Harold R. Peat
6. *Outwitting the Hun*, Lieut. Pat O'Brien
7. *Face to Face with Kaiserism*, James W. Gerard
8. *Carry On*, Coningsby Dawson
9. *Out to Win*, Coningsby Dawson
10. *Under Fire*, Henri Barbusse

1919

Fiction

1. *The Four Horsemen of the Apocalypse*, V. Blasco Ibañez
2. *The Arrow of Gold*, Joseph Conrad
3. *The Desert of Wheat*, Zane Grey
4. *Dangerous Days*, Mary Roberts Rinehart
5. *The Sky Pilot in No Man's Land*, Ralph Connor
6. *The Re-creation of Brian Kent*, Harold Bell Wright
7. *Dawn*, Gene Stratton Porter
8. *The Tin Soldier*, Temple Bailey
9. *Christopher and Columbus*, "Elizabeth"

10. *In Secret*, Robert W. Chambers

Nonfiction
1. *The Education of Henry Adams*, Henry Adams
2. *The Years Between*, Rudyard Kipling
3. *Belgium*, Brand Whitlock
4. *The Seven Purposes*, Margaret Cameron
5. *In Flanders Fields*, John McCrae
6. *Bolshevism*, John Spargo

1920

Fiction
1. *The Man of the Forest*, Zane Grey
2. *Kindred of the Dust*, Peter B. Kyne
3. *The Re-creation of Brian Kent*, Harold Bell Wright
4. *The River's End*, James Oliver Curwood
5. *A Man for the Ages*, Irving Bacheller
6. *Mary-Marie*, Eleanor H. Porter
7. *The Portygee*, Joseph C. Lincoln
8. *The Great Impersonation*, E. Phillips Oppenheim
9. *The Lamp in the Desert*, Ethel M. Dell
10. *Harriet and the Piper*, Kathleen Norris

Nonfiction
1. *Now It Can Be Told*, Philip Gibbs
2. *The Economic Consequences of the Peace*, John M. Keynes
3. *Roosevelt's Letters to His Children*, Joseph B. Bishop, editor
4. *Theodore Roosevelt*, William Roscoe Thayer
5. *White Shadows in the South Seas*, Frederick O'Brien
6. *An American Idyll*, Cornelia Stratton Parker

1921

Fiction
1. *Main Street*, Sinclair Lewis
2. *The Brimming Cup*, Dorothy Canfield
3. *The Mysterious Rider*, Zane Grey
4. *The Age of Innocence*, Edith Wharton
5. *The Valley of Silent Men*, James Oliver Curwood
6. *The Sheik*, Edith M. Hull
7. *A Poor Wise Man*, Mary Roberts Rinehart
8. *Her Father's Daughter*, Gene Stratton Porter
9. *The Sisters-in-Law*, Gertrude Atherton
10. *The Kingdom Round the Corner*, Coningsby Dawson

Nonfiction
1. *The Outline of History*, H. G. Wells
2. *White Shadows in the South Seas*, Frederick O'Brien

3. *The Mirrors of Downing Street*, A Gentleman with a Duster (pseudonym for Harold Begbie)
4. *The Autobiography of Margot Asquith*, Margot Asquith
6. *Peace Negotiations*, Robert Lansing

1922

Fiction
1. *If Winter Comes*, A. S. M. Hutchinson
2. *The Sheik*, Edith M. Hull
3. *Gentle Julia*, Booth Tarkington
4. *The Head of the House of Coombe*, Frances Hodgson Burnett
5. *Simon Called Peter*, Robert Keable
6. *The Breaking Point*, Mary Roberts Rinehart
7. *This Freedom*, A. S. M. Hutchinson
8. *Maria Chapdelaine*, Louis Hémon
9. *To the Last Man*, Zane Grey
10. *Babbitt*, Sinclair Lewis (tie)
10. *Helen of the Old House*, Harold Bell Wright (tie)

Nonfiction
1. *The Outline of History*, H. G. Wells
2. *The Story of Mankind*, Hendrik Willem Van Loon
3. *The Americanization of Edward Bok*, Edward Bok
4. *Diet and Health*, Lulu Hunt Peters
5. *The Mind in the Making*, James Harvey Robinson
6. *The Outline of Science*, J. Arthur Thomson
7. *Outwitting Our Nerves*, Josephine A. Jackson and Helen M. Salisbury
8. *Queen Victoria*, Lytton Strachey
9. *Mirrors of Washington*, anonymous (Clinton W. Gilbert)
10. *Painted Windows*, A Gentleman with a Duster (pseudonym for Harold Begbie)

1923

Fiction
1. *Black Oxen*, Gertrude Atherton
2. *His Children's Children*, Arthur Train
3. *The Enchanted April*, "Elizabeth"
4. *Babbitt*, Sinclair Lewis
5. *The Dim Lantern*, Temple Bailey
6. *This Freedom*, A. S. M. Hutchinson
7. *The Mine with the Iron Door*, Harold Bell Wright
8. *The Wanderer of the Wasteland*, Zane Grey
9. *The Sea-Hawk*, Rafael Sabatini
10. *The Breaking Point*, Mary Roberts Rinehart

Nonfiction
1. *Etiquette*, Emily Post
2. *The Life of Christ*, Giovanni Papini
3. *The Life and Letters of Walter H. Page*, Burton J. Hendrick, editor
4. *The Mind in the Making*, James Harvey Robinson
5. *The Outline of History*, H. G. Wells
6. *Diet and Health*, Lulu Hunt Peters
7. *Self-Mastery Through Conscious Auto-Suggestion*, Emile Coué
8. *The Americanization of Edward Bok*, Edward Bok
9. *The Story of Mankind*, Hendrik Willem Van Loon
10. *A Man from Maine*, Edward Bok

1924

Fiction
1. *So Big*, Edna Ferber
2. *The Plastic Age*, Percy Marks
3. *The Little French Girl*, Anne Douglas Sedgwick
4. *The Heirs Apparent*, Philip Gibbs
5. *A Gentleman of Courage*, James Oliver Curwood
6. *The Call of the Canyon*, Zane Grey
7. *The Midlander*, Booth Tarkington
8. *The Coast of Folly*, Coningsby Dawson
9. *Mistress Wilding*, Rafael Sabatini
10. *The Homemaker*, Dorothy Canfield Fisher

Nonfiction
1. *Diet and Health*, Lulu Hunt Peters
2. *The Life of Christ*, Giovanni Papini
3. *The Boston Cooking School Cook Book*, rev. ed., Fannie Farmer, editor
4. *Etiquette*, Emily Post
5. *Ariel*, André Maurois
6. *The Cross Word Puzzle Books*, Prosper Buranelli, et al.
7. *Mark Twain's Autobiography*, Mark Twain
8. *Saint Joan*, Bernard Shaw
9. *The New Decalogue of Science*, Albert E. Wiggam
10. *The Americanization of Edward Bok*, Edward Bok

1925

Fiction
1. *Soundings*, A. Hamilton Gibbs
2. *The Constant Nymph*, Margaret Kennedy
3. *The Keeper of the Bees*, Gene Stratton Porter
4. *Glorious Apollo*, E. Barrington
5. *The Green Hat*, Michael Arlen

6. *The Little French Girl*, Anne Douglas Sedgwick
7. *Arrowsmith*, Sinclair Lewis
8. *The Perennial Bachelor*, Anne Parrish
9. *The Carolinian*, Rafael Sabatini
10. *One Increasing Purpose*, A. S. M. Hutchinson

Nonfiction
1. *Diet and Health*, Lulu Hunt Peters
2. *The Boston Cooking School Cook Book*, rev. ed., Fannie Farmer, editor
3. *When We Were Very Young*, A. A. Milne
4. *The Man Nobody Knows*, Bruce Barton
5. *The Life of Christ*, Giovanni Papini
6. *Ariel*, André Maurois
7. *Twice Thirty*, Edward Bok
8. *Twenty-five Years*, Lord Grey
9. *Anatole France Himself*, J. J. Brousson
10. *The Cross Word Puzzle Books*, Prosper Buranelli, et al.

1926

Fiction
1. *The Private Life of Helen of Troy*, John Erskine
2. *Gentlemen Prefer Blondes*, Anita Loos
3. *Sorrell and Son*, Warwick Deeping
4. *The Hounds of Spring*, Sylvia Thompson
5. *Beau Sabreur*, P. C. Wren
6. *The Silver Spoon*, John Galsworthy
7. *Beau Geste*, P. C. Wren
8. *Show Boat*, Edna Ferber
9. *After Noon*, Susan Ertz
10. *The Blue Window*, Temple Bailey

Nonfiction
1. *The Man Nobody Knows*, Bruce Barton
2. *Why We Behave Like Human Beings*, George A. Dorsey
3. *Diet and Health*, Lulu Hunt Peters
4. *Our Times*, Vol. I, Mark Sullivan
5. *The Boston Cooking School Cook Book*, rev. ed., Fannie Farmer, editor
6. *Auction Bridge Complete*, Milton C. Work
7. *The Book Nobody Knows*, Bruce Barton
8. *The Story of Philosophy*, Will Durant
9. *The Light of Faith*, Edgar A. Guest
10. *Jefferson and Hamilton*, Claude G. Bowers

1927

Fiction
1. *Elmer Gantry*, Sinclair Lewis
2. *The Plutocrat*, Booth Tarkington
3. *Doomsday*, Warwick Deeping
4. *Sorrell and Son*, Warwick Deeping
5. *Jalna*, Mazo de la Roche
6. *Lost Ecstasy*, Mary Roberts Rinehart
7. *Twilight Sleep*, Edith Wharton

8. *Tomorrow Morning*, Anne Parrish
9. *The Old Countess*, Anne Douglas Sedgwick
10. *A Good Woman*, Louis Bromfield

Nonfiction
1. *The Story of Philosophy*, Will Durant
2. *Napoleon*, Emil Ludwig
3. *Revolt in the Desert*, T. E. Lawrence
4. *Trader Horn*, Vol. I, Alfred Aloysius Horn and Ethelreda Lewis
5. *We*, Charles A. Lindbergh
6. *Ask Me Another*, Julian Spafford and Lucien Esty
7. *The Royal Road to Romance*, Richard Halliburton
8. *The Glorious Adventure*, Richard Halliburton
9. *Why We Behave Like Human Beings*, George A. Dorsey
10. *Mother India*, Katherine Mayo

1928

Fiction
1. *The Bridge of San Luis Rey*, Thornton Wilder
2. *Wintersmoon*, Hugh Walpole
3. *Swan Song*, John Galsworthy
4. *The Greene Murder Case*, S. S. Van Dine
5. *Bad Girl*, Viña Delmar
6. *Claire Ambler*, Booth Tarkington
7. *Old Pybus*, Warwick Deeping
8. *All Kneeling*, Anne Parrish
9. *Jalna*, Mazo de la Roche
10. *The Strange Case of Miss Annie Spragg*, Louis Bromfield

Nonfiction
1. *Disraeli*, André Maurois
2. *Mother India*, Katherine Mayo
3. *Trader Horn*, Vol. I, Alfred Aloysius Horn and Ethelreda Lewis
4. *Napoleon*, Emil Ludwig
5. *Strange Interlude*, Eugene O'Neill
6. *We*, Charles A. Lindbergh
7. *Count Luckner, the Sea Devil*, Lowell Thomas
8. *Goethe*, Emil Ludwig
9. *Skyward*, Richard E. Byrd
10. *The Intelligent Woman's Guide to Socialism and Capitalism*, George Bernard Shaw

1929

Fiction
1. *All Quiet on the Western Front*, Erich Maria Remarque
2. *Dodsworth*, Sinclair Lewis
3. *Dark Hester*, Anne Douglas Sedgwick

4. *The Bishop Murder Case*, S. S. Van Dine
5. *Roper's Row*, Warwick Deeping
6. *Peder Victorious*, O. E. Rölvaag
7. *Mamba's Daughters*, DuBose Heyward
8. *The Galaxy*, Susan Ertz
9. *Scarlet Sister Mary*, Julia Peterkin
10. *Joseph and His Brethren*, H. W. Freeman

Nonfiction
1. *The Art of Thinking*, Ernest Dimnet
2. *Henry the Eighth*, Francis Hackett
3. *The Cradle of the Deep*, Joan Lowell
4. *Elizabeth and Essex*, Lytton Strachey
5. *The Specialist*, Chic Sale
6. *A Preface to Morals*, Walter Lippmann
7. *Believe It or Not*, Robert L. Ripley
8. *John Brown's Body*, Stephen Vincent Benét
9. *The Tragic Era*, Claude G. Bowers
10. *The Mansions of Philosophy*, Will Durant

1930

Fiction
1. *Cimarron*, Edna Ferber
2. *Exile*, Warwick Deeping
3. *The Woman of Andros*, Thornton Wilder
4. *Years of Grace*, Margaret Ayer Barnes
5. *Angel Pavement*, J. B. Priestley
6. *The Door*, Mary Roberts Rinehart
7. *Rogue Herries*, Hugh Walpole
8. *Chances*, A. Hamilton Gibbs
9. *Young Man of Manhattan*, Katharine Brush
10. *Twenty-four Hours*, Louis Bromfield

Nonfiction
1. *The Story of San Michele*, Axel Munthe
2. *The Strange Death of President Harding*, Gaston B. Means and May Dixon Thacker
3. *Byron*, André Maurois
4. *The Adams Family*, James Truslow Adams
5. *Lone Cowboy*, Will James
6. *Lincoln*, Emil Ludwig
7. *The Story of Philosophy*, Will Durant
8. *The Outline of History*, H. G. Wells
9. *The Art of Thinking*, Ernest Dimnet
10. *The Rise of American Civilization*, Charles and Mary Beard

1931

Fiction
1. *The Good Earth*, Pearl S. Buck
2. *Shadows on the Rock*, Willa Cather
3. *A White Bird Flying*, Bess Streeter Aldrich

4. *Grand Hotel*, Vicki Baum
5. *Years of Grace*, Margaret Ayer Barnes
6. *The Road Back*, Erich Maria Remarque
7. *The Bridge of Desire*, Warwick Deeping
8. *Back Street*, Fannie Hurst
9. *Finch's Fortune*, Mazo de la Roche
10. *Maid in Waiting*, John Galsworthy

Nonfiction
1. *Education of a Princess*, Grand Duchess Marie
2. *The Story of San Michele*, Axel Munthe
3. *Washington Merry-Go-Round*, anonymous (Drew Pearson and Robert S. Allen)
4. *Boners: Being a Collection of School-boy Wisdom, or Knowledge as It Is Sometimes Written*, compiled by Alexander Abingdon; illustrated by Dr. Seuss
5. *Culbertson's Summary*, Ely Culbertson
6. *Contract Bridge Blue Book*, Ely Culbertson
7. *Fatal Interview*, Edna St. Vincent Millay
8. *The Epic of America*, James Truslow Adams
9. *Mexico*, Stuart Chase
10. *New Russia's Primer*, Mikhail Ilin

1932

Fiction
1. *The Good Earth*, Pearl S. Buck
2. *The Fountain*, Charles Morgan
3. *Sons*, Pearl S. Buck
4. *Magnolia Street*, Louis Golding
5. *The Sheltered Life*, Ellen Glasgow
6. *Old Wine and New*, Warwick Deeping
7. *Mary's Neck*, Booth Tarkington
8. *Magnificent Obsession*, Lloyd C. Douglas
9. *Inheritance*, Phyllis Bentley
10. *Three Loves*, A. J. Cronin

Nonfiction
1. *The Epic of America*, James Truslow Adams
2. *Only Yesterday*, Frederick Lewis Allen
3. *A Fortune to Share*, Vash Young
4. *Culbertson's Summary*, Ely Culbertson
5. *Van Loon's Geography*, Hendrik Willem Van Loon
6. *What We Live By*, Ernest Dimnet
7. *The March of Democracy*, James Truslow Adams
8. *Washington Merry-Go-Round*, anonymous (Drew Pearson and Robert S. Allen)

9. *The Story of My Life*, Clarence Darrow
10. *More Merry-Go-Round*, anonymous (Drew Pearson and Robert S. Allen)

1933

Fiction
1. *Anthony Adverse*, Hervey Allen
2. *As the Earth Turns*, Gladys Hasty Carroll
3. *Ann Vickers*, Sinclair Lewis
4. *Magnificent Obsession*, Lloyd C. Douglas
5. *One More River*, John Galsworthy
6. *Forgive Us Our Trespasses*, Lloyd C. Douglas
7. *The Master of Jalna*, Mazo de la Roche
8. *Miss Bishop*, Bess Streeter Aldrich
9. *The Farm*, Louis Bromfield
10. *Little Man, What Now?*, Hans Fallada

Nonfiction
1. *Life Begins at Forty*, Walter B. Pitkin
2. *Marie Antoinette*, Stefan Zweig
3. *British Agent*, R. H. Bruce Lockhart
4. *100,000,000 Guinea Pigs*, Arthur Kallet and F. J. Schlink
5. *The House of Exile*, Nora Waln
6. *Van Loon's Geography*, Hendrik Willem Van Loon
7. *Looking Forward*, Franklin D. Roosevelt
8. *Contract Bridge Blue Book of 1933*, Ely Culbertson
9. *The Arches of the Years*, Halliday Sutherland
10. *The March of Democracy*, Vol. II, James Truslow Adams

1934

Fiction
1. *Anthony Adverse*, Hervey Allen
2. *Lamb in His Bosom*, Caroline Miller
3. *So Red the Rose*, Stark Young
4. *Good-Bye, Mr. Chips*, James Hilton
5. *Within This Present*, Margaret Ayer Barnes
6. *Work of Art*, Sinclair Lewis
7. *Private Worlds*, Phyllis Bottome
8. *Mary Peters*, Mary Ellen Chase
9. *Oil for the Lamps of China*, Alice Tisdale Hobart
10. *Seven Gothic Tales*, Isak Dinesen

Nonfiction
1. *While Rome Burns*, Alexander Woollcott
2. *Life Begins at Forty*, Walter B. Pitkin
3. *Nijinsky*, Romola Nijinsky

4. *100,000,000 Guinea Pigs*, Arthur Kallet and F. J. Schlink
5. *The Native's Return*, Louis Adamic
6. *Stars Fell on Alabama*, Carl Carmer
7. *Brazilian Adventure*, Peter Fleming
8. *Forty-two Years in the White House*, Ike Hoover
9. *You Must Relax*, Edmund Jacobson
10. *The Life of Our Lord*, Charles Dickens

1935

Fiction
1. *Green Light*, Lloyd C. Douglas
2. *Vein of Iron*, Ellen Glasgow
3. *Of Time and the River*, Thomas Wolfe
4. *Time Out of Mind*, Rachel Field
5. *Good-Bye, Mr. Chips*, James Hilton
6. *The Forty Days of Musa Dagh*, Franz Werfel
7. *Heaven's My Destination*, Thornton Wilder
8. *Lost Horizon*, James Hilton
9. *Come and Get It*, Edna Ferber
10. *Europa*, Robert Briffault

Nonfiction
1. *North to the Orient*, Anne Morrow Lindbergh
2. *While Rome Burns*, Alexander Woollcott
3. *Life with Father*, Clarence Day
4. *Personal History*, Vincent Sheean
5. *Seven Pillars of Wisdom*, T. E. Lawrence
6. *Francis the First*, Francis Hackett
7. *Mary Queen of Scotland and the Isles*, Stefan Zweig
8. *Rats, Lice and History*, Hans Zinsser
9. *R. E. Lee*, Douglas Southall Freeman
10. *Skin Deep*, M. C. Phillips

1936

Fiction
1. *Gone with the Wind*, Margaret Mitchell
2. *The Last Puritan*, George Santayana
3. *Sparkenbroke*, Charles Morgan
4. *Drums Along the Mohawk*, Walter D. Edmonds
5. *It Can't Happen Here*, Sinclair Lewis
6. *White Banners*, Lloyd C. Douglas
7. *The Hurricane*, Charles Nordhoff and James Norman Hall
8. *The Thinking Reed*, Rebecca West
9. *The Doctor*, Mary Roberts Rinehart
10. *Eyeless in Gaza*, Aldous Huxley

Nonfiction
1. *Man the Unknown*, Alexis Carrel
2. *Wake Up and Live!*, Dorothea Brande

3. *The Way of a Transgressor*, Negley Farson
4. *Around the World in Eleven Years*, Patience, Richard, and Johnny Abbe
5. *North to the Orient*, Anne Morrow Lindbergh
6. *An American Doctor's Odyssey*, Victor Heiser
7. *Inside Europe*, John Gunther
8. *Live Alone and Like It*, Marjorie Hillis
9. *Life with Father*, Clarence Day
10. *I Write As I Please*, Walter Duranty

1937

Fiction

1. *Gone with the Wind*, Margaret Mitchell
2. *Northwest Passage*, Kenneth Roberts
3. *The Citadel*, A. J. Cronin
4. *And So—Victoria*, Vaughan Wilkins
5. *Drums Along the Mohawk*, Walter D. Edmonds
6. *The Years*, Virginia Woolf
7. *Theatre*, W. Somerset Maugham
8. *Of Mice and Men*, John Steinbeck
9. *The Rains Came*, Louis Bromfield
10. *We Are Not Alone*, James Hilton

Nonfiction

1. *How to Win Friends and Influence People*, Dale Carnegie
2. *An American Doctor's Odyssey*, Victor Heiser
3. *The Return to Religion*, Henry C. Link
4. *The Arts*, Hendrik Willem Van Loon
5. *Orchids on Your Budget*, Marjorie Hillis
6. *Present Indicative*, Noel Coward
7. *Mathematics for the Million*, Lancelot Hogben
8. *Life with Mother*, Clarence Day
9. *The Nile*, Emil Ludwig
10. *The Flowering of New England*, Van Wyck Brooks

1938

Fiction

1. *The Yearling*, Marjorie Kinnan Rawlings
2. *The Citadel*, A. J. Cronin
3. *My Son, My Son!*, Howard Spring
4. *Rebecca*, Daphne du Maurier
5. *Northwest Passage*, Kenneth Roberts
6. *All This, and Heaven Too*, Rachel Field
7. *The Rains Came*, Louis Bromfield
8. *And Tell of Time*, Laura Krey
9. *The Mortal Storm*, Phyllis Bottome
10. *Action at Aquila*, Hervey Allen

Nonfiction

1. *The Importance of Living*, Lin Yutang
2. *With Malice Toward Some*, Margaret Halsey
3. *Madame Curie*, Eve Curie
4. *Listen! The Wind*, Anne Morrow Lindbergh
5. *The Horse and Buggy Doctor*, Arthur E. Hertzler
6. *How to Win Friends and Influence People*, Dale Carnegie
7. *Benjamin Franklin*, Carl Van Doren
8. *I'm a Stranger Here Myself*, Ogden Nash
9. *Alone*, Richard E. Byrd
10. *Fanny Kemble*, Margaret Armstrong

1939

Fiction

1. *The Grapes of Wrath*, John Steinbeck
2. *All This, and Heaven Too*, Rachel Field
3. *Rebecca*, Daphne du Maurier
4. *Wickford Point*, John P. Marquand
5. *Escape*, Ethel Vance
6. *Disputed Passage*, Lloyd C. Douglas
7. *The Yearling*, Marjorie Kinnan Rawlings
8. *The Tree of Liberty*, Elizabeth Page
9. *The Nazarene*, Sholem Asch
10. *Kitty Foyle*, Christopher Morley

Nonfiction

1. *Days of Our Years*, Pierre van Paassen
2. *Reaching for the Stars*, Nora Waln
3. *Inside Asia*, John Gunther
4. *Autobiography with Letters*, William Lyon Phelps
5. *Country Lawyer*, Bellamy Partridge
6. *Wind, Sand and Stars*, Antoine de Saint-Exupéry
7. *Mein Kampf*, Adolf Hitler
8. *A Peculiar Treasure*, Edna Ferber
9. *Not Peace but a Sword*, Vincent Sheean
10. *Listen! The Wind*, Anne Morrow Lindbergh

1940

Fiction

1. *How Green Was My Valley*, Richard Llewellyn
2. *Kitty Foyle*, Christopher Morley
3. *Mrs. Miniver*, Jan Struther
4. *For Whom the Bell Tolls*, Ernest Hemingway
5. *The Nazarene*, Sholem Asch
6. *Stars on the Sea*, F. van Wyck Mason
7. *Oliver Wiswell*, Kenneth Roberts
8. *The Grapes of Wrath*, John Steinbeck
9. *Night in Bombay*, Louis Bromfield
10. *The Family*, Nina Fedorova

Nonfiction

1. *I Married Adventure*, Osa Johnson
2. *How to Read a Book*, Mortimer Adler
3. *A Smattering of Ignorance*, Oscar Levant
4. *Country Squire in the White House*, John T. Flynn
5. *Land Below the Wind*, Agnes Newton Keith
6. *American White Paper*, Joseph W. Alsop Jr. and Robert Kintnor
7. *New England: Indian Summer*, Van Wyck Brooks
8. *As I Remember Him*, Hans Zinsser
9. *Days of Our Years*, Pierre van Paassen
10. *Bet It's a Boy*, Betty B. Blunt

1941

Fiction

1. *The Keys of the Kingdom*, A. J. Cronin
2. *Random Harvest*, James Hilton
3. *This Above All*, Eric Knight
4. *The Sun Is My Undoing*, Marguerite Steen
5. *For Whom the Bell Tolls*, Ernest Hemingway
6. *Oliver Wiswell*, Kenneth Roberts
7. *H. M. Pulham, Esquire*, John P. Marquand
8. *Mr. and Mrs. Cugat*, Isabel Scott Rorick
9. *Saratoga Trunk*, Edna Ferber
10. *Windswept*, Mary Ellen Chase

Nonfiction

1. *Berlin Diary*, William L. Shirer
2. *The White Cliffs*, Alice Duer Miller
3. *Out of the Night*, Jan Valtin
4. *Inside Latin America*, John Gunther
5. *Blood, Sweat and Tears*, Winston S. Churchill
6. *You Can't Do Business with Hitler*, Douglas Miller
7. *Reading I've Liked*, Clifton Fadiman, editor
8. *Reveille in Washington*, Margaret Leech
9. *Exit Laughing*, Irvin S. Cobb
10. *My Sister and I*, Dirk van der Heide

1942

Fiction

1. *The Song of Bernadette*, Franz Werfel
2. *The Moon Is Down*, John Steinbeck
3. *Dragon Seed*, Pearl S. Buck
4. *And Now Tomorrow*, Rachel Field
5. *Drivin' Woman*, Elizabeth Pickett
6. *Windswept*, Mary Ellen Chase
7. *The Robe*, Lloyd C. Douglas
8. *The Sun Is My Undoing*, Marguerite Steen
9. *Kings Row*, Henry Bellamann

10. *The Keys of the Kingdom*, A. J. Cronin

Nonfiction
1. *See Here, Private Hargrove*, Marion Hargrove
2. *Mission to Moscow*, Joseph E. Davies
3. *The Last Time I Saw Paris*, Elliot Paul
4. *Cross Creek*, Marjorie Kinnan Rawlings
5. *Victory Through Air Power*, Major Alexander P. de Seversky
6. *Past Imperfect*, Ilka Chase
7. *They Were Expendable*, W. L. White
8. *Flight to Arras*, Antoine de Saint-Exupéry
9. *Washington Is Like That*, W. M. Kiplinger
10. *Inside Latin America*, John Gunther

1943

Fiction
1. *The Robe*, Lloyd C. Douglas
2. *The Valley of Decision*, Marcia Davenport
3. *So Little Time*, John P. Marquand
4. *A Tree Grows in Brooklyn*, Betty Smith
5. *The Human Comedy*, William Saroyan
6. *Mrs. Parkington*, Louis Bromfield
7. *The Apostle*, Sholem Asch
8. *Hungry Hill*, Daphne du Maurier
9. *The Forest and the Fort*, Hervey Allen
10. *The Song of Bernadette*, Franz Werfel

Nonfiction
1. *Under Cover*, John Roy Carlson
2. *One World*, Wendell L. Willkie
3. *Journey Among Warriors*, Eve Curie
4. *On Being a Real Person*, Harry Emerson Fosdick
5. *Guadalcanal Diary*, Richard Tregaskis
6. *Burma Surgeon*, Lt. Col. Gordon Seagrave
7. *Our Hearts Were Young and Gay*, Cornelia Otis Skinner and Emily Kimbrough
8. *U. S. Foreign Policy*, Walter Lippmann
9. *Here Is Your War*, Ernie Pyle
10. *See Here, Private Hargrove*, Marion Hargrove

1944

Fiction
1. *Strange Fruit*, Lillian Smith
2. *The Robe*, Lloyd C. Douglas
3. *A Tree Grows in Brooklyn*, Betty Smith
4. *Forever Amber*, Kathleen Winsor
5. *The Razor's Edge*, W. Somerset Maugham
6. *The Green Years*, A. J. Cronin
7. *Leave Her to Heaven*, Ben Ames Williams

8. *Green Dolphin Street*, Elizabeth Goudge
9. *A Bell for Adano*, John Hersey
10. *The Apostle*, Sholem Asch

Nonfiction
1. *I Never Left Home*, Bob Hope
2. *Brave Men*, Ernie Pyle
3. *Good Night, Sweet Prince*, Gene Fowler
4. *Under Cover*, John Roy Carlson
5. *Yankee from Olympus*, Catherine Drinker Bowen
6. *The Time for Decision*, Sumner Welles
7. *Here Is Your War*, Ernie Pyle
8. *Anna and the King of Siam*, Margaret Landon
9. *The Curtain Rises*, Quentin Reynolds
10. *Ten Years in Japan*, Joseph C. Grew

1945

Fiction
1. *Forever Amber*, Kathleen Winsor
2. *The Robe*, Lloyd C. Douglas
3. *The Black Rose*, Thomas B. Costain
4. *The White Tower*, James Ramsey Ullman
5. *Cass Timberlane*, Sinclair Lewis
6. *A Lion Is in the Streets*, Adria Locke Langley
7. *So Well Remembered*, James Hilton
8. *Captain from Castile*, Samuel Shellabarger
9. *Earth and High Heaven*, Gwethalyn Graham
10. *Immortal Wife*, Irving Stone

Nonfiction
1. *Brave Men*, Ernie Pyle
2. *Dear Sir*, Juliet Lowell
3. *Up Front*, Bill Mauldin
4. *Black Boy*, Richard Wright
5. *Try and Stop Me*, Bennett Cerf
6. *Anything Can Happen*, George and Helen Papashvily
7. *General Marshall's Report*, U.S. War Department General Staff
8. *The Egg and I*, Betty MacDonald
9. *The Thurber Carnival*, James Thurber
10. *Pleasant Valley*, Louis Bromfield

1946

Fiction
1. *The King's General*, Daphne du Maurier
2. *This Side of Innocence*, Taylor Caldwell
3. *The River Road*, Frances Parkinson Keyes
4. *The Miracle of the Bells*, Russell Janney
5. *The Hucksters*, Frederic Wakeman

6. *The Foxes of Harrow*, Frank Yerby
7. *Arch of Triumph*, Erich Maria Remarque
8. *The Black Rose*, Thomas B. Costain
9. *B.F.'s Daughter*, John P. Marquand
10. *The Snake Pit*, Mary Jane Ward

Nonfiction
1. *The Egg and I*, Betty MacDonald
2. *Peace of Mind*, Joshua L. Liebman
3. *As He Saw It*, Elliott Roosevelt
4. *The Roosevelt I Knew*, Frances Perkins
5. *Last Chapter*, Ernie Pyle
6. *Starling of the White House*, Thomas Sugrue and Col. Edmund Starling
7. *I Chose Freedom*, Victor Kravchenko
8. *The Anatomy of Peace*, Emery Reves
9. *Top Secret*, Ralph Ingersoll
10. *A Solo in Tom-Toms*, Gene Fowler

1947

Fiction
1. *The Miracle of the Bells*, Russell Janney
2. *The Moneyman*, Thomas B. Costain
3. *Gentleman's Agreement*, Laura Z. Hobson
4. *Lydia Bailey*, Kenneth Roberts
5. *The Vixens*, Frank Yerby
6. *The Wayward Bus*, John Steinbeck
7. *House Divided*, Ben Ames Williams
8. *Kingsblood Royal*, Sinclair Lewis
9. *East Side, West Side*, Marcia Davenport
10. *Prince of Foxes*, Samuel Shellabarger

Nonfiction
1. *Peace of Mind*, Joshua L. Liebman
2. *Information Please Almanac, 1947*, John Kieran, editor
3. *Inside U.S.A.*, John Gunther
4. *A Study of History*, Arnold J. Toynbee
5. *Speaking Frankly*, James F. Byrnes
6. *Human Destiny*, Pierre Lecomte du Noüy
7. *The Egg and I*, Betty MacDonald
8. *The American Past*, Roger Butterfield
9. *The Fireside Book of Folk Songs*, Margaret B. Boni, editor
10. *Together*, Katharine T. Marshall

1948

Fiction
1. *The Big Fisherman*, Lloyd C. Douglas
2. *The Naked and the Dead*, Norman Mailer
3. *Dinner at Antoine's*, Frances Parkinson Keyes
4. *The Bishop's Mantle*, Agnes Sligh Turnbull
5. *Tomorrow Will Be Better*, Betty Smith

6. *The Golden Hawk*, Frank Yerby
7. *Raintree County*, Ross Lockridge Jr.
8. *Shannon's Way*, A. J. Cronin
9. *Pilgrim's Inn*, Elizabeth Goudge
10. *The Young Lions*, Irwin Shaw

Nonfiction
1. *Crusade in Europe*, Dwight D. Eisenhower
2. *How to Stop Worrying and Start Living*, Dale Carnegie
3. *Peace of Mind*, Joshua L. Liebman
4. *Sexual Behavior in the Human Male*, A. C. Kinsey, et al.
5. *Wine, Women and Words*, Billy Rose
6. *The Life and Times of the Shmoo*, Al Capp
7. *The Gathering Storm*, Winston Churchill
8. *Roosevelt and Hopkins*, Robert E. Sherwood
9. *A Guide to Confident Living*, Norman Vincent Peale
10. *The Plague and I*, Betty MacDonald

1949

Fiction
1. *The Egyptian*, Mika Waltari
2. *The Big Fisherman*, Lloyd C. Douglas
3. *Mary*, Sholem Asch
4. *A Rage to Live*, John O'Hara
5. *Point of No Return*, John P. Marquand
6. *Dinner at Antoine's*, Frances Parkinson Keyes
7. *High Towers*, Thomas B. Costain
8. *Cutlass Empire*, Van Wyck Mason
9. *Pride's Castle*, Frank Yerby
10. *Father of the Bride*, Edward Streeter

Nonfiction
1. *White Collar Zoo*, Clare Barnes Jr.
2. *How to Win at Canasta*, Oswald Jacoby
3. *The Seven Storey Mountain*, Thomas Merton
4. *Home Sweet Zoo*, Clare Barnes Jr.
5. *Cheaper by the Dozen*, Frank B. Gilbreth Jr. and Ernestine Gilbreth Carey
6. *The Greatest Story Ever Told*, Fulton Oursler
7. *Canasta, the Argentine Rummy Game*, Ottilie H. Reilly
8. *Canasta*, Josephine Artayeta de Viel and Ralph Michael
9. *Peace of Soul*, Fulton J. Sheen
10. *A Guide to Confident Living*, Norman Vincent Peale

1950

Fiction
1. *The Cardinal*, Henry Morton Robinson
2. *Joy Street*, Frances Parkinson Keyes
3. *Across the River and into the Trees*, Ernest Hemingway
4. *The Wall*, John Hersey
5. *Star Money*, Kathleen Winsor
6. *The Parasites*, Daphne du Maurier
7. *Floodtide*, Frank Yerby
8. *Jubilee Trail*, Gwen Bristow
9. *The Adventurer*, Mika Waltari
10. *The Disenchanted*, Budd Schulberg

Nonfiction
1. *Betty Crocker's Picture Cook Book*
2. *The Baby*
3. *Look Younger, Live Longer*, Gayelord Hauser

4. *How I Raised Myself from Failure to Success in Selling*, Frank Bettger
5. *Kon-Tiki*, Thor Heyerdahl
6. *Mr. Jones, Meet the Master*, Peter Marshall
7. *Your Dream Home*, Hubbard Cobb
8. *The Mature Mind*, H. A. Overstreet
9. *Campus Zoo*, Clare Barnes Jr.
10. *Belles on Their Toes*, Frank Gilbreth Jr. and Ernestine Gilbreth Carey

1951

Fiction
1. *From Here to Eternity*, James Jones
2. *The Caine Mutiny*, Herman Wouk
3. *Moses*, Sholem Asch
4. *The Cardinal*, Henry Morton Robinson
5. *A Woman Called Fancy*, Frank Yerby
6. *The Cruel Sea*, Nicholas Monsarrat
7. *Melville Goodwin, U.S.A.*, John P. Marquand
8. *Return to Paradise*, James A. Michener
9. *The Foundling*, Cardinal Spellman
10. *The Wanderer*, Mika Waltari

Nonfiction
1. *Look Younger, Live Longer*, Gayelord Hauser
2. *Betty Crocker's Picture Cook Book*
3. *Washington Confidential*, Jack Lait and Lee Mortimer
4. *Better Homes and Gardens Garden Book*
5. *Better Homes and Gardens Handyman's Book*
6. *The Sea Around Us*, Rachel L. Carson
7. *Thorndike-Barnhart Comprehensive Desk Dictionary*, Clarence L. Barnhart, editor
8. *Pogo*, Walt Kelly
9. *Kon-Tiki*, Thor Heyerdahl
10. *The New Yorker Twenty-fifth Anniversary Album*

1952

Fiction
1. *The Silver Chalice*, Thomas B. Costain
2. *The Caine Mutiny*, Herman Wouk
3. *East of Eden*, John Steinbeck
4. *My Cousin Rachel*, Daphne du Maurier
5. *Steamboat Gothic*, Frances Parkinson Keyes
6. *Giant*, Edna Ferber
7. *The Old Man and the Sea*, Ernest Hemingway
8. *The Gown of Glory*, Agnes Sligh Turnbull
9. *The Saracen Blade*, Frank Yerby
10. *The Houses in Between*, Howard Spring

THE LONGEST WORDS

Though most of us will never attempt to use them, these are the longest unhyphenated words in that linguists' Bible, the *Oxford English Dictionary*.

	WORD	LETTERS
1.	pneumonoultramicroscopicsilicovolcanoconiosis	45
2.	supercalifragilisticexpialidocious	34
3.	pseudopseudohypoparathyroidism	30
4.	floccinaucinihilipilification	29
4.	triethylsulphonemethylmethane	29
6.	antidisestablishmentarianism	28
6.	octamethylcyclotetrasiloxane	28
6.	tetrachlorodibenzoparadioxin	28
9.	hepaticocholangiogastronomy	27
10.	radioimmunoelectrophoresis	26
10.	radioimmunoelectrophoretic	26

Nonfiction
1. *The Holy Bible: Revised Standard Version*
2. *A Man Called Peter*, Catherine Marshall
3. *U.S.A. Confidential*, Jack Lait and Lee Mortimer
4. *The Sea Around Us*, Rachel L. Carson
5. *Tallulah*, Tallulah Bankhead
6. *The Power of Positive Thinking*, Norman Vincent Peale
7. *This I Believe*, Edward P. Morgan, editor; Edward R. Murrow, foreword
8. *This Is Ike*, Wilson Hicks, editor
9. *Witness*, Whittaker Chambers
10. *Mr. President*, William Hillman

1953

Fiction
1. *The Robe*, Lloyd C. Douglas
2. *The Silver Chalice*, Thomas B. Costain
3. *Désirée*, Annemarie Selinko
4. *Battle Cry*, Leon M. Uris
5. *From Here to Eternity*, James Jones
6. *The High and the Mighty*, Ernest K. Gann
7. *Beyond This Place*, A. J. Cronin
8. *Time and Time Again*, James Hilton
9. *Lord Vanity*, Samuel Shellabarger
10. *The Unconquered*, Ben Ames Williams

Nonfiction
1. *The Holy Bible: Revised Standard Version*
2. *The Power of Positive Thinking*, Norman Vincent Peale
3. *Sexual Behavior in the Human Female*, Alfred C. Kinsey, et al.
4. *Angel Unaware*, Dale Evans Rogers
5. *Life Is Worth Living*, Fulton J. Sheen
6. *A Man Called Peter*, Catherine Marshall
7. *This I Believe*, Edward P. Morgan, editor; Edward R. Murrow, foreword
8. *The Greatest Faith Ever Known*, Fulton Oursler and G. A. O. Armstrong
9. *How to Play Your Best Golf*, Tommy Armour
10. *A House Is Not a Home*, Polly Adler

1954

Fiction
1. *Not as a Stranger*, Morton Thompson
2. *Mary Anne*, Daphne du Maurier
3. *Love Is Eternal*, Irving Stone
4. *The Royal Box*, Frances Parkinson Keyes
5. *The Egyptian*, Mika Waltari
6. *No Time for Sergeants*, Mac Hyman
7. *Sweet Thursday*, John Steinbeck

8. *The View from Pompey's Head*, Hamilton Basso
9. *Never Victorious, Never Defeated*, Taylor Caldwell
10. *Benton's Row*, Frank Yerby

Nonfiction
1. *The Holy Bible: Revised Standard Version*
2. *The Power of Positive Thinking*, Norman Vincent Peale
3. *Better Homes and Gardens New Cook Book*
4. *Betty Crocker's Good and Easy Cook Book*
5. *The Tumult and the Shouting*, Grantland Rice
6. *I'll Cry Tomorrow*, Lillian Roth, Gerold Frank, and Mike Connolly
7. *The Prayers of Peter Marshall*, Catherine Marshall, editor
8. *This I Believe, 2*, Raymond Swing, editor
9. *But We Were Born Free*, Elmer Davis
10. *The Saturday Evening Post Treasury*, Roger Butterfield, editor

1955

Fiction
1. *Marjorie Morningstar*, Herman Wouk
2. *Auntie Mame*, Patrick Dennis
3. *Andersonville*, MacKinlay Kantor
4. *Bonjour Tristesse*, Françoise Sagan
5. *The Man in the Gray Flannel Suit*, Sloan Wilson
6. *Something of Value*, Robert Ruark
7. *Not As a Stranger*, Morton Thompson
8. *No Time for Sergeants*, Mac Hyman
9. *The Tontine*, Thomas B. Costain
10. *Ten North Frederick*, John O'Hara

Nonfiction
1. *Gift from the Sea*, Anne Morrow Lindbergh
2. *The Power of Positive Thinking*, Norman Vincent Peale
3. *The Family of Man*, Edward Steichen
4. *A Man Called Peter*, Catherine Marshall
5. *How to Live 365 Days a Year*, John A. Schindler
6. *Better Homes and Gardens Diet Book*
7. *The Secret of Happiness*, Billy Graham
8. *Why Johnny Can't Read*, Rudolf Flesch
9. *Inside Africa*, John Gunther
10. *Year of Decisions*, Harry S Truman

1956

Fiction
1. *Don't Go Near the Water*, William Brinkley
2. *The Last Hurrah*, Edwin O'Connor
3. *Peyton Place*, Grace Metalious
4. *Auntie Mame*, Patrick Dennis
5. *Eloise*, Kay Thompson
6. *Andersonville*, MacKinlay Kantor
7. *A Certain Smile*, Françoise Sagan
8. *The Tribe That Lost Its Head*, Nicholas Monsarrat
9. *The Mandarins*, Simone de Beauvoir
10. *Boon Island*, Kenneth Roberts

Nonfiction
1. *Arthritis and Common Sense*, rev. ed., Dan Dale Alexander
2. *Webster's New World Dictionary of the American Language*, concise ed., David B. Guralnik
3. *Betty Crocker's Picture Cook Book*, 2nd. ed.
4. *Etiquette*, Frances Benton
5. *Better Homes and Gardens Barbecue Book*
6. *The Search for Bridey Murphy*, Morey Bernstein
7. *Love or Perish*, Smiley Blanton, M.D.
8. *Better Homes and Gardens Decorating Book*
9. *How to Live 365 Days a Year*, John A. Schindler
10. *The Nun's Story*, Kathryn Hulme

1957

Fiction
1. *By Love Possessed*, James Gould Cozzens
2. *Peyton Place*, Grace Metalious
3. *Compulsion*, Meyer Levin
4. *Rally Round the Flag, Boys!*, Max Shulman
5. *Blue Camellia*, Frances Parkinson Keyes
6. *Eloise in Paris*, Kay Thompson
7. *The Scapegoat*, Daphne du Maurier
8. *On the Beach*, Nevil Shute
9. *Below the Salt*, Thomas B. Costain
10. *Atlas Shrugged*, Ayn Rand

Nonfiction
1. *Kids Say the Darndest Things!*, Art Linkletter
2. *The FBI Story*, Don Whitehead
3. *Stay Alive All Your Life*, Norman Vincent Peale
4. *To Live Again*, Catherine Marshall
5. *Better Homes and Gardens Flower Arranging*

6. *Where Did You Go? Out. What Did You Do? Nothing*, Robert Paul Smith
7. *Baruch: My Own Story*, Bernard M. Baruch
8. *Please Don't Eat the Daisies*, Jean Kerr
9. *The American Heritage Book of Great Historic Places*
10. *The Day Christ Died*, Jim Bishop

1958

Fiction

1. *Doctor Zhivago*, Boris Pasternak
2. *Anatomy of a Murder*, Robert Traver
3. *Lolita*, Vladimir Nabokov
4. *Around the World with Auntie Mame*, Patrick Dennis
5. *From the Terrace*, John O'Hara
6. *Eloise at Christmastime*, Kay Thompson
7. *Ice Palace*, Edna Ferber
8. *The Winthrop Woman*, Anya Seton
9. *The Enemy Camp*, Jerome Weidman
10. *Victorine*, Frances Parkinson Keyes

Nonfiction

1. *Kids Say the Darndest Things!*, Art Linkletter
2. *'Twixt Twelve and Twenty*, Pat Boone
3. *Only in America*, Harry Golden
4. *Masters of Deceit*, Edgar Hoover
5. *Please Don't Eat the Daisies*, Jean Kerr
6. *Better Homes and Gardens Salad Book*
7. *The New Testament in Modern English*, J. P. Phillips, trans.
8. *Aku-Aku*, Thor Heyerdahl
9. *Dear Abby*, Abigail Van Buren
10. *Inside Russia Today*, John Gunther

1959

Fiction

1. *Exodus*, Leon Uris
2. *Doctor Zhivago*, Boris Pasternak
3. *Hawaii*, James Michener
4. *Advise and Consent*, Allen Drury
5. *Lady Chatterley's Lover*, D. H. Lawrence
6. *The Ugly American*, William J. Lederer and Eugene L. Burdick
7. *Dear and Glorious Physician*, Taylor Caldwell
8. *Lolita*, Vladimir Nabokov
9. *Mrs. 'Arris Goes to Paris*, Paul Gallico
10. *Poor No More*, Robert Ruark

Nonfiction

1. *'Twixt Twelve and Twenty*, Pat Boone
2. *Folk Medicine*, D. C. Jarvis

3. *For 2¢ Plain*, Harry Golden
4. *The Status Seekers*, Vance Packard
5. *Act One*, Moss Hart
6. *Charley Weaver's Letters from Mamma*, Cliff Arquette
7. *The Elements of Style*, William Strunk Jr. and E. B. White
8. *The General Foods Kitchens Cookbook*
9. *Only in America*, Harry Golden
10. *Mine Enemy Grows Older*, Alexander King

1960

Fiction

1. *Advise and Consent*, Allen Drury
2. *Hawaii*, James A. Michener
3. *The Leopard*, Giuseppe di Lampedusa
4. *The Chapman Report*, Irving Wallace
5. *Ourselves to Know*, John O'Hara
6. *The Constant Image*, Marcia Davenport
7. *The Lovely Ambition*, Mary Ellen Chase
8. *The Listener*, Taylor Caldwell
9. *Trustee from the Toolroom*, Nevil Shute
10. *Sermons and Soda-Water*, John O'Hara

Nonfiction

1. *Folk Medicine*, D. C. Jarvis
2. *Better Homes and Gardens First Aid for Your Family*
3. *The General Foods Kitchens Cookbook*
4. *May This House Be Safe from Tigers*, Alexander King
5. *Better Homes and Gardens Dessert Book*
6. *Better Homes and Gardens Decorating Ideas*
7. *The Rise and Fall of the Third Reich*, William L. Shirer
8. *The Conscience of a Conservative*, Barry Goldwater
9. *I Kid You Not*, Jack Paar
10. *Between You, Me and the Gatepost*, Pat Boone

1961

Fiction

1. *The Agony and the Ecstasy*, Irving Stone
2. *Franny and Zooey*, J. D. Salinger
3. *To Kill a Mockingbird*, Harper Lee
4. *Mila 18*, Leon Uris
5. *The Carpetbaggers*, Harold Robbins
6. *Tropic of Cancer*, Henry Miller
7. *Winnie Ille Pu*, Alexander Lenard, trans.
8. *Daughter of Silence*, Morris West

9. *The Edge of Sadness*, Edwin O'Connor
10. *The Winter of Our Discontent*, John Steinbeck

Nonfiction

1. *The New English Bible: The New Testament*
2. *The Rise and Fall of the Third Reich*, William Shirer
3. *Better Homes and Gardens Sewing Book*
4. *Casserole Cook Book*
5. *A Nation of Sheep*, William Lederer
6. *Better Homes and Gardens Nutrition for Your Family*
7. *The Making of the President, 1960*, Theodore H. White
8. *Calories Don't Count*, Dr. Herman Taller
9. *Betty Crocker's New Picture Cook Book: New Edition*
10. *Ring of Bright Water*, Gavin Maxwell

1962

Fiction

1. *Ship of Fools*, Katherine Anne Porter
2. *Dearly Beloved*, Anne Morrow Lindbergh
3. *A Shade of Difference*, Allen Drury
4. *Youngblood Hawke*, Herman Wouk
5. *Franny and Zooey*, J. D. Salinger
6. *Fail-Safe*, Eugene Burdick and Harvey Wheeler
7. *Seven Days in May*, Fletcher Knebel and Charles W. Bailey II
8. *The Prize*, Irving Wallace
9. *The Agony and the Ecstasy*, Irving Stone
10. *The Reivers*, William Faulkner

Nonfiction

1. *Calories Don't Count*, Dr. Herman Taller
2. *The New English Bible: The New Testament*
3. *Better Homes and Gardens Cook Book: New Edition*
4. *O Ye Jigs & Juleps!*, Virginia Cary Hudson
5. *Happiness Is a Warm Puppy*, Charles M. Schulz
6. *The Joy of Cooking: New Edition*, Irma S. Rombauer and Marion Rombauer Becker
7. *My Life in Court*, Louis Nizer
8. *The Rothschilds*, Frederic Morton
9. *Sex and the Single Girl*, Helen Gurley Brown
10. *Travels with Charley*, John Steinbeck

1963

Fiction

1. *The Shoes of the Fisherman*, Morris L. West
2. *The Group*, Mary McCarthy
3. *Raise High the Roof Beam, Carpenters, and Seymour—An Introduction*, J. D. Salinger
4. *Caravans*, James A. Michener
5. *Elizabeth Appleton*, John O'Hara
6. *Grandmother and the Priests*, Taylor Caldwell
7. *City of Night*, John Rechy
8. *The Glass-Blowers*, Daphne du Maurier
9. *The Sand Pebbles*, Richard McKenna
10. *The Battle of the Villa Fiorita*, Rumer Godden

Nonfiction

1. *Happiness Is a Warm Puppy*, Charles M. Schulz
2. *Security Is a Thumb and a Blanket*, Charles M. Schulz

3. *J.F.K.: The Man and the Myth*, Victor Lasky
4. *Profiles in Courage: Inaugural Edition*, John F. Kennedy
5. *O Ye Jigs & Juleps!*, Virginia Cary Hudson
6. *Better Homes and Gardens Bread Cook Book*
7. *The Pillsbury Family Cookbook*
8. *I Owe Russia $1200*, Bob Hope
9. *Heloise's Housekeeping Hints*
10. *Better Homes and Gardens Baby Book*

1964

Fiction

1. *The Spy Who Came in from the Cold*, John le Carré
2. *Candy*, Terry Southern and Mason Hoffenberg
3. *Herzog*, Saul Bellow
4. *Armageddon*, Leon Uris
5. *The Man*, Irving Wallace
6. *The Rector of Justin*, Louis Auchincloss

7. *The Martyred*, Richard E. Kim
8. *You Only Live Twice*, Ian Fleming
9. *This Rough Magic*, Mary Stewart
10. *Convention*, Fletcher Knebel and Charles W. Bailey II

Nonfiction

1. *Four Days*, American Heritage and United Press International
2. *I Need All the Friends I Can Get*, Charles M. Schulz
3. *Profiles in Courage: Memorial Edition*, John F. Kennedy
4. *In His Own Write*, John Lennon
5. *Christmas Is Together-Time*, Charles M. Schulz
6. *A Day in the Life of President Kennedy*, Jim Bishop
7. *The Kennedy Wit*, compiled by Bill Adler
8. *A Moveable Feast*, Ernest Hemingway
9. *Reminiscences*, General Douglas MacArthur
10. *The John F. Kennedys*, Mark Shaw

LITERATURE GOES TO THE MOVIES

It's no secret that many movies, both good and bad, are based on books. This list presents a small sampling of unusual, delightful, and surprising books by leading writers that were turned into well-known movies. (The dates after the titles indicate the year of the film version's release.)

American Hero (released as *Wag the Dog*, 1997), Larry Beinhart
Awakenings (1990), Oliver Sacks
The Blue Angel (1930, 1959), Heinrich Mann
The Body Snatcher (1945), Robert Louis Stevenson
Breakfast at Tiffany's (1961), Truman Capote
Burning Patience (released as *Il Postino (The Postman)*, 1995), Antonio Skarmeta
Chitty, Chitty, Bang, Bang (1968), Ian Fleming
The Death and Life of Dith Pran (released as *The Killing Fields*, 1984), Sidney Schanberg
Deliverance (1972), James Dickey
Do Androids Dream of Electric Sheep? (released as *Blade Runner*, 1982), Philip K. Dick
Donnie Brasco: My Undercover Life in the Mafia (released as *Donnie Brasco*, 1997), Joseph D. Pistone with Richard Woodley
Don't Look Now (1971), Daphne du Maurier
Dream Story (released as *Eyes Wide Shut*, 1999), Arthur Schnitzler
The Executioners (released as *Cape Fear*, 1962, 1991), J. D. MacDonald
The Grifters (1990), Jim Thompson
The Hamlet (originally *The Long, Hot Summer*, 1957) William Faulkner
Jumanji (1995), Chris Van Allsburg

The Killer Angels (released as *Gettysburg*, 1993), Michael Shaara
L.A. Confidential (1997), James Ellroy
The Last Picture Show (1971), Larry McMurtry
Legends of the Fall (1994), Jim Harrison
Lost Moon (released as *Apollo 13*, 1995), Jim Lovell and Jeffrey Kluger
The Magnificent Ambersons (1942), Booth Tarkington
The Maltese Falcon (1941; also released as *Satan Met a Lady*, 1937), Dashiell Hammett
Mildred Pierce (1945), James M. Cain
The Natural (1984), Bernard Malamud
The Postman Always Rings Twice (1946, 1981), James M. Cain
Psycho (1960), Robert Bloch
Rum Punch (released as *Jackie Brown*, 1997), Elmore Leonard
The Seven Pillars of Wisdom (released as *Lawrence of Arabia*, 1962), T. E. Lawrence
Seven Years in Tibet (1997), Heinrich Harrar
Starship Troopers (1997), Robert A. Heinlein
Tales from the South Pacific (produced as the musical *South Pacific* and later released as a film, 1958), James Michener
The Turn of the Screw (released as *The Innocents*, 1961), Henry James
Two Hours to Doom (released as *Dr. Strangelove*, 1964), Peter George

1965

Fiction

1. *The Source*, James A. Michener
2. *Up the Down Staircase*, Bel Kaufman
3. *Herzog*, Saul Bellow
4. *The Looking Glass War*, John le Carré
5. *The Green Berets*, Robin Moore
6. *Those Who Love*, Irving Stone
7. *The Man with the Golden Gun*, Ian Fleming
8. *Hotel*, Arthur Hailey
9. *The Ambassador*, Morris West
10. *Don't Stop the Carnival*, Herman Wouk

Nonfiction

1. *How to Be a Jewish Mother*, Dan Greenburg
2. *A Gift of Prophecy*, Ruth Montgomery
3. *Games People Play*, Eric Berne, M.D.
4. *World Aflame*, Billy Graham
5. *Happiness Is a Dry Martini*, Johnny Carson
6. *Markings*, Dag Hammarskjöld
7. *A Thousand Days*, Arthur Schlesinger Jr.
8. *My Shadow Ran Fast*, Bill Sands
9. *Kennedy*, Theodore C. Sorensen
10. *The Making of the President, 1964*, Theodore H. White

1966

Fiction

1. *Valley of the Dolls*, Jacqueline Susann
2. *The Adventurers*, Harold Robbins
3. *The Secret of Santa Vittoria*, Robert Crichton
4. *Capable of Honor*, Allen Drury
5. *The Double Image*, Helen MacInnes
6. *The Fixer*, Bernard Malamud
7. *Tell No Man*, Adela Rogers St. Johns
8. *Tai-Pan*, James Clavell
9. *The Embezzler*, Louis Auchincloss
10. *All in the Family*, Edwin O'Connor

Nonfiction

1. *How to Avoid Probate*, Norman F. Dacey
2. *Human Sexual Response*, William Howard Masters and Virginia E. Johnston
3. *In Cold Blood*, Truman Capote
4. *Games People Play*, Eric Berne, M.D.
5. *A Thousand Days*, Arthur M. Schlesinger Jr.
6. *Everything but Money*, Sam Levenson
7. *The Random House Dictionary of the English Language*
8. *Rush to Judgment*, Mark Lane
9. *The Last Battle*, Cornelius Ryan
10. *Phyllis Diller's Housekeeping Hints*, Phyllis Diller

1967

Fiction

1. *The Arrangement*, Elia Kazan
2. *The Confessions of Nat Turner*, William Styron (tie)
2. *The Chosen*, Chaim Potok (tie)
4. *Topaz*, Leon Uris
5. *Christy*, Catherine Marshall
6. *The Eighth Day*, Thornton Wilder
7. *Rosemary's Baby*, Ira Levin
8. *The Plot*, Irving Wallace
9. *The Gabriel Hounds*, Mary Stewart
10. *The Exhibitionist*, Henry Sutton

Nonfiction

1. *Death of a President*, William Manchester
2. *Misery Is a Blind Date*, Johnny Carson
3. *Games People Play*, Eric Berne, M.D.
4. *Stanyan Street and Other Sorrows*, Rod McKuen
5. *A Modern Priest Looks at His Outdated Church*, Father James Kavanaugh
6. *Everything but Money*, Sam Levenson
7. *Our Crowd*, Stephen Birmingham
8. *Edgar Cayce—The Sleeping Prophet*, Jess Stearn (tie)
8. *Better Homes and Gardens Favorite Ways with Chicken* (tie)
8. *Phyllis Diller's Marriage Manual*, Phyllis Diller (tie)

1968

Fiction

1. *Airport*, Arthur Hailey
2. *Couples*, John Updike
3. *The Salzburg Connection*, Helen MacInnes
4. *A Small Town in Germany*, John Le Carré
5. *Testimony of Two Men*, Taylor Caldwell
6. *Preserve and Protect*, Allen Drury
7. *Myra Breckinridge*, Gore Vidal
8. *Vanished*, Fletcher Knebel
9. *Christy*, Catherine Marshall
10. *The Tower of Babel*, Morris L. West

Nonfiction

1. *Better Homes and Gardens New Cook Book*
2. *The Random House Dictionary of the English Language: College Edition*, Laurence Urdang, editor
3. *Listen to the Warm*, Rod McKuen
4. *Between Parent and Child*, Haim G. Ginott
5. *Lonesome Cities*, Rod McKuen
6. *The Doctor's Quick Weight Loss Diet*, Erwin M. Stillman and Samm Sinclair Baker
7. *The Money Game*, Adam Smith
8. *Stanyan Street and Other Sorrows*, Rod McKuen
9. *The Weight Watcher's Cook Book*, Jean Nidetch
10. *Better Homes and Gardens Eat and Stay Slim*

1969

Fiction

1. *Portnoy's Complaint*, Philip Roth
2. *The Godfather*, Mario Puzo
3. *The Love Machine*, Jacqueline Susann
4. *The Inheritors*, Harold Robbins
5. *The Andromeda Strain*, Michael Crichton
6. *The Seven Minutes*, Irving Wallace
7. *Naked Came the Stranger*, Penelope Ashe
8. *The Promise*, Chaim Potok
9. *The Pretenders*, Gwen Davis
10. *The House on the Strand*, Daphne du Maurier

Nonfiction

1. *American Heritage Dictionary of the English Language*, William Morris, editor
2. *In Someone's Shadow*, Rod McKuen
3. *The Peter Principle*, Laurence J. Peter and Raymond Hull
4. *Between Parent and Teenager*, Dr. Haim G. Ginott
5. *The Graham Kerr Cookbook*, The Galloping Gourmet
6. *The Selling of the President, 1968*, Joe McGinniss
7. *Miss Craig's 21-Day Shape-Up Program for Men and Women*, Marjorie Craig
8. *My Life and Prophecies*, Jeane Dixon with René Noorbergen
9. *Linda Goodman's Sun Signs*, Linda Goodman
10. *Twelve Years of Christmas*, Rod McKuen

1970

Fiction

1. *Love Story*, Erich Segal
2. *The French Lieutenant's Woman*, John Fowles
3. *Islands in the Stream*, Ernest Hemingway
4. *The Crystal Cave*, Mary Stewart
5. *Great Lion of God*, Taylor Caldwell
6. *QB VII*, Leon Uris

7. *The Gang That Couldn't Shoot Straight*, Jimmy Breslin
8. *The Secret Woman*, Victoria Holt
9. *Travels with My Aunt*, Graham Greene
10. *Rich Man, Poor Man*, Irwin Shaw

Nonfiction

1. *Everything You Always Wanted to Know About Sex but Were Afraid to Ask*, David Reuben, M.D.
2. *The New English Bible*
3. *The Sensuous Woman*, "J"
4. *Better Homes and Gardens Fondue and Tabletop Cooking*
5. *Up the Organization*, Robert Townsend
6. *Ball Four*, Jim Bouton
7. *American Heritage Dictionary of the English Language*, William Morris
8. *Body Language*, Julius Fast
9. *In Someone's Shadow*, Rod McKuen
10. *Caught in the Quiet*, Rod McKuen

1971

Fiction

1. *Wheels*, Arthur Hailey
2. *The Exorcist*, William P. Blatty
3. *The Passions of the Mind*, Irving Stone
4. *The Day of the Jackal*, Frederick Forsyth
5. *The Betsy*, Harold Robbins
6. *Message from Malaga*, Helen MacInnes
7. *The Winds of War*, Herman Wouk
8. *The Drifters*, James A. Michener
9. *The Other*, Thomas Tryon
10. *Rabbit Redux*, John Updike

Nonfiction

1. *The Sensous Man*, "M"
2. *Bury My Heart at Wounded Knee*, Dee Brown
3. *Better Homes and Gardens Blender Cook Book*
4. *I'm O.K., You're O.K.*, Thomas Harris
5. *Any Woman Can!*, David Reuben, M.D.
6. *Inside the Third Reich*, Albert Speer
7. *Eleanor and Franklin*, Joseph P. Lash
8. *Wunnerful, Wunnerful!*, Lawrence Welk
9. *Honor Thy Father*, Gay Talese
10. *Fields of Wonder*, Rod McKuen

1972

Fiction

1. *Jonathan Livingston Seagull*, Richard Bach
2. *August, 1914*, Alexander Solzhenitsyn
3. *The Odessa File*, Frederick Forsyth

4. *The Day of the Jackal*, Frederick Forsyth
5. *The Word*, Irving Wallace
6. *The Winds of War*, Herman Wouk
7. *Captains and the Kings*, Taylor Caldwell
8. *Two from Galilee*, Marjorie Holmes
9. *My Name Is Asher Lev*, Chaim Potok
10. *Semi-Tough*, Dan Jenkins

Nonfiction

1. *The Living Bible*, Kenneth Taylor
2. *I'm O.K., You're O.K.*, Thomas Harris
3. *Open Marriage*, Nena and George O'Neill
4. *Harry S. Truman*, Margaret Truman
5. *Dr. Atkins' Diet Revolution*, Robert C. Atkins
6. *Better Homes and Gardens Menu Cook Book*
7. *The Peter Prescription*, Laurence J. Peter
8. *A World Beyond*, Ruth Montgomery
9. *Journey to Ixtlan*, Carlos Castaneda
10. *Better Homes and Gardens Low-Calorie Desserts*

1973

Fiction

1. *Jonathan Livingston Seagull*, Richard Bach
2. *Once Is Not Enough*, Jacqueline Susann
3. *Breakfast of Champions*, Kurt Vonnegut
4. *The Odessa File*, Frederick Forsyth
5. *Burr*, Gore Vidal
6. *The Hollow Hills*, Mary Stewart
7. *Evening in Byzantium*, Irwin Shaw
8. *The Matlock Paper*, Robert Ludlum
9. *The Billion Dollar Sure Thing*, Paul E. Erdman
10. *The Honorary Consul*, Graham Greene

Nonfiction

1. *The Living Bible*, Kenneth Taylor
2. *Dr. Atkins' Diet Revolution*, Robert C. Atkins
3. *I'm O.K., You're O.K.*, Thomas Harris
4. *The Joy of Sex*, Alex Comfort
5. *Weight Watchers Program Cookbook*, Jean Nidetch
6. *How to Be Your Own Best Friend*, Mildred Newman, et al.
7. *The Art of Walt Disney*, Christopher Finch
8. *Better Homes and Gardens Home Canning Cookbook*
9. *Alistair Cooke's America*, Alistair Cooke
10. *Sybil*, Flora R. Schreiber

1974

Fiction

1. *Centennial*, James A. Michener
2. *Watership Down*, Richard Adams
3. *Jaws*, Peter Benchley
4. *Tinker, Tailor, Soldier, Spy*, John le Carré
5. *Something Happened*, Joseph Heller
6. *The Dogs of War*, Frederick Forsyth
7. *The Pirate*, Harold J. Robbins
8. *I Heard the Owl Call My Name*, Margaret Craven
9. *The Seven-Per-Cent Solution*, John H. Watson, M.D., Nicholas Meyer, editor
10. *The Fan Club*, Irving Wallace

Nonfiction

1. *The Total Woman*, Marabel Morgan
2. *All the President's Men*, Carl Bernstein and Bob Woodward
3. *Plain Speaking: An Oral Biography of Harry S. Truman*, Merle Miller
4. *More Joy: A Lovemaking Companion to The Joy of Sex*, Alex Comfort
5. *Alistair Cooke's America*, Alistair Cooke
6. *Tales of Power*, Carlos A. Castaneda
7. *You Can Profit from a Monetary Crisis*, Harry Browne
8. *All Things Bright and Beautiful*, James Herriot
9. *The Bermuda Triangle*, Charles Berlitz with J. Manson Valentine
10. *The Memory Book*, Harry Lorayne and Jerry Lucas

1975

Fiction

1. *Ragtime*, E. L. Doctorow
2. *The Moneychangers*, Arthur Hailey
3. *Curtain*, Agatha Christie
4. *Looking for Mister Goodbar*, Judith Rossner
5. *The Choirboys*, Joseph Wambaugh
6. *The Eagle Has Landed*, Jack Higgins
7. *The Greek Treasure: A Biographical Novel of Henry and Sophia Schliemann*, Irving Stone
8. *The Great Train Robbery*, Michael Crichton
9. *Shogun*, James Clavell
10. *Humboldt's Gift*, Saul Bellow

Nonfiction

1. *Angels: God's Secret Agents*, Billy Graham
2. *Winning Through Intimidation*, Robert Ringer

3. *TM: Discovering Energy and Overcoming Stress*, Harold H. Bloomfield
4. *The Ascent of Man*, Jacob Bronowski
5. *Sylvia Porter's Money Book*, Sylvia Porter
6. *Total Fitness in 30 Minutes a Week*, Laurence E. Morehouse and Leonard Gross
7. *The Bermuda Triangle*, Charles Berlitz with J. Manson Valentine
8. *The Save-Your-Life Diet*, David Reuben
9. *Bring on the Empty Horses*, David Niven
10. *Breach of Faith: The Fall of Richard Nixon*, Theodore H. White

1976

Fiction
1. *Trinity*, Leon Uris
2. *Sleeping Murder*, Agatha Christie
3. *Dolores*, Jacqueline Susann
4. *Storm Warning*, Jack Higgins
5. *The Deep*, Peter Benchley
6. *1876*, Gore Vidal
7. *Slapstick: or, Lonesome No More!*, Kurt Vonnegut
8. *The Lonely Lady*, Harold Robbins
9. *Touch Not the Cat*, Mary Stewart
10. *A Stranger in the Mirror*, Sidney Sheldon

Nonfiction
1. *The Final Days*, Bob Woodward and Carl Bernstein
2. *Roots*, Alex Haley
3. *Your Erroneous Zones*, Dr. Wayne W. Dyer

AMERICA'S POETS LAUREATE

To honor America's greatest poets, the Librarian of Congress names a poet laureate. The anointed:

Robert Penn Warren	1986–87
Richard Wilbur	1987–88
Howard Nemerov	1988–90
Mark Strand	1990–91
Joseph Brodsky	1991–92
Mona Van Duyn	1992–93
Rita Dove	1993–95
Robert Hass	1995–97
Robert Pinsky	1997–00
Stanley Kunitz	2000–

4. *Passages: The Predictable Crises of Adult Life*, Gail Sheehy
5. *Born Again*, Charles W. Colson
6. *The Grass Is Always Greener over the Septic Tank*, Erma Bombeck
7. *Angels: God's Secret Agents*, Billy Graham
8. *Blind Ambition: The White House Years*, John Dean
9. *The Hite Report: A Nationwide Study of Female Sexuality*, Shere Hite
10. *The Right and the Power: The Prosecution of Watergate*, Leon Jaworski

1977

Fiction
1. *The Silmarillion*, J. R. R. Tolkien; Christopher Tolkien
2. *The Thorn Birds*, Colleen McCullough
3. *Illusions: The Adventures of a Reluctant Messiah*, Richard Bach
4. *The Honourable Schoolboy*, John le Carré
5. *Oliver's Story*, Erich Segal
6. *Dreams Die First*, Harold Robbins
7. *Beggarman, Thief*, Irwin Shaw
8. *How to Save Your Own Life*, Erica Jong
9. *Delta of Venus: Erotica*, Anaïs Nin
10. *Daniel Martin*, John Fowles

Nonfiction
1. *Roots*, Alex Haley
2. *Looking Out for #1*, Robert Ringer
3. *All Things Wise and Wonderful*, James Herriot
4. *Your Erroneous Zones*, Dr. Wayne W. Dyer
5. *The Book of Lists*, David Wallechinsky, Irving Wallace, and Amy Wallace
6. *The Possible Dream: A Candid Look at Amway*, Charles Paul Conn
7. *The Dragons of Eden: Speculations on the Evolution of Human Intelligence*, Carl Sagan
8. *The Second Ring of Power*, Carlos Castaneda
9. *The Grass Is Always Greener over the Septic Tank*, Erma Bombeck
10. *The Amityville Horror*, Jay Anson

1978

Fiction
1. *Chesapeake*, James A. Michener
2. *War and Remembrance*, Herman Wouk
3. *Fools Die*, Mario Puzo
4. *Bloodlines*, Sidney Sheldon
5. *Scruples*, Judith Krantz
6. *Evergreen*, Belva Plain
7. *Illusions: The Adventures of a Reluctant Messiah*, Richard Bach

8. *The Holcroft Covenant*, Robert Ludlum
9. *Second Generation*, Howard Fast
10. *Eye of the Needle*, Ken Follett

Nonfiction
1. *If Life Is a Bowl of Cherries—What Am I Doing in the Pits?*, Erma Bombeck
2. *Gnomes*, Wil Huygen and Rien Poortvliet
3. *The Complete Book of Running*, James Fixx
4. *Mommie Dearest*, Christina Crawford
5. *Pulling Your Own Strings*, Dr. Wayne W. Dyer
6. *RN: The Memoirs of Richard Nixon*, Richard Nixon
7. *A Distant Mirror: The Calamitous Fourteenth Century*, Barbara Tuchman
8. *Faeries*, Brian Froud and Alan Lee
9. *In Search of History: A Personal Adventure*, Theodore H. White
10. *The Muppet Show Book*, The Muppet People

1979

Fiction
1. *The Matarese Circle*, Robert Ludlum
2. *Sophie's Choice*, William Styron
3. *Overload*, Arthur Hailey
4. *Memories of Another Day*, Harold Robbins
5. *Jailbird*, Kurt Vonnegut
6. *The Dead Zone*, Stephen King
7. *The Last Enchantment*, Mary Stewart
8. *The Establishment*, Howard Fast
9. *The Third World War: August 1985*, Gen. Sir John Hackett, et al.
10. *Smiley's People*, John le Carré

Nonfiction
1. *Aunt Erma's Cope Book*, Erma Bombeck
2. *The Complete Scarsdale Medical Diet*, Herman Tarnower, M.D., and Samm Sinclair Baker
3. *How to Prosper During the Coming Bad Years*, Howard J. Ruff
4. *Cruel Shoes*, Steve Martin
5. *The Pritikin Program for Diet and Exercise*, Nathan Pritikin and Patrick McGrady Jr.
6. *White House Years*, Henry Kissinger
7. *Lauren Bacall: By Myself*, Lauren Bacall
8. *The Brethren: Inside the Supreme Court*, Bob Woodward and Scott Armstrong
9. *Restoring the American Dream*, Robert J. Ringer
10. *The Winner's Circle*, Charles Paul Conn

1980

Fiction
1. *The Covenant*, James A. Michener
2. *The Bourne Identity*, Robert Ludlum
3. *Rage of Angels*, Sidney Sheldon
4. *Princess Daisy*, Judith Krantz
5. *Firestarter*, Stephen King
6. *The Key to Rebecca*, Ken Follett
7. *Random Winds*, Belva Plain
8. *The Devil's Alternative*, Frederick Forsyth
9. *The Fifth Horseman*, Larry Collins and Dominique Lapierre
10. *The Spike*, Arnaud de Borchgrave and Robert Moss

Nonfiction
1. *Crisis Investing: Opportunities and Profits in the Coming Great Depression*, Douglas R. Casey
2. *Cosmos*, Carl Sagan
3. *Free to Choose: A Personal Statement*, Milton and Rose Friedman
4. *Anatomy of an Illness as Perceived by the Patient*, Norman Cousins
5. *Thy Neighbor's Wife*, Gay Talese
6. *The Sky's the Limit*, Dr. Wayne W. Dyer
7. *The Third Wave*, Alvin Toffler
8. *Craig Claiborne's Gourmet Diet*, Craig Claiborne with Pierre Franey
9. *Nothing Down*, Robert Allen
10. *Shelley: Also Known as Shirley*, Shelley Winters

1981

Fiction
1. *Noble House*, James Clavell
2. *The Hotel New Hampshire*, John Irving
3. *Cujo*, Stephen King
4. *An Indecent Obsession*, Colleen McCullough
5. *Gorky Park*, Martin Cruz Smith
6. *Masquerade*, Kit Williams
7. *Goodbye, Janette*, Harold Robbins
8. *The Third Deadly Sin*, Lawrence Sanders
9. *The Glitter Dome*, Joseph Wambaugh
10. *No Time for Tears*, Cynthia Freeman

Nonfiction
1. *The Beverly Hills Diet*, Judy Mazel
2. *The Lord God Made Them All*, James Herriot
3. *Richard Simmons' Never-Say-Diet Book*, Richard Simmons
4. *A Light in the Attic*, Shel Silverstein
5. *Cosmos*, Carl Sagan
6. *Better Homes & Gardens New Cook Book*

7. *Miss Piggy's Guide to Life*, Miss Piggy as told to Henry Beard
8. *Weight Watchers 365-Day Menu Cookbook*
9. *You Can Negotiate Anything*, Herb Cohen
10. *A Few Minutes with Andy Rooney*, Andrew A. Rooney

1982

Fiction
1. *E.T., the Extra-Terrestrial Storybook*, William Kotzwinkle
2. *Space*, James A. Michener
3. *The Parsifal Mosaic*, Robert Ludlum
4. *Master of the Game*, Sidney Sheldon
5. *Mistral's Daughter*, Judith Krantz
6. *The Valley of Horses*, Jean M. Auel
7. *Different Seasons*, Stephen King
8. *North and South*, John Jakes
9. *2010: Odyssey Two*, Arthur C. Clarke
10. *The Man from St. Petersburg*, Ken Follett

Nonfiction
1. *Jane Fonda's Workout Book*, Jane Fonda
2. *Living, Loving and Learning*, Leo Buscaglia
3. *And More by Andy Rooney*, Andrew A. Rooney
4. *Better Homes & Gardens New Cookbook*
5. *Life Extension: Adding Years to Your Life and Life to Your Years—A Practical Scientific Approach*, Durk Pearson and Sandy Shaw
6. *When Bad Things Happen to Good People*, Harold S. Kushner
7. *A Few Minutes with Andy Rooney*, Andrew A. Rooney
8. *The Weight Watchers Food Plan Diet Cookbook*, Jean Nidetch
9. *Richard Simmons' Never-Say-Diet Cookbook*, Richard Simmons
10. *No Bad Dogs: The Woodhouse Way*, Barbara Woodhouse

1983

Fiction
1. *Return of the Jedi Storybook*, Joan D. Vinge, adapt.
2. *Poland*, James A. Michener
3. *Pet Sematary*, Stephen King
4. *The Little Drummer Girl*, John le Carré
5. *Christine*, Stephen King
6. *Changes*, Danielle Steel
7. *The Name of the Rose*, Umberto Eco
8. *White Gold Wielder: Book Three of The Second Chronicles of Thomas Covenant*, Stephen R. Donaldson
9. *Hollywood Wives*, Jackie Collins
10. *The Lonesome Gods*, Louis L'Amour

Nonfiction
1. *In Search of Excellence: Lessons from America's Best-Run Companies*, Thomas J. Peters and Robert H. Waterman Jr.
2. *Megatrends: Ten New Directions Transforming Our Lives*, John Naisbitt
3. *Motherhood: The Second Oldest Profession*, Erma Bombeck
4. *The One Minute Manager*, Kenneth Blanchard and Spencer Johnson
5. *Jane Fonda's Workout Book*, Jane Fonda
6. *The Best of James Herriot*, James Herriot
7. *The Mary Kay Guide to Beauty: Discovering Your Special Look*
8. *On Wings of Eagles*, Ken Follett
9. *Creating Wealth*, Robert G. Allen
10. *The Body Principal: The Exercise Program for Life*, Victoria Principal

1984

Fiction
1. *The Talisman*, Stephen King and Peter Straub
2. *The Aquitaine Progression*, Robert Ludlum
3. *The Sicilian*, Mario Puzo
4. *Love and War*, John Jakes
5. *The Butter Battle Book*, Dr. Seuss
6. *". . . And the Ladies of the Club,"* Helen Hooven Santmyer
7. *The Fourth Protocol*, Frederick Forsyth
8. *Full Circle*, Danielle Steel
9. *The Life and Hard Times of Heidi Abromowitz*, Joan Rivers
10. *Lincoln: A Novel*, Gore Vidal

Nonfiction
1. *Iacocca: An Autobiography*, Lee Iacocca with William Novak
2. *Loving Each Other*, Leo Buscaglia
3. *Eat to Win: The Sports Nutrition Bible*, Robert Haas, M.D.
4. *Pieces of My Mind*, Andrew A. Rooney
5. *Weight Watchers Fast and Fabulous Cookbook*
6. *What They Don't Teach You at Harvard Business School: Notes from a Street-Smart Executive*, Mark H. McCormack
7. *Women Coming of Age*, Jane Fonda with Mignon McCarthy
8. *Moses the Kitten*, James Herriot
9. *The One Minute Salesperson*, Spencer Johnson, M.D., and Larry Wilson
10. *Weight Watchers Quick Start Program Cookbook*, Jean Nidetch

1985

Fiction
1. *The Mammoth Hunters*, Jean M. Auel
2. *Texas*, James A. Michener
3. *Lake Wobegon Days*, Garrison Keillor
4. *If Tomorrow Comes*, Sidney Sheldon
5. *Skeleton Crew*, Stephen King
6. *Secrets*, Danielle Steel
7. *Contact*, Carl Sagan
8. *Lucky*, Jackie Collins
9. *Family Album*, Danielle Steel
10. *Jubal Sackett*, Louis L'Amour

Nonfiction
1. *Iacocca: An Autobiography*, Lee Iacocca with William Novak
2. *Yeager: An Autobiography*, Gen. Chuck Yeager and Leo Janos
3. *Elvis and Me*, Priscilla Beaulieu Presley with Sandra Harmon
4. *Fit for Life*, Harvey and Marilyn Diamond
5. *The Be-Happy Attitudes*, Robert Schuller
6. *Dancing in the Light*, Shirley MacLaine
7. *A Passion for Excellence: The Leadership Difference*, Thomas J. Peters and Nancy K. Austin
8. *The Frugal Gourmet*, Jeff Smith
9. *I Never Played the Game*, Howard Cosell with Peter Bonventre
10. *Dr. Berger's Immune Power Diet*, Stuart M. Berger, M.D.

1986

Fiction
1. *It*, Stephen King
2. *Red Storm Rising*, Tom Clancy
3. *Whirlwind*, James Clavell
4. *The Bourne Supremacy*, Robert Ludlum
5. *Hollywood Husbands*, Jackie Collins
6. *Wanderlust*, Danielle Steel
7. *I'll Take Manhattan*, Judith Krantz
8. *Last of the Breed*, Louis L'Amour
9. *The Prince of Tides*, Pat Conroy
10. *A Perfect Spy*, John le Carré

Nonfiction
1. *Fatherhood*, Bill Cosby
2. *Fit for Life*, Harvey and Marilyn Diamond
3. *His Way: The Unauthorized Biography of Frank Sinatra*, Kitty Kelley
4. *The Rotation Diet*, Martin Katahn
5. *You're Only Old Once*, Dr. Seuss
6. *Callanetics: Ten Years Younger in Ten Hours*, Callan Pinckney
7. *The Frugal Gourmet Cooks with Wine*, Jeff Smith

8. *Be Happy—You Are Loved!*, Robert H. Schuller
9. *Word for Word*, Andrew A. Rooney
10. *James Herriot's Dog Stories*, James Herriot

1987

Fiction
1. *The Tommyknockers*, Stephen King
2. *Patriot Games*, Tom Clancy
3. *Kaleidoscope*, Danielle Steel
4. *Misery*, Stephen King
5. *Leaving Home: A Collection of Lake Wobegon Stories*, Garrison Keillor
6. *Windmills of the Gods*, Sidney Sheldon
7. *Presumed Innocent*, Scott Turow
8. *Fine Things*, Danielle Steel
9. *Heaven and Hell*, John Jakes
10. *The Eyes of the Dragon*, Stephen King

Nonfiction
1. *Time Flies*, Bill Cosby
2. *Spycatcher: The Candid Autobiography of a Senior Intelligence Officer*, Peter Wright with Paul Greengrass
3. *Family: The Ties That Bind . . . and Gag!*, Erma Bombeck
4. *Veil: The Secret Wars of the CIA, 1981–1987*, Bob Woodward
5. *A Day in the Life of America*, Rick Smolan and David Cohen
6. *The Great Depression of 1990*, Ravi Batra
7. *It's All in the Playing*, Shirley MacLaine
8. *Man of the House: The Life and Political Memoirs of Speaker Tip O'Neill*, Thomas P. O'Neill Jr. with William Novak
9. *The Frugal Gourmet Cooks American*, Jeff Smith
10. *The Closing of the American Mind*, Allan Bloom

1988

Fiction
1. *The Cardinal of the Kremlin*, Tom Clancy
2. *The Sands of Time*, Sidney Sheldon
3. *Zoya*, Danielle Steel
4. *The Icarus Agenda*, Robert Ludlum
5. *Alaska*, James A. Michener
6. *Till We Meet Again*, Judith Krantz
7. *The Queen of the Damned*, Anne Rice
8. *To Be the Best*, Barbara Taylor Bradford
9. *One: A Novel*, Richard Bach
10. *Mitla Pass*, Leon Uris

Nonfiction
1. *The 8-Week Cholesterol Cure*, Robert E. Kowalski
2. *Talking Straight*, Lee Iacocca with Sonny Kleinfield
3. *A Brief History of Time: From the Big Bang to Black Holes*, Steven W. Hawking
4. *Trump: The Art of the Deal*, Donald J. Trump with Tony Schwartz
5. *Gracie: A Love Story*, George Burns
6. *Elizabeth Takes Off*, Elizabeth Taylor
7. *Swim with the Sharks Without Being Eaten Alive*, Harvey MacKay
8. *Christmas in America*, David Cohen, editor
9. *Weight Watchers Quick Success Program Book*, Jean Nidetch
10. *Moonwalk*, Michael Jackson

1989

Fiction
1. *Clear and Present Danger*, Tom Clancy
2. *The Dark Half*, Stephen King
3. *Daddy*, Danielle Steel
4. *Star*, Danielle Steel
5. *Caribbean*, James A. Michener
6. *The Satanic Verses*, Salman Rushdie
7. *The Russia House*, John le Carré
8. *The Pillars of the Earth*, Ken Follet
9. *California Gold*, John Jakes
10. *While My Pretty One Sleeps*, Mary Higgins Clark

Nonfiction
1. *All I Really Need to Know I Learned in Kindergarten: Uncommon Thoughts on Common Things*, Robert Fulghum
2. *Wealth Without Risk: How to Develop a Personal Fortune Without Going Out on a Limb*, Charles J. Givens
3. *A Woman Named Jackie*, C. David Heymann
4. *It Was on Fire When I Lay Down on It*, Robert Fulghum
5. *Better Homes and Gardens New Cook Book*
6. *The Way Things Work*, David Macaulay
7. *It's Always Something*, Gilda Radner
8. *Roseanne: My Life as a Woman*, Roseanne Barr
9. *The Frugal Gourmet Cooks Three Ancient Cuisines: China, Greece, and Rome*, Jeff Smith
10. *My Turn: The Memoirs of Nancy Reagan*, Nancy Reagan with William Novak

1990

Fiction
1. *The Plains of Passage*, Jean M. Auel
2. *Four Past Midnight*, Stephen King
3. *The Burden of Proof*, Scott Turow
4. *Memories of Midnight*, Sidney Sheldon
5. *Message from Nam*, Danielle Steel
6. *The Bourne Ultimatum*, Robert Ludlum
7. *The Stand: The Complete and Uncut Edition*, Stephen King
8. *Lady Boss*, Jackie Collins
9. *The Witching Hour*, Anne Rice
10. *September*, Rosamunde Pilcher

Nonfiction
1. *A Life on the Road*, Charles Kuralt
2. *The Civil War*, Geoffrey C. Ward with Ric Burns and Ken Burns
3. *The Frugal Gourmet on Our Immigrant Heritage: Recipes You Should Have Gotten from Your Grandmother*, Jeff Smith
4. *Better Homes and Gardens New Cook Book*
5. *Financial Self-Defense: How to Win the Fight for Financial Freedom*, Charles J. Givens
6. *Homecoming: Reclaiming and Championing Your Inner Child*, John Bradshaw
7. *Wealth Without Risk: How to Develop a Personal Fortune Without Going Out on a Limb*, Charles J. Givens
8. *Bo Knows Bo*, Bo Jackson and Dick Schaap
9. *An American Life: An Autobiography*, Ronald Reagan
10. *Megatrends 2000: Ten New Directions for the 1990s*, John Naisbitt and Patricia Aburdene

1991

Fiction
1. *Scarlett: The Sequel to Margaret Mitchell's "Gone with the Wind,"* Alexandra Ripley
2. *The Sum of All Fears*, Tom Clancy
3. *Needful Things*, Stephen King
4. *No Greater Love*, Danielle Steel
5. *Heartbeat*, Danielle Steel
6. *The Doomsday Conspiracy*, Sidney Sheldon
7. *The Firm*, John Grisham
8. *Night Over Water*, Ken Follet
9. *Remember*, Barbara Taylor Bradford
10. *Loves Music, Loves to Dance*, Mary Higgins Clark

Nonfiction
1. *Me: Stories of My Life*, Katharine Hepburn
2. *Nancy Reagan: The Unauthorized Biography*, Kitty Kelley
3. *Uh-Oh: Some Observations from Both Sides of the Refrigerator Door*, Robert Fulghum
4. *Under Fire: An American Story*, Oliver North with William Novak
5. *Final Exit: The Practicalities of Self-Deliverance and Assisted Suicide for the Dying*, Derek Humphry
6. *When You Look Like Your Passport Photo, It's Time to Go Home*, Erma Bombeck
7. *More Wealth Without Risk*, Charles J. Givens
8. *Den of Thieves*, James B. Stewart
9. *Childhood*, Bill Cosby
10. *Financial Self-Defense*, Charles J. Givens

1992

Fiction
1. *Dolores Claiborne*, Stephen King
2. *The Pelican Brief*, John Grisham
3. *Gerald's Game*, Stephen King
4. *Mixed Blessings*, Danielle Steel
5. *Jewels*, Danielle Steel
6. *The Stars Shine Down*, Sidney Sheldon
7. *Tale of the Body Thief*, Anne Rice
8. *Mexico*, James A. Michener
9. *Waiting to Exhale*, Terry McMillan
10. *All Around the Town*, Mary Higgins Clark

Nonfiction
1. *The Way Things Ought to Be*, Rush Limbaugh
2. *It Doesn't Take a Hero: The Autobiography*, Gen. H. Norman Schwarzkopf
3. *How to Satisfy a Woman Every Time*, Naura Hayden
4. *Every Living Thing*, James Herriot
5. *A Return to Love*, Marianne Williamson
6. *Sam Walton: Made in America*, Sam Walton
7. *Diana: Her True Story*, Andrew Morton
8. *Truman*, David McCullough
9. *Silent Passage*, Gail Sheehy
10. *Sex*, Madonna

1993

Fiction
1. *The Bridges of Madison County*, Robert James Waller
2. *The Client*, John Grisham
3. *Slow Waltz at Cedar Bend*, Robert James Waller
4. *Without Remorse*, Tom Clancy
5. *Nightmares and Dreamscapes*, Stephen King

6. *Vanished*, Danielle Steel
7. *Lasher*, Anne Rice
8. *Pleading Guilty*, Scott Turow
9. *Like Water for Chocolate*, Laura Esquivel
10. *The Scorpio Illusion*, Robert Ludlum

Nonfiction
1. *See, I Told You So*, Rush Limbaugh
2. *Private Parts*, Howard Stern
3. *Seinlanguage*, Jerry Seinfeld
4. *Embraced by the Light*, Betty J. Eadie with Curtis Taylor
5. *Ageless Body, Timeless Mind*, Deepak Chopra
6. *Stop the Insanity*, Susan Powter
7. *Women Who Run with the Wolves*, Clarissa Pinkola Estes
8. *Men Are from Mars, Women Are from Venus*, John Gray
9. *The Hidden Life of Dogs*, Elizabeth Marshall Thomas
10. *And If You Play Golf, You're My Friend*, Harvey Penick with Bud Shrake

1994

Fiction
1. *The Chamber*, John Grisham
2. *Debt of Honor*, Tom Clancy
3. *The Celestine Prophecy*, James Redfield
4. *The Gift*, Danielle Steel
5. *Insomnia*, Steven King
6. *Politically Correct Bedtime Stories*, James Finn Garner
7. *Wings*, Danielle Steel
8. *Accident*, Danielle Steel
9. *The Bridges of Madison County*, Robert James Waller
10. *Disclosure*, Michael Crichton

Nonfiction
1. *In the Kitchen with Rosie*, Rosie Daley
2. *Men Are from Mars, Women Are from Venus*, John Gray
3. *Crossing the Threshold of Hope*, John Paul II.
4. *Magic Eye I*, N.E. Thing Enterprises
5. *The Book of Virtues*, William J. Bennett
6. *Magic Eye II*, N.E. Thing Enterprises
7. *Embraced by the Light*, Betty J. Eadie with Curtis Taylor
8. *Don't Stand Too Close to a Naked Man*, Tim Allen
9. *Couplehood*, Paul Reiser
10. *Magic Eye III*, N.E. Thing Enterprises

1995

Fiction
1. *The Rainmaker*, John Grisham
2. *The Lost World*, Michael Crichton

3. *Five Days in Paris*, Danielle Steel
4. *The Christmas Box*, Richard Paul Evans
5. *Lightning*, Danielle Steel
6. *The Celestine Prophecy*, James Redfield
7. *Rose Madder*, Stephen King
8. *Silent Night*, Mary Higgins Clark
9. *Politically Correct Holiday Stories*, James Finn Garner
10. *The Horse Whisperer*, Nicholas Evans

Nonfiction

1. *Men Are from Mars, Women Are from Venus*, John Gray
2. *My American Journey*, Colin Powell with Joseph Persico
3. *Miss America*, Howard Stern
4. *The Seven Spiritual Laws of Success*, Deepak Chopra
5. *The Road Ahead*, Bill Gates
6. *Charles Kuralt's America*, Charles Kuralt
7. *Mars and Venus in the Bedroom*, John Gray
8. *To Renew America*, Newt Gingrich
9. *My Point...and I Do Have One*, Ellen DeGeneres
10. *The Moral Compass*, William J. Bennett

1996

Fiction

1. *The Runaway Jury*, John Grisham
2. *Executive Orders*, Tom Clancy
3. *Desperation*, Stephen King
4. *Airframe*, Michael Crichton
5. *The Regulators*, Richard Bachman
6. *Malice*, Danielle Steel
7. *Silent Honor*, Danielle Steel
8. *Primary Colors*, anonymous
9. *Cause of Death*, Patricia Cornwell
10. *The Tenth Insight*, James Redfield

Nonfiction

1. *Make the Connection*, Oprah Winfrey and Bob Greene
2. *Men Are from Mars, Women Are from Venus*, John Gray
3. *The Dilbert Principle*, Scott Adams
4. *Simple Abundance*, Sarah Ban Breathnach
5. *The Zone*, Barry Sears with Bill Lawren
6. *Bad As I Wanna Be*, Dennis Rodman
7. *In Contempt*, Christopher Darden
8. *A Reporter's Life*, Walter Cronkite
9. *Dogbert's Top Secret Management Handbook*, Scott Adams
10. *My Sergei: A Love Story*, Ekaterina Gordeeva with E. M. Swift

1997

Fiction

1. *The Partner*, John Grisham
2. *Cold Mountain*, Charles Frazier
3. *The Ghost*, Danielle Steel
4. *The Ranch*, Danielle Steel
5. *Special Delivery*, Danielle Steel
6. *Unnatural Exposure*, Patricia Cornwell
7. *The Best Laid Plans*, Sidney Sheldon
8. *Pretend You Don't See Her*, Mary Higgins Clark
9. *Cat & Mouse*, James Patterson
10. *Hornet's Nest*, Patricia Cornwell

Nonfiction

1. *Angela's Ashes*, Frank McCourt
2. *Simple Abundance*, Sarah Ban Breathnach
3. *Midnight in the Garden of Good and Evil*, John Berendt
4. *The Royals*, Kitty Kelley
5. *Joy of Cooking*, Irma S. Rombauer, Marion Rombauer Becker, and Ethan Becker
6. *Diana: Her True Story*, Andrew Morton
7. *Into Thin Air*, Jon Krakauer
8. *Conversations with God, Book I*, Neale Donald Walsch
9. *Men Are from Mars, Women Are from Venus*, John Gray
10. *Eight Weeks to Optimum Health*, Andrew Weil

1998

Fiction

1. *The Street Lawyer*, John Grisham
2. *Rainbow Six*, Tom Clancy
3. *Bag of Bones*, Stephen King
4. *A Man in Full*, Tom Wolfe
5. *Mirror Image*, Danielle Steel
6. *The Long Road Home*, Danielle Steel
7. *The Klone and I*, Danielle Steel
8. *Point of Origin*, Patricia Cornwell
9. *Paradise*, Toni Morrison
10. *All Through the Night*, Mary Higgins Clark

Nonfiction

1. *The 9 Steps to Financial Freedom*, Suze Orman
2. *The Greatest Generation*, Tom Brokaw
3. *Sugar Busters!*, H. Leighton Steward, Morrison C. Bethea, Sam S. Andrews, and Luis A. Balart
4. *Tuesdays with Morrie*, Mitch Albom
5. *The Guinness Book of Records 1999*
6. *Talking to Heaven*, James Van Praagh
7. *Something More: Excavating Your Authentic Self*, Sarah Ban Breathnach

8. *In the Meantime*, Iyanla Vanzant
9. *A Pirate Looks at Fifty*, Jimmy Buffett
10. *If Life Is a Game These Are the Rules*, Cherie Carter-Scott, Ph.D.

1999

1. *The Testament*, John Grisham
2. *Hannibal*, Thomas Harris
3. *Assassins*, Jerry B. Jenkins & Tim LaHaye
4. *Star Wars: Episode 1, The Phantom Menace*, Terry Brooks
5. *Timeline*, Michael Crichton
6. *Hearts in Atlantis*, Stephen King
7. *Apollyon*, Jerry B. Jenkins & Tim LaHaye
8. *The Girl Who Loved Tom Gordon*, Stephen King
9. *Irresistible Forces*, Danielle Steel
10. *Tara Road*, Maeve Binchy

Nonfiction

1. *Tuesdays with Morrie*, Mitch Albom
2. *The Greatest Generation*, Tom Brokaw
3. *Guinness World Records 2000: Millennium Edition*
4. *'Tis*, Frank McCourt
5. *Who Moved My Cheese?*, Spencer Johnson
6. *The Courage to Be Rich*, Suze Orman
7. *The Greatest Generation Speaks*, Tom Brokaw
8. *Sugar Busters!*, H. Leighton Steward, Morrison C. Bethea, Sam S. Andrews and Luis A. Balart
9. *The Art of Happiness*, the Dalai Lama and Howard C. Cutler
10. *The Century*, Peter Jennings & Todd Brewster

THE PEOPLE BOOKSHELF

PEOPLE hasn't been reviewing books long enough to hazard a best-of-the-century list, but here are the books we loved the most over the years.

FICTION

Absolute Power, David Baldacci
The Accidental Tourist, Anne Tyler
All the Pretty Horses, Cormac McCarthy
Amy and Isabelle, Elizabeth Strout
Anagrams, Lorrie Moore
Anton the Dove Fancier, Bernard Gotfryd
August, Judith Rossner
Be Cool, Elmore Leonard
Before and After, Rosellen Brown
Beloved, Toni Morrison
Birds of America, Lorrie Moore
Birdy, William Wharton
The Blooding, Joseph Wambaugh
The Blue Afternoon, William Boyd
Body and Soul, Frank Conroy
The Bonfire of the Vanities, Tom Wolfe
Breathing Lessons, Anne Tyler
Bridget Jones's Diary, Helen Fielding
Cat's Eye, Margaret Atwood
Clockers, Richard Price
The Cloister Walk, Kathleen Norris
Cold Mountain, Charles Frazier
Collaborators, Janet Kauffman
The Collected Stories, Isaac Bashevis Singer
The Color Purple, Alice Walker
Come to Grief, Dick Francis
A Confederacy of Dunces, John Kennedy Toole
Damascus Gate, Robert Stone
Dinner at the Homesick Restaurant, Anne Tyler
The Dragons of Eden, Carl Sagan
Dutch Shea Jr., John Gregory Dunne
East Is East, T. Coraghessan Boyle
Ellis Island, Mark Helprin
Enchantment, Daphne Merkin
Eye of the Needle, Ken Follett
Fanny, Erica Jong
The Farming of Bones, Edwidge Danticat
Final Payments, Mary Gordon
The Firm, John Grisham

The First Man in Rome, Colleen McCullough
For Love, Sue Miller
Foreign Affairs, Alison Lurie
A Gesture Life, Chang-Rae Lee
Get Shorty, Elmore Leonard
The Girls' Guide to Hunting and Fishing, by Melissa Bank
The Glass House, Laura Furman
The God of Small Things, Arundhati Roy
Gone, Baby, Gone, Dennis Lehane
The Good Mother, Sue Miller
Gorky Park, Martin Cruz Smith
The Green Mile, Stephen King
Happy to Be There, Garrison Keillor
Her First American, Lore Segal
The Honourable Schoolboy, John Le Carré
The House of the Spirits, Isabel Allende
Illumination Night, Abbie Hoffman
An Indecent Obsession, Colleen McCollough
Independence Day, Richard Ford
Juneteenth, Ralph Ellison
Kolymsky Heights, Lionel Davidson
Krik? Krak!, Edwidge Danticat
Labrava, Elmore Leonard
Lake Wobegon Days, Garrison Keillor
Lancelot, Walker Percy
A Lesson Before Dying, Ernest J. Gaines
The Liar's Club, Mary Karr
Libra, Don DeLillo
A Light in the Attic, Shel Silverstein
Life Its Ownself, Dan Jenkins
Love in the Time of Cholera, Gabriel García Márquez
The Love Letter, Cathleen Schine
Machine Dreams, Jayne Anne Phillips
The Mambo Kings Play Songs of Love, Oscar Hijuelos
A Man in Full, Tom Wolfe
A Map of the World, Jane Hamilton
Maus: A Survivor's Tale, II: And Here My Troubles Begin, Art Spiegelman

Me and My Baby View the Eclipse, Lee Smith
Memoirs of an Invisible Man, H. F. Saint
Monkeys, Susan Minot
Monsignor Quixote, Graham Greene
More Die of Heartbreak, Saul Bellow
Music for Chameleons, Truman Capote
The Natural Man, Ed McClanahan
Noble House, James Clavell
Owning Jolene, Shelby Hearon
The Palace Thief, Ethan Canin
Patrimony, Philip Roth
Perfume, Patrick Süskind
Plainsong, Kent Haruf
Poodle Springs, Raymond Chandler and Robert B. Parker
The Pope of Greenwich Village, Vincent Park
Presumed Innocent, Scott Turow
The Progress of Love, Alice Munro
Quinn's Book, William Kennedy
Rabbit at Rest, John Updike
The Robber Bride, Margaret Atwood
Roger's Version, John Updike
Rose, Martin Cruz Smith
The Russia House, John Le Carré
Salvador, Joan Didion
The Secret History, Donna Tartt
Seventh Heaven, Alice Hoffman
She's Come Undone, Wally Lamb
The Sicilian, Mario Puzo
Smilla's Sense of Snow, Peter Hoeg
A Soldier of the Great War, Mark Helprin
Sophie's Choice, William Styron
Stormy Weather, Carl Hiaasen
Talking to the Dead, Sylvia Watanabe
Tooth Imprints on a Corn Dog, Mark Leyner
Tracks, Louise Erdrich
The Tree of Life, Hugh Nissenson
True Confessions, John Gregory Dunne
The Twenty-Seventh City, Jonathan Franzen
Typical American, Gish Jen

NONFICTION

BOOKS OF THE CENTURY

To commemorate the New York Public Library's 100th anniversary, the librarians of this venerable institution identified books that, from their varying perspectives, have played defining roles in the making of the 20th century. Included are books that influenced the course of events, for good and for bad; books that interpreted new worlds; and books that simply delighted millions of patrons.

LANDMARKS OF MODERN LITERATURE

The Three Sisters, Anton Chekhov (1901)

Remembrance of Things Past, Marcel Proust (1913-27)

Tender Buttons, Gertrude Stein (1914)

The Metamorphosis, Franz Kafka (1915)

Renascence and Other Poems, Edna St. Vincent Millay (1917)

The Wild Swans at Coole, William Butler Yeats (1917)

Six Characters in Search of an Author, Luigi Pirandello (1921)

The Waste Land, T. S. Eliot (1922)

Ulysses, James Joyce (1922)

The Magic Mountain, Thomas Mann (1924)

The Great Gatsby, F. Scott Fitzgerald (1925)

To the Lighthouse, Virginia Woolf (1927)

Gypsy Ballads, Frederico García Lorca (1928)

Native Son, Richard Wright (1940)

The Age of Anxiety: A Baroque Eclogue, W. H. Auden (1947)

Invisible Man, Ralph Ellison (1952)

Lolita, Vladimir Nabokov (1955)

Fictions, Jorge Luis Borges (1944; 2nd augmented edition 1956)

One Hundred Years of Solitude, Gabriel García Márquez (1967)

Song of Solomon, Toni Morrison (1977)

PROTEST AND PROGRESS

The Battle with the Slum, Jacob Ritts (1902)

The Souls of Black Folk, W. E. B. Du Bois (1903)

The Jungle, Upton Sinclair (1906)

Twenty Years at Hull-House, Jane Addams (1910)

The House on Henry Street, Lillian Wald (1915)

The Autobiography of Lincoln Steffens, Lincoln Steffens (1931)

U.S.A., John Dos Passos (1937)

The Grapes of Wrath, John Steinbeck (1939)

Let Us Now Praise Famous Men, James Agee and Walker Evans (1941)

Strange Fruit, Lillian Smith (1944)

Growing Up Absurd, Paul Goodman (1960)

The Fire Next Time, James Baldwin (1963)

The Autobiography of Malcolm X, Malcolm X (1965)

And the Band Played On, Randy Shilts (1987)

There Are No Children Here, Alex Kotlowitz (1991)

POPULAR CULTURE & MASS ENTERTAINMENT

Dracula, Bram Stoker (1897)

The Turn of the Screw, Henry James (1898)

The Hound of the Baskervilles, Arthur Conan Doyle (1902)

Tarzan of the Apes, Edgar Rice Burroughs (1912)

Riders of the Purple Sage, Zane Grey (1912)

The Mysterious Affair at Styles, Agatha Christie (1920)

How to Win Friends and Influence People, Dale Carnegie (1936)

Gone with the Wind, Margaret Mitchell (1936)

The Big Sleep, Raymond Chandler (1939)

The Day of the Locust, Nathanael West (1939)

Peyton Place, Grace Metalious (1956)

The Cat in the Hat, Dr. Seuss (1957)

Stranger in a Strange Land, Robert A. Heinlein (1961)

Catch-22, Joseph Heller (1961)

In Cold Blood: A True Account of a Multiple Murder and Its Consequences, Truman Capote (1965)

Ball Four: My Life and Times Throwing the Knuckleball in the Big Leagues, Jim Bouton (1970)

Carrie, Stephen King (1974)

The Bonfire of the Vanities, Tom Wolfe (1987)

WOMEN RISE

The Age of Innocence, Edith Wharton (1920)

Woman Suffrage and Politics: The Inner Story of the Suffrage Movement, Carrie Chapman Catt and Nettie Rogers Shuler (1923)

My Fight for Birth Control, Margaret Sanger (1931)

Dust Tracks on a Dirt Road, Zora Neale Hurston (1942)

The Second Sex, Simone de Beauvoir (1949)

The Golden Notebook, Doris Lessing (1962)

The Feminine Mystique, Betty Friedan (1963)

I Know Why the Caged Bird Sings, Maya Angelou (1969)

Sisterhood Is Powerful: An Anthology of Writings from the Women's Liberations Movement, edited by Robin Morgan (1970)

Against Our Will: Men, Women and Rape, Susan Brownmiller (1975)

The Color Purple, Alice Walker (1982)

ECONOMICS & TECHNOLOGY

The Theory of the Leisure Class: An Economic Study of Institutions, Thorstein Veblen (1899)

The Protestant Ethic and the Spirit of Capitalism, Max Weber (1904–1905)

The Education of Henry Adams, Henry Adams (1907)

The General Theory of Employment, Interest and Money, John Meynard Keynes (1936)

A Theory of the Consumption Function, Milton Friedman (1957)

The Affluent Society, John Kenneth Galbraith (1958)

The Death and Life of Great American Cities, Jane Jacobs (1961)

Superhighway—Super Hoax, Helen Leavitt (1970)

Small Is Beautiful: A Study of Economics As If People Mattered, E. F. Schumacher (1973)

The Whole Internet: User's Guide and Catalogue, Ed Krol (1992)

MIND & SPIRIT

Suicide: A Study in Sociology, Emile Durkheim (1897)

The Interpretation of Dreams, Sigmund Freud (1900)

Studies in the Psychology of Sex, Havelock Ellis (1901–28)

The Varieties of Religious Experience: A Study in Human Nature, Wiilliam James (1902)

The Prophet, Kahlil Gibran (1923)

Why I Am Not a Christian, Bertrand Russell (1927)

Coming of Age in Samoa, Margaret Mead (1928)

Being and Nothingness, Jean-Paul Sartre (1943)

The Common Sense Book of Baby Care, Dr. Benjamin Spock (1946)

The Holy Bible, Revised Standard Version (1952)

The Courage to Be, Paul Tillich (1952)

One Flew over the Cuckoo's Nest, Ken Kesey (1962)

The Politics of Ecstasy, Timothy Leary (1968)

On Death and Dying, Elisabeth Kübler-Ross (1969)

The Uses of Enchantment, Bruno Bettelheim (1976)

MORE BOOKS THAT SHAPE LIVES

The Library of Congress established its Center for the Book in 1977 to stimulate public interest in books, reading, and libraries. Here is its list of the 25 books that have had the greatest impact on readers' lives.

The Adventures of Huckleberry Finn, Mark Twain

Atlas Shrugged, Ayn Rand

The Autobiography of Benjamin Franklin

The Bible

The Catcher in the Rye, J. D. Salinger

Charlotte's Web, E. B. White

The Diary of a Young Girl, Anne Frank

Don Quixote, Miguel de Cervantes

Gone with the Wind, Margaret Mitchell

Hiroshima, John Hersey

How to Win Friends and Influence People, Dale Carnegie

I Know Why the Caged Bird Sings, Maya Angelou

Invisible Man, Ralph Ellison

The Little Prince, Antoine de Saint-Exupéry

Little Women, Louisa May Alcott

The Lord of the Rings, J. R. R. Tolkien

Roots, Alex Haley

The Secret Garden, Frances Hodgson Burnett

To Kill a Mockingbird, Harper Lee

Treasure Island, Robert Louis Stevenson

Walden, Henry David Thoreau

War and Peace, Leo Tolstoy

What Color Is Your Parachute? Richard Nelson Bolles

THE MODERN LIBRARY FICTION LIST

Get out your pencils and get ready to quibble. Last year the Modern Library released its list of the top 100 English-language novels of the century (so never mind that manuscript in progress), 59 of which happen to be available in Modern Library editions. The hue and cry was heard even in hushed libraries. Objectors noted the panel of 10 was 90% male, all white, with an average age of just under 69, and a clear distaste for the contemporary. But at least they got us talking—and reading.

Rank	Book, Author (original publication date)
1.	*Ulysses*, James Joyce (1922)
2.	*The Great Gatsby*, F. Scott Fitzgerald (1925)
3.	*A Portrait of the Artist as a Young Man*, James Joyce (1916)
4.	*Lolita*, Vladimir Nabokov (1955)
5.	*Brave New World*, Aldous Huxley (1932)
6.	*The Sound and the Fury*, William Faulkner (1929)
7.	*Catch-22*, Joseph Heller (1961)
8.	*Darkness at Noon*, Arthur Koestler (1941)
9.	*Sons and Lovers*, D. H. Lawrence (1913)
10.	*The Grapes of Wrath*, John Steinbeck (1939)
11.	*Under the Volcano*, Malcolm Lowry (1947)
12.	*The Way of All Flesh*, Samuel Butler (1903)
13.	*1984*, George Orwell (1949)
14.	*I, Claudius*, Robert Graves (1934)
15.	*To the Lighthouse*, Virginia Woolf (1927)
16.	*An American Tragedy*, Theodore Dreiser (1925)
17.	*The Heart Is a Lonely Hunter*, Carson McCullers (1940)
18.	*Slaughterhouse Five*, Kurt Vonnegut, Jr. (1969)
19.	*Invisible Man*, Ralph Ellison (1952)
20.	*Native Son*, Richard Wright (1940)
21.	*Henderson the Rain King*, Saul Bellow (1959)
22.	*Appointment in Samarra*, John O'Hara (1934)
23.	*U.S.A.* (trilogy), John Dos Passos (1936)
24.	*Winesburg, Ohio*, Sherwood Anderson (1919)
25.	*A Passage to India*, E. M. Forster (1924)
26.	*The Wings of the Dove*, Henry James (1902)
27.	*The Ambassadors*, Henry James (1903)
28.	*Tender Is the Night*, F. Scott Fitzgerald (1934)
29.	*Studs Lonigan* (trilogy), James T. Farrell (1935)
30.	*The Good Soldier*, Ford Madox Ford (1915)
31.	*Animal Farm*, George Orwell (1945)
32.	*The Golden Bowl*, Henry James (1904)
33.	*Sister Carrie*, Theodore Dreiser (1900)
34.	*A Handful of Dust*, Evelyn Waugh (1934)
35.	*As I Lay Dying*, William Faulkner (1934)
36.	*All the King's Men*, Robert Penn Warren (1946)
37.	*The Bridge of San Luis Rey*, Thornton Wilder (1927)
38.	*Howards End*, E. M. Forster (1910)
39.	*Go Tell It on the Mountain*, James Baldwin (1953)
40.	*The Heart of the Matter*, Graham Greene (1948)
41.	*Lord of the Flies*, William Golding (1954)
42.	*Deliverance*, James Dickey, (1970)
43.	*A Dance to the Music of Time* (series), Anthony Powell (1975)
44.	*Point Counter Point*, Aldous Huxley (1928)
45.	*The Sun Also Rises*, Ernest Hemingway (1926)
46.	*The Secret Agent*, Joseph Conrad (1907)
47.	*Nostromo*, Joseph Conrad (1904)
48.	*The Rainbow*, D. H. Lawrence (1915)
49.	*Women in Love*, D. H. Lawrence (1920)
50.	*Tropic of Cancer*, Henry Miller (1934)

Rank	Book, Author (original publication date)
51.	*The Naked and the Dead*, Norman Mailer (1948)
52.	*Portnoy's Complaint*, Philip Roth (1969)
53.	*Pale Fire*, Vladimir Nabokov (1962)
54.	*Light in August*, William Faulkner (1932)
55.	*On the Road*, Jack Kerouac (1957)
56.	*The Maltese Falcon*, Dashiell Hammett (1930)
57.	*Parade's End*, Ford Madox Ford (1928)
58.	*The Age of Innocence*, Edith Wharton (1920)
59.	*Zuleika Dobson*, Max Beerbohm (1911)
60.	*The Moviegoer*, Walker Percy (1961)
61.	*Death Comes for the Archbishop*, Willa Cather (1927)
62.	*From Here to Eternity*, James Jones (1951)
63.	*The Wapshot Chronicle*, John Cheever (1957)
64.	*The Catcher in the Rye*, J. D. Salinger (1951)
65.	*A Clockwork Orange*, Anthony Burgess (1962)
66.	*Of Human Bondage*, W. Somerset Maugham (1915)
67.	*Heart of Darkness*, Joseph Conrad (1902)
68.	*Main Street*, Sinclair Lewis (1920)
69.	*The House of Mirth*, Edith Wharton (1905)
70.	*The Alexandria Quartet*, Lawrence Durrell (1960)
71.	*A High Wind in Jamaica*, Richard Hughes (1929)
72.	*A House for Mr. Biswas*, V. S. Naipaul (1961)
73.	*The Day of the Locust*, Nathanael West (1939)
74.	*A Farewell to Arms*, Ernest Hemingway (1929)
75.	*Scoop*, Evelyn Waugh (1938)
76.	*The Prime of Miss Jean Brodie*, Muriel Spark (1961)
77.	*Finnegans Wake*, James Joyce (1939)
78.	*Kim*, Rudyard Kipling (1901)
79.	*A Room with a View*, E. M. Forster (1908)
80.	*Brideshead Revisited*, Evelyn Waugh (1945)
81.	*The Adventures of Augie March*, Saul Bellow (1971)
82.	*Angle of Repose*, Wallace Stegner (1971)
83.	*A Bend in the River*, V. S. Naipaul (1979)
84.	*The Death of the Heart*, Elizabeth Bowen (1938)
85.	*Lord Jim*, Joseph Conrad (1900)
86.	*Ragtime*, E. L. Doctorow (1975)
87.	*The Old Wives' Tale*, Arnold Bennett (1908)
88.	*The Call of the Wild*, Jack London (1903)
89.	*Loving*, Henry Green (1945)
90.	*Midnight's Children*, Salman Rushdie (1981)
91.	*Tobacco Road*, Erskine Caldwell (1932)
92.	*Ironweed*, William Kennedy (1983)
93.	*The Magus*, John Fowles (1966)
94.	*Wide Sargasso Sea*, Jean Rhys (1966)
95.	*Under the Net*, Iris Murdoch (1954)
96.	*Sophie's Choice*, William Styron (1979)
97.	*The Sheltering Sky*, Paul Bowles (1949)
98.	*The Postman Always Rings Twice*, James M. Cain (1934)
99.	*The Ginger Man*, J. P. Donleavy (1955)
100.	*The Magnificent Ambersons*, Booth Tarkington (1918)

THE MODERN LIBRARY NONFICTION LIST

This year the Modern Library struck again, with a selection of the century's best nonfiction. The panel was slightly younger and a little more balanced for gender and race, and the final results were a tad less controversial. The primary dispute was whether these books are important to read or just plain important (case in point, Whitehead and Russell's *Principia Mathematica*). Read, and judge, for yourself.

Rank	Book, Author
1.	*The Education of Henry Adams*, Henry Adams
2.	*The Varieties of Religious Experience*, William James
3.	*Up from Slavery*, Booker T. Washington
4.	*A Room of One's Own*, Virginia Woolf
5.	*Silent Spring*, Rachel Carson
6.	*Selected Essays, 1917–1932*, T. S. Eliot
7.	*The Double Helix*, James D. Watson
8.	*Speak, Memory*, Vladimir Nabokov
9.	*The American Language*, H. L. Mencken
10.	*The General Theory of Employment, Interest, and Money*, John Maynard Keynes
11.	*The Lives of a Cell*, Lewis Thomas
12.	*The Frontier in American History*, Frederick Jackson Turner
13.	*Black Boy*, Richard Wright
14.	*Aspects of the Novel*, E. M. Forster
15.	*The Civil War*, Shelby Foote
16.	*The Guns of August*, Barbara Tuchman
17.	*The Proper Study of Mankind*, Isaiah Berlin
18.	*The Nature and Destiny of Man*, Reinhold Niebuhr
19.	*Notes of a Native Son*, James Baldwin
20.	*The Autobiography of Alice B. Toklas*, Gertrude Stein
21.	*The Elements of Style*, William Strunk and E. B. White
22.	*An American Dilemma*, Gunnar Myrdal
23.	*Principia Mathematica*, Alfred North Whitehead and Bertrand Russell
24.	*The Mismeasure of Man*, Stephen Jay Gould
25.	*The Mirror and the Lamp*, Meyer Howard Abrams
26.	*The Art of the Soluble*, Peter B. Medawar
27.	*The Ants*, Bert Hölldobler and Edward O. Wilson
28.	*A Theory of Justice*, John Rawls
29.	*Art and Illusion*, Ernest H. Gombrich
30.	*The Making of the English Working Class*, E. P. Thompson
31.	*The Souls of Black Folk*, W. E. B. Du Bois
32.	*Principia Ethica*, G. E. Moore
33.	*Philosophy and Civilization*, John Dewey
34.	*On Growth and Form*, D'Arcy Thompson
35.	*Ideas and Opinions*, Albert Einstein
36.	*The Age of Jackson*, Arthur Schlesinger Jr.
37.	*The Making of the Atomic Bomb*, Richard Rhodes
38.	*Black Lamb and Grey Falcon*, Rebecca West
39.	*Autobiographies*, W. B. Yeats
40.	*Science and Civilization in China*, Joseph Needham
41.	*Goodbye to All That*, Robert Graves
42.	*Homage to Catalonia*, George Orwell
43.	*The Autobiography of Mark Twain*, Mark Twain
44.	*Children of Crisis*, Robert Coles
45.	*A Study of History*, Arnold J. Toynbee
46.	*The Affluent Society*, John Kenneth Galbraith
47.	*Present at the Creation*, Dean Acheson
48.	*The Great Bridge*, David McCullough
49.	*Patriotic Gore*, Edmund Wilson
50.	*Samuel Johnson*, Walter Jackson Bate
51.	*The Autobiography of Malcolm X*, Alex Haley and Malcolm X
52.	*The Right Stuff*, Tom Wolfe
53.	*Eminent Victorians*, Lytton Strachey
54.	*Working*, Studs Terkel
55.	*Darkness Visible*, William Styron
56.	*The Liberal Imagination*, Lionel Trilling
57.	*The Second World War*, Winston Churchill
58.	*Out of Africa*, Isak Dinesen
59.	*Jefferson and His Time*, Dumas Malone
60.	*In the American Grain*, William Carlos Williams
61.	*Cadillac Desert*, Marc Reisner
62.	*The House of Morgan*, Ron Chernow
63.	*The Sweet Science*, A. J. Liebling
64.	*The Open Society and Its Enemies*, Karl Popper
65.	*The Art of Memory*, Frances A. Yates
66.	*Religion and the Rise of Capitalism*, R. H. Tawney
67.	*A Preface to Morals*, Walter Lippmann
68.	*The Gate of Heavenly Peace*, Jonathan D. Spence
69.	*The Structure of Scientific Revolutions*, Thomas S. Kuhn
70.	*The Strange Career of Jim Crow*, C. Vann Woodward
71.	*The Rise of the West*, William H. McNeill
72.	*The Gnostic Gospels*, Elaine Pagels
73.	*James Joyce*, Richard Ellmann
74.	*Florence Nightingale*, Cecil Woodham-Smith
75.	*The Great War and Modern Memory*, Paul Fussell
76.	*The City in History*, Lewis Mumford
77.	*Battle Cry of Freedom*, James M. McPherson
78.	*Why We Can't Wait*, Martin Luther King Jr.
79.	*The Rise of Theodore Roosevelt*, Edmund Morris
80.	*Studies in Iconography*, Erwin Panofsky
81.	*The Face of Battle*, John Keegan
82.	*The Strange Death of Liberal England*, George Dangerfield
83.	*Vermeer*, Lawrence Gowing
84.	*A Bright Shining Lie*, Neil Sheehan
85.	*West with the Night*, Beryl Markham
86.	*This Boy's Life*, Tobias Wolff
87.	*A Mathematician's Apology*, G. H. Hardy
88.	*Six Easy Pieces*, Richard P. Feynman
89.	*Pilgrim at Tinker Creek*, Annie Dillard
90.	*The Golden Bough*, James George Frazer
91.	*Shadow and Act*, Ralph Ellison
92.	*The Power Broker*, Robert A. Caro
93.	*The American Political Tradition*, Richard Hofstadter
94.	*The Contours of American History*, William Appleman Williams
95.	*The Promise of American Life*, Herbert Croly
96.	*In Cold Blood*, Truman Capote
97.	*The Journalist and the Murderer*, Janet Malcolm
98.	*The Taming of Chance*, Ian Hacking
99.	*Operating Instructions*, Anne Lamott
100.	*Melbourne*, Lord David Cecil

LITERARY AWARDS

NATIONAL BOOK AWARDS

Fiction

1950 Nelson Algren
The Man with the Golden Arm
1951 William Faulkner
The Collected Stories of William Faulkner
1952 James Jones
From Here to Eternity
1953 Ralph Ellison
Invisible Man
1954 Saul Bellow
The Adventures of Augie March
1955 William Faulkner
A Fable
1956 John O'Hara
Ten North Frederick
1957 Wright Morris
The Field of Vision
1958 John Cheever
The Wapshot Chronicle
1959 Bernard Malamud
The Magic Barrel
1960 Philip Roth
Goodbye, Columbus
1961 Conrad Richter
The Waters of Kronos
1962 Walker Percy
The Moviegoer
1963 J. F. Powers
Morte D'Urban
1964 John Updike
The Centaur
1965 Saul Bellow
Herzog
1966 Katherine Anne Porter
The Collected Stories of Katherine Anne Porter
1967 Bernard Malamud
The Fixer
1968 Thornton Wilder
The Eighth Day
1969 Jerzy Kosinski
Steps
1970 Joyce Carol Oates
Them
1971 Saul Bellow
Mr. Sammler's Planet
1972 Flannery O'Connor
The Complete Stories of Flannery O'Connor
1973 John Barth
Chimera
John Williams
Augustus
1974 Thomas Pynchon
Gravity's Rainbow
Isaac Bashevis Singer
A Crown of Feathers and Other Stories

1975 Robert Stone
Dog Soldiers
Thomas Williams
The Hair of Harold Roux
1976 William Gaddis
JR
1977 Wallace Stegner
The Spectator Bird
1978 Mary Lee Settle
Blood Ties
1979 Tim O'Brien
Going After Cacciato
1980 William Styron (hardcover)
Sophie's Choice
John Irving (paperback)
The World According to Garp
1981 Wright Morris (hardcover)
Plains Song
John Cheever (paperback)
The Stories of John Cheever
1982 John Updike (hardcover)
Rabbit Is Rich
William Maxwell (paperback)
So Long, See You Tomorrow
1983 Alice Walker (hardcover)
The Color Purple
Eudora Welty (paperback)
Collected Stories of Eudora Welty
1984 Ellen Gilchrist
Victory over Japan: A Book of Stories
1985 Don DeLillo
White Noise
1986 E. L. Doctorow
World's Fair
1987 Larry Heinemann
Paco's Story
1988 Pete Dexter
Paris Trout
1989 John Casey
Spartina
1990 Charles Johnson
Middle Passage
1991 Norman Rush
Mating
1992 Cormac McCarthy
All the Pretty Horses
1993 E. Annie Proulx
The Shipping News
1994 William Gaddis
A Frolic of His Own
1995 Philip Roth
Sabbath's Theater
1996 Andrea Barrett
Ship Fever and Other Stories
1997 Charles Frazier
Cold Mountain
1998 Alice McDermott
Charming Billy
1999 Ha Jin
Waiting

Nonfiction

1950 Ralph L. Rusk
Ralph Waldo Emerson
1951 Newton Arvin
Herman Melville
1952 Rachel Carson
The Sea Around Us
1953 Bernard A. De Voto
The Course of an Empire
1954 Bruce Catton
A Stillness at Appomattox
1955 Joseph Wood Krutch
The Measure of Man
1956 Herbert Kubly
An American in Italy
1957 George F. Kennan
Russia Leaves the War
1958 Catherine Drinker Bowen
The Lion and the Throne
1959 J. Christopher Herold
Mistress to an Age: A Life of Madame de Stael
1960 Richard Ellmann
James Joyce
1961 William L. Shirer
The Rise and Fall of the Third Reich
1962 Lewis Mumford
The City in History: Its Origins, Its Transformations and Its Prospects
1963 Leon Edel
Henry James, Vol. II: The Conquest of London. Henry James, Vol. III: The Middle Years
No general nonfiction prize awarded 1964–79
1980 Tom Wolfe (hardcover)
The Right Stuff
Peter Matthiessen (paperback)
The Snow Leopard
1981 Maxine Hong Kingston (hardcover)
China Men
Jane Kramer (paperback)
The Last Cowboy
1982 Tracy Kidder (hardcover)
The Soul of a New Machine
Victor S. Navasky (paperback)
Naming Names
1983 Fox Butterfield (hardcover)
China: Alive in the Bitter Sea
James Fallows (paperback)
National Defense
1984 Rovert V. Remini
Andrew Jackson and the Course of American Democracy, 1833–1845
1985 J. Anthony Lukas
Common Ground: A Turbulent Decade in the Lives of Three American Families

1986   Barry Lopez
       Arctic Dreams
1987   Richard Rhodes
       The Making of the Atom Bomb
1988   Neil Sheehan
       *A Bright Shining Lie: John Paul
       Vann and America in Vietnam*
1989   Thomas L. Friedman
       From Beirut to Jerusalem
1990   Ron Chernow
       *The House of Morgan: An Ameri-
       can Banking Dynasty and the
       Rise of Modern Finance*
1991   Orlando Patterson
       Freedom
1992   Paul Monette
       *Becoming a Man: Half a Life
       Story*
1993   Gore Vidal
       *United States: Essays
       1952–1992*
1994   Sherwin B. Nuland
       *How We Die: Reflections on Life's
       Final Chapter*
1995   Tina Rosenberg
       *The Haunted Land: Facing
       Europe's Ghosts After
       Communism*
1996   James Caroll
       An American Requiem
1997   Joseph J. Ellis
       *American Sphinx: The Character
       of Thomas Jefferson*
1998   Edward Ball
       Slaves in the Family
1999   John W. Dower
       *Embracing Defeat: Japan in the
       Wake of World War II*

Poetry

1950   William Carlos Williams
       *Paterson: Book III and Selected
       Poems*
1951   Wallace Stevens
       The Auroras of Autumn
1952   Marianne Moore
       Collected Poems
1953   Archibald MacLeish
       Collected Poems, 1917–1952
1954   Conrad Aiken
       Collected Poems
1955   Wallace Stevens
       *The Collected Poems of Wallace
       Stevens*
1956   W. H. Auden
       The Shield of Achilles
1957   Richard Wilbur
       Things of This World
1958   Robert Penn Warren
       Promises: Poems, 1954–1956
1959   Theodore Roethke
       Words for the Wind
1960   Robert Lowell
       Life Studies

1961   Randall Jarrell
       *The Woman at the
       Washington Zoo*
1962   Alan Dugan
       Poems
1963   William Strafford
       Traveling Through the Dark
1964   John Crowe Ransom
       Selected Poems
1965   Theodore Roethke
       The Far Field
1966   James Dickey
       Buckdancer's Choice: Poems
1967   James Merrill
       Nights and Days
1968   Robert Bly
       The Light Around the Body
1969   John Berryman
       His Toy, His Dream, His Rest
1970   Elizabeth Bishop
       The Complete Poems
1971   Mona Van Duyn
       To See, To Take
1972   Howard Moss
       Selected Poems
       Frank O'Hara
       *The Collected Poems of
       Frank O'Hara*
1973   A. R. Ammons
       Collected Poems, 1951–1971
1974   Allen Ginsberg
       *The Fall of America: Poems of
       These States*
       Adrienne Rich
       *Diving into the Wreck: Poems
       1971–1972*
1975   Marilyn Hacker
       Presentation Piece
1976   John Ashbery
       Self-Portrait in a Convex Mirror
1977   Richard Eberhart
       Collected Poems, 1930–1976
1978   Howard Nemerov
       *The Collected Poems of Howard
       Nemerov*
1979   James Merrill
       Mirabell: Book of Numbers
1980   Philip Levine
       Ashes
1981   Lisel Mueller
       The Need to Hold Still
1982   William Bronk
       *Life Supports: New and
       Collected Poems*
1983   Galway Kinnell
       Selected Poems
       Charles Wright
       *Country Music: Selected Early
       Poems*
1991   Philip Levine
       What Work Is
1992   Mary Oliver
       New and Selected Poems
1993   A. R. Ammons

       Garbage
1994   James Tate
       A Worshipful Company of Fletchers
1995   Stanley Kunitz
       *Passing Through: The Later
       Poems New and Selected*
1996   Hayden Carruth
       Scrambled Eggs and Whiskey
1997   William Meredith
       *Effort at Speech: New and
       Selected Poems*
1998   Gerald Stern
       *This Time: New and Selected
       Poems*
1999   Ai
       Vice: New and Selected Poems

Young People's Literature

1996   Victor Martinez
       Parrot in the Oven: Mi Vida
1997   Han Dolan
       Dancing on the Edge
1998   Louis Sachar
       Holes
1999   Kimberly Willis Holt
       *When Zachary Beaver Came to
       Town*

NEWBERY MEDAL BOOKS

For children's literature

1922   Hendrik van Loon
       The Story of Mankind
1923   Hugh Lofting
       The Voyages of Doctor Dolittle
1924   Charles Hawes
       The Dark Frigate
1925   Charles Finger
       Tales from Silver Lands
1926   Arthur Chrisman
       Shen of the Sea
1927   Will James
       Smoky, the Cowhorse
1928   Dhan Mukerji
       Gay Neck, the Story of a Pigeon
1929   Eric P. Kelly
       The Trumpeter of Krakow
1930   Rachel Field
       Hitty, Her First Hundred Years
1931   Elizabeth Coatsworth
       The Cat Who Went to Heaven
1932   Laura Armer
       Waterless Mountain
1933   Elizabeth Lewis
       Young Fu of the Upper Yangtze
1934   Cornelia Meigs
       Invincible Louisa
1935   Monica Shannon
       Dobry
1936   Carol Brink
       Caddie Woodlawn
1937   Ruth Sawyer
       Roller Skates
1938   Kate Seredy

The White Stag
1939 Elizabeth Enright
Thimble Summer
1940 James Daugherty
Daniel Boone
1941 Armstrong Sperry
Call It Courage
1942 Walter Edmonds
The Matchlock Gun
1943 Elizabeth Gray
Adam of the Road
1944 Esther Forbes
Johnny Tremain
1945 Robert Lawson
Rabbit Hill
1946 Lois Lenski
Strawberry Girl
1947 Carolyn Bailey
Miss Hickory
1948 William Pène du Bois
The Twenty-One Balloons
1949 Marguerite Henry
King of the Wind
1950 Marguerite de Angeli
The Door in the Wall
1951 Elizabeth Yates
Amos Fortune, Free Man
1952 Eleanor Estes
Ginger Pye
1953 Ann Nolan Clark
Secret of the Andes
1954 Joseph Krumgold
...And Now Miguel
1955 Meindert DeJong
The Wheel on the School
1956 Jean Lee Latham
Carry On, Mr. Bowditch
1957 Virginia Sorenson
Miracles on Maple Hill
1958 Harold Keith
Rifles for Watie
1959 Elizabeth George Speare
The Witch of Blackbird Pond
1960 Joseph Krumgold
Onion John
1961 Scott O'Dell
Island of the Blue Dolphins
1962 Elizabeth George Speare
The Bronze Bow
1963 Madeleine L'Engle
A Wrinkle in Time
1964 Emily Neville
It's Like This, Cat
1965 Maia Wojciechowska
Shadow of a Bull
1966 Elizabeth Borton de Trevino
I, Juan de Pareja
1967 Irene Hunt
Up a Road Slowly
1968 E. L. Konigsburg
From the Mixed-Up Files of Mrs. Basil E. Frankweiler

1969 Lloyd Alexander
The High King
1970 William H. Armstrong
Sounder
1971 Betsy Byars
Summer of the Swans
1972 Robert C. O'Brien
Mrs. Frisby and the Rats of NIMH
1973 Jean Craighead George
Julie of the Wolves
1974 Paula Fox
The Slave Dancer
1975 Virginia Hamilton
M. C. Higgins, the Great
1976 Susan Cooper
The Grey King
1977 Mildred D. Taylor
Roll of Thunder, Hear My Cry
1978 Katherine Paterson
Bridge to Terabithia
1979 Ellen Raskin
The Westing Game
1980 Joan W. Blos
A Gathering of Days
1981 Katherine Paterson
Jacob Have I Loved
1982 Nancy Willard
A Visit to William Blake's Inn: Poems for Innocent and Experienced Travelers
1983 Cynthia Voight
Dicey's Song
1984 Beverly Cleary
Dear Mr. Henshaw
1985 Robin McKinley
The Hero and the Crown
1986 Patricia MacLachlan
Sarah, Plain and Tall
1987 Sid Fleischman
The Whipping Boy
1988 Russell Freedman
Lincoln: A Photobiography
1989 Paul Fleischman
Joyful Noise: Poems for Two Voices
1990 Lois Lowry
Number the Stars
1991 Jerry Spinelli
Maniac Magee
1992 Phyllis Reynolds Naylor
Shiloh
1993 Cynthia Rylant
Missing May
1994 Lois Lowry
The Giver
1995 Sharon Creech
Walk Two Moons
1996 Karen Cushman
The Midwife's Apprentice
1997 E. L. Konigsburg
The View from Saturday
1998 Karen Hesse
Out of Dust

1999 Louis Sachar
Holes

CALDECOTT MEDAL BOOKS

For children's picture books

1938 Helen Dean Fish, ill. by Dorothy P. Lathrop
Animals of the Bible
1939 Thomas Handforth
Mei Li
1940 Ingri and Edgar Parin d'Aulaire
Abraham Lincoln
1941 Robert Lawson
They Were Strong and Good
1942 Robert McCloskey
Make Way for Ducklings
1943 Virginia Lee Burton
The Little House
1944 James Thurber, ill. by Louis Slobodkin
Many Moons
1945 Rachel Field, ill. by Elizabeth Orton Jones
Prayer for a Child
1946 Maude and Mishka Petersham
The Rooster Crows
1947 Golden MacDonald, ill. by Leonard Weisgard
The Little Island
1948 Alvin Tresselt, ill. by Roger Duvoisin
White Snow, Bright Snow
1949 Berta and Elmer Hader
The Big Snow
1950 Leo Politi
Song of the Swallows
1951 Katherine Milhous
The Egg Tree
1952 Will Lipkind, ill. by Nicolas Mordvinoff
Finders Keepers
1953 Lynd Ward
The Biggest Bear
1954 Ludwig Bemelmans
Madeline's Rescue
1955 Marcia Brown
Cinderella
1956 John Langstaff, ill. by Feodor Rojankovsky
Frog Went A-Courtin'
1957 Janice Udry, ill. by Marc Simont
A Tree Is Nice
1958 Robert McCloskey
Time of Wonder
1959 Barbara Cooney
Chanticleer and the Fox
1960 Marie Hall Ets and Aurora Labastida
Nine Days to Christmas
1961 Ruth Robbins, ill. by Nicolas Sidjakov
Baboushka and the Three Kings

1962	Marcia Brown	
	Once a Mouse	
1963	Ezra Jack Keats	
	The Snowy Day	
1964	Maurice Sendak	
	Where the Wild Things Are	
1965	Beatrice Schenk de Regniers, ill.	
	by Beni Montresor	
	May I Bring a Friend?	
1966	Sorche Nic Leodhas, ill. by Nonny	
	Hogrogian	
	Always Room for One More	
1967	Evaline Ness	
	Sam, Bangs & Moonshine	
1968	Barbara Emberley, ill. by Ed	
	Emberley	
	Drummer Hoff	
1969	Arthur Ransome, ill. by Uri	
	Shulevitz	
	The Fool of the World and the	
	Flying Ship	
1970	William Steig	
	Sylvester and the Magic Pebble	
1971	Gail E. Haley	
	A Story a Story	
1972	Nonny Hogrogian	
	One Fine Day	
1973	Lafcadio Hearn, retold by Arlene	
	Mosel, ill. by Blair Lent	
	The Funny Little Woman	
1974	Harve Zemach, picts. by Margot	
	Zemach	
	Duffy and the Devil	
1975	Gerald McDermott	
	Arrow to the Sun	
1976	Verna Aardema, picts. by Leo	
	and Diane Dillon	
	Why Mosquitoes Buzz in People's	
	Ears	
1977	Margaret Musgrove, picts. by Leo	
	and Diane Dillon	
	Ashanti to Zulu	
1978	Peter Spier	
	Noah's Ark	
1979	Paul Goble	
	The Girl Who Loved Wild Horses	
1980	Donald Hall, picts. by Barbara	
	Cooney	
	Ox-Cart Man	
1981	Arnold Lobel	
	Fables	
1982	Chris Van Allsburg	
	Jumanji	
1983	Blaise Cendrars, trans. and ill.	
	by Marcia Brown	
	Shadow	
1984	Alice and Martin Provensen	
	The Glorious Flight: Across the	
	Channel with Louis Blériot	
1985	Margaret Hodges, ill. by Trina	
	Schart Hyman	
	Saint George and the Dragon	
1986	Chris Van Allsburg	
	The Polar Express	

1987	Arthur Yorinks, ill. by Richard
	Egielski
	Hey, Al
1988	Jane Yolen, ill. by John Schoenherr
	Owl Moon
1989	Karen Ackerman, ill. by Stephen
	Gammell
	Song and Dance Man
1990	Ed Young
	Lon Po Po
1991	David Macaulay
	Black and White
1992	David Wiesner
	Tuesday
1993	Emily Arnold McCully
	Mirette on the High Wire
1994	Allen Say
	Grandfather's Journey
1995	Eve Bunting, ill. by David Diaz
	Smoky Night
1996	Peggy Rathmann
	Officer Buckle and Gloria
1997	David Wisniewski
	Golem
1998	Paul O. Zelinsky
	Rapunzel
1999	Mary Azarian
	Snowflake Bentley

BOLLINGEN PRIZE IN POETRY

1949	Wallace Stevens
1950	John Crowe Ransom
1951	Marianne Moore
1952	Archibald MacLeish
	William Carlos Williams
1953	W. H. Auden
1954	Leonie Adams
	Louise Bogan
1955	Conrad Aiken
1956	Allen Tate
1957	E. E. Cummings
1958	Theodore Roethke
1959	Delmore Schwartz
1960	Yvor Winters
1961	Richard Eberhart
	John Hall Wheelock
1962	Robert Frost
1965	Horace Gregory
1967	Robert Penn Warren
1969	John Berryman
	Karl Shapiro
1971	Richard Wilbur
	Mona Van Duyn
1973	James Merrill
1975	A. R. Ammons
1977	David Ignatow
1979	W. S. Merwin
1981	May Swenson
	Howard Nemerov
1983	Anthony E. Hecht
	John Hollander

1985	John Ashbery
	Fred Chappell
1987	Stanley Kunitz
1989	Edgar Bowers
1991	Laura (Riding) Jackson
	Donald Justice
1993	Mark Strand
1995	Kenneth Koch
1997	Gary Snyder
1999	Robert White Creeley

PEN/FAULKNER AWARD

Best American work of fiction

1981	Walter Abish
	How German Is It?
1982	David Bradley
	The Chaneysville Incident
1983	Toby Olson
	Seaview
1984	John Edgar Wideman
	Sent for You Yesterday
1985	Tobias Wolff
	The Barracks Thief
1986	Peter Taylor
	The Old Forest
1987	Richard Wiley
	Soldiers in Hiding
1988	T. Coraghessan Boyle
	World's End
1989	James Salter
	Dusk
1990	E. L. Doctorow
	Billy Bathgate
1991	John Edgar Wideman
	Philadelphia Fire
1992	Don DeLillo
	Mao II
1993	E. Annie Proulx
	Postcards
1994	Philip Roth
	Operation Shylock
1995	David Guterson
	Snow Falling on Cedars
1996	Richard Ford
	Independence Day
1997	Gina Berriault
	Women in Their Beds
1998	Rafi Zabor
	The Bear Comes Home
1999	Michael Cunningham
	The Hours

BOOKER PRIZE

British award for fiction

1969 P. H. Newby
Something to Answer For
1970 Bernice Rubens
The Elected Member
1971 V. S. Naipaul
In a Free State
1972 John Berger
G
1973 J. G. Farrell
The Siege of Krishnapur
1974 Nadine Gordimer
The Conservationist
1975 Ruth Prawer Jhabvala
Heat and Dust
1976 David Storey
Saville
1977 Paul Scott
Staying On
1978 Iris Murdoch
The Sea, the Sea
1979 Penelope Fitzgerald
Offshore
1980 William Golding
Rites of Passage
1981 Salman Rushdie
Midnight's Children
1982 Thomas Keneally
Schindler's Ark
1983 J. M. Coetzee
Life and Times of Michael K
1984 Anita Brookner
Hotel du Lac
1985 Keri Hulme
The Bone People
1986 Kingsley Amis
The Old Devils
1987 Penelope Lively
Moon Tiger
1988 Peter Carey
Oscar and Lucinda
1989 Kazuo Ishiguro
The Remains of the Day
1990 A. S. Byatt
Possession
1991 Ben Okri
The Famished Road
1992 Michael Ondaatje
The English Patient
Barry Unsworth
Sacred Hunger
1993 Roddy Doyle
Paddy Clark Ha Ha Ha
1994 James Kelman
How Late It Was, How Late
1995 Pat Barker
The Ghost Road
1996 Graham Swift
Last Orders
1997 Arundhati Roy
The God of Small Things
1998 Ian McEwan
Amsterdam
1999 J. M Coetzee
Disgrace

NOBEL PRIZE FOR LITERATURE

1901 Rene-Francois-Armend Prudhomme
France
1902 Bjornstjerne Bjornson
Norway
1903 Christian Mommsen
Germany
1904 Jose Echegaray y Eizaguirre
Spain
Frederic Mistral
France
1905 Henryk Sienkiewicz
Poland
1906 Giosue Carducci
Italy
1907 Joseph Rudyard Kipling
Great Britain
1908 Rudolph Eucker
Germany
1909 Selma Lagerlof
Sweden
1910 Paul Ludwig von Heyse
Germany
1911 Maurice Maeterlinck
Belgium
1912 Gerhart Hauptmann
Germany
1913 Sir Rabindranath Tagore
India
1915 Roland Romain
France
1916 Carl Gustof Verner Von
Heidenstam
Sweden
1917 Karl Adolph Gjellerup
Denmark
Henrik Pontoppidan
Denmark
1918 Erik Axel Karlfeldt
Sweden
1919 Carl Spitteler
Switzerland
1920 Knut Hamsun
Norway
1921 Anatole France
France
1922 Jacinto Benaventi y Martinez
Spain
1923 William Butler Yeats
Ireland
1924 Wladylaw Reymont
Poland
1925 George Bernard Shaw
Ireland
1926 Grazia Deledda
Italy
1927 Henri Bergson
France
1928 Sigrid Undset
Norway
1929 Paul Mann
Germany

1930 Henry Sinclair Lewis
United States
1931 Erik Axel Karlfeldt
Sweden
1932 John Galsworthy
Great Britain
1933 Ivan Bunin
Russia
1934 Luigi Pirandello
Italy
1936 Eugene O'Neill
United States
1937 Roger Martin du Gard
France
1938 Pearl S. Buck
United States
1939 Frans Sillanpaa
Finland
1944 Johannes Jensen
Denmark
1945 Gabriela Mistral
Chile
1946 Herman Hesse
Germany
1947 Andre Gide
France
1948 Thomas Stearns Eliot
United States
Isaac Singer
Poland
1949 William Faulkner
United States
1950 Bertrand Russell
Great Britain
1951 Par Fabian Lagerkirst
Sweden
1952 Francois Mauriac
France
1953 Sir Winston Churchill
Great Britain
1954 Ernest Hemingway
United States
1955 Halldor Laxness
Iceland
1956 Juan Jimenez
Spain
1957 Albert Camus
France
1958 Boris Pasternak
Russia
1959 Salvatore Quasimodo
Italy
1960 Saint-John Perse
France
1961 Ivo Andric
Yugoslavia
1962 John Steinbeck
United States
1963 Giorgos Seferis
Greece
1964 Jean-Paul Sartre
France
1965 Mikhail Sholokov
Russia

1966 Shmuel Agnon
     Austria
     Leonie Sachs
     Germany
1967 Miguel Asturias
     Guatemala
1968 Yasunari Kawabata
     Japan
1969 Samuel Beckett
     Ireland
1970 Alexander Solzhenitsyn
     Russia
1971 Pablo Neruda
     Chile
1972 Heinrich Boll
     Germany
1973 Patrick White
     Australia
1974 Euyind Johnson
     Sweden
1975 Eugenio Montale
     Italy
1976 Saul Bellow
     United States
1977 Vicente Aleixandre y Merlo
     Spain
1978 Isaac Bashevis Singer
     United States
1979 Odysseus Elytis
     Greece
1980 Czeslaw Milosz
     Poland
1981 Elias Canetti
     Bulgaria
1982 Gabriel Jose García Márquez
     Colombia
1983 William Golding
     Great Britain
1984 Jaroslav Seifert
     Czechoslovakia
1985 Claude Simon
     France
1986 Wole Soyinka
     Nigeria
1987 Joseph Brodsky
     Russia
1988 Naguib Mahfouz
     Egypt
1989 Camilo Jose Cela
     Spain
1990 Octavio Paz
     Mexico
1991 Nadine Gordimer
     South Africa
1992 Derek Walcott
     St. Lucia
1993 Toni Morrison
     United States
1994 Kenzaburo Oe
     Japan
1995 Seamus Heaney
     Ireland
1996 Wislawa Szymborska
     Poland

1997 Dario Fo
     Italy
1998 José Saramago
     Portugal
1999 Günter Grass
     Germany

NATIONAL MAGAZINE AWARD

Public Service/Public Interest

1970 Life
1971 The Nation
1972 Philadelphia
1973 [not awarded]
1974 Scientific American
1975 Consumer Reports
1976 Business Week
1977 Philadelphia
1978 Mother Jones
1979 New West
1980 Texas Monthly
1981 Reader's Digest
1982 The Atlantic Monthly
1983 Foreign Affairs
1984 The New Yorker
1985 The Washingtonian
1986 Science 85
1987 Money
1988 The Atlantic Monthly
1989 California
1990 Southern Exposure
1991 Family Circle
1992 Glamour
1993 The Family Therapy Network
1994 Philadelphia
1995 The New Republic
1996 Texas Monthly
1997 Fortune
1998 The Atlantic Monthly
1999 Time

Specialized Journalism

1970 Philadelphia
1971 Rolling Stone
1972 Architectural Record
1973 Psychology Today
1974 Texas Monthly
1975 Medical Economics
1976 United Mine Workers Journal
1977 Architectural Record
1978 Scientific American
1979 National Journal
1980 IEEE Spectrum

Design/Visual Excellence

1970 Look
1971 Vogue
1972 Esquire
1973 Horizon
1974 Newsweek
1975 Country Journal
     National Lampoon

1976 Horticulture
1977 Rolling Stone
1978 Architectural Digest
1979 Audubon
1980 GEO
1981 Attenzione
1982 Nautical Quarterly
1983 New York
1984 House & Garden
1985 Forbes
1986 Time
1987 Elle
1988 Life
1989 Rolling Stone
1990 Esquire
1991 Condé Nast Traveler
1992 Vanity Fair
1993 Harper's Bazaar
1994 Allure
1995 Martha Stewart Living
1996 Wired
1997 I.D. Magazine
1998 Entertainment Weekly
1999 ESPN: The Magazine

Reporting (Excellence)/News Reporting

1970 The New Yorker
1971 The Atlantic Monthly
1972 The Atlantic Monthly
1973 New York
1974 The New Yorker
1975 The New Yorker
1976 Audubon
1977 Audubon
1978 The New Yorker
1979 Texas Monthly
1980 Mother Jones
1981 National Journal
1982 The Washingtonian
1983 Institutional Investor
1984 Vanity Fair
1985 Texas Monthly
1986 Rolling Stone
1987 Life
1988 Baltimore Magazine
     The Washingtonian
1989 The New Yorker
1990 The New Yorker
1991 The New Yorker
1992 The New Republic
1993 IEEE Spectrum
1994 The New Yorker
1995 The Atlantic Monthly
1996 The New Yorker
1997 Outside
1998 Rolling Stone
1999 Newsweek

General Excellence
(Under 100,000 circulation)

1981 ARTnews
1982 Camera Arts
1983 Louisiana Life

1984	The American Lawyer	
1985	Manhattan, inc.	
1986	New England Monthly	
1987	New England Monthly	
1988	The Sciences	
1989	The Sciences	
1990	7 Days	
1991	The New Republic	
1992	The New Republic	
1993	Lingua Franca	
1994	Print	
1995	I.D. Magazine	
1996	The Sciences	
1997	I.D. Magazine	
1998	DoubleTake	
1999	I.D. Magazine	

General Excellence (100,000–400,000)

1981	Audubon
1982	Rocky Mountain Magazine
1983	Harper's Magazine
1984	Outside
1985	American Heritage
1986	3-2-1 Contact
1987	Common Cause
1988	Hippocrates
1989	American Heritage
1990	Texas Monthly
1991	Interview
1992	Texas Monthly
1993	American Photo
1994	Wired
1995	Men's Journal
1996	Civilization
1997	Wired
1998	Preservation
1999	Fast Company

General Excellence (400,000–1,000,000)

1981	Business Week
1982	Science 81
1983	Science 82
1984	House & Garden
1985	American Health
1986	Discover
1987	Elle
1988	Fortune
1989	Vanity Fair
1990	Metropolitan Home
1991	Condé Nast Traveler
1992	Mirabella
1993	The Atlantic Monthly
1994	Health
1995	The New Yorker
1996	Outside
1997	Outside
1998	Outside
1999	Condé Nast Traveler

General Excellence (over 1,000,000)

1981	Glamour
1982	Newsweek

1983	Life
1984	National Geographic
1985	Time
1986	Money
1987	People Weekly
1988	Parents
1989	Sports Illustrated
1990	Sports Illustrated
1991	Glamour
1992	National Geographic
1993	Newsweek
1994	Business Week
1995	Entertainment Weekly
1996	Business Week
1997	Vanity Fair
1998	Rolling Stone
1999	Vanity Fair

Essays and Criticism

1978	Esquire
1979	Life
1980	Natural History
1981	Time
1982	The Atlantic Monthly
1983	The American Lawyer
1984	The New Republic
1985	Boston
1986	The Sciences
1987	Outside
1988	Harper's Magazine
1989	Harper's Magazine
1990	Vanity Fair
1991	The Sciences
1992	The Nation
1993	The American Lawyer
1994	Harper's Magazine
1995	Harper's Magazine
1996	The New Yorker
1997	The New Yorker
1998	The New Yorker
1999	The Atlantic Monthly

Fiction

1978	The New Yorker
1979	The Atlantic Monthly
1980	Antaeus
1981	The North American Review
1982	The New Yorker
1983	The North American Review
1984	Seventeen
1985	Playboy
1986	The Georgia Review
1987	Esquire
1988	The Atlantic
1989	The New Yorker
1990	The New Yorker
1991	Esquire
1992	Story
1993	The New Yorker
1994	Harper's Magazine
1995	Story
1996	Harper's Magazine

1997	The New Yorker
1998	The New Yorker
1999	Harper's Magazine

Single Topic Issue

1979	Progressive Architecture
1980	Scientific American
1981	Business Week
1982	Newsweek
1983	IEEE Spectrum
1984	Esquire
1985	American Heritage
1986	IEEE Spectrum
1987	Bulletin of the Atomic Scientists
1988	Life
1989	Hippocrates
1990	National Geographic
1991	The American Lawyer
1992	Business Week
1993	Newsweek
1994	Health
1995	Discover
1996	Bon Appétit
1997	Scientific American
1998	The Sciences
1999	The Oxford American

Personal Service/Service to the Individual

1974	Sports Illustrated
1975	Esquire
1976	Modern Medicine
1977	Harper's Magazine
1978	Newsweek
1979	The American Journal of Nursing
1980	Saturday Review
1982	Philadelphia
1983	Sunset
1984	New York
1985	The Washingtonian
1986	Farm Journal
1987	Consumer Reports
1988	Money
1989	Good Housekeeping
1990	Consumer Reports
1991	New York
1992	Creative Classroom
1993	Good Housekeeping
1994	Fortune
1995	SmartMoney
1996	SmartMoney
1997	Glamour
1998	Men's Journal
1999	Good Housekeeping

Special Interests

1986	Popular Mechanics
1987	Sports Afield
1988	Condé Nast Traveler
1989	Condé Nast Traveler
1990	Arts & Antiques
1991	New York
1992	Sports Afield

1993	Philadelphia
1994	Outside
1995	Gentlemen's Quarterly
1996	Saveur
1997	Smithsonian Magazine
1998	Entertainment Weekly
1999	PC Computing

Photography

1985	Life
1986	Vogue
1987	National Geographic
1988	Rolling Stone
1989	National Geographic
1990	Texas Monthly
1991	National Geographic
1992	National Geographic
1993	Harper's Bazaar
1994	Martha Stewart Living
1995	Rolling Stone
1996	Saveur
1997	National Geographic
1998	W
1999	Martha Stewart Living

Feature Writing

1988	The Atlantic Monthly
1989	Esquire
1990	The Washingtonian
1991	U.S. News & World Report
1992	Sports Illustrated
1993	The New Yorker
1994	Harper's Magazine
1995	Gentlemen's Quarterly
1996	Gentlemen's Quarterly
1997	Sports Illustrated
1998	Harper's Magazine
1999	The American Scholar

New Media

| 1999 | Cigar Aficionado |

PULITZER PRIZE

Fiction

1918	Ernest Poole
	His Family
1919	Booth Tarkington
	The Magnificent Ambersons
1920	No award
1921	Edith Wharton
	The Age of Innocence
1922	Booth Tarkington
	Alice Adams
1923	Willa Cather
	One of Ours
1924	Margaret Wilson
	The Able McLaughlins
1925	Edna Ferber
	So Big
1926	Sinclair Lewis (refused prize)
	Arrowsmith

1927	Louis Bromfield
	Early Autumn
1928	Thornton Wilder
	Bridge of San Luis Rey
1929	Julia M. Peterkin
	Scarlet Sister Mary
1930	Oliver LaFarge
	Laughing Boy
1931	Margaret Ayer Barnes
	Years of Grace
1932	Pearl S. Buck
	The Good Earth
1933	T. S. Stribling
	The Store
1934	Caroline Miller
	Lamb in His Bosom
1935	Josephine W. Johnson
	Now in November
1936	Harold L. Davis
	Honey in the Horn
1937	Margaret Mitchell
	Gone with the Wind
1938	John P. Marquand
	The Late George Apley
1939	Marjorie Kinnan Rawlings
	The Yearling
1940	John Steinbeck
	The Grapes of Wrath
1941	No award
1942	Ellen Glasgow
	In This Our Life
1943	Upton Sinclair
	Dragon's Teeth
1944	Martin Flavin
	Journey in the Dark
1945	John Hersey
	A Bell for Adano
1946	No award
1947	Robert Penn Warren
	All the King's Men
1948	James A. Michener
	Tales of the South Pacific
1949	James Gould Cozzens
	Guard of Honor
1950	A. B. Guthrie, Jr.
	The Way West
1951	Conrad Richter
	The Town
1952	Herman Wouk
	The Caine Mutiny
1953	Ernest Hemingway
	The Old Man and the Sea
1954	No award
1955	William Faulkner
	A Fable
1956	MacKinlay Kantor
	Andersonville
1957	No award
1958	James Agee
	A Death in the Family
1959	Robert Lewis Taylor
	The Travels of Jaimie McPheeters
1960	Allen Drury
	Advise and Consent

1961	Harper Lee
	To Kill a Mockingbird
1962	Edwin O'Connor
	The Edge of Sadness
1963	William Faulkner
	The Reivers
1964	No award
1965	Shirley Ann Grau
	The Keepers of the House
1966	Katherine Anne Porter
	The Collected Stories of Katherine Anne Porter
1967	Bernard Malamud
	The Fixer
1968	William Styron
	The Confessions of Nat Turner
1969	N. Scott Momaday
	House Made of Dawn
1970	Jean Stafford
	Collected Stories
1971	No award
1972	Wallace Stegner
	Angle of Repose
1973	Eudora Welty
	The Optimist's Daughter
1974	No award
1975	Michael Shaara
	The Killer Angels
1976	Saul Bellow
	Humboldt's Gift
1977	No award
1978	James Alan McPherson
	Elbow Room
1979	John Cheever
	The Stories of John Cheever
1980	Norman Mailer
	The Executioner's Song
1981	John Kennedy Toole
	A Confederacy of Dunces
1982	John Updike
	Rabbit Is Rich
1983	Alice Walker
	The Color Purple
1984	William Kennedy
	Ironweed
1985	Alison Lurie
	Foreign Affairs
1986	Larry McMurtry
	Lonesome Dove
1987	Peter Taylor
	A Summons to Memphis
1988	Toni Morrison
	Beloved
1989	Anne Tyler
	Breathing Lessons
1990	Oscar Hijuelos
	The Mambo Kings Play Songs of Love
1991	John Updike
	Rabbit at Rest
1992	Jane Smiley
	A Thousand Acres
1993	Robert Olen Butler
	A Good Scent from a Strange Mountain

1994 E. Annie Proulx
The Shipping News
1995 Carol Shields
The Stone Diaries
1996 Richard Ford
Independence Day
1997 Steven Millhauser
Martin Dressler: The Tale of an American Dreamer
1998 Philip Roth
American Pastoral
1999 Michael Cunningham
The Hours

Nonfiction

1962 Theodore H. White
The Making of the President, 1960
1963 Barbara W. Tuchman
The Guns of August
1964 Richard Hofstadter
Anti-Intellectualism in American Life
1965 Howard Mumford Jones
O Strange New World
1966 Edwin Way Teale
Wandering Through Winter
1967 David Brion Davis
The Problem of Slavery in Western Culture
1968 Will Durant and Ariel Durant
Rousseau and Revolution: The Tenth and Concluding Volume of The Story of Civilization
1969 Norman Mailer
The Armies of the Night
Rene Jules Dubos
So Human an Animal
1970 Erik H. Erikson
Gandhi's Truth
1971 John Toland
The Rising Sun
1972 Barbara W. Tuchman
Stilwell and the American Experience in China, 1911–1945
1973 Robert Coles
Children of Crisis, Vols. II and III
Francis FitzGerald
Fire in the Lake: The Vietnamese and the Americans in Vietnam
1974 Ernest Becker
The Denial of Death
1975 Annie Dillard
Pilgrim at Tinker Creek
1976 Robert N. Butler
Why Survive?: Being Old in America
1977 William W. Warner
Beautiful Swimmers
1978 Carl Sagan
The Dragons of Eden
1979 Edward O. Wilson
On Human Nature
1980 Douglas R. Hofstadter
Gödel, Escher, Bach: An Eternal Golden Braid

1981 Carl E. Schorske
Fin-de-Siecle Vienna: Politics and Culture
1982 Tracy Kidder
The Soul of a New Machine
1983 Susan Sheehan
Is There No Place on Earth for Me ?
1984 Paul Starr
The Social Transformation of American Medicine
1985 Studs Terkel
The Good War: An Oral History of World War Two
1986 J. Anthony Lukas
Common Ground: A Turbulent Decade in the Lives of Three American Families
Joseph Lelyveld
Move Your Shadow
1987 David K. Shipler
Arab and Jew: Wounded Spirits in a Promised Land
1988 Richard Rhodes
The Making of the Atomic Bomb
1989 Neil Sheehan
A Bright Shining Lie: John Paul Vann and America in Vietnam
1990 Dale Maharidge and Michael Williamson
And Their Children After Them
1991 Bert Holdobler and Edward O. Wilson
The Ants
1992 Daniel Yergin
The Prize: The Epic Quest for Oil, Money, and Power
1993 Garry Wills
Lincoln at Gettysburg
1994 David Remnick
Lenin's Tomb
1995 Jonathan Weiner
The Beak of the Finch: A Story of Evolution in Our Time
1996 Tina Rosenberg
The Haunted Land: Facing Europe's Ghosts After Communism
1997 Richard Kluger
Ashes to Ashes: America's Hundred-Year Cigarette War, the Public Health, and the Unabashed Triumph of Philip Morris
1998 Jared Diamond
Guns, Germs, and Steel: The Fates of Human Societies
1999 John A. McPhee
Annals of the Former World

Poetry

1918 Sara Teasdale
Love Songs
1919 Carl Sandburg
Corn Huskers
Margaret Widemer
Old Road to Paradise

1920 No award
1921 No award
1922 Edwin Arlington Robinson
Collected Poems
1923 Edna St. Vincent Millay
The Ballad of the Harp-Weaver; A Few Figs from Thistles; Eight Sonnets in American Poetry, 1922; A Miscellany
1924 Robert Frost
New Hampshire: A Poem with Notes and Grace Notes
1925 Edwin Arlington Robinson
The Man Who Died Twice
1926 Amy Lowell
What's O'Clock
1927 Leonora Speyer
Fiddler's Farewell
1928 Edwin Arlington Robinson
Tristram
1929 Stephen Vincent Benet
John Brown's Body
1930 Conrad Aiken
Selected Poems
1931 Robert Frost
Collected Poems
1932 George Dillon
The Flowering Stone
1933 Archibald MacLeish
Conquistador
1934 Robert Hillyer
Collected Verse
1935 Audrey Wurdemann
Bright Ambush
1936 Robert P. Tristram Coffin
Strange Holiness
1937 Robert Frost
A Further Range
1938 Marya Zaturenska
Cold Morning Sky
1939 John Gould Fletcher
Selected Poems
1940 Mark Van Doren
Collected Poems
1941 Leornard Bacon
Sunderland Capture
1942 William Rose Benet
The Dust Which Is God
1943 Robert Frost
A Witness Tree
1944 Stephen Vincent Benet
Western Star
1945 Karl Shapiro
V-Letter and Other Poems
1946 No award
1947 Robert Lowell
Lord Weary's Castle
1948 W. H. Auden
The Age of Anxiety
1949 Peter Viereck
Terror and Decorum
1950 Gwendolyn Brooks
Annie Allen

1951	Carl Sandburg *Complete Poems*	1967	Anne Sexton *Live or Die*	1984	Mary Oliver *American Primitive*
1952	Marianne Moore *Collected Poems*	1968	Anthony Hecht *The Hard Hours*	1985	Carolyn Kizer *Yin*
1953	Archibald MacLeish *Collected Poems 1917–1952*	1969	George Oppen *Of Being Numerous*	1986	Henry Taylor *The Flying Change*
1954	Theodore Roethke *The Waking*	1970	Richard Howard *Untitled Subjects*	1987	Rita Dove *Thomas and Beulah*
1955	Wallace Stevens *Collected Poems*	1971	W. S. Merwin *The Carrier of Ladders*	1988	William Meredith *Partial Accounts: New and Selected Poems*
1956	Elizabeth Bishop *Poems, North and South*	1972	James Wright *Collected Poems*	1989	Richard Wilbur *New and Collected Poems*
1957	Richard Wilbur *Things of This World*	1973	Maxine Kumin *Up Country*	1990	Charles Simic *The World Doesn't End*
1958	Robert Penn Warren *Promises: Poems 1954–1956*	1974	Robert Lowell *The Dolphin*	1991	Mona Van Duyn *Near Changes*
1959	Stanley Kunitz *Selected Poems 1928–1958*	1975	Gary Snyder *Turtle Island*	1992	James Tate *Selected Poems*
1960	W. D. Snodgrass *Heart's Needle*	1976	John Ashbery *Self-Portrait in a Convex Mirror*	1993	Louise Gluck *The Wild Iris*
1961	Phyllis McGinley *Times Three: Selected Verse from Three Decades*	1977	James Merrill *Divine Comedies*	1994	Yusef Komunyakaa *Neon Vernacular*
1962	Alan Dugan *Poems*	1978	Howard Nemerov *Collected Poems*	1995	Philip Levine *The Simple Truth*
1963	William Carlos Williams *Pictures from Breughel*	1979	Robert Penn Warren *Now and Then*	1996	Jorie Graham *The Dream of the Unified Field*
1964	Louis Simpson *At the End of the Open Road*	1980	Donald Justice *Selected Poems*	1997	Lisel Mueller *Alive Together*
1965	John Berryman *77 Dream Songs*	1981	James Schuyler *The Morning of the Poem*	1998	Charles Wright *Black Zodiac*
1966	Richard Eberhart *Selected Poems*	1982	Sylvia Plath *The Collected Poems*	1999	Mark Strand *Blizzard of One*
		1983	Galway Kinnell *Selected Poems*		

STAGE

BROADWAY SHOWS OF THE 1999–2000 SEASON

This year on the Great White Way, plays staged a comeback, making up nearly half of the new openings—and providing the season's hot ticket, Philip Seymour Hoffman and John C. Reilly in the Broadway bow of Sam Shepard's *True West*. (Source: *Variety*)

NEW PRODUCTIONS

Aida (M)
Amadeus (R)
Copenhagen
Contact (M)
Dame Edna: The Royal Tour (Sp)
Dirty Blonde
Epic Proportions
The Green Bird
*Jackie Mason: Much Ado About
    Everything (Sp-So)*
James Joyce's The Dead (M)
Jesus Christ Superstar (M-R)
Kat and the Kings (M)
Kiss Me Kate (M-R)
Marie Christine (M)
Minnelli on Minnelli (Sp)
A Moon for the Misbegotten (R)
The Music Man (M-R)
The Price (R)
Putting It Together (M)
The Rainmaker (R)
The Real Thing (R)
The Ride Down Mt. Morgan
Riverdance-On Broadway (M-Rev)
Rose
Saturday Night Fever (M)
Squonk (Sp)

Swing! (M)
Taller than a Dwarf
Tango Argentino (Sp)
True West
Uncle Vanya (R)
Voices in the Dark
Waiting in the Wings
The Wild Party (M)
Wrong Mountain

HOLDOVERS

Annie Get Your Gun (M-R)
Beauty and the Beast (M)
Cabaret (M-R)
Cats (M)
Chicago (M-R)
The Civil War (M)
Closer
Death of a Salesman (R)
Footloose (M)
Fosse (M)
It Ain't Nothin' but the Blues (M)
Jekyll & Hyde (M)
Les Misérables (M)
The Lion King (M)
The Lonesome West
Miss Saigon (M)
Not About Nightingales

The Phantom of the Opera (M)
Ragtime (M)
Rent (M)
The Scarlet Pimpernel (M)
Side Man
Smokey Joe's Cafe (M-Rev)
The Sound of Music (M-R)
The Weir
*You're a Good Man, Charlie Brown
    (M-R)*

(M) denotes musical
(R) denotes revival
(So) denotes solo performance
(Rev) denotes revue
(Sp) denotes special attraction

THAT'S SHOW BIZ

Watch out for that dip in the road! After years of outshining Times Square at the box office, Broadway's touring productions took it on the chin this season. Are the new megamusicals less magnetic than well-seen warhorses like *Phantom* or *Les Miz*? (Source: *Variety*)

Season	Broadway box office/ total shows during most profitable week	Road box office/ total shows during most profitable week
1982–83	$203.1 million/27 shows	$184.3 million/24 shows
1987–88	$253.5 million/21 shows	$223.0 million/24 shows
1992–93	$327.7 million/21 shows	$620.6 million/34 shows
1993–94	$356.0 million/21 shows	$687.7 million/30 shows
1994–95	$406.3 million/23 shows	$694.6 million/33 shows
1995–96	$436.1 million/28 shows	$762.3 million/27 shows
1996–97	$499.4 million/27 shows	$752.9 million/27 shows
1997–98	$557.3 million/32 shows	$794.1 million/26 shows
1998–99	$588.1 million/30 shows	$711.4 million/26 shows
1999–00	$602.6 million/36 shows	$584.5 million/23 shows

LONGEST-RUNNING SHOWS ON BROADWAY

"Now and Forever" is no more. After 18 years, *Cats* has closed in New York—but not before clawing its way to the top of our list of Broadway's longest-running shows. Positions are based on the number of performances as of September 10, 2000. (M) stands for musical and (R) for revival. (Source: *Variety*)

Cats (M) (1982–00)	7,485	*Same Time, Next Year* (1976–78)	1,453
A Chorus Line (M) (1975–90)	6,137	*Arsenic and Old Lace* (1941–44)	1,444
Oh! Calcutta! (M-R) (1976–89)	5,852	*The Sound of Music* (M) (1959–63)	1,443
Les Misérables (M) (1987–)	5,562	*Me and My Girl* (M-R) (1986–89)	1,420
The Phantom of the Opera (M) (1988–)	5,270	*How to Succeed in Business*	
Miss Saigon (M) (1991–)	3,920	*Without Really Trying* (M) (1961–65)	1,417
42nd Street (M) (1980–89)	3,486	*Jekyll & Hyde* (1997–)	1,407
Grease (M) (1972–80)	3,388	*Hellzapoppin* (M) (1938–41)	1,404
Fiddler on the Roof (M) (1964–72)	3,242	*The Music Man* (M) (1957–61)	1,375
Life with Father (1939–47)	3,224	*Funny Girl* (M) (1964–67)	1,348
Tobacco Road (1933–41)	3,182	*Mummenschanz* (M) (1977–80)	1,326
Hello, Dolly! (M) (1964–70)	2,844	*Oh! Calcutta!* (M) (1969–72)	1,314
My Fair Lady (M) (1956–62)	2,717	*Angel Street* (1941–44)	1,295
Beauty and the Beast (M) (1994–)	2,591	*Lightnin'* (1918–21)	1,291
Annie (M) (1977–83)	2,377	*Promises, Promises* (M) (1968–72)	1,281
Man of La Mancha (M) (1965–71)	2,328	*The King and I* (M) (1951–54)	1,246
Abie's Irish Rose (1922–27)	2,327	*Cactus Flower* (1965–68)	1,234
Oklahoma! (M) (1943–48)	2,212	*Grease* (M-R) (1993–98)	1,231
Smokey Joe's Cafe (M) (1995–2000)	2,036	*Torch Song Trilogy* (1982–85)	1,222
Pippin (M) (1972–77)	1,944	*Sleuth* (1970–73)	1,222
South Pacific (M) (1949–54)	1,925	*1776* (M) (1969–72)	1,217
The Magic Show (M) (1974–78)	1,920	*Equus* (1974–77)	1,209
Rent (M) (1996–)	1,825	*Sugar Babies* (M) (1979–82)	1,208
Deathtrap (1978–82)	1,792	*Guys and Dolls* (M) (1950–53)	1,200
Gemini (1977–81)	1,788	*The Lion King* (M) (1997–)	1,182
Harvey (1944–49)	1,775	*Amadeus* (1980–83)	1,181
Dancin' (M) (1978–82)	1,774	*Cabaret* (M) (1966–69)	1,165
La Cage aux folles (M) (1983–87)	1,761	*Mister Roberts* (1948–51)	1,157
Hair (M) (1968–72)	1,750	*Annie Get Your Gun* (M) (1946–49)	1,147
The Wiz (M) (1975–79)	1,672	*Guys and Dolls* (M-R) (1992–95)	1,143
Born Yesterday (1946–49)	1,642	*The Seven Year Itch* (1952–55)	1,141
Crazy for You (1992-96)	1,622	*Butterflies Are Free* (1969–72)	1,128
Ain't Misbehavin' (M) (1978–82)	1,604	*Pins and Needles* (M) (1937–40)	1,108
Chicago (M-R) (1996–)	1,602	*Plaza Suite* (1968–70)	1,097
Best Little Whorehouse in Texas (M) (1978–82)	1,584	*They're Playing Our Song* (M) (1979–81)	1,082
Mary, Mary (1961–64)	1,572	*Kiss Me, Kate* (M) (1948–51)	1,070
Evita (M) (1979–83)	1,567	*Don't Bother Me, I Can't*	
Voice of the Turtle (1943–48)	1,557	*Cope* (M) (1972–74)	1,065
Barefoot in the Park (1963–64)	1,530	*The Pajama Game* (M) (1954–56)	1,063
Brighton Beach Memoirs (1983–86)	1,530	*Shenandoah* (M) (1975–77)	1,050
Dreamgirls (M) (1981–85)	1,521	*Teahouse of the August Moon* (1953–56)	1,027
Mame (M) (1966–70)	1,508		

BROADWAY'S FAVORITES: PLACE THAT TUNE

Know the song but can't place the musical in which it originally appeared? Here is a checklist of some Great White Way melodies that linger on.

SONG	SHOW
"Almost Like Being in Love"	Brigadoon
"And I Am Telling You I'm Not Going"	Dreamgirls
"Anything You Can Do"	Annie Get Your Gun
"Bali Ha'i"	South Pacific
"The Ballad of Mack the Knife"	The Threepenny Opera
"Bewitched, Bothered, and Bewildered"	Pal Joey
"A Bushel and a Peck"	Guys and Dolls
"Climb Ev'ry Mountain"	The Sound of Music
"Everything's Coming Up Roses"	Gypsy
"Getting to Know You"	The King and I
"I Am What I Am"	La Cage aux folles
"I Cain't Say No"	Oklahoma!
"I Could Have Danced All Night"	My Fair Lady
"I Don't Know How to Love Him"	Jesus Christ Superstar
"I Feel Pretty"	West Side Story
"I Get a Kick Out of You"	Anything Goes
"I Got Plenty o' Nothin' "	Porgy and Bess
"I Got Rhythm"	Girl Crazy
"I Got the Sun in the Morning"	Annie Get Your Gun
"I Whistle a Happy Tune"	The King and I
"If Ever I Would Leave You"	Camelot
"It Ain't Necessarily So"	Porgy and Bess
"I've Grown Accustomed to Her Face"	My Fair Lady
"Let the Sunshine In"	Hair
"Lover, Come Back to Me"	The New Moon
"Luck Be a Lady"	Guys and Dolls
"Maria"	West Side Story
"Memory"	Cats

SONG	SHOW
"The Music of the Night"	The Phantom of the Opera
"My Favorite Things"	The Sound of Music
"Oh, What a Beautiful Mornin' "	Oklahoma!
"Ol' Man River"	Show Boat
"One Night in Bangkok"	Chess
"On the Street Where You Live"	My Fair Lady
"The Quest (The Impossible Dream)"	Man of La Mancha
"Seasons of Love"	Rent
"Seventy-Six Trombones"	The Music Man
"Shall We Dance?"	The King and I
"Smoke Gets in Your Eyes"	Roberta
"Some Enchanted Evening"	South Pacific
"The Sound of Music"	The Sound of Music
"Summertime"	Porgy and Bess
"Sunrise, Sunset"	Fiddler on the Roof
"Tea for Two"	No, No, Nanette
"Thank Heaven for Little Girls"	Gigi
"There Is Nothin' Like a Dame"	South Pacific
"There's No Business Like Show Business"	Annie Get Your Gun
"This Is the Army, Mr. Jones"	This Is the Army
"This is the Moment"	Jekyll & Hyde
"Till There Was You"	The Music Man
"Tomorrow"	Annie
"Tonight"	West Side Story
"You'll Never Walk Alone"	Carousel
"You're the Top"	Anything Goes
"We Need a Little Christmas"	Mame
"What I Did for Love"	A Chorus Line

SCHOOLS FOR STARS

Even some of the most talented thespians have honed their gifts in the classroom, as indicated by the alumni rolls of these five career-nurturing institutions.

CARNEGIE MELLON SCHOOL OF DRAMA

Shari Belafonte, actor
Steven Bochco, producer
Albert Brooks, actor/director
Ted Danson, actor
Iris Rainier Dart, novelist
Barbara Feldon, actor
Mark Frost, producer
Mariette Hartley, actor
Holly Hunter, actor
Jack Klugman, actor
Judith Light, actor
Burke Moses, actor
John Pasquin, director
George Peppard, actor
George Romero, director
Laura San Giacomo, actor
Ellen Travolta, actor
Michael Tucker, actor
Blair Underwood, actor
John Wells, producer

JUILLIARD SCHOOL DRAMA DIVISION

Christine Baranski, actor
Andre Braugher, actor
Kelsey Grammer, actor
William Hurt, actor
Laura Linney, actor
Patti LuPone, actor/singer
Val Kilmer, actor
Kevin Kline, actor/director
Linda Kozlowski, actor
Kelly McGillis, actor
Elizabeth McGovern, actor
Mandy Patinkin, actor/singer
Christopher Reeve, actor
Ving Rhames, actor
Kevin Spacey, actor
Jeanne Tripplehorn, actor
Robin Williams, actor

NEW YORK UNIVERSITY, TISCH SCHOOL OF THE ARTS

Alec Baldwin, actor
Barry Bostwick, actor
Joel Coen, screenwriter
Billy Crudup, actor
Kathryn Erbe, actor
Bridget Fonda, actor
Lisa Gay Hamilton, actor
Marcia Gay Harden, actor
Kristen Johnston, actor
Tony Kushner, playwright
Eriq LaSalle, actor
Spike Lee, director/screenwriter/actor
Camryn Manheim, actor
Andrew McCarthy, actor
Jerry O'Connell, actor
Adam Sandler, actor
Kevin Spacey, actor
Stephen Spinella, actor
D. B. Sweeney, actor
Skeet Ulrich, actor
George C. Wolfe, director

NORTHWESTERN UNIVERSITY SCHOOL OF SPEECH

Ann-Margret, actor/dancer
Warren Beatty, actor
Richard Benjamin, actor
Karen Black, actor
Brad Hall, actor
Charlton Heston, actor
Sherry Lansing, producer
Shelly Long, actor
Julia Louis-Dreyfus, actor
Dermot Mulroney, actor
Patricia Neal, actor
Jerry Orbach, actor
Paula Prentiss, actor
Tony Randall, actor
Tony Roberts, actor
David Schwimmer, actor
Peter Strauss, actor
Kimberly Williams, actor

YALE SCHOOL OF DRAMA

Angela Bassett, actor
Robert Brustein, director/writer
David Duchovny, actor
Christopher Durang, playwright
Charles S. Dutton, actor
Jill Eikenberry, actor
David Alan Grier, actor
John Guare, playwright
A. R. Gurney, playwright
Julie Harris, actor
Tama Janowitz, writer
Elia Kazan, director
Stacy Keach, actor
Mark Linn-Baker, actor
Santo Loquasto, set designer
Frances McDormand, actor
Paul Newman, actor
Carrie Nye, actor
Tony Shalhoub, actor
Talia Shire, actor
Meryl Streep, actor
Ted Tally, playwright/screenwriter
John Turturro, actor/director
Joan Van Ark, actor
Courtney B. Vance, actor
Wendy Wasserstein, playwright
Sigourney Weaver, actor
Edmund Wilson, writer
Henry Winkler, actor/director

MAJOR SHOWS THAT BEGAN IN REGIONAL THEATERS

Beginning in the '70s, the creative impetus in American drama began to shift away from the increasingly expensive Broadway venues and toward regional and nonprofit theaters. While most major playwrights once wrote directly for Broadway production, regional theaters have more commonly become the place of origination for America's most important plays. The following productions may have gone on to national and even international fame, but they all began in regional theaters.

American Buffalo, by David Mamet, Goodman Theater, Chicago

Angels in America, by Tony Kushner, Eureka Theatre Company, San Francisco

Annie, by Thomas Meehan, Martin Charnin, and Charles Strouse, Goodspeed Opera House, East Haddam, Connecticut

Big River, adapted by William Hauptman from Mark Twain, La Jolla Playhouse, La Jolla, California

Buried Child, by Sam Shepard, Magic Theater, San Francisco

California Suite, by Neil Simon, Hartman Theatre, Stamford, Connecticut

Children of a Lesser God, by Mark Medoff, Mark Taper Forum, Los Angeles

The Colored Museum, by George C. Wolfe, Crossroads Theatre Company, New Brunswick, New Jersey

Conversations with My Father, by Herb Gardner, Seattle Repertory Theatre

Crimes of the Heart, by Beth Henley, Actors Theatre of Louisville

Eastern Standard, by Richard Greenberg, Seattle Repertory Theatre

Fences, by August Wilson, Yale Repertory Theatre, New Haven, Connecticut

The Gin Game, by D. L. Coburn, Long Wharf Theatre, New Haven, Connecticut

Glengarry Glen Ross, by David Mamet, Goodman Theatre, Chicago

The Heidi Chronicles, by Wendy Wasserstein, Seattle Repertory Theatre

How to Succeed in Business Without Really Trying, La

BROADWAY: PRICEY, DICEY, BUT FILLING SEATS

Theater attendance actually declined for the first time in years, as prices jumped than they have in years. (Source: *Variety*)

Year	Average Ticket Price	Attendance	Year	Average Ticket Price	Attendance
1975-76	$9.86	7,181,898	1987-88	$31.65	8,142,722
1976-77	10.60	8,815,095	1988-89	32.88	7,968,273
1977-78	12.05	8,621,262	1989-90	35.24	8,039,106
1978-79	14.02	9,115,613	1990-91	36.53	7,314,138
1979-80	15.29	9,380,648	1991-92	39.69	7,365,528
1980-81	17.97	10,822,324	1992-93	41.71	7,856,727
1981-82	22.07	10,025,788	1993-94	43.87	8,116,031
1982-83	25.07	8,102,262	1994-95	44.92	9,044,763
1983-84	28.68	7,898,765	1995-96	46.06	9,468,210
1984-85	29.06	7,156,683	1996-97	48.40	10,318,217
1985-86	29.20	6,527,498	1997-98	49.39	11,283,378
1986-87	29.74	6,968,277	1998-99	50.68	11,605,278
			1999-2000	53.02	11,365,309

Jolla Playhouse, La Jolla, California

I'm Not Rappaport, by Herb Gardner, Seattle Repertory Theatre

In the Belly of the Beast, adapted by Adrian Hall from Jack Henry Abbott, Trinity Repertory Company, Providence, Rhode Island

Into the Woods, by James Lapine and Stephen Sondheim, Old Globe Theatre, San Diego

Jekyll & Hyde, by Frank Wildhorn, Alley Theatre, Houston, Texas

Jelly's Last Jam, by George C. Wolfe, Jelly Roll Morton, and Susan Birkenhead, Mark Taper Forum, Los Angeles

Joe Turner's Come and Gone, by August Wilson, Yale Repertory Theatre, New Haven, Connecticut

Love Letters, by A. R. Gurney, Long Wharf Theatre, New Haven, Connecticut

Ma Rainey's Black Bottom, by August Wilson, Yale Repertory Theatre, New Haven, Connecticut

Master Class, by Terrence McNally, Philadelphia Theater Company, Pennsylvania

"Master Harold"...and the Boys, by Athol Fugard, Yale Repertory Theatre, New Haven, Connecticut

'Night, Mother, by Marsha Norman, American Repertory Theatre, Cambridge, Massachusetts

Prelude to a Kiss, by Craig Lucas, South Coast Repertory, Costa Mesa, California

Quilters, by Molly Newman and Barbara Damashek, Denver Center Theatre Company

Streamers, by David Rabe, Long Wharf Theatre, New Haven, Connecticut

Twilight, by Anna Deavere Smith, Mark Taper Forum, Los Angeles, California

True West, by Sam Shepard, Steppenwolf Theatre Company, Chicago

Two Trains Running, by August Wilson, Yale Repertory Theatre, New Haven, Connecticut

The Wake of Jamey Foster, by Beth Henley, Hartford Stage Company, Hartford, Connecticut

The Who's "Tommy," by Pete Townshend and Wayne Cilento, La Jolla Playhouse, La Jolla, California

THE TONY AWARDS

	1947	**1948**	**1949**
Actor (Dramatic)	Fredric March, *Years Ago*; José Ferrer, *Cyrano de Bergerac*	Basil Rathbone, *The Heiress*; Henry Fonda, *Mister Roberts*; Paul Kelly, *Command Decision*	Rex Harrison, *Anne of the Thousand Days*
Actress (Dramatic)	Helen Hayes, *Happy Birthday*; Ingrid Bergman, *Joan of Lorraine*	Jessica Tandy, *A Streetcar Named Desire*; Judith Anderson, *Medea*; Katharine Cornell, *Antony and Cleopatra*	Martita Hunt, *The Madwoman of Chaillot*
Supporting Actor (Dramatic)	—	—	Arthur Kennedy, *Death of a Salesman*
Supporting Actress (Dramatic)	Patricia Neal, *Another Part of the Forest*	—	Shirley Booth, *Goodbye, My Fancy*
Play	—	*Mister Roberts*	*Death of a Salesman*
Actor (Musical)	—	Paul Hartman, *Angel in the Wings*	Ray Bolger, *Where's Charley?*
Actress (Musical)	—	Grace Hartman, *Angel in the Wings*	Nanette Fabray, *Love Life*
Supporting Actor (Musical)	David Wayne, *Finian's Rainbow*	—	—
Supporting Actress (Musical)	—	—	—
Musical	—	—	*Kiss Me Kate*
Director	Elia Kazan, *All My Sons*	—	Elia Kazan, *Death of a Salesman*
Score	—	—	Cole Porter, *Kiss Me Kate*
Author (Dramatic)	—	Thomas Heggen and Joshua Logan, *Mister Roberts*	Arthur Miller, *Death of a Salesman*
Author (Musical)	—		Bella and Samuel Spewack, *Kiss Me Kate*
Scenic Designer	—	Horace Armistead, *The Medium*	Jo Mielziner, *Sleepy Hollow; Summer and Smoke; Anne of the Thousand Days; Death of a Salesman; South Pacific*
Costume Designer	—	—	Lemuel Ayers, *Kiss Me Kate*
Choreographer	Agnes de Mille, *Brigadoon*; Michael Kidd, *Finian's Rainbow*	Jerome Robbins, *High Button Shoes*	Gower Champion, *Lend an Ear*
Producer (Dramatic)	—	Leland Hayward, *Mister Roberts*	Kermit Bloomgarden and Walter Fried, *Death of a Salesman*
Producer (Musical)	—	—	Saint-Subber and Lemuel Ayers, *Kiss Me Kate*
Conductor and Musical Director	—	—	Max Meth, *As the Girls Go*
Stage Technician	—	George Gebhardt; George Pierce	—

1950	1951	1952	1953
Sydney Blackmer, *Come Back, Little Sheba*	Claude Rains, *Darkness at Noon*	Jose Ferrer, *The Shrike*	Tom Ewell, *The Seven Year Itch*
Shirley Booth, *Come Back, Little Sheba*	Uta Hagen, *The Country Girl*	Julie Harris, *I Am a Camera*	Shirley Booth, *Time of the Cuckoo*
—	Eli Wallach, *The Rose Tattoo*	John Cromwell, *Point of No Return*	John Williams, *Dial M for Murder*
—	Maureen Stapleton, *The Rose Tattoo*	Marian Winters, *I Am a Camera*	Beatrice Straight, *The Crucible*
The Cocktail Party	*The Rose Tattoo*	*The Fourposter*	*The Crucible*
Ezio Pinza, *South Pacific*	Robert Alda, *Guys and Dolls*	Phil Silvers, *Top Banana*	Thomas Mitchell, *Hazel Flagg*
Mary Martin, *South Pacific*	Ethel Merman, *Call Me Madam*	Gertrude Lawrence, *The King and I*	Rosalind Russell, *Wonderful Town*
Myron McCormick, *South Pacific*	Russell Nype, *Call Me Madam*	Yul Brynner, *The King and I*	Hiram Sherman, *Two's Company*
Juanita Hall, *South Pacific*	Isabel Bigley, *Guys and Dolls*	Helen Gallagher, *Pal Joey*	Sheila Bond, *Wish You Were Here*
South Pacific	*Guys and Dolls*	*The King and I*	*Wonderful Town*
Joshua Logan, *South Pacific*	George S. Kaufman, *Guys and Dolls*	Jose Ferrer, *The Shrike; The Fourposter; Stalag 17*	Joshua Logan, *Picnic*
Richard Rodgers, *South Pacific*	Frank Loesser, *Guys and Dolls*	—	Leonard Bernstein, *Wonderful Town*
T.S. Eliot, *The Cocktail Party*	Tennessee Williams, *The Rose Tattoo*	—	Arthur Miller, *The Crucible*
Oscar Hammerstein II and Joshua Logan, *South Pacific*	Jo Swerling and Abe Burrows, *Guys and Dolls*	—	Joseph Fields and Jerome Chodorov, *Wonderful Town*
Jo Mielziner, *The Innocents*	Boris Aronson, *The Rose Tattoo; The Country Girl; Season in the Sun*	Jo Mielziner, *The King and I*	Raoul Pene du Bois, *Wonderful Town*
Aline Bernstein, *Regina*	Miles White, *Bless You All*	Irene Sharaff, *The King and I*	Miles White, *Hazel Flagg*
Helen Tamiris, *Touch and Go*	Michael Kidd, *Guys and Dolls*	Robert Alton, *Pal Joey*	Donald Saddler, *Wonderful Town*
Gilbert Miller, *The Cocktail Party*	Cheryl Crawford, *The Rose Tattoo*	—	Kermit Bloomgarden, *The Crucible*
Richard Rodgers, Oscar Hammerstein II, Leland Hayward, and Joshua Logan, *South Pacific*	Cy Feuer and Ernest H. Martin, *Guys and Dolls*	—	Robert Fryer, *Wonderful Town*
Maurice Abravanel, *Regina*	Lehman Engel, *The Consul*	Max Meth, *Pal Joey*	Lehman Engel, *Wonderful Town; Gilbert and Sullivan Season*
Joe Lynn, master propertyman, *Miss Liberty*	Richard Raven, *The Autumn Garden*	Peter Feller, master carpenter, *Call Me Madam*	Abe Kurnit, *Wish You Were Here*

	1954	1955	1956
Actor (Dramatic)	David Wayne, *The Teahouse of the August Moon*	Alfred Lunt, *Quadrille*	Paul Muni, *Inherit the Wind*
Actress (Dramatic)	Audrey Hepburn, *Ondine*	Nancy Kelly, *The Bad Seed*	Julie Harris, *The Lark*
Featured/Supporting Actor (Dramatic)	John Kerr, *Tea and Sympathy*	Francis L. Sullivan, *Witness for the Prosecution*	Ed Begley, *Inherit the Wind*
Featured/Supporting Actress (Dramatic)	Jo Van Fleet, *The Trip to Bountiful*	Patricia Jessel, *Witness for the Prosecution*	Una Merkel, *The Ponder Heart*
Play	*The Teahouse of the August Moon*	*The Desperate Hours*	*The Diary of Anne Frank*
Actor (Musical)	Alfred Drake, *Kismet*	Walter Slezak, *Fanny*	Ray Walston, *Damn Yankees*
Actress (Musical)	Dolores Gray, *Carnival in Flanders*	Mary Martin, *Peter Pan*	Gwen Verdon, *Damn Yankees*
Featured/Supporting Actor Role (Musical)	Harry Belafonte, *John Murray Anderson's Almanac*	Cyril Ritchard, *Peter Pan*	Russ Brown, *Damn Yankees*
Featured/Supporting Actress (Musical)	Gwen Verdon, *Can-Can*	Carol Haney, *The Pajama Game*	Lotte Lenya, *The Threepenny Opera*
Musical	*Kismet*	*The Pajama Game*	*Damn Yankees*
Director	Alfred Lunt, *Ondine*	Robert Montgomery, *The Desperate Hours*	Tyrone Guthrie, *The Matchmaker; Six Characters in Search of an Author; Tamburlaine the Great*
Director (Dramatic)	—	—	—
Director (Musical)	—	—	—
Score	Alexander Borodin, *Kismet*	Richard Adler and Jerry Ross, *The Pajama Game*	Richard Adler and Jerry Ross, *Damn Yankees*
Author (Dramatic)	John Patrick, *The Teahouse of the August Moon*	Joseph Hayes, *The Desperate Hours*	Frances Goodrich and Albert Hackett, *The Diary of Anne Frank*
Author (Musical)	Charles Lederer and Luther Davis, *Kismet*	George Abbott and Richard Bissell, *The Pajama Game*	George Abbott and Douglass Wallop, *Damn Yankees*
Scenic Designer	Peter Larkin, *Ondine; The Teahouse of the August Moon*	Oliver Messel, *House of Flowers*	Peter Larkin, *Inherit the Wind; No Time for Sergeants*
Costume Designer	Richard Whorf, *Ondine*	Cecil Beaton, *Quadrille*	Alvin Colt, *The Lark/Phoenix '55/ Pipe Dream*
Choreographer	Michael Kidd, *Can-Can*	Bob Fosse, *The Pajama Game*	Bob Fosse, *Damn Yankees*
Producer (Dramatic)	Maurice Evans and George Schaefer, *The Teahouse of the August Moon*	Howard Erskine and Joseph Hayes, *The Desperate Hours*	Kermit Bloomgarden, *The Diary of Anne Frank*
Producer (Musical)	Charles Lederer, *Kismet*	Frederick Brisson, Robert Griffith, and Harold S. Prince, *The Pajama Game*	Frederick Brisson, Robert Griffith, Harold S. Prince in association with Albert B. Taylor, *Damn Yankees*
Conductor and Musical Director	Louis Adrian, *Kismet*	Thomas Schippers, *The Saint of Bleecker Street*	Hal Hastings, *Damn Yankees*
Stage Technician	John Davis, *Picnic*	Richard Rodda, *Peter Pan*	Harry Green, electrician and sound man, *The Middle of the Night; Damn Yankees*

1957 | 1958 | 1959 | 1960

1957	1958	1959	1960
Fredric March, *Long Day's Journey into Night*	Ralph Bellamy, *Sunrise at Campobello*	Jason Robards Jr., *The Disenchanted*	Melvyn Douglas, *The Best Man*
Margaret Leighton, *Separate Tables*	Helen Hayes, *Time Remembered*	Gertrude Berg, *A Majority of One*	Anne Bancroft, *The Miracle Worker*
Frank Conroy, *The Potting Shed*	Henry Jones, *Sunrise at Campobello*	Charlie Ruggles, *The Pleasure of His Company*	Roddy McDowall, *The Fighting Cock*
Peggy Cass, *Auntie Mame*	Anne Bancroft, *Two for the Seesaw*	Julie Newmar, *The Marriage-Go-Round*	Anne Revere, *Toys in the Attic*
Long Day's Journey into Night	*Sunrise at Campobello*	*J.B.*	*The Miracle Worker*
Rex Harrison, *My Fair Lady*	Robert Preston, *The Music Man*	Richard Kiley, *Redhead*	Jackie Gleason, *Take Me Along*
Judy Holliday, *Bells Are Ringing*	Gwen Verdon, *New Girl in Town;* Thelma Ritter, *New Girl in Town*	Gwen Verdon, *Redhead*	Mary Martin, *The Sound of Music*
Sydney Chaplin, *Bells Are Ringing*	David Burns, *The Music Man*	Russell Nype, *Goldilocks;* cast of *La Plume de ma tante*	Tom Bosley, *Fiorello!*
Edith Adams, *Li'l Abner*	Barbara Cook, *The Music Man*	Pat Stanley, *Goldilocks;* cast of *La Plume de ma tante*	Patricia Neway, *The Sound of Music*
My Fair Lady	*The Music Man*	*Redhead*	*Fiorello!*
Moss Hart, *My Fair Lady*	—	Elia Kazan, *J.B.*	—
—	Vincent J. Donehue, *Sunrise at Campobello*	—	Arthur Penn, *The Miracle Worker*
—	—	—	George Abbott, *Fiorello!*
Frederick Loewe, *My Fair Lady*	Meredith Willson, *The Music Man*	Albert Hague, *Redhead*	Jerry Bock, *Fiorello!;* Richard Rodgers, *The Sound of Music*
Eugene O'Neill, *Long Day's Journey into Night*	Dore Schary, *Sunrise at Campobello*	Archibald MacLeish, *J.B.*	William Gibson, *The Miracle Worker*
Alan Jay Lerner, *My Fair Lady*	Meredith Willson and Franklin Lacey, *The Music Man*	Herbert and Dorothy Fields, Sidney Sheldon, and David Shaw, *Redhead*	Jerome Weidman and George Abbott, *Fiorello!;* Howard Lindsay and Russel Crouse, *The Sound of Music*
Oliver Smith, *A Clearing in the Woods; Candide; Auntie Mame; My Fair Lady; Eugenia; A Visit to a Small Planet*	Oliver Smith, *West Side Story*	Donald Oenslager, *A Majority of One*	Howard Bey, *Toys in the Attic* (Dramatic); Oliver Smith, *The Sound of Music* (Musical)
Cecil Beaton, *Little Glass Clock/ My Fair Lady*	Motley, *The First Gentleman*	Robert Ter-Arutunian, *Redhead*	Cecil Beaton, *Saratoga*
Michael Kidd, *Li'l Abner*	Jerome Robbins, *West Side Story*	Bob Fosse, *Redhead*	Michael Kidd, *Destry Rides Again*
Leigh Connell, Theodore Mann, and Jose Quintero, *Long Day's Journey into Night*	Lawrence Langner, Theresa Helburn, Armina Marshall, and Dore Schary, *Sunrise at Campobello*	Alfred de Liagre, Jr., *J.B.*	Fred Coe, *The Miracle Worker*
Herman Levin, *My Fair Lady*	Kermit Bloomgarden, Herbert Greene, Frank Productions, *The Music Man*	Robert Fryer and Lawrence Carr, *Redhead*	Robert Griffith and Harold Prince, *Fiorello!;* Leland Hayward and Richard Halliday, *The Sound of Music*
Franz Allers, *My Fair Lady*	Herbert Greene, *The Music Man*	Salvatore Dell'Isola, *Flower Drum Song*	Frederick Dvonch, *The Sound of Music*
Howard McDonald (posthumous), carpenter, *Major Barbara*	Harry Romar, *Time Remembered*	Sam Knapp, *The Music Man*	John Walters, chief carpenter, *The Miracle Worker*

	1961	1962	1963
Actor (Dramatic)	Zero Mostel, *Rhinoceros*	Paul Scofield, *A Man for All Seasons*	Arthur Hill, *Who's Afraid of Virginia Woolf?*
Actress (Dramatic)	Joan Plowright, *A Taste of Honey*	Margaret Leighton, *Night of the Iguana*	Uta Hagen, *Who's Afraid of Virginia Woolf?*
Featured/Supporting Actor (Dramatic)	Martin Gabel, *Big Fish, Little Fish*	Walter Matthau, *A Shot in the Dark*	Alan Arkin, *Enter Laughing*
Featured/Supporting Actress (Dramatic)	Colleen Dewhurst, *All the Way Home*	Elizabeth Ashley, *Take Her, She's Mine*	Sandy Dennis, *A Thousand Clowns*
Play	*Becket*	*A Man for All Seasons*	*Who's Afraid of Virginia Woolf?*
Actor (Musical)	Richard Burton, *Camelot*	Robert Morse, *How to Succeed in Business Without Really Trying*	Zero Mostel, *A Funny Thing Happened on the Way to the Forum*
Actress (Musical)	Elizabeth Seal, *Irma La Douce*	Anna Maria Alberghetti, *Carnival*	Vivien Leigh, *Tovarich*
Featured/Supporting Actor (Musical)	Dick Van Dyke, *Bye, Bye Birdie*	Charles Nelson Reilly, *How to Succeed in Business Without Really Trying*	David Burns, *A Funny Thing Happened on the Way to the Forum*
Featured/Supporting Actress (Musical)	Tammy Grimes, *The Unsinkable Molly Brown*	Phyllis Newman, *Subways Are for Sleeping*	Anna Quayle, *Stop the World—I Want to Get Off*
Musical	*Bye, Bye Birdie*	*How to Succeed in Business Without Really Trying*	*A Funny Thing Happened on the Way to the Forum*
Director (Dramatic)	John Gielgud, *Big Fish, Little Fish*	Noel Willman, *A Man for All Seasons*	Alan Schneider, *Who's Afraid of Virginia Woolf?*
Director (Musical)	Gower Champion, *Bye, Bye Birdie*	Abe Burrows, *How to Succeed in Business Without Really Trying*	George Abbott, *A Funny Thing Happened on the Way to the Forum*
Score	—	Richard Rodgers, *No Strings*	Lionel Bart, *Oliver!*
Author (Dramatic)	Jean Anouilh, *Becket*	Robert Bolt, *A Man for All Seasons*	—
Author (Musical)	Michael Stewart, *Bye, Bye Birdie*	Abe Burrows, Jack Weinstock, and Willie Gilbert, *How to Succeed in Business Without Really Trying*	Burt Shevelove and Larry Gelbart, *A Funny Thing Happened on the Way to the Forum*
Scenic Designer	Oliver Smith, *Becket* (Dramatic); Oliver Smith, *Camelot* (Musical)	Will Steven Armstrong, *Carnival*	Sean Kenny, *Oliver!*
Costume Designer	Motley, *Becket;* Adrian and Tony Duquette, *Camelot*	Lucinda Ballard, *The Gay Life*	Anthony Powell, *The School for Scandal*
Choreographer	Gower Champion, *Bye, Bye Birdie*	Agnes de Mille, *Kwamina;* Joe Layton, *No Strings*	Bob Fosse, *Little Me*
Producer (Dramatic)	David Merrick, *Becket*	Robert Whitehead and Roger L. Stevens, *A Man for All Seasons*	Richard Barr and Clinton Wilder, Theatre 1963, *Who's Afraid of Virginia Woolf?*
Producer (Musical)	Edward Padula, *Bye, Bye Birdie*	Cy Feuer and Ernest Martin, *How to Succeed in Business Without Really Trying*	Harold Prince, *A Funny Thing Happened on the Way to the Forum*
Conductor and Musical Director	Franz Allers, *Camelot*	Elliot Lawrence, *How to Succeed in Business Without Really Trying*	Donald Pippin, *Oliver!*
Stage Technician	Teddy Van Bemmel, *Becket*	Michael Burns, *A Man for All Seasons*	—

1964	1965	1966	1967
Alec Guinness, *Dylan*	Walter Matthau, *The Odd Couple*	Hal Holbrook, *Mark Twain Tonight!*	Paul Rogers, *The Homecoming*
Sandy Dennis, *Any Wednesday*	Irene Worth, *Tiny Alice*	Rosemary Harris, *The Lion in Winter*	Beryl Reid, *The Killing of Sister George*
Hume Cronyn, *Hamlet*	Jack Albertson, *The Subject Was Roses*	Patrick Magee, *Marat/Sade*	Ian Holm, *The Homecoming*
Barbara Loden, *After the Fall*	Alice Ghostley, *The Sign in Sidney Brustein's Window*	Zoe Caldwell, *Slapstick Tragedy*	Marian Seldes, *A Delicate Balance*
Luther	*The Subject Was Roses*	*Marat/Sade*	*The Homecoming*
Bert Lahr, *Foxy*	Zero Mostel, *Fiddler on the Roof*	Richard Kiley, *Man of La Mancha*	Robert Preston, *I Do! I Do!*
Carol Channing, *Hello, Dolly!*	Liza Minnelli, *Flora, the Red Menace*	Angela Lansbury, *Mame*	Barbara Harris, *The Apple Tree*
Jack Cassidy, *She Loves Me*	Victor Spinetti, *Oh, What a Lovely War!*	Frankie Michaels, *Mame*	Joel Grey, *Cabaret*
Tessie O'Shea, *The Girl Who Came to Supper*	Maria Karnilova, *Fiddler on the Roof*	Beatrice Arthur, *Mame*	Peg Murray, *Cabaret*
Hello, Dolly!	*Fiddler on the Roof*	*Man of La Mancha*	*Cabaret*
Mike Nichols, *Barefoot in the Park*	Mike Nichols, *Luv; The Odd Couple*	Peter Brook, *Marat/Sade*	Peter Hall, *The Homecoming*
Gower Champion, *Hello, Dolly!*	Jerome Robbins, *Fiddler on the Roof*	Albert Marre, *Man of La Mancha*	Harold Prince, *Cabaret*
Jerry Herman, *Hello, Dolly!*	Jerry Bock and Sheldon Harnick, *Fiddler on the Roof*	Mitch Leigh and Joe Darion, *Man of La Mancha*	John Kander and Fred Ebb, *Cabaret*
John Osborne, *Luther*	Neil Simon, *The Odd Couple*	—	—
Michael Stewart, *Hello, Dolly!*	Joseph Stein, *Fiddler on the Roof*	—	—
Oliver Smith, *Hello, Dolly!*	Oliver Smith, *Baker Street; Luv; The Odd Couple*	Howard Bay, *Man of La Mancha*	Boris Aronson, *Cabaret*
Freddy Wittop, *Hello, Dolly!*	Patricia Zipprodt, *Fiddler on the Roof*	Gunilla Palmstierna-Weiss, *Marat/Sade*	Patricia Zipprodt, *Cabaret*
Gower Champion, *Hello, Dolly!*	Jerome Robbins, *Fiddler on the Roof*	Bob Fosse, *Sweet Charity*	Ronald Field, *Cabaret*
Herman Shumlin, *The Deputy*	Claire Nichtern, *Luv*	—	—
David Merrick, *Hello, Dolly!*	Harold Prince, *Fiddler on the Roof*	—	—
Shepard Coleman, *Hello, Dolly!*	—	—	—
—	—	—	—

	1968	1969	1970
Actor (Dramatic)	Martin Balsam, *You Know I Can't Hear You When the Water's Running*	James Earl Jones, *The Great White Hope*	Fritz Weaver, *Child's Play*
Actress (Dramatic)	Zoe Caldwell, *The Prime of Miss Jean Brodie*	Julie Harris, *Forty Carats*	Tammy Grimes, *Private Lives*
Featured/Supporting Actor (Dramatic)	James Patterson, *The Birthday Party*	Al Pacino, *Does a Tiger Wear a Necktie?*	Ken Howard, *Child's Play*
Featured/Supporting Actress (Dramatic)	Zena Walker, *Joe Egg*	Jane Alexander, *The Great White Hope*	Blythe Danner, *Butterflies Are Free*
Play	*Rosencrantz and Guildenstern Are Dead*	*The Great White Hope*	*Borstal Boy*
Actor (Musical)	Robert Goulet, *The Happy Time*	Jerry Orbach, *Promises, Promises*	Cleavon Little, *Purlie*
Actress (Musical)	Leslie Uggams, *Hallelujah, Baby!*; Patricia Routledge, *Darling of the Day*	Angela Lansbury, *Dear World*	Lauren Bacall, *Applause*
Featured/Supporting Actor (Musical)	Hiram Sherman, *How Now, Dow Jones*	Ronald Holgate, *1776*	Rene Auberjonois, *Coco*
Featured/Supporting Actress (Musical)	Lillian Hayman, *Hallelujah, Baby!*	Marian Mercer, *Promises, Promises*	Melba Moore, *Purlie*
Musical	*Hallelujah, Baby!*	*1776*	*Applause*
Director (Dramatic)	Mike Nichols, *Plaza Suite*	Peter Dews, *Hadrian VII*	Joseph Hardy, *Child's Play*
Director (Musical)	Gower Champion, *The Happy Time*	Peter Hunt, *1776*	Ron Field, *Applause*
Book (Musical)	—	—	—
Score	Jule Styne, Betty Comden, and Adolph Green, *Hallelujah, Baby!*	—	—
Scenic Designer	Desmond Heeley, *Rosencrantz and Guildenstern Are Dead*	Boris Aronson, *Zorba*	Howard Bay, *Cry for Us All*; Jo Mielziner, *Child's Play*
Costume Designer	Desmond Heeley, *Rosencrantz and Guildenstern Are Dead*	Louden Sainthill, *Canterbury Tales*	Cecil Beaton, *Coco*
Lighting Designer	—	—	Jo Mielziner, *Child's Play*
Choreographer	Gower Champion, *The Happy Time*	Joe Layton, *George M!*	Ron Field, *Applause*
Producer (Dramatic)	The David Merrick Arts Foundation, *Rosencrantz and Guildenstern Are Dead*	—	—
Producer (Musical)	Albert Selden, Hal James, Jane C. Nusbaum, and Harry Rigby, *Hallelujah, Baby!*	—	—

1971	1972	1973	1974
Brian Bedford, *The School for Wives*	Cliff Gorman, *Lenny*	Alan Bates, *Butley*	Michael Moriarty, *Find Your Way Home*
Maureen Stapleton, *The Gingerbread Lady*	Sada Thompson, *Twigs*	Julie Harris, *The Last of Mrs. Lincoln*	Colleen Dewhurst, *A Moon for the Misbegotten*
Paul Sand, *Story Theatre*	Vincent Gardenia, *The Prisoner of Second Avenue*	John Lithgow, *The Changing Room*	Ed Flanders, *A Moon for the Misbegotten*
Rae Allen, *And Miss Reardon Drinks a Little*	Elizabeth Wilson, *Sticks and Bones*	Leora Dana, *The Last of Mrs. Lincoln*	Frances Sternhagen, *The Good Doctor*
Sleuth	*Sticks and Bones*	*That Championship Season*	*The River Niger*
Hal Linden, *The Rothschilds*	Phil Silvers, *A Funny Thing Happened on the Way to the Forum* (Revival)	Ben Vereen, *Pippin*	Christopher Plummer, *Cyrano*
Helen Gallagher, *No, No, Nanette*	Alexis Smith, *Follies*	Glynis Johns, *A Little Night Music*	Virginia Capers, *Raisin*
Keene Curtis, *The Rothschilds*	Larry Blyden, *A Funny Thing Happened on the Way to the Forum* (Revival)	George S. Irving, *Irene*	Tommy Tune, *Seesaw*
Patsy Kelly, *No, No, Nanette*	Linda Hopkins, *Inner City*	Patricia Elliot, *A Little Night Music*	Janie Sell, *Over Here!*
Company	*Two Gentlemen of Verona*	*A Little Night Music*	*Raisin*
Peter Brook, *Midsummer Night's Dream*	Mike Nichols, *The Prisoner of Second Avenue*	A. J. Antoon, *That Championship Season*	Jose Quintero, *A Moon for the Misbegotten*
Harold Prince, *Company*	Harold Prince and Michael Bennett, *Follies*	Bob Fosse, *Pippin*	Harold Prince, *Candide*
George Furth, *Company*	John Guare and Mel Shapiro, *Two Gentlemen of Verona*	Hugh Wheeler, *A Little Night Music*	Hugh Wheeler, *Candide*
Stephen Sondheim, *Company*	Stephen Sondheim, *Follies*	Stephen Sondheim, *A Little Night Music*	Frederick Loewe (Music); Alan Jay Lerner (Lyrics), *Gigi*
Boris Aronson, *Company*	Boris Aronson, *Follies*	Tony Walton, *Pippin*	Franne and Eugene Lee, *Candide*
Raoul Pene du Bois, *No, No, Nanette*	Florence Klotz, *Follies*	Florence Klotz, *A Little Night Music*	Franne Lee, *Candide*
H. R. Poindexter, *Story Theatre*	Tharon Musser, *Follies*	Jules Fisher, *Pippin*	Jules Fisher, *Ulysses in Nighttown*
Donald Saddler, *No, No, Nanette*	Michael Bennett, *Follies*	Bob Fosse, *Pippin*	Michael Bennett, *Seesaw*
Helen Bonfils, Morton Gottlieb, and Michael White, *Sleuth*	—	—	—
Harold Prince, *Company*	—	—	—

	1975	1976	1977
Actor (Dramatic)	John Kani and Winston Ntshona, *Sizwe Banzi Is Dead & The Island*	John Wood, *Travesties*	Al Pacino, *The Basic Training of Pavlo Hummel*
Actress (Dramatic)	Ellen Burstyn, *Same Time, Next Year*	Irene Worth, *Sweet Bird of Youth*	Julie Harris, *The Belle of Amherst*
Featured Actor (Dramatic)	Frank Langella, *Seascape*	Edward Herrmann, *Mrs. Warren's Profession*	Jonathan Pryce, *Comedians*
Featured Actress (Dramatic)	Rita Moreno, *The Ritz*	Shirley Knight, *Kennedy's Children*	Trazana Beverley, *For Colored Girls Who Have Considered Suicide/When the Rainbow Is Enuf*
Play	*Equus*	*Travesties*	*The Shadow Box*
Actor (Musical)	John Cullum, *Shenandoah*	George Rose, *My Fair Lady*	Barry Bostwick, *The Robber Bridegroom*
Actress (Musical)	Angela Lansbury, *Gypsy*	Donna McKechnie, *A Chorus Line*	Dorothy Loudon, *Annie*
Featured Actor (Musical)	Ted Ross, *The Wiz*	Sammy Williams, *A Chorus Line*	Lenny Baker, *I Love My Wife*
Featured Actress (Musical)	Dee Dee Bridgewater, *The Wiz*	Carole Bishop, *A Chorus Line*	Delores Hall, *Your Arms Too Short to Box with God*
Musical	*The Wiz*	*A Chorus Line*	*Annie*
Director (Dramatic)	John Dexter, *Equus*	Ellis Rabb, *The Royal Family*	Gordon Davidson, *The Shadow Box*
Director (Musical)	Geoffrey Holder, *The Wiz*	Michael Bennett, *A Chorus Line*	Gene Saks, *I Love My Wife*
Book (Musical)	James Lee Barrett, *Shenandoah*	James Kirkwood and Nicholas Dante, *A Chorus Line*	Thomas Meehan, *Annie*
Score	Charlie Smalls (Music & Lyrics), *The Wiz*	Marvin Hamlisch (Music); Edward Kleban (Lyrics), *A Chorus Line*	Charles Strouse (Music); Martin Charnin (Lyrics), *Annie*
Scenic Designer	Carl Toms, *Sherlock Holmes*	Boris Aronson, *Pacific Overtures*	David Mitchell, *Annie*
Costume Designer	Geoffrey Holder, *The Wiz*	Florence Klotz, *Pacific Overtures*	Theoni V. Aldredge, *Annie;* Santo Loquasto, *The Cherry Orchard*
Lighting Designer	Neil Patrick Jampolis, *Sherlock Holmes*	Tharon Musser, *A Chorus Line*	Jennifer Tipton, *The Cherry Orchard*
Choreographer	George Faison, *The Wiz*	Michael Bennett and Bob Avian, *A Chorus Line*	Peter Gennaro, *Annie*
Reproduction of a Play or Musical	—	—	*Porgy and Bess*

1978	1979	1980	1981
Barnard Hughes, *Da*	Tom Conti, *Whose Life Is It Anyway?*	John Rubinstein, *Children of a Lesser God*	Ian McKellen, *Amadeus*
Jessica Tandy, *The Gin Game*	Constance Cummings, *Wings;* Carole Shelley, *The Elephant Man*	Phyllis Frelich, *Children of a Lesser God*	Jane Lapotaire, *Piaf*
Lester Rawlins, *Da*	Michael Gough, *Bedroom Farce*	David Rounds, *Morning's at Seven*	Brian Backer, *The Floating Light Bulb*
Ann Wedgeworth, *Chapter Two*	Joan Hickson, *Bedroom Farce*	Dinah Manoff, *I Ought to Be in Pictures*	Swoosie Kurtz, *Fifth of July*
Da	*The Elephant Man*	*Children of a Lesser God*	*Amadeus*
John Cullum, *On the Twentieth Century*	Len Cariou, *Sweeney Todd*	Jim Dale, *Barnum*	Kevin Kline, *The Pirates of Penzance*
Liza Minnelli, *The Act*	Angela Lansbury, *Sweeney Todd*	Patti LuPone, *Evita*	Lauren Bacall, *Woman of the Year*
Kevin Kline, *On the Twentieth Century*	Henderson Forsythe, *The Best Little Whorehouse in Texas*	Mandy Patinkin, *Evita*	Hinton Battle, *Sophisticated Ladies*
Nell Carter, *Ain't Misbehavin'*	Carlin Glynn, *The Best Little Whorehouse in Texas*	Priscilla Lopez, *A Day in Hollywood, a Night in the Ukraine*	Marilyn Cooper, *Woman of the Year*
Ain't Misbehavin'	*Sweeney Todd*	*Evita*	*42nd Street*
Melvin Bernhardt, *Da*	Jack Hofsiss, *The Elephant Man*	Vivian Matalon, *Morning's at Seven*	Peter Hall, *Amadeus*
Richard Maltby Jr., *Ain't Misbehavin'*	Harold Prince, *Sweeney Todd*	Harold Prince, *Evita*	Wilford Leach, *The Pirates of Penzance*
Betty Comden and Adolph Green, *On the Twentieth Century*	Hugh Wheeler, *Sweeney Todd*	Tim Rice, *Evita*	Peter Stone, *Woman of the Year*
Cy Coleman (Music); Betty Comden and Adolph Green (Lyrics), *On the Twentieth Century*	Stephen Sondheim (Music & Lyrics), *Sweeney Todd*	Andrew Lloyd Webber (Music); Tim Rice (Lyrics), *Evita*	John Kander (Music); Fred Ebb (Lyrics), *Woman of the Year*
Robin Wagner, *On the Twentieth Century*	Eugene Lee, *Sweeney Todd*	John Lee Beatty, *Talley's Folly;* David Mitchell, *Barnum*	John Bury, *Amadeus*
Edward Gorey, *Dracula*	Franne Lee, *Sweeney Todd*	Theoni V. Aldredge, *Barnum*	Willa Kim, *Sophisticated Ladies*
Jules Fisher, *Dancin'*	Roger Morgan, *The Crucifer of Blood*	David Hersey, *Evita*	John Bury, *Amadeus*
Bob Fosse, *Dancin'*	Michael Bennett and Bob Avian, *Ballroom*	Tommy Tune and Thommie Walsh, *A Day in Hollywood, a Night in the Ukraine*	Gower Champion, *42nd Street*
Dracula	—	Elizabeth I. McCann, Nelle Nugent, Ray Larsen, producers, *Morning's at Seven*	Joseph Papp, producer, *The Pirates of Penzance*

	1982	**1983**	**1984**
Actor (Dramatic)	Roger Rees, *The Life and Adventures of Nicholas Nickleby*	Harvey Fierstein, *Torch Song Trilogy*	Jeremy Irons, *The Real Thing*
Actress (Dramatic)	Zoë Caldwell, *Medea*	Jessica Tandy, *Foxfire*	Glenn Close, *The Real Thing*
Featured Actor (Dramatic)	Zakes Mokae, *"Master Harold"...and the Boys*	Matthew Broderick, *Brighton Beach Memoirs*	Joe Mantegna, *Glengarry Glen Ross*
Featured Actress (Dramatic)	Amanda Plummer, *Agnes of God*	Judith Ivey, *Steaming*	Christine Baranski, *The Real Thing*
Play	*The Life and Adventures of Nicholas Nickleby*	*Torch Song Trilogy*	*The Real Thing*
Actor (Musical)	Ben Harney, *Dreamgirls*	Tommy Tune, *My One and Only*	George Hearn, *La Cage aux folles*
Actress (Musical)	Jennifer Holliday, *Dreamgirls*	Natalia Makarova, *On Your Toes*	Chita Rivera, *The Rink*
Featured Actor (Musical)	Cleavant Derricks, *Dreamgirls*	Charles "Honi" Coles, *My One and Only*	Hinton Battle, *The Tap Dance Kid*
Featured Actress (Musical)	Liliane Montevecchi, *"Nine"*	Betty Buckley, *Cats*	Lila Kedrova, *Zorba*
Musical	*"Nine"*	*Cats*	*La Cage aux folles*
Director (Dramatic)	Trevor Nunn and John Caird, *The Life and Adventures of Nicholas Nickleby*	Gene Saks, *Brighton Beach Memoirs*	Mike Nichols, *The Real Thing*
Director (Musical)	Tommy Tune, *"Nine"*	Trevor Nunn, *Cats*	Arthur Laurents, *La Cage aux folles*
Book (Musical)	Tom Eyen, *Dreamgirls*	T. S. Eliot, *Cats*	Harvey Fierstein, *La Cage aux folles*
Score	Maury Yeton (Music & Lyrics), *"Nine"*	Andrew Lloyd Webber (Music); T. S. Eliot (Lyrics), *Cats*	Jerry Herman (Music & Lyrics), *La Cage aux folles*
Scenic Designer	John Napier and Dermot Hayes, *The Life and Adventures of Nicholas Nickleby*	Ming Cho Lee, *K2*	Tony Straiges, *Sunday in the Park with George*
Costume Designer	William Ivey Long, *"Nine"*	John Napier, *Cats*	Theoni V. Aldredge, *La Cage aux folles*
Lighting Designer	Tharon Musser, *Dreamgirls*	David Hersey, *Cats*	Richard Nelson, *Sunday in the Park with George*
Choreographer	Michael Bennett and Michael Peters, *Dreamgirls*	Thommie Walsh and Tommy Tune, *My One and Only*	Danny Daniels, *The Tap Dance Kid*
Reproduction of a Play or Musical	Barry and Fran Weissler, CBS Video Enterprises, Don Gregory, producers, *Othello*	Alfred De Liagre Jr., Roger L. Stevens, John Mauceri, Donald R. Seawell, Andre Pastoria, producers, *On Your Toes*	Robert Whitehead, Roger L. Stevens, producers, *Death of a Salesman*

1985	1986	1987	1988
Derek Jacobi, *Much Ado About Nothing*	Judd Hirsch, *I'm Not Rappaport*	James Earl Jones, *Fences*	Ron Silver, *Speed-the-Plow*
Stockard Channing, *Joe Egg*	Lily Tomlin, *The Search for Signs of Intelligent Life in the Universe*	Linda Lavin, *Broadway Bound*	Joan Allen, *Burn This*
Barry Miller, *Biloxi Blues*	John Mahoney, *The House of Blue Leaves*	John Randolph, *Broadway Bound*	B. D. Wong, *M. Butterfly*
Judith Ivey, *Hurlyburly*	Swoosie Kurtz, *The House of Blue Leaves*	Mary Alice, *Fences*	L. Scott Caldwell, *Joe Turner's Come and Gone*
Biloxi Blues	*I'm Not Rappaport*	*Fences*	*M. Butterfly*
—	George Rose, *The Mystery of Edwin Drood*	Robert Lindsay, *Me and My Girl*	Michael Crawford, *The Phantom of the Opera*
—	Bernadette Peters, *Song & Dance*	Maryann Plunkett, *Me and My Girl*	Joanna Gleason, *Into the Woods*
Ron Richardson, *Big River*	Michael Rupert, *Sweet Charity*	Michael Maguire, *Les Misérables*	Bill McCutcheon, *Anything Goes*
Leilani Jones, *Grind*	Bebe Neuwirth, *Sweet Charity*	Frances Ruffelle, *Les Misérables*	Judy Kaye, *The Phantom of the Opera*
Big River	*The Mystery of Edwin Drood*	*Les Misérables*	*The Phantom of the Opera*
Gene Saks, *Biloxi Blues*	Jerry Zaks, *The House of Blue Leaves*	Lloyd Richards, *Fences*	John Dexter, *M. Butterfly*
Des McAnuff, *Big River*	Wilford Leach, *The Mystery of Edwin Drood*	Trevor Nunn and John Caird, *Les Misérables*	Harold Prince, *The Phantom of the Opera*
William Hauptman, *Big River*	Rupert Holmes, *The Mystery of Edwin Drood*	Alain Boublil and Claude-Michel Schönberg, *Les Misérables*	James Lapine, *Into the Woods*
Roger Miller (Music & Lyrics), *Big River*	Rupert Holmes (Music & Lyrics), *The Mystery of Edwin Drood*	Claude-Michel Schönberg (Music); Herbert Kretzmer, and Alain Boublil (Lyrics), *Les Misérables*	Stephen Sondheim (Music & Lyrics), *Into the Woods*
Heidi Landesman, *Big River*	Tony Walton, *The House of Blue Leaves*	John Napier, *Les Misérables*	Maria Bjornson, *The Phantom of the Opera*
Florence Klotz, *Grind*	Patricia Zipprodt, *Sweet Charity*	John Napier, *Starlight Express*	Maria Bjornson, *The Phantom of the Opera*
Richard Riddell, *Big River*	Pat Collins, *I'm Not Rappaport*	David Hersey, *Starlight Express*	Andrew Bridge, *The Phantom of the Opera*
—	Bob Fosse, *Big Deal*	Gillian Gregory, *Me and My Girl*	Michael Smuin, *Anything Goes*
The Shubert Organization, Emanuel Azenberg, Roger Berlind, Ivan Bloch, MTM Enterprises, Inc., producers, *Joe Egg*	Jerome Minskoff, James M. Nederlander, Arthur Rubin, Joseph Harris, producers, *Sweet Charity*	Jay H. Fuchs, Steven Warnick, Charles Patsos, producers, *All My Sons*	Lincoln Center Theater, Gregory Mosher, Bernard Gersten, producers, *Anything Goes*

	1989	1990	1991
Actor (Dramatic)	Philip Bosco, *Lend Me a Tenor*	Robert Morse, *Tru*	Nigel Hawthorne, *Shadowlands*
Actress (Dramatic)	Pauline Collins, *Shirley Valentine*	Maggie Smith, *Lettice & Lovage*	Mercedes Ruehl, *Lost in Yonkers*
Featured Actor (Dramatic)	Boyd Gaines, *The Heidi Chronicles*	Charles Durning, *Cat on a Hot Tin Roof*	Kevin Spacey, *Lost in Yonkers*
Featured Actress (Dramatic)	Christine Baranski, *Rumors*	Margaret Tyzack, *Lettice & Lovage*	Irene Worth, *Lost in Yonkers*
Play	*The Heidi Chronicles*	*The Grapes of Wrath*	*Lost in Yonkers*
Actor (Musical)	Jason Alexander, *Jerome Robbins' Broadway*	James Naughton, *City of Angels*	Jonathan Pryce, *Miss Saigon*
Actress (Musical)	Ruth Brown, *Black and Blue*	Tyne Daly, *Gypsy*	Lea Salonga, *Miss Saigon*
Featured Actor (Musical)	Scott Wise, *Jerome Robbins' Broadway*	Michael Jeter, *Grand Hotel, the Musical*	Hinton Battle, *Miss Saigon*
Featured Actress (Musical)	Debbie Shapiro, *Jerome Robbins' Broadway*	Randy Graff, *City of Angels*	Daisy Eagan, *The Secret Garden*
Musical	*Jerome Robbins' Broadway*	*City of Angels*	*The Will Rogers Follies*
Director (Dramatic)	Jerry Zaks, *Lend Me a Tenor*	Frank Galati, *The Grapes of Wrath*	Jerry Zaks, *Six Degrees of Separation*
Director (Musical)	Jerome Robbins, *Jerome Robbins' Broadway*	Tommy Tune, *Grand Hotel, the Musical*	Tommy Tune, *The Will Rogers Follies*
Book (Musical)	—	Larry Gelbart, *City of Angels*	Marsha Norman, *The Secret Garden*
Score	—	Cy Coleman (Music); David Zippel (Lyrics), *City of Angels*	Cy Coleman (Music); Betty Comden and Adolph Green (Lyrics), *The Will Rogers Follies*
Scenic Designer	Santo Loquasto, *Cafe Crown*	Robin Wagner, *City of Angels*	Heidi Landesman, *The Secret Garden*
Costume Designer	Claudio Segovia, Hector Orezzoli, *Black and Blue*	Santo Loquasto, *Grand Hotel, the Musical*	Willa Kim, *The Will Rogers Follies*
Lighting Design	Jennifer Tipton, *Jerome Robbins' Broadway*	Jules Fisher, *Grand Hotel, the Musical*	Jules Fisher, *The Will Rogers Follies*
Choreographer	Cholly Atkins, Henry LeTang, Frankie Manning, Fayard Nicholas, *Black and Blue*	Tommy Tune, *Grand Hotel, the Musical*	Tommy Tune, *The Will Rogers Follies*
Reproduction of a Play or Musical	Lincoln Center Theater, Gregory Mosher, Bernard Gersten, producers, *Our Town*	Barry and Fran Weissler, Kathy Levin, Barry Brown, producers, *Gypsy*	Barry and Fran Weissler, Pace Theatrical Group, producers, *Fiddler on the Roof*

1992	1993	1994	1995
Judd Hirsch, *Conversations with My Father*	Ron Leibman, *Angels in America: Millennium Approaches*	Stephen Spinella, *Angels in America: Perestroika*	Ralph Fiennes, *Hamlet*
Glenn Close, *Death and the Maiden*	Madeline Kahn, *The Sisters Rosensweig*	Diana Rigg, *Medea*	Cherry Jones, *The Heiress*
Larry Fishburne, *Two Trains Running*	Stephen Spinella, *Angels in America: Millennium Approaches*	Jeffrey Wright, *Angels in America: Perestroika*	John Glover, *Love! Valour! Compassion!*
Brid Brennan, *Dancing at Lughnasa*	Debra Monk, *Redwood Curtain*	Jane Adams, *An Inspector Calls*	Frances Sternhagen, *The Heiress*
Dancing at Lughnasa	*Angels in America: Millennium Approaches*	*Angels in America: Perestroika*	*Love! Valour! Compassion!*
Gregory Hines, *Jelly's Last Jam*	Brent Carver, *Kiss of the Spider Woman—The Musical*	Boyd Gaines, *She Loves Me*	Matthew Broderick, *How to Succeed in Business Without Really Trying*
Faith Prince, *Guys and Dolls*	Chita Rivera, *Kiss of the Spider Woman—The Musical*	Donna Murphy, *Passion*	Glenn Close, *Sunset Boulevard*
Scott Waara, *The Most Happy Fella*	Anthony Crivello, *Kiss of the Spider Woman—The Musical*	Jarrod Emick, *Damn Yankees*	George Hearn, *Sunset Boulevard*
Tonya Pinkins, *Jelly's Last Jam*	Andrea Martin, *My Favorite Year*	Audra Ann McDonald, *Carousel*	Gretha Boston, *Show Boat*
Crazy for You	*Kiss of the Spider Woman—The Musical*	*Passion*	*Sunset Boulevard*
Patrick Mason, *Dancing at Lughnasa*	George C. Wolfe, *Angels in America: Millennium Approaches*	Stephen Daldry, *An Inspector Calls*	Gerald Gutierrez, *The Heiress*
Jerry Zaks, *Guys and Dolls*	Des McAnuff, *The Who's Tommy*	Nicholas Hynter, *Carousel*	Harold Prince, *Show Boat*
William Finn and James Lapine, *Falsettos*	Terrence McNally, *Kiss of the Spider Woman—The Musical*	James Lapine, *Passion*	Christopher Hampton and Don Black, *Sunset Boulevard*
William Finn, *Falsettos*	John Kander (Music), Fred Ebb (Lyrics), *Kiss of the Spider Woman—The Musical*; Pete Townshend (Music and Lyrics), *The Who's Tommy*	Stephen Sondheim, *Passion*	Andrew Lloyd Webber (music), Christopher Hampton and Don Black (lyrics), *Sunset Boulevard*
Tony Walton, *Guys and Dolls*	John Arnone, *The Who's Tommy*	Bob Crowley, *Carousel*	John Napier, *Sunset Boulevard*
William Ivey Long, *Crazy for You*	Florence Klotz, *Kiss of the Spider Woman—The Musical*	Ann Hould-Ward, *Beauty and the Beast*	Florence Klotz, *Show Boat*
Jules Fisher, *Jelly's Last Jam*	Chris Parry, *The Who's Tommy*	Rick Fisher, *An Inspector Calls*	Andrew Bridge, *Sunset Boulevard*
Susan Stroman, *Crazy for You*	Wayne Cilento, *The Who's Tommy*	Kenneth McMillan, *Carousel*	Susan Stroman, *Show Boat*
Dodger Productions, Roger Berlind, Jujamcyn Theaters/TV Asahi, Kardana Productions, John F. Kennedy Center for the Performing Arts, producers, *Guys and Dolls*	Roundabout Theatre Company, Todd Haimes, producers, *Anna Christie*	Noel Pearson, the Shubert Organization, Capital Cities/ABC, Joseph Harris, producers, *An Inspector Calls* (Dramatic); Lincoln Center Theater, Andre Bishop, Bernard Gersten, the Royal National Theater, Cameron Mackintosh, the Rodgers & Hammerstein Organization, producers, *Carousel* (Musical)	Lincoln Center Theater, Andre Bishop, Bernard Gersten, producers, *The Heiress* (Dramatic); Livent (U.S.) Inc., producer, *Show Boat* (Musical)

	1996	1997	1998
Actor (Dramatic)	George Grizzard, *A Delicate Balance*	Christopher Plummer, *Barrymore*	Anthony LaPaglia, *A View from the Bridge*
Actress (Dramatic)	Zoë Caldwell, *Master Class*	Janet McTeer, *A Doll's House*	Marie Mullen, *The Beauty Queen of Leenane*
Featured Actor (Dramatic)	Ruben Santiago-Hudson, *Seven Guitars*	Owen Teale, *A Doll's House*	Tom Murphy, *The Beauty Queen of Leenane*
Featured Actress (Dramatic)	Audra McDonald, *Master Class*	Lynne Thigpen, *An American Daughter*	Anna Manahan, *The Beauty Queen of Leenane*
Play	*Master Class*	*The Last Night of Ballyhoo*	*Art*
Actor (Musical)	Nathan Lane, *A Funny Thing Happened on the Way to the Forum*	James Naughton, *Chicago*	Alan Cumming, *Cabaret*
Actress (Musical)	Donna Murphy, *Passion*	Bebe Neuwirth, *Chicago*	Natasha Richardson, *Cabaret*
Featured Actor (Musical)	Wilson Jermain Heredia, *Rent*	Chuck Cooper, *The Life*	Ron Rifkin, *Cabaret*
Featured Actress (Musical)	Ann Duquesnay, *Bring in 'Da Noise, Bring in 'Da Funk*	Lillias White, *The Life*	Audra McDonald, *Ragtime*
Musical	*Rent*	*Titanic*	*The Lion King*
Director (Dramatic)	Gerald Gutierrez, *A Delicate Balance*	Anthony Page, *A Doll's House*	Garry Hynes, *The Beauty Queen of Leenane*
Director (Musical)	George C. Wolfe, *Bring in 'Da Noise, Bring in 'Da Funk*	Walter Bobbie, *Chicago*	Julie Taymor, *The Lion King*
Book (Musical)	Jonathan Larson, *Rent*	Peter Stone, *Titanic*	Terrence McNally, *Ragtime*
Score	Jonathan Larson, *Rent*	Maury Yeston, *Titanic*	Stephen Flaherty (music); Lynn Ahrens (lyrics), *Ragtime*
Scenic Designer	Brian Thomson, *The King and I*	Stewart Laing, *Titanic*	Richard Hudson, *The Lion King*
Costume Designer	Roger Kirk, *The King and I*	Judith Dolan, *Candide*	Julie Taymor, *The Lion King*
Lighting Designer	Jules Fisher and Peggy Eisenhauer, *Bring in 'Da Noise, Bring in 'Da Funk*	Ken Billington, *Chicago*	Donald Holder, *The Lion King*
Choreographer	Savion Glover, *Bring in 'Da Noise, Bring in 'Da Funk*	Ann Reinking, *Chicago*	Garth Fagan, *The Lion King*
Orchestration	—	Jonathan Tunick, *Titanic*	William David Brohn, *Ragtime*
Reproduction of a Play or Musical	Lincoln Center Theater, producer, *A Delicate Balance* (Dramatic); Dodger Productions, the John F. Kennedy Center for the Performing Arts, James M. Nederlander, Perseus Productions, John Frost, The Adelaide Festival Center, the Rodgers and Hammerstein Organization, producers, *The King and I* (Musical)	Bill Kenwright, Thelma Holt, producers, *A Doll's House* (Dramatic); Barry Weissler, Fran Weissler, Kardana Prods. Inc., producers, *Chicago* (Musical)	Roundabout Theater Co., Todd Haimes, Ellen Richard, Roger Berlind, James M. Nederlander, Nathaniel Kramer, Elizabeth Ireland McCann, Roy Gabay, Old Ivy Prods., producers, *A View from the Bridge* (Dramatic); Roundabout Theater Co., Todd Haimes, Ellen Richard, *Cabaret* (Musical)

1999 | 2000

1999	2000
Brian Dennehy, *Death of a Salesman*	Stephen Dillane, *The Real Thing*
Judi Dench, *Amy's View*	Jennifer Ehle, *The Real Thing*
Frank Wood, *Side Man*	Roy Dotrice, *A Moon for the Misbegotton*
Elizabeth Franz, *Death of a Salesman;* Claire Bloom, *Electra*	Blair Brown, *Copenhagen*
Side Man	*Copenhagen*
Martin Short, *Little Me*	Brian Stokes Mitchell, *Kiss Me Kate*
Bernadette Peters, *Annie Get Your Gun*	Heather Headley, *Aida*
Roger Bart, *You're a Good Man, Charlie Brown*	Boyd Gaines, *Contact*
Kristin Chenoweth, *You're a Good Man, Charlie Brown*	Karen Ziemba, *Contact*
Fosse	*Contact*
Robert Falls, *Death of a Salesman*	Michael Blakemore, *Copenhagen*
Matthew Bourne, *Swan Lake*	Michael Blakemore, *Kiss Me Kate*
Alfred Uhry, *Parade*	James Joyce's *The Dead*
Jason Robert Brown, *Parade*	Elton John, *Aida*
Richard Hoover, *Not About Nightingales*	Bob Crowley, *Aida*
Lez Brotherston, *Swan Lake*	Martin Pakledinaz, *Kiss Me, Kate*
Andrew Bridge, *Fosse*	Natasha Katz, *Aida*
Matthew Bourne, *Swan Lake*	Susan Stroman, *Contact*
Ralph Burns & Douglas Besterman, *Fosse*	Don Sebesky, *Kiss Me, Kate*
Death of a Salesman (Dramatic); *Annie Get Your Gun* (Musical)	*The Real Thing* (Dramatic); *Kiss Me, Kate* (Musical)

A POP CULTURE TIMELINE OF THE 20TH CENTURY

Here is a selective chronicle of the events and inventions, milestones and hallmarks, people and productions that have entertained us and changed life in our century.

1900

THE BROWNIE BOX CAMERA, the first consumer-oriented camera, is introduced by Eastman Kodak. It sells for $1.

PHILOSOPHER FRIEDRICH NIETZSCHE dies after 11 years of madness.

THE HOT DANCE around the nation is the cake walk, invented by African Americans in the late 18th century.

STAGE ACTRESS SARAH BERNHARDT, 56, makes her film debut in *Hamlet's Duel.* She plays Hamlet.

BOOKER T. WASHINGTON publishes his autobiography, *Up from Slavery.*

FERDINAND VON ZEPPELIN'S famous airship makes its first flight on July 20.

1901

VICTORIA, Queen of England and Ireland, and Empress of India, dies on January 22 at age 82, marking the end of the Victorian Era.

THE VICTOR TALKING MACHINE COMPANY is formed by Emile Berliner and Eldridge

Johnson. "His Master's Voice" is the registered trademark for their gramophones, called Victrolas.

1902

BEATRIX POTTER creates the first of her legendary Peter Rabbit children's stories.

1903

THE GREAT TRAIN ROBBERY, starring Max Anderson, is released, marking the debut of the first male movie star.

THE WORLD SERIES is launched, pitting the winners of the National and the American Leagues against each other: this year, the Boston Red Stockings triumph over the Pittsburgh Pirates.

ORVILLE AND WILBUR WRIGHT fly the first powered, heavier-than-air airplane at Kitty Hawk, N.C., on December 17.

1904

HELEN KELLER graduates with honors from Radcliffe, thanks to years of devoted assistance from Anne Sullivan, who will go down in history as the Miracle Worker.

FREUD introduces the idea of neuroses in *The Psychopathology of Everyday Life,* his first major work on psychoanalysis.

THE TEDDY BEAR makes its debut. Created by the German Richard Sterb, it is inspired by President Theodore Roosevelt, who refused to kill a bear cub on a hunting trip.

1905

THE WORLD'S FIRST all-motion picture theater opens in Pittsburgh. The cost is 10¢ for a showing of *Poor But Honest.*

ALBERT EINSTEIN publishes his theory of the photoelectric effect, which is later essential in the development of the TV camera.

Sarah Bernhardt.

1906

Jelly Roll Morton at the piano.

FERDINAND "JELLY ROLL" MORTON, jazz's first great composer, writes "The King Porter Stomp."

THE SAN FRANCISCO EARTHQUAKE kills hundreds on April 18 and causes hundreds of millions of dollars in damage throughout the Bay Area as the city crashes and burns.

UPTON SINCLAIR publishes *The Jungle*, his exposé of the meat-packing industry, which prompts Congress to pass labor reform laws in addition to the Pure Food and Drug Act and the Meat Packing Act of 1906.

1907

FLORENZ ZIEGFELD offers his first version of the *Ziegfeld*

Follies, an extravaganza that will continue for 24 years.

HENRY ADAMS'S masterful autobiography, *The Education of Henry Adams*, is published privately; the Nobel Prize for Biography will be awarded to Adams posthumously in 1919.

COLOR PHOTOGRAPHY becomes practical for the first time due to the development of a new method by the brothers Auguste and Louis Lumière.

THE FIRST MOTION PICTURE with both sound and color is shown in Cleveland.

THE RINGLING BROTHERS buy out their archrivals, Barnum and Bailey, although the two circuses will be operated separately until 1919.

1908

A L'ECU D'OR becomes the earliest dated pornographic film.

THE FIRST MODEL T, known as the Tin Lizzy, is produced on October 1 at Ford's Detroit plant.

THE FIRST COMMERCIAL COLOR FILM, G. A. Smith's *A Visit to the Seaside* (Britain), is released.

1909

ROLLER COASTERS become increasingly popular in amusement parks all over the country.

VITAGRAPH'S *Les Misérables* becomes the first feature film produced in the United States.

THE FIRST ANIMATED CARTOON, *Gertie the Dinosaur*, is released.

ROBERT EDWIN PEARY becomes the first person ever to reach the North Pole.

1910

AUTHOR MARK TWAIN (Samuel Longhorne Clemens) dies at 74.

Mark Twain.

THOMAS EDISON demonstrates his "kinetophone," which successfully displays talking motion pictures.

THE BOY SCOUTS OF AMERICA is founded by William D. Boyce, who takes his inspiration from the English program started by Sir Robert Baden-Powell.

T. S. ELIOT writes *Love Song of J. Alfred Prufrock* while a Harvard undergraduate; it becomes one of the seminal works of the Modernist movement when it is published in 1915.

1911

JEAN, Larry Trimble's pet collie, becomes the first canine star on the big screen. Hired by Vitagraph, she earns $10 more per week than Trimble earns as an actor-writer.

IRVING BERLIN writes "Alexander's Ragtime Band," melding the rhythms of black ragtime into American popular music.

1912

SEIZING ON A CRAZE that has millions of Americans doing the tango, the turkey trot, the hesitation waltz, and the one-step, Victor releases a series of recordings intended for dancing.

THE *TITANIC* sinks after hitting an iceberg on April 14, drowning 1,595 people.

ZANE GREY publishes his most famous Western, *Riders of the Purple Sage*.

THE FIRST BLUES SONG is published by W. C. Handy. Originally called "Memphis Blues," it becomes a hit as "Mr. Crump."

PERHAPS THE BEST ALL-AROUND ATHLETE in history, Native American track-and-field star Jim Thorpe dominates the Olympics, winning gold medals for both the pentathlon and the decathlon. But his medals are taken away from him when it is discovered that he played semi-pro baseball two years before.

STUNT FLYING becomes a staple across the country, taking a terrible toll on pioneering aviators.

1913

DUKE ELLINGTON writes his first song, "Soda Fountain Rag," at the age of 14.

BILLBOARD magazine publishes its first song-popularity chart

by listing leading songs in vaudeville as well as bestselling sheet music.

THE FIRST CROSSWORD puzzle is published in the *New York World*.

1914

CHARLIE CHAPLIN creates the legendary Little Tramp in his second film, *Kid's Auto Races*.

BERT WILLIAMS, a popular vaudevillian, stars in *Darktown Jubilee*, one of the first movies to use an African American actor rather than white actors in blackface. The movie causes a riot in Brooklyn, N.Y.

THE TARZAN SAGA begins with the publication of *Tarzan of the Apes* by Edgar Rice Burroughs.

ASCAP—the American Society of Composers, Authors, and Publishers—is formed to empower artists to collect fees for the performances and use of their work.

THE PANAMA CANAL opens on May 18.

WORLD WAR I breaks out on July 28. One of the many consequences is that movie production outside of

the United States will be suspended, allowing American filmmakers to dominate the industry.

1915

ALBERT EINSTEIN proposes the General Theory of Relativity.

AUDREY MUNSON reveals all as she becomes the first leading lady to appear on the screen nude in *Inspiration*.

MARGARET SANGER is jailed for writing about birth control in her book *Family Limitation*.

THE MOST FAMOUS MOVIE of the silent era, D. W. Griffith's *The Birth of a Nation*, opens in New York City to great success, but is bitterly criticized for its racism.

THE DIVINE Sarah Bernhardt finally faces what appears to be the end of her stage career when her leg is amputated at the age of 71; the next year, however, she stages what proves at last to be her final one-for-the-road, this time playing Portia in *The Merchant of Venice* with an artificial leg.

THE PROVINCETOWN PLAYERS are organized in Massa-

chusetts and become the first to present the works of playwright Eugene O'Neill. The next year the group moves its already highly influential theater to New York where it begins the off-Broadway theater movement.

USING VACUUM TUBES, AT&T introduces long-distance service between New York and San Francisco.

THE MOVIE BUSINESS takes root in Hollywood, California, land of good weather and cheap labor. By 1915, half of all American films are made there.

1916

NOTORIOUS SIBERIAN MONK GRIGORY RASPUTIN is murdered. Rasputin had been a confidant and

Grigory Rasputin.

advisor to the Czarina after using his hypnotic powers to "cure" the Empress's heir, Alexis, of hemophilia.

TWO VERY DIFFERENT major American writers die—action-adventure writer Jack London, author of *Call of the Wild*, and expatriate novelist Henry James, author of *Portrait of a Lady*.

THE DADA MOVEMENT is founded in Zurich as an anti-art, anti-literature protest against the atrocities of the Great War.

1917

"THE DIXIE JAZZ BAND ONE-STEP" by Nick LaRocca's Original Dixieland Jazz Band, a group of white musicians, is the first jazz record to be released in the United States.

MATA HARI, a Dutch dancer, is executed by the French as a spy for Germany.

THE FIRST PULITZER PRIZES are awarded, in the categories of biography, history, and journalism. The award for drama is added the following year.

1918

PRESIDENT WOODROW WILSON proclaims his Fourteen Points for world peace; World War I comes to an end on November 11.

DAYLIGHT SAVINGS TIME is introduced in America.

1919

JACK DEMPSEY, known as the Manassa Mauler, wins the world heavyweight boxing championship.

Mata Hari.

1920

PROHIBITION begins with the enactment of the Eighteenth Amendment, which makes it illegal to produce, sell, or drink alcoholic beverages.

HERCULE POIROT is introduced in Agatha Christie's first novel, *The Mysterious Affair at Styles.*

MAMIE SMITH becomes the first African-American singer to record a vocal blues performance with "Crazy Blues."

THE NATION'S FIRST RADIO stations—KDKA, Pittsburgh and WWJ, Detroit—hit the airwaves.

1921

THE FIRST MISS AMERICA pageant is held on September 9, won by Margaret Gorman, Miss Washington, D.C.

READER'S DIGEST begins publication.

1922

THE FIRST 3-D feature film is released when Nat Deverich creates *Power of Love.*

NANOOK OF THE NORTH by Robert J. Flaherty is released and comes to be regarded as one of the greatest documentaries ever filmed.

THE TECHNICOLOR film process makes its initial successful run.

JAMES JOYCE'S *Ulysses* is published in Paris by the expatriate American Sylvia Beach; though one of the greatest novels of the century, it remains banned in the United States until December 6, 1933, when a judge rules that the book does not contain "the leer of a sensualist."

1923

LEE DEFOREST devises a method of recording sound directly on film. Producers utilize the technology to create vaudeville shorts.

THE COVERED WAGON, the first of the great Western epics, is released to huge success.

TIME magazine begins publication, providing the news in a flavorful, succinct format.

1924

STAGE LEGENDS Alfred Lunt and Lynn Fontanne first appear together as a team in a play called *The Guardsman.*

THE FIRST MILLION-SELLERS in America are instrumentals: Paul Whiteman's *Whispering* and Ben Selvin's *Dardanella.*

NATHAN LEOPOLD and Richard Loeb are tried for the "thrill killing" of 14-year-old Robert Franks; Clarence Darrow's pioneering insanity plea saves them from execution.

THE LITTLE ORPHAN ANNIE comic strip is created by Harold Gray.

1925

THE FIRST national spelling bee is held.

THE AGE OF THE CHARLESTON bounces into dancehalls across America.

THE NEW YORKER is founded on February 21, edited by Harold Ross. The first issue bears the image of Eustace Tilley, who will come to serve as the magazine's unofficial symbol and patriarch.

THE WSM BARN DANCE—renamed the *Grand Ole Opry* in 1928—premieres in November.

THE CLASSIC NOVEL of the Jazz Age, *The Great Gatsby* by F. Scott Fitzgerald, is published.

1926

TELEVISION is invented in Scotland by John Logie Baird, but the Depression and World War II stifle development of the industry until the '50s.

DEFORD BAILEY is the first African American musician to appear on Nashville's *Grand Ole Opry* show. He becomes nationally known as "The Harmonica Wizard,"

and remains a regular until 1941.

RUDOLPH VALENTINO, the most popular of all male silent film stars and a worldwide sex symbol, dies at age 31 of a ruptured appendix and a gastric ulcer.

Rudolph Valentino.

NBC RADIO is founded.

NEW YORK talks to London in the first successful transatlantic radiotelephone conversation.

MAE WEST writes and stars in a play called *Sex;* the performance that launches her

Mae West.

career as the greatest sex symbol of the era also inspires the police to close the show and sentence West to 10 days in a workhouse.

THE BOOK-OF-THE-MONTH CLUB is founded, the first of the mail-order book programs. The first offering is Sylvia Townsend Warner's novel, *Lolly Willowes.*

MINIATURE GOLF is introduced in Lookout Mountain, Tenn., and from there it expands to over 40,000 courses within three years.

THE SUN ALSO RISES, the classic novel of disillusionment in the postwar years, is written by Ernest Hemingway.

1927

THE AGE OF THE TALKIES arrives with the Warner Bros. release of the wildly successful film *The Jazz Singer,* starring Al Jolson.

THE FIRST CAR RADIOS are introduced.

CHARLES LINDBERGH makes the first nonstop solo flight across the Atlantic, from New York to Paris.

Charles Lindbergh and his famous plane.

1928

TELEVISION comes to a home in Schenectady, N.Y., and begins receiving regularly scheduled broadcasts, three afternoons a week, on its one and one-half-inch screen.

WOMEN COMPETE in the Olympics (in Amsterdam) for the first time.

AMELIA EARHART becomes the first woman to fly across the Atlantic Ocean when she lands in London.

MICKEY MOUSE debuts in Walt Disney's first cartoon, *Plane Crazy*. The public however, first meets him in *Steamboat Willie*, which is released before its progenitor.

1929

THE FIRST ACADEMY AWARDS are presented at the Hollywood Roosevelt Hotel in Los Angeles, May 16. Douglas Fairbanks Sr. presents all of the awards in five minutes. The first winner for Best Picture is the now-forgotten Clara Bow vehicle, *Wings*.

VIRGINIA WOOLF publishes her feminist classic, *A Room of One's Own.*

CBS (Columbia Broadcasting System) is founded by William S. Paley, age 27.

THE MUSEUM OF MODERN ART (MOMA) opens in New York with an exhibition of works by Cezanne, Gaugin, Seurat, and Van Gogh.

ON BLACK THURSDAY, October 24, the stock market crashes, abruptly beginning the transition from the Roaring Twenties to the Great Depression.

KODAK introduces 16mm color movie film.

1930

SINCLAIR LEWIS becomes the first American to win the Nobel Prize for Literature.

THE FIRST SUPERMARKET opens in Queens, N.Y., offering low prices, and a huge selection; it achieves tremendous success overnight.

THE HAYS OFFICE creates a production code to enforce self-censorship in the film business. **GRANT WOOD** paints *American Gothic.*

GARBO TALKS, in Eugene O'Neill's *Anna Christie,* her first speaking role.

Garbo poses.

1931

THE WORLD'S TALLEST BUILDING, the Empire State Building, is opened to the public. RCA and NBC install a TV transmitter atop the building.

AL "SCARFACE" CAPONE, all-time great American gangster, goes to jail for tax evasion.

THE WHITNEY MUSEUM, founded by sculptor and railroad heiress Gertrude Vanderbilt Whitney, opens in New York City.

SCRABBLE is invented by New York architect Alfred Butts, but the game is turned down by every manufacturer; not until 1948 is Scrabble widely distributed, and not until 1952 does word of mouth turn it into a bonanza.

1932

THE LINDBERGH BABY is kidnapped on May 1, only to be discovered dead 12 days later, after the parents pay a $50,000 ransom.

OF THEE I SING, a musical comedy written by George and Ira Gershwin with book by George S.

Kaufman and Morrie Ryskind, becomes the first musical to win a Pulitzer Prize.

BIG-TIME VAUDEVILLE begins its final fade-out as the last two-a-day show opens at the Palace on Broadway.

ECSTASY, in which Hedy Lamarr appears nude, becomes the first film in which a sexual experience is depicted.

FRANCES PERKINS becomes the first woman to hold a Cabinet post when she is appointed secretary of labor by Franklin Delano Roosevelt.

THE FIRST DRIVE-IN cinema is built in Camden, N.J., accommodating 400 cars, and opens with *Wife Beware.*

PRESIDENT ROOSEVELT holds the first Fireside Chat on March 12, a radio address to the entire nation.

PROHIBITION is repealed with the ratification of the 21st Amendment on December 5. The watering holes that soon cover the country—bars, saloons, cocktail lounges—have a new feature, the jukebox.

THE FIRST NATIONAL FOOTBALL LEAGUE championship play-off pits the Chicago Bears against the New York Giants on December 17. The Bears win, 23–21.

1934

THE APOLLO THEATRE stages its first live show in Harlem.

BENNY GOODMAN begins his radio show *Let's Dance,* establishing himself as the "King of Swing."

JOHN DILLINGER, Public Enemy No. 1, is gunned down in chicago by FBI agents.

1935

THE FEDERAL THEATRE PROJECT is instituted by Congress as part of the Works Progress Administration. An attempt to assist an ailing theater community hit badly by the Depression, it is disbanded in 1939.

BECKY SHARP, the first full-length color feature film, opens.

THE FIRST NIGHT BASEBALL game in the major leagues is played between the Cincinnati Reds and

the Philadelphia Phillies. Cincinnati wins, 2–1.

GEORGE AND DOROTHY GERSHWIN'S opera *Porgy and Bess* opens at Boston's Colonial Theater.

1936

JESSE OWENS wins four gold medals in track events at the Berlin Olympics, infuriating German Chancellor Adolf Hitler,who preaches the mental and physical supremacy of Aryan whites over all other races.

MARGARET MITCHELL'S *Gone with the Wind*

is published, selling a million copies in six months and winning the Pulitzer Prize in 1937. It will be her only book.

FRANKLIN DELANO ROOSEVELT is reelected president in the greatest Democratic landslide ever, carrying 48 states.

EUGENE O'NEILL, the great American dramatist, is awarded the Nobel Prize for Literature.

1937

VENTRILOQUIST EDGAR BERGEN and Charlie McCarthy premiere on NBC. They will

Jesse Owens in gold-medal form.

remain hugely popular with audiences when the show makes the move from radio to TV.

JOHN STEINBECK'S *Of Mice and Men* is published.

THE FIRST worldwide radio broadcast to be received in the United States brings us the coronation of King George VI of England on May 12.

1938

WALT DISNEY'S *Snow White and the Seven Dwarfs* tops the movie charts, making Disney internationally famous, and goes on to become an all-time classic.

OUR TOWN, by Thornton Wilder, is produced (and not in a high school theater). It wins a Pulitzer.

HEAVYWEIGHT BOXING champion Joe Louis defends his title with a first-round knockout of German boxer Max Schmeling, a Nazi hero who symbolizes the notion of Aryan superiority. His victory is viewed as a triumph both for African Americans and for democracy.

THE DIRIGIBLE *Hindenburg* bursts into flames as it lands in New Jersey on May

Joe Louis.

6, marking the virtual end of lighter-than-air transportation. Simultaneously, the first coast-to-coast radio broadcast is conducted by Herbert Morrison, who reports on the disaster.

THE RADIO PLAY *War of the Worlds* (based on the novel by H.G. Wells) is broadcast on October 30 by Orson Welles, causing widespread panic among listeners who believe its story of an invasion from Mars.

1939

THE FIRST GOLDFISH is swallowed by a Harvard undergrad, beginning a fad that quickly sweeps across the nation and sets off such variations on the theme as eating light bulbs and biting snakes' heads off.

MARIAN ANDERSON, world-famous African American contralto, is denied permission to sing in Washington D.C.'s Constitution Hall by the Daughters of the American Revolution. Undaunted, she is sponsored by Eleanor Roosevelt in a triumphant performance on the steps of the Lincoln Memorial in front of 75,000 fans.

ROBERT KANE creates the cartoon character Batman.

THE GOLDEN GATE Exposition is held in San Francisco.

LOU NOVA squares off against Max Baer in the first televised prizefight, direct from Yankee Stadium. Nova wins in 11 rounds.

RHETT BUTLER'S infamous declaration in the film version of *Gone with the Wind,* "Frankly, my dear, I don't give a damn," breaks the taboo against cursing in the movies.

AT THE NEW YORK WORLD'S FAIR thousands ogle RCA TV sets featuring a 12-inch screen reflected in a cabinet-lid mirror.

1940

RICHARD WRIGHT'S masterpiece, *Native Son,* is published to wide acclaim; it is later adapted for a successful Broadway run.

A WORKABLE COLOR TV is announced by Peter Goldmark, chief television engineer at CBS.

THE COTTON CLUB, Harlem's famous jazz nightclub, closes down.

CONGRESS passes the Selective Service Act, the first U.S. peacetime draft law ever.

1941

THE FIRST TV AD comes on the air, marking the advent of commercial television; the spot, for Bulova watches, lasts 10 seconds and costs the company $9.

PEARL HARBOR is bombed by Japan on December 7, a day of infamy that ushers the U.S. into World War II.

1942

RODGERS AND HAMMERSTEIN transform the musical comedy

with their production of *Oklahoma!*

PHYSICISTS John Atanasoff and Clifton Berry develop the first fully electronic computer.

CAPITOL RECORDS is launched by Glenn Wallichs, who invents the art of record promotion by sending copies of new record releases to prominent disc jockeys.

BING CROSBY releases "White Christmas," from the film *Holiday Inn*, and it becomes the biggest-selling song from a movie in history.

1943

FRANK LLOYD WRIGHT begins work on the Solomon R. Guggenheim Museum in New York. Founded in 1939 as the Museum of Non-Objective Painting, the building opens its doors in 1959.

GEORGE WASHINGTON CARVER, 81, dies in Tuskegee, Ala. Born into slavery, he developed inventive uses for peanuts, soybeans, and other traditional Southern crops, which proved to be a boon to agriculture in the region.

BILLBOARD introduces the first country music charts, first called "Most-Played Juke Box Hillbilly Records" and then changed to "Folk Records" before being relabeled "Country & Western" in 1949.

PAPER SHORTAGES during World War II force the publishing business to experiment with softcover bindings for its books, with stunning success.

SMELL-O-VISION is created by Swiss inventor Hans E. Laube, who develops a "smell pack" that is stimulated by TV waves to produce an odor to accompany what is being shown on the screen.

WORLD WAR II comes to an end. Germany surrenders on May 8 (V-E Day). The only atomic bombs ever to be used in war are dropped by the U.S. on Hiroshima on August 6 and Nagasaki three days later, leading to the surrender of Japan on August 15 (V-J Day).

DR. BENJAMIN SPOCK revolutionizes the way Americans raise their families with his *Common Sense Book of Baby and Child Care.*

WINSTON CHURCHILL coins the term "iron curtain" in a speech at Westminster College in Missouri.

THE U.S. detonates a nuclear bomb on Bikini Atoll on July 5 in the South Pacific. Five days later, designer Louis Reard commemorates the blast at a fashion show in Paris, where a certain itsy-bitsy, teeny-weeny two-piece bathing suit makes its first appearance.

THE CANNES FILM FESTIVAL premieres in September.

THE FIRST TV SOAP OPERA, *Faraway Hill,* debuts on the DuMont network.

CONSUMERS RUSH to buy the new 10-inch RCA TV set for $375. This "Model T of television" ushers in the TV age.

THE POLAROID Land camera is patented by Dr. Edwin Land, providing prints that develop inside the camera within a minute. It enters the market the following year, selling for $90.

JACKIE ROBINSON becomes the first African American to sign with a major-league baseball team. His first game with the Brooklyn Dodgers is an exhibition game against the New York Yankees.

NBC'S *KRAFT TELEVISION THEATRE* introduces serious drama. Overnight, cheese sales soar and Madison Avenue melts.

FLYING SAUCER! The first sighting is reported on June 25, according to one source.

THE WORLD SERIES is broadcast on TV for the first time and four million baseball fans watch the New York Yankees and the Brooklyn Dodgers battle it out. The Yanks go on to win the series.

THE FIRST ANTOINETTE PERRY (TONY) AWARDS for excellence in theater are handed out. No best play award is included, but José Ferrer wins as Best Actor, and Best Actress awards go to Ingrid Bergman and Helen Hayes.

THE TRANSISTOR is invented by Bell

Telephone Laboratories; it becomes one of the most significant advances in the history of consumer electronics, paving the way for miniature TV sets, radios, and gear like CD players that haven't yet been invented.

1948

TED MACK'S *THE ORIGINAL AMATEUR HOUR* premieres in January. By year's end the first "ratings sweep" declares it the most popular show on TV.

THE PHONOGRAPH RECORDING market is fraught with competition as companies come up with improvements on the old 78 rpm disks. Columbia introduces the first long-playing commercial record, the 33⅓ rpm disk, and RCA releases the 45.

LEE STRASBERG takes over the Actors Studio, introducing the Method acting techniques that will profoundly influence such students as Marlon Brando, Paul Newman, James Dean, and Marilyn Monroe.

THE MOTORCYCLE CLAN Hell's Angels is formed.

THE ED SULLIVAN SHOW premiers to an initially poor viewer response. The influential variety program will stay on the air until 1971.

THE TERM "COLD WAR" is popularized by a speech before the Senate War Investigation Committee.

TV SET SALES skyrocket, with an estimated 250,000 sets installed every month.

NORMAN MAILER'S first novel, *The Naked and the Dead*, comes out. It remains one of the most important fictional works about World War II.

1949

CHIC YOUNG'S *BLONDIE* is the most popular comic strip in the world.

THE FIRST CABLE television systems go into homes.

ARTHUR MILLER'S play *Death of a Salesman*, the first dramatic tragedy to feature a common man as a protagonist, wins a Pulitzer Prize.

UNERRING *CRUSADER RABBIT* debuts as the first made-for-TV animated cartoon.

1950

GWENDOLYN BROOKS is the first African American to win a Pulitzer Prize, for her work *Annie Allen*.

MCCARTHYISM begins in February when the obscure U.S. senator Joseph McCarthy alleges that the federal government is infested with Communists.

GOOD OL' CHARLIE BROWN enters American culture as Charles Schulz creates the legendary comic strip *Peanuts*.

TELEVISION takes it first late-night variety plunge with *Broadway Open House*, and "dumb blonde" Dagmar (Jennie Lewis) becomes the first boob-tube sex symbol.

THE FIRST AMERICAN TROOPS land in Korea on July 1 after soldiers from North Korea invade South Korea. Although the move is described as a United Nations action, American soldiers comprise the vast majority of foreign troops. With news footage being aired on American TVs, it is also the first living-room war.

HOLLYWOOD buys its first million-dollar property: Columbia

acquires the rights to the successful Broadway play *Born Yesterday* from the writer Garson Kanin.

A. C. NIELSEN begins gathering ratings data for TV, employing electronic viewing records along with written logs to determine the popularity of shows.

BELL LABORATORIES and Western Electric create the first telephone answering machine.

THE SITCOM laugh track is introduced on *The Hank McCune Show*, a program that has the added distinction of being canceled midseason.

THE FIRST CREDIT CARD is introduced through the Diners Club.

THE CISCO KID, starring Duncan Renaldo and Leo Carillo, is the first TV series filmed in color. At the time, there are fewer than 100 experimental sets in the U.S.

THE 1949 NOBEL PRIZE for Literature is retroactively awarded to William Faulkner. No prize had been awarded the previous year because none of the candidates had won a majority of the votes.

1951

PAY-PER-VIEW dies a premature death after Zenith begins testing its "Phonevision" in Chicago. Viewers can dial a phone number and watch a recent feature film for $1. But skittish movie studios decide not to make first-run films available, fearing the consequences.

SENATE HEARINGS on organized crime rivet the nation. Mobster Frank Costello allows only his hands to be shown.

UNIVAC I, the first commercially built computer, goes into operation at the Census Bureau in Philadelphia.

CBS broadcasts the first commercial color telecast on June 25 with a one-hour special from New York to four other cities.

NBC begins the first network coast-to-coast programming.

AMOS 'N' ANDY bows with TV's first all-black cast. Though canceled in 1953, reruns air until 1966, when protests about racial stereotyping force withdrawal of the show from syndication.

I LOVE LUCY debuts to tremendous success, creating the mold for TV sitcoms.

CLEVELAND DJ Alan Freed, the first to introduce black R&B to a white audience on station WJW, coins the term "rock and roll."

CBS debuts its "unblinking eye," which evolves into TV's most famous logo.

GIAN CARLO MENOTTI'S *Amahl and the Night Visitors* becomes the first made-for-TV opera on Christmas Eve. It becomes a perennial seasonal favorite.

1952

THE REVISED STANDARD edition of the Old Testament, only the third authorized Protestant revision in 341 years, becomes a No. 1 bestseller and sets records by selling 1.6 million copies in eight weeks; the old record was held by *Gone with the Wind*, which sold 1 million books in six months.

THE MOUSETRAP, originally a play created by Agatha Christie for the 80th birthday of Britain's Queen Mary, premieres in London. It will become the longest-

running theatrical work of all time.

MAD **MAGAZINE** and the *National Enquirer* make their debuts.

UNIDENTIFIED FLYING OBJECTS capture the imagination of Americans. No longer looked on as simply science fiction, the national fascination with UFOs even prompts the U.S. Air Force to publish possible photographs of the phenomenon.

THE FIRST HYDROGEN BOMB is detonated on November 1, and Americans' fear of complete annihilation intensifies.

BWANA DEVIL leads a resurgence of popularity for 3-D movies, Hollywood's attempt to combat the appeal of "free" TV.

PANTY RAIDS occur in epic proportions at college sororities across the nation.

TWO OF TELEVISION'S biggest all-time hits—*Today,* hosted by Dave Garroway, and *Guiding Light*—begin broadcasting on NBC and CBS, respectively; both programs are still going strong today.

THE MARILYN MONROE image crystallizes with four film releases, helping movie theaters draw

Marilyn Monroe.

Americans away from their TV sets.

ART LINKLETTER tosses a *House Party* on September 1, and the bash lasts longer (17 years) than any daytime variety show.

VEEP HOPEFUL Richard Nixon makes a politician's first direct TV appeal on September 23, citing his dog, Checkers, in his successful quest to beat fund-misuse charges and save his career.

CHRISTINE JORGENSON returns from Denmark where she had undergone the first publicized sex-change operation.

1953

I LOVE LUCY features the birth of Little Ricky on January 19 as the real Lucille Ball gives birth to Desi Arnaz Jr. The landmark show draws a 92 percent share of TV sets in use, or 44 million viewers—a record to date. Turns out the "dual birth" was no happy accident, since Desi Junior was born by a scheduled caesarean section. The event received more media attention than Dwight Eisenhower's inauguration, which took place the following day. Eisenhower and Nixon form the first Republican administration in 24 years.

DESI JR. scores again when the first issue of *TV Guide* is published, featuring him on the cover.

AT AGE 27, Queen Elizabeth II is crowned as England's monarch.

JULIUS AND ETHEL ROSENBERG are executed, the only American civilians ever to receive such a penalty for espionage.

THE DISC JOCKEY Top 40 radio format is established on KOWH, an Omaha station. It features a limited number of records played over and over, hourly news breaks, and sporadic chatter from the announcer.

CINEMASCOPE premieres with *The Robe*, and its wide-screen format becomes a huge hit with filmgoers.

PLAYBOY MAGAZINE is founded by 27-year-old Hugh Hefner with a first issue featuring the nude Marilyn Monroe on its cover.

THE FIRST ROCK AND ROLL song hits the Billboard charts: Bill Haley and His Comets' "Crazy, Man, Crazy."

THE RCA compatible color television is approved by the FCC and becomes the industry standard.

HOUSTON'S KUHT debuts as the country's first noncommercial educational TV station; within 10 years there will be 75 other such stations.

1954

MARILYN MONROE marries former New York Yankees star Joe DiMaggio, a second marriage for both. Alas, the match is not meant to be—Marilyn files for divorce nine months later.

TELEVISION JOURNALIST Edward R. Murrow launches the first major attack on Joseph McCarthy's witch-hunt tactics on CBS's *See It Now*,

Hugh Hefner.

inspiring a groundswell of support for the senator's critics and ultimately precipitating his downfall.

SEGREGATION in schools is declared unconstitutional on May 14 in the landmark case, *Brown vs. Board of Education*.

ELVIS PRESLEY cuts his first record, the double-sided 45 "That's All Right (Mama)"/"Blue Moon of Kentucky."

THE FIRST COLOR TV sets and the first

Elvis Presley.

transistor radios are marketed.

TONIGHT!, later known as *The Tonight Show*, premieres with Steve Allen as host.

SWANSON brings out the very first TV dinners—ominously, turkey—for 69¢.

1955

CONTRALTO MARIAN ANDERSON becomes the first African American to sing a major role at the Metropolitan Opera, appearing as Ulrica in Verdi's *Masked Ball*.

A NEW ERA in domestic politics is launched with the first filmed presidential press conference. Both TV and motion picture newsreel photographers cover the event.

WALT DISNEY'S TV show, *Disneyland*, first appears on ABC and quickly becomes one of the most successful programs on the tube. One segment, "Davy Crockett, Indian Fighter," instigates a full-blooded Davy Crockett mania, which sweeps the country. Over 3,000 Crockett-related items sell in crazy numbers, from coonskin caps to Bill Hayes's song "Ballad of Davy Crockett," which rises to the top of the charts.

ANN LANDERS launches her advice column in the *Chicago Sun-Times.*

BILL HALEY and His Comets' "Rock Around the Clock" goes to No. 1 on *Billboard*'s charts on June 6, marking the indisputable ascent of rock and roll.

DISNEYLAND, the first theme amusement park, opens south of Los Angeles in Anaheim.

JAMES DEAN stars in *Rebel Without a Cause*, his second and penultimate starring role before crashing his Porsche later in the year and dying at age 26. His death gives rise to his enduring status as a cult hero, embodying the spirit of rebelliousness so sought after by

America's younger generation.

BOB KEESHAN debuts as the Captain on *Captain Kangaroo*, which goes on to become the longest-running kids' show. *The Mickey Mouse Club* begins as well.

IN ONE OF THE greatest record deals of all time, RCA buys Elvis's contract—for an unprecedented $40,000—from Sam Phillips's Sun Records.

COMIC BOOK popularity reaches unprecedented heights, with sales soaring beyond a billion copies. Concern over their violent content increases in due measure, prompting New York State to ban the sale of certain graphic comics to minors.

1956

ACTOR GRACE KELLY retires from Hollywood and marries Prince Rainier III of Monaco, a member of the thousand-year-old Grimaldi dynasty, in one of the most publicized marriages of the century.

BEAT POET ALAN GINSBERG'S *"Howl" and Other Poems* is released and its publisher is promptly brought up on

obscenity charges that are later successfully defended in court.

MARILYN MONROE weds husband No. 3, Pulitzer- and Tony Award-winning playwright Arthur Miller (it's his second marriage). The two are divorced in 1961.

DEAN MARTIN and Jerry Lewis are a team no more. They split on July 25, exactly 10 years after they first appeared together in Atlantic City.

NBC'S Huntley and Brinkley are TV's first co-anchors: "Goodnight, Chet." "Goodnight, David."

IN HIS FIRST YEAR OF stardom, Elvis releases "Don't Be Cruel"/ "Hound Dog," a 45 that becomes the biggest hit of all time on *Billboard*'s charts. His appearance on Ed Sullivan's *Toast of the Town* on September 9, shot discreetly above the pelvis, earns the highest rating for any regularly scheduled program, drawing an estimated audience of 50 million people. He also appears in his first movie, *Love Me Tender*.

1957

Slick Jerry Lee Lewis.

LEONARD BERNSTEIN is named the first American musical director of the New York Philharmonic.

JERRY LEE LEWIS scandalizes the nation when he marries his 13-year-old cousin, Myra Gale Brown—also committing bigamy by failing to divorce wife, Jane Mitcham.

BOBBY FISCHER, 14, wins the U.S. chess championship.

THE HULA HOOP is introduced and takes America by storm, selling over 45 million by 1958.

DICK CLARK'S *American Bandstand* moves from a local Philadelphia station to its national debut on ABC. It becomes TV's longest-running variety show.

THE SOVIET UNION launches *Sputnik*, and the space race.

LEAVE IT TO BEAVER debuts on CBS, presenting the audience with the most typically American family to date.

THE NAT "KING" COLE SHOW, the first major series with an African American host, is canceled after a year, for lack of a national sponsor.

1958

ALVIN AILEY founds the American Dance Theatre.

BILLBOARD begins its Hot 100 chart; the first No. 1 record is "Poor Little Fool" by Ricky Nelson.

VLADIMIR NABOKOV'S sensational novel *Lolita* is published by Putnam after being rejected as too obscene by four other American publishers.

DEEJAYS AT ST. LOUIS' KWK radio station complete their "Record Breaking Week" when, at the insistence of the management, "undesirable" records are given a final play on the airwaves and then ceremoniously destroyed. Most of the sacrificed recordings are of rock and roll music.

SCIENTISTS at the ESSO Gas Research Center—now EXXON—announce on July 28 that they have found that drivers waste gas when they listen to rock and roll because they tend to jiggle the pedals in time with the beat.

VAN CLIBURN becomes the first American to win a gold medal at the Tchaikovsky International Piano Festival. His subsequent recording of the composer's *Piano Concerto No. 1* is the first classical record to go gold.

THE BROOKLYN DODGERS and the New York Giants move to California, bringing major-league baseball to the West Coast.

THE GRAMMY AWARDS are launched. Ignoring the rising predominance of rock and roll, the organizers present Best Album of the Year to Henry Mancini and name "Volaré" by Domenico Modugno as Best Song.

QUIZ SHOW scandals erupt with an initial investigation of answer-feeding on a program called *Dotto* prompted by a complaint by contestant Eddie Hilgemeier. By the end of the year most quiz shows are pulled off the air.

1959

BUDDY HOLLY, Ritchie Valens, and The Big Bopper are tragically killed in February when their single-engine light aircraft crashes in a snowstorm about 10 minutes after takeoff.

BARBIE is introduced to the toy world, created by Ruth and Elliot Handler, who founded Mattel in 1945. The doll's proportions, if copied on a human scale, would be 33-18-28. Barbie was named for the Handlers' daughter, Barbara, just as their son, Ken, was later honored when his parents created a male companion doll.

ISLAND IN THE SUN, starring James Mason, Dorothy Dandridge, Harry Belafonte, and Joan Fontaine, becomes the first film to portray interracial romance.

THE U.S. POSTMASTER GENERAL bans *Lady Chatterley's Lover* by D. H. Lawrence, but sales skyrocket after courts hold that the book is not obscene.

AMERICANS SEE THE WORLD from a new perspective as *Explorer VI* sends down the first photograph of Earth taken from outer space.

THE TELEPHONE-BOOTH JAMMING fad hits this year and fades almost as quickly. The fad first catches hold on the West Coast and moves quickly across the country, the record being set with 32 squashed students at Modesto Junior College in California.

MOTOWN RECORDS is founded in Detroit by songwriter Berry Gordy Jr.

IS TELEVISION KING? In December, for the first time, TV rings up more in commercial sales ($1.24 billion) than Hollywood cashes in box-office receipts ($1.235 billion).

1960

ELVIS PRESLEY'S army career, which began in March of 1958, comes to a close.

A CONGRESSIONAL investigation into payola determines that radio deejays have been receiving payments from record companies to play their disks. Dick Clark and Alan Freed are the particular focus of allegations, and Freed eventually loses his job.

SMELL-O-VISION hits theaters as Michael

Todd Jr.'s film *Scent of Mystery* is released to general indifference.

Master director Alfred Hitchcock.

PSYCHO, directed by Alfred Hitchcock, sets new movie attendance records and earns a mint as one of the most frightening films ever made.

THE TWIST is introduced by 19-year-old Chubby Checker.

BEN-HUR collects a record 11 Oscars out of 12 nominations.

THE FANTASTICKS debuts May 3. It will become the longest-running off-Broadway show ever, hitting its 14,000th performance on March 2, 1994—and still going strong at the Sullivan Street Playhouse in Greenwich Village. Since its beginning, notable performers have included Kevin Kline, Richard Chamberlain, and Jerry Orbach.

THE FLINTSTONES debuts as prime time's first animated sitcom.

BIRTH CONTROL PILLS become available for widespread use as the FDA approves the public sale of Enovid at $10 to $11 for a month's supply.

THE FIRST FRENCH KISS on the Hollywood big screen takes place between Natalie Wood and Warren Beatty in *Splendor in the Grass*.

SOPRANO LEONTYNE PRICE, 34, debuts at New York's Metropolitan Opera House in *Il Trovatore* and receives a 45-minute ovation.

BOB DYLAN gives his first solo performance, opening for blues musician John Lee Hooker in New York City's Gerde's Folk City.

ABC'S WIDE WORLD OF SPORTS with Jim McKay is introduced and runs on Saturday afternoons, showing us "the thrill of victory and the agony of defeat."

ALAN B. SHEPARD JR. becomes the first American astronaut

Jacqueline Kennedy lights up the White House.

to go into space on May 5.

SATURDAY NIGHT AT THE MOVIES debuts as the first regular TV showcase for major motion pictures.

JACQUELINE KENNEDY takes the country on a televised tour of the White House.

THE FIRST USE OF NUDITY in advertising appears in *Harper's Bazaar* in a bare-breasted photo by Richard Avedon.

THE FIRST JAMES BOND movie, *Dr. No*, is released. Starring as

007 is Sean Connery, 32.

DIRECT-DIAL long-distance telephone service begins in the United States.

MARILYN MONROE dies of a barbiturate overdose at age 36 on August 5.

THE VIRGINIAN makes its debut as the first 90-minute TV series. In a nine-year run, its cast includes Lee Majors, David Hartman, and Lee J. Cobb as a frontier judge.

JOHNNY CARSON takes over *The Tonight Show* where he will reign as King of Television until he retires in 1992.

1963

WEIGHT WATCHERS enters the market, turning dieting into big business.

POP ART is given its first major show at the Guggenheim Museum in New York. Artists include Andy Warhol, Jasper Johns, and Roy Lichtenstein.

BETTY FRIEDAN publishes her landmark feminist tract, *The Feminine Mystique.*

JULIA CHILD bubbles up on *The French Chef* and becomes public TV's first star; she'll keep TV cooking for the next 10 years.

WHISKEY A-GO-GO opens in Los Angeles, beginning its tenure as Hollywood's longest-lived club devoted to cutting-edge rock music.

THE BEATLES release their first single in the U.S., "Please Please Me," in February along with their LP *Introducing The Beatles.*

CLEOPATRA, with Elizabeth Taylor and Richard Burton, scores as both the top money-maker of the year and one of the biggest flops in movie history as its vast costs far overrun its huge budget; Tay-lor alone receives $1.75 million for her participation.

PEBBLES FLINTSTONE is born to parents Wilma and Fred on February 22 at the Bedrock Rockapedia Hospital.

TROLLS are introduced. Billed as good-luck charms, their ugliness is a charm indeed, producing sales in the millions.

THE FUGITIVE debuts September 17; David Janssen runs. He'll catch the one-armed man—and a then record prime-time audience—in the '67 finale. That episode still ranks as the third-most-watched episode of a television series ever.

PRESIDENT JOHN F. KENNEDY, 46, is assassinated in

Elizabeth Taylor as Cleopatra.

Dallas on November 22. The immediacy of television's coverage of the surrounding events transforms TV into a witness to history and binds together a nation in mourning.

1964

FIVE THOUSAND SCREAMING FANS greet The Beatles at Kennedy Airport in New York on February 7, when the band arrives for its first American tour. Two days later the Fab Four appear on *The Ed Sullivan Show.* They draw an estimated 75 percent of all TV viewers, making it the most-watched hour of television to date. Songs include "All My Loving," "She Loves You," and "I Want To Hold Your Hand."

THE MOOG, the first commercial music synthesizer, is developed.

ELIZABETH TAYLOR finally meets her match, again, as she marries husband No. 5, Richard Burton, just 10 days after getting a divorce from Eddie Fisher. The two had met on the set of *Cleopatra.*

THE HOME VIDEO RECORDER is invented in Japan by the Sony Corporation.

MARSHALL MCLUHAN declares that the "medium is the message" in his book *Understanding Media.* Nobody gets it, but everybody talks about it.

LYNDON B. JOHNSON'S "daisy" campaign spot airs once on September 7, suggesting that Republican opponent Goldwater is nuke-happy. Fallout: LBJ wins in a landslide.

PEYTON PLACE airs September 15 as the first prime-time soap and becomes a smash hit.

G.I. JOE is introduced by Hasbro and sells for $4.

MARTIN LUTHER KING JR. receives the Nobel Peace Prize. Jean-Paul Sartre is awarded the Nobel Prize for Literature and becomes the first person to reject the honor.

1965

SOUPY SALES asks his loyal young viewers to send him "those little green pieces of paper" from dad's wallet, "and I'll send you a postcard from

Puerto Rico." The January 1 stunt draws a big enough response to get Sales suspended by the station, but viewers protest and he is reinstated.

BELL-BOTTOMS grace the nation's hips, and lava lamps make a splash, selling 2.5 million units this year alone.

THE FIRST AMERICAN COMBAT TROOPS not deployed in an advisory capacity land in South Vietnam, turning a local conflict into an undeclared large-scale international war.

THE NATIONAL ENDOWMENT for the Arts and Humanities is established by Congress.

"(I CAN'T GET NO) SATISFACTION," the classic Rolling Stones tune, becomes a No. 1 hit in the United States, sealing the British invasion as one of the dominant musical developments of the decade.

THE BEATLES play before 55,000 fans at New York's Shea Stadium on August 15 to open their third U.S. tour.

THE SOUND OF MUSIC is released, eventually overtaking *Gone With the Wind* to rank for a time as the top box-office earner ever.

GO-GO DANCING and its accompanying little white boots quickly wax and then wane in popularity among discotheque goers.

CINEMA'S 34-year rule against nudity is broken when a scene in *The Pawnbroker* is approved by the ratings board as essential to the plot.

CBS AND NBC adopt virtually all-color formats starting with the fall season.

BILL COSBY becomes the first African American TV star, in *I Spy*.

SONY introduces the first commercial home video tape recorder. The size of an overnight bag, it costs $995.

1966

"YESTERDAY," the most recorded song in the history of popular music, is released by Paul McCartney in the first solo by a Beatle. The record label, however, still reads "Beatles."

CINEMA'S BLUE LANGUAGE ban finally falls with *Who's Afraid of Virginia Woolf?*

THE SUPREMES become the first female group to top the U.S. album chart with *Supremes a Go Go*.

JOHN LENNON makes his most infamous remark on August 5 by saying that he and his Beatles bandmembers are "more popular than Jesus." Subsequently radio stations across the country take Beatles songs off the air.

LSD is pulled off the market by its manufacturer, Sandoz Pharmaceuticals, after being banned by the government in response to controversy over the hallucinogen's recreational uses.

STAR TREK is launched in September 8 and remains on the air until 1969. It will become one of the few series to be more popular in syndication than in its network run.

"PAUL IS DEAD." For those who believe, November 9 marks the date of the Beatle's supposed decapitation.

STEREO CASSETTE TAPE RECORDERS are introduced, a breakthrough for tape cartridges.

1967

THE FIRST SUPER BOWL is held on January 15, broadcast in color on both CBS and NBC; setting a model for future contests, the Green Bay Packers defeat the Kansas City Chiefs in a lopsided game, 35–10.

THE BLACK PANTHER PARTY is founded in Oakland by Huey Newton and Bobby Seale.

OTIS REDDING, 26, dies in a plane crash in December. One month later, his biggest hit, the chart-topping "Sittin' on the Dock of the Bay," is released.

ELVIS PRESLEY weds Priscilla Beaulieu on May 1 at the Aladdin Hotel in Las Vegas.

THE MONTEREY INTERNATIONAL POP FESTIVAL in California features such performers as Janis Joplin, Jimi Hendrix, and the Grateful Dead.

RIOTING breaks out in Detroit as racial tension builds; over 17,000 people are arrested in what proves to be the worst U.S. riot of the century.

FOLKSINGER PETE SEEGER is finally allowed to appear on

TV (on *The Smothers Brothers Comedy Hour*) after having been blacklisted for 17 years for his leftist politics.

HAIR has its off-Broadway premiere at the Public Theatre in New York.

ROLLING STONE magazine begins publication under the direction of 21-year-old Jann Wenner.

PRESIDENT LYNDON B. JOHNSON signs a law insuring federal support for public TV, and the Corporation for Public Broadcasting is created.

THE FIRST WITH SO-CALLED SPAGHETTI WESTERN, Sergio Leone's *A Fistful of Dollars*, is released in the United States. Filmed in 1964, it stars Clint Eastwood.

INTERRACIAL ROMANCE unfolds on TV as Mia and Paul fall for each other on *Love Is a Many Splendored Thing.*

BOXER MUHAMMAD ALI is stripped of his heavyweight title after refusing to serve in the army during the Vietnam War.

THE FIRST HUMAN HEART TRANSPLANT is performed by Dr. Christiaan Barnard in South Africa on Louis Washkansky, who lives for 18 days.

Martin Luther King Jr. giving his famous "I have a dream" speech in Washington, D.C.

MAO TSE-TUNG'S QUOTATIONS, better known as the Red Book, is the biggest-selling read in the world this year.

CARDIGAN-CARRYING MISTER ROGERS opens his Neighborhood February 19, beginning a 27-year run that will establish a PBS record.

MOVIE RATINGS are introduced by the Motion Picture Association of America. The original classifications are G, M (mature audience), R, and X. M is changed to GP two years later, and then PG (parental guidance) a year after that.PG-13 is invented in 1984 as the result of a dispute over the vio-lence in *Gremlins* and *Indiana Jones and the Temple of Doom,* and in 1990 the nefarious X is replaced by NC-17.

ARTHUR CLARKE and Stanley Kubrick's *2001: A Space Odyssey* is released, introducing the evil computer, Hal, an antihero who becomes a cultural icon.

THE EARLIEST-KNOWN HEIDI scandal: With 50 seconds left and the New York Jets leading the Oakland Raiders, NBC cuts from the game to the movie *Heidi*. The Raiders go on to win by scoring two touchdowns in nine seconds.

CIVIL RIGHTS LEADER Martin Luther King Jr. is assassinated on April 4 at age 39 on the balcony outside of his motel room in Memphis, Tenn. Many American cities erupt in riots.

ROBERT F. KENNEDY, 42, is assassinated June 5 by Sirhan Sirhan in a Los Angeles hotel after winning the California presidential primary. In response, David Crosby writes "A Long Time Coming."

AT THE SUMMER OLYMPIC GAMES in Mexico City, American runners Tommy Smith and John Carlos give the black power salute as they receive their gold and bronze medals, resulting in their suspension from competition.

PRESIDENTIAL CANDIDATE Richard Nixon appears on *Laugh-In* and says,"Sock it to me!"

JULIA, premiering September 17, is the first TV series to star a black woman in a non-menial role as Diahann Carroll plays a nurse who is also a single parent.

MIKE WALLACE and Harry Reasoner start grilling as *60 Minutes* starts ticking on September 24; the news program will eventually top the ratings.

1969

THE BEATLES stage their last public performance on January 30 from a rooftop in London.

JIM MORRISON, lead singer for The Doors, is arrested for lewd and lascivious behavior after exposing himself at a concert in Miami.

DIANA ROSS invites 350 special guests to the trendy Daisy Club in Beverly Hills to see the new Motown act, The Jackson Five.

JOHN LENNON and Yoko Ono tie the knot on Gibraltar March 20.

THE FIRST FULL-FRONTAL male nudity appears in film with Alan Bates and Oliver Reed in Ken Russell's *Women in Love.*

THE ALTAMONT FESTIVAL—starring such acts as The Rolling Stones, Santana, Jefferson Airplane, and Crosby, Stills, Nash & Young—is struck by tragedy when the Hell's Angels security force beats to death an 18-year-old boy.

CAST MEMBERS of the play *Oh! Calcutta!* are arrested for indecent exposure in Los Angeles.

THE SUPREME COURT rules that laws prohibiting the private possession of obscene material by adults are unconstitutional.

PRINCE CHARLES is officially titled Prince of Wales.

UPON WALKING ON THE MOON on July 20, Neil Armstrong proclaims, "That's one small step for a man, one giant leap for mankind."

ACTRESS SHARON TATE, wife of director Roman Polanski, is found murdered along with four others—victims of Charles Manson's cult, known as The Family. Although not present at the house that night, would-be rock musician and psychopath Manson is convicted of the grisly killings and imprisoned.

THE WOODSTOCK Music and Art Festival is held August 15–17 in upstate New York. Playing before an audience of around 400,000, featured performers include The Who, Grateful Dead, Janis Joplin, Joe Cocker, Santana, Jimi Hendrix, Jefferson Airplane, and Crosby, Stills, Nash & Young.

SESAME STREET debuts, starring Big Bird, Oscar, Bert,

Jimi Hendrix.

Ernie, Cookie Monster, Grover, and Kermit; it marks a radical breakthrough for children's TV programming.

TINY TIM marries Miss Vickie before 45 million witnesses on *The Tonight Show.*

1970

RECORDING TOGETHER for the last time, the Beatles cut "I Me Mine" on January 3. The historic breakup happens on April 10, when Paul McCartney announces that he will not record with John Lennon again. By the end of the year, John, Paul, George, and Ringo have all released albums of their own.

EVERYTHING You Always Wanted to Know About Sex, but Were Afraid To Ask by Dr. David Reuben becomes a No. 1 bestseller.

JIMI HENDRIX and Janis Joplin both die drug-related deaths this year at age 27.

THE FILM VERSION OF *M*A*S*H,* with Elliott Gould and Donald Sutherland, is officially banned from military installations for "reducing the conventions and paraphernalia of war to total idiocy."

MIDNIGHT COWBOY is the first and only X-rated film to win Best Picture at the Academy Awards.

MASTERPIECE THEATRE is introduced on National Educational Television, hosted by Alistair Cooke, featuring BBC dramas.

TV'S PARTRIDGE FAMILY records "I Think I Love You," which becomes a smash hit first in the show's story line and then in real life, and makes David Cassidy a teen idol.

WATERBEDS hit the market, and although technical problems often produce flooding, sales skyrocket.

MONDAY NIGHT FOOTBALL takes its bow September 21 (with the New York Jets vs. the Cleveland Browns) and strains U.S. marriages, but Don Meredith, Howard Cosell, and Frank Gifford will boost ABC's ratings.

1971

CIGARETTE ADS are banned January 2 and TV networks lose $200 million in annual advertising.

CBS'S controversial *All in the Family* is introduced, featuring the bigoted Archie Bunker, whose offensive diatribes and hilarious family members drive the show's great popularity.

EXCERPTS FROM THE PENTAGON PAPERS, leaked by Daniel Ellsberg, are published in the *New York Times*, showing that presidential administrations had indeed recognized the futility of the Vietnam War but escalated involvement anyway and then lied about it. The Nixon administration attempts to block publication but the Supreme Court rules in favor of the newspaper on First Amendment grounds.

BILL GRAHAM closes down Fillmore East in New York City and Fillmore West in San Francisco, unable to pay the increasing prices charged by the musicians he has showcased for so long.

MUHAMMAD ALI'S conviction for draft evasion is overturned by the Supreme Court, which rules that the boxer's pacifist religious convictions were sincere.

JIM MORRISON, 27, dies in a bathtub in Paris on July 3.

HOSTED BY GEORGE HARRISON, the Concert for Bangladesh initiates the rise of the celebrity fundraiser. The concert features Ringo Starr, Eric Clapton, and Bob Dylan, but while its success is great, only a small fraction of its proceeds ever reach the starving people of Bangladesh.

LEGENDARY ALLMAN BROTHERS Band member Duane Allman is killed on October 29 in a motorcycle accident near Macon, Ga.

1972

MS., edited by Gloria Steinem, publishes its premiere issue in January.

RECLUSIVE MULTIMILLIONAIRE Howard Hughes exposes as a hoax an upcoming "autobiography" supposedly written with, but actually forged by, author Clifford Irving.

PONG, the first commercial computer game, is created by Atari.

BURT REYNOLDS poses nude for the centerfold of *Cosmopolitan*.

AT THE SUMMER OLYMPICS in Munich, 11 Israeli Olympians are killed by Arab terrorists, and the games are suspended for the first time in history.

JONATHAN LIVINGSTON SEAGULL establishes itself as the best-selling book since *Gone with the Wind*.

DEEP THROAT becomes one of the most successful porn films ever made; produced on a budget of $40,000, it goes on to gross around $40 million.

THE HOME BOX OFFICE cable channel goes on the air in Wilkes-Barre, Pa., with 365 subscribers. The first offering is a Paul Newman movie, *Sometimes a Great Notion.*

1973

ROE V. WADE is upheld by the Supreme Court, legalizing unrestricted abortion in the first trimester of pregnancy.

A CEASE-FIRE agreement is signed on January 27 that essentially ends the Vietnam War.

Marlon Brando as the Godfather.

SACHEEN LITTLEFEATHER refuses Marlon Brando's Oscar for Best Actor on his behalf to protest the treatment of Native Americans. (Brando had been nominated for *The Godfather*.)

PBS'S *STEAMBATH* takes on a taboo as Valerie Perrine becomes the first woman to bare her breasts in a dramatic TV program.

AT THE AGE OF 38, Seiji Ozawa becomes the youngest permanent conductor of the Boston Symphony.

A BREAK-IN at Democratic party headquarters at the Watergate Hotel is discovered, eventually leading to the only resignation of a sitting president in American history when Richard Nixon is forced to leave office on August 9 of the following year.

PUNK/NEW WAVE club CBGB and OMFUG (which stands for Country, Bluegrass, Blues, and Other Music for Uplifting Gourmandizers) opens its doors on Manhattan's divey Bowery, becoming home to such performers as Blondie, Talking Heads, Patti Smith, The Ramones, The Police, Joan Jett, and Sid Vicious. As Joey Ramone put it 20 years later, "It's a birthplace. It's like a big womb there. It's very primitive, very primal."

BILLIE JEAN KING trounces male chauvinist Bobby Riggs in tennis's ballyhooed "Battle of the Sexes."

THE AMERICAN PSYCHIATRIC ASSOCIATION reverses its traditional position and declares that homosexuality is not a mental illness.

1974

THE AUTOBIOGRAPHY OF MISS JANE PITTMAN, starring Cicely Tyson, becomes one of TV's most highly praised and successful special programs, going on to win nine Emmys.

HEIRESS PATRICIA HEARST is kidnapped by the Symbionese Liberation Army, which she later joins and with which she commits a robbery. Nineteen months after her kidnapping, Hearst is captured and convicted.

AFTER 10 YEARS OF MARRIAGE, Cher files for divorce from her husband and performing partner Sonny Bono. She marries Gregg Allman of the Allman Brothers Band only four days after the divorce is finalized.

PEOPLE magazine, featuring Mia Farrow on the cover, is launched by Time, Inc., in February.

EVEL KNIEVEL fails his attempt to jump the Snake River Canyon on his motorcycle, but survives.

ONE THOUSAND FANS at a David Cassidy concert in London are injured during a frenzy following the teen idol's appearance. One concertgoer dies.

FLORIDA TV commentator Chris Chubbuck announces her own suicide at the end of the news broadcast, and proceeds to shoot herself in the head on the air.

ALEKSANDR SOLZHENITSYN is expelled from Russia for his dissident writings; this year *The Gulag Archipelago* is also published in the West.

STREAKING becomes a momentary fad, primarily on college campuses, although the madness eventually extends to telecasts of the Academy Awards and *The Tonight Show.*

RUSSIAN DANCER EXTRAORDINAIRE Mikhail Barishnikov defects to the West, electrifying the American dance scene.

KAREN SILKWOOD is killed in a suspicious car crash on November 13. A laboratory worker at the Kerr-McGee plutonium plant, she dies on her way to meet with a reporter to discuss safety hazards at her workplace.

Sonny and Cher, before the divorce.

1975

THE VIETNAM WAR officially comes to an end.

JOHN LENNON wins a four-year-long battle against American immigration authorities when they drop his case for humanitarian reasons due to the pregnancy of Yoko Ono.

SATURDAY NIGHT LIVE hits the airwaves from New York City, with guest host George Carlin.

RICHARD BURTON and Elizabeth Taylor marry for the second time, only a year after their divorce.

THE VIDEOCASSETTE recorder/player is introduced by Sony.

MOOD RINGS are introduced and reach their peak in only a few months, selling more than 20 million before passing from popular fancy. Meanwhile, maintenance-free pet rocks also hit the short-term big time.

1976

THE MINISERIES comes to commercial TV, as *Rich Man, Poor Man* airs, starring Peter Strauss,

Susan Blakely, and Nick Nolte.

BRITAIN'S PRINCESS MARGARET scandalizes the world with an illicit liaison on the island of Mustique with brewery heir Roddy Llewellyn. She and her husband, Lord Snowdon, separate later this year.

GONE WITH THE WIND is telecast over two evenings on NBC, earning the highest ratings to date.

1977

ALEX HALEY'S novel *Roots*, a story of his quest for his ancestors in Africa and America, is made into the most successful miniseries in history. It wins a record nine Emmys, and mesmerizes the country for over a week, drawing approximately 130 million people to watch at least one of its eight episodes.

STUDIO 54 opens its doors in New York, becoming the quintessential glamorous nightclub until owners Steve Rubell and Ian Shrager are arrested for tax evasion in 1980.

GEORGE LUCAS releases *Star Wars*, which becomes the highest-grossing movie of all time until

John Travolta strikes the pose that made him famous.

dethroned by *E. T., the Extra-Terrestrial* five years later.

THE KING IS DEAD: Elvis Presley, 42, passes on at Graceland, his palatial estate in Memphis, Tenn., on August 16.

SOAP introduces prime time's first gay character–Billy Crystal as Jodie Dallas.

RONALD ZAMORA, 15, confesses to murder and claims TV made him do it; he will be convicted in the first televised trial.

SATURDAY NIGHT FEVER premieres in New York on December 14, launching the disco era.

1978

FORMER FIRST LADY Betty Ford helps break the stigma of addiction by entering a rehabilitation clinic.

THE WORLD'S FIRST test-tube baby, Louise Brown, is born July 25 in England.

AT 25 HOURS and $25 million, the dramatization of James Michener's *Centennial* is the most outsized program yet produced for TV.

JIM JONES leads his followers to a mass death in Jonestown, Guyana, on November 18. 1,914 of his cult commit suicide or kill each other.

SONY invents the revolutionary Walkman, the first portable cassette player.

1979

RAP MUSIC is ushered into the commercial age when the Sugarhill Gang releases "Rapper's Delight." Earlier in the year a Brooklyn group called The Fatback Band had produced "King Tim III (Personality Jock)," a disk widely regarded as the first rap record.

WHILE THE WOMEN on TV's *Charlie's Angels* changed outfits on average eight times per show, a guest appearance this year by Farrah Fawcett (who left the show in 1977) easily breaks the record: In one hour-long program she changes clothes 12 times.

1980

THE U.S. HOCKEY TEAM beats the Soviet Union during the Winter Olympics at Lake Placid, on their way to winning their first gold medal since 1960—and only their second gold since the Olympics began.

President Ronald Reagan.

POST-IT NOTES enter the market, revolutionizing the office and the refrigerator.

TED KOPPEL'S *Nightline*, begun as an ABC series following the status of U.S. hostages in Iran, brings hard news in the wee hours.

COMEDIAN RICHARD PRYOR is badly burned when a flammable drug mixture used to make "freebase," a cocaine derivative, explodes in his face.

WITH SUCH BLOCKBUSTER musicals as *A Chorus Line, Oh! Calcutta!*, and *Evita* on the boards, Broadway box offices collect almost $200 million, a dramatic increase over a five-year period. Road shows during this period experience an even greater success.

TV'S FIRST ALL-NEWS SERVICE begins with Ted Turner's Cable News Network on

June 1. Broadcasting 24 hours a day, the network loses $16 million in a year, but grabs seven million viewers.

HALF THE NATION'S VIEWERS tune in to *Dallas* on November 21 to find out "Who Shot J.R.?," more viewers than for any other single TV show in history.

MARK DAVID CHAPMAN shoots and kills John Lennon on December 8 outside the singer's apartment in New York City.

1981

HOMOSEXUAL MEN across the country are struck down by a wave of cancer and pneumonia that is traced to a mysterious breakdown in the body's disease-fighting system. It will be referred to later as Acquired Immune Deficiency Syndrome, or AIDS.

HILL STREET BLUES premieres.

TICKETS TO BROADWAY'S *The Life and Adventures of Nicholas Nickleby* go on sale at the Plymouth Theatre for a record-setting $100 each.

PRESIDENT RONALD REAGAN is shot in an assassination

attempt on March 30 that leaves his press secretary, James Brady, paralyzed for life. John Hinckley apparently undertakes the assassination in an attempt to impress Jodie Foster.

THE VIDEO GAME PAC MAN devours the market as young people everywhere are seized with acute Pacmania.

CHARLES, PRINCE OF WALES, and Lady Diana Spencer are married on July 29 at Saint Paul's Cathedral in London.

MTV unveils music for your eyes on August 1. The channel's opener: "Video Killed the Radio Star," by The Buggles.

SANDRA DAY O'CONNOR becomes the first woman Supreme Court justice in U.S. history.

PRIVATE SATELLITE DISHES sprout after the FCC gives them the okay. By the end of the '80s, there will be two million nationwide.

1982

OZZY OSBOURNE bites the head off a live bat thrown at him during a performance on January 20, a moment that is immortalized in heavy metal chronicles.

THE REVEREND SUN MYUNG MOON performs a mass ceremony at Madison Square Garden, marrying some 4,150 of his followers, the "Moonies."

MICHAEL JACKSON'S *Thriller* is released. Selling over 20 million copies in 1983 and 1984 alone, it becomes the biggest-selling album in history.

JOHN BELUSHI dies March 5 of an overdose of cocaine and heroin in a Hollywood hotel room.

CHARLES AND DI produce their first offspring, Prince William, on June 21, the latest heir to the British throne.

PRINCESS GRACE dies on September 14 after an automobile accident.

THE WATCHMAN, Sony's portable microtelevision, is invented.

THE FIRST ARTIFICIAL HEART is transplanted into Barney C. Clark, age 61, in Utah. He lives for 112 days.

CABLE TV subscribers reach the 30 million mark.

SINGER KAREN CARPENTER dies of anorexia nervosa on February 4.

*M*A*S*H* ends its 11-year, 14-Emmy run with the largest audi-

ence ever to watch a single TV show.

ASTRONAUT SALLY RIDE becomes the first american woman in space as she blasts off on June 18 with four colleagues aboard the space shuttle *Challenger.*

VANESSA WILLIAMS becomes the first African American to win the Miss America pageant. She relinquishes her title two months before her term ends in 1984, when it is discovered that revealing nude photos of the singer are going to be published in *Penthouse.*

THE CHILLING TV DRAMA *The Day After*, with Jason Robards, explores the aftermath of nuclear war, harden-

ing both pro- and anti-freeze positions.

CABBAGE PATCH DOLLS, introduced by Coleco Industries, become the holy grail of the holiday season.

HOME TAPING OF TV programming is held not to be in violation of copyright law by the Supreme Court, which throws out a suit brought against Sony by MCA and Walt Disney.

SURROGATE CONCEPTION is successful for the first time in California.

GERALDINE FERRARO becomes the first woman to run for vice president as presidential candidate Walter Mondale names the Queens congresswoman as his running mate; the pair lose the election to President Reagan and Vice President George Bush in a landslide.

GYMNAST MARY LOU RETTON wins two gold, two silver, and two bronze Olympic medals for the U.S.

SIDNEY BIDDLE BARROWS is arrested. Known as the Mayflower Madam, she included numerous famous and pow-

Vice-presidential candidate Geraldine Ferraro.

erful people among her clients.

THE COSBY SHOW premieres, becoming the most popular series of the decade before going off the air in 1993.

THE FIRST ALL-RAP RADIO format is introduced by KDAY in Los Angeles.

RUN-DMC becomes the first rap group to have an album—*Run-DMC*—certified gold.

BOB GELDOF and Band Aid's "Do They Know It's Christmas" raise money to help feed the starving people of Africa.

"WE ARE THE WORLD" is recorded by 45 pop music superstars under the auspices of USA for Africa.

CRACK COCAINE hits the streets, further devastating already blighted urban areas.

PIANO MAN BILLY JOEL and supermodel Christie Brinkley tie the knot.

MADONNA begins her road debut, The Virgin Tour, on April 10.

THE MUSIC INDUSTRY'S benefit for African famine relief, Live Aid, is staged in London and Philadelphia

and beamed all over the world.

ROCK HUDSON becomes the first major public figure to die of AIDS, at 59, on October 2.

1986

THE SPACE SHUTTLE *CHALLENGER* explodes January 28 shortly after launching, killing everyone on board, including schoolteacher Christa McAuliffe, the first private citizen to go into space.

FILIPINO FIRST LADY Imelda Marcos is found to possess 2,700 pairs of shoes.

ARNOLD SCHWARZENEGGER and Maria Shriver are married.

JOHNNY CARSON stops talking to Joan Rivers when she accepts an offer to host a late-night show on the Fox network.

CAROLINE KENNEDY marries artist-designer Edwin Schlossberg.

PRINCE ANDREW marries Sarah Ferguson in London on July 23.

THE OPRAH WINFREY SHOW, originally a local program called *A.M. Chicago*, goes

national on September 8. Its host soon establishes herself as one of the most successful personalities in show business.

TURNER BROADCASTING colorizes black-and-white classics and directors, stars and movie buffs see red. First to run: Jimmy Cagney's *Yankee Doodle Dandy*.

1987

JESSICA HAHN is implicated in a scandal with TV evangelist Jim Bakker.

VAN GOGH'S "Irises" is auctioned at $53.9 million, the highest price ever paid for a painting at the time.

PRINCE CHARLES and Diana begin leading separate lives in March as their marriage starts to deteriorate.

PRESIDENTIAL CANDIDATE Gary Hart's connection with model Donna Rice destroys his political aspirations, and he is forced to withdraw from the race.

GARRISON KEILLOR broadcasts his last radio show, *A Prairie Home Companion*, from Lake Wobegon on June 13 and moves to New York City.

PORN QUEEN CICCIOLINA wins a seat in the Italian parliament on June 16.

BRUCE WILLIS and Demi Moore are married November 21 in Las Vegas.

1988

TV PREACHER JIMMY SWAGGART admits his involvement with pornography and prostitutes. His February 21 statement, "I have sinned," deals a serious setback to electronic evangelism.

COMPACT DISCS outsell vinyl albums for the first time: the Recording Industry Association of America reports unit sales of 149.7 million CDs to 72.4 million records.

SONNY BONO is elected mayor of Palm Springs, California.

THE VERY LAST Playboy Club in America closes July 30 in Lansing, Mich.

ACTRESS ROBIN GIVENS files for divorce on October 7 from world heavyweight champion Mike Tyson, claiming that the fighter is violent.

TALK SHOW HOST Phil Donahue wears a

dress on November 18 to boost his ratings.

BENAZIR BHUTTO of Pakistan becomes the first woman to lead an Islamic nation.

PAN AM FLIGHT 103 explodes over Lockerbie, Scotland, killing all 259 passengers.

THE ERA of the personal video arrives when Sony introduces the Video Walkman, an ultracompact VCR with a three-inch color screen.

1989

LATE-NIGHT TV gets its first regular African-American host on January 3 with comedian Arsenio Hall.

VIRTUAL REALITY, the term as well as the equipment to achieve it, is invented by Jaron Lanier.

NOVELIST SALMAN RUSHDIE is forced into hiding after a death threat is issued by Islamic militants angry over what they see as sacrilege in his book *The Satanic Verses.*

KIM BASINGER steps in to rescue near-bankrupt Braselton, Ga., by buying the town for a reported $20 million.

LUCILLE BALL, perhaps the most beloved television star in history, dies on April 26.

ACTOR ROB LOWE is identified by Fulton County, Ga. officials in a homemade porn video with an underaged girl.

PLAYBOY **FOUNDER** Hugh Hefner marries former *Playboy* Playmate Kimberley Conrad.

JOSE MENENDEZ AND his wife, Kitty, are found murdered August 20 in their $4 million Beverly Hills mansion. Their sons, Lyle and Erik, will later be accused of murdering their parents for money, though at their trials the brothers claim that years of sexual and psychological abuse by their parents drove them to kill in self-defense.

PETE ROSE, Cincinnati Reds manager and one of the greatest baseball players in history, is banned from the game for life for gambling.

TV GUIDE boasts a picture on the cover of the newly slim Oprah Winfrey, but the image turns out to be a composite of Oprah's head and Ann-Margret's body.

PRINCESS ANNE issues a palace statement

on August 31 that she is officially separating from her husband, Mark Phillips.

THE BERLIN WALL falls on November 9.

SAN FRANCISCO GIANTS pitcher Dave Dravecky retires after an aborted comeback attempt from cancer in his pitching arm.

1990

THE SIMPSONS spins off from *The Tracey Ullman Show* and makes the fledgling Fox network a real contender as a fourth network.

NELSON MANDELA is released from prison after 27 years of incarceration for leading a campaign against the South African government.

"ICE ICE BABY" by Vanilla Ice becomes the first rap record to top the U.S. singles chart.

SONY creates the first portable compact disc player, the Discman.

M. C. HAMMER releases *Please Hammer Don't Hurt 'Em,* which becomes the biggest-selling rap record in history.

DONALD AND IVANA TRUMP divorce.

MILLI VANILLI is accused of fraud for using voices other than its own on its Grammy-winning album, *Girl You Know It's True.* The group is forced to surrender the award.

IN THE FIRST such ruling against a music group in the U. S., a Florida judge declares 2 Live Crew's album *As Nasty As They Wanna Be* obscene and bans all sales of the rap recording to minors. The move ignites a campaign against censorship in the music business.

TWIN PEAKS debuts on ABC as a two-hour movie with limited commercial interruption.

SEINFELD, a show about "nothing," quietly debuts on May 31.

AMERICA RELIVES the war between the states with Ken Burns's indelible PBS documentary *The Civil War.*

IN AN EFFORT to raise money for AIDS research, the *Red Hot & Blue* album is released on October 30, featuring such stars as U2, David Byrne, and The Neville Brothers performing Cole Porter songs.

1991

OPERATION DESERT SHIELD turns into Desert Storm on January 16 as the Allied forces attack Iraq to liberate Kuwait. CNN's Bernard Shaw, Peter Arnett, and John Holliman broadcast live to the world from downtown Baghdad.

THE GODFATHER OF SOUL, James Brown, is released from a Georgia prison after serving two years of a six-year sentence for aggravated assault, not stopping for police, and carrying a gun.

RODNEY KING'S beating by Los Angeles police is recorded by an observer with a home video camera on March 3.

DR. JACK KEVORKIAN'S attempts to help people commit suicide first come to light.

WILLIAM KENNEDY SMITH, nephew of Ted Kennedy, is accused of rape by a Florida woman; after a harrowing trial, he is exonerated.

PAUL REUBENS, creator of the much-admired *Pee-wee's Playhouse* and the character Pee-wee Herman, is busted in Florida for indecent exposure.

Paul Reubens, a.k.a. Pee-wee Herman, after his infamous arrest.

LIZ TAYLOR marries husband number seven, 39-year-old Larry Fortensky, a carpenter she met at the Betty Ford Center. The wedding, held on Michael Jackson's estate, draws such guests as Nancy Reagan.

THE ANITA HILL/ CLARENCE THOMAS hearings galvanize the nation with charges of sexual harassment against the Supreme Court nominee; Thomas is narrowly approved for the post.

MAGIC JOHNSON announces his retirement from professional basketball because he has tested positive for the HIV virus.

MEDIA MOGUL Ted Turner and actress-cum-fitness-guru Jane Fonda are married.

1992

ARTHUR ASHE, tennis star and beloved public figure, dies of AIDS.

MIKE TYSON is convicted of raping beauty contestant Desiree Washington and is jailed in the Indiana Youth Center in Plainfield, Ohio until 1995. While in prison, Tyson studied the Koran intensely, and has embraced its teachings.

TAMMY FAYE BAKKER files for divorce from husband Jim, who's still in prison on a fraud conviction and not eligible for parole for another three years.

FERGIE AND ANDY separate after six years of marriage.

A *MURPHY BROWN* segment in which the unmarried Murphy gives birth, spurs the wrath of Vice President Dan Quayle and instigates a nationwide debate over family values.

LONG ISLAND TEENAGER Amy Fisher shoots Mary Jo Buttafuoco.

JOHNNY CARSON ends his reign over late-night talk shows on May 22 with his last appearance on *The Tonight Show.*

CANDIDATE BILL CLINTON appears on *The Arsenio Hall Show,* complete with dark shades and saxophone, to perform "Heartbreak Hotel" with the show's "posse."

WOODY ALLEN AND MIA FARROW begin a bitter custody battle over their son Satchel, 4, and two children they adopted together, Moses, 14, and daughter Dylan, 7. The dispute is fueled by Allen's affair with Farrow's adopted daughter Soon-Yi Previn.

THE TORONTO BLUE JAYS become the first non-American team to win that most American of sports championships, the World Series, with a 4–2 series win over Ted Turner's Atlanta Braves.

PRINCE CHARLES and Princess Diana formally serparate.

1993

THE U.S. POSTAL SERVICE releases its commemorative Elvis stamp, featuring the youthful Elvis, the overwhelming selection of the voting public.

BILL WYMAN leaves The Rolling Stones in January. He is 56.

DR. DRE'S album *The Chronic* (named after a very potent form of marijuana) reaches No. 1 on the *Billboard* charts and becomes the most successful hard-core rap album to date.

MICHAEL JACKSON tells interviewer Oprah Winfrey that his lightened skin color is due to a rare skin disease, and says that he is in love with Brooke Shields. Later in the year Jackson is accused of having fondled a 13-year-old Los Angeles boy.

PRINCE, born Prince Rogers Nelson, turns 35 and, in a most confusing commemoration, changes his name to a symbol that no one knows how to pronounce, He is now "The Artist Formally Known as Prince.".

JULIA ROBERTS, 25, and Lyle Lovett, 35, wed.

ACTOR RIVER PHOENIX, 23, dies on October 31. The young actor had a reputation for clean living, but coroners find high levels of cocaine and morphine as well as Valium and marijuana in Phoenix's system.

NANCY KERRIGAN is attacked in January by a club-wielding assailant, but battles back from the resulting knee injury to win a silver medal in the Winter Olympics.

MICHAEL JORDAN quits basketball and signs with the Chicago White Sox, fulfilling his childhood dream of becoming a baseball player. Playing for the Birmingham Barons, a Class AA team, he hits .202 for the season.

STEVEN SPIELBERG finally claims Oscars for Best Picture and Best Director with *Schindler's List*, which receives a total of seven awards. *Jurassic Park* wins another three. Later in the year, Spielberg forms Dreamworks SKG, the first new major studio in 55 years, with record mogul David Geffen and former Disney executive Jeffrey Katzenberg.

KURT COBAIN takes his own life with a shotgun on April 8 in his Seattle-area lakeside home. He joins a long and sad list of fellow rock stars: Janis Joplin, Jimi Hendrix, Jim Morrison—all dead at 27.

JACQUELINE BOUVIER KENNEDY ONASSIS dies at age 64 on May 19. She had been diagnosed just four months before with non-Hodgkin's lymphoma, a cancer of the lymphatic system.

NICOLE BROWN SIMPSON, 35, and Ronald Goldman, 25, are brutally murdered in front of Simpson's Brentwood condominium. After an eerie low-speed chase watched live on television by 95 million people, Nicole's ex-husband O.J. Simpson surrenders to police and is charged with the murders.

NEVERLAND meets Graceland as Michael Jackson and Lisa Marie Presley get hitched in a secret ceremony in the Dominican Republic.

WOODSTOCK '94 is held on the 25th anniversary of the original with acts old (the Allman Brothers Band, Bob Dylan) and new (Green Day, Nine Inch Nails).

GEORGE FOREMAN, 45, recaptures the heavyweight title he lost to Muhammad Ali 20 years ago. He defeats Michael Moore in Las Vegas with a 10th-round knockout.

1995

O.J. SIMPSON is found not guilty of the murders of Nicole Brown Simpson and Ronald Goldman.

OLYMPIC DIVER GREG LOUGANIS discloses to Barbara Walters and readers of his memoirs that "I do have AIDS."

EAZY-E, (a.k.a. Eric Wright), 31, the founder of rap group N.W.A. and president of Ruthless Records, dies of AIDS.

MICHAEL JORDAN resumes his basketball career. Dismayed by the baseball strike, he dons a new basketball jersey, #45, and leads the Chicago Bulls to another run of three straight championships.

TOUTED AS LATIN MUSIC'S Madonna, the Texas-born singer Selena is killed by her fan club president Yolanda Saldvar, 34, whom she was about to confront for embezzling funds.

CHRISTOPHER REEVE suffers a tragic accident on a cross-country jumping course, when his 7-year-old chestnut Thoroughbred Eastern Express refuses a fence. Though he is wearing a protective vest and helmet, the fall causes multiple fractures in his spinal column, leaving the actor paralyzed.

THE KING OF POP and his princess go live with Diane Sawyer and draw over 60 million viewers. The combination inter-

O. J. Simpson tries on the infamous black glove in his 1995 murder trial.

view/publicity opportunity includes an answer to fans' most frequently asked question: Do Lisa-Marie and Michael have sex? The answer: "Yes, yes, yes," answers the Mrs. Presley-Jackson.

HUGH GRANT is arrested for engaging in a "lewd act" with Sunset Strip prostitute Divine Brown. Grant soon begins his tour of contrition with a *Tonight Show* appearance that draws the show its third-highest ratings ever.

THE WALT DISNEY COMPANY announces that it's buying Capital Cities/ABC for $19 million. The day after Disney's acquisition, Westinghouse Electric announces its agreement to pur-

chase CBS for $5.4 billion.

LEGENDARY GRATEFUL DEAD guru Jerry Garcia, 53, dies of an apparent heart attack. To many who have idolized the band from its formation in 1966, it is a sad ending to the "feel good" era that the Dead carried well into the '90s with their record-grossing tours.

NEW YORK YANKEE GREATS gather in Dallas to lay to rest Mickey Mantle, dead of cancer, in a funeral filled with warm memories.

AFTER 10 YEARS IN THE PLANNING, the $92 million I. M. Pei–designed Rock and Roll Hall of Fame and Museum opens in Cleveland, Ohio, paying tribute to 40 years of rock

and to the jazz, blues, and gospel artists who laid down the roots of the genre.

HE WAS THE FIRST TALK show host to invite the audience into the act, but after 29 years, Phil Donahue calls it quits. He was seen in 200 television markets at the height of his popularity, winning 20 Emmys along the way.

THEODORE JOHN KACZYNSKI, 53, the former Berkeley math professor suspected of being the Unabomber, is charged with possessing a partially completed pipe bomb.

JACKIE KENNEDY ONASSIS'S belongings are auctioned off during a four-day sale at Sotheby's New York. The least expensive item, an etching of Washington, D.C., valued no higher than $30, sells for $2,070. A walnut cigar humidor smokes out $574,500.

EIGHT CLIMBERS ON MOUNT EVEREST become victims in one of the worst tragedies to strike the 29,028-foot Himalayan peak since it was first scaled in 1953.

GYMNAST KERRI STRUG, 18, limps to the gold after her heart-stopping final vault clinches top honors—the first ever—for the U.S. women's team. The Tucson, Arizona, native had to be carried to the medal stand by coach Bela Karolyi.

PRINCESS DIANA and Prince Charles's divorce becomes official in late August.

JOHN F. KENNEDY JR. and Calvin Klein publicist Carolyn Bessette surprise everyone with a secret wedding on Cumberland Island, off the Georgia coast.

THE MATERNAL GIRL'S newest release, born in October, is a daughter: Lourdes Maria Ciccone Leon. Her father is Carlos Leon, Madonna's personal trainer and companion.

1997

A SANTA MONICA CIVIL JURY finds O. J. Simpson liable in the 1994 deaths of Ron Goldman and Nicole Brown Simpson. According to Goldman's father, the family—which is awarded $8.5 million—"is grateful for a verdict of responsibility."

TARA LIPINSKI, 14, becomes the youngest U.S. figure skating champion ever.

SCOTTISH RESEARCHERS introduce a new star to biology—Dolly, a 7-month-old Finn-Dorset lamb that began life not like any other lamb but as a speck of DNA from a mature female sheep, of which she is now a perfect copy.

MEMBERS OF THE HEAVEN'S GATE CULT, who believed their deaths would give them passage aboard a UFO trailing the Hale-Bopp Comet, commit mass suicide.

TIGER WOODS, 21, becomes the youngest golfer to win the Masters and the first African American to win a major golf championship—while breaking the tournament record at 18 under par.

FRANK GIFFORD, 66, is caught on hidden video in an intimate encounter with a flight attendant, tarnishing the image of an idyllic marriage put forth by his wife, talk show queen Kathie Lee Gifford.

ELLEN DEGENERES and her character on ABC's *Ellen* both come out of the closet.

TIMOTHY MCVEIGH is found guilty on 11 federal charges, including seven counts of murder, relating to 1995's Oklahoma City blast. He is sentenced to death.

CATS becomes the longest-running show in Broadway history.

MIKE TYSON is banned from the ring after biting off part of heavyweight champion Evander Holyfield's earlobe during a bout.

ITALIAN DESIGNER GIANNI VERSACE, 50, is shot to death outside his South Beach mansion in Miami Beach, Florida. He is gunned down by suspected gay serial killer Andrew Philip Cunanan, 27, who later shoots himself to death.

THE WORLD MOURNS the death of Princess Diana, victim of an early morning car crash in a tunnel below Paris's Seine River. Her funeral at Westminster Abbey is watched by 2 billion viewers.

CHRIS FARLEY, 33, is found dead in his Chicago condominium. An autopsy reports the death is from an accidental cocaine overdose.

LOUISE WOODWARD, 19, a British au pair, is convicted of the second degree murder of 8-month-old Matthew Eappen. Her conviction is reduced to manslaughter by the judge, who sentences her to 279 days, the time already served while awaiting trial.

1998

ALLEGATIONS FIRST COME TO LIGHT in early January that President Clinton, 51, engaged in an affair with a White House intern, Monica Lewinsky, 24. In September, special prosecutor Kenneth Starr provides Congress with a shockingly detailed account of the President's alleged trespasses, and a videotape of Clinton's grand jury testimony is televised nationwide.

ER, prime time's No. 1–rated TV show, is renewed by NBC for a reported record $13 million an episode.

RANDOM HOUSE book publishers is sold by tycoon Si Newhouse to the giant German media company Bertelsmann, for a reported $1.5 billion.

FRANK SINATRA, the 82-year-old singer, movie actor, producer, record and casino mogul, and controversial figure, considered by many to be the Voice of the Century, dies on May 14.

SEINFELD, the hit sitcom of the decade, signs off the air, but only after much hype.

PHIL HARTMAN, 50, the *NewsRadio* actor-comedian, is shot multiple times and killed by his wife, Brynn, as he sleeps. After confessing to a friend, Brynn, 40, returns home and shoots herself in the head.

GERI "GINGER SPICE" HALLIWELL, 25,

announces she is leaving the Spice Girls, just before the group begins a sold-out U.S. tour.

HIGH-PROFILE COUPLE Bruce Willis, 41, and Demi Moore, 35, split up after 11 years of marriage. Moore will have custody of the couple's three daughters, ages 4 to 9.

BARBRA STREISAND, 56, and actor James Brolin, 57, tie the knot on the second anniversary of their first date. They are married at her Malibu estate, among a glittering background of stars.

NEW YORKER **MAGAZINE EDITOR** (since 1992) Tina Brown, 44, leaves her post to start a co-venture with Miramax Films that will launch *Talk* magazine, produce feature films and TV programs, and publish books.

ST. LOUIS CARDINAL MARK MCGWIRE, 34, breaks Roger Maris's record for the most home runs hit in a single baseball season, finishing with 70.

1999

LAURYN HILL grabs five Grammy Awards, including Album of the Year and Best New Artist. The 23-year-old soul diva breaks Carole King's 1971 record for most awards nabbed by a female artist in a single night.

BARBARA WALTERS airs two hours of a "very full and frank" discussion with Monica Lewinsky to an estimated audience of 70 million people, drawing ratings just below those for OprahWinfrey's prime-time interview of Michael Jackson in 1993. Lewinsky will tell her children, "Mommy made a big mistake."

AMERICAN HERO JOE DIMAGGIO, baseball's legendary "Yankee Clipper," dies at his home in Harbour Island, Fla. at age 84, after a six-month battle with lung cancer.

BROOKE SHIELDS AND ANDRE AGASSI announce that they are divorcing after almost two years of marriage.

WAYNE GRETZKY, 38, ends his National Hockey League career, finishing with

an assist (his 1,963rd, to go along with his 894 goals) as his New York Rangers lose to Pittsburgh 2–1 in overtime.

SEAN "PUFFY" COMBS is charged with second-degree assault in connection with an alleged attack on music executive Steve Stoute. He later pleads guilty to a reduced charge of harassment, and settles a civil suit with Stoute.

THE JENNY JONES SHOW is found negligent in the slaying of gay guest Scott Amedure, who admitted to having a crush on another man, Jonathan Schmitz, in an episode of the show taped (but never aired) in 1995. The producers are ordered to pay more than $25 million in damages.

STAR WARS: EPISODE I—THE PHANTOM MENACE smashes its way to box-office records after months of pre-opening hype.

SUSAN LUCCI finally wins the Best Actress trophy at the Daytime Emmys after receiving 19 nominations over the years.

STEPHEN KING, 51, is struck by an out-of-control minivan while walking along a road

in North Lovell, Maine. After five operations, he begins a slow recovery.

NBC'S SOAP *ANOTHER WORLD* airs its last episode after 35 years.

JOHN F. KENNEDY JR., 38, plunges to his death in the Atlantic Ocean while piloting his private plane. His wife Carolyn, 33, and her sister Lauren Bessette, 34, also perish.

GEORGE HARRISON, 56, receives a near-fatal stab wound to the chest in a struggle with an intruder at his English estate.

PEOPLE
EXTRAS

THE MOST INTRIGUING PEOPLE: 1974–PRESENT

Every December, in the Christmas double issue, the PEOPLE editors single out the 25 most intriguing people of the past year. We reprint here the complete roll of honorees, with a brief description for each, to remind readers of the notable and notorious from the past 26 years.

1974

Gerald Ford	The new president copes.
Patty Hearst	Kidnapped heiress turns terrorist.
Joe Hirshhorn	Establishes Smithsonian's new Hirshhorn Museum.
Kay Graham	Publisher of the Watergate-breaking *Washington Post* prevails.
Yasir Arafat	Addresses the United Nations.
Faye Dunaway	Stars in *Chinatown*, *The Towering Inferno*, and *Three Days of the Condor*.
Alexander Solzhenitsyn	Russian exile wins the Nobel.
Nelson Rockefeller	The vice president–elect gets a financial grilling from Congress.
Leon Jaworski	The Watergate prosecutor.
Erica Jong	Author scores with *Fear of Flying*.
Francis Ford Coppola	*Godfather II* confirms him as cinema's creative king.
Muhammad Ali	The champ wants another son.
Pat Nixon	The former First Lady deals stoically.
John Glenn	Could the Ohio senator be the Ike of the '70s?
Sherlock Holmes	He's the most omnipresent literary figure of 1974.
Carter Heyward	One of 11 women ordained as Episcopal priests.
Stevie Wonder	A blind artist brings soul to his music.
Alexander Calder	It seems every U.S. city must have one of his mobiles.
Charlie Finley	The fiery owner of World Series–winning Oakland A's.
Ella Grasso	The first woman to capture a governorship without inheriting it from her husband.
J. Kenneth Jamieson	Exxon's chief has big profits and big problems.
Jimmy Connors	He catches fire; his romance catches cold.
Gunnar Myrdal	Nobel Prize winner in economics.
Valerie Harper	Rhoda's a winner on her own.
Mikhail Baryshnikov	The former Kirov Ballet star defects to Toronto.

1975

Betty Ford	The president's secret weapon.
Richard Zanuck	Son of Darryl F. makes his own name coproducing *Jaws*.
Frank E. Fitzsimmons	The boss of 2.2 million Teamsters.
Charles Manson	May have influenced Squeaky Fromme in her failed assassination attempt on President Ford.
Daniel Patrick Moynihan	Fighting Irishman at the U.N. talks tough.
James Coleman	The University of Chicago professor blamed for busing says it backfired.
Indira Gandhi	After six months of rule in India, her popularity soars.
Cher Bono Allman	The new First Lady of splitsville.
Andrei Sakharov	The Nobel Peace Prize winner.
Teng Hsiao-Ping	China's tough, blunt, outspoken leader.
Patty Hearst	Was she a terrorist or a victim?
Christina Onassis	The daughter of the late shipping magnate Aristotle Onassis marries her father's rival.
Leonard Matlovich	An Air Force sergeant is discharged after admitting his homosexuality.
Dolly Parton	Nashville's new queen-in-waiting.
Fred Lynn	All-American boy dazzles baseball in his miraculous rookie year.
Frank Borman	Ex-astronaut gets Eastern Airlines off the ground.
Rosemary Rogers	The master of the erotic gothic.
Werner Erhard	The smooth guru of est.
Woody Allen	Now a triple creative threat—actor, director, and author.
Marabel Morgan	The housewife behind *The Total Woman* cashes in on the antifeminist backlash.
Jerry Brown	California loves its young governor.
Don King	A flashy ex-con turned promoter is the new lord of the rings.
Hercule Poirot	The famed Belgian detective is killed by Dame Agatha Christie after 55 years.
Anwar Sadat	Egyptian president opens the Suez Canal, closed since the Six-Day War in 1967.
Gelsey Kirkland	The prima ballerina of the American Ballet dances a triumphant *Giselle*.

1976

Jimmy Carter	He wants to be the "citizen president."
Farrah Fawcett-Majors	An "Angel" turns into a star.
Andrew Wyeth	Is he America's most popular painter? The thought grieves some critics.
Betty Williams	An anguished mother asks Ulster to give peace a chance.
Andrew Young	The first black U.S. ambassador to the U.N.
Juan Carlos I	Spain's new king empowers the people.
Linda Ronstadt	From vagabond to country rock's First Lady.
Reverend Sun Myung Moon	Troubles build for the mysterious head of the Unification Church.
Bert Jones	Pro football's man with the golden arm.
Julius Nyerere	Tanzania's superstar of African diplomacy.
Carl Sagan	Viking I's expedition to Mars thrills would-be space explorer.
Fred Silverman	TV's superprogrammer switches to ABC.
Liz Ray	After affair with Representative Wayne Hays, she brings out a book and gets religion.
C. W. McCall	His "Convoy" is the year's bestselling single.
Shere Hite	Hotly read reporter on women's sexuality.
Donald Kendall	Pepsico's chief sells his drink to Soviets.
Vivian Reed	The star of *Bubbling Brown Sugar* proves that black is beautiful on Broadway.
Ron Kovic	Disabled Vietnam veteran turned antiwar activist was *Born on the Fourth of July*.
Chevy Chase	*Saturday Night*'s stumblebum is hot.
Regine	The queen mother of the disco craze.
Har Gobind Khorana	Gives world a man-made working gene.
Nadia Comaneci	The Romanian Olympic champion.
Robert Redford	Turns producer with *All the President's Men*.
Don Shomron	Led the Entebbe raid to save 105 hostages.
King Kong	Returning, courtesy of Dino De Laurentis.

PEOPLE'S COVER CHAMPS

Their fame far exceeded the usual 15 minutes. The saga of their lives held readers rapt. Here are the titleholders for the most times featured on the cover of PEOPLE.

Personality	Number of Covers
Princess Diana	52
Elizabeth Taylor	14
Sarah Ferguson	13
Michael Jackson	13
Jacqueline Kennedy Onassis	13
Cher	11

1977

Jimmy Carter	The first year at 1600: he likes it.
Diane Keaton	Woody's flaky foil is *Looking for Mr. Goodbar*.
General Omar Torrijos	Ratify the canal treaties or bring in the marines, says Panama's strongman.
Steven Ross	The chairman-impresario of Warner Communications.
Midge Costanza	The president's pipeline to the people.
Anwar Sadat and Menachem Begin	The president of Egypt and the prime minister of Israel strive for peace.
Ted Turner	Cable entrepreneur and ball team owner.
Margaret Trudeau	Runaway wife of Canada's prime minister.
Robert Byrd	A self-made fiddler calls the tunes in the world's most exclusive club.
Susanne Albrecht	A brutal murder of an old friend makes her the dark queen of German terrorism.
Lily Tomlin	Wins a Tony for her one-woman show, *Appearing Nightly*.
Billy Carter	Ad spokesman to the masses.
Anita Bryant	After a *très* un-gay year, she's still praising God and passing the orange juice.
Shaun Cassidy	*Hardy Boy* moonlights as a pop star.
Jacqueline Onassis	Quits her editor's job and gets $25 million from stepdaughter Christina Onassis.
Jasper Johns	The enigmatic master of pop art.
Toni Morrison	Flies into the literary top rank.
Dr. Robert Linn	His liquid protein diet has him in fat city.
Tracy Austin	At 14, Wimbledon's youngest invitee ever.
Rosalyn Yalow	Winner of 1977's Nobel Prize for medicine.
Reggie Jackson	Yankee hot dog turns into a hero.
Stevie Nicks	Rock singer-songwriter casts a sexy spell.
George Lucas	A new "force" in film.
Princess Caroline	Grace and Rainier's girl will wed Junot.

1978

Jimmy Carter	Negotiates peace between Egypt and Israel, and looks for antidotes to rising inflation.
Pope John Paul II	A tough, ebullient Pole remolds the papacy.
Queen Noor al-Hussein	This blue-jeaned American queen is ready for a child.
G. William Miller	Fearless chairman of the Federal Reserve.
Teng Hsiao-Ping	The tough vice-premier of China.
Brooke Shields	Three movies, beaucoup bucks, no beau.
Melvin Gottlieb	The dream this Princeton physicist pursues is limitless energy from nuclear fusion.
Louise Brown	The first test-tube baby is doing just fine.
Reverend Jim Jones	Feeling threatened, he offers a deadly communion to his followers.
John Belushi	A hard act to outgross—in every way.

Jim Fixx — His *The Complete Book of Running* is a run-away bestseller.

Garry Marshall — TV writer and producer of *Laverne and Shirley* , *Happy Days*, and *Mork and Mindy*.

Arlene Blum — The biochemist who led the first all-woman expedition up Annapurna, loses two fellow climbers.

Howard Jarvis — A crusader against high property taxes sees his Proposition 13 endorsed in California

Miss Piggy — The famed Muppet pig wants it all.

Luciano Pavarotti — It's supertenor, opera's newest sex symbol.

Cheryl Tiegs — This model aims to survive in the TV jungle.

Meat Loaf — Rock's newest (and heftiest) hero.

Sir Freddie Laker — The founder of the Skytrain revolutionized air fares with cheap transatlantic flights.

Nancy Lopez — Rookie Player and Golfer of the Year.

John Travolta — A solitary new superstar, besieged by fans.

James Crosby — Brings big-time gambling to Atlantic City.

John Irving — Down-to-earth Vermonter is on the best-seller list with *The World According to Garp*.

Donna Summer — The queen of disco is softening her act.

Burt Reynolds — A star working on a new image: sensitivity.

1979

Rosalynn Carter — The First Lady skirts the charge that she is involved in government policy formation.

Aleksandr Godunov — Volatile Russian dancer defects to the U.S.

Marvin Mitchelson — The divorce lawyer introduces "palimony."

Bo Derek — This *10* is bringing sex back to films.

Lee Iacocca — Struggles valiantly to get Chrysler into gear under the threat of bankruptcy.

Sly Stallone — His *Rocky II* is the biggest movie of the year.

Megan Marshack — Former vice president Nelson Rockefeller's secretary and companion on the night of his death is back in New York.

Mani Said al-Otaiba — Poetry-writing leader of a tamer OPEC.

Joan Kennedy — Sobers up to campaign alongside Ted.

Johnny Carson — Plans to give up his 17-year reign at NBC.

Ayatollah Khomeini — Iran's ruler leads his nation toward chaos.

Tom Wolfe — *The Right Stuff* is his latest and biggest.

Joan Baez — The brave anti-warrior raises her voice for the boat people and refugees of Cambodia.

Sebastian Coe — British runner prepares for the Olympics.

Gloria Vanderbilt — Her top-grossing jeans bring a new chic.

Bruce Babbitt — The Arizona governor and Three Mile Island investigator believes nuclear power is a necessary evil.

Meryl Streep — A big year for our most intelligent actress.

Willie Stargell — The beloved Pittsburgh Pirate is voted MVP.

Pope John Paul II — A fine first year for the new pope.

Paul Volcker — The frugal chairman of the Federal Reserve.

Jesse Jackson — Offers support and often inflammatory statements around the world.

Dan Aykroyd — Brilliant actor/writer moves on to movies.

Margaret Thatcher — The first female prime minister of England.

William Webster — America's top cop de-Hooverizes the FBI.

Deborah Harry — Taking disco to a new wavelength.

1980

Ronald Reagan — He wins the presidency by a landslide.

Goldie Hawn — *Private Benjamin* liberates a beloved ding-a-ling.

Lech Walesa — An unemployed electrician turns working-class hero to Poland—and the free world.

Colonel Charlie Beckwith — Heroic commander of the failed mission to rescue American hostages in Iran.

Herbert Boyer — Makes new strides in genetic engineering.

Mary Cunningham — Blond, beautiful, and no longer at Bendix, she's looking for room at the top.

Fidel Castro — Faces a new problem: Reagan.

Mel Weinberg — Con artist sets up Abscam for the FBI.

Sugar Ray Leonard — Tough little man wins boxing championship.

Robert Redford — Superstar directs a fine debut film.

Jean Harris — Was the death of Scarsdale Diet's Dr. Tarnower an accident? Only she knows.

Stephen King — Mild down-easter finds terror is the ticket.

Grete Waitz — The swift Norwegian runner leads the pack.

Baron St. Helens — English diplomat lives on—as a volcano.

The Reverend Jerry Falwell — A TV preacher sells America on flag, family, and freedom, of sorts.

Pat Benatar — Rock finds its missing lynx.

Lee Rich — The producer behind *Dallas*.

Sonia Johnson — A Mormon feminist in the ERA battle.

Sam Shepard — Mr. Funk of off-Broadway.

Richard Pryor — Having been through the fire, he's back with a new self.

Eudora Welty — Critics bow to this master Southern writer.

Soichiro Honda — The Henry Ford of Japanese autos.

Beverly Sills — Begins bossing the New York City Opera.

Dan Rather — Can he hold Walter Cronkite's CBS audience?

Brooke Shields — Nothing comes between her and success.

1981

Ronald Reagan — Survives an assassination attempt.

Elizabeth Taylor — Claims Tony nomination for her Broadway debut.

Lech Walesa — Poland's patriarch of Solidarity.

Bradford Smith — His Voyager project took us to the planets.

PEOPLE'S MOST BEAUTIFUL PEOPLE

Every year PEOPLE faces the difficult task of choosing only 50 of the most stunning celebrities we've seen all year. Here is the face of beauty in 2000, led by six-timer Tom Cruise, and a look at the stars who have dazzled their way onto more than one of our Most Beautiful People lists.

6-TIMERS
Tom Cruise
Michelle Pfeiffer

5-TIMERS
Mel Gibson
John F. Kennedy Jr.
Julia Roberts

4-TIMERS
Halle Berry
Denzel Washington

3-TIMERS
Antonio Banderas
George Clooney
Kevin Costner
Nicole Kidman
Demi Moore
Brad Pitt
Claudia Schiffer

2-Timers
Ben Affleck
Tyra Banks
Juliette Binoche
Toni Braxton
Pierce Brosnan
Sandra Bullock
Cindy Crawford
Daniel Day-Lewis
Princess Diana
Leonardo DiCaprio
Emme

Whitney Houston
Helen Hunt
Matt Lauer
Jared Leto
Jennifer Lopez
Paul Newman
Gwyneth Paltrow
Freddie Prinze Jr.
Paulina Porizkova
Jason Priestley
Rebecca Romijn-Stamos
Isabella Rossellini
Winona Ryder
Jaclyn Smith
Hunter Tylo
Meredith Vieira
Katarina Witt

2000'S PICKS
Ben Affleck
Joshua Bell
Candice Bergen
Billy Campbell
Neve Campbell
Nick Carter
George Clooney
Tom Cruise
Penelope Cruz
Cristián de la Fuente
Alison Deans
Bo Derek
Kate Dillon
Scott Erickson
Rupert Everett
Jan-Michael Gambill
Galen Gering

Heather Graham
Faith Hill
Amy Holmes
Iman
Ashley Judd
Ashton Kutcher
Michelle Kwan
Jude Law
Matt LeBlanc
Ananda Lewis
Nia Long
Rob Lowe
Andie MacDowell
Ricky Martin
Dylan McDermott
Soledad O'Brien
Amanda Peet
Tracy Pollan
Freddie Prinze Jr.
Queen Rania of Jordan
Julia Roberts
Brooke Shields
Henry Simmons
Hilary Swank
T-Boz
Charlize Theron
Ming Tsai
Tina Turner
Shania Twain
Blair Underwood
Goran Visnjic
Denzel Washington
Catherine Zeta-Jones

Bryant Gumbel	The new *Today* show host.
Crown Prince Fahd	The Saudi heir-apparent works for peace.
Rabbit Angstrom	John Updike's fictional hero returns.
Ted Turner	Stares down the big guns of network TV.
Princess Diana	Kindergarten teacher becomes princess.
Gloria Monty	Producer of ABC's *General Hospital*.
David Stockman	Reagan's budget director is nearly done in.
Lena Horne	How does the old broad do it? With glamour.
John McEnroe	The tennis superbrat is number one.
Edgar Bronfman	Seagram's liquor baron enlivens a year of corporate merger mania.
Barbara Mandrell	A new country queen takes on TV and wins.
Thomas Sowell	Reagan's favorite black intellectual doesn't like all the attention.
Wolfgang Amadeus Mozart	After two centuries, Austria's child prodigy has become the world's favorite composer.
Tom Selleck	The modest heartthrob of *Magnum P.I.*
Mick Jagger	Finds satisfaction with rock's richest tour.
Richard Viguerie	New Right's fundraiser purges Senate of Democrats.
Nicholas Nickleby	A $100-a-seat Broadway smash by Dickens.
Sandra Day O'Connor	A woman justice's work is never done.
Harrison Ford	The new breed of action star.
Fernando Valenzuela	Mexican rookie conjures baseball magic.
Elizabeth McGovern	A talented beauty soars to stardom.

1982

Ronald Reagan	Enjoys "confinement" in the White House.
Joan Jett	Rocks latest leading lady earns her stripes.
Ariel Sharon	Defiant Israeli defense minister battles on.
Princess Stephanie	Numbed by her mother's death.
Jessica Lange	Talented beauty breaks through in *Tootsie* and *Frances*.
Herschel Walker	Georgia's got football's best running back.
Larry Gelbart	After *M*A*S*H*, he writes the hit *Tootsie*.
Margaret Thatcher	Triumphs in a nasty war in the Falklands.
Dr. William DeVries	A surgeon installs the artificial heart.
Princess Diana	Britain's darling may have newlywed blues.
Yuri Andropov	Master spy takes over Brezhnev's Kremlin.
George Wallace	Seeks blacks' votes and forgiveness.
Paolo Rossi	Leads Italy to the World Cup.
Randall Forsberg	A scholar sounds call to (freeze) arms.
Norma Kamali	Fashion's Greta Garbo.
E.T.	An alien finds his home in Hollywood.
Richard Gere	*Officer* makes a star of a movie maverick.
Sam Knox	Offers consoling facts to herpes victims.
Andrew Lloyd Webber	Broadway's hottest composer strikes all the right notes.
Evelyn Waugh	*Brideshead Revisited* is the year's TV event.

Barbra Streisand	The Brooklyn songbird directs *Yentl*.
Ted Koppel	Revolutionizes night-owl journalism.
Kiri Te Kanawa	Opera diva claims title and acts nothing like a dame.
Reverend Sun Myung Moon	The Unification Church leader is convicted of tax evasion, but he still wins converts.
Paul Newman	*The Verdict* may win him elusive Oscar gold.
Bill Agee and Mary Cunningham	The Bendix takeover didn't take, but this couple makes one merger that works.

1983

Ronald Reagan	Bombs Syrian antiaircraft nests in the mountains east of Beirut.
Debra Winger	Hollywood star scores on her own *Terms*.
Fidel Castro	The aging lion pulls in his claws.
The Cabbage Patch Kids	Glassy of eye and poker of face, this chubby horde masks a plot to take over the planet.
Jesse Jackson	His campaign breeds fusion and fission for Democrats.
William Gates	A computer software whiz makes hard cash.
Sam Shepard	Stage and screen laureate wants anonymity.
Chun Byung In	Pilot of Korean Air Lines flight 007, shot down over Soviet airspace in August.
Mr. T	The show-business maniac of the year.
Ben Lexcen	Impish Aussie wins the America's Cup.
Joan Rivers	*Tonight Show* guest host skewers guests.
Robert Mastruzzi	A demanding Bronx high school principal.
Eddie Murphy	He makes folks mad, but he's got it made.
Matthew Broderick	Buttoned-down leader of young Hollywood.
Barbara McClintock	Discoverer of "jumping genes" wins Nobel.
Harvey Fierstein	Takes theater on a gay whirl with *La Cage*.
Philip Johnson	The grand old man of architecture.
Vanessa Williams	The first black Miss America.
Richard Chamberlain	The public hails the king of miniseries.
Michael Jackson	*Thriller* makes him the biggest star in pop.
Rei Kawakubo	Designs atonal, asymmetric sad rags.
Konrad Kujau	Nearly fools world with fake Führer's diaries.
Alice Walker	*The Color Purple* brings her a Pulitzer.
Alfred Hitchcock	Five buried treasures from the master of suspense are the movie event of 1983.
Jennifer Beals	A dancing Yalie changes into a flashy star.

1984

Geraldine Ferraro	A pioneer loses the battle for vice president.
Bruce Springsteen	The Boss becomes a symbol of America.
Andrei Gromyko	The poker face of Soviet foreign policy.
José Napoleón Duarte	El Salvador's gutsy president is its hope for emerging from a nightmare civil war.

Mary Lou Retton	The Olympian is Madison Avenue's million-dollar baby.
Richard Gere	His silence marks him as an enigma.
Peter Ueberroth	Organized the L.A. Olympic Games.
Joe Kittinger	Flies the Atlantic solo in a hot-air balloon.
Farrah Fawcett	This mother-to-be's career surges.
Clint Eastwood	Reveals darker dimensions in *Tightrope*.
Betty Ford	Publicly tackles her addiction problems.
John Malkovich	A versatile young Chicago actor stars on Broadway and in film.
John Henry	Geriatric equine trots coast to coast.
Sparky Anderson	Manages the Tigers to World Series victory.
Tina Turner	A "Soul Survivor" strides back into rock.
William Kennedy	Author collects a Pulitzer and a MacArthur.
Lee Iacocca	Chrysler's blunt philosopher offers a plan to fix the economy.
Vanessa Williams	The discovery that she had posed nude forces her resignation as Miss America.
Kathleen Turner	The hottest actress since Streep.
James Baker	Reagan's ageless but his chief of staff, perhaps coincidentally, is not.
Kathleen Morris	A controversial Minnesota prosecutor fights against sexual abuse of children.
John Torrington	Discovery of a 19th-century explorer sheds new light on the chilling fate of Britain's ill-fated Franklin expedition.
Bill Murray	Star of the year's biggest box-office hit.
Baby Fae	A child with a transplanted baboon heart.
Michael Jackson	PEOPLE ran five covers on him during 1984.

1985

Bob Geldof	Raises a cry with song to save the hungry.
Joe Kennedy	Bobby's eldest son announces for the congressional seat once held by Uncle Jack.
Corazon Aquino	Philippine housewife and presidential widow rides an emotional swell to political prominence.
Steven Rosenberg	Making big steps toward a cancer cure.
Rambo	His deeds are the stuff of cinema legend.
Akira Kurosawa	Japan's feisty grand old man of the movies triumphs with *Ran*.
Nelson Mandela	Imprisoned black leader may yet save South Africa from the horror of racial war.
William Perry	308-pound surprise of the football season.
Uli Derickson	TWA Flight 847's flight attendant becomes the heroine of a hijacking.
Bernhard Goetz	NY's subway vigilante: victim or criminal?
William Hurt	Oscar favorite for *Kiss of the Spider Woman*.
Hulk Hogan	The World Wrestling Federation's heavyweight champion.
Cathleen Webb	Faked a rape that sent a man to prison.
Madonna	Rich, famous, and married to Sean Penn.

Rupert Murdoch	Now an American citizen, the publisher builds his media empire.
Dwight Gooden	Baseball's best pitcher is quiet but deadly.
Don Johnson	America's Friday night vice.
Princess Diana	Embodies dreams and looks like a princess.
Mel Fisher	Pulls 34 tons of Spanish silver from Key West.
Michael J. Fox	The boy king of Hollywood.
Mengele's Bones	Discovery of this Nazi's remains ends the intense manhunt.
Whoopi Goldberg	She's been on welfare and now she's on-screen in *The Color Purple*.
Rock Hudson	The most famous person to die of AIDS.
The Springsteens	A storybook year for Beauty and the Boss.
Gracie Mansion	A hip gallery owner brings fame to the art of Manhattan's East Village.

1986

Sarah, Duchess of York	A commoner wins a nation's heart without losing her independent personality.
Ivan Boesky	Inside tips make him a Wall Street demon.
Dr. Seuss	*You're Only Old Once!* makes oldsters hoot.
Bette Midler	Becomes a movie draw and a mother.
David Letterman	The askew host of *Late Night*.
Pat Robertson	TV preacher makes a bid to move to the White House.
Daniel Ortega	Nicaragua's president bedevils Reagan.
Raymond Hunthausen	Seattle's progressive archbishop believes he's keeping the faith.
Bob Hoskins	The Cockney Cagney is the actor of the year.
Oliver North	Reagan's marine: hero or loose cannon?
Terry Waite	Church's envoy obtains freedom for hostages in Beirut.
Paul Hogan	Makes *Crocodile Dundee* a U.S. favorite.
Howard the Duck	Turns out to be a turkey for George Lucas.
Greg LeMond	America's first Tour de France winner.
Run–D.M.C.	Rapper tells us to *Walk This Way*.
Debi Thomas	Figure-skating champion finds time to study microbiology at Stanford.
Helga	Posed for previously unknown Wyeth paintings.
Vanna White	*Wheel of Fortune*'s letter-turning bombshell rakes in endorsements and writes a book.
Beth Henley	A Mississippi playwright goes Hollywood.
Jerome P. Horwitz	Developed drug AZT now used to combat AIDS.
David Byrne	Celebrates a wacky America in *True Stories*.
William Rehnquist	The new chief justice of the Supreme Court.
Tom Cruise	The box-office *Top Gun* of 1986.
Max Headroom	A nonhuman talk-show host.
Whitney Houston	Pop's prettiest new commercial monster.

1987

Ronald Reagan	Completes his term with a Hollywood finish.
Mikhail Gorbachev	The Russian leader takes the West by storm and ushers in an age of optimism.
Baby Jessica McClure	After her rescue from a Midland, Texas well, she gets on with a normal toddler's life.
Gary Hart	Re-enters the 1988 presidential race.
Oliver North	Charms his way through the Iran-Contra hearings.
Michael Douglas	Kirk's son steps into the spotlight.
Patient Zero	French Canadian Gaetan Dugas, identified as a major transmitter of the AIDS virus.
Donald Trump	Real estate mogul emerges as an icon for the '80s.
Cher	Soars with new movie roles.
Christian Lacroix	A whimsical, chic new fashion designer.
Oprah Winfrey	Uses television to fight apartheid and racism at home.
Vincent Van Gogh	The most marketable Postimpressionist of the century.
Magic Johnson	Smiling as he leads the Lakers to the top.
The Church Lady	*Saturday Night Live*'s biting holy roller.
Princess Diana	Tests limits of acceptable royal behavior.
Donna Fawn Hahn	Rice, Hall, and Jessica: Three faces of Eve.
Bono	Rock musician struggles with hero status.
Brigitte Nielsen	Stallone's ex remains notorious for her leggy sexuality and questionable motives in love.
Tracey Ullman	Host of delightful, astonishing show on Fox.
Jerry Garcia	Singing to a new generation of Deadheads.
Glenn Close	At 40, she is a siren onscreen in *Fatal Attraction*.
Garrison Keillor	The creator of National Public Radio's *A Prairie Home Companion*.
William Casey	Reagan's CIA director dies before he can testify in Iran-Contra hearings.
Dennis Quaid	Ignites the screen in *The Big Easy*
Tammy Faye Bakker	America's most unusual makeup consumer makes herself a national joke on *Nightline*.

PEOPLE'S BEST AND WORST DRESSED

Who are the biggest fashion victors and victims? The following lists the most recent winners and sinners, along with PEOPLE's new Best Dressed and Worst Dressed of All Time.

BEST OF ALL TIME	WORST OF ALL TIME	2000'S BEST AND WORST
Fred Astaire	Mariah Carey	**10 Best Dressed**
Warren Beatty	Pamela Anderson Lee	Jennifer Aniston
Coco Chanel	Tammy Faye Bakker Messner	Pierce Brosnan
Bill Cosby	Dolly Parton	George Clooney
Tom Cruise	Dennis Rodman	Samuel L. Jackson
Princess Diana	Roseanne	Heather Locklear
Richard Gere	Queen Elizabeth II	Freddie Prinze Jr.
Carey Grant	Elizabeth Taylor	Kevin Spacey
Audrey Hepburn		Britney Spears
Katharine Hepburn	**IN A LEAGUE OF THEIR OWN**	Charlize Theron
Lena Horne		Prince William
Peter Jennings	Cher	
Grace Kelly	Madonna	**10 Worst Dressed**
John F. Kennedy		Christina Aguilera
Jackie Onassis		Lara Flynn Boyle
Babe Paley		Jennifer Love Hewitt
Barbara Walters		Lauren Holly
The Duchess and Duke of Windsor		Lil' Kim
		Lucy Liu
		Bebe Neuwirth
		Portia de Rossi
		Bruce Willis
		Renee Zellweger

1988

George Bush	The president-elect.
Jodie Foster	Makes a comeback in *The Accused*.
Roseanne Barr	A larger-than-life housewife, both on and off the small screen.
Athina Roussel	Money won't buy the love she lost with the death of her mother, Christina Onassis.
The Cyberpunk	Hackers wreak havoc on info networks.
Florence Griffith Joyner	Wins four medals as a sprinter at the Seoul Olympics.
Lisa Marie Presley	Marries a sober fellow and settles down.
Benazir Bhutto	Pakistani discovers the challenges of being the first woman to lead an Islamic nation.
Liz Taylor	Autobiography, AIDS advocacy, and addiction: another rollercoaster year for Liz.
Michelle Pfeiffer	This actress is more than just a pretty face.
Jesse Jackson	His presidential campaign shows that he is a political force to be reckoned with.
Phantom of the Opera	Beguiles us again with a vision of the tragic depths of love.
Merv Griffin	Takes over ownership of Trump's resorts.
Anne Tyler	Reclusive novelist faces an adoring public.
Orel Hershiser	Uncompromising World Series MVP pitcher.
Shi Peipu	Inspires Tony-winning play, *M. Butterfly*.
Kevin Costner	Sends hearts aflutter with *Bull Durham*.
Tracy Chapman	Serious black folk musician enjoys success.
David Hockney	His bright canvases are the talk of the art scene.
Jessica Rabbit	The hottest woman on celluloid is a 'toon.
Stephen Hawking	Unwinds mysteries of the universe in his bestselling book.
Tom Hanks	A familiar face hits the *Big* time.
Fergie	Year One with the Windsors is no fairy tale.
Mike Tyson	Heavyweight champion and husband to the beautiful Robin Givens.
Sage Volkman	Young burn survivor gets back her smile.

1989

George and Barbara Bush	George turns his gaze to domestic matters, while Barbara helps Millie write her book.
Jack Nicholson	The Joker fits him like white grease paint.
Arsenio Hall	The hippest night owl of them all.
Julio Berumen	Pluckiest survivor of the Bay Area quake.
Princess Anne	The least-liked royal turns object of desire.
Mikhail Gorbachev	Proves he's serious about *perestroika*.
Salman Rushdie	For publishing *The Satanic Verses* he now lives with the threat he'll perish.
John Goodman	The TV Barr-tender is an extra-large hit.

Gaia	The Greek goddess lends her name to the daring theory that the planet itself is alive.
Manuel Noriega	The Panamanian dictator gives American leaders fits.
Michael Milken	Junk bond entrepreneur's indictment brings an end to an era.
Paula Abdul	No longer just Janet Jackson's footwork coach, she's a song-and-dance sensation.
Deborah Gore Dean	As the HUD scandal unravels, it's clear that she saw government as a game show and helped her friends win valuable prizes.
Robert Fulghum	Author of unlikely bestseller, *All I Really Need to Know I Learned in Kindergarten*.
Madonna	Irks some Christians, splits from Sean, dallies with Warren, and gets canned by Pepsi.
Spike Lee	The director raises a ruckus—and important questions—with *Do the Right Thing*.
Ellen Barkin	Tough, vulnerable, smart, very sexy, and riveting on-screen.
Billy Crystal	Becomes a genuine sex symbol in *When Harry Met Sally....*
Pete Rose	Battles bad press, baseball commissioner A. Bartlett Giamatti, and his own demons.
Pablo Escobar	A Colombian drug lord markets death while evading an outraged citizenry.
Michelle Pfeiffer	In *The Fabulous Baker Boys* she adds a dash of hot pepper to a delicious dish.
Elizabeth Morgan	Jailed for shielding her daughter from alleged sexual abuse, she is freed at last.
Robert Mapplethorpe	The photographer rattles the art world and Jesse Helms with a shocking retrospective.
Captain Al Haynes	In crash-landing a crippled DC-10 in Iowa, he saves lives with grit and cool.
Donna Karan	High fashion's newest mogul scores with DKNY.

1990

George Bush	Faces a sea of troubles.
Sinead O'Connor	Her haunting rebel voice is heard.
Julia Roberts	The first hit female star of the '90s.
Ken Burns	Produces the 11-hour epic *The Civil War*.
Patrick Swayze	Every woman's dream of a heavenly *Ghost*.
Neil Bush	His questionable involvement with a Denver S&L puts a First Family face on the $500-billion S&L scandal.
Delta Burke	She has unkind words for her *Designing Women* producers.
Saddam Hussein	His invasion of Kuwait brings the world to the brink of war.
Michael Ovitz	The man everyone in Hollywood would like to know spins gold out of tinsel.
Nancy Cruzan	Off life support after years in a coma, she dramatizes the need for living wills.
Colin Powell	Raises the world's shield against Hussein.

Fidel Castro	The world's lone, defiant Communist.
Effi Barry	A model of decorum as husband Marion, Washington's mayor, goes up in smoke.
Dr. Anthony Fauci	America's point man in the fight against AIDS.
M.C. Hammer	Brings showbiz flash and footwork to rap.
Bart Simpson	TV's intemperate urchin gives authority figures a cow.
Nancy Ziegenmeyer	A housewife and rape victim goes public.
Nelson Mandela	He steps from the dim recesses of jail into the harsh reality of freedom.
Francis Ford Coppola	The acclaimed director stages *The Godfather, Part III*.
Keenan Ivory Wayans	His *In Living Color* brings howls of laughter and out-Foxes the network establishment.
Claudia Schiffer	A German supermodel, via Bardot.
William Styron	*Darkness Visible* helps fellow depressives.
Laura Palmer	The Girl Most Likely to Pique on *Twin Peaks*.
Bo Jackson	Hits, runs, and scores on Madison Avenue.
Princess Caroline	Monaco's First Lady copes with her husband's violent death.

1991

George and Barbara Bush	The First Couple's first concerns are war, peace, and their kids.
Jodie Foster	The first-time director commands respect with *Little Man Tate*.
Magic Johnson	Tests HIV-positive and competes against AIDS.
Julia Roberts	After a busted engagement and a box-office bust, she flies away.
Luke Perry	The hunk of *Beverly Hills 90210*.
Anita Hill	Starts a debate on sexual harassment.
Garth Brooks	Lassos the attention of all America.
Princess Diana	Surviving digs at her marriage and her AIDS activism, she turns a very regal 30.
William Kennedy Smith	He beats a charge of rape, but his famous family may never be the same again.
Terry Anderson	Emerges after seven years as a Beirut hostage.
Boris Yeltsin	Russia's new voice.
Kenneth Branagh	Goes Hollywood with *Dead Again*.
Anjelica Huston	Recovering from loss, she emerges as Morticia, the *Addams*'s coolest ghoul.
Jeffrey Dahmer	His confession could not explain why his grisly killings went so long undetected.
Elizabeth Taylor	Will altar trip No. 8 be her last?
Robert Bly	*Iron John*'s readers go ape for him.
John Singleton	*Boyz N the Hood* opens middle-class eyes.
Naomi Campbell	This diva reigns over high-fashion runways.
Axl Rose	Guns N' Roses' lead pistol.

The 4,600-Year-Old Man	Freed from an Alpine deep freeze.
Mariah Carey	Pop's queen shares her *Emotions*.
Derek Humphry	His *Final Exit* ignites debate about suicide.
Pee-Wee Herman	Loses his image at an X-rated theater.
Norman Schwarzkopf	Gulf hero faces life after the army.
Jimmy Connors	Tennis "has-been" defiantly returns.

1992

Bill Clinton	The president-elect recoups from a rough campaign.
Hillary Clinton	A savvy lawyer determined to make a difference.
Cindy Crawford	Becomes a video celebrity.
Ross Perot	Trying to crash the two major parties, he goes from can-do to quitter and back.
Denzel Washington	As *Malcolm X* he catapults to superstardom.
Princess Diana	She dumps her hubby.
Woody Allen	His breakup with Mia Farrow is ballistic.
Larry King	*Larry King Live* is the whistle-stop that White House contenders must visit this year.
Barney	Purple dino gives kid-vid a Jurassic spark.
Billy Ray Cyrus	He's raising Nashville's pulse.
Terry McMillan	Her *Waiting to Exhale* is a surprise smash.
Gregory K.	Sets legal precedents by divorcing his mom.
Desiree Washington	Scores a knockout in court over Mike Tyson.
Diane English	Makes *Murphy Brown* a single mom and herself a lightning rod.
Madonna	She bares her bod and blankets the media.
George Smoot	He finds the missing ripples that confirm the universe began with a Big Bang.
Katie Couric	She boosts the *Today* show.
Fabio	Once a fantasy figure on romance-novel covers, he actually moves and speaks.
Arthur Ashe	He brings eloquence, guts, and grace to his instructive fight against AIDS.
Dana Carvey	Whether he's doing Bush, Perot, or *Wayne*'s Garth, he's always hilariously on target.
Bernadine Healy	The first woman to head the National Institutes of Health.
Carol Moseley Braun	The first black woman to be a U.S. senator.
Henri Matisse	This glorious painter has crowds in line.
Whoopi Goldberg	More prolific than some Hollywood studios.
Sharon Stone	Shows a *Basic Instinct* for sensuality.

1993

Bill Clinton	Faces tough issues and a skeptical nation.
Hillary Rodham Clinton	Reflects on family life while heading the committee on health care reform.

Princess Diana	She still has a place in Britons' hearts.
Michael Jackson	Can't hide from allegations of child abuse.
Yasir Arafat	PLO leader makes peace with his enemy.
Oprah Winfrey	Becomes the world's highest-paid entertainer, sheds 60 pounds, and stays single.
Andrew Wiles	A Princeton prof awes math's great minds.
David Letterman	He's now the leader of the late-night pack.
Janet Reno	Wows Washington with her guts and candor.
Susan Powter	Her hot *Stop the Insanity!* suggests anger might be the best weight-loss prescription.
Howard Stern	Exposes his *Private Parts.*
Baby Jessica	Focuses us on parental rights arguments.
Lyle Lovett	Country's wry specialist in heartache and rue wins the hand of Julia Roberts.
Ol' Man River	The Mississippi inspires awe and rage.
Jerry Seinfeld	He's got TV's most buzzed-about sitcom.
Katherine Ann Power	In facing her bloody past she prompts a rethinking of '60s ideals.
Eddie Vedder	His hellbound vocals make Pearl Jam jell.
Vincent Foster	His suicide brings sadness and self-examination to Clinton's inner circle.
Sheik Omar Abdel Rahmen	A blind cleric is accused of inciting his U.S. followers to bomb and kill.
Michael Jordan	Announces a surprise retirement.
Rush Limbaugh	He bashes liberals for fun and profit.
Shannen Doherty	The feisty actress runs amok.
Tommy Lee Jones	He's a must-find in *The Fugitive.*
Lorena Bobbitt	She provokes the national imagination with an act few could view with detachment.
Tom Hanks	Three diverse, challenging roles this year.

1994

Bill Clinton	Strives to restore voter confidence.
Tim Allen	Has a hit film, book, and sitcom.
O. J. Simpson	Murder suspect of the decade.
The Pope	Delivers his message to millions in a book.
Princess Diana	She tries to resume private life amid allegations of adultery and instability.
Gerry Adams	The Sinn Fein leader calls for his Irish countrymen to lay down their arms.
Shannon Faulkner	Fights tenaciously to become the Citadel's first female cadet.
Michael Fay	In Singapore, the American teen is charged with vandalism and sentenced to a caning.
Whitney Houston	Top songstress walks a rocky path at home.
Ricki Lake	Trounces her competition, marries, and lands in jail for an anti-fur protest.
Vinton Cerf	The hearing-impaired Father of the Internet.
Michael Jordan	Basketball's king graces baseball.
Heather Locklear	Sizzling *Melrose Place* star plans marriage.
Jim Carrey	Shows off rare slapstick style.

YEAR-BY-YEAR, THE BEST- (AND WORST-) SELLING PEOPLE ISSUES

Here are the regular weekly issues that have fared best and worst at the newsstand.

	Best Seller	Worst Seller
1974	The Johnny Carsons	J. Paul Getty
1975	Cher & Gregg Allman	Liv Ullmann
1976	Cher, Gregg, & Baby	Nancy Reagan
1977	Tony Orlando's Breakdown	Julie Andrews
1978	Olivia Newton-John	Vice President & Mrs. Mondale
1979	A Readers' Poll/ 5th Anniversary	Fleetwood Mac
1980	John Lennon, A Tribute	Paul Simon
1981	Charles & Diana's Wedding	Justice Sandra Day O'Connor
1982	Princess Grace, A Tribute	*Annie,* the musical
1983	Karen Carpenter's Death	Sally Ride, America's First Woman in Space
1984	Michael Jackson	How to Make Your Kid a Star
1985	The Other Life of Rock Hudson	Bisset & Godunov
1986	Andrew & Fergie's Wedding	The Raid on Libya
1987	The Follies of Fergie & Di	Michael Caine
1988	Burt & Loni's Wedding	Our American Hostages
1989	Lucy, A Tribute	Abbie Hoffman, Death of a Radical
1990	Patrick Swayze	Campus Rape
1991	Jeffrey Dahmer	Richard & Jeramie Dreyfuss
1992	Princess Diana	Betty Rollin: "I Helped My Mother Die"
1993	Julia Robert's Wedding	Hillary Clinton
1994	The Nicole Simpson Murders	Kelsey Grammer
1995	David Smith	Larry Hagman
1996	Margaux Hemingway's Death	Audrey Meadows and Gene Kelly: Tributes
1997	Goodbye Diana	The Fight Against Child Abuse
1998	Barbra's Wedding Album	Emmy's 50th Birthday
1999	J.F.K. Jr. & Carolyn Bessette Kennedy, Charmed Life/ Tragic Death	Dr. Jerri Nielsen

Tonya Harding	Feisty figure skater slides into scandal.
Jeffrey Katzenberg	The Disney exec ditches Mickey and Pluto for Spielberg and Geffen.
Nadja Auermann	This year's supermodel.
Aldrich Ames	Rogue CIA agent caught betraying the U.S.
Christine Todd Whitman	New Jersey's new governor becomes a GOP darling.
James Redfield	*The Celestine Prophecy* breathes new life into New Age.
Andre Agassi	Tennis's reformed bad boy has Brooke in his court.
Liz Phair	Alternative rock's hottest star.
Power Rangers	Six multicultural teenage superheroes.
John Travolta	With *Pulp Fiction*, he's Hollywood's most durable comeback kid.
Newt Gingrich	Tough-talking new Speaker of the House.

1995

Bill Clinton	Takes on Bosnia and the budget.
Princess Diana	Makes stunning confession to BBC.
Christopher Reeve	Finds a new role: inspirational spokesperson.
Elizabeth Hurley	Actress, model, and Hugh Grant's better half.
Colin Powell	Decides to stay above the presidential fray.
Nicole Kidman	*To Die For* gives birth to a star.
O. J. Simpson	After the verdict, the unsettling image of a fallen idol remains.
Marcia Clark	Loses the O. J. trial but wins over the public.
Susan Smith	Sentenced to life for drowning her sons.
Jay Leno	Mr. Nice Guy becomes late night's top dog.
C. Delores Tucker	Alarmed by gangsta rap, she declares war on media giant Time Warner—and wins.
Jane Austen	Novel Brit wit makes her hot in Hollywood.
Shania Twain	A Canadian honky-tonker watches her fortunes change in Nashville.
Brad Pitt	*Seven* proves he's more than skin-deep.
Babe	The sty's no limit to a charming porker.
Louis Farrakhan	Demagogue takes a step from hate to healing.
Ted Turner	Hitches his wagon to Time Warner.
Hootie & the Blowfish	Fun-loving frat band finds sweet success.
The Unabomber	Issues another bomb, more threats, and a "manifesto."
Jennifer Aniston	Makes *Friends* and influences hairstyles.
JFK Jr.	With *George*, a political prince gets focused.
Monica Seles	A leading lady of tennis returns to court.
R. L. Stine	He gives young readers *Goosebumps*.
Selena	The late Latina takes *Tejano* mainstream.
Cal Ripken Jr.	Plays 2,131 consecutive baseball games.

1996

Rosie O'Donnell	The Queen of Nice cleans up the talk show.
Ted Kaczynski	A Harvard-educated hermit is charged as the Unabomber.
Carolyn Bessette Kennedy	She weds JFK Jr. and becomes America's most watched woman.
Dennis Rodman	Nude, lewd, and tattooed—and all Bull?
Princess Diana	Out of the palace and into the world.
George Clooney	New Batman battles stalkerazzi.
Richard Jewell	Cleared as a bombing suspect, he struggles to restore his name
Binta-Jua	A gorilla with a humanitarian streak.
Jenny McCarthy	MTV's rising star.
Christopher Reeve	Works tirelessly for the disabled.
Kathie Lee Gifford	Pushed to put an end to sweatshops.
Dilbert	Scott Adams's cartoon office drudge.
Gwyneth Paltrow	Hot new actress gets Brad Pitt too.
Marian Wright Edelman	Fighting for children's rights, she loses a White House ally.
Tom Cruise	Mission Accomplished: two blockbusters.
Alanis Morissette	The pied piper of teen angst.
Shannon Lucid	A working mom logs 188 days in space.
Brooke Shields	Comeback kid turns to comedy.
Conan O'Brien	He's the big man of the wee small hours.
Carolyn McCarthy	A victim of tragedy wins a seat in Congress.
Madonna	Is reinvented by Lourdes and Evita.
Tiger Woods	Golf gets a Gen-X superstar.
Goldie Hawn	At 51, her movie career is still golden.
Chelsea Clinton	The First Daughter takes the stage.
Bob Dole	Loses presidential bid, wins on Letterman.

1997

Princess Diana	Her sudden death becomes the year's defining event.
Bill Cosby	Copes with the slaying of his only son and the extortion trial of his would-be daughter.
Ellen DeGeneres	Reshaping TV's take on sexual identity.
Leonardo DiCaprio	In *Titanic*, he swims toward big-star status.
Kathie Lee Gifford	Adds cheating husband to her list of travails.
Rudolph W. Giuliani	The antagonistic mayor cleans up NYC.
Elton John	Mourning friends, he finds new inspiration.
Sheryl Swoopes	Basketball star is in control.
Beck	A fresh, ambitious voice in pop music.
Andrew Cunanan	A killing binge ending with the murder of Gianni Versace makes a chilling stranger an all-too-familiar face.
Michael Moore	Big Tobacco's worst headache wins billions in Medicaid costs.

Lucy Lawless	As Xena, she clears the path for powerful female role models.
Tommy Hilfiger	His bright, relaxed styles prove their cross-cultural appeal.
Frank McCourt	In childhood misery, a writer finds wisdom—and poetry.
Brenda Hoster	Blows the whistle on sexual harassment in the army.
John F. Kennedy Jr.	Successful and settled, he comes into his own.
Bobbi McCaughey	She makes history with healthy septuplets.
Madeleine Albright	Uses magnetism and muscle for diplomacy.
Drew Carey	TV's average Joe bares a long-held secret.
Bill McCartney	A onetime coach exhorts men to tackle their familial and spiritual duties.
Jewel	Folk music gets a '90s poster girl.
Joseph Hartzler	Wins a swift guilty verdict against Oklahoma bomber Timothy McVeigh.
Julia Roberts	Rediscovers her roots in romantic comedy.
Dolly	Poor little lamb—she's all a clone.
Bill Clinton	Faces a full docket of controversies.

1998

Mark McGwire	Hits 70 glorious home runs.
Cameron Diaz	Sweet center of a giddily vulgar comedy.
Kenneth Starr	He turns up the heat on Clinton so high, his own reputation gets scorched.
Lauryn Hill	Goes solo and takes hip-hop to new heights.
John Glenn	His triumphant return to space puts the country in orbit as well.
Katie Couric	Rocked by the death of her husband, Jay, she carries on with courage and strength.
Chris Rock	His edgy comic candor makes him a major player.
Edward Fugger	His quest to help you choose your baby's sex bares fruit.
Geri Halliwell	On her own, she emerges as a surprisingly admirable post–Spice Woman.
The WWII Soldier	Wins the gratitude of a new generation when brought to vivid life on the big screen.
James Brolin	Steals Barbra's heart with an easy confidence, but he'll never be Mr. Streisand.
Camryn Manheim	Triumphs as a fully rounded Emmy winner.
Judy Blume	The queen of preteen fiction hits home with grown-up fans.
David Kaczynski	A concerned brother reaches out to the Unabomber's victims.
Michael J. Fox	Courageously shares his battle with Parkinson's disease
Oprah Winfrey	She brings a *Beloved* project to completion.
Alan Greenspan	Fed chief holds the world's markets steady.

Leonardo DiCaprio	To *Titanic* fanfare, he takes a puzzling break.
Matt Drudge	This wired Walter Winchell spreads gossip that all too often becomes news.
Calista Flockhart	She faces scrutiny of body and role.
Adam Sandler	Sophomoric humor makes him head of the Hollywood class.
Joan Kroc	She quietly shares her wealth.
Emeril Legasse	The star chef is hotter than haute.
Hillary Rodham Clinton	In a difficult year, she embraces dignity.
The American People	Whether voting, viewing, or investing, we defy expectations.

1999

John F. Kennedy Jr.	He leaves the world grieving for what might have been.
Ashley Judd	Scores with *Double Jeopardy*.
Ricky Martin	Pop crowns a new king of the sexy swivel.
Serena Williams	Claims center court with beads, brilliance, and brawn.
Jesse Ventura	Wrestles political pundits to the mat as Minnesota's new governor.
Julia Roberts	The ever-Pretty Woman is Hollywood's runaway hitmaker.
Dr. Robert Atkins	Weight watchers love his low-carb diet.
George W. Bush	Aims to follow his father's footsteps.
Sara Jane Olsen	California fugitive lives an alleged double life as a Minnesota mom.
Tiger Woods	He blasts into the record books.
Bill Gates	Under attack for raking it in, he excels at giving it away.
Judge Judy	TV's supreme jurist rules with a smart mouth.
Chris Spielman	Football player leaves the game for the family he cherishes.
Jennifer Lopez	Music, movies, modeling—all her way.
David E. Kelley	With an Emmy sweep, he rules TV.
J. K. Rowling	Enchants readers with Harry Potter.
Lance Armstrong	His Tour de France makes him a hero.
JonBenet Ramsey	Becomes a symbol of judicial failure as her murder remains unsolved.
Bruce Willis	Uses his *Sixth Sense* to scare up a hit.
Mike Myers	His *Austin Powers* sequel is shagadelic.
Pokémon	They captivate kids and confound parents.
Brandi Chastain	Gives women's soccer a grand kick start.
Regis Philbin	Asks *Who Wants to Be a Millionaire* and a nation answers.
Dr. Martin Citron	Finds a chemical key that could lead to a treatment for Alzheimer's.
Hillary Clinton	Rebounds with a New York State of mind.

MIND YOUR E-MANNERS

Staff writer Samantha Miller answers readers' questions about Net dos and don'ts in PEOPLE'S weekly Internet Manners column. Here are answers to some problems that pop up most often.

1. What's the proper salutation for business e-mail?

In today's khaki-clad office scene, we're almost all on a first-name basis, so inter-cubicle missives can start with a cheery "Hi, Bob!" "Bob:" or nothing at all. The same goes for outside contacts you're already acquainted with, unless you're a peon and they're big cheeses ("Dear Mr. Gates..."). Don't know your recipient? Stick with Mr. or Ms. Traditionalists won't bristle, and whippersnappers will be tickled.

2. How should I sign e-mail?

Like TV news anchors, Netizens love signature sign-offs. Hippies use "Peace"; gen Y, "C-ya L8R"; acronym addicts, "TTFN." ("Ta-ta for now.") Some savvy users scorn cutesiness and simply sign their names or initials. We say creativity is no crime, but be original—or you'll look as pretentious as non-Italians who double-cheek kiss a ciao.

3. Can I use e-mail to send thank-you notes for my holiday loot?

Nice try, lazybones. You think a few electrons can repay Grandma for battling the shopping-mall hordes (never mind those Amazon.com boxes in her trash)? Pick up a pen—retro is trendy! E-mail is okay for informal notes to pals and in geek enclaves like Silicon Valley, where folks e-mail wedding invitations (!). But when in doubt, write it out.

4. I got an e-mail warning me about a computer virus. Should I forward it to everyone I know?

We know you mean well. But your Net-savvy pals will cringe as if you coughed on them. Most of these scares are hoaxes that waste more time than computer solitaire. If you're worried, check with your office tech-support squad or a hoax-busting Web site like kumite.com/myths. If only the flu were as easy to avoid.

5. Can I ask for a first date via e-mail?

A casual "met you last night, wanna have dinner?" note is a fine way for the tongue-tied to break the ice—though it doesn't exactly signal a hunk of burnin' love, so hope your fun e-Valentine digs shy types. One tip: spell-check.

THE MOST BEAUTIFUL PEOPLE ON THE WEB

Every year, PEOPLE's print editors name the 50 Most Beautiful People in the World. People.com, meanwhile, asks Web surfers to nominate their own favorites. Herewith the drop-dead adorables who received the most online votes in 2000.

1. Justin Timberlake
2. Britney Spears
3. Scott Cohen
4. Nick Carter
5. Roy Dupuis
6. Oded Fehr
7. Gillian Anderson
8. Julia Roberts
9. Angelina Jolie
10. Tori Amos

6. Why is it bad to type in all capital letters? What about all small letters?

Net tradition dictates that all caps denotes shouting: PIPE DOWN! As for the e.e. cummings mode, it's fine for speed in chat rooms, but ease up on the accelerator for e-mail.

7. How do I get my friends to stop e-mailing me lists of jokes?

Would-be Jay Lenos, listen up: This seems to be readers' top e-etiquette peeve. As for those of you who don't like being drafted into Open Mike Night, begin by trying a polite "Thanks, but no thanks." If that doesn't work, say you just don't have time. Worried about being rude? How rude are your so-called friends to clog your in-box in the first place?

8. Is it okay to send e-mail full of spelling errors?

look over emale before u sned it. its only commn curtesy. How annoying was that to read? Very—which is why the "I'm so busy I can't take time to spellcheck" attitude has got to go. It's rude to recipients. They're busy too.

9. I stumbled across some intimate e-mail sent to my significant other. I believe exchanging sexy e-mail is a form of cheating. What do you think?

As any world leader would tell you, it depends on your definition of "cheating." But while a strictly cyber affair obviously isn't as bad as the real thing, it's bad enough, even if it was "just for fun"—a frequently deployed excuse that only raises disturbing questions. And don't get roped into an argument with your s.o. about whether e-dallying really is cheating. If snookums got steamy with someone else and has the gall to debate the technicalities, maybe it's time for both of you to cut your losses and head to the singles chat room.

10. When I'm sending e-mail back and forth with one person, how often should I change the subject line?

Well, if you and your steady are discussing which wedding caterer to hire and the subject still reads, "Re: Nice Meeting You," it's time to freshen it up. But using a new heading on every note can get confusing. So switch when the rest of the message no longer has anything to do with the subject—just say non to non sequiturs.

THE SEXIEST MAN ALIVE

PEOPLE has honored someone with this title beginning in 1985. Here is a look at the magazine's hunks of the year. Discerning readers will recall the drought of 1994, when no one made the honor roll.

1985
Mel Gibson

1986
Mark Harmon

1987
Harry Hamlin

1988
John F. Kennedy Jr.

1989
Sean Connery

1990
Tom Cruise

1991
Patrick Swayze

1992
Nick Nolte

1993
Richard Gere and
Cindy Crawford
(The Sexiest Couple Alive)

1994
No winner

1995
Brad Pitt

1996
Denzel Washington

1997
George Clooney

1998
Harrison Ford

1999
Richard Gere

CYBERWORLD: 20 ESSENTIAL BOOKMARKS

Some Web sites are good for a one-time giggle, and some will have you going back again and again. PEOPLE staff writer Samantha Miller selects some of the best—the useful, the dishy, and the downright indispensable:

1. Yahoo! (www.yahoo.com)
Yahoo! breaks down the Web like a card catalog, sorting through sites by subject. It's the perfect starting point for any Web expedition—or you can stay on the site for the news stories, stock tickers, and other extras. Bonus: If you want to search the Web itself, Yahoo! puts you in the capable hands of Google, a search engine that really works.

2. Ask Jeeves (ask.com)
A different way to search the Web. Just type a question using regular language—i.e. "What is Mongolia's biggest export?"—and this plucky butler does his best to serve up sites that answer it.

3. About.com
A network of hundreds of sites dedicated to particular topics—gardening, adoption, horror movies—each run by an expert guide. A great way to get up to speed on anything, pronto.

4. FAQs (faqs.org)
One of many sites archiving Frequently Asked Questions lists—one of the great inventions of geek culture—from the Net's multitudes of freewheeling Usenet message boards dedicated to topics from lemurs to David Letterman.

2000 WEBBY AWARD WINNERS

These "Oscars of the Internet," awarded to the best Web sites in a range of categories as judged by a panel of technology-world professionals, were handed out in a ceremony in San Francisco on May 11, 2000.

Activism: AdBusters (adbusters.org)

Arts: WebStalker (backspace.org/iod/iod4Winupdates.html)

Broadband: Video Farm (videofarm.com)

Commerce: BabyCenter (babycenter.com)

Community: Café Utne (cafe.utne.com/cafe)

Education: Merriam-Webster Word Central (wordcentral.com)

Fashion: Paul Smith (paulsmith.co.uk)

Film: Atom Films (atomfilms.com)

Finance: Gomez.com (gomez.com)

Games: Gamespy Industries (gamespy.com)

Health: ThriveOnline (thriveonline.com)

Humor: The Onion (theonion.com)

Kids: Scholastic.com (scholastic.com)

Living: Epicurious (epicurious.com)

Music: Napster (napster.com)

News: Jim Romenesko's Media News (poynter.org/medianews)

Personal Web Sites: Cocky Bastard (cockybastard.com)

Politics and Law: Politics.com (politics.com)

Print and Zines: Nerve (nerve.com)

Radio: Lost and Found Sound (lostandfoundsound.com)

Science: The Cave of Lascaux (culture.fr/culture/arcnat/lascaux)

Services: Evite (evite.com)

Sports: ESPN.com (espn.go.com)

Technical Achievement: Google (google.com)

Travel: Outside Online (outsidemag.com)

Television: MSNBC (msnbc.com)

Weird: Stile Project (stileproject.com)

5. eHow (ehow.com)
Need to know how to change a tire? How to sew on a button? How to conceal a hickey? Get it done with help from this collection of thousands of how-tos.

6. Amazon.com (www.amazon.com)
You don't have to spend, spend, spend at this ever-expanding shopping site (although it's sooo easy…). Browsing its well-written and artfully designed book, music, and video info—plus reviews from users around the world—is free.

7. eBay (eBay.com)
The one, the only—the Web's most dangerous site (for auction addicts, anyway). So what if you get carried away and overpay? It's entertainment.

8. MySimon (mysimon.com)
About to splurge on something? This site will scour the Web to see if you can get it cheaper.

9. Infospace (www.infospace.com)
National yellow pages, white pages, e-mail address directories, and more—all the better to help you track down that old buddy or lost love.

10. The Internet Movie Database (us.imdb.com)
Everything you ever wanted to know about nearly every movie ever made. Cast, crew, reviews, release dates, and more—all

linked so you can play your own version of Six Degrees of Kevin Bacon.

11. ESPN.com
Whether your pleasure is baseball or roller hockey, this site dishes out more up-to-the-minute stats and scores than you can shake a stick (bat, racquet, javelin . . .) at.

12. Weather.com
A stormy paradise for weather junkies—minus the Muzak. And handy for anyone without a window office.

13. The Obscure Store and Reading Room (www.obscurestore.com)
One guy's daily roundup of wacky and/or provocative tidbits from the nation's newspapers. If a blind golfer scores a hole in one—or a crook in drag holds up a bank—this site is sure to have a link.

14. The Drudge Report (www.drudgereport.com)
See ground zero of the Monica Lewinsky mess—the snappy, salacious site of one-man gossip machine Matt Drudge.

15. Ain't It Cool News (www.aint-it-cool-news.com)
Proprietor Harry Knowles commands an army of moles who attend advance movie screenings, providing early dish and perturbing Hollywood execs.

16. The Onion (www.theonion.com)
A humor magazine that's actually funny. Long a Net pleasure, it made the big time with its bestselling book, *Our Dumb Century*.

17. Epicurious (epicurious.com)
Whether you cook or just like to eat, this foodie fave has the recipe for success, with a searchable 11,000-recipe database (chiefly taken from *Gourmet* and *Bon Appetit* magazines) and tons of tips.

18. MapQuest (www.mapquest.com)
Another great thing about the Net: enter any two places in the United States and get free personalized point-to-point driving instructions.

19. Microsoft Expedia (expedia.msn.com)
If you're picky about your travel plans—and who isn't?—it pays to book your own plane tickets. Here and on other sites (but, hey, Bill Gates really needs the money) you can shop from a full range of flights and pick your own seat assignment.

20. People.com
Head to the Web outpost of our mother magazine for daily celeb news, in-depth profiles of your favorite stars, and lots more.

MOST POPULAR WEB SITES

Ranking the popularity of Web sites is far from an exact science. One method follows the approach of TV's Neilsen ratings—following a bunch of selected surfers to see where they're clicking. For this June 2000 survey, Internet measurement company Media Metrix tracked 55,000 computer users to see which sites were visited most.

TOP NEWS SITES
1. MSNBC.com
2. About.com
3. Weather.com
4. CNN.com
5. Time.com
6. CBS.com
7. ABCNews.com
8. Discovery.com
9. NYTimes.com
10. USAToday.com

TOP ENTERTAINMENT SITES
1. Real.com
2. Snap.com
3. About.com
4. Disney.com
5. Speedyclick.com
6. Freelotto.com
7. Entertaindom.com
8. Uproar.com
9. Webstakes.com
10. Macromedia.com

TOP SEARCH SITES
1. Altavista.com
2. Looksmart.com
3. Askjeeves.com
4. Goto.com
5. Google.com

TOP PORTALS
1. Yahoo.com
2. MSN.com
3. AOL.com
4. Lycos.com
5. Go.com

TOP TRAVEL SITES
1. Expedia.com
2. Travelocity.com
3. MapQuest.com
4. Priceline.com
5. Southwest.com
6. ITN.net
7. Delta-air.com
8. AA.com
9. Lowestfare.com
10. Cheaptickets.com

TOP SHOPPING SITES
1. Amazon.com
2. Americangreetings.com
3. Mypoints.com
4. Webstakes.com
5. Barnesandnoble.com
6. Bizrate.com
7. BMGMusicservice.com
8. Directhit.com
9. CDNow.com
10. Freeshop.com

TOP SPORTS SITES
1. ESPN.com
2. SportsLine.com
3. CNNSI.com
4. Majorleaguebaseball.com
5. NASCAR.com
6. NBA.com
7. Sandbox.com
8. FOXSports.com
9. Seasonticket.com
10. Gorp.com

TOP HEALTH SITES
1. Onhealth.com
2. WebMD.com
3. Planetrx.com
4. EDiets.com
5. Drkoop.com
6. Drugstore.com
7. More.com
8. Thriveonline.com
9. Healthmall.com
10. Discoveryhealth.com

CYBERSPACE'S MOST WANTED

Search sites help Web crawlers find sites devoted to their favorite stars and shows. Here's what people sought out most often at Lycos (lycos.com) from January 1 through August 10, 2000:

TOP FEMALE ACTORS
1. Jennifer Lopez
2. Carmen Electra
3. Alyssa Milano
4. Jennifer Love Hewitt
5. Jenny McCarthy
6. Angelina Jolie
7. Sarah Michelle Gellar
8. Shannon Elizabeth
9. Denise Richards
10. Salma Hayek

TOP ACTORS
1. Russell Crowe
2. Brad Pitt
3. Bruce Lee
4. Leonardo DiCaprio
5. Tom Cruise
6. Will Smith
7. Mel Gibson
8. Keanu Reeves
9. Ryan Phillippe
10. Tom Green

TOP MOVIES
1. X-Men
2. Gladiator
3. Mission: Impossible 2
4. American Beauty
5. Romeo Must Die
6. Scream 3
7. The Blair Witch Project
8. Coyote Ugly
9. Toy Story 2
10. Scary Movie

TOP TV SHOWS
1. Survivor
2. Big Brother
3. Buffy the Vampire Slayer
4. Who Wants To Be a Millionaire
5. The X-Files
6. The Oprah Winfrey Show
7. Friends
8. Charmed
9. Ally McBeal
10. ER

TOP MUSIC ARTISTS
1. Britney Spears
2. 'N Sync
3. Jennifer Lopez
4. Eminem
5. Christina Aguilera
6. Backstreet Boys
7. Korn
8. Metallica
9. Mariah Carey
10. Blink 182

FASHION AWARDS

CFDA AWARDS

Since 1981 the Council of Fashion Designers of America has presented annual awards to honor the best design talent. In the earlier years a single award designation was bestowed upon from five to thirteen fashion luminaries. The present categories began to take shape in 1986 with the inception of the Perry Ellis Award. Over the years a number of special awards and special categories have been recognized. The following list culls some of the most prominent categories and long-lived award designations over the years.

1986

Perry Ellis Award: David Cameron
Lifetime Achievement: Bill Blass and Marlene Dietrich

1987

Designer (menswear): Ronaldus Shamask
Perry Ellis Award: Marc Jacobs
Lifetime Achievement: Giorgio Armani, Horst, and Eleanor Lambert

1988

Designer (menswear): Bill Robinson
Perry Ellis Award: Isaac Mizrahi
Lifetime Achievement: Richard Avedon and Nancy Reagan

1989

Designer (womenswear): Isaac Mizrahi
Designer (menswear): Joseph Abboud
Accessory: Paloma Picasso
Perry Ellis Award: Gordon Henderson

Lifetime Achievement: Oscar de la Renta

1990

Designer (womenswear): Donna Karan
Designer (menswear): Joseph Abboud
Accessory: Manolo Blahnik

Perry Ellis Award: Christian Francis Roth
Lifetime Achievement: Martha Graham

1991

Designer (womenswear): Isaac Mizrahi
Designer (menswear): Roger Forsythe
Accessory: Karl Lagerfeld for House of Chanel
Perry Ellis Award: Todd Oldham
Lifetime Achievement: Ralph Lauren

1992

Designer (womenswear): Marc Jacobs
Designer (menswear): Donna Karan
Accessory: Chrome Hearts
Perry Ellis Award: Anna Sui
International: Gianni Versace
Lifetime Achievement: Pauline Trigère

1993

Designer (womenswear): Calvin Klein
Designer (menswear): Calvin Klein
Perry Ellis Award (womenswear): Richard Tyler
Perry Ellis Award (menswear): John Bartlett
Perry Ellis Award (accessories): Kate Spade
Lifetime Achievement: Judith Leiber and Polly Anne Mellen

1994

Designer (womenswear): Richard Tyler
Perry Ellis Award (womenswear): Victor Alfaro and Cynthia Rowley (tie)
Perry Ellis Award (menswear): Robert Freda
Perry Ellis Award (accessories): Kate Spade
Lifetime Achievement: Carrie Donova, Nonnie Moore, and Bernadine Morris

1995

Designer (womenswear): Ralph Lauren
Designer (menswear): Tommy Hilfiger
Perry Ellis Award (womenswear): Marie-Ane Oudejans for Tocca
Perry Ellis Award (menswear): Richard Tyler, Richard Bengtsson, and Edward Pavlick for Richard Edwards
Perry Ellis Award (accessories): Kate Spade
International: Tom Ford
Lifetime Achievement: Hubert de Givenchy

1996

Designer (womenswear): Donna Karan
Designer (menswear): Ralph Lauren
Designer (accessories): Elsa Peretti for Tiffany
Perry Ellis Award (womenswear): Daryl Kerrigan for Daryl K.
Perry Ellis Award (menswear): Gene Myer
Perry Ellis Award (accessories): Kari Sigerson and Miranda Morrison for Sigerson Morrison
International: Helmut Lang
Lifetime Achievement: Arnold Scaasi

1997

Designer (womenswear): Marc Jacobs
Designer (menswear): John Bartlett
Designer (accessories): Kate Spade
Perry Ellis Award (womenswear): Narciso Rodriguez
Perry Ellis Award (menswear): Sandy Dalal
International: John Galliano
Lifetime Achievement: Geoffrey Beene

1998/99

Designer (womenswear): Michael Kors
Designer (menswear): Calvin Klein
Designer (accessories): Marc Jacobs
Perry Ellis Award (womenswear): Josh Patner and Bryan Bradley for Tuleh
Perry Ellis Award (menswear): Matt Nye
Perry Ellis Award (accessories): Tony Valentine
International: Yohji Yamamoto
Lifetime Achievement: Yves Saint Laurent

2000

Designer (womenswear): Oscar de la Renta
Designer (menswear): Helmut Lang
Designer (accessories): Richard Lambertson and John Truex
Perry Ellis Award (womenswear): Miguel Adrover
Perry Ellis Award (menswear): John Varvatos
Perry Ellis Award (accessories): Dean Harris
International: Jean-Paul Gaultier
Most Stylish Dot-com: Issey Miyake's Pleats Please
Lifetime Achievement Award: Valentino

VH1 FASHION AWARDS

For the last five years, VH1 has bestowed fashion awards (combined with music awards in the first year), and in 1999 the channel joined forces with *Vogue* magazine in the presentation. Here are names who paraded down the presentation catwalk:

1995

Designer: Miuccia Prada
New Designer: Tom Ford for Gucci
Model (female): Shalom Harlow
Model (male): Tyson Beckford
Most Fashionable Artist: Madonna
Ongoing Life Achievement: Karl Lagerfeld
Frock 'N' Rock: Gianni Versace.
Catwalk to Sidewalk: Tommy Hilfiger
Stylist for a Music Video: Lori Goldstein, Madonna's "Take a Bow"

1996

Designer: Tom Ford for Gucci
Model (female): Kate Moss
Model (male): Mark Vanderloo (Hugo Boss)
Most Fashionable Artist: Elton John
Best Personal Style (female): Gwyneth Paltrow
Best Personal Style (male): Dennis Rodman

1997

Designer (womenswear): John Galliano
Designer (menswear): Helmut Lang;
Model (female): Karen Elson
Model (male): Charlie Speed
Most Fashionable Artist: Beck
Best Personal Style (female): Courtney Love
Best Personal Style (male): Will Smith
Best Second Collection: Donatella Versace, for Versus

Most Stylish Music Video: Fiona Apple, "Criminal"

1998

Designer (womenswear): Marc Jacobs
Designer (menswear): Prada
Avant Garde Designer: Alexander McQueen
New Designer: Veronique Branquinho
Model (female): Carolyn Murphy
Model (male): Scott Barnhill
Most Fashionable Artist: Madonna
Best Personal Style (female): Cameron Diaz
Best Personal Style (male): Chris Rock
Photographer: Steven Meisel
Most Stylish Music Video: Janet Jackson, "Gone Till It's Gone"

1999

Designer: Tom Ford
Avant Garde Designer: Alexander McQueen
Model: Gisele Bundchen
Most Fashionable Artist (female): Jennifer Lopez
Most Fashionable Artist (male): Lenny Kravitz
Celebrity Style (female): Heather Graham
Celebrity Style (male): Rupert Everett

THE PEOPLE 600

Previous editions of the *Almanac* have assembled essential dossiers and fascinating facts on an imaginary guest list of the 400 most compelling, fastest-rising, and indisputably established stars and starmakers, for a fantasy party to put Mrs. Astor's original 400 to shame. Last year we expanded the guest list to 500, and to accommodate the new millennium's infinitely expanding galaxy of pop culture stars, we've made room at the Ball for another 100 hotly contested seats. Join us for the richest feast of star stats ever, and welcome our newest guests.

A HEARTY WELCOME

Christina Aguilera
Christian Bale
Maria Bartiromo
Lance Bass
Victoria Beckham
Jessica Biel
Amy Brenneman
Melanie Brown
Joy Browne
Emma Bunton
Gabriel Byrne
Michael Caine
Billy Campbell
Nick Carter
Kim Cattrall
J. C. Chasez
Don Cheadle
Kenny Chesney
Melanie Chisholm
Chyna
Russell Crowe
Penelope Cruz
Carson Daly
D'Angelo
Kristin Davis
Vin Diesel
Howie Dorough
Illeana Douglas
Kirsten Dunst
Eminem
Edie Falco
Jon Favreau
Jamie Foxx

Joseph Fatone
Liam Gallagher
Macy Gray
Tom Green
Angie Harmon
Steve Harvey
Kate Hudson
John Irving
Joshua Jackson
Jay-Z
Kid Rock
Chris Kirkpatrick
Anna Kournikova
Diana Krall
Lenny Kravitz
Jude Law
Tommy Lee
John Leguizamo
Jet Li
Brian Littrell
Lisa Lopes
Shelby Lynne
Norm MacDonald
Tobey Maguire
Aimee Mann
Shirley Manson
A. J. McLean
Janet McTeer
Matthew Modine
Julianne Moore
Mandy Moore
Frankie Muniz
Cynthia Nixon
Donny Osmond

Marie Osmond
Amanda Peet
Bijou Phillips
Maury Povich
Kathleen Quinlan
Denise Richards
Kevin Richardson
J. K. Rowling
Geoffrey Rush
Carlos Santana
Chloe Sevigny
Charles Sheen
Martin Sheen
Martin Short
Jessica Simpson
Gary Sinise
Sisqo
Jimmy Smits
Leelee Sobieski
John Stossel
Mena Suvari
Hilary Swank
Rozonda Thomas
Justin Timberlake
Donatella Versace
Goran Visnjic
Christopher Walken
Sela Ward
Tionne Watkins
Emily Watson
Forest Whitaker
Barry White
Michelle Williams

BEN AFFLECK

Birthplace: Berkeley, CA
Birthdate: 8/15/72
Occupation: Actor, screenwriter
Education: Attended University of Vermont and Occidental College
Debut: (Film) *Mystic Pizza*, 1988
Signature: *Good Will Hunting,* 1997
Facts: Became friends with Matt Damon in elementary school. By high school, the pair held "business meeting lunches" in the cafeteria to plot their future acting careers.

Wrote *Good Will Hunting* with Damon out of frustration when they weren't getting many acting jobs. Eventually sold the script to Miramax for $800,000.

Owns vintage Ms. Pac-Man and Millipede video arcade games.

Owns 5 motorcycles.
Famous Relative: Casey Affleck, actor, brother
Major Award: Oscar, Best Original Screenplay, *Good Will Hunting*, 1997
Quote: "I feel like fame is wasted on me. I already feel like I don't want to have sex five times a day. It's kind of depressing."

CHRISTINA AGUILERA

Birthplace: Staten Island, NY
Birthdate: 12/18/80
Occupation: Singer
Education: High school
Debut: (Album) *Christina Aguilera*, 1999
Signature: "What a Girl Wants"
Facts: Born to an Ecuadoran-born army sergeant and Irish-American mother, she lived in Texas, Japan, New Jersey, and Pennsylvania.

At eight, she appeared on *Star Search*, winning runner-up for her rendition of Whitney Houston's "The Greatest Love of All."

Sang National Anthem at a Pittsburgh Steelers game at age 10.

At age 12 joined the *New Mickey Mouse Club* with Britney Spears, Justin Timberlake, J. C. Chasez, and Keri Russell.

Still sleeps with lights on because she is afraid of the dark.

Reportedly has been in relationships with Carson Daly, Eminem, and Limp Bizkit's Fred Durst.

Talent scout Ruth Imus, who claims to be her former manager filed a $7 million lawsuit against her mother and others in 2000, alleging breach of contract and accusing them of cheating her out of her share of the star's fortune.
Relationship: Jorge Santos, dancer
Major Award: Grammy, Best New Artist, 1999
Quote: "I think everybody should have a great Wonderbra. There's so many ways to enhance them, everybody does it."

JASON ALEXANDER

Real Name: Jay Scott Greenspan
Birthplace: Newark, NJ
Birthdate: 9/23/59
Occupation: Actor
Education: Boston University
Debut: (Film) *The Burning,* 1981; (TV) *Senior Trip!,* 1981
Signature: *Seinfeld*
Facts: *Seinfeld* creator Larry David modeled the George character after himself.

Is an accomplished dancer and operatic tenor.
Marriage: Daena E. Title, 1979
Child: Gabriel, 1992; Noah, 1996
Major Awards: Tony, Best Actor, *Jerome Robbins' Broadway,* 1989; Grammy, Best Cast Show Album, *Jerome Robbins' Broadway* (with others), 1989
Quote: "I started losing my hair when I was a wee kid of 16."

TIM ALLEN

Real Name: Tim Allen Dick
Birthplace: Denver, CO
Birthdate: 6/13/53
Occupation: Comedian, actor
Education: Western Michigan University

Debut: (TV) *Showtime Comedy Club All-Stars II*
Signature: *Home Improvement*
Facts: Has nine brothers and sisters.

Appeared in Mr. Goodwrench commercials.

Provided the voice for Buzz Lightyear in *Toy Story*, 1995.

Paid $2 million for 26 acres of Michigan campground with the intention of keeping it in its natural, undeveloped state.
Infamy: He served 28 months in jail in 1978 for attempting to sell cocaine.

Pled guilty to impaired driving in 1997. When stopped by police, Allen failed four sobriety tests, including counting backward and reciting the alphabet.
Original Job: Creative director for an advertising agency
Marriage: Laura Deibel, 1978 (separated, 1999)
Child: Kady, 1990

WOODY ALLEN

Real Name: Allen Stewart Konigsberg; legal name Heywood Allen
Birthplace: Brooklyn, NY
Birthdate: 12/1/35
Occupation: Actor, director, writer
Education: New York University, City College of New York
Debut: (Film) *What's New Pussycat?,* 1965 [see page 102 for a complete filmography]
Signature: *Annie Hall,* 1977
Facts: Played clarinet every Monday night at Michael's Pub in Manhattan. Missed the Academy Awards ceremony for *Annie Hall* because it was on a Monday night. Now plays at the Café Carlyle.

Among his many neuroses: won't take showers if the drain is in the middle.

Was suspended from New York University for inattention to his work.

His daughters are both named after jazz greats.
Infamy: After details became known

of his affair with Soon-Yi, Mia Farrow's oldest adopted daughter, Farrow accused him of sexual abuse of her younger children. In 1993, he was denied custody of their adopted children, Dylan (since renamed Malone) and Moses, and biological son Satchel (since renamed Seamus).

After Allen adopted a daughter with wife Soon-Yi, Farrow commented: "I don't know how the courts permitted this, especially in light of a judge not allowing Mr. Allen to see his own children."

Original Job: During high school, he supplied comic snippets to newspaper columnists Walter Winchell and Earl Wilson; he later became a hired gag-writer on a retainer of $25 a week.
Marriages: Harlene Rosen (divorced), Louise Lasser (divorced); Soon-Yi Previn, 1997
Children: Moses,1978 (adopted); Malone, 1985 (originally Dylan, changed to Eliza, changed again; adopted); Seamus, 1987 (formerly Satchel); (with Mia Farrow). Bechet Dumaine, 1998 (adopted); Manzie Tio, 2000 (adopted)
Major Awards: Oscar, Best Director, *Annie Hall,* 1977; Oscar, Best Original Screenplay, *Annie Hall,* 1977; Oscar, Best Original Screenplay, *Hannah and Her Sisters,* 1986
Quote: "I've never had an audience in any medium."

TORI AMOS

Real Name: Myra Ellen Amos
Birthdate: 8/22/63
Occupation: Singer, songwriter
Education: High school
Debut: (Album) *Y Kant Tori Read?,* 1988
Signature: "Crucify," 1992
Facts: She started playing the piano at age three. At age 5 she won a scholarship to study piano in a conservatory in Baltimore but was kicked out by age 11 for refusing to practice.

Father was an evangelical preacher, a fact that figures heavily into her sex-laden lyrics in songs like "Leather" and "God."
Original Job: Piano player in Los Angeles lounges
Marriage: Mark Hawley, 1998
Child: daughter, 2000 (name not released at press time)
Quote: "I have vivid memories of being a prostitute in another life."

GILLIAN ANDERSON

Birthplace: Chicago, IL
Birthdate: 8/9/68
Occupation: Actor
Education: DePaul University
Debut: (Stage) *Absent Friends,* 1991
Signature: *The X-Files*
Facts: Lived in London during her childhood.

As a teenager smitten by British punk rock, she spiked her hair, pierced her nose, put a safety pin through her cheek, and dated a rock musician almost a decade her senior.

To hide her pregnancy, Anderson wore bulky trench coats and took three episodes off during an alleged alien abduction.

Believes in UFOs, ESP, and other paranormal phenomena.

Thousands of male fans have formed an online Gillian Anderson Testosterone Brigade.

Has raised about $250,000 for the nonprofit Neurofibromatosis Inc., by auctioning off X-Files memorablilia on the Web. The disease affects 100,000 Americans, including her 19-year-old brother, Aaron.
Marriage: Clyde Klotz, 1994 (separated, 1996); Rodney Rowland (relationship)
Child: Piper, 1994
Major Award: Emmy, Best Actress in a Drama Series, *The X-Files,* 1997

PAMELA ANDERSON

Birthplace: Comox, Canada
Birthdate: 7/1/67
Occupation: Actor
Education: High school

Debut: (TV) *Home Improvement,* 1991; (Film) *Barb Wire,* 1995
Signature: *V.I.P*
Facts: Got her first commercial job after her image was projected on a giant scoreboard screen at a Canadian football game in 1989.

Says her mother encouraged her to pose for her several *Playboy* covers, telling her it was a compliment (8 in all—a record).

Writes fairy tales and poetry and regularly keeps a dream diary.

Married Mötley Crüe drummer Tommy Lee in Cancun, Mexico, in 1995 wearing a tiny white bikini. (Lee wore white Bermuda shorts.)

Lost a court request to halt distribution of a homemade video showing her and then-husband Tommy Lee having sex; the two claim the tape was stolen from their home.

Filed for divorce from Lee on grounds of spousal abuse. He spent 3 months in jail for kicking her and was put on probation.

In 1999, had her silicone breast implants removed, going from a size 34 D to a 34 C. (Surgery revealed that the implants had been leaking.)

Shared a New Year's drink with Lee in 2000 which resulted in an extension of his probation until May 2003 for violating his parole.
Original Job: Beer company spokesmodel
Marriage: Tommy Lee (1995; divorced, 1998; remarried, 1999; separated, 2000); Markus Schenkenburg, model (relationship)
Child: Brandon Thomas, 1996; Dylan Jagger, 1997
Quote: "Tommy has been fixed. Actually, he has been neutered or spayed. What do you call it?"

JULIE ANDREWS

Birthplace: Walton-on-Thames, England
Birthdate: 10/1/35
Occupation: Actor, singer
Education: High school

Debut: (Stage) *Starlight Roof*, 1947; (Film) *Mary Poppins*, 1964
Signature: *Mary Poppins*
Facts: By age 8, had a fully formed adult throat and a four-octave voice.

The 1965 film *The Sound of Music*, in which she played Maria Von Trapp, was the highest-grossing film of its day.

She and husband Edwards adopted two Vietnamese girls during the war.

Under married name Julie Edwards, wrote two children's books in the 1970s, *Mandy* and *The Last of the Really Great Whangdoodles*.

Before starring in *Victor/Victoria*, was last on Broadway 33 years ago.

Rejected her 1996 Tony award nomination for best actress for *Victor/Victoria* because the show was snubbed in all other categories.

Surgery to remove noncancerous throat nodules in June 1997 has silenced her professional singing voice. In 1999, she filed a negligence complaint against Dr. Scott M. Kessler and Dr. Jeffrey D. Libin, claiming she wasn't informed that the surgery carried the risk of permanent hoarseness and "irreversible loss of vocal quality." The suit was settled for undisclosed terms in 2000.
Infamy: Tried to shed *Mary Poppins* image by baring her breasts in 1981's *S.O.B.*
Original Job: Toured from age 12 with mother and alcoholic stepfather in a vaudeville act.
Marriages: Tony Walton, 1959 (divorced, 1968); Blake Edwards, 1969
Children: Emma, 1962 (with Tony Walton). Jennifer (stepdaughter); Geoffrey (stepson); Amy Leigh, 1974 (adopted); Joanna Lynne, 1975 (adopted).
Major Award: Oscar, Best Actress, *Mary Poppins*, 1964

MAYA ANGELOU

Real Name: Margueritte Annie Johnson
Birthplace: St. Louis, MO
Birthdate: 4/4/28
Occupation: Writer, actor, singer, dancer
Education: California Labor School
Debut: (Film) *Calypso Heatwave*, 1957
Signature: *I Know Why the Caged Bird Sings*, 1979
Facts: Nicknamed "Maya" by her brother, who called her "My" or "Mine."

At age 7, she was raped by her mother's boyfriend. Sever al days after her testimony at the trial, her assailant was found dead—killed by her uncles. She blamed herself for the death and did not speak for the next five years.

Tried to join the army in the late 1940s, but was turned down after a security check revealed that the California Labor School was listed as subversive.

Has received over 30 honorary degrees.

Read the inaugural poem at President Clinton's inauguration ceremony.
Infamy: In the late 1950s, she worked as a madam, managing two prostitutes in San Diego. Her guilty conscience caused her to quit after only a short stint.
Original job: The first black—and the first female—streetcar conductor in San Francisco at age 16.
Marriages: Tosh Angelou (divorced, c. 1952); Vusumze Make (divorced); Paul Du Feu, 1973 (divorced, 1981)
Child: Guy Johnson, 1945
Major Award: Grammy, Best Spoken Word Recording, *On the Pulse of Morning*, 1993

JENNIFER ANISTON

Birthplace: Sherman Oaks, CA
Birthdate: 2/11/69
Occupation: Actor
Education: High School of Performing Arts
Debut: (TV movie) *Camp Cucamonga*, 1990
Signature: *Friends*
Facts: Actor Telly Savalas was her godfather.

Like her *Friends* character, Aniston worked as a waitress after graduating from school.

The rail-thin Aniston actually used to be fat. When she realized that was keeping her from landing acting parts, she went on the Nutri/System diet and lost 30 pounds.

Because of her often-emulated shag, she was dubbed America's First Hairdo by *Rolling Stone* magazine.

In 2000, along with *Friends* costars, received a salary increase from $125,000 to $750,000 per episode.
Infamy: Caused a stir in 1996 when she posed nude in *Rolling Stone*.

In 2000, sued *High Society* and *Celebrity Skin* for publishing pictures of her while she sunbathed topless in her backyard.
Marriage: Brad Pitt, 2000
Famous Relative: John Aniston, actor, father

MARC ANTHONY

Real Name: Antonio Marco Muniz
Birthplace: East Harlem, New York City
Birthdate: 9/16/69
Occupation: Salsa singer
Education: High school
Debut: (Album) *When the Night Is Over*, 1991; (Film) *Hackers*, 1995; (Broadway) *The Capeman*, 1998
Signature: *Contra la Corriente (Against the Flood)*, 1997
Facts: Was discovered at age 12 by commercial producer David Harris.

First exposed to salsa music in his family's kitchen, where his father would play with a salsa band.

Changed his name not only because his listeners were primarily English-speaking but also because there was a known Mexican singer with the same name.

His first solo salsa album, *Otra nota,* which included "El ultimo beso," a song written by his father, went gold five months after its release in 1992.

Rejecting the typical flashy salsa dress, he often wears a pair of jeans, a T-shirt, and a baseball cap on stage.

During his performances, he always pays a tribute to the Puerto Rican flag.

Original Job: Backup singer for TV commercials
Marriage: Dayanara Torres, 2000
Child: Arianna, 1994 (with Debbie Rosado)
Famous Relative: Felipe Muniz, Puerto Rican jibaro guitarist, father
Quote: "I still don't know how to pick up panties in front of thousands of people and be cool about it. I gotta call Tom Jones and ask his advice."

FIONA APPLE

Real Name: Fiona Apple McAfee Maggart
Birthplace: New York, NY
Birthdate: 9/13/77
Occupation: Singer-songwriter
Education: High school
Debut: (Album) *Tidal,* 1996
Signature: "Criminal," 1997
Facts: Named after a character in *Brigadoon.*

A rape by a stranger at age 12 precipitated years of therapy and inspired the lyrics to her song "Sullen Girl."

After her parents divorced, she lived with her mother and sister in New York City. Leaving school to join her father in Los Angeles, she finished her high school requirements through a correspondence course.

Lack of a driver's education course has kept her from earning her diploma. She still doesn't have a driver's license.

Regarded as a loner in high school and was nicknamed "Dog" by classmates.

Began taking piano lessons when she was about 8 years old and debuted an original composition at her first recital.

At age 18, she produced a demo tape for a publicist and was instantly signed by a manager.

Follows a vegetarian diet and her typical preperformance meal is split pea soup.

Infamy: Used profanity at the 1997 *MTV Video Music Awards* show.
Relationship: Paul Thomas Anderson, writer-director
Famous Relative: Brandon Maggart, actor, father; Diana McAfee, singer, dancer, mother
Major Awards: Grammy, Best Rock Vocal—Female, "Criminal," 1997
Quote: "If I'm going to end up a role model, then I'd rather not end up being the kind of role model that pretends to be perfect and pretends that she always has the right thing to say."

CHRISTINA APPLEGATE

Birthplace: Los Angeles, CA
Birthdate: 11/25/71
Occupation: Actor
Debut: (TV) *Days of Our Lives,* 1971; (Film) *Jaws of Satan,* 1979
Signature: *Married...With Children*
Facts: When she was 3 months old, she appeared in her mother's arms on *Days of Our Lives.*

During her period of "image-experimentation," she appeared on a poster wearing battered cut-offs and a black leather vest with nothing underneath. A falcon is sitting on one arm and a snake is wrapped around the other.

Bought her first house when she was 11 years old, using her investment money.

Her mother, poor and at one time on food stamps, took her along on casting calls.

She has 3 tattoos.

Relationship: Jonathan Schaech, actor (1998)
Famous Relative: Nancy Priddy, actor, mother
Quote: "As a kid, I was pretty wild. Now I think I'm boring."

GIORGIO ARMANI

Birthplace: Piacenza, Italy
Birthdate: 7/11/34
Occupation: Fashion designer
Facts: Entered medical school but after two years decided to join the military.

Designed uniforms for the Italian Air Force (1980).

Original Job: Medical assistant for Italian military, window dresser in a Milan department store
Major Awards: Neiman-Marcus Award, Distinguished Service in the Field of Fashion, 1979; Cutty Sark Award, Outstanding International Designer, 1981

COURTENEY COX ARQUETTE

Birthplace: Birmingham, AL
Birthdate: 6/15/64
Occupation: Actor
Education: Mt. Vernon College (Washington, DC)
Debut: (TV) *Misfits of Science,* 1985; (Film) *Down Twisted,* 1987
Signature: *Friends*
Facts: Discovered in 1984 Brian De Palma video "Dancing in the Dark" with Bruce Springsteen.

Played Michael J. Fox's girlfriend on *Family Ties* and Jim Carrey's love interest in *Ace Ventura: Pet Detective.*

Had LASIK eye surgery (to correct nearsightedness).

In 2000, along with *Friends* costars, received a salary increase from $125,000 to $750,000 per episode.

Original Job: Model
Marriage: David Arquette, 1999
Famous Relatives: Patricia Arquette, sister-in-law, actor; Rosanna Arquette, sister-in-law, actor

ROWAN ATKINSON

Birthplace: Newcastle-upon-Tyne, England
Birthdate: 1/6/55
Occupation: Actor, comedian, writer
Education: Newcastle University, Oxford University
Debut: (Stage) *Beyond a Joke,* 1978; (TV) BBC series *Not the Nine O'Clock News,* 1979; (Film) *Bean,* 1997
Signature: Mr. Bean
Facts: Earned a B.S. in electrical engineering but was rejected for a job at the BBC. Later earned a masters degree in computer engineering.

His middle name is Sebastian.

In elementary school, his fellow students referred to him as "Moon Man," "Doopie," and "Zoonie."

He drives go-carts, collects classic sports cars, and has written for automobile magazines.

His one-man Broadway show closed after only 14 performances.

He met his wife on the set of *The Black Adder;* she was a make-up artist at the time.

In 1994, he won raves for his well-known comical cameo as the misspeaking vicar in *Four Weddings and a Funeral.*

He is very protective of his private life and reveals very little about his family in interviews.
Original Job: Actor
Marriage: Sunetra Sastry, 1990
Children: Two children
Quote: "I am essentially a rather quiet, dull person who just happens to be a performer."

STEVE AUSTIN

Real Name: Steven Williams
Birthplace: Austin, TX
Birthdate: 12/18/64
Occupation: Wrestler
Education: Attended University of North Texas
Facts: Dropped out of school in 1987, a few credits short of a degree in physical education.

Began wrestling in 1989 for $20 per day.

Known as "Stone Cold" Steve Austin, he once shouted in a fight against Bible-quoting Jake "The Snake" Roberts, "Talk about your psalms, talk about John 3:16; Austin 3:16 says I just whipped your [butt]!" Since then, he sells some 1 million self-designed T-shirts each month, with his Austin 3:16 logo.

Before he married Jeannie Clark, she was his valet, Lady Blossom.

His stats are listed at 6'2", 252 pounds.

He wrestles 180 shows a year.

Suffered a spinal injury in 1997 after wrestler Owen Hart landed on his head in a "tombstone piledriver," which left him unsure of his future with the WWF.

In 2000, he underwent spinal surgery to remove bone spurs in his neck vertebrae from years of body slamming.
Original Job: Loaded trucks at a freight terminal
Marriage: Jeannie Clark (separated)
Children: Jade, 1981 (step-daughter); Stephanie, 1992; Cassidy, 1996
Quote: "A lot of people relate to me. Look, I dumped my boss on his head. I think that everybody would like to do that."

DAN AYKROYD

Birthplace: Ottawa, Canada
Birthdate: 7/1/52
Occupation: Actor, writer
Education: Carleton University
Debut: (TV) *Saturday Night Live,* 1975; (Film) *1941,* 1979
Signature: *Ghostbusters,* 1984
Facts: His grandfather was a Mountie.

Was expelled for delinquency from St. Pious X Preparatory Seminary.

Had a cameo role in *Indiana Jones and the Temple of Doom,* 1984.

A police buff, he rides an Ontario Provincial Police motorcycle, collects police badges, sometimes rides shotgun with detectives in squad cars, and owns, in partnership with

several Toronto police officers, a Toronto bar called Crooks.

He is very interested in the supernatural and has an extensive collection of books on the subject. He admits, "I've never seen a full apparition, but I once saw what could be termed ectoplasmic light, and that scared the hell out of me."

Co-founder of the House of Blues restaurant/music club chain.
Original Job: Stand-up comedian
Marriages: Maureen Lewis (divorced), Donna Dixon, 1983
Children: Oscar; Mark; Lloyd; (with Maureen Lewis). Danielle Alexandra, 1989; Belle Kingston, 1993; Stella Irene Augustus, 1998
Major Award: Emmy, Best Writing in a Comedy, Variety, or Music Series, *Saturday Night Live,* 1977

BURT BACHARACH

Birthplace: Kansas City, MO
Birthdate: 5/12/28
Occupation: Songwriter, composer, producer, arranger
Education: Attended Mannes College of Music, New York City
Debut: (First No. 1 hit) "The Story of My Life," 1957; (First film as composer of theme song) *The Sad Sack,* 1957
Signature: "I'll Never Fall in Love Again," 1960
Facts: He toured army bases as a concert pianist from 1950 to 1952.

Following army service, he was accompanist for Polly Bergen, Georgia Gibbs, the Ames Brothers, Imogene Coca, Joel Grey, and Paula Stewart.

Once he's left the recording studio, he does not want to hear the record again.

Unwillingly studied piano during childhood to please his mother.

As a child, he attempted to grow taller and fulfill his dream of becoming a football player by eating jars of peanut butter.

In 1957, he met lyricist Hal David and began years of collaboration—

some 150 songs—and No. 1 hits, including "Magic Moments" (Perry Como, 1958).

Bacharach and David teamed with Dionne Warwick in 1962, and they had 39 chart records in 10 years, eight of which made it to the Top 10.

He cowrote with Carole Bayer Sager the Grammy-winning song "That's What Friends Are For," which became the popular anthem for the struggle against AIDS.

By the mid-1990s, his music enjoyed a revival, and five of his songs were used in the 1997 film *My Best Friend's Wedding*.

Bacharach now enjoys breeding and racing thoroughbred race horses.

Original Jobs: Pianist
Marriages: Paula Stewart (divorced); Angie Dickinson, 1965 (divorced, 1981); Carole Bayer Sager, 1981 (divorced, c. 1991); Jane Hanson, 1991
Children: Lea Nikki, 1966 (with Dickinson). Cristopher Elton, c. 1986 (adopted); Oliver, c. 1993; Raleigh, c. 1996 (with Sager)
Famous Relative: Bert Bacharach, men's fashion columnist and author, father
Major Awards: Grammy Award, Best Instrumental Arrangement, "Alfie," 1967; Academy Award, Best Original Music Score, *Butch Cassidy and the Sundance Kid,* 1969; Academy Award, Best Original Song, "Raindrops Keep Fallin' on My Head," *Butch Cassidy and the Sundance Kid,* 1969; Grammy Award, Best Original Score Written for Motion Picture, *Butch Cassidy and the Sundance Kid,* 1969; Grammy Award, Best Score from an Original Cast Album, *Promises, Promises,* 1969; Emmy Award, Outstanding Single Program, Variety or Musical, *Singer Presents Burt Bacharach,* 1970/71; Academy Award, Best Song, "Best That You Can Do," *Arthur,* 1984; Grammy Award, Song of the Year, "That's What Friends Are For," 1986; Grammy Award, Pop Collaboration With Vocals, "I Still Have That Other Girl" (with Elvis Costello), 1999

Quote: "With technology today, you can make perfect garage music, but when you peel it back, maybe what's missing is melody."

KEVIN BACON

Birthplace: Philadelphia, PA
Birthdate: 7/8/58
Occupation: Actor
Education: Manning St. Actor's Theatre, Circle in the Square Theater School
Debut: (Film) *National Lampoon's Animal House,* 1978 [see page 102 for a complete filmography]
Signature: *Footloose,* 1984
Facts: Nervous about Bacon's sex appeal, Paramount's Dawn Steel took his photo around the studio when casting *Footloose* asking everyone, "Is this guy f--kable?" (Obviously he was; he got the teen idol part in the 1984 film.)

For *Murder in the First,* went on a 600 calorie-a-day diet, shaved his head, and wore uncomfortable contacts that completely covered his eyes. When filming the "dungeon" scenes, he put crickets in his hair (to simulate lice) and got welts from being hit with a leather blackjack.

In 1994, formed band the Bacon Brothers with Emmy-winning composer, older brother Michael.
Marriage: Kyra Sedgwick, 1988
Children: Travis, 1989; Sosie Ruth, 1992
Famous Relatives: Michael Bacon, composer, brother
Quote: "My groupies are now between 40 and 50. But that's cool. I'll take them where I can get them."

ERYKAH BADU

Real Name: Erica Wright
Birthplace: Dallas, TX
Birthdate: 2/26/71
Occupation: Singer, songwriter
Education: Attended Grambling State University
Debut: (Album) *Baduizm,* 1997; (Film) *The Cider House Rules,* 1999

Signature: *Baduizm*
Facts: As a teen, wanted to change her "slave name"; when her mother objected, respelled her first name, with the *y* symbolizing "origin" and the *kah,* ancient Egyptian for "pure inner light." Later changed her surname, choosing a riff she favored.

Is influenced by "mathematics," a type of numerology that equates numbers with personal growth and self-knowledge.

Formed the group Erykah Free with cousin Robert "Free" Bradford, but she alone was signed by a label. To symbolize his presence, she began lighting a candle at her concerts.

Gave birth to son, Seven (named because that number cannot be divided by anything but itself), in a planned home birth.
Original Jobs: Teacher, waiter
Relationship: Andre "Dre" Benjamin
Child: Seven Sirius, 1997
Major Awards: Grammy, Best R&B Album, *Baduizm,* 1997; Grammy, Best Female R&B Vocal Performance, "On and On," 1997; Grammy, Best Rap Performance–Duo or Group, "You Got Me" (with the Roots), 1999

ALEC BALDWIN

Real Name: Alexander Rae Baldwin III
Birthplace: Massapequa, NY
Birthdate: 4/3/58
Occupation: Actor
Education: New York University, Lee Strasberg Theatre Institute
Debut: (TV) *The Doctors,* 1963
Signature: *The Hunt for Red October,* 1990
Facts: He is not naturally tall, dark, and handsome—he dyes his fair hair black.

Originally wanted to be a lawyer.

Was engaged to Janine Turner (*Northern Exposure*); she had the wedding dress ready and the invitations were sent out when they broke up.
Infamy: Was taken to court for assaulting a paparazzo, who had staked out the actor's house for a

photo of his newborn; Baldwin's acquittal was applauded weeks later by the audience at the Oscars.
Original Job: Waiter and doorman at Studio 54
Marriage: Kim Basinger, 1993
Child: Ireland Eliesse, 1995
Famous Relatives: Daniel Baldwin, actor, brother; William Baldwin, actor, brother; Stephen Baldwin, actor, brother

CHRISTIAN BALE

Birthplace: Pembrokeshire, Wales
Birthdate: 1/30/74
Occupation: Actor
Debut: (TV) *Anastasia: The Mystery of Anna*, 1986; (Film) *Empire of the Sun*, 1987
Signature: *American Psycho*, 2000
Facts: He began his acting career in a commercial for Pac-Man cereal in 1983.

His mother was a circus dancer; his grandfather was a stand-up comedian and ventriloquist.

In 1987, Steven Spielberg picked Bale out of 4,000 hopefuls to star in *Empire of the Sun*.

Almost lost his role in *American Psycho* to Leonardo DiCaprio. He won the role back when DiCaprio accepted a role in *The Beach*.

In 2000 his father married Gloria Steinem.
Marriage: Sandra (Sibi) Blazic, free-lance producer, 2000
Quote: "The more high-profile I get, the less I can surprise people anymore. I've managed it very well. Nobody has a clue who I am, so it's worked."

ANTONIO BANDERAS

Birthplace: Málaga, Spain
Birthdate: 8/10/60
Occupation: Actor
Education: School of Dramatic Art, Málaga, Spain
Debut: (Stage) *Los Tarantos,* 1981; (Film) *Labyrinth of Passion,* 1982
Signature: *The Mask of Zorro,* 1998

Facts: Modeled for Ralph Lauren and Gucci.

Would love to play the Hunchback of Notre Dame, but thinks he won't be able to because of his good looks.

Studied fencing with the U.S. National Olympic Team.
Original Job: Model, waiter
Marriages: Ana Leza (divorced), Melanie Griffith, 1996
Child: Estela del Carmen, 1996
Quote: "I thought to myself, 'Oh my God. How disgusting.' Then I went to the first rehearsal and it was...so easy. I didn't lose my fingers, my ear didn't fall down. Nothing happens if you're sure of who you are." (On his first kiss in a role as a homosexual, in the 1988 Almodóvar movie *Law of Desire*.)

TYRA BANKS

Birthplace: Inglewood, CA
Birthdate: 12/4/73
Occupation: Model, actor
Education: High school
Debut: (TV) *Fresh Prince of Bel Air*, 1994; (Film) *Higher Learning*, 1995
Facts: The August before she was to enroll in college, she was asked by a French modeling agent to work at the couture shows in Paris. Within a week of that first stroll, "Miss Tyra" (as the fashion cognoscenti call her) had accumulated 25 more bookings.

Became the second-ever black model (Lana Ogilvie was the first) under contract with Cover Girl Cosmetics.

Director John Singleton saw her on the cover of *Essence* and felt she'd be perfect for a part in his *Higher Learning*. He arranged for an audition, and during the drawn-out casting process they fell in love for a spell.
Relationship: Craig Taylor

DREW BARRYMORE

Birthplace: Los Angeles, CA
Birthdate: 2/22/75
Occupation: Actor
Education: High school dropout

Debut: (Film) *Altered States,* 1980
Signature: *The Wedding Singer,* 1998
Facts: Starred in a TV commercial for Gainsburgers when she was 11 months old.

After drug rehabilitation, she starred in *Fifteen and Getting Straight* (1989), a TV movie about drug abuse, and wrote her own autobiography, *Little Lost Girl,* at age 14 to clear the air. Credits musician David Crosby for helping her get over drugs.
Infamy: Began drinking at age 9 and started taking drugs at 10.

In 1992, posed nude for *Interview* magazine.

In 1995, posed nude for *Playboy.*

While on the *Late Show with David Letterman* in 1995, pulled down her trousers to display tattoos on her behind, then pulled up her shirt and flashed her breasts at Letterman. She has six tattoos.
Marriage: Jeremy Thomas (divorced, 1994); Tom Green (engaged, 2000)
Famous Relatives: John Barrymore Jr., actor and director, father; Ethel Barrymore, actor, great-aunt; Lionel Barrymore, actor, great-uncle; John Barrymore Sr., actor, grandfather
Quote: "I was born 10 years old."

MARIA BARTIROMO

Birthplace: Brooklyn, NY
Birthdate: 9/11/67
Occupation: TV financial journalist
Education: New York University

Signature: The Money Honey
Facts: She hired a speech therapist to erase her Brooklyn accent.

In her senior year of college, began work as an intern at CNN *Business News*.

In 1995, she was the first TV journalist to report live from the floor of the New York Stock Exchange.

The Maria Bartiromo Market Hairdex is a website devoted to the correlation between her hair style and the market flux.

She laughs in her sleep.
Marriage: Jonathan Steinberg, 1999
Quote: "There's no reason to believe this stuff is over your head. A woman, particularly a woman, needs to know. It's not brain surgery."

KIM BASINGER

Birthplace: Athens, GA
Birthdate: 12/8/53
Occupation: Actor
Education: University of Georgia
Debut: (Film) *Hard Country,* 1981
Signature: *9¹/₂ Weeks,* 1986
Facts: Filed for bankruptcy in May 1993 after an $8.1 million verdict was rendered against her in favor of Main Line Pictures, after she dropped out of the movie *Boxing Helena*. Had to limit her monthly living expenses to $10,000 under bankruptcy plan. An appeals court later reversed the verdict, setting the stage for another trial.

Developed agoraphobia while a model.

Threw her modeling portfolio off the Brooklyn Bridge.

Was involved with Prince before marrying Alec Baldwin.
Infamy: In 1983, she appeared in an eight-page *Playboy* spread.

Bought Braselton, a town in Georgia, for $20 million in 1989, with plans to develop it into a tourist attraction. Dumped her interest in the town after she declared bankruptcy, leaving residents angry and fearful for their futures.
Original Job: Breck shampoo model,

then a Ford model; pursued a singing career under the nom-de-chant Chelsea
Marriages: Ron Britton (divorced), Alec Baldwin, 1993
Child: Ireland Eliesse, 1995
Major Award: Oscar, Best Actress, *L.A. Confidential,* 1997
Quote: On *L.A. Confidential:* "It's great to be in a movie where people come up to me and say something besides, 'Uh, what were you thinking?' "

LANCE BASS

Real Name: James Lance Lantsen Bass
Birthplace: Laurel, MS
Birthdate: 5/4/79
Occupation: Singer
Debut: (Single) "I Want You Back," 1996; (Album) *NSYNC, 1996 (American release, 1998)
Signature: *No Strings Attached,* 2000
Facts: Was a choirboy in his Baptist church.

Was recruited to join 'N Sync because his deep voice rounded out their sound.

Manages country music acts.

Reportedly raised the first red flags about the group's contract with their ex-manager.

Acted on an episode of *7th Heaven.*
Infamy: When the fivesome felt they weren't getting a fair share of the money they were generating, they left RCA Records and former manager Lou Pearlman. Pearlman responded with a $150 million lawsuit; the band countersued for $25 million. The parties reached a private, out-of-court settlement, allegedly in 'N Sync's favor.
Original Job: Day care worker
Quote: "With your second album, people think, 'I guess there must be something to their music because they lasted.' "

ANGELA BASSETT

Birthplace: New York, NY
Birthdate: 8/16/58
Occupation: Actor
Education: Yale University
Debut: (Film) *F/X,* 1986
Signature: *What's Love Got to Do With It,* 1993
Facts: Helped integrate her high school, where she was on the honor roll and the cheerleading squad. Went to college on a scholarship.
Original Job: Hair stylist, photo researcher at *U.S. News and World Report*
Marriage: Courtney B. Vance, 1997

KATHY BATES

Real Name: Kathleen Doyle Bates
Birthplace: Memphis, TN
Birthdate: 6/28/48
Occupation: Actor
Education: Southern Methodist University
Debut: (Film) *Taking Off,* 1971; (Stage) *Casserole,* 1975; (TV) *The Love Boat,* 1977
Signature: *Misery,* 1990
Facts: She lost the screen roles of characters she originated on the stage (Frankie in *Frankie and Johnny in the Claire de Lune* and Lenny McGrath in *Crimes of the Heart*) to Michelle Pfeiffer and Diane Keaton.

Terrence McNally created the character Frankie (in *Frankie and Johnny in the Claire de Lune*) with her in mind.
Original Job: Singing waitress in the Catskills, cashier in the gift shop of Museum of Modern Art in New York
Marriage: Tony Campisi (divorced, 1997)
Major Award: Oscar, Best Actress, *Misery,* 1990

WARREN BEATTY

Real Name: Henry Warren Beaty
Birthplace: Richmond, VA
Birthdate: 3/30/37
Occupation: Actor, producer, director, screenwriter

Education: Northwestern University
Debut: (Film) *Splendor in the Grass,* 1961
Signature: *Shampoo,* 1975
Facts: Rejected football scholarships to go to drama school.

Is famed for his reluctance to do interviews and his tendency to pause for a minute or more before giving a yes or no answer.

The longtime womanizer broke the hearts of many famous actresses, including Natalie Wood, Leslie Caron, and Joan Collins. (Collins even had a wedding dress hanging in a wardrobe for almost a year.)

A behind-the-scenes political player and auteur of *Bulworth,* made noises about seeking the 2000 Democratic presidential nomination.
Original Job: Bricklayer, dishwasher, construction worker, piano player
Marriage: Annette Bening, 1992
Children: Kathlyn, 1992; Benjamin, 1994; Isabel, 1997; Ella Corinne, 2000
Famous Relative: Shirley MacLaine, actor, sister
Major Award: Oscar, Best Director, *Reds,* 1981.
Quote: "For me, the highest level of sexual excitement is in a monogamous relationship."

BECK

Real Name: Beck Hansen
Birthplace: Los Angeles, CA
Birthdate: 7/8/70
Occupation: Singer, songwriter
Education: High school dropout
Debut: (Album) *Mellow Gold,* 1994
Signature: *Odelay,* 1996
Facts: In 1993, making just four dollars an hour, lived in a rat-infested shed behind a house.

Mellow Gold, which includes "Loser," was recorded for $500, mostly at his friend's house.

Hung out in New York's East Village in the late '80s, where the "anti-folk scene" convinced him that there are no restrictions on subject matter for songs.

Mom was once a regular at Andy Warhol's Factory.
Original Jobs: Painting signs, moving refrigerators, taking ID photos at New York's YMCA, clerking in a video store
Relationship: Leigh Limon
Famous Relatives: Bibbe Hansen, guitarist, mother; Al Hansen, artist, grandfather
Major Awards: Grammy, Best Rock Vocal—Male, "Where It's At," 1996; Grammy, Best Alternative Album, *Odelay,* 1996; Grammy, Best Alternative Performance, *Mutations,* 1999

VICTORIA BECKHAM

Birthplace: Goff's Oak, Hertfordshire, England
Birthdate: 4/17/74
Occupation: Singer
Education: Performing arts college in Epsom, England
Debut: (Album) *Spice,* 1996; (Movie) *Spice World,* 1997 (American release, 1998)
Signature: "Wannabe," (1996) / Posh Spice
Facts: Was nicknamed "Acne Face" as a child.

Was awarded £100,000 from British Airways after they misplaced her four matching Louis Vuitton bags.

Named her son after the city in which he was conceived.

Her lavish wedding featured a £100,000 tiara, an 18-piece orchestra, and a turkey dinner.

Made her catwalk debut in 2000.

Was the last Spice Girl to release a solo single ("Out of Your Mind").

The British Press accused her of anorexia; she denied having a weight problem.

Caused a stir by characterizing her husband as "an animal in bed."

She and her husband sued to stop the publication of a book by a former employee in 2000, but subsequently settled and allowed publication to proceed.

Marriage: David Beckham, 1999, soccer star
Child: Brooklyn David Beckham, 1999
Quote: "I'm not that desperate to be liked."

GIL BELLOWS

Birthplace: Vancouver, British Columbia, Canada
Birthdate: 6/28/67
Occupation: Actor
Education: American Academy of Dramatic Arts
Debut: (Film) *The First Season* (Canadian), 1987; (TV) *Law & Order,* 1991; (Stage) *True West*
Signature: *Ally McBeal*
Facts: First appeared in several low-budget films, one-act plays, and Off-Broadway shows. In 1995, he enjoyed his first lead in the TV movie *The Silver Strand.*

Proposed to his wife on Valentine's Day.

Landed a 10-minute role in 1994's *Shawshank Redemption,* playing the pivotal part of the thief who provided information about the murder of Tim Robbins's wife.

Co-founded a small theater group called Seraphim.

His first child was born in his home; a mirror fell and shattered as the baby let out her first screams.
Original Job: Hotel doorman
Marriage: Rya Kihlstedt, actress, 1994
Child: Ava Emmanuelle, 1999

ROBERTO BENIGNI

Birthplace: Arezzo, Tuscany, Italy
Birthdate: 10/27/52
Occupation: Actor, comedian, screenwriter, director, producer
Education: Accounting school, Prado, Italy
Debut: (U.S. Film) *Down by Law,* 1986
Signature: *Life Is Beautiful,* 1998
Facts: Originally planning to become a priest, he attended a

seminary in Florence, Italy, but left when the building was damaged by a flood.

The idea for *Life Is Beautiful* came from Benigni's father, who was imprisoned in Bergen-Belsen concentration camp for two years before being liberated in 1945. His father always added humor in the telling of his story.

When he was a child, his family spent three weeks sleeping in a friend's stable.

He was discovered at age 16 by the director of an experimental theater group while delivering an improvised, satirical, political speech in a Tuscan town square.

At 19 he began acting with a theater group in Rome while doing stand-up comedy.

In 1983, *You Disturb Me* launched his career as an actor-writer-director. It was also his first of many collaborations with Nicoletta Braschi, whom he later married.

A passionate Dantista as a youth, he could recite *The Divine Comedy* by heart.

The number Benigni wears on his concentration camp uniform in *Life Is Beautiful* is the same number that his role model, Charlie Chaplin, wore in *The Great Dictator*.

Infamy: In 1980, he mocked Pope John Paul II on Italian TV, and, facing obscenity charges, was fined and given a one-year suspended sentence. Years later, he exuberantly kissed Pope John Paul II instead of his papal ring during an audience and private screening of *Life Is Beautiful*.

Original Jobs: Musician, clown, magician's assistant

Marriage: Nicoletta Braschi, actor, 1991

Major Awards: Oscars, Best Actor and Best Foreign Film, *Life Is Beautiful*, 1998

Quote: "I am so full of joy. Every organ in my body is moving in a very bad way."

ANNETTE BENING

Birthplace: Topeka, KS
Birthdate: 5/29/58
Occupation: Actor
Education: San Diego Mesa College, San Francisco State University, American Conservatory Theater, San Francisco
Debut: (Stage) *Coastal Disturbances*, 1986; (Film) *The Great Outdoors*, 1988
Signature: *The Grifters*, 1990
Fact: Originally cast as Catwoman in *Batman Returns*, she got pregnant and lost the role to Michelle Pfeiffer.
Original Job: Cook on a charter boat for a year, to pay for college
Marriages: Steve White (divorced, 1991), Warren Beatty, 1992
Children: Kathlyn, 1992; Benjamin, 1994; Isabel, 1997; Ella Corinne, 2000

TONY BENNETT

Real Name: Anthony Dominick Benedetto
Birthplace: Astoria, NY
Birthdate: 8/3/26
Occupation: Singer
Education: Manhattan's School of Industrial Art
Debut: (Album) *The Boulevard of Broken Dreams*, 1950
Signature: "I Left My Heart in San Francisco," 1962
Facts: Marched with Martin Luther King Jr. in Selma in 1965 at the urging of Harry Belafonte.

Used the name Joe Bari until Bob Hope introduced him as Tony Bennett in 1949.

Served two years as an infantryman in Europe during World War II.

An avid painter, his works have been exhibited in galleries around the country.

Had released 98 albums as of 1999.

Original Job: Singing waiter
Marriages: Patricia Beech, 1952

(divorced, 1971); Sandra Grant, 1971 (divorced, 1984)
Children: D'andrea (Danny), 1954; Daegal, 1955 (with Patricia Beech). Joanna, 1970; Antonia, 1974
Major Awards: Grammy, Best Pop Vocal—Male, "I Left My Heart in San Francisco," 1962; Grammy, Record of the Year, "I Left My Heart in San Francisco," 1962; Grammy, Album of the Year, *MTV Unplugged*, 1994; Grammy, Best Traditional Pop Vocal Performance, *MTV Unplugged*, 1994; Grammy, Best Traditional Pop Vocal Performance, *Tony Bennett on Holiday*, 1997; Grammy, Best Traditional Pop Vocal Performance, *Bennett Sings Ellington—Hot & Cool*, 1999

CANDICE BERGEN

Birthplace: Beverly Hills, CA
Birthdate: 5/9/46
Occupation: Actor, photojournalist
Education: University of Pennsylvania
Debut: (Film) *The Group*, 1966
Signature: *Murphy Brown*
Facts: Her father's puppet, Charlie McCarthy, had a bigger bedroom and more clothes than she did as a child.

As a photojournalist, was published in *Life* and *Playboy*.

Wrote a play, *The Freezer,* which is included in *Best Short Plays of 1968.*

Original Job: Model
Marriage: Louis Malle, 1981 (deceased, 1995); Marshall Rose, 2000
Child: Chloe, 1985
Famous Relative: Edgar Bergen, ventriloquist, father
Major Awards: Emmy, Best Actress in a Comedy Series, *Murphy Brown*, 1989, 1990, 1992, 1993, 1995

HALLE BERRY

Birthplace: Cleveland, OH
Birthdate: 8/14/66
Occupation: Actor
Education: Cuyahoga Community College

Debut: (TV) *Living Dolls,* 1989
Signature: *Boomerang,* 1992
Facts: Elected prom queen her senior year in high school, she was accused of stuffing the ballot box. Was forced to share the title with a "white, blond, blue-eyed, all-American girl."

Raised by her white mother after her black father left when she was four years old.

Lost 80 percent of the hearing in her left ear from an injury sustained from a physically abusive lover. (She rarely wears her hearing aid.)

Learned she was a diabetic when she collapsed in a coma while filming the TV series *Living Dolls.*

She was first runner-up in the 1986 Miss USA pageant.

Played a crackhead in Spike Lee's *Jungle Fever* (1991) and did not bathe for days to prepare for the role.
Infamy: Sued by a Chicago dentist (and former boyfriend) who claims she never repaid the $80,000 she borrowed from him. Refused to settle and, spending $50,000 defending herself, won in court.

In 2000 was indicted on charges of leaving the scene of an accident, when she struck another motorist with her car after running through a red light. After pleading no contest to charges, she was sentenced to three years probation, fined $13,500 and ordered to serve 200 hours of community service. The victim, Hetal Raythatha, also filed a civil lawsuit for "gross negligence."
Original Job: Model
Marriage: David Justice (divorced, 1996); Eric Benet (engaged, 1999) R&B singer

JESSICA BIEL

Birthplace: Ely, MN
Birthdate: 3/3/82
Occupation: Actor, model
Education: Young Actors Space, Los Angeles
Debut: (TV) *7th Heaven,* 1996; (Film) *Ulee's Gold,* 1997
Signature: *7th Heaven*

Facts: She credits her complexion to her Choctaw blood. She is German, French, English, and American Indian.

Was a teen model for two years, making her first TV commercial for Pringles potato chips.

Enjoys mountain biking, snowboarding, gymnastics, soccer and basketball.
Infamy: Posed topless in 2000 for *Gear* magazine, attempting to change her wholesome image. *7th Heaven* producer Aaron Spelling filed a $100 million lawsuit against the magazine, claiming that the magazine had defamed him by alleging that he had prevented Biel from securing film work.
Quote: "Sex is overrated. People make such a big deal out of it."

JULIETTE BINOCHE

Birthplace: Paris, France
Birthdate: 3/9/64
Occupation: Actor
Education: Attended Paris's National Conservatory of Dramatic Arts
Debut: (Film) *La Vie de famille,* 1984
Signature: *The English Patient,* 1996
Facts: A big star in France, she is known simply as "la Binoche."

Was replaced in the title role of *Lucie Aubrac* while filming was already underway; Binoche felt some of her lines were out of character and wanted to rewrite them.

Her lucrative Lancôme deal requires only 10 working days a year.

Her parents divorced when she was four; grew up shuttling between each parent and a Catholic boarding school.
Relationship: Olivier Martinez
Child: Raphael, 1993 (with Andre Halle)
Major Awards: Cesar (France's Oscar), Best Actress, *Blue,* 1994; Oscar, Best Supporting Actress, *The English Patient,* 1996

CATE BLANCHETT

Birthplace: Melbourne, Australia
Birthdate: 5/14/69
Occupation: Actor
Education: Attended Melbourne University
Debut: (TV) *Police Rescue,* 1994; (Film) *Paradise Road,* 1997; (Stage) *Plenty,* 1999
Signature: *Elizabeth,* 1998
Facts: Her father died of a heart attack when she was 10 years old.

Dropped out of college after two years to attend drama school in Sydney.

After leaving England due to an improper visa, she found a job as an extra in a boxing movie filmed in Egypt.

She bites her nails.

Director Shekhar Kapur decided that he wanted Cate for the lead role in *Elizabeth* based on the trailer for 1997's *Oscar and Lucinda.*
Marriage: Andrew Upton, 1997
Quote: "Growing up in Australia, I always bemoaned the fact that I wasn't a bronzed surfer chick."

BILLY BLANKS

Birthplace: Erie, Pennsylvania
Birthdate: 9/1/55
Occupation: Fitness expert, actor
Debut: (Film) *Bloodfist,* 1989
Signature: Tae-Bo fitness program
Facts: Grew up with 14 brothers and sisters.

Inspired by Bruce Lee as Kato on TV's *The Green Hornet,* he took karate lessons and ultimately became an international karate champion.

Has trained Paula Abdul, Brooke Shields, Shaquille O'Neal, Ashley Judd, and Carmen Electra, among others.

Has been diagnosed with dyslexia.

He developed Tae-Bo, which combines aerobics, jazz, dance, karate, and boxing, to introduce women to martial arts.

Tae-Bo is an acronym that stands for *T*otal *A*wareness, *E*xcellence, *B*ody *O*bedience.

415

Billy Blanks World Training Center in Sherman Oaks, Calif., is the only place where the patented and copy-righted Tae-Bo is taught.

Was paid $1.5 million for his book.

By early 1999, his workout video had grossed $75 million.

Original Job: Garbage man
Marriage: Gayle Godfrey
Children: Shellie (stepdaughter); Billy Jr., 1976
Quote: "If you want to sweat, go sit in a whirlpool. I want you to get some power, I want you to feel like you can overcome anything."

MARY J. BLIGE

Birthplace: Bronx, NY
Birthdate: 1/11/71
Occupation: Singer, songwriter
Education: High school dropout
Debut: (Album) *What's the 411?*, 1992
Signature: "I'm Goin' Down"
Facts: Her father left the family when she was 4, leaving her mother to raise Blige and three siblings in a Yonkers, N.Y., housing project.

While hanging out with buddies at a suburban New York mall, made a karaoke-style recording of an Anita Baker song. That tape found its way to Uptown Records' CEO, who signed her to his label.

This Queen of Hip-Hop Soul has been dubbed the Aretha Franklin of Generation X.
Infamy: Developed a reputation for having an "attitude problem" after being sullen, withdrawn, and even nasty during interviews.

Sued for $1 million by her ex-managers for breach of contract, who claimed Blige was a "selfish artist" who forgot the people who worked to make her a success.
Relationship: Jodeci lead singer K-Ci (engaged)
Major Award: Grammy, Best Rap Performance by a Duo or Group, "I'll Be There for You/You're All I Need to Get By" 1995

ANDREA BOCELLI

Birthplace: Lajatico, Italy
Birthdate: 9/22/58
Occupation: Opera singer
Education: University of Pisa
Debut: (U.S.) Kennedy Center, Spring Gala, 1998
Signature: "Con te partiro," ("Time to Say Goodbye") 1995
Facts: Took piano, saxophone, and flute lessons in his youth.

Born with visually debilitating glaucoma, he was left fully blind by a brain hemorrhage at age 12 after hitting his head playing soccer.

His parents own a farm with a small vineyard from which his father still produces Chianti Bocelli.

Obtained law degree while singing professionally in piano bars; he then studied opera.

Big break came in 1992 when he recorded "Miserere" with Italian rock star Zucchero Fornaciari.

In December 1997, PBS aired an *In the Spotlight* special of "Andrea Bocelli: Romanza in Concert." He reached a huge pop audience with this concert of opera renditions in Pisa.

Loves horseback riding and skiing.

With over 20 million albums sold worldwide by early 1999, he ranks as one of the bestselling classical recording artists of all time.
Original Job: Lawyer, piano bar entertainer
Marriage: Enrica Cenzatti, 1992
Children: Amos, Matteo, 1997
Quote: "I don't feel I'm really credible enough yet as an opera singer. I still have to suffer a little while longer."

STEVEN BOCHCO

Birthplace: New York, NY
Birthdate: 12/16/43
Occupation: Producer, screenwriter
Education: Carnegie Institute of Technology
Debut: (TV) *A Fade to Black*, 1967
Signature: *NYPD Blue*

Facts: *Hill Street Blues* won 26 Emmys.

His father, Rudolph Bochco, was a child prodigy violinist who later played with orchestras in Broadway shows and with leading artists at Carnegie Hall.

Wrote material for *Ironside* and was the story editor for *Columbo*.

Turned down the presidency of CBS Entertainment in 1987.
Original Job: Assistant to the head of the story department at Universal Studios
Marriage: One prior marriage, divorced, 1966; Barbara Bosson, 1969 (divorced, 1998); Dayna Flanagan, 2000
Children: Melissa, 1970; Jesse, 1975 (with Barbara Bosson)
Famous Relative: Alan Rachins, actor, former brother-in-law
Major Awards: Emmy, Outstanding Drama Series, *Hill Street Blues*, 1981, 1982, 1983, 1984; Emmy, Outstanding Drama Series, *L.A. Law*, 1987, 1989, 1990, 1991

MICHAEL BOLTON

Real Name: Michael Bolotin
Birthplace: New Haven, CT
Birthdate: 2/26/53
Occupation: Singer, songwriter
Education: High school dropout
Debut: (EP) *Blackjack* (with Black-jack), 1979; (Album) *Michael Bolton* (solo), 1983
Facts: Wrote ballads and love songs for other artists, including Laura Branigan, Cher, The Pointer Sisters, and Barbra Streisand.

After the breakup of his band, Blackjack, he began recording solo in 1983.

In the mid '80s, he was a regular opening act for metal acts such as Ozzy Osbourne and Krokus.

A research library in the New York Medical College was dedicated to him in 1993 for his work as honorary chairman of This Close for Cancer Research.
Infamy: After a two-week trial in

1994, a jury ruled that Bolton's "Love Is a Wonderful Thing" is remarkably similar to the Isley Brothers song "Love Is a Wonderful Thing." In 2000, a federal appeals court upheld the $7 million ruling against him and rejected his request for a new trial. Bolton attempted to buy the Isley Brothers' publishing rights from a bankruptcy court in 2000, but he was passed over in favor of another bidder.

Marriage: Maureen McGuire, 1975 (divorced, 1991); Ashley Judd (relationship)

Children: Isa, 1975; Holly, 1977; Taryn, 1979; (with Maureen McGuire).

Major Awards: Grammy, Best Pop Vocal—Male, "How Am I Supposed to Live Without You," 1989; Grammy, Best Pop Vocal—Male, "When a Man Loves a Woman," 1991

HELENA BONHAM CARTER

Birthplace: London, England
Birthdate: 5/26/66
Occupation: Actor
Education: Attended Westminster School
Debut: (TV) *A Pattern of Roses,* 1982; (Film) *Lady Jane,* 1985
Facts: Lived with her parents until she was 30, helping care for her paralyzed father.

As a child, she wanted to be a spy because she loved *Charlie's Angels.*

At age 13, she entered a national writing contest and used the money that she won to pay for her entry into the actors' directory *Spotlight.*

Has made four films based on E. M. Forster novels *(A Room with a View; Maurice; Where Angels Fear to Tread; Howard's End).*

Famous Relatives: Herbert Henry Asquith, Britain's prime minister, 1908–1916, great-grandfather; Anthony "Puffin" Asquith, director, screenwriter, great-uncle; Lady Violet Bonham Carter, a.k.a. Baroness Asquith, grandmother
Quote: "Period movies are my

destiny. I should get a few ribs taken out, because I'll be in a corset for the rest of my life."

JON BON JOVI

Real Name: John Bongiovi
Birthplace: Sayreville, NJ
Birthdate: 3/2/62
Occupation: Singer, songwriter
Education: High school
Debut: (Album) *Bon Jovi,* 1984
Signature: Bon Jovi
Facts: Polygram executives gave the band a contract with the following conditions: John Bongiovi would become Jon Bon Jovi and only he would be given a contract. The other four members of the band would become Jon Bon Jovi's employees.

His first solo album, *Blaze of Glory* (1990), was "written for and inspired by" the film *Young Guns II,* in which he had a cameo role.

Title of Bon Jovi's album, *7800° Fahrenheit,* refers to the temperature of an exploding volcano.

Infamy: Had a legal dispute with cousin Tony Bongiovi, who owned the Record Plant, a New York City recording studio, over the extent to which Tony had aided his cousin's career. In 1984, Tony brought a lawsuit against Bon Jovi, the outcome of which gave him a producer's credit, a fee, royalties from Bon Jovi's first album, a cash award, and a one percent royalty from the group's next two albums.
Original Job: Floor sweeper at the Record Plant
Marriage: Dorothea Hurley, 1989
Children: Stephanie Rose, 1993; Jesse James Louis, 1995

BONO

Real Name: Paul Hewson
Birthplace: Dublin, Ireland
Birthdate: 5/10/60
Occupation: Singer, songwriter
Education: High school
Debut: (EP) *U2:3* (with U2), 1979
Signature: U2

Facts: Got his nickname from a billboard advertising Bono Vox, a hearing aid retailer.

In November 1987, U2 opened for themselves at the L.A. Coliseum as the country-rock group The Dalton Brothers.

His efforts to reduce the debt owed by Third World nations to the major industrial powers has resulted in the forgiving of tens of billions of dollars in loans.

Infamy: Was the first winner in Grammy history to say "f--k"during its live telecast (1994).
Marriage: Ali Hewson, 1982
Children: Jordan, 1989; Eve, c. 1993; Elijah Bob, 1999
Major Awards: Grammy, Album of the Year, *The Joshua Tree,* 1987; Grammy, Best Rock Performance—Duo or Group, *The Joshua Tree,* 1987; Grammy, Best Video—Long Form, *Where the Streets Have No Name,* 1988; Grammy, Best Rock Performance—Duo or Group, "Desire," 1988; Grammy, Best Rock Performance—Duo or Group, *Achtung Baby,* 1992; Grammy, Best Alternative Performance, *Zooropa,* 1993

DAVID BOREANAZ

Birthplace: Buffalo, NY
Birthdate: 5/16/71
Occupation: Actor
Education: Ithaca College
Debut: (TV) *Married…With Children,* 1993
Signature: *Angel*
Facts: He majored in film moved to L.A. after graduation to find work behind the cameras.

College classmates called him Q-Tip Head because of his unruly hair.

Formed MoBo Films in 1999 with actor Jarrod Moses.

Was chased out of the Creative Arts Agency in 1993 for dropping by unannounced with copies of his résumé
Original Job: Props department assistant, house painter, parking attendant

Marriage: Ingrid Quinn, screen-writer, 1997 (divorced, 1999)
Quote: "I'm a petit prince, as my sister would say."

KENNETH BRANAGH

Birthplace: Belfast, Northern Ireland
Birthdate: 12/10/60
Occupation: Actor, director
Education: Royal Academy of Dramatic Arts
Debut: (Stage) *Another Country,* 1982
Signature: *Henry V,* 1989
Facts: Grew up in poverty in the shadow of a tobacco factory in Belfast.

Co-founded England's Renaissance Theater Company.

To prepare for *Henry V,* Branagh received an audience with Prince Charles to gain insight on being heir to the throne.
Marriage: Emma Thompson (divorced, 1996)

MARLON BRANDO

Birthplace: Omaha, NE
Birthdate: 4/3/24
Occupation: Actor
Education: Expelled from Shattuck Military Academy, attended New School for Social Research
Debut: (Stage) *I Remember Mama,* 1944; (Film) *The Men,* 1950
Signature: *The Godfather,* 1972
Fact: Exiled himself to his private island, Tetiaroa, near Tahiti, which he bought after filming *Mutiny on the Bounty* there in 1960.

Wrote an autobiography, *Brando: Songs My Mother Taught Me* (1994) to raise money for son Christian's legal fees, but the book was panned for omitting his many wives and lovers, the latter including Shelley Winters and Rita Moreno.
Infamy: Son Christian killed daughter Cheyenne's boyfriend and served time for manslaughter (1990). Distraught, Cheyenne took her own life in 1995.

Original Job: Tile fitter, elevator operator
Marriages: Anna Kashfi, 1957 (divorced, 1959); Movita Castenada, 1960 (annulled); Tarita Teripia, 1966 (divorced)
Children: Christian Devi, 1958 (with Anna Kashfi). Sergio, 1960 (a.k.a. Miko; with Movita Castenada). Teihotu Teripaia, 1963. Maya Gabriella Cui, 1963 (with Marie Cui). Tarita Cheyenne, 1970 (deceased, 1995), (with Tarita Teriipaia). Rebecca, 1966; Pietra Barrett, 1970 (adopted; birth father as James Clavell). Ninna Priscilla, 1989 (with Cristina Ruiz).
Major Awards: Oscar, Best Actor, *On the Waterfront,* 1955, Oscar, Best Actor, *The Godfather,* 1972; Emmy, Best Supporting Actor in a Limited Series, *Roots,* 1979

BRANDY

Real Name: Brandy Norwood
Birthplace: McComb, MS
Birthdate: 2/11/79
Occupation: Singer, actor
Education: Pepperdine University
Debut: (Album) *Brandy,* 1994
Signature: "The Boy is Mine," 1998
Facts: From ages 12 to 14, sang backup for the R&B group Immature.

Brandy's famous braids are styled every three weeks, with fake hair extensions added for thickness, in an eight-hour process.

Before starring in UPN's *Moesha,* played the daughter in the short-lived 1993 TV comedy, *Thea.*

Her dad was choir director at their church, so as a child Brandy was always showcased as a featured singer.

Wasn't allowed to date until she was 16, but her mother/manager did provide her with a $500/week allowance.

Enjoys jelly-and-fried-egg sandwiches.
Infamy: Sued by a management and production company for $5 million

for allegedly breaking an oral contract to represent her.
Relationship: Wanya Morris
Famous Relative: Ray-J, actor, singer, brother
Major Award: Grammy, R&B Performance—Duo or Group with vocal, "The Boy Is Mine" (with Monica), 1998.

BENJAMIN BRATT

Birthplace: San Francisco, CA
Birthdate: 12/16/63
Occupation: Actor
Education: University of California, Santa Barbara
Debut: (Stage) Utah Shakespeare Festival, 1987; (TV) *Knightwatch,* 1988; (Film) *Bright Angel,* 1990
Signature: *Law & Order*
Facts: He is of Peruvian and German-English lineage.

At age 5, he participated in a takeover of Alcatraz Island with his Peruvian mother and Native American activists. He has remained active on behalf of Native Americans.

Was nicknamed "Scarecrow" in high school for being too thin.

Graduated with honors from college but left the masters program at American Conservatory Theater to begin his career.
Relationship: Julia Roberts
Famous Relative: George Bratt, Broadway actor, grandfather

TONI BRAXTON

Birthplace: Severn, MD
Birthdate: 10/7/66
Occupation: Singer
Education: Bowie State University
Signature: "Breathe Again," 1994
Fact: Learned to sing in a church choir. Her three sisters sing backup vocals on her albums. She and her sisters were only allowed to listen to gospel music, but she would "sneak into empty rooms to watch *Soul Train.*"

Declared bankruptcy in 1998.

Some observers saw the move as a tactic to dissolve her recording contract, from which she had sought legal release on grounds of a low royalty rate.

Relationship: Keri Lewis, musician
Major Awards: Grammy, Best New Artist, 1993; Grammy, Best R&B Vocal—Female, "Another Sad Love Song," 1993; Grammy, Best R&B Vocal—Female, "Breathe Again," 1994; Grammy, Best Pop Vocal—Female, "Un-break My Heart," 1996; Grammy, Best R&B Vocal—Female, "You're Makin' Me High," 1996

AMY BRENNEMAN

Birthplace: New London, CT
Birthdate: 6/22/64
Occupation: Actor, producer
Education: Harvard University, 1987
Debut: (TV) *Middle Ages*, 1992; (Film) *Bye, Bye, Love*, 1995
Signature: *Judging Amy*
Facts: Graduated high school a year early and worked in France as an au pair.

Founded the Cornerstone Theater Company and traveled with the group for five years. She is currently its chairman.

In 1993, she landed the role of Officer Janice Licalsi in *NYPD Blue* and is best remembered for her nude scene with David Caruso.

Her *Judging Amy* role is based partly on her mother Frederica, now a Connecticut State Supreme Court judge.

Marriage: Bradley Silberling, director, 1995
Quote: "People always talk about how they don't like shooting love scenes. I really don't mind it. I don't know what that says about me."

JEFF BRIDGES

Birthplace: Los Angeles, CA
Birthdate: 12/4/49
Occupation: Actor
Education: High school, Herbert Berghof Studio
Debut: (Film) *The Company She Keeps*, 1950; (TV) *Sea Hunt*, 1957
Signature: *The Fabulous Baker Boys*, 1989
Facts: Joined the Coast Guard Reserves in 1968 to avoid the draft.

At age 16, he wrote a song included on the soundtrack of the 1969 film *John and Mary*, which starred Dustin Hoffman and Mia Farrow, and sold two compositions to Quincy Jones. To date, he has written over 200 songs.

Has exhibited his paintings and photographs in art galleries.
Infamy: In high school, developed a dependency on marijuana. He joined DAWN (Developing Adolescents Without Narcotics) and kicked the habit.
Marriage: Susan Gaston, 1977
Children: Isabelle, 1982; Jessica, 1984; Hayley, 1988
Famous Relatives: Lloyd Bridges, actor, father; Beau Bridges, actor, brother

CHRISTIE BRINKLEY

Birthplace: Malibu, CA
Birthdate: 2/2/54
Occupation: Supermodel
Education: UCLA
Debut: (Film) *National Lampoon's Vacation*, 1983
Signature: Cover Girl Cosmetics model
Facts: An avid Francophile, Brinkley transferred from her local high school to the Lycée Français in Los Angeles.

She later dropped out of college and worked at odd jobs selling ice cream, clothes, and plants to earn money for a ticket to Paris.

Designed the cover for Billy Joel's *River of Dreams* album.

Married Taubman atop a ski mountain, a symbolic acknowledgment of the helicopter crash they both survived while heli-skiing in 1994.
Original Job: Painter
Marriages: Jean Francois Allaux (divorced); Billy Joel (divorced); Rick Taubman (divorced); Peter Cook, 1996
Children: Alexa Ray, 1985 (with Billy Joel). Jack Paris, 1995 (with Ricky Taubman). Sailor Lee, 1998
Famous Relative: David Brinkley, scriptwriter, producer, father

MATTHEW BRODERICK

Birthplace: New York, NY
Birthdate: 3/21/62
Occupation: Actor
Debut: (Stage) *Torch Song Trilogy*, 1982; (Film) *Max Dugan Returns*, 1983
Signature: *Ferris Bueller's Day Off*, 1986
Fact: Was heavily influenced by father James Broderick, who played the father in the TV series *Family* and died of cancer in 1982.
Infamy: While on vacation in Northern Ireland in 1987 with his then-girlfriend, actress Jennifer Grey, Broderick suffered a broken leg when the car he was driving collided with another automobile, killing its two occupants. Broderick was acquitted of one count of manslaughter and reckless driving.
Marriage: Sarah Jessica Parker, 1997
Famous Relative: James Broderick, character actor, father
Major Awards: Tony, Best Featured Actor (Dramatic), *Brighton Beach Memoirs*, 1983; Tony, Best Actor (Musical), *How To Succeed in Business Without Really Trying*, 1995

TOM BROKAW

Birthplace: Yankton, SD
Birthdate: 2/6/40
Occupation: Anchor, correspondent, managing editor
Education: University of South Dakota
Debut: (TV) KTIV, Sioux City, IA, 1960
Signature: *NBC Nightly News*
Facts: Served as president of high school student body. Also met future wife who became Miss South Dakota in high school.

Began with NBC as their White House correspondent in 1973.

Was the only network anchor present at the collapse of the Berlin Wall in 1989.
Marriage: Meredith, 1962
Children: Jennifer, 1966; Andrea, 1968; Sarah, 1970
Major Awards: 6 News and Documentary Emmys: 4 as anchor, 1 as interviewer, 1 as managing editor

GARTH BROOKS

Real Name: Troyal Garth Brooks
Birthplace: Tulsa, OK
Birthdate: 2/7/62
Occupation: Singer, songwriter
Education: Oklahoma State University
Debut: (Album) *Garth Brooks,* 1989
Signature: *Ropin' the Wind,* 1991
Facts: In 1990 at age 28, Garth became the youngest member of Nashville's Grand Ole Opry.

Brooks met his future wife while working as a bouncer. (He threw her out for fighting.)

In 1991, *Ropin' the Wind* became the first country album ever to reach No. 1 on the *Billboard* pop chart.

The video for "The Thunder Rolls," about a cheating husband shot by his battered wife after coming home drunk, was banned by Country Music Television and The Nashville Network. Thousands of shelters for battered women in America used the video in group counseling sessions.

Brooks' half sister is his bassist, his brother handles the books, and a

college roommate is one of his guitarists.

Refused the Artist of the Year title from the American Music Awards in 1996, later explaining "I just couldn't accept it, just out of the love of the fellow musicians. I think we're all one."

Took time off from music to try and play professional baseball. He joined the San Diego Padres in 1999 for spring training but did not make the team. Playing left field, Brooks went 1 for 22 at the plate.

In 2000, he joined the New York Mets for their spring training.

Wanted to buildhimself a Graceland-like museum on his 20-acre Blue Rose Estate in a Nashville suburb, but was shot down by his neighbors.
Original Job: Bouncer in a nightclub
Marriage: Sandy Mahl, 1986
Children: Taylor Mayne Pearl, 1992; August Anna, 1994; Allie Colleen, 1996
Famous Relative: Colleen Carroll, singer, mother
Major Awards: Grammy, Best Country Vocal—Male, *Ropin' the Wind,* 1991; Grammy, Best Country Vocal—Collaboration, "In Another's Eyes" (with Trisha Yearwood), 1997

JAMES L. BROOKS

Birthplace: North Bergen, NJ
Birthdate: 5/9/40
Occupation: Producer, director, actor, screenwriter
Education: New York University
Debut: (TV) *Room 222,* 1969; (Film) *Starting Over,* 1979
Signature: *The Mary Tyler Moore Show*
Facts: Founded Gracie Films, which produces *The Simpsons,* in 1984.

With fellow writer Allan Burns, created *The Mary Tyler Moore Show* in 1970.
Original Job: Copyboy for CBS News
Marriages: Marianne Catherine Morrissey (divorced), Holly Beth Holmberg, 1978 (separated, 2000)

Children: Amy Lorraine, 1971 (with Morrissey); Chloe, c. 1984; Cooper, c. 1986; Joseph, c. 1993 (with Holmberg)
Major Awards: Emmy, Best Writing in a Comedy Series, *The Mary Tyler Moore Show,* 1971, 1977; Emmy, Best Comedy Series, *The Mary Tyler Moore Show,* 1975, 1976, 1977; Emmy, Best Comedy Series, *Taxi,* 1979, 1980, 1981; Oscar, Best Director, *Terms of Endearment,* 1983; Oscar, Best Adapted Screenplay, *Terms of Endearment,* 1983; Emmy, Outstanding Variety, Music, or Comedy Program, *The Tracey Ullman Show,* 1989; Emmy, Outstanding Animated Program, *The Simpsons,* 1990, 1991

MEL BROOKS

Real Name: Melvin Kaminsky
Birthplace: Brooklyn, NY
Birthdate: 6/28/26
Occupation: Actor, writer, director, producer
Education: Boston College
Debut: (Stage) *Broadway Revue,* 1949; (TV) *Your Show of Shows,* 1950
Signature: *Blazing Saddles,* 1974
Facts: Fought in Battle of the Bulge during World War II.

Co-creator of the TV series *Get Smart.*
Original Job: Drummer
Marriages: Florence Baum, 1950 (divorced); Anne Bancroft, 1964
Children: Stephanie; 1951; Nicholas, 1952; Edward, 1953; (with Florence Baum). Maximillian, 1972
Major Awards: Emmy, Best Writing in a Variety or Music Program, *Howard Morris Special,* 1967; Oscar, Best Original Screenplay, *The Producers,* 1968; Emmy, Best Guest Actor in a Comedy Series, *Mad About You,* 1997; Grammy, Best Comedy Album, *The 2000 Year Old Man In The Year 2000* (with Carl Reiner), 1998

PIERCE BROSNAN

Birthplace: Navan, County Meath, Ireland
Birthdate: 5/16/52
Occupation: Actor
Debut: (Stage) *Wait Until Dark,* 1976; (Film) *The Mirror Crack'd,* 1980; (TV) *Remington Steele,* 1982
Signature: *Tomorrow Never Dies,* 1997
Facts: Wife, Cassandra (best known for playing Countess Lisl in *For Your Eyes Only,* 1981), introduced Brosnan to Albert Broccoli, producer of the 007 series. Brosnan almost replaced Roger Moore as James Bond, but couldn't get out of his contract with NBC's *Remington Steele.*

In 1995, he finally played Bond in *Goldeneye,* and is credited with helping to revive the then-ailing series.

Ran away with the circus as a fire eater in his teens.
Original Job: Commercial artist
Marriages: Cassandra Harris, 1977 (deceased, 1991); Keely Shaye-Smith (engaged, 2000).
Children: Charlotte, 1971 (step-daughter); Christopher, 1972 (stepson); Sean William, 1984; (with Cassandra Harris). Dylan Thomas, 1997
Quote: "I'd like to see him killed off. I want to have a death scene with Bond. Now that would be something."

MELANIE BROWN

Birthplace: Leeds, Yorkshire, England
Birthdate: 5/29/75
Occupation: Singer
Debut: (Album) *Spice,* 1996; (Movie) *Spice World,* 1997 (American release, 1998)
Signature: "Wannabe," (1996) / Scary Spice
Facts: Tensions between Brown and Geri Halliwell were cited for Halliwell's departure from the group.

Her ex-husband was a dancer on a Spice Girls tour.

During downtime from her music career, has worked as a VJ for Pure Naughty on BBC2.

Her favorite movie star is Wesley Snipes.
Marriage: Jimmy Gulzar, 1998 (divorced, 2000)
Child: Phoenix Chi, 1999
Quote: "You can make life what you want it to be."

JOY BROWNE

Birthplace: New Orleans, LA
Birthdate: 10/24/50
Occupation: On-air psychologist
Education: Rice University; North-eastern University, Ph.D.
Facts: In 1982, she hit the Boston airwaves, and in 1984 moved to San Francisco where she was an on-air psychologist.

Author of *Dating for Dummies* (1998), *9 Fantasies That Will Ruin Your Life* (1998), *It's a Jungle Out There, Jane! Understanding the Male Animal* (1999)
Relationship: Divorced
Child: Daughter, 1977, marine biologist
Quote: "I want Oprah's warmth, Donahue's energy, Springer's excitement, Geraldo's IQ, Ricki Lake's exuberance, Sally's caring, and Montel's baldness."

KOBE BRYANT

Birthplace: Philadelphia, PA
Birthdate: 8/23/78
Occupation: Basketball player
Education: High school
Debut: (N.B.A.) Los Angeles Lakers, 1996
Facts: Was named for the Kobe steak house in suburban Philadelphia.

His family moved to Italy for eight years when he was six; there his father played pro ball.

In high school, shattered all of Wilt Chamberlain's Pennsylvania school scoring records by more than 500 points.

Took *Moesha*'s Brandy to his prom.

Has written "spiritual rap" with the rap group Cheizaw. His hip-hop name is "Kobe One Kenobe the Eighth."
Marriage: Vanessa Laine (engaged, 2000)
Famous Relative: Joe "Jelly Bean" Bryant, basketball player, father

JIMMY BUFFETT

Birthplace: Pascagoula, MS
Birthdate: 12/25/46
Occupation: Singer, songwriter
Education: University of Southern Mississippi
Debut: (Album) *Down to Earth,* 1970
Signature: "Margaritaville"
Facts: Has chaired Florida's Save the Manatee Club since its inception in 1981. In 1992, sued the parent Florida Audubon Society for independent control of the club, arguing that the society was "too cozy" with many of the businesses he felt were polluters.

Wrote a children's book, *The Jolly Man,* with his eight-year-old daughter in 1987. Also wrote two novels, including *Tales from Margaritaville* (1989) and a bestselling memoir, *A Pirate Looks at Fifty.* Received a $3-million advance for a collection of tropical short stories.

In 1991, four Cuban exiles seeking political asylum swam to Buffett's Florida house. He handed them over to the authorities after offering them refreshments.

Also owns the Margaritaville Cafe franchise.
Original Job: Reviewer for *Billboard* magazine and freelance writer for *Inside Sports* and *Outside* magazines
Marriage: Jane Slagsvol, 1977
Children: Savannah Jane, 1979; Sarah, 1992; Cameron Marley (adopted).

SANDRA BULLOCK

Birthplace: Arlington, VA
Birthdate: 7/26/64
Occupation: Actor
Education: East Carolina University, Neighborhood Playhouse with Sanford Meisner
Debut: (TV) *Bionic Showdown: The Six Million Dollar Man and the Bionic Woman*, 1989; (Film) *Hangmen*, 1987 [see page 102 for a complete filmography]
Signature: *Speed*, 1994
Facts: Her mother was a European opera singer, so as a child Bullock shuttled between Austria, Germany, and the U.S.

Was a cheerleader in high school.

Played lead actress in the short-lived TV series *Working Girl*.

Her role in *While You Were Sleeping* was originally offered to Demi Moore, whose salary demands were out of reach.

Formerly involved in a relationship with Matthew McConaughey.

Spent time at a Rehabilitation Clinic in 2000 to prepare for her role in *28 Days*.
Original Job: Waitress
Famous Relative: Helga Bullock, mother, opera singer

EMMA BUNTON

Birthplace: North Finchley, North London, England
Birthdate: 1/21/76
Occupation: Singer
Debut: (Album) *Spice*, 1996; (Movie) *Spice World*, 1997 (American release, 1998)
Signature: "Wannabe," (1996) / Baby Spice
Facts: Was not an original member of the band that became Spice Girls; one of the singers chosen left the group early, and Ms. Bunton stepped in.

Prince William designated her his favorite Spice.

Describes herself as part

"mummy's girl" and part "hot, sexy bitch."

Writes poetry.

Her debut solo single, released in England, was a remake of Edie Brickell's "What I Am."
Infamy: When the band fired their manager in 1997, rumors put the blame on his "nasty affair" with Bunton.

ED BURNS

Birthplace: Valley Stream, NY
Birthdate: 1/29/68
Occupation: Director, actor, writer
Education: Attended Hunter College
Debut: (Film) *The Brothers McMullen*, 1995
Signature: *The Brothers McMullen*
Facts: His first seven screenplays were rejected by agents and producers.

The Brothers McMullen was shot in eight months for around $20,000 (primarily a loan from dad), with Burns's parents' home the principal set.

Won the Catholic Daughters of America Poetry Award in sixth grade for a poem "about Jesus and a tree."

Bought JFK Jr.'s Tribeca loft for an estimated $2 million plus.

Formerly involved in a relationship with Heather Graham.
Original Job: Production assistant, *Entertainment Tonight*
Quote: "I try not to read reviews unless they're absolutely glowing. I don't read mixed or negative at all, because life's too short."

STEVE BUSCEMI

Birthplace: Brooklyn, NY
Birthdate: 12/13/57
Occupation: Actor, director
Education: Attended Nassau Community College and Lee Strasberg Institute
Debut: (Film) *The Way It Is, or Eurydice in the Avenues*, 1984; (TV) *Miami Vice*, 1988
Signature: *Fargo*, 1996

Facts: Was hit by a bus when he was a child and received a settlement that he later used to finance acting lessons.

His wife, a performance artist-choreographer-filmmaker, has cast him in several of her performances.

Directed and starred in *Trees Lounge* in 1996, a film based on what his life on Long Island would have been be like if he'd never moved to Manhattan to pursue acting. Also directed TV commercials for Nike, and a 1998 episode of *Homicide*, and a series of episodes of HBO's *Oz* for the 1999–2000 season.
Infamy: When he was 16, he was arrested for trespassing in a Burger King parking lot.

He used to squeeze through the back window of a bar to steal crates of beer for his friends.
Original Jobs: Ice cream truck driver, comedian, firefighter
Marriage: Jo Andres
Child: Lucian, 1991
Famous Relatives: Michael Buscemi, actor, brother
Quote: "I guess I sometimes get frustrated about having played too many seedy, ratty guys. But, I'm working."

GABRIEL BYRNE

Birthplace: Dublin, Ireland
Birthdate: 5/12/50
Occupation: Actor, producer, director, screenwriter
Education: University College, Dublin
Debut: (TV) *The Riordans*, 1981; (Film) *Excalibur*, 1981; (Book) *Pictures in My Head*
Signature: *Miller's Crossing*, 1990
Facts: When he was 8, he played the accordion in a local pub with his uncle.

Began studying at an English seminary at age 12 and was expelled at age 16 after being caught smoking in a graveyard.

Founded the Irish-based production company Mirabilis Films in 1990.

Original Job: author, archaeologist, teacher, messenger, toy factory worker, plumber's assistant, apprentice chef
Marriage: Ellen Barkin, 1988 (divorced, 1999)
Children: Jack, 1989; Romey Marion, 1992

NICOLAS CAGE

Real Name: Nicholas Coppola
Birthplace: Long Beach, CA
Birthdate: 1/7/64
Occupation: Actor
Education: High school dropout
Debut: (TV) *The Best of Times*, 1980; (Film) *Valley Girl*, 1983 [see page 102 for a complete filmography]
Signature: *Con Air*, 1997
Facts: Was expelled from elementary school.

Changed his last name to have an identity independent of his famous uncle. He assumed the name Cage in admiration of the avant-garde composer John Cage and comic-book character Luke Cage.

His method-acting techniques have involved having wisdom teeth removed without Novocaine for his role as a wounded war veteran in *Birdy,* slashing his arm with a knife in *Racing with the Moon,* and consuming a live cockroach for *Vampire's Kiss.*

Eight years before marrying Patricia Arquette, Cage proposed to her by volunteering to go on "a quest" for her. When he came up with a few of her chosen items—including J. D. Salinger's signature and a (spray-painted) black orchid—Arquette called off the deal to wed.

Then, according to court papers from his 2000 divorce filing, he and his wife separated only 9 months after their marriage. But in April 2000, they got back together again and Cage asked the court to dismiss the case.
Infamy: In 1999 was criticized by friend Sean Penn, who said Cage "is no longer an actor . . . now he's more

like a . . . performer." Nick Nolte and Stephen Baldwin added their own complaints about Cage's recent oeuvre.
Marriage: Kirsten Zang (engaged, never married); Patricia Arquette, 1995 (separated, 1996; reconciled, 2000)
Child: Weston, 1990 (by ex-girlfriend Kristina Fulton)
Famous Relatives: Francis Ford Coppola, director, uncle; Talia Shire, actor, aunt
Major Award: Oscar, Best Actor, *Leaving Las Vegas*, 1995.
Quote: "I've seen a lot of actors get high on their own importance with the Academy Award, and they snob themselves right out of the industry."

MICHAEL CAINE

Name: Maurice Joseph Micklewhite Jr.
Birthplace: Bermondsey, England
Birthdate: 3/14/33
Occupation: Actor, producer
Debut: (Film) *A Hill in Korea*, 1956; (U.S. Film) *Gambit*, 1966
Signature: *The Cider House Rules*, 1999
Facts: When he was a child, his mother pasted his ears to his head to prevent them from sticking out.

In his 1992 autobiography, Caine revealed that his mother concealed another son in a mental institution for forty years.

In 1951, he was drafted for National Service and spent two years in West Berlin and in combat in Korea.

His original stage name was Michael Scott, but when joining Actors Equity that name was taken. Seeing a marquee announcing *The Caine Mutiny*, he took Caine as his surname.

Saw his wife Shakira for the first time in a coffee commercial and called her for 12 days before she agreed to go out with him. She was Miss Guyana 1967.

In 1976, opened Langen's Brasserie, a London restaurant. He

now owns six restaurants worldwide.

Knighted by Queen Elizabeth II in 2000.

He is an avid gardener.
Original Job: Production office assistant, cement mixer, driller
Marriages: Patricia Haines, 1955 (divorced, 1957); Shakira Baksh, 1973
Children: Dominique, 1956 (with Patricia Haines); Natasha, 1973
Major Awards: Oscar, Best Supporting Actor, *Hannah and Her Sisters*, 1986; Oscar, Best Supporting Actor, *Cider House Rules*, 1999
Quote: "I used to do films where I got the girl. Now I just get the part."

JAMES CAMERON

Birthplace: Kapuskasing, Ontario
Birthdate: 8/16/54
Occupation: Director, producer, screenwriter, editor
Education: Attended California State University
Debut: (Film) *Piranha II: The Spawning,* 1981
Signature: *Titanic*, 1997
Facts: After seeing *Star Wars,* the physics-majoring college dropout knew what he wanted for his career. Following frequent trips to the USC library, he acquired camera equipment, built a dolly track in his living room, and began making a film.

When the Italian producers who hired him to direct his first film prepared the final cut without him, he flew to Rome, broke into the editing room, and secretly recut the film himself.

Co-founded his own special effects company, Digital Domain.

Went so far over budget for *Terminator 2* that distributor Carolco had to file for bankruptcy. When he again vastly exceeded his budget for *Titanic,* he voluntarily relinquished all pay except for screenwriting. After it became the biggest box-office grosser of all time, studio executives reinstated his original contract terms.

Infamy: A perfectionist, is known to be verbally abusive to his crew during filming, which frequently runs months behind schedule and tens of millions over budget.

Original Jobs: Machinist, truck driver, school-bus driver

Marriages: first wife (divorced); Gale Anne Hurd (divorced); Kathryn Bigelow (divorced); Linda Hamilton, 1981 (filed for divorce, 1999); Suzy Amis, 2000

Child: Dalton Abbott, 1989 (stepson); Josephine Archer, 1993 (with Linda Hamilton)

Major Award: Oscar, Best Director, *Titanic,* 1997

BILLY CAMPBELL

Birthplace: Charlottesville, VA
Birthdate: 7/7/59
Education: American Academy of Art
Debut: *Family Ties,* 1982; (Film) *Call From Space,* 1989; (TV) (Broadway) *Hamlet,* 1993
Facts: Repeated senior year in high school.

An heir to the Champion spark plug fortune, he received an inheritance at age 18.

Originally wanted to be a comic-book artist.

Had a recurring role as a gay man on *Dynasty* in the 1984—85 season.

Stands 6'4".

Was once engaged to actor Jennifer Connelly, but they never married.

Still has a plus Pooh bear in his bedroom from when he was child.

Famous Relatives: David, brother, actor; John, brother, screenwriter

NAOMI CAMPBELL

Birthplace: London, England
Birthdate: 5/22/70
Occupation: Supermodel
Education: London School of Performing Arts
Debut: (Magazine) *British Elle,* 1985
Facts: In an effort to extend her

talents beyond her modeling career, she wrote a novel, *Swan,* starred in the movie *Miami Rhapsody,* and recorded an album for Epic Records.

Has been romantically involved with Mike Tyson, Robert De Niro, and U2's Adam Clayton.

Opened the now-defunct Fashion Cafe in 1995 in New York City with fellow supermodels Elle MacPherson and Claudia Schiffer.

Infamy: Staged an impromptu stripping episode during lesbian night at a Manhattan bar.

Pleaded guilty in 2000 to misdemeanor assault for roughing up former assistant Georgina Galanis in 1998, and was let off with a warning. In 1999, Campbell settled a related case with Galanis for undisclosed terms.

Relationship: Muhammad Al Habtoor

NEVE CAMPBELL

Birthplace: Guelph, Ontario
Birthdate: 10/3/73
Occupation: Actor
Education: National Ballet School of Canada
Debut: (Stage) Toronto production, *Phantom of the Opera,* 1988; (TV) *Catwalk,* 1992
Signature: *Party of Five*
Facts: Beat out 300 other actors for her *Po5* role.

At age 9, joined the prestigious National Ballet of Canada. Is also trained in jazz, modern, flamenco, and hip-hop.

Drama may be in her blood: her mother once owned a dinner theater and her father was a high school drama teacher. They divorced when she was a toddler.

Her first name is her mother's Dutch maiden name and means "snow."

Auditioned for *Baywatch.* The casting director turned her down, in part, because "she is pale."

Original Job: Ballerina, model

Marriage: Jeff Colt, 1995 (divorced, 1997); John Cusack (relationship)

Famous Relative: Christian, actor, brother

DREW CAREY

Birthplace: Cleveland, OH
Birthdate: 5/23/58
Occupation: Actor, comedian, writer
Education: Attended Kent State University
Debut: (TV) *Star Search,* 1987
Signature: *The Drew Carey Show*
Facts: Served in the marines for six years.

Got into comedy when a DJ friend paid him to write some comedy material; Carey decided to try out the jokes himself on stage.

Battled depression for years, stemming from his grief over his father's death from a brain tumor when Drew was 8. Attempted suicide on several occasions.

Raised $500,000 for the Ohio Library Foundation by appearing as a contestant on *Who Wants to Be a Millionaire.*

Original Job: Waiter at Las Vegas Denny's

MARIAH CAREY

Birthplace: New York, NY
Birthdate: 3/27/69
Occupation: Singer
Education: High school
Debut: (Album) *Mariah Carey,* 1990; (Film) *The Bachelor,* 1999
Signature: "Vision of Love," 1990
Facts: Her vocal range spans five octaves.

Her wedding cost half a million dollars. She watched tapes of the 1981 wedding of Charles and Diana in preparation.

Bought Marilyn Monroe's white lacquered baby grand piano (it originally belonged to Marilyn's mother) at auction for $662,500.

In 1999, her $20 million former mansion in Westchester County, NY was completely destroyed by fire in what an insurance official termed "the most expensive single-family-home fire ever."

Claims a rude remark by Joan Rivers at the 1999 Oscars inspired her to diet.

Is fascinated with Guam—she started a recent world tour there, and named one of her Jack Russell terriers after the island.
Infamy: Sued by her stepfather in 1992 for failing to share profits from her 1990 album.
Original Jobs: Waitress, hat checker, restaurant hostess
Marriage: Tommy Mottola, 1993 (divorced, 1998); Luis Miguel (relationship)
Major Awards: Grammy, Best Pop Vocal—Female, "Vision of Love," 1990; Grammy, Best New Artist, 1990

MARY CHAPIN CARPENTER

Birthplace: Princeton, NJ
Birthdate: 2/21/58
Occupation: Singer, songwriter, guitarist
Education: Brown University
Debut: (Album) *Hometown Girl*, 1988
Signature: "He Thinks He'll Keep Her"
Facts: Father, Chapin Carpenter, was a high-level *Life* magazine executive, so she spent her youth in Princeton, Tokyo, and Washington, DC.

Goes by the name Chapin, not Mary.

After college, considered music something to do for extra cash until she found her real career. Only after landing a nine-to-five job did she realize how much music meant to her, and began to focus on it.

Wrote Wynonna Judd's hit "Girls with Guitars" and co-wrote Cyndi Lauper's "Sally's Pigeon."
Infamy: Became an alcoholic after performing for years in bars.
Major Awards: Grammy, Best Country Vocal—Female, "Down at the Twist and Shout," 1991; Grammy, Best Country Vocal—Female, "I Feel

Lucky," 1992; Grammy, Best Country Vocal—Female, "Passionate Kisses," 1993; Grammy, Best Country Vocal—Female, "Shut Up and Kiss Me," 1994; Grammy, Best Country Album, *Stones in the Road*, 1994

JIM CARREY

Birthplace: Jacksons Point, Canada
Birthdate: 1/17/62
Occupation: Actor
Debut: (TV) *The Duck Factory*, 1984; (Film) *Finders Keepers,* 1984
Signature: *Ace Ventura: Pet Detective*, 1994 [see page 103 for a complete filmography]
Fact: When his accountant father was laid off, he quit high school to make money doing janitorial work.

His $20 million paycheck for *The Cable Guy* was the highest salary yet paid to a comedian.

A coalition of fire prevention groups demanded that his Fire Marshall Bill sketches on *In Living Color* be taken off the air because of the negative effect they were having on children.

Gave Zellwegger a $200,000 "friendship" ring in early 2000.
Marriages: Melissa Womer, 1987 (divorced, 1993); Lauren Holly, 1996 (divorced, 1997); Renee Zellweger (relationship)
Child: Jane, 1987 (with Melissa Womer).
Quote: "I'm the Tom Hanks of the Golden Globes."

JOHNNY CARSON

Birthplace: Corning, IA
Birthdate: 10/23/25
Occupation: Talk show host
Education: University of Nebraska
Debut: (TV) *Carson's Cellar,* 1951
Signature: *The Tonight Show*
Facts: Declined role to play lead in the series that became *The Dick Van Dyke Show.*

As a 12-year-old, performed at local parties as "The Great Carsoni."

His son Richard was killed when his car plunged off a road.

Third wife Joanna Holland received $20 million in cash and property in a 1983 divorce settlement.

Served with the U.S. Naval Reserve during World War II.

Suffered a heart attack and underwent quadruple-bypass surgery in 1999.
Original Job: Radio announcer, ventriloquist, magician
Marriages: Jody Wolcott, 1949 (divorced, 1963); Joanne Copeland, 1963 (divorced, 1972); Joanna Holland, 1972 (divorced, 1983); Alexis Maas, 1987
Children: Christopher, 1950; Richard, 1952 (deceased, 1991); Cory, 1953; (with Jody Wolcott).
Major Awards: Elected to the Emmy Hall of Fame in 1987; Kennedy Center honoree, 1993

NICK CARTER

Birthplace: Jamestown, NY
Birthdate: 1/28/80
Occupation: Singer
Debut: (Single) "We've Got It Goin' On," 1995; (Album) *Backstreet Boys,* 1995 (American version, 1997)
Signature: "Everybody (Backstreet's Back),"1997
Facts: One of his early idols was Steve Perry from Journey.

Turned down *Mickey Mouse Club* for Backstreet Boys.

The band is named after Orlando, Florida's Backstreet Market, a popular teen hangout.

The group's debut was a hit in 26 countries before *Backstreet Boys* was released in the U.S.

Collects Beanie Babies.

Bandmates consider his attention span the shortest.

With Stan "Spider-man" Lee, has created a comic featuring the band as superheroes.

Is a certified scuba diver.
Infamy: Band filed suit against former manager Lou Pearlman, claiming he had made $10 million from their labor while they had received $300,000.

Quote: "Each one of us is extremely talented. A lot of groups might utilize one or two of the group's voices for the lead vocals. We use every single one."

JOHNNY CASH

Real Name: J. R. Cash
Birthplace: Kingsland, AR
Birthdate: 2/26/32
Occupation: Singer, songwriter
Debut: (Song) "Hey Porter," 1955
Signature: "I Walk The Line," 1955
Facts: Cash is one-fourth Cherokee Indian.

He cannot read music.

Created 75 cuts for his 1994 album, produced by Rick Rubin (of Beastie Boys fame), which included songs written for him by Red Hot Chili Pepper Flea and Glenn Danzig.

Known as "the Man in Black," which is the title of his 1975 autobiography. Cash adopted this persona while working in a trio that only wore matching black outfits.

Wrote a novel, *Man in White,* in 1986.

He chose John as a first name when the military wouldn't accept initials.

Has Parkinson's disease.
Infamy: Cash was addicted to Dexadrine in the '60s.
Original Job: Door-to-door appliance salesman, factory worker
Marriages: Vivian Liberto, 1954 (divorced, 1967); June Carter, 1968
Children: Rosanne, 1955; Kathleen, 1956; Cindy, 1958; Tara, 1961; (with Vivian Liberto). John Carter, 1970; Rebecca Carlene (stepdaughter); Rozanna Lea (stepdaughter).
Major Awards: Grammy, Best Country Performance—Duo or Group, "Jackson" (with June Carter), 1967; Grammy, Best Country Vocal—Male, "Folsom Prison Blues," 1968; Grammy, Best Country Vocal—Male, "A Boy Named Sue," 1969; Grammy, Best Country Performance—Duo or Group, "If I Were a Carpenter" (with June Carter), 1970; elected to Country

Music Hall of Fame, 1980; Grammy, Best Spoken Word Recording, *Interviews from the Class of '55* (with others), 1986; Grammy, Legend Award, 1991; elected to the Rock and Roll Hall of Fame, 1992; Grammy, Best Contemporary Folk Album, *American Recordings,* 1994; Grammy, Best Country Album, *Unchained,* 1997

ROSANNE CASH

Birthplace: Memphis, TN
Birthdate: 5/24/55
Occupation: Singer, songwriter
Education: State Community College; Vanderbilt University and Lee Strasberg Theatre Institute
Debut: (Song) "Blue Moon with Heartache," 1979
Signature: "I Don't Know Why You Don't Want Me," 1985
Fact: Never intended to become a musician. Her original ambition was to become a serious fiction writer.
Infamy: In 1982, entered a drug rehabilitation program for a cocaine dependency she had developed in 1979.
Original Job: Worked in wardrobe department during her father's tour. One day the tour managers asked her to come on stage and sing harmony.
Marriage: Rodney J. Crowell, 1979 (divorced, 1992); John Leventhal
Children: Caitlin Rivers, c. 1980; Chelsea Jane, 1982; Carrie Kathleen, 1988 (with Rodney J. Crowell). Jakob William, 1999
Famous Relatives: Johnny Cash, country singer, father; June Carter Cash, country singer, stepmother; Carlene Carter, country singer, stepsister
Major Award: Grammy, Best Country Vocal—Female, "I Don't Know Why You Don't Want Me," 1985

KIM CATTRALL

Birthplace: Liverpool, England
Birthdate: 8/21/56
Occupation: Actor
Education: American Academy of

Dramatic Arts
Debut: (Film) *Rosebud,* 1975; (Stage) *The Rocky Horror Show,* 1975; (TV) *Good Against Evil,* 1977; (Broadway) *Wild Honey,* 1986
Signature: *Sex and the City*
Facts: Originally turned down her role in *Sex and the City* because she was afraid that it would interfere with her film career.
Marriages: Andreas Lyson, 1982 (divorced 1989); Daniel Benzali (engaged, never married); Mark Levinson, 1998.
Quote: "I love my curves and my softness and my breasts. I think they're beautiful, so I don't have a problem showing them."

JACKIE CHAN

Real Name: Chan Kwong-Sang
Birthplace: Hong Kong
Birthdate: 4/7/54
Occupation: Actor, writer, producer, director
Education: Chinese Opera Research Institute
Debut: *Big and Little Wong Tin Bar,* 1962; American debut, *The Big Brawl,* 1980
Signature: *Rumble in the Bronx,* 1995
Facts: Considered the biggest non-Hollywood movie star in the world; has been in more than 40 Asian action comedies. His fan club once topped 10,000 mostly young-girl members, one of whom killed herself when she read Chan was involved with someone.

His first attempts to break into Hollywood in the early '80s led to movie flops.

Nearly died making a 1986 film, when, leaping from a castle to a tree, he fell nearly 40 feet and broke his skull. He's also broken his jaw, shoulder, fingers and nose three times making movies.

To perfect his comic approach, studied old Hollywood Buster Keaton movies.

Impoverished parents left him at the Chinese Opera Institute at age 7 when they moved to Australia. During this militaristic-type training, he was beaten nearly every day.

Original Job: Stuntman
Marriage: Lin Feng-Chiao, 1983 (separated)
Child: Chan Cho-Ming, 1982
Quote: "I have a few rules that I tell my manager: No sex scenes! No make love! The kids who like me don't need to see it. It would gross them out."

J. C. CHASEZ

Real Name: Joshua Scott Chasez
Birthplace: Washington, DC
Birthdate: 8/8/76
Occupation: Singer
Debut: (Single) "I Want You Back," 1996; (Album) *NSYNC*, 1996 (American release, 1998)
Signature: *No Strings Attached*, 2000
Facts: As a boy, wanted to be a carpenter.

Claims he didn't start listening to music until he was "13 or 14."

After his years on TV's *Mickey Mouse Club,* waited tables to make ends meet.

His nickname is "Mr. Sleepy."

Is viewed as the most serious of the 'N Sync personalities.
Infamy: 'N Sync broke with their original record label and management over compensation. Suits and countersuits flew before a settlement was reached, allegedly favoring the band.
Quote: "I wouldn't go on TV grabbing this, that or the other and have my parents looking at that. That's just the way I was raised."

DON CHEADLE

Birthplace: Kansas City, MO
Birthdate: 11/29/64
Occupation: Actor
Education: California Institute of the Arts
Debut: (Film) *Moving Violations*, 1985; (TV) *Hill Street Blues*, 1987
Signature: *Devil in a Blue Dress*,

1995
Facts: Was offered scholarships to four arts colleges; two in art and two in theater.

Once acted in a production of *Hamlet* staged in a skid row parking lot.

Founded Elemental Prose, a company of artists aiming to pass down oral history through words and music.

An accidental meeting with director Carl Franklin in a doctor's office landed him an audition for *Devil in a Blue Dress*.

A trained jazz musician, he plays the saxophone and writes his own music. Learned to play the drums and the trumpet and to twirl a gun for his role as Sammy Davis Jr. in 1998's *The Rat Pack*.

Has been trying to develop a film version of *Groomed*, a play he wrote. He's also written the screenplay for an updated version of the 1973 film, *Cleopatra Jones*
Relationship: Bridgid Coulter, actor
Children: daughter, c. 1995; daughter, c. 1997
Famous relative: Colin Cheadle, brother, actor
Quote: "I'm not hot, I'm lukewarm. I'm making money and I'm saving my money and trying to be good in everything I do."

KENNY CHESNEY

Birthplace: Luttrell, TN
Birthdate: 3/26/68
Occupation: Country singer, songwriter
Education: East Tennessee State University
Debut: (Album) *In My Wildest Dreams*, 1994
Signature: "You Had Me from Hello," 2000
Facts: Majored in advertising and marketing, moved to Nashville.

Used to be a full-time songwriter and first hit the charts in country music in the early 1990s with "When I Close My Eyes."

His tour manager and concert sales director are childhood friends.
Infamy: A minor police altercation ensued after Chesney rode off on a policeman's horse in Erie County, NY while there for his concert tour. He had permission to sit in the saddle, but not to ride off. Tim McGraw went to his music friend's aid and tried to hold back the officers as they attempted to pull Chesney off the horse.
Relationship: Mandy Weals
Quote: "There's still tons of people, millions of people out there who don't know who I am."

CHER

Real Name: Cherilyn Sarkisian La Piere
Birthplace: El Centro, CA
Birthdate: 5/20/46
Occupation: Actor, singer
Education: High school dropout
Debut: (Film) *Wild on the Beach*, 1965; (TV) *The Sonny and Cher Comedy Hour*, 1971; (Stage) *Come Back to the Five and Dime, Jimmy Dean, Jimmy Dean*, 1981
Signature: "I Got You Babe," 1965
Facts: Abandoned by father when she was a few months old and placed in a home until her mother, who is part Cherokee, could save money to support her, she was eventually adopted by her mother's fifth husband, Gilbert La Piere.

Quit school as a teenager, ran away from home, and landed in L.A.

In 1964 began performing with Sonny Bono as Caesar & Cleo. The following year they changed their names to Sonny and Cher.

At one point, sold hair products by infomercial, was the spokesperson for the sweetener Equal, and started her own mail-order home decor business.

Has been linked to many famous men, including David Geffen, Mark Hudson, Gene Simmons, Val Kilmer, and Richie Sambora.

Nine days after her marriage to

427

Gregg Allman, she filed for divorce.

Nominated for Best Supporting Actress Oscar for her role in 1983's *Silkwood,* she formed Isis, her own film production company, two years later and soon found herself in acclaimed roles in *Mask* (1985) and *Moonstruck* (1987).

Her daughter, Chastity Bono, a lesbian activist, was outed in 1990 by a tabloid and later wrote a book, *Family Outing.*

Enjoyed yet another comeback with her 1999 hit single "Believe."

Is seeking a share of Sonny's estate, claiming he owed her back alimony payments.

Original Job: Background vocalist for the Crystals and Ronettes
Marriage: Sonny Bono, 1964 (divorced,1975); Gregg Allman, 1975 (divorced,1977)
Children: Chastity, 1969 (with Bono); Elijah Blue, 1976 (with Allman)
Major Awards: Oscar, Best Actress, *Moonstruck,* 1987; Grammy, Best Dance Recording, "Believe," 1999
Quote: "I still feel pretty kick-ass. I'm pretty vital. I have my truck and my motorcycle."

MELANIE CHISHOLM

Birthplace: Widnes, Cheshire, England
Birthdate: 1/12/74
Occupation: Singer
Debut: (Album) *Spice,* 1996; (Movie) *Spice World,* 1997 (American release, 1998)
Signature: "Wannabe," (1996) / Sporty Spice
Facts: As a child, imitated Madonna and studied ballet.

Regarded as the Spice Girl with the best vocal chops, she contests barbs that claim her bandmates can't sing.

The Chinese characters tattooed on her arm translate to "girl power."

Surfs, kick-boxes, practices yoga, and can do a backward somersault from a standing start.

Favorite film is *Toy Story.*
Owns over 200 pairs of sneakers.
Her solo album *Northern Star* (2000) veered from Spice Girls pop by including jazz balladry and industrial rock.
Infamy: A British tabloid ran an old photo of her at a party where other guests could be seen taking drugs.
Quote: "I think I'm pretty good, especially compared to some of the crap that's out there. And everyone likes Spice Girls records when they are drunk."

DEEPAK CHOPRA

Birthplace: India
Birthdate: April 1947
Occupation: Author
Education: All-India Institute of Medicine
Signature: *Ageless Body, Timeless Mind*
Facts: Was a mainstream endocrinologist and chief of staff at New England Memorial Hospital before embracing alternative healing methods.

Dr. Chopra practices a form of Ayurvedic medicine called Maharishi Ayur-Veda, named after the Indian spiritual leader who taught transcendental meditation to the Beatles. The system is based on a 5,000-year-old Indian holistic health system involving herbal remedies, massage, yoga, and transcendental meditation. (Ayur-Veda is derived from the Sanskrit roots for "life" and "knowledge.")
Marriage: Rita, c. 1970
Children: Gautama, Mallika

CHYNA

Real Name: Joanie Laurer
Birthplace: Rochester, NY
Birthdate: 12/27/69
Occupation: Wrestler
Education: University of Tampa (Florida)
Signature: WWF

Facts: Majored in Spanish literature in college.

While growing up with an alcoholic father, Chyna began following Jane Fonda's workout tapes, then moved on to weight lifting at a gym.

A basement kennel for her two schnauzers served as a makeshift wrestling ring for Chyna's older brother and wrestling soon became a source of inspiration.

She starred in high school productions of *Die Fledermaus* and *Grease.* Had reconstructive surgery on her jaw because of an underbite. Initially inspired to be an actor, she worked out too hard and developed a very muscular body.

After winning a United Nations scholarship for students with special abilities in languages, she spent her senior year in Madrid before entering University of Tampa.

Stands 6' 3", weighing in at some 200 pounds, Chyna likes to describe herself as "an empowered woman who kicks guys in the nuts for a living."
Original Job: Waitress, beeper salesperson
Relationship: Paul "Hunter Hearst Helmsley" Levesque, wrestler
Quote: "Chyna didn't just happen overnight. I took years to literally mold this character into this beautiful kick-ass woman."

TOM CLANCY

Birthplace: Baltimore, MD
Birthdate: 4/12/47
Occupation: Author
Debut: (Book) *The Hunt for Red October,* 1984
Facts: First short story was rejected by *Analog* science fiction magazine. Had just one article (on the MX missile system) to his credit when *Hunt for Red October* was published.

In the U.S. Army Reserve Officers' Training Corps, his poor eyesight kept him from serving in the Vietnam War.

Part-owner of the Baltimore Orioles, he also led the effort to bring an NFL expansion team to Baltimore for the 1994 season. He was successful, and is now part-owner of the Baltimore Ravens.

Clear and Present Danger was the bestselling book of the '80s.
Original Job: Insurance agent
Marriage: Wanda Thomas (divorced, 1999); Alexandra Llewellyn, 1999
Children: Michelle, 1973; Christine, 1974; Tom, c. 1983; Kathleen, 1985
Quote: "What do I care if someone reads my books a hundred years from now? I will be dead. And it's kind of hard to make money when you're dead."

ERIC CLAPTON

Real Name: Eric Clapp
Birthplace: Ripley, England
Birthdate: 3/30/45
Occupation: Singer, guitarist, songwriter
Education: Kingston Art School
Debut: (Album) *The Yardbirds,* 1963
Signature: "Layla," 1992
Facts: At the Ealing Club in London, occasionally substituted for lead singer Mick Jagger in Blues, Inc.

Earned the nickname "Slowhand" because his powerful playing regularly broke his guitar strings, which he then changed onstage to the accompaniment of a slow handclap from listeners.

The song "Layla" was reportedly inspired by an affair that Clapton had at the time with George Harrison's wife Patti, and was dedicated "to the wife of my best friend."

Tragedy struck in 1991, when his 4-year-old son died in a fall from Clapton's ex-girlfriend's apartment. The song "Tears in Heaven" is a tribute to him.

Was among 1,080 Britons recognized on Queen Elizabeth's honors list at the end of 1994.

In 1999, sold 100 of his guitars at auction for over $5 million, to benefit Crossroads Center, a clinic he founded in Antigua to treat drug and alcohol abuse.

Infamy: After release of *Layla and Other Assorted Love Songs* (1970), dropped out of sight for two-and-a-half years because of a heroin addiction. He was brought out of seclusion by Pete Townshend of The Who. A bout with alcoholism followed. Now, he says he hasn't touched a drink since 1987.
Original Job: Construction worker
Marriage: Patricia Anne Boyd-Harrison (divorced, 1988)
Child: Conor (deceased)
Major Awards: Grammy, Album of the Year, *The Concert for Bangladesh* (with George Harrison and Friends), 1972; Grammy, Best Rock Vocal—Male, "Bad Love," 1990; Grammy, Album of the Year, *Unplugged,* 1992; Grammy, Best Rock Vocal—Male, "Layla," 1992; Grammy, Record of the Year, Song of the Year, and Best Pop Vocal—Male, "Tears in Heaven," 1992; Grammy, Best Traditional Blues Album, *From the Cradle,* 1994; Grammy, Record of the Year, "Change the World," 1996; Grammy, Best Pop Vocal—Male, "Change the World," 1996; Grammy, Best Pop Vocal—Male, "My Father's Eyes," 1998; Grammy, Best Rock Instrumental Performance, "The Calling" (with Santana), 1999

GEORGE CLOONEY

Birthplace: Lexington, KY
Birthdate: 5/6/61
Occupation: Actor
Education: Northern Kentucky University
Debut: (TV) *E/R,* 1984
Signature: *ER*
Facts: In high school, was on the basketball team.

Got his Hollywood break playing a medical intern on the short-lived CBS comedy series *E/R,* set in a Chicago hospital emergency room. On NBC's *ER,* also set in a Chicago hospital emergency room, he graduated to full-fledged doctor.

Appeared as Roseanne's boss and

Jackie's boyfriend during the first season of *Roseanne.*
Original Jobs: Sold insurance door to door; cut tobacco
Marriage: Talia Balsam, 1989 (divorced, 1992); Brooke Langton, actress (relationship)
Famous Relatives: Rosemary Clooney, singer, aunt; Nick Clooney, TV host, father; Miguel Ferrer, actor, cousin

GLENN CLOSE

Birthplace: Greenwich, CT
Birthdate: 3/19/47
Occupation: Actor
Education: The College of William and Mary
Debut: (Stage) *Love for Love,* 1974; (TV) *Too Far To Go,* 1979; (Film) *The World According to Garp,* 1982 [see page 103 for a complete filmography]
Signature: *Fatal Attraction,* 1987
Facts: When she was 13, her father opened a clinic in the Belgian Congo (now Zaire) and ran it for 16 years. During most of that time, the Close children lived alternately in Africa and at boarding schools in Switzerland.

Her voice was dubbed over that of Andie MacDowell in the her starring role in *Greystoke: The Legend of Tarzan, Lord of the Apes.* Fifteen years later, Close's voice was used in Disney's animated *Tarzan* (1999).

Chosen by Andrew Lloyd Webber to replace Patti LuPone in *Sunset Boulevard,* 1994.

Collects costumes from her films.
Infamy: When she went on a two-week vacation from *Sunset Boulevard* in 1995, the production company released erroneous box-office figures implying that Close's absence had no effect on ticket sales. Close sent a scathing letter of complaint to composer-producer Andrew Lloyd Webber, which was obtained and published in the media.
Original Job: Toured Europe and the U.S. as a member of Up With People
Marriages: Cabot Wade, 1969

(divorced, 1971); James Marlas, 1984 (divorced, 1987); Steve Beers (engaged, 1995)
Child: Annie Maude Starke, 1988 (from relationship with John Starke)
Major Awards: Tony, Best Actress (Dramatic), *The Real Thing,* 1984; Tony, Best Actress (Dramatic), *Death and the Maiden,* 1992; Tony, Best Actress (Musical), *Sunset Boulevard,* 1995; Emmy, Best Actress in a Miniseries or Special, *Serving in Silence: The Margarethe Cammermeyer Story,* 1995

PAULA COLE

Birthplace: Manchester, CT
Birthdate: 4/5/68
Occupation: Singer, songwriter
Education: Berklee College of Music
Debut: (Album) *Harbinger,* 1994
Signature: "Where Have All the Cowboys Gone?" 1996
Facts: In high school, was a self-proclaimed "goody two-shoes," holding posts as three-time class president and junior prom queen.

Had a nervous breakdown and contemplated suicide while in college. Wrote "Bethlehem" during that period.

This Fire's seven Grammy nominations included one for best producer, the first ever for a woman.
Relationship: Seyi Sonuga
Major Award: Grammy, Best New Artist, 1997

SHAWN COLVIN

Birthplace: Vermillion, SD
Birthdate: 1/10/56
Occupation: Singer, songwriter, guitarist
Education: Southern Illinois University
Debut: Shawn Colvin Band, 1976
Signature: "Sunny Came Home," 1997
Facts: At a young age, she sang in the church choir, learned guitar, and designed album covers.

Played folk and rock during her college years, and later played small clubs in California and with the country rock group Dixie Diesels in Texas.

Had to quit in 1978 to let her throat heal after years of singing hard rock with the Shawn Colvin Band.

Sang back-up on Suzanne Vega's 1987 hit "Luka," which led to a tour and signing with Vega's manager.
Marriage: Simon Tassano (divorced, 1995); Mario Erwin, 1997
Child: Caledonia Jean-Marie, 1998
Major Awards: Grammy, Best Contemporary Folk Recording, *Steady On,* 1991; Grammies, Song of the Year and Record of the Year, "Sunny Came Home," 1998
Quote: "I think at best my voice sounds honest."

SEAN "PUFFY" COMBS

Birthplace: New York, NY
Birthdate: 11/4/69
Occupation: Rap singer, producer, executive
Education: Attended Howard University
Debut: (Album) *No Way Out,* 1997
Signature: Puff Daddy
Facts: His father died when Combs was 3; until age 14, he believed it was in a car accident, but later discovered it likely resulted from involvement in illegal street activities.

While in college in Washington, D.C., would ride a four-hour train to New York on weekends to intern at Uptown Records. Was named VP there at age 21. Became CEO of Bad Boy Entertainment at age 24.

Got the nickname "Puffy" as a child because he would huff and puff when angry.

His clothes label, Sean John, is monikered after his first and middle names.
Infamy: Nine people died during a stampede at a hip-hop celebrity basketball game Combs organized in 1991; he was later cleared of criminal charges but settled private lawsuits with the families after a report revealed he had delegated most of the arrangements to inexperienced assistants.

In 1996, was found guilty of criminal mischief after threatening a *New York Post* photographer.

Was arrested in April 1999 on charges that he and his bodyguards beat up Interscope Records executive Steve Stoute. He pleaded guilty to a reduced violation, and was sentenced to a day of "anger management." A civil suit settlement is being negotiated.

Indicted in 2000 for allegedly trying to bribe his driver, Wardell Fenderson, to claim ownership of a gun police say was discovered in Combs's car shortly after a Dec. 27, 1999 nightclub shooting.
Relationship: Jennifer Lopez
Children: Justin Dior, 1993 (with ex–girlfriend Tanieka Misa Hylton); Christopher Casey, 1998 (with Kim Porter)
Major Awards: Grammy, Best Rap Album, *No Way Out,* 1997; Grammy, Best Rap Performance By Duo Or Group, "I'll Be Missing You," 1997

SEAN CONNERY

Real Name: Thomas Connery
Birthplace: Edinburgh, Scotland
Birthdate: 8/25/30
Occupation: Actor
Debut: (Stage) *South Pacific,* 1951 [see page 103 for a complete filmography]
Signature: James Bond
Facts: Connery grew up in a poor, industrial district of Scotland. At age 7, he took a job delivering milk before school, and by age 13 he quit school.

Served in the British Navy from 1947 to 1950. Was discharged due to ulcers.

In 1950, represented Scotland in London's Mr. Universe competition.

Was denied for knighthood in 1998.

New Woman voted him sexiest man of the century.

Knighted by Queen Elizabeth II in Scotland in 2000.
Original Jobs: Lifeguard, milkman, bricklayer, plasterer, coffin polisher, and usher
Marriages: Diane Cilento, 1962 (divorced, 1973); Micheline Roquebrune, 1975
Child: Jason Joseph, 1963 (with Diane Cilento)
Major Awards: Oscar, Best Supporting Actor, *The Untouchables*, 1987; Tony, Best Play, *Art* (coproducer), 1997

HARRY CONNICK JR.

Birthplace: New Orleans, LA
Birthdate: 9/11/67
Occupation: Singer
Education: Loyola University, Hunter College, Manhattan School of Music
Debut: (Album) *Harry Connick, Jr.,* 1987
Signature: "It Had To Be You"
Facts: Performed annually at the New Orleans Jazz & Heritage Festival from the time he was 8.

He also recorded two albums of Dixieland music on little-known labels—the first when he was nine and the second when he was 10.

Learned jazz music from Ellis Marsalis, the patriarch of the Marsalis family at the New Orleans Center for the Creative Arts.
Infamy: Arrested for having a gun in his luggage at New York's JFK airport.
Marriage: Jill Goodacre, 1994
Children: Georgia Tatom, 1996; Sara Kate, 1997
Major Awards: Grammy, Best Jazz Vocal—Male, *When Harry Met Sally*, 1989; Grammy, Best Jazz Vocal—Male, "We Are in Love," 1990

DAVID COPPERFIELD

Real Name: David Kotkin
Birthplace: Metuchen, NJ
Birthdate: 9/16/56
Occupation: Magician
Education: Fordham University

Debut: (TV) *The Magic of ABC,* 1977
Facts: In his act, has levitated a Ferrari, walked through the Great Wall of China, and made the Statue of Liberty disappear. He has also extricated himself from a safe in a building about to be demolished by explosives and a steel box on a raft heading for Niagara Falls.

By age 12, had performed at local birthday parties for a fee of five dollars, under the name "Davino, the Boy Magician."

In 1982 developed Project Magic, a program designed to help people with physical and mental disabilities by teaching them magic.

Was engaged to Claudia Schiffer, but they never married.

Honored as a Living Legend by the Library of Congress in 2000. The library owns half of Harry Houdini's original library while Copperfield owns the other half—80,000 different items which he keeps in a "secret location" near his Las Vegas home.
Relationship: Amber Frisque, model

FRANCIS FORD COPPOLA

Birthplace: Detroit, MI
Birthdate: 4/7/39
Occupation: Director and writer
Education: Hofstra University, UCLA Film School
Debut: (Film) *Dementia 13,* 1963
Signature: *The Godfather,* 1972
Facts: First dreamed of becoming a filmmaker at age 10, while bedridden with polio. He put on shows for himself using puppets, a tape recorder, a film projector, and a television set.

Coppola's interest in producing a film about the automaker Preston Tucker—*Tucker: The Man and His Dream* (1988)—began when his father invested and lost $5,000 in the automaker's company.

Directed Michael Jackson in the 15-minute Epcot Center feature *Captain EO.*

First son, Gian Carlo, was killed in a boating accident in 1986.

Owns a vineyard in California's Napa Valley. Also owns a restaurant in San Francisco and property in Belize; he hopes to make that country the hub for a huge telecommunications center.

Successfully sued Warner Bros. for thwarting his attempts to develop "dream project," a new version of *Pinocchio,* at another studio; Coppola was awarded $80 million.

Filed a lawsuit against the late science writer Carl Sagan and Warner Bros. for a portion of the earnings of the 1997 movie version of Sagan's 1985 book "Contact," claiming that it was based upon an idea of his. The case was dismissed in 2000 on the grounds that it was filed too late.
Original Job: Worked for famous B-movie producer/director Roger Corman as dialogue director, sound man, and associate producer
Marriage: Eleanor Neil, 1962
Children: Gian Carlo, 1963 (deceased, 1986); Roman, 1965; Sofia, 1971
Famous Relatives: Talia Shire, actor, sister; Nicholas Cage, actor, nephew; Jason Schwartzman, actor/musician, nephew; Spike Jonze, director/actor, son-in-law
Major Awards: Oscar, Best Original Screenplay, *Patton* (with Edmund H. North), 1970; Oscar, Best Adapted Screenplay, *The Godfather* (with Mario Puzo), 1972; Oscar, Best Director, *The Godfather Part II*, 1974; Oscar, Best Adapted Screenplay, *The Godfather Part II* (with Mario Puzo), 1974

PATRICIA CORNWELL

Real Name: Patricia Daniels
Birthplace: Miami, FL
Birthdate: 6/9/56
Occupation: Author
Education: Davidson College
Signature: Kay Scarpetta, hero of her medical examiner–crime series

Facts: After her father had abandoned her and her siblings, her mother sought help from neighbors—evangelist Billy Graham and his wife, Ruth—who placed the children with Christian missionaries.

Her first book was an authorized biography of Ruth Graham, which strained their friendship for several years because of a "misunderstanding."

As a teenager, Cornwell was hospitalized for anorexia.

She married her English professor, 16 years her senior, after college.

Was a cartoonist for her college newspaper.

She travels with at least two bodyguards and hires armed, off-duty police officers for book signings.

She owns a .357 Colt Python, a .380 Walther semi-automatic, and a .38 Smith & Wesson.

Has a history of impulse buying and once spent $27,000 on a furniture shopping spree.

Was rescued by a jaws of life tool after her Mercedes crashed into a stalled van and flipped over three times.

She was known to behave erratically and suffered manic depression, which went undiagnosed for several years. In 1993, she checked into a clinic for recovering alcoholics.

Thoroughly researches technical details for her novels. Has attended approximately 600 autopsies for these purposes.

Gave $1.5 million to help the state of Virginia create an institute to train forensic scientists and pathologists.

Infamy: In 1992, had a lesbian affair with a married F.B.I. agent whose husband, also with the F.B.I., tried to ambush and kill his estranged wife.

Original Jobs: Police reporter for the *Charlotte Observer;* computer analyst in Richmond, Virginia, morgue

Marriage: Charles Cornwell (divorced, 1990)

Famous Relatives: Descendant of Harriet Beecher Stowe, author

Major Award: Mystery Writers of America, for *Post Mortem,* 1990

Quote: "I have this very cagey way of worming myself in; I'm an infection. You try to pacify me, and before you know it, you can't get me out of your system."

BILL COSBY

Birthplace: Philadelphia, PA
Birthdate: 7/12/37
Occupation: Actor, comedian, producer, author
Education: Temple University; Doctor of Education, University of Massachusetts at Amherst
Debut: (TV) *I Spy,* 1965; (Film) *Hickey and Boggs,* 1971
Signature: *The Cosby Show*
Facts: Grew up in a housing project in Philadelphia.

A gifted athlete, he was noticed by a scout for the Green Bay Packers.

Has played the drums since he was 11. A jazz aficionado, is president of the Rhythm and Blues Hall of Fame.

Infamy: In 1997, Cosby admitted having an adulterous "rendezvous" with Shawn Thompson in the early 1970s. The one-night stand came to light when Thompson's daughter, Autumn Jackson, threatened to tell the media that Cosby was her father unless he gave her $40 million. Jackson, whose education was financed by the entertainer, was convicted of extortion and sentenced to 26 months in jail, though a federal appeals court subsequently overturned the conviction. Unlike Cosby, Jackson reportedly never submitted DNA samples, thereby precluding a conclusive paternity test.

Original Job: Shined shoes, delivered groceries

Marriage: Camille Hanks

Children: Erika Ranee, 1965; Erinn Charlene, 1966; Ennis William, 1969 (deceased); Ensa Camille, 1973; Evin Harrah, 1976

Major Awards: Grammy, Best Comedy Recording, *I Started Out as a Child,* 1964; Grammy, Best Comedy Recording, *Why Is There Air,* 1965; Grammy, Best Comedy Recording, *Wonderfulness,* 1966; Grammy, Best Comedy Recording, *Revenge,* 1967; Emmy, Best Actor in a Drama Series, *I Spy,* 1966, 1967, 1968; Grammy, Best Comedy Recording, *To Russell, My Brother, Whom I Slept With,* 1968; Grammy, Best Comedy Recording, *Bill Cosby,* 1969; Emmy, *Bill Cosby Special,* 1969; Grammy, Best Recording for Children, *Bill Cosby Talks to Kids About Drugs,* 1971; Grammy, Best Recording for Children, *The Electric Company* (with Lee Chamberlin and Rita Moreno), 1972; NAACP Image Award, 1976; Emmy, *The New Fat Albert Show,* 1981; Emmy, Best Comedy Series, *The Cosby Show,* 1985; Grammy, Best Comedy Recording, *Those of You with or without Children, You'll Understand,* 1986; elected to the Emmy Hall of Fame, 1991

ELVIS COSTELLO

Real Name: Declan Patrick McManus
Birthplace: London, England
Birthdate: 8/25/54
Occupation: Singer, songwriter
Education: High school dropout
Debut: (Album) *My Aim Is True,* 1977
Signature: "Alison"
Facts: "Costello" is his mother's maiden name.

Began playing guitar at age 15 after testing out the violin, among other instruments.

Strongly influenced by American songwriters John Prine and Lowell George.

Got his first contract with CBS Records by performing on the sidewalk in front of the hotel where the label's sales conference was in progress. Was arrested for disturbing the peace but achieved his purpose.

From 1977 to 1986, he performed with the Attractions, including a tour in the U.S. and a spot on

Saturday Night Live. He was asked on the show to perform "Less Than Zero" after the Sex Pistols cancelled. Instead, he played "Radio, Radio," a song that comments on media manipulation. Many thought the appearance would end his career.

His album *King of America* identifies him by his real name, adding on the imaginary second middle name "Aloysius."

Composed "She," the Charles Aznavour ballad from *Notting Hill.*
Infamy: In a drunken argument in 1979, used racial epithets in referring to Ray Charles and James Brown. American disc jockeys took his records off their playlists, and he received numerous death threats.
Original Job: Computer programmer at Elizabeth Arden's factory in England
Marriage: Mary, 1974 (divorced, c. 1985); Caitlin O'Riordan, 1986
Child: Matthew, c. 1973 (with Mary)
Famous Relatives: Ross McManus, jazz singer with Joe Loss Band, father
Major Awards: Grammy Pop Collaboration with Vocals (with Burt Bacharach) "I Still Have That Other Girl," 1998
Quote: "I'm not interested in courting people. If people don't like me, there's no way I'm going to be nice to them so they do like me. All I want is for the records to be heard. I'm not out there saying, 'Love me, love me.'"

KEVIN COSTNER

Birthplace: Lynwood, CA
Birthdate: 1/18/55
Occupation: Actor, director, producer
Education: California State University at Fullerton
Debut: (Film) *Sizzle Beach,* 1979 [see page 103 for a complete filmography]
Signature: *The Untouchables,* 1987
Facts: At 18, built a canoe and paddled down the same rivers that

Lewis and Clark had navigated on their way to the Pacific.

As a teenager, he sang in the church choir.

Turned down the leading role in *War Games* (played by Matthew Broderick) to play Alex, the character who commits suicide, in *The Big Chill.* Only two weeks before the film's release, Alex's part was cut. But director Lawrence Kasdan promised Costner that he would write a part for him in another film, and tailored the role of Jake in *Silverado* (1985) for Costner.
Infamy: In February 1995, Costner and his brother Dan began building an entertainment complex in the Black Hills of South Dakota, on land that the Lakota Indians consider sacred and have been trying to recover since 1887. Costner had been made an honorary Lakota in 1990 after working with them on *Dances with Wolves.*
Original Job: Worked in marketing, stage-managed Raleigh Studios in L.A.
Marriage: Cindy Silva (divorced, 1995)
Children: Annie, c. 1984; Lily, c. 1986; Joe, c. 1988; (with Cindy Silva). Liam, 1996 (with Bridget Rooney).
Major Awards: Oscar, Best Director, *Dances with Wolves,* 1990; Oscar, Best Picture, *Dances with Wolves* (produced with Jim Wilson), 1990.

KATIE COURIC

Birthplace: Arlington, VA
Birthdate: 1/7/57
Occupation: Broadcast journalist
Education: University of Virginia
Signature: *Today*
Fact: Was a cheerleader in high school.

After hearing Couric read a report on the air, the president of CNN banned the young assignment editor from further television appearances, complaining about her high-pitched, squeaky voice. Keeping her spirits,

Couric began working with a voice coach.
Original Job: Desk assistant at ABC News in Washington, DC
Marriage: Jay Monahan, 1989 (deceased, 1998); Tom Werner, television producer (relationship)
Children: Elinor Tully, 1991; Caroline, 1996
Quote: "Bob Costas is short and cute, but I've never heard him being called 'perky.'"
Major Awards: Daytime Emmy Outstanding Special Class Program, *Macy's Thanksgiving Day Parade,* 1996, 1997, 1998 (shared awards)

CINDY CRAWFORD

Birthplace: De Kalb, IL
Birthdate: 2/20/66
Occupation: Supermodel
Education: Northwestern University
Debut: (Film) *Fair Game,* 1995
Facts: Crawford was the valedictorian of her high school class, and received a full scholarship to study chemical engineering in college. There, a professor accused Crawford of cheating after she received a perfect score on a calculus midterm exam.

Supports P-FLAG (Parents and Friends of Lesbians and Gays) and leukemia research (her brother died of the disease at age 3).

Had LASIK eye surgery (to correct nearsightedness).
Infamy: Posed for the cover of *Vanity Fair* shaving lesbian singer k.d. lang, prompting a renewal of international rumors she and then-husband Richard Gere were each homosexual and maintained the marriage for appearances only. In May 1994, the couple took out a $30,000 ad in the *Times* of London denying the rumors.
Original Job: Spent summers during high school detasseling corn in fields
Marriages: Richard Gere (divorced, 1994); Rande Gerber, 1998
Child: Presley Walker Gerber, 1999

433

MICHAEL CRICHTON

Real Name: John Michael Crichton
Birthplace: Chicago, IL
Birthdate: 10/23/42
Occupation: Writer, director, producer
Education: Harvard, Harvard Medical School
Debut: (Book) *Odds On* (under the pseudonym John Lange), 1966; (Film) *Westworld*, 1973
Signature: *Jurassic Park*
Facts: Published a travel article in *The New York Times* when he was 14.

Developed FilmTrak, a computer program for film production, and is creator of the computer game Amazon.

As a college student, turned in a paper written by George Orwell to test whether or not a professor was grading him fairly. The professor, who had been giving Crichton C-plusses, gave the Orwell paper in Crichton's name a B-minus.
Infamy: In 1974 was fired as screenwriter of the film adaptation of *The Terminal Man* when his screenplay deviated too much from the book.
Original Job: Anthropology professor
Marriages: Joan Radam, 1965 (divorced, 1970); Kathy St. Johns, 1978 (divorced, 1980); Suzanne Childs (divorced); Anne–Marie Martin, 1987
Child: Taylor, 1989

SHERYL CROW

Birthplace: Kennett, MO
Birthdate: 2/11/62
Occupation: Singer, songwriter
Education: University of Missouri
Debut: (Album) *Tuesday Night Music Club*, 1994
Signature: "All I Wanna Do," 1994
Facts: Her mother and father played piano and trumpet, respectively, with a big band on weekends. Their four children were encouraged to learn music and often practiced on

the four pianos in the house simultaneously.

In high school, she ran the hurdles in the Missouri state track meet.

Sang backup for Michael Jackson's 18-month *Bad* tour and, later, for Don Henley.

Went through a severe depression in the late '80s and didn't get out of bed for six months.

Played at Woodstock '94.
Relationship: Owen Wilson
Major Awards: Grammy, Record of the Year, "All I Wanna Do," 1994; Grammy, Best New Artist, 1994; Grammy, Best Pop Vocal—Female, "All I Wanna Do," 1994; Grammy, Best Rock Vocal—Female, "If It Makes You Happy," 1996; Grammy, Best Rock Album, *The Globe Sessions*, 1998; Grammy, Best Rock Vocal—Female, "Sweet Child O' Mine," 1999

RUSSELL CROWE

Birthplace: Wellington, New Zealand
Birthdate: 4/7/64
Occupation: Actor, musician
Debut: (TV) *Spyforce*, 1970; (Film) *Blood Oath*, 1990; (Album) *The Photograph Kills*, 1996
Signature: *Gladiator*, 2000
Facts: He is one-sixteenth Maori.

In 1980, he recorded a single "I Want to Be Like Marlon Brando," billing himself as Rus La Roq, and formed the band Roman Antix, which later became 30 Odd Foot of Grunts.

Had a tooth knocked out at age 10 and did not replace it until he was 25.

His grandfather was a cinematographer of war documentaries.

Gained 48 pounds to play Dr. Jeffrey Wigand for 1999's *The Insider*.

Tickets for his 30 Odd Foot of Grunts concert in Austin, TX in 2000 sold for over $500 on eBay.

Lives on a 560-acre farm north of Sydney, Australia. He recently purchased 129 cows.
Original Job: Street performer,

waiter, bingo caller, fruit picker, bartender
Relationship: Meg Ryan

TOM CRUISE

Real Name: Thomas Cruise Mapother IV
Birthplace: Syracuse, NY
Birthdate: 7/3/62
Occupation: Actor
Education: High school dropout
Debut: (Film) *Endless Love*, 1981 [see page 104 for a complete filmography]
Signature: *Jerry Maguire*, 1996
Facts: Dyslexia put him in remedial reading courses in school, but Cruise proved himself in sports.

At age 14, enrolled in a seminary to become a priest. Dropped out after one year.

Took up acting after losing his place on a high school wrestling team due to a knee injury.

Member of the Church of Scientology.

Developed an ulcer while filming *Eyes Wide Shut*.

Has saved three lives, rescuing people in Santa Monica, London, and off the island of Capri.

Likes to skydive and pilot his Pitts Special S-2B stunt plane.
Infamy: Author Anne Rice publicly criticized David Geffen for casting Cruise in *Interview with a Vampire* in 1994. After Rice saw the film she admitted Geffen had been right.

Won $580,000 in libel damages in 1998 from Britain's *Express on Sunday* for a story that claimed Cruise and his wife might be closet gays in a sham marriage.

Sued the *Star* in 1999 for claiming that sex experts had to coach Cruise and his wife in the art of lovemaking for *Eyes Wide Shut*.
Original Job: Busboy
Marriages: Mimi Rogers (divorced), Nicole Kidman, 1990
Children: Isabella Jane, 1993; Connor Antony, 1995; (both adopted).
Quote: "I'm not the Stanislavski kind

of actor. I just want to communicate with the people in the scene."

PENELOPE CRUZ

Birthplace: Madrid, Spain
Birthdate: 4/28/74
Occupation: Actor
Education: National Conservatory, Madrid
Debut: (Film) *The Greek Labyrinth*, 1991; (TV) *Framed*, 1993
Signature: *All About My Mother*, 1999
Facts: Donated her salary from 1998's *The Hi-Lo Country* to Mother Theresa's children's sanctuary in Calcutta after volunteering there for a week.

Became a vegetarian in 2000 after filming *All the Pretty Horses*.

Her sister, Monica, is professional flamenco dancer.
Original Job: Ballet dancer, model
Quote: "It is impossible to sustain an acting career longer than two or three years when you are known only for your beauty."

BILLY CRYSTAL

Birthplace: New York, NY
Birthdate: 3/14/48
Occupation: Comedian, actor
Education: Marshall University, Nassau Community College; New York University
Debut: (TV) *Soap*, 1977; (Film) *Rabbit Test*, 1978

Signature: *When Harry Met Sally...*, 1989
Facts: Went to college on a baseball scholarship and hosted a campus-radio talk show.

First theater job as a house manager for *You're a Good Man Charlie Brown*, 1968.

Studied directing under Martin Scorsese at New York University.
Infamy: Walked off the set of his first *Saturday Night Live* appearance after his seven-minute monologue was cut from the show.
Original Job: Substitute teacher, writer
Marriage: Janice Goldfinger, 1970
Children: Jennifer, 1973; Lindsay, 1977
Famous Relative: Milt Gabler, founded Commodore Records and later headed Decca Records, uncle
Major Awards: Emmy, Best Writing in a Variety or Music Program, *Midnight Train to Moscow*, 1990; Emmy, Best Individual Performance in a Variety or Music Program, *The 63rd Annual Oscars*, 1991; *The 70th Annual Academy Awards*, 1998; Emmy, Best Writing in a Variety or Music Program, *The 63rd Annual Oscars*, 1991; Emmy, Best Writing in a Variety or Music Program, *The 64th Annual Oscars*, 1992
Quote: "My father used to bring home jazz musicians at Passover. We had swinging seders."

JAMIE LEE CURTIS

Birthplace: Los Angeles, CA
Birthdate: 11/22/58
Occupation: Actor
Education: Choate; University of the Pacific
Debut: (TV) *Operation Petticoat*, 1977; (Film) *Halloween*, 1978
Signature: *A Fish Called Wanda*, 1988
Facts: Very athletic, Curtis was trained as a dancer and appeared on *Circus of the Stars* as an acrobat.

Curtis became interested in her husband Christopher Guest when

she saw his picture in *Rolling Stone*. She gave him her home number through an agent.

When her husband inherited his grandfather's English peerage title, Curtis earned the right to be addressed as "Lady Haden-Guest."

She has authored several best-selling children's books, including *When I Was Little: A 4-Year-Old's Memoir of Her Youth* and *Today I Feel Silly and Other Moods That Make My Day*.
Infamy: Admitted to using cocaine, even with her father, although not abusing it. She quit completely in 1983.
Marriage: Christopher Guest, 1983
Children: Annie, 1986; Thomas Haden, 1996 (adopted)
Famous Relatives: Tony Curtis, actor, father; Janet Leigh, actor, mother

JOHN CUSACK

Birthplace: Evanston, IL
Birthdate: 6/28/66
Occupation: Actor, writer, producer
Education: Attended New York University
Debut: (Film) *Class*, 1983
Signature: *Grosse Pointe Blank*, 1997
Facts: Grew up in a tightknit Irish Catholic family, always putting on neighborhood plays. Four of the five kids appear in *Grosse Pointe Blank*, which Cusack wrote and produced.

His parents were active in the anti-war and social protest movements; today he chooses most roles with an eye towards their social statements. During the Gulf War, he even wrote an op-ed for the *Chicago Sun-Times* protesting "police brutality" during an anti-war rally outside a rap concert.

At 20, started his own Chicago theater group, New Crime Productions.
Relationship: Neve Campbell
Famous Relative: Joan Cusack, actor, sister
Quote: "I was a teen star. That's disgusting enough."

CARSON DALY

Birthplace: Santa Monica, CA
Birthdate: 6/22/73
Occupation: MTV veejay
Education: Attended Loyola Marymount University
Signature: *Total Request Live* (*TRL*)
Facts: A devout Catholic, he contemplated priesthood.

Once played with Tiger Woods in the American Junior Golf Association. He received a partial scholarship to college, but left the following year hoping to turn pro.

Landed a job at KROQ-FM, L.A.'s leading modern-rock station. Previously host of *MTV Live* and *Total Request*, Daly became the host of *TRL*, a combination of the two, in 1998.

Tall, dark, and handsome, he has a wide knowledge of music and performers.

He learned of his breakup with Jennifer Love Hewitt while listening to the *Howard Stern Show*.

Reported to have dated pop star Christina Aguilera.
Relationship: Tara Reid, actor
Original Job: Radio deejay, KROQ-FM
Quote: "I'm nothing more than the Willy Wonka of MTV."

MATT DAMON

Birthplace: Cambridge, MA
Birthdate: 10/8/70
Occupation: Actor, screenwriter
Education: Attended Harvard University

Debut: (Film) *Mystic Pizza*, 1988
Signature: *Good Will Hunting*, 1997
Facts: As a teenager, occasionally break-danced for money in Harvard Square.

Left Harvard two semesters shy of an English degree.

Good Will Hunting, co-written with Ben Affleck, grew out of a scene Damon wrote for a Harvard playwriting class.

Lost 40 pounds in three months to play heroin addict in *Courage Under Fire*, creating an anorexia-like medical condition that injured his adrenal glands, requiring months of medication.

Formerly involved in a relationship with Winona Ryder for two years.
Major Award: Oscar, Best Original Screenplay, *Good Will Hunting*, 1997

CLAIRE DANES

Birthplace: New York, NY
Birthdate: 4/12/79
Occupation: Actor
Education: Attending Yale University
Debut: (TV) *Law & Order*, 1992; (Film) *Little Women*, 1995
Signature: *My So-Called Life*
Facts: Winona Ryder was so taken with Danes's portrayal of Angela Chase on *My So-Called Life* that she called her director on *Little Women* to suggest Danes for the part of Beth.

First auditioned for *My So-Called Life* when she was 13, but it took two more years for the show to get a firm commitment from ABC.
Relationship: Ben Lee, musician

D'ANGELO

Real name: Michael D'Angelo Archer
Birthplace: Richmond, VA
Birthdate: 1974
Occupation: R&B singer
Debut: (Single) "U Will Know," 1994; (Album) *Brown Sugar*, 1995
Signature: *Voodoo*, 2000
Facts: His father and grandfather were both Pentecostal Ministers.

Played piano at age 3 and learned the organ at age 4.

Started his first band, Michael Archer and Precise, when he was 16 and learned the drums, sax, guitar, bass, and keyboards.

In 1992, he was a three-time winner at Amateur Night at Harlem's Apollo Theater.

By 19, having moved to New York, he gave a three-hour impromptu piano recital for an EMI records executive, who signed him to a record deal.

The mother of his first child was his writing partner on his inaugural album.
Children: Michael, Jr. (with Angie Stone); Imani, 1999 (mother unreported)

JEFF DANIELS

Real Name: Jeffrey Daniels
Birthplace: Athens, GA
Birthdate: 2/19/55
Occupation: Actor
Education: Attended Central Michigan University
Debut: (Stage) *Fifth of July*, 1980; (TV) *A Rumor of War*, 1980; (Film) *Ragtime*, 1981
Signature: *Dumb and Dumber*, 1995
Facts: Starred in McDonald's commercials as a child.

He married his high school sweetheart on Friday the 13th because he used to wear the number 13 on his baseball uniform.

He won an Obie in 1982 for his one-man show, *Johnny Got His Gun*.

Worked four summers in his dad's lumber company in Chelsea, Michigan, and eventually moved there with his family. In 1990, he founded and financed Purple Rose Theater Company in Chelsea, where several of his original plays have been produced.

Learned how to moonwalk for the high school reunion scene in *Something Wild*.

During *The Fifth of July,* he shared a stage kiss, in successive productions, with William Hurt and

Christopher Reeve.

His most prized possessions are an autographed Al Kaline–Norm Cash baseball and a 1968 Kaline trading card.

Marriage: Kathleen Traedo, 1979
Children: Benjamin, 1984; Lucas, 1987; Nellie, 1990
Quote: "Sometimes you have to do things that will put the kids through college, in an industry that will spit you out tomorrow and forget your name."

TED DANSON

Real Name: Edward Bridge Danson III
Birthplace: San Diego, CA
Birthdate: 12/29/47
Occupation: Actor
Education: Stanford University, Carnegie-Mellon University
Debut: (TV) *Somerset*, 1975; (Film) *The Onion Field*, 1979
Signature: *Cheers*
Facts: Father was the director of a local Native American museum.

In 1981, was the Aramis man on TV ads for cologne and men's toiletry products.

While at Stanford, followed a good-looking waitress to an audition "just to be near her" and ended up winning a part.

Tap dances.
Infamy: Appeared at then-companion Whoopi Goldberg's 1993 Friars Club roast in blackface.
Marriages: Randall Lee Gosch (divorced), Casey Coates (divorced), Mary Steenburgen, 1995
Children: Kate, 1979 (with Casey Coates). Alexis, 1985
Major Awards: Emmy, Best Actor in a Comedy Series, *Cheers,* 1990, 1993; Golden Globe, Best Actor in a Comedy Series, *Cheers,* 1990, 1991

GEENA DAVIS

Real Name: Virginia Davis
Birthplace: Wareham, MA
Birthdate: 1/21/56
Occupation: Actor

Education: Boston University
Debut: (Film) *Tootsie,* 1982; (TV) *Buffalo Bill,* 1983
Signature: *Thelma & Louise,* 1991
Facts: Six-foot Davis, two inches taller than the cutoff established by professional modeling agencies, worked as a waitress to pay her bills. Finally she lied about her height and was accepted by the Zoli agency.

While working as a saleswoman at Anne Taylor, Davis got a job as a human mannequin in the store window.

Tried to qualify for the U.S. women's Olympic archery team in 1999.
Marriages: Richard Emmolo (divorced); Jeff Goldblum (divorced); Renny Harlin, 1993 (divorced, 1997).
Major Award: Oscar, Best Supporting Actress, *The Accidental Tourist,* 1988

KRISTIN DAVIS

Birthplace: Boulder, CO
Birthdate: 2/23/65
Occupation: Actor
Education: Rutgers University
Debut: (Film) *Doom Asylum*, 1987; (TV) *Another World*; 1987 (TV movie) *N.Y.P.D. Mounted*, 1991.
Signature: *Sex and the City*
Facts: Played a recurring role on *General Hospital*. Gained notice in 1995 for her recurring role as Brooke Armstrong on *Melrose Place*.

Appeared in numerous commercials, including one for Odor-Eaters (her most embarrassing).

Guest starred on *Seinfeld* as the girl whose toothbrush Jerry drops in the toilet.

Does yoga.
Original Job: Waitress
Quote: "I don't want to be taking my clothes off as an actress. My mother wouldn't be very happy."

DANIEL DAY-LEWIS

Birthplace: London, England
Birthdate: 4/29/57
Occupation: Actor

Education: Old Vic Theatre School
Debut: (Film) *Sunday, Bloody Sunday,* 1971
Signature: *My Left Foot,* 1989
Fact: At 16, accidentally overdosed on migraine medicine and suffered from two weeks of hallucinations. Because of this, he was mistakenly diagnosed as a heroin addict and placed in a mental hospital. To escape, he had to put on his "greatest performance of sanity."
Original Job: Loaded trucks
Marriage: Rebecca Miller, 1996
Child: Gabriel Kane, 1995 (with Isabelle Adjani). son, 1998
Famous Relatives: C. Day-Lewis, former poet laureate of Britain, father; Sir Michael Balcon, producer, grandfather; Jane Balcon, actress, mother
Major Award: Oscar, Best Actor, *My Left Foot,* 1989

ELLEN DEGENERES

Birthplace: New Orleans, LA
Birthdate: 1/26/58
Occupation: Actor, comedian
Signature: *Ellen*
Facts: Considered becoming a professional golfer.

In the 1980s the Showtime cable network, looking to name someone Funniest Person in America, found DeGeneres at a comedy club in New Orleans. She was given the title, and toured the country in a Winnebago with a big nose above the front bumper. It earned her the scorn of other comics, who thought she received the title undeservedly.

Was the first female comic ever to be invited to sit on Carson's couch in her first appearance on *The Tonight Show.*

Ellen's title character became the first uncloseted TV lead when she declared herself a lesbian; weeks before the "coming out" episode aired, DeGeneres herself did the same.

Formerly involved in a relationship with Anne Heche.

Original Job: Vacuum cleaner saleswoman, waitress
Major Award: Emmy, Best Writing in a Comedy Series, *Ellen,* 1997

JUDI DENCH

Real Name: Judith Olivia Dench
Birthplace: York, England
Birthdate: 12/9/34
Occupation: Actor, director
Education: Central School of Speech and Drama, London
Debut: (London stage) *Hamlet,* 1957; (Broadway) *Henry V,* 1958; (Film) *The Third Secret,* 1964
Signature: *Shakespeare in Love,* 1998
Facts: A much heralded actress, a member of the Old Vic Theatre Company since 1957 and the Royal Shakespeare Company since 1969, she has received numerous awards in England for her performances.

When she was young, she attended the Mount School and became a Quaker, a decision that she stands by to this day.

She has portrayed a wide range of characters, from Shakespeare's Ophelia and Lady Macbeth to historic queens Victoria and Elizabeth I to M, James Bond's boss in *GoldenEye* and *Tomorrow Never Dies.*

In 1980, she was awarded an Order of the British Empire and in 1987, named a Dame Commander of the British Empire.

Was the original choice to play Grizabella in *Cats.*

Was on screen for only eight minutes in *Shakespeare in Love,* for which she won an Academy Award.

She, along with Audrey Hepburn, is one of only a few actresses who have won an Oscar and a Tony in the same year.
Marriage: Michael Williams, actor, 1971
Child: Finty, a.k.a. Tara Cressida Frances, actor, 1972
Famous Relatives: Jeffrey Dench, actor, brother
Major Awards: Oscar, Best Supporting Actress, *Shakespeare In*

Love, 1999; Tony, Best Actress (Dramatic), *Amy's View,* 1999
Quote: "If anyone called me Judith they'd get a black eye. Judi, Judi, I like best."

ROBERT DE NIRO

Birthplace: New York, NY
Birthdate: 8/17/43
Occupation: Actor
Education: Attended the High School of Music and Art and dropped out, studied at the Dramatic Workshop, the Luther James Studio, the Stella Adler Studio, and the Actor's Studio
Debut: (Film) *Greetings,* 1969
Signature: *Taxi Driver,* 1976
Facts: Although commonly regarded as Italian-American, De Niro is more Irish in ancestry.

First acting experience was playing the Cowardly Lion in a Public School 41 production of *The Wizard of Oz.*

Co-owns Rubicon, a San Francisco restaurant, with Francis Ford Coppola.

The pop group Bananarama recorded a song (1984) called "Robert De Niro's Waiting." They originally wanted to use Al Pacino's name, but Pacino refused to let them.

De Niro grew up in New York City's Little Italy, just a few blocks away from his future friend, Martin Scorsese.

Three years after their breakup, De Niro was sperm donor for his ex-girlfriend Toukie Smith; a surrogate mother delivered her twin boys, Aaron and Julian

Was questioned by French police for nine hours regarding an international prostitution ring. Charging that the detectives' only reason for interrogating him was to heighten their profile, De Niro won a defamation case against the paper that printed the investigators' leak, returned his Legion of Honor medal, and vowed never to return to France.
Marriages: Diahnne Abbott (divorced, 1988), Grace Hightower, 1997 (separated, 1999)

Children: Drena, 1967; Raphael, c. 1976 (with Diahnne Abbott). Aaron, 1995; Julian, 1995; (with Toukie Smith). Elliot, 1998
Major Awards: Oscar, Best Supporting Actor, *The Godfather Part II,* 1974; Oscar, Best Actor, *Raging Bull,* 1980.

BRIAN DENNEHY

Birthplace: Bridgeport, CT
Birthdate: 7/9/38
Occupation: Actor
Education: Columbia University; attended Yale University, graduate program
Debut: (Stage) *Streamers,* 1976; (Film) *Semi-Tough,* 1977; (TV) *It Happened at Lakewood Manor,* 1977
Signature: *Death of a Salesman,* 1999
Facts: Was in the Marines for over five years and served eight months in Vietnam before returning home because of shrapnel wounds and a concussion.

He made his TV screenwriting-directing debut in 1994, with *Jack Reed: A Search for Justice.*

Attended college on football scholarship and, although he loved the theater, never auditioned because he was a member of the team.

Admits to being a "functional alcoholic" in the beginning of his career.

Owns a cottage on the coast of Ireland.

Collects art and enjoys sailing.
Infamy: Arrested for drunk driving while with actor Steve Guttenberg.
Original Jobs: Meat truck driver, bartender, salesman
Marriage: Judy (divorced); Jennifer Arnott, 1988
Children: Elizabeth, 1960; Kathleen, 1962; Deirdre, 1964 (with Judy). Cormack, 1993 (adopted; with Arnott); Sarah, 1995 (adopted, biological sister of Cormack; with Arnott).
Famous Relatives: Edward Dennehy Jr., acting teacher, theater director, brother
Major Award: Tony, Best Actor

(Dramatic), *Death of a Salesman,* 1999

Quote: "People always ask me if my size has helped or hurt me in this business. It's pretty much an even split."

JOHNNY DEPP

Birthplace: Owensboro, KY
Birthdate: 6/9/63
Occupation: Actor
Education: High school dropout
Debut: (Film) *Nightmare on Elm Street,* 1984
Signature: *21 Jump Street*
Facts: Dropped out of school at age 16 and joined a series of garage bands, one of which (The Kids) opened for Iggy Pop. Moved to L.A., where his ex-wife introduced him to actor Nicolas Cage, who spawned Depp's career.

Once owned a painting of a clown by executed serial killer John Wayne Gacy; now Depp has a pathological fear of clowns.

Tattoos: "Betty Sue" and "Wino Forever" (formerly "Winona Forever").

Co-owns the Viper Room, the '30s-style nightclub in L.A., outside of which River Phoenix died (1994).

Member of the band P, with ex-Sex Pistol Steve Jones and Red Hot Chili Pepper Flea.

Infamy: Charged with trashing a $1,200/night hotel room in New York City in September 1994. He agreed to pay the $9,767.12 in damages.
Original Jobs: Rock guitarist, sold pens over the phone
Marriages: Lori Anne Allison (divorced); Sherilyn Fenn (engaged, never married); Jennifer Grey (engaged, never married); Winona Ryder (engaged, never married); Vanessa Paradis (relationship)
Child: Lily-Rose Melody, 1999
Quote: "I've built a career at being a failure. I'm always shocked when I get a job."

PORTIA DE ROSSI

Real Name: Amanda Rogers
Birthplace: Melbourne, Australia
Birthdate: 1/31/73
Occupation: Actor
Education: Attended Melbourne University
Debut: (Film) *Sirens,* 1994
Signature: *Ally McBeal*
Facts: Began modeling at 11 and took professional name at 14.

Attended college as law major but dropped out to pursue career. She still holds on to *Black's Law Dictionary* for reference.

Modeled and appeared in TV commercials in Melbourne to pay tuition when a local film producer suggested she audition for *Sirens.*

Nicknamed "Portia de Froggy" after an episode of *Ally McBeal* where she had several scenes involving frogs.
Original Job: Model
Quote: "I think playing a lawyer alleviates some of my guilt at not becoming one."

DANNY DEVITO

Birthplace: Neptune, NJ
Birthdate: 11/17/44
Occupation: Actor, director, producer
Education: American Academy of Dramatic Arts
Debut: (Stage) *The Man with a Flower in His Mouth,* 1969
Signature: *Taxi*
Facts: After high school he worked in his sister's hair salon and was known as "Mr. Danny."

Got his part in *One Flew Over the Cuckoo's Nest* (1975) through producer Michael Douglas, whom DeVito had met in summer stock a few years before. Kirk Douglas had directed DeVito in *Scalawag* in 1973. At one point, the two were roommates in New York City.
Original Jobs: Hairdresser, theatrical makeup artist, valet
Marriage: Rhea Perlman, 1982
Children: Lucy Chet, 1983; Gracie

Fan, 1985; Jake Daniel Sebastian, 1987
Major Award: Emmy, Best Supporting Actor in a Comedy Series, *Taxi,* 1981

CAMERON DIAZ

Birthplace: San Diego, CA
Birthdate: 8/30/72
Occupation: Actor, model
Education: High school
Debut: (Film) *The Mask,* 1994
Signature: *There's Something About Mary,* 1998
Facts: The 5' 9" beauty signed with the Elite Modeling Agency at age 16; as a teen, made up to $2,000 a day.

Was a cheerleader in high school.

Says she "nearly killed herself" with her excessive drinking as she traveled the world as a successful —and fun-loving—model.

Nicknamed "Skeletor" as a child for being so skinny.

Competed in the Long Beach celebrity Grand Prix.

Since her only acting experience was in a school play, she originally auditioned for the smaller part of a reporter in *The Mask;* she was called back 12 times before snaring the lead.

Her looks spring from a combination of her dad's Cuban ethnicity and her mother's heritage of German, English, and American Indian. First name means "crooked stream" in Gaelic.

Her favorite authors are Charles Bukowski and Raymond Carver.
Relationship: Jared Leto
Quote: " 'Model turned actress' is a silly phrase. People just assume you don't have the capacity to think."

LEONARDO DICAPRIO

Birthdate: 11/11/74
Occupation: Actor
Debut: (TV) *Romper Room;* (Film) *Poison Ivy,* 1992
Signature: *Titanic,* 1997
Facts: Rejected by a talent agent

when he was 10 years old for having a bad haircut.

First memory is of wearing red-and-yellow tap shoes and being lifted onto a stage by his father to entertain people waiting for a concert.

First acting experience was in a Matchbox car commercial.

Successfully sued *Playgirl* to block publication of unauthorized nude photos.

Plays pick-up basketball with Tobey Maguire, Freddie Prinze Jr., Will Smith, and Mark Wahlberg.

Interviewed President Clinton about the state of the environment for an Earth Day 2000 special.

Relationship: Gisele Bundchen
Famous Relative: Adam Farrar, actor, stepbrother
Quote: "I used to think that famous people were so full of crap."

VIN DIESEL

Birthplace: New York, NY
Birthdate: 7/18/67
Occupation: Actor, director, screen-writer, producer
Education: Attended Hunter College
Facts: His first name is Vincent; he hasn't revealed his true last name.

Started acting at age 7 with the Theatre for New York City.

In 1992 he began writing scripts, and directed the film short *Multi-Facial*, which was shown in 1995 at the Cannes Film Festival. Two years later, his first full-length feature (which he wrote, coproduced and starred in), *Strays*, premiered in the Sundance Film Festival competition.

His script *Doorman* is based on his experiences as a New York City bouncer.

Original Job: Bouncer
Famous relative: Paul Vincent, film editor, twin brother
Quote: "I don't think I'm a man yet. I'm learning and I'm getting a little bit closer every day, but I'm not there yet."

TAYE DIGGS

Birthplace: Essex County, NJ
Birthdate: 1/2/71
Occupation: Actor
Education: Syracuse University
Debut: (Stage) *Carousel*, 1994; (TV) *New York Undercover*, 1996; (Film) *How Stella Got Her Groove Back*, 1998
Signature: *How Stella Got Her Groove Back*, 1998
Facts: Spent nine months singing and dancing in the *Caribbean Revue* at Tokyo's Disneyland.

Landed feature role in Broadway's *Rent* and continued TV spots in *Guiding Light*.

Upon learning he landed the *Stella* role, he ran naked through the aisles of *Rent*'s theater.

Costarred in the 1999 films *Go* and *The Wood*.

Relationship: Idina Menzel, singer
Quote: "If you could have seen me in high school, you would laugh. I loved sports and I loved women, but I was always a little too small and geeky."

CELINE DION

Birthplace: Charlemagne, Canada
Birthdate: 3/30/68
Occupation: Singer
Education: High school dropout
Signature: "My Heart Will Go On," 1997
Fact: Celine had nine best-selling French albums behind her before she recorded *Unison* in 1990.

She has over 500 pairs of shoes, with not letup in sight.

Announced she would retire after her 1999 tour, in part to focus on having children.

Renewed her vows with husband Rene Angelil in 2000 at Caesars Palace. The ballroom was trans-formed into a scene from "1001 Arabian Nights" with camels, exotic birds, singers, belly dancers jugglers and Berber tents.

Infamy: In 1990, refused to accept a Quebec music award as anglophone artist of the year, declaring she was

"proud to be Quebecoise." The anglophone press criticized her harshly for exploiting the incident for its publicity value.

Marriage: Rene Angélil, 1994 (renewed their vows in 2000)
Major Awards: Grammy, Best Pop Performance—Duo or Group, "Beauty and the Beast" (with Peabo Bryson), 1992; Grammy, Best Song Written Specifically for a Movie, "Beauty and the Beast" (with Peabo Bryson), 1992; Grammy, Record of the Year, "My Heart Will Go On," 1998; Grammy, Best Pop Vocal—Female, "My Heart Will Go On," 1998.

SHANNEN DOHERTY

Birthplace: Memphis, TN
Birthdate: 4/12/71
Occupation: Actor
Education: High school
Debut: (Film) *Night Shift*, 1982; (TV) *Father Murphy*, 1982
Signature: *Beverly Hills, 90210*
Facts: Before her role on *90210*, she starred in *Little House on the Prairie* with Melissa Gilbert and *Our House* with Wilfred Brimley.

Gained attention as a teen lead in *90210* for her temperamental behavior.

Subject of *I Hate Brenda* newsletter.

Reteamed with Aaron Spelling for *Charmed* in 1998.

Led the Pledge of Allegiance at the Republican National Convention in 1992.

Was asked to audition for *The Class of Beverly Hills* (a.k.a. *Beverly Hills, 90210*) based on her perfor-mance in *Heathers*.

She has three dogs.

Met ex-husband, Ashley Hamilton, only two weeks before they were married.

At her backyard wedding, Doherty wore a silk bathrobe and went barefoot.

Infamy: Highly volatile, she engaged in a bar fight with an aspiring actress and several public brawls with boyfriends.

Cited for thousands of dollars in unpaid rent.

Admits to abusing drugs and alcohol.

Marriage: Dean Factor (engaged, 1990; never married); Chris Foufas (engaged, 1991; never married); Ashley Hamilton (divorced, 1994); Rob Weiss (engaged, never married).

Quote: "Don't judge me for who I am, because everybody makes mistakes."

HEATHER DONAHUE

Birthplace: Upper Darby, PA
Birthdate: 12/22/73
Occupation: Actor
Education: University of the Arts, Philadelphia
Debut: (Film) *The Blair Witch Project,* 1999
Signature: *The Blair Witch Project,* 1999
Facts: After growing up in Philadelphia, Donahue landed a role in the spooky hit independent film *Blair Witch.* Left to their own devices, with their own handheld cameras, the cast had little contact with the film's directors.
Original Job: Office temp
Relationship: Gregor Hrynisdak, writer-photographer
Quote: "When you know you look like crap, you roll with it after a while. What was I going to do? Start putting on mascara?"

HOWIE DOROUGH

Birthplace: Orlando, FL
Birthdate: 8/22/73
Occupation: Singer
Education: Valencia Community College
Debut: (Single) "We've Got It Goin' On," 1995; (Album) *Backstreet Boys,* 1995 (American version, 1997)
Signature: "Everybody (Backstreet's Back),"1997
Facts: Took jazz, tap, and ballet classes as a child.

Missed the final cut to be a member of Menudo.

'N Sync's Chris Kirkpatrick was in his college graduating class.

The band is named after Orlando, Florida's Backstreet Market, a popular teen hangout.

The group's debut was a hit in 26 countries before *Backstreet Boys* was released in the U.S.

Backstreet's very first gig was at Sea World.

Labeled the "friendliest," "sweetest" Backstreet Boy.

Develops condos on the east coast of Florida.

Established the Caroline Dorough-Cochran Lupus Memorial Foundation in memory of his late sister.

Acted in an episode of *Roswell.*
Infamy: Band filed suit against former manager Lou Pearlman, claiming he had made $10 million from their labor while they had received $300,000.
Original Job: Actor in commercials
Quote: "We want [our music] to be for everybody. Our audience is not just teenagers—it's mothers and daughters, boyfriends and girlfriends, people my age and older than me."

ILLEANA DOUGLAS

Birthplace: Massachusetts
Birthdate: 7/25/65
Occupation: Actor, screenwriter, director, producer
Education: American Academy of Dramatic Art, NY
Debut: (Film) *New York Stories,* 1989; (TV) *Homicide: Life on the Street,* 1995
Signature: *To Die For,* 1995
Facts: As a child, she created anti-pollution shows while in the third grade. Also sent sketches to *Saturday Night Live* on spec, and tape-recorded movies on TV to replay and mimic.

Had a relationship with Martin

Scorsese from 1988 to 1997. First auditioned for him while working as an assistant for PR maven Peggy Siegal.

Loves to drive by famous people's houses.
Original Job: Comic, publicist
Marriage: Jonathan Axelrod, producer, 1998
Child: Sam Axelrod (stepson), 1990
Famous relatives: Melvyn Douglas, actor, grandfather; Rosalind Hightower, actor, grandmother
Quote: "When you're an actress in Hollywood, playing a hooker is the highest form of flattery. I'm serious. It's like when men get asked to play Hamlet."

MICHAEL DOUGLAS

Birthplace: New Brunswick, NJ
Birthdate: 9/25/44
Occupation: Actor, producer, director
Education: University of California, Santa Barbara
Debut: (TV) *The Experiment,* 1969; (Film) *Hail, Hero!,* 1969
Signature: *Fatal Attraction,* 1987
Facts: His film company produced *One Flew over the Cuckoo's Nest* (1975) and *The China Syndrome* (1979), in which he starred.

Directed two episodes of TV show *The Streets of San Francisco,* in which he costarred.

Flunked out of college during his freshman year.

Shared an apartment in New York City with Danny DeVito when both were struggling actors.

Is a UN Ambassador on nuclear disarmament.
Marriage: Diandra Luker, 1977 (separated, 1995); Catherine Zeta-Jones (engaged, 1999)
Children: Cameron, 1978 (with Diandra Luker); Dylan Michael, 2000
Famous Relatives: Kirk Douglas, actor, father; Diana Dill, actress, mother; Eric Douglas, comedian, half brother
Major Award: Oscar, Best Actor, *Wall Street,* 1987

ROMA DOWNEY

Birthplace: Derry, Northern Ireland
Birthdate: 5/6/60
Occupation: Actor
Education: London Drama Studio
Debut: (Stage) *The Circle*, 1989; (TV) *A Woman Named Jackie*, 1991
Signature: *Touched by an Angel*
Facts: An Irish Catholic, was raised in war-torn Northern Ireland, where she sometimes heard gunshots in the night.

Her mother collapsed from a heart attack in front of her when she was 10. Her father died from a heart attack 11 years later.

Turned down for a grant to attend drama school; her tuition was paid by a local theater director and two other teachers who believed in her talent.

Angel costar Della Reese, a minister, officiated at her Salt Lake City wedding, then entertained guests with a jazzy, romantic set.
Marriage: One prior marriage; David Anspaugh, 1995 (divorced, 1998).
Child: Reilly Marie, 1996

ROBERT DOWNEY JR.

Birthplace: New York, NY
Birthdate: 4/4/65
Occupation: Actor
Education: High school dropout
Debut: (Film) *Pound*, 1970; (TV) *Mussolini: The Untold Story*, 1985
Signature: *Chaplin*, 1992
Facts: His middle name is John.

At age 5, he played a puppy in his father's film *Pound*.

Was the live-in companion of Sarah Jessica Parker for seven years.

In 1985, he took a turn as a regular cast member on *Saturday Night Live*.

To play the part of Charlie Chaplin, Downey learned to pantomime, speak two British dialects, and play left-handed tennis.

An avid musician, Downey plays the piano and sings opera. He composed the closing theme song for *Two Girls and a Guy* as well as recording a version of "Smile" for *Chaplin*.
Infamy: In 1987, he began therapy at a substance rehabilitation center.

Arrested in 1996 on charges of driving while under the influence, carrying a concealed weapon, and drug possession.

Arrested a month later for criminal trespass and leaving a court-ordered rehab, he spent time in a drug clinic and, in 1997, was sentenced to time served and three years' probation.

Arrested again in June 1999 for admitting that he was still doing drugs, he was sentenced to 3 years in prison for violating his probation. With credit for time spent in county jail and treatment centers, he was released just over a year later.
Marriage: Deborah Falconer (separated, 1996)
Child: Indio, 1993
Famous Relatives: Robert Downey, actor, director, screenwriter, father; Elsie Downey, actor, singer, mother; Laura Downey, screenwriter, stepmother
Quote: "Stopping isn't hard. Not starting again is."

FRAN DRESCHER

Birthplace: Queens, NY
Birthdate: 9/30/57
Occupation: Actor
Education: Queens College
Debut: (Film) *Saturday Night Fever*, 1977
Signature: *The Nanny*
Facts: Her husband (since 1979) is a writer and executive producer of *The Nanny*.

Her five-line part in *Saturday Night Fever* included memorably asking John Travolta, "Are you as good in bed as you are on the dance floor?"

Before pursuing acting, went to beauty school to have a profession to fall back on. Uses that knowledge to do her own "AstroTurf of hairdos—nothing can hurt it": first mousse, then gel, then voluminize.

Studied with a vocal coach to lose her accent, but gave that up when she stopped getting acting work.

During the writer's strike in the late '80s, started a gourmet crouton business, a product that recently grossed seven figures annually.
Marriage: Peter Marc Jacobson, 1978 (separated, 1997); Michael Angelo (relationship).

MINNIE DRIVER

Real Name: Amelia Driver
Birthplace: Barbados
Birthdate: 1/31/70
Occupation: Actor
Education: England's Webber-Douglas Academy of Dramatic Art
Debut: (Film) *Circle of Friends*, 1995
Signature: *Good Will Hunting*, 1997
Facts: Grew up in the Caribbean until age 9, when she was sent to an English boarding school.

Gained over 20 pounds for *Circle of Friends*, then shed every ounce to play a thin Bond woman in *Goldeneye*.

Stands 5'10".
Original Jobs: Jazz singer, guitarist
Relationship: Josh Brolin

MATT DRUDGE

Birthplace: Tacoma Park, MD
Birthdate: 10/27/66
Occupation: Cybercolumnist, television commentator
Education: High school
Signature: *Drudge Report*
Facts: He reportedly graduated 325th of 350 in his high school class.

When he was younger, he watched television talk shows, listened to talk radio, and sat in his bedroom with a microphone and tape recorder, narrating his own show.

After moving to L.A., he managed a CBS Studio Center gift shop, and in 1995 began his Internet column with tidbits garnered from trash-cans.

He works out of his Hollywood apartment.

In 1997, he posted items about Kathleen Willey, the former Clinton campaign worker who would later allege unwanted sexual advances from the Oval Office, and the following year he reported that *Newsweek* held back on a story about intimacies between Clinton and Monica Lewinsky.

Infamy: In 1997, his unsubstanti-ated report accusing White House aide Sidney Blumenthal of wife-beating was retracted, but because Drudge would not divulge his sources, he was slapped with a $30 million defamation suit, which remains unresolved.

Original Job: Night shift manager at 7-Eleven.

Quote: "I know it's unethical as hell, but it's fun."

DAVID DUCHOVNY

Birthplace: New York, NY
Birthdate: 8/7/60
Occupation: Actor
Education: Princeton; master's degree from Yale
Debut: (Film) *Working Girl*, 1988
Signature: *The X-Files*
Facts: As a six-year-old, Duchovny wanted to be a bathtub.

Duchovny was working on his Ph.D. dissertation, "Magic and Technology in Contemporary Fiction," when he got his first acting job in a Lowen-brau beer commercial.

Played Denise the transvestite detective on *Twin Peaks,* 1990–91.

America Online has two separate folders devoted to messages about him; as one fan explained, "the drool is too heavy to be confined to one."
Infamy: In 1999, filed suit against 20th Century Fox, alleging that the studio has cheated him out of millions of dollars in profits from his TV series, of which he owns a

percentage. The lawsuit was settled in 2000.
Original Jobs: Teaching assistant at Yale, bartender
Marriage: Téa Leoni, 1997
Child: Madelaine West, 1999
Quote: "Seven years of trying to find my sister is enough already. For me as an actor, there's nothing left."

KIRSTEN DUNST

Name: Kirsten Caroline Dunst
Birthplace: Point Pleasant, NJ
Birthdate: 4/30/82
Occupation: Actor, model
Debut: (Film) *Oedipus Wrecks* of *New York Stories,* 1989; (TV) *Darkness Before Dawn,* 1993
Signature: *Interview with the Vampire,* 1994
Facts: While growing up in New York City, she appeared in TV commer-cials (eventually appearing in more than 70) and signed with a modeling agency.

Was 10 when she played Claudia in *Interview with the Vampire,* which brought a Golden Globe nomination.

Plans on starting her own produc-tion company, with her mother, to be named Wooden Spoon Productions (because her grandmother always carried one to keep the grandkids in line). Also aspires to have a fashion and makeup line.
Relationship: Jake Hoffman, actor (son of Dustin Hoffman)
Quote: "On my down time, I am a clean fanatic. I love to clean. It's a sick thing. I clean more than my mom. Scrubbing helps me get out my stress. I love Windex."

BOB DYLAN

Real Name: Robert Zimmerman
Birthplace: Duluth, MN
Birthdate: 5/24/41
Occupation: Singer, songwriter
Education: University of Minnesota
Debut: (Album) *Bob Dylan,* 1961
Signature: "Blowin' in the Wind," 1963

Facts: Took stage name from Dylan Thomas.

His backup band, The Hawks, later evolved into The Band.

Motorcycle crash in July 1966 led to a brief retirement.

Became a born-again Christian in 1979.
Infamy: Sued by Ruth Tryangiel in 1994. She claims she was his lover on and off for 19 years, and that she cowrote much of his music and helped manage his career. The lawsuit asks for $5 million plus damages and palimony.
Original Job: Performed with a Texas carnival
Marriage: Sarah Lowndes (divorced, 1977)
Children: Jesse, 1966; Maria, 1961 (stepdaughter, adopted); Samuel, 1968; Anna, 1967; Jakob, 1969
Major Awards: Grammy, Album of the Year, *The Concert for Bangladesh* (with George Harrison and Friends), 1972; Grammy, Best Rock Vocal—Male, "Gotta Serve Somebody," 1979; Grammy, Lifetime Achievement Award, 1991; Grammy, Best Traditional Folk Album, *World Gone Wrong,* 1994; Grammy, Album of the Year, *Time Out of Mind,* 1997; Grammy, Best Rock Vocal—Male, "Cold Irons Bound," 1997; Grammy, Best Contemporary Folk Album, *Time Out of Mind,* 1997

JAKOB DYLAN

Birthplace: New York, NY
Birthdate: 12/9/69
Occupation: Singer, songwriter
Education: Attended Parsons School of Design
Debut: (Album) *The Wallflowers,* 1992
Signature: The Wallflowers
Facts: The youngest of five children, is rumored to be the inspiration for his father's classic "Forever Young." As a child, often went on the road with dad.

Lived with his mother, Sarah Lowndes, after parents' bitter 1977 divorce. In an incident during a custody suit, Sarah tried to take Jakob and his siblings out of school, chasing them down the halls and even assaulting an uncooperative teacher.

Had a D average in high school. Began career wearing anonymous knit caps for seven years, playing L.A.'s clubs and delis without identifying himself as Dylan's son.

Having grown up the protected child of a famous celebrity, Dylan says privacy and security are crucial to his own family as well: he won't even reveal his son's first name.

Debut album bombed at only 40,000 copies, causing Virgin Records to drop him; took more than a year to find a new label.

Marriage: Paige
Child: Son
Famous Relative: Bob Dylan, singer, songwriter, father
Major Awards: Grammy, Best Rock Vocal—Duo or Group, "One Headlight" (with the Wallflowers), 1997; Grammy, Best Rock Song, "One Headlight," 1997

CLINT EASTWOOD

Birthplace: San Francisco, CA
Birthdate: 5/31/30
Occupation: Actor, director
Education: Los Angeles City College
Debut: (Film) *Revenge of the Creature,* 1955 [see page 104 for a complete filmography]
Signature: *Dirty Harry,* 1972
Facts: He was drafted in 1951 but en route to Korea his plane crashed. He swam miles to shore and was made swimming instructor at a boot camp, where he met actors Martin Milner and David Janssen, who sparked his acting career.

Elected mayor of Carmel, CA, in 1986; reelected in 1988.

Jazz musician and self-taught piano player, he plays three songs in the movie *In the Line of Fire.* Also composed two Cajun-inspired instrumentals for *A Perfect World.*

Has own beer "Pale Rider Ale," named for his 1985 Western *Pale Rider.*

Reportedly had a son and a daughter with Jacelyn Reeves. Names were not released.

Is a part-owner of the famed golf courses at Pebble Beach.
Infamy: Slapped with palimony suit by former lover Sondra Locke.
Original Job: Lumberjack, forest-fire fighter, steelworker
Marriages: Maggie Johnson (divorced); Dina Ruiz, 1996
Children: Kimber, 1964 (with Roxanne Tunis). Kyle, 1968; Alison, 1972; (with Maggie Johnson). Francesca, 1993 (with Frances Fisher). Morgan, 1996
Major Awards: Oscar, Best Picture, *Unforgiven,* 1992, Academy of Motion Pictures Arts and Sciences, Irving G. Thalberg Memorial Award, 1995

ROGER EBERT

Birthplace: Urbana, IL
Birthdate: 6/18/42
Occupation: Film critic, writer
Education: University of Illinois; University of Cape Town, South Africa; University of Chicago
Debut: Film critic for the *Chicago Sun-Times,* 1967
Signature: Siskel & Ebert
Facts: While at the University of Illinois, was editor of the *Daily Illini* and president of the U.S. Student Press Association, 1963–64.

Wrote the screenplay for *Beyond the Valley of the Dolls,* 1970. Also wrote a novel, *Behind the Phantom's Mask,* which was released in 1993.

Is a member of the Studebaker Drivers' Club.
Marriage: Chaz Hammel-Smith, 1993
Major Award: Pulitzer Prize for Distinguished Criticism, 1975

KENNETH "BABYFACE" EDMONDS

Birthplace: Indianapolis, IN
Birthdate: 4/10/58
Occupation: Singer, songwriter, producer
Debut: (Album) *Lovers,* 1989
Facts: While in ninth grade, phoned concert promoters pretending to be his teacher, asking if musicians would grant his gifted young charge—actually himself—an interview. Through this ruse, chatted with Stevie Wonder, the Jackson 5, and Earth, Wind and Fire.

Given his moniker in the early '80s by funk guitarist Bootsy Collins because of his youthful looks.

Has written or produced hits for Mariah Carey, Whitney Houston, Bobby Brown, TLC, Boyz II Men, and Toni Braxton.

Produced the movie *Soul Food* with his wife; they both cameo as film executives in *Hav Plenty.*
Marriages: Denise (divorced); Tracey McQuarn, 1992
Major Awards: Grammy, Best R&B Song, "End of the Road" (with L.A. Reid and Daryl Simmons), 1992; Grammy, Producer of the Year (with L.A. Reid), 1992; Grammy, Album of the Year (producer), *The Bodyguard,* 1993; Grammy, Best R&B Song, "I'll Make Love to You," 1994; Grammy, Best R&B Vocal—Male, "When Can I See You," 1994; Grammy, Producer of the Year, 1995; Grammy, Record of the Year, "Change the World," 1996; Best R&B Song, "Exhale (Shoop Shoop)," 1996; Grammy, Producer of the Year, 1996; Grammy, Producer of the Year, 1997

ANTHONY EDWARDS

Birthplace: Santa Barbara, CA
Birthdate: 7/19/62
Occupation: Actor
Education: University of Southern California
Debut: (TV) *The Killing of Randy*

Webster, 1981; (Film) *Heart Like a Wheel*, 1982
Signature: *ER*
Facts: His classmates at USC included Forest Whitaker and Ally Sheedy.

Played a burnt-out surfer in 1982's *Fast Times at Ridgemont High*, and one of the two head nerds in 1984's *Revenge of the Nerds*.

Somewhat bored with acting, he was planning to direct a low-budget children's feature, *Charlie's Ghost Story*, when he was called for *ER*. Originally turned down the *ER* role when production dates for the two projects initially overlapped.
Original Job: Actor in commercials for McDonald's and Country Time Lemonade
Marriage: Jeanine Lobell, 1995
Child: Bailey, 1994; Esme, 1997

CARMEN ELECTRA

Real Name: Tara Leigh Patrick
Birthplace: Cincinnati, OH
Birthdate: 4/20/72
Occupation: Actor, model, singer, dancer
Education: High school
Debut: (Album) *Carmen Electra,* 1992; (TV) *Baywatch Nights,* 1994
Signature: *Baywatch*
Facts: As a protégé of The Artist Formerly Known As Prince, she changed her name and flopped with her debut album. She later scored with *Playboy*, replaced Jenny McCarthy in 1997 as cohost of *Singled Out,* then played a *Baywatch* lifeguard when Pamela Anderson left the hit show, and is now a regular on *Hyperion Bay*.

She's the youngest of five children.

She lost her mother and her sister within a week of each other.

Wore Capri pants, a black Mark Wong Nark shirt, and black high-heel platform shoes to her wedding.

After marrying her in Las Vegas, Dennis Rodman sought an annulment of their marriage, issuing a statement that claimed he was drunk at the time. They remained married for months thereafter, though. Even after Rodman filed for divorce, the two were still linked.
Infamy: Posed nude for *Playboy* in 1996 and appeared in the video *Playboy Cheerleaders*
Original Job: Model
Marriage: Dennis Rodman, 1998 (filed for divorce, 1999)
Quote: "I love being in front of an audience. It's so stimulating. You get that adrenaline rush in your body and there's nothing like it in the world. I also love to barbecue."

JENNA ELFMAN

Real name: Jenna Butala
Birthplace: Los Angeles, CA
Birthdate: 9/30/71
Occupation: Actor, dancer
Education: Attended Cal State University and Beverly Hills Playhouse
Debut: (Film) *Grosse Pointe Blank*, 1997
Signature: *Dharma & Greg*
Facts: Became a member of the Church of Scientology in 1991.

Trained in classical dance from age 5, she considered joining Seattle's Pacific Northwest Ballet.

Was a chorus line tap dancer at the 1991 Academy Awards and a "Legs Girl" in ZZ Top's 1994 World Tour.
Marriage: Bodhi Elfman, 1994
Famous Relative: Danny Elfman, composer, rocker, uncle-in-law

EMINEM

Name: Marshall Mathers III
Birthplace: Kansas City, MO
Birthdate: 10/17/72
Occupation: Rap artist
Education: High school dropout
Debut: (Album) *Infinite*, 1997
Signature: "The Real Slim Shady," 2000
Facts: Never knew his father.

Failed the ninth grade three times.

His 2000 album *The Marshall Mathers LP* is the fastest-selling rap CD ever.

Musicians ribbed in his music include Christina Aguilera, Britney Spears, 'N Sync, the Spice Girls, and Vanilla Ice.
Infamy: Sued by his mother for depicting her in interviews as "pill-popping" and "lawsuit-happy." She's also a subject of his song "Kill You."

The Gay and Lesbian Alliance Against Defamation announced that his lyrics may provoke hate crimes against gays.

Police reports state Eminem threatened Insane Clown Posse rapper Douglas Dali with an unloaded revolver.

Had a rocky eight-year relationship with his ex-wife Kim. Eminem sports a "Kim: Rot in Pieces" tattoo on his chest, and his songs "97 Bonnie and Clyde" and "Kim" present tales of killing her.

In 2000, Eminem was charged with pistol-whipping a man he claims he found kissing his wife.

Soon after, his wife attempted suicide. In a matter of weeks, Eminem filed for divorce; his wife then filed civil suit, seeking $10 million and charging "intentional infliction of emotional distress."

Marriage: Kimberly, 1999 (separated, 2000)

Child: Hallie Jade, 1995

Major Awards: Grammy, Best Rap Album, *The Slim Shady LP*, 1999; Grammy, Best Rap Solo Performance, "My Name Is," 1999

Quote: "I do feel like I'm coming from a standpoint where people don't realize there are a lot of poor white people."

NORA EPHRON

Birthplace: New York, NY
Birthdate: 5/19/41
Occupation: Screenwriter, director
Education: Wellesley College
Debut: (Book) *Wallflower at the Orgy*, 1970; (TV) *Perfect Gentleman*, 1978
Signature: *Sleepless in Seattle*, 1993
Facts: She was the subject of the play *Take Her, She's Mine,* written by her parents.

Her autobiographical novel *Heartburn* was adapted into a 1986 movie starring Jack Nicholson and Meryl Streep. Wrote screenplays for *Silkwood* and *When Harry Met Sally...*

Marriages: Dan Greenburg, 1967 (divorced); Carl Bernstein, 1976 (divorced, 1979); Nicholas Pileggi, 1987
Children: Jacob, 1978; Max, 1979; (with Carl Bernstein).
Famous Relatives: Henry Ephron, screenwriter, father; Phoebe Ephron, screenwriter, mother; Delia Ephron, writer, sister
Quote: "No matter how cynical I get, I just can't keep up."

MELISSA ETHERIDGE

Birthplace: Leavenworth, KS
Birthdate: 5/29/61
Occupation: Singer, songwriter, guitarist
Education: Berklee College of Music
Debut: *Melissa Etheridge,* 1988
Facts: Played in women's bars around L.A. for six years beginning in 1982.

Came out by leaping onstage at one of Bill Clinton's presidential inaugural bashes, kissing cult figure Elvira, and proclaiming herself a proud lifelong lesbian.

David Crosby was the sperm donor for her children.

Her former partner, Julie Cypher, was once married to Lou Diamond Phillips.

Children: Bailey Jean, 1997; Beckett, 1998
Major Awards: Grammy, Best Rock Vocal—Female, "Ain't It Heavy," 1992; Grammy, Best Rock Vocal—Female, "Come to My Window," 1994
Quote: "I like to bring the sexual energy out by seducing the audience, and, when it's there, building on it. I would like to say that, maybe, going to a concert of mine is like foreplay."

RUPERT EVERETT

Birthplace: Norfolk, England
Birthdate: 5/29/59
Occupation: Actor
Education: High school dropout
Debut: (Film) *A Shocking Accident,* 1982; (TV) *Princess Daisy,* 1983; (American stage) *The Vortex,* 1991
Signature: *My Best Friend's Wedding,* 1997
Facts: As a child, he was very thin with huge buck teeth.

Was expelled for insubordination from Central School of Speech and Drama.

At his all-male, Catholic boarding schools, he was often cast in female roles in plays.

While a struggling actor, he supported himself as a male prostitute. Everett publicly disclosed his homosexuality in 1989.

Scenes from *My Best Friend's Wedding* were reshot to give him more screen time after focus groups praised his performance.

In 1991, he published his first novel, *Hello Darling, Are You Working?*
Original Job: Model
Quote: "I don't think anyone's particularly shocked by anything any more. Are they? We are all such old sluts now."

EDIE FALCO

Birthplace: Brooklyn, NY
Birthdate: 7/5/63
Occupation: Actor
Education: SUNY, Purchase
Debut: (Film) *The Unbelievable Truth,* 1989; (TV) *Homicide: Life on the Street,* 1993 (Stage) *Side Man,* 1999
Signature: *The Sopranos*
Facts: Her full name is Edith.

In college, she studied with fellow drama majors Parker Posey, Wesley Snipes, Stanley Tucci, and Sherry Stringfield.

Played Sheriff Marge Gunderson in a pilot based on the film *Fargo,* directed by Kathy Bates.

Has her own Aunt Carmela.
Relationship: John Devlin, actor/director
Major award: Emmy, Best Actress in a Drama Series, *The Sopranos,* 1999

MIA FARROW

Birthplace: Los Angeles, CA
Birthdate: 2/9/45
Occupation: Actor
Education: Marymount in Los Angeles and Cygnet House in London
Debut: (Stage) *The Importance of Being Earnest,* 1963
Signature: *Rosemary's Baby,* 1968
Facts: Mother—biological or adoptive—of 15 kids.

Was on first cover of PEOPLE, March 4, 1974.

At age 12, son Seamus became the youngest student at Simon's Rock College of Bard.
Infamy: Was awarded custody of the two children she and Woody Allen adopted, as well as their biological son, after a highly publicized case involving allegations of molestation by Allen.
Marriages: Frank Sinatra, 1966 (divorced, 1968); André Previn 1970 (divorced, 1977).
Children: Matthew, 1970; Sascha, 1970; Soon-Yi, 1970 (adopted); Lark, 1973 (adopted); Fletcher, 1974; Daisy, 1974 (adopted); (with André Previn).

Moses, 1978 (adopted); Tam, c. 1981 (adopted by Mia alone; deceased 2000); Malone, 1985 (originally Dylan, changed to Eliza, changed again; adopted); Seamus (formerly Satchel), 1987; (with Woody Allen).
Thaddeus, c. 1989 (adopted); Frankie-Minh, c. 1991 (adopted); Isaiah Justus, 1992 (adopted); Kaeli-Shea, 1994 (adopted); Gabriel Wilk (adopted); (by Mia alone)
Famous Relatives: Maureen O'Sullivan, actor, mother; John Farrow, director, father

JOEY FATONE

Birthplace: Brooklyn, NY
Birthdate: 1/28/77
Occupation: Singer
Debut: (Single) "I Want You Back," 1996; (Album) **NSYNC,* 1996

(American release, 1998)
Signature: *No Strings Attached,* 2000
Facts: Had a bit part in the 1993 film *Matinee.*

Was a singing star in high school in a quartet named The Big Guys.

Worked as the Wolfman at Universal Studios Florida.

His dancing clinched his invitation to join 'N Sync.

When in public, he and his bandmates wear matching bracelets engraved with "WWJD"—standing for "What Would Jesus Do?"

Describes self as the "ladies' man" of the five.

Along with Lance Bass, has written a screenplay for the band's movie debut.
Infamy: 'N Sync broke with their original record label and management over compensation. Suits and countersuits flew before a settlement was reached, allegedly favoring the band.
Quote: "You'll never find an ad in some old newspaper saying, 'Looking for a group.' We put this group together ourselves."

JON FAVREAU

Birthplace: Queens, NY
Birthdate: 10/19/66
Occupation: Actor, screenwriter
Education: Attended Queens College
Debut: (Film) *Folks!,* 1992
Signature: *Swingers,* 1996
Facts: Once overweight (he's since lost 75 pounds), he was inspired by Chris Farley when he was at Second City. He wrote his first script, *Swingers,* in two weeks and eventually sold the rights with the provision that he and friend, actor Vince Vaughn, would play leading roles.

His TV guest appearances include *Seinfeld, Chicago Hope, Friends,* and *The Sopranos.*

Wrote the script for *The Marshal of Revelation,* about an Hasidic gunslinger.

Original Job: Maintenance worker
Quote: "Write an inexpensive movie, get famous friends to be in it, and you get to do whatever you want."

SALLY FIELD

Birthplace: Pasadena, CA
Birthdate: 11/6/46
Occupation: Actor
Education: Columbia Pictures Workshop, Actor's Studio
Debut: (TV) *Gidget,* 1965
Signature: *The Flying Nun*
Facts: Was a cheerleader in high school.

Won the lead role in *Gidget* from among 150 other finalists.

Though entertaining, *The Flying Nun* discouraged people from thinking of her as a serious actress; the producers of the movie *True Grit* refused even to give her an audition. She was paid $4,000 a week for the television show.

According to PEOPLE's Pop Profiles for 3 consecutive years, Field was among the top three female celebrities most appreciated by the public.
Marriages: Steve Craig (divorced); Alan Greisman (divorced, 1994)
Children: Peter, 1969; Elijah, 1972; (with Steve Craig). Samuel, 1987
Famous Relatives: Mary Field Mahoney, actor, mother; Jock Mahoney, actor, stepfather
Major Awards: Emmy, *Sybil,* 1977; Oscar, Best Actress, *Norma Rae,* 1979; Oscar, Best Actress, *Places in the Heart,* 1984

JOSEPH FIENNES

Birthplace: Wiltshire, England
Birthdate: 5/27/70
Occupation: Actor
Education: Guildhall School of Music and Drama
Debut: (Stage) *A Month in the Country,* 1994; (TV) *The Vacillations of Poppy Carew,* 1995; (Film) *Stealing Beauty,* 1996
Signature: *Shakespeare in Love,* 1998

Facts: His middle name is Alberic.
He has a fraternal twin.

He began his career on stage with Helen Mirren and the Royal Shakespeare Company.
Original Job: Dresser, National Theatre
Famous Relatives: Ralph Fiennes, actor, brother; Martha Fiennes, director, sister; Magnus Hubert Fiennes, musician, brother; Sophie Victoria Fiennes, producer, sister; Jennifer Lash, mother, novelist (deceased)

RALPH FIENNES

Birthplace: Suffolk, England
Birthdate: 12/22/62
Education: London's Royal Academy of Dramatic Art
Debut: (Film) *Wuthering Heights,* 1992
Signature: *Schindler's List,* 1993
Facts: Fiennes gained 28 pounds to play Amon Goeth in *Schindler's List,* 1993. He was chosen for the role after director Steven Spielberg saw Fiennes's performance in the British TV movie *A Dangerous Man: Lawrence After Arabia.*

His name is pronounced "Rafe."
Marriage: Alex Kingston (divorced, 1997); Francesca Annis (relationship)
Famous Relative: Joseph, actor, brother; Martha Fiennes, director, sister; Magnus Hubert Fiennes, musician, brother; Sophie Victoria Fiennes, producer, sister; Jennifer Lash, mother, novelist (deceased)
Major Award: Tony, Best Actor (Dramatic), *Hamlet,* 1995

LAURENCE FISHBURNE

Birthplace: Augusta, GA
Birthdate: 7/30/61
Occupation: Actor
Education: Lincoln Square Academy
Debut: (Stage) *Section D,* 1975; (Film) *Cornbread, Earl and Me,* 1975
Signature: *Boyz N the Hood,* 1991
Facts: Appeared regularly on soap

opera *One Life to Live* for four years starting when he was 9.

At 14, went with his mother to the Philippines for what was supposed to be a three-month shoot for *Apocalypse Now;* the shoot lasted 18 months.

A theater buff, he wrote, directed, and starred in a play, *Riff Raff,* in 1994.
Marriage: Hanja Moss, 1985 (divorced, c. 1993)
Children: Langston, 1987; Montana, 1991
Major Awards: Tony, Featured Actor (Dramatic), *Two Trains Running,* 1992; Emmy, Best Guest Actor in a Drama, *Tribeca,* 1993

CARRIE FISHER

Birthplace: Burbank, CA
Birthdate: 10/21/56
Occupation: Actor, novelist, screenwriter
Education: Dropped out of Beverly Hills High School, attended Sarah Lawrence College and Central School of Speech and Drama, London
Debut: (Stage) *Irene,* 1972; (Book) Postcards from the Edge
Signature: *Star Wars,* 1977
Facts: Sang in her mother's Las Vegas nightclub act.

Her first public appearance was in a *Life* magazine photograph with her mother shortly after her father had run off to marry Elizabeth Taylor.
Infamy: Was a user of LSD and Percodan; almost overdosed, 1985.
Marriage: Paul Simon, 1983 (divorced, 1984)
Child: Billie Catherine Lourd, 1992
Famous Relatives: Debbie Reynolds, actress, mother; Eddie Fisher, singer, father
Quote: "You find me a kid that thinks he got enough affection and attention as a child and I'll show you Dan Quayle."

CALISTA FLOCKHART

Birthplace: Freeport, IL
Birthdate: 11/11/64
Occupation: Actor
Education: Rutgers University
Debut: (TV) *Darrow,* 1991
Signature: *Ally McBeal*
Facts: Named after her greatgrandmother, "Calista" means "most beautiful" in Greek.

Was a cheerleader in high school.
Has performed in several lead roles on Broadway.

In 1992, she joined Malaparte, a small Manhattan theater group headed by Ethan Hawke.

Turned down an audition for *Ally McBeal* because she was busy with theater and reluctant to do TV. The producers were persistent and she eventually agreed, flying to L.A. between the Sunday-matinee and Monday-evening performances. She was hired on the spot.

After a local TV station aired an unconfirmed report that she was anorexic, a flurry of rumors led her to publicly declare, "Am I anorexic?...No."
Quote: "I live vicariously through my rumors."

BRIDGET FONDA

Birthplace: Los Angeles, CA
Birthdate: 1/27/64
Occupation: Actor
Education: New York University, studied at the Lee Strasberg Institute and with Harold Guskin
Debut: (Film) *Aria,* 1987; (TV) *21 Jump Street,* 1989
Signature: *Singles,* 1992
Facts: Named after Bridget Hayward, a woman her father had loved who had committed suicide.

Her movie debut was in *Aria,* in which she stripped naked, had sex, then committed suicide during her eight minutes on screen with no dialogue.

Dated Eric Stoltz for eight years.
Relationship: Dwight Yoakam

Famous Relatives: Peter Fonda, actor, father; Susan Brewer, actor, mother; Henry Fonda, actor, grandfather; Jane Fonda, actor, aunt

JANE FONDA

Birthplace: New York, NY
Birthdate: 12/21/37
Occupation: Actor, political activist, fitness instructor
Education: Vassar College, studied method acting in Lee Strasberg's Actors Studio
Debut: (Film) *Tall Story,* 1960
Signature: *Barbarella,* 1968
Facts: Mother committed suicide in a sanitarium in 1953.

Jane Fonda's Workout is the best-selling nondramatic video in history.

Spent much of the '70s speaking for the Black Panthers and against the Vietnam War and was almost arrested for treason, earning her the nickname "Hanoi Jane."

Reportedly has an adopted daughter whom she refuses to speak about.
Marriages: Roger Vadim, 1965 (divorced, 1973); Tom Hayden, 1973 (divorced, 1990); Ted Turner, 1991 (separated, 2000)
Children: Vanessa, 1968 (with Vadim); Troy Garrity, 1973 (with Hayden)
Famous Relatives: Henry Fonda, actor, father; Peter Fonda, actor, brother; Bridget Fonda, actor, niece
Major Awards: Oscar, Best Actress, *Klute,* 1971; Oscar, Best Actress, *Coming Home,* 1978; Emmy, Lead Actress in a Limited Series or Special, *The Dollmaker,* 1983
Quote: "The disease to please a man goes deep. I had to reach my sixties to find my voice again…. If you're not convinced of your self-worth, you won't be respected."

HARRISON FORD

Birthplace: Chicago, IL
Birthdate: 7/13/42
Occupation: Actor, director
Education: Ripon College

Debut: (Film) *Dead Heat on a Merry-Go-Round,* 1966 [see page 104 for a complete filmography]
Signature: Indiana Jones
Fact: Scar beneath his lower lip is the result of a motorcycle accident.

Ford had his ear pierced at age 54, explaining that he had always wanted one; he was accompanied by already-pierced old friends Jimmy Buffett and Ed Bradley.

Owns a Bell 206 helicopter and three planes. In 1999, he crashed his chopper while practicing emergency landings and, in 2000, he missed the runway when landing his Beech Bonanza plane.
Original Job: Carpenter
Marriages: Mary Marquardt (divorced), Melissa Mathison, 1983
Children: Benjamin, 1966; Willard, 1969; (with Mary Marquardt). Malcolm, 1987; Georgia, 1990
Quote: "I feel physically fit—and capable of pretending to be fitter."

JODIE FOSTER

Real Name: Alicia Christian Foster
Birthplace: Los Angeles, CA
Birthdate: 11/19/62
Occupation: Actor, director
Education: Yale University
Debut: (TV) *Mayberry RFD,* 1968; (Film) *Napoleon and Samantha,* 1972 [see page 104 for a complete filmography]
Signature: *The Silence of the Lambs,* 1991
Facts: Started at 3 years old as the bare-bottomed Coppertone child in the then ubiquitous advertisement. She got the job when, too young to wait in the car, she was noticed at her brother's casting call. By age 8, she had appeared in over 40 commercials.

At 13, played a hooker in *Taxi Driver.* Because she was so young, the film's producers hired her sister Constance to double for her in a nude scene. Before she got the role, she had to pass psychological tests. "I spent four hours with a shrink to

prove I was normal enough to play a hooker. Does that make sense?"

As valedictorian in high school, she gave her graduation speech in French.

Object of would-be presidential assassin John Hinckley's obsession.

Has not identified the father of her child.
Child: Charles, 1998
Famous Relative: Buddy Foster, actor, brother
Major Awards: Oscar, Best Actress, *The Accused,* 1988; Oscar, Best Actress, *The Silence of the Lambs,* 1991

MATTHEW FOX

Birthplace: Crowheart, WY
Birthdate: 7/14/66
Occupation: Actor
Education: Columbia University
Debut: (TV) *Freshman Dorm,* 1992
Signature: *Party of Five*
Facts: Grew up on a 120-acre Wyoming ranch, attending a one-room schoolhouse until the fourth grade.

Pondered becoming a farmer like his father, but dad suggested he go east for college. During a year of prep at Massachusetts' Deerfield Academy, snooty classmates voted him "Most Likely to Appear on *Hee-Haw.*"

Played football at college, where he was wide receiver and an economics major.
Original Job: Model
Marriage: Margherita Ronchi, 1992
Child: Kyle Allison, 1997

MICHAEL J. FOX

Birthplace: Edmonton, Canada
Birthdate: 6/9/61
Occupation: Actor
Education: High school dropout
Debut: (TV) *Palmerstown, U.S.A,* 1980; (Film) *Midnight Madness,* 1980
Signature: *Family Ties*
Facts: When he got the audition for *Family Ties,* he was $35,000 in debt, living on macaroni and cheese, and

had been forced to sell off a sectional couch piece by piece to raise money.

Eric Stoltz was first cast in *Back to the Future,* but when he proved to be "too intense for the comedy," Fox got the role. For seven weeks he played Alex on *Family Ties* by day, then transformed himself into Marty McFly for the film.

Heavy smoker, but asks not to be photographed smoking to avoid becoming a negative role model for his younger fans.

Announced in 1998 that he suffers from Parkinson's Disease. First diagnosed seven years prior, he underwent brain surgery to alleviate his tremors.

Purchased two of Eric Clapton's guitars at auction for $79,300.

In 2000, he left TV show *Spin City* to spend time with his family and to head the Michael J. Fox Foundation for Parkinson's Research which is merging with the Parkinson's Action Network.

Is eligible to vote for the first time in 2000, having recently become a US citizen.
Marriage: Tracy Pollan, 1988
Children: Sam Michael, 1989; Aquinnah Kathleen, 1995; Schuyler Frances, 1995
Major Awards: Emmy, Best Actor in a Comedy Series, *Family Ties,* 1985, 1986, 1987, 1988, *Spin City,* 1999

VIVICA A. FOX

Birthplace: Indianapolis, IN
Birthdate: 7/30/64
Occupation: Actor
Education: High school
Debut: (TV) *Days of Our Lives;* (Film) *Born on the Fourth of July,* 1989
Signature: *Independence Day,* 1996
Facts: She was a cheerleader in high school.

Her nickname for her husband is "Big Daddy."

Her middle name is Agnetta.

She has two cats named Tiger and Snookie.

She got her first big break in 1988

when a producer saw her in a restaurant and recommended an agent.

Appeared in *Days of Our Lives; Family Matters; Matlock; Beverly Hills, 90210; The Fresh Prince of Bel-Air;* and *The Young and the Restless* before being tapped to play Will Smith's girlfriend in *Independence Day.*

She and Christopher Harvest arrived at their wedding in a horse-drawn carriage. She wore a diamond tiara and was presented with a thousand red roses from her husband.
Original Job: Model, waitress
Marriage: Christopher Harvest (a.k.a. SixxNine),1998

JAMIE FOXX

Real Name: Eric Bishop
Birthplace: Terrell, TX
Birthdate: 12/13/67
Occupation: Actor, comedian, singer
Education: attended U.S. International University
Debut: (TV) *In Living Color,* 1991; (Film) *Toys,* 1992; (Album) *Peep This,* 1994
Signature: *The Jamie Foxx Show,* 1996
Facts: His college major was classical music.

First tried stand-up on a dare from his girlfriend.

Chose his androgynous stage name when he saw female comics getting preference at open-micro-

phone nights.

Doing stand-up after *In Living Color* was cancelled, Foxx talked up his next project, *The Jamie Foxx Show*—even though it existed only as a name in his head.

His show was initially branded as stereotypical by the NAACP; since then, however, Foxx has earned three nominations for NAACP Image Awards in three years.

Won acclaim for his dramatic turn in *Any Given Sunday.*
Original Job: Shoe salesman
Child: Corinne, 1995

ARETHA FRANKLIN

Birthplace: Memphis, TN
Birthdate: 3/25/42
Occupation: Singer
Education: High school dropout
Debut: (Song) "Rock-A-Bye Your Baby with a Dixie Melody," 1961
Signature: "Respect," 1967
Facts: Started out as a gospel singer in her father's Baptist church in Detroit in the '50s. Her father was minister of the New Bethel Baptist Church, one of the largest pastorates in the U.S., until 1979, when he went into a coma after being shot in his home by a burglar.
Infamy: Was sued for breach of contract in 1984 when she was unable to open in the Broadway musical *Sing, Mahalia, Sing,* mainly because of her fear of flying.
Marriages: Ted White (divorced), Glynn Turman, 1978 (divorced, 1984).
Children: Edward, 1957; Clarence, c. 1958;(father undisclosed). Theodore Jr., 1963 (with Ted White). Kecalf, 1970 (with Ken Cunningham).
Major Awards: Grammy, Best Rhythm and Blues Song, "Respect," 1967; Grammy, Best R&B Vocal—Female, "Respect," 1967; Grammy, Best R&B Vocal—Female, "Chain of Fools," 1968; Grammy, Best R&B Vocal—Female, "Share Your Love with Me," 1969; Grammy, Best R&B Vocal—

Female, "Don't Play That Song," 1970; Grammy, Best R&B Vocal—Female, "Bridge over Troubled Water," 1971; Grammy, Best R&B Vocal—Female, *Young, Gifted, & Black,* 1972; Grammy, Best R&B Vocal—Female, "Master of Eyes," 1973; Grammy, Best R&B Vocal—Female, "Ain't Nothing Like the Real Thing," 1974; Grammy, Best R&B Vocal—Female, "Hold On I'm Comin'," 1981; Grammy, Best R&B Vocal—Female, "Freeway of Love," 1985; Grammy, Best R&B Vocal—Female, *Aretha,* 1987; Grammy, Best R&B Duo or Group, "I Knew You Were Waiting (For Me)" (with George Michael), 1987; Grammy Legend Award, 1991; inducted into the Rock and Roll Hall of Fame, 1987; NARAS Lifetime Achievement Award, 1994

DENNIS FRANZ

Birthplace: Chicago, IL
Birthdate: 10/28/44
Occupation: Actor
Debut: (TV) *Chicago Story,* 1981
Signature: *NYPD Blue*
Facts: Claims he was the "worst postman in the history of the post office" before becoming an actor. "I used to start my route at daybreak, and I would finish long after dark. I'd stop for donuts, I'd play with animals, I'd go home with my bag of mail and just lay around the house a bit."
Served 11 months in Vietnam with an elite Airborne division.
Marriage: Joanie Zeck, 1995
Children: Tricia, 1974 (stepdaughter); Krista, 1976 (stepdaughter)
Major Awards: Emmy, Best Actor in a Drama Series, *NYPD Blue,* 1994, 1996, 1997, 1999

BRENDAN FRASER

Birthplace: Indianapolis, IN
Birthdate: 12/3/68
Occupation: Actor
Education: Cornish College of the Arts
Debut: (Film) *Dogfight,* 1991

Signature: *The Mummy,* 1999
Facts: His Canadian-tourism-exec father had the family moving every three years. As a child, lived in Cincinnati, Detroit, Ottawa, Holland and Toronto, among others.
Stands 6'3".
Underwent six months of intensive weight training and a strict high-protein, low carb diet to beef up for his *George of the Jungle* role.
Marriage: Afton Smith, 1998
Quote: "Rather than dumb, I think these characters [the ones he plays] are more of an exploration of wide-eyed availableness."

MORGAN FREEMAN

Birthplace: Memphis, TN
Birthdate: 6/1/37
Occupation: Actor, director
Education: Attended Los Angeles City College
Debut: (Stage, Broadway) *Hello, Dolly,* 1967; (Film) *Brubaker,* 1980
Signature: *Driving Miss Daisy,* 1989
Facts: Got his show business start as a dancer at the 1964 New York World's Fair. He had studied ballet, tap, and jazz.
Played Easy Reader for five years in the 1970s on the PBS series *Electric Company.*
Moved from New York City, where he lived for 25 years, to a Mississippi farm. Is raising one of his nine grandchildren there.
Marriage: Jeanette Adair Bradshaw (divorced), Myrna Colley-Lee, 1984
Children: Alphonse; Saifoulaye; Deena (adopted); Morgana

LIAM GALLAGHER

Birthplace: Manchester, England
Birthdate: 9/21/72
Occupation: Musician
Education:
Debut: (Album) *Definitely Maybe,* 1994
Signature: Oasis
Facts: With the British pop band Oasis, Gallagher, famous for a quick

temper, is wont to stalk the stage and glare at his audience.
Known as a drinker, along with his brother and bandmate Noel, Gallagher went on the wagon while recording *Standing on the Shoulder of Giants.*
Was voted Best Dressed Man in Britain by *GQ* magazine.
Infamy: Cathay Pacific airlines banned Liam Gallagher and his brother Neil in 1998 after rowdy behavior on a 747 flying from Hong Kong to Australia.
Was sued in civil court by a man who alleged he suffered a broken nose after being butted in the head by Gallagher while taking his photograph.
Marriage: Patsy Kensit, 1997 (divorced, 2000)
Child: Lennon
Famous relative: Noel Gallagher, brother, fellow bandmate
Quote: "To be really big in America, to tell you the truth, mate, you've got to f- - -ing put a lot of work into it. You've gotta spend a lot of time there, y'know, and I don't personally want to."

JOEY FATONE

Birthplace: Brooklyn, NY
Birthdate: 1/28/77
Occupation: Singer
Debut: (Single) "I Want You Back," 1996; (Album) **NSYNC,* 1996 (American release, 1998)
Signature: *No Strings Attached,* 2000
Facts: Had a bit part in the 1993 film *Matinee.*
Was a singing star in his high school in a quartet named The Big Guys.
Worked as the Wolfman at Universal Studios Florida.
His dancing clinched his invitation to join 'N Sync.
When in public, he and his bandmates wear matching bracelets engraved with "WWJD"—standing for "What Would Jesus Do?"

Describes self as the "ladies' man" of the five.

Along with Lance Bass, has written a screenplay for the band's movie debut.

Infamy: 'N Sync broke with their original record label and management over compensation. Suits and countersuits flew before a settlement was reached, allegedly favoring the band.

Quote: "You'll never find an ad in some old newspaper saying, 'Looking for a group.' We put this group together ourselves."

JAMES GANDOLFINI

Birthplace: Westwood, NY
Birthdate: 9/18/61
Occupation: Actor
Education: Rutgers University
Debut: (Broadway) A Streetcar Named Desire, 1992; (Film) A Stranger Among Us, 1992; (TV) The Sopranos, 1999
Signature: The Sopranos
Facts: Began as a theater actor before Hollywood found him.

He plays the trumpet and saxophone.

Got a late start as an actor when a friend took him to his first acting class in the late 1980s.

Having never been in therapy, he struggles with the therapy scenes of his character, Tony Soprano.

Original Jobs: Bouncer, night club manager, truck driver
Major Award: Emmy, Best Actor in a Drama Series, The Sopranos, 1999
Quote: "Human frailty and confusion are what interest me. The more sensitive the character and the more he's in touch with things, the more confusion there is."

ANDY GARCIA

Real Name: Andres Arturo Garcia-Menendez
Birthplace: Havana, Cuba
Birthdate: 4/12/56

Occupation: Actor, director, songwriter
Education: Florida International University
Debut: (TV) Hill Street Blues, 1981; (Film) Blue Skies Again, 1983
Signature: The Godfather Part III, 1990
Facts: His family moved to Florida from Cuba after the Bay of Pigs invasion. He was 5 years old at the time and claims to have vivid memories of the event.

He was athletic as a child, until he was sidelined by a case of mononucleosis and began to take an interest in performing.

After college, he went to L.A. and waited tables while working improv and the Comedy Store.

In 1993, he produced and directed a documentary about Cuban mambo artist Cachao, called Cachao: Like His Rhythm, There Is No Other.

He wrote and performed several songs for 1995's Steal Little, Steal Big. His daughter Dominik made an appearance in this film.

He proposed to his wife on the first night he met her. They were married seven years later.

He produced, helped score, and starred in 1999's Just the Ticket.

Owns 25 conga drums, collects hats, and wears a beret in the winter.

Wore his father's pearl tie-pin, his most personal keepsake from Cuba, in When a Man Loves a Woman.

Original Job: Waiter
Marriage: Maria (Marvi) Victoria Lorido, 1982
Children: Dominik, 1984; Daniella, 1988; Alessandra, 1991
Quote: "First and foremost, I am a father—who just happens to act."

JANEANE GAROFALO

Birthplace: New Jersey
Birthdate: 9/28/64
Occupation: Actor, comedian
Education: Providence College

Debut: (TV) The Ben Stiller Show, 1992; (Film) Reality Bites, 1994
Signature: The Truth About Cats and Dogs, 1996
Facts: Has "Think" tattooed on her arm.

Does the voice for the never-seen character Sally on Felicity.

Original Jobs: Bike messenger, receptionist
Marriage: Rob Cohn (divorced); Craig Bierko (relationship)
Quote: "I really am not full of self-loathing. People think that because the name of my company is I Hate Myself Productions."

BILL GATES

Birthplace: Seattle, WA
Birthdate: 10/28/55
Occupation: Computer software entrepreneur-executive
Education: Harvard University
Signature: Microsoft Windows
Facts: After learning how to crash an operating system while a high school student, did it to the Control Data Corporation. Their reprimand caused him to abandon computers for a year.

Formed a company to sell a computerized traffic counting system to cities, which made $20,000 its first year. Business fell off when customers learned Gates was only 14.

Became the youngest billionaire ever at age 31.

As head of fast-growing Microsoft, took a total of six vacation days in the company's first six years.

Owns the Bettmann Archive, one of the world's greatest collections of documentary images.

His $100 million "smart house" in Lake Washington features a 20-vehicle garage; dining space for 100; and music, artwork, lighting, and TV shows that follow individuals from room to room.

Infamy: Accused by competitors of using clout from operating systems software to quash software competitors.

Marriage: Melinda French, 1994
Child: Jennifer Katharine, 1996; Rory John, 1999

SARAH MICHELLE GELLAR

Birthplace: New York, NY
Birthdate: 4/14/77
Occupation: Actor, model
Education: Professional Children's High School
Debut: (TV movie) *Invasion of Privacy*, 1983
Signature: *Buffy the Vampire Slayer*
Facts: At age 4, she chided McDonald's for their skimpy patties in a Burger King ad, for which BK was sued for libel. Gellar appeared in court, though the case was soon settled. Has appeared in more than100 commercials.

Has five holes in each earlobe and one for a navel ring. Tattooed the Chinese character for integrity on her lower back.

Possesses a brown belt in tae kwon do, and was a competitive figure skater as a child.
Relationship: Freddie Prinze Jr.
Major Award: Emmy, Outstanding Younger Actress, *All My Children*, 1994
Quote: "It's really hard to be a vampire slayer if you're scared of cemeteries."

RICHARD GERE

Birthplace: Philadelphia, PA
Birthdate: 8/31/49
Occupation: Actor
Education: attended University of Massachusetts, Amherst
Debut: (Film) *Report to the Commissioner*, 1975
Signature: *Pretty Woman*, 1990
Facts: Won a gymnastics scholarship to the University of Massachusetts.

In 1973, first studied the "middle way" of Siddhartha Gotama Buddha as preached by a Japanese sect. In 1982, switched faith to the Tibetan

school of Buddhism. In 1986, became a student of the exiled Dalai Lama.

First three big film roles (*Days of Heaven,* 1978, *American Gigolo,* 1980, and *An Officer and a Gentleman,* 1982) were roles turned down by John Travolta.

His photographs were published in the book *Pilgrims.*

His son's middle name, Jigme, means "fearless" in Tibetan.

Girlfriend Lowell was formerly married to Griffin Dunne, father of their daughter, Hannah.
Infamy: Took out a $30,000 ad with then-wife Cindy Crawford in the *Times* of London in May 1994 denying rumors of their homosexuality.
Original Job: Rock musician
Marriage: Cindy Crawford (divorced, 1994); Carey Lowell (relationship)
Child: Homer James Jigme, 2000
Quote: "I think most actors go into acting because there's a lot of self-loathing and confusion."

MEL GIBSON

Birthplace: Peekskill, NY
Birthdate: 1/3/56
Occupation: Actor, director
Education: University of New South Wales
Debut: (Film) *Summer City,* 1977 [see page 105 for a complete filmography]
Signature: *Lethal Weapon,* 1987
Facts: Father moved the family from New York to Australia in the '60s so his sons wouldn't be drafted.

The night before his audition for *Mad Max,* he got into a barroom fight in which his face was badly beaten, an accident that won him the role.

Took up acting only because his sister submitted an application to the National Institute of Dramatic Art behind his back.

For *Lethal Weapon 4,* was dragged on a freeway at 35 mph.
Marriage: Robyn Moore, 1980
Children: Hannah, c. 1980; Edward, 1982; Christian, 1982; Will, 1984;

Louis, 1987; Milo, 1989; Tommy, 1999
Famous Relative: Eva Mylott, opera singer, grandmother
Major Awards: Oscars for Best Director and Best Picture, *Braveheart,* 1995

KATHIE LEE GIFFORD

Real Name: Kathie Epstein
Birthplace: Paris, France
Birthdate: 8/16/53
Occupation: Talk show host, singer
Education: Oral Roberts University
Debut: (TV) *$100,000 Name That Tune,* 1976
Signature: *Live with Regis and Kathie Lee*
Facts: Despite having a Jewish father, became a born-again Christian at age 11.

Won the Maryland Junior Miss Pageant at age 17.

Organized a folk singing group while at Oral Roberts University.

Was a cheerleader in high school.

Named her dog Regis.

In 2000, decided to leave "Live with Regis & Kathie Lee" after 11 years.
Infamy: A human rights crusader accused Gifford's Honduran-manufactured clothing line of using exploitative child labor.
Original Job: Gospel singer
Marriages: Paul Johnson (divorced); Frank Gifford, 1986
Children: Cody Newton, 1990; Cassidy Erin, 1993
Quote: "I am irreverent, I am opinionated, but I'm not perky."

VINCE GILL

Birthplace: Norman, OK
Birthdate: 4/12/57
Occupation: Singer, songwriter, guitarist
Education: High school
Debut: (Song) "Turn Me Loose," 1984
Signature: "When I Call Your Name," 1990
Facts: After high school, contem-

plated a career as a pro golfer, but dropped that idea when offered a spot in a top progressive bluegrass group, Bluegrass Alliance.

Joined the band Sundance to play with its great fiddler, Bryon Berline; later joined The Cherry Bombs to be with singer-songwriter Rodney Crowell.

Lead singer for Pure Prairie League in the late '70s.

In the 1980s, worked in Nashville as a studio session vocalist and musician with such stars as Bonnie Raitt, Rosanne Cash, and Patty Loveless.

Dubbed "The Benefit King," he sponsors his own pro-celebrity golf tournament and annual celebrity basketball game and concert.
Marriage: Janis Oliver, 1980 (divorced, 1997); Amy Grant 2000
Child: Jennifer, 1982 (with Janis Oliver)
Major Awards: Grammy, Best Country Vocal—Male, "When I Call Your Name," 1990; Grammy, Best Country Vocal Collaboration (with Steve Wariner and Ricky Skaggs), "Restless," 1991; Grammy, Best Country Song, "I Still Believe in You" (with John Barlow Jarvis), 1992; Grammy, Best Country Vocal—Male, "I Still Believe in You," 1992; Grammy, Best Country Instrumental "Red Wing" (with Asleep at the Wheel), 1993; Grammy, Best Country Vocal—Male, "When Love Finds You," 1994; Grammy, Best Country Vocal—Male, "Go Rest High on That Mountain," 1995; Grammy, Best Country Song, "Go Rest High on That Mountain," 1995; Grammy, Best Country Vocal—Male, "Worlds Apart," 1996; Grammy, Best Country Vocal—Male, "Pretty Little Adriana," 1997; Grammy, Best Country Vocal—Male, "If You Ever Have Forever In Mind," 1998; Grammy, Best Country Instrumental Performance, "A Soldier's Joy" (with Randy Scruggs), 1998, Grammy, Best Country Instrumental Performance, "Bob's

Breakdowns" (with Asleep at the Wheel), 1999

SAVION GLOVER

Birthplace: Newark, NJ
Birthdate: 11/19/73
Occupation: Dancer, choreographer
Education: Newark Arts High School
Debut: (Stage) *The Tap Dance Kid*, 1984; (Film) *Tap*, 1989
Signature: *Bring In 'Da Noise, Bring in 'Da Funk*, 1996
Facts: At age 7, played drums in a band.

Made choreography debut at age 16 at New York's Apollo Theater.

Began a featured run on *Sesame Street* in 1990 as a character also named Savion.

His name is his mother's variation on the word "savior."
Infamy: Arrested in late 1995 for driving under the influence of marijuana and criminal possession of bags of marijuana, hidden in his socks. Pled guilty to the reduced charge of disorderly conduct.
Famous Relatives: Yvette Glover, actress and singer, mother
Major Award: Tony, Best Choreography, *Bring In 'Da Noise, Bring in 'Da Funk*, 1996

GOLDBERG

Real Name: Bill Goldberg
Birthplace: Tulsa, OK
Birthdate: 12/27/66
Occupation: Wrestler
Education: University of Georgia
Debut: (Film) *Universal Soldier, the Return*, 1999
Facts: Attended World Championship Wrestling Power Plant training school.

On scholarship at University of Georgia, he majored in psychology and was an all-conference nose tackle before going into pro football.

An eleventh round draft pick in 1990 for the Los Angeles Rams, he was cut after pulling a hamstring muscle and spent three seasons as

a defensive lineman for the Atlanta Falcons. He finally opted for wrestling after an abdominal injury.

He dips snuff.

He weighs in at some 285 pounds.

He enjoys fishing and collects vintage muscle cars.

His signature finishing move is the "Jackhammer," in which he drives his opponent headfirst into the mat.

His girlfriend of six years is a former "Diamond Doll," who used to escort wrestler Diamond Dallas Page to and from the ring.
Original Job: Bouncer
Relationship: Lisa Shekter
Famous Relatives: Ethel Goldberg, concert violinist with Oklahoma City Philharmonic, mother
Quote: "I never aspired to wrestle. But here I am, wearing my underwear on national television in front of millions of people."

WHOOPI GOLDBERG

Real Name: Caryn Johnson
Birthplace: New York, NY
Birthdate: 11/13/49
Occupation: Actor, comedian
Education: School for the Performing Arts, New York
Debut: (Film) *The Color Purple*, 1985 [see page 105 for a complete filmography]
Signature: *Ghost*, 1990
Facts: Kicked a heroin addiction in the '70s.

Began performing at age 8 with the Helena Rubenstein Children's Theater and later enrolled in the Hudson Guild children's arts program.

Co-owns the West Hollywood restaurant Eclipse with Steven Seagal and Joe Pesci.

She hates to fly and travels on a customized bus.
Infamy: Was roasted by black-faced companion Ted Danson at a Friars Club event, 1993.
Original Jobs: Bricklayer, hair-

dresser, bank teller, and makeup artist for a funeral parlor
Marriages: One prior marriage, David Claessen (divorced); Lyle Trachtenberg (divorced, 1995)
Child: Alexandrea Martin, 1974
Major Awards: Grammy, Best Comedy Recording, *Whoopi Goldberg,* 1985; Oscar, Best Supporting Actress, *Ghost,* 1990

JEFF GOLDBLUM

Birthplace: Pittsburgh, PA
Birthdate: 10/22/52
Occupation: Actor
Education: Trained at Sanford Meisner's Neighborhood Playhouse
Debut: (Stage) *Two Gentlemen of Verona,* 1971; (Film) *Death Wish,* 1974
Signature: *The Big Chill,* 1983
Facts: Brother Rick died at 23 from a rare virus picked up on a North African trip.

Starred as a stockbroker-turned-P.I. with Ben Vereen in the TV series *Tenspeed and Brownshoe,* 1980.
Marriages: Patricia Gaul (divorced), Geena Davis (divorced)

CUBA GOODING JR.

Birthplace: Bronx, NY
Birthdate: 1/2/68
Occupation: Actor
Education: High school dropout
Debut: (Film) *Coming to America,* 1988
Signature: *Jerry Maguire,* 1996
Facts: His first professional job was at age 16, breakdancing with Lionel Richie at the 1984 Olympic Games.

Big money came to his family when Cuba was a child, after his father's band (The Main Ingredient) hit it big with "Everybody Plays the Fool," but dad split two years later (they have since reunited), leaving mom and the kids on welfare.

Became a born-again Christian at age 13.
Original Jobs: Construction worker, busboy

Marriage: Sara Kapfer, 1994
Children: Spencer, 1994; Mason, 1996
Famous Relative: Cuba Gooding, singer, father
Quote: "The first time I saw myself naked in a school locker room, I was like, 'Wow.' After that, everything had to be trimmed, oiled, and together."
Major Awards: Oscar, Best Supporting Actor, *Jerry Maguire,* 1996

JOHN GOODMAN

Birthplace: Afton, MO
Birthdate: 6/20/52
Occupation: Actor
Education: Southwest Missouri State University
Debut: (Film) *Eddie Macon's Run,* 1983
Signature: *Roseanne*
Facts: Made a living doing dinner and children's theater before Broadway debut in 1979 in *Loose Ends.*

Acted in college with Kathleen Turner and Tess Harper.

Appeared in commercials for Coors beer, Crest toothpaste, and 7UP.
Original Job: Bouncer
Marriage: Anna Beth Hartzog, 1989
Child: Molly, 1990
Major Award: Golden Globe, Best Actor in a Comedy Series, *Roseanne,* 1993

JEFF GORDON

Birthplace: Vallejo, CA
Birthdate: 8/4/71
Occupation: Race car driver
Education: High school
Facts: Began racing at age five when his stepfather bought him a race car. By age eight he was a national champion. By age 11, he won 25 of 25 races in the go-cart division.

After donning his racing suit, he always puts right glove on first.
In 1993 Gordon, the first rookie in 30

years to win Daytona's 125-mile qualifying race, went on to become Rookie of the Year in the Winston Cup Series, and the first driver to win rookie honors in NASCAR's two top divisions.

Polite, slim, and slight, Gordon loses some eight pounds during a race. After races, his eye sockets ache.
Major Awards: Three-time NASCAR Winston Cup winner
Marriage: Brooke

HEATHER GRAHAM

Birthplace: Milwaukee, WI
Birthdate: 1/29/70
Occupation: Actor, model
Education: Attended UCLA
Debut: (Film) *License to Drive,* 1988
Signature: *Boogie Nights,* 1997
Facts: Raised in a religious Catholic household; her parents once encouraged her to become a nun.

Had a year-long romance with actor James Woods, who was twice her age at the time. Also was involved with Ed Burns.

Regularly practices Transcendental Meditation.
Original Job: Usher at Hollywood Bowl
Relationship: Heath Ledger
Famous Relative: Aimee Graham, actor, sister
Quote: "I love telling dirty jokes. Sex is funny."

KELSEY GRAMMER

Birthplace: St. Thomas, Virgin Islands
Birthdate: 2/21/55
Occupation: Actor
Education: Juilliard School
Debut: (TV) *Another World,* 1983
Signature: *Frasier*
Facts: Father and sister were murdered; his two half brothers died in a scuba accident.

His unborn child died when his ex-wife attempted suicide.

Was nominated five times before finally winning an Emmy in 1994. **Infamy:** Arrested for driving under the influence of drugs in 1987; failed to show up for two arraignments for a cocaine arrest in 1988; sentenced to community service and 30 days in prison in 1990.

In 1995, faced allegations of sexual assault by a 17-year-old, who claimed they had had sex when she was 15. The New Jersey grand jury declined to charge him.

In 1996, crashed his Viper and wound up in the Betty Ford Clinic. **Original Job:** Theatrical painter **Marriages:** Doreen Alderman (divorced), Leigh-Anne Csuhany (divorced), Camille Donatucci, 1997 **Children:** Spencer,1985 (with Doreen Alderman). Greer, 1992 (with Barrie Buckner) **Major Awards:** Emmy, Best Actor in a Comedy, *Frasier*, 1994, 1995, 1998

HUGH GRANT

Birthplace: London, England
Birthdate: 9/9/60
Occupation: Actor
Education: New College, Oxford University
Debut: (Film) *Privileged*, 1982
Signature: *Four Weddings and a Funeral*, 1994
Facts: Grant opted not to do a nude scene with Andie MacDowell in *Four Weddings and a Funeral* when a makeup artist asked if he wanted definition painted on his body.

While at Oxford, formed a revue group, The Jockeys of Norfolk.

Grant is very popular in Japan, and there are two books on him published there, *Hugh Grant Vol. 1* and *Hugh Grant Vol. 2*.

Split with girlfriend Elizabeth Hurley after 13 years in 2000. The two continue to co-own Simian Films and maintain their two London homes.
Infamy: Arrested in June 1995 in Hollywood for picking up a prostitute. Was sentenced to two years' proba-

tion, fined $1,180 (which included court costs), and ordered to complete an AIDS education program.
Quote: "So many dogs have their day. I'm having mine now—and though I'd love it to go on and on, I suspect I'll be back doing BBC radio drama next spring."

MACY GRAY

Real Name: Natalie McIntyre
Birthplace: Canton, OH
Birthdate: 9/6/67
Occupation: Singer
Education: attended USC
Debut: (Album) *On How Life Is,* 1999; (Single) "Do Something," 1999
Signature: "I Try"
Facts: Was kicked out of boarding school—she says it was because she reported a Dean who made improper physical contact.

Played basketball, volleyball, swam, and ran track in high school. She wears size 11 shoes.

Left film school a few credits short of a degree.

Made a Super-8 film of a strait-jacketed woman in a psychiatric ward.

A classmate asked her to write some lyrics for his music, then asked her to sing the song for his demo recording. The publisher liked her voice. She eventually signed with Epic.

Was dropped from her original recording contract and moved home, planning to become a teacher.

Sang "Winter Wonderland" for the BabyGap ad in 1998.

Wrote all the lyrics for her debut album. Also wrote songs for Fatboy Slim, Rod Stewart, and Guru.

Worked behind the scenes on videos by Tupac Shakur and others.

Took her stage name from a neighbor who played pool with her father.
Marriage: Married 1993, divorced 1998
Children: Happy, 1995; Aanisah,

1995; Mel, 1997
Quote: "I won't say that I've had a bad life, but I've definitely gone through a lot."

TOM GREEN

Birthplace: Pembroke, Ontario, Canada
Birthdate: 7/71
Occupation: Comedian
Education: Algonquin College of Applied Arts and Technology
Debut: (TV) MTV's *Tom Green Show*, 1999; (Video) *Something Smells Funny*, 1999, (Film) *Charlie's Angels*, 2000
Signature: *Tom Green Show*
Facts: At 15, began performing on amateur night at a comedy club. He dropped out of a college radio and TV program to form his rap-spoof group Organized Rhyme. The group won an A&M record deal.

In 1990, became a cohost on a nighttime college radio show. Five years later he launched the *Tom Green Show* on community access cable.

Notorious for his sometimes cruel and grotesque pranks and his taste-less humor, which frequently targets his parents. Green has painted their house plaid, brought animals into their home, and had a pornographic picture airbrushed on their car. He also put a severed cow's head in their bed. He once conned his grandmother into licking a sex toy on television.

In March 2000, he had surgery for testicular cancer and taped the procedure for *the Tom Green Cancer Special*. Then started the Tom Green's Nuts Cancer Fund
Original Job: Musician
Relationship: Drew Barrymore (engaged)
Quote: "I think people under the age of 30 get this. Once you get over 40, there are people who really don't understand why it's funny. It just doesn't register as comedy to them, which to me is hilarious. That's what it's all about, confusing conservative people

MELANIE GRIFFITH

Birthplace: New York, NY
Birthdate: 8/9/57
Occupation: Actor
Education: Pierce College
Debut: (Film) *Night Moves,* 1975
Signature: *Working Girl,* 1988
Facts: Alfred Hitchcock, who was in love with Griffith's mother, gave Melanie a tiny wooden coffin containing a wax replica of her mother, outfitted in the same clothes she had worn in *The Birds,* on her sixth birthday.

At 14, left home to move in with Don Johnson, who was then 22. She married him at 18 and was divorced a year later. In 1988, on her way to the Hazelden Clinic for rehab, she called Don from the plane and renewed their love.

Was clawed in the face by a lioness in the filming of *Roar* (1981).
Infamy: Was addicted to drugs and alcohol in the late '70s and early '80s, and studio executives refused to speak with her. In 1980, she was hit by a car while crossing Sunset Boulevard. She suffered a broken leg and arm, but her doctor said that if she hadn't been so drunk she probably would have been killed.
Original Job: Model
Marriages: Don Johnson (divorced), Steven Bauer (divorced), Don Johnson (divorced), Antonio Banderas, 1996

Children: Alexander, 1985 (with Steven Bauer). Dakota, 1989 (with Don Johnson). Stella del Carmen, 1996
Famous Relatives: Tippi Hedren, actor, mother; Tracy Griffith, actor, half-sister
Quote: "I'm done with stupid movies—I want to be taken seriously again."

JOHN GRISHAM

Birthplace: Arkansas
Birthdate: 2/8/55
Occupation: Author
Education: Mississippi State, University of Mississippi Law School
Debut: (Book) *A Time To Kill,* 1989
Signature: *The Firm*
Facts: Little League baseball coach. Wife edits his books as he writes them.

Was inspired to write *A Time To Kill* by testimony he heard at the De Soto County courthouse from a 10-year-old girl who was testifying against a man who had raped her and left her for dead.

Served as a Democrat in the Mississippi State Legislature for seven years (1983–90).

Shaves only once a week, before church on Sunday.

In 1989 formed Bongo Comics Group.

A 16th cousin of Bill Clinton.
Original Job: Attorney
Marriage: Renee Jones, 1981
Children: Ty, c. 1983; Shea, c. 1986

CHARLES GRODIN

Real Name: Charles Grodinsky
Birthplace: Pittsburgh, PA
Birthdate: 4/21/35
Occupation: Actor, writer
Education: University of Miami, Pittsburgh Playhouse School, studied with Lee Strasberg and Uta Hagen
Debut: (Stage) *Tchin-Tchin,* 1962
Signature: *Midnight Run,* 1988
Facts: Grodin was almost cast in the

lead role in *The Graduate* but lost it due to an argument with the producers over salary.

Only leases white or gray Cadillac DeVille sedans because he doesn't like to attract attention.

Took his "self-parodying loutishness," as one reviewer called it, to his own cable TV talk show in 1995, to entertaining results.
Marriages: Julia (divorced), Elissa, 1985
Children: Marion, 1960 (with Julia). Nicky, c. 1987
Quote: On a *Tonight Show* appearance, Grodin told Johnny Carson, "It's hard for me to answer a question from someone who really doesn't care about the answer." Carson banned Grodin from the show.

MATT GROENING

Birthplace: Portland, OR
Birthdate: 2/15/54
Occupation: Cartoonist
Education: Evergreen College
Debut: (Comic Strip) *Life in Hell* (in the *Los Angeles Reader),* April 1980
Signature: *The Simpsons*
Facts: Elected student-body president in high school. Once elected, tried to rewrite the student government constitution to switch absolute power to himself.

In Los Angeles, ghostwrote the autobiography of an elderly film director who also employed him as a chauffeur, and worked as a landscaper for a sewage treatment plant.

The members of the Simpson family bear the same names as members of Groening's family (although Bart is an anagram for brat).

Groening's home in Venice, CA, is near a canal so he can canoe easily.
Original Job: Writer, rock critic
Marriage: Deborah Caplin, 1986 (separated, 1999)
Children: Homer, 1989; Abraham, 1991

Major Award: Emmy, Outstanding Animated Program, *The Simpsons,* 1990, 1991

GENE HACKMAN

Birthplace: San Bernardino, CA
Birthdate: 1/30/30
Occupation: Actor
Education: Pasadena Playhouse, University of Illinois, School of Radio Technique in NY
Debut: (Stage) *Any Wednesday,* 1964; (Film) *Lillith,* 1964; (Novel) *Wake of the Perdido Star,* 1999
Signature: *The French Connection,* 1971
Facts: Did his own driving in the car-chase scenes in *The French Connection.*

At the Pasadena Playhouse, he and classmate Dustin Hoffman were voted the two least likely to succeed.
Original Jobs: Doorman, truck driver, shoe salesman, soda jerk, furniture mover, dog license-checker
Marriages: Faye Maltese (divorced, 1986), Betsy Arakawa, 1991
Children: Christopher, 1960;Elizabeth, 1962; Leslie, 1966; (with Faye Maltese)
Major Awards: Oscar, Best Actor, *The French Connection,* 1971; Oscar, Best Supporting Actor, *Unforgiven,* 1992

GERI HALLIWELL

Real Name: Geraldine Estolle Halliwell
Birthplace: Watford, England
Birthdate: 8/6/72
Education: College graduate, UK
Debut: (Album) *Spice,* 1997; (Solo album) *Schizophonic,* 1999
Signature: Ginger Spice
Facts: After leaving the Spice Girls, auctioned her performance clothing, earning $246,000 for charity.

Had a benign lump in her breast when she was 18, which inspired in part her current role as a Goodwill Ambassador of the United Nations Population Fund, promoting popula-

tion control and reproductive health care.

At Prince Charles's 50th birthday party, she sang in a manner reminiscent of Marilyn Monroe's famous serenade of John F. Kennedy.

Lived with friend George Michael and his boyfriend for three months after leaving the Spice Girls.

Was a game-show host on Turkish television.
Infamy: Was first photographed nude by Sebastian Amengual when she was 17, and subsequently posed nude for numerous other photographers. She also appeared nude in *Playboy.*
Relationship: Chris Evans, television host
Quote: "I am more creative when I don't have sex."

TOM HANKS

Birthplace: Concord, CA
Birthdate: 7/9/56
Occupation: Actor
Education: Chabot College, California State University–Sacramento
Debut: (Film) *He Knows You're Alone,* 1980 [see page 105 for a complete filmography]
Signature: *Forrest Gump,* 1994
Facts: Attended at least five different elementary schools.

In high school, became a born-again Christian for a couple of years. Converted to Greek Orthodox after marrying Wilson.

After a one-shot guest spot on *Happy Days,* producer Ron Howard asked him to read for a secondary part in *Splash,* but he got the lead instead.

Played Michael J. Fox's alcoholic uncle on the sitcom *Family Ties.*

Doesn't like to talk on the phone, is a bit of a hermit at times.

Collects 1940s typewriters.
Marriages: Samantha Lewes (divorced), Rita Wilson, 1988
Children: Colin, 1977; Elizabeth, 1982; (with Samantha Lewes).

Chester, 1990; Truman Theodore, 1995
Major Awards: Oscar, Best Actor, *Philadelphia,* 1993; Oscar, Best Actor, *Forrest Gump,* 1994

ANGIE HARMON

Birthplace: Dallas, TX
Birthdate: 8/10/72
Occupation: Actor, model
Education: High school graduate
Debut: (TV) *Baywatch Nights,* 1995; (Film) *Lawn Dogs,* 1997
Signature: *Law & Order*
Facts: Began her career as a newborn, in *How to Give Your Baby a Bath,* a hospital-made film. Both of her parents were models.

After working as a child model, she won a *Seventeen* magazine cover model contest at age 17, beating out 63,000 contestants.

Was a runway model for major designers, including Calvin Klein, Giorgio Armani, and Donna Karan.

Was cast in *Baywatch Nights* after being discovered on an airplane by David Hasselhoff.

Organizes her 75 boxes of shoes by taping Polaroid pictures on the boxes.

Her fiancé proposed to her on *The Tonight Show* with Jay Leno.
Original Job: Model
Marriage: Jason Sehorn, professional football player (engaged, 2000)
Quote: "This life is so much fun. I keep waiting, like in the cartoons, for an anvil to drop on my head."

WOODY HARRELSON

Real Name: Woodrow Tracy Harrelson
Birthplace: Midland, TX
Birthdate: 7/23/61
Occupation: Actor
Education: Hanover College
Debut: (Film) *Wildcats,* 1986
Signature: *Cheers*
Facts: A hyperactive child, sometimes prone to violence, he was

placed in a school for problem students. "Violence was almost an aphrodisiac for me." Took Ritalin.

His absent father was convicted of murdering a federal judge and sentenced to life in prison when Woody was a freshman in college.

Sang and composed for a 10-piece "blues-a-billy" band, Manly Moondog and the Three Kool Kats.

Dated Brooke Shields, Carol Kane, Glenn Close, and Moon Unit Zappa.

Infamy: Admits to having been a sex addict.

Arrested for marijuana possession when he planted four hemp seeds in July 1996 to challenge a state law making it illegal to grow industrial hemp. After a four-year court battle, a Kentucky jury cleared him.

Arrested November 1996 for climbing the Golden Gate Bridge. Harrelson was intending to hang banners calling for federal protection for 60,000 acres of redwood trees in Northern California. He was charged with trespassing, being a public nuisance, and failing to obey a peace officer. Agreed to pay a $1,000 fine and spend 25 hours teaching children about the environment.

Original Job: Claims he had over 17 different jobs in one year, including waiting tables and short-order cooking, and was fired from almost all of them

Marriages: Nancy Simon (divorced), Laura Louie, 1998

Children: Deni Montana, 1993; Zoe, 1996

Major Award: Emmy, Best Supporting Actor in a Comedy Series, *Cheers,* 1989

ED HARRIS

Birthplace: Tenafly, NJ
Birthdate: 11/28/50
Occupation: Actor
Education: California Institute of the Arts
Debut: (Film) *Coma,* 1978
Signature: *Apollo 13,* 1995
Facts: Twelve years before *Apollo 13,*

appeared in the space film *The Right Stuff.*

His highly lauded *Apollo* scene where he reacts to the astronauts' splashing down was perfected in a single take.

Played more than 20 film roles in 17 years.

Marriage: Amy Madigan, 1983
Child: Lily, 1993

THOMAS HARRIS

Birthplace: Jackson, TN
Birthdate: 9/22/40
Occupation: Author
Education: Baylor University
Debut: (Novel) *Black Sunday,* 1973
Signature: *Silence of the Lambs,* 1988
Facts: As a seemingly shy crime reporter for the *Waco Herald Tribune* after college, he tooled off to assignments on his motorcycle. One such story involved a Mexican child-prostitution racket, which some consider the beginning of his interest in the darker side.

While working at the Associated Press in New York, he and two colleagues came up with a premise for a thriller about terrorists, which soon became *Black Sunday.*

A reclusive perfectionist, he meticulously researches his material.

He refuses to lecture, promote his books, or grant interviews. (He stopped giving interviews in the early '80s after he was asked if you had to be a homicidal psycho to write about serial killers.)

Original Job: Newspaper copy boy
Marriage: One prior marriage (divorced); Pace Barnes (relationship)
Child: Anne, c. 1962
Quote: "I think really everything that I know is in my books."

MELISSA JOAN HART

Birthplace: Sayville, NY
Birthdate: 4/18/76
Occupation: Actor

Education: Attended New York University
Debut: (TV) *The Lucie Arnaz Show,* 1984
Signature: *Sabrina, the Teenage Witch*
Facts: By age five, had already appeared in 22 commercials. In the next few years she would star in more than a hundred.

She was so young at the time of her 1984 performance on *Saturday Night Live* that she couldn't stay up for the entire show.

Her mom developed *Sabrina,* and became its executive producer.

Relationship: Bryan Kirkwood, soap opera actor
Famous Relatives: Emily, actor, half-sister; Alexandra Hart-Gilliams, actor, half-sister
Quote: "If your butt looks good, your outfit looks good."

STEVE HARVEY

Birthplace: Cleveland, OH
Birthdate: 10/20/60
Occupation: Comedian
Education: Attended Kent State University
Debut: (TV) *It's Showtime at the Apollo*
Signature: *The Steve Harvey Show*
Facts: Hosts the syndicated TV series *It's Showtime at the Apollo,* and used to host a morning radio show in Chicago.

Has criticized his network, the WB, for not supporting his show and others that appeal to black audiences. His show is the highest-rated on the network.

His own show, in which he stars as Steve Hightower, a former '70s R&B singer who became a high school music teacher, is the top-rated sitcom in African-American homes. He signed a book deal for his autobiography.

The Kings of Comedy tour, featuring Harvey, D. L. Hughley, Bernie Mac, and Cedric "The Entertainer," is the highest grossing comedy tour ever, and has taken in tens of millions of dollars. Spike Lee made a feature film of a performance.

Marriage: One prior marriage; Mary Lee

Child: Twin daughters, c. 1982 (from first marriage); Wynton, 1997

Quote: "America is not yet where it needs to be in race relations for all of us, toward one another. If you had to explain to your children why their faces aren't on television or why we're not in many movies, then you would feel the exact same way yourself."

DAVID HASSELHOFF

Birthplace: Baltimore, MD
Birthdate: 7/17/52
Occupation: Actor
Education: California Institute of the Arts
Debut: (TV) *The Young and the Restless*, 1975
Signature: *Knight Rider*, 1991
Facts: Hasselhoff is a successful recording star in Europe, and has toured Germany and Austria. He performed a concert in front of 500,000 people at the Berlin Wall.

Baywatch was the first American show to appear in mainland China. It is the most watched show on the planet, seen by almost a billion people every day.

Marriages: Catherine Hickland (divorced), Pamela Bach, 1989
Children: Taylor Ann, 1990; Hayley Amber, 1992

ETHAN HAWKE

Birthplace: Austin, TX
Birthdate: 11/6/70
Occupation: Actor, director, writer
Education: New York University, studied acting at the McCarter Theatre in Princeton, the British Theatre Association, and Carnegie-Mellon University
Debut: (Film) *Explorers*, 1985; (Stage) *The Seagull*, 1992
Signature: *Dead Poets Society*, 1989

Facts: Was seen out drinking and dancing with the married Julia Roberts in April 1994. He claims they were just discussing a possible movie project.

Starred in *Explorers* when he was 14 with River Phoenix.

His own singing was featured in the *Reality Bites* soundtrack.

Dropped out of Carnegie Mellon after two months to act in *Dead Poets Society*.

Co-founded the New York theater company Malaparte.

Raised eyebrows when *The Hottest State*, his first published novel, attracted advance payments much higher than other novice authors'.

Marriage: Uma Thurman, 1998
Child: Maya Ray Thurman-Hawke, 1998
Quote: "I didn't realize how selfish I was until I had a baby."

GOLDIE HAWN

Birthplace: Takoma Park, MD
Birthdate: 11/21/45
Occupation: Actor
Education: American University
Debut: (Film) *The One and Only Genuine Family Band*, 1968
Signature: *Private Benjamin*, 1980
Facts: Discovered while dancing in the chorus of an Andy Griffith TV special in 1967. Became a regular on *Laugh-In*.

Father performed as a musician at the White House.

Hobbies include knitting.
Original Job: Go-go dancer
Marriages: Gus Trikonis (divorced, 1976); Bill Hudson (divorced, 1982); Kurt Russell (relationship)
Children: Oliver Rutledge, 1976; Kate Garry, 1979; (with Bill Hudson). Wyatt, 1986
Major Award: Oscar, Best Supporting Actress, *Cactus Flower*, 1969

SALMA HAYEK

Birthplace: Coastzacoalcos, Veracruz, Mexico
Birthdate: 9/2/66
Occupation: Actor
Education: Attended National University of Mexico and Stella Adler Conservatory
Debut: (TV) *Nurses*, 1992; (TV movie) *Roadracers*, 1994; (Film) *Mi vida loca ("My Crazy Life")*, 1993
Signature: *Desperado*, 1995
Facts: Attained stardom on Mexican TV, then moved to L.A. in 1991 to study English and acting.

She is of Lebanese descent.

As a child, her grandmother frequently shaved Salma's head and clipped her eyebrows, believing that it would add body to her dark, thick hair.

She finished high school in two years, but her mother was afraid of "college boys" and made her live in Houston until the age of 17.

Discovered by director Robert Rodriguez on a Spanish-language cable-access talk show while he was channel surfing.

Has two pet monkeys, a gift from friend Antonio Banderas.
Infamy: Expelled from a boarding school in Louisiana for setting alarm clocks back three hours.
Relationship: Ed Norton
Famous Relatives: Diana Hayek, opera singer, mother
Quote: "When I was a little girl, they told me I couldn't wear tiaras to school. Now I get to wear whatever I want!"

ANNE HECHE

Birthplace: Aurora, OH
Birthdate: 5/25/69
Occupation: Actor
Education: High school
Debut: (TV) *Another World*, 1988; (Film) *The Adventures of Huck Finn*, 1993
Signature: *Volcano*, 1969
Facts: Her father was a Baptist church choir director who was

secretly gay; Heche found out at age 12 when he was dying of AIDS.

The same year her father died, her brother was killed in a car accident. To help support her family while in junior high school, Heche sang in a local dinner theater.

Was asked to be in a soap opera by a Procter & Gamble talent scout who happened to see her in a high school play.

Dated Steve Martin, costar of her film *A Simple Twist of Fate* for two years until she broke it off.

Formerly involved in a relationship with Ellen DeGeneres.

Infamy: Shortly after her relationship with Ellen DeGeneres was announced, the pair was criticized for nuzzling and hugging during the annual White House Correspondents' Dinner.

Quote: "I put a very high premium on honesty. If you don't accept your own sexuality, it will kill you."

Major Awards: Emmy, Outstanding Younger Actress, *Another World*, 1990

KATHARINE HEPBURN

Birthplace: Hartford, CT
Birthdate: 5/12/07
Occupation: Actor
Education: Bryn Mawr College
Debut: (Stage) *The Czarina*, 1928; (Film) *A Bill of Divorcement*, 1932
Signature: *The African Queen*, 1951
Facts: In her strict New England home, where her father was a surgeon and her mother a militant suffragette, Hepburn and her siblings took cold showers every morning.

Since she was considered too much of a tomboy, she was educated by home tutors.

Decided to take up acting once she realized there was little opportunity for a woman to become a doctor.

According to a 1995 biography, she settled for Tracy after her true love, Catholic director John Ford, couldn't get a divorce from his wife.

Original Job: Sold balloons
Marriages: Ludlow Ogden Smith (divorced, 1934), Spencer Tracy (relationship, deceased)
Major Awards: Oscar, Best Actress, *Morning Glory*, 1933; Oscar, Best Actress, *Guess Who's Coming to Dinner*, 1967; Oscar, Best Actress, *The Lion in Winter*, 1968; Emmy, Best Actress in a Drama Special, *Love Among the Ruins*, 1975; Oscar, Best Actress, *On Golden Pond*, 1981; Kennedy Center Honor for Lifetime Achievement, 1990
Quote: "I am revered rather like an old building."

JENNIFER LOVE HEWITT

Birthplace: Waco, TX
Birthdate: 2/21/79
Occupation: Actor, dancer, singer
Education: High school
Debut: (Film) *Sister Act 2*, 1993
Signature: *Party of Five*
Facts: Made her acting debut at age 6 in a pig barn at a Texas livestock show.

Her debut CD, *Love Songs*, was released in Japan, but not the U.S., when she was 13.

The "starstruck" star has a large celebrity autograph collection.

She sang "How Do I Deal" on the soundtrack for *I Still Know What You Did Last Summer*.

Sent Gwyneth Paltrow, who she looks up to, three dozen roses the night she won an Oscar.

Relationship: Rich Cronin, musician in the group LFO

TOMMY HILFIGER

Birthplace: Elmira, NY
Birthdate: 3/24/51
Occupation: Designer
Education: High school
Debut: (Clothes line) Tommy Hilfiger, 1985
Facts: As a child, struggled with dyslexia and, consequently, was a poor student.

Opened his first store, People's

Place, selling bell bottoms and other trendy clothes, at age 18. After expanding to several cities, the chain went bankrupt.

Sales of his clothes went up $90 million in 1994, the year Snoop Dogg wore his oversized jersey on *Saturday Night Live*.

Bought a blimp in 1998.
Marriage: Susie, 1980 (separated, 2000)
Children: Alexandra, c. 1985; Richard; Elizabeth; Kathleen Anne, 1995
Major Award: Council of Fashion Designers of America, Menswear Designer of the Year, 1995

FAITH HILL

Real Name: Audrey Faith Hill
Birthplace: Jackson, MI
Birthdate: 9/21/67
Occupation: Country singer
Education: High school
Debut: (Album) *Take Me As I Am*, 1993
Signature: *This Kiss*, 1998
Facts: Adopted and raised in Star, Mississippi, she sang in church and formed her first country band by age 16, performing first at a Tobacco Spit competition and eventually at rodeos and country fairs.

Her break came when a talent scout heard her sing harmony with Gary Burr at the Bluebird Cafe.

After some 150 performances in 1994, she endured vocal surgery, followed by three weeks of complete silence.

At the last minute, she was asked to join Tina Turner, Elton John, Cher, and Whitney Houston for the *VH1 Divas Live* concert event.

Husband Tim McGraw proposed to her in his trailer during 1996's "Spontaneous Combustion" tour. She responded by scrawling "I'm going to be your wife" on the mirror while he was performing on stage.
Marriage: Dan Hill (divorced); Scott Hendricks (engaged, 1995; never married); Tim McGraw, 1996

Children: Gracie Katherine, 1997; Maggie Elizabeth, 1998
Quotes: "I'm not even sure I know what a diva is. But I'm very glad I was there."

LAURYN HILL

Birthplace: South Orange, NJ
Birthdate: 5/25/75
Occupation: Singer
Education: Attended Columbia University
Debut: (Album) *Blunted on Reality*, 1993
Signature: *The Miseducation of Lauryn Hill*, 1998
Facts: Originally called Tranzlator Crew, the group changed their name to The Fugees when a long-forgotten 1980s new-wave act called Translator objected.

The Fugees sprang from the trio's feeling of being refugees from mainstream culture and even hip-hop, and from their sense that they found refuge in the music they made.

Hill met fellow group member Pras Michel when the two attended the same high school. Wyclef Jean, who soon joined forces with them, is Michel's cousin.

Her five-Grammy haul for *The Miseducation of Lauryn Hill* tied her with Carole King for most trophies by a female artist in a single year.

Her fiancé is an ex-college football star and the son of the late Bob Marley.
Relationship: Rohan Marley (engaged)
Children: Zion David, 1997; Selah Louise, 1998
Major Award: Grammy, Best R&B Group with Vocal, "Killing Me Softly," 1996; Grammy, Album of the Year, *The Miseducation of Lauryn Hill*, 1998; Grammy, Best New Artist, 1998; Grammy, Best R&B Song, "Doo Wop (That Thing)," 1998; Grammy, Best R&B Vocal—Female, "Doo Wop (That Thing)," 1998; Grammy, Best R&B Album, *The Miseducation of Lauryn Hill,* 1998.

DUSTIN HOFFMAN

Birthplace: Los Angeles, CA
Birthdate: 8/8/37
Occupation: Actor
Education: Los Angeles Conservatory of Music, Santa Monica City College; studied at the Pasadena Playhouse and the Actor's Studio
Debut: (Stage) *Yes Is for a Very Young Man,* 1960; (Film) *Tiger Makes Out,* 1967
Signature: *The Graduate,* 1967
Facts: Played Tiny Tim in junior high school.

Slept on Gene Hackman's kitchen floor while looking for work.

Achieved Ratso's distinctive walk in *Midnight Cowboy* by putting pebbles in his shoe.

When taking the screen test for *The Graduate,* Hoffman said, "I don't think I'm right for the role. He's a kind of Anglo-Saxon, tall, slender, good-looking chap. I'm short and Jewish." During the screen test he forgot his lines and was nervous and clumsy.

Hoffman originally wanted to be a concert pianist. Also studied to be a doctor.

Los Angeles magazine paid Hoffman $1.5 million for running a computer-altered image of him in an evening dress and high heels. The judge said the magazine violated Hoffman's publicity rights.
Original Job: Washing dishes, checking coats, waiting tables, cleaning a dance studio, selling toys at Macy's, attendant in a psychiatric institution
Marriages: Anne Byrne (divorced); Lisa Gottsegen, 1980
Children: Karina, 1966; Jenna, 1970; (with Anne Byrne). Jacob, 1981; Rebecca, 1983; Max, 1984; Alexandra, 1987
Major Awards: Oscar, Best Actor, *Kramer vs. Kramer,* 1979; Oscar, Best Actor, *Rain Man,* 1988; Emmy, Best Actor in a Made-for-TV Movie, *Death of a Salesman,* 1986
Quote: "I kept all the dresses from Tootsie. I wear them every Thursday night."

LAUREN HOLLY

Birthplace: Geneva, NY
Birthdate: 10/28/63
Occupation: Actor
Education: Sarah Lawrence College
Debut: (Film) *Band of the Hand,* 1986
Signature: *Picket Fences* (TV series)
Facts: Personal tragedy struck in 1992 when her parents ended their 30-year marriage and, a short time later, her 14-year-old brother died in a house fire.

Her very public 1994 divorce from Anthony Quinn's struggling actor son, Danny, had him claiming that her careless spending squandered their fortune and her accusing him of having affairs and refusing to work.

Roomed with Robin Givens in college.
Marriages: Danny Quinn (divorced); Jim Carrey (divorced, 1997); Marc Grace, baseball player for Chicago Cubs (relationship)

KATIE HOLMES

Real Name: Kate Noelle Holmes
Birthplace: Toledo, OH
Birthdate: 12/18/78
Occupation: Actor
Education: High school
Debut: (Film) *The Ice Storm,* 1997; (TV) *Dawson's Creek,* 1998
Signature: *Dawson's Creek*
Facts: Was cast as Joey Potter on *Dawson's Creek* based on a videotape that she made in her basement.

She grew up in a strict Catholic household as the youngest of five children.

The Ice Storm was the first movie she ever auditioned for.

Her mother sent her to modeling school at age 10 to expose her to the field and to teach her how to be graceful. At 16 she attended a modeling convention in New York City, but she never pursued the career.

Earned a 4.0 average in high

school and graduated in 1997, deferring enrollment twice at Columbia University.
Relationship: Chris Klein
Quote: "It isn't my fault that I come from a really normal, dream family."

ANTHONY HOPKINS

Birthplace: Port Talbot, South Wales
Birthdate: 12/31/37
Occupation: Actor
Education: Welsh College of Music and Drama, Royal Academy of Dramatic Art, London
Debut: (Stage) *Julius Caesar,* 1964; (Film) *The Lion in Winter,* 1968 [see page 105 for a complete filmography]
Signature: *The Silence of the Lambs,* 1991
Facts: Debuted as conductor with the New Symphony Orchestra at Royal Albert Hall, 1982.

Was knighted by Queen Elizabeth in 1993.

Understudied for Laurence Olivier in *Dance Of Death,* 1966.

Wrote the music for his 1996 film *August.*

Became a US citizen in 2000.
Infamy: Had a long bout with alcohol addiction.
Original Job: Steelworker
Marriages: Petronella Barker, 1967 (divorced, 1972); Jennifer Ann Lynton, 1973
Child: Abigail, 1968 (with Petronella Barker)
Major Awards: Emmy, Best Actor in a Drama or Comedy Special, *The Lindbergh Kidnapping Case,* 1976; Emmy, Best Actor in a Miniseries, *The Bunker,* 1981; Oscar, Best Actor, *The Silence of the Lambs,* 1991
Quote: "I don't like slow movies. I don't like *Masterpiece Theater.*"

WHITNEY HOUSTON

Birthplace: Newark, NJ
Birthdate: 8/9/63
Occupation: Singer
Education: High school

Debut: (Album) *Whitney Houston,* 1985
Signature: "The Greatest Love of All," 1987
Facts: Got her start at age 8 singing in the New Hope Baptist Junior Choir.

Sang backup for Chaka Khan, Lou Rawls, and Dionne Warwick.

As a model, appeared on the cover of *Seventeen.*

Was an actress in her early days, appearing on *Silver Spoons* and *Gimme a Break.*
Infamy: In 2000 was found with 15.2 grams of marijuana in her pocketbook at a Hawaii airport security checkpoint. She departed before local police arrived, but was later charged with a misdemeanor.
Original Job: Model
Marriage: Bobby Brown, 1992
Child: Bobbi Kristina, 1993
Famous Relatives: Cissy Houston, singer, mother; Thelma Houston, singer, aunt; Dionne Warwick, singer, cousin
Major Awards: Emmy, Best Individual Performance in a Variety or Music Program, *The 28th Annual Grammy Awards,* 1986; Grammy, Best Pop Vocal—Female, "Saving All My Love for You," 1985; Grammy, Best Pop Vocal—Female, "I Wanna Dance with Somebody," 1987; Grammy, Best Pop Vocal—Female, "I Will Always Love You," 1993; Grammy, Record of the Year, "I Will Always Love You," 1993; Grammy, Album of the Year, *The Bodyguard Soundtrack,* 1993; Grammy, Best R&B Vocal—Female, "It's Not Right But It's Okay," 1999

RON HOWARD

Birthplace: Duncan, OK
Birthdate: 3/1/54
Occupation: Actor, director, producer
Education: University of Southern California
Debut: (Film) *Frontier Woman,* 1956; (TV) *Playhouse 90, 1959*
Signature: *Cocoon,* 1985

Facts: Starred on *The Andy Griffith Show* as Opie when just 6 years old.

The long-running hit *Happy Days* actually struggled in the ratings when it focused mostly on the misadventures of Howard's teenage character; it took off a year later when Henry Winkler's Fonzie became the star.

First directing effort, 1977's *Grand Theft Auto,* was shot in 20 days for $602,000; grossed $15 million.

True to his All-American persona, married his high school sweetheart.
Marriage: Cheryl Alley, 1975
Children: Bryce, 1980; Jocelyn, 1985; Paige, 1985; Reed, 1987
Famous Relatives: Rance Howard, actor, father; Jean Howard, actor, mother; Clint Howard, actor, brother

KATE HUDSON

Birthplace: Los Angeles, CA
Birthdate: 4/19/79
Education: High school graduate
Occupation: Actor
Debut: (TV) *Party of Five,* 1996; (Film) *Desert Blue,* 1999
Signature: *Almost Famous,* 2000
Facts: Her middle name is Garry. Brother Oliver calls her Hammerhead Shark (because of the space between her eyes) and Dumbo.

Turned down the title role in *Felicity* to continue her education.

Was in a relationship with Eli Craig, son of Sally Field.

Is estranged from her natural father.
Relationship: Chris Robinson, musician
Famous relatives: Goldie Hawn, mother, actor; Bill Hudson, father, comedian-musician; Kurt Russell, "adoptive father," actor; Wyatt Russell, half-brother, actor; Oliver Hudson, brother, actor,
Quote: "I'm not the cool, hard, independent-movie-chick—the grungy outfit, reading Dostoyevsky. I like to look nice and dress nice. I'm very Betty Crocker."

D. L. HUGHLEY

Real Name: Darryl Lynn Hughley
Birthplace: Los Angeles, CA
Birthdate: 3/6/63
Occupation: Comedian
Education: High school
Debut: (TV) *Def Comedy Jam*
Signature: *The Hughleys*
Facts: Urged by his barber to enter a stand-up comedy contest, then booked on the so-called "Chitlin Circuit." Big break came after 10 years and a million frequent-flyer miles as a stand-up comic.

Expelled from high school in tenth grade for fighting, he later completed his GED.

Sitcom *The Hughleys* is based on his personal experiences living in a white neighborhood.
Infamy: One-time member of the notorious L.A. gang the Bloods, he turned his life around after his cousin, a member of rival gang the Crips, was murdered.
Original Job: Telemarketer for *Los Angeles Times*
Marriage: LaDonna, 1986
Children: Ryan, 1987; Kyle, 1989; Tyler, 1991
Quote: "I don't sing, I don't dance, I don't do impressions. I'm just a guy who gets up there and talks trash."

SAMMO HUNG

Real Name: Samo Hung Kam-Bo
Birthplace: Hong Kong
Birthdate: 1/7/52
Occupation: Actor, director, producer, fight choreographer
Education: Chinese Opera Research Institute
Debut: (Film) *Education of Love,* 1961; (Directorial) *The Iron-Fisted Monk,* 1978; (TV) *Martial Law,* 1998
Signature: *Martial Law*
Facts: Inspired to be an actor, he studied at the Beijing Opera School, combining physical conditioning with dramatic study, and became star member of the Seven Little Fortunes children's troupe, performing in local nightclubs.

Instructed younger classmates, including Jackie Chan, in Opera-style martial arts, earning him the nickname of "Big Brother."

He's completely colorblind.

His wife, who also acts as his dialogue coach, is a former Miss Hong Kong.

His trademark scar, that runs from the side of his nose to the top of his lip, is the result of being slashed with a cracked soda bottle at age 16.

With some 140 films to his credit in Hong Kong, he is best known in America for his fight with Bruce Lee at the beginning of 1973's *Enter the Dragon.*
Marriages: Jo Yuen Ok, 1973 (divorced,1994); Joyce Mina Godenzi, 1995
Children: Timmy, c. 1974; Jimmy, c. 1975; Sammy, c. 1979; Stephanie, c. 1983 (with Jo Yuen Ok)
Quote: "A sprained ankle to me is like a paper cut to you."

HELEN HUNT

Birthplace: Los Angeles, CA
Birthdate: 6/15/63
Occupation: Actor
Education: UCLA
Debut: (TV) *The Mary Tyler Moore Show,* 1970; (Film) *Rollercoaster,* 1977 [see page 105 for a complete filmography]
Signature: *Mad About You*
Facts: Hunt studied acting, got an agent, and got a part in the TV movie *Pioneer Woman* by age 9.

Began a two-year romance with actor Matthew Broderick while working on *Project X* (1986).

Played Murray Slaughter's daughter on *The Mary Tyler Moore Show.*

Autograph Collector named her as 1999's Worst Signer. If she does give you an autograph, complains the publication, it's "just an H with a sloppy line after it."
Marriage: Hank Azaria, 1999 (separated, 2000)
Famous Relatives: Gordon Hunt, director, father; Peter Hunt, director, uncle

Major Awards: Emmy, Best Actress in a Comedy Series, *Mad About You,* 1996, 1997, 1998, 1999; Oscar, Best Actress, *As Good As It Gets,* 1997

HOLLY HUNTER

Birthplace: Conyers, GA
Birthdate: 3/20/58
Occupation: Actor
Education: Carnegie Mellon University
Debut: (Film) *The Burning,* 1981; (Stage) *Crimes of the Heart,* 1981
Signature: *Broadcast News*
Facts: Director Jane Campion was originally looking for a tall, statuesque Sigourney Weaver type for the lead in *The Piano.*

Youngest of seven children, grew up on a cattle and hay farm in Georgia, where she drove a tractor.

Appeared in pilot for television series *Fame* (1982).
Marriage: Janusz Kaminski, 1995
Major Awards: Emmy, Best Actress in a Miniseries, *Roe vs. Wade,* 1989; Emmy, Best Actress in a Miniseries, *The Positively True Adventures of the Alleged Texas Cheerleader-Murdering Mom,* 1993; Oscar, Best Actress, *The Piano,* 1993

ELIZABETH HURLEY

Birthplace: Hampshire, England
Birthdate: 6/10/65
Occupation: Actor, model
Education: London Studio Centre
Debut: (Stage) *The Man Most Likely To...,* (Film) *Rowing in the Wind,* 1986
Signature: *Austin Powers: International Man of Mystery,* 1997
Facts: Long recognized only as actor Hugh Grant's girlfriend. In 1995 when she accompanied Grant on a guest appearance on *The Joan Rivers Show,* Rivers asked, "And who are you?" The two broke up in 2000 after dating for 13 years.

At the opening of Grant's movie *Four Weddings and a Funeral,* she wore a

Versace dress held together by 24 safety pins.

Replaced Paulina Porizkova as the face of Estée Lauder cosmetics. Defied conventional stardom by beginning as an actor and becoming a supermodel at age 29.

Characterizes herself as an army brat; her father was a major.

Notorious in her early 20s for her punk-rock phase. She pierced her nose, spiked and painted her hair pink and frequented punk rock bars.

Needlepoint is one of her favorite pastimes.

Was a candidate for the position of ambassador for the United Nations High Commissioner for Refugees.

Won a libel suit against a London paper that claimed she could be "hired" for private functions. Money she has been awarded from such suits has funded an island preserve for abandoned or abused chimpanzees.

Infamy: Was expelled from the London Studio Centre after leaving school and going to a Greek Island.

Angered SAG members in 2000 by shooting a non-union commercial for Estee Lauder during a strike. She apologized to the union, claiming that she was unaware of the situation because she does not live in the country.

Quote: "I've always wanted to be a spy, and frankly I'm a little surprised that British intelligence has never approached me."

ICE CUBE

Real Name: O'Shea Jackson
Birthplace: Los Angeles, CA
Birthdate: 6/15/69
Occupation: Rap artist, actor
Education: Phoenix Institute of Technology
Debut: (Album) *Boyz N the Hood* (with N.W.A.), 1986; (Album) *Amerikkka's Most Wanted* (solo), 1990
Signature: *Boyz N the Hood*, 1991

Facts: Former lyricist of the rap group N.W.A. His 1991 album, *Death Certificate,* stirred controversy because it contained racist attacks on Koreans and called for the murder of a Jewish man.

Began writing rap lyrics at age 14.
Marriage: Kim
Child: Darrell, 1986 (stepson); O'Shea Jackson Jr., 1991; Kareema, 1994
Quote: "Rap is the network newscast black people never had."

ENRIQUE IGLESIAS

Birthplace: Madrid, Spain
Birthdate: 5/8/75
Occupation: Singer
Education: Attended University of Miami
Debut: (Album) *Enrique Iglesias,* 1995; (Single) "Si Tu Te Vas," 1995
Facts: After parents divorced in 1979 and his grandfather had been kidnapped in Spain, he went to Miami to live with his father, Julio, not only to learn English but also for safety.

Began singing and writing music at 15 with a couple of older musicians in a Morales basement studio. He kept these meetings secret from his family.

He hates to have his picture taken.

When he first began performing, he was known only as Enrique because he wanted to succeed (or fail) on his own. Walked out of a New York radio interview because he was introduced as Julio's son, and, for the same reason, turned down a spot on Oprah's scheduled show about sons of famous fathers.

Dubbed Sexiest Man by *PEOPLE en Español.*

He loves to windsurf.

Booked himself on Howard Stern's radio show in 2000 after hearing Stern suggest that he could not sing. After appearing on the show, Stern changed his mind and agreed to play Iglesias's songs for several days.

Major Awards: Grammy, Best Latin Pop Performer, 1997
Famous Relatives: Julio Iglesias, singer, father; Julio Jose, actor, model, brother; Chabelli, Spanish television personality, sister
Quote: "I say stuff in my music that I would never dare say face-to-face; I'd be too embarrassed."

NATALIE IMBRUGLIA

Birthplace: Campsie, Sydney, Australia
Birthdate: 2/4/75
Occupation: Singer, actor
Education: High school dropout
Debut: (TV, Australia) *Neighbours,* 1992; (Album) *Left of the Middle,* 1998
Signature: "Torn," 1998
Facts: Started dance lessons at age 2 and attended six days a week.

At 14 she turned down the offer of an Australian entrepreneur for a solo recording act.

She left parochial high school at 16, did some commercials, attended a performing arts college in Sydney, and landed a role in *Neighbours,* an Australian teen-oriented soap.

"Torn" was originally recorded by Ednaswap, an L.A. punk band, though it received no airplay.

DON IMUS

Real Name: John Donald Imus Jr.
Birthplace: Riverside, CA
Birthdate: 7/23/40
Occupation: Radio talk-show host
Education: High school dropout
Debut: KUTY, Palmdale, CA, 1968
Signature: "Imus in the Morning"
Facts: Fired from an early window dressing job for staging striptease shows with mannequins to amuse passersby.

Once called a fast-food restaurant while on the air and ordered 1,200 specially-prepared hamburgers to go, an incident that contributed to an FCC ruling that DJs must identify themselves when phoning listeners.

Wrote the novel *God's Other Son*, based on his lecherous evangelist radio character. Originally published in 1981, it was reissued in 1994 and hit the bestseller list for 13 weeks.

Hospitalized in 2000 with numerous broken bones and a punctured lung after being thrown by his horse.

Infamy: Caused a stir among media members when his jokes insulted Bill and Hillary Clinton during a televised correspondents' dinner.

Had a severe alcohol and cocaine abuse problem, for which he was fired from his New York station in 1977. Finally kicked the habit in 1987, after a nine-day drinking binge scared him into a treatment center.

Original Job: Department store window dresser

Marriage: Harriet (divorced, 1979); Deirdre Coleman, 1994

Children: Nadine, 1960 (stepdaughter); Antoinette, 1962 (stepdaughter); Elizabeth, 1966; Ashleigh, 1967; (with Harriet). Fredric Wyatt, 1998

Major Award: Inducted into the Broadcast Hall of Fame, 1996

JEREMY IRONS

Birthplace: Isle of Wight, England
Birthdate: 9/19/48
Occupation: Actor
Education: Bristol Old Vic Theatre School
Debut: (Stage) *Godspell*, 1972
Signature: *The French Lieutenant's Woman*, 1982
Facts: At school, excelled at rugby, the fiddle, and clarinet and headed the cadet corps.

Made his mark with the BBC series *Brideshead Revisited*, 1981.

Played a dual role as twin brothers in *Dead Ringers*, a 1988 movie he considers his best work.

Original Job: Housecleaner, gardener, assistant stage manager, busker (singing and playing guitar outside movie theaters)

Marriage: Sinéad Moira Cusack, 1978
Children: Samuel James, 1978; Maximilian Paul, 1985
Major Awards: Tony, Best Actor (Dramatic), *The Real Thing*, 1984; Oscar, Best Actor, *Reversal of Fortune*, 1990

JOHN IRVING

Birthplace: Exeter, NH
Birthdate: 3/2/42
Education: University of New Hampshire, BA; University of Iowa, MFA
Occupation: Novelist, screenwriter, actor, college instructor
Debut: (Novel) *Setting Free the Bears*, 1969
Signature: *The World According to Garp*, 1978
Facts: His father taught at Phillips Exeter Academy.

Was dyslexic as a child.

Studied under Günter Grass for a year at the Institute of European Studies in Vienna, Austria. Also studied with Kurt Vonnegut

Played a wrestling referee in the movie version of *The World According to Garp*.

When starting a new novel, he typically writes the last line first.

His son Colin, an actor, appeared in the movie versions of *The Cider House Rules* and *The Hotel New Hampshire*.

Was so unhappy with changes made in the 1998 film *Simon Birch* that he demanded the credit, "suggested by *A Prayer for Owen Meany*."

The Cider House Rules was his screenwriting debut. His grandfather, a noted obstetrician at Boston's Lying-In Hospital, was one of the models for Dr. Larch. (He had a cameo as the stationmaster in the film.)

In 1999, Irving published *My Movie Business: A Memoir*, about his film experiences.

Original Job: English instructor
Marriages: Shyla Leary Irving, 1964 (divorced 1981); Janet Turnbull, 1987
Children: Colin, c. 1965; Brendan, c. 1969 (with Shyla Irving); Everett, 1991
Quote: "I write about characters I love. I want the readers or the audience to love them or at least to sympathize with them, too. If that's sentimental, then I'm guilty."
Major Award: Oscar, Best Adapted Screenplay, *The Cider House Rules*, 1999

ALAN JACKSON

Birthplace: Newnan, GA
Birthdate: 10/17/58
Occupation: Singer, songwriter
Education: South Georgia College
Debut: (Album) *Here in the Real World*, 1989
Signature: "Neon Rainbow"
Facts: In 1985, his wife got Jackson his big break. A flight attendant, she cornered Glen Campbell in the Atlanta airport and asked him to listen to her husband's tape.

Started wearing his trademark white Stetson to hide scars above his left eyebrow (a result of a childhood accident with a coffee table).

Original Job: Forklift operator, car salesman, home builder
Marriage: Denise, 1979
Children: Mattie, 1990; Alexandra, 1993; Dani Grace, 1997

JANET JACKSON

Birthplace: Gary, IN
Birthdate: 5/16/66
Occupation: Singer, actor
Debut: (TV) *Good Times*, 1977
Signature: *Control*, 1986
Facts: With 1986 song "When I Think of You," she and brother Michael became the first siblings in the rock era to have No. 1 songs as soloists.

Paula Abdul was Janet's choreographer before starting her own career.

Played Charlene DuPrey on the TV series *Diff'rent Strokes*.

Marriages: James DeBarge, 1984

(annulled, 1985); Johnny Gill (relationship)

Famous Relatives: Michael, singer, brother; La Toya, singer, sister; Tito, singer, brother; Randy, singer, brother; Marlon, singer, brother; Jermaine, singer, brother; Jackie, singer, brother

Major Awards: Grammy, Best Music Video—Long Form, *Rhythm Nation 1814,* 1989; Grammy, Best R&B Song, "That's the Way Love Goes," 1993; Grammy, Best Short Form Music Video, "Got 'Till It's Gone," 1997

Quote: "It was always my dream for no one to know I was a Jackson."

JOSHUA JACKSON

Real name: Joshua Carter Jackson
Birthplace: British Columbia, Canada
Birthdate: 6/11/78
Education: High school equivalency
Occupation: Actor
Debut: (Film) *Crooked Hearts,* 1991
Signature: *Dawson's Creek*
Facts: By age nine, Jackson had lived in Vancouver, the U.S. and in Dublin, Ireland, moving 10 different times.

Was expelled from two different high schools, once for poor attendance and once for "being mouthy."

His mother is a casting director. In 1987, he begged her to send him out on auditions and he soon landed a commercial for British Columbia Tourism. She also cast him in his movie debut.

In 1999, he and a friend saved two girls from drowning; the girls then sold the story to *The Star.*

He would eventually like to find time for college. Philosophy is his favorite subject.

Briefly dated Katie Holmes.

Has been estranged from his father for years.

Relationship: Brittany Daniel, actor
Quote: "I'm really a normal guy with an abnormal job."

MICHAEL JACKSON

Birthplace: Gary, IN
Birthdate: 8/29/58
Occupation: Singer, songwriter, actor
Debut: (Stage) Mr. Lucky's, Gary, IN (with Jackson 5), 1966
Signature: *Thriller,* 1983
Facts: Built amusement park on property and maintains a menagerie of animals including Bubbles the Chimp.

Gave Elizabeth Taylor away at her marriage to Larry Fortensky in 1991.

Surgery includes four nose jobs, two nose adjustments, and cleft put in his chin. J. Randy Taraborrelli's unauthorized biography claims that Michael had the surgery to avoid resembling his abusive father as much as possible.

Bought the Best Picture statuette awarded by the Academy for *Gone with the Wind* at auction for $1.54 million.

Plans to build a $500 million dollar amusement park in Warsaw, Poland were stalled when the local citizenry protested the proposed site of the park. After planning to visit Warsaw to discuss the location, he cancelled his trip and financial discussions with a private investor have reportedly stalled.

Infamy: Settled out of court a civil lawsuit alleging child molestation. The boy then refused to testify in a criminal proceeding, so prosecutors declined to press charges.

Accused of including anti-Semitic lyrcs in his song "They Don't Care About Us" on *HIStory;* to stem the controversy, the offending lines were altered on later pressings.

In 1999, an Italian judge ruled that he plagiarized the work of songwriter Al Bano when composing the 1991 song, "Will You Be There." An appeals court ruled in Jackson's favor in 2000, but a related second case is still pending.

Famous Relatives: Janet, singer, sister; LaToya, singer, sister; Tito, singer, brother; Randy, singer, brother; Marlon, singer, brother; Jermaine, singer, brother; Jackie, singer, brother

Marriage: Lisa Marie Presley

(divorced); Debbie Rowe, 1997 (separated, 1999)

Children: Prince Michael Jr, 1997; Paris Michael Katherine, 1998

Major Awards: Grammy, Best R&B Vocal—Male, "Don't Stop Till You Get Enough," 1979; Grammy, Album of the Year, *Thriller,* 1983; Grammy, Best Pop Vocal—Male, *Thriller,* 1983; Grammy, Best R&B Song, "Billie Jean," 1983; Grammy, Best R&B Vocal—Male, "Billie Jean," 1983; Grammy, Best Recording for Children, *E.T., the Extra-Terrestrial,* 1983; Grammy, Record of the Year, "Beat It," 1984; Grammy, Best Pop Vocal—Male, "Beat It," 1984; Grammy, Song of the Year, "We Are the World" (with Lionel Richie), 1985; Grammy, Best Music Video, Short Form, *Leave Me Alone,* 1989; Grammy, Legend Award, 1993; Grammy, Best Music Video, "Scream," 1995

Quote: "The press exaggerated the plastic surgery. It's just my noes, you know. Elvis had his nose done—Lisa Marie told m.

SAMUEL L. JACKSON

Birthplace: Chattanooga, TN
Birthdate: 12/21/48
Occupation: Actor
Education: Morehouse College
Debut: (Film) *Ragtime,* 1981
Signature: *Pulp Fiction,* 1994
Facts: Angry at Morehouse College's lack of African-American studies and its control by a white governing body, he participated in a protest involving locking up the school's board of trustees, and was expelled in 1969. He later returned to graduate.

In 1991's *Jungle Fever,* Jackson's performance as crackhead Gator won him the first-ever supporting actor award given by the Cannes Film Festival.

Was Bill Cosby's stand-in for three years on *The Cosby Show.*

Infamy: Had a problem with drugs and alcohol for several years. Ironically, his first role after taking a vow of sobriety was as the crack addict Gator.

Original Job: Security guard
Marriage: LaTanya Richardson, 1980
Child: Zoe, 1982

MICK JAGGER

Birthplace: Dartford, England
Birthdate: 7/26/43
Occupation: Singer, songwriter
Education: London School of Economics
Debut: (Song) "Come On" (cover of Chuck Berry original), 1963
Signature: The Rolling Stones
Facts: Went to elementary school with guitarist Keith Richards but lost touch with him until they met again on a London train in 1960.

Sang backup on Carly Simon's 1973 hit, "You're So Vain."

Co-owned the Philadelphia Furies, a soccer team, with Peter Frampton, Rick Wakeman, and Paul Simon.

In agreeing to an annullment, Hall capitulated to Jagger's claim that their 1990 Hindu wedding on Bali was invalid due to incomplete paperwork. She received a reported settlement of $15 million and ownership of their $8 million, 26-room London mansion.

Denied fathering son Lucas until a blood test proved paternity. In 2000, he was ordered to pay $10,000 per month in temporary support to Luciana Morad.

Marriages: Bianca Perez Morena de Macias (divorced); Jerry Hall, 1990 (annulled, 1999); Vanessa Neumann (relationship)
Children: Karis, 1970 (with Marsha Hunt). Jade, 1971 (with Bianca Jagger). Elizabeth Scarlett, 1984; James Leroy Augustine, 1985; Georgia May Ayeesha, 1992; Gabriel Luke Beauregard, 1997 (with Jerry Hall). Lucas Maurice, 1999 (with Luciana Morad)
Major Awards: Grammy, Best Album Package, *Tattoo You* (with the Rolling Stones), 1981; Grammy, NARAS Lifetime Achievement Award, 1986; inducted into the Rock and Roll Hall of

Fame (with the Rolling Stones), 1989; Grammy, Best Rock Album, *Voodoo Lounge* (with the Rolling Stones), 1994
Quote: "It's a good way of making a living. I think we'll just keep right on doing it."

JAY-Z

Real name: Shawn Carter
Birthplace: Brooklyn, NY
Birthdate: 12/4/70
Occupation: Rap artist
Debut: (Single) "In My Lifetime," 1995; (Album) *Reasonable Doubt*, 1996
Signature: "Money Ain't a Thang," 1998
Facts: Grew up in the Marcy Projects in Brooklyn, near the J and Z subway lines.

Was a high-school friend of the late Notorious B.I.G.

Began producing albums for other artists in 1994, and has collaborated with Puff Daddy, Timbaland, and Jermaine Dupri.

Was featured on Mariah Carey's "Heartbreaker."

In 1997, released *Vol. 1...In My Lifetime*—his second album, title notwithstanding.

The chorus of his song "Hard Knock Life," describing life in the ghetto, samples singing children from the family musical *Annie*.

Co-headlined the Hard Knock Life tour, which became rap's biggest-grossing ever—and surprised naysayers by proceeding without any violent incidents.

Is preparing his Roc-a-Wear clothing line.
Infamy: Was a crack cocaine dealer.

In December, 1999, was charged with first-degree assault in a stabbing incident in a New York City nightclub. He was also charged with two earlier assaults at other nightclubs. After turning himself in and pleading not guilty, he was released on $50,000 bail. He and his attorney later claimed to have a videotape taken at the time of the stabbing that would clear Jay-Z of the charge.

As of press time, details of any resolution have not been made public.
Major Awards: Grammy, Best Rap Album, *Vol. 2... Hard Knock Life,* 1998
Quote: "When you're part of rap, anything that happens definitely is going to be related back to rap, which is unfair."

WYCLEF JEAN

Real Name: Nelust Wyclef Jean
Birthplace: Port-au-Prince, Haiti
Birthdate: 10/17/69
Education: High school
Occupation: Rap artist, guitarist
Debut: (Album) *Blunted on Reality*, 1993; (Solo Album) *The Carnival*, 1997
Signature: The Fugees
Facts: At age nine, he came to the U.S. with his family, as his Baptist preacher father fled the reign of "Baby Doc" Duvalier.

His mother bought him an acoustic guitar to keep him off the streets. He mastered it—along with the organ, drums, and bass.

Learned English by listening to rap music.

His devout parents would not allow him to listen to any music that was not religious.

Bandmate Prakazrel "Pras" Michel is his cousin; Lauryn Hill he knew from high school.

Originally called Tranzlator Crew, the group changed their name to The Fugees when a long-forgotten 1980s new-wave act called Translator objected.

The Fugees sprang from the trio's feeling of being refugees from mainstream culture and even hip-hop, and from their sense that they found refuge in the music they made.

At one performance, he played the guitar with his teeth, then put on a hockey mask (like Jason from *Friday the 13th*) to thrill the crowd.

Sang at the memorial service for John F. Kennedy Jr. in 1999.
Major Awards: Grammy Award, R&B Vocal by a Duo or Group, "Killing Me

Softly with His Song," 1997; Grammy Award, Best Rap Album, 1997

Quote: "My father would whup my ass for playing rap."

PETER JENNINGS

Birthplace: Toronto, Canada
Birthdate: 7/29/38
Occupation: Anchor, senior editor
Education: Carleton University and Rider College
Debut: At age nine, hosted *Peter's People,* a CBC radio show for children, 1947
Signature: *ABC's World News Tonight*
Facts: At 26, was the youngest network anchor ever. ABC removed him after three years. Took over as permanent anchor in 1983.
Original Job: Bank teller and late-night radio host
Marriages: First marriage (divorced); Valerie Godsoe (divorced); Kati Marton (divorced); Kayce Freed, 1997
Children: Elizabeth, 1979; Christopher, c. 1982; (with Kati Marton).
Famous Relative: Charles Jennings, vice president of programming at CBC, father

JEWEL

Real Name: Jewel Kilcher
Birthplace: Payson, UT
Birthdate: 5/23/74
Occupation: Singer, songwriter
Education: Interlochen Arts Academy High School
Debut: (Album) *Pieces of You,* 1995; (TV) *The Wizard of Oz in Concert;* (Film) *Ride With the Devil,* 1999
Signature: *Pieces of You*
Facts: Was raised by her father in a log cabin on an 800-acre farm near Homer, Alaska, with no running water, an outhouse for a bathroom, and only a coal stove for heat.

Before they divorced, her parents, Atz and Nedra Kilcher, recorded two LPs as a folk duo.

Jewel has been a crackerjack

yodeler since she was a small child; experts told her parents it was supposed to be impossible for someone so young to yodel, since the vocal cords aren't well developed.

As a teenager, she spelled her name, "Juel."

When she began singing at coffeehouses, she and her mom lived in adjacent vans, surviving on fruit from nearby orchards and free happy-hour fare from bars.

Ex-boyfriend Sean Penn directed the video for "You Were Meant for Me"; Jewel had it refilmed after their breakup.

Still suffers from a past kidney infection that hospitals refused to treat due to Jewel's then-low income.
Infamy: Is being sued by former manager, Inga Vainshtein, for $10 million. The suit includes charges that Jewel's mother and current manager, Nedra Carroll, consulted channeler Jackie Snyder on business decisions. Snyder, a friend of Jewel's, died of cancer in 1998.
Original Job: Restaurant worker
Relationship: Ty Murray, rodeo champion
Quote: "I'm just this cute blonde folk singer who should be patted on the head. My motto is, 'Candy bars for everybody.'"

BILLY JOEL

Birthplace: Bronx, NY
Birthdate: 5/9/49
Occupation: Singer, songwriter, piano player
Education: High school
Debut: (Song) "You Got Me Hummin'" (cover of Sam and Dave original, with The Hassles), 1965
Signature: "Piano Man," 1973
Facts: Had a suicidal period when he was in his early 20s; after taking pills and swallowing furniture polish, he spent three weeks in Meadowbrook Hospital.

As a Long Island teenager, was a local welterweight boxing champion.

Wrote "New York State of Mind"

within 20 minutes of returning home from California in 1975.
Original Job: Rock critic for *Changes* magazine
Marriages: Elizabeth Weber (divorced); Christie Brinkley (divorced, 1994)
Child: Alexa Ray, 1985
Major Awards: Grammy, Record of the Year, "Just the Way You Are," 1978; Grammy, Song of the Year, "Just the Way You Are," 1978; Grammy, Album of the Year, *Billy Joel,* 1979; Grammy, Best Pop Vocal—Male, *52nd Street,* 1979; Grammy, Best Rock Vocal—Male, *Glass Houses,* 1980; Grammy, Best Recording for Children, *In Harmony 2* (with others), 1982; Grammy, Legend Award, 1991; inducted into Rock and Roll Hall of Fame, 1999

ELTON JOHN

Real Name: Reginald Kenneth Dwight
Birthplace: Pinner, England
Birthdate: 3/25/47
Occupation: Singer, songwriter, piano player
Education: Royal Academy of Music, London
Debut: (Album) *Come Back Baby* (with Bluesology), 1965
Signature: "Candle in the Wind"
Facts: Took his name from first names of Bluesology members Elton Dean and John Baldry.

Wrote "Philadelphia Freedom" in 1975 for Billie Jean King.

Is godfather to Sean Lennon.

Attended London's Royal Academy of Music but quit three weeks before final exams.

Has donated more than $5.5 million—profits from his singles—to his nonprofit care and education foundation.

"Candle in the Wind" is the best-selling single of all time, having sold over 35 million copies.

Had a pacemaker installed in 1999.

Was knighted by Queen Elizabeth in 1998.

Infamy: In 1994, *Star* magazine alleged that he was in a romantic relationship with an Atlanta man. He denied being involved with the man and sued the magazine over the article.

Original Job: Worked at Mills Music Publishers

Marriage: Renate Blauer (divorced, 1988); David Furnish (relationship)

Major Awards: Grammy, Best Pop Performance—Duo or Group, "That's What Friends Are For" (with Dionne & Friends), 1986; Grammy, Best Pop Vocal Performance—Male, "Can You Feel the Love Tonight," 1994; inducted into the Rock and Roll Hall of Fame, 1994; Oscar, Best Original Song, "Can You Feel the Love Tonight," 1994; Grammy, Best Pop Vocal—Male, "Candle in the Wind 1997," 1997; Tony, Best Score, *Aida*, 2000

DON JOHNSON

Birthplace: Flat Creek, MO
Birthdate: 12/15/49
Occupation: Actor
Education: University of Kansas, studied at the American Conservatory Theater in San Francisco
Debut: (Stage) *Fortunes and Men's Eyes*, 1969; (Film) *The Magic Garden of Stanley Sweetheart*, 1970
Signature: *Nash Bridges*
Facts: At age 12, seduced his babysitter. At 16, moved out of his dad's place and moved in with a 26-year-old cocktail waitress. At the University of Kansas, became romantically involved with a drama professor.

Owns a successful race horse, Penny Blues.

Infamy: When he was 12, was caught stealing a car and sent to a juvenile detention home.

Admits to having been addicted to alcohol and cocaine. Says he was sober for ten years, but was treated again for a drinking problem in 1994.

Original Job: Worked in a meat-packing plant

Marriages: a first and second marriage; Melanie Griffith (divorced, remarried, divorced); Kelley Phleger, 1999

Children: Jesse, 1982 (with Patti D'Arbanville). Dakota, 1989 (with Melanie Griffith). Atherton Grace, 1999.

MAGIC JOHNSON

Real Name: Earvin Johnson
Birthplace: Lansing, MI
Birthdate: 8/14/59
Occupation: Basketball player (retired)
Education: Michigan State University
Facts: On November 7, 1991, announced that he was retiring from basketball after being diagnosed HIV positive. Was diagnosed only months after marrying longtime friend Earleatha "Cookie" Kelly, who was in the early stages of pregnancy. Neither Cookie nor the child have tested positive for the disease.

After his diagnosis, became one of the world's major fundraisers and spokesmen for AIDS.

Given his nickname in high school by a local sportswriter after a game in which he scored 36 points and had 18 rebounds.

Hosted short-lived late-night talk show in 1998.

Now a leading businessman, he has helped launch movie theaters in urban locations in Los Angeles and other cities; owns Starbucks and TGIFriday's franchises, has a music management agency with such clients as Boys II Men and Mase, and a music label with MCA Records.

Infamy: In 1992, admitted he caught the AIDS virus from "messing around with too many women."

Marriage: Earleatha "Cookie" Kelly, 1991

Children: Andre, 1982; Earvin III, 1992; Elisa, 1995 (adopted)

Major Awards/Titles: MVP, National

Collegiate Athletic Association Final Four playoff tournament, 1979; MVP, NBA Finals, 1980, 1982, 1987; 3 Time NBA Regular Season MVP; 9 Time All-NBA First Team; 11 Time NBA All-Star; Olympic Gold Medal 1992; Grammy, Best Spoken Word Album, *What You Can Do To Avoid AIDS* (with Robert O'Keefe), 1992

ANGELINA JOLIE

Real Name: Angelina Jolie Voight
Birthplace: Los Angeles, CA
Birthdate: 6/4/75
Occupation: Actor
Education: Attended New York University
Debut: (Film) *Lookin' to Get Out*, 1982. (Stage) *Room Service*
Signature: *Gia*, 1998
Facts: Collects daggers, reads about Vlad the Impaler, and has the Japanese word for death tattooed on her shoulder. Other tatoos include a cross, a dragon, the letter H, and the newest, "Billy Bob."

Six years after film debut, began studying acting at age 11.

Originally wanted to be a funeral director.

Dropped last name to develop individual identity.

Appeared in numerous music videos, including some by Meat Loaf, The Lemonheads, and the Rolling Stones.

First lead in a theatrical release was *Hackers*, which costarred her future husband, Jonny Lee Miller.

For her first wedding, she wore black rubber pants and a white shirt with Miller's name written in blood across the back.

Nominated for an Emmy for her roles in *George Wallace* and *Gia*.

She never goes anywhere without Blistex lip balm.

Original Job: Model

Marriages: Jonny Lee Miller (divorced, 1999); Billy Bob Thornton, 2000

Famous Relatives: Jon Voight, actor, father; Marcheline Bertrand, actor, mother; James Haven Voight, director, brother

Major Award: Oscar, Best Supporting Actress, *Girl Interrupted,* 1999

Quote: "I'm never concerned about going too far. I don't even care if I'm judged."

JAMES EARL JONES

Birthplace: Arkabutla, MS
Birthdate: 1/17/31
Occupation: Actor
Education: Attended University of Michigan
Debut: (Broadway) *The Egghead,* 1957 (understudy); (Film) *Dr. Strangelove,* 1964; (TV) *As the World Turns,* 1966
Facts: Raised by his maternal grandparents after his father left home before he was born and his mother left when he was very young.

He developed a serious stutter at age six, which necessitated communication through written notes in school.

Was drawn to acting after seeing a magazine photo of his father appearing in a Broadway play.

One of his favorite roles was in 1989's *Field of Dreams.*

He was one of the first black regulars on a daytime drama.

Original Jobs: Floor waxer, janitor
Marriages: Julienne Marie Hendricks (divorced); Cecilia Hart, 1982
Child: Flynn Earl Jones, 1983
Famous Relatives: Robert Earl Jones, prizefighter (known as "Battling Bill Stovall") and actor, father
Major Awards: Tony, Outstanding Actor in a Play, *The Great White Hope,* 1969; Grammy, Best Spoken Word Recording, *Great American Documents,* 1976 (with Orson Welles, Helen Hayes, and Henry Fonda); Tony, Best Actor in a Play, *Fences,* 1987; Emmy, *Gabriel's Fire,* 1990; Emmy, Outstanding Supporting Actor in a Miniseries or Special, *Heatwave,* 1990.
Quote: "I was a stutterer, a stam-

merer, totally impaired vocally, and I still am. I worked on it all my life and I still do. From the beginning of high school through the end of college, my extracurricular activity was using my voice."

QUINCY JONES

Birthplace: Chicago, IL
Birthdate: 3/14/33
Occupation: Composer, producer
Education: Seattle University; Berklee College of Music, Boston Conservatory
Debut: Trumpeter, arranger, for Lionel Hampton Orchestra, 1950
Signature: Produced *Off the Wall, Thriller,* and *Bad*
Facts: Established his own label, Qwest, in 1981 and founded *Vibe* magazine.

Scored the TV series *Roots* in 1977.

Has worked with many prominent pop and jazz artists, including Ray Charles, Miles Davis, Ella Fitzgerald, Dizzy Gillespie, Ice-T, Chaka Khan, and Sarah Vaughan.

Middle name is Delight.

Marriages: Jeri Caldwell (divorced); Ulla Anderson (divorced); Peggy Lipton (divorced, 1989); Donya Fiorentino (relationship)
Children: Jolie, 1953 (with Jeri Caldwell). Martina, 1966; Quincy III, 1968 (with Ulla Anderson). Kidada, 1974; Rashida, 1976 (with Peggy Lipton). Kenya, 1993 (with Nastassja Kinski)
Major Award: Grammy, Album of the Year, *Back on the Block,* 1991; Oscar, Jean Hersholt Humanitarian Award, 1995

TOMMY LEE JONES

Birthplace: San Saba, TX
Birthdate: 9/15/46
Occupation: Actor
Education: Harvard University
Debut: (Stage) *A Patriot for Me,* 1969; (TV) *One Life To Live,* 1969; (Film) *Love Story,* 1970
Signature: *The Fugitive,* 1993

Facts: Roomed with Vice President Al Gore while attending Harvard.

Is a champion polo player.

Raises Black Angus cattle on his ranch in San Antonio.

Original Job: Worked in oil fields
Marriages: Katherine Lardner (divorced); Kimberlea Gayle Cloughley (divorced, 1995); Dawn Laurel (relationship)
Children: Austin, c. 1992; Victoria, c. 1991 (with Cloughley)
Major Awards: Emmy, Best Actor in a Miniseries, *The Executioner's Song,* 1983; Oscar, Best Supporting Actor, *The Fugitive,* 1993
Quote: "I like to cook. I'm really interested in killing things and eating them."

MICHAEL JORDAN

Birthplace: Brooklyn, NY
Birthdate: 2/17/63
Occupation: Basketball player
Education: University of North Carolina
Signature: Ability to fly.
Facts: He was cut from the varsity basketball team in high school.

Though he said, "This is my dream," after hitting his first homer playing professional baseball in the minor leagues, he soon left baseball to return to basketball.

In his first game back as a Bull against archrival Knicks in 1995, some fans paid scalpers more than $1,000 a ticket. They were not disappointed; he scored 55 points.

An agreement with the Washington Wizards gave him control of the team's basketball operations in 2000.

Launched Hidden Beach Recordings, a new record label, in 2000.

Marriage: Juanita Vanoy, 1989
Children: Jeffrey Michael, 1988; Marcus James, 1990; Jasmine Mickael, 1992
Major Awards/Titles: NCAA College Player of the Year 1984; MVP NBA Finals, 1991, 1992, 1993, 1996, 1998; four-time NBA Regular Season MVP;

eight-time All NBA First Team; ten-time NBA All-Star; eight-time Winner of NBA Scoring Title; Gold Medal at 1984 and 1992 Olympics.

ASHLEY JUDD

Birthplace: Los Angeles, CA
Birthdate: 4/19/68
Occupation: Actor
Education: University of Kentucky
Debut: (Film) *Kuffs*, 1992; (TV) *Sisters*, 1995
Signature: *Double Jeopardy*, 1999
Facts: Grew up dirt poor in various Kentucky homes lacking electricity, running water or a telephone. Was shuttled around to 12 different schools while Naomi and Wynonna tried to make it in the music business.

As a teenager she cleaned her sister and mother's tour bus for $10 a day.

Graduated Phi Beta Kappa from college.

Suffered a severe depression in 1996 that lasted for several months.

Used to date Matthew McConaughey and Michael Bolton.
Relationship: Dario Franchitti, race car driver (engaged, 2000)
Famous Relatives: Naomi Judd, singer, mother; Wynonna, singer, sister

MIKE JUDGE

Birthplace: Guayaqyuil, Ecuador
Birthdate: 10/17/62
Occupation: Animator, voice actor
Education: University of California at San Diego
Debut: (Film short) *Office Space* 1991; (TV) *Beavis and Butt-head*, 1993; (Film) *Beavis and Butt-head Do America*, 1996
Signature: *Beavis and Butt-head*
Facts: Grew up in Albuquerque, New Mexico, with his father, an archaeology professor, and his school librarian mother.

Was employee of the month at Whataburger, a fast-food emporium, in June 1979. He drew on his early

experiences in such jobs to form Beavis and Butt-head.

While studying physics in college, he took a year off to play bass. After receiving his degree and suffering tedium of two engineering jobs, he moved to Texas to briefly try his hand as a blues musician.

After its 1993 debut, *Beavis and Butt-head* was blamed for several destructive acts committed by young people. MTV eventually responded by moving the program to a later time slot and requesting that Judge tone down references to pyromania and animal cruelty.

He taught himself animation, drawing on books from the library and using an old Bolex 16mm movie camera with his own system of track reading.
Original Jobs: Electrical engineer, professional musician
Marriage: Francesca Morocco, 1989

Children: Julia, 1991; daughter, 1994
Quote: "Sometimes the truth comes out if you let yourself be simple-minded."

MELINA KANAKAREDES

Birthplace: Akron, OH
Birthdate: 4/23/67
Occupation: Actor
Education: Attended Ohio State University, Point Park College
Debut (Film) *Bleeding Hearts,* 1994; (TV) *One Life to Live,* 1989
Signature: *Providence*
Facts: Growing up, she spent many hours in her family's candy store.

First performed at age 8 in a local community theater and was a runner-up in the Miss Ohio beauty pageant.

Had a recurring role as Jimmy Smits's reporter girlfriend on *NYPD Blue* before landing *Providence*.

Known for researching her projects, she visited a coroner's office for *Leaving L.A.* and plastic surgeons for *Providence*.

Her extended family is so large that she and her husband invited 550 guests to their wedding.

She was cast for *Providence* without an audition and the other members of the cast were chosen on the basis of their chemistry with her.

She never leaves home without her Braun electric toothbrush.

Met her husband at Ohio State in Sigma Epsilon Phi, a group that tried to get Greek-American kids to socialize with the hope that they will eventually marry.
Original Jobs: Singer, dancer, model, waitress on World Yacht
Marriage: Peter Constantinides, 1992
Child: Zoe, 2000
Quote: "My sanity is my family. Actually, my sanity and my insanity is my family. I'm Greek, and togetherness is a big part of our culture."

DONNA KARAN

Real Name: Donna Faske
Birthplace: Forest Hills, NY
Birthdate: 10/2/48
Occupation: Fashion designer
Education: Parsons School of Design
Signature: DKNY clothes
Facts: While in college, worked for designers Chuck Howard and Liz Claiborne.

After serving a long apprenticeship with the Anne Klein collection, at age 26 was given full creative control by the principal owner of the firm after Anne Klein died of cancer in 1974.

Close personal friend to many stars including Barbra Streisand.
Original Job: Sales clerk at a Long Island dress shop
Marriages: Mark Karan (divorced), Stephen Weiss, 1983
Child: Cory, 1955 (stepson); Lisa, 1957 (stepdaughter); Gabrielle, 1974 (with Mark Karan)
Major Awards: Coty Award, 1977, 1981; named to Coty Hall of Fame, 1984

HARVEY KEITEL

Birthplace: Brooklyn, NY
Birthdate: 5/13/39
Occupation: Actor, producer
Education: Studied with Lee Strasberg at the Actor's Studio and Stella Adler
Debut: (Film) *Who's That Knocking at My Door?*, 1968
Signature: *The Piano*
Facts: Joined the U.S. Marine Corps at age 16 and served in Lebanon.

Answered a newspaper ad placed by Martin Scorsese, then an NYU student director, seeking actors for his first film in 1965, which started their professional relationship.

Was cast as the lead in *Apocalypse Now*, but had a falling out with director Francis Ford Coppola and was fired on location in the Philippines. He was replaced by Martin Sheen.

As a child, Keitel had a severe stutter.

Unusual among Hollywood actors for his willingness to show frontal nudity in his films *(The Piano, Bad Lieutenant).*
Infamy: Was asked to leave the Alexander Hamilton Vocational School in Brooklyn because of truancy.

His ex-wife filed for Chapter 11 protection in 1999, and claimed that her protracted custody battle (she was awarded sole custody in 1996, now being challenged) with Keitel was the cause after paying nearly $2 million in legal fees.
Original Job: Shoe salesman
Marriage: Lorraine Bracco (divorced, 1992)
Child: Stella, 1986

DAVID E. KELLEY

Birthplace: Waterville, ME
Birthdate: 4/4/56
Occupation: Producer, scriptwriter
Education: Princeton University, Boston University Law School
Debut: (TV writing) *L.A. Law*, 1986
Signature: *Ally McBeal*

Facts: While working at a law firm, wrote a screenplay about young lawyers which an agent sent to Steven Bochco. Soon hired for the then-fledgling *L.A. Law*, he took a leave from his firm rather than resign.

Simultaneously wrote every episode of *Chicago Hope* and *Picket Fences* in 1994 and *Ally McBeal* and *The Practice* several years later.

Signed a deal with Fox TV in 2000 that will make him the highest-paid TV producer ever. His gross over a 6-year contract will be over $300 million.
Original Job: Attorney
Marriage: Michelle Pfeiffer, 1993
Children: Claudia Rose, 1993 (adopted); John Henry, 1994
Major Awards: Emmy, Outstanding Drama Series, *L.A. Law,* 1989; Emmy, Outstanding Drama Series, *L.A. Law,* 1990; Emmy, Outstanding Writing in a Drama Series, *L.A. Law,* 1990; Emmy, Outstanding Drama Series, *L.A. Law,* 1991; Emmy, Outstanding Writing in a Drama Series, *L.A. Law,* 1991; Emmy, Outstanding Drama Series, *Picket Fences,* 1993; Emmy, Outstanding Drama Series, *Picket Fences,* 1994; Emmy, Outstanding Drama Series, *The Practice,* 1998, 1999; Emmy, Outstanding Comedy Series, *Ally McBeal,* 1999

KID ROCK

Real Name: Robert James Ritchie
Birthplace: Rome, MI
Birthdate: c. 1972
Occupation: Rapper, rock musician
Debut: *Grit Sandwiches for Breakfast,* 1990
Signature: *Devil Without a Cause,* 1998
Facts: Despite his act's celebration of "white trash," Rock grew up in a lakefront home with six acres of land.

Learned to scratch with turntables at urban house parties. The mostly black crowds gave him his stage name by crying, "Look at that white kid rock!"

His mother kicked him out of the house when he wouldn't support his brother in rehab.

When preparing *Devil Without a Cause,* clashed with record labels executives over his emphasis on rap, his disposition toward ballads, and the title cut's "I'm going platinum" boast.

Has a contract rider demanding Pabst Blue Ribbon in his dressing room.

His stage show featured an eight-foot-tall middle finger.

Describes his cleanliness as "anal."
Infamy: Sold crack as a teen.

The FCC declared "Yodeling in the Valley" from his debut "obscene, indecent and profane."
Child: Robert Jr., 1993 (with Kelly Russell)

Quote: "I've been into this music since I was eleven years old—purchased it, played it, loved it. If people are going to have a problem with me performing it, I'm like, 'F—- you and your black and white s—.' "

NICOLE KIDMAN

Birthplace: Hawaii
Birthdate: 6/20/67
Occupation: Actor
Education: St. Martin's Youth Theatre, Melbourne, Australia
Debut: (Film) *Bush Christmas*, 1983 [see page 105 for a complete filmography]
Signature: *To Die For*, 1995
Facts: Became an overnight star in Australia with her performance in the miniseries *Vietnam*, 1988.

Joined the Church of Scientology, of which husband Cruise is a devoted member.

Her husband calls her "Nic."
Infamy: Won $580,000 in libel damages in 1998 from Britain's *Express on Sunday* for a story that claimed Kidman and her husband might be closet gays in a sham marriage.

Appeared nude on stage (for approximately 14 seconds) in a limited-run Broadway production of David Hare's *The Blue Room* in 1999.

Sued the *Star* in 1999 for claiming that sex experts had to coach Kidman and her husband in the art of lovemaking for *Eyes Wide Shut*.
Marriage: Tom Cruise, 1990
Children: Isabella Jane, 1993; Connor Antony, 1995; (both adopted)

CRAIG KILBORN

Birthplace: Hastings, MN
Birthdate: 8/24/62
Occupation: Comedian, sports announcer
Education: Montana State University
Debut: (TV) Salinas, CA's KCBA-TV sports anchor, 1987
Signature: *The Daily Show*
Facts: After college, was offered a

spot on a professional basketball team in Luxembourg. Turned down the $600/month job to try his luck in Hollywood.

Stands 6'4".

Daily Show's "5 Questions" was inspired by a failed pickup line he once used in a Manhattan bar.
Infamy: Long-running feud with *Daily Show* female head writer resulted in his one-week suspension after he called her and other female staffers a derogatory name in *Esquire* magazine and suggested that she would perform a sex act on him if requested.

In 1999, admitted to having an 11-year-old son after a tabloid prepared to break the story.
Original Job: Traffic school instructor
Child: son

VAL KILMER

Birthplace: Los Angeles, CA
Birthdate: 12/31/59
Occupation: Actor
Education: Hollywood Professional School, Juilliard
Debut: (Stage) *Slab Boys*, 1983; (TV) *One Too Many*, 1985; (Film) *Top Secret!*, 1984
Signature: *The Doors*, 1991
Facts: Grew up in Chatsworth, CA, across the road from the Roy Rogers ranch. Was the middle child of three boys.

His younger brother, Wesley, drowned right before he left for Juilliard.

At 17, was the youngest person ever accepted to Juilliard's drama school. Cowrote a play with Juilliard classmates, *How It All Began;* starred in an off-Broadway production at the New York Shakespeare Festival.

Met Joanne Whalley on the set of *Willow* in 1988. Pursued her persistently until she finally agreed to marry him.

Provided much of the vocals for the film *The Doors.*

Lives in a cabin in Tesuque, NM. Is

part Cherokee and spends his leisure time exploring the Southwest.
Infamy: On the set of *The Island of Dr. Moreau,* Kilmer burned a cameraman's face with a cigarette.
Marriage: Joanne Whalley (divorced, 1995)
Children: Mercedes, 1991; Jack, 1995
Famous Relatives: Joyce Kilmer, poet, second cousin twice removed
Quote: "I don't make any pretense about being normal. I'm not."

LARRY KING

Real Name: Lawrence Harvey Zeiger
Birthplace: Brooklyn, NY
Birthdate: 11/19/33
Occupation: Talk show host
Facts: Father died of a heart attack when he was 10, and he grew up on public assistance.

As a teenager, ran away to get married. Had the ceremony annulled shortly thereafter.

Graduated from high school just one point above passing.

In February of 1992, Ross Perot announced his bid for the presidency on *Larry King Live.*
Infamy: In December of 1971, he was arrested for stealing money a financier had given him for the New Orleans D.A.'s investigation into the death of John F. Kennedy. King had used the money to pay taxes after he had blown his own money on Cadillacs, expensive restaurants, and gambling debts. The charge was eventually dropped.
Original Job: Janitor at a local AM radio station in Florida
Marriages: Frada Miller, c. 1953 (annulled); Alene Akins, c. 1961 (divorced, remarried, divorced, 1963); Mickey Sutphin, 1964 (divorced, 1968); Sharon Leporte, 1976 (divorced, 1983); Julie Alexander, 1989 (divorced, 1992); Rama Fox (engaged, 1992; never married); Deanna Lund (engaged,

1995; never married); Shawn Southwick, 1997

Children: Andy (adopted); Chaia, 1967; (with Alene Akins). Larry Jr., 1961 (mother unknown). Kelly (with Mickey Sutphin). Chance Armstrong, 1999; Cannon Edward, 2000

Major Award: One News and Documentary Emmy, as interviewer

STEPHEN KING

Birthplace: Portland, ME
Birthdate: 9/21/47
Occupation: Author
Education: University of Maine
Debut: (Book) *Carrie*, 1974
Signature: *The Shining*
Facts: Family was deserted by father, who went out for a pack of cigarettes and never returned.

Wrote first short story at age 7.

Had his first story published in a comic book fan magazine, *Comics Review*, in 1965.

Was working as a high school English teacher at Hampden Academy, in Maine, when his first book was published.

Used the pseudonym Richard Bachman for five novels, including *The Running Man* (made into an Arnold Schwarzenegger film, 1987).

His tales have been turned into seven TV movies and 27 feature films.

Rob Reiner's production company Castle Rock is named after the fictional Maine town in which many King tales are set.

Underwent 5 operations to set broken bones after he was hit by Bryan Smith, an out-of-control motorist, in 1999 while walking alongside the road in Maine. Criticized prosecutors in 2000 for allowing Smith to plead guilty to a lesser charge of driving to endanger, calling the plea agreement "irresponsible public business."

His e-book, "Riding the Bullet," racked up 400,000 orders during its first 24 hours for sale.

In 2000, he started posting installments of a rewritten serialized novel, *The Plant*, on his Web site and asked readers to pay for each installment on the honor system.

Original Job: Laborer in an industrial laundry
Marriage: Tabitha Spruce, 1971
Children: Naomi, 1970; Joe, 1972; Owen, 1977

GREG KINNEAR

Birthplace: Logansport, IN
Birthdate: 6/17/63
Occupation: Actor
Education: University of Arizona
Debut: (TV) *Movietime*, 1987; (Film) *Sabrina*, 1995
Signature: *As Good As It Gets*, 1997
Facts: Lived in Beirut, Lebanon, with family and then evacuated to Athens, Greece, when the Lebanese civil war broke out.

Worked on the advertising campaigns for such films as *Space Sluts in the Slammer, The Imp,* and the *Ghoulies* series.

Hosted syndicated action game show, *College Mad House*.
Marriage: Helen Labdon, 1999

CHRIS KIRKPATRICK

Birthplace: Clarion, PA
Birthdate: 10/17/71
Occupation: Singer
Education: Valencia Community College
Debut: (Single) "I Want You Back," 1996; (Album) **NSYNC*, 1996 (American release, 1998)
Signature: *No Strings Attached*, 2000
Facts: Grew up in near-poverty.

Graduated from college with Backstreet Boy Howie Dorough.

When the band switched record labels, they scrapped months' worth of work to make a completely new beginning.

No Strings Attached smashed CD sales records, moving 1.13 million copies on the day of its release and 2.4 million within a week.

Would like to launch a clothing line.

Infamy: 'N Sync broke with their original record label and management over compensation. Suits and countersuits flew before a settlement was reached, allegedly favoring the band.
Original Job: Performer at Universal Studios Florida theme park
Quote: "We're not going to pierce everything that we have and paint our faces trying to get a different market."

CALVIN KLEIN

Real Name: Richard Klein
Birthplace: New York, NY
Birthdate: 11/19/42
Occupation: Fashion designer
Education: Fashion Institute of Technology
Facts: Rescued his daughter from kidnappers in 1978.

As a boy in the Bronx, grew up around the corner from Ralph Lifshitz (now Ralph Lauren).

Former junk bond czar Michael Milken issued $80 million in high-interest Klein bonds in the '80s.
Infamy: Was addicted to valium and alcohol in the '80s, and attended a Minnesota rehabilitation center for 31 days in 1988.
Marriages: Jayne Centre, 1964 (divorced, 1974); Kelly Rector, 1986 (separated, 1996)
Child: Marci, 1966 (with Jayne Centre)
Major Awards: Coty Award, 1973, 1974, 1975; elected to American Fashion Critics Circle Hall of Fame, 1975; Council of Fashion Designers of America Award, 1994
Quote: "Anything I've ever wanted to do, I've done. Anyone I've wanted to be with, I've had."

HEIDI KLUM

Birthplace: Germany
Birthdate: 1973
Occupation: Model

Facts: She was the 1998 *Sports Illustrated* swimsuit-issue cover girl.

Has been nicknamed "The Body." She's 5'9".

Her husband proposed to her atop the Empire State Building.

Marriage: Ric Pipino, 1997

Quote: "On the runway you always wish your body was a little tighter, and you worry that if you walk too fast things start to jiggle."

TED KOPPEL

Birthplace: Lancashire, England
Birthdate: 2/8/40
Occupation: Broadcast journalist
Education: Syracuse University, Stanford University
Debut: (Radio) WMCA radio
Signature: *Nightline*
Facts: Author, *Adlai Stevenson: In the National Interest*.

When he joined ABC in 1963, he was the youngest news reporter ever to join a network.

Emigrated to the U.S. from England in 1953.

Marriage: Grace Anne Dorney, 1963
Children: Andrea, 1963; Deidre, 1965; Andrew, 1970; Tara, 1971
Major Award: Elected to the Emmy Hall of Fame, 1991

ANNA KOURNIKOVA

Birthplace: Moscow, Russia
Birthdate: 6/7/81
Occupation: Tennis player
Facts: At age nine, she left Russia for Florida, to live and train at Nick Bollettieri's Tennis Academy. She broke away from Bollettieri in 1997, made the semifinals in her Wimbledon debut and became the No. 1 junior player in the world.

Her father was a Greco-Roman wrestling champion, and her mother ran the 400 meters.

Won the doubles title with Martina Hingis at the Australian Open in 1999, her only major title.

Has not cut her waist-length hair since she was seven.

Is the most downloaded athlete on the Web, far outpacing Michael Jordan. There are an estimated 18,000 Web pages devoted to her.

With multiple endorsement deals, she earns an estimated $10 to $14 million a year (less than a million of which is from playing tennis).

Formerly involved with hockey player Sergei Fedorov.

Relationship: Pavel Bure, hockey player

Quote: "I'm still a virgin. I do not let anyone even have a peep in my bed…not for love [or] affection."

JANE KRAKOWSKI

Birthplace: Parsippany, NJ
Birthdate: 9/11/68
Occupation: Actor, singer, dancer
Education: Professional Children's School
Debut: (Film) *National Lampoon's Vacation*, 1983; (TV) *Search for Tomorrow*, 1984; (Stage) *Starlight Express*, 1987
Facts: Twice nominated for a Daytime Emmy for her role in *Search for Tomorrow*, which she landed at age 14.

Made her broadway debut in *Starlight Express* at the age of 18. She was one of only four cast members to stay for its two-year run.

Earned a Tony nomination for her role in *Grand Hotel* in 1990.

She has recorded music by Sondheim, Burt Bacharach, and Paul Simon, and recently signed a contract for a new solo album.

Original Job: Performing at industrial fashion shows
Relationship: Charles Hart

DIANA KRALL

Birthplace: Nanaimo, Canada
Birthdate: 4/16/64
Occupation: Singer, pianist
Education: Berklee School of Music
Debut: (Album) *Stepping Out*, 1993; (Movie) *At First Sight*, 1999
Signature: "Peel Me a Grape," 1997

Facts: Major influences include Shirley Horn, Willie Nelson, and her father's record collection.

Regularly played lounge piano jobs in Nanaimo at 15.

As a student in Boston, had a moonlighting gig playing "to nobody" for four years. "They didn't care. They just wanted to have someone in there, playing."

Made recurring appearances on *Melrose Place*.

Music video "Why Should I Care?" was directed by Clint Eastwood.

Her album *When I Look Into Your Eyes* is one of the few jazz albums to ever be nominated for an Album of the Year Grammy.

Is currently the bestselling jazz artist in the world.

Major Award: Grammy, Jazz Vocal Album of the Year, 1999

Quote: "Hey, I'm a cowgirl who loves to ride horses on the beach, but I'm also a girl who likes clothes and likes to look nice. So why shouldn't I have a beautiful [album] cover? I'm confident enough in my music that I don't have to apologize for that."

LENNY KRAVITZ

Birthplace: Brooklyn, NY
Birthdate: 5/24/64
Occupation: Singer, songwriter, musician
Debut: *Let Love Rule,* 1989
Signature: "It Ain't Over 'Til It's Over"
Facts: As a child, sang in the California Boys Choir.

Though he jams with musicians on tour, in the studio he prefers to play all parts himself.

Cowrote Madonna's "Justify My Love" and Aerosmith's "Line Up."

Cut off his distinctive long dreadlocks "to change my energy… It had to do with getting rid of that baggage from the last 10 years."

Marriage: Lisa Bonet (divorced)
Children: Zoe, 1988
Famous Relative: Roxie Roker, actor, mother, deceased 1995
Major Award: Grammy, Best Rock

Vocal—Male, "Fly Away," 1998
Quote: "Maybe someday I'll do something that no one's heard, I don't know. But at least I'm doing what God put in me to come out."

LISA KUDROW

Birthplace: Encino, CA
Birthdate: 7/30/63
Occupation: Actor
Education: Vassar College
Debut: (TV) *Cheers,* 1982
Signature: *Friends*
Facts: Earned her B.S. in sociobiology, intent on being a doctor like her father, a renowned headache expert. Decided to become a comic actor when she saw Jon Lovitz, her brother's childhood friend, make it on *Saturday Night Live.*

Was on the tennis team in college.

Her movie debut in 1990's *Impulse* ended up completely cut from the film. Later, she was hired but soon fired as Roz on the pilot for *Frasier.*

Grew up with a pool table in her house and is something of a pool shark, able to perform many difficult trick shots.

In 2000, along with *Friends* costars, received a salary increase from $125,000 to $750,000 per episode.
Marriage: Michel Stern, 1995
Child: Julian Murray, 1998
Major Award: Emmy, Best Supporting Actress in a Comedy Series, *Friends,* 1998

EMERIL LAGASSE

Birthplace: Fall River, MA
Birthdate: 10/15/59
Occupation: Chef, television show host
Education: Johnson and Wales University
Debut: (TV) *Essence of Emeril,* 1993
Signature: "Whoo!" "Bam!" "Pow!"
Facts: Interest in cooking began when he was growing up with his French-Canadian father and Portuguese mother.

Had taught himself how to play

trombone, trumpet, flute, and drums, played in a Portuguese band, but turned down a scholarship to the New England Conservatory of Music to pursue culinary arts.

Raises hogs to produce farm-fresh andouille sausage, bacon, and ham, and is a firm believer in organically grown produce.
Original Job: Dishwasher in a Portuguese bakery
Marriages: Elizabeth (divorced, c. 1982); Tari Hohn (divorced, 1996); Alden Lovelace, 2000
Children: Jessica, c. 1980; Jillian, c. 1982 (with Elizabeth)
Quote: "I've been a big Spam fan for a long time."

RICKI LAKE

Birthplace: New York, NY
Birthdate: 9/21/68
Occupation: Actor, talk show host
Education: Ithaca College
Debut: (Film) *Hairspray,* 1988
Signature: *The Ricki Lake Show*
Facts: This once-dumpy star of John Waters' cult films like *Cry Baby* lost 125 pounds over a three-year period.

Plays the flute, piccolo, clarinet, and piano.
Infamy: Arrested in 1994 for criminal mischief for her part in a People for the Ethical Treatment of Animals attack on the offices of designer Karl Lagerfeld.
Original Job: Cabaret singer, appeared off-Broadway in 1983
Marriage: Rob Sussman, 1994
Child: Milo Sebastian, 1997

NATHAN LANE

Real Name: Joseph Lane
Birthplace: Jersey City, NJ
Birthdate: 2/3/56
Occupation: Actor
Education: High school
Debut: (Stage) *A Midsummer Night's Dream,* 1978; (Film) *Ironweed,* 1987
Signature: *The Birdcage,* 1996
Facts: Took the name Nathan at age 22 after playing Nathan Detroit in a

Guys and Dolls dinner-theater show, since there was another Joe Lane in Actors' Equity.

His truckdriver father drank himself to death when Lane was 11. Lane, too, had a drinking problem for two decades, one he kicked only a few years ago.

Playwright Terrence McNally wrote several plays specifically for him.

Played the voice of Timon, the wisecracking meerkat in *The Lion King.*
Original Job: Police bail interviewer
Major Award: Tony, Best Actor (Musical), *A Funny Thing Happened on the Way to the Forum,* 1996

K.D. LANG

Real Name: Katherine Dawn Lang
Birthplace: Consort, Canada
Birthdate: 11/2/61
Occupation: Singer, songwriter
Education: Attended college in Red Deer, Alberta, Canada
Debut: (Album) *A Truly Western Experience,* 1984
Signature: "Constant Craving," 1992
Facts: Acted in the movie *Salmonberries,* 1991.

Recorded a duet with Roy Orbison on a remake of his song "Crying" in 1988, shortly before he died.

Her recordings have been boycotted in the conservative areas of the South and cattle ranching areas of central Canada because she is a lesbian and an animal rights activist.
Original Job: Performance artist
Relationship: Leisha Hailey
Major Awards: Grammy, Best Country Vocal—Collaboration, "Crying" (with Roy Orbison), 1988; Grammy, Best Country Vocaynl—Female, "Absolute Torch and Twang," 1989; Grammy, Best Pop Vocal—Female, "Constant Craving," 1992
Quote: "I have a little bit of penis envy. They're ridiculous, but they're cool."

JESSICA LANGE

Birthplace: Cloquet, MN
Birthdate: 4/20/49
Occupation: Actor
Education: University of Minnesota
Debut: (Film) *King Kong*, 1976
Signature: *Frances*, 1982
Facts: Raised in a depression-prone family with an alcoholic father who moved the family repeatedly, Lange adopted a full-blown, travel-and-party lifestyle as a young adult.

Had a relationship (and a child) with Mikhail Baryshnikov.

The 1994 film *Blue Sky*, for which she won a best actress Academy Award (after four previous nominations), languished in a bank vault after it was made in 1991 because its studio, Orion Pictures, had declared bankruptcy.
Original Jobs: Dancer, model
Marriage: Paco Grande (divorced, 1982); Sam Shepard (relationship)
Children: Alexandra,1981 (with Mikhail Baryshnikov). Hannah Jane, 1985; Samuel Walker, 1987
Major Awards: Oscar, Best Supporting Actress, *Tootsie*, 1982; Oscar, Best Actress, *Blue Sky*, 1994
Quote: "I did bail on the glamor thing early. And now I look back and think oh, hell, I should have done it for another five or 10 years…I'm tired of thinking I have to rip my heart out for every character."

ANGELA LANSBURY

Birthplace: London, England
Birthdate: 10/16/25
Occupation: Actor
Education: Webber-Douglas School of Singing and Dramatic Art, Feagin School of Drama and Radio
Debut: (Film) *Gaslight*, 1944
Signature: *Murder, She Wrote*
Facts: Immigrated with her family to the U.S. when the Germans began to bomb London in World War II.

In 1943, went to MGM to audition for *The Picture of Dorian Gray* and was told the studio was looking for someone to play the role of the maid in *Gaslight*. She auditioned and got it.

In the seven years she was under contract to MGM, she appeared in 70 films.
Original Job: Ticket-taker in the theater in which her mother worked, clerk in department store
Marriages: Richard Cromwell (divorced); Peter Pullen Shaw, 1949
Children: David, 1944 (stepson); Anthony Peter, 1952; Deidre Angela, 1953
Famous Relatives: Moyna McGill, actor, mother; David Lansbury, actor, nephew
Major Awards: Tony, Best Actress (Musical), *Mame*, 1966; Tony, Best Actress (Musical), *Dear World*, 1969; Tony, Best Actress (Musical), *Gypsy*, 1975; Tony, Best Actress (Musical), *Sweeney Todd*, 1979

ERIQ LASALLE

Birthplace: Hartford, CT
Birthdate: 7/23/62
Occupation: Actor, director
Education: New York University; attended Julliard
Debut: (Film) *Coming to America*, 1988
Signature: *ER*
Facts: Was once a competitor in martial arts.

After four years of unsuccessfully shopping a screenplay he wrote and wanted to direct, he borrowed $140,000 and some equipment and filmed a short version of the work himself.

Along with the four other original, continuing *ER* cast members, received a $1 million bonus in 1998 from Warner Bros. Television.
Marriage: Angela Johnson (engaged; never married)

MATT LAUER

Birthplace: New York, NY
Birthdate: 12/30/57
Occupation: Newscaster, producer
Education: Ohio University
Debut: (TV) WOWK-TV, Huntington, WV, 1980
Signature: *Today*
Facts: Quit college for a TV job four credits shy of graduation in 1979; finally got the degree 18 years later by writing a paper on his work experience.

Hosted *9 Broadcast Plaza,* a low-budget tabloid talk show, for two years, but was fired when he refused to do live commercials during the program. Months later, desperate for a job, he applied for a tree-trimming position in upstate New York. When the phone rang, however, it was NBC, asking him to host a local news show.

Appeared 150 times as guest-host of *Today* before landing the permanent slot.

Has an impressive 8 handicap in golf.
Marriages: Nancy Alspaugh (divorced); Annette Roque

RALPH LAUREN

Real Name: Ralph Lifshitz
Birthplace: Bronx, NY
Birthdate: 10/14/39
Occupation: Designer
Education: Attended City College of New York
Facts: Growing up in the Moshulu Park area of New York, Lauren lived two blocks from Calvin Klein.

As a youth, he was drawn to movies and the novels of F. Scott Fitzgerald.

While attending high school in the Bronx, he worked part-time as a department store stockboy and spent most of his earnings on clothes.

After a stint in the army, he was hired as a designer by Beau Brummell Ties. His unusual, wider products sold well, and within a year he formed his own company—Polo—with a loan of $50,000.

He is the only American designer who manufactures and licenses his own designs.

Met his wife when he went to get his eyes tested—she was the optician's receptionist.
Original Job: Salesman
Marriage: Ricky Low Beer, 1964
Children: Andrew, 1969; David, 1971; Dylan, 1974
Quote: "Being comfortable is more important than being slinky."

JUDE LAW

Real Name: David Jude Law
Birthplace: Lewisham, London, England
Birthdate: 12/29/72
Occupation: Actor
Education: Attended Alleyns, Dulwich, England
Debut: (TV) *The Tailor of Gloucester*, 1990; (Film) *Shopping*, 1994
Signature: *The Talented Mr. Ripley*, 1998
Facts: He decided on an acting career at age 4.

Began six years of National Youth Music Theater training at age 12. Played lead in their production *of Joseph and the Amazing Technicolor Dreamcoat.*

Met pal Ewen McGregor at a 1990 audition when, to see how the actors would get along, the director paid them to get drunk together.

Has "Sexy Sadie" tattooed on his arm.

Appeared nude on Broadway during the 1995 run of *Indiscretions.*

Made his directorial debut in 1999 with a segment of the TV movie *Tube Tales.*

Is one of the British actors who formed the film production company Natural Nylon.

He and his wife's film contracts specify they must be released on days of their children's school events.
Marriage: Sadie Frost, 1997
Children: Finlay, c.1990 (stepson); Rafferty, c.1996
Quote: "I model each character on me, really."

LUCY LAWLESS

Birthplace: Mount Albert, Auckland, New Zealand
Birthdate: 3/28/68
Occupation: Actor
Education: Attended Auckland University
Debut: (TV) *Funny Business,* 1988
Signature: *Xena: Warrior Princess*
Facts: Got the part of Xena when the original actor became ill and the producers needed someone to fill in quickly. They turned to Lawless, who had been cast in bit parts in the show.

Stands at 5' 11".
Original Jobs: Picking grapes along Germany's Rhine River, working a gold mine in Australia.
Marriages: Garth Lawless (divorced); Rob Tapert, 1998
Children: Daisy, 1988 (with Garth Lawless); Julius Robert Bay, 1999

MARTIN LAWRENCE

Birthplace: Frankfurt, Germany
Birthdate: 4/16/65
Occupation: Actor
Education: High school
Debut: (TV) *What's Happening Now,* 1985; (Film) *Do the Right Thing,* 1989
Signature: *Martin*
Facts: He was a *Star Search* winner, a street performer in Washington Square Park, and a stand-up comedian at the Improv's open-mike night.

Worked at Sears in Queens with Salt-N-Pepa and Kid 'N Play.
Infamy: After a 1994 appearance on *Saturday Night Live* in which he told women to "put a Tic-Tac in your ass" to remain clean, Lawrence was banned from all NBC productions.

Yelled at passersby and brandished a pistol in the middle of a busy L.A. intersection. Tried to board a plane while carrying a Baretta.

In 1997, former *Martin* costar Tisha Campbell filed a suit claiming that he groped and kissed her, among other things, in front of the cast and crew.
Original Jobs: Gas station attendant, store clerk
Marriage: Patricia Southall, 1995 (divorced, 1996)
Child: Jasmine Page, 1996

DENIS LEARY

Birthplace: Worcester, MA
Birthdate: 8/18/57
Occupation: Actor
Education: Emerson College
Debut: (Off-Broadway) *No Cure for Cancer,* 1991; (Film) *Strictly Business,* 1992
Signature: *Dennis Leary: Lock 'n' Load,* 1997
Facts: Co-founded Comedy Workshop in Boston before moving to New York City in 1990, where he formed Apostle Productions.

Made Fiona Apple cry with a joke about her MTV Awards speech in his HBO special *Lock 'n' Load.*

Known as a "bad boy of comedy" for his aggressive smoking and politically incorrect jokes.

To make extra money while teaching drama, he drove a delivery truck and worked in a sulfuric-acid plant.

During a weekend trip to London with his wife, their first son was born prematurely and they were forced to live there for five months.
Original Job: Acting teacher
Marriage: Ann Lembeck, c. 1990
Children: Jack, c. 1990; Devin, c. 1992

Famous Relative: Conan O'Brien, talk-show host, cousin
Quote: "I have a lot of anger about the loss of the way things used to be. Like how you can't get coffee-flavored coffee anymore because everything is frappuccino or mochaccino."

MATT LEBLANC

Birthplace: Newton, MA
Birthdate: 7/25/67
Occupation: Actor
Education: Wentworth Institute of Technology
Debut: (TV) *TV 101,* 1988
Signature: *Friends*
Facts: First big breaks were in TV commercials, including an award-winning Heinz spot that ran four years.

Actually of mixed heritage—Italian, French, English, Irish, and Dutch—though usually cast as Italian.

After receiving his first motorcycle at age 8, began entering amateur competitions with hopes of racing professionally, a dream his mother quickly quashed.

A passion for landscape photography has taken him all over the world.

Before *Friends,* starred in three TV flops; interest in him soon cooled, and he sold his truck and motorcycle and moved to a smaller apartment to stay afloat financially.

In 2000, along with *Friends* costars, received a salary increase from $125,000 to $750,000 per episode.
Marriage: Melissa McKnight (engaged, 1999)

VIRGINIE LEDOYEN

Birthplace: Aubervilliers, France
Birthdate: 11/15/76
Occupation: Actor, model
Education: L'Ecole des Enfants du Spectacle
Debut: (Stage) *L'affaire du courrier*

de Lyon, c. 1987; (Film) *The Exploits of a Young Don Juan,* 1987
Signature: *The Beach,* 2000
Facts: Did TV commercials as a child.

Likes the subway, existential literature, Agnes B. clothes, and Leonard Cohen's music.

Her idol is Jeanne Moreau.

Secretary General of "Pour le Tibet," a charity that brings medical aid to Tibetan centers in the Himalayas and North India.
Quote: "I do like to play girls who are independent, who have a lot of character and a story to tell. They aren't there just to be pretty."

SPIKE LEE

Real Name: Shelton Lee
Birthplace: Atlanta, GA
Birthdate: 3/20/57
Occupation: Filmmaker, director
Education: Morehouse College, New York University
Debut: (Film) *She's Gotta Have It,* 1986 [see page 106 for a complete filmography]
Signature: *Do the Right Thing,* 1989
Facts: Known as an unofficial New York Knick, sitting courtside and shouting out to players on both teams. During the 1994 Eastern Conference Championships, some fans felt that his harassment of an Indiana Pacer caused the player to score the most points in the game and defeat the Knicks.

Taught at Harvard as a visiting professor in 1992.

A film he made at NYU, *Joe's Barbershop: We Cut Heads,* was the first student work ever selected for Lincoln Center's "New Directors, New Films" showcase and won a student award from the Academy of Motion Pictures Arts and Sciences.
Infamy: Accused by the Anti-Defamation League of B'Nai Brith of fostering anti-Semitism through his films, most notably via his portrayal of two Jewish nightclub owners in *Mo' Better Blues.*

Original Job: Advertising copywriter
Marriage: Tonya Linette Lewis, 1993
Children: Satchel Lewis, 1994; Jackson Lewis, 1997

TOMMY LEE

Real Name: Thomas Lee Bass
Birthplace: Athens, Greece
Birthdate: 10/3/62
Occupation: Rock drummer, singer
Debut: *Too Fast for Love,* 1981 (with Mötley Crüe)
Signature: *Dr. Feelgood,* 1989 (with Mötley Crüe)
Facts: His band Mötley Crüe was an early target of Tipper Gore's music watchdog group, the PMRC.

Proposed to Pamela Anderson after four days of dating.

He and Anderson once unwound by water-skiing nude on Lake Mead.

Spent a night in jail with Robert Downey, Jr.

Among his tattoos are "eather"—a now-defaced tribute to his first wife—and "mayhem," which marks his stomach.

Credits prison stint with helping him break substance abuse habits.

Now playing in the rock-rap hybrid Methods of Mayhem.
Infamy: In a failed attempt to get high, once injected Jack Daniels into his arm.

Arrested in 1993 for possession of a semiautomatic weapon.

Arrested in 1994 for injuring his then live-in fiancée, Bobbi Brown.

In 1996, a homemade video of Lee and then-wife Pamela Anderson enjoying their honeymoon made its way to the public.

In 1998, pleaded no contest to kicking Lee once in the buttocks and once in the back; served four months in prison.

In 2000, jailed for five days for violating his probation by drinking alcohol.
Marriages: Heather Locklear, 1984 (divorced, 1994); Pamela Anderson, 1995 (divorced, 1998; reunited, 1999; separated, 2000)

Children: Brandon Thomas, 1996; Dylan Jagger, 1998
Quote: "You see everything thrown on stage: money, shoes, bottles of pee. I thought I'd pretty much seen it all until this cow's eye came up and stuck in my drum riser."

JOHN LEGUIZAMO

Birthplace: Bogota, Colombia
Birthdate: 7/22/64
Occupation: Actor, comedian, playwright, producer
Education: Attended New York University
Debut: (Film) *Mixed Blood*, 1984; (Television) *Miami Vice*, 1984; (One man show) *Mambo Mouth*, 1990
Signature: *To Wong Foo, Thanks for Everything, Julie Newmar* 1995

Facts: Named after actor John Saxon (now best known for *Enter the Dragon* and *A Nightmare on Elm Street*).
Grew up in Jackson Heights, Queens. Would imitate TV comics to make his "painfully serious" father laugh.
Voted "Most Talkative" in high school.
His leading inspirations are Lily Tomlin, Jonathan Winters, and especially Richard Pryor.
Attracted note in *Casualties of War*, but got few meaty roles until he created *Freak* and *Spic-o-Rama*, solo shows drawing from his stand-up experience and eye on Hispanic culture.
Created, executive produced, wrote for, and starred in "House of Buggin' ", a Latino-oriented sketch comedy show.
Infamy: Arrested at 15 for broadcasting a comedy routine about his sex life over a subway public address system. Was also once arrested for truancy.
Major Award: Emmy, Individual Performance—Variety or Music Program, *Freak*, 1999
Marriages: Yelba Matamoros, 1994 (filed for divorce, 1996); Justine Maurer (relationship)

Children: Allegra Sky, 1999
Quote: "As long as a director or an actor understands and observes life, you can capture anybody."

JENNIFER JASON LEIGH

Real Name: Jennifer Leigh Morrow
Birthplace: Los Angeles, CA
Birthdate: 2/5/62
Occupation: Actor
Education: High school dropout
Debut: (TV) *The Young Runaways*, 1978; (Film) *Eyes of a Stranger*, 1980; (Off Broadway) *Sunshine*, 1989
Signature: *Single White Female*, 1992
Facts: Dropped out of high school six weeks before graduation to act in her debut film.
Since another Jennifer Leigh was already registered with the Screen Actors Guild, she added Jason in honor of family friend Jason Robards.
For her role in 1981 as an anorexic teen in TV's *The Best Little Girl in the World,* she dropped her weight to 86 pounds.
Her father was killed in a helicopter accident on the set of *Twilight Zone: The Movie.*
She is very shy and dreads parties. As a result, she spends her free time reading or going to movies.
Famous Relatives: Barbara (Freedman) Turner, TV scriptwriter, mother; Vic Morrow, actor, father; Mina Badie, actor, half-sister
Quote: "I like the idea of being able to play anything from waif to prostitute."

JACK LEMMON

Birthplace: Boston, MA
Birthdate: 2/8/25
Occupation: Actor
Education: Harvard University
Debut: (Film) *It Should Happen to You,* 1954
Signature: *Odd Couple*, 1968
Facts: Underwent three ear surgeries as a boy, forcing him to miss a

year of school.
Son of a top donut executive, he went to the elite Phillips Academy in Andover. (He was a cheerleade there.)
At Harvard, was president of the Hasty Pudding Club.
Has made more than 60 films in almost 50 years.
Was handed the 1997 TV drama Golden Globe award by actor Ving Rhames who believed Lemmon deserved it even though he won.
Odd Couple II marked the tenth movie with pal Walter Matthau.
Infamy: Had a longtime problem with alcohol abuse, eventually sobering up through AA.
Marriages: Cynthia Stone, 1950 (divorced); Felicia Farr, 1962
Children: Christopher, 1954 (with Cynthia Stone). Courtney, 1966
Major Awards: Oscar, Best Supporting Actor, *Mister Roberts*, 1955; Oscar, Best Actor, *Save the Tiger*, 1973

JAY LENO

Real Name: James Leno
Birthplace: New Rochelle, NY
Birthdate: 4/28/50
Occupation: Talk show host, comedian
Education: Emerson College
Debut: (TV) *The Marilyn McCoo & Billy Davis Jr. Show,* 1977; (Film) *Silver Bears,* 1978
Signature: *The Tonight Show*
Facts: Collects antique cars and motorcycles.
Made his first appearance on *The Tonight Show* in 1977.
While in grade school, Leno executed such pranks as flushing tennis balls down the toilet and hiding a dog in his locker. His fifth grade teacher wrote on his report card, "If Jay spent as much time studying as he does trying to be a comedian, he'd be a big star."
Was made a contributing editor at *Popular Mechanics* magazine in

1999. He pens the "Jay Leno's Garage" column.
Original Jobs: Rolls-Royce mechanic, deliveryman
Marriage: Mavis Nicholson, 1980

TÉA LEONI

Birthplace: New York, NY
Birthdate: 2/25/66
Occupation: Actor
Education: Sarah Lawrence College
Debut: (TV) *Santa Barbara*, 1984; (Film) *Switch*, 1994
Signature: *Deep Impact*, 1998
Facts: A sufferer of stage fright, was so nervous shooting the pilot for *The Naked Truth* she threw up five times.

Got into acting when, on a dare, entered a mass audition for the remake of *Charlie's Angels* and was chosen, although the show never aired.

Caused a stir when *The Naked Truth* producer Chris Thompson left his wife and children to date her.
Original Job: Teaching Japanese men how to interact with American women
Marriages: One prior marriage; David Duchovny, 1997
Child: Madelaine West, 1999

DAVID LETTERMAN

Birthplace: Indianapolis, IN
Birthdate: 4/12/47
Occupation: Talk show host
Education: Ball State University
Debut: (TV) *The Starland Vocal Band Show*, 1977
Signature: *Late Show with David Letterman*
Facts: While working as a weather announcer at a local TV station, he congratulated a tropical storm on being upgraded to a hurricane.

Was the announcer for the late-night movie program *Freeze Dried Movies*. On the program, he blew up a model of the television station at which he was working.

Margaret Ray stalked him at his New Canaan, Conn., home. She was caught at or in his home eight times from 1988 to 1993.

Underwent quintuple bypass surgery at age 52. When he returned to the *Late Show* he received his best ratings in six years.
Original Jobs: TV announcer, weatherman
Marriage: Michelle Cook (divorced, 1977); Regina Lasko (relationship)
Major Awards: Emmy, Best Host of a Daytime Variety Series, *The David Letterman Show*, 1981; Emmy, Writing in a Variety or Music Show, *Late Night with David Letterman*, 1984, 1985, 1986, 1987

JET LI

Real Name: Li Lian-jie
Birthplace: Beijing, China
Birthdate: 4/26/63
Occupation: Actor, martial artist
Education: Beijing Martial Art Troupe
Debut: *Shaolin Temple*, 1982
Signature: *Romeo Must Die*, 2000
Facts: Began his study of martial arts at age 7 to overcome a sickly childhood.

At 11, performed at the Nixon White House. When warned that his hotel room might be bugged, he told the furnishings what kinds of foods he liked—and found them waiting upon his return.

Won China's gold medal for *wu shu* (a type of martial art he performs) four times.

Has directed (*Born to Defend*) and produced (*Bodyguard from Beijing*).

For Hong Kong film fans, Li's signature is the recent *Once Upon a Time in China* films. Li made the lead role of real-life folk hero Wong Fei-hung his own—even though it had previously been played by others onscreen nearly a hundred times.

Was initially left off the *Lethal Weapon 4* print ads and posters. When his fans deluged the movie's web site with complaints, he was included with the five heroes—even though he played the villain.
Marriages: Qiuyan Huang, 1987 (divorced, c. 1989); Nina Li, 1999
Children: Two daughters (with Qiuyan Huang); Jane, 2000
Quote: "I want to give a smart and positive image to martial arts, not this bloody, fight-for-no-reason image."

RUSH LIMBAUGH

Birthplace: Cape Girardeau, MO
Birthdate: 1/12/51
Occupation: Political commentator, radio and TV broadcaster, author
Education: Elkins Institute of Radio and Technology; attended Southeastern Missouri State University
Facts: After dropping out of college, he left home in 1971 in pursuit of a big-time radio career. Fired from various stations, he left radio seven years later and worked in the public relations office of the Kansas City Royals baseball team.

He targets radical-liberals, environmentalists, do-gooders, and anyone further left than he.

More than 300 "Rush rooms" have opened in restaurants nationwide for the purpose of broadcasting Rush Limbaugh's programs to patrons.

Met his wife, Marta, via electronic mail on CompuServe Information Service. They were married by Supreme Court Justice Clarence Thomas.

He named his radio web The Excellence in Broadcasting Network, which began with 56 AM stations and 250,000 listeners. Within three years, his broadcast had an estimated 2 million listeners at any given moment
Infamy: His recurring AIDS Update enraged activists. He ultimately apologized, withdrew the segment, and donated $10,000 to the Pediatric AIDS Foundation.

In February 1994, the Florida Citrus Commission advertised orange juice on Limbaugh's show.

The ads generated 7,500 calls to the commission protesting their choice of such a controversial figure to promote their product. The National Organization for Women, as well as various gay and lesbian groups, urged people to boycott Florida orange juice. Meanwhile, about 30 Rush supporters bought out the entire supply of orange juice at an Orlando, Florida, store in counter-protest.

Original job: Apprentice at KGMO radio station

Marriages: Roxie Maxine McNeely (divorced); Michelle Sixta (divorced); Marta Fitzgerald

Famous Relatives: Rush Limbaugh Sr., President Eisenhower's ambassador to India, grandfather; Stephen Limbaugh, federal judge appointed by Ronald Reagan, uncle.

Quote: "My first real interest in radio can be traced to a dislike for school."

LAURA LINNEY

Birthplace: New York, NY
Birthdate: 2/5/64
Occupation: Actor
Education: Attended Northwestern University, Brown University, Juilliard School
Debut: (Stage) *Six Degrees of Separation*, 1990; (Film) *Lorenzo's Oil*, 1992; (TV) *Class of '61*, 1993
Signature: *The Truman Show*, 1998
Facts: First recognized in 1994 for her portrayal of Mary Ann Singleton in *Armistead Maupin's Tales of the City*.

Her middle name is Legett.

During her years at Juilliard, she suffered from severe stage fright.

She is afraid to fly.

In elementary school she tried to con her teachers into letting her act out book reports instead of writing them.

Based on her performance in *Primal Fear*, she was handpicked by Clint Eastwood to star in 1997's *Absolute Power*.

Original Job: Backstage hand in New England theaters
Marriage: David Adkins, 1995
Famous Relative: Romulus Linney, playwright
Quote: "I have the Cindy Brady complex. You know that episode of *The Brady Bunch* where Cindy goes catatonic when she appears on a TV show? That was me."

TARA LIPINSKI

Birthplace: Sewell, NJ
Birthdate: 6/10/82
Occupation: Ice skater
Debut: (TV) *The Young and the Restless*, 1999
Facts: At age 11, she and her mother left Texas so she could train year-round with prestigious coaches.

Practiced only two weeks before landing her signature triple-loop combination—the first ice skater ever to do so.

Stood 4'10" and weighed 82 pounds when she won her Olympic medal.

At age 14, she was the youngest-ever winner of the U.S. Figure Skating Championship.

Major Award: Olympics, Gold medal, women's figure skating, 1998

JOHN LITHGOW

Birthplace: Rochester, NY
Birthdate: 10/19/45
Occupation: Actor
Education: Harvard University, London Academy of Music and Dramatic Arts
Debut: (Film) *Dealing: or The Berkeley-to-Boston Forty-Brick Lost-Bag Blues*, 1972; (TV) *Mom, the Wolfman and Me*, 1980
Signature: *3rd Rock from the Sun*
Facts: His father ran the Antioch Shakespeare Festival, and John had small parts in the plays from early childhood.

Stars in a children's videotape, *John Lithgow's Kid-Size Concert*.

Some years ago he read the book

Forrest Gump and wanted to acquire the movie rights so he could play the lead, but he didn't get around to it.

Known as a serious dramatic actor, but actually did more than 40 comedies on stage.

Son Ian appears in *3rd Rock* as Professor Solomon's slowest student.

Marriage: Jean Taynton, 1966 (divorced); Mary Yeager, 1981
Children: Ian, 1972 (with Jean Taynton). Phoebe, 1982; Nathan, c. 1984
Major Awards: Tony, Best Supporting Actor (Dramatic), *The Changing Room*, 1973; Emmy, Outstanding Guest Performance in a Drama Series, *Amazing Stories*, 1986; Emmy, Best Actor in a Comedy Series, *3rd Rock from the Sun*, 1996, 1997, 1999
Quote: "God bless television."

BRIAN LITTRELL

Birthplace: Lexington, KY
Birthdate: 2/20/75
Occupation: Singer
Education: High school dropout
Debut: (Single) "We've Got It Goin' On," 1995; (Album) *Backstreet Boys*, 1995 (American version, 1997)
Signature: "Everybody (Backstreet's Back),"1997
Facts: Is cousin to Backstreet Boy Kevin Richardson.

Before joining the band, was planning to attend Cincinnati Bible College.

Got the call to join the band while sitting in history class during the last hour of his junior year.

The band is named after Orlando, Florida's Backstreet Market, a popular teen hangout.

The group's debut was a hit in 26 countries before *Backstreet Boys* was released in the U.S.

Underwent surgery to fix a congenital hole in his heart at the age of 22. Was onstage again in eight weeks, with oxygen tents waiting in the wings.

Wrote the song "The Perfect Fan" for his mother.

Has a chihuahua named Little Tyke.

Plays basketball, tennis, and golf to relax.

Infamy: Band filed suit against former manager Lou Pearlman, claiming he had made $10 million from their labor while they had received $300,000.

Original Job: Employee of Long John Silver's

Marriage: Leighanne Wallace, 2000

Quote: "I don't want a Backstreet Boys cereal."

LUCY LIU

Birthplace: New York, NY
Birthdate: 12/2/67
Occupation: Actor
Education: Attended New York University; University of Michigan
Debut: (TV) *Beverly Hills, 90210,* 1991; (Film) *Jerry Maguire,* 1996
Signature: *Ally McBeal*
Facts: Her middle name is Alexis.

While earning her B.A. in Chinese language and culture, Liu became serious about acting when she played the lead in a campus production of *Alice in Wonderland.*

Her mixed-media photo collages have been exhibited frequently in New York and Los Angeles. After her show at SoHo's Cast Iron Gallery, she was awarded a grant in 1994 to study in China.

She was originally signed on to *Ally McBeal* for only six episodes but her popularity among audiences won her a recurring role.

She practices martial arts.

She treats her long hair with olive oil and lavender.

Nickname among friends is "Curious George."

Original Job: Artist, caterer, aerobics instructor

Quote: "I wanted to be Barbie and I was as opposite to Barbie as you could get."

HEATHER LOCKLEAR

Birthplace: Los Angeles, CA
Birthdate: 9/25/61
Occupation: Actor
Education: UCLA
Debut: (TV) *Dynasty,* 1981
Signature: *Melrose Place*
Facts: Served over six years as the spokesperson for the Health and Tennis Corporation of America.

Played officer Stacy Sheridan on the crime drama series *T.J. Hooker* with William Shatner, 1982–87.

When she joined the cast of *Melrose Place,* the series's audience jumped 50 percent.

Marriage: Tommy Lee (divorced), Richie Sambora, 1994

Child: Ava Elizabeth, 1997

LISA LOPES

Birthplace: Philadelphia, PA
Birthdate: 5/27/71
Occupation: Singer, songwriter
Debut: *Ooooooohhh…On the TLC Tip,* 1992
Signature: "Waterfalls," 1995 / "Left Eye"
Facts: Taught herself to play piano by age five.

Grew up with a physically abusive father who beat her and introduced her to alcohol.

Her nickname comes from the condom she regularly wore over the left lens of her glasses.

Hosted MTV fashion show, *The Cut.*

When third album *Fanmail* was released, Lopes repeatedly aired misgivings about TLC's musical and business decisions. When her bandmates counterattacked with charges of unprofessional behavior, Lopes challenged them to produce solo albums in order to compete against the one she was planning

Infamy: In 1993, was arrested in Atlanta for fighting with police.

Charged with disorderly conduct at the Georgia Dome football stadium.

Turned herself in for burning down

boyfriend Andre Rison's mansion. She entered an alcohol rehab clinic soon after, and intimated that she was being battered by Rison.

Relationship: Sean Newman

Major Awards: Grammy, Best R&B Album, *Crazysexycool,* 1995; Grammy, Best R&B Vocal—Duo or Group, "Creep," 1995; Grammy, Best R&B Album, *Fanmail,* 1999; Grammy, Best R&B Vocal—Duo or Group, "No Scrubs," 1999

JENNIFER LOPEZ

Birthplace: Bronx, NY
Birthdate: 7/24/70
Occupation: Actor, singer
Debut: (TV) *In Living Color,* 1990; (Film) *Mi Familia ("My Family"),* 1995; (Album) *On the 6,* 1999
Signature: *The Cell,* 2000; "If You Had My Love," 1999
Facts: The daughter of Puerto Rican parents, she danced for music videos and on stage, and then was selected to be a Fly Girl for TV's *In Living Color.*

Her role as Selena was protested by some Latinos because she is of Puerto Rican rather than Mexican descent.

She is the highest paid Latina actress in history.

When she was younger she wanted to be a hairstylist.

On the 6 is named for the subway line that she took to Manhattan when she was growing up.

Original Job: Dancer

Marriage: Ojani Noa (divorced,

1998); Sean "Puffy" Combs (relationship)

Quote: "I'm a typical Latino. I scream and shout about things. Some men can't handle that."

SOPHIA LOREN

Real Name: Sophia Villani Scicolone
Birthplace: Rome, Italy
Birthdate: 9/20/34
Education: Catholic parochial school, Teachers' Institute
Occupation: Actor
Debut: (Film) *Variety Lights*, 1950; (TV) *The World of Sophia Loren*, 1962
Signature: *Two Women*, 1961
Facts: Although her parents never married, her father, Ricardo Scicolone, granted her the legal right to use his last name.

Growing up poor with her sister and mother in Pozzuoli, a small industrial town near Naples, Italy, she attended a Catholic school, where she has said she was plain, thin, and nicknamed *"Stecchetto"* ("the stick") or *"Stuzzicadenti"* ("toothpick").

At age 12, she enrolled in the Teachers' Institute, where she studied teaching for three years.

Met producer and future husband Carlo Ponti during a beauty contest where he was a judge and she was a contestant. She was 15 years old.

She and her mother worked as extras in *Quo Vadis*, earning a total income of $33.

Sophia began modeling for Italian magazines and in 1952 was given the name Sophia Loren by a director.

She did her famous striptease in 1963 in the film *Yesterday, Today and Tomorrow*, which she reprised in 1994's *Ready to Wear* at age 59.

Suffered two miscarriages and two difficult pregnancies.

Her marriage to Ponti was annulled due to charges by the Italian government that Ponti was a bigamist, claiming that his divorce from a previous wife was invalid. They were married again in 1966.

She is the only actress to have won an Oscar for a foreign-language film.

Infamy: Spent 17 days in jail in 1982 for underpaying her taxes in Italy.

Original Job: Model
Marriage: Carlo, 1957 (annulled in 1962; remarried, 1966)
Children: Carlo Ponti Jr., 1968; Eduardo, 1972
Major Awards: Academy Award, Best Actress, *Two Women*, 1961; Honorary Academy Award, as "one of the genuine treasures of world cinema," 1990
Quote: "I am not a sexy pot."

JULIA LOUIS-DREYFUS

Birthplace: New York, NY
Birthdate: 1/13/61
Occupation: Actor
Education: Northwestern University
Debut: (TV) *Saturday Night Live*, 1982; (Film) *Hannah and Her Sisters*, 1986
Signature: *Seinfeld*
Facts: Parents were divorced when she was only 1 year old.

Met husband in college and worked with him on *Saturday Night Live*.

Her role in *Seinfeld* was not in the original mix created by Jerry Seinfeld and Larry David, but was imposed by the network, which felt a female perspective was needed.

Original Job: Member of the Second City comedy troupe
Marriage: Brad Hall, 1987
Child: Henry, 1992; Charles, 1997
Major Award: Emmy, Best Supporting Actress, *Seinfeld*, 1996

COURTNEY LOVE

Real Name: Love Michelle Harrison
Birthplace: San Francisco, CA
Birthdate: 7/9/64
Occupation: Singer, songwriter, actor
Education: High school dropout
Debut: (Film) *Sid and Nancy*, 1986; (Album) *Pretty on the Inside*, 1991

Signature: Hole
Facts: Ran away to Europe at 15; her grandfather's death left her a millionaire.

Mother was the psychologist who examined Katherine Anne Power ('60s radical and fugitive who recently confessed to being an accessory to bank robbery).

Appeared in the film *Straight to Hell*, 1987.

Before founding Hole, Love was lead vocalist for the rock band Faith No More in the early '80s "for about a week" (before they found Chuck Mosely). She also played with Kat Bjelland of the Minneapolis all-girl band Babes in Toyland and future L7 member Jennifer Finch in Sugar Baby Doll.

Named daughter after the '30s actress Frances Farmer, who is the subject of Nirvana song "Frances Farmer Will Have Her Revenge on Seattle."

Infamy: In her early teens, was sent to a juvenile detention center after stealing a Kiss T-shirt from a department store.

A *Vanity Fair* article described Love as shooting heroin while pregnant. Though she denied the charge, child-welfare authorities temporarily removed the baby after she was born.

Arrested in 1995 for verbally abusing a flight attendant aboard an Australian flight. She was not convicted, but ordered to remain on good behavior for one month.

Sued by David Geffen of Geffen Records for breach of contract in 2000. Geffen is claiming that Hole still owes his company 5 albums and is seeking unspecified damages as well as an injunction barring Hole from recording for any other label.

Original Job: Danced in strip joints in L.A. and Alaska
Marriages: James Moreland, 1989 (divorced, 1989); Kurt Cobain, 1992 (deceased, 1994); Jim Barber (relationship)
Child: Frances Bean, 1992
Famous Relatives: Linda Carroll,

psychologist, mother; Hank Harrison, author, father

Quote: "Once you've cleared a million bucks, excuse me, you're not a punk anymore"

LYLE LOVETT

Birthplace: Klein, TX
Birthdate: 11/1/57
Occupation: Singer, songwriter
Education: Texas A&M
Debut: (Album) *Lyle Lovett*, 1986
Facts: Played guitar in coffee shops while in college.

Lives in a clapboard house built by his grandparents.

Is afraid of cows.

Marriage: Julia Roberts, 1993 (divorced, 1995)
Major Awards: Grammy, *Lyle Lovett and His Large Band*, 1989; Grammy, Best Pop Vocal Collaboration, "Funny How Time Slips Away" (with Al Green), 1994; Grammy, Best Country Group Performance with Vocal, "Blues for Dixie" (with Asleep at the Wheel), 1994

ROB LOWE

Birthplace: Charlottesville, VA
Birthdate: 3/17/64
Occupation: Actor
Education: High school
Debut: (TV) *A New Kind of Family*, 1978; (Film) *The Outsiders*, 1983; (Broadway) *A Little Hotel on the Side*, 1992
Signature: *The West Wing*, 1999
Facts: His middle name is Helper.

While in high school, he appeared in Super 8 movies made by classmates Sean Penn and Charlie Sheen.

He is deaf in his right ear.

As the "crown prince" of the Brat Pack, he was romantically linked to Melissa Gilbert, Chynna Phillips, and Princess Stephanie of Monaco.

Wears a gold cross and a gold medallion around his neck with the Serenity Prayer used in 12-step recovery programs, both given to

him by his wife.

Infamy: After being caught on videotape with two young women, one of whom was only 16, while attending 1988's Democratic National Convention in Atlanta, he avoided prosecution by agreeing to perform 20 hours of community service.

During the 1989 Academy Awards, in a disastrously bad number, he crooned "Proud Mary" with a Snow White impostor. The Academy apologized to the Walt Disney Company for the potential trademark infringement.

Original Job: Actor in TV commercials
Marriage: Sheryl Berkoff, 1991
Children: Matthew Edward, 1993; John Owen, 1995
Famous Relative: Chad Lowe, actor, brother; Hilary Swank, actor, sister-in-law
Quote: "I drank too much. I had no sense of what should be private and what should be public. And I was very unfocused and not even aware of how the onrush of really being a *man*—as opposed to a young man—was scaring me."

GEORGE LUCAS

Birthplace: Modesto, CA
Birthdate: 5/14/44
Occupation: Director, producer, screenwriter
Education: University of Southern California
Debut: (Film) *THX-1138*, 1971
Signature: *Star Wars*, 1977
Facts: Has sold more than $3 billion in licensed *Star Wars* merchandise, money Lucas got to keep because licensing rights were thrown into his contract in exchange for his having given up an extra director's fee (he forfeited the higher fee to ensure that 20th Century Fox would bankroll his sequel).

His empire includes the Industrial Light & Magic special effects firm, LucasArts interactive media, and a

group selling his advanced THX theater sound system.

Still writes scripts in longhand, using the same three-ring binder he used in college.

As an 18-year-old, nearly killed himself while joyriding on a country road when his Fiat hit a car, flipped over, and crashed into a tree. He survived only because his seat belt broke and threw him from the car before impact.

Has received permission from the government to develop 23 acres of land at the former Presidio Army base in San Francisco for his Letterman Digital Arts Center, which will house part of Lucas's film and technology empire.

Marriage: Marcia Griffin (divorced, 1983)
Children: Amanda, 1981; Katie, 1988; Jett, 1993; (all adopted).
Major Award: Academy of Motion Pictures Arts and Sciences, Irving Thalberg Award, 1992

SUSAN LUCCI

Birthplace: Scarsdale, NY
Birthdate: 12/23/46
Education: Marymount College
Debut: (TV) *All My Children*, 1969
Signature: *All My Children*
Facts: Was nominated 19 times for the best actress in a daytime series Emmy, and finally won in 1999. **In 2000, she was overlooked for a nomination but served as the event's host.**

Was a cheerleader in high school.

Made the semifinals in New York State Miss Universe pageant, 1968. Dropped out of the competition to finish her college exams.

As Erica Kane, Lucci has impersonated a nun, been kidnapped, rescued a lover from prison using a helicopter, and stared down a grizzly bear.

Daughter Liza appears on the new daytime drama, *Passions*.

Original Job: "Color girl" for CBS, sitting for cameras as a new

lighting system for color TV was being developed
Marriage: Helmut Huber, 1969
Children: Liza Victoria, actor, 1975; Andreas Martin, 1980
Major Award: Emmy, Best Actress in a Daytime Drama Series, *All My Children,* 1998–99

LORETTA LYNN

Real Name: Loretta Webb
Birthplace: Butcher Hollow, KY
Birthdate: 4/14/35
Occupation: Singer, songwriter
Debut: (Single) "Honky Tonk Girl," 1960
Signature: "Coal Miner's Daughter"
Facts: First woman to earn a certified gold country album.

While her kids were still young, her husband gave her a guitar to accompany the singing she did around the house. She taught herself to play.

Her first No. 1 single, "Don't Come Home A-Drinkin' (With Lovin' on Your Mind)" was banned from several stations. Many of her songs have been banned, including "Rated X" and "The Pill."

Married when she was 13. "By the time I was 17, I had four kids, and I had never been anywhere." She was a grandmother at 31, one year after her twins (her last children) were born.
Marriage: Oliver Vanetta Lynn Jr., 1948 (deceased, 1996)
Children: Betty Sue Lynn Markworth, c. 1948; Jack Benny, 1949 (deceased, 1984); Ernest Ray, 1953; Clara Marie Lynn Lyell, 1954; Peggy, 1964; Patsy, 1964
Famous Relative: Crystal Gayle, singer, sister
Major Awards: Grammy, Best Country Performance—Duo or Group, "After the Fire Is Gone" (with Conway Twitty), 1971; Grammy, Best Recording for Children, *Sesame Country* (with others), 1981; inducted into the Country Music Hall of Fame, 1988

SHELBY LYNNE

Birthplace: Quantico, VA
Birthdate: 10/22/68
Occupation: Country-soul singer
Debut: (Album) *Sunrise,* 1988
Signature: *I AM Shelby Lynne,* 1999
Facts: Raised by a grandmother after her father killed her mother before turning the gun on himself.

Married her high school sweetheart at 18. She and her then-husband moved to Nashville, where a cable-TV appearance encouraged Tammy Wynette's retired writer-producer to help Lynne's career.

Sang with George Jones on her debut single.

Made five albums with three different labels by 1997. Now disavows her Nashville hits.

When branded a complainer and a troublemaker, Lynne left Nashville to work on new songs in Alabama. She re-emerged with fresh music that became *I AM Shelby Lynne.* It was first released in England, where her musical and personal differences with Nashville would less of an obstacle to creating buzz. The strategy worked.

Drives a 1968 Cadillac Coupe de Ville.
Marriage: One marriage (divorced)
Famous Relative: Allison Moorer, singer-songwriter, sister
Quote: "I am proud of all my albums, but I'm not gonna sit around and study them or anything, man. They're just not that good, and it's not where I am any more. Those hairstyles haunt me, but hey, what are you gonna do?"

NORM MACDONALD

Birthplace: Quebec, Canada
Birthdate: 10/4/62
Occupation: Comedian, actor, screenwriter
Debut: (TV) *Saturday Night Live,* 1993; (Film) *Billy Madison,* 1995
Signature: *The Norm Show,* 1999
Facts: Once conned reporters into believing that he played pro hockey in Ottawa.

Was removed from his *SNL* "Weekend Update" post in 1998. Speculation attributed it to his constant on-air jabs at O. J. Simpson, a friend of NBC West Coast president Don Ohlmeyer. Macdonald disputes the theory, offering that NBC brass simply didn't find him funny. Soon after Macdonald's ousting, NBC refused to air advertisements for *Dirty Work,* written by and starring Macdonald.

Declined an offer to host his own late-night show out of deference to his idol, David Letterman.

Played Michael "Kramer" Richards in *Man on the Moon.*
Infamy: Used the F-word in an April 1997 live *SNL* broadcast.

His off-color stand-up show shocked the University of Iowa so much it apologized to its students. A similar response followed his hosting an ESPN awards ceremony.
Original Job: Stand-up comic, writer for *The Dennis Miller Show* and *Roseanne*
Marriage: Connie (separated)
Child: Dylan, 1992
Quote: "I'm not a versatile actor. I have no idea how to act. I can specifically write for myself and be funny."

ANDIE MACDOWELL

Real Name: Rosalie Anderson MacDowell
Birthplace: Gaffney, SC
Birthdate: 4/21/58
Occupation: Actor
Education: Attended Winthrop College
Debut: (Film) *Greystoke: The Legend of Tarzan, Lord of the Apes,* 1984
Signature: *Sex, Lies and Videotape,* 1989
Facts: After *Greystoke* was filmed, MacDowell's part was overdubbed with a British accent provided by Glenn Close.

Played Jimi Hendrix's "Angel" at her wedding.

Original Job: McDonald's, Elite model
Marriage: Paul Qualley, 1986 (separated, 1999)
Children: Justin, 1986; Rainey, 1989; Sarah Margaret, 1994

SHIRLEY MACLAINE

Real Name: Shirley MacLean Beaty
Birthplace: Richmond, VA
Birthdate: 4/24/34
Occupation: Actor, author
Education: Washington School of Ballet
Debut: (Stage) *Oklahoma!*, 1950
Signature: *Terms of Endearment*, 1983
Facts: Starred in her own TV series, *Shirley's World* (1971–72).

Was performing with the Washington School of Ballet by the time she was 12, but soon grew too tall to be a ballerina.

Following a showbiz cliché, she got the lead in the 1954 Broadway show *The Pajama Game* when the lead hurt her ankle.

As a young girl, often had to come with fists blazing to the aid of her bookish and picked-on younger brother.
Infamy: Ridiculed for her oft-expressed beliefs in reincarnation, detailed in her best-selling books *Out on a Limb* and *Dancing in the Light*. Satirized herself in the "Pavilion of Former Lives" in the film *Defending Your Life* (1991).

Had an open marriage with husband Parker, but was stunned to learn from a channeler (later confirmed by a private eye) that he had transferred millions of dollars to his girlfriend's account.

Wrote a tell-all book in 1995, detailing how Debra Winger mooned her and broke wind, and describing Frank Sinatra as "a perpetual kid" and "someone who muscled others." Sinatra's response to the book: "It's amazing what a broad will do for a buck."
Original Job: Dancer
Marriage: Steve Parker (divorced, 1983); Andrew Peacock (relationship)

Child: Stephanie Sachiko, 1956
Famous Relative: Warren Beatty, actor, brother
Major Awards: Emmy, Outstanding Comedy-Variety or Musical Special, *Shirley MacLaine: If They Could See Me Now*, 1974; Emmy, Outstanding Comedy-Variety or Musical Special, *Gypsy in My Soul*, 1976; Emmy, Outstanding Writing of Variety or Music Program, *Shirley MacLaine... Every Little Movement*, 1980; Oscar, Best Actress, *Terms of Endearment*, 1983

PETER MACNICOL

Birthplace: Texas
Birthdate: 4/10/58
Education: Attended University of Minnesota
Occupation: Actor
Debut: (Film) *Dragonslayer*, 1981; (Stage) *Crimes of the Heart*
Signature: *Ally McBeal*
Facts: Originally planned a career in paleontology.

After his first movie experience, he left New York and traveled around Europe and the United States without telling anyone where he was going. When he finally called his agent, he found out that he had an audition for *Sophie's Choice*.
Marriage: Marsue Cumming

ELLE MACPHERSON

Real Name: Eleanor Gow
Birthplace: Sydney, Australia
Birthdate: 3/29/64
Occupation: Supermodel, actor
Debut: *Sports Illustrated* swimsuit model, (Film) *Sirens*, 1994
Facts: Appeared in every issue of *Elle* magazine from 1982 to 1988.

Launched a designer lingerie line in Australia and New Zealand in 1991.

Opened Fashion Cafe in New York City in 1995 with supermodels Claudia Schiffer and Naomi Campbell.

Named the world's wealthiest model by *Business Age* in 1998.

Marriage: Gilles Bensimon (divorced, 1989); Arpad Busson (relationship)
Children: Arpad Flynn, 1998

WILLIAM H. MACY

Birthplace: Miami, FL
Birthdate: 3/13/50
Occupation: Actor, stage director, screenwriter
Education: Goddard College
Debut: (Broadway) *Our Town*, 1988; (TV) *The Awakening Land*, 1978; (Film) *House of Games*, 1987
Signature: *Fargo*, 1996
Facts: Initially planning on a career in veterinary medicine, he transferred from Bethany College to major in theater at Goddard, where he studied under David Mamet.

Moved to Chicago with Mamet and Steven Schacter and founded the St. Nicholas Theater, where he appeared in 1975 in its first production, *American Buffalo*, and landed small roles in TV.

Is actively involved with Boy Scout Troop 184 in L.A.

His middle name is Hall.

During the 1980s, he performed in more than 50 Broadway and Off-Broadway productions. He and Mamet founded the Atlantic Theatre Company in New York in 1983.
Original Jobs: Musician, acting teacher
Marriage: Felicity Huffman, actor, 1997
Child: Sofia Grace, 2000
Quote: "I'm sort of an odd duck. I look really odd sometimes, then other times I look okay. I tend to get cast for who I am, which is a white guy who can talk a good game."

MADONNA

Real Name: Madonna Louise Veronica Ciccone
Birthplace: Bay City, MI
Birthdate: 8/16/58
Occupation: Singer
Education: University of Michigan
Debut: Dancer, Alvin Ailey Dance Company, 1979

Signature: "Material Girl"
Facts: Was a cheerleader in high school.

She starred in an exploitation film called *A Certain Sacrifice* in 1980.

Early in her career, posed nude for a New York photographer. Those photos later appeared in *Playboy*.

She appears in a nightclub scene from the 1983 movie *Vision Quest*, singing "Crazy for You" in the background.

Her hobby is making scrapbooks.

Has been drinking "kabbalah water," blessed by a rabbi versed in the Jewish mystical tradition to help with her insomnia.
Infamy: In 1994, swore 14 times while on *The Late Show with David Letterman*, to get revenge for his many jokes at her expense. She also handed Letterman a pair of her panties and told him to smell them.

Her video for "Justify My Love" (1990) was banned from MTV.

Her book *Sex* (1992) was originally banned in Japan, where it is against the law to show pubic hair. Officials eventually relented since the book was being distributed anyway.
Original Jobs: Model, worked in a doughnut shop
Marriage: Sean Penn (divorced, 1988); Guy Ritchie, director (relationship)
Child: Lourdes Maria Ciccone Leon, 1996 (with Carlos Leon); Rocco Ritchie, 2000
Major Awards: Grammy, Best Music Video—Long Form, *Madonna—Blonde Ambition World Tour Live*, 1991; Grammy, Best Dance Recording, "Ray of Light," 1998; Grammy, Best Shortform Music Video, "Ray of Light," 1998; Grammy, Best Pop Album, *Ray of Light*, 1998; Grammy, Best Song written for a Motion Picture/Television, "Beautiful Stranger" (with William Orbit), *Austin Powers: The Spy Who Shagged Me*, 1999
Quote: "I don't think that having a child has made me unsexy. There's nothing sexier than a mother."

TOBEY MAGUIRE

Birthplace: Santa Monica, CA
Birthdate: 6/27/75
Occupation: Actor
Education: High school dropout; earned a GED
Debut: (TV) *On Location: Rodney Dangerfield—"Opening Night at Rodney's Place"*; (Film) *This Boy's Life*, 1995
Signature: *Pleasantville*, 1998
Facts: Grew up "super-duper poor." Was planning to take culinary arts in school until his mother offered him $100 to try the drama elective.

Auditioned for the lead in *This Boy's Life*, but choked over acting with Robert DeNiro; pal Leonardo DiCaprio got the part.

Played Joan Allen's son in both *The Ice Storm* and *Pleasantville*.

Does not drink, smoke, take drugs, or eat meat. Does do yoga.
Infamy: He and DiCaprio were sued by the makers of an improvisational film they acted in, *Don's Plum*. The producers claimed the duo were unhappy with their performances and conspired to block the film's release; the actors claimed their participation was based on the movie not being a feature-length theatrical release. Terms of settlement were undisclosed, but the film cannot be released in the U.S. or Canada.
Relationship: Rashida Jones
Quote: "I think I'm going somewhere between Tom Hanks and John Malkovich."

BILL MAHER

Birthplace: New York, NY
Birthdate: 1/20/56
Occupation: Comedian, talk show host
Education: Cornell University
Debut: *The Tonight Show*, 1982
Signature: *Politically Incorrect*
Facts: Says the most politically incorrect thing he ever did was to say "f--k" in front of the president.

Originally did stand-up on the New York club circuit with other up-and-coming comics, including Jerry Seinfeld and Paul Reiser.

Wrote *True Story: A Comedy Novel.*

JOHN MALKOVICH

Birthplace: Christopher, IL
Birthdate: 12/9/53
Occupation: Actor
Education: Eastern Illinois University, Illinois State University
Debut: (Stage) *True West*, 1982
Signature: *Dangerous Liaisons*, 1988
Facts: Played football and tuba in high school.

Took up acting in college when he fell for a female drama student.

Co-founded the Steppenwolf Theatre in Chicago, in 1976.
Original Job: Enrolled in Eastern Illinois University with plans of becoming an environmentalist
Marriages: Glenne Headly, 1982 (divorced, c. 1988); Nicoletta Peyran (relationship)
Children: Amandine, 1990; Lowey, 1992
Major Award: Emmy, Best Supporting Actor in a Made-for-TV Movie, *Death of a Salesman*, 1986

DAVID MAMET

Birthplace: Chicago, IL
Birthdate: 11/30/47
Occupation: Writer, director
Education: Goddard College, studied at the Neighborhood Playhouse in New York

Debut: (Stage) *The Duck Variations*, 1972

Signature: *Glengarry Glen Ross*, 1984

Facts: Has written several books and children's plays, including *Revenge of the Space Pandas, or Binky Rudich and the Two-Speed Clock.*

Has worked as a busboy, driven a cab, worked at *Oui* magazine, and waited tables. Was an assistant office manager for a real estate company and taught drama at Yale, New York University, and the University of Chicago.

Wrote the screenplays for *The Postman Always Rings Twice* (1981), *The Verdict* (1982), and *The Untouchables* (1987).

Published his first novel, *The Village*, in 1994.

Still writes on a '70s manual typewriter and uses a pencil.

Co-founded the Atlantic Theater Company as a summer workshop in Vermont for his NYU students.

Original Job: Worked backstage at the Hull House Theatre in Chicago

Marriages: Lindsay Crouse, 1977 (divorced); Rebecca Pidgeon, 1991

Children: Willa, 1982; Zosia, 1988; (with Lindsay Crouse). Clara, 1994; Noah, 1999

Major Award: Pulitzer Prize, *Glengarry Glen Ross*, 1984

CAMRYN MANHEIM

Real Name: Debra Manheim
Birthplace: Caldwell, NJ
Birthdate: 3/8/61
Occupation: Actor
Education: Cabrillo Junior College; University of California at Santa Cruz; New York University (MFA)
Debut: (Stage) *Hydriotaphia*, 1987; (Film) *The Bonfire of the Vanities*, 1990; (TV) *Law & Order*, 1991
Signature: *The Practice*
Facts: While at NYU she took crystal methedrine to lose weight, became addicted, and accidentally overdosed.

Between sporadic acting gigs in New York, she was a sign language interpreter for the deaf in theaters and hospitals.

The success in 1993 of her one-woman Off-Broadway show, *Wake Up, I'm Fat!*, caught the eye of David E. Kelley, who cast her in the series pilot of *The Practice.*

Has 12 piercings in her right ear, a tattoo of Pegasus above her ankle, and drives a motorcycle.

Accepting her Emmy Award in 1998, she held it up and said, "This is for all the fat girls!"

Influenced by her activist parents, she was once arrested for marching in a pro-choice demonstartion.

Original Job: Sign language interpreter, improvisation teacher

Major Award: Emmy Award, Outstanding Supporting Actress in Drama Series, *The Practice,* 1998

Quote: "I'm a five-foot-ten Amazon who isn't afraid to be naked or to kiss men or to be sexual anymore."

AIMEE MANN

Birthplace: Richmond, VA
Birthdate: 8/9/60
Occupation: Singer, songwriter
Education: Attended Berklee School of Music
Debut: *Voices Carry,* 1985 (with 'Til Tuesday)
Signature: *Magnolia* soundtrack
Facts: Was abducted to Europe at age 4 by her mother. After a year, Mann's father tracked down his ex-wife and regained their daughter.

Took up music when recovering from mononucleosis.

Majored in bass at Berklee. Says that "no one could teach me how to sing."

Her first band was a postpunk group called the Young Snakes. She quit when she realized her attraction to melodic music.

When her record label went bankrupt, Warner Bros. offered to release her upcoming solo album as a personal favor to her old label

head. Mann declined, citing lack of commitment to her and her music.

Her song "Deathly" inspired the screenplay of *Magnolia.*

Marriage: Michael Penn, 1998
Famous Relatives: Sean Penn, actor, brother-in-law; Chris Penn, actor, brother-in-law
Quote: "I think the role of artists and songwriters is to say, 'Maybe you can't do this, but I'll do it for you...' I'll try to sing, out loud, the truth."

MARILYN MANSON

Real Name: Brian Hugh Warner
Birthplace: Canton, OH
Birthdate: 1/5/69
Occupation: Singer, band leader
Education: High school
Debut: (Album) *Portrait of an American Family,* 1994
Facts: An only child, he was sent to a private conservative Christian school for the best possible education, but he resented the restrictions and the warnings about evil rock music. He eventually caused sufficient trouble to be expelled and finished his last two years in a public school.

He formed his band in 1990 and created his alter ego based on Marilyn Monroe and Charles Manson, considering them the most popular personalities of the 1960s.

For his music and stage show, he drew from pornography, horror films, and Satanism because they were the forbidden items of youth.

The title of his album *Antichrist Superstar* is a twist on Andrew Lloyd Webber's *Jesus Christ Superstar.*

He proposed to Rose on Valentine's Eve with an antique diamond ring.

After candlelight vigils and bomb threats at some venues, Manson had a hard time getting booked in certain cities.

Infamy: His group was banned in Salt Lake City after he ripped apart a Mormon Bible on stage.

He sold T-shirts imprinted "Kill God...Kill Your Mom and Dad...Kill Yourself."

During a 1998 rampage in Poughkeepsie, NY, he trashed and burned his dressing room and destroyed four hotel rooms.
Relationship: Rose McGowan (engaged)
Quote: "To the people who are afraid of things like me, the answer is to raise your kids to be more intelligent."

SHIRLEY MANSON

Birthplace: Edinburgh, Scotland
Birthdate: 8/26/66
Education: High school dropout
Occupation: Singer, guitarist
Debut: (Album) *Garbage*, 1995
Signature: *Version 2.0*, 1998
Facts: Learned to play violin, clarinet and piano.

Left school at 16 to work in a clothing store.

Joined the band Goodbye Mr. McKenzie after she had a crush on the lead singer. Ten years later, around 1994, she left the band to form her own group, Angelfish.
Marriage: Eddie Farrell, sculptor, 1996
Quote: "I was born with rage. What can I say? Under the Chinese calendar I'm a fire horse."

JULIANNA MARGULIES

Birthplace: Spring Valley, NY
Birthdate: 6/8/66
Occupation: Actor
Education: Sarah Lawrence College
Debut: (Film) *Out for Justice*, 1991
Signature: *ER*
Facts: Her father was the ad executive who wrote the Alka Seltzer "Plop, plop, fizz, fizz" jingle.

Her parents divorced early, and her mother, a former dancer with the American Ballet Theatre, moved her to Paris and then London.

A perfectionist in high school, once threw a 50-page, illustrated research report into the mud because it got an A-minus.

While waiting for an acting break, waitressed at some of New York's trendiest restaurants.

Turned down a $27 million two-year contract offer when she left *ER*.
Relationship: Ron Eldard
Major Award: Emmy, Best Supporting Actress (Drama), *ER*, 1995

WYNTON MARSALIS

Birthplace: New Orleans, LA
Birthdate: 10/18/61
Occupation: Trumpeter
Education: Attended Juilliard on a full scholarship
Debut: (Band) Art Blakey's Jazz Messengers, 1980
Facts: His first trumpet was a hand-me-down from bandleader Al Hirt.

Played with New Orleans Philharmonic at age 14.

Released his first classical album, *Trumpet Concertos,* in 1983. Was first artist ever to receive—or be nominated for—awards in both jazz and classical categories in a single year.
Children: Wynton, 1990; Simeon, 1992; Jasper Armstrong, 1996
Famous Relatives: Ellis Marsalis, musician, father; Branford Marsalis, musician, brother
Major Awards: Grammy, Best Jazz Performance—Soloist, "Think of One," 1983; Grammy, Best Jazz Performance—Soloist, "Hot House Flowers," 1984; Grammy, Best Jazz Performance—Soloist, "Black Codes from the Underground," 1985; Grammy, Best Jazz Performance—Group, "Black Codes from the Underground," 1985; Grammy, Best Jazz Performance—Group, "J Mood," 1986; Grammy, Best Jazz Performance—Group, *Marsalis Standard Time Volume I,* 1987; Pulitzer Prize, *Blood on the Fields,* 1997; Grammy, Best Spoken Word Album for Children, *Listen to the Storyteller* (with Graham Greene and Kate Winslet), 1999

PENNY MARSHALL

Real Name: Carole Penny Marshall
Birthplace: New York, NY
Birthdate: 10/15/43
Occupation: Actor, director
Education: University of New Mexico
Debut: (TV) *The Danny Thomas Hour,* 1967
Signature: *Laverne and Shirley*
Facts: Even though the family was Congregationalist, Marshall's mother was convinced that Jewish men make the best husbands, so she sent Penny to a Jewish summer camp each year.

Lost the part of Gloria on TV's *All in the Family* to Sally Struthers.

Was first woman director to have a film take in more than $100 million at the box office (*Big*).
Original Jobs: Dance instructor, secretary
Marriages: Michael Henry (divorced); Rob Reiner, 1971 (divorced, 1979)
Child: Tracy Lee, 1964
Famous Relatives: Garry Marshall, director, producer, brother; Tony Maschiarelli, producer, father

RICKY MARTIN

Real Name: Enrique José Martin Morales
Birthplace: San Juan, PR
Birthdate: 12/24/71
Occupation: Singer
Education: High school
Debut: (Solo Album) *Ricky Martin,* 1988; (Solo English-Language Album) *Ricky Martin,* 1999; (TV) *Getting By,* 1993; (Broadway) *Les Misérables,* 1996
Signature: "Livin' La Vida Loca"
Facts: At age six, he began appearing in local television commercials.

When he first tried out the singing group Menudo, he was considered too short. By 1984, he joined as its youngest member, and took "mandatory retirement" before turning 18.

In 1985, legally changed his name from Enrique to Ricky

Played a singing bartender in the soap *General Hospital* in 1993 and by 1994, he had a regular role.

Considers himself a "spiritual" person, is a student of yoga and Buddhism, and shaved his head in India in December, 1998.

Sang the Spanish-language version of the theme to Disney's *Hercules*.

Ricky Martin (1999) has sold over 5 million copies in the U.S. and is the best-selling album ever by a Latin artist.

Major Award: Grammy, Best Latin Pop Performance, *Vuelve*, 1999

Quote: "I have no butt. Everybody tells me that. It's tiny…not even rock climbing helps."

STEVE MARTIN

Birthplace: Waco, TX
Birthdate: 8/14/45
Occupation: Actor, writer
Education: Long Beach State College, UCLA
Debut: (TV) *The Smothers Brothers Comedy Hour,* 1967
Signature: "A wild and crazy guy"
Facts: Lived behind Disneyland and got his start there performing magic tricks and playing the banjo.

Was a cheerleader in high school. Is a dedicated art collector.

Dated Anne Heche for two years before she broke it off.

Has published sophisticated satirical pieces in *The New Yorker* and the book *Pure Drivel.*

Original Job: Sold guidebooks at Disneyland

Marriage: Victoria Tennant (divorced, 1993); Ellen Ladowsky, writer (relationship)

Major Awards: Emmy, Best Writing in a Comedy, Variety, or Music Program, *The Smothers Brothers Comedy Hour,* 1969; Grammy, Best Comedy Recording, *Let's Get Small,* 1977; Grammy, Best Comedy

Recording, *A Wild and Crazy Guy,* 1978

Quote: "I became an actor because I was fearful of becoming a has-been standup comic working Las Vegas. And I became a standup comic because I was fearful of becoming a has-been TV writer. Fear is a very constructive force."

MASTER P

Real Name: Percy Miller
Birthplace: New Orleans, LA
Birthdate: 2/9/69
Occupation: Rapper, actor, movie producer, record and film company executive
Education: Junior college
Debut: (Album) *The Ghetto's Tryin' to Kill Me,* 1994
Signature: No Limit
Facts: The eldest of five children, he grew up in a housing project in an area with a high crime rate and a reputation for violence.

Attended University of Houston on a basketball scholarship but left when he was sidelined with a leg injury.

Moved to Richmond, Virginia, and opened a small record store, No Limits, which has become a very successful independent record company and has made him a multi-millionaire.

He sold his debut album out of the trunk of his car in Oakland and New Orleans. It became an underground hit, selling 200,000 copies without radio play.

His film, *I'm 'Bout It,* which he produced, directed, and acted in, was a fictionalized version of his brother's murder.

He tried out for the Continental Basketball Association's team in 1998 and signed on as a free agent, earning $1,000 per week with a $15 per day allowance. Several months later, he tried out for the Charlotte Hornets, an NBA team, but did not make the cut.

In 1997 he started No Limit Sports Management, a company that repre-

sented young NBA players, including Ron Mercer (Boston Celtics) and Derek Anderson (Cleveland Cavaliers).

In 1998 *Forbes* ranked him as the tenth highest paid entertainer.

Original Job: Record store owner
Marriage: Sonya Miller
Children: Four children
Quote: "What I learned in the ghetto is that everybody wants more for their money. You gotta be able to give your customers more for their money, 'cause that's how you're going to keep them coming back to you."

PAUL MCCARTNEY

Real Name: James Paul McCartney
Birthplace: Liverpool, England
Birthdate: 6/18/42
Occupation: Singer, songwriter, bassist
Education: High school
Debut: Formed the Quarry Men, Moondogs, and the Silver Beatles with John Lennon and George Harrison, 1956–1962
Signature: The Beatles
Facts: When he wanted to use "Yesterday" in his 1984 film *Give My Regards to Broad Street,* he had to apply to the publishers for its use; he no longer owned the copyright of the most recorded song in history (over 2,500 cover versions exist).

Was the first Beatle to quit in 1970, releasing his solo album *McCartney* almost simultaneously with the band's release of *Let It Be.*

His version of "Mary Had a Little Lamb" hit No. 9 on the British charts in June 1972.

In the Paul McCartney Kindergarten in Krakow, Poland, children are taught English through McCartney's songs.

Was knighted by Queen Elizabeth in 1996.

Inherited his wife's fortune after her death and, although no monetary value was placed on the trust, it is estimated that he is now worth $1.1 billion.

Infamy: Admitted to taking LSD and was arrested numerous times with Linda for possession of marijuana and for growing it at their Scotland farmhouse. Because of this, his application for a U.S. passport was refused many times.
Marriage: Linda Eastman, 1969 (deceased, 1998); Heather Mills (relationship)
Children: Heather, 1962 (step-daughter); Mary, 1969; Stella, 1971; James, 1977
Major Awards: Grammy, Best New Artist (with The Beatles), 1964; Grammy, Best Pop Vocal—Duo or Group, *A Hard Day's Night* (with The Beatles), 1964; Grammy, Song of the Year, "Michelle" (with John Lennon), 1966; Grammy, Best Rock Vocal, "Eleanor Rigby," 1966; Grammy, Album of the Year, *Sgt. Pepper's Lonely Hearts Club Band* (with The Beatles), 1967; Grammy, Best Score, *Let It Be* (with The Beatles), 1970; Grammy, Best Pop Performance—Duo or Group, *Band on the Run* (with Wings), 1974; Grammy, Hall of Fame Winner, *Sgt. Pepper's Lonely Hearts Club Band* (with The Beatles), 1992; Oscar, Best Score, *Let It Be* (with The Beatles), 1970; inducted into the Rock and Roll Hall of Fame (with The Beatles), 1988; NARAS Lifetime Achievement Award, 1990; Grammy, Best Pop Vocal, Duo or Group with Vocal, "Free as a Bird" (with The Beatles), 1996; inducted into Rock and Roll Hall of Fame, 1999.

STELLA MCCARTNEY

Birthplace: England
Birthdate: 9/13/71
Occupation: Fashion designer
Education: Central St. Martin's College of Art and Design
Facts: At 15 she worked at Patou, the French couture house, but left because she was opposed to the use of fur in fashion.

Apprenticed with a Savile Row tailor, enabling her to sew as well as to design.

Her graduation fashion show for St. Martin's featured a song by her father, and her clothes were modeled by friends Kate Moss, Yasmin Le Bon, and Naomi Campbell.

A brief stint running her own company failed, and she was hired by Chloe. Now head designer, she has revitalized the house's line.

Like her parents, she is an active member of PETA, and narrated a video about animal cruelty at fur ranches.

Her father advised her, "Nobody is Beatle-proof."
Famous Relatives: Linda Eastman McCartney, photographer/musician, mother (deceased 1998); Paul McCartney, ex-Beatle, father
Quote: "Of course my name opens doors. But they can close just as quickly if I don't deliver."

MATTHEW MCCONAUGHEY

Birthplace: Uvalde, TX
Birthdate: 11/4/69
Occupation: Actor
Education: University of Texas
Debut: (Film) *Dazed and Confused,* 1993
Signature: *A Time To Kill,* 1996
Facts: College friend of Rene Zellweger's, they appeared together in school productions.

Endlessly rereads the motivational book, *The Greatest Salesman in the World.* Used its techniques to sell his talents to get acting parts.

Was cast in *Kill* after executives vetoed Kevin Costner, Keanu Reeves, Val Kilmer and others in a year-long search. Received just $200,000 to play the part.
Quote: "There are certain nights you and your image just aren't in the same bed."

DYLAN MCDERMOTT

Birthplace: Waterbury, CT
Birthdate: 10/26/61
Occupation: Actor
Education: Fordham University; also

trained under Sanford Meisner at the Neighborhood Playhouse
Debut: (Theater) *Biloxi Blues,* 1985; (Film) *Hamburger Hill,* 1987
Signature: *The Practice*
Facts: Moved to Greenwich Village as a teen to live with his father. His playwright-stepmother soon wrote a part for him.

Engagement to Julia Roberts was broken off by her after she fell for Kiefer Sutherland on a movie set.
Original job: Busboy
Marriage: Shiva Afshar, 1995
Child: Colette, 1996
Famous Relative: Eve Ensler, playwright, stepmother
Quote: "My theory about actors is, we're all walking milk cartons. Expiration dates everywhere."

FRANCES MCDORMAND

Birthplace: Illinois
Birthdate: 6/23/57
Occupation: Actor
Education: Bethany College, Yale Drama School
Debut: (Film) *Blood Simple,* 1984
Signature: *Fargo,* 1996
Facts: Born to a Disciples of Christ preacher. The family moved repeatedly throughout the Midwest when she was a child.

Met Holly Hunter when the two studied at Yale. After graduation, Hunter told her she had auditioned for "two weird guys" (the Coen brothers) and that McDormand should too. After repeated failed attempts to get an audition, McDormand finally succeeded. *Blood Simple* not only launched her (and Hunter's) career, it introduced her to future husband Joel.

Was nominated in 1988 for Oscar's best supporting actress (for *Mississippi Burning*), the same year she was also nominated for a Tony for *A Streetcar Named Desire.*
Marriage: Joel Coen, 1994
Child: Pedro, c. 1994 (adopted)
Famous Relative: Ethan Coen,

writer, director, producer, brother-in-law
Major Award: Oscar, Best Actress, *Fargo*, 1996

REBA MCENTIRE

Birthplace: Chockie, OK
Birthdate: 3/28/55
Occupation: Singer, songwriter
Education: Southeastern State University
Debut: (Song) "I Don't Want To Be a One-Night Stand," 1976
Signature: "Is There Life Out There?"
Facts: As a teenager, performed with her siblings in the Singing McEntires. Their first single was a tribute to her grandfather, rodeo rider John McEntire.

Appeared in the 1990 movie *Tremors,* as well as other film and TV roles.

Her longtime tour manager and seven of her band members died in a plane crash in 1991.
Original Job: Cattle rancher, rodeo barrel racer
Marriages: Charlie Battles (divorced), Narvel Blackstock, 1989
Child: Shelby, 1990 (with Blackstock)
Major Awards: Grammy, Best Country Vocal—Female, "Whoever's in New England," 1986; Grammy, Best Country Female Vocalist, 1987; Grammy, Best Country Vocal—Collaboration, "Does He Love You" (with Linda Davis), 1993

TIM MCGRAW

Birthplace: Jacksonville, FL
Birthdate: 5/11/66
Occupation: Singer
Education: Attended Northeast Louisiana University
Debut: (Album) *Tim McGraw,* 1993
Signature: *Not a Moment Too Soon*
Facts: Mom Betty was an 18-year-old dancer when she and then bachelor Tug consummated their summer romance while Tug was in baseball camp. Tim learned who his

father was only when he found his birth certificate at age 11. Tim met Tug but had little contact until high school, when Tug agreed to help pay for his son's college education.

Started his own management company, Breakfast Table Management, to launch other groups.

The lyrics to his "Indian Outlaw" outraged some Native American groups, who had it banned from radio stations in several states.
Infamy: Charged with a felony count of second degree assault after attacking officers who were trying to remove fellow performer Kenny Chesney from a police horse after a concert in Buffalo, NY.
Marriage: Faith Hill, 1996
Child: Gracie Katherine, 1997; Maggie Elizabeth, 1998
Famous Relative: Tug McGraw, baseball player, father

EWAN MCGREGOR

Birthplace: Crieff, Scotland
Birthdate: 3/31/71
Occupation: Actor
Education: Attended London's Guildhall School of Music and Drama
Debut: (Film) *Being Human,* 1993
Signature: *Star Wars: Episode 1—The Phantom Menace,* 1999
Facts: Inspired by his uncle, knew he wanted to be in theater at age 9. Left home at 16 to work backstage at Scotland's Perth Repertory Theatre.

Lost nearly 30 pounds and shaved his head for his role in *Trainspotting.* Debated trying to shoot heroin but decided that it would be disrespectful to the recovering addicts acting as technical advisors to the film.
Marriage: Eve Maurakis, 1995
Child: Clara Mathilde, 1996
Famous Relative: Dennis Lawson, actor, uncle

MARK MCGWIRE

Birthplace: Pomona, CA
Birthdate: 10/1/63
Occupation: Baseball player
Education: University of Southern California
Debut: (Major League Baseball) Oakland Athletics, 1986
Signature: Record-setting home-run hitter
Facts: Began playing Little League baseball at 8. Hit a home run in his first at-bat, against a 12-year-old pitcher.

Has 4 brothers, all of whom are over 6 feet tall and weigh more than 200 pounds.

His ex-wife was a bat girl at USC.

Brother Dan played quarterback for the Seattle Seahawks and the Miami Dolphins.

Was drafted by the Montreal Expos out of high school, but when they offered a signing bonus of only $8,500, he opted for college, where he intended to be a pitcher.

Was rookie of the year in 1987, hitting 49 home runs, the most ever for a rookie.

In 1998 smashed Roger Maris's legendary record of 61 home runs in a season, finishing with a total of 70.

His biceps are 20 inches wide.

Hit 500 home runs sooner in his career than any other slugger.

Loves classical music and watching the Learning Channel.

His on-again, off-again girlfriend runs the Mark McGwire Foundation.

Very close to his son, who fills in as a St. Louis Cardinal's batboy and is contractually guaranteed a seat on the team plane with his father.
Infamy: Has admitted to taking androstenedione pills. Though legal and allowed in baseball, this testosterone-producing substance is banned by the NFL and IOC. Also took creatine, a muscle-building substance.
Marriage: Kathy Williamson (divorced, 1988); Ali Dickson (relationship)
Child: Matthew, 1987

SARAH MCLACHLAN

Birthplace: Halifax, Nova Scotia, Canada
Birthdate: 1/28/68
Occupation: Singer, songwriter, concert promoter
Education: Attended Nova Scotia College of Art and Design
Debut: (Album) *Touch,* 1988
Signature: Lilith Fair
Facts: She and two brothers were adopted; at age 19, met her birth mother by coincidence.

Offered a chance to record demo tapes for a Vancouver independent label while in high school, but her parents refused to let her.

Was harassed for years by an obsessive fan, with his letters inspiring the song "Possession." Recognizing his words, he sued, but committed suicide before the matter was resolved.

Named the Lilith concert after Adam's first wife in Jewish mythology, a woman tossed out of Eden for being too independent and forced to make it alone.
Marriage: Ashwin Sood, 1997
Major Awards: Grammy, Best Female Pop Vocal Performance, "Building a Mystery," 1997; Grammy, Best Pop Instrumental Performance, "Last Dance," 1997; Grammy, Best Pop Vocal Performance—Female, "I Will Remember You," 1999
Quote: "Don't think I don't count the horseshoes on my ass daily."

A. J. MCLEAN

Real Name: Alexander James McLean
Birthplace: West Palm Beach, FL
Birthdate: 1/9/78
Occupation: Singer
Debut: (TV) *Hi Honey, I'm Home,* 1991; (Single) "We've Got It Goin' On," 1995; (Album) *Backstreet Boys,* 1995 (American version, 1997)
Signature: "Everybody (Backstreet's Back)," 1997

Facts: Has a strong background in theater.

The band is named after Orlando, Florida's Backstreet Market, a popular teen hangout.

The group's debut was a hit in 26 countries before *Backstreet Boys* was released in the U.S.

The "edgy" Backstreet Boy.

Has at least eight tattoos.

His lucky number is 69.

His favorite restaurant is McDonald's.

Spends a half-hour each morning sculpting his goatee.

Has never blown his nose: "When it comes to anything mucus-oriented or phlegm or someone spitting, I gag."

His mother manages his career.

Sometimes performs solo as his British alter ego "Johnny No Name," who covers songs by Stone Temple Pilots and the Commodores.
Infamy: Band filed suit against former manager Lou Pearlman, claiming he had made $10 million from their labor while they had received $300,000.
Original Job: Actor
Quote: "I'm the complete opposite of every clean-cut, decent-looking guy you could think of, yet I have the biggest heart in the world."

JANET MCTEER

Birthplace: Newcastle, England
Birthdate: 5/8/61
Occupation: Actor
Education: Royal Academy of Dramatic Art
Debut: (Stage) *Mother Courage and Her Children,* 1984; (Film) *Half Moon Street,* 1984
Signature: *Tumbleweeds,* 1999
Facts: Was "tiny" until she was 13, when she shot up six inches in a year; her knees were bandaged to cope with the growing pains. She now stands 6'1".

Became a British celebrity when she played Virginia Woolf's lover in a BBC made-for-television movie.

While shooting in North Africa, caught a virus which robbed her right eye of its central vision.

Despite her size, is such a chameleon that she was brushed aside by theatergoers waiting for her outside *A Doll's House.*

To nail her *Tumbleweeds* accent, spent three months in South Carolina and watched *Coal Miner's Daughter* "32 million times."
Original Job: Coffee seller at Theatre Royal
Major Award: Tony, Best Actress (Dramatic), *A Doll's House,* 1997
Quote: "Let's face it, there aren't many wonderful scripts for women over the age of 10."

NATALIE MERCHANT

Birthplace: Jamestown, NY
Birthdate: 10/26/63
Occupation: Singer
Education: High school dropout
Debut: (Album, with 10,000 Maniacs) *Human Conflict No. 5;* (Solo album) *Tigerlily,* 1995
Signature: "Carnival"
Facts: After her mother remarried, the family moved to a commune: "I fell in love with those people."

At 16 she dropped out of high school, took college courses, and worked three jobs, including one at a whole foods bakery.

Frequently in the audience for 10,000 Maniacs' performances, she was suddenly invited up to sing, and at 17 joined the group as lead singer. Quit the group in 1992 to go solo.

Dated R.E.M.'s Michael Stipe on and off for three years.
Quote: "People need to change within first, with their hearts before their minds. Now, instead of wanting to change people, I just want to move them."

DEBRA MESSING

Birthplace: Brooklyn, NY
Birthdate: 8/15/68
Occupation: Actor
Education: Brandeis University, New York University (MFA)
Debut: (Off-Broadway) *Four Dogs and a Bone*; (TV) *NYPD Blue*, 1994; (Film) *A Walk in the Clouds*, 1995
Signature: *Will & Grace*
Facts: Graduated summa cum laude from college.

She won her own series, *Ned and Stacey*, after four episodes of *NYPD Blue*.

Appeared twice on *Seinfeld* as Jerry's unavailable crush.
Marriage: Daniel Zelman, 2000
Major Award: Emmy, Best Actress in a Comedy Series, *Will & Grace*, 2000

BETTE MIDLER

Birthplace: Honolulu, HI
Birthdate: 12/1/45
Occupation: Singer, comedian, actor, producer
Education: Attended University of Hawaii
Debut: (Album) *The Divine Miss M*, 1972; (Film) *Hawaii*, 1966
Signature: "Wind Beneath My Wings," 1989
Facts: Named after Bette Davis, which her mother mistakenly thought was pronounced "Bet."

Spent her first 21 years in Hawaii, then worked carefully to cultivate a New Yorker image.

Was married in a Las Vegas chapel by an Elvis impersonator.

Wrote a best-selling children's book, *The Saga of Baby Divine*.
Infamy: Became a gay icon in the 1970s by singing at New York's bath houses, often with then-unknown Barry Manilow as her pianist.
Original Jobs: Pineapple cannery worker, radio station secretary, go-go dancer
Marriage: Martin Von Haselburg, 1984
Child: Sophie, 1986

Major Awards: Grammy, Best New Artist, 1973; Grammy, Best Contemporary/Pop Female Solo Vocal, *The Rose*, 1980; Grammy, Best Children's Recording, *In Harmony, A Sesame Street Record*, 1980; Grammy, Record of the Year, "Wind Beneath My Wings,"1989; Grammy, Song of the Year, "Wind Beneath My Wings," 1989; Grammy, Song of the Year, "From a Distance," 1990; Emmy, Best Individual Performance—Variety or Music Show, *The Tonight Show Starring Johnny Carson*, 1992; Emmy, Outstanding Special — Comedy, Variety, or Music, *Ol' Red Hair Is Back*, 1978; Emmy, Best Individual Performance—Variety or Music Show, *Diva Las Vegas*, 1997; Tony, special award, 1974

ALYSSA MILANO

Birthplace: Brooklyn, NY
Birthdate: 12/19/72
Occupation: Actor
Education: High school dropout
Debut: (Stage) *Annie*, 1980; (Film) *Old Enough*, 1982; (TV) *Who's the Boss*, 1984
Signature: *Who's the Boss*
Facts: Began acting at age eight, as Molly in a national touring company production of *Annie*.

Made an exercise video, *Teen Steam*, and released three albums in Japan.

Says she is "obsessed with religious art" and has an impressive collection of Madonnas, cruicifixes, statues, and rosaries. Also collects Barbie and Madame Alexander dolls.

Her tattoos include an angel, a sacred heart, a garland of flowers, a fairy kneeling in grass, and rosary beads.
Infamy: Successfully sued multiple parties to get images of herself, including both real and fake nude photos, removed from the Internet, and contributed the settlements toward funding Web site www.safe-searching.com, which she developed with her mother to direct surfers to celebrity sites.
Marriage: Scott Wolf (engaged; never married); Cinjun Tate, singer and guitarist for rock band Remy Zero, 1999 (separated, 1999)
Quote: "Every part I play, I change my hair."

MATTHEW MODINE

Birthplace: Loma Linda, CA
Birthdate: 3/22/59
Occupation: Actor
Education: Attended Brigham Young University
Debut: (TV) *Amy and the Angel*, 1982; (Film) *Baby, It's You*, 1983; (Stage) *Breaking Up*, 1990
Signature: *Married to the Mob*, 1988
Facts: Was raised as a Mormon.

He and his siblings worked at their father's drive-in movie theaters.

Feeling connected to the characters in the musical *Oliver!*, he took up tapdancing.

Was kicked out of at least two high schools.

Married his wife at a Halloween-night costume ceremony at New York City's Plaza Hotel.

Played Vietnam vets in *Birdy* and *Full Metal Jacket*, but turned down the lead in *Top Gun* because of its cold-warrior worldview.

Passionate about horticulture, he is planting hundreds of trees at his upstate NY farm.
Original Job: Drive-in theater worker, electrician, rock band gofer, macrobiotic chef
Marriage: Caridad Rivera, 1980
Children: Ruby, 1990; Boman, c. 1996

JAY MOHR

Real Name: Jon Ferguson Mohr
Birthplace: Verona, NJ
Birthdate: 8/23/71
Occupation: Actor, comedian
Education: High school
Debut: (TV) MTV's *Lip Service*, 1991; (Film) *For Better or Worse*, 1995

Signature: *Jerry Maguire* (1996)
Facts: After graduating from high school in 1988, Mohr spent two years racking up 10 national comedy shows.

In 1993 he began a two-year stint on *Saturday Night Live,* known for his impersonations of Tony Bennett and Christopher Walken. Though well known for his time on the show, he complains about "All that waiting around for a glimmer of stage time, just getting angry every week…It was just an oppressive, horrible, horrible place to be. I went to work feeling nauseous."

The inside of his left arm is tattooed with "Will 12-27," in honor of his cousin who was killed by a drunk driver in 1995, two days after Christmas.
Wife: Nicole Chamberlain, model, actor, 1998
Quote: "Hey, I'm no nancy boy. I've got my bitchin' truck and my rottweiler. I'm a dude…But I still admit to my girlfriend when I'm wrong."

MONICA

Real Name: Monica Arnold
Birthplace: College Park, GA
Birthdate: 12/24/80
Occupation: Singer
Education: High school
Debut: (Single) "Don't Take It Personal," 1995; (Album) *Miss Thang,* 1995; (TV) *Living Single*
Signature: "The Boy Is Mine" (1998)
Facts: Began to sing publicly in church at age 2, and at 12 was discovered at a talent show.

At age 14 with her debut single became the youngest artist to top the Billboard charts. Her 1998 album, *The Boy Is Mine,* produced three consecutive No. 1 singles.

Had a 4.0 average at Atlanta County Day School.

Rapper Queen Latifah is her manager.
Major Award: Grammy, R&B Performance—Duo or Group with vocal,

"The Boy Is Mine" (with Brandy), 1998

DEMI MOORE

Real Name: Demetria Guynes
Birthplace: Roswell, NM
Birthdate: 11/11/62
Occupation: Actor
Education: Left high school to model in Europe, studied with Zina Provendie
Debut: (Film) *Choices,* 1981; (TV) *General Hospital,* 1981 [see page 106 for a complete filmography]
Signature: *Ghost,* 1990
Facts: Was cross-eyed as a child and had an operation to correct it, wearing a patch over one eye.

Decided to become an actor in high school when she lived in the same building as Nastassja Kinski.

In order to play coke addict Jules in the 1985 movie *St. Elmo's Fire,* she had to sign a contract stipulating that she would stop her own alcohol and drug abuse, an agreement that caused her to turn her life around.

Was engaged to Emilio Estevez.

She and Bruce Willis were married by singer Little Richard.
Infamy: Posed nude and pregnant on the cover of *Vanity Fair.*
Original Job: Model
Marriages: Freddy Moore (divorced), Bruce Willis, 1987 (separated, 1998); Oliver Whitcomb (relationship)
Children: Rumer Glenn, 1988; Scout Larue, 1991; Tallulah Belle, 1994

JULIANNE MOORE

Real Name: Julie Anne Smith
Birthplace: Fort Bragg, NC
Birthdate: 12/3/60
Occupation: Actor
Education: Boston University
Debut: (TV) *Edge of Night,* 1983; (Film) *Tales from the Darkside: The Movie,* 1990
Signature: *Boogie Nights,* 1997
Facts: Was an Army brat.

Played good and evil twins Frannie and Sabrina on *As the World Turns.*

Has vowed not to gorge or starve for a part after weight loss for *Safe* left her sick for a year.

Is a self-described "library girl" and "magazine addict."

Credits her love of reading with providing an eye for good scripts.
Original Job: Waitress
Marriages: John Gould Rubin, c. 1984 (divorced, 1995); Bart Freundlich (relationship)
Child: Caleb, 1997
Quote: "I have an ability to hear characters, it's an aural thing. If I can't hear the voice then I can't do the part."

MANDY MOORE

Birthplace: Nashua, NH
Birthdate: 4/10/84
Occupation: Singer
Debut: *So Real,* 1999
Signature: "Candy"
Facts: Decided to become a performer after seeing a stage revival of *Oklahoma!* at age 6.

Was Orlando's "National Anthem Girl" because of her frequent gigs opening sporting matches.

Was discovered by a FedEx man who had a friend at Epic Records.

Aims to do Broadway.

Is learning to play guitar.
Quote: "I don't think I have to dress sexy or provocative to get my point across. I don't sing about stuff I haven't experienced yet."

ALANIS MORISSETTE

Birthplace: Ottawa, Canada
Birthdate: 6/1/74
Occupation: Singer, songwriter
Education: High school
Debut: (Album) *Alanis,* 1991
Signature: "You Oughta Know," 1995
Facts: At age 10, appeared as a sweet little girl on Nickelodeon's *You Can't Do That on Television.* At 17, was a Queen of Disco, dubbed the Canadian Debbie Gibson.

During her dance pop days, toured with Vanilla Ice.

Has a twin brother, Wade.

Claimed it took 15 to 45 minutes

to write most of the songs on *Jagged Little Pill.*
Major Awards: Grammy, Album of the Year, *Jagged Little Pill,* 1995; Grammy, Best Rock Album, *Jagged Little Pill,* 1995; Grammy, Best Female Rock Vocalist, "You Oughta Know," 1995; Grammy, Best Rock Song, "You Oughta Know," 1995; Grammy, Best Long Form Music Video, *Jagged Little Pill Live,* 1997; Grammy, Best Rock Song, "Uninvited," 1998

TONI MORRISON

Real Name: Chloe Anthony Wofford
Birthplace: Lorain, OH
Birthdate: 2/18/31
Occupation: Author
Education: Howard University, Cornell University
Debut: (Book) *The Bluest Eye,* 1969
Signature: *Beloved*
Facts: Has served as an editor at Random House, helping to publish the works of other black Americans like Toni Cade Bambara, Angela Davis, and Muhammad Ali.

Has taught at Harvard, Yale, and Princeton.
Original Job: Textbook editor
Marriage: Harold Morrison, 1958 (divorced, 1964)
Children: Harold Ford, 1961; Slade Kevin, 1965
Major Awards: National Book Critics Circle Award, *Song of Solomon,* 1977; Pulitzer Prize, *Beloved,* 1988; Nobel Prize for Literature, 1993
Quote: "Although we women are coming into our own, we still love you men for what you are, just to let you know."

VAN MORRISON

Real Name: George Ivan Morrison
Birthplace: Belfast, Northern Ireland.
Birthdate: 8/31/45
Occupation: Singer, songwriter
Education: High school dropout

Debut: (Song) "Don't Start Crying" (with Them), 1964
Signature: "Brown Eyed Girl"
Facts: Was lead singer of Them from 1964 to 1967 and has worked solo ever since.

In 1965, wrote "Gloria," which achieved moderate success but didn't hit the U.S. top ten until it was covered by The Shadows of Knight in 1966.
Marriage: Janet Planet, 1968 (divorced, 1973)
Child: Shana, 1970
Major Award: Grammy, Best Pop Vocal Collaboration (with Sinead O'Connor and the Chieftains), "Have I Told You Lately That I Love You," 1995

FRANKIE MUNIZ

Birthplace: Wood Ridge, NJ
Birthdate: c. 1985
Occupation: Actor
Debut: (TV) *To Dance with Olivia,* 1997; (Film) *My Dog Skip,* 2000
Signature: *Malcolm in the Middle,* 2000
Facts: When money from *Malcolm* came in, Muniz rewarded himself with golf clubs and a new computer.

Is keeping a video record of his life and career.

Counts his appearance on the cover of *Super Teen* magazine as the culmination of a dream.
Quote: "Acting classes, I guess, are good, and I would like to maybe sometime take one, but I would feel

like I'm learning someone else's technique. I like mine."

EDDIE MURPHY

Birthplace: Hempstead, NY
Birthdate: 4/3/61
Occupation: Actor
Education: Nassau Community College
Debut: (TV) *Saturday Night Live*, 1980
Signature: *Beverly Hills Cop*, 1984
Facts: Father was a policeman who died when Eddie was 5.

Was voted most popular at Roosevelt Jr.-Sr. High School in Roosevelt, NY.

Created and produced the TV series *The Royal Family*, which was cut short upon the sudden death of the star Redd Foxx.

Co-created the controversial animated comedy *The PJ's* (complaints, from Spike Lee among others, arose about its racial depictions, though TV reviewers found it hilarious)and provides the voice of lead character Thurgood Stubbs

Co-owns the L.A. restaurant Georgia with Denzel Washington.
Infamy: In May 1997, police tracking a transvestite prostitute pulled Murphy's Toyota over at 4:45 a.m.; police arrested the prostitute and immediately released Murphy, who explained he was only giving the streetwalker a lift. In the aftermath Murphy sued the *National Enquirer* for publishing interviews with transvestite prostitutes claiming to have had sex with Murphy; the suit was eventually dropped.
Original Job: Shoe store clerk
Marriage: Nicole Mitchell, 1992
Children: Ashlee, 1987; Bria, 1989; (with Nicolle Rader). Eddie Jr., c. 1989; (with Paulette McNeeley). Christian Edward, 1990 (with Tamara Hood). Miles Mitchell, 1992; Shayne Audra, 1994; Zola Ivy, 1999
Major Award: Grammy, Best Comedy Recording, *Eddie Murphy—Comedian*, 1983

Quote: "You get born only once in this business, but you can die over and over again. Then you make comebacks."

BILL MURRAY

Birthplace: Wilmette, IL
Birthdate: 9/21/50
Occupation: Actor, writer
Education: Loyola Academy, Regis College, Second City Workshop in Chicago
Debut: (TV) *Saturday Night Live*, 1977
Signature: *Ghostbusters*, 1984
Facts: Was a pre-med student at St. Regis College.

Provided the voice of Johnny Storm, the Human Torch, on Marvel Comics' radio show, *The Fantastic Four*. This is where he was heard by the producers of *Saturday Night Live*.

Bill's son, Homer Banks, is named after legendary Chicago Cub Ernie Banks.

In 1981, performed the song "The Best Thing (Love Song)" for John Waters' *Polyester*.
Original Job: Pizza maker
Marriage: Margaret Kelly (divorced, 1996)
Children: Homer, 1982; Luke, 1985
Famous Relative: Brian Doyle-Murray, actor, brother
Major Award: Emmy, Best Writing in a Comedy Series, *Saturday Night Live*, 1977

MIKE MYERS

Birthplace: Scarborough, Canada
Birthdate: 5/25/63
Occupation: Actor, writer
Education: High school
Debut: (TV) *Mullarkey & Myers*, 1984; (Film) *Elvis Stories*, 1989
Signature: Austin Powers
Facts: When he was a child, Myers's comedy-loving father would wake his three sons at night to watch *Monty Python*.

First appeared in TV commercials when he was 4, and at 8 he did a commercial with Gilda Radner. Also

appeared as a kid on Canadian TV programs such as the dance show, *Boogie Junior*.

Modeled his *Saturday Night Live* character Linda "Coffee Talk" Richman on his mother-in-law.

Wrote the script for the original *Austin Powers* in three weeks.

Started a retro-mod band, Ming Tea.

Hobbies include watching old war footage and painting toy soldiers.
Marriage: Robin Ruzan, 1993
Major Awards: Emmy, Outstanding Writing in a Comedy Series, *Saturday Night Live*, 1989

LIAM NEESON

Birthplace: Ballymena, Northern Ireland
Birthdate: 6/7/52
Occupation: Actor
Debut: (Stage) *In the Risen*, 1976; (Film) *Excalibur*, 1981
Signature: *Schindler's List*, 1993
Facts: At age 9, joined a boxing team run by a priest. Nose was broken during an early match, and had it set on site by his manager. Quit boxing at age 17.

First starring role was the disfigured hero of the film *Darkman*, 1990.

Chipped his pelvis in 2000 after hitting a deer while riding his motorcycle.
Original Job: Forklift operator, architect's assistant, amateur boxer
Marriage: Natasha Richardson, 1994
Children: Micheál, 1995; Daniel Jack N., 1996
Quote: "You have these people in therapy 25 years because, what, their moms didn't cuddle them? I'm sorry. Get a f---in' life."

WILLIE NELSON

Birthplace: Abbott, TX
Birthdate: 4/30/33
Occupation: Singer, songwriter, guitarist, actor
Education: Baylor University
Debut: (Album) *...And Then I Wrote*,

1962; (Film) *The Electric Horseman,* 1979
Signature: "Mamas, Don't Let Your Babies Grow Up To Be Cowboys," 1978
Facts: Nelson taught at Baptist Sunday school until officials objected to him playing in seedy bars.

Sold his first song, "Family Bible," for $50 to feed his family; it became a huge hit, performed by more than 70 country artists.

Organized Farm Aid concerts to help midwestern farmers stricken by drought and threatened with foreclosure.

Began writing songs at age 7.
Infamy: In 1991, after a seven-year dispute with the IRS over $16.7 million in back taxes, the government seized most of Nelson's possessions (country club, recording studio, 44-acre ranch, 20 other properties in four states, instruments, recordings, and memorabilia).

Arrested in 1994 for possession of marijuana. Charges were later dismissed.
Original Jobs: Janitor, door-to-door salesman (Bibles, encyclopedias, vacuum cleaners, sewing machines), hosted country music shows on Texas radio stations
Marriages: Martha Matthews, 1952 (divorced, 1962); Shirley Collie, 1963 (divorced, 1971); Connie Koepke (divorced, 1989); Annie D'Angelo, 1991
Children: Lana, 1953; Susie, 1957; Billy, 1958 (deceased, 1991); (with Martha Matthews). Paula Carlene, 1969; Amy, 1973; (with Connie Koepke). Lukas Autry, 1988; Jacob Micah, 1990
Major Awards: Grammy, Best Country Vocal—Male, "Blue Eyes Cryin' in the Rain," 1975; Grammy, Best Country Vocal—Male, "Georgia on My Mind," 1978; Grammy, Best Country Performance—Duo or Group, "Mamas Don't Let Your Babies Grow Up To Be Cowboys" (with Waylon Jennings), 1978;

Grammy, Best Country Song, "On the Road Again," 1980; Grammy, Best Country Vocal—Male, "Always on My Mind," 1982; Grammy, Best Country Song, "Always on My Mind," 1982; Grammy, Legend Award, 1990; inducted into the Country Music Hall of Fame in 1993

PAUL NEWMAN

Birthplace: Cleveland, OH
Birthdate: 1/26/25
Occupation: Actor, director, producer
Education: Kenyon College, Yale School of Drama, Actors Studio
Debut: (Film) *The Silver Chalice,* 1954
Signature: *The Hustler,* 1961
Facts: Briefly attended Ohio University and was allegedly asked to leave for crashing a beer keg into the president's car.

The Newman's Own food company he founded in 1987 with writer friend A.E. Hochner has donated more than $100 million to charity.

Has worked on more than nine movies with actor wife Joanne Woodward.

A die-hard, marching liberal, he invested in the leftist opinion-making magazine, *The Nation.*

Is a professional race car driver.
Marriages: Jacqueline Witte (divorced), Joanne Woodward, 1958
Children: Scott, 1950 (deceased); Susan, 1953; Stephanie, 1955; (with Jacqueline Witte). Elinor "Nell" Teresa, 1959; Melissa Steward, 1961; Claire Olivia, 1965
Major Awards: Oscar, Jean Hersholt Humanitarian Award, 1993; Oscar, Lifetime Achievement, 1985; Oscar, Best Actor, *The Color of Money,* 1986;

WAYNE NEWTON

Birthplace: Norfolk, VA
Birthdate: 4/3/42
Occupation: Entertainer
Education: High school dropout
Debut: (TV) *Jackie Gleason and His*

American Scene Magazine, 1962; (Film) *80 Steps to Jonah,* 1969
Signature: "Danke Schoen"
Facts: Protégé of Jackie Gleason.

Partly Native American.

In 1999, signed a multimillion-dollar deal to perform seven shows a week, 40 weeks a year, for up to 10 years in a new showroom bearing his name at the Stardust Hotel in Las Vegas.
Infamy: In 1992, declared bankruptcy, listing debts of more than $20 million.

In 1994 his creditors again went to court, charging that, despite millions in current earnings, he continued spending lavishly on himself (including a reported $75,000 repairing his home pond for his pet penguins) and made little effort to pay what he owed them.
Marriages: Elaine Okamura (divorced, 1985); Kathleen McCrone, 1994
Child: Erin, 1976 (with Elaine Okamura)

JACK NICHOLSON

Birthplace: Neptune, NJ
Birthdate: 4/22/37
Occupation: Actor, director, producer, screenwriter
Education: Studied with the Players Ring acting group
Debut: (Stage) *Tea and Sympathy,* 1957; (Film) *Cry-Baby Killer,* 1958
Signature: *One Flew Over the Cuckoo's Nest,* 1975 [see page 106 for a complete filmography]
Facts: Recorded *The Elephant's Child,* a children's record, with Bobby McFerrin (1987).

Abandoned by his father in childhood, he was raised believing his grandmother was his mother and his real mother was his older sister. The truth was revealed to him years later when a *Time* magazine researcher uncovered the truth while preparing a story on the star.

Has been nominated 11 times for the Academy Award.

Infamy: Known for being a ladies' man, Nicholson had a 17-year relationship with actress Anjelica Huston that ended in 1990 when Nicholson revealed that actor Rebecca Broussard, his daughter's best friend, was carrying his child.

During a later two-year falling out period with Broussard, he dated a 20-year-old and allegedly fathered her baby girl.

Was accused of using a golf club to strike the windshield of a '69 Mercedes that had cut him off in traffic in 1994. The driver's civil suit was settled out of court.

Admitted the paternity of Caleb Goddard, an adult New York City producer and writer. The public acknowledgment arose out of a messy civil battle between Nicholson and Goddard's mother, actress Susan Anspach.
Original Job: Office boy in MGM's cartoon department
Marriage: Sandra Knight, 1961 (divorced, 1966)
Children: Jennifer Norfleet, c. 1964 (with Sandra Knight). Caleb Goddard, 1970 (with Susan Anspach). Lorraine, 1990; Raymond, 1992 (with Rebecca Broussard)
Major Awards: Oscar, Best Actor, *One Flew over the Cuckoo's Nest,* 1975; Oscar, Best Supporting Actor, *Terms of Endearment,* 1983; Grammy, Best Recording for Children, *The Elephant's Child,* 1987; Oscar, Best Actor, *As Good As It Gets,* 1997
Quote: "More good times—that's my motto."

LESLIE NIELSEN

Real Name: Leslie Nielsen
Birthplace: Regina, Saskatchewan
Birthdate: 2/11/26
Occupation: Actor
Education: Lorne Greene's Academy of Radio Arts, Toronto
Debut: (TV) *Studio One's Battleship Bismarck,* 1950; (Film) *The Vagabond King,* 1956
Signature: *The Naked Gun*

Facts: Spent his childhood 100 miles from the Arctic Circle.

Father was a Royal Canadian Mountie.

A prolific actor, he appeared on countless television programs—over 45 live dramas in 1950 alone, and over 1,500 shows to date—including everything from *Playhouse 90, Wagon Train, Dr. Kildare,* and *Bonanza* to *M*A*S*H* and *The Love Boat.*

Comedic career was launched with *Airplane!*

Author of *The Naked Truth* (1993) and *Bad Golf My Way* (1996).
Original Job: Royal Canadian Air Force; D.J. and radio announcer
Marriages: Monica Boyer, singer (1950; divorced 1955); Alisand "Sandy" Ullman (1958; divorced, 1974); Brooks Nielsen (divorced, 1982), Barbaree Earl (relationship, since 1981)
Children: Thea, 1961; Maura, 1963 (with Ullman)
Famous Relative: Jean Hersholt, character actor, uncle.
Quote: "At this stage of my life, I don't give a damn. If they want to type me, let 'em. I just want to maintain whatever celebrity status I have, so they'll keep inviting me to golf tournaments."

CYNTHIA NIXON

Birthplace: New York, NY
Birthdate: 4/9/66
Occupation: Actor
Education: Barnard College; Yale Drama School
Debut: (TV) *The Seven Wishes of a Rich Kid,* 1979; (Film) *Little Darlings,* 1980; (Stage) *The Philadelphia Story,* 1980
Signature: *Sex and the City*
Facts: Met her husband in junior high school.

When filming *Amadeus* in Prague, flew back and forth five times so she wouldn't miss high school classes.

In 1984, appeared on Broadway at the same time in both *The Real Thing*

and *Hurlyburly,* two blocks apart.

Co-founded The Drama Dept., whose members include Billy Crudup and Sarah Jessica Parker.
Marriage: Danny Mozes
Child: Samantha, 1996
Quote: "I have very nice men in my life. But I see men all around me who shock and horrify me."

NICK NOLTE

Real Name: Nicholas King Nolte
Birthplace: Omaha, NE
Birthdate: 2/8/41
Occupation: Actor, producer
Debut: (TV) *The Framing of Billy the Kid,* 1973; (Film) *Return to Macon County,* 1975
Signature: *Prince of Tides,* 1991
Facts: Did runway and print modeling and appeared on Clairol box for many years.

Was 35 before gaining attention for his role in *Rich Man, Poor Man.*

Known to show up in public wearing pajama bottoms.

Has openly admitted lying to the press to create a persona. He has lied about his educational background, claiming that he won football scholarships to several different universities, and once told a reporter, as a lark, that his ex-wife had been a high-wire circus performer.
Infamy: Convicted in 1962 for selling fake draft cards.

Was sued for palimony by longtime companion Karen Louise Eklund; suit was settled out of court.
Original Jobs: Model, ironworker
Marriages: Sheila Page (divorced 1971); Sharon Haddad (divorced 1983); Rebecca Linger (divorced 1991); Vicki Lewis (relationship)
Children: Brawley King, 1986 (with Linger)
Quote: "Early on I decided that I was going to lie to the press. The best approach to talking about my personal life was to lie."

EDWARD NORTON

Birthplace: Columbia, MD
Birthdate: 8/18/69
Occupation: Actor
Education: Yale University
Debut: (Film) *Primal Fear,* 1996
Signature: *Primal Fear*
Facts: Was on the baseball team in high school.

When Leonardo DiCaprio dropped out of *Primal Fear,* Paramount launched an international search of 2,100 actors with no success. Costar Richard Gere was ready to walk from the project until Norton read for the part.

Grandfather James Rouse designed Boston's Faneuil Hall and New York's South Street Seaport. Father Ed Sr., a lawyer, was a federal prosecutor under Jimmy Carter.

Studied astronomy and Japanese (he's fluent) in college before getting a degree in history.
Original Jobs: Proofreader, waiter, low-income housing worker
Relationship: Salma Hayek
Famous Relative: James Rouse, architect, grandfather

CONAN O'BRIEN

Birthplace: Brookline, MA
Birthdate: 4/18/63
Occupation: Talk show host
Education: Harvard University
Debut: (TV) *Not Necessarily the News,* 1985
Signature: *NBC's Late Night with Conan O'Brien*
Facts: Has written for *Saturday Night Live* and *The Simpsons.*

While at Harvard, served as president of *The Harvard Lampoon* for two years, the first person to do so since Robert Benchley in 1912.

First TV producing credit was *Lookwell* (1991), a sitcom pilot starring Adam West as a former TV detective who becomes a real cop.

Once dated Lisa Kudrow, who he met while performing with the Groundlings.
Famous Relative: Denis Leary, actor, cousin
Major Award: Emmy, Best Writing in a Variety or Music Program, *Saturday Night Live,* 1989
Quote: "The nightmare is that you spend the rest of your life being funny at parties and people say, 'Why didn't you do *that* when you were on television?' "

CHRIS O'DONNELL

Birthplace: Chicago, IL
Birthdate: 6/26/70
Occupation: Actor
Education: Boston College, UCLA
Debut: (TV) *Jack and Mike,* 1986; (Film) *Men Don't Leave,* 1990
Signature: *Scent of a Woman,* 1992
Facts: Youngest of seven children (four sisters and two brothers), grew up in Winnetka, IL.

Began modeling and appearing in commercials in 1983, at age 13. Appeared in a McDonald's commercial opposite Michael Jordan.

Was 17 when he auditioned for *Men Don't Leave.* His mother had to promise him a new car to get him to try out. He is still waiting for that car.

Originally cast as Barbra Streisand's son in *Prince of Tides,* but she decided to have her real-life son play the role instead.

Took time off from pursuing a degree in marketing from Boston College in order to work with Al Pacino on *Scent of a Woman.*
Marriage: Caroline Fentress, 1997
Child: Lily Anne, 1999

ROSIE O'DONNELL

Birthplace: Commack, NY
Birthdate: 3/21/62
Occupation: Actor, comedian
Education: Dickinson College and Boston University
Debut: (TV) *Gimme a Break,* 1986; (Film) *A League of Their Own,* 1992; (Stage) *Grease,* 1994
Signature: *The Rosie O'Donnell Show*
Facts: Won the *Star Search* comedy competition five times.

Fascinated with the blue-collar mundane, she began extensively collecting McDonald's Happy Meal figurines.

Against her agent's advice, she auditioned for—and won—the role of Betty Rizzo in the Broadway revival of *Grease* in 1994. She had no theater experience and says she'd never sung in public before.

In a 1999 interview with Tom Selleck, who once filmed a commercial for the NRA, she began a heated debate about gun control. Selleck finally declared, "I didn't come on your show to have a debate, I came on your show to plug a movie."

In 2000, her producers sued radio station Rosie 105 (KRSK-FM) in Portland, Ore. over the name and a logo they said is similar to theirs.

Helped contestant Jerry Halpin win $32,000 as a phone friend on *Who Wants to Be a Millionaire.* Before giving her final answer, she promised Halpin that if she were wrong, she would pay him the money out of guilt.

Appearing on *Millionaire* as a contestant, she raised $500,000 for the For All Kids Foundation.
Children: Parker Jaren, 1995; Chelsea Belle, 1997; Blake Christopher, 1999; Maria, c. 1997 (all adopted).
Major Awards: Emmy, Best Host—Talk or Service Show, *The Rosie O'Donnell Show,* 1995–96; Emmy, Best Host—Talk or Service Show, *The Rosie O'Donnell Show,* 1996–97; Emmy, Best Host—Talk or Service Show, *The Rosie O'Donnell Show,* 1997–98; 1998–99; 1999-00

ASHLEY OLSEN

Birthdate: 6/13/86
Occupation: Actor
Debut: (TV) *Full House,* 1987
Facts: Two minutes older than fraternal twin sister Mary-Kate and has a freckle under her nose.

Their mother says, "When they need

someone to be more active or emotional, they let Ashley do it."

The twins' commercial empire includes Olsen Twins books (100-plus titles), videos (over 20), game cartridges for Nintendo and Playstation, and a popular Web site, www.marykateandashley.com, plus a pair of Olsen Barbie dolls and a clothing line from Wal-Mart. How is she different from her twin? "My voice is deeper."

Famous Relative: Jamie Olsen, former dancer with the Los Angeles Ballet, mother

MARY-KATE OLSEN

Birthdate: 6/13/86
Occupation: Actor
Debut: (TV) *Full House,* 1987
Facts: Wants to be a candymaker or a cowgirl when she grows up.

The twins' commercial empire includes Olsen Twins books (100-plus titles), videos (over 20), game cartridges for Nintendo and Playstation, and a popular Web site, www.marykateandashley.com, plus a pair of Olsen Barbie dolls and a clothing line from Wal-Mart.

"Mary-Kate is more serious, so she gets the serious lines to do," says her mother.

Famous Relative: Jamie Olsen, former dancer with the Los Angeles Ballet, mother

SHAQUILLE O'NEAL

Birthplace: Newark, NJ
Birthdate: 3/6/72
Occupation: Basketball player
Education: Louisiana State University
Facts: His rap album, *Shaq Diesel,* sold more than one million copies. Got his rap start by singing on "What's Up Doc," a song put out in 1993 by his favorite rap group, FU-Schnickens.

He stands seven feet one inch, weighs 303 pounds, and wears size 21 triple-E shoes.

His first name translates, ironically, to "little one."

Spent most of his adolescence in Germany, where his stepfather was an army sergeant.
Relationship: Arnetta (engaged)
Children: Tahaera, 1996
Major Awards: NBA Rookie of the Year, 1993; 4 Time NBA All-Star; Winner of NBA Scoring Title 1995; Gold Medal at 1996 Olympics

SUZE ORMAN

Real Name: Suzie Orman
Birthdate: 6/5/51
Occupation: Author, financial guru
Education: University of Illinois at Urbana-Champaign
Signature: *Nine Steps to Financial Freedom* (1997)
Facts: As a child, her parents lost their boardinghouse in a liability suit, and 10 years later her father's deli burned down. He suffered third-degree burns on his arms after he ran inside to save the cash register. She claims that incident taught her that money is "more important than life."

During college, she roomed with John Belushi and his wife, Judy. "I told Judy he'd never amount to anything. Shows you what I know about picking husbands."

Her degree is in social work.

After college, she waitressed at the Buttercup Bakery in Berkeley, Califonia, for seven years before talking her way into a stockbroker's job at Merrill Lynch. One of the first female brokers in northern California, she sought out unusual clients, like truck drivers and waitresses, and consulted a crystal on investment decisions.

In 1987 opened her own investment/financial advisory firm, which failed in six months because of an employee dispute over commissions, which was finally settled in court.

Receives up to $20,000 for lecture appearances. Is the most successful personality ever on PBS pledge drives.

She lives alone in the same one-bedroom, one-story home she bought 23 years ago, and drives a 1987 BMW.
Quote: "I don't care that I don't look like a hotshot and my English isn't always proper. People can relate to that. I've helped people realize their dreams."

OZZY OSBOURNE

Real Name: John Michael Osbourne
Birthplace: Birmingham, England
Birthdate: 12/3/48
Occupation: Singer
Debut: (Album) *Black Sabbath,* 1969; (Solo album) *Blizzard of Oz,* 1980
Signature: Godfather of heavy metal
Facts: Was the vocalist with Black Sabbath until he was kicked out of the band in 1979.

The original band members reunited in 1997 for a series of concerts in Birmingham and to record an album.

Gave a facelift to his favorite bulldog Baldrick, whose face wrinkles produced sores.

Collects art, particularly Victorian nudes.

A member of the Church of England, he kneels to pray backstage before performances.

Has 15 tattoos.
Infamy: He spent years on various drugs, was often in a clinic to kick his addictions. Doctors determined he has a chemical imbalance resulting from years of alcohol and drugs, and he has been drug- and alcohol-free since 1991.

In 1982 he bit off the head of a live bat, thinking it was made of rubber, but when it bit him back and lashed his face with its wings, he rushed for a rabies shot.

Bit the head off a white dove in front of American businessmen.

Shot his ex-wife's 17 cats.

Was arrested in San Antonio for urinating on the Alamo (he was drunk and wearing a dress).

In 1989 he was charged with attempted manslaughter after allegedly trying to strangle his wife, Sharon, but she later dropped the charges.

In the mid-'80s, he was taken to court by parents who accused him of recording subliminal messages urging teens to commit suicide.

Original Jobs: Car-horn assembly-line worker; slaughterhouse worker

Marriages: Thelma (divorced 1981); Sharon Arden, 1982

Children: Elliott, c. 1966; Jessica, c. 1972; Louis, c. 1975 (with Thelma; Elliott was her son from a previous relationship but took Osbourne's name). Aimee, 1983; Kelly, c. 1984; Jack, c. 1985.

Major Award: Grammy, Best Heavy Metal Performance, "I Don't Want to Change the World," 1994

Quote: "I used to be an alcoholic drug addict, now I'm a workaholic. I've gotta keep moving all the time."

DONNY OSMOND

Real Name: Donald Clark Osmond
Birthplace: Ogden, Utah
Birthdate: 12/9/57
Occupation: Singer, keyboardist, actor, TV host
Education:
Debut: (TV) The Andy Williams Show, 1963; (Album) One Bad Apple, 1971; (Film) Goin' Coconuts, 1978; (Stage) Little Johnny Jones, 1982
Signature: "One Bad Apple," 1971
Facts: Joined his singing brothers on The Andy Williams Show at age six.

Had his first solo gold record with 1971's Go Away Little Girl, and his 1972 single, "Puppy Love," also went gold.

In 1989 had a comeback hit with his somewhat edgier rock recording "Soldier of Love."

In the 90s, toured as the lead in Joseph and the Amazing Technicolor Dreamcoat.

Joked about Rosie O'Donnell's weight on her talk show in 1996,

and came back to apologize dressed in dog suit, serenading her with "Puppy Love."

Provided the singing voice in Mulan and teamed with sister Marie for a syndicated daily talk show.

In 1999, he published his autobiography Life Is Just What You Make It: My Life So Far.

Marriage: Debra Glenn, 1978
Children: Donald, 1979; Jeremy, 1981; Brandon, 1985; Christopher, 1990; Joshua, 1998
Famous relatives: Alan, Wayne, Merrill, Jay, entertainers, brothers (The Osmond Brothers); Marie, singer, sister
Quote: "We've had life experiences. Now, granted, we may not have been in the ditches like a lot of people who had drug problems or were fired from jobs. But when I quit the old Donny and Marie show, that was the toughest time in my life. I couldn't even get arrested."

MARIE OSMOND

Real Name: Olive Marie Osmond
Birthplace: Ogden, Utah
Birthdate: 10/13/59
Occupation: Singer, actor, TV host
Debut: (TV) The Andy Williams Show, 1963; (Film) Goin' Coconuts, 1978; (Stage) The King and I, 1998
Signature: "Paper Roses," 1975
Facts: The only girl in a family of nine children, she made her TV debut at age three, and by 12, had recorded her first No. 1 hit on the country charts, "Paper Roses."

Toured as Maria in The Sound of Music from 1994–95, and made her Broadway debut in 1998. That same year, she and bother Donny co-hosted a daily talk show, Donny & Marie.

Has had her own line of cosmetics, issued a line of clothing patterns and published Marie Osmond's Guide to Beauty, Health and Style. Since 1991, she has also marketed own line of porcelain dolls on QVC, with total sales of over 1

million units.

Reportedly turned down the role of Sandy in the film version of Grease because she thought the script was too racy.

She suffered a severe bout of postpartum depression, which she openly discussed on Oprah Winfrey in 1999.

Is the cofounder of the Children's Miracle Network, which has raised $1.5 billion for children's hospitals across the country.

Marriages: Steve Craig, 1982 (divorced, 1985); Brian Blosil, record producer, 1986 (separated, then reconciled, 2000)
Children: Stephen (with Steve Craig), 1983; Jessica, adopted, c. 1988; Rachel, 1989; Michael, c. 1991; Brandon, c. 1996; Brianna, daughter, c. 1997; Matthew, 1999
Famous relatives: Alan, Wayne, Merrill, Jay and Donny, entertainers, brothers (The Osmond Brothers)
Quote: "I learned early on that choices have consequences. You can either plan for the long-term or grab the short-term fix."

AL PACINO

Real Name: Alfredo James Pacino
Birthplace: New York, NY
Birthdate: 4/25/40
Occupation: Actor
Education: attended High School of the Performing Arts, Actor's Studio
Debut: (Stage) The Peace Creeps, 1966; (Film) Me, Natalie, 1969
Signature: The Godfather, 1972
Facts: Has been involved with actresses Jill Clayburgh, Marthe Keller, and Diane Keaton.

Is so shy that in 1999 he appeared on the Rosie O'Donnell Show only on the condition that no audience be present.

Original Jobs: Mail deliverer at Commentary magazine, messenger, movie theater usher, building superintendent
Relationship: Beverly D'Angelo

Child: Julie Marie, 1989 (with Jan Tarrant)

Major Awards: Tony, Best Supporting Actor (Dramatic), *Does a Tiger Wear a Necktie?*, 1969; Tony, Best Actor (Dramatic), *The Basic Training of Pavlo Hummel*, 1977; Oscar, Best Actor, *Scent of a Woman*, 1992

SE RI PAK

Birthplace: Taejon, South Korea
Birthdate: 9/28/77
Occupation: Golfer
Education: Student at David Leadbetter Golf Academy
Facts: Was avid track athlete before turning to golf at age 14.

Her father, who admits to being a thug in his past, occasionally left her alone in a dark cemetery to develop her courage.

At 20, was the youngest winner of a major women's golf tournament in 30 years.

Major Awards: Winner, U.S. Women's Open, 1998; Winner, McDonald's LPGA Championship, 1998

GWYNETH PALTROW

Birthplace: Los Angeles, CA
Birthdate: 9/27/72
Occupation: Actor
Education: University of California, Santa Barbara
Debut: (Film) *Shout*, 1991 [see page 106 for a complete filmography]
Signature: *Shakespeare in Love*, 1998
Facts: Nude pictures of her and former beau Brad Pitt that were taken with a telephoto lens while the couple vacationed in privacy in St. Bart's were circulated on the Internet and published in the tabloids. Pitt filed suit against the photographer. The couple split in 1997 after more than two years together.

Says a major goal for her life is to have babies.

Infamy: Was named in a personal injury lawsuit in 2000, alleging that a year prior Paltrow's rental car collided with the plaintiff's vehicle. The plaintiff is allegedly seeking $62,000 from Paltrow and Midway Rent-a-Car to cover medical expenses and repairs.

Famous Relatives: Blythe Danner, actor, mother; Bruce Paltrow, producer, father; Jake Paltrow, actor, director, brother; Hillary Danner, actor, cousin

Major Award: Academy Award, Best Actress, *Shakespeare In Love*, 1998

Quote: "I'm so sick of myself, my boring voice and my stupid sound bites."

SARAH JESSICA PARKER

Birthplace: Nelsonville, OH
Birthdate: 3/25/65
Occupation: Actor
Education: American Ballet Theater, Professional Children's School in New York
Debut: (TV) *The Little Match Girl*, 1973; (Stage) *The Innocents*, 1976
Signature: *Sex in the City*
Facts: Sang in Metropolitan Opera productions of *Hansel and Gretel*, *Cavalleria Rusticana*, *Pagliacci*, and *Parade*.

Starred as nerdy Patty Green on the CBS TV sitcom *Square Pegs*, 1982–83.

Played Annie in the Broadway musical, 1979–80.

Lived with Robert Downey Jr. for seven years.

Wears a size two.

Original Job: Dancer with Cincinnati Ballet and the American Ballet Theatre

Marriage: Matthew Broderick, 1997

DOLLY PARTON

Birthplace: Sevierville, TN
Birthdate: 1/19/46
Occupation: Singer, songwriter
Education: High school
Debut: (Song) "Puppy Love," 1956
Signature: "9 to 5," 1981

Facts: Met her husband in the Wishy Washy laundromat.

Has her own theme park, Dollywood, located in Gatlinburg at the edge of the Smoky Mountains. In her hometown of Sevierville, Tennessee, there is a statue of her on the Sevier County Courthouse lawn.

Marriage: Carl Dean, 1966

Major Awards: Grammy, Best Country Vocal—Female, *Here You Come Again*, 1978; Grammy, Best Country Vocal—Female, "9 to 5," 1981; Grammy, Best Country Performance—Duo or Group, *Trio* (with Linda Rondstadt and Emmylou Harris), 1987; Grammy, Best Country Vocal–Collaboration, *After the Gold Rush* (with Linda Ronstadt and Emmylou Harris), 1999

Quote: "Left to my own, I'd rather look like trash. I love tacky clothes. My look came from a very serious honest place, and that was a country girl's idea of what glamour was."

JANE PAULEY

Real Name: Margaret Jane Pauley
Birthplace: Indianapolis, IN
Birthdate: 10/31/50
Occupation: Broadcast journalist
Education: Indiana University
Debut: (TV) WISH-TV, Indiana, 1972
Signature: *Dateline NBC*
Facts: Succeeded Barbara Walters on the *Today* show two weeks shy of her 26th birthday in 1976; left 13 years later in a controversy over Deborah Norville's role that generated enormous sympathy for Pauley.

Limited her children's TV viewing to one hour a day.

Marriage: Garry Trudeau, 1980
Children: Richard Ross,1983; Rachel Grandison, 1983; Thomas Moore, 1986
Major Awards: 3 News and Documentary Emmys: 2 as correspondent, 1 as writer

LUCIANO PAVAROTTI

Birthplace: Modena, Italy
Birthdate: 10/12/35
Occupation: Singer
Education: Istituto Magistrale Carlo Sigonio
Debut: (Stage) *La Bohème,* 1961
Facts: Established Opera Company of Philadelphia/ Luciano Pavarotti Vocal Company, 1980.

Makes at least $100,000 per concert. His fortune is estimated to be between $25 and $50 million.

Dreads the anticipation of singing more than singing itself. "The 10 minutes before the performance you wouldn't wish on your worst enemies."

Half a billion people saw the televised "Three Tenors" concert (with Placido Domingo and José Carreras) in 1990.

In 1990, the only musicians who sold more recordings than Pavarotti were Madonna and Elton John.
Infamy: He was sued by the BBC when it found out that a 1992 Pavarotti concert it had bought for broadcast had really been lip-synched.

An ongoing affair with his 26-year old secretary, Nicoletta Mantovani, led to his separation.

In 2000, agreed to pay nearly $12 million in back taxes and interest to the Italian government.
Original Jobs: Elementary school teacher, salesman
Marriage: Adua Veroni (separated, 1996); Nicoletta Mantovani (relationship)
Children: Lorenza, Cristina, Giuliana
Major Awards: Grammy, Best Classical Vocal Performance, *Luciano Pavarotti—Hits from London Center,* 1978; Grammy, Best Classical Vocal Performance, *O Sole Mio (Favorite Neapolitan Songs),* 1979; Grammy, Best Classical Vocal Performance, *Live from Lincoln Center—Sutherland—Horne—Pavarotti* (with Joan Sutherland and Marilyn Horne), 1981; Grammy, Best Classical Vocal Performance, *Luciano Pavarotti in Concert,* 1988; Grammy, Best Classical Vocal Performance, *Carreras, Domingo, Pavarotti in Concert* (with José Carreras and Placido Domingo), 1990

BILL PAXTON

Birthplace: Ft. Worth, TX
Birthdate: 5/17/55
Occupation: Actor
Education: New York University
Debut: (Film) *Mortuary,* 1981
Signature: *Twister,* 1996
Facts: Spent much of his career making B-grade movies like *Pass the Ammo* and *Brain Dead.*

For his *Mortuary* character's wardrobe, Paxton bought second-hand sweaters, from which he caught scabies.

Directed *Fishheads,* a cult music video that aired on MTV in the early 1980s.

Has had several long bouts of depression that sometimes took months to shake.

Wife is 10 years younger than he is. They met when he followed her onto a bus.
Original Job: Set dresser
Marriages: First wife (divorced), Louise Newbury, 1985
Children: James, 1994; Lydia, 1997

AMANDA PEET

Birthplace: New York, NY
Birthdate: 1/11/72
Occupation: Actor
Education: Columbia University, 1995
Debut: (TV) *One Life to Live,* 1994; (Film) *Grind,* 1994
Signature: *The Whole Nine Yards,* 2000
Facts: While a junior in college, she began studying theater with actor Uta Hagen.

Is able to recite the entire dialogue from *Tootsie* and *A Chorus Line.*
Relationship: Brian Van Holt, actor
Quote: "I'm a perennial stress ball. I find it really hard to be Zen and take a deep breath."

ROBIN WRIGHT PENN

Real Name: Robin Wright
Birthplace: Dallas, TX
Birthdate: 4/8/66
Occupation: Actor
Education: High school
Debut: (TV) *The Yellow Rose,* 1984; (Film) *Hollywood Vice Squad,* 1986
Signature: *Forrest Gump,* 1994
Facts: Began modeling after a talent scout spotted her roller-skating.

She was waiting tables in Hawaii when she found out that she had won the role of Kelly on NBC soap opera *Santa Barbara*; received two daytime Emmy nominations for her work on the show.

Met future husband, Sean Penn, at a coffee shop where he bummed a cigarette off of her. He was married to Madonna at the time.

Paired with Sean in 1990's *State of Grace,* directed by him in 1995 in *The Crossing Guard,* then costarred with him again in *She's So Lovely,* 1997.

Was the victim of a carjacking in front of her home in 1996.

On Oscar night, 1996, she needed emergency gall bladder surgery and Sean skipped the ceremony to be with her.

Son, Hopper Jack, is named after Dennis Hopper and Jack Nicholson.
Original Job: Model
Marriages: Dane Witherspoon (divorced); Sean Penn, 1996
Children: Dylan Frances, 1991; Hopper Jack, 1993
Quote: "I don't want my daughter to think she should go to the front of the line just because her daddy is Sean Penn. I want us to wait like everybody else."

SEAN PENN

Birthplace: Burbank, CA
Birthdate: 8/17/60
Occupation: Actor, director, writer
Education: High school
Debut: (Film) *Taps*, 1981
Signature: *Dead Man Walking*, 1995
Facts: In high school, was on the tennis team. Rob Lowe and Charlie Sheen were his classmates.

His lavish house burned to the ground in the 1993 Malibu brush-fires. Rather than rebuilding, he put a 27 1/ foot trailer on the land and moved in there.

Wears a tattoo saying "NOLA deliver me!," a reference to a fright-ening night spent in New Orleans (the NOLA) after drinking a glass of water spiked with seven hits of acid.

While growing up, his director father was blacklisted as a Commu-nist, and had trouble getting work for years.
Infamy: Punched several photogra-phers attempting to take his picture, and allegedly fired a gun at a hovering helicopter covering his first wedding. Spent 34 days in jail in 1987 for smacking a film extra while on probation for hitting someone who tried to kiss then wife Madonna.

Was so volatile during his marriage to Madonna she called a SWAT team to help her retrieve her possessions. Now says he "was drunk all the time" during their marriage.
Marriages: Elizabeth McGovern (engaged, never married); Madonna, 1985 (divorced,1989); Robin Wright, 1996
Children: Dylan Frances, 1991; Hopper Jack, 1993
Famous Relatives: Leo Penn, director, father; Eileen Ryan, actor, mother; Christopher Penn, actor, brother; Aimee Mann, sister-in-law
Quote: "I'm not an alcoholic. I'm just a big drinker, and there's a difference."

MATTHEW PERRY

Birthplace: Williamstown, MA
Birthdate: 8/19/69
Occupation: Actor, writer
Education: High school
Debut: (Film) *A Night in the Life of Jimmy Reardon*, 1988
Signature: *Friends*
Facts: His father is best known for Old Spice commercials.

Moved to his mother's native Ottawa after his parents split when he was a year old. His journalist mother became press aide to Canadian Prime Minister Pierre Trudeau.

An avid tennis player, at 13 was ranked the No. 2 junior player in Ottawa.

Frustrated by the lack of good parts, he and a friend wrote a sitcom about six twentysomethings, which interested NBC. When the network ultimately decided to go with a similar sitcom, *Friends,* Perry decided since he couldn't beat 'em, he'd join 'em.

In 2000, along with *Friends* costars, received a salary increase from $125,000 to $750,000 per episode.

Withdrew his name from the Emmy ballot in 2000 after learning that he had been placed in the leading man column rather than in the supporting category with the rest of the cast of *Friends.*
Infamy: Checked into rehab to overcome addiction to prescription painkillers.
Relationship: Rene Ashton
Famous Relative: John Bennett Perry, actor, father
Quote: "I describe my dating style as 'basic stupidity.' I'll take a woman and try to impress her with my sense of humor to the level that my head will almost implode. I also juggle if all else fails."

JOE PESCI

Birthplace: Newark, NJ
Birthdate: 2/9/43
Occupation: Actor
Education: High school dropout
Debut: (Radio) *Star Kids*, 1947; (Film) *Hey, Let's Twist!*, 1961
Signature: *My Cousin Vinny*, 1992
Facts: Played guitar for Joey Dee and The Starliters.

At age 5 appeared in Broadway musicals and Eddie Dowling plays. At age 10 became a regular on TV's *Star Time Kids* doing impersonations and singing.

Was managing a restaurant in the Bronx when called by Robert De Niro and Martin Scorsese to play Jake LaMotta's brother in *Raging Bull,* 1978.

He appears in some of his films under the psuedonym Joe Ritchie.
Original Jobs: Nightclub singer, stand-up comedian, barber, postal worker, delivery boy, produce manager, answering service worker, and restaurant manager
Marriages: Two prior marriages; Martha Haro, 1988 (divorced, 1991).
Child: Tiffany, 1966
Major Award: Oscar, Best Supporting Actor, *GoodFellas,* 1990

BERNADETTE PETERS

Real Name: Bernadette Lazzara
Birthplace: Ozone Park, Queens, NY
Birthdate: 2/28/48
Occupation: Actress, comedian, singer, dancer
Education: Quintano's School for Young Professionals, New York City
Debut: (TV) *Juvenile Jury,* 1951; (Stage) *Most Happy Fella,* 1959; (Broadway) *Johnny No Trump,* 1967; (Film) *Ace Eli and Rodger of the Skies,* 1973
Signature: *Sunday in the Park with George*
Facts: At age 3 appeared on a TV game show; two years later, won $800 on *Name That Tune.*

At 9, joined Actors' Equity, and

when she was 10, she changed her name (after her father's first name); by 15 she was in a national tour of *Gypsy*.

Her Broadway debut closed after one performance.

First attained success in *Dames at Sea*, a 1967 Off-Broadway spoof.

In 1999, after a five-year absence from the theater, she returned to the stage to star in a remake of the 1946 Irving Berlin classic *Annie Get Your Gun*.

Marriage: Michael Wittenberg, 1997
Major Awards: Tony Award, *Song and Dance*, 1985
Quotes: "I've done it all—everything but circus acrobatics."

TOM PETTY

Birthplace: Gainesville, FL
Birthdate: 10/20/50
Occupation: Singer, songwriter, guitarist
Education: High school dropout
Debut: *Tom Petty and the Heartbreakers*, 1977
Signature: "Free Fallin' "
Facts: Toured for two years as Bob Dylan's backing band.

Recorded two albums with The Traveling Wilburys, comprised of George Harrison, Bob Dylan, Roy Orbison, Jeff Lynne, and Petty.

Marriage: Jane (divorced, 1996)
Children: Adria, Anna Kim

MICHELLE PFEIFFER

Birthplace: Santa Ana, CA
Birthdate: 4/29/58
Occupation: Actor
Education: Golden West College and Whitley College for Court Reporting
Debut: (TV) *Delta House*, 1979; (Film) *The Hollywood Knights*, 1980 [see page 107 for a complete filmography]
Signature: *The Fabulous Baker Boys*, 1989
Facts: Had one line on TV show *Fantasy Island*.

Got her first break by winning the

Miss Orange County Beauty Pageant.

In 1993, she decided to be a single mother and adopted a baby girl, who was given the last name Kelley after Pfeiffer married.

Had the leading role in *Grease 2*, 1982.

Original Job: Supermarket cashier, court reporter, model
Marriages: Peter Horton (divorced); David E. Kelley, 1993
Children: Claudia Rose, 1993 (adopted); John Henry, 1994
Famous Relatives: DeDee Pfeiffer, actor, sister

REGIS PHILBIN

Birthplace: New York, NY
Birthdate: 8/25/31
Occupation: Talk show host
Education: University of Notre Dame
Debut: (TV) KOGO news anchor, San Diego, 1960
Signature: *Live With Regis and Kathie Lee*
Facts: Named after Regis High, a Manhattan Catholic boys' school and his father's alma mater.

Son Dan was born with two malformed legs, which were later amputated.

Between 1970 and 1990, hosted nearly a dozen talk and game shows and went through a series of co-hosts before clicking with Kathie Lee.

Finished last twice on *Celebrity Jeopardy!*.

Closed a deal with ABC in 2000 that yielded him $20 million a year for hosting *Who Wants to Be a Millionaire*.

Marriages: Kay Faylan, 1955 (divorced,1968); Joy Senese, 1970
Children: Amy, 1958; Dan, 1965; (with Kay Faylan). Joanna, 1973; Jennifer, 1974
Quote: "I've worked with Kathie Lee for 15 years. That builds stamina and endurance. A lesser man would be in his grave by now."

RYAN PHILLIPPE

Birthplace: Iowa
Birthdate: 9/10/74
Occupation: Actor
Education: High school
Debut: (TV) *One Life to Live*, 1992; (Film) *Crimson Tide*, 1995
Signature: *54*, 1998
Facts: Was getting a haircut when a stranger approached him and suggested that he consider an acting career. The man gave him the name of an agent whom Phillippe met and signed with shortly afterward. He had no acting experience at the time.

Played first openly gay male on daytime TV in *One Life to Live*.

Marriage: Reese Witherspoon, 1999
Child: Ava Elizabeth, 1999

BIJOU PHILLIPS

Birthplace: Greenwich, CT
Birthdate: 4/1/80
Occupation: Actor, model, singer, songwriter
Debut: (Film) *Sugar Town*, 1999; (Album) *I'd Rather Eat Glass*, 1999
Signature: *Black and White*, 2000
Facts: When her musician father was touring, he placed her in foster homes.

Began modeling at 13; a year later she declared herself emancipated and began living on her own. At 15, participated in the controversial Calvin Klein ads featuring underage models and was a regular on the party scene. At 17, she entered rehab.

Had a very public affair with Evan Dando when she was 16. Also was formerly involved with Elijah Blue Allman, daughter of Cher.

In the film *Black and White*, she is featured in a same-sex scene. Posed in a *Playboy* pictorial, and appeared on the cover in April 2000.

Claims to have "Daddy" tattooed on her behind.

Wrote a song called "When I Hated Him" about her father, and another called "Little Dipper" about her mother.

Infamy: At 20, she "borrowed" a car from a Miss USA winner and cut off a lounge patron's fingertip with a cigar cutter, later saying it was a magic trick.

Famous relatives: John Phillips, musician, founding member of the pop group The Mamas and the Papas, father; Genevieve Waite, actor, painter, mother; Mackenzie Phillips, actor, half-sister; Chynna Phillips, actor, singer, half-sister

Quote: "I don't regret anything that I did. If I had stayed home and gone to school and done the normal *Brady* [*Bunch*] thing, I would have been a total idiot. My whole thing is that I was stupid, but I was 14 and everybody's stupid at that age, so it's fine."

JOAQUIN PHOENIX

Real Name: Joaquin Rafael Bottom
Birthplace: Puerto Rico
Birthdate: 10/28/74
Occupation: Actor
Education: Dropped out of ninth grade; home-schooled
Signature: *To Die For* (1995)
Debut: (TV musical) *Seven Brides for Seven Brothers,* (with brother River) 1982; (Film) *Space Camp,* 1986
Facts: The son of missionaries for the Children of God, he traveled throughout Puerto Rico, Mexico, South America, Venezuela, and, returning to the U.S., lived in Florida. When siblings Rainbow and River won talent contests, the family moved to Los Angeles.

Changed his name to Leaf around age 6 or 7; changed it back to Joaquin as a teenager.

Has been a strict vegan since he was 3. (He turned down a part as a bullfighter.)

Drives a yellow '72 Pontiac LeMans.

Was in a relationship with Liv Tyler.

Infamy: Made the 911 call as his brother River suffered a drug overdose on Sunset Strip.

Original Job: Model
Famous Relatives: River Phoenix, a.k.a. River Jude Bottom, who died of a drug overdose in 1993, actor, brother; Rain Joan of Arc Phoenix, a.k.a. Rainbow Phoenix, actor, sister; Liberty Butterfly Phoenix, former actor, sister; Summer Joy Phoenix, actor, sister

Quote: "The reason why I keep making movies—which is the reason why I keep doing interviews—is because I hate the last thing that I did. I'm always trying to rectify my wrongs."

DAVID HYDE PIERCE

Birthplace: Saratoga Springs, NY
Birthdate: 4/3/59
Occupation: Actor
Education: Yale University
Debut: (Stage) *Beyond Therapy,* 1982; (Film) *The Terminator,* 1984; (TV) *Powers That Be,* 1991
Signature: *Frasier*
Facts: Realized he had a strong resemblance to his TV brother Frasier (Kelsey Grammer) after being mistaken for Grammer many times before he even accepted the role. In the original storyline for *Frasier,* Pierce's character (Niles) didn't exist but was added after producers, who saw Pierce in *The Powers That Be,* noticed the resemblance.
Original Job: Clothing salesman, church organist
Major Award: Emmy, Best Supporting Actor in a Comedy Series, *Frasier,* 1995, 1998, 1999

BRAD PITT

Real Name: William Bradley Pitt
Birthplace: Shawnee, OK
Birthdate: 12/18/63
Occupation: Actor
Education: University of Missouri at Columbia, studied acting with Roy London
Debut: (TV) *Dallas;* (Film) *Cutting*

Class, 1989 [see page 107 for a complete filmography]
Signature: *Legends of the Fall,* 1994
Facts: Graduated from Kickapoo High, where he was on the tennis team.

Got his big break when he was seen in a sexy Levi's TV ad in 1989. Was cast as the hitchhiker in the 1991 movie *Thelma and Louise* only after William Baldwin turned down the role, choosing to star in *Backdraft* instead.

Dated Robin Givens for six months when they both acted in the TV series *Head of the Class.* Also lived with Juliette Lewis for several years; was engaged to Gwyneth Paltrow.

While at college, posed shirtless for a campus fundraising calendar.

His earliest movie work was filmed in Yugoslavia and lost during its civil war; eight years later, in 1996, the producer finally found all the scattered footage.

In 1997, sued *Playgirl* to force them to recall an issue that contained nude photos of him.

Had LASIK eye surgery (to correct nearsightedness).

Infamy: Aspiring actress Athena Marie Rolando, 19, broke into his home in 1999. A three-year restraining order bars any communication with Pitt and requires that she stay at least 100 yards away from him.

Marriage: Jennifer Aniston, 2000
Original Job: Chauffeur for Strip-O-Gram women, dressed up as the El Pollo Loco restaurant chicken
Quote: "Being a sex symbol all the time hampers my work."

SARA POLLEY

Birthplace: Toronto, Ontario, Canada
Birthdate: 1/8/79
Occupation: Actor, singer
Education: High School drop-out
Debut: (Film) *One Magic Christmas,* 1985; (TV) *Ramona/The Ramona Series,* 1988

Signature: *The Sweet Hereafter*, 1997

Facts: Began acting at age five, and made her film debut in 1985.

From 1990 to 1996, she costarred in the Canadian TV series *The Road to Avonlea*, which also aired in the U.S. as *Avonlea*.

At 14, she moved out of her parents' home, with their blessings.

In 1994, she had major surgery for scoliosis, during which a steel rod was inserted into her back.

Dropped out of high school in her senior year to devote all her time to political activism, joining the Ontario Coalition Against Poverty.

Wrote, coproduced, and directed a film short, *Don't Think Twice*, which was shown at Sundance in 2000.

Famous relatives: Michael Polley, actor, father; Diane Polley, actor and casting director, mother (deceased)

Quote: "When people ask me what I do, acting is usually the furthest thing from my mind."

NATALIE PORTMAN

Real Name: Has been kept from the press

Birthplace: Jerusalem, Israel

Birthdate: 6/9/81

Occupation: Actor, model

Education: High school

Debut: (Film) *The Professional*, 1994; (Broadway) *The Diary of Anne Frank*, 1997

Signature: *Star Wars: Episode I— The Phantom Menace* (1999)

Facts: After spending her first four years in Israel, she and her parents moved to the U.S., eventually settling on Long Island.

Was discovered by a Revlon scout in a pizza parlor in 1991.

Her first professional acting job was as an understudy in the Off-Broadway show *Ruthless*.

Turned down the title role in the *Lolita* remake, heeding her father's advice to do on screen only what she had experienced in real life.

A high school honor student, she is fluent in Hebrew and has studied French and Japanese.

Calls acting her "extra-curricular activity."

Role models include the late AIDS activist Elisabeth Glaser and the late prime minister of Israel Yitzhak Rabin. Favorite actor is Ben Kingsley.

Her last name has been kept from the press to protect the privacy of her and her family.

Is committed to play Queen Amidala in Episodes II and III of *Star Wars*.

Relationship: Lukas Haas, actor

Quote: "I'm going to college. I don't care if it ruins my career. I'd rather be smart than a movie star."

PARKER POSEY

Birthplace: Baltimore, MD

Birthdate: 11/8/68

Occupation: Actor

Education: Attended North Carolina School for the Arts and State University of New York, Purchase

Debut: (Film) *Dazed and Confused*, 1993

Signature: *House of Yes*

Facts: Was named after the supermodel Suzy Parker.

Roomed with *ER*'s Sherry Stringfield while at SUNY. Left school three weeks short of graduation to appear on *As the World Turns*.

Appeared in more than 20 films, the vast majority independents, in a five-year period.

Has a twin brother.

MAURY POVICH

Birthplace: Washington, D.C.

Birthdate: 1/17/39

Occupation: Talk show host, newscaster

Education: University of Pennsylvania

Debut: (TV) *Panorama*, 1969; (Film) *The Imagemaker*, 1986

Signature: *A Current Affair*

Facts: His father Shirley was a well-known sports writer for the *Washington Post*.

Started in broadcasting as as a general assignment and sports reporter in Washington, D.C.,

Briefly worked as a coanchor with Connie Chung in 1977.

In 1986, Povich was the first anchor of a TV tabloid show when he began *A Current Affair*.

In 1989, Povich hosted the prime-time, tongue-in-cheek show *Confessions of Mr. Tabloid*. In 1991, he began the daytime talk show, *The Maury Povich Show*, which aired until 1998.

In 1991, he coauthored a book, *Current Affairs: Life on the Edge*, with Ken Gross.

Marriages: Phyllis Minkoff, c. 1962; Connie Chung, 1984

Children: Susan, c. 1964; Amy, c. 1967 (with Phyllis Minkoff); Matthew Jay, c. 1995 (adopted)

Quote: "Connie has always made a lot more money. There have been times when I would have pangs about it, but whenever they surfaced, I would just put a stake in them."

LISA MARIE PRESLEY

Birthplace: Memphis, TN

Birthdate: 2/1/68

Facts: Daughter of Elvis and Priscilla Presley

Inherited an estate of upwards of $100 million from her father.

When Lisa Marie once said she had never seen snow, Elvis flew her to Utah. She also received a tiny mink coat from her father and $100 bills from the Tooth Fairy.

Is a devoted follower of the Church of Scientology.

Marriages: Danny Keough (divorced); Michael Jackson (divorced, 1996); John Oszajca, musician (engaged, 2000)

Children: Danielle, 1989; Benjamin, 1992

PRINCE

Real Name: Prince Rogers Nelson
Birthplace: Minneapolis, MN
Birthdate: 6/7/58
Occupation: Singer, songwriter, actor
Education: High school dropout
Debut: (Album) *For You,* 1978
Signature: *Purple Rain,* 1984
Facts: Named after the Prince Roger Trio, a jazz group led by his father.

Can play over two dozen instruments.

Returned to using the name Prince in 2000, after his publishing contract with Warner-Chappell expired. He had previously been known as a symbol, or referred to as "The Artist Formerly Known as Prince," sometimes abbreviated to "TAFKA," in order to free himself from "undesirable relationships."

After annulling his marriage, he said he believes marriage contracts "guarantee the possibility of divorce," though he did remain with his Mayte.

Marriage: Mayte Garcia, 1996 (annulled, 1999; relationship)
Child: deceased (name unreported)
Major Awards: Grammy, Best Rock Performance—Duo or Group, *Purple Rain* (with The Revolution), 1984; Grammy, Best Rhythm and Blues Song, "I Feel for You," 1984; Grammy, Best Soundtrack Album, *Purple Rain* (with The Revolution, John L. Nelson, Lisa & Wendy), 1984; Oscar, Best Original Song Score, *Purple Rain,* 1984; Grammy, Best R&B Duo or Group, "Kiss" (with The Revolution), 1986

FREDDIE PRINZE JR.

Birthplace: Los Angeles, CA
Birthdate: 3/8/76
Occupation: Actor
Education: High school
Debut: (TV) *Family Matters,* 1994; (Film) *To Gillian on Her 37th Birthday,* 1996
Signature: *She's All That* (1999)
Facts: His father committed suicide when Freddie was 10 months old (his father nicknamed him "Pie").

His mother is of English, Irish, and Native American descent.
Relationship: Sarah Michelle Gellar
Famous Relative: Freddie Prinze, comedian, actor (*Chico and the Man*), father; high on prescription drugs and despondent over divorce from his wife, he committed suicide in 1977.
Quote: "I know one day I'm going to be the best father in the world. Me not having a father makes me want to be a great one. I have so much love I wanted to give him, and I'll be damned if I don't give it to a child of mine."

DENNIS QUAID

Birthplace: Houston, TX
Birthdate: 4/9/54
Occupation: Actor
Education: University of Houston
Debut: (Film) *September 30, 1955,* 1978
Signature: *The Big Easy,* (1987)
Fact: Wrote songs for three of his films: *The Night the Lights Went Out in Georgia* in 1981, *Tough Enough* in 1983, and *The Big Easy* in 1987.

Shed 47 pounds over a three-month period before playing the scrawny Doc Holliday in 1994's *Wyatt Earp.*

In 2000, filed for divorce from Meg Ryan after nine years, citing irreconcilable differences and asking for joint custody of their son, Jack.
Infamy: Admitted to having a cocaine addiction, a problem he overcame with help from then girlfriend Meg Ryan.
Marriages: Pamela Jayne Soles (divorced), Meg Ryan, 1991 (filed for divorce, 2000)
Child: Jack Henry, 1992
Famous Relative: Randy Quaid, actor, brother

QUEEN LATIFAH

Real Name: Dana Owens
Birthplace: East Orange, NJ
Birthdate: 3/18/70
Occupation: Rap artist, actor
Education: High school
Debut: (Album) *All Hail the Queen,* 1989; (TV) *The Fresh Prince of Bel-Air,* 1991; (Film) *Jungle Fever,* 1991
Facts: Was a power forward on two state championship basketball teams in high school.

Trained in karate and use of firearms by her policeman father.

CEO of Flavor Unit, a management and production company whose clients have included Naughty by Nature and FU-Schnickens.

Brother Lance Owens Jr. died at age 24 in a motorcycle accident in 1992; "Winky's Theme" on the album *Black Reign* was dedicated to him.

Starred in sitcom *Living Single.*
Infamy: Charged in a municipal misdemeanor complaint in 1995 after 240 illegally copied tapes were found in a video store she had sold in 1994.

Arrested by California Highway Patrolman in west L.A. and cited for speeding, driving under the influence, carrying a concealed firearm, carrying a loaded firearm, and possession of marijuana.
Original Jobs: Worked at Burger King, cashier at the Wiz
Major Award: Grammy, Best Rap Solo Performance, "U.N.I.T.Y.", 1994

KATHLEEN QUINLAN

Birthplace: Pasadena, CA
Birthdate: 11/19/54
Occupation: Actor
Education:
Debut: (Film) *American Graffiti,* 1973; (TV) *Where Have All the People Gone?,* 1974
Signature: *Family Law*
Facts: Suffered allergy-induced asthma as a child.

Her original aspiration was to each gymnastics. She's a longtime surfer.

Appeared as a diving double for Trish Van Devere in 1972's *One Is a Lonely Number* .

George Lucas spotted her at high school and cast her a very small part in 1973's *American Graffiti.*

Had a three-year relationship with Al Pacino in the late '70s and early '80s.

Marriages: One previous marriage; Bruce Abbott, actor, 1994

Children: Dalton Abbott, stepson, 1989; Tyler Abbott, 1990

Famous relative: Robert Quinlan, TV sportscaster, father (deceased)

Quote: "I was not ambitious. Never have been."

BONNIE RAITT

Birthplace: Burbank, CA
Birthdate: 11/8/49
Occupation: Singer, songwriter
Education: Radcliffe College
Debut: (Album) *Bonnie Raitt,* 1971
Signature: "Something To Talk About," 1991
Facts: Grew up in a Quaker family in L.A.

Got her first guitar for Christmas when she was eight.

Founded the annual Rhythm & Blues Awards, to provide money to deserving R&B stars who may have been cheated in the early days by managers and/or record labels.

Infamy: Was an avid drinker until giving up all alcohol and drugs a decade ago.

Marriage: Michael O'Keefe, 1991 (separated, 1999)

Child: One son

Famous Relative: John Raitt, actor, father

Major Awards: Grammies, Album of the Year, Best Rock Vocal—Female, and Best Pop Vocal—Female, "Nick of Time," 1989; Grammy, Best Pop Vocal—Female, "Something To Talk About," 1991; Grammy, Best Rock Vocal—Female, "Luck of the Draw," 1991; Grammy, Best Rock Duo with Vocal, "Good Man, Good Woman"

(with Delbert McClinton), 1991; Grammy, Best Pop Album, *Longing in Their Hearts,* 1994

DAN RATHER

Birthplace: Wharton, TX
Birthdate: 10/31/31
Occupation: Anchor, correspondent, editor
Education: Sam Houston State College
Debut: (TV) KHOU-TV, Houston, 1960
Signature: *CBS Evening News with Dan Rather*
Facts: Succeeded Walter Cronkite in anchoring the evening news upon Cronkite's retirement in 1981.

In his 1994 book, *The Camera Never Blinks Twice,* he devotes less than a page to his former co-anchor Connie Chung.

Was attacked on the street by two men who called him "Kenneth" and repeatedly demanded "What's the frequency?" R.E.M. used the cryptic phrase as a song title and later performed the tune with Rather on *Late Show with David Letterman.*

Infamy: Angry over a delay in the start of the news, he walked off the set, leaving TV screens blank for six minutes. He also had a stormy pre-election interview with then vice-president George Bush in 1988.

Marriage: Jean Goebel, 1958
Children: Robin, 1958; Danjack, 1960
Major Awards: 28 News and Documentary Emmys: 19 as correspondent, 9 as anchor

ROBERT REDFORD

Real Name: Charles Robert Redford Jr.
Birthplace: Santa Monica, CA
Birthdate: 8/18/36
Occupation: Actor, director, producer
Education: University of Colorado, Pratt Institute of Design, the American Academy of Dramatic Arts
Debut: (Stage) *Tall Story,* 1959; (Film) *War Hunt,* 1962

Signature: *Butch Cassidy and the Sundance Kid,* 1969
Facts: In 1959, his first child died of Sudden Infant Death Syndrome.

Went to college on a baseball scholarship but lost it due to alcohol abuse. Left school in 1957 to go to Europe; lived in Paris and Florence as a painter.

Was burned in effigy in 1976 for opposing a $3.5 billion power plant.

Founded the nonprofit Sundance Institute in Park City, UT, which sponsors an annual film festival and provides support for independent film production.

Infamy: As a teenager, Redford stole and resold hubcaps.

Original Job: Carpenter, shop assistant, oil field worker

Marriage: Lola Van Wagenen (divorced, 1985); Sibylle Szaggars (relationship)

Children: Shauna, 1960; James, 1962; Amy, 1970

Major Awards: Oscar, Best Director, *Ordinary People,* 1980; Cecil B. DeMille Lifetime Achievement Award, 1994

CHRISTOPHER REEVE

Birthplace: New York, NY
Birthdate: 9/25/52
Occupation: Actor
Education: Cornell University, Juilliard graduate program
Debut: (Film) *Gray Lady Down,* 1977
Signature: *Superman,* 1978
Facts: While studying at Juilliard under John Houseman, shared an apartment with then-unknown Robin Williams.

Turned down a lucrative offer to do cigarette commericals in Japan in 1990.

Says the accident that fractured his first and second vertebrae happened on an easy jump, when his Thoroughbred Eastern Express suddenly halted and his hands became entangled in the bridle so he couldn't break his fall.

Completely paralyzed, though with

some sensation in his left leg, he gets around by motorized wheelchair, which he directs by puffing air through a tube.

A television ad featuring a computer generated Reeves walking, which debuted on the 2000 Super Bowl broadcast, caused considerable controversy.

Marriage: Dana Morosini, 1992
Children: Matthew, 1979; Alexandra, 1983; (with Gae Exton). Will, 1992
Major Award: Grammy, Best Spoken Word Album, *Still Me*, 1998

KEANU REEVES

Birthplace: Beirut, Lebanon
Birthdate: 9/2/64
Occupation: Actor
Education: High school dropout; studied with Jasper Deeter
Debut: (Film) *Youngblood*, 1986; (Album) *Happy Ending*, 2000
Signature: *The Matrix*, 1999
Facts: His father is Chinese-Hawaiian and his mother is English.

Hasn't seen his father, who is currently serving a ten-year prison term in Hawaii for cocaine possession, since he was 13.

His first name means "cool breeze over the mountains" in Hawaiian.

Had traveled around the world by the time he was 2 years old.

Was the MVP on his high school hockey team in Toronto. A skilled goalie, Reeves earned the name "The Wall."

Turned down the Al Pacino/Robert De Niro film *Heat* to play Hamlet on stage in Winnipeg, Canada. The February 1995 sold-out run was critically acclaimed.

He plays bass in the band Dogstar.

His mother was a costume designer for rock stars.

His child was reportedly stillborn in late 1999.

Relationship: Jennifer Syme

PAUL REISER

Birthplace: New York, NY
Birthdate: 3/30/56
Occupation: Actor, comedian
Education: SUNY-Binghamton
Debut: (Film) *Diner,* 1982
Signature: *Mad About You*
Facts: Has appeared in several hit films, including *Beverly Hills Cop* (1984), *Aliens* (1986), and *Beverly Hills Cop II* (1987).

Dubbed by reporters as part of the Four Funniest Men in the World Club, which includes Jerry Seinfeld, Larry Miller, and Mark Schiff. The members meet every New Year's Day for lunch (once they even met in London when Reiser was there filming *Aliens*).

Original Job: Health food distributor
Marriage: Paula, 1988
Child: Ezra Samuel, 1995

GLORIA REUBEN

Birthplace: Toronto, Canada
Birthdate: 6/9/65
Occupation: Actor
Education: Attended Canadian Royal Conservatory
Debut: (TV) *The Round Table*, 1988
Signature: *ER*
Facts: Her father, who died when she was 11, was a white Jamaican while her mother is a black Jamaican.

Studied ballet and jazz dancing at a prestigious music college, and plays classical piano.

In 2000, toured with Tina Turner as a backup singer.

Original Job: Model
Marriage: Wayne Isaak, VH1 executive, 1999
Famous Relative: Denis Simpson, brother, actor

BURT REYNOLDS

Birthplace: Waycross, GA
Birthdate: 2/11/36
Occupation: Actor, director
Education: Attended Florida State University, Palm Beach Junior College and Hyde Park Playhouse
Debut: (Stage) *Mister Roberts*, 1956; (Film) *Angel Baby*, 1961
Signature: *Smokey and the Bandit*, 1977
Facts: Was signed to play football with the Baltimore Colts, but a car accident derailed that career and led him to acting.

Has dated Dinah Shore (19 years his senior), Chris Evert, and Sally Field.

Is part Cherokee, part Italian.

Infamy: Appeared nude in *Cosmopolitan* magazine centerfold in 1972.

Untrue rumors circulated in the late 1980s that Reynolds had AIDS; he was actually suffering from a joint disorder.

Ugly divorce from Loni Anderson cost him fans and product endorsement contracts, partly contributing to a 1996 bankruptcy filing.

Original Jobs: Bouncer, dishwasher, stuntman
Marriages: Judy Carne (divorced); Loni Anderson (divorced, 1993); Pam Seals (engaged)
Child: Quentin, c. 1988 (adopted)
Major Award: Emmy, Best Actor in a Comedy Series, *Evening Shade*, 1991

TRENT REZNOR

Birthplace: Mercer, PA
Birthdate: 5/17/65
Occupation: Singer, keyboardist
Education: Allegheny College
Debut: (Album) *Pretty Hate Machine*, 1989
Signature: Nine Inch Nails
Facts: Reznor makes all Nine Inch Nails albums himself, using a band only for live shows.

In 1990, misplaced video footage of a half-naked Reznor being thrown from a building landed in the hands of the FBI, who thought it was an actual murder. They led an investigation and found Reznor, alive and well and on tour. The publicity helped put Nine Inch Nails in the spotlight.

Mixed the soundtrack LP for Oliver Stone's film *Natural Born Killers* in 1994.

Lived for a year in the Benedict Canyon, CA, house where Sharon Tate and others were murdered by Charles Manson followers.

In what he says was possibly an unconscious attempt to identify with Woodstock '94 fans, he tripped his guitar player on the way to the stage, who fell flat in the mud and started the whole band in a mud match. They performed covered in the stuff.

Original Job: Odd jobs—including cleaning toilets—at a recording studio
Major Awards: Grammy, Best Metal Performance, "Wish," 1992

CHRISTINA RICCI

Birthplace: Santa Monica, CA
Birthdate: 2/12/80
Occupation: Actor
Education: Professional Children's School
Debut: (Film) *Mermaids*, 1990
Signature: *The Opposite of Sex*, 1998
Facts: While starring in her second-grade pageant, she caught the eye of a local movie critic in the audience, who told her parents to get her an agent.

Was a schoolmate of Macaulay Culkin.

Fellow teen actress Natalie Portman was initially approached for the role in *The Ice Storm*, but her parents decided it was too sexual.
Quote: "Basically, I'm like a whore. I'll give people whatever they want so they'll like me."

ANNE RICE

Real Name: Howard Allen O'Brien
Birthdate: 10/4/41
Occupation: Writer
Education: North Texas State

University, San Francisco State College
Debut: (Book) *Interview with a Vampire,* 1976
Facts: Is the author of a series of pornographic novels under the name A. N. Roquelaure (which means "cloak").

Is afraid of the dark.

Was originally named after her father and mother's maiden name; changed name to Anne by the time she was in first grade.

In 1972 her six-year-old daughter died of leukemia.
Original Job: Waitress, cook, insurance claims adjuster
Marriage: Stan Rice, 1961
Children: Michelle, 1966 (deceased, 1972); Christopher, 1978

DENISE RICHARDS

Birthplace: Downers Grove, IL
Birthdate: 2/17/71
Occupation: Actor
Education: High school
Debut: (TV) *Life Goes On*, 1990; (Film) *National Lampoon's Loaded Weapon 1*, 1993
Signature: *Wild Things*, 1998
Facts: Was called Fish Lips in junior high school.

Played a recurring role (beauty contestant Brandy Carson) in *Melrose Place*.
Original Job: Model
Relationship: Patrick Muldoon, actor
Quote: "It's always fun to be a bad girl and get away with it."

MICHAEL RICHARDS

Birthplace: Culver City, CA
Birthdate: 7/24/49
Occupation: Actor
Education: Los Angeles Valley College, California Insitute of the Arts
Debut: (TV) *Fridays,* 1980
Signature: *Seinfeld*
Facts: Has appeared in guest spots on *Hill Street Blues* and *Miami Vice.*

Starred with Weird Al Yankovic in the film *UHF,* 1989.

He was drafted at the height of the Vietnam War in 1970: "When the drill sergeant yelled at me on the first day, I tried to explain the duffel bag was too heavy."
Original Job: Postal worker, schoolbus driver
Marriages: Cathleen (divorced, 1993); Ann Talman (relationship)
Child: Sophia, 1975
Major Award: Emmy, Best Supporting Actor in a Comedy Series, *Seinfeld,* 1992, 1993, 1997

KEVIN RICHARDSON

Birthplace: Lexington, KY
Birthdate: 10/3/72
Occupation: Singer
Debut: (Single) "We've Got It Goin' On," 1995; (Album) *Backstreet Boys,* 1995 (American version, 1997)
Signature: "Everybody (Backstreet's Back),"1997
Facts: Is cousin to Backstreet Boy Kevin Littrell.

Has played the piano since he was 9.

Was football captain at Estill County High in Lexington.

Spent eight years of his life in a log cabin.

After high school, played piano and sang in a band named Paradise. Their covers included Journey and Bobby Brown tunes.

Played a Ninja Turtle at the Disney-MGM Studios theme park. Met his wife in the park's cafeteria.

The band is named after Orlando, Florida's Backstreet Market, a popular teen hangout.

The group's debut was a hit in 26 countries before *Backstreet Boys* was released in the U.S.
Seen as the most business-minded Backstreet Boy.

Since PEOPLE named him "Sexiest Pop Star" in 1999, his bandmates call him "Mr. Sexy."
Infamy: Band filed suit against former manager Lou Pearlman, claim-

ing he had made $10 million from their labor while they had received $300,000.
Original Job: MGM Studios guide
Marriage: Kristin Willits, 2000
Quote: "You know, we do more than just sing and dance. We've got a brain, too."

NATASHA RICHARDSON

Birthplace: London, England
Birthdate: 5/11/63
Occupation: Actor
Education: Central School for Speech and Drama
Debut: (Stage) *On the Razzle,* 1983
Signature: *The Handmaid's Tale,* 1990
Facts: At age 4, appeared as a bridesmaid of Vanessa Redgrave in *The Charge of the Light Brigade.*
  Was named after the heroine in Tolstoy's *War and Peace.*
Marriages: Robert Fox (divorced); Liam Neeson, 1994
Children: Micheál, 1995; Daniel Jack N., 1996
Famous Relatives: Vanessa Redgrave, actor, mother; Tony Richardson, director, father; Joely Richardson, actor, sister; Lynn Redgrave, actor, aunt
Quote: "I've spent half my life trying to get away from being Vanessa Redgrave's daughter, and now I've got to get away from being Liam Neeson's wife."
Major Award: Tony, Best Actress (Musical), *Cabaret,* 1998

LEANN RIMES

Birthplace: Flowood, MS
Birthdate: 8/28/82
Occupation: Singer
Debut: (Album) *Blue,* 1996
Signature: *Blue*
Facts: Was singing songs like "Jesus Loves Me"—on pitch—at 18 months. Appeared on *Star Search* at age 8 and signed a major record deal at 11.
  "Blue" was actually written for

Patsy Cline in 1963 but was never recorded because she died that year. When songwriter Bill Mack heard Rimes sing the "Star-Spangled Banner" at a Texas Rangers game he was so impressed he sent her the tune.
  Filed a lawsuit against her father and former co-manager in 2000, claiming that the two are responsible for spending more than $7 million of her earnings.
Major Awards: Grammy, Best New Artist, 1996; Grammy, Best Country Vocal—Female, "Blue," 1996

GERALDO RIVERA

Birthplace: New York, NY
Birthdate: 7/4/43
Occupation: Broadcast journalist, talk show host
Education: University of Arizona; J.D., Brooklyn School of Law; Columbia Journalism School post-graduate
Debut: (TV) *Eyewitness News,* WABC-TV, New York, 1968
Signature: *Geraldo!*
Facts: In the late '60s was involved with a Latino activist group, the Young Lords. Appeared so many times on the evening news the station eventually hired him as a temporary reporter—a good way to satisfy federal minority hiring quotas.
  Was fired from ABC-TV in 1985 when the network tired of his sensationalist style and arrogance. At the time, was making $800,000 a year.
  In the late '80s, promised a junior high school class he would pay for their college education. Five years later paid $180,000 for nine of the graduates' schooling.
  In 1993, opened the Broadcast Boxing Club fitness center in New York.
Infamy: Arrested several times at demonstrations, as well as at a TV filming of a rally, when he got into a scuffle with a Ku Klux Klansman.
  Accused of leading talk shows into the gutter. Once even had his nose broken during a brawl on his show.

Original Job: Attorney
Marriage: Linda Coblentz, c. 1965 (divorced); Edith Bucket Vonnegut, 1971 (divorced); Sherryl Raymond, 1976 (divorced, 1984); C. C. Dyer, 1987 (separated, 1999)
Children: Gabriel Miguel, 1979 (with Sherryl Raymond); Cruz, 1987 (born after a brief liaison); Isabella Holmes, 1992; Simone Cruickshank, 1994 (with Dyer)
Major Awards: 3 national and 4 local Emmy Awards

JOAN RIVERS

Real Name: Joan Alexandra Molinsky
Birthplace: Brooklyn, NY
Birthdate: 6/8/33
Occupation: Talk show host
Education: Connecticut College for Women, Barnard College
Debut: (TV) *The Tonight Show,* 1965
Facts: Wrote for *Candid Camera* and *The Ed Sullivan Show.*
Original Job: Publicist at Lord & Taylor, fashion coordinator for Bond Clothing Stores, temporary office secretary, syndicated columnist
Marriage: Edgar Rosenberg, 1965 (deceased); Orin Lehman (relationship)
Child: Melissa, 1968
Major Award: Emmy, Best Host of a Talk Show, *The Joan Rivers Show,* 1990

TIM ROBBINS

Birthplace: West Covina, CA
Birthdate: 10/16/58
Occupation: Writer, director, actor
Education: New York University, SUNY-Plattsburgh, and UCLA
Debut: (Film) *No Small Affair,* 1984
Signature: *The Player,* 1992
Facts: Was kicked off the hockey team in high school for fighting.
  Founded Los Angeles theater group Actors' Gang.
  Has been an outspoken political activist and peace advocate.
Original Job: Factory worker
Relationship: Susan Sarandon

Children: Jack Henry, 1989; Miles, 1992

JULIA ROBERTS

Birthplace: Smyrna, GA
Birthdate: 10/28/67
Occupation: Actor
Education: High school
Debut: (TV) *Crime Story*, 1986 [see page 107 for a complete filmography]
Signature: *Pretty Woman*, 1990
Facts: Originally wanted to be a veterinarian.

Her middle name is Fiona.

In 1986, she played opposite her brother (actor Eric Roberts) in the film *Blood Red*.

Was set to marry Kiefer Sutherland in 1991, but canceled the wedding at the last minute with virtually no explanation. And she had taken up with Sutherland after breaking off an engagement to Dylan McDermott.

Has also been linked to Liam Neeson, Jason Patric, Daniel Day-Lewis, Ethan Hawke, and Matthew Perry.

Hobbies include knitting.

Has a 51-acre ranch in Taos. N.M.

Filed a lawsuit against entrepreneur Russell Boyd, who had been the first to register juliaroberts.com as an Internet domain, in 2000 and won back her own name.
Original Job: Worked in a shoe store and an ice cream shop
Marriage: Lyle Lovett, 1993 (divorced, 1995); Benjamin Bratt (relationship)
Famous Relatives: Eric Roberts, actor, brother; Lisa Roberts, actor, sister
Quote: "I used to think I was weird. Now I think I'm just interesting."

CHRIS ROCK

Birthplace: Brooklyn, NY
Birthdate: 2/7/65
Occupation: Actor, comedian
Education: High school dropout (later got his GED)

Debut: (Film) *Beverly Hills Cop II*, 1987; (TV) *Saturday Night Live*, 1990
Signature: *The Chris Rock Show*
Facts: Grew up in Brooklyn's Bedford-Stuyvesant but was bused to an all-white grade school in Bensonhurst, where he was often the victim of racial violence and discrimination.

Discovered by Eddie Murphy at age 18 during open-mike night at a New York comedy club.

Created the voice of the Little Penny puppet on the Penny Hardaway Nike ads.
Marriage: Malaak Compton
Major Awards: Emmy, Best Writing in a Variety or Music Program, *Chris Rock: Bring the Pain*, 1997; Grammy, Best Spoken Comedy Album, *Roll With the New*, 1997; Emmy, Best Writing in a Variety or Music Program, *The Chris Rock Show*, 1999; Grammy, Best Comedy Album, *Bigger and Blacker*, 1999
Quote: "Cool is comedy's biggest enemy."

AL ROKER

Birthplace: Queens, NY
Birthdate: 8/20/54
Occupation: TV host, weatherman
Education: SUNY, Oswego
Debut: (TV) WTVH in Syracuse, NY, 1974
Signature: *Today*
Facts: While a sophomore in college, Roker worked as a weatherman for a Syracuse station and found his calling. After graduation, he was a weathercaster in Washington, D.C., (where he befriended Willard Scott), then Cleveland, where he was a pioneer in the use of computer graphics for weather forcasts.

Has hosted *Remember This?*, a college quiz show (MSNBC) and *The Al Roker Show*. His production company produced *Savage Skies* (PBS), a weather documentary series, and *Going Places* (PBS), a series on time- and cost-efficient vacations.

Received the American Meteorological Society's Seal of Approval, awarded to fewer than 2 percent of TV weather reporters.

Won Cleveland's "International Rib Burn-Off" cooking contest twice.

Has served on the board of Outward Bound.

For his website, roker.com, he creates "Rokertoon of the Day" cartoons.

His wife used to think he was "kind of annoying, overly chatty."

His ancestors were slaves on a plantation on the Caribbean island of Exuma, which he has visited. Relatives still live on the island.
Marriages: Alice (divorced); second wife (divorced); Deborah Ann Roberts, NY correspondent for ABC's *20/20*, 1995
Children: Courtney Roker, c. 1988 (with Alice); Leila Ruth, 1998
Major Awards: Daytime Emmys, Outstanding Special Class Program, *Macy's Thanksgiving Day Parade*, 1996, 1997, 1998
Quote: "I really wanted to write comedy or direct. But my college professors told me that I had the perfect face for radio."

RAY ROMANO

Birthplace: Queens, NY
Birthdate: 12/21/57
Occupation: Actor, comedian
Education: High school
Debut: (TV, stand-up) *The Tonight Show Starring Johnny Carson*, 1991; (TV) *Dr. Katz: Professional Therapist*, cartoon voice, 1995
Signature: *Everybody Loves Raymond*
Facts: While working a variety of jobs, he appeared at clubs as a stand-up comic.

Lived in the basement of his parents' home in Forest Hills, New York, until he was 29.

Was replaced by Joe Rogan after two days of rehearsal on *NewsRadio*.

David Letterman's production company developed the sitcom

Everybody Loves Raymond.

Published his autobiography, *Everything and a Kite,* in 1998.

Original Job: Gas station attendant, futon delivery man

Marriage: Anna Scarpulla, 1987

Children: Alexandra, 1990; twins Matthew and Gregory, 1993; Joseph, 1998

Quote: "Whenever my wife complains about material we use on the show, I tell her to go cry on a bag of money."

REBECCA ROMIJN-STAMOS

Birthdate: 11/6/72

Occupation: Model, actor

Education: University of California, Santa Cruz

Debut: (TV) *House of Style*

Signature: *Sports Illustrated* swimsuit issue cover

Facts: Was nicknamed "Jolly Blonde Giant" in high school.

Likes craft projects, including building an elaborate dollhouse.

Marriage: John Stamos, actor, 1998

Quote: "Fashion is intimidating, and I'm intimidated by most designers I meet. It's a scary thing, and I think other women are intimidated too."

ROSEANNE

Birthplace: Salt Lake City, UT

Birthdate: 11/3/52

Occupation: Actor

Education: High school dropout

Debut: (TV) *Funny,* 1983; (Film) *She-Devil,* 1989

Signature: *Roseanne*

Facts: Dropped out of high school to hitchhike cross country, landing in a Colorado artists' colony at age 18.

Had cosmetic surgery and weight reduction in 1993. Breasts were reduced from 40DD to 38C.

Had a tattoo on her upper right thigh that read: "Property of Tom Arnold." When the pair split, she tattooed over it with a flying fairy and flowers.

Claims she was physically and

sexually abused as a child and that she suppressed memory of the abuse until an adult.

Gave up first baby girl, Brandi, for adoption at age 18.

Born to Jewish parents but raised as a Mormon in Salt Lake City. Her dad sold crucifixes door to door.

In 1999, four of her children developed an animated autobiographical comedy pilot: "The kids live off her money and have to do what she says," described ringleader Jenny.

Infamy: Grabbed her crotch, spat, and screeched while singing the national anthem at a San Diego baseball game in 1990.

Original Job: Window dresser, cocktail waitress

Marriages: Bill Pentland, 1974 (divorced, 1990); Tom Arnold (divorced); Ben Thomas, 1995 (separated, 1998)

Children: Brandi Brown, 1971. Jessica, 1975; Jennifer, 1976; Jake, c. 1978; (with Bill Pentland). Buck, 1995

Major Award: Emmy, Best Actress in a Comedy Series, *Roseanne,* 1993

DIANA ROSS

Real Name: Diane Ernestine Ross

Birthplace: Detroit, MI

Birthdate: 3/26/44

Occupation: Singer, actor

Education: High school

Debut: *The Primettes,* 1959; (TV) *Tarzan,* 1968; (Film) *Lady Sings the Blues,* 1972

Signature: *Ain't No Mountain High Enough,* 1970

Facts: Sung with the Primettes as a teenager until the group was reformed as the Supremes in 1961 and signed on with Motown. Six years later the group, then called Diana Ross and the Supremes, became the most successful black recording artists of their time. Nominated for an Oscar for her first feature film role in 1972's *Lady Sings the Blues,* she went on to appear in 1978's *The Wiz,* which

proved unsuccessful and ended her movie career.

She often insists that subordinates address her as "Miss Ross."

Received rave reviews in 1994 for her role as a paranoid schizophrenic in the TV movie *Out of Darkness.*

In the late 1970s, she turned down the role that would become Whitney Houston's in *The Bodyguard.*

Her 2000 "Return to Love" concert tour, without the other two original Supremes, was cut short due to lackluster ticket sales.

Infamy: Kept secret the fact that Motown mogul Berry Gordy fathered her first child.

Original Job: Fashion designer, cafeteria busgirl

Marriage: Robert Ellis Silberstein (divorced, 1976); Arne Naess, 1986 (divorced, 2000)

Children: Rhonda Suzanne, 1971 (with Berry Gordy). Tracee Joy, 1972; Chudney Lane, 1975 (with Silberstein). Ross Arne, 1987; Evan, 1988 (with Naess).

Major Awards: Grammy, Best Vocal (Contemporary) Performance by a Female, "Ain't No Mountain High Enough," 1970; Special Tony for *An Evening with Diana Ross,* 1977

Quote: "I never thought this little Detroit girl would ever go to Nepal, climb the Himalayas, or be in the bush country in Africa".

GAVIN ROSSDALE

Birthplace: London, England

Birthdate: 10/30/67

Occupation: Singer, songwriter, guitarist

Education: High school

Debut: (Album) *Sixteen Stone,* 1994

Signature: Bush

Facts: His parents divorced when he was eleven. He lived with his physician father in the well-heeled North London Kilburn district, attending the posh Westminster high school. After graduating, became a regular party animal at London's clubs.

As a teen, played semi-pro soccer in

London and even tried out for a top pro team, Chelsea.

His former band, the pop-oriented Midnight, had a record deal in the mid-1980s but produced no hits.

Originally signed by Disney's Hollywood Records, but exec Frank G. Wells, a major fan, was killed in a helicopter crash just as *Sixteen Stone* was completed. Other execs deemed the album unacceptable, so it went into limbo until being rescued by Interscope.

Original Job: Music video production assistant
Relationship: Gwen Stefani

J. K. ROWLING

Real Name: Joanne Kathleen Rowling
Birthplace: Bristol, England
Birthdate: 7/31/65
Occupation: Author
Education: Exeter University
Debut: (UK) *Harry Potter and the Philosopher's Stone*, 1997 (*Harry Potter and the Sorcerer's Stone*, 1998, in U.S.)
Signature: Harry Potter
Facts: Wanted to be a writer from age six.

Her last name is pronounced "ROE-ling."

Originally worked in London at Amnesty International, then at the Chamber of Commerce in Manchester.

Following her divorce from a Portuguese journalist, Rowling returned to England in 1993 with no money, no job, and a young child. She qualified for public assistance, but not for child care, so she was forced to remain unemployed.

Wrote her first book in a coffee shop as her daughter napped. She first thought of the series in 1990, and conceived portions of all seven books from the start.

Received an advance of $4,000 for the first Harry Potter book.

Harry Potter and the Goblet of Fire was the fastest-selling book of all time in the U.S., practically selling out its 3-million copy first printing in its first week on sale. Her books have been translated into at least 28 languages.

Original Job: Teacher
Marriage: Jorge Arantes, 1992 (divorced, 1995)
Children: Jessica, 1993
Quote: "It's going to break my heart when I stop writing about Harry."

GEOFFREY RUSH

Birthplace: Toowoomba, Queensland, Australia
Birthdate: 7/6/51
Occupation: Actor, theater director, playwright, musician
Education: University of Queensland
Debut: (Film) *Hoodwink*, 1981
Signature: *Shine*, 1996
Facts: Played Snoopy in *You're a Good Man, Charlie Brown*. ("One of my first big hits. I was a very good dog.")

Studied for two years at Jacques Lecoq School of Mime, Movement and Theater in Paris.

Made his stage directing debut in 1978 with the Queensland Theatre Company.

Appeared with Mel Gibson in *Waiting for Godot*. They were roommates for four months in 1980 during the production.

In 1992, he suffered a breakdown, which was attributed to his hectic schedule.

Marriage: Jane Menelaus, actor, 1988
Children: Angelica, c. 1992; James, c. 1995
Quote: "My career has been in theater for 23 years, with spits and coughs in bits and pieces of films."
Major award: Oscar, Best Actor, *Shine*, 1996

KERI RUSSELL

Birthplace: Fountain Valley, CA
Birthdate: 3/23/76
Occupation: Actor

Education: High school
Debut: (TV) Disney Channel's *All New Mickey Mouse Club*, 1991; (Film) *Honey, I Blew Up the Kid,* 1992
Signature: *Felicity*
Facts: A successful audition in Denver led to her three-year stint as a Mouseketeer, launching her career and her long romance with Tony Lucca, with whom she also costarred in TV's 1996 *Malibu Shores.*

Her middle name is Lynn.

At age 17 she set off on her own to L.A. and got a role right away on Dudley Moore's sitcom *Daddy's Girl.*

Producers originally thought she was too pretty for the role of Felicity—even though she dressed down for the audition to make herself look plain.

Her favorite things are massages, fresh flowers, live music, and trips to Ireland and Big Sur.

Original Job: Model
Relationship: Scott Speedman
Quote: "You gotta be low maintenance."

KURT RUSSELL

Birthplace: Springfield, MA
Birthdate: 3/17/51
Occupation: Actor, screenwriter, producer
Education: High school
Debut: (Film) *The Absent-Minded Professor*, 1960
Signature: *Stargate*, 1994
Facts: At 12, starred in his own Western series, *The Travels of Jaimie McPheeters,* featuring Charles Bronson and the very young Osmond brothers.

Left acting in 1971 to play minor league baseball. Returned to acting two years later after tearing a shoulder muscle.

His actor father played the sheriff for 14 years on *Bonanza.*

Marriages: Season Hubley, 1979 (divorced, 1983); Goldie Hawn (relationship)

Children: Boston, 1980 (with Season Hubley). Wyatt, 1986
Famous Relatives: Bing Russell, actor, father

RENE RUSSO

Birthplace: Burbank, CA
Birthdate: 2/17/54
Occupation: Actor
Education: High school dropout
Debut: (Film) *Major League*, 1989
Signature: *Lethal Weapon 3*, 1992
Facts: Considered herself unattractive as a teen because she wore a body cast to correct a curved spine from ages 10 to 14. Shy and uninterested in school (where high school classmates included Ron Howard), she dropped out in 10th grade and worked in an eyeglass factory.

Was discovered by a modeling agent in the parking lot following a Rolling Stones concert. A few weeks later, she was in New York shooting a Revlon ad with Richard Avedon.

At age 30, depressed by being too old to model, she discovered Christian theology, which she spent the next three years studying. Religion gave her the confidence to try an acting career.

Met her future husband on the set of *Freejack*, a film for which she had originally turned down an acting role and for which Gilroy had originally rejected the job of script rewriting.
Original Job: Supermodel
Marriage: Danny Gilroy (divorced)
Child: Rose, 1993
Quote: (on her nude scenes in *The Thomas Crown Affair*): "It never really dawned on me that, gee, I'm 45 and I'm taking off my clothes."

JERI RYAN

Real Name: Jeri Lynn Zimmerman
Birthplace: Munich, Germany
Birthdate: 2/22/68
Occupation: Actor
Education: Northwestern University
Debut: (TV movie) *Nightmare in Columbia County*, 1991

Signature: Seven of Nine in *Star Trek: Voyager*
Facts: From 1993 to 1997, she appeared in episodes of *Who's the Boss*; *Murder, She Wrote*; *Diagnosis Murder*; *Melrose Place*; and the short-lived *Dark Skies*.

Was a National Merit Scholar.

Her original *Voyager* suit was so tight that she passed out four times and required oxygen on the set.
Marriage: Jack Ryan (John Clemens Ryan), 1991 (separated, 1998)
Child: Alex Ryan, c. 1994
Quote: "I don't mind being called a babe. It's better than being called a dog."

MEG RYAN

Real Name: Margaret Hyra
Birthplace: Fairfield, CT
Birthdate: 11/19/61
Occupation: Actor
Education: New York University
Debut: (Film) *Rich and Famous*, 1981; (TV) *As the World Turns*, 1983 [see page 107 for a complete filmography]
Signature: *When Harry Met Sally...*, 1989
Fact: Became high school homecoming queen when the original queen was suspended.

Her strained relationship with her mother became tabloid-show fodder when her stepfather wrote an article about the pair's discord in a magazine in 1992. Ryan subsequently ended all contact with them.

Met husband Quaid on the set of the comedy film, *Innerspace*, in 1987. A year later, they professionally reunited for the unsuccessful film *D.O.A.*
Marriage: Dennis Quaid, 1991 (filed for divorce, 2000); Russell Crowe (relationship)
Child: Jack Henry, 1992
Quote: "I have remained consistently and nauseatingly adorable. In fact, I have been known to cause diabetes."

WINONA RYDER

Real Name: Winona Laura Horowitz
Birthplace: Winona, MN
Birthdate: 10/29/71
Occupation: Actor
Education: High school
Debut: (Film) *Lucas*, 1986 [see page 107 for a complete filmography]
Signature: *Beetlejuice*, 1988
Facts: Her childhood home in Elk, CA, had no electricity.

In junior high school, was attacked and beaten by fellow students during her first week at a new school, apparently because they mistook her for a boy.

Her natural hair color is blond. She's been a brunette since she auditioned for *Lucas* in 1986.

Has read *The Catcher in the Rye* countless times, and travels with a copy.

Dated Christian Slater, David Pirner, and Matt Damon; was engaged to Johnny Depp. Is rumored to have also dated Daniel Day-Lewis, Stephan Jenkins, and Evan Dando.

Timothy Leary, the famous psychologist and countercultural philosopher, was her godfather.

ADAM SANDLER

Birthplace: Brooklyn, NY
Birthdate: 9/9/66
Occupation: Comedian, actor
Education: New York University
Debut: (TV) *The Cosby Show*, 1987; (Film) *Shakes the Clown*, 1992
Signature: *Big Daddy*, 1999
Facts: Became a writer for *Saturday Night Live* in 1990, but his sketches were often too eccentric for others to make their own. He soon became a "featured player" doing those skits and, after the success of his Opera Man, became a regular cast member.

As a developing comic, was so taken by Rodney Dangerfield he memorized many of Dangerfield's routines.

Original Job: Stand-up comedian
Relationship: Margaret Ruden (engaged, never married); Jackie Titone
Quote: "If you don't get the best grades, don't fret—I didn't do too well in school and I'm a multimillionaire."

CARLOS SANTANA

Birthplace: Autlan de Navarro, Mexico
Birthdate: 7/20/47
Occupation: Musician, bandleader
Debut: (Album) *Santana*, 1969
Signature: "Smooth," 1999
Facts: His father, a traditional violinist, played mariachi music, and began teaching music theory to his son, then five.

Began playing in night clubs when he was just 11.

Five years later, the family moved to San Francisco.

Was mentored by the Grateful Dead's Jerry Garcia before forming the Santana Blues Band. The band played at Woodstock in 1969, even though they didn't have an album out at the time. Their appearance on *The Ed Sullivan Show* landed them a deal with Columbia Records.

In the early '70s he became a follower of Sri Chimnoy, and in 1973 changed his name to Devadip (meaning the light of the lamp of the Supreme). He discontinued the association in 1982.

In 1988, helped organize the "Blues for Salvador" concert in California, to benefit children of El Salvador.

Founded a record label, Guts and Grace, in 1994.

The eight Grammy wins for *Supernatural* tied it with Michael Jackson's 1983 *Thriller* for most awards in a single night.
Original Job: Dishwasher
Marriage: Deborah King, 1973
Children: Salvador, 1984; Stella, 1985; Angelica, 1990
Major Awards: Grammy, Best Rock Instrumental Performance of Blues, *Salvador*, 1988; Grammy, Record of the Year, "Smooth," 1999; Grammy, Song of the Year, "Smooth," 1999; Grammy, Pop Collaboration with Voals, "Smooth," 1999; Grammy, Album of the Year, *Supernatural*, 1999; Grammy, Rock Album, *Supernatural*, 1999; Grammy, Pop Instrumental Performance, "El Farol," 1999; Grammy, Rock Performance by a Due or Group with Vocal, "Put Your Lights on," 1999; Grammy, Rock Instrumental Performance, "The Calling," 1999
Quote: "A lot of people didn't want to work with be because I'm too old."

SUSAN SARANDON

Real Name: Susan Abigail Tomaling
Birthplace: New York, NY
Birthdate: 10/4/46
Occupation: Actor
Education: Catholic University of America
Debut: (Film) *Joe*, 1970 [see page 107 for a complete filmography]
Signature: *Thelma & Louise*, 1991
Facts: Her background is Welsh-Italian. Was one of nine children, and attended Catholic school.

Is 12 years older than beau Tim Robbins.

An activist for numerous political, cultural, and health causes, she digressed during her 1991 Academy Awards presentation to speak for a half-minute on behalf of Haitian refugees with AIDS.

Starred in cult classic *The Rocky Horror Picture Show*.

She and Robbins keep all their awards in the "famous bathroom."
Original Job: While in college, worked in the drama department, modeled, and cleaned apartments.
Marriages: Chris Sarandon, 1967 (divorced, 1979); Tim Robbins (relationship)
Children: Eva Maria Livia, 1985 (with Franco Amurri). Jack Henry, 1989; Miles, 1992 (with Tim Robbins)
Major Awards: Oscar, Best Actress, *Dead Man Walking*, 1995

DIANE SAWYER

Birthplace: Glasgow, KY
Birthdate: 12/22/45
Occupation: Broadcast journalist
Education: Wellesley College
Debut: (TV) WLKY-TV, Louisville, 1967
Signature: *Primetime Live*
Facts: Was national Junior Miss, largely on the strength of her interview and essays.

Dated Bill Bradley in college.

As a weathercaster in Louisville, KY, she spruced up forecasts with quotes from her favorite poems.

Served as staff assistant to former President Nixon and helped him research his memoirs.
Marriage: Mike Nichols, 1988
Major Awards: 10 News and Documentary Emmys: 9 as correspondent, 1 as anchor

CLAUDIA SCHIFFER

Birthplace: Dusseldorf, Germany
Birthdate: 8/25/70
Occupation: Supermodel
Education: High school
Facts: Tripped during her runway modeling debut in 1990.

Earns as much as $50,000 a day.

Opened Fashion Cafe in New York City in 1995 with fellow supermodels

Elle MacPherson and Naomi Campbell.

Was engaged to David Copperfield, but they never married.

Marriage: Tim Jeffries (engaged, 2000)

Quote: "I actually don't meet very many men because they are, I guess, afraid to approach me or think that I'm from another planet."

LAURA SCHLESSINGER

Birthdate: 1947
Occupation: Radio talk show host
Education: SUNY, Stony Brook; Columbia University, Ph.D. in physiology; University of Southern California, post-doctoral certificate in marriage and family therapy
Debut: (Radio) *The Dr. Laura Schlessinger Show,* 1990
Signature: "Dr. Laura"
Facts: Had a tubal ligation at age 30, which she later had reversed.

Has been estranged from her mother since before the birth of her son.

Converted to Judaism in 1994.

Her house burned almost entirely in an electrical fire in 1992.

Has a black belt in Karate.

Her radio call-in show now has an audience of some 20 million listeners on 450 U.S. stations and 30 Canadian stations, and is even heard in South Africa.

In addition to her adult bestsellers, recently began writing children's picture books, her first entitled *Why Do You Love Me?*

Owns a Harley and a rose-colored Mercedes-Benz.

Her radio show was sold in 1997 for $71.5 million, 40 percent more than an earlier deal for Rush Limbaugh's show.

It's estimated that 60,000 people call into to her show every day.

She encountered a firestorm of protest in 2000 after making comments on the air that characterized homosexuality as deviant behavior

and a biological error. A successful boycott pressured advertisers to stay away from her television talk show, launched in the fall, prompting her to run a full-page apology in *Variety.*
Infamy: In 1998 tried unsuccessfully to have a court keep a dozen nude photos of her, taken by a former lover decades earlier, from being posted on the Internet.
Marriages: First husband (divorced, 1978); Lewis Bishop, 1984
Child: Deryk Schlessinger, 1986
Quotes: "I do not see it as my mission to make anybody feel better. I want them to get better."

RICK SCHRODER

Birthplace: Staten Island, NY
Birthdate: 4/13/70
Occupation: Actor
Education: Mesa State College
Debut: (Film) *The Champ,* 1979; (TV) *Silver Spoons,* 1982
Signature: *Silver Spoons*
Facts: "Ricky" began making TV commercials as a toddler, appearing in some 60 by age 7.

Won a Golden Globe when he was 9 for his role as boxer Jon Voight's son in *The Champ,* directed by Franco Zeffirelli.

Following his youthful sitcom run, he landed his first starring role in the TV movie *Something So Right* in 1982. He later won a key role in the miniseries *Lonesome Dove* and its sequel.

Owns 800 head of cattle, quarter horses, 2,000 deer, and 3 trout lakes on his 45,000-acre Colorado ranch.

He takes time out of his days to indulge in yoga and receives weekly massages.

He wishes he were taller.
Original Job: Model
Marriage: Andrea Bernard, 1992
Children: Holden, 1992; Luke, 1993; Cambrie, 1996
Major Awards: Golden Globe Award, New Star of the Year, *The Champ,* 1979
Quote: "I guess I've come to terms

with myself and what I look like. These are the cards I was dealt, so I play 'em the best I know how."

ARNOLD SCHWARZENEGGER

Birthplace: Graz, Austria
Birthdate: 7/30/47
Occupation: Actor, director, bodybuilder
Education: University of Wisconsin
Debut: (Film) *Hercules in New York,* 1969 [see page 108 for a complete filmography]
Signature: *The Terminator,* 1984
Facts: After coming to the U.S. in the '60s, founded a bricklaying business, Pumping Bricks, to finance his bodybuilding career.

Won the Austrian Junior Olympic weightlifting championship as well as Junior Mr. Europe and several curling titles.

In 1974, acted in *Happy Anniversary and Goodbye,* an unsold CBS sitcom pilot starring Lucille Ball and Art Carney.

Has killed over 275 people on screen.
Infamy: Named in a 1995 paternity suit by a Texas woman who claims he fathered her daughter 12 years earlier.
Original Job: Managed a Munich health club
Marriage: Maria Owings Shriver, 1986
Children: Katherine Eunice, 1989; Christina Maria Aurelia, 1991; Patrick, 1993; Christopher, 1997
Quote: "Everything I have ever done in my life has always stayed. I've just added to it...But I will not change. Because when you are successful and you change, you are an idiot."

DAVID SCHWIMMER

Birthplace: Queens, NY
Birthdate: 11/2/66
Occupation: Actor
Education: Northwestern University
Debut: (TV movie) *A Deadly Silence,*

1989; (Film) *Crossing the Bridge*, 1992
Signature: *Friends*
Facts: His mother is the attorney who handled Roseanne's first divorce. Since his father is also an attorney, he flirted with becoming one before settling on acting.

Appeared in the 1994 Henry Winkler flop, *Monty*.

Started Chicago's Lookingglass Theater Company in 1988 with seven other Northwestern graduates.

In 2000, along with *Friends* costars, received a salary increase from $125,000 to $750,000 per episode.
Relationship: Mili Avital

MARTIN SCORSESE

Birthplace: New York, NY
Birthdate: 11/17/42
Occupation: Director
Education: New York University
Debut: (Film) *Boxcar Bertha*, 1972 [see page 108 for a complete filmography]
Signature: *Taxi Driver*, 1976
Facts: Collaborated on the production of Michael Jackson's *Bad* video in 1987.

Was originally enrolled as an English major before switching to film.
Original Job: Faculty assistant and instructor in film department at NYU
Marriages: Larraine Marie Brennan, 1965 (divorced); Julia Cameron, 1975 (divorced); Isabella Rosellini, 1979 (divorced, 1983); Barbara DeFina, 1985 (divorced); Helen Morris, 1999
Children: Catherine Terese, 1965 (with Larraine Marie Brennan). Domenica Elizabeth, 1976 (with Julia Cameron). Francesca, 1999 (with Helen Morris).
Major Award: Cannes Film Festival, Palme d'Or, *Taxi Driver*, 1976

STEVEN SEAGAL

Birthplace: Lansing, MI
Birthdate: 4/10/52
Occupation: Actor, producer
Education: Orange Coast College
Debut: (Film) *Above the Law*, 1988
Signature: *Hard To Kill*, 1990
Facts: Founder, Aikido Ten Shin Dojo, Los Angeles.

First non-Asian to successfully open a martial arts academy in Japan.

In 1968, moved to Japan, where he taught English and wrote articles for Japanese magazines and newspapers.

Organized security for the departure of the Shah's family from Iran.

Commands the title of Shihan (Master of Masters).

The high lama of the Nyingma school of Buddhism ceremonially recognized Seagal as a *tulku*—a reincarnated holy man.
Infamy: Was sued by a film assistant for sexual harassment. Paid money to settle out of court in 1990.

Was married to both his first and second wives simultaneously.

Scriptwriter Lars Hansson claimed in 1994 that Seagal threatened him with death after he refused to sell him film rights to a CIA hit-man story.

In 1995, was accused by ex-girlfriend Cheryl Shuman of harassing her. A judge threw out her lawsuit, calling it unintelligible.
Original Job: Martial arts instructor, bodyguard
Marriages: Miyako Fujitani (divorced); Adrienne LaRussa (annulled); Kelly LeBrock, 1994; Arissa Wolf (relationship)
Children: Justice (a.k.a. Kentaro), 1975; Ayako, c. 1980; (with Miyako Fujitani). Anna-lisa, c. 1987; Dominick San Rocco, 1990; Arissa, 1993; (with Kelly LeBrock). Savannah, 1996
Quote: "I just care about bringing joy into this world in my little way."

SEAL

Real Name: Sealhenry Samuel
Birthplace: Paddington, England
Birthdate: 2/19/63
Occupation: Singer, songwriter
Education: High school dropout
Debut: (Album) *Seal*, 1991
Signature: "Kiss from a Rose," 1995
Facts: His name comes from his Brazilian father's custom of having the grandparents select the name (they chose Seal) coupled with his parents' fascination with British royalty (they wanted Henry).

As an infant, lived with a white foster family until his Nigerian mother reclaimed him. When she became ill several years later, went to his father's, whom he says beat him mercilessly.

Plays a six-string guitar upside down; left-handed, learned on guitars borrowed from studios and they were all right-handed.

The scars on his face are remnants of lupus contracted at age 23.
Major Awards: Grammy, Record of the Year, "Kiss from a Rose," 1995; Grammy, Song of the Year, "Kiss from a Rose," 1995; Grammy, Best Male Pop Vocal Performance, "Kiss from a Rose," 1995

JERRY SEINFELD

Birthplace: Brooklyn, NY
Birthdate: 4/29/54
Occupation: Actor, comedian
Education: Queens College
Debut: (Stand-up) Catch a Rising Star, Manhattan, 1976
Signature: *Seinfeld*
Facts: At his first stage appearance, he was so nervous he forgot his routine and only mumbled the words "The beach. Driving. Shopping. Parents," and walked off.

Owns several dozen pairs of sneakers, including a custom pair of "Air Seinfelds."

Has practiced yoga for 20 years and is a strict vegetarian.

His TV series *Seinfeld* was one of

15 stamps depicting 90s pop culture issued in 2000.

Infamy: Created a stir when he began dating 18-year-old Shoshanna Lonstein in 1993. They broke up in 1997.

His relationship with newlywed Jessica Sklar, 27, broke up her marriage

Marriage: Jessica Sklar, 1999

Original Job: Sought the worst jobs possible, including selling light bulbs over the phone and costume jewelry on the streets of New York, to force himself to succeed at comedy

Major Award: Emmy, Best Comedy Series, *Seinfeld,* 1993

Quote: "I'm hardly interested in my own life. I don't know how you could be interested."

CHLOE SEVIGNY

Birthplace: Darien, CT
Birthdate: 11/18/74
Occupation: Actor
Education: High School
Debut: (Film) *Kids,* 1994
Signature: *Boys Don't Cry,* 1999
Facts: Met screenwriter Harmony Korine as a teenager while hanging out in New York City's Washington Square park. They dated for a while, and she lives next door to Korine in Darien, CT now.

Interned at *Sassy* magazine.

Jay McInerney heralded her as Manhattan's It girl in a 1994 *New Yorker* profile, prior to the release of *Kids.*

She likes to sail.

Original Job: Salesgirl, model
Quote: "I've questioned issues of gender and sexuality since I was a teenager, and I did some experimenting. Its not my thing now, but I've always questioned it."

JANE SEYMOUR

Real Name: Joyce Frankenberg
Birthplace: Hillingdon, England
Birthdate: 2/15/51
Occupation: Actor

Education: Arts Educational School, London

Debut: (Film) *Oh, What a Lovely War,* 1968

Signature: *Dr. Quinn, Medicine Woman*

Facts: Danced with the London Festival Ballet at 13.

Named Honorary Citizen of Illinois by Governor Thompson in 1977.

Original Job: Ballet dancer

Marriages: Michael Attenborough (divorced); Geoffrey Planer (divorced); David Flynn (divorced); James Keach, 1993

Children: Kalen; 1977 (stepson, with James Keach). Jennifer, 1980; Katie, 1982; Sean, 1985 (with David Flynn). John, 1995; Kristopher, 1995

Major Awards: Emmy, Best Supporting Actress in a Miniseries, *Onassis,* 1988

GARRY SHANDLING

Birthplace: Chicago, IL
Birthdate: 11/29/49
Occupation: Actor, writer, comedian
Education: University of Arizona
Debut: (TV) *Sanford & Son,* 1976
Signature: *The Larry Sanders Show*
Fact: Wrote for *Sanford & Son, Welcome Back, Kotter,* and *Three's Company.*

Named *The Tonight Show*'s permanent guest host in 1986 and was widely expected to be Johnny Carson's successor, but decided he didn't enjoy it enough so he left.

Infamy: A former co-star sued Shandling for sexual harassment; she claimed her firing from *Sanders* was tied to the break-up of their relationship.

In 1998, Shandling sued his 18-year friend and manager, Brad Grey, for $100 million, claiming that Grey didn't protect his interests and built a management/production empire on Shandling's talents. Grey counter-sued for $10 million, alleging breach of contract and fiduciary duty. They settled their respective suits in 1999 by

exchanging "certain interests in various television properties."

Major Award: Emmy, Writing for a Comedy Series, *The Larry Sanders Show,* 1998

Quote: "It's really to the point now, when I envision myself walking down the aisle with a woman in white, it's a nurse."

WILLIAM SHATNER

Birthplace: Montreal, Canada
Birthdate: 3/22/31
Occupation: Actor, author, producer, director
Education: McGill University
Debut: (TV) *Goodyear TV Playhouse,* 1956
Signature: *Star Trek*
Facts: Has written a series of books, beginning with *TekWar,* which were turned into movies in which he stars.

Most celebrated pre-*Trek* experience was as a guest on one of the most famous *Twilight Zone* episodes, "Nightmare at 20,000 Feet," in 1963.

One of his leisure activities is breeding horses.

Became CEO of a special effects company, CORE Digital Pictures, in 1995.

Original Job: Novelist

Marriages: Gloria Rand (divorced); Marcy Lafferty, 1973 (divorced, 1996); Nerine Kidd, 1997 (deceased)

Children: Leslie, 1958; Lisabeth, 1961; Melanie, 1964; (with Gloria Rand).

CHARLES SHEEN

Real name: Carlos Irwin Estevez
Birthplace: Los Angeles CA
Birthdate: 9/3/65
Occupation: Actor, screenwriter, producer, poet
Education: High school dropout
Debut: (TV) *Silence of the Heart,* 1984; (Film) *Grizzly II-The Predator,* 1984; (Book) *A Peace of Mind,* poetry, 1991
Signature: *Platoon,* 1986

Facts: The third son of actor Martin Sheen, he lost his college baseball scholarship because of poor grades, and failed to graduate high school.

At age 9 appeared as extra in a TV movie, *The Execution of Private Slovik*, starring his father. Appeared as an extra in *Apocalypse Now*.

Since childhood, has created over 200 Super-8 and video film shorts, and the 16mm film *R.P.G.*

Was friendly in high school with classmates Sean Penn and Rob Lowe.

Had a child out of wedlock with his high school girlfriend.

In 1990, he checked into a drug and alcohol rehab center after reportedly suffering from exhaustion.

Has his own $1.5 million custom-designed bus with a full-size master bedroom and three satellite TVs to take on the set with him.

Infamy: While in high school, he was arrested for marijuana possession and credit card forgery.

In 1995, he admitted paying Heidi Fleiss more than $53,000 for 27 trysts with her employees.

Assault charges were filed against him by companion Brittany Ashland in 1996; he pleaded no contest and received a one-year suspended sentence with two years probation.

In 1998, he was hospitalized following a drug overdose. After walking out of rehab, his father asked prosecutors to file probation violation charges. A judge extended his probation and ordered him into rehab.

In 1999, he was sued by two female adult movie actors who claimed his bodyguard had assaulted them.

Marriages: Kelly Preston (engaged, never married); Donna Peele, 1995 (divorced 1996)

Child: Cassandra Sheen, 1984 (with Paula Profitt)

Famous relatives: Martin Sheen, actor, director, father; Renee Pilar Estevez, actor, sister; Emilio Estevez, actor, director, screenwriter, brother;

Ramon Estevez, actor, brother

Quote: "What do you do when you've got studio heads that won't hire you, even though you screwed the same whores? Yet they pull you aside at a party and say that you're their hero for the things that you do.... I feel like Vicarious Man. I am Vicarious Man!"

MARTIN SHEEN

Real Name: Ramon G. Estevez
Birthplace: Dayton, OH
Birthdate: 8/3/40
Occupation: Actor, producer, director
Education: High school
Debut: (Stage) *The Connection*, 1959; (TV) *The Defenders*, 1961; (Film) *The Incident*, 1967
Signature: *Apocalypse Now*, 1979
Facts: His father was Spanish and his mother Irish (she was sent to the U.S. as a child for safety, since her father and brothers were very involved with the IRA).

A forceps delivery crushed his left shoulder, and he is still handicapped by it.

At 11, he worked as a caddy at a local country club, but was fired when he tried to start a union.

Read poetry and scripture on a local Dayton TV program and won a trip to New York for an audition.

Took his stage name from the last names of CBS's casting director Robert Dale Martin and Bishop Fulton Sheen.

Was featured on *As the World Turns* in the early 60s.

A play he wrote, *Down the Morning Line*, was performed at New York City's Public Theater in 1969.

Sons Charlie Sheen and Emilio Estevez both became fathers at young ages, and out of wedlock. He bought houses for both mothers and set up trusts for the grandchildren.

Was made honorary mayor of Malibu, California in 1989.

Made his feature film screenwriting and directing debut in 1990's *Cadence*, which starred his

sons Charlie Sheen and Ramon Estevez.

A longtime activist, he was arrested in 1996 for trespassing at a New York think tank which was thought to be contributing to nuclear weapons programs.

Marriage: Janet, 1961

Children: Emilio Estevez, actor, son, 1962; Ramon Estevez, actor, son, 1963; Charlie Sheen, actor, son, 1965; Renee Estevez, actor, daughter, 1967

Famous Relative: Joe Estevez, brother, actor

Major Awards: Daytime Emmy for Outstanding Direction in Children's Programming for *Babies Having Babies*, 1986; Emmy, guest appearance, *Murphy Brown*, 1993

Quote: "I'm not a purist. I've been at this for 31 years, and most of the work I've done has been crap.... But I did it for the money. I'm not proud of it."

JUDITH SHEINDLIN

Real Name: Judy Blum
Birthplace: Brooklyn, NY
Birthdate: 10/21/42
Occupation: TV judge
Education: American University, New York Law School
Signature: *Judge Judy*
Facts: Married while in law school and the only woman in the graduating class of 1965, she practiced law for a few years before staying home to care for her young children.

Returned to work in 1972 as a prosecutor in New York's family court, then served as family court judge in New York for 24 years.

Following publication of her 1996 book, *Don't Pee on My Leg and Tell Me It's Raining*, she began her successful courtroom TV show.

Original Job: Lawyer

Marriage: Ronald Levy, 1964 (divorced, 1976); Jerry Sheindlin, 1978

Children: Adam (with Levy); Jamie Hartwright (with Sheindlin)

Quote: "I'm rough on people. I say what's on my mind. If that's not the law in your jurisdiction, it ought to be."

BROOKE SHIELDS

Birthplace: New York, NY
Birthdate: 5/31/65
Occupation: Actor
Education: Princeton University
Debut: (Film) *Alice, Sweet Alice*, 1978
Signature: *Suddenly Susan*
Facts: Began her career as an Ivory Snow baby when she was 11 months old. Appeared on more than 30 magazine covers at age 16.

Says now that her overbearing ex-manager stage-mother, Teri, was an alcoholic. Shields was conceived out of wedlock and her father was around only for the first few months of her life.

Has previously been linked romantically to Liam Neeson, Prince Albert of Monaco, George Michael, Michael Bolton, and Michael Jackson.

Her divorce papers cited "incompatible tastes [and] temperament."
Infamy: As the 12-year-old star of *Pretty Baby*, played a prostitute in various states of undress.
Original Job: Model
Marriage: André Agassi, 1997 (separated, 1999); Chris Henchy (engaged, 2000)
Quote: "Every time I go to the doctor I say, 'Can I still make a baby?... How much time do I have? What am I going to have to do, find a sire?'"

MARTIN SHORT

Birthplace: Hamilton, Ontario, Canada
Birthdate: 3/26/50
Occupation: Actor
Education: McMaster University
Debut: (Stage) *Godspell*, 1972; (Movie) *Lost and Found*, 1979
Signature: *Saturday Night Live*, 1984
Facts: As a child, used to produce his own mock talk show in his family's attic; he had his own syndicated talk show in 1999.

Majored in social work in college.

His first acting job was as a giant Visa card for a television commercial.

A lively talk-show guest, he once did his Bette Davis imitation while the actress was next to him on Johnny Carson's couch.

Has received the Order of Canada, which is the equivalent of Britain's knighthood.
Marriage: Nancy Dolman, 1980
Children: Oliver, c. 1986; Henry, c. 1990
Major Awards: Emmy, Outstanding Writing in a Variety or Music Program, *SCTV Network*, 1983; Tony, Best Actor (Musical), *Little Me*, 1999
Quote: "I am a timeless imp with endless energy."

ELISABETH SHUE

Birthplace: Wilmington, DE
Birthdate: 10/6/63
Occupation: Actor
Education: attended Wellesley College, Harvard University
Debut: (Film) *The Karate Kid*, 1984
Signature: *Leaving Las Vegas*, 1995
Facts: Admits to drinking heavily and going to class stoned while in high school.

Encouraged her baby brother Andrew to join her in acting.

Broke into show business as a teenager appearing on a series of 20 Burger King commercials.

Older brother Will died in a swimming accident on a family vacation at age 27.

In 2000, returned to Harvard to finish course work toward a political science degree (she left school one semester shy of graduation in the 1980s).
Marriage: Davis Guggenheim, 1994
Child: Miles William, 1997
Famous Relatives: Andrew Shue, actor, brother

ALICIA SILVERSTONE

Birthplace: San Francisco, CA
Birthdate: 10/4/76
Occupation: Actor
Education: High school equivalency
Debut: (Film) *The Crush*, 1993
Signature: *Clueless*, 1995
Facts: Filed for emancipation from her parents at 15 so she could work in films as an adult.

Was a cheerleader in high school.

Won MTV's Villain of the Year award in 1993 for her performance as the lovestruck psychopath in *The Crush*.
Relationship: Chris Jarecki, musician
Quote: "People who say I'm sexy don't really understand what sexy means. I'm always dirty and always in sweats. That's the real me."

NEIL SIMON

Real Name: Marvin Neil Simon
Birthplace: Bronx, NY
Birthdate: 7/4/27
Occupation: Playwright, screenwriter, producer
Education: New York University
Debut: (Stage) *Adventures of Marco Polo: A Musical Fantasy*, 1959; (Film) *After the Fox*, 1966
Signature: *The Odd Couple*, 1965
Facts: Flew in the U.S. Air Force, 1945–46.

Met his third wife in 1985 when she was handing out perfume samples at the Beverly Hills Neiman Marcus store.

Owns Eugene O'Neill Theatre in New York.

Has written nearly 30 Broadway shows.

Was nicknamed Doc by older brother Danny after Simon took to a toy doctor's kit.
Original Job: Mail room clerk
Marriages: Joan Baim (deceased); Marsha Mason (divorced, 1983); Diane Lander (divorced, remarried, divorced, 1998); Elaine Joyce, 1999
Children: Ellen, 1957; Nancy, 1963;

(with Joan Biam). Bryn, c. 1984 (stepdaughter)
Major Awards: Tony, Best Author (Dramatic), *The Odd Couple,* 1965; Tony, Special Award, 1975, Tony, Best Play, *Biloxi Blues,* 1985; Tony, Best Play, *Lost in Yonkers,* 1991; Pulitzer Prize, Best Play, *Lost in Yonkers,* 1991

PAUL SIMON

Birthplace: Newark, NJ
Birthdate: 10/13/41
Occupation: Singer, songwriter
Education: Queens College, Brooklyn Law School
Debut: (Song) "Hey Schoolgirl" (with Art Garfunkel, under the name Tom and Jerry), 1957
Signature: *Graceland,* 1986
Facts: In sixth grade, he played the White Rabbit to Garfunkel's Cheshire Cat in *Alice in Wonderland.*

Co-owned the Philadelphia Furies, a soccer team, with Mick Jagger, Peter Frampton, and Rick Wakeman.

Composed music and cowrote book for *The Capeman,* a Broadway show that played briefly in 1998.
Marriages: Peggy Harper (divorced), Carrie Fisher (divorced), Edie Brickell, 1992
Children: Harper,1992; Adrian Edward, 1993; Lulu, 1995
Famous Relative: Louis Simon, bassist, father
Major Awards: Grammy, Record of the Year, "Mrs. Robinson" (with Simon & Garfunkel), 1968; Grammy, Best Pop Performance—Duo or Group, "Mrs. Robinson" (with Simon & Garfunkel), 1968; Grammy, Best Soundtrack Album, *The Graduate* (with Dave Grusin), 1968; Grammy, Record of the Year, "Bridge over Troubled Water" (with Simon & Garfunkel), 1970; Grammy, Album of the Year, *Bridge over Troubled Water* (with Simon & Garfunkel), 1970; Grammy, Song of the Year, "Bridge over Troubled Water," 1970; Grammy, Best Rock/Contemporary Song, "Bridge over Troubled Water," 1970;

Grammy, Album of the Year, *Still Crazy After All These Years,* 1975; Grammy, Best Pop Vocal—Male, "Still Crazy After All These Years," 1975; Grammy, Album of the Year, *Graceland,* 1986; Emmy, Best Writing in a Comedy, Variety, or Music Special, *The Paul Simon Special,* 1978; inducted into the Rock and Roll Hall of Fame (with Art Garfunkel), 1990

JESSICA SIMPSON

Birthplace: Dallas, TX
Birthdate: 7/10/80
Education: High school
Debut: (Album) *Sweet Kisses,* 1999
Signature: "I Wanna Love You Forever""
Facts: Auditioned for *The New Mickey Mouse Club* at age 12 but lost out to Christina Aguilera and Britney Spears.

Performed in her church choir was discovered at a church summer camp. Her initial success came on the Christian Yourth Conference circuit.

Her father was a Baptist minister; now he's her manager.
Relationship: Nick Lachey of 98 Degrees
Quote: "My virginity is something I stand strong in."

SINBAD

Real Name: David Adkins
Birthplace: Benton Harbor, MI
Birthdate: 11/10/56
Occupation: Actor, comedian
Education: University of Denver
Debut: (TV) *Comedy Tonight,* 1985; (Film) *That's Adequate,* 1989
Signature: *A Different World*
Facts: Finalist in the comedy competition on *Star Search* in 1984.

Original dream was to play pro basketball.
Infamy: While in the Air Force, imper-sonated officers and went AWOL.
Marriage: Meredith Adkins (divorced, 1992)

Children: Paige, c. 1986; Royce, c. 1989

GARY SINISE

Birthplace: Blue Island, IL
Birthdate: 3/17/55
Occupation: Actor, director, producer
Education: High school graduate
Debut: (TV) *Knots Landing,* 1980; (Film) *A Midnight Clear,* 1992; (Film, as director) *Miles from Home,* 1988
Signature: *Forrest Gump,* 1994
Facts: Co-founded Steppenwolf Theater in 1974 (at age 18) in the basement of a church with John Malkovich, Terry Kinney, Jeff Perry, and Moira Harris (whom he later married).

First appeared on TV as an extra in *General Hospital.*

His TV directorial debut came in 1987, with a two-part episode of *Crime Story.* Two years later he directed a couple of episodes of *thir-tysomething.*

In 1997, formed the band The Bonsoir Boys, playing bass and singing.
Marriage: Moira Harris, 1981
Children: Sophie, c. 1988; McCanna, c. 1990; Ella, c. 1992
Major Award: Emmy, Lead Actor in a Miniseries or Movie, for *George Wallace,* 1997

SISQÓ

Real Name: Mark Andrews
Birthplace: Baltimore, MD
Birthdate: 11/9/75
Occupation: Singer
Debut: (Album) *Dru Hill,* 1996; (Solo Album) *Unleash the Dragon,* 2000
Signature: "Thong Song," 2000
Facts: His Baltimore-based R&B group Dru Hill, which includes high school friends Woody (James Green), Nokio (Tamir Ruffin) and Jazz (Larry Anthony Jr.) was spotted at a talent show when Sisqó was a high school junior.

His name is pronounced "SIS-co."

Fans regularly throw Victoria's

Secret g-strings at him when he performs.

Now hosts his own MTV dance competition show.

Designs his own clothes with Jonathan Logan. The dragon, which he calls his alter ego, always appears on his clothes. Also has a penchant for exotic belt buckles.

Sprays his hair every day to make it platinum.

Infamy: He was jailed twice as a teenager for fight-related incidents.
Child: Shaione, 1995 (with Tera Thomas); Shaione appears in his "Thong Song" video
Quote: "I'm still looking for that celebrity chick that's gonna take my career to the next level."

CHRISTIAN SLATER

Real Name: Christian Hawkins
Birthplace: New York, NY
Birthdate: 8/18/69
Occupation: Actor
Education: Dalton School, Professional Children's School
Debut: (TV) *One Life To Live,* 1976; (Film) *The Legend of Billie Jean,* 1985
Signature: *Heathers,* 1989
Facts: Began his career in the stage revival of *The Music Man,* at the age of 9.

Dated Winona Ryder, Christy Turlington, and Samantha Mathis.

Was born on the final day of Woodstock.
Infamy: Arrested twice for drunk driving, served ten days in jail in 1990.

Arrested in 1994 for attempting to carry a 9mm pistol through an airport metal detector. He was ordered to spend three days working with homeless children on a plea-bargained misdemeanor charge in 1995.

Was sued in 1995 for palimony seeking $100,000 plus property worth $2 million by ex-fiancée Nina Peterson Huang, who claims she had an agreement with Slater to put her career on hold during their five

years of living together. Four months after they got engaged, Huang left the volatile actor and broke off the relationship.

Was arrested in 1997 for assault and battery for acts which encompassed stomach-biting; later admitted to being on alcohol, heroin, and cocaine at the time. He served 59 days in jail and 90 days of community service.
Marriage: Ryan Haddon, 2000
Child: Jaden Christopher, 1999
Famous Relatives: Mary Jo Slater, casting director, mother; Michael Gainsborough, stage and soap actor, father

JADA PINKETT SMITH

Birthplace: Baltimore, MD
Birthdate: 9/18/71
Occupation: Actor
Education: Attended North Carolina School for the Arts
Debut: (TV) *A Different World,* 1991; (Film) *Menace II Society,* 1993
Signature: *The Nutty Professor*
Facts: Her parents divorced around the time of her birth. She was raised in a rough Baltimore neighborhood by her mother and grandmother.

In addition to acting, has directed rap music videos, performed poetry readings, appeared at inner-city schools as a motivational speaker, and started a mail-order clothing line of T-shirts and dresses bearing feminist slogans.

Five feet tall and just 100 pounds, she often buys her clothes from stores' children's departments.

Reportedly gave $100,000 bail to rapper/actor friend Tupac Shakur to gain his release from jail while awaiting an appeal on a sexual abuse conviction.
Marriage: Will Smith, 1997
Child: Jaden Christopher Syre, 1998

WILL SMITH

Birthplace: Philadelphia, PA
Birthdate: 9/25/68
Occupation: Actor, rap artist
Education: High school
Debut: Rapper as part of DJ Jazzy Jeff & The Fresh Prince
Signature: *Men In Black,* 1997
Facts: Turned down a scholarship to MIT to pursue music.

By 1989 had made and lost his first million dollars, the latter due to excessive spending.

Earned his nickname, the Prince, from a teacher in Overbrook High School because of his regal attitude and ability to talk his way out of difficult situations.
Original Job: Rap artist
Marriages: Sheree Zampino (divorced); Jada Pinkett, 1997
Children: Willard C. "Trey" III, 1992 (with Sheree Zampino). Jaden Christopher Syre, 1998
Major Awards: Grammy, Best Rap Performance—Solo, "Parents Just Don't Understand" (with D.J. Jazzy Jeff & The Fresh Prince), 1988; Grammy, Best Rap Performance—Duo or Group, "Summertime" (with D.J. Jazzy Jeff & The Fresh Prince), 1991; Grammy, Best Rap Performance—Solo, "Men in Black," 1997; Grammy, Best Rap Performance—Solo, "Gettin' Jiggy Wit It," 1998
Quote: "I have no idea what my limits are. I believe that if I set my mind to it, within the next 15 years, I would be the President of the United States."

JIMMY SMITS

Birthplace: New York, NY
Birthdate: 7/9/55
Occupation: Actor
Education: Brooklyn College, 1980; Cornell University, MFA in theater, 1982
Debut: (Off-Broadway) *Hamlet,* 1982; (TV) *Miami Vice,* 1984; (Film) *Running Scared,* 1986
Signature: *NYPD Blue*

Facts: His mother is Puerto Rican; his father is from the former Dutch colony of Suriname.

Played linebacker on his high school football team.

Was producer Steven Bochco's original choice for the costarring role in *NYPD Blue* first filled by David Caruso, but the timing was not right for Smits. (Smits appeared in Bochco's earlier hit, *L.A. Law*.)

Is an investor in L.A.'s dance club and restaurant, The Conga Room, along with Jennifer Lopez, Paul Reiser, and others.

Original Job: Community organizer
Marriage: Barbara, 1981 (divorced 1987); Wanda De Jesus, actor (engaged)
Children: Taiana, c. 1973; Joaquin, c. 1983
Major Award: Emmy, Best Supporting Actor, *L.A. Law*, 1990

WESLEY SNIPES

Birthplace: Orlando, FL
Birthdate: 7/31/62
Occupation: Actor
Education: New York City's High School of the Performing Arts, SUNY-Purchase
Debut: (Film) *Wildcats*, 1985
Signature: *New Jack City*, 1991
Facts: Has studied martial arts, including the African/Brazilian version Capoeira, since his youth.

Was "in the Girl Scouts when I was 9 or 10"—in a helper capacity. "I sold cookies like anybody else, so I could get to go on the field trip."

Appeared in commercials for Levi's 501 Jeans and Coca-Cola Classic.

Snipes came to director Spike Lee's attention when he played a young punk who threatens Michael Jackson in the Martin Scorsese–directed video *Bad*, 1987.

Infamy: Arrested in 1994 for reckless driving for speeding at up to 120 mph on his motorcycle in Florida, leading state troopers on a 30-mile chase. Sentenced to eighty hours of community service, six months'

probation, and $7,000 in fines and court costs.

Original Jobs: Street and puppet theater in his troupe, Struttin' Street Stuff, telephone installer, parking attendant
Marriages: One marriage (divorced), Donna Wong (relationship)
Child: Jelani Asar, 1988
Quote: "What I may be lacking in terms of my physical beauty, I make up for in personality and experience."

SNOOP DOGG

Real Name: Cordozar "Calvin" Broadus
Birthplace: Long Beach, CA
Birthdate: 10/20/71
Occupation: Rap artist
Education: High school
Debut: (Album) *Doggystyle*, 1993
Facts: Nickname "Snoop" was given to him by his mother; "Doggy Dogg" came from a cousin who used to call himself Tate Doggy Dog. In 1999 he shortened his moniker, dropping the "Doggy."

Says his musical heroes are Al Green, Curtis Mayfield, and L. J. Reynolds of the Dramatics.

He's 6'4".

Infamy: One month after graduating from Long Beach Polytechnic High School, was arrested and incarcerated on a drug charge.

Dogg went on trial for the murder of L.A. gang member Phil Wolde-mariam; Snoop was driving the Jeep from which his bodyguard fired two fatal gunshots. The two were found not guilty of murder; the jury deadlocked on manslaughter charges and a mistrial was declared.

In 1994, was arrested in Lake Charles, La., when deputies attempting to deliver civil court papers smelled marijuana outside his hotel room. Charged with possession of marijuana and drug paraphernalia.
Original Job: Sold candy, delivered newspapers, bagged groceries
Marriage: Shanté Taylor, 1997

Child: Cordé, c. 1994; Cordell, 1997

TOM SNYDER

Birthplace: Milwaukee, WI
Birthdate: 5/12/36
Occupation: Talk show host
Education: Marquette University
Debut: (Radio) WRIT-AM, Milwaukee; (TV) KNBC-TV News, Los Angeles, 1970
Signature: *Late Late Show with Tom Snyder*
Facts: David Letterman, whose company produces Snyder's new late-night talk show, *Late Late Show with Tom Snyder*, is the one who took over Snyder's time slot when NBC dropped *Tomorrow* in 1982.
Marriage: One marriage (divorced)
Child: Anne Marie, 1964
Major Award: Emmy, Best Host, *Tomorrow*, 1974

LEELEE SOBIESKI

Real Name: Liliane Rudabet Gloria Elsveta Sobieski
Birthplace: New York, NY
Birthdate: 6/10/82
Occupation: Actor, model
Debut: (TV) *Reunion*, 1994; (Film) *Jungle2Jungle*, 1997
Signature: *Joan of Arc*, 1999 (TV version)
Facts: Born to French painter Jean and novelist Elizabeth, Leelee grew up on a ranch in the Carmarque region of France and in New York. Her father once acted in Westerns; her mother is working on a script for her.

Was spotted in her school by a casting director when she was 10.

Claimed to be the first virgin to play virgin Joan of Arc.

Plans to attend college every other semester to continue her education and her acting career.
Quote: "[My opinions are] the opinions of a teenage girl whose ideas have been borrowed or stolen from others and infiltrated by those of her parents."

STEPHEN SONDHEIM

Birthplace: New York, NY
Birthdate: 3/22/30
Occupation: Composer, lyricist
Education: Williams College
Debut: (Stage) *Girls of Summer,* 1956
Signature: *West Side Story*
Facts: In May 1992, turned down the NEA's Medal of Arts Award, claiming the agency is "a symbol of censorship and repression rather than encouragement and support."

When Sondheim left home at age 15, he was taken in by Oscar Hammerstein II (lyricist of *Oklahoma!*), who taught him how to structure songs.
Original Jobs: Wrote for *Topper* TV series, 1953, crossword puzzle writer
Major Awards: Grammy, Best Cast Show Album, *Company,* 1970; Tony, Best Score, *Company,* 1971; Tony, Best Score; *Follies,* 1972; Tony, Best Score, *A Little Night Music,* 1973; Grammy, Best Cast Show Album, *A Little Night Music,* 1973; Grammy, Song of the Year, "Send in the Clowns," 1975; Tony, Best Score, *Sweeney Todd,* 1979; Grammy, Best Cast Show Album, *Sweeney Todd,* 1979; Grammy, Best Cast Show Album, *Sunday in the Park with George,* 1984; Pulitzer Prize, Best Play, *Sunday in the Park with George,* 1985; Grammy, Best Cast Show Album, *West Side Story,* 1985; Grammy, Best Cast Show Album *Follies in Concert,* 1986; Tony, Best Score, *Into the Woods,* 1988; Grammy, Best Cast Show Album, *Into the Woods,* 1988; Oscar, Best Song, "Sooner or Later (I Always Get My Man)," 1990; Tony, Best Score, *Passion,* 1994
Quote: "I like neurotic people. I like troubled people. Not that I don't like squared away people, but I prefer neurotic people...Songs can't develop uncomplicated characters or unconflicted people. You can't just tell the sunny side and have a story with any richness to it."

KEVIN SORBO

Real Name: Kevin Sorbo
Birthplace: Bound, MN
Birthdate: 9/24/58
Occupation: Actor
Education: Attended University of Minnesota
Debut: (TV) *Murder, She Wrote,* 1993; (Film) *Kull, the Conqueror*
Signature: *Hercules*
Facts: Sorbo, who aspired to act from age 11, joined a theater group in Dallas after dropping out of college.

During the 1980s he filmed numerous TV commercials, including Diet Coke, Budweiser, BMW, and Lexus, before heading for Hollywood in 1987.

Lost the role of Superman in *Lois and Clark: The New Adventures of Superman* after seven auditions.
Original Job: Model
Marriage: Sam Jenkins, actor, 1998
Quote: "I've paid my dues. It's not like I was an accountant and all of a sudden I said, 'Hey, I want a series.'"

MIRA SORVINO

Birthplace: Tenafly, NJ
Birthdate: 9/28/67
Occupation: Actor
Education: Harvard University
Debut: (Film) *Amongst Friends,* 1993
Signature: *Mighty Aphrodite,* 1995
Facts: The East Asian Studies major speaks fluent Chinese Mandarin.

Discouraged from acting by her father, took up ballet and performed in a professional production of *The Nutcracker* at age 12.

In addition to playing the female in *Amongst Friends,* was casting director and third assistant director.
Original Job: Script reader
Relationship: Olivier Martinez
Famous Relative: Paul Sorvino, actor, father
Major Award: Oscar, Best Supporting Actress, *Mighty Aphrodite,* 1995

SAMMY SOSA

Birthplace: San Pedro de Macoris, Dominican Republic
Birthdate: 11/10/68
Occupation: Baseball player
Debut: (Major League Baseball) Texas Rangers, 1989
Signature: record-breaking home-run hitter
Facts: As a child, after his father died when he was 7, Sosa sold oranges, shined shoes, and worked as a janitor to help support his family.

His first "baseball glove" was made out of a milk carton.

Signed with the Philadelphia Phillies when he was 15, but the contract was voided because he was too young. Signed the following year with the Texas Rangers, and gave the $3,500 bonus to his mother after buying himself a bicycle.

In 1993, was the first Chicago Cubs players to have 30 home runs and 30 stolen bases in a season.

His hometown was also produced major leaguers George Bell, Pedro Guerrero, and Tony Fernandez.

Wears number 21 on his jersey in honor of Roberto Clemente.

In 1998 smashed Roger Maris's legendary record of 61 home runs in a season, hitting 66, but lost the record to Mark McGwire, who hit 70.
Marriage: Sonia
Children: Keysha; Kenia; Sammy; Michael
Major Award: National League Most Valuable Player, 1998
Quote: "My life is kind of like a miracle."

KEVIN SPACEY

Birthplace: South Orange, NJ
Birthdate: 7/26/59
Occupation: Actor
Education: Los Angeles Valley College, Juilliard
Debut: (Film) *Heartburn,* 1986
Signature: *Seven,* 1995
Facts: Kicked out of a military

academy as a kid for hitting a classmate with a tire.

Worked in New York theater in classic Shakespeare, Chekhov, and O'Neill roles before coming to Hollywood.

Was once considered not talented enough to appear on *The Gong Show*.

Major Awards: Tony, Best Featured Actor (Dramatic), *Lost in Yonkers*, 1991; Oscar, Best Supporting Actor, *The Usual Suspects*, 1995; Oscar, Best Actor, *American Beauty,* 1999

DAVID SPADE

Birthplace: Birmingham, MI
Birthdate: 7/22/64
Occupation: Comedian, actor
Education: Attended Arizona State University
Debut: (Film) *Police Academy 4,* 1987
Signature: *Just Shoot Me*
Facts: His father abandoned the family when he was 5.

In his debut year on *Saturday Night Live* he appeared on camera just three times.

Infamy: Many criticized his decision not to attend friend Chris Farley's funeral.

Original Job: Skateboard shop employee

Famous Relative: Kate Spade, handbag designer, sister-in-law

BRITNEY SPEARS

Birthplace: Kentwood, LA
Birthdate: 12/2/81
Occupation: Singer
Education: home-schooled
Debut: (Album) *[Hit Me]...Baby One More Time,* 1998; (Song) "[Hit Me]...Baby One More Time," 1998
Signature: "[Hit Me]...Baby One More Time"
Facts: Was turned away from *The Mickey Mouse Club* at age 9 as too young, but admitted 2 years later, joining such future stars as 'N Sync's JC Chasez and Justin Timber-

lake, Christina Aguilera, and Felicity's Keri Russell.

In 1991, was in the off-Broadway show *Ruthless*.

Was a *Star Search* champion in 1992.

Had arthroscopic surgery on her left knee in 1999 to remove cartilage damaged while rehearsing for a video.

Misses eating crawfish when she is on tour.

Favorite authors include Danielle Steel and Jackie Collins.

Her hometown has a population of approximately 2,500.

Has a pierced belly-button.

A Baptist, she jots her daily prayers in a journal she calls her Bible Book.

Plans for the Spears Museum, an addition to the existing Kentwood Museum, have been proposed by two fans in Kentwood, LA as a means of boosting tourism in their town.

Set a new benchmark in 2000 for first week sales for a single female artist or group with *Oops! I Did It Again*.

Relationship: Justin Timberlake
Quote: "I have really strong morals, and just because I look sexy on the cover of *Rolling Stone* doesn't mean that I'm a naughty girl."

AARON SPELLING

Birthplace: Dallas, TX
Birthdate: 4/22/23
Occupation: Producer, writer
Education: The Sorbonne, Southern Methodist University
Signature: *Beverly Hills 90210*
Facts: Served in U.S. Army Air Force, 1942–45; awarded the Bronze Star and Purple Heart with Oak Leaf Cluster.

In 1969, founded Thomas-Spelling Productions with actor Danny Thomas.

Has produced network hit series such as *The Mod Squad, Starsky and Hutch, S.W.A.T., Charlie's Angels,*

Family, Dynasty, Beverly Hills 90210, and *Melrose Place*.
Original Job: Actor
Marriage: Carole Gene Marer, 1968
Children: Victoria "Tori" Davey, 1973; Randall Gene, 1976
Famous Relative: Tori Spelling, actor, daughter
Major Awards: Emmy, Outstanding Drama/Comedy Special, *Day One,* 1989; Emmy, Outstanding Made-for-TV Movie, *And the Band Played On,* 1993
Quote: "I just got tired of the critics saying that I was the master of schlock. It didn't bother me until my kids began growing up and reading it. Well, I'm proud of those entertainment shows they call schlock."

STEVEN SPIELBERG

Birthplace: Cincinnati, OH
Birthdate: 12/18/46
Occupation: Director, producer
Education: California State College at Long Beach
Debut: (TV) *Night Gallery,* 1969 [see page 108 for a complete filmography]
Signature: *E.T., the Extra-Terrestrial,* 1982
Facts: Made the film *Firelight* at age 16, about the reflecting telescope he made himself, and his father hired a Phoenix, AZ, movie house to show it.

Became a TV director at Universal Pictures at age 20 after finding an empty office and pretending he belonged there.

Was not accepted by the University of Southern California's film department.

Co-owns the Las Vegas restaurant Dive! with Jeffrey Katzenberg.

A 22-minute film he made in college, *Amblin'*, brought him the attention of Sidney Sheinberg, at the time head of Universal Television. It also provided the name for his production company.

Directed the first episode of *Columbo*, as well as installments of *Marcus Welby, M.D.*

Marriages: Amy Irving (divorced); Kate Capshaw, 1991
Children: Jessica, 1976 (step-daughter); Max, 1985 (with Amy Irving); Theo, 1988 (adopted); Sasha, 1990; Sawyer, 1992; Mikaela George, 1996 (adopted); Destry Allyn, 1996
Famous Relative: Anne Spielberg, screenwriter, sister
Major Awards: Academy of Motion Picture Arts and Sciences, Irving G. Thalberg Award, 1986; Oscar, Best Director, *Schindler's List*, 1993; American Film Institute Lifetime Achievement Award, 1995; Oscar, Best Director, *Saving Private Ryan*, 1998

JERRY SPRINGER

Birthplace: London, England
Birthdate: 2/13/44
Occupation: Talk-show host
Education: Tulane University, Northwestern Law School
Signature: *The Jerry Springer Show*
Facts: His family emigrated from London when he was 5.

Elected mayor of Cincinnati at age 33; later ran for governor of Ohio but lost.

Was a serious news anchor and commentator before hosting his talk show.

His daughter was born without nasal passages and is legally blind and deaf in one ear.
Infamy: Early in his career while vice mayor of Cincinnati, police found his check to a whorehouse and he resigned in disgrace.

A Chicago TV station's offer that he do commentaries for the news prompted the resignation of two esteemed anchors.

Several ex-guests accused his show of staging dialogue, situations, and those notorious fights —charges Springer denied.
Original Job: Presidential campaign worker for Robert Kennedy
Marriage: Micki Velton, 1973 (divorced 1994)

Child: Katie, 1976
Major Awards: Seven local Emmys for nightly news commentaries

BRUCE SPRINGSTEEN

Birthplace: Freehold, NJ
Birthdate: 9/23/49
Occupation: Singer, songwriter
Education: Ocean City Community College
Debut: (Album) *Greetings from Asbury Park*, 1973
Signature: *Born in the USA*
Facts: E Street Band, formed in 1973, was named after the road in Belmar, NJ, where keyboardist David Sancious's mother lives.

After a 1976 Memphis concert, was caught climbing over the wall to Graceland.

Gave the song "Because the Night" to Patti Smith's producer, who was working in the adjacent recording studio.

In 1986, he rejected a $12-million offer from Lee Iococca to use "Born in the U.S.A." for Chrysler commercials.
Marriages: Julianne Phillips (divorced); Patti Scialfa, 1991
Children: Evan, 1990; Jessica, 1991; Sam, 1994
Major Awards: Grammy, Best Recording for Children, *In Harmony 2* (with others), 1982; Grammy, Best Rock Vocal, "Dancing in the Dark," 1984; Grammy, Best Rock Vocal, "Tunnel of Love," 1987; Oscar, Best Song, "Streets of Philadelphia," 1993; Grammy, Song of the Year, "Streets of Philadelphia," 1994; Grammy, Best Rock Vocal—Male, "Streets of Philadelphia," 1994; Grammy, Best Rock Song, "Streets of Philadelphia," 1994; Grammy, Best Song Written for a Motion Picture, "Streets of Philadelphia," 1994; Grammy, Best Contemporary Folk Recording, *The Ghost of Tom Joad*, 1996; inducted into Rock and Roll Hall of Fame, 1999

SYLVESTER STALLONE

Birthplace: Hell's Kitchen, New York
Birthdate: 7/6/46
Occupation: Actor, writer, director
Education: American School of Switzerland, University of Miami
Debut: (Film) *Bananas,* 1971 [see page 108 for a complete filmography]
Signature: *Rocky*, 1976
Facts: When he was born, the forceps severed a nerve in his face and partially paralyzed his lip, chin, and half of his tongue.

Had rickets as a child.

In high school he played football, fenced, and threw discus.

His paintings have been featured in galleries.

In *Bananas* (1971), played a goon who was thrown off a subway by Woody Allen.

As a boy was kicked out of fourteen schools in eleven years.

In 1971 appeared in a soft-core porn film, *A Party at Kitty & Stud's*.

Finally completed his degree at the University of Miami nearly 30 years after he dropped out.
Infamy: In March 1994, dumped longtime girlfriend Jennifer Flavin via letter sent FedEx. They have since reconciled.

Romanced Janice Dickinson, until DNA tests revealed that her newborn daughter wasn't his. She claimed to be pregnant by him again, then miscarried.
Original Jobs: Usher, fish salesman, zoo attendant, bookstore detective, teacher at American School of Switzerland.
Marriages: Sasha Czack (divorced); Brigitte Nielsen (divorced); Jennifer Flavin, 1997
Children: Sage, 1976; Seargeoh, 1979; (with Sasha Czack). Sophia Rose, 1996; Sistine Rose, 1998
Famous Relative: Frank Stallone, musician, brother; Jacqueline Stallone, astrologer, mother

DANIELLE STEEL

Real Name: Danielle Schuelein-Steel
Birthplace: New York, NY
Birthdate: 8/14/47
Occupation: Writer
Education: Lycée Français, Parsons School of Design, New York University
Debut: (Book) *Going Home,* 1973
Facts: Wrote over 30 best-selling novels in 20 years, including *The Ring* (1980), *Secrets* (1985), and *Daddy* (1989).

Vowed to wear only black until the one-year anniversary of her son's death.
Infamy: Two of her ex-husbands were convicts; she married one while he was still in prison, the other when she was eight months pregnant with his child.
Original Job: Vice president of public relations and new business for Supergirls, Ltd., a PR and ad agency
Marriages: Claude-Eric Lazard (divorced); Danny Zugelder (divorced); Bill Toth (divorced); John Traina (divorced); Tom Perkins, 1998 (separated, 1999)
Children: Beatrix, 1968 (with Claude-Eric Lazard). Nicholas, 1978 (deceased, 1997); (with Bill Toth). Samantha, 1982; Victoria, 1983; Vanessa, 1984; Max, 1986; Zara, 1987 (with John Traina).

GWEN STEFANI

Birthplace: Anaheim, CA
Birthdate: 10/3/69
Occupation: Singer, songwriter
Education: Attended California State—Fullerton
Debut: (Album) *No Doubt,* 1992
Signature: No Doubt
Facts: Older brother Eric recruited her in 1986 to sing in the band he formed with his Dairy Queen coworker John Spence, their flamboyant front man who the following year fatally shot himself in a local park. Gwen was eventually encouraged to step out front so the group could continue.

The bouncy group gave away kazoos at the album-release party for their first record. Released at the height of grunge's popularity, the album bombed.

Started wearing the stick-on *pottu* dots, the jewel-like Hindi forehead decoration, when she dated fellow band member Tony Kanal, whose parents are Indian. Many of the songs on *Tragic Kingdom* reflect her distress about their breakup after seven years.
Relationship: Gavin Rossdale

HOWARD STERN

Birthplace: New York, NY
Birthdate: 1/12/54
Occupation: Radio DJ
Education: Boston University
Signature: *The Howard Stern Show*
Facts: 1994 Libertarian gubernatorial candidate in New York but dropped out of race before the elections.

Once fired for referring to station management as "scumbags" on the air during a salary dispute.

Practices transcendental meditation each morning in the limo ride to work.
Infamy: After angry listeners provided the FCC with transcripts of Stern's show about masturbating to thoughts of Aunt Jemima and having rough sex with actress Michelle Pfeiffer, the commission fined Infinity Broadcasting, which owns WNBC-New York, $600,000.

Stern made fun of singer Selena Quintanilla Perez after her murder in April 1995, playing her music with sounds of gunfire in the background and parodying her mourners. The League of United Latin American Citizens said it intended to drive Stern's program off the air. Stern later apologized for his conduct.

Refusing to apologize for calling French-speakers "scumbags," Stern reasoned, "I can't imagine anybody would take what I say seriously."

In 1999, he signed a deal to produce his own animated cartoon series about people in motor homes

searching for family values in post–apocalyptic America.
Marriage: Alison Berns, 1978 (separated, 1999)
Children: Emily, Debra, Ashley Jade, 1993

JON STEWART

Real Name: Jon Stuart Liebowitz
Birthplace: Lawrence, NJ
Birthdate: 11/28/62
Occupation: Comedian, actor
Education: College of William and Mary
Debut: (TV) *Short Attention Span Theater,* 1991
Signature: *The Daily Show, with Jon Stewart*
Facts: Got the idea to do stand-up at age 24, when using puppets to teach schoolkids about disabled people—a gig that honed his prop-wielding skills. Went on the road doing stand-up for the next six years.

His parents divorced when he was 9, and his relationship with his dad became increasingly strained over the years as Stewart gleefully aired the family's dirty laundry in his club acts.
Original Jobs: Bartender, bike mechanic, porter in a bakery, research lab assistant
Quote: "As long as I can remember, I wanted to sleep late, stay up late, and do nothing in between."

MARTHA STEWART

Birthplace: Nutley, NJ
Birthdate: 8/3/41
Occupation: Entertainment and lifestyle consultant
Education: Barnard College
Debut: (Book) *Entertaining,* 1981
Signature: *Martha Stewart Living*
Facts: Has published nearly 30 books on entertaining.

Discovered her love for decorating, gardening, and cooking when she and her husband bought a Connecticut farmhouse and fixed it up themselves in 1971. Over the years, she added a barn-turned-party-room, a greenhouse, pool, vegetable gardens, orchards, an English border garden, and beehives, turkeys, chickens, and cats.

Sleeps four hours a night with the lights on so when she wakes up she can get right to work.

Has filed an extortion, coercion, and defamation suit against a landscaper who claims she and her car pinned him against a security box.

After the IPO of her company Martha Stewart Living Omnimedia in 1999 (and before the stock slid the following year) was worth over $1 billion on paper.

Infamy: Ordered by NY Division of Tax Appeals to pay $221,677 in back homeowner's taxes for 1991 and 1992. She plans to appeal, claiming that she has been a resident of Connecticut since 1971.
Original Jobs: Model, stockbroker, take-out gourmet food store owner
Marriage: Andy Stewart (divorced, 1990)
Child: Alexis, 1965

PATRICK STEWART

Birthplace: Mirfield, England
Birthdate: 7/13/40
Occupation: Actor, writer
Education: Bristol Old Vic Theatre School
Debut: (Stage) *Treasure Island*, 1959
Signature: *Star Trek: The Next Generation*
Facts: Was so sure that he was going to be fired from the initial season of *Star Trek: The Next Generation* that he didn't unpack his bags for six weeks.

In 2000, complained from the stage after a performance of Arthur Miller's *The Ride Down Mt. Morgan* that his producers, the Shuberts, weren't supporting the show. After receiving a complaint, Actors Equity

ordered him to make a public apology to the Shuberts.

A doll based on his Professor X character in *X-Men* was "resculpted to add to the realism" after he complained that it looked nothing like him.
Original Job: Journalist
Marriage: Sheila Falconer, 1966 (divorced, 1990); Wendy Neuss, 2000
Children: Daniel Freedom, 1968; Sophie Alexandra, 1973
Quote: "I was brought up in a very poor and very violent household. I spent much of my childhood being afraid."

BEN STILLER

Birthplace: New York, NY
Birthdate: 11/30/65
Occupation: Actor, director
Education: UCLA
Debut: (Film) *Empire of the Sun*, 1987
Signature: *Reality Bites*, 1994
Facts: At age 10, began making Super-8 movies about getting revenge on bullies in his neighborhood.

Learned swimming from the Pips, Gladys Knight's backup vocalists.

His short film parody of *The Color of Money* landed him a job at *Saturday Night Live* and his own show on MTV.

Was once engaged to Jeanne Tripplehorn.
Marriage: Christine Taylor, actress (engaged, 1999)
Famous Relatives: Jerry Stiller, comedian, father; Anne Meara, comedian, mother; Amy Stiller, actor, sister
Major Award: Emmy, Best Writing in Variety or Music Program, *The Ben Stiller Show* (with others), 1992

R. L. STINE

Real Name: Robert Lawrence Stine
Birthplace: Columbus, OH
Birthdate: 10/8/43
Occupation: Writer
Education: Ohio State University, New York University

Signature: The Goosebumps series
Facts: Noted author of the Goosebumps and Fear Street series of books for children among others, he has sold over 170 million books.

Before hitting it big, wrote everything from coloring books to bubble gum cards.

Types only with his left index finger.

In 1997 he published his autobiography, *It Came from Ohio*.

Has written under the pseudonyms Eric Affabee, Zachary Blue, Jovial Bob Stine.
Original Jobs: Social studies teacher; magazine editor
Marriage: Jane Waldhorn, 1969
Children: Matthew, 1980
Quote: "I've been called a literary training bra for Stephen King."

STING

Real Name: Gordon Matthew Sumner
Birthplace: Newcastle upon Tyne, England
Birthdate: 10/2/51
Occupation: Singer, songwriter, actor
Education: Warwick University
Debut: (Song) "Fall Out" (with The Police), 1977
Signature: The Police
Facts: Rejected the villain role in James Bond film *A View to a Kill*.

He gained his nickname by wearing a black-and-yellow striped shirt, like a bee.

Received a seaman's card and worked as a bass player with The Ronnie Pierson Trio on Princess Cruise Lines at age 17.

Claimed in a 1993 *Rolling Stone* interview that by practicing meditation, he can make love for more than five hours at a time.

In 2000, he was unable to gain ownership of the Internet address www.sting.com because he had never registered the name Sting as a trademark. He is the first celebrity

to lose such a case at the World Intellectual Property Organization.
Original Jobs: Teacher, construction worker, clerk for Inland Revenue
Marriages: Frances Eleanor Tomelty (divorced); Trudie Styler, 1996
Children: Joseph, 1977; Katherine "Kate," 1982 (with Tomelty); Michael "Mickey," 1984; Jake, 1985; Eliot Pauline "Coco," 1990; Giacomo Luke, 1995 (with Styler)
Major Awards: Grammy, Best Rock Performance—Duo or Group, "Don't Stand So Close to Me" (with The Police), 1981; Grammy, Song of the Year, "Every Breath You Take," 1983; Grammy, Best Pop Performance—Duo or Group, "Every Breath You Take" (with The Police), 1983; Grammy, Best Pop Vocal—Male, "Bring On the Night," 1987; Grammy, Best Rock Song/Vocal Performance, "Soul Cages," 1991; Grammy, Best Pop Vocal—Male, "If I Ever Lose My Faith in You," 1993; Grammy, Best Music Video—Long Form, *Ten Summoner's Tales,* 1993; Grammy, Best Pop Vocal—Male, "Brand New Day," 1999; Grammy, Best Pop Album, *Brand New Day,* 1999

MICHAEL STIPE

Birthplace: Decatur, GA
Birthdate: 1/4/60
Occupation: Singer, songwriter
Education: Southern Illinois University, University of Georgia
Debut: *Chronic Town* (with R.E.M.), 1982
Signature: R.E.M.
Facts: In the early years of R.E.M., traveled to 49 states by the time he was 24.

Planned to record with friend Kurt Cobain. Cobain had tickets to come to Stipe's in Atlanta but called to cancel, and committed suicide soon after.

Was rumored to have AIDS because, he says, he is thin, has bad skin, and is sexually ambiguous. He denies being HIV-positive.

Major Awards: Grammy, Best Alternative Performance, *Out of Time,* 1991; Grammy, Best Pop Vocal—Group, "Losing My Religion," 1991

OLIVER STONE

Birthplace: New York, NY
Birthdate: 9/15/46
Occupation: Director, writer, producer
Education: Yale University, New York University film school
Debut: (Film) *Seizure,* 1974
Signature: *Platoon,* 1986
Facts: Served in the U.S. Merchant Marine, 1966; in the Army in Vietnam, 1967–68. Awarded Bronze Star and Purple Heart with Oak Leaf Cluster.

Made acting debut as a bum in *The Hand* (1981), which he wrote and directed.

Infamy: At least 10 real killings were linked to his ode to violence, *Natural Born Killers,* with one 14-year-old decapitator even telling friends he wanted to be famous like the killers in the movie.

Was arrested in 1999 for allegedly driving under the influence and possession of hashish. Plead no contest on the DUI count and guilty to possession, and was ordered to enter drug and alchohol treatment programs.

Original Jobs: Taxi driver in New York City, teacher at Free Pacific Institute in South Vietnam
Marriages: Majwa Sarkis (divorced); Elizabeth Burkit Cox (divorced, 1993)
Children: Sean, 1984; Michael, 1991; (with Elizabeth Cox Stone) Tara, 1995 (with Chong Son Chong).
Major Awards: Oscar, Best Adapted Screenplay, *Midnight Express,* 1978; Oscar, Best Director, *Platoon,* 1986; Oscar, Best Director, *Born on the Fourth of July,* 1991

SHARON STONE

Birthplace: Meadville, PA
Birthdate: 3/10/58
Occupation: Actor
Education: Edinboro State University
Debut: (Film) *Stardust Memories,* 1981 [see page 108 for a complete filmography]
Signature: *Basic Instinct,* 1992
Facts: She has an I.Q. of 154.

Between 1977 and 1980, became one of the top 10 models at the Ford Agency.
Infamy: Posed nude for *Playboy* just days after finishing *Total Recall,* 1990.
Original Job: Model
Marriages: Michael Greenburg (divorced), Phil Bronstein, 1998
Child: Roan Joseph, 2000 (adopted)
Famous Relative: Michael Stone, actor, brother
Quote: "I'm naked at the drop of a hat.... Why not? Why pretend? Be happy they're interested."

JOHN STOSSEL

Birthplace: Illinois
Birthdate: 3/47
Occupation: News correspondent, producer
Education: Princeton University
Debut: KGW, Portland, Oregon
Signature: (TV series) *20/20,* 1981; (TV Special) *Are We Scaring Ourselves to Death?,* 1994
Facts: Was a stutterer. The disability was severe enough to earn him a draft deferment.

Finally found a successful treatment for his stutter—but only after he struggling through on-camera news work.

His transition from a consumer activist who supported government regulation into a challenger of alarmist reporting and overintervention has provoked former allies like Ralph Nader to castigate him as "lazy and dishonest."

Surfs and coaches soccer.
Infamy: ABC News made him apolo-

gize on *20/20* for citing a nonexistent study stating that the level of pesticide residue on organic foods was no less than that on conventionally grown foods.
Original Job: Television newsroom researcher
Marriage: One marriage
Children: Two children
Major Awards: Nineteen Emmy awards for reporting
Quote: "When I started consumer reporting I was a typical left-wing, Ivy League graduate. Now I lean toward liberty."

GEORGE STRAIT

Birthplace: Pearsall, TX
Birthdate: 5/18/52
Occupation: Singer, songwriter
Education: Southwest Texas State
Debut: (Album) *Let's Get Down To It*, 1976
Signature: "Carrying Your Love With Me"
Facts: Grew up on a Texas ranch his family owned for decades.
Before joining the army, eloped with his high school sweetheart.
Frustrated by his lack of success, gave up singing in 1979 and went back to his agriculture roots. Returned soon after to give it one more try.
Original Job: Cattle-pen employee
Marriage: Norma
Children: Jenifer (deceased); George Jr.

MERYL STREEP

Real Name: Mary Louise Streep
Birthplace: Summit, NJ
Birthdate: 6/22/49
Occupation: Actor
Education: Vassar College; MFA, Yale University
Debut: (Stage) *Trelawny of the Wells*, NY Shakespeare Festival, 1975; (Film) *Julia*, 1977 [see page 109 for a complete filmography]
Signature: *Sophie's Choice*, 1982
Facts: When she was 12, began

studying with vocal coach Estelle Liebling, who had also taught diva Beverly Sills.
In high school, was a cheerleader and homecoming queen.
Formed a child support group with Annette Bening, Carrie Fisher, and Tracey Ullman, in which they watch each other's children.
When New York theater giant Joseph Papp—who ran New York's Public Theater and Shakespeare in the Park—knew he was dying, he asked Streep to succeed him; she turned him down so she could devote more time to her family.
Is tied with Katharine Hepburn for most Oscar nominations for acting.
Original Job: Waitress
Marriage: Don Gummer, 1978
Children: Henry, 1979; Mary Willa, 1983; Grace Jane, 1986; Louisa Jacobson, 1991
Major Awards: Emmy, Best Actress in a Miniseries, *Holocaust*, 1978; Oscar, Best Supporting Actress, *Kramer vs. Kramer*, 1979; Oscar, Best Actress, *Sophie's Choice*, 1982
Quote: "My own kids haven't seen most of my movies. Too upsetting: Mommy dies."

BARBRA STREISAND

Real Name: Barbara Streisand
Birthplace: Brooklyn, NY
Birthdate: 4/24/42
Occupation: Singer, actor, director
Education: Yeshiva University
Debut: (Stage) *Another Evening with Harry Stoones*, 1961; (Film) *Funny Girl*, 1968
Signature: "The Way We Were"
Facts: Her father died when she was 15 months old.
She graduated from high school two years early.
Although she had never sung before an audience before, she won a talent contest in a Greenwich Village bar and won a singing job at another bar.
Her Academy Award for *Funny Girl* (1968) was shared with Katharine

Hepburn for *A Lion in Winter;* it's only tie for the Best Actress Oscar to date.
Reportedly has a pet name from her husband: "Beezer."
She's only the second artist (after Elvis Presley) to claim 40 gold albums. Her *Christmas Album* is the only vocal holiday album to sell over 5 million copies.
Her 1999/2000 New Year's Eve sell-out show at MGM Grand in Las Vegas set a U.S. box-office record for a single concert, grossing $14.7 million.
Original Jobs: Theater usher, switchboard operator, waitress
Marriages: Elliot Gould (divorced); James Brolin, 1998
Child: Jason Emanuel, 1966 (with Elliot Gould)
Famous Relative: Roslyn Kind, singer, sister
Major Awards: Grammy, Best Female Pop Vocalist 1963–65; Emmy, Outstanding Program Achievements in Entertainment, *My Name Is Barbra*, 1965; Oscar, Best Actress, *Funny Girl*, 1968; Tony, Special Award, 1970; Oscar, Best Song, "Evergreen" (with Paul Williams), 1976; Grammy, Best Songwriter (with Paul Williams), 1977; Grammy, Best Female Pop Vocalist, 1977, 1986; Grammy, Legend Award, 1992; Emmy, Best Individual Performance in a Variety or Music Program, *Barbra Streisand: The Concert*, 1995
Quote: "I don't like performing. I feel like I'm in a beauty pageant, like I'm 18 and strutting around on stage."

MENA SUVARI

Birthplace: Newport, RI
Birthdate: 2/13/79
Occupation: Actor
Education: High school
Debut: (TV) *Boy Meets World*, 1996; (Film) *Nowhere*, 1997
Signature: *American Beauty*, 1999
Facts: She is of Estonian and Greek descent.

Signed with Wilhelmina modeling agency in seventh grade and modeled for five years.

Has three brothers, all of whom went to the Citadel and joined the U.S. Army.

Did her own singing when playing a chorus member in *American Pie*.
Original Job: Model
Marriage: Robert Brinkmann, cinematographer, 2000
Quote: "Early on, I told my agent, 'I'm not interested in being popular, the flavor of the week. I want meaty, challenging parts.'"

HILARY SWANK

Birthplace: Lincoln, NB
Birthdate: 7/30/74
Occupation: Actor
Education: Santa Monica City College
Debut: (TV) *Harry and the Hendersons*, 1990; (Film) *Buffy the Vampire Slayer*, 1992.
Signature: *Boys Don't Cry*, 1999
Facts: She is part Spanish, part Native American.

Competed in the Junior Olympics and the Washington State championships in swimming, and ranked fifth in her state's gymnastics competitions.

After her parents separated, she and her mother endured hardship, at times living out of their car.

She played recurring roles in *Growing Pains* and *Evening Shade*.

To prepare for her role in *Boys Don't Cry*, she spent almost a month living as a man in Los Angeles.
Marriage: Chad Lowe, actor,1997
Major award: Oscar, Best Actress, *Boys Don't Cry*, 1999
Quote: "It's so boring to play the pretty girl."

QUENTIN TARANTINO

Birthplace: Knoxville, TN
Birthdate: 3/27/63
Occupation: Director, writer, actor
Education: High school dropout
Debut: (Film) *Reservoir Dogs,* 1992 (writer, director, and actor)
Signature: *Pulp Fiction*, 1994

Facts: Studied movies while working at an L.A. video store for four years. Got the idea for *Reservoir Dogs* when he saw that no one had made a heist movie in a long time.

Once played an Elvis impersonator on *The Golden Girls*.

Is said to have an I.Q. of 160.

Had already tried his hand at screenwriting as a teenager, penning *Captain Peachfuzz and the Anchovy Bandit*.
Infamy: Once went to jail for failing to pay his parking tickets.

Physically attacked *Natural Born Killers* producer Don Murphy in an L.A. restaurant; recounted the episode on Keenan Ivory Wayans's talk show as a "bitch-slap." Got into another bar brawl in the spring of 1998.
Original Job: Video sales clerk
Major Awards: Cannes Film Festival, Palme d'Or, *Pulp Fiction*, 1994; Oscar, Best Original Screenplay, *Pulp Fiction,* 1994
Quote: "People ask me if I went to film school. And I tell them, 'No, I went to films.' "

ELIZABETH TAYLOR

Birthplace: London, England
Birthdate: 2/27/32
Occupation: Actor
Education: Byron House, Hawthorne School, Metro-Goldwyn-Mayer School
Debut: (Film) *There's One Born Every Minute,* 1942
Signature: *Cleopatra*
Facts: Almost died from pnuemonia and had an emergency tracheotomy in 1961.

When she was three years old she danced before Queen Elizabeth and Princess Margaret.

After friend Rock Hudson died from AIDS, became the founding chair of the American Foundation for AIDS Research (AMFAR) in 1985.

She met construction worker Larry Fortensky, whom she married in 1992, at the Betty Ford Clinic.

Was made a Dame by Queen Eliz-

abeth in 2000 in a London ceremony.

Infamy: Checked herself into the Betty Ford Clinic to overcome alcohol dependency, 1983. Returned in 1988 to overcome painkiller dependency.

Marriages: Nicholas Conrad Hilton Jr. (divorced); Michael Wilding (divorced); Mike Todd (deceased); Eddie Fisher (divorced); Richard Burton (divorced, remarried, divorced); John Warner (divorced); Larry Fortensky (divorced, 1996)

Children: Michael, 1953; Christopher, 1955; (with Michael Wilding). Liza, 1957 (with Mike Todd). Maria Carson, c. 1961 (adopted with Richard Burton).

Major Awards: Oscar, Best Actress, *Butterfield 8*, 1960; Oscar, Best Actress, *Who's Afraid of Virginia Woolf*, 1966; Oscar, Jean Hersholt Humanitarian Award, 1992; American Film Institute Lifetime Achievement Award, 1993

Quote: "I've been known to swim in my emeralds."

JOHN TESH

Birthplace: Garden City, NY
Birthdate: 7/9/52
Occupation: Television host, composer, pianist
Education: Attended Juilliard during high school, North Carolina State University
Signature: *Entertainment Tonight*
Facts: Anchored local TV news in Durham, N.C.; Orlando; Nashville; and New York before signing with CBS Sports and, in 1986, *Entertainment Tonight*.

An incurable romantic, he proposed to Selleca by reserving an entire Monterey restaurant; hiring a string quartet to serenade her with a song he had written, "Concetta"; and arranging for a fireworks display outside the window.

He and Selleca, who pledged to avoid premarital sex during their year-long courtship, starred in a

late-night infomercial for a series of videos about relationships.

Composed songs for sporting events he was covering for CBS, including the Tour de France and the Pan-American Games, both of which won Emmys.

His own recording label, GTS Records, has sold more than two million of his CDs. His *Romantic Christmas,* with Selleca, went gold, selling more than 500,000 copies.

Whenever Tesh performs a concert, the event's promoters are contractually bound to provide at least one World Wrestling Foundation action figure for his dressing room.

In 1998 he graced 12 million Kellogg's Complete Oat Bran Flakes cereal boxes (his late parents both suffered from heart-related ailments).

Original Job: TV reporter
Marriages: Julie Wright (divorced); Connie Selleca, 1992
Child: Prima, 1994
Major Awards: Emmy, Best Musical Composition for a Sports Program, Pan-American Games, 1983; Emmy, Best Musical Score, Tour de France, 1987

CHARLIZE THERON

Birthplace: Benoni, South Africa
Birthdate: 8/7/75
Occupation: Actor, model
Debut: (Film) *Two Days in the Valley,* 1996
Facts: Had a pet goat as a child.

Afrikaans was her first language. She mastered English by watching television.

Her father was French, her mother German.

At 16 entered a modeling contest on a whim and won. After a brief modeling stint, she studied with the Joffrey Ballet until a knee injury halted her career.

By 1994 she settled in Los Angeles and caught the attention of a personal manager when she caused

a fuss because a bank would not cash her check.

She and her mother have matching fish tattoos.

Original Job: Model
Relationships: Stephan Jenkins, musician with Third Eye Blind, 1998
Quotes: "A nice pair of pumps, a skirt that goes to your knees, that Vargas-red-lipstick glamour—to me, that's what a girl is."

JONATHAN TAYLOR THOMAS

Real Name: Jonathan Weiss
Birthplace: Bethlehem, PA
Birthdate: 9/8/81
Occupation: Actor
Debut: (TV) *The Bradys,* 1990
Signature: *Home Improvement*
Facts: Was the voice of Simba in *The Lion King,* as well as several other characters in kids' cartoons.

Got straight A's when attending public school during breaks in filming.

At one point received nearly 50,000 pieces of fan mail a month.

Original Job: Model
Quote: "On occasion, I've taken the test that's been in the teen magazines about me and I've failed. Isn't that scary?"

KRISTIN SCOTT THOMAS

Birthplace: Redruth, Cornwall, England
Birthdate: 5/24/60
Occupation: Actor
Education: Attended London's Central School of Speech and Drama and Paris's Ecole Nationale des Arts et Techniques de Theatre
Debut: (Film) *Under the Cherry Moon,* 1986
Signature: *The English Patient,* 1996
Facts: Her father, a naval pilot, was killed in a flying accident when she was 5. Some years later her stepfather, another naval pilot, was killed in a nearly identical crash.

At 16, enrolled in a convent school with aspirations to be a nun.

Was married in Dorset, a beautiful part of England made famous by novelist Thomas Hardy. Two days of ceremonies included one civil and one before a rabbi and a priest (she's Catholic).

Marriage: François Oliviennes
Children: Hannah, c. 1989; Joseph, 1991; George, 2000
Famous Relative: Serena Scott Thomas, model, actor, sister

ROZONDA THOMAS

Birthplace: Atlanta, GA
Birthdate: 2/27/71
Occupation: Singer, songwriter
Education: Attended Georgia Southern University
Debut: *Oooooooohhh…On the TLC Tip*, 1992
Signature: "Waterfalls," 1995 / "Chilli"
Facts: Wanted to be in fashion, but when given the choice between managing a clothing store and dancing for hip-hop artist Damian Dane, she tried the latter.

Was a replacement for TLC's original "C," named Crystal.

Choreographs the band's videos and live performances.

In 1997, met her father for the first time as part of the *Sally Jessy Raphael Show.*

After researching breast implants, decided against them—as dramatized in the "Unpretty" video.

Appeared in the movies *House Party 3, Hav Plenty,* and *Snow Day.*
Relationship: Dallas Austin
Child: Tron, 1997
Major Awards: Grammy, Best R&B Album, *Crazysexycool*, 1995; Grammy, Best R&B Vocal—Duo or Group, "Creep," 1995; Grammy, Best R&B Album, *Fanmail*, 1999; Grammy, Best R&B Vocal—Duo or Group, "No Scrubs," 1999

EMMA THOMPSON

Birthplace: London, England
Birthdate: 4/15/59
Occupation: Actor
Education: Cambridge University
Debut: (Film) *Henry V,* 1989
Signature: *Howards End,* 1992
Facts: Wrote screenplay adaptation of *Sense and Sensibility* by Jane Austen, whose novels she began reading at age 9.

When first met her ex-husband, Kenneth Branagh, she "thought he had strange hair."

Lives on the street on which she was raised, opposite her mother and down the street from her younger sister, Sophie.
Marriage: Kenneth Branagh (divorced, 1996); Greg Wise (relationship)
Child: Gaia Romilly Wise, 1999 (with Greg Wise)
Famous Relatives: Eric Thompson, producer, father; Phyllida Law, actor, mother; Sophie Thompson, actor, sister
Major Awards: Oscar, Best Actress, *Howards End,* 1992; Oscar, Best Adapted Screenplay, *Sense and Sensibility,* 1995

COURTNEY THORNE-SMITH

Birthplace: San Francisco, CA
Birthdate: 11/8/67
Occupation: Actor
Education: High school
Debut: (Film) *Lucas,* 1986; (TV) *Fast Time,* 1986
Signature: *Melrose Place*
Facts: Her hyphenated name is a combination of her mother's maiden name, Thorne, and her father's name, Smith.

Drew attention with her recurring role in *L.A. Law* in 1990.

Used to date actor Andrew Shue.

Hobbies include knitting.
Marriage: Andrew Conrad, 2000

BILLY BOB THORNTON

Birthplace: Alpine, AR
Birthdate: 8/4/55
Occupation: Actor, screenwriter, director
Education: Attended Henderson State University
Debut: (Film) *Hunter's Blood,* 1986
Signature: *Sling Blade,* 1996
Facts: Grew up in a rural area with coal-oil lamps and an outhouse, where supper was whatever grandpa happened to shoot.

Mother Virginia was a psychic, who once predicted that Thornton would work with Burt Reynolds, which he did on *Evening Shade* in 1990.

Broke for years in L.A., he ate nothing but potatoes during a particularly bleak period in 1984, which resulted in nearly fatal heart failure.

Sling Blade's character Karl came to Thornton in 1985 while in a B-movie trailer awaiting his four-line part. The character later appeared in his 1994 short film *Some Folks Call It a Sling Blade,* a forerunner to the feature.

Terrified of flying, he got distributor Miramax to drive him to the New York Film Festival from L.A. in a limousine.
Original Job: Drummer (one of his bands, Tres Hombres, once opened for Hank Williams Jr.), singer, screen-door factory worker, pizza maker
Marriage: Melissa Lee Gatlin, 1978 (divorced, 1980); Toni Lawrence, 1986 (divorced, 1988); Cynda Williams (divorced, 1992); Pietra Dawn Cherniak, 1993 (divorced, 1997); Angelina Jolie, 2000
Children: Amanda, 1979 (with Melissa Lee Gatlin). William Langston, 1993; Harry James, 1994; (with Pietra Dawn Cherniak).
Major Award: Oscar, Best Adapted Screenplay, *Sling Blade,* 1996
Quote: "I prefer eating with plastic—I can't use real silver. Swear to God. I think some big old

mad king used to use it or something."

UMA THURMAN

Birthplace: Boston, MA
Birthdate: 4/29/70
Occupation: Actor
Education: Professional Children's School
Debut: (Film) *Kiss Daddy Good Night,* 1987
Signature: *Pulp Fiction,* 1994
Facts: Her father, Robert, an eminent professor of Asian religion, named her Uma after a Hindu goddess.

Her Swedish mother, a psychotherapist, was once married to Timothy Leary.

The nearly six-foot actress quit school and headed for New York at age 16. Modeling jobs and movies quickly followed.
Original Job: Model, dishwasher
Marriages: Gary Oldman (divorced); Ethan Hawke, 1998
Child: Maya Ray Thurman-Hawke, 1998

JUSTIN TIMBERLAKE

Birthplace: Memphis, TN
Birthdate: 1/31/81
Occupation: Singer
Debut: (Single) "I Want You Back," 1996; (Album) **NSYNC,* 1996 (American release, 1998)
Signature: *No Strings Attached,* 2000
Facts: Lost on *Star Search* at the age of 4.

Like bandmate J C Chasez, is a former Mouseketeer.

His mother came up with 'N Sync's name.

The band was successful in Europe before its first album was released in America.

Set up the Justin Timberlake Foundation to support arts programs in U.S. public schools.

Acted in 2000 TV movie *Model Behavior.*

Is so popular that a piece of french toast that he didn't finish eating was auctioned on eBay. It went for $1,025.

Though Eminem rails against 'N Sync, Timberlake loves him, saying: "He's a supertalented artist."
Infamy: 'N Sync broke with their original record label and management over compensation. Suits and countersuits flew before a settlement was reached, allegedly favoring the band.
Relationship: Britney Spears
Quote: "We're like Frosted Flakes. The parents don't like to admit they enjoy the music."

JOHN TRAVOLTA

Birthplace: Englewood, NJ
Birthdate: 2/18/54
Occupation: Actor
Education: High school dropout
Debut: (Stage) *Who Will Save the Plow,* 1966; (Film) *The Devil's Rain,* 1975; (TV) *Welcome Back, Kotter,* 1975 [see page 109 for a complete filmography]
Signature: *Saturday Night Fever,* 1977
Facts: Holds the record for the most *Rolling Stone* covers for an actor: four.

An avid flyer since the age of 16, he turned down the lead in *An Officer and a Gentleman,* a part reportedly written for him, because the shooting conflicted with his attendance of American Airlines' month-long jet pilot training school. In 1995, a plane he owns and was piloting lost electrical power over Washington, DC, and had a mid-air near-miss with a commercial jetliner.

His first love, actor Diana Hyland, was 18 years older than the then 22-year-old Travolta. Nine months into the romance she died of cancer—in Travolta's arms.

Languished for nearly a decade in forgettable and/or unpopular films until *Pulp Fiction* restored him to Hollywood's A-list. He earned just

$140,000 for his part in the film, far less than the millions-per-picture he once commanded and now receives again.

Has been a member of the Church of Scientology for more than 20 years.
Marriage: Kelly Preston, 1991
Child: Jett, 1992; Ella Bleu, 2000
Famous Relatives: Ellen Travolta, actor, sister; Joey Travolta, actor, brother

CHRIS TUCKER

Birthplace: Atlanta, GA
Birthdate: 8/31/71
Occupation: Comedian, actor
Education: High school
Debut: (Film) *House Party 3,* 1994
Signature: *Fifth Element*
Facts: Is the youngest of six children.

Was voted Most Humorous in his high school, dubbed a Little Eddie Murphy.

Personally rewrote or improvised most of his trademark quick dialogue in *Money Talks.*

TANYA TUCKER

Birthplace: Seminole, TX
Birthdate: 10/10/58
Occupation: Singer
Education: High school dropout
Debut: (Album) *Delta Dawn,* 1972
Signature: "Delta Dawn"
Facts: Her family moved to Las Vegas when she was 12, on the theory that it was a good city to launch a new entertainer. Within two years she had a hit in "Delta Dawn," a $1.5 million record deal, and a cover story in *Rolling Stone.*

High-profile romances included Merle Haggard, Don Johnson, the late Andy Gibb, and Glen Campbell.

Has released more than 30 country albums.

A reported $700,000 advance and the prodding of friends convinced her to write the tell-all, *Nickel Dreams.*
Infamy: Began drinking in her late teens and quickly developed a reputation as a wild party girl. The

cocaine, alcohol, and violence that was integral to her 1980 relationship with Glen Campbell became a national symbol of celebrity excess (the pair split in 1981, and Tucker continued her drinking and drugging until entering the Betty Ford clinic in 1988).

In 1997, with a TV crew in attendance to film a *Dateline* profile segment, Tucker flashed her breasts to a roomful of Nashville music-industry partygoers.

Relationship: Jerry Laseter (engaged)

Children: Presley Tanita, 1989; Beau Grayson, 1991 (both with Ben Reed)

CHRISTY TURLINGTON

Birthplace: Walnut Creek, CA
Birthdate: 1/2/69
Occupation: Supermodel
Education: New York University
Facts: Her face was used on mannequins at the Metropolitan Museum of Art's costume galleries.

Dated screenwriter Roger Wilson for seven years; they had a Buddhist service together, though they were never officially married. Also dated Jason Patric.

Plans to attend graduate school—possibly in a writing program.

TED TURNER

Real Name: Robert Edward Turner III
Birthplace: Cincinnati, OH
Birthdate: 11/19/38
Occupation: Media executive, owner of Atlanta Braves and Hawks
Education: Brown University
Debut: In 1970, bought failing Atlanta TV station, which he turned into WTBS
Signature: CNN
Facts: Won the America's Cup in his yacht, *Courageous,* in 1977.

Interested in owning a major TV network, he made a failed bid for CBS in 1985, and launched negotia-

tions with NBC in 1994 that ultimately broke down.

Owns four bison ranches out west, making him America's largest private bison rancher.

Infamy: Was "asked to leave" Brown University in 1967 for having a girl in his room after hours; was later awarded an honorary degree.

Original Job: Selling space on billboards in family business

Marriages: Judy Nye (divorced), Janie Shirley Smith (divorced), Jane Fonda, 1991 (separated, 2000)

Children: Laura Seydel, 1961; Robert Edward IV, 1963; (with Judy Nye). Rhett, 1965; Beau, 1968; Sara Jean "Jennie," 1969; (with Janie Shirley Smith).

Major Award: Elected to the Emmy Hall of Fame, 1991

Quote: "You don't have to be smart to make a lot of money."

TINA TURNER

Real Name: Anna Mae Bullock
Birthplace: Nutbush, TN
Birthdate: 11/26/39
Occupation: Singer, actor
Debut: (Song) "Fool in Love," 1960
Signature: "What's Love Go to Do with It?" 1984
Facts: "River Deep, Mountain High" (1966) was No. 1 in Britain and earned The Ike and Tina Turner Revue the chance to open for The Rolling Stones in 1969.

Became a Buddhist in the early '80s.

Endured years of physical abuse and extramarital affairs by then husband Ike.

Marriages: Ike Turner, 1956 (divorced, 1978); Erwin Bach (relationship)

Children: Raymond Craig Hill, 1958 (with Raymond Hill); Ronald Renelle "Ronnie," 1960 (with Ike Turner)

Major Awards: Grammy, Best R&B Duo or Group, "Proud Mary" (with Ike Turner), 1972; Grammy, Record of the Year and Best Pop Vocal—Female, "What's Love Got to Do with It?,"

1984; Grammy, Best Rock Vocal of the Year, "Better Be Good to Me," 1985; Grammy, Best Rock Vocal of the Year, "One of the Living," 1986; Grammy, Best Rock Vocal of the Year, "Back Where You Started," 1986; Grammy, Best Rock Vocal of the Year, *Tina Live in Europe,* 1988; inducted into Rock and Roll Hall of Fame, 1991

SHANIA TWAIN

Real name: Eileen Regina Twain
Birthplace: Windsor, Ontario
Birthdate: 8/28/65
Occupation: Singer, songwriter
Education: High school
Debut: (Album) *Shania Twain,* 1993
Signature: *Come on Over,* 1997
Facts: Grew up so poor her Canadian family often went without heat.

Says she's of Ojibwa Indian ancestry, but was actually adopted by her Indian stepfather. Shania means "I'm on my way" in Ojibwa dialect.

Raised her three younger siblings after her parents died in an auto accident when she was 21.

Come on Over is the best-selling album by a female artist ever, as well as the top country album of all time.

Original job: secretary
Marriage: Robert "Mutt" Lange, 1993
Major Awards: Grammy, Best Country Album, *The Woman in Me,* 1995; Best Country Song, "You're Still The One" (with Robert John "Mutt" Lange), 1998; Grammy, Best Country Vocal—Female, "You're Still The One," 1998; Grammy, Best Country Song, "Come on Over" (with Robert John "Mutt" Lange), 1999; Grammy, Best Country Vocal—Female, "Man! I Feel Like A Woman," 1999

LIV TYLER

Birthplace: New York, NY
Birthdate: 7/1/77
Occupation: Actor

Education: High school
Debut: (Film) *Silent Fall*, 1994
Signature: *Armageddon*, 1998
Facts: First came to the world's attention as the girl wearing a silver bra in the Aerosmith's 1994 video "Crazy," which also starred Alicia Silverstone.

As a child, believed her father was rocker Todd Rundgren, who was married to her mother, '70s Playboy Playmate Bebe Buell. But at an Aerosmith concert at age 11, she realized she greatly resembled Steven Tyler.

Likes to shop with her father: "We both wear the same size, and we'll just try on clothes for hours."

Was in a relationship with Joaquin Phoenix.
Original Job: Model
Famous Relative: Steve Tyler, Aerosmith lead singer, father
Quote: "It's important to surround yourself with beautiful friends and family who will say, 'You are a dork today.'"

STEVEN TYLER

Real Name: Steven Tallarico
Birthplace: Boston, MA
Birthdate: 3/26/48
Education: High school dropout
Debut: (Album) *Aerosmith*, 1973
Signature: Aerosmith
Facts: Met future Aerosmith members Joe Perry and Tom Hamilton at Lake Sunapee, NH, where their families had vacation houses.

Seriously injured in a motorcycle accident in 1981, capping a long period of discord and debauchery among band members. "I lay there in the hospital crying and flipping out, knowing some other group was going to step into our space. Through the stupor of my medication, I pictured a spotlight. We walked out of it."

When the band reformed in 1984, they got a contract with Geffen but had to audition first.

Aerosmith co-owns the West Holly-wood restaurant House of Blues with Dan Aykroyd and Jim Belushi.
Infamy: Alcohol and drug use including heroin addiction.

Sued his ex-wife in 1999 in an attempt to get her to return photographs taken of him in the nude after reading that she intended to publish them.
Marriages: Cyrinda Fox (divorced); Kathleen Tallarico (divorced, 1987); Theresa Barrick
Children: Liv, 1977 (with Bebe Buell). Mia, 1978 (with Cyrinda Fox). Chelsea, 1988; Taj, 1992.
Major Awards: Grammy, Best Rock Performance by a Duo or Group with Vocal, "Janie's Got a Gun," 1990; Grammy, Best Rock Performance by a Duo or Group with Vocal, "Crazy," 1994; Grammy, Best Rock Performance by a Duo or Group with Vocal, "Pink," 1998
Quote: On what is left for his band to accomplish: "I'm looking to be the lounge act on the space shuttle so I can sing 'Walk This Way' on the ceiling."

JOHN UPDIKE

Birthplace: Shillington, PA
Birthdate: 3/18/32
Occupation: Writer
Education: Harvard College, Oxford University
Debut: (Book) *The Carpentered Hen and Other Tame Creatures*, 1958
Signature: *Rabbit, Run*
Fact: Collects Walt Disney comic books.
Marriages: Mary Entwhistle Pennington, 1953 (divorced, 1974); Martha R. Bernhard, 1977
Children: Elizabeth, c. 1955; David, c. 1957; Michael, c. 1959; Miranda, c. 1960; (with Pennington). Three stepchildren
Major Awards: Pulitzer Prize, *Rabbit Is Rich*, 1982, *Rabbit at Rest*, 1991; American Book Award, *Rabbit Is Rich*, 1982

USHER

Real Name: Usher Raymond IV
Birthplace: Chattanooga, TN
Birthdate: 10/14/78
Occupation: Singer, songwriter, actor
Education: High school
Debut: (Album) *Usher*, 1994
Signature: *My Way*
Facts: Appeared on *Star Search* at age 13 and won as best teen vocalist.

Was signed by a record label while still in high school.

When he travels, decoys dressed like the singer head for packs of screaming fans so he can quietly escape.

Does up to 1,000 stomach crunches a day.
Quote: "I'm a ladies' man. But it really shocks me how attached women are to their emotions, whereas a man thinks more in terms of realities."

JAMES VAN DER BEEK

Birthplace: Cheshire, CT
Birthdate: 3/8/77
Occupation: Actor
Education: Attended Drew University
Debut: (Film) *Angus*, 1995
Signature: *Dawson's Creek*
Facts: Was identified as dyslexic in kindergarden and learned to read in a special class. Later became an honors student.

In eighth grade, he was sidelined from football with a concussion and discovered acting in community theater.

Depressed after reading about successful up-and-comers when he was unemployed, he went backpacking in Europe for six weeks. Upon returning, was offered a movie, play, and *Dawson's Creek*.

LUTHER VANDROSS

Birthplace: New York, NY
Birthdate: 4/20/51
Occupation: Singer, songwriter

Education: Attended Western Michigan University
Debut: (Song) "Everybody Rejoice (A Brand New Day)" from *The Wiz*, 1978
Signature: "Here and Now," 1990
Facts: Started playing the piano at age 3.

Sister was a member of the '50s group The Crests.

His first group, Listen My Brother, formed while he was a high school student, played at the Apollo and appeared on the first episode of *Sesame Street*.

He fights a continuous battle with his weight; he has seesawed between189 and 340 pounds.

His middle name is Ronzoni, the only food his mother could keep down during a diffcult pregnancy.

At one point, supported himself singing jingles for Pepsi-Cola, Juicy Fruit gum, and the U.S. Army.
Original Job: S&H Green Stamp defective-merchandise clerk
Major Awards: Grammy, Best R&B Vocal—Male, "Here and Now," 1990; Grammy, Best R&B Song, "Power of Love/Love Power," 1991; Grammy, Best R&B Vocal—Male, *Power of Love*, 1991; Grammy, Best R&B Vocal—Male, "Your Secret Love," 1996

VINCE VAUGHN

Birthplace: Buffalo Grove, IL
Birthdate: 3/28/70
Occupation: Actor
Education: High school
Debut: (TV) *China Beach*, 1989; (Film) *Rudy*, 1993
Signature: *Swingers*
Facts: First film role was a sex-education short, in which he played a guy trying to persuade his girl-friend to have sex with him.

Met *Swingers* writer and star Jon Favreau while filming *Rudy*. Favreau based the script on his late-night adventures in L.A. with Vaughn.

His father is named Vernon, and both of his sisters and all three

family dogs have names beginning with "V."

Stands 6' 5".
Relationship: Jody Lauren Adams, actor
Quote: "I made an independent movie thinking I'll have chicks crawling all over me. Instead, I got guys who emulate me because they—wrongly—think I'm some kind of real swinger."

DONATELLA VERSACE

Birthplace: Reggio di Calabria, Italy
Birthdate: 5/2/55
Occupation: Designer, businessperson
Education: University of Florence
Facts: Began working with her brother Gianni's rising fashion business in 1978. Her contributions include the design of ad campaigns and the introduction of a rock-and-roll sensibility to the clothes.

In the 1990s she created Versace's youthful Versus line and led the making of the perfume Blonde; she was the face in the fragrance's advertisements.

Became chief designer of the Versace empire upon her brother's murder; she had 12 weeks to finish a spring collection and mount the show.

Her influence has resulted in softer, sleeker business suits, with a greater emphasis on shape and color.

Has been recruited to spruce up the image of Prince Charles's companion, Camilla Parker Bowles.

Chain smokes.

Never eats until noon.
Marriage: Paul Beck, c. 1982
Children: Allegra, c. 1986; Daniel, c. 1991
Famous Relative: Gianni Versace, brother, deceased 1997
Quote: "For me, there's no middle way—I live my life in extremes…. If [a skirt is] tight, it should be super-tight. If I want to be blonde, it has to be platinum!"

GORAN VISNIJC

Birthplace: Sibenik, Croatia
Birthdate: 9/9/72
Occupation: Actor
Education: Academy of Dramatic Arts, Zagreb, Croatia
Debut: (TV) *Alistair MacLean's Night Watch*, 1995; (Film) *The Peacemaker*, 1997
Signature: *ER*
Facts: Served a mandatory tour in the Yugoslavian army as a paratrooper, and volunteered for another three months in the Croatian army during the Balkan conflict.

Is widely known in Croatia for playing Hamlet on the stage for years (he won the Croatian equivalent of a Tony award when he was 21).

His name is pronounced "GOR-an VISH-nick."

He is 6', 4".
Marriage: Ivana, sculptor

MARK WAHLBERG

Birthplace: Dorchester, MA
Birthdate: 6/5/71
Occupation: Actor, model, rap artist
Education: High school dropout
Debut: (Album) *Music for the People*, 1991; (Film) *Renaissance Man*, 1994
Signature: *Boogie Nights*, 1997
Facts: Left school at 14 to hustle on the street.

An original member with older brother in New Kids on the Block, he dropped out after six months.

Debut album under nom de rap.

Marky Mark was produced by his brother with his brother's money.

Has a third nipple, which was airbrushed out of Calvin Klein underwear ads.

Wore a 13-inch prosthetic penis and lost 30 pounds for his role in *Boogie Nights*.

Infamy: Convicted at age 16 for his involvement in the beating of two Vietnamese men during a robbery. Served 45 days in jail.

Was arrested on two occasions for yelling racial epithets at black schoolchildren. Gays and Asian-Americans also accused him of bias.

His public misconduct included a catfight with Madonna and an alleged assault on a security guard.

Famous Relative: Donnie Wahlberg, singer (original New Kids on the Block member), brother

CHRISTOPHER WALKEN

Real Name: Ronald Walken
Birthplace: New York
Birthdate: 3/31/43
Occupation: Actor
Education: Attended Hofstra University
Debut: (TV) *The Guiding Light*, 1954; (Film) *Me and My Brother*, 1968
Signature: *The Deer Hunter*, 1978
Facts: Studied dance as a child.

Spent the summer of 1960 as an assistant lion tamer.

Changed his name when a singer remarked, "I see you more as a Christopher."

Tested for the lead in *Love Story* and played Romeo in 1970.

Made a splash—and started his creepy public image—as Diane Keaton's mild yet deranged brother in *Annie Hall*.

In 1995, performed in one-man stage play he wrote, *Him*, about Elvis Presley.

A Christopher Walken mask outsold the Freddy Krueger mask in Halloween, 1996.

Is scared of guns and does not like to use them as props.

Original Job: Catalog model
Marriage: Georgianne, 1968
Major Award: Oscar, Best Supporting Actor, *The Deer Hunter*, 1978
Quote: "I'm such a pussycat in real life. I'm a song-and-dance man who played a few scary parts and got mistaken for the characters he plays."

BARBARA WALTERS

Birthplace: Boston, MA
Birthdate: 9/25/31
Occupation: Broadcast journalist
Education: Sarah Lawrence College
Debut: (TV) *The Today Show*, 1974
Signature: *20/20*
Facts: In 1957, Don Hewitt, now executive producer of *60 Minutes*, told Walters: "You're marvelous, but stay out of television."

Walters was the only woman reporter in the press group that accompanied President Nixon on his historic trip to China in 1972.

Original Job: Intent on becoming a teacher, went for her master's in education while working as a secretary
Marriages: Robert Henry Katz (annulled); Lee Guber (divorced); Merv Adelson (divorced, 1992); Sen. John Warner (relationship)
Child: Jacqueline Dena, 1968
Major Awards: Emmy, Best Host on a Talk Show, *Today*, 1975; Emmy, Best Interviewer, *The Barbara Walters Show*, 1982; 4 News and Documentary Emmys as correspondent; elected to the Television Hall of Fame, 1990

VERA WANG

Birthplace: New York, NY
Birthdate: 6/27/49
Occupation: Designer
Education: Sarah Lawrence College
Signature: Mariah Carey's wedding dress
Facts: Her parents emigrated from China and built a multimillion-dollar oil and pharmaceutical company in the U.S.

Competed in figure skating at the U.S. national championship in 1968.

Began designing bridal gowns after she saw a niche when she couldn't find anything mature and elegant for her own nuptials. Has designed wedding-wear for Sharon Stone, Holly Hunter, Uma Thurman and Chynna Phillips.

Original Job: *Vogue* fashion editor
Marriage: Arthur Becker, 1989
Children: Cecilia, 1990; Josephine, 1993; (both adopted).

SELA WARD

Birthplace: Meridian, MS
Birthdate: 7/11/56
Occupation: Actress
Education: University of Alabama
Debut: (Film) *The Man Who Loved Women*, 1983
Signature: *Once and Again*, 1999
Facts: Her name is from the Bible; it means "hallelujah" or "amen."

Was a cheerleader and homecoming queen in college.

Modeled before studying acting.

Was engaged to Peter "Robocop" Weller.

Appeared as Harrison Ford's murdered wife in *The Fugitive*.

Her favorite thing in life: a candle-lit bubblebath with her husband.

Original Job: Advertising art director
Marriage: Howard Sherman, 1992
Children: Austin Ward, 1994;

Anabella Raye, 1998
Major Awards: Emmy, Best Actress in a Drama Series, *Sisters,* 1994; Emmy, Best Actress in a Drama Series, *Once and Again,* 2000
Quote: "At the age of 43, I have never felt better in my life. Much more grounded, and very sexy. I feel like a juicy piece of fruit."

DENZEL WASHINGTON

Birthplace: Mt. Vernon, NY
Birthdate: 12/28/54
Occupation: Actor
Education: Fordham University, studied acting at the American Conservatory Theatre, San Francisco
Debut: (Film) *Carbon Copy,* 1981
Signature: *Malcolm X,* 1992 [see page 109 for a complete filmography]
Facts: Played Malcolm X in *When The Chickens Come Home To Roost* on Broadway, as well as in the 1992 Spike Lee movie.

In college, played football and basketball and wrote poetry before deciding to try acting.
Original Job: Drama instructor
Marriage: Pauletta Pearson, 1983
Children: John David, 1984; Katia, 1987; Malcolm, 1991; Olivia, 1991
Major Award: Oscar, Best Supporting Actor, *Glory,* 1989

WENDY WASSERSTEIN

Birthplace: Brooklyn, NY
Birthdate: 10/18/50
Occupation: Playwright
Education: Mount Holyoke College, City College of New York, Yale University School of Drama
Debut: (Stage) *Any Woman Can't,* 1973
Signature: *The Heidi Chronicles*
Facts: Almost enrolled in business school rather than pursuing drama.

Brother sent her a note prior to a premiere: "Can't come to play tonight. Am buying Nabisco."
Child: Lucy Jane, 1999

Famous Relative: Bruce Wasserstein, investment banking star, brother
Major Awards: Pulitzer Prize, *The Heidi Chronicles,* 1988; Tony, Best Play, *The Heidi Chronicles,* 1989

TIONNE WATKINS

Birthplace: Des Moines, IA
Birthdate: 4/26/70
Occupation: Singer, songwriter
Debut: (Album) *Oooooooohhh ... On the TLC Tip,* 1992; (Book) *Thoughts,* 1999
Signature: "Waterfalls," 1995 / "T-Boz"
Facts: TLC's original look featured colorful, baggy clothes, a hip-hop style previously reserved for men.

Suffers from sickle cell anemia; her bandmates didn't know until she collapsed during a 1995 concert.

The band's sophomore effort, *Crazysexycool,* is the bestselling album ever by a female group.

Soon after *Crazysexycool,* the band declared bankruptcy, blaming a low royalty clause in their contract.

Appeared in the movies *House Party 3* and *Belly.*

Thoughts contains her poetry and essays.
Original Jobs: Hair model, shampoo girl, manicurist
Marriage: D'Mon Rolison, 2000 (aka Mack 10, rap artist)
Major Awards: Grammy, Best R&B Album, *Crazysexycool,* 1995; Grammy, Best R&B Vocal—Duo or Group, "Creep," 1995; Grammy, Best R&B Album, *Fanmail,* 1999; Grammy, Best R&B Vocal—Duo or Group, "No Scrubs," 1999
Quote: "We stand up for the girl groups who always wanted to dress like this, but couldn't. We didn't show a stitch of our skin and we made it."

EMILY WATSON

Birthplace: London, England
Birthdate: 1/14/67
Occupation: Actress
Education: Bristol University, Eng-

land; London Drama Studio
Debut: (Film) *Breaking the Waves,* 1996
Signature: *Breaking the Waves,* 1996
Facts: At age 4, modeled for Laura Ashley.

Her parents didn't allow television in her childhood home.

Was a member of the Royal Shakespeare Company, which is where she met her husband.

For her role as Jacqueline du Pre in *Hilary and Jackie,* Watson first learned to play the cello, then to physically mimic du Pre's playing.

Is a devoted Londoner.
Original Jobs: Waitress; photocopier
Marriage: Jack Waters, 1995
Quote: "To be famous for pretending to be someone else is quite anonymous, in a way."

DAMON WAYANS

Birthplace: New York, NY
Birthdate: 9/4/60
Occupation: Comedian, actor, writer, director
Education: High school
Debut: (Film) *Beverly Hills Cop,* 1984; (TV) *Saturday Night Live,* 1985
Signature: *In Living Color*
Facts: Grew up poor as one of 11 children.

Began career performing stand-up in clubs.
Marriage: Lisa
Children: Damon Jr., 1983; Michael, 1985; Cara Mia, c. 1987; Kyla, c. 1990
Famous Relatives: Keenan Ivory Wayans, actor/producer/writer/ director, brother; Kim Wayans, actor, sister; Marlon Wayans, actor, brother; Shawn Wayans, actor, brother

SIGOURNEY WEAVER

Real Name: Susan Weaver
Birthplace: New York, NY
Birthdate: 10/8/49

Occupation: Actor
Education: Stanford University; Yale University (MFA)
Debut: (Stage) *The Constant Wife* (with Ingrid Bergman), 1974
Signature: *Alien*
Facts: Took her name from a character in *The Great Gatsby*.

As a senior at Stanford, she dressed as an elf and lived in a treehouse with her boyfriend.

Accepted at Yale Drama School as "Mr." Sigourney Weaver.
Marriage: Jim Simpson, 1984
Child: Charlotte, 1990
Famous Relatives: Sylvester "Pat" Weaver, president of NBC, father; Elizabeth Inglis, actor, mother

VERONICA WEBB

Birthplace: Detroit, MI
Birthdate: 2/25/65
Occupation: Model, writer, actor
Education: Attended New School for Social Research
Signature: *Veronica Webb Sight*
Facts: Was a cashier in a SoHo boutique when spotted by a makeup artist for the Click modeling agency. Fearing he was a fraud, she resisted calling him back until she was fired from her job.

While a top model for Chanel and Revlon, wrote articles for *Esquire*, *Details*, and other magazines.

Broke the color barrier in modeling when she became a multimillion-dollar Revlon model.
Original Job: Cashier

ANDREW LLOYD WEBBER

Birthplace: London, England
Birthdate: 3/22/48
Occupation: Composer, producer
Education: Magdelen College of Oxford University, Royal Academy of Music, Oxford, Guildhall School of Music, Royal College of Music
Debut: (Stage) *Joseph and the Amazing Technicolor Dreamcoat*, 1968

Signature: *The Phantom of the Opera*
Fact: In 1969, was commissioned by RCA to write an opera based on a single, "Jesus Christ Superstar."
Infamy: After firing Faye Dunaway from the play *Sunset Boulevard* in 1994 because, he said, she couldn't sing, Webber wrote a confidential letter of apology that he then allowed the *London Standard* to print in its entirety. Dunaway, claiming she could indeed sing, sued, and settled for a reported $1.5 million.
Marriages: Sarah Jane Tudor Hugill (divorced); Sarah Brightman (divorced); Madeleine Astrid Gurdon, 1991
Children: Nicholas; Imogen; Alastair, 1992; Richard, 1993; Billy, 1994; Isabella Aurora, 1996
Famous Relative: William Webber, London College of Music director, father
Major Awards: Grammy, Best Cast Show Album, *Evita* (with Tim Rice), 1980; Grammy, Best Cast Show Album, *Cats*, 1983; Grammy, Legend Award, 1990; New York Drama Critics Award, *Evita*, 1980; Tony, Best Score, *Evita* (music; Tim Rice, lyrics), 1980; Tony, Best Score, *Cats* (music; T. S. Eliot, lyrics), 1983; Tony, Best Musical, *The Phantom of the Opera*, 1988; Academy Award, Best Song, "You Must Love Me," (music; Tim Rice, lyrics), 1996

FOREST WHITAKER

Birthplace: Longview, TX
Birthdate: 7/15/61
Occupation: Actor, director, producer
Education: USC
Debut: (Film) *Fast Times at Ridgemont High*, 1982; (TV) *North and South*, 1985; (Film, directing) *Waiting to Exhale*, 1995
Signature: *The Crying Game*, 1992
Facts: Growing up in the Compton area of south central Los Angeles, he was an All-league defensive tackle on his high school football

team.

First attended college on a full sports scholarship; then switched schools, intending to be a classical tenor, on a Levar Burton Scholarship.
Marriage: Keisha Nash, 1996
Children: Ocean Alexander, c. 1990 (from a previous relationship); Autumn, stepdaughter, c. 1991; Sonnet Noel, 1996; True Isabella Summer, 1998
Famous relative: Damon Whitaker, actor, brother

BARRY WHITE

Birthplace: Galveston, TX
Birthdate: 9/12/44
Occupation: Singer, songwriter
Education: High school dropout
Debut: "Love's Theme" (with the Love Unlimited Orchestra, 1971)
Signature: "Can't Get Enough of Your Love, Babe," 1974
Facts: His birth certificate read "Barry Eugene Carter," but when White's unmarried father caught a look at his son's birth certificate, he had the name changed.

Credits his mother, who taught him how to harmonize at age 4, with providing his core of personal values.

According to his autobiography, White was an amateur couples therapist at the age of 14.

Went to jail for stealing tires at 14; claimed hearing Elvis's "It's Now or Never" in his cell convinced him to turn his life around.

After singing in vocal groups and a drumming stint, teenage White toiled as a songwriter, record producer, and label A&R man.

Wrote two songs for the kids show *The Banana Splits*.

His nicknames include The Maestro, The Prince of Pillow Talk, and Dr. Love.

Designs his own clothes and handpicks the tailors.
Original Jobs: News vendor, fry cook, construction worker

Marriages: Mary Smith (divorced); Glodean James, 1973 (divorced, 1988); Katherine Denton (relationship, 1994)
Children: Eight children
Major Awards: Grammy, Best R&B Vocal—Male, *Staying Power*, 1999
Quote: "Once my voice changed, there was no escaping its power."

ROBIN WILLIAMS

Birthplace: Chicago, IL
Birthdate: 7/21/51
Occupation: Actor
Education: Claremont Men's College, College of Marin, Juilliard
Debut: (TV) *Laugh-In*, 1977 [see page 109 for a complete filmography]
Signature: *Mork and Mindy*
Facts: Grew up on a 30-room estate in Bloomfield Hills, MI.

Spent most of childhood playing with his 2,000 toy soldiers.

Second wife was a former nanny of Robin's children and his personal assistant. She served as a producer for *Mrs. Doubtfire*, 1994.

In 2000, launched a weekly web-based show at RobinWilliams@audible.com.
Infamy: Sued for $6.2 million in 1986 by former companion Michelle Tish Carter, who claimed that he gave her herpes during their two-year relationship. Williams countersued for extortion. The suits were settled out of court for an undisclosed amount.

Shared cocaine with John Belushi only a few hours before Belushi's death.
Original Job: Street mime
Marriages: Valeri Velardi (divorced, 1978); Marsha Garces, 1989
Children: Zachary, 1983 (with Valeri Velardi). Zelda, 1989; Cody Alan, 1991
Major Awards: Grammy, Best Comedy Recording, *Reality...What a Concept*, 1979; Emmy, Best Individual Performance in a Variety or Music Program, *A Carol Burnett Special*, 1987; Grammy, Best Comedy Recording, *A Night at the Met*, 1987; Emmy, Best Individual Performance in a Variety or Music Program, *ABC Presents a Royal Gala*, 1988; Grammy, Best Comedy Recording, *Good Morning, Vietnam*, 1988; Grammy, Best Recording for Children, *Pecos Bill*, 1988; Oscar, Best Supporting Actor, *Good Will Hunting*, 1997

MICHELLE WILLIAMS

Birthplace: Kalispell, Montana
Birthdate: 9/9/80
Occupation: Actor
Education: High school
Debut: (TV) *Baywatch*, 1989; (Film) *Lassie*, 1994
Signature: *Dawson's Creek*
Facts: At 16, was legally emancipated from her parents so she could live on her own in Burbank, Calif.

Her father, a Republican, ran for the U.S. Senate twice in Montana.

Her favorite authors are Ayn Rand and Fyodor Dostoyevsky.

Cowrote a feature script set in a brothel with two friends.
Relationship: Morgan J. Freeman, director, screenwriter
Quote: "I can't imagine why anyone would want to be a sex symbol. It's so surface, so uninteresting and so boring. Sex symbols are a dime a dozen; you can find one on any street in Los Angeles."

VANESSA WILLIAMS

Birthplace: New York, NY
Birthdate: 3/18/63
Occupation: Singer, actor
Education: Syracuse University
Debut: (Album) *The Right Stuff*, 1988; (Film) *The Pick-Up Artist*, 1987
Signature: *Kiss of the Spider Woman*
Facts: Was the first black Miss America. Got hate mail from white-supremacist groups and also from blacks claiming she was too white.

Her debut album sold more than 500,000 copies.
Infamy: Forced to resign as Miss America in 1984, after *Penthouse* printed nude photos of her in leather bondage gear with another woman that had been taken several years earlier.
Marriage: Ramon Hervey, 1988 (divorced, 1996); Rick Fox, professional basketball player, 1999
Children: Melanie, 1987; Jillian, 1989; Devin, 1993 (with Ramon Hervey). Sasha Gabriella, 2000
Quote: "I've had four children. Going topless is no longer an option."

KEVIN WILLIAMSON

Birthplace: Bern, NC
Birthdate: 3/14/65
Occupation: Screenwriter, director, executive producer
Education: Attended East Carolina State University
Debut: (Filmwriting) *Scream*, 1996
Signature: *Dawson's Creek*
Facts: In high school, an English teacher told him he had little talent and shouldn't consider a writing career.

The real Dawson's Creek is located a few miles from his childhood home and was a favored hangout.

Like Dawson, Williamson has memorized many lines from *Jaws*.
Original Jobs: Actor, music-video director's assistant, dog-walker

BRUCE WILLIS

Real Name: Walter Bruce Willis
Birthplace: Idar-Oberstein, Germany
Birthdate: 3/19/55
Occupation: Actor
Education: Montclair State College
Debut: (Stage) *Heaven and Earth*, 1977
Signature: *Die Hard*, 1988
Facts: Was student council president in high school.

The stammer he'd had since childhood disappeared whenever he performed.

Willis and Demi Moore were married by singer Little Richard.

Has his own band, Bruno.

He and his family live in once sleepy Hailey, Idaho, in the Rockies. Attempting to revitalize the town, Willis bought nearly every building on Main Street.

Infamy: During his senior year in high school, was expelled after a racial disturbance and was only permitted to graduate because his father hired an attorney to get him reinstated.

Original Jobs: Du Pont plant worker, bartender, commercial actor for Levi's 501 jeans

Marriage: Demi Moore, 1987 (separated, 1998); Maria Bravo, model (relationship)

Children: Rumer Glenn, 1988; Scout Larue, 1991; Tallulah Belle, 1994

Major Award: Emmy, Best Actor in a Drama Series, *Moonlighting,* 1987; Emmy, Guest Actor, *Friends,* 2000

Quote: "Being famous, it's like alcohol—whatever you are, it's just a little more of that. If you're an ---hole, you're more of an ---hole; if you're a nice guy, you're more of a nice guy."

AUGUST WILSON

Real Name: Frederick August Kittel
Birthplace: Pittsburgh, PA
Birthdate: 4/27/45
Education: High school dropout
Occupation: Playwright
Debut: (Play) *Ma Rainey's Black Bottom,* 1981
Signature: *The Piano Lesson,* 1990
Fact: Founded the black activist theater company Black Horizon on the Hill in the 1960s.
Marriages: One prior marriage, Judy Oliver (divorced), Constanza Romero, 1994
Child: Sakina Ansari, 1970
Major Awards: Tony, Best Play, *Fences,* 1987; Pulitzer Prize, Best Play, *Fences,* 1987; Pulitzer Prize, Best Play, *The Piano Lesson,* 1990

CASSANDRA WILSON

Birthplace: Jackson, Mississippi
Birthdate: 12/4/55
Occupation: Jazz singer, composer
Education: attended Millsaps College; Jackson State University
Debut: (Album) *Point of View,* 1985
Signature: *New Moon Daughter,* 1995
Facts: Widely considered one of the top jazz singers of the 1990s, she studied classical piano for six years, then learned acoustic guitar. By age 15, she had written some 20 songs.

After moving to New York, joined forces with the Brooklyn-based M-Base movement (stands for macro-basic array of structured extemporizations), which tried to create music inspired from jazz and the contemporary urban scene.

Was selected by Wynton Marsalis for the lead vocal role in his jazz oratorio *Blood on the Fields,* which won the 1997 Pulitzer Prize for Music.

Original Job: Television station public-affairs assistant
Marriage: Bruce Lincoln (divorced); Isaach de Bankole, actor (engaged)
Child: Jeris, 1990
Major Award: Grammy, Best Jazz Vocal Recording, *New Moon Daughter,* 1995
Quote: "People don't see things in streams, they don't see what tends to connect us all together. That's what I see. That's what I try to get to."

OPRAH WINFREY

Birthplace: Kosciusko, MS
Birthdate: 1/29/54
Occupation: Talk show host
Education: Tennesee State University
Debut: (Radio Reporter) WVOL, Nashville, 1971–72
Signature: *The Oprah Winfrey Show*
Facts: Delivered Easter sermon to congregation when she was 2 years old.

Once approached Aretha Franklin as she was stepping out of a limo and convinced Franklin that she had been abandoned. Aretha gave her $100, which Oprah used to stay in a hotel.

After being sexually abused at age 9 by an older cousin and later by a family friend, she ran away from home at age 13.

She bore a child when she was 14, though the baby died as an infant.

As a college sophomore, was the first African-American news co-anchor on a local TV station.

In college, won the title of Miss Tennessee and competed in the Miss Black America contest.

She left college in 1975, just a few credits shy of her degree. She finally received a B.S. in communications and theater in 1987, at age 33.

Formed Oxygen Media with Marcy Carsey and Geraldine Laybourne. She says she'll give up her talk show in 2002 and focus on the female-oriented channel.

Along with her fiance, taught a course entitled "Dynamics of Leadership" to 110 graduate students at Northwestern University in 1999. Giving herself a grade of B, she is due to teach the class again in 2000.
Original Jobs: News reporter, WVOL radio, WTVF television, Nashville, TN
Relationship: Stedman Graham (engaged)
Major Awards: Emmy, Best Host of a Talk Show, *The Oprah Winfrey Show,* 1986, 1990, 1991, 1992, 1993, 1994, 1997

KATE WINSLET

Birthplace: Reading, England
Birthdate: 10/5/75
Occupation: Actor
Education: High school
Debut: (Film) *Heavenly Creatures,* 1994
Signature: *Titanic,* 1997
Facts: Her grandparents ran a local repertory theater, where uncle Robert Bridges and father Roger Winslet both worked as actors.

Appeared in a breakfast cereal commercial frolicking with a "honey monster" creature at age 11. By age 17, starred in her first feature film.

Weighing 180 pounds in high school, she had the unhappy nickname Blubber. Went on Weight Watchers to drop 50 pounds.

Original Job: Delicatessen worker
Marriage: Jim Threapleton, 1998
Major Award: Grammy, Best Spoken Word Album for Children, *Listen to the Storyteller* (with Wynton Marsalis and Graham Greene), 1999

REESE WITHERSPOON

Real Name: Laura Jean Reese Witherspoon
Birthplace: New Orleans, LA
Birthdate: 3/22/76
Occupation: Actor
Education: Attended Stanford University
Debut: (Film) *The Man in the Moon*, 1991; (TV) *Wildflower*, 1991
Signature: *Election*, 1999
Facts: She began acting and modeling at age 7.

Won a 10-state talent search and, at age 15 debuted in *The Man in the Moon*. By 23 she had appeared in 10 films.

Met future husband, Ryan Phillippe, at her twenty-first birthday party before they became an on-screen couple in 1999's *Cruel Intentions*.

Original Job: Model
Marriage: Ryan Phillippe, 1999
Child: Ava Elizabeth, 1999
Quote: "Thank God none of my movies have made any money. God forbid they should ever make any money."

SCOTT WOLF

Birthplace: Boston, MA
Birthdate: 6/4/68
Occupation: Actor
Education: George Washington University
Debut: (TV) *Evening Shade*, 1990
Signature: *Party of Five*
Facts: Majored in finance in college.

Played doubles tennis with Tony the Tiger in a long-running early 1990s Frosted Flakes commercial.

Proposed to actress Alyssa Milano by hiding a 1940s-vintage diamond engagement ring in a pumpkin, getting down on one knee to pop the question, then carving the gourd with a big heart. The pair subsequently broke off their engagement. For a time after, Wolf dated fellow *Po5* costar Paula Devicq.

ELIJAH WOOD

Birthplace: Cedar Rapids, IA
Birthdate: 1/28/81
Occupation: Actor
Debut: (Film) *Back to the Future II*, 1989
Signature: *The War*, 1994
Facts: His first acting role was when he was seven, playing the pint-sized executive in Paula Abdul's "Forever Your Girl" video.

Has appeared in more than 15 national commercials.

Gets more than 700 fan letters every week from adoring teenage girls.

Favorite actors include Tim Roth and Gary Oldman.

Original Job: Model, commercial actor

JAMES WOODS

Birthplace: Vernal, UT
Birthdate: 4/18/47
Occupation: Actor
Education: Massachusetts Institute of Technology
Debut: (Film) *The Visitors*, 1972
Signature: *Ghosts of Mississippi*
Facts: Majored in political science in college. His mother was also interested in politics and was once asked to run for lieutenant governor of Rhode Island, though she declined.

Modeled his voice as Hades for Disney's *Hercules* after an oily William Morris agent he knows.

Was formerly involved in a relationship with Heather Graham.
Infamy: He and then fiancé Sarah Owen were allegedly the objects of harassment in the late 1980s by actress Sean Young, with whom Woods supposedly had an affair. Hate mail and gifts of mutilated dolls arrived, though nothing was ever proven. After Owen split with Woods following their four-month marriage, she accused him in the tabloids of spousal abuse. Woods countered by saying that Owen had been the one staging the earlier harassment.
Marriage: Kathryn Greko, 1980 (divorced, 1983); Sarah Owen, 1989 (divorced, 1990); Missy Crider (twice engaged, never married); Alexis Thorpe (relationship)
Major Awards: Emmy, Best Actor in a Miniseries, *The Promise*, 1986; Emmy, Best Actor in a Special, *My Name Is Bill W*, 1988

TIGER WOODS

Real Name: Eldrick Woods
Birthplace: Cypress, CA
Birthdate: 12/30/75
Occupation: Golfer
Education: Attended Stanford University
Facts: Was introduced to golf by his athletic father at nine months; by age 2 had outputt Bob Hope on *The Mike Douglas Show*, by 6 had hit his first hole-in-one, and by 8 had broken 80.

Began listening to subliminal tapes at age 6, featuring such messages as "I believe in me," and "My will moves mountains."

A gifted athlete, is also a switch-hitter in baseball, plays shooting guard in basketball, runs 400-meter track, and has played wide receiver in football.

His ethnicity includes parts African-American, Thai, Chinese, and Indian. On applications requesting ethnic identity, he has described himself as Asian.

The nickname Tiger comes from father Earl's Green Beret army past; it was the moniker of a South Vietnamese officer who saved Earl's life on several occasions.

In 2000, won his sixth consecutive tournament, tying Ben Hogan for the second-longest winning streak. He finished in a tie for second in his seventh outing, but did claim the all-time money-winning crown.

Also in 2000, won the U.S. Open by a record-setting 15 strokes, and captured the British Open and the PGA championship as well. He is the first player to win three straight majors since Ben Hogan in 1953, and the first golfer to win back-to-back PGA titles since Denny Shute repeated in 1937.

Later in 2000, he signed a new five-year contract with Nike said to be worth $85 million or more.
Relationship: Joanna Jagoda
Major Awards: U.S. Golf Association National Junior Amateur Champion, 1991-1993; U.S. Amateur Golf Champion, 1994-1996; Masters Tournament winner, 1997; PGA Championship winner, 1999; U.S. Open winner, 2000; British Open winner, 2000; PGA Championship winner, 2000

NOAH WYLE

Birthplace: Los Angeles, CA
Birthdate: 6/4/71
Occupation: Actor
Education: High school
Debut: (TV) *Blind Faith*, 1990
Signature: *ER*
Facts: Is a Civil War buff.

Was given George Clooney's 1960 Oldsmobile Dynamic 88, with the hope that his so-called makeoutmobile would be as lucky for him as it had been for Clooney.

Plays billiards like a pool shark at the Hollywood Athletic Club and at his pool table at home.
Marriage: Tracy Warbin, 2000

WYNONNA

Real Name: Christina Claire Ciminella
Birthplace: Ashland, KY
Birthdate: 5/3/64
Occupation: Singer
Education: High school
Debut: (Song) "Had a Dream" (with The Judds), 1984
Signature: *Wynonna*
Facts: Drives a 1957 Chevy and a turquoise Harley-Davidson.

Had asthma as a child.

Adopted her name after the town of Wynona, OK, mentioned in the song "Route 66."

The Judds got their first recording contract when mother Naomi, a nurse, gave a tape to patient Diana Maher, daughter of record producer Brent Maher.
Marriage: Arch Kelley III, 1996 (divorced, 1999)
Children: Elijah, 1995; Pauline Grace, 1996
Famous Relatives: Naomi Judd, country singer, mother; Ashley Judd, actor, sister
Major Awards: Best Country Performance by a Group or Duo, "Mama He's Crazy," 1984; "Why Not Me," 1985; "Grandpa (Tell Me 'Bout the Good Old Days)," 1986; "Give a Little Love," 1988; "Love Can Build a Bridge," 1991; Grammy, Best Country Song, "Love Can Build a Bridge," 1991

YANNI

Real Name: Yanni Chrysomallis
Birthplace: Kalamata, Greece
Birthdate: 11/4/54
Occupation: Musician, pianist
Education: University of Minnesota
Debut: (Album) *Optimystique*, 1986
Facts: Former member of the Greek National Swimming Team.

Toured with the cult rock band Chameleon.

His music has been used on broadcasts of numerous sporting events, including the Tour de France, the Olympic Games, and the World Series.

Spent nine years as Linda Evans's signficant other.

RENEE ZELLWEGER

Birthplace: Katy, TX
Birthdate: 4/25/69
Occupation: Actor
Education: University of Texas
Debut: (Film) *The Texas Chainsaw Massacre 2*, 1986
Signature: *Jerry Maguire*, 1996
Facts: Her Texas hometown was so small it had neither a movie theater nor cable television.

Signed up for her first drama class in college simply because she needed the credit to complete her English degree. Fell in love with acting and declared herself a professional actor upon graduation.

Was a star cheerleader in high school.

Was a college friend of Matthew McConaughey; they appeared together in school productions.

Though practically every well-known actress under age 35 auditioned during a four-month hunt for the *Jerry Maguire* part, the relatively obscure Zellweger impressed Tom Cruise and writer Cameron Crowe with her freshness and offbeat quality—and the fact that she wasn't intimidated by her sizzling co-star.

Recevied a $200,000 "friendship" ring from Carrey.
Original Job: Bartender assistant
Relationship: Jim Carrey

CATHERINE ZETA-JONES

Birthplace: Swansea, Wales
Birthdate: 9/25/69
Occupation: Actor
Signature: *The Mask of Zorro*, 1998
Debut: (Film) *Sheherazade/Les 1001 Nuits*, 1990; (TV) *The Young Indiana Jones Chronicles*, 1992
Facts: As an infant, she contracted a virus which caused difficulty breathing, and has a tracheotomy scar.

As a child, she appeared on the stage in various British musicals, starting with Annie.

Was a major television star in the U.K. in the early '90s for her role in *The Darling Buds of May.* Moved to Hollywood to avoid the British press.

Zeta, her grandmother's Christian name, was added to distinguish herself from another Catherine Jones in Actors Equity.

Reportedly turned down producer and former studio chief Jon Peters' marriage proposal in 1996 because "I want to be known as an actress rather than a Hollywood wife."

Douglas gave her a vintage 1920s 10-carat, marquis-cut diamond engagement ring.

Relationship: Angus Macfadyen, actor (engaged, never married); Michael Douglas (engaged, 2000)
Child: Dylan Michael Douglas, 2000
Quote: "I think I came out of the womb loving makeup."

THE REGISTER OF THOUSANDS

Here's a celebrity database covering the multitudes of shakers and shapers, the near-great and notorious, those who grace the screen and the tube, the page and the stage—a resource to discover the real names, birthdates, birthplaces, occupations, and claims to fame of a large slice of pop culture. Those who are coy about their birthdates or are too new on the scene to be sufficiently well documented have been passed over for this year's list—but stay tuned.

AAMES, WILLIE (Willie Upton). Los Angeles, CA, 7/15/60. Actor. *Eight Is Enough.*

ABBOTT, JIM. Flint, MI, 9/19/67. One-handed baseball pitcher.

ABDUL, PAULA. Los Angeles, CA, 6/19/62. Singer, dancer, choreographer, divorced from Emilio Estevez. "Straight Up."

ABRAHAM, F. MURRAY. Pittsburgh, PA, 10/24/39. Actor. *Amadeus.*

ABRAHAMS, JIM. Milwaukee, WI, 5/10/44. Producer, writer, director. *Airplane!; The Naked Gun.*

ABRAHAMS, MICK. Luton, England, 4/7/43. Guitarist. Jethro Tull.

AD-ROCK, KING (Adam Horovitz). New York, NY, 10/31/66. Rap artist. The Beastie Boys.

ADAMS, BROOKE. New York, NY, 2/8/49. Actor. *Invasion of the Body Snatchers.*

ADAMS, BRYAN. Kingston, Canada, 11/5/59. Singer, songwriter. "(Everything I Do) I Do It for You."

ADAMS, DON. New York, NY, 4/19/26. Actor. Maxwell Smart on *Get Smart.*

ADAMS, DOUGLAS. Cambridge, England, 3/11/52. Novelist. *The Hitchhiker's Guide to the Galaxy.*

ADAMS, EDIE (Elizabeth Edith Enke). Kingston, PA, 4/16/29. Actor. *The Ernie Kovacs Show.*

ADAMS, MAUD (Maud Wikstrom). Lulea, Sweden, 2/12/45. Actor. *Octopussy.*

ADAMS, VICTORIA. 4/7/74. Singer. Posh Spice of the Spice Girls.

ADAMSON, STUART (William Adamson). Manchester, England, 4/11/58. Guitarist, singer. Big Country.

ADJANI, ISABELLE. Paris, France, 6/27/55. Actor. *Camille Claudel.*

AGAR, JOHN. Chicago, IL, 1/31/21. Actor, formerly married to Shirley Temple. *The Sands of Iwo Jima.*

AGASSI, ANDRÉ Las Vegas, NV, 4/29/70. Tennis Player.

AGNEW, PETE. Scotland, 9/14/46. Bassist, singer. Nazareth.

AGUTTER, JENNY. Taunton, England, 12/20/52. Actor. *Logan's Run.*

AIELLO, DANNY. New York, NY, 6/20/33. Actor, writer. *Moonstruck.*

AIKMAN, TROY KENNETH. Cerritos, CA, 11/21/66. Football player. Quarterback for the Dallas Cowboys.

AIMEE, ANOUK (Françoise Soyra Dreyfus). Paris, France, 4/27/32. Actor. *A Man and a Woman.*

AKERS, KAREN. New York, NY, 10/13/45. Cabaret singer.

ALBERT, EDDIE (Eddie Albert Heimberger). Rock Island, IL, 4/22/08. Actor, father of Edward. Oliver Wendell Douglas on *Green Acres.*

ALBERT, EDWARD. Los Angeles, CA, 2/20/51. Actor, son of Eddie. *Midway.*

ALBERT, MARV. 6/12/41.

Sportscaster.

ALBRECHT, BERNIE (Bernard Dicken). Salford, England, 1/4/56. Guitarist. Joy Division; New Order.

ALDA, ALAN (Alphonso D'Abruzzo). New York, NY, 1/28/36. Actor, writer, director, son of Robert Alda. Benjamin Franklin "Hawkeye" Pierce on *M*A*S*H.*

ALDRIN, BUZZ (Edwin Eugene Aldrin Jr.). Montclair, NJ, 1/20/30. Astronaut, businessman.

ALEXANDER, GARY. Chattanooga, TN, 9/25/43. Singer, guitarist. The Association.

ALEXANDER, JANE (Jane Quigley). Boston, MA, 10/28/39. Actor. *All the President's Men.* Head of the National Endowment for the Arts.

ALI, MUHAMMAD (Cassius Clay). Louisville, KY, 1/17/42. Boxing great.

ALLEN, DEBBIE. Houston, TX, 1/16/50. Choreographer, actor, sister of Phylicia Rashad. *Fame.*

ALLEN, DUANE. Taylortown, TX, 4/29/43. Singer. The Oak Ridge Boys.

ALLEN, JOAN. Rochelle, IL, 8/20/56. Actor. *Face/Off.*

ALLEN, KAREN. Carrollton, IL, 10/5/51. Actor. *Raiders of the Lost Ark.*

ALLEN, NANCY. New York, NY, 6/24/50. Actor. *Robocop.*

ALLEN, PAPA DEE (Thomas Allen). Wilmington, DE, 7/18/31. Keyboardist, singer. War.

ALLEN, RICK. Sheffield, England, 11/1/63. One-armed drummer. Def Leppard.

ALLEN, ROD (Rod Bainbridge). Leicester, England, 3/31/44. Bassist, singer. The Fortunes.

ALLEN, STEVE. New York, NY, 12/26/21. Writer, performer, variety show host, husband of Jayne Meadows. *The Steve Allen Show.*

ALLEN, VERDEN. Hereford, England, 5/26/44. Keyboardist. Mott The Hoople.

ALLEY, KIRSTIE. Wichita, KS, 1/12/51. Actor. Formerly married to Parker Stevenson. Rebecca Howe on *Cheers.*

ALLISON, JERRY. Hillsboro, TX, 8/31/39. Drummer. Buddy Holly & The Crickets.

ALLMAN, GREGG. Nashville, TN, 12/8/47. Keyboardist, guitarist, singer, formerly married to Cher. The Allman Brothers Band.

ALLSUP, MIKE. Modesto, CA, 3/8/47. Guitarist. Three Dog Night.

ALLYSON, JUNE (Ella Geisman). Westchester, NY, 10/7/17. Actor. *The Dupont Show Starring June Allyson; Lassie.*

ALMOND, MARC (Peter Almond). Southport, England, 7/9/59. Singer. Soft Cell.

ALONSO, MARIA CONCHITA. Cuba, 6/29/56. Actor. *The Running Man.*

ALPERT, HERB. Los Angeles, CA, 3/31/35. Trumpeter, band leader, cofounder of

A&M Records. The Tijuana Brass.

ALSTON, BARBARA. Brooklyn, NY, 1945. Singer. The Crystals.

ALSTON, SHIRLEY (Shirley Owens). Passaic, NJ, 6/10/41. Singer. The Shirelles.

ALT, CAROL. Queens, NY, 8/18/60. Supermodel.

ALTMAN, ROBERT. Kansas City, MO, 2/20/25. Director, writer, producer. *The Player.*

ALVARADO, TRINI. New York, NY, 1/10/67. Actor. *Rich Kids.*

AMIS, SUZY. Oklahoma City, OK, 1/5/61. Actor. *Titanic.*

AMOS, JOHN. Newark, NJ, 12/27/41. Actor. James Evans on *Good Times.*

AMOS, WALLY JR. Tallahassee, FL, 7/1/36. Business executive. Famous Amos chocolate chip cookies.

ANDERSON, ALFA. 9/7/46. Singer. Chic.

ANDERSON, HARRY. Newport, RI, 10/14/52. Actor. Judge Harry Stone on *Night Court.*

ANDERSON, IAN. Edinburgh, Scotland, 8/10/47. Singer, flautist. Jethro Tull.

ANDERSON, JON. Lancashire, England, 10/25/44. Singer, drummer. Yes.

ANDERSON, KEVIN. Illinois, 1/13/60. Actor. *Sleeping with the Enemy.*

ANDERSON, LAURIE. Chicago, IL, 6/5/47. Singer, performance artist.

ANDERSON, LONI. St. Paul, MN, 8/5/45. Actor. Receptionist Jennifer Marlowe on *WKRP in Cincinnati.*

ANDERSON, MELISSA SUE. Berkeley, CA, 9/26/62. Actor. Mary Ingalls Kendall on *Little House on the Prairie.*

ANDERSON, MELODY. Edmonton, Canada, 1/3/55. Actor. Dale Arden in *Flash Gordon.*

ANDERSON, RICHARD. Long Branch, NJ, 8/8/26. Actor.

Oscar Goldman on *The Six Million Dollar Man* and *The Bionic Woman.*

ANDERSON, RICHARD DEAN. Minneapolis, MN, 1/23/50. Actor. *MacGyver.*

ANDERSON, RICK. St. Paul, MN, 8/1/47. Bassist. The Tubes.

ANDERSON, TERRY. 10/27/47. Journalist, former hostage.

ANDERSSON, BENNY (Goran Andersson). Stockholm, Sweden, 12/16/46. Keyboards, singer. Abba.

ANDERSSON, BIBI. Stockholm, Sweden, 11/11/35. Actor. *The Seventh Seal.*

ANDES, MARK. Philadelphia, PA, 2/19/48. Bassist. Spirit.

ANDRESS, URSULA. Berne, Switzerland, 3/19/36. Actor. *Dr. No.*

ANDRETTI, MARIO. Montona Trieste, Italy, 2/28/40. Auto racer.

ANDREW, PRINCE. London, England, 2/19/60. British royalty, son of Queen Elizabeth II.

ANDREWS, ANTHONY. London, England, 1/12/48. Actor. *Brideshead Revisited.*

ANDREWS, BARRY. London, England, 9/12/56. Keyboardist. XTC.

ANKA, PAUL. Ottawa, Canada, 7/30/41. Singer, songwriter. "Diana."

ANN-MARGRET (Ann-Margret Olsson). Valsjobyn, Sweden, 4/28/41. Actor, singer. *Viva Las Vegas.*

ANNAUD, JEAN-JACQUES. Draveil, France, 10/1/43. Writer, director. *Quest for Fire; The Lover.*

ANNE, PRINCESS. London, England, 8/15/50. British royalty, daughter of Queen Elizabeth II.

ANSPACH, SUSAN. New York, NY, 11/23/42. Actor. *Five Easy Pieces.*

ANT, ADAM (Stewart Goddard). London, England, 11/3/54. Singer. Adam &

The Ants.

ANTHONY, MICHAEL. Chicago, IL, 6/20/55. Bassist. Van Halen.

ANTON, SUSAN. Oak Glen, CA, 10/12/50. Actor, singer. *Goldengirl.*

ANWAR, GABRIELLE. Laleham, England, 2/4/70. Actor. Tangoed with Al Pacino in *Scent of a Woman.*

APPICE, CARMINE. New York, NY, 12/15/46. Drummer. Vanilla Fudge.

AQUINO, CORAZON. Tarlac, Philippines, 1/25/33. Political leader. Former president of the Philippines.

ARAFAT, YASIR. Cairo, Egypt, 8/24/29. Political leader. Head of the PLO.

ARCHER, ANNE. Los Angeles, CA, 8/25/47. Actor. Wife of Michael Douglas in *Fatal Attraction.*

ARENHOLZ, STEPHEN. The Bronx, NY, 4/29/69. Actor.

ARGENT, ROD. St. Albans, England, 6/14/45. Keyboardist. The Zombies.

ARKIN, ALAN. New York, NY, 3/26/34. Actor, director, writer, folk singer, member of Second City, father of Adam Arkin (*Chicago Hope*). *The In-Laws.*

ARMATRADING, JOAN. Basseterre, West Indies, 12/9/50. Singer, songwriter. "Me, Myself, I."

ARMSTRONG, BESS. Baltimore, MD, 12/11/53. Actor. Julia Peters on *On Our Own.*

ARMSTRONG, BILLIE JOE Rodeo, CA, 2/17/72, Singer, songwriter, guitrarist, Green Day.

ARMSTRONG, NEIL. Wapakoneta, OH, 8/5/30. Astronaut.

ARNAZ, DESI JR. Los Angeles, CA, 1/19/53. Actor, singer, son of Lucille Ball and Desi Arnaz. *Here's Lucy.*

ARNAZ, LUCIE. Los Angeles, CA, 7/17/51. Actor, daughter of Lucille Ball and Desi

Arnaz, married to Laurence Luckinbill. *Here's Lucy.*

ARNESS, JAMES (James Aurness). Minneapolis, MN, 5/26/23. Actor, brother of Peter Graves. *Gunsmoke.*

ARNOLD, TOM Ottumwa, IA, 3/6/59. Actor, ex-husband of Roseanne. *Roseanne, True Lies.*

ARQUETTE, PATRICIA. New York, NY, 4/8/68. Actor, granddaughter of Cliff Arquette, sister of Rosanna, David and Alexis. *True Romance.*

ARQUETTE, ROSANNA. New York, NY, 8/10/59. Actor, granddaughter of Cliff Arquette, sister of Patricia, and inspiration for Toto song "Rosanna." *Desperately Seeking Susan.*

ARTHUR, BEATRICE (Bernice Frankel). New York, NY, 5/13/26. Actor. *Maude.*

ASH, DANIEL. 7/31/57. Guitarist, singer. Bauhaus; Love and Rockets.

ASHER, PETER. London, England, 6/22/44. Singer. Peter and Gordon.

ASHFORD, NICKOLAS. Fairfield, SC, 5/4/42. Singer. Ashford and Simpson.

ASHFORD, ROSALIND. Detroit, MI, 9/2/43. Singer. Martha & The Vandellas.

ASHLEY, ELIZABETH (Elizabeth Ann Cole). Ocala, FL, 8/30/39. Actor. *Evening Shade.*

ASNER, EDWARD. Kansas City, KS, 11/15/29. Actor. *Lou Grant.*

ASSANTE, ARMAND. New York, NY, 10/4/49. Actor. *The Doctors.*

ASTBURY, IAN. Heswall, England, 5/14/62. Singer. The Cult.

ASTIN, JOHN. Baltimore, MD, 3/30/30. Actor, formerly married to Patty Duke, father of Sean Astin. Gomez Addams on *The Addams Family.*

ASTIN, SEAN. Santa Monica,

CA, 2/25/71. Actor, son of John Astin and Patty Duke. *Encino Man.*

ASTLEY, RICK. Warrington, England, 2/6/66. Singer, songwriter. "Never Gonna Give You Up."

ASTON, JAY. London, England, 5/4/61. Singer. Bucks Fizz.

ASTON, JOHN. England, 11/30/57. Guitarist. Psychedelic Furs.

ATKINS, CHET. Luttrell, TN, 6/20/24. Virtuoso guitarist.

ATKINS, CHRISTOPHER. Rye, NY, 2/21/61. Actor. *The Blue Lagoon.*

ATKINSON, PAUL. Cuffley, England, 3/19/46. Guitarist. The Zombies.

ATTENBOROUGH, RICHARD. Cambridge, England, 8/29/23. Actor, producer, director. *Gandhi.*

ATWOOD, MARGARET. Ottawa, Canada, 11/18/39. Author, poet. *The Handmaid's Tale.*

AUBERJONOIS, RENE. New York, NY, 6/1/40. Actor. Security Chief Odo on *Deep Space Nine.*

AUERMANN, NADJA. Berlin, Germany, 1971. Supermodel.

AUTRY, ALAN. Shreveport, LA, 7/31/52. Actor. Bubba Skinner on *In the Heat of the Night.*

AVALON, FRANKIE (Francis Thomas Avallone). Philadelphia, PA, 9/18/40. Singer, actor. *Beach Blanket Bingo.*

AVORY, MICK. London, England, 2/15/44. Drummer. The Kinks.

AZARIA, HANK. 4/25/64. Actor. *The Simpsons.*

AZNAVOUR, CHARLES (Shahnour Varenagh Aznourian). Paris, France, 5/22/24. Singer, songwriter, actor. *Shoot the Piano Player.*

BACALL, LAUREN (Betty Perske). New York, NY, 9/16/24. Actor, widow of

Humphrey Bogart, formerly married to Jason Robards. *Key Largo.*

BACH, BARBARA. Queens, NY, 8/27/47. Actor, married to Ringo Starr. *The Spy Who Loved Me.*

BACHMAN, RANDY. Winnipeg, Canada, 9/27/43. Guitarist, singer. Bachman-Turner Overdrive; The Guess Who.

BACHMAN, ROBBIE. Winnipeg, Canada, 2/18/53. Drummer. Bachman-Turner Overdrive.

BADANJEK, JOHN. 1948. Drummer. Mitch Ryder & The Detroit Wheels.

BAEZ, JOAN. Staten Island, NY, 1/9/41. Folk singer and songwriter, peace and civil rights activist.

BAILEY, PHILIP. Denver, CO, 5/8/51. Singer, conga player, percussionist. Earth, Wind & Fire.

BAILEY, TOM. Halifax, England, 6/18/57. Singer, keyboardist. Thompson Twins.

BAIN, BARBARA. Chicago, IL, 9/13/31. Actor. *Mission: Impossible.*

BAIO, SCOTT. Brooklyn, NY, 9/22/61. Actor. Charles "Chachi" Arcola on *Happy Days.*

BAIUL, OKSANA. 11/16/77. Figure skater. Olympic Gold Medalist.

BAKER, ANITA. Detroit, MI, 12/20/57. R&B singer.

BAKER, CARROLL. Johnstown, PA, 5/28/31. Actor. *Kindergarten Cop.*

BAKER, CHERYL (Rita Crudgington). London, England, 3/8/54. Singer. Bucks Fizz.

BAKER, GINGER (Peter Baker). Lewisham, England, 8/19/40. Drummer. Cream; Blind Faith.

BAKER, JOE DON. Groesbeck, TX, 2/12/36. Actor. *Walking Tall.*

BAKER, KATHY. Midland, TX, 6/8/50. Actor. *Picket Fences.*

BAKER, MICKEY (McHouston Baker). Louisville, KY, 10/15/25. Singer. Mickey & Sylvia.

BAKKER, JIM. Muskegon, MI, 1/2/40. TV evangelist, participant in the PTL scandal.

BAKSHI, RALPH. Haifa, Palestine, 10/29/38. Animator, writer, director. *Fritz the Cat.*

BAKULA, SCOTT. St. Louis, MO, 10/9/55. Actor. *Quantum Leap.*

BALABAN, BOB. Chicago, IL, 8/16/45. Actor. *Midnight Cowboy, Little Man Tate.*

BALDWIN, ADAM. Chicago, IL, 2/27/62. Actor. *My Bodyguard.*

BALDWIN, DANIEL.. Massapequa, NY, 10/5/60. Actor. *Homicide.*

BALDWIN, STEPHEN. Massapequa, NY, 5/12/66. Actor. *Threesome.*

BALDWIN, WILLIAM. Massapequa, NY, 2/21/63. Actor, married to Chynna Phillips. *Backdraft.*

BALIN, MARTY (Martyn Jerel Buchwald). Cincinnati, OH, 1/30/43. Singer. Jefferson Airplane/Starship.

BALL, DAVID. Blackpool, England, 5/3/59. Keyboardist. Soft Cell.

BALL, ROGER. Dundee, Scotland, 6/4/44. Alto and baritone saxophonist. Average White Band.

BALLARD, HANK. Detroit, MI, 11/18/36. Singer/songwriter. "Work with Me Annie."

BALLARD, KAYE (Catherine Gloria Balotta). Cleveland, OH, 11/20/26. Actor, singer.

BALSLEY, PHILIP. 8/8/39. Singer. Kingsmen; Statler Brothers.

BAMBAATAA, AFRIKA. The Bronx, NY, 1958. Rap/hip-hop DJ.

BAN BREATHNACH, SARAH. 5/5/47. Author. *Simple Abundance.*

BANALI, FRANKIE.

11/14/55. Musician. Quiet Riot.

BANANA (Lowell Levinger). Cambridge, MA, 1946. Keyboardist, guitarist. The Youngbloods.

BANCROFT, ANNE (Anna Maria Italiano). The Bronx, NY, 9/17/31. Actor. Mrs. Robinson in *The Graduate.*

BANKS, TONY. East Heathly, England, 3/27/51. Keyboardist. Genesis.

BARANSKI, CHRISTINE Buffalo, NY, 5/2/52. Actor. *Cybill.*

BARBATA, JOHN. 4/1/45. Drummer. The Turtles; Jefferson Starship.

BARBEAU, ADRIENNE. Sacramento, CA, 6/11/45. Actor. Carol on *Maude.*

BARBIERI, RICHARD. 11/30/57. Keyboardist. Japan.

BARDOT, BRIGITTE (Camille Javal). Paris, France, 9/28/34. Sex goddess. *And God Created Woman.*

BARGERON, DAVE. Massachusetts, 9/6/42. Trombonist. Blood, Sweat and Tears.

BARKER, BOB. Darrington, WA, 12/12/23. Game show host. *The Price Is Right.*

BARKER, CLIVE. Liverpool, England, 10/5/52. Author. *The Inhuman Condition.*

BARKIN, ELLEN. The Bronx, NY, 4/16/54. Actor. Separated from Gabriel Byrne. *Sea of Love.*

BARNES, LEO. 10/5/55. Musician. Hothouse Flowers.

BARRE, MARTIN. 11/17/46. Guitarist. Jethro Tull.

BARRERE, PAUL. Burbank, CA, 7/3/48. Lead guitarist. Little Feat.

BARRETT, ASTON. Kingston, Jamaica, 11/22/46. Bassist. Bob Marley & The Wailers.

BARRETT, MARCIA. St. Catherine's, Jamaica, 10/14/48. Singer. Boney M.

BARRETT, RONA. New York, NY, 10/8/36. News correspondent, columnist.

BARRETT, SYD (Roger Barrett). Cambridge, England, 1/6/46. Singer, guitarist. Pink Floyd.

BARRY, DAVE. 7/3/47. Columnist, author. *Dave's World*.

BARRY, MARION. Itta Bena, MS, 3/6/36. Mayor of Washington, served six-month prison term for cocaine possession.

BARRYMORE, JOHN DREW. Beverly Hills, CA, 6/4/32. Actor, father of Drew Barrymore.

BARSON, MIKE. England, 5/21/58. Keyboardist. Madness.

BARTHOL, BRUCE. Berkeley, CA, 1947. Bassist. Country Joe & The Fish.

BARYSHNIKOV, MIKHAIL. Riga, Latvia, 1/28/48. Dancer, actor. *White Nights*.

BATEMAN, JASON. Rye, NY, 1/14/69. Actor, brother of Justine. David on *The Hogan Family*.

BATEMAN, JUSTINE. Rye, NY, 2/19/66. Actor, sister of Jason. Mallory Keaton on *Family Ties*.

BATES, ALAN. Allestree, England, 2/17/34. Actor. *An Unmarried Woman*.

BATTLE, KATHLEEN. Portsmouth, OH, 8/13/48. Opera singer.

BAUER, JOE. Memphis, TN, 9/26/41. Drummer. The Youngbloods.

BAUER, STEVEN (Steven Echevarria). Havana, Cuba, 12/2/56. Actor, formerly married to Melanie Griffith. *Wiseguy*.

BAUMGARTNER, STEVE. Philadelphia, PA, 10/28/67. Writer. *The Rogue Element*.

BAXTER, JEFF "SKUNK." Washington, DC, 12/13/48. Lead Guitarist. Steely Dan; The Doobie Brothers.

BAXTER, KEITH. Monmouthshire, Wales, 4/29/33. Actor.

BAXTER, MEREDITH. Los Angeles, CA, 6/21/47. Actor, formerly married to David Birney. Elyse Keaton on *Family Ties*.

BAY, WILLOW. 12/28/63. Model, television journalist.

BEACHAM, STEPHANIE. Hertfordshire, England, 2/28/47. Actor. Sable Scott Colby on *The Colbys*.

BEAKY (John Dymond). Salisbury, England, 7/10/44. Guitarist. Dave Dee, Dozy, Beaky, Mick and Tich.

BEALS, JENNIFER. Chicago, IL, 12/19/63. Actor. *Flashdance*.

BEARD, FRANK. Dallas, TX, 12/10/49. Drummer. ZZ Top.

BEASLEY, ALLYCE. Brooklyn, NY, 7/6/54. Actor. Agnes Dipesto on *Moonlighting*.

BEATRICE, PRINCESS. London, England, 8/8/88. British royalty, daughter of Prince Andrew and the Duchess of York.

BEATTY, NED. Lexington, KY, 7/6/37. Actor. *Deliverance*.

BECK, JEFF. Wallington, England, 6/24/44. Guitarist. The Yardbirds; The Jeff Beck Group; The Jan Hammer Group.

BECK, JOHN. Chicago, IL, 1/28/43. Actor. Mark Graison on *Dallas*.

BECK, MICHAEL. Memphis, TN, 2/4/49. Actor. *The Warriors*.

BECKER, BORIS. Liemen, Germany, 11/22/67. Tennis player.

BECKER, WALTER. New York, NY, 2/20/50. Bassist. Steely Dan.

BECKLEY, GERRY. Texas, 9/12/52. Singer, guitarist. America.

BEDELIA, BONNIE. New York, NY, 3/25/48. Actor. *Presumed Innocent*.

BEDFORD, MARK. London, England, 8/24/61. Bassist. Madness.

BEEFHEART, CAPTAIN (Don Van Vliet). Glendale, CA,

1/15/41. Singer, high school friend of Frank Zappa. Captain Beefheart & The Magic Band.

BEERS, GARY. 6/22/57. Bassist, singer. INXS

BEGLEY, ED JR. Los Angeles, CA, 9/16/49. Actor. Dr. Victor Ehrlich on *St. Elsewhere*.

BEL GEDDES, BARBARA New York, NY, 10/31/22. Actor. *Dallas*.

BELAFONTE, HARRY. New York, NY, 3/1/27. Actor, singer, father of Shari. "The Banana Boat Song."

BELAFONTE, SHARI. New York, NY, 9/22/54. Actor, daughter of Harry. *Hotel*.

BELL, ANDY. Peterborough, England, 4/25/64. Singer. Erasure.

BELL, RICKY. Boston, MA, 9/18/67. Singer. New Edition.

BELL, ROBERT. Youngstown, OH, 10/8/50. Bassist. Kool & The Gang.

BELL, RONALD. Youngstown, OH, 11/1/51. Saxophonist. Kool & The Gang.

BELLADONNA, JOEY. Oswego, NY. Singer. Anthrax.

BELLAMY, GEORGE. Sunderland, England, 10/8/41. Guitarist. The Tornados.

BELLAMY, TONY. Los Angeles, CA, 9/12/40. Singer, guitarist. Redbone.

BELLO, FRANK. 7/9/65. Bassist. Anthrax.

BELMONDO, JEAN-PAUL. Paris, France, 4/9/33. Actor. *Breathless*.

BELUSHI, JIM. Chicago, IL, 6/15/54. Actor, brother of late John Belushi. *K-9*.

BENATAR, PAT (Pat Andrzejewski). Brooklyn, NY, 1/10/53. Singer. "Heartbreaker."

BENBEN, BRIAN. Newburgh, NY. Actor. Dream On. Married to Madeline Stowe.

BENEDICT, DIRK (Dirk Niewoehner). Helena, MT, 3/1/45. Actor. Lt. Templeton

Peck on *The A-Team*.

BENJAMIN, RICHARD. New York, NY, 5/22/38. Actor, director. *Love at First Bite; Goodbye, Columbus*.

BENNETT, BRIAN. London, England, 2/9/40. Drummer. The Shadows.

BENNETT, ESTELLE. New York, NY, 7/22/44. Singer. The Ronettes.

BENNETT, PATRICIA. New York, NY, 4/7/47. Singer. The Chiffons.

BENSON, GEORGE. Pittsburgh, PA, 3/22/43. Singer, guitarist. "Give Me the Night."

BENSON, RENALDO. Detroit, MI, 1947. Singer. The Four Tops.

BENSON, ROBBY (Robby Segal). Dallas, TX, 1/21/56. Actor, writer, director. *Ice Castles*.

BERENDT, JOHN. 12/5/39. Author. *Midnight in the Garden of Good and Evil*.

BERENGER, TOM. Chicago, IL, 5/31/49. Actor. *Platoon*.

BERENSON, MARISA. New York, NY, 2/15/47. Actor. *Barry Lyndon*.

BERGEN, POLLY (Nellie Paulina Burgin). Knoxville, TN, 7/14/30. Singer, actor. *The Winds of War*.

BERGER, ALAN. 11/8/49. Bassist. Southside Johnny & The Asbury Jukes.

BERGMAN, INGMAR. Uppsala, Sweden, 7/14/18. Writer, director. *The Silence*.

BERKLEY, ELIZABETH. 7/28/72. Actor. *Showgirls*.

BERKOWITZ, DAVID. New York, NY, 6/1/53. Serial killer. Son of Sam.

BERLE, MILTON (Milton Berlinger). New York, NY, 7/12/08. Actor. *The Milton Berle Show*.

BERNHARD, SANDRA. Flint, MI, 6/6/55. Actor, singer. *Roseanne*.

BERNSEN, CORBIN. Los Angeles, CA, 9/7/54. Actor, married to Amanda Pays.

Arnie Becker on *L.A. Law.*

BERRI, CLAUDE (Claude Langmann). Paris, France, 7/1/34. Actor, director, producer of films.

BERRY, BILL. Hibbing, MN, 7/31/58. Drummer. R.E.M.

BERRY, CHUCK. San Jose, CA, 10/18/26. Rock and Roll legend, singer and guitarist. "Johnny B. Goode."

BERRY, JAN. Los Angeles, CA, 4/3/41. Singer. Jan & Dean.

BERTINELLI, VALERIE. Wilmington, DE, 4/23/60. Actor, married to Eddie Van Halen. Barbara Cooper Royer on *One Day at a Time.*

BETTS, DICKEY. West Palm Beach, FL, 12/12/43. Guitarist, singer. The Allman Brothers Band.

BIALIK, MAYIM. San Diego, CA, 12/12/75. Actor. *Blossom.*

BIEHN, MICHAEL. Anniston, AL, 7/31/56. Actor. *The Terminator.*

BIG FIGURE, THE (John Martin). 1947. Drummer. Dr. Feelgood.

BILLINGSLEY, BARBARA. Los Angeles, CA, 12/22/22. Actor. June Cleaver on *Leave It to Beaver.*

BILLINGSLEY, PETER. New York, NY, 1972. Child actor. *A Christmas Story.*

BILLINGSLEY, RAY. Wake Forest, NC, 7/25/57. Cartoonist. *Curtis.*

BIRD, LARRY. West Baden, IN, 12/7/56. Basketball great. Boston Celtics.

BIRNEY, DAVID. Washington, DC, 4/23/39. Actor, formerly married to Meredith Baxter. *St. Elsewhere.*

BIRRELL, PETE. Manchester, England, 5/9/41. Bassist. Freddie & The Dreamers.

BIRTLES, BEEB (Gerard Birtlekamp). Amsterdam, the Netherlands, 11/28/48. Guitarist. The Little River Band.

BISHOP, JOEY (Joseph Gotl-

lieb). The Bronx, NY, 2/3/18. Actor. *The Joey Bishop Show.*

BISSET, JACQUELINE. Waybridge, England, 9/13/44. Actor. *The Deep.*

BISSET, JOSIE. Seattle, WA, 10/5/70. Actor. *Melrose Place.*

BIVINS, MICHAEL. 8/10/68. Singer. New Edition, Bell Biv DeVoe.

BLACK, CILLA (Cilla White). Liverpool, England, 5/27/43. Singer, TV personality.

BLACK, JET (Brian Duffy). England, 8/26/58. Drummer. The Stranglers.

BLACK, KAREN (Karen Ziegler). Park Ridge, IL, 7/1/42. Actor. *Easy Rider.*

BLACK, LISA HARTMAN. 6/1/56. Actor, married to Clint Black. *Knot's Landing.*

BLACKMON, LARRY. New York, 5/29/56. Singer, drummer. Cameo.

BLACKMORE, RITCHIE. Weston-Super-Mare, England, 4/14/45. Guitarist. Deep Purple; Rainbow.

BLADD, STEPHEN JO. Boston, MA, 7/13/42. Drummer, singer. The J. Geils Band.

BLADES, RUBEN. Panama City, Panama, 7/16/48. Actor, singer. *The Milagro Beanfield War.*

BLAIR, BONNIE. Cornwall, NY, 3/18/64. Speed skater.

BLAIR, LINDA. Westport, CT, 1/22/59. Actor. *The Exorcist.*

BLAKE, ROBERT (Michael Gubitosi). Nutley, NJ, 9/18/33. Actor. *Baretta.*

BLAKELY, SUSAN. Frankfurt, Germany, 9/7/50. Actor. *Rich Man, Poor Man.*

BLAKLEY, ALAN. Bromley, England, 4/1/42. Guitarist. Brian Poole & The Tremeloes.

BLAND, BOBBY. Rosemark, TN, 1/27/30. Singer.

BLASS, BILL. Ft. Wayne, IN, 6/22/22. Fashion designer.

BLEDSOE, TEMPESTT. Chicago, IL, 8/1/73. Actor.

Vanessa Huxtable on *The Cosby Show.*

BLEETH, YASMINE. 6/14/68. Actor. *Baywatch.*

BLOOM, CLAIRE. London, England, 2/15/31. Actor. *Richard III.*

BLOOM, ERIC. Long Island, NY, 12/1/44. Lead guitarist, keyboardist. Blue Öyster Cult.

BLOW, KURTIS (Kurtis Walker). New York, NY, 8/9/59. DJ, rapper. "The Breaks."

BLUECHEL, TED JR. San Pedro, CA, 12/2/42. Singer, drummer. The Association.

BLUME, JUDY. Elizabeth, NJ, 2/12/38. Novelist. *Are You There God? It's Me Margaret.*

BLUNSTONE, COLIN. Hatfield, England, 6/24/45. Singer. The Zombies.

BOBBY G. (Bobby Gubby). London, England, 8/23/53. Singer. Bucks Fizz.

BOGERT, TIM. Richfield, NJ, 8/27/44. Bassist. Vanilla Fudge.

BOGLE, BOB. Portland, OR, 1/16/37. Guitarist, bassist. The Ventures.

BOGOSIAN, ERIC. Woburn, MA, 4/24/53. Actor, writer. *Talk Radio.*

BOLDER, TREVOR. 6/9/50. Bassist. Spiders from Mars; Uriah Heep.

BOLOGNA, JOSEPH. Brooklyn, NY, 12/30/34. Actor. *Chapter Two.*

BONADUCE, DANNY. 8/13/59. Actor, radio personality. Danny on *The Partridge Family.*

BOND, RONNIE (Ronnie Bullis). Andover, England, 5/4/43. Drummer. The Troggs.

BONDS, GARY (Gary Anderson). Jacksonville, FL, 6/6/39. Singer.

BONET, LISA. San Francisco, CA, 11/16/67. Actor, formerly married to Lenny Kravitz. Denise Huxtable on

The Cosby Show.

BONNER, FRANK. Little Rock, AR, 2/28/42. Actor. Herb Tarlek on *WKRP in Cincinnati.*

BONO, CHASTITY. Los Angeles, CA, 3/4/69. Daughter of Sonny and Cher.

BONSALL, BRIAN. 12/3/82. Child actor. *Family Ties.*

BONSALL, JOE. Philadelphia, PA, 5/18/48. Singer. The Oak Ridge Boys.

BOONE, PAT. Jacksonville, FL, 6/1/34. Singer, actor. *The Pat Boone Show.*

BOONE, STEVE. North Carolina, 9/23/43. Bassist, singer. The Lovin' Spoonful.

BOOTHE, POWERS. Snyder, TX, 6/1/49. Actor. *Guyana Tragedy: The Story of Jim Jones.*

BORGNINE, ERNEST (Ernest Borgnino). Hamden, CT, 1/24/17. Actor. *McHale's Navy.*

BOSSON, BARBARA. Charleroi, PA, 11/1/39. Actor, married to producer Steven Bochco. Fay Furillo on *Hill Street Blues.*

BOSTWICK, BARRY. San Mateo, CA, 2/24/45. Actor. *The Rocky Horror Picture Show.*

BOTTOMS, JOSEPH. Santa Barbara, CA, 4/22/54. Actor. *The Black Hole.*

BOTTOMS, SAM. Santa Barbara, CA, 10/17/55. Actor. *Apocalypse Now.*

BOTTOMS, TIMOTHY. Santa Barbara, CA, 8/30/51. Actor. *Johnny Got His Gun.*

BOTTUM, RODDY. Los Angeles, CA, 7/1/63. Keyboardist. Faith No More.

BOUCHARD, JOE. Long Island, NY, 11/9/48. Bassist, singer. Blue Öyster Cult.

BOWE, RIDDICK. New York, NY, 8/10/67. Boxer, former heavyweight champion of the world.

BOWERS, TONY. 10/31/56. Bassist. Simply Red.

BOWIE, DAVID (David Jones). Brixton, England, 1/8/47. Singer, actor, married to Iman. *Ziggy Stardust and the Spiders from Mars.*

BOX, MICK. London, England, 6/8/47. Guitarist, songwriter. Uriah Heep.

BOXLEITNER, BRUCE. Elgin, IL, 5/12/50. Actor, married to Melissa Gilbert. *Scarecrow and Mrs. King.*

BOY GEORGE (George O'Dowd). Eltham, England, 6/14/61. Singer. Culture Club.

BOYLE, LARA FLYNN. Davenport, IA, 3/24/70. Actor. *Twin Peaks.*

BOYLE, PETER. Philadelphia, PA, 10/18/33. Actor. *Young Frankenstein.*

BRACCO, LORRAINE. Brooklyn, NY, 10/2/54. Actor. *GoodFellas.*

BRADBURY, RAY. Waukegan, IL, 8/22/20. Novelist. *The Martian Chronicles.*

BRAGG, BILLY (Steven Bragg). Barking, England, 12/20/57. Punk/R&B singer, songwriter.

BRAID, LES (William Braid). Liverpool, England, 9/15/41. Bassist. The Swinging Blue Jeans.

BRAMLETT, BONNIE. Acton, IL, 11/8/44. Singer. Delaney & Bonnie.

BRAMLETT, DELANEY. Pontotoc County, MS, 7/1/39. Guitarist, singer. Delaney & Bonnie.

BRANDAUER, KLAUS MARIA. Altaussee, Austria, 6/22/44. Actor. *Out of Africa.*

BRATTON, CREED. Sacramento, CA, 2/8/43. Guitarist. The Grass Roots.

BRAUNN, ERIK. Boston, MA, 8/11/50. Guitarist, singer. Iron Butterfly.

BREATHED, BERKE. Encino, CA, 6/21/57. Cartoonist. *Bloom County.*

BRENNAN, EILEEN. Los Angeles, CA, 9/3/34. Actor. *Private Benjamin.*

BRENNER, DAVID. Philadelphia, PA, 2/4/45. Stand-up comedian. *Nightlife.*

BREWER, DONALD. Flint, MI, 9/3/48. Drummer. Grand Funk Railroad.

BRICKELL, EDIE. Oak Cliff, TX, 1966. Singer, songwriter, married to Paul Simon. Edie Brickell and New Bohemians.

BRIDGES, BEAU (Lloyd Vernet Bridges III). Los Angeles, CA, 12/9/41. Actor, director, brother of Jeff. *The Fabulous Baker Boys.*

BRIDGES, TODD. San Francisco, CA, 5/27/65. Actor. Willis Jackson on *Diff'rent Strokes.*

BRIGATI, EDDIE. Garfield, NJ, 10/22/46. Singer, percussionist. The (Young) Rascals.

BRIGGS, DAVID. Melbourne, Australia, 1/26/51. Guitarist. The Little River Band.

BRILEY, ALEX. 4/12/56. Singer. The Village People.

BRIMLEY, WILFORD. Salt Lake City, UT, 9/27/34. Actor. *Cocoon.*

BRINKLEY, DAVID. Wilmington, NC, 7/10/20. Pioneer news journalist and anchor. *This Week with David Brinkley.*

BRIQUETTE, PETE (Patrick Cusack). Ireland, 7/2/54. Bassist, singer. The Boomtown Rats.

BRITTANY, MORGAN (Suzanne Cupito). Los Angeles, CA, 12/5/51. Actor. Katherine Wentworth on *Dallas.*

BRITTON, CHRIS. Watford, England, 6/21/45. Guitarist. The Troggs.

BROLIN, JAMES (James Bruderlin). Los Angeles, CA, 7/18/40. Actor, father of Josh. Dr. Steven Kiley on *Marcus Welby, M.D.*

BRONSON, CHARLES (Charles Buchinsky). Ehrenfield, PA, 11/3/21. Actor, widower of Jill Ireland.

Death Wish.

BROOKER, GARY. Southend, England, 5/29/45. Singer, keyboardist. Procol Harum.

BROOKS, ALBERT (Albert Einstein). Los Angeles, CA, 7/22/47. Actor, writer, director. *Defending Your Life.*

BROOKS, LALA. Brooklyn, NY, 1946. Singer. The Crystals.

BROTHERS, JOYCE (Joyce Bauer). New York, NY, 10/20/27. Psychologist.

BROWN, BLAIR. Washington, DC, 1948. Actor. *The Days and Nights of Molly Dodd.*

BROWN, BOBBY. Boston, MA, 2/5/69. Singer, dancer. "My Perogative."

BROWN, BRYAN. Panania, Australia, 6/23/47. Actor, married to Rachel Ward. *FX.*

BROWN, DAVID. Houston, TX, 2/15/47. Bassist. Santana.

BROWN, ERROL. Kingston, Jamaica, 11/12/48. Singer. Hot Chocolate.

BROWN, GEORG STANFORD. Havana, Cuba, 6/24/43. Actor. *Colossus: The Forbin Project.*

BROWN, GEORGE. Jersey City, NJ, 1/5/49. Drummer. Kool and The Gang.

BROWN, HAROLD. Long Beach, CA, 3/17/46. Drummer. War.

BROWN, IAN. Sale, England, 2/20/63. Singer. Stone Roses.

BROWN, JAMES. Augusta, GA, 5/3/33. The Godfather of Soul.

BROWN, JIM. St. Simons Island, GA, 2/17/36. Football player, actor. *The Dirty Dozen.*

BROWN, JIMMY. Birmingham, England, 11/20/57. Drummer. UB40.

BROWN, MELANIE. 5/29/75. Singer. Scary Spice of the Spice Girls.

BROWN, MICHAEL (Michael Lookofsky). New York, NY,

4/25/49. Keyboardist. The Left Banke.

BROWNE, JACKSON. Heidelberg, Germany, 10/9/48, Singer, songwriter.

BRUCE, JACK. Glasgow, Scotland, 5/14/43. Singer, bassist. Cream.

BRUCE, MICHAEL. 3/16/48. Guitarist, keyboardist. Alice Cooper.

BRUFORD, BILL. London, England, 5/17/48. Drummer. Yes.

BRYAN, DAVID (David Rashbaum). New Jersey, 2/7/62. Keyboardist. Bon Jovi.

BRYON, DENNIS. Cardiff, Wales, 4/14/49. Drummer. Amen Corner.

BRYSON, PEABO. (Robert Peabo Bryson), Greenville, SC, 4/13/51, Singer.

BRZEZICKI, MARK. Slough, England, 6/21/57. Drummer. Big Country.

BUCHANAN, PAUL. Scotland. Singer, synthesizer player. Blue Nile.

BUCHHOLZ, FRANCIS. 2/19/50. Guitarist. Scorpions.

BUCK, PETER. Athens, GA, 12/6/56. Guitarist. R.E.M.

BUCK, ROBERT. Guitarist. 10,000 Maniacs.

BUCKINGHAM, LINDSEY. Palo Alto, CA, 10/3/47. Guitarist, singer. Fleetwood Mac.

BUCKLER, RICK (Paul Buckler). 12/6/56. Drummer, singer. The Jam.

BUCKLEY, BETTY. Big Spring, TX, 7/3/47. Actor. *Eight Is Enough.*

BUJOLD, GENEVIEVE. Montreal, Canada, 7/1/42. Actor. *Dead Ringers.*

BUNKER, CLIVE. Blackpool, England, 12/12/46. Drummer. Jethro Tull.

BUNNELL, DEWEY. Yorkshire, England, 1/19/51. Singer, guitarist. America.

BUNTON, EMMA. 1/21/76. Singer. Baby Spice of the Spice Girls.

BURCHILL, CHARLIE. Glasgow, Scotland, 11/27/59. Guitarist. Simple Minds.

BURDEN, IAN. 12/24/57. Synthesizer player. Human League.

BURDON, ERIC. Walker-on-Tyne, England, 5/11/41. Singer, songwriter. The Animals; War.

BURGHOFF, GARY. Bristol, CT, 5/24/43. Actor. Radar O'Reilly on *M*A*S*H*.

BURKE, DELTA. Orlando, FL, 7/30/56. Actor, married to Gerald McRaney. *Designing Women*.

BURKE, SOLOMON. Philadelphia, PA, 1936. Country-gospel-R&B singer, songwriter.

BURNEL, JEAN-JACQUES. London, England, 2/21/52. Bassist. The Stranglers.

BURNETT, CAROL. San Antonio, TX, 4/26/33. Actor. *The Carol Burnett Show*.

BURNS, BOB. Drummer. Lynyrd Skynyrd.

BURR, CLIVE. 3/8/57. Drummer. Iron Maiden.

BURRELL, BOZ (Raymond Burrell). Lincoln, England, 1946. Bassist. Bad Company.

BURROWS, DARREN E. Winfield, KS, 9/12/66. Actor. Ed Chigliak on *Northern Exposure*.

BURSTYN, ELLEN (Edna Rae Gillooly). Detroit, MI, 12/7/32. Actor. *Alice Doesn't Live Here Anymore*.

BURT, HEINZ. Hargin, Germany, 7/24/42. Bassist. The Tornados.

BURTON, LEVAR. Landstuhl, Germany, 2/16/57. Actor. Geordi LaForge on *Star Trek: The Next Generation*.

BURTON, TIM. 8/25/58. Director. *Edward Scissorhands*.

BURTON, TREVOR. Aston, England, 3/9/44. Lead guitarist. The Move.

BUSEY, GARY. Goose Creek, TX, 6/29/44. Actor. *The Buddy Holly Story*.

BUSFIELD, TIMOTHY. Lansing, MI, 6/12/57, Actor, *thirtysomething*.

BUSH, BARBARA. Rye, NY, 6/8/25. Former First Lady, married to George Bush.

BUSH, GEORGE. Milton, MA, 6/12/24. Political leader, husband of Barbara. Forty-first president of the U.S.

BUSH, KATE. Bexleyheath, England, 7/30/58. Singer, songwriter.

BUSHY, RONALD. Washington, DC, 9/23/45. Drummer. Iron Butterfly.

BUTKUS, DICK. Chicago, IL, 12/9/42. Football player, actor. *My Two Dads*.

BUTLER, GEEZER (Terry Butler). Birmingham, England, 7/17/49. Bassist. Black Sabbath.

BUTLER, JERRY. Sunflower, MS, 12/8/39. Singer. The Impressions.

BUTLER, BRETT Montgomery, AL, 1/30/58. Actor, comedian. *Grace Under Fire*.

BUTLER, JOE. Glen Cove, NY, 9/16/43. Drummer, singer. The Lovin' Spoonful.

BUTLER, RICHARD. Surrey, England, 6/5/56. Singer, lyricist. Psychedelic Furs.

BUTLER, TONY. Ealing, England, 2/13/57. Bassist. Big Country.

BUTTAFUOCO, JOEY. Massapequa, NY. 3/11/56. Mechanic. Had affair with Amy Fisher.

BUXTON, GLEN. Akron, OH, 11/10/47. Guitarist. Alice Cooper.

BUZZI, RUTH. Westerly, RI, 7/24/36. Actor. *Laugh-In*.

BYRNE, DAVID. Dumbarton, Scotland, 5/14/52, Singer, songwriter, director, Talking Heads.

BYRON, DAVID. Essex, England, 1/29/47. Singer. Uriah Heep.

CAAN, JAMES. The Bronx, NY, 3/26/40. Actor. *The Godfather*.

CADDY, ALAN. London, England, 2/2/40. Guitarist. The Tornados; Johnny Kidd & The Pirates.

CAESAR, SID. Yonkers, NY, 9/8/22. Performer. *Your Show of Shows*.

CAFFEY, CHARLOTTE. Santa Monica, CA, 10/21/53. Singer. The Go-Gos.

CAIN, DEAN Mt. Clemens, MI, 7/31/66. Actor. *Lois & Clark: The New Adventures of Superman*.

CAIN, JONATHAN. Chicago, IL, 2/26/50. Keyboardist. Journey.

CALABRO, THOMAS. 2/3/59. Actor. Michael Mancini on *Melrose Place*.

CALE, JOHN. Garnant, Wales, 3/9/42. Bassist, keyboardist, violist, singer. The Velvet Underground.

CALIFORNIA, RANDY (Randy Wolfe). Los Angeles, CA, 2/20/51. Guitarist, singer. Spirit.

CALLOW, SIMON. London, England, 6/15/49. Actor. *A Room with a View*.

CALVERT, BERNIE. Burnley, England, 9/16/43. Bassist. The Hollies.

CAMERON, KIRK. Panorama City, CA, 10/12/70. Actor, brother of Candace. Mike Seaver on *Growing Pains*.

CAMP, COLLEEN. San Francisco, CA, 1953. Actor. Kristin Shepard on *Dallas*.

CAMPBELL, ALI (Alastair Campbell). Birmingham, England, 2/15/59. Lead singer, guitarist. UB40.

CAMPBELL, BRUCE. Royal Oak, MI, 6/22/58. Actor, producer, screenwriter. *The Adventures of Briscoe County Jr.*

CAMPBELL, GLEN. Delight, AR, 4/22/36. Actor, singer. *The Glen Campbell Goodtime Hour*.

CAMPBELL, MIKE. Panama City, FL, 2/1/54. Guitarist. Tom Petty & The Heartbreakers.

CAMPBELL, ROBIN. Birmingham, England, 12/25/54. Lead guitarist, singer. UB40.

CAMPBELL, TISHA. Oklahoma City, OK, 10/13/70. Actor. *Martin*.

CAMPION, JANE. Wellington, New Zealand, 4/30/54. Director, screenwriter, daughter of Richard and Edith. *The Piano*.

CANN, WARREN. Victoria, Canada, 5/20/52. Drummer. Ultravox.

CANNON, DYAN (Samille Diane Friesen). Tacoma, WA, 1/4/39. Actor. *Bob & Carol & Ted & Alice*.

CAPALDI, JIM. Evesham, England, 8/24/44. Drummer, singer. Traffic.

CAPRIATI, JENNIFER. Long Island, NY, 3/29/76. Tennis player

CAPSHAW, KATE (Kathleen Sue Nail). Ft. Worth, TX, 11/3/53. Actor, married to Steven Spielberg. *Indiana Jones and the Temple of Doom*.

CARA, IRENE. New York, NY, 3/18/59. Actor, singer. *Fame*.

CARDIN, PIERRE. Venice, Italy, 7/7/22. Fashion designer.

CARDINALE, CLAUDIA. Tunis, Tunisia, 4/15/39. Actor. *The Pink Panther*.

CAREY, TONY. 10/16/53. Keyboardist. Rainbow.

CARLIN, GEORGE. New York, NY, 5/12/37. Actor. "Seven Dirty Words."

CARLISLE, BELINDA. Hollywood, CA, 8/17/58. Singer, songwriter.

CARLOS, BUN (Brad Carlson). Rockford, IL, 6/12/51. Drummer. Cheap Trick.

CARMEN, ERIC. Cleveland, OH, 8/11/49. Singer. The Raspberries.

CARNE, JUDY (Joyce Botterill). Northampton, England, 3/27/39. Actor. *Laugh-In*.

CARNEY, ART. Mt. Vernon,

NY, 11/4/18. Actor and comedian. Ed Norton on *The Honeymooners*.

CAROLINE, PRINCESS. Monte Carlo, Monaco, 1/23/57. Daughter of Princess Grace of Monaco.

CARON, LESLIE. Paris, France, 7/1/31. Actor. *Lili*.

CARPENTER, JOHN. Carthage, NY, 1/16/48. Director, writer. *Halloween*.

CARPENTER, RICHARD. New Haven, CT, 10/15/46. Keyboardist, singer. The Carpenters.

CARR, DAVID. Leyton, England, 8/4/43. Keyboardist. The Fortunes.

CARRACK, PAUL. Sheffield, England, 4/21/51. Singer, songwriter. Squeeze; Ace; Mike and the Mechanics.

CARRADINE, DAVID. Hollywood, CA, 12/8/36. Actor, son of John Carradine, brother of Keith and Robert. *Kung Fu*.

CARRADINE, KEITH. San Mateo, CA, 8/8/49. Actor, son of John, brother of David and Robert, father of Martha Plimpton. *The Will Rogers Follies*.

CARRADINE, ROBERT. Hollywood, CA, 3/24/54. Actor, son of John, brother of David and Keith. *Revenge of the Nerds*.

CARRERA, BARBARA. Managua, Nicaragua, 12/31/47. Model, actor. *Dallas*.

CARROLL, DIAHANN (Carol Diahann Johnson). New York, NY, 7/17/35. Actor, singer, married to Vic Damone. *I Know Why the Caged Bird Sings*.

CARRY, JULIUS. Actor. Mitchell Baldwin on *Murphy Brown*.

CARTER, DIXIE. McLemoresville, TN, 5/25/39. Actor. Julia Sugarbaker on *Designing Women*.

CARTER, JIMMY. Plains, GA, 10/1/24. Political leader. Thirty-ninth president of the

U.S.

CARTER, LYNDA. Phoenix, AZ, 7/24/51. Actor. *Wonder Woman*.

CARTER, NELL. Birmingham, AL, 9/13/48. Actor, singer. *Gimme a Break*.

CARTERIS, GABRIELLE. 1/2/61. Actor. Andrea Zuckerman on *Beverly Hills 90210*.

CARTWRIGHT, VERONICA. Bristol, England, 1950. Actor. *Alien*.

CARVEY, DANA. Missoula, MT, 4/2/55. Actor. *Saturday Night Live, Wayne's World*.

CARUSO, DAVID. Queens, NY, 1/17/56, Actor, *NYPD Blue*.

CASADY, JACK. Washington, DC, 4/13/44. Bass guitarist. Jefferson Airplane/Starship.

CASEY, HARRY WAYNE (Harold Casey). Hialeah, FL, 1/31/51. Singer, keyboardist. KC & The Sunshine Band.

CASS, PEGGY (Mary Margaret Cass). Boston, MA, 5/21/24. Actor. Panelist on *To Tell the Truth*.

CASSIDY, DAVID. New York, NY, 4/12/50. Actor, half brother of Shaun, son of Jack, step-son of Shirley Jones. Keith in *The Partridge Family*.

CASSIDY, ED. Chicago, IL, 5/4/31. Drummer. Spirit.

CASSIDY, JOANNA. Camden, NJ, 8/2/44. Actor. Jo Jo White on *Buffalo Bill*.

CASTRO, FIDEL (Fidel Ruz). Mayari, Cuba, 8/13/26. Political leader. President of Cuba.

CATES, PHOEBE. New York, NY, 7/16/63. Actor, married to Kevin Kline. *Fast Times at Ridgemont High*.

CATHERALL, JOANNE. Sheffield, England, 9/18/62. Singer. Human League.

CATTINI, CLEM. 8/28/39. Drummer. Johnny Kidd & The Pirates; Tornados.

CAVALIERE, FELIX. Pelham,

NY, 11/29/44. Singer, keyboardist. The (Young) Rascals.

CAVETT, DICK. Gibbon, NE, 11/19/36. Actor, talk show host. *The Dick Cavett Show*.

CEASE, JEFF. Nashville, TN, 6/24/67. Guitarist. The Black Crowes.

CETERA, PETER. Chicago, IL, 9/13/44. Singer, songwriter. Chicago.

CHABERT, LACEY. 9/30/82. Actor. *Party of Five*.

CHADWICK, LES (John Chadwick). Liverpool, England, 5/11/43. Bassist. Gerry & The Pacemakers.

CHAMBERLAIN, RICHARD (George Chamberlain). Los Angeles, CA, 3/31/34. Actor. *Dr. Kildare*.

CHAMBERS, GEORGE. Flora, MS, 9/26/31. Bassist, singer. The Chambers Brothers.

CHAMBERS, JOE. Scott County, MS, 8/24/42. Guitarist, singer. The Chambers Brothers.

CHAMBERS, LESTER. Flora, MS, 4/13/40. Harmonicist, singer. The Chambers Brothers.

CHAMBERS, MARTIN. Hereford, England, 9/4/51. Drummer. The Pretenders.

CHAMBERS, TERRY. England, 7/18/55. Drummer. XTC.

CHAMBERS, WILLIE. Flora, MS, 3/3/38. Guitarist, singer. The Chambers Brothers.

CHANDLER, GENE (Gene Dixon). Chicago, IL, 7/6/37. Singer, songwriter.

CHANNING, CAROL. Seattle, WA, 1/31/21. Actor. *Hello, Dolly!*

CHANNING, STOCKARD (Susan Williams Antonia Stockard). New York, NY, 2/13/44. Actor. *Grease*.

CHAO, ROSALIND. Los Angeles, CA. Actor. Soon-Lee on *M*A*S*H*.

CHAPLIN, GERALDINE.

Santa Monica, CA, 7/31/44. Actor. *Dr. Zhivago*.

CHAPMAN, ROGER. Leicester, England, 4/8/44. Singer. Family.

CHAPMAN, TRACY. Cleveland, OH, 3/30/64. Folk singer, songwriter.

CHAQUICO, CRAIG. 9/26/54. Singer, guitarist. Jefferson Starship.

CHARISSE, CYD (Tula Ellice Finklea). Amarillo, TX, 3/8/22. Actor. *Brigadoon*.

CHARLES, RAY (Ray Robinson). Albany, GA, 9/23/30. Singer, songwriter. "Georgia on My Mind."

CHARLTON, MANUEL. 7/25/41. Guitarist, singer, songwriter. Nazareth.

CHARO. Murcia, Spain, 1/15/41. Actor, singer. *The Love Boat*.

CHASE, CHEVY (Cornelius Crane Chase) New York, NY, 10/8/43, Actor, *National Lampoon's Vacation* movies.

CHECKER, CHUBBY (Ernest Evans). Spring Gulley, SC, 10/3/41. Singer, songwriter. Popularized the Twist and Limbo.

CHERRY, NENEH. Stockholm, Sweden, 3/10/64. Rap/pop singer, songwriter.

CHILD, JULIA. Pasadena, CA, 8/15/12. TV chef, author. *Mastering the Art of French Cooking*.

CHILES, LOIS. Alice, TX, 4/15/47. Model, actor. *The Way We Were*.

CHILTON, ALEX. Memphis, TN, 12/28/50. Guitarist, singer. The Box Tops; Big Star.

CHISHOLM, MELANIE. 1/12/74. Singer. Sporty Spice of the Spice Girls.

CHONG, RAE DAWN. Vancouver, Canada, 1962. Actor, daughter of Thomas Chong. *The Color Purple*.

CHONG, THOMAS. Edmonton, Canada, 5/24/38. Singer, actor, writer, director, former partner of

Cheech Marin, father of Rae Dawn Chong. *Up in Smoke.*

CHRISTIAN, GARRY. Merseyside, England, 2/27/55. Singer. The Christians.

CHRISTIAN, ROGER. 2/13/50. Singer. The Christians.

CHRISTIAN, RUSSELL. 6/8/56. Singer. The Christians.

CHRISTIE, JULIE. Chukua, India, 4/14/41. Actor. *Dr. Zhivago.*

CHRISTIE, LOU (Lugee Sacco). Glenwillard, PA, 2/19/43. Singer, songwriter. "Lightnin' Strikes."

CHRISTO (Christo Javacheff). Gabrovo, Bulgaria, 6/13/35. Artist. The Umbrellas.

CHRISTOPHER, WILLIAM. Evanston, IL, 10/20/32. Actor. Father Francis Mulcahy on *M*A*S*H.*

CHUCK D. (Charles Ridenhour). 1960. Rap artist. Public Enemy.

CHUNG, CONNIE (Constance Yu-Hwa Chung) Washington, DC, 8/20/46, TV journalist, CBS.

CHURCHILL, CHICK. Mold, Wales, 1/2/49. Keyboardist. Ten Years After.

CIPOLLINA, JOHN. Berkeley, CA, 8/24/43. Guitarist. Quicksilver Messenger Service.

CLAIBORNE, LIZ (Elisabeth Claiborne). Brussels, Belgium, 3/31/29. Fashion designer.

CLARK, ALAN. Durham, NC, 3/5/52. Keyboardist. Dire Straits.

CLARK, DAVE. Tottenham, England, 12/15/42. Drummer. The Dave Clark Five.

CLARK, DICK. Mt. Vernon, NY, 11/30/29. Producer, music/game show host. *American Bandstand.*

CLARK, GRAEME. Glasgow, Scotland, 4/15/66. Bassist. Wet Wet Wet.

CLARK, NEIL. 7/3/55. Guitarist. Lloyd Cole & The Commotions.

CLARK, PETULA. Surrey, England, 11/15/32. Actor, singer. *Downtown.*

CLARK, ROY. Meherrin, VA, 4/15/33. Country singer, songwriter. *Hee Haw.*

CLARK, STEVE. Hillsborough, England, 4/23/60. Guitarist. Def Leppard.

CLARKE, ALLAN (Harold Clarke). Salford, England, 4/5/42. Singer. The Hollies.

CLARKE, EDDIE. 10/5/50. Guitarist. Motörhead.

CLARKE, MICHAEL (Michael Dick). New York, NY, 6/3/44. Drummer. The Byrds.

CLARKE, VINCE. Basildon, England, 7/3/61. Keyboardist. Erasure.

CLAY, ANDREW DICE. Brooklyn, NY, 1958. Actor. *The Adventures of Ford Fairlaine.*

CLAYBURGH, JILL. New York, NY, 4/30/44. Actor. *An Unmarried Woman.*

CLAYTON, ADAM. Ireland, 3/13/60. Bassist. U2.

CLAYTON-THOMAS, DAVID (David Thomsett). Surrey, England, 9/13/41. Lead singer. Blood, Sweat & Tears.

CLEESE, JOHN. Weston-Super-Mare, England, 10/27/39. Actor. *Monty Python's Flying Circus.*

CLIFF, JIMMY (Jimmy Chambers). Somerton, Jamaica, 1949. Reggae singer, songwriter.

CLIFFORD, DOUG. Palo Alto, CA, 4/24/45. Drummer. Creedence Clearwater Revival.

CLINTON, BILL. Hope, AK, 8/19/46. Husband of Hillary Rodham, father of Chelsea. 42nd President of the United States.

CLINTON, CHELSEA. Arkansas, 2/27/80. Daughter of Bill and Hillary.

CLINTON, GEORGE. Kannapolis, NC, 7/22/41. Funk pioneer, singer. Parliament; Funkadelic.

CLINTON, HILLARY RODHAM. Park Ridge, IL, 10/26/47. Wife of Bill, mother of Chelsea. First Lady.

CLOONEY, NICK. 1/13/35. Actor, father of George Clooney. American Movie Classics.

CLOONEY, ROSEMARY. Maysville, KY, 5/23/28. Actor, singer, aunt of George Clooney.

CLYDE, JEREMY. England, 3/22/44. Singer, guitarist. Chad & Jeremy.

COBURN, JAMES. Laurel, NE, 8/31/28. Actor. *The Magnificent Seven.*

COCA, IMOGENE. Philadelphia, PA, 11/18/08. Actor. *Your Show of Shows.*

COCHRANE, TOM. 5/14/53. Singer, guitarist. Red Rider.

COCKER, JOE (John Cocker). Sheffield, England, 5/20/44. Singer.

COEN, ETHAN. St. Louis Park, MN, 1958. Director, writer. Brother of Joel. *Raising Arizona.*

COEN, JOEL. St. Louis Park, MN, 1955. Director, writer. Brother of Ethan. *Fargo.*

COGHLAN, JOHN. Dulwich, England, 9/19/46. Drummer. Status Quo.

COHEN, DAVID. Brooklyn, NY, 1942. Keyboardist. Country Joe & The Fish.

COHEN, LEONARD. Montreal, Canada, 9/21/34. Singer, songwriter, poet.

COLE, BRIAN. Tacoma, WA, 9/8/42. Singer, bassist. The Association.

COLE, LLOYD. Derbyshire, England, 1/31/61. Singer, guitarist. Lloyd Cole & The Commotions.

COLE, NATALIE (Stephanie Natalie Maria Cole). Los Angeles, CA, 2/6/50. Singer. *Unforgettable.*

COLEMAN, DABNEY. Austin, TX, 1/3/32. Actor. *Buffalo Bill.*

COLEMAN, GARY. Zion, IL, 2/8/68. Actor. Arnold Jackson on *Diff'rent Strokes.*

COLEY, DORIS. Passaic, NJ, 8/2/41. Singer. The Shirelles.

COLLA, JOHNNY. California, 7/2/52. Saxophonist, guitarist. Huey Lewis & The News.

COLLEN, PHIL. London, England, 12/8/57. Guitarist. Def Leppard.

COLLINS, ALLEN. Jacksonville, FL, 7/19/52. Guitarist. Lynyrd Skynyrd.

COLLINS, GARY. Boston, MA, 4/30/38. Actor, talk show host. *Home.*

COLLINS, JACKIE. 10/4/39. Author. *Lucky.*

COLLINS, JOAN. London, England, 5/23/33. Actor. Alexis Carrington Colby on *Dynasty.*

COLLINS, JUDY. Seattle, WA, 5/1/39. Folk/rock guitarist, singer, songwriter. "Send in the Clowns."

COLLINS, PHIL. Chiswick, England, 1/30/51. Singer, drummer. Genesis.

COLLINS, STEPHEN. Des Moines, IA, 10/1/47. Actor. *Tales of the Gold Monkey.*

COLOMBY, BOBBY. New York, NY, 12/20/44. Drummer, singer. Blood, Sweat & Tears.

COLT, JOHNNY. Cherry Point, NC, 5/1/66. Bassist. The Black Crowes.

COLUMBUS, CHRIS. Spangler, PA, 9/10/58. Director. *Home Alone.*

CONAWAY, JEFF. New York, NY, 10/5/50. Actor. Bobby Wheeler on *Taxi.*

CONNELLY, JENNIFER. New York, NY, 12/12/70. Actor. *The Rocketeer.*

CONNOLLY, BRIAN. Hamilton, Scotland, 10/5/49. Singer. Sweet.

CONNORS, JIMMY. Belleville, IL, 9/2/52. Tennis player.

CONNORS, MIKE (Krekor Ohanian). Fresno, CA, 8/15/25. Actor. *Mannix.*

CONROY, KEVIN. Westport, CT, 11/30/55. Actor. Voice of Batman in *Batman: The Animated Series.*

CONROY, PAT. 10/26/45. Author. *Prince of Tides.*

CONSTANTINE, MICHAEL (Constantine Joanides). Reading, PA, 5/22/27. Actor. *Room 222.*

CONTI, TOM. Paisley, Scotland, 11/22/41. Actor. *Reuben Reuben.*

CONWAY, KEVIN. New York, NY, 5/29/42. Actor. *Slaughterhouse Five.*

CONWAY, TIM (Thomas Daniel Conway). Willoughby, OH, 12/15/33. Actor. *The Carol Burnett Show.*

COODER, RY (Ryland Cooder). Los Angeles, CA, 3/15/47. Folk blues guitarist, composer.

COOK, JEFF. Fort Payne, AL, 8/27/49. Singer, fiddler, guitarist, keyboardist. Alabama.

COOK, NORMAN (Quentin Cook). Sussex, England, 7/31/63. Singer. The Housemartins.

COOK, PAUL. London, England, 7/20/56. Drummer. The Sex Pistols.

COOK, STU. Oakland, CA, 4/25/45. Bassist. Creedence Clearwater Revival.

COOLIO Los Angeles,CA, 8/1/63. Rap Artist. "Gangsta's Paradise."

COONCE, RICKY. Los Angeles, CA, 8/1/47. Drummer. The Grass Roots.

COOPER, ALICE (Vincent Furnier). Detroit, MI, 2/4/48. Singer, songwriter. Alice Cooper.

COOPER, JACKIE (John Cooper Jr.). Los Angeles, CA, 9/15/22. Actor, director. *Superman.*

COPE, JULIAN. Bargoed, Wales, 10/21/57. Singer, bassist. The Teardrop Explodes.

COPELAND, STEWART. Alexandria, Egypt, 7/16/52. Drummer, singer. The Police.

CORBIN, BARRY. Dawson County, TX, 10/16/40. Actor. Maurice Minnifield on *Northern Exposure.*

CORGAN, BILLY. Chicago, IL, 3/17/67. Singer, songwriter, guitarist. Smashing Pumpkins.

CORLEY, PAT. Dallas, TX, 6/1/30. Actor. Phil the bartender on *Murphy Brown.*

CORNELL, CHRIS. Seattle, WA, 7/20/64. Singer, songwriter, drummer. Soundgarden.

CORNICK, GLENN. Barrow-in-Furness, England, 4/24/47. Bassist. Jethro Tull.

CORNISH, GENE. Ottowa, Canada, 5/14/45. Guitarist. The (Young) Rascals.

CORNWELL, HUGH. London, England, 8/28/49. Singer, guitarist. The Stranglers.

CORT, BUD (Walter Edward Cox). New Rochelle, NY, 3/29/48. Actor. *Harold and Maude.*

COSTELL, DAVID. Pittsburgh, PA, 3/15/44. Bassist. Gary Lewis and the Playboys.

COULIER, DAVID. Detroit, MI. Actor. Joey Gladstone on *Full House.*

COVERDALE, DAVID. Saltburn-by-the-Sea, England, 9/22/49. Singer. Whitesnake.

COWSILL, BARRY. Newport, RI, 9/14/54. Bassist, singer. The Cowsills.

COWSILL, BILL. Newport, RI, 1/9/48. Guitarist, singer. The Cowsills.

COWSILL, BOB. Newport, RI, 8/26/49. Guitarist, singer. The Cowsills.

COWSILL, JOHN. Newport, RI, 3/2/56. Drummer. The Cowsills.

COWSILL, PAUL. Newport, RI, 11/11/52. Keyboardist, singer. The Cowsills.

COWSILL, SUE. Newport, RI, 5/20/60. Singer. The Cowsills.

COX, ANDY. Birmingham, England, 1/25/60. Guitarist. Fine Young Cannibals.

COX, RONNY. Cloudcroft, NM, 8/23/38. Actor. *Beverly Hills Cop.*

COYOTE, PETER (Peter Cohon). New York, NY, 1942. Actor. *Jagged Edge.*

CRAIG, MIKEY. Hammersmith, England, 2/15/60. Bassist. Culture Club.

CRAVEN, WES. Cleveland, OH, 8/2/39. Director, novelist. *A Nightmare on Elm Street.*

CRAWFORD, JOHN. 1/17/60. Bassist, singer. Berlin.

CRAWFORD, MICHAEL (Michael Dumble-Smith). Salisbury, England, 1/19/42. Actor, singer. *The Phantom of the Opera.*

CRAWFORD, RANDY (Veronica Crawford). Macon, GA, 2/18/52. Rock-R&B singer, songwriter.

CRAY, ROBERT. Columbus, GA, 8/1/53. Contemporary blues singer, songwriter. "Smoking Gun."

CREGAN, JIM. 3/9/46. Guitarist. Steve Harley & Cockney Rebel.

CREME, LOL. Manchester, England, 9/19/47. Singer, guitarist. 10cc; Godley & Creme.

CRENNA, RICHARD. Los Angeles, CA, 11/30/27. Actor. *Rambo: First Blood Part II.*

CREWSDON, ROY. Manchester, England, 5/29/41. Guitarist. Freddie & The Dreamers.

CRISS, PETER (Peter Crisscoula). Brooklyn, NY, 12/27/47. Drummer, singer. Kiss.

CROFTS, DASH. Cisco, TX, 8/14/40. Singer, guitarist, mandolinist. Seals & Crofts.

CRONIN, KEVIN. Evanston, IL, 10/6/51. Singer. REO Speedwagon.

CRONKITE, WALTER. St. Joseph, MO, 11/4/16. News journalist and anchor. *CBS Evening News.*

CRONYN, HUME. London, Canada, 7/18/11. Actor, writer, director, widower of Jessica Tandy. *The Postman Always Rings Twice.*

CROPPER, STEVE. Willow Springs, MO, 10/21/41. Guitarist. Booker T. & The MG's.

CROSBY, CATHY LEE. Los Angeles, CA, 12/2/49. Actor. *That's Incredible!*

CROSBY, DAVID (David Van Cortland). Los Angeles, CA, 8/14/41. Singer, guitarist. The Byrds; Crosby, Stills, Nash & Young.

CROSBY, DENISE. Hollywood, CA, 1958. Actor, granddaughter of Bing Crosby. *Star Trek: The Next Generation.*

CROSBY, HARRY. Los Angeles, CA, 8/8/58. Actor, singer.

CROSS, BEN. London, England, 12/16/48. Actor. *Chariots of Fire.*

CROSS, CHRIS (Chris St. John). London, England, 7/14/52. Bassist, synthesizer player. Ultravox.

CROSS, CHRISTOPHER (Christopher Geppert). San Antonio, TX, 5/3/51. Guitarist, singer, songwriter. "Ride Like the Wind."

CROUSE, LINDSAY. New York, NY, 5/12/48. Actor. *The Verdict.*

CRYER, JON. New York, NY, 4/16/65. Actor. *Pretty in Pink.*

CULKIN, MACAULAY. New York, NY, 8/26/80. Actor. *Home Alone, My Girl.*

CULLIMORE, STAN. Hull, England, 4/6/62. Bassist. The Housemartins.

CULLUM, JOHN. Knoxville, TN, 3/2/30. Actor. Holling Vincoeur on *Northern Exposure.*

CULP, ROBERT. Oakland, CA, 8/16/30. Actor. *I Spy.*

CUMMINGS, BURTON. Winnipeg, Canada, 12/31/47. Singer, keyboardist. The Guess Who.

CUMMINGS, GEORGE. Meridian, MS, 7/28/38. Lead guitarist. Dr. Hook.

CUNNINGHAM, BILL. Memphis, TN, 1/23/50. Bassist, pianist. The Box Tops; Big Star.

CUNNINGHAM, TOM. Glasgow, Scotland, 6/22/65. Drummer. Wet Wet Wet.

CUOMO, MARIO. Queens, NY, 6/15/32. Political leader. Former Governor of New York.

CURRIE, ALANNAH. Auckland, New Zealand, 9/20/59. Singer, saxophonist, percussionist. Thompson Twins.

CURRIE, BILLY. Huddersfield, England, 4/1/52. Synthesizer player, keyboardist. Ultravox.

CURRIE, CHERIE. Los Angeles, CA, 1960. Singer, married to Robert Hays. The Runaways.

CURRY, TIM. Cheshire, England, 4/19/46. Actor. *The Rocky Horror Picture Show.*

CURTIN, JANE. Cambridge, MA, 9/6/47. Actor. *Kate & Allie.*

CURTIS, CHRIS (Chris Crummy). Oldham, England, 8/26/41. Singer, drummer. The Searchers.

CURTIS, SONNY. Meadow, TX, 5/9/37. Guitarist. Buddy Holly & The Crickets.

CURTIS, TONY (Bernard Schwartz). New York, NY, 6/3/25. Actor, father of Jamie Lee Curtis, formerly married to Janet Leigh. *Some Like It Hot.*

CUSACK, JOAN. Evanston, IL, 10/11/62. Actor. *Working Girl.*

CUSACK, SINEAD. Ireland, 2/18/48. Actor, married to Jeremy Irons, daughter of

Cyril Cusack.

CYRUS, BILLY RAY. Flatwoods, NY, 8/25/61. Singer, son of politician Ronald Ray Cyrus. "Achy-Breaky Heart."

D'ABO, OLIVIA. 1/22/69. Actor. *The Wonder Years.*

D'ALEO, ANGELO. The Bronx, NY, 2/3/41. Singer. Dion & The Belmonts.

D'ANGELO, BEVERLY. Columbus, OH, 11/15/51. Actor. *Hair.*

D'ARBANVILLE, PATTI. 5/25/51. Actress

D'ARBY, TERENCE TRENT. New York, NY, 3/15/62. R&B singer, songwriter. "Wishing Well."

D'ONOFRIO, VINCENT. 6/30/59. Actor. *The Newton Boys.*

DAFOE, WILLEM. Appleton, WI, 7/22/55. Actor. *Mississippi Burning.*

DALE, GLEN (Richard Garforth). Deal, England, 4/2/43. Guitarist, singer. The Fortunes.

DALEY, ROSIE. South Seaville, NJ, 1961. Chef. *In the Kitchen with Rosie.*

DALLIN, SARAH. Bristol, England, 12/17/61. Singer. Bananarama.

DALTON, TIMOTHY. Colwyn Bay, Wales, 3/21/44. Actor. James Bond in *The Living Daylights.*

DALTREY, ROGER. London, England, 3/1/44. Lead singer. The Who.

DALY, GARY. Merseyside, England, 5/5/62. Singer. China Crisis.

DALY, TIMOTHY. New York, NY, 3/1/56. Actor. *Wings.*

DALY, TYNE (Ellen Tyne Daly). Madison, WI, 2/21/46. Actor. *Cagney & Lacey.*

DAMMERS, JERRY (Jerry Dankin). 5/22/54. Keyboardist. The Specials.

DAMONE, VIC (Vito Farinola). Brooklyn, NY, 6/12/28. Singer, married to Diahann Caroll. *The Vic Damone Show.*

DANCE, CHARLES. Worcestershire, England, 10/10/46. Actor. *The Jewel in the Crown.*

DANDO, EVAN. 3/4/67. Musician. The Lemonheads.

DANELLI, DINO. New York, NY, 7/23/45. Drummer. The (Young) Rascals.

DANGERFIELD, RODNEY (Jacob Cohen). Babylon, NY, 11/22/21. Actor. *Back to School.*

DANIEL, JEFFREY. Los Angeles, CA, 8/24/55. Singer. Shalamar.

DANIELS, WILLIAM. Brooklyn, NY, 3/31/27. Actor. *St. Elsewhere.*

DANNER, BLYTHE. Philadelphia, PA, 2/3/43. Actor. *The Prince of Tides.*

DANTE, MICHAEL (Ralph Vitti). Stamford, CT, 1935. Actor. Crazy Horse in *Custer.*

DANZA, TONY. Brooklyn, NY, 4/21/51. Actor. Tony Micelli on *Who's the Boss?*

DAVIDOVICH, LOLITA. Ontario, Canada, 7/15/61. Actor. *Blaze.*

DAVIDSON, JAYE. Riverside, CA, 1967. Actor. *The Crying Game.*

DAVIDSON, JOHN. Pittsburgh, PA, 12/13/41. Game show host. *Hollywood Squares.*

DAVIDSON, LENNY. Enfield, England, 5/30/44. Guitarist. The Dave Clark Five.

DAVIES, DAVE. Muswell Hill, England, 2/3/47. Singer, guitarist. The Kinks.

DAVIES, IVA. Australia, 5/22/55. Guitarist, singer. Icehouse.

DAVIES, RAY. Muswell Hill, England, 6/21/44. Singer, guitarist. The Kinks.

DAVIES, RICHARD. England, 7/22/44. Singer, keyboardist. Supertramp.

DAVIS, BILLY JR. St. Louis, MO, 6/26/38. Singer. The 5th Dimension.

DAVIS, CLIFTON. Chicago, IL, 10/4/45. Actor, singer,

composer. *Never Can Say Goodbye.*

DAVIS, JIM. Marion, IN, 7/28/45. Cartoonist. *Garfield.*

DAVIS, MAC (Morris Mac Davis). Lubbock, TX, 1/21/42. Singer, songwriter, actor. *The Mac Davis Show.*

DAVIS, MARTHA. Berkeley, CA, 1/15/51. Singer. The Motels.

DAVIS, OSSIE. Cogdell, GA, 12/18/17. Actor, writer. *Evening Shade.*

DAVIS, PAUL. Manchester, England, 3/7/66. Keyboardist. Happy Mondays.

DAVIS, ROB. Carshalton, England, 10/1/47. Lead guitarist, singer. Mud.

DAVIS, SPENCER. Swansea, Wales, 7/17/42. Guitarist. The Spencer Davis Group.

DAVIS, WILLIE. 1940. Drummer. Joey Dee and the Starliters.

DAWBER, PAM. 10/18/50. Actor. Married to Mark Harmon. *Mork and Mindy.*

DAY, DORIS (Doris von Kappelhoff). Cincinnati, OH, 4/3/24. Actor, performer. *The Doris Day Show.*

DAY, MARK. Manchester, England, 12/29/61. Guitarist. Happy Mondays.

DE BURGH, CHRIS (Chris Davidson). Argentina, 10/15/48. Singer, songwriter. "Lady in Red."

DE HAVILLAND, OLIVIA. Tokyo, Japan, 7/1/16. Actor. *Gone with the Wind.*

DE LAURENTIS, DINO. Torre Annunziata, Italy, 8/8/19. Producer. *King Kong; Conan the Barbarian.*

DEACON, JOHN. Leicester, England, 8/19/51. Bassist. Queen.

DEAN, JIMMY. Plainview, TX, 8/10/28. Performer. *The Jimmy Dean Show.*

DEBARGE, EL (Eldra DeBarge). Grand Rapids, MI, 6/4/61. Singer, keyboardist, record producer.

DEE, DAVE (Dave Harman). Salisbury, England, 12/17/43. Lead singer, tambourinist. Dave Dee, Dozy, Beaky, Mick and Tich.

DEE, JOEY (Joey DiNicola). Passaic, NJ, 6/11/40. Singer. Joey Dee and the Starliters.

DEE, KIKI. Bradford, England, 3/6/47. Pop singer.

DEE, RUBY. Cleveland, OH, 10/27/24. Actor. *Do the Right Thing.*

DEE, SANDRA (Alexandra Zuck). Bayonne, NJ, 4/23/42. Actor. *Gidget.*

DEFOREST, CALVERT. Brooklyn, NY, 1923. Actor, Larry "Bud" Melman.

DEKKER, DESMOND (Desmond Dacris). Kingston, Jamaica, 7/16/42. Reggae singer, songwriter.

DELANEY, KIM. 11/29/61. Actress. *NYPD Blue.*

DELANY, DANA. New York, NY, 3/11/56. Actor. *China Beach.*

DELON, ALAIN. Sceaux, France, 11/8/35. Actor. *Le Samourai.*

DELP, BRAD. Boston, MA, 6/12/51. Guitarist, singer. Boston.

DELUISE, DOM. Brooklyn, NY, 8/1/33. Actor. *The Dom DeLuise Show.*

DELUISE, PETER. Hollywood, CA, 1967. Actor. Doug Penhall on *21 Jump Street.*

DEMME, JONATHAN. Rockville Centre, MD, 2/22/44. Director, producer, writer. *The Silence of the Lambs.*

DEMORNAY, REBECCA. Santa Rosa, CA, 8/29/59. Actor. *The Hand That Rocks the Cradle.*

DEMPSEY, PATRICK. Lewiston, ME, 1/13/66. Actor. *Loverboy.*

DENEUVE, CATHERINE (Catherine Dorleac). Paris, France, 10/22/43. Actor. *Belle de Jour.*

DENSMORE, JOHN. Los Angeles, CA, 12/1/44. Drummer. The Doors.

DENVER, BOB. New Rochelle, NY, 1/9/35. Actor. Gilligan on *Gilligan's Island.*

DEPARDIEU, GERARD. Chateauroux, France, 12/27/48. Actor. *Green Card.*

DEREK, BO (Mary Cathleen Collins). Long Beach, CA, 11/20/56. Actor, married to John Derek. *10.*

DERN, BRUCE. Chicago, IL, 6/4/36. Actor, father of Laura. *Coming Home.*

DERN, LAURA. Los Angeles, CA, 2/10/67. Actor, daughter of Bruce Dern and Diane Ladd, engaged to Jeff Goldblum. *Jurassic Park.*

DERRINGER, RICK (Richard Zehringer). Fort Recovery, OH, 8/5/47. Singer, songwriter, producer. The McCoys.

DESTRI, JIMMY. 4/13/54. Keyboardist. Blondie.

DEVANE, WILLIAM. Albany, NY, 9/5/39. Actor. Greg Sumner in *Knots Landing.*

DEVITO, TOMMY. Montclair, NJ, 6/19/36. Singer, guitarist. The Four Seasons.

DEVOE, RONALD. 11/17/67. Singer. New Edition; Bell Biv DeVoe.

DEY, SUSAN. Pekin, IL, 12/10/52. Actor. *L.A. Law.*

DEYOUNG, CLIFF. Inglewood, CA, 2/12/45. Actor. *The Hunger.*

DEYOUNG, DENNIS. Chicago, IL, 2/18/47. Singer, keyboardist. Styx.

DIAMOND, NEIL (Noah Kaminsky). New York, NY, 1/24/41. Singer, songwriter. *The Jazz Singer.*

DIAMONDE, DICK (Dingeman Van Der Sluys). Hilversum, Holland, 12/28/47. Bassist. The Easybeats.

DICKEN (Jeff Pain). 4/4/50. Singer. Mr. Big.

DICKERSON, B. B. (Morris Dickerson). Torrance, CA, 8/3/49. Bassist, singer. War.

DICKINSON, ANGIE (Angie Brown). Kulm, ND, 9/30/32. Actor. *Police Woman.*

DICKINSON, BRUCE (Paul Dickinson). Worksop, England, 8/7/58. Singer. Iron Maiden.

DIDDLEY, BO (Otha Bates). McComb, MS, 12/30/28. Legendary blues guitarist, singer, songwriter.

DIFFORD, CHRIS. London, England, 11/4/54. Singer, guitarist. Squeeze.

DILLER, PHYLLIS (Phyllis Driver). Lima, OH, 7/17/17. Actor. *The Phyllis Diller Show.*

DILLON, KEVIN. Mamaroneck, NY, 8/19/65. Actor. *The Doors.*

DILLON, MATT. New Rochelle, NY, 2/18/64. Actor. *The Outsiders.*

DIMAGGIO, JOE. Martinez, CA, 11/25/14. Baseball great. New York Yankees. Once married to Marilyn Monroe.

DIMUCCI, DION. The Bronx, NY, 7/18/39. Lead singer. Dion & The Belmonts.

DIO, RONNIE JAMES. Cortland, NY, 7/10/48. Singer. Rainbow; Black Sabbath.

DITKA, MIKE. Carnegie, PA, 10/18/39. NFL football player, coach.

DIXON, DONNA. Alexandria, VA, 7/20/57. Actor, married to Dan Aykroyd. *Bosom Buddies.*

DOBSON, KEVIN. New York, NY, 3/18/43. Actor. *Knots Landing.*

DOHERTY, DENNY. Halifax, Canada, 11/29/41. Singer. The Mamas and the Papas.

DOLENZ, MICKEY (George Dolenz). Los Angeles, CA, 3/8/45. Singer, drummer. The Monkees.

DOMINO, FATS (Antoine Domino). New Orleans, LA, 2/26/28. Legendary singer, songwriter.

DONAHUE, PHIL. Cleveland, OH, 12/21/35. Talk show host.

DONAHUE, TROY (Merle Johnson). New York, NY, 1/27/36. Actor. *Hawaiian Eye.*

DONALDSON, SAM. El Paso, TX, 3/11/34. News reporter and anchor. *Prime Time Live.*

DONEGAN, LAWRENCE. 7/13/61. Bassist. Lloyd Cole & The Commotions.

DONEGAN, LONNIE (Anthony Donegan). Glasgow, Scotland, 4/29/31. Folk/blues guitarist, banjoist, and singer.

DONOVAN (Donovan Leitch). Glasgow, Scotland, 2/10/46. Folk/psychedelic singer, songwriter, father of Ione Skye and Donovan Leitch. "Mellow Yellow."

DONOVAN, JASON. Malvern, Australia, 6/1/68. Singer, actor.

DORMAN, LEE. St. Louis, MO, 9/19/45. Bassist. Iron Butterfly.

DOUGHTY, NEAL. Evanston, IL, 7/29/46. Keyboardist. REO Speedwagon.

DOUGLAS, BUSTER (James Douglas). Columbus, OH, 4/7/60. Boxer. Defeated Mike Tyson.

DOUGLAS, DONNA (Dorothy Bourgeois). Baywood, LA, 9/26/35. Actor. Elly May Clampett on *The Beverly Hillbillies.*

DOUGLAS, KIRK (Issur Danielovitch). Amsterdam, NY, 12/9/16. Actor, producer, father of Michael. *Spartacus.*

DOW, TONY. Hollywood, CA, 4/13/45. Actor. Wally Cleaver on *Leave It to Beaver.*

DOWN, LESLEY-ANN. London, England, 3/17/54. Actor. *Dallas.*

DOWNEY, BRIAN. Dublin, Ireland, 1/27/51. Drummer. Thin Lizzy.

DOWNEY, MORTON JR. 12/9/33. Controversial talk

show host, actor.

DOWNS, HUGH. Akron, OH, 2/14/21. Host, actor, commentator. *20/20*.

DOZY (Trevor Davies). Enford, England, 11/27/44. Bassist. Dave Dee, Dozy, Beaky, Mick and Tich.

DRAGON, DARYL. Los Angeles, CA, 8/27/42. Keyboardist. The Captain & Tennille.

DR. DRE Compton, CA, 1965. Rap artist, record producer. *The Chronic*.

DREJA, CHRIS. Surbiton, England, 11/11/44. Guitarist. The Yardbirds.

DREYFUSS, RICHARD. Brooklyn, NY, 10/29/47. Actor. *Close Encounters of the Third Kind*.

DRYDEN, SPENCER. New York, NY, 4/7/38. Drummer. Jefferson Airplane/Starship.

DUBROW, KEVIN. 10/29/55. Lead singer. Quiet Riot.

DUDIKOFF, MICHAEL. Redondo Beach, CA, 10/8/54. Actor. *American Ninja*.

DUFFY, BILLY. 5/12/61. Lead guitarist. The Cult.

DUFFY, JULIA. Minneapolis, MN, 6/27/51. Actor. *Newhart*.

DUFFY, KAREN. 5/23/61. TV personality. MTV.

DUFFY, PATRICK. Townsend, MT, 3/17/49. Actor. Bobby Ewing on *Dallas*.

DUKAKIS, OLYMPIA. Lowell, MA, 6/20/31. Actor. *Moonstruck*.

DUKE, DAVID. Tulsa, OK, 1951. White supremacist, politician.

DUKE, PATTY (Anna Marie Duke). New York, NY, 12/14/46. Actor, formerly married to John Astin, mother of Sean Astin. *The Patty Duke Show*.

DUKES, DAVID. San Francisco, CA, 6/6/45. Actor. *Sisters*.

DULLEA, KEIR. Cleveland, OH, 5/30/36. Actor. *2001: A Space Odyssey*.

DUNAWAY, DENNIS. Cottage Grove, OR, 12/9/48. Bassist. Alice Cooper.

DUNAWAY, FAYE. Bascom, FL, 1/14/41. Actor. *Mommie Dearest*.

DUNCAN, GARY (Gary Grubb). San Diego, CA, 9/4/46. Guitarist. Quicksilver Messenger Service.

DUNCAN, SANDY. Henderson, TX, 2/20/46. Actor. *Funny Face*.

DUNN, DONALD. Memphis, TN, 11/24/41. Bassist. Booker T. & The MG's.

DUNN, LARRY. Colorado, 6/19/53. Keyboardist. Earth, Wind & Fire.

DUNNE, GRIFFIN. New York, NY, 6/8/55. Actor, director, son of Dominick. *After Hours*.

DUNST, KIRSTEN. 4/30/82. Actor. *Interview With A Vampire*.

DURBIN, DEANNA (Edna Durbin). Winnipeg, Canada, 12/4/21. Actor. *One Hundred Men and a Girl*.

DURNING, CHARLES. Highland Falls, NY, 2/28/23. Actor. *Evening Shade*.

DUTTON, CHARLES. Baltimore, MD, 1/30/51. Actor. *Roc*.

DUVALL, ROBERT. San Diego, CA, 1/5/31. Actor. *Tender Mercies*.

DUVALL, SHELLEY. Houston, TX, 7/7/49. Actor, producer. *The Shining*.

DYSART, RICHARD. Brighton, MA, 3/30/29. Actor. Leland McKenzie on *L.A. Law*.

EARLE, STEVE. Fort Monroe, VA, 1/17/55. Country/rock singer, songwriter. Guitar Town.

EASTON, ELLIOT (Elliot Shapiro). Brooklyn, NY, 12/18/53. Guitarist. The Cars.

EASTON, SHEENA (Sheena Orr). Bellshill, Scotland, 4/27/59. Rock/R&B singer.

EBSEN, BUDDY (Christian Ebsen Jr.). Belleville, IL, 4/2/08. Actor. Jed Clampett on *The Beverly Hillbillies*.

ECHOLS, JOHN. Memphis, TN, 1945. Lead guitarist. Love.

EDDY, DUANE. Corning, NY, 4/26/38. Legendary rock guitarist.

EDEN, BARBARA (Barbara Huffman). Tucson, AZ, 8/23/34. Actor. Jeannie in *I Dream of Jeannie*.

EDGE, GRAEME. Rochester, England, 3/30/42. Drummer. The Moody Blues.

EDGE, THE (David Evans). Wales, 8/8/61. Guitarist. U2.

EDMONTON, JERRY. Canada, 10/24/46. Drummer. Steppenwolf.

EDWARD, PRINCE. London, England, 3/10/64. British royalty, son of Queen Elizabeth II.

EDWARDS, BERNARD. Greenville, NC, 10/31/52. Bassist. Chic.

EDWARDS, BLAKE (William Blake McEdwards). Tulsa, OK, 7/26/22. Writer, director. The *Pink Panther* series. Married to Julie Andrews.

EDWARDS, NOKIE. Washington, DC, 5/9/39. Lead guitarist. The Ventures.

EGGAR, SAMANTHA. London, England, 3/5/39. Actor. *The Collector*.

EIKENBERRY, JILL. New Haven, CT, 1/21/47. Actor. Ann Kelsey on *L.A. Law*.

EKBERG, ANITA. Malmo, Sweden, 9/29/31. Actor. *La Dolce Vita*.

EKLAND, BRITT. Stockholm, Sweden, 10/6/42. Actor. *After the Fox*.

ELIZONDO, HECTOR. New York, NY, 12/22/36. Actor. *Pretty Woman*.

ELLERBEE, LINDA. Bryan, TX, 8/15/44. News commentator. *Our World*.

ELLIOTT, BOBBY. Burnley, England, 12/8/42. Drum-

mer. The Hollies.

ELLIOTT, CHRIS. New York, NY, 1960. Comedy writer, actor. *Get a Life*.

ELLIOTT, DENNIS. London, England, 8/18/50. Drummer. Foreigner.

ELLIOTT, JOE. Sheffield, England, 8/1/59. Singer. Def Leppard.

ELLIOTT, SAM. Sacramento, CA, 8/9/44. Actor. *Tombstone*.

ELLIS, RALPH. Liverpool, England, 3/8/42. Guitarist, singer. The Swinging Blue Jeans.

ELMORE, GREG. San Diego, CA, 9/4/46. Drummer. Quicksilver Messenger Service.

ELSWIT, RIK. New York, NY, 7/6/45. Guitarist, singer. Dr. Hook.

ELVIRA (Cassandra Peterson). Manhattan, KS, 9/17/51. Horror film hostess.

ELWES, CARY. London, England, 10/26/62. Actor. *The Princess Bride*.

EMERSON, KEITH. Todmorden, England, 11/1/44. Keyboardist. Emerson, Lake & Palmer.

ENGEL, SCOTT (Noel Engel). Hamilton, OH, 1/9/44. Singer. The Walker Brothers.

ENGLUND, ROBERT. Hollywood, CA, 6/6/49. Actor. Freddie Krueger in *Nightmare on Elm Street* series.

ENNIS, RAY. Liverpool, England, 5/26/42. Lead guitarist, singer. The Swinging Blue Jeans.

ENO, BRIAN. Woodbridge, England, 5/15/48. Synthesizer player, producer. Cofounder of Roxy Music.

ENTNER, WARREN. Boston, MA, 7/7/44. Singer, guitarist. The Grass Roots.

ENTWISTLE, JOHN. Chiswick, England, 10/9/44. Bassist. The Who.

ENYA (Eithne Ni Bhraona). Gweedore, Ireland, 1962.

Singer, composer.

ERRICO, GREG. San Francisco, CA, 9/1/46. Drummer. Sly & The Family Stone.

ERVING, JULIUS. Roosevelt, NY, 2/22/50. Basketball great. Philadelphia 76ers.

ESIASON, BOOMER (Norman Julius Esiason Jr.). West Islip, NY, 4/17/61. NFL football player.

ESPOSITO, GIANCARLO. Copenhagen, Denmark, 4/26/61. Actor. *Do the Right Thing.*

ESSEX, DAVID (David Cook). Plaistow, England, 7/23/47. Drummer, singer, songwriter, actor. *Stardust.*

ESTEFAN, GLORIA (Gloria Fajardo). Havana, Cuba, 9/1/57. Latin pop singer. The Miami Sound Machine.

ESTEVEZ, EMILIO. New York, NY, 5/12/62. Actor, writer, divorced from Paula Abdul, son of Martin Sheen. *Repo Man.*

ESTRADA, ERIK. New York, NY, 3/16/49. Actor. Frank "Ponch" Poncherello on *CHiPS.*

EUGENIE, PRINCESS. London, England, 3/23/90. British royalty, daughter of Prince Andrew and the Duchess of York.

EVANGELISTA, LINDA. Canada, 5/10/65. Supermodel.

EVANS, DALE (Francis Smith). Uvalde, TX, 10/31/12. Actor. *The Yellow Rose of Texas.*

EVANS, LINDA (Linda Evanstad). Hartford, CT, 11/18/42. Actor. *Dynasty.*

EVANS, MARK. Melbourne, Australia, 3/2/56. Bassist. AC/DC.

EVANS, MIKE (Michael Jonas Evans). Salisbury, NC, 11/3/49. Actor. Lionel on *The Jeffersons.*

EVERETT, CHAD (Raymond Lee Cramton). South Bend, IN, 6/11/36. Actor. *Medical Center.*

EVERLY, DON (Isaac Everly). Brownie, KY, 2/1/37. Singer, guitarist. The Everly Brothers.

EVERLY, PHIL. Chicago, IL, 1/19/39. Singer, guitarist. The Everly Brothers.

EVERT, CHRIS. Ft. Lauderdale, FL, 12/21/54. Tennis player.

EVIGAN, GREG. South Amboy, NJ, 10/14/53. Actor. *B.J. and the Bear.*

FABARES, SHELLEY (Michelle Marie Fabares). Santa Monica, CA, 1/19/44. Actor, married to Mike Farrell, niece of Nanette Fabray. Christine Armstrong on *Coach.*

FABIAN (Fabian Forte). Philadelphia, PA, 2/6/43. Singer, actor. *American Bandstand.*

FABIO (Fabio Lanzoni). Milan, Italy, 3/15/61. Model.

FABRAY, NANETTE (Ruby Nanette Fabares). San Diego, CA, 10/27/20. Actor, aunt of Shelley Fabares. *One Day at a Time.*

FAGEN, DONALD. Passaic, NJ, 1/10/48. Singer, keyboardist. Steely Dan.

FAHEY, SIOBHAN. 9/10/60. Singer. Bananarama.

FAIRCHILD, MORGAN (Patsy McClenny). Dallas, TX, 2/3/50. Actor. *Falcon Crest.*

FAIRWEATHER-LOW, ANDY. Ystrad Mynach, Wales, 8/8/50. Singer, guitarist. Amen Corner.

FAITH, ADAM (Terence Nelhams). Acton, England, 6/23/40. Singer, actor, financial adviser.

FAITHFULL, MARIANNE. Hampstead, England, 12/29/46. Folk/rock singer.

FAKIR, ABDUL. Detroit, MI, 12/26/35. Singer. The Four Tops.

FALANA, LOLA (Loletha Elaine Falana). Philadelphia, PA, 9/11/43. Singer.

FALCONER, EARL. Birmingham, England, 1/23/59.

Bassist. UB40.

FALK, PETER. New York, NY, 9/16/27. Actor. *Columbo.*

FALTSKOG, AGNETHA. Jonkoping, Sweden, 4/5/50. Singer. Abba.

FAMBROUGH, HENRY. 5/10/38. Singer. The (Detroit) Spinners.

FAME, GEORGIE (Clive Powell). Leigh, England, 9/26/43. Singer, keyboardist. Georgie Fame & The Blue Flames.

FARENTINO, JAMES. Brooklyn, NY, 2/24/38. Actor. *Dynasty.*

FARINA, DENNIS. Chicago, IL, 2/29/44. Actor. *Crime Story.*

FARNER, MARK. Flint, MI, 9/29/48. Singer, guitarist. Grand Funk Railroad.

FARR, JAMIE (Jameel Joseph Farah). Toledo, OH, 7/1/34. Actor. Maxwell Klinger on *M*A*S*H.*

FARRAKHAN, LOUIS (Louis Eugene Walcott). New York, NY, 5/11/33. Controversial Muslim minister.

FARRELL, BOBBY. Aruba, West Indies, 10/6/49. Singer. Boney M.

FARRELL, MIKE. St. Paul, MN, 2/6/39. Actor, writer, director, married to Shelley Fabares. B.J. Hunnicutt on *M*A*S*H.*

FARRIS, STEVE. 5/1/57. Guitarist. Mr. Mister.

FARRISS, ANDREW. Perth, Australia, 3/27/59. Keyboardist. INXS.

FARRISS, JON. Perth, Australia, 8/10/61. Drummer, singer. INXS.

FAULKNER, ERIC. Edinburgh, Scotland, 10/21/55. Guitarist. The Bay City Rollers.

FAWCETT, FARRAH. Corpus Christi, TX, 2/2/47. Actor. Jill Munroe on *Charlie's Angels.*

FELDMAN, COREY. Reseda, CA, 7/16/71. Actor. *Stand By Me.*

FELDON, BARBARA (Barbara

Hall). Pittsburgh, PA, 3/12/41. Actor. Agent 99 on *Get Smart.*

FELDSHUH, TOVAH. New York, NY, 12/27/53. Actor. *The Idolmaker.*

FELICIANO, JOSE. Lares, Puerto Rico, 9/10/45. Singer, guitarist. *Chico and the Man.*

FENN, SHERILYN. Detroit, MI, 2/1/65. Actor. *Twin Peaks.*

FERGUSON, JAY (John Ferguson). Burbank, CA, 5/10/47. Singer. Spirit.

FERGUSON, LARRY. Nassau, Bahamas, 4/14/48. Keyboardist. Hot Chocolate.

FERGUSON, SARAH. London, England, 10/15/59. Duchess of York. Formerly married to Prince Andrew.

FERRARO, GERALDINE. Newburgh, NY, 8/26/35. Politician, first woman vice-presidential candidate.

FERRER, MEL (Melchor Gaston Ferrer). Elberon, NJ, 8/25/12. Producer, director, actor, formerly married to Audrey Hepburn. *Falcon Crest.*

FERRER, MIGUEL. Santa Monica, CA, 2/7/54. Actor, son of Jose Ferrer and Rosemary Clooney. *Twin Peaks.*

FERRIGNO, LOU. Brooklyn, NY, 11/9/52. Actor, bodybuilder. *The Incredible Hulk.*

FERRIS, BARBARA. London, England, 10/3/40. Actor. *The Strauss Family.*

FERRY, BRYAN. Durham, England, 9/26/45. Singer, songwriter. Roxy Music.

FIEGER, DOUG. Detroit, MI, 8/20/52. Singer, guitarist. The Knack.

FIELDER, JIM. Denton, TX, 10/4/47. Bassist. Blood, Sweat & Tears.

FIELDS, KIM. Los Angeles, CA, 5/12/69. Actor. Dorothy "Tootie" Ramsey on *The Facts of Life.*

FIERSTEIN, HARVEY. Brooklyn, NY, 6/6/54. Actor, writer.

Mrs. Doubtfire.

FILIPOVIC, ZLATA. Sarajevo, Bosnia-Herzegovina, 12/3/81. Author. *Zlata's Diary.*

FINCH, RICHARD. Indianapolis, IN, 1/25/54. Bassist. KC & The Sunshine Band.

FINER, JEM. Ireland. Banjoist. The Pogues.

FINGERS, JOHNNIE (Johnnie Moylett). Ireland, 9/10/56. Keyboardist, singer. The Boomtown Rats.

FINN, TIM (Te Awamutu). New Zealand, 6/25/52. Singer, keyboardist. Split Enz.

FINNEY, ALBERT. Salford, England, 5/9/36. Actor. *Tom Jones.*

FIORENTINO, LINDA (Clorinda Fiorentino). Philadelphia, PA, 3/9/58. Actor. *The Last Seduction.*

FIRTH, COLIN. Grayshott, England, 9/10/60. Actor. *Another Country.*

FISH (Derek Dick). Dalkeith, Scotland, 4/25/58. Singer. Marillion.

FISHER, AMY. New York, NY, 1974. The "Long Island Lolita."

FISHER, EDDIE. Philadelphia, PA, 8/10/28. Singer, formerly married to Debbie Reynolds, Elizabeth Taylor, and Connie Stevens, father of Carrie Fisher. *The Eddie Fisher Show.*

FISHER, JOELY. 10/29/67. Actor, daughter of Eddie Fisher. *Ellen.*

FISHER, MATTHEW. Croydon, England, 3/7/46. Keyboardist. Procol Harum.

FISHER, ROGER. Seattle, WA, 2/14/50. Guitarist. Heart.

FITZGERALD, GERALDINE. Dublin, Ireland, 11/24/14. Actor. *Wuthering Heights.*

FLACK, ROBERTA. Black Mountain, NC, 2/10/40. Pop singer. "The First Time Ever I Saw Your Face."

FLATLEY, MICHAEL. 7/16/58. Dancer. *Lord of the Dance.*

FLEA (Michael Balzary). Melbourne, Australia. Singer, bassist. The Red Hot Chili Peppers.

FLEETWOOD, MICK. London, England, 6/24/42. Drummer. Fleetwood Mac.

FLEMING, PEGGY. San Jose, CA, 7/27/48. Ice skater. Olympic gold medalist.

FLETCHER, ANDY. Basildon, England, 7/8/60. Keyboardist. Depeche Mode.

FLETCHER, LOUISE. Birmingham, AL, 7/22/34. Actor. *One Flew over the Cuckoo's Nest.*

FLOYD, EDDIE. Montgomery, AL, 6/25/35. R&B singer, songwriter.

FOGELBERG, DAN. Peoria, IL, 8/13/51. Guitarist, singer, songwriter.

FOGERTY, JOHN. Berkeley, CA, 5/28/45. Singer, guitarist. Creedence Clearwater Revival.

FOLLOWS, MEGAN. Toronto, Canada, 3/14/68. Actor. *Anne of Green Gables.*

FONDA, PETER. New York, NY, 2/23/40. Actor, son of Henry Fonda, brother of Jane, father of Bridget. *Easy Rider.*

FONTAINE, JOAN (Joan de Havilland). Tokyo, Japan, 10/22/17. Actor, sister of Olivia de Havilland. *Suspicion.*

FONTANA, WAYNE (Glyn Ellis). Manchester, England, 10/28/40. Singer. Wayne Fontana & The Mindbenders.

FORD, FAITH. Alexandria, LA, 9/14/64. Actor. Corky Sherwood Forrest on *Murphy Brown.*

FORD, FRANKIE (Frankie Guzzo). Gretna, LA, 8/4/40. Singer.

FORD, LITA. London, England, 9/23/59. Lead guitarist. The Runaways.

FOREMAN, CHRIS. England, 8/8/58. Guitarist. Madness.

FOREMAN, GEORGE. Marshall, TX, 1/10/49. Boxer, actor. *George.*

FORSSI, KEN. Cleveland, OH, 1943. Bassist. Love.

FORSTER, ROBERT. Rochester, NY, 7/13/41. Actor. *Jackie Brown.*

FORSYTHE, JOHN (John Freund). Penns Grove, NJ, 1/29/18. Actor. Blake Carrington on *Dynasty.*

FORTUNE, JIMMY. Newport News, VA, 3/1/55. Musician. Statler Brothers.

FORTUNE, NICK (Nick Fortuna). Chicago, IL, 5/1/46. Bassist. The Buckinghams.

FOSTER, MEG. Reading, PA, 5/14/48. Actor. *Cagney and Lacey.*

FOX, JACKIE. California, 1960. Bassist. The Runaways.

FOX, JAMES. London, England, 5/19/39. Actor. *The Loneliness of the Long Distance Runner.*

FOX, SAMANTHA. England, 4/15/66. Singer. "Naughty Girls (Need Love Too)."

FOX, TERRY (Terrance Stanley Fox). Winnipeg, Canada, 7/28/58. Track athlete, fund-raiser.

FOXTON, BRUCE. Woking, Surrey England, 9/1/55. Guitarist. The Jam.

FOXWORTH, ROBERT. Houston, TX, 11/1/41. Actor. Chase Gioberti on *Falcon Crest.*

FOXWORTHY, JEFF Hapeville, GA, 9/6/58. Comedian, actor. "You Might Be a Redneck If..."

FRAKES, JONATHAN. Bethlehem, PA, 8/19/52. Actor. Commander William Riker on *Star Trek: The Next Generation.*

FRAME, RODDY. East Kilbride, Scotland, 1/29/64. Singer, guitarist. Aztec Camera.

FRAMPTON, PETER KEN-

NETH. Beckenham, England, 4/22/50. Guitarist, singer, songwriter.

FRANCIOSA, ANTHONY (Anthony Papaleo). New York, NY, 10/25/28. Actor. *The Long Hot Summer.*

FRANCIS, ANNE. Ossining, NY, 9/16/30. Actor, former child model.

FRANCIS, BILL. Mobile, AL, 1/16/42. Keyboardist, singer. Dr. Hook.

FRANCIS, CONNIE (Concetta Franconero). Newark, NJ, 12/12/38. Singer. "Where the Boys Are."

FRANCIS, GENIE. 5/26/62. Actor. *General Hospital.*

FRANKEN, AL. 5/21/51. Actor, author. *Rush Limbaugh's a Big Fat Idiot.*

FRANKLIN, BONNIE. 1/6/44. Actor. *One Day At A Time.*

FRANTZ, CHRIS (Charlton Frantz). Fort Campbell, KY, 5/8/51. Drummer. Talking Heads.

FRASER, ANDY. London, England, 8/7/52. Bassist. Free.

FRAZIER, JOE. Beaufort, SC, 1/17/44. Boxer, former heavyweight champ.

FREDRIKSSON, MARIE. Sweden, 5/30/58. Singer. Roxette.

FREEMAN, BOBBY. San Francisco, CA, 6/13/40. Singer, songwriter.

FREEMAN, MORGAN. Memphis, TN, 6/1/37. Actor. *Driving Miss Daisy.*

FREHLEY, ACE (Paul Frehley). The Bronx, NY, 4/22/51. Guitarist, singer. Kiss.

FREIBERG, DAVID. Boston, MA, 8/24/38. Bassist. Quicksilver Messenger Service.

FREWER, MATT. Washington, DC, 1/4/58. Actor. *Max Headroom.*

FREY, GLENN. Detroit, MI, 11/6/48. Singer, songwriter. The Eagles.

FRICKER, BRENDA. Dublin,

Ireland, 2/17/45. Actor. *My Left Foot.*

FRIPP, ROBERT. Wimborne Minster, England, 1946. Guitarist. King Crimson.

FROST, CRAIG. Flint, MI, 4/20/48. Keyboardist. Grand Funk Railroad.

FRY, MARTIN. Manchester, England, 3/9/58. Singer. ABC.

FUNICELLO, ANNETTE. Utica, NY, 10/22/42. Actor, Mouseketeer. *Beach Blanket Bingo.*

FURAY, RICHIE. Yellow Springs, OH, 5/9/44. Singer, guitarist. Buffalo Springfield; Poco.

FURUHOLMEN, MAGS. Oslo, Norway, 11/1/62. Keyboardist, singer. a-ha.

G, KENNY. 6/5/56. Musician. *Breathless.*

GABLE, JOHN CLARK. Los Angeles, CA, 3/20/61. Actor. Son of Clark Gable.

GABOR, ZSA ZSA (Sari Gabor). Budapest, Hungary, 2/6/17. Actor. *Moulin Rouge.*

GABRIEL, PETER. Cobham, England, 2/13/50. Singer, songwriter. Genesis.

GAHAN, DAVE. Epping, England, 5/9/62. Singer. Depeche Mode.

GAIL, MAXWELL. Derfoil, MI, 4/5/43. Actor. Sergeant Stanley Wojohowicz on *Barney Miller.*

GALLAGHER, PETER. Armonk, NY, 8/19/55. Actor. *sex, lies and videotape.*

GARDNER, CARL. Tyler, TX, 4/29/27. Lead singer. The Coasters.

GARFAT, JANCE. California, 3/3/44. Bassist, singer. Dr. Hook.

GARFUNKEL, ART. New York, NY, 11/5/41. Singer, actor, former partner of Paul Simon. *Carnal Knowledge.*

GARLAND, BEVERLY. Santa Cruz, CA, 10/17/26. Actor. *My Three Sons.*

GARNER, JAMES (James Baumgarner). Norma, OK,

4/7/28. Actor, producer. *The Rockford Files.*

GARR, TERI. Lakewood, OH, 12/11/44. Actor. *Tootsie.*

GARRETT, BETTY. St. Joseph, MO, 5/23/19. Actor. *All in the Family.*

GARRITY, FREDDIE. Manchester, England, 11/14/40. Singer. Freddie & The Dreamers.

GARTH, JENNIE. Champaign, IL, 4/3/72. Actor. Kelly Taylor on *Beverly Hills 90210.*

GARTSIDE, GREEN (Green Strohmeyer-Gartside). Cardiff, Wales, 6/22/56. Singer. Scritti Politti.

GARY, BRUCE. Burbank, CA, 4/7/52. Drummer. The Knack.

GATES, DAVID. Tulsa, OK, 12/11/40. Keyboardist, singer. Bread.

GATLIN, RUDY. 8/20/52. Singer. The Gatlin Brothers.

GATLIN, STEVE. 4/4/51. Singer. The Gatlin Brothers.

GAUDIO, BOB. The Bronx, NY, 11/17/42. Singer, organist. The Four Seasons.

GAYLE, CRYSTAL (Brenda Webb). Paintsville, KY, 1/9/51. Country singer.

GAYLORD, MITCH. Van Nuys, CA, 1961. Gymnast.

GAYNOR, MITZI (Francesca Marlene Von Gerber). Chicago, IL, 9/4/31. Actor. *Anything Goes.*

GAZZARA, BEN (Biago Gazzara). New York, NY, 8/28/30. Actor. *Inchon.*

GEARY, ANTHONY. Coalville, UT, 5/29/47. Actor. Luke Spencer on *General Hospital.*

GEARY, CYNTHIA. Jackson, MS, 3/21/66. Actor. *Northern Exposure.*

GEFFEN, DAVID Brooklyn, NY, 2/21/43. Procucer, executive. Geffen Records, Dreamworks SKG.

GEILS, J. (Jerome Geils). New York, NY, 2/20/46. Guitarist. The J. Geils Band.

GELDOF, BOB. Dublin, Ireland, 10/5/54. Singer. The Boomtown Rats.

GERARD, GIL. Little Rock, AR, 1/23/43. Actor. *Buck Rogers in the 25th Century.*

GERARDO. Ecuador, 1965. Rap artist. "Rico Suave."

GERTZ, JAMI. Chicago, IL, 10/28/65. Actor. *Less Than Zero; Twister.*

GESSLE, PER. 1/12/59. Guitarist, singer. Roxette.

GETTY, BALTHAZAR. 1/22/75. Actor, grandson of J. Paul Getty. *Where the Day Takes You.*

GETTY, ESTELLE. New York, NY, 7/25/23. Actor. Sophia Petrillo on *The Golden Girls.*

GHOSTLEY, ALICE. Eve, MO, 8/14/26. Actor. *Bewitched.*

GIAMMARESE, CARL. Chicago, IL, 8/21/47. Guitarist. The Buckinghams.

GIANNINI, GIANCARLO. Spezia, Italy, 8/1/42. Actor. *Seven Beauties.*

GIBB, BARRY. Isle of Man, England, 9/1/46. Singer, guitarist. The Bee Gees.

GIBB, CYNTHIA. Bennington, VT, 12/14/63. Actor. *Madman of the People.*

GIBB, MAURICE. Manchester, England, 12/22/49. Singer, bassist. The Bee Gees.

GIBB, ROBIN. Manchester, England, 12/22/49. Singer. The Bee Gees.

GIBBINS, MIKE. Swansea, Wales, 3/12/49. Drummer. Badfinger.

GIBBONS, BILLY. Houston, TX, 12/16/49. Guitarist, singer. ZZ Top.

GIBBONS, LEEZA. 3/26/57. TV personality. *Entertainment Tonight.*

GIBBS, MARLA (Margaret Bradley). Chicago, IL, 6/14/31. Actor. Florence Johnston on *The Jeffersons.*

GIBSON, DEBORAH. Long Island, NY, 8/31/70. Singer, songwriter, actor. "Foolish Beat."

GIBSON, HENRY. Germantown, PA, 9/21/35. Actor. Poet from *Laugh-In.*

GIFFORD, FRANK. Santa Monica, CA, 8/16/30. Football player turned sports commentator, married to Kathie Lee Gifford. *Monday Night Football.*

GIFT, ROLAND. Birmingham, England, 5/28/62. Singer. Fine Young Cannibals.

GIGUERE, RUSS. Portsmouth, NH, 10/18/43. Singer, guitarist. The Association.

GILBERT, GILLIAN. Manchester, England, 1/27/61. Keyboardist. New Order.

GILBERT, MELISSA. Los Angeles, CA, 5/8/64. Actor, daughter of Robert and Barbara Crane. *Little House on the Prairie.*

GILBERT, SARA (Rebecca Sara MacMahon). Santa Monica, CA, 1/29/75. Actor, sister of Melissa and Jonathan Gilbert. Darlene Conner on *Roseanne.*

GILES, MIKE. Bournemouth, England, 1942. Drummer. King Crimson.

GILL, PETER. Liverpool, England, 3/8/64. Drummer. Frankie Goes to Hollywood.

GILLAN, IAN. Hounslow, England, 8/19/45. Singer. Deep Purple.

GILLIAM, TERRY. Minneapolis, MN, 11/22/40. Writer, director, actor. *Monty Python and the Holy Grail.*

GILMORE, JIMMIE DALE. Tulia, TX, 1945. Country singer. "Dallas."

GILMOUR, DAVID. Cambridge, England, 3/6/44. Singer, guitarist. Pink Floyd.

GINTY, ROBERT. New York, NY, 11/14/48. Actor. *Baa Baa Black Sheep.*

GILPIN, PERI. 5/27/61. Actor. *Frasier.*

GIVENS, ROBIN. New York, NY, 11/27/64. Actor, formerly married to Mike Tyson. *Head of the Class.*

GLASER, PAUL MICHAEL. Cambridge, MA, 3/25/43. Actor, director. Det. Dave Starsky on *Starsky and Hutch.*

GLASS, RON. Evansville, IN, 7/10/45. Actor. *Barney Miller.*

GLEASON, JOANNA. Winnipeg, Canada, 6/2/50. Actor, daughter of Monty Hall. *Into the Woods.*

GLENN, SCOTT. Pittsburgh, PA, 1/26/42. Actor. *Urban Cowboy.*

GLESS, SHARON. Los Angeles, CA, 5/31/43. Actor. Chris Cagney on *Cagney and Lacey.*

GLITTER, GARY (Paul Gadd). Banbury, England, 5/8/40. Singer, songwriter.

GLOVER, CRISPIN. New York, NY, 9/20/64. Actor. George McFly in *Back to the Future.*

GLOVER, DANNY. San Francisco, CA, 7/22/47. Actor. *Lethal Weapon.*

GLOVER, JOHN. Kingston, NY, 8/7/44. Actor. *Shamus.*

GLOVER, ROGER. Brecon, Wales, 11/30/45. Bassist. Deep Purple.

GOBLE, GRAHAM. Adelaide, Australia, 5/15/47. Guitarist. Little River Band.

GODLEY, KEVIN. Manchester, England, 10/7/45. Singer, drummer. 10cc; Godley & Creme.

GOLD, TRACEY. New York, NY, 5/16/69. Actor. *Growing Pains.*

GOLDEN, WILLIAM LEE. Brewton, AL, 1/12/39. Singer. The Oak Ridge Boys.

GOLDING, LYNVAL. Coventry, England, 7/24/51. Guitarist. The Specials.

GOLDTHWAIT, BOBCAT. Syracuse, NY, 5/26/62. Actor. *Police Academy* series.

GOLDWYN, TONY. Los Angeles, CA, 5/20/60. Actor. *Ghost.*

GOLINO, VALERIA. Naples, Italy, 10/22/66. Actor. *Rain Man.*

GOODALL, JANE. London, England, 4/3/34. Author, anthropologist. *In the Shadow of Man.*

GOODEN, SAM. Chattanooga, TN, 9/2/39. Singer. The Impressions.

GORBACHEV, MIKHAIL. Privolnoye, Russia, 3/2/31. Former leader of the USSR.

GORE, ALBERT JR. Washington, DC, 3/31/48. Vice president of the United States.

GORE, LESLEY. New York, NY, 5/2/46. Singer. "It's My Party."

GORE, MARTIN. Basildon, England, 7/23/61. Keyboardist. Depeche Mode.

GORHAM, SCOTT. Santa Monica, CA, 3/17/51. Guitarist. Thin Lizzy.

GORMAN, STEVE. Hopkinsville, KY, 8/17/65. Drummer. The Black Crowes.

GORME, EYDIE. New York, NY, 8/16/32. Singer. Steve and Eydie.

GORRIE, ALAN. Perth, Scotland, 7/19/46. Singer, bassist. Average White Band.

GORSHIN, FRANK. Pittsburgh, PA, 4/5/33. Actor. The Riddler on *Batman.*

GOSSETT, LOUIS JR. Brooklyn, NY, 5/27/37. Actor. *An Officer and a Gentleman.*

GOTTI, JOHN. New York, NY, 10/27/41. Reputed mob leader.

GOUDREAU, BARRY. Boston, MA, 11/29/51. Guitarist. Boston.

GOULD, BILLY. Los Angeles, CA, 4/24/63. Bassist. Faith No More.

GOULD, BOON. 3/14/55. Guitarist. Level 42.

GOULD, ELLIOTT (Elliott Goldstein). Brooklyn, NY, 8/29/38. Actor. Formerly married to Barbra Streisand. *Bob & Carol & Ted & Alice.*

GOULD, PHIL. 2/28/57. Drummer. Level 42.

GOULDMAN, GRAHAM. Manchester, England, 5/10/45. Singer, guitarist. 10cc.

GOULET, ROBERT (Stanley Applebaum). Lawrence, MA, 11/26/33. Singer, actor. *Blue Light.*

GRAF, STEFFI. Bruhl, Germany, 6/14/69. Tennis player, youngest woman to win French Open.

GRAHAM, BILLY. Charlotte, NC, 11/7/18. Evangelist. *Billy Graham Crusades.*

GRAHAM, LARRY. Beaumont, TX, 8/14/46. Bass guitarist. Sly & The Family Stone.

GRAMM, LOU. Rochester, NY, 5/2/50. Singer. Foreigner.

GRANDMASTER FLASH (Joseph Saddler). New York, NY, 1958. Rap artist. Grandmaster Flash; Melle Mel & The Furious Five.

GRANDY, FRED. Sioux City, IA, 6/29/48. Actor, politician. Burl "Gopher" Smith on *The Love Boat.*

GRANGER, FARLEY. San Jose, CA, 7/1/25. Actor. *Strangers on a Train.*

GRANT, AMY. Augusta, GA, 11/25/60. Singer. *Age to Age.*

GRANT, EDDY (Edmond Grant). Plaisance, Guyana, 3/5/48. Reggae singer, songwriter.

GRANT, LEE (Lyova Rosenthal). New York, NY, 10/31/27. Actor, mother of Dinah Manoff. *Peyton Place.*

GRANTHAM, GEORGE. Cordell, OK, 11/20/47. Drummer, singer. Poco.

GRATZER, ALAN. Syracuse, NY, 11/9/48. Drummer. REO Speedwagon.

GRAVES, PETER (Peter Aurness). Minneapolis, MN, 3/18/26. Actor, brother of James Arness. Jim Phelps on *Mission: Impossible.*

GRAY, EDDIE. 2/27/48. Gui-

tarist. Tommy James & The Shondells.

GRAY, LES. Carshalton, England, 4/9/46. Singer. Mud.

GRAY, LINDA. Santa Monica, CA, 9/12/40. Actor. *Dallas.*

GRAY, SPALDING. Barrington, RI, 6/5/41. Actor, writer, performance artist. *The Killing Fields.*

GREBB, MARTY. Chicago, IL, 9/2/46. Keyboardist. The Buckinghams.

GREEN, AL (Al Greene). Forrest City, AR, 4/13/46. R&B singer, songwriter.

GREEN, BRIAN AUSTIN. 7/15/73. Actor. *Beverly Hills 90210.*

GREEN, KARL. Salford, England, 7/31/47. Bassist. Herman's Hermits.

GREENAWAY, PETER. Newport, Wales, 4/5/42. Director, writer. *The Cook, the Thief, His Wife and Her Lover.*

GREENFIELD, DAVE. Keyboardist. The Stranglers.

GREENSPOON, JIMMY. Los Angeles, CA, 2/7/48. Organist. Three Dog Night.

GREENWOOD, ALAN. New York, NY, 10/20/51. Keyboardist. Foreigner.

GREGG, BRIAN. Bassist. Johnny Kidd & The Pirates.

GREGORY, GLENN. Sheffield, England, 5/16/58. Singer. Heaven 17.

GRETZKY, WAYNE. Brantford, Canada, 1/26/61. Hockey player.

GREY, JENNIFER. New York, NY, 3/26/60. Actor, daughter of Joel. *Dirty Dancing.*

GREY, JOEL (Joel Katz). Cleveland, OH, 4/11/32. Musical comedy performer, father of Jennifer. *Cabaret.*

GRIER, DAVID ALAN. Detroit, MI, 6/30/55. Actor. *In Living Color.*

GRIER, PAM. 5/26/49. Actor. *Jackie Brown.*

GRIER, ROSEY (Roosevelt Grier). Cuthbert, GA, 7/14/32. Football player, actor.

GRIFFEY, KEN JR. 11/21/69. Baseball player.

GRIFFITH, ANDY. Mt. Airy, NC, 6/1/26. Actor, writer, producer. *The Andy Griffith Show.*

GRIFFITH, NANCI. Austin, TX, 7/6/53. Singer, songwriter. "From a Distance."

GRILL, ROB. Los Angeles, CA, 11/30/44. Bassist, singer. The Grass Roots.

GROSS, MARY. Chicago, IL, 3/25/53. Actor, sister of Michael. *Saturday Night Live.*

GROSS, MICHAEL. Chicago, IL, 6/21/47. Actor, brother of Mary. Steven Keaton on *Family Ties.*

GRUNDY, HUGH. Winchester, England, 3/6/45. Drummer. The Zombies.

GUCCIONE, BOB. New York, NY, 12/17/30. Publisher, founder of *Penthouse.*

GUEST, CHRISTOPHER. New York, NY, 2/5/48. Actor, writer, married to Jamie Lee Curtis. *This Is Spinal Tap.*

GUEST, LANCE. Saratoga, CA, 7/21/60. Actor. *Knots Landing.*

GUEST, WILLIAM. Atlanta, GA, 6/2/41. Singer. Gladys Knight & The Pips.

GUILLAUME, ROBERT (Robert Williams). St. Louis, MO, 11/30/27. Actor. Benson DuBois on *Soap.*

GUISEWITE, CATHY. 9/5/50. Cartoonist. *Cathy.*

GULAGER, CLU. Holdenville, OK, 11/16/28. Actor. *The Last Picture Show.*

GUMBEL, BRYANT. New Orleans, LA, 9/29/48. News show host and sportscaster. *Today.*

GUSTAFSON, KARIN. Miami, FL, 6/23/59. Actor. *Taps.*

GUSTAFSON, STEVEN. Bassist. 10,000 Maniacs.

GUTHRIE, ARLO. New York, NY, 7/10/47. Folk singer, songwriter. "Alice's Restaurant."

GUTTENBERG, STEVE. Brooklyn, NY, 8/24/58. Actor. *Three Men and a Baby.*

GUY, BILLY. Attasca, TX, 6/20/36. Baritone. The Coasters.

GUY, BUDDY (George Guy). Lettsworth, LA, 7/30/36. Blues guitarist.

GUY, JASMINE. Boston, MA, 3/10/62. Actor. Whitley Gilbert on *A Different World.*

HAAS, LUKAS. West Hollywood, CA, 4/16/76. Actor. *Witness.*

HACK, SHELLEY. Greenwich, CT, 7/6/52. Actor. *Charlie's Angels.*

HACKETT, BUDDY (Leonard Hacker). Brooklyn, NY, 8/31/24. Actor. *It's a Mad Mad Mad Mad World; The Love Bug.*

HADLEY, TONY. Islington, England, 6/2/59. Singer. Spandau Ballet.

HAGAR, SAMMY. Monterey, CA, 10/13/47. Singer, guitarist. Van Halen.

HAGERTY, JULIE. Cincinnati, OH, 6/15/55. Actor. *Airplane!*

HAGMAN, LARRY (Larry Hageman). Fort Worth, TX, 9/21/31. Actor, son of Mary Martin. J. R. Ewing on *Dallas.*

HAHN, JESSICA. Massapequa, NY, 7/7/59. *Playboy* model, involved in PTL/Jim Bakker scandal.

HAID, CHARLES. San Francisco, CA, 6/2/43. Actor, director, producer. Andrew Renko on *Hill Street Blues.*

HAIM, COREY. Toronto, Canada, 12/23/71. Actor. *The Lost Boys.*

HALE, BARBARA. DeKalb, IL, 4/18/22. Actor, mother of William Katt. Della Street on *Perry Mason.*

HALFORD, ROB. Birmingham, England, 8/25/51. Singer. Judas Priest.

HALL, ANTHONY MICHAEL. Boston, MA, 4/14/68. Actor. *Sixteen Candles.*

HALL, ARSENIO. Cleveland, OH, 2/12/56. Actor. *The Arsenio Hall Show.*

HALL, BRIDGET. Dallas, TX, 12/14/77. Supermodel.

HALL, BRUCE. Champaign, IL, 5/3/53. Bassist. REO Speedwagon.

HALL, DARYL (Daryl Hohl). Pottstown, PA, 10/11/46. Singer, guitarist. Hall & Oates.

HALL, DEIDRE. 10/31/47. Actor. Marlena Evans on *Days of Our Lives.*

HALL, FAWN. Annandale, VA, 9/4/59. Secretary for Oliver North. Iran-Contra scandal.

HALL, JERRY. 7/2/56. Model, married to Mick Jagger.

HALL, MONTY. Winnipeg, Canada, 8/25/21. TV personality. *Let's Make a Deal.*

HALL, TERRY. Coventry, England, 3/19/59. Singer. The Specials.

HAM, GREG. Australia, 9/27/53. Saxophonist, keyboardist, flautist. Men at Work.

HAM, PETE. Swansea, Wales, 4/27/47. Guitarist, pianist, singer. Badfinger.

HAMEL, VERONICA. Philadelphia, PA, 11/20/43. Actor. Joyce Davenport on *Hill Street Blues.*

HAMILL, DOROTHY. Chicago, IL, 7/26/56. Ice skater. Olympic gold medalist.

HAMILL, MARK. Oakland, CA, 9/25/51. Actor. Luke Skywalker in *Star Wars* trilogy.

HAMILTON, GEORGE. Memphis, TN, 8/12/39. Actor. *Love at First Bite.*

HAMILTON, LINDA. Salisbury, MD, 9/26/56. Actor. Sarah Connor in *The Terminator.* Separated from James Cameron.

HAMILTON, SCOTT. Haverford, PA, 8/28/58. Ice skater.

HAMILTON, TOM. Colorado Springs, CO, 12/31/51. Bassist. Aerosmith.

HAMLIN, HARRY. Pasadena, CA, 10/30/51. Actor. *L.A. Law.*

HAMLISCH, MARVIN. New York, NY, 6/2/44. Composer. *The Way We Were; The Sting.*

HAMMER, MC. (Stanley Kirk Burrell). Oakland, CA, 3/30/62. Rap artist, dancer. *Please Hammer Don't Hurt 'Em.*

HAMMETT, KIRK. 11/18/62. Guitarist. Metallica.

HAMPSHIRE, SUSAN. London, England, 5/12/41. Actor. *The Forsythe Saga.*

HANCOCK, HERBIE. Chicago, IL, 4/12/40. Jazz pianist, composer. "Rockit."

HANNAH, DARYL. Chicago, IL, 12/3/60. Actor. *Splash.*

HANSON, ISAAC. 11/17/80. Singer. "MMMbop."

HANSON, TAYLOR. 3/14/83. Singer. "MMMbop."

HANSON, ZAC. 10/22/85. Singer. "MMMbop."

HARDING, TONYA. Portland, OR, 11/12/70. Figure skater. Pled guilty to hindering prosecution in Nancy Kerrigan attack.

HARDISON, KADEEM. Brooklyn, NY, 7/24/66. Actor. Dwayne Wayne on *A Different World.*

HAREWOOD, DORIAN. Dayton, OH, 8/6/50. Actor. *Roots—The Next Generation.*

HARKET, MORTEN. Konigsberg, Norway, 9/14/59. Lead singer. a-ha.

HARLEY, STEVE (Steve Nice). London, England, 2/27/51. Singer. Steve Harley & Cockney Rebel.

HARLIN, RENNY. 3/15/58. Director, formerly married to Geena Davis.

HARMON, MARK. Los Angeles, CA, 9/2/51. Actor. *Chicago Hope.* Married to Pam Dawber.

HARPER, JESSICA. Chicago, IL, 10/10/49. Actor.

HARPER, TESS (Tessie Jean

Washam). Mammoth Spring, AR, 8/15/50. Actor. *Crimes of the Heart.*

HARPER, VALERIE. Suffern, NY, 8/22/39. Actor. Rhoda Morgenstern on *The Mary Tyler Moore Show.*

HARRINGTON, PAT. New York, NY, 8/13/29. Actor. Dwayne Schneider on *One Day at a Time.*

HARRIS, BARBARA (Sandra Markowitz). Evanston, IL, 7/25/35. Actor. *Family Plot.*

HARRIS, JULIE. Grosse Point, MI, 12/2/25. Actor. *Knots Landing.*

HARRIS, EMMYLOU. 4/2/47. Singer.

HARRIS, MEL (Mary Ellen Harris). Bethlehem, PA, 7/12/56. Actor. Hope Murdoch Steadman on *thirtysomething.*

HARRIS, RICHARD. Limerick, Ireland, 10/1/33. Actor. *A Man Called Horse.*

HARRISON, BILLY. Belfast, Ireland, 10/14/42. Lead guitarist. Them.

HARRISON, GEORGE. Liverpool, England, 2/25/43. Singer, lead guitarist. The Beatles.

HARRISON, GREGORY. Catalina Island, CA, 5/31/50. Actor. *Trapper John, MD.*

HARRISON, JENILEE. Northridge, CA, 6/12/59. Actor. Jamie Ewing Barnes on *Dallas.*

HARRISON, JERRY. Milwaukee, WI, 2/21/49. Keyboardist. Talking Heads.

HARRISON, NOEL. London, England, 1/29/34. Singer, actor. *The Girl from U.N.C.L.E.*

HARRY, DEBORAH. Miami, FL, 7/1/45. Singer. Blondie.

HART, MARY. Sioux Falls, SD, 11/8/51. TV hostess. *Entertainment Tonight.*

HART, MICKY (Michael Hart). New York, NY, 9/11/44. Drummer, songwriter. Grateful Dead.

HARTLEY, MARIETTE. New York, NY, 6/21/40. Actor. *Peyton Place.*

HARTMAN, DAVID. Pawtucket, RI, 5/19/35. Actor, talk show host. *Good Morning America.*

HARTMAN, JOHN. Falls Church, VA, 3/18/50. Drummer. The Doobie Brothers.

HASSAN, NORMAN. Birmingham, England, 11/26/57. Percussionist. UB40.

HATCHER, TERI. 12/8/64. Actor. *Lois and Clark: The New Adventures of Superman.*

HATFIELD, BOBBY. Beaver Dam, WI, 8/10/40. Singer. The Righteous Brothers.

HATTON, BILLY. Liverpool, England, 6/9/41. Bassist. The Fourmost.

HAUER, RUTGER. Breukelen, Netherlands, 1/23/44. Actor. *Blade Runner.*

HAVENS, RICHIE. Brooklyn, NY, 1/21/41. Folk/blues guitarist, singer, songwriter.

HAWKING, STEPHEN. Oxford, England, 1/8/42. Theoretical physicist, author of *A Brief History of Time.*

HAY, COLIN. Scotland, 6/29/53. Singer. Men at Work.

HAY, ROY. Southend, England, 8/12/61. Guitarist, keyboardist. Culture Club.

HAYDOCK, ERIC. Stockport, England, 2/3/42. Bassist. The Hollies.

HAYES, CHRIS. California, 11/24/57. Lead guitarist. Huey Lewis & The News.

HAYES, ISAAC. Covington, TN, 8/20/42. R&B/rock saxophonist, keyboardist, singer, songwriter, radio personality, actor. *South Park.*

HAYS, ROBERT. Bethesda, MD, 7/24/47. Actor, married to Cherie Currie. *Airplane!*

HAYWARD, JUSTIN. Wiltshire, England, 10/14/46. Singer, songwriter. The Moody Blues.

HEADLY, GLENNE. New London, CT, 3/13/55. Actor, formerly married to John Malkovich. *Dirty Rotten Scoundrels.*

HEADON, NICKY. Bromley, England, 5/30/55. Drummer. The Clash.

HEALEY, JEFF. Toronto, Canada, 1966. Singer, songwriter, guitarist.

HEARD, JOHN. Washington, DC, 3/7/46. Actor. Father in *Home Alone.*

HEATON, PAUL. Birkenhead, England, 5/9/62. Singer, guitarist. The Housemartins.

HEDREN, TIPPI (Natalie Kay Hedren). New Ulm, MN, 1/19/35. Actor. Mother of Melanie Griffith. *The Birds.*

HEFNER, HUGH. Chicago, IL, 4/9/26. Publisher, founder of *Playboy.*

HELL, RICHARD (Richard Myers). Lexington, KY, 10/2/49. Bassist. Television.

HELLIWELL, JOHN. England, 2/15/45. Saxophonist. Supertramp.

HELM, LEVON. Marvell, AR, 5/26/42. Drummer, singer. The Band.

HELMSLEY, LEONA. New York, NY, 7/4/20. Hotel executive. Convicted of tax evasion.

HEMINGWAY, MARIEL. Ketchum, ID, 11/22/61. Actor, granddaughter of Ernest Hemingway, sister of Margaux. *Manhattan.*

HEMSLEY, SHERMAN. Philadelphia, PA, 2/1/38. Actor. George on *The Jeffersons.*

HENDERSON, ALAN. Belfast, Ireland, 11/26/44. Bassist. Them.

HENDERSON, BILLY. Detroit, MI, 8/9/39. Singer. The (Detroit) Spinners.

HENDERSON, FLORENCE. Dale, IN, 2/14/34. Actor. Carol Brady on *The Brady Bunch.*

HENLEY, DON. Linden, TX,

7/22/47. Singer, songwriter, drummer, guitarist. The Eagles.

HENNER, MARILU. Chicago, IL, 4/6/52. Actor. Elaine Nardo on *Taxi.*

HENRIKSEN, LANCE. New York, NY, 5/5/40. Actor. *Aliens.*

HENRY, BUCK (Buck Zuckerman). New York, NY, 12/9/30. Actor, writer. *Get Smart; That Was the Week That Was.*

HENRY, CLARENCE. Algiers, LA, 3/19/37. Singer. "Ain't Got No Home."

HENRY, JUSTIN. Rye, NY, 5/25/71. Actor. *Kramer vs. Kramer.*

HENRY, PRINCE. London, England, 8/15/84. British royalty, son of Prince Charles and Princess Diana.

HENSLEY, KEN. England, 8/24/45. Keyboardist, guitarist, singer, percussionist. Uriah Heep.

HENSLEY, PAMELA. Los Angeles, CA, 10/3/50. Actor. C. J. Parsons on *Matt Houston.*

HENSTRIDGE, NATASHA. 8/15/74. Actor. *Species.*

HERMAN, PEE-WEE (Paul Reubens). Peekskill, NY, 8/27/52. Children's performer. *Pee-Wee's Playhouse.*

HERRMANN, EDWARD. Washington, DC, 7/21/43. Actor. *The Paper Chase.*

HERSHEY, BARBARA (Barbara Herzstein). Hollywood, CA, 2/5/48. Actor. *Hannah and Her Sisters.*

HERVEY, JASON. Los Angeles, CA, 4/6/72. Actor. Wayne Arnold on *The Wonder Years.*

HESSEMAN, HOWARD. Salem, OR, 2/27/40. Actor. Dr. Johnny Fever on *WKRP in Cincinnati.*

HESTON, CHARLTON (Charles Carter). Evanston, IL, 10/4/24. Actor. *The Ten Commandments.*

HETFIELD, JAMES. 8/3/63. Singer, guitarist. Metallica.

HEWETT, HOWARD. Akron, OH, 10/1/55. Singer. Shalamar.

HEYWARD, NICK. Kent, England, 5/20/61. Guitarist, singer. Haircut 100.

HICKS, CATHERINE. New York, NY, 8/6/51. Actor. *7th Heaven.*

HICKS, TONY. Nelson, England, 12/16/43. Guitarist. The Hollies.

HILL, ANITA. Tulsa, OK, 7/30/56. Lawyer, law professor. Accused Supreme Court nominee Clarence Thomas of sexual harrassment.

HILL, ARTHUR. Saskatchewan, Canada, 8/1/22. Actor. *Owen Marshall, Counsellor at Law.*

HILL, DAVE. Fleet Castle, England, 4/4/52. Guitarist. Slade.

HILL, DUSTY. Dallas, TX, 5/19/49. Bassist, singer. ZZ Top.

HILL, STEVEN. Seattle, WA, 2/24/22. Actor. *Law and Order.*

HILLERMAN, JOHN. Denison, TX, 12/20/32. Actor. Jonathan Quayle Higgins III on *Magnum P.I.*

HILLERMAN, TONY. Sacred Heart, OK, 5/27/25. Novelist.

HILLMAN, CHRIS. Los Angeles, CA, 12/4/42. Singer, bassist. The Byrds.

HINES, GREGORY. New York, NY, 2/14/46. Actor, dancer. *The Cotton Club.*

HINGLE, PAT (Martin Patterson Hingle). Denver, CO, 7/19/23. Actor. *Gunsmoke.*

HINSLEY, HARVEY. Northampton, England, 1/19/48. Guitarist. Hot Chocolate.

HIRSCH, GARY "CHICKEN." England, 1940. Drummer. Country Joe & The Fish.

HIRSCH, JUDD. New York,

NY, 3/15/35. Actor. Alex Rieger on *Taxi.*

HITCHCOCK, RUSSELL. Melbourne, Australia, 6/15/49. Singer. Air Supply.

HO, DON. Kakaako, HI, 8/13/30. Singer. "Tiny Bubbles."

HOBBS, RANDY. 3/22/48. Bassist. The McCoys.

HODGE, PATRICIA. Lincolnshire, England, 9/29/46. Actor. *The Elephant Man.*

HODGSON, ROGER. Portsmouth, England, 3/21/50. Guitarist. Supertramp.

HODO, DAVID. 7/7/50. Singer. The Village People.

HOFFS, SUSANNA. Newport Beach, CA, 1/17/57. Guitarist, singer. The Bangles.

HOGAN, HULK (Terry Gene Bollea). Augusta, GA, 8/11/53. Wrestler, former World Federation heavyweight champion.

HOGAN, PAUL. Lightning Ridge, Australia, 10/8/39. Actor. *Crocodile Dundee.*

HOLBROOK, HAL. Cleveland, OH, 2/17/25. Actor. *All the President's Men.*

HOLDER, NODDY (Neville Holder). Walsall, England, 6/15/50. Guitarist, singer. Slade.

HOLLAND, JOOLS (Julian Holland). 1/24/58. Keyboardist. Squeeze.

HOLLIMAN, EARL. Delhi, LA, 9/11/28. Actor. *Police Woman.*

HOLLIS, MARK. Tottenham, England, 1955. Singer, guitarist, keyboardist. Talk Talk.

HOLM, CELESTE. New York, NY, 4/29/19. Actor. *All About Eve.*

HOLMES, LARRY. Cuthbert, GA, 11/3/49. Boxer. Former heavyweight champ.

HOOK, PETER. Salford, England, 2/13/56. Bassist. Joy Division; New Order.

HOOKER, JOHN LEE. Clarks-

dale, MS, 8/22/17. Legendary blues guitarist, singer, songwriter.

HOOKS, JAN. Decatur, GA, 4/23/57. Actor. Carlene Frazier Dobber on *Designing Women.*

HOPE, BOB (Leslie Hope). Eltham, England, 5/29/03. Actor, performer for overseas troops. *The Road* movies with Bing Crosby.

HOPE, DAVE. Kansas, 10/7/49. Bassist. Kansas.

HOPKIN, MARY. Pontardawe, Wales, 5/3/50. Singer, discovered by the Beatles. "Those Were the Days."

HOPKINS, TELMA. Louisville, KY, 10/28/48. Singer, actor, former member of Tony Orlando & Dawn. *Family Matters.*

HOPPER, DENNIS. Dodge City, KS, 5/17/36. Actor, director. *Easy Rider.*

HOPPER, SEAN. California, 3/31/53. Keyboardist. Huey Lewis & The News.

HOPWOOD, KEITH. Manchester, England, 10/26/46. Guitarist. Herman's Hermits.

HORNE, LENA. Brooklyn, NY, 6/30/17. Singer, actor.

HORNSBY, BRUCE. Williamsburg, VA, 11/23/54. Singer, keyboardist, accordionist. Bruce Hornsby & The Range.

HOSKINS, BOB. Bury St. Edmunds, England, 10/26/42. Actor. *Who Framed Roger Rabbit.*

HOWARD, ALAN. Dagenham, England, 10/17/41. Bassist. Brian Poole & The Tremeloes.

HOWARD, ARLISS. Independence, MO, 1955. Actor. *Full Metal Jacket.*

HOWARD, KEN. El Centro, CA, 3/28/44. Actor. *The White Shadow.*

HOWE, STEVE. London, England, 4/8/47. Guitarist, singer. Yes; Asia.

HUCKNALL, MICK "RED." Manchester, England, 6/8/60. Singer. Simply Red.

HUDLIN, REGINALD. Centerville, IL, 12/15/61. Director, writer, producer, brother of Warrington. *House Party.*

HUDLIN, WARRINGTON. East St. Louis, IL, 1952. Producer, director, brother of Reginald. *House Party.*

HUDSON, GARTH. London, Canada, 8/2/37. Organist. The Band.

HUGG, MIKE. Andover, England, 8/11/42. Drummer. Manfred Mann.

HUGHES, GLENN. 7/18/50. Singer. The Village People.

HULCE, TOM. White Water, WI, 12/6/53. Actor. *Amadeus.*

HUMPERDINCK, ENGELBERT (Arnold Dorsey). Madras, India, 5/2/36. Pop singer. *The Engelbert Humperdinck Show.*

HUMPHREYS, PAUL. London, England, 2/27/60. Keyboardist. Orchestral Manoeuvres in the Dark (OMD).

HUNT, BILL. 5/23/47. Keyboardist. Electric Light Orchestra (ELO).

HUNT, LINDA. Morristown, NJ, 4/2/45. Actor. *The Year of Living Dangerously.*

HUNTER, IAN. Shrewsbury, England, 6/3/46. Singer, guitarist. Mott The Hoople.

HUNTER, TAB (Arthur Gelien). New York, NY, 7/11/31. Actor. *Damn Yankees.*

HUPPERT, ISABELLE. Paris, France, 3/16/55. Actor. *Entre Nous.*

HURT, JOHN. Shirebrook, England, 1/22/40. Actor. *The Elephant Man.*

HURT, MARY BETH (Mary Beth Supinger). Marshalltown, IA, 9/26/48. Actor, formerly married to William Hurt. *The World According to Garp.*

HURT, WILLIAM. Washington, DC, 3/20/50. Actor, formerly married to Mary Beth Hurt. *Children of a Lesser God.*

HUSSEIN, SADDAM. Tikrit, Iraq, 4/28/37. Leader of Iraq.

HUSSEY, WAYNE. Bristol, England, 5/26/59. Guitarist, singer. The Mission.

HUSTON, ANJELICA. Santa Monica, CA, 7/8/51. Actor, daughter of John Huston. *Prizzi's Honor.*

HUTTER, RALF. Krefeld, Germany, 1946. Keyboardist, drummer, singer. Kraftwerk.

HUTTON, DANNY. Buncrana, Ireland, 9/10/42. Singer. Three Dog Night.

HUTTON, LAUREN (Mary Hutton). Charleston, SC, 11/17/43. Actor, model. *American Gigolo.*

HUTTON, TIMOTHY. Malibu, CA, 8/16/60. Actor, director. *Ordinary People.*

HUXLEY, RICK. Dartford, England, 8/5/42. Guitarist. The Dave Clark Five.

HYNDE, CHRISSIE. Akron, OH, 9/7/51. Singer, divorced from Jim Kerr. The Pretenders.

IACOCCA, LEE (Lido Anthony Iacocca). Allentown, PA, 10/15/24. Auto executive, author. *Iacocca.*

IAN, JANIS (Janis Fink). New York, NY, 4/7/51. Folk/rock singer, songwriter.

ICE-T Newark, NJ, 2/16/58. Rap artist, actor. *New Jack City, Breakin'.*

IDLE, ERIC. Durham, England, 3/29/43. Actor. *Monty Python's Flying Circus.*

IDOL, BILLY (Billy Broad). Stanmore, England, 11/30/55. Singer, songwriter.

IGLESIAS, JULIO. Madrid, Spain, 9/23/43. Pop singer, songwriter.

ILLSLEY, JOHN. Leicester, England, 6/24/49. Bassist. Dire Straits.

IMAN. Mogadishu, Somalia,

7/25/55. Model, married to David Bowie.

INGELS, MARTY. Brooklyn, NY, 3/9/36. Actor, agent, married to Shirley Jones. *The Pruitts of Southampton.*

INGLE, DOUG. Omaha, NE, 9/9/46. Singer, keyboardist. Iron Butterfly.

INGRAM, JAMES. Akron, OH, 2/16/56. R&B singer, songwriter.

INNES, NEIL. Essex, England, 12/9/44. Singer, keyboardist. The Bonzo Dog Doo-Dah Band.

INNIS, ROY. Saint Croix, Virgin Islands, 6/6/34. Civil rights leader.

IOMMI, TONY. Birmingham, England, 2/19/48. Guitarist. Black Sabbath.

IRELAND, KATHY. Santa Barbara, CA, 3/20/63. Model, sister of Mary and Cynthia. *Sports Illustrated* swimsuit cover girl.

IRELAND, PATRICIA. Oak Park, IL, 10/19/45. Political activist. President of NOW.

IRVING, AMY. Palo Alto, CA, 9/10/53. Actor. *Yentl.*

IRWIN, BILL. Santa Monica, CA, 4/11/50. Actor. *Eight Men Out.*

ISAAK, CHRIS. Stockton, CA, 6/26/56. Singer, songwriter, actor. "Wicked Game".

ISLEY, O'KELLY. Cincinnati, OH, 12/25/37. Singer. The Isley Brothers.

ISLEY, RONALD. Cincinnati, OH, 5/21/41. Lead singer. The Isley Brothers.

ISLEY, RUDOLPH. Cincinnati, OH, 4/1/39. Singer. The Isley Brothers.

IVEY, JUDITH. El Paso, TX, 9/4/51. Actor. *Designing Women.*

IVORY, JAMES. Berkeley, CA, 6/7/28. Director, producer. *Howards End.*

JABS, MATTHIAS. 10/25/56. Guitarist. Scorpions.

JACKEE (Jackee Harry). Winston-Salem, NC, 8/14/56. Actor. *227.*

JACKSON, BO. Bessemer, AL, 11/30/62. Pro football, baseball player.

JACKSON, EDDIE. 1/29/61. Bassist, singer. Queensryche.

JACKSON, FREDDIE. New York, NY, 10/2/56. R&B singer, songwriter.

JACKSON, GLENDA. Birkenhead, England, 5/9/36. Actor, member of British Parliament. *Women in Love.*

JACKSON, JACKIE (Sigmund Jackson). Gary, IN, 5/4/51. Singer, brother of Michael and Janet Jackson. The Jacksons.

JACKSON, JERMAINE. Gary, IN, 12/11/54. Singer, brother of Michael and Janet. The Jacksons.

JACKSON, JESSE. Greenville, SC, 10/8/41. Civil rights leader, politician. Founded the Rainbow Coalition.

JACKSON, JOE. Burton-on-Trent, England, 8/11/55. Singer, songwriter.

JACKSON, KATE. Birmingham, AL, 10/29/48. Actor. Sabrina Duncan on *Charlie's Angels.*

JACKSON, LATOYA. 5/29/56. Sister of Michael and Janet.

JACKSON, MARLON. Gary, IN, 3/12/57. Singer, brother of Michael and Janet. The Jacksons.

JACKSON, PERVIS. 5/17/38. Singer. The (Detroit) Spinners.

JACKSON, TITO (Toriano Jackson). Gary, IN, 10/15/53. Singer, brother of Michael and Janet. The Jacksons.

JACKSON, TONY. Liverpool, England, 7/16/40. Singer, bassist. The Searchers.

JACKSON, VICTORIA. Miami, FL, 8/2/59. Actor. *Saturday Night Live.*

JACOBI, DEREK. London, England, 10/22/38. Actor. *The Day of the Jackal.*

JACOBI, LOU. Toronto, Canada, 12/28/13. Actor.

Irma La Douce.

JAGGER, BIANCA. Managua, Nicaragua, 5/2/45. Socialite, actor. Divorced from Mick Jagger.

JAM MASTER JAY (Jason Mizell). New York, NY, 1965. DJ. Run-D.M.C.

JAMES, CLIFTON. Portland, OR, 5/29/25. Actor. *Cool Hand Luke.*

JAMES, ETTA. Los Angeles, CA, 1/25/38. Singer. Bridged R&B and rock.

JAMES, RICK (James Johnson). Buffalo, NY, 2/1/48. Funk singer, songwriter. "Super Freak."

JAMES, TOMMY (Tommy Jackson). Dayton, OH, 4/29/47. Singer. Tommy James & The Shondells.

JANIS, CONRAD. New York, NY, 2/11/28. Actor, musician. Frederick McConnell on *Mork and Mindy.*

JARDINE, AL. Lima, OH, 9/3/42. Guitarist, singer. The Beach Boys.

JARREAU, AL. Milwaukee, WI, 3/12/40. Jazz singer, sang theme song to *Moonlighting.*

JAZZIE B. (Beresford Romeo). London, England, 1/26/63. Rap artist. Soul II Soul.

JEFFRIES, LIONEL. London, England, 6/10/26. Actor, director. *The Water Babies.*

JENNER, BRUCE. Mount Kisco, NY, 10/28/49. Track athlete, sportscaster. Olympic gold medalist.

JENNINGS, WAYLON. Littlefield, TX, 6/15/37. Country singer, songwriter. *The Dukes of Hazzard* theme song.

JETER, MICHAEL. Lawrenceburg, TN, 8/26/52. Actor. *Evening Shade.*

JETT, JOAN. Philadelphia, PA, 9/22/58. Singer, guitarist. "I Love Rock 'n' Roll."

JILLIAN, ANN (Anne Nauseda). Cambridge, MA, 1/29/51. Actor. *It's a Living.*

JOHANSEN, DAVID. Staten Island, NY, 1/9/50. Actor, singer, a.k.a. Buster Poindexter. *Scrooged.*

JOHN, DR. (Malcolm Rebennack). New Orleans, LA, 11/21/41. Rock/cajun/blues singer, songwriter. "Right Place Wrong Time."

JOHN PAUL II, POPE. Wadowice, Poland, 5/18/20. First non-Italian pope since the Renaissance.

JOHNS, GLYNIS. Durban, South Africa, 10/5/23. Actor. *Glynis.*

JOHNSON, ARTE. Benton Harbor, MI, 1/20/29. Actor. *Laugh-In.*

JOHNSON, BEVERLY. Buffalo, NY, 10/13/52. Model, actor.

JOHNSON, HOLLY (William Johnson). Khartoum, Sudan, 2/19/60. Singer. Frankie Goes to Hollywood.

JOHNSON, HOWIE. Washington, DC, 1938. Drummer. The Ventures.

JOHNSON, LADY BIRD. Karnack, TX, 12/22/12. Former First Lady, wife of Lyndon.

JOHNSON, MATT. 8/15/61. Singer, guitarist. The The.

JOHNSON, VAN. Newport, RI, 8/25/16. Actor. *The Caine Mutiny.*

JOHNSON, WILKO (John Wilkinson). 1947. Guitarist. Dr. Feelgood.

JON, JOHN. 2/26/61. Musician. Bronski Beat.

JONES, ALAN. Swansea, Wales, 2/6/47. Baritone saxophonist. Amen Corner.

JONES, BOOKER T. Memphis, TN, 12/11/44. Keyboardist. Booker T. & The MG's.

JONES, DAVY. Manchester, England, 12/30/45. Singer, actor. The Monkees.

JONES, DEAN. Decatur, AL, 1/25/31. Actor. *The Shaggy D.A.*

JONES, GRACE. Spanishtown, Jamaica, 5/19/52. Singer, actor. *A View to a Kill.*

JONES, GRAHAM. North Yorkshire, England, 7/8/61. Guitarist. Haircut 100.

JONES, HOWARD. Southampton, England, 2/23/55. Singer, songwriter.

JONES, JEFFREY. Buffalo, NY, 9/28/47. Actor. Principal Ed Rooney in *Ferris Bueller's Day Off.*

JONES, JENNIFER (Phyllis Isley). Tulsa, OK, 3/2/19. Actor. *The Song of Bernadette.*

JONES, JOHN PAUL (John Paul Baldwin). Sidcup, England, 1/31/46. Bassist. Led Zeppelin.

JONES, KENNY. London, England, 9/16/48. Drummer. The Small Faces.

JONES, MICK. Brixton, England, 6/26/55. Guitarist, singer. The Clash; Big Audio Dynamite.

JONES, MICK. London, England, 12/27/44. Guitarist. Foreigner.

JONES, NEIL. Llanbradach, Wales, 3/25/49. Guitarist. Amen Corner.

JONES, PAUL (Paul Pond). Portsmouth, England, 2/24/42. Singer, harmonicist. Manfred Mann.

JONES, RANDY. 9/13/52. Singer. The Village People.

JONES, RAY. Oldham, England, 10/22/39. Bassist. Billy J. Kramer & The Dakotas.

JONES, RICKIE LEE. Chicago, IL, 11/8/54. Rock/jazz singer, songwriter.

JONES, SAM J. Chicago, IL, 8/12/54. Actor. *Flash Gordon.*

JONES, SHIRLEY. Smithton, PA, 3/31/34. Actor, married to Marty Ingels. *The Partridge Family.*

JONES, STAR. 3/24/62. TV host. *The View.*

JONES, STEVE. London, England, 9/3/55. Guitarist. The Sex Pistols.

JONES, TERRY. Colwyn Bay, Wales, 2/1/42. Actor, director, writer. *Monty Python's Life of Brian.*

JONES, TOM (Tom Woodward). Pontypridd, Wales, 6/7/40. Pop singer.

JORDAN, LONNIE (Leroy Jordan). San Diego, CA, 11/21/48. Keyboardist, singer. War.

JOURARD, JEFF. 1955. Guitarist. The Motels.

JOURDAN, LOUIS (Louis Gendre). Marseilles, France, 6/19/19. Actor. *Gigi.*

JOVOVICH, MILLA. 12/17/75. Actor. *The Fifth Element.*

JOYCE, MIKE. Manchester, England, 6/1/63. Drummer. The Smiths.

JOYNER-KERSEE, JACKIE. St. Louis, IL, 3/3/62. Track athlete. Olympic gold medalist.

JUDD, NAOMI (Diana Judd). Ashland, KY, 1/11/46. Country singer, mother of Wynonna and Ashley. The Judds.

JUMP, GORDON. Dayton, OH, 4/1/32. Actor. Arthur Carlson on *WKRP in Cincinnati.*

JUSTMAN, SETH. Washington, DC, 1/27/51. Keyboardist, singer. The J. Geils Band.

KALE, JIM. 8/11/43. Bassist. The Guess Who.

KANE, BIG DADDY. New York, NY, 9/10/68. Rap artist, songwriter. "Long Live the Kane."

KANE, CAROL. Cleveland, OH, 6/18/52. Actor. Simka Graves on *Taxi.*

KANTNER, PAUL. San Francisco, CA, 3/12/42. Guitarist. Jefferson Airplane; Starship.

KAPRISKY, VALERIE. Paris, France, 1963. Actor. *Breathless.*

KARPOV, ANATOLY. Zlatoust, Russia, 5/23/51. Chess player. International grandmaster, world champion.

KARRAS, ALEX. Gary, IN, 7/15/35. Former football player, actor. *Webster.*

KASPAROV, GARRY. Baku, Russia, 4/13/63. Chess player. International grandmaster, world champion.

KATH, TERRY. Chicago, IL, 1/31/46. Guitarist. Chicago.

KATT, WILLIAM. Los Angeles, CA, 2/16/55. Actor, son of Barbara Hale. *The Greatest American Hero.*

KATZ, STEVE. New York, NY, 5/9/45. Guitarist, harmonicist, singer. Blood, Sweat & Tears.

KATZENBERG, JEFFREY. New York, NY, 12/21/50. Studio executive.

KAUKONEN, JORMA. Washington, DC, 12/23/40. Guitarist. Jefferson Airplane; Hot Tuna.

KAVNER, JULIE. Los Angeles, CA, 9/7/50. Actor. Voice of Marge Simpson on *The Simpsons; Rhoda.*

KAY, JOHN (Joachim Krauledat). Tilsit, Germany, 4/12/44. Guitarist, singer. Steppenwolf.

KAYLAN, HOWARD (Howard Kaplan). New York, NY, 6/22/47. Singer, saxophonist. The Turtles.

KAZURINSKY, TIM. Johnstown, PA, 3/3/50. Actor. *Saturday Night Live.*

KEACH, STACY (William Keach Jr.). Savannah, GA, 6/2/41. Actor. *Mickey Spillane's Mike Hammer.*

KEANE, BIL. Philadelphia, PA, 10/5/22. Cartoonist. *The Family Circus.*

KEATON, DIANE (Diane Hall). Los Angeles, CA, 1/5/46. Actor. *Annie Hall.*

KEATON, MICHAEL (Michael Douglas). Coraopolis, PA, 9/9/51. Actor. *Batman.*

KEEBLE, JON. London, England, 7/6/59. Drummer. Spandau Ballet.

KEEL, HOWARD (Harold Leek). Gillespie, IL, 4/13/17. Actor. Clayton Farlow on *Dallas.*

KEENAN, BRIAN. New York, NY, 1/28/44. Drummer. The

Chambers Brothers; Manfred Mann.

KEESHAN, BOB (Robert James Keeshan). Lynbrook, NY, 6/27/27. TV personality, author. *Captain Kangaroo.*

KEFFORD, ACE (Christopher Kefford). Mosely, England, 12/10/46. Bassist. The Move.

KEILLOR, GARRISON. 8/7/42. Author, radio personality. *Lake Wobegon Days.*

KEITH, DAVID. Knoxville, TN, 5/8/54. Actor. *An Officer and a Gentleman.*

KELLER, MARTHE. Basel, Switzerland, 1/28/45. Actor. *Marathon Man.*

KELLERMAN, SALLY. Long Beach, CA, 6/2/37. Actor. Hot Lips in the movie *M*A*S*H.*

KELLEY, DEFOREST. Atlanta, GA, 1/20/20. Actor. Dr. Leonard "Bones" McCoy on *Star Trek.*

KELLEY, KITTY. Spokane, WA, 4/4/42. Unauthorized biographer.

KELLING, GRAEME. Paisley, Scotland, 4/4/57. Guitarist. Deacon Blue.

KELLY, MARK. Dublin, Ireland, 4/9/61. Keyboardist. Marillion.

KELLY, MOIRA. 1968. Actor. *The Cutting Edge.*

KEMP, GARY. Islington, England, 10/16/60. Guitarist, brother of Martin. Spandau Ballet.

KEMP, MARTIN. London, England, 10/10/61. Bassist, brother of Gary. Spandau Ballet.

KENDRICKS, EDDIE. Birmingham, AL, 12/17/39. Singer. The Temptations.

KENNEDY, GEORGE. New York, NY, 2/18/25. Actor. *Cool Hand Luke.*

KENNEDY, TED. Brookline, MA, 2/22/32. Politician, brother of John and Robert.

KENNIBREW, DEE DEE (Dolores Henry). Brooklyn, NY, 1945. Singer. The Crystals.

KENNY G (Kenneth Gorelick). Seattle, WA, 6/5/56. Jazz saxophone player.

KENSIT, PATSY. London, England, 3/4/68. Actor, formerly married to Jim Kerr; married to Liam Gallagher. *Lethal Weapon 2.*

KERNS, JOANNA (Joanna De Varona). San Francisco, CA, 2/12/53. Actor. Maggie Seaver on *Growing Pains.*

KERR, DEBORAH. Helensburg, Scotland, 9/30/21. Actor. *The King and I.*

KERR, JIM. Glasgow, Scotland, 7/9/59. Singer. Simple Minds.

KERRIGAN, NANCY. Stoneham, MA, 10/13/69. Figure skater. Olympic silver medalist, victim of knee attack.

KHAN, CHAKA (Yvette Marie Stevens). Great Lakes, IL, 3/23/53. Singer. Rufus.

KIDD, JOHNNY (Frederick Heath). London, England, 12/23/39. Singer. Johnny Kidd & The Pirates.

KIDDER, MARGOT. Yellow Knife, Canada, 10/17/48. Actor. Lois Lane in *Superman.*

KIEDIS, ANTHONY. Grand Rapids, MI, 11/1/62. Singer. Red Hot Chili Peppers.

KIEL, RICHARD. Detroit, MI, 9/13/39. Actor. Jaws in *The Spy Who Loved Me.*

KILPATRICK, JAMES JR. Oklahoma City, OK, 11/1/20. Journalist. *60 Minutes.*

KIMBALL, BOBBY (Bobby Toteaux). Vinton, LA, 3/29/47. Lead singer. Toto.

KING, ALAN (Irwin Kniberg). Brooklyn, NY, 12/26/27. Producer, comedian. *The Andersen Tapes.*

KING, B. B. (Riley King). Itta Bena, MS, 9/16/25. Legendary blues guitarist, singer, songwriter.

KING, BEN E. (Ben E. Nelson). Henderson, NC, 9/23/38. Singer. The Drifters.

KING, BILLIE JEAN. Long Beach, CA, 11/22/43. Tennis player.

KING, CAROLE (Carole Klein). Brooklyn, NY, 2/9/42. Singer, songwriter.

KING, CORETTA SCOTT. Marion, AL, 4/29/27. Author, lecturer, widow of Martin Luther King Jr.

KING, DON. Cleveland, OH, 8/20/31. Boxing promoter.

KING, MARK. Isle of Wight, England, 10/20/58. Singer, bassist. Level 42.

KING, PERRY. Alliance, OH, 4/30/48. Actor. Cody Allen on *Riptide.*

KING, WILLIAM. Alabama, 1/30/49. Trumpeter, keyboardist. The Commodores.

KINGSLEY, BEN (Krishna Bhanji). Snaiton, England, 12/31/43. Actor. *Gandhi.*

KINSKI, NASTASSJA (Nastassja Nakszynski). Berlin, Germany, 1/24/61. Actor, daughter of Klaus Kinski. *Cat People.*

KIRBY, BRUNO (Bruce Kirby Jr.). New York, NY, 4/28/49. Actor. *City Slickers.*

KIRKE, SIMON. Wales, 7/28/49. Drummer. Bad Company; Free.

KIRKLAND, SALLY. New York, NY, 10/31/41. Actor. *Anna.*

KIRKMAN, TERRY. Salina, KS, 12/12/41. Singer, keyboardist. The Association.

KIRKPATRICK, JEANE. Duncan, OK, 11/19/26. Diplomat. Former U.S. representative to the U.N.

KISSINGER, HENRY. Fuerth, Germany, 5/27/23. Richard Nixon's secretary of state.

KITT, EARTHA. North, SC, 1/17/27. Actor, singer. *The Mark of the Hawk.*

KLEIN, DANNY. New York, NY, 5/13/46. Bassist. The J. Geils Band.

KLEIN, ROBERT. New York, NY, 2/8/42. Actor. *Comedy Tonight.*

KLEMPERER, WERNER. Cologne, Germany, 3/22/20. Actor. Colonel Wilhelm Klink on *Hogan's Heroes.*

KLINE, KEVIN. St. Louis, MO, 10/24/47. Actor, married to Phoebe Cates. *The Big Chill.*

KLUGMAN, JACK. Philadelphia, PA, 4/27/22. Actor. Oscar Madison on *The Odd Couple.*

KNIGHT, GLADYS. Atlanta, GA, 5/28/44. Singer. Gladys Knight & The Pips.

KNIGHT, JONATHAN. Boston, MA, 11/29/69. Singer. New Kids on the Block.

KNIGHT, JORDAN. Boston, MA, 5/17/71. Singer. New Kids on the Block.

KNIGHT, MERALD. Atlanta, GA, 9/4/42. Singer. Gladys Knight & The Pips.

KNIGHT, MICHAEL E. Princeton, NJ, 5/7/59. Actor. Tad Martin on *All My Children.*

KNIGHT, SHIRLEY. Goessell, KS, 7/5/36. Actor. *The Dark at the Top of the Stairs.*

KNIGHT, SUGE. 4/19/65. Musician.

KNIGHTS, DAVE. Islington, England, 6/28/45. Bassist. Procol Harum.

KNOPFLER, DAVID. Glasgow, Scotland, 12/27/52. Guitarist. Dire Straits.

KNOPFLER, MARK. Glasgow, Scotland, 8/12/49. Singer, guitarist. Dire Straits.

KNOTTS, DON. Morgantown, WV, 7/21/24. Actor. Barney Fife on *The Andy Griffith Show.*

KNUDSEN, KEITH. Ames, IA, 10/18/52. Drummer, singer. The Doobie Brothers.

KOCH, ED. New York, NY, 12/12/24. Former mayor of New York.

KOENIG, WALTER. Chicago, IL, 9/14/36. Actor, writer, director, producer. Pavel Chekov on *Star Trek.*

KOOL ROCK (Damon Wimbley). 11/4/66. Rap artist. Fat Boys.

KOPELL, BERNIE. New York,

NY, 6/21/33. Actor. Dr. Adam Bricker on *The Love Boat.*

KORMAN, HARVEY. Chicago, IL, 2/15/27. Actor. *The Carol Burnett Show.*

KOSSOFF, PAUL. London, England, 9/14/50. Guitarist. Free.

KOTTO, YAPHET. New York, NY, 11/15/39. Actor. *Live and Let Die.*

KRABBE, JEROEN. Amsterdam, The Netherlands, 12/5/44. Actor. *The Fugitive.*

KRAMER, BILLY J. (Billy J. Ashton). Bootle, England, 8/19/43. Singer. Billy J. Kramer & The Dakotas.

KRAMER, JOEY. New York, NY, 6/21/50. Drummer. Aerosmith.

KRANTZ, JUDITH. New York, NY, 1/9/28. Novelist. *Scruples.*

REUTZMANN, BILL JR. Palo Alto, CA, 5/7/46. Drummer. Grateful Dead.

KRIEGER, ROBBIE. Los Angeles, CA, 1/8/46. Guitarist. The Doors.

KRIGE, ALICE. Upington, South Africa, 6/28/55. Actor. *Chariots of Fire.*

KRISTOFFERSON, KRIS. Brownsville, TX, 6/22/36. Singer, songwriter, actor. *Amerika.*

KUHLKE, NORMAN. Liverpool, England, 6/17/42. Drummer. The Swinging Blue Jeans.

KURTZ, SWOOSIE. Omaha, NE, 9/6/44. Actor. *Sisters.*

KWAN, NANCY. Hong Kong, 5/19/39. Actor. *The World of Suzie Wong.*

LABELLE, PATTI (Patricia Holt). Philadelphia, PA, 10/4/44. Pop/soul singer.

LADD, CHERYL (Cheryl Stoppelmoor). Huron, SD, 7/12/51. Actor. Kris Munroe on *Charlie's Angels.*

LADD, DIANE (Diane Ladner). Meridian, MS, 11/29/39. Actor, mother of Laura Dern. *Alice Doesn't Live Here Anymore.*

LAGASSE, EMERIL. 10/15/59. Chef, author, TV personality.

LAGERFELD, KARL Hamburg, Germany, 9/10/38. Fashion designer. Chanel.

LAHTI, CHRISTINE. Birmingham, MI, 4/4/50. Actor. *Swing Shift.*

LAINE, DENNY (Brian Hines). Jersey, England, 10/29/44. Singer, guitarist. The Moody Blues.

LAKE, GREG. Bournemouth, England, 11/10/48. Bassist, singer. Emerson, Lake & Palmer; King Crimson.

LAMAS, LORENZO. Los Angeles, CA, 1/20/58. Actor. Lance Cumson on *Falcon Crest.*

LAMBERT, CHRISTOPHER. New York, NY, 3/29/57. Actor. *Greystoke: The Legend of Tarzan, Lord of the Apes.*

LAMM, ROBERT. New York, NY, 10/13/44. Singer, keyboardist. Chicago.

LANCASTER, ALAN. London, England, 2/7/49. Bassist. Status Quo.

LANDAU, MARTIN. Brooklyn, NY, 6/20/28. Actor. *Mission: Impossible.*

LANDERS, AUDREY. Philadelphia, PA, 7/18/59. Actor. Afton Cooper on *Dallas.*

LANDESBERG, STEVE. The Bronx, NY, 11/3/45. Actor. Detective Arthur Dietrich on *Barney Miller.*

LANDIS, JOHN. Chicago, IL, 8/3/50. Director. *Twilight Zone—The Movie.*

LANE, ABBE. Brooklyn, NY, 12/14/34. Actor, formerly married to Xavier Cugat. *Xavier Cugat Show.*

LANE, CHARLES. New York, NY, 12/5/53. Director. *Sidewalk Stories.*

LANE, DIANE. New York, NY, 1/22/65. Actor. *Rumble Fish.*

LANG, BOB. Manchester, England, 1/10/46. Bassist. Wayne Fontana & The Mind-

benders.

LANGE, HOPE. Redding Ridge, CT, 11/28/31. Actor. *The Ghost and Mrs. Muir.*

LANGE, TED. Oakland, CA, 1/5/47. Actor. Isaac Washington on *The Love Boat.*

LANGELLA, FRANK. Bayonne, NJ, 1/1/38. Actor. *Dracula.*

LANIER, ALLEN. 6/25/46. Guitarist, keyboardist. Blue Öyster Cult.

LANSING, ROBERT (Robert Brown). San Diego, CA, 6/5/29. Actor. *The Man Who Never Was.*

LAPREAD, RONALD. Alabama, 9/4/50. Bassist, trumpeter. The Commodores.

LARDIE, MICHAEL. 9/8/58. Musician. Great White.

LARROQUETTE, JOHN. New Orleans, LA, 11/25/47. Actor. *Night Court.*

LARUE, FLORENCE. Pennsylvania, 2/4/44. Singer. The 5th Dimension.

LASSER, LOUISE. New York, NY, 4/11/39. Actor, formerly married to Woody Allen. *Bananas.*

LAUDER, ESTEE. New York, NY, 7/1/08. Fashion designer.

LAUPER, CYNDI. New York, NY, 6/22/53. Singer, actor, professional wrestling promoter. *She's So Unusual.*

LAURIE, PIPER (Rosetta Jacobs). Detroit, MI, 1/22/32. Actor. Mother in *Carrie.*

LAVERN, ROGER (Roger Jackson). Kidderminster, England, 11/11/38. Keyboardist. The Tornados.

LAVIN, LINDA. Portland, ME, 10/15/37. Actor, singer. *Alice.*

LAWRENCE, CAROL (Carol Laraia). Melrose Park, IL, 9/5/34. Actor, singer. *West Side Story.*

LAWRENCE, JOEY. Montgomery, PA, 4/20/76. Actor, singer. *Blossom.*

LAWRENCE, VICKI. Ingle-

wood, CA, 3/26/49. Actor. *Mama's Family.*

LAWSON, LEIGH. Atherston, England, 7/21/45. Actor. *Tess.*

LAWTON, JOHN. 6/11/46. Singer. Uriah Heep.

LEA, JIMMY. Melbourne Arms, England, 6/14/52. Bassist, keyboardist, violinist. Slade.

LEACH, ROBIN. London, England, 8/29/41. TV host. *Lifestyles of the Rich and Famous.*

LEACHMAN, CLORIS. Des Moines, IA, 4/30/26. Actor. Phyllis Lyndstrom on *The Mary Tyler Moore Show.*

LEADON, BERNIE. Minneapolis, MN, 7/19/47. Guitarist, singer. The Eagles.

LEAR, NORMAN. New Haven, CT, 7/27/22. Producer, director, formerly married to Frances. *All in the Family.*

LEARNED, MICHAEL. Washington, DC, 4/9/39. Actor. Olivia on *The Waltons.*

LEBON, SIMON. Bushey, England, 10/27/58. Lead singer. Duran Duran.

LEBROCK, KELLY. 3/22/60. Actor, married to Steven Seagal. *Weird Science.*

LEE, ALVIN. Nottingham, England, 12/19/44. Guitarist, singer. Ten Years After.

LEE, ARTHUR. Memphis, TN, 1945. Guitarist, singer. Love.

LEE, BARBARA. New York, NY, 5/16/47. Singer. The Chiffons.

LEE, BEVERLY. Passaic, NJ, 8/3/41. Singer. The Shirelles.

LEE, BRENDA (Brenda Tarpley). Lithonia, GA, 12/11/44. Singer.

LEE, GEDDY. Willowdale, Canada, 7/29/53. Singer, bassist. Rush.

LEE, JASON SCOTT. Los Angeles, CA, 1966. Actor. *Dragon: The Bruce Lee Story.*

LEE, JOHNNY. Texas City, TX, 7/3/46. Singer. "Lookin' for Love."

LEE, MICHELE (Michele Dusiak). Los Angeles, CA, 6/24/42. Actor. Karen Fairgate MacKenzie on *Knots Landing.*

LEE, PEGGY (Norma Delores Egstrom). Jamestown, ND, 5/26/20. Actor, singer. *The Jazz Singer.*

LEE, RIC. Cannock, England, 10/20/45. Drummer. Ten Years After.

LEE, STAN. New York, NY, 12/28/22. Artist, writer, Marvel Comics legend.

LEEDS, GARY. Glendale, CA, 9/3/44. Drummer. The Walker Brothers.

LEESE, HOWARD. Los Angeles, CA, 6/13/51. Keyboardist, guitarist. Heart.

LEEVES, JANE. East Grinstead, England, 4/18/61. Actor. Daphne Moon on *Frasier.*

LEEWAY, JOE. London, England, 1957. Percussionist. Thompson Twins.

LEIBMAN, RON. New York, NY, 10/11/37. Actor. *Kaz.*

LEIFER, CAROL. 7/27/56. Comic. *Alright Already.*

LEIGH, JANET (Jeannette Helen Morrison). Merced, CA, 7/6/27. Actor, mother of Jamie Lee Curtis. *Psycho.*

LEIGHTON, LAURA (Laura Miller). Iowa City, IA, 7/24/68. Actor. *Melrose Place.*

LEITCH, DONOVAN. 8/16/67. Actor, son of folk singer Donovan, brother of Ione Skye.

LEMAT, PAUL. Rahway, NJ, 9/22/52. Actor. *American Graffiti.*

LEMIEUX, MARIO. Montreal, Canada, 10/5/65. NHL hockey player. Pittsburgh Penguins.

LEMMON, CHRIS. Los Angeles, CA, 1/22/54. Actor, son of Jack Lemmon. *Swing Shift.*

LEMMY (Ian Kilmister). Stoke-on-Trent, England, 12/24/45. Bassist, singer. Motorhead.

LEMON, MEADOWLARK. Wilmington, NC, 4/25/32. Basketball player. Harlem Globetrotters.

LENNON, JULIAN (John Charles Julian Lennon). Liverpool, England, 4/8/63. Singer, songwriter, son of John Lennon. Half brother of Sean.

LENNON, SEAN. 10/9/75. Musician. Son of John Lennon and Yoko Ono. Half brother of Julian Lennon.

LENNOX, ANNIE. Aberdeen, Scotland, 12/25/54. Singer, songwriter. Eurythmics.

LEONARD, ROBERT SEAN. Westwood, NJ, 2/28/69. Actor. *Dead Poets Society.*

LEONARD, SUGAR RAY. Wilmington, NC, 5/17/56. Boxer.

LERNER, MICHAEL. Brooklyn, NY, 6/22/41. Actor. *Barton Fink.*

LESH, PHIL (Phil Chapman). Berkeley, CA, 3/15/40. Bassist. Grateful Dead.

LESTER, ROBERT "SQUIRREL." 1/13/30. Singer. The Chi-Lites.

LEVERT, EDDIE. Canton, OH, 6/16/42. Singer. The O'Jays.

LEVIN, DRAKE. Guitarist. Paul Revere & The Raiders.

LEVY, EUGENE. Hamilton, Canada, 12/17/46. Actor, writer. *SCTV.*

LEWINSKY, MONICA. 7/23/73. Former White House intern, had "inappropriate" relationship with Bill Clinton.

LEWIS, AL (Alexander Meister). New York, NY, 4/30/10. Actor. *The Munsters.*

LEWIS, CARL (Carl Frederick Carlton). Birmingham, AL, 7/1/61. Track athlete. Olympic gold medalist.

LEWIS, EMMANUEL. New York, NY, 3/9/71. Actor. Webster Long on *Webster.*

LEWIS, GARY (Gary Levitch). New York, NY, 7/31/46. Singer, drummer, son of Jerry Lewis. Gary Lewis & The Playboys.

LEWIS, HUEY (Hugh Cregg III). New York, NY, 7/5/50. Singer. Huey Lewis & The News.

LEWIS, JERRY (Joseph Levitch). Newark, NJ, 3/16/26. Actor, father of Gary Lewis. *The Nutty Professor.*

LEWIS, JERRY LEE. Ferriday, LA, 9/29/35. Legendary rock keyboardist, singer, songwriter.

LEWIS, JULIETTE. San Fernando Valley, CA, 6/21/73. Actor. *Cape Fear.*

LEWIS, PETER. Los Angeles, CA, 7/15/45. Guitarist, singer. Moby Grape.

LEWIS, RICHARD. 6/29/47. Comic. *Anything But Love.*

LIDDY, G. GORDON. New York, NY, 11/30/30. Watergate participant, talk show host. *The G. Gordon Liddy Show.*

LIFESON, ALEX. Fernie, Canada, 8/27/53. Guitarist. Rush.

LIGHT, JUDITH. Trenton, NJ, 2/9/49. Actor. Angela on *Who's the Boss?*

LIGHTFOOT, GORDON. Orillia, Canada, 11/17/38. Folk guitarist, singer, songwriter.

LINCOLN, ABBEY (Anna Marie Woolridge). Chicago, IL, 8/6/30. Singer, actor. *For Love of Ivy.*

LINDEN, HAL (Hal Lipshitz). The Bronx, NY, 3/20/31. Actor. *Barney Miller.*

LINDES, HAL. Monterey, CA, 6/30/53. Guitarist. Dire Straits.

LINDSAY, MARK. Eugene, OR, 3/9/42. Singer, saxophonist. Paul Revere & The Raiders.

LINDUP, MIKE. 3/17/59. Keyboardist, singer. Level 42.

LINKLETTER, ART. Moose Jaw, Canada, 7/17/12. TV personality. *People Are Funny.*

LINN-BAKER, MARK. St. Louis, MO, 6/17/54. Actor. Cousin Larry Appleton on *Perfect Strangers.*

LIOTTA, RAY. Newark, NJ, 12/18/54. Actor. *GoodFellas.*

LIPNICKI, JONATHAN. 10/22/90. Actor. *Jerry Maguire.*

LITTLE EVA (Eva Narcissus Boyd). Bellhaven, NC, 6/29/45. Singer. "The Loco-Motion."

LITTLE RICHARD (Richard Penniman). Macon, GA, 12/5/32. Legendary singer, songwriter.

LIVGREN, KERRY. Kansas, 9/18/49. Guitarist. Kansas.

L.L. COOL J (James Todd Smith). New York, NY, 1/14/68. Rap artist.

LLOYD, CHRISTOPHER. Stamford, CT, 10/22/38. Actor. "Reverend Jim" Ignatowski on *Taxi.*

LLOYD, EMILY. London, England, 9/29/70. Actor. *Wish You Were Here.*

LOCKE, JOHN. Los Angeles, CA, 9/25/43. Keyboardist. Spirit.

LOCKE, SONDRA. Shelbyville, TN, 5/28/47. Actor. *The Gauntlet.*

LOCKHART, JUNE. New York, NY, 6/25/25. Actor. *Lost in Space.*

LOCKWOOD, GARY. Van Nuys, CA, 2/21/37. Actor. *2001: A Space Odyssey.*

LOCORRIERE, DENNIS. Union City, NJ, 6/13/49. Lead singer. Dr. Hook.

LODGE, JOHN. Birmingham, England, 7/20/45. Bassist. The Moody Blues.

LOEB, LISA. 3/11/68. Singer. "Stay."

LOFGREN, NILS. Chicago, IL, 6/21/51. Guitarist, keyboardist, singer, songwriter.

LOGGIA, ROBERT. Staten Island, NY, 1/3/30. Actor. *Mancuso, FBI.*

LOGGINS, KENNY. Everett,

WA, 1/7/48. Singer, songwriter.

LOLLOBRIGIDA, GINA. Subiaco, Italy, 7/4/27. Actor. *Circus.*

LOM, HERBERT. Prague, Czechoslovakia, 1/9/17. Actor. *Spartacus.*

LONG, SHELLEY. Ft. Wayne, IN, 8/23/49. Actor. Diane Chambers on *Cheers.*

LONGMUIR, ALAN. Edinburgh, Scotland, 6/20/53. Bassist. The Bay City Rollers.

LONGMUIR, DEREK. Edinburgh, Scotland, 3/19/55. Drummer. The Bay City Rollers.

LORD, JON. Leicester, England, 6/9/41. Keyboardist. Deep Purple.

LORDS, TRACI (Norma Kuzma). Steubenville, OH, 5/7/68. Actor, former porn star. *Melrose Place.*

LOUGANIS, GREG. El Cajon, CA, 1/29/60. Diver. Olympic gold medalist.

LOUGHNANE, LEE. Chicago, IL, 10/21/46. Trumpeter. Chicago.

LOUISE, TINA (Tina Blacker). New York, NY, 2/11/34. Actor. Ginger Grant on *Gilligan's Island.*

LOVE, MIKE. Baldwin Hills, CA, 3/15/41. Singer. The Beach Boys.

LOVELADY, DAVE. Liverpool, England, 10/16/42. Drummer. The Fourmost.

LOVELESS, PATTY. Belcher Holler, KY, 1/4/57 Singer.

LOVITZ, JON. Tarzana, CA, 7/21/57. Actor. *Saturday Night Live.*

LOWE, CHAD. Dayton, OH, 1/15/68. Actor, brother of Rob Lowe. *Life Goes On.*

LOWE, CHRIS. Blackpool, England, 10/4/59. Keyboardist. Pet Shop Boys.

LUCIA, PETER. 2/2/47. Drummer. Tommy James & The Shondells.

LUCKINBILL, LAURENCE. Fort Smith, AR, 11/21/34.

Actor, married to Lucie Arnaz. *The Boys in the Band.*

LUDLUM, ROBERT. New York, NY, 5/25/27. Novelist, actor, producer. *The Gemini Contenders.*

LUFT, LORNA. Los Angeles, CA, 11/21/52. Actor, half-sister of Liza Minnelli, daughter of Judy Garland. *Where the Boys Are.*

LUKATHER, STEVE. Los Angeles, CA, 10/21/57. Lead guitarist. Toto.

LULU (Marie Lawrie). Glasgow, Scotland, 11/3/48. Singer, actor. *To Sir with Love.*

LUNDEN, JOAN. Fair Oaks, CA, 9/19/50. Host. *Good Morning America.*

LUNDGREN, DOLPH. Stockholm, Sweden, 11/3/59. Actor. *Rocky IV.*

LUPONE, PATTI. Northport, NY, 4/21/49. Actor. *Life Goes On.*

LUPUS, PETER. Indianapolis, IN, 6/17/37. Actor. Willie Armitage on *Mission: Impossible.*

LWIN, ANNABELLA (Myant Aye). Rangoon, Burma, 10/31/65. Singer. Bow Wow Wow.

LYDON, JOHN. London, England, 1/31/56. Singer, a.k.a. Johnny Rotten. The Sex Pistols; Public Image Ltd.

LYNCH, STAN. Gainesville, FL, 5/21/55. Drummer. Tom Petty & The Heartbreakers.

LYNGSTAD, FRIDA (Anni-Frid Lyngstad). Narvik, Sweden, 11/15/45. Singer. Abba.

LYNNE, JEFF. Birmingham, England, 12/30/47. Singer, guitarist. Electric Light Orchestra (ELO).

LYNOTT, PHIL. Dublin, Ireland, 8/20/51. Singer, bassist. Thin Lizzy.

LYONS, LEO. Standbridge, England, 11/30/43. Bassist. Ten Years After.

LYTE, MC. New York, NY, 1971. Rap artist.

MA, YO-YO. Paris, France, 10/7/55. Cello virtuoso.

MACARTHUR, JAMES. Los Angeles, CA, 12/8/37. Actor, son of Helen Hayes. Danny Williams on *Hawaii Five-O.*

MACCHIO, RALPH. Long Island, NY, 11/4/62. Actor. *The Karate Kid.*

MACCORKINDALE, SIMON. Cambridge, England, 2/12/52. Actor. *Falcon Crest.*

MACDONALD, EDDIE. St. Asaph, Wales, 11/1/59. Bassist. The Alarm.

MACDONALD, ROBIN. Nairn, Scotland, 7/18/43. Guitarist. Billy J. Kramer & The Dakotas.

MACGOWAN, SHANE. Kent, England, 12/25/57. Guitarist, singer. The Pogues.

MACGRAW, ALI. Pound Ridge, NY, 4/1/38. Actor. *Love Story.*

MACKAY, ANDY. London, England, 7/23/46. Saxophonist, woodwindist. Roxy Music.

MACKAY, DUNCAN. 7/26/50. Keyboardist. Steve Harley & Cockney Rebel.

MACLACHLAN, KYLE. Yakima, WA, 2/22/59. Actor. *Twin Peaks.*

MACLEAN, BRYAN. Los Angeles, CA, 1947. Guitarist, singer. Love.

MACLEOD, GAVIN. Mt. Kisco, NY, 2/28/31. Actor. Captain Stubing of *The Love Boat.*

MACNAUGHTON, ROBERT. New York, NY, 12/19/66. Actor. *E.T., the Extra-Terrestrial.*

MACNEE, PATRICK. London, England, 2/6/22. Actor. *The Avengers.*

MACNEIL, ROBERT. Montreal, Canada, 1/19/31. Broadcast journalist. *MacNeil/Lehrer Report.*

MACNELLY, JEFF. New York, NY, 9/17/47. Cartoonist. *Shoe.*

MADDEN, JOHN. Austin, MN, 4/10/36. Sportscaster, football analyst.

MADIGAN, AMY. Chicago, IL, 9/11/51. Actor. *Places in the Heart.*

MADSEN, MICHAEL. Chicago, IL, 1959. Actor, brother of Virginia. *Reservoir Dogs.*

MADSEN, VIRGINIA. Winnetka, IL, 9/11/61. Actor, sister of Michael. *Electric Dreams.*

MAGNUSON, ANN. Charleston, WV, 1/4/56. Actor. Catherine Hughes on *Anything but Love.*

MAGUIRE, LES. Wallasey, England, 12/27/41. Keyboardist, saxophonist. Gerry & The Pacemakers.

MAHONEY, JOHN. Manchester, England, 6/20/40. Actor. Father of Dr. Crane on *Cheers* and *Frasier.*

MAJORS, LEE (Harvey Lee Yeary II). Wyandotte, MI, 4/23/39. Actor, formerly married to Farrah Fawcett. *The Six Million Dollar Man.*

MAKEPEACE, CHRIS. Montreal, Canada, 4/22/64. Actor. *My Bodyguard.*

MAKO (Makoto Iwamatsu). Kobe, Japan, 12/10/33. Actor. *The Sand Pebbles.*

MALDEN, KARL (Mladen Sekulovich). Gary, IN, 3/22/12. Actor, American Express spokesperson. *The Streets of San Francisco.*

MALONE, DOROTHY. Chicago, IL, 1/30/25. Actor. *Written on the Wind.*

MALTIN, LEONARD. New York, NY, 12/18/50. Film critic. *Entertainment Tonight.*

MANDEL, HOWIE. Toronto, Canada, 11/29/55. Actor. Dr. Wayne Fiscus on *St. Elsewhere.*

MANDELA, NELSON. Umtata, South Africa, 7/18/18. President of South Africa.

MANDELA, WINNIE. Transkei, South Africa, 9/26/34. Political activist, formerly married to Nelson

Mandela.

MANDRELL, BARBARA. Houston, TX, 12/25/48. Country singer. Barbara Mandrell & The Mandrell Sisters.

MANETTI, LARRY. Chicago, IL, 7/23/47. Actor. Rick on *Magnum, P. I.*

MANILOW, BARRY (Barry Alan Pincus). Brooklyn, NY, 6/17/43. Singer, songwriter. *I Write the Songs.*

MANN, MANFRED (Michael Lubowitz). Johannesburg, South Africa, 10/21/40. Keyboardist. Manfred Mann.

MANN, TERRENCE. Kentucky, 1945. Actor. *Les Misérables.*

MANOFF, DINAH. New York, NY, 1/25/56. Actor, daughter of Lee Grant. Carol Weston on *Empty Nest.*

MANSON, CHARLES. Cincinnati, OH, 11/12/34. Murderer, cult leader.

MANTEGNA, JOE. Chicago, IL, 11/13/47. Actor. *The Godfather, Part III.*

MANZANERA, PHIL. London, England, 1/31/51. Guitarist. Roxy Music.

MANZAREK, RAY. Chicago, IL, 2/12/39. Keyboardist. The Doors.

MARCEAU, MARCEL. Strasbourg, France, 3/22/23. Actor, pantomimist. *Bip.*

MARCOS, IMELDA. Talcoban, the Philippines, 7/2/31. Wife of late Ferdinand Marcos.

MARCOVICCI, ANDREA. New York, NY, 11/18/48. Actor, singer. *Trapper John, MD.*

MARGO, MITCH. Brooklyn, NY, 5/25/47. Tenor singer. The Tokens.

MARGO, PHIL. Brooklyn, NY, 4/1/42. Bass singer. The Tokens.

MARIN, CHEECH (Richard Marin). Los Angeles, CA, 7/13/46. Actor, writer, former partner of Tommy Chong. *Up in Smoke.*

MARINARO, ED. New York,

NY, 3/31/50. Actor, football player. *Hill Street Blues.*

MARLEY, ZIGGY (David Marley). Jamaica, 10/17/68. Singer, songwriter, son of Bob Marley. Ziggy Marley & The Melody Makers.

MARR, JOHNNY. Manchester, England, 10/31/63. Guitarist. The Smiths.

MARRIOTT, STEVE. Bow, England, 1/30/47. Singer, guitarist. The Small Faces.

MARS, MICK (Bob Deal). Terre Haute, IN, 4/4/55. Guitarist. Mötley Crüe.

MARSALIS, BRANFORD. Breaux Bridge, LA, 8/26/60. Jazz musician, bandleader, saxophonist. Brother of Wynton Marsalis. Former musical director of *The Tonight Show.*

MARSDEN, FREDDIE. Liverpool, England, 10/23/40. Drummer. Gerry & The Pacemakers.

MARSDEN, GERRY. Liverpool, England, 9/24/42. Singer, lead guitarist. Gerry & The Pacemakers.

MARSH, IAN. Sheffield, England, 11/11/56. Keyboardist. The Human League; Heaven 17.

MARSHALL, PETER (Pierre La Cock). Huntington, WV, 3/30/30. TV personality. Host of *The Hollywood Squares.*

MARTELL, VINCE. New York, NY, 11/11/45. Guitarist. Vanilla Fudge.

MARTIN, ANDREA. Portland, ME, 1/15/47. Writer, actor. *SCTV.*

MARTIN, DEWEY. Chesterville, Canada, 9/30/42. Singer, drummer. Buffalo Springfield.

MARTIN, DICK. Battle Creek, MI, 1/30/22. Actor. Cohost of *Laugh-In.*

MARTIN, JIM. Oakland, CA, 7/21/61. Guitarist. Faith No More.

MARTIN, PAMELA SUE.

Westport, CT, 1/15/53. Actor. *Dynasty.*

MARTINDALE, WINK (Winston Conrad Martindale). Bells, TN, 12/4/34. TV personality. Host of *Tic Tac Dough* and *Debt.*

MARTINI, JERRY. Colorado, 10/1/43. Saxophonist. Sly & The Family Stone.

MARVIN, HANK (Brian Rankin). Newcastle, England, 10/28/41. Lead guitarist. The Shadows.

MARX, RICHARD. Chicago, IL, 9/16/63. Singer, songwriter.

MASON, DAVE. Worcester, England, 5/10/47. Singer, guitarist. Traffic.

MASON, JACKIE. Sheboygan, WI, 6/9/34. Actor. *Chicken Soup.*

MASON, MARSHA. St. Louis, MO, 4/3/42. Actor. *The Goodbye Girl.*

MASON, NICK. Birmingham, England, 1/27/45. Drummer. Pink Floyd.

MASSI, NICK (Nick Macioci). Newark, NJ, 9/19/35. Singer, bassist. The Four Seasons.

MASTELOTTO, PAT. 9/10/55. Drummer. Mr. Mister.

MASTERSON, MARY STUART. Los Angeles, CA, 6/28/66. Actor, daughter of Peter. *Fried Green Tomatoes.*

MASTERSON, PETER. Houston, TX, 6/1/34. Actor, writer, director, father of Mary Stuart. *The Exorcist.*

MASTRANGELO, CARLO. The Bronx, NY, 10/5/39. Bass singer. Dion & The Belmonts.

MASTRANTONIO, MARY ELIZABETH. Oak Park, IL, 11/17/58. Actor. *The Color of Money.*

MASUR, RICHARD. New York, NY, 11/20/48. Actor, Screen Actors Guild president. *One Day at a Time.*

MATHERS, JERRY. Sioux City, IA, 6/2/48. Actor. Theodore "Beaver" Cleaver on *Leave It to Beaver.*

MATHESON, TIM. Glendale, CA, 12/31/47. Actor. *National Lampoon's Animal House.*

MATHEWS, DENISE (formerly Vanity). Niagara, Canada, 1/3/63. Former singer and actor (a.k.a. D.D. Winters), now Christian Evangelist, bible student, married to L.A. Raiders defensive end Anthony Smith. *The Last Dragon.*

MATHIS, JOHNNY. San Francisco, CA, 9/30/35. Pop singer.

MATLOCK, GLENN. 8/27/56. Bassist. The Sex Pistols.

MATTHEWS, IAN (Ian McDonald). Lincolnshire, England, 6/16/45. Singer, guitarist. Matthew's Southern Comfort.

MAUS, JOHN. New York, NY, 11/12/43. Singer. The Walker Brothers.

MAXFIELD, MIKE. Manchester, England, 2/23/44. Lead guitarist. Billy J. Kramer & The Dakotas.

MAY, BRIAN. Twickenham, England, 7/19/47. Guitarist. Queen.

MAY, ELAINE (Elaine Berlin). Philadelphia, PA, 4/21/32. Actor, director, writer. *Ishtar.*

MAY, PHIL. Dartford, England, 11/9/44. Singer. The Pretty Things.

MAYALL, JOHN. Macclesfield, England, 11/29/33. Singer, keyboardist, harmonicist. The Bluesbreakers.

MAYS, WILLIE. Fairfield, AL, 5/6/31. Baseball player. San Francisco Giants.

MAZAR, DEBI. Queens, NY, 1964. Actor. *Civil Wars; L.A. Law.*

MAZURSKY, PAUL. Brooklyn, NY, 4/25/30. Producer, director, writer, actor. *Down and Out in Beverly Hills.*

M.C. ERIC. 8/19/70. Rap artist. Technotronic.

MCA (Adam Yauch). Brooklyn, NY, 8/15/67. Rap artist. The Beastie Boys.

MCBRIDE, MARTINA.
Sharon, KS, 7/29/66. Singer.

MCCALLUM, DAVID. Glasgow, Scotland, 9/19/33. Actor. *The Great Escape.*

MCCARTHY, ANDREW. Westfield, NJ, 11/29/62. Actor. *Less Than Zero.*

MCCARTHY, JENNY Chicago, IL, 11/1/72. *Singled Out.*

MCCARTHY, KEVIN. Seattle, WA, 2/15/14. Actor. *Invasion of the Body Snatchers.*

MCCARTY, JIM. Liverpool, England, 7/25/44. Drummer. The Yardbirds; Mitch Ryder & The Detroit Wheels.

MCCAULEY, JACKIE. Coleraine, Ireland, 12/14/46. Keyboardist. Them.

MCCAULEY, PATRICK. Northern Ireland, 3/17/44. Drummer. Them.

MCCLANAHAN, RUE. Healdton, OK, 2/21/34. Actor. Blanche Devereaux on *The Golden Girls.*

MCCLARY, THOMAS. 10/6/50. Lead guitarist. The Commodores.

MCCLINTON, DELBERT. Lubbock, TX, 11/4/40. Singer, songwriter.

MCCLURG, EDIE. Kansas City, MO, 7/23/50. Actor. *The Hogan Family.*

MCCLUSKEY, ANDY. Wirral, England, 6/24/59. Singer. Orchestral Manoeuvres in the Dark (OMD).

MCCOO, MARILYN. Jersey City, NJ, 9/30/43. Singer, cohost of *Solid Gold.* The 5th Dimension.

MCCREADY, MIKE. 4/5/66. Guitarist. Pearl Jam.

MCCULLOCH, IAN. Liverpool, England, 5/5/59. Singer. Echo & The Bunnymen.

MCDANIELS, DARRYL D. New York, NY, 1964. Rap artist. Run-D.M.C.

MCDONALD, COUNTRY JOE. El Monte, CA, 1/1/42. Guitarist, singer. Country Joe & The Fish.

MCDONALD, IAN. London, England, 6/25/46. Saxophonist. King Crimson.

MCDONALD, MICHAEL. St. Louis, MO, 12/2/52. Singer, songwriter, keyboardist. The Doobie Brothers.

MCDONALD, PAT. 8/6/52. Musician. Timbuk 3.

MCDONNELL, MARY. Ithaca, NY, 1952. Actor. *Dances with Wolves.*

MCDOWELL, MALCOLM. Leeds, England, 6/19/43. Actor. *A Clockwork Orange.*

MCENROE, JOHN JR. Wiesbaden, Germany, 2/16/59. Tennis player. Formerly married to Tatum O'Neal, relationship with Patty Smyth.

MCFADDEN, CYNTHIA. 5/27/56. Television journalist.

MCFERRIN, BOBBY. New York, NY, 3/11/50. Singer. "Don't Worry, Be Happy."

MCGAVIN, DARREN. Spokane, WA, 5/7/22. Actor. *The Night Stalker.*

MCGEOCH, JOHN. Guitarist. Siouxsie & The Banshees.

MCGILLIS, KELLY. Newport Beach, CA, 7/9/57. Actor. *Witness.*

MCGOVERN, ELIZABETH. Evanston, IL, 7/18/61. Actor. *Ragtime.*

MCGOVERN, MAUREEN. Youngstown, OH, 7/27/49. Singer, actor. "The Morning After."

MCGUINN, ROGER "JIM" (James Joseph McGuinn). Chicago, IL, 7/13/42. Singer, guitarist. The Byrds.

MCGUINNESS, TOM. Wimbledon, England, 12/2/41. Bassist. Manfred Mann.

MCINTOSH, LORRAINE. Glasgow, Scotland, 5/13/64. Singer. Deacon Blue.

MCINTYRE, FRITZ. 9/2/58. Keyboardist. Simply Red.

MCINTYRE, JOE. Needham, MA, 12/31/73. Singer. New Kids on the Block.

MCINTYRE, ONNIE. Lennox Town, Scotland, 9/25/45. Guitarist. Average White Band.

MCJOHN, GOLDY. 5/2/45. Organist. Steppenwolf.

MCKAGAN, DUFF ROSE (Michael McKagan). Seattle, WA. Bassist. Guns N' Roses.

MCKEAN, MICHAEL. New York, NY, 10/17/47. Actor, writer. Lenny Kosnowski on *Laverne & Shirley.*

MCKELLAR, DANICA. 1/3/75. La Jolla, CA. Actor. Winnie Cooper on *The Wonder Years.*

MCKELLEN, IAN. Burnley, England, 5/25/39. Shakespearian actor.

MCKEON, NANCY. Westbury, NY, 4/4/66. Actor. Jo Polniaczek on *The Facts of Life.*

MCKEOWN, LESLIE. Edinburgh, Scotland, 11/12/55. Singer. The Bay City Rollers.

MCKUEN, ROD. Oakland, CA, 4/29/33. Poet. *Laugh-In.*

MCLAGAN, IAN. England, 5/12/46. Keyboardist. The Faces.

MCLEAN, DON. New Rochelle, NY, 10/2/45. Singer, songwriter.

MCLEMORE, LAMONTE. St. Louis, MO, 9/17/39. Singer. The 5th Dimension.

MCMAHON, ED. Detroit, MI, 3/6/23. Announcer and host. *The Tonight Show; Star Search.*

MCNALLY, JOHN. Liverpool, England, 8/30/41. Singer, guitarist. The Searchers.

MCNEIL, MICK. Scotland, 7/20/58. Keyboardist. Simple Minds.

MCNICHOL, KRISTY. Los Angeles, CA, 9/11/62. Actor. Barbara Weston on *Empty Nest.*

MCPHERSON, GRAHAM. Hastings, England, 1/13/61. Singer. Madness.

MCVIE, CHRISTINE (Christine Perfect). Birmingham, England, 7/12/44. Keyboardist, singer. Fleetwood Mac.

MCVIE, JOHN. London, England, 11/26/45. Bassist. Fleetwood Mac.

MEADOWS, JAYNE (Jayne Cotter). Wu Chang, China, 9/27/24. Actor, quiz show regular, married to Steve Allen, sister of Audrey.

MEANEY, COLM. Dublin, Ireland, 1953. Actor. Miles O'Brien on *Star Trek: The Next Generation.*

MEARA, ANNE. Brooklyn, NY, 9/20/29. Actor, partner/married to Jerry Stiller, mother of Ben Stiller. *The Out-of-Towners.*

MEAT LOAF (Marvin Lee Aday). Dallas, TX, 9/27/51. Singer. *Bat out of Hell.*

MEDLEY, BILL. Santa Ana, CA, 9/19/40. Singer. The Righteous Brothers.

MEDRESS, HANK. Brooklyn, NY, 11/19/38. Tenor singer. The Tokens.

MEHTA, ZUBIN. Bombay, India, 4/29/36. Conductor.

MEINE, KLAUS. 5/25/48. Singer. Scorpions.

MEISNER, RANDY. Scottsbluff, NE, 3/8/47. Bassist, singer. The Eagles; Poco.

MELLENCAMP, JOHN. Seymour, IN, 10/7/51. Guitarist, singer, songwriter.

MENDOZA, MARK. Long Island, NY, 6/13/54. Bassist. Twisted Sister.

MENKEN, ALAN. New Rochelle, NY, 1949. Composer. *Beauty and the Beast.*

MERCHANT, JIMMY. New York, NY, 2/10/40. Singer. Frankie Lymon & The Teenagers.

MESSINA, JIM. Maywood, CA, 12/5/47. Guitarist, singer. Poco.

MESSNER, TAMMY FAYE. International Falls, MN, 3/7/42. Former wife of PTL founder Jim Bakker.

METCALF, LAURIE. Edwardsville, IL, 6/16/55. Actor. Jackie Conner Harris on *Roseanne.*

METHENY, PAT. Lee's Summit, MO, 8/12/54. Jazz guitarist. "Offramp."

MEYERS, ARI. San Juan, Puerto Rico, 4/6/69. Actor. Emma McArdle on *Kate & Allie*.

MEYERS, AUGIE. San Antonio, TX, 5/31/40. Keyboardist. Texas Tornados.

MIALL, TERRY LEE. England, 11/8/58. Drummer. Adam & The Ants.

MICHAEL, GEORGE (Georgios Kyriacou Panayiotou). London, England, 6/25/63. Singer, songwriter. Wham!

MICHAELS, LORNE Toronto, Canada, 11/17/44. Producer, writer. *Saturday Night Live*.

MICK (Michael Wilson). Amesbury, England, 3/4/44. Drummer. Dave Dee, Dozy, Beaky, Mick and Tich.

MIDORI. Osaka, Japan, 10/25/71. Violinist.

MIKE D. (Mike Diamond). New York, NY, 11/20/65. Rap artist. The Beastie Boys.

MILANO, FRED. The Bronx, NY, 8/26/40. Tenor singer. Dion & The Belmonts.

MILES, SARAH. Ingatestone, England, 12/31/41. Actor. *Ryan's Daughter*.

MILES, SYLVIA. New York, NY, 9/9/34. Actor. *Midnight Cowboy*.

MILES, VERA (Vera Ralston). Boise City, OK, 8/23/30. Actor. *Psycho*.

MILKEN, MICHAEL. Van Nuys, CA, 1946. Financier. Convicted of securities violations.

MILLER, ANN (Lucille Ann Collier). Chireno, TX, 4/12/23. Actor. *On the Town*.

MILLER, CHARLES. Olathe, KS, 6/2/39. Saxophonist, clarinetist. War.

MILLER, DENNIS. Pittsburgh, PA, 11/3/53. TV personality. *Saturday Night Live*.

MILLER, JERRY. Tacoma, WA, 7/10/43. Guitarist. Moby Grape.

MILLER, PENELOPE ANN.

Santa Monica, CA, 1/13/64. Actor. *Carlito's Way*.

MILLER, STEVE. Milwaukee, WI, 10/5/43. Singer, guitarist. The Steve Miller Band.

MILLS, HAYLEY. London, England, 4/18/46. Actor, daughter of John Mills, sister of Juliet Mills. *The Parent Trap*.

MILLS, JOHN. Suffolk, England, 2/22/08. Actor, father of Hayley and Juliet Mills. *Ryan's Daughter*.

MILLS, JULIET. London, England, 11/21/41. Actor, daughter of John Mills, sister of Hayley Mills. *Nanny and the Professor*.

MILLS, MIKE. 12/17/58. Bassist. R.E.M.

MILLS, STEPHANIE. New York, NY, 3/22/57. Actor, singer. *The Wiz*.

MILLWARD, MIKE. Bromborough, England, 5/9/42. Guitarist, singer. The Fourmost.

MIMIEUX, YVETTE. Los Angeles, CA, 1/8/42. Actor. *The Black Hole*.

MINNELLI, LIZA. Los Angeles, CA, 3/12/46. Singer, actor, daughter of Vincente Minnelli and Judy Garland, half-sister of Lorna Luft. *Cabaret; The Sterile Cuckoo*.

MINOGUE, KYLIE. Melbourne, Australia, 5/28/68. Actor, singer.

MIOU-MIOU (Sylvette Hery). Paris, France, 2/22/50. Actor. *Going Places*.

MIRABELLA, GRACE. Maplewood, NJ, 6/10/29. Fashion editor, publishing executive. *Mirabella*.

MIRREN, HELEN. 7/26/45. Actor. *Prime Suspect*.

MITCHELL, JONI (Roberta Anderson). Fort McLeod, Canada, 11/7/43. Folk singer, songwriter.

MITCHELL, LIZ. Clarendon, Jamaica, 7/12/52. Singer. Boney M.

MITCHELL, MITCH (John Mitchell). Middlesex, England, 7/9/46. Drummer. The Jimi Hendrix Experience.

MITCHELL, NEIL. Helensborough, Scotland, 6/8/67. Keyboardist. Wet Wet Wet.

MITCHUM, JAMES. Los Angeles, CA, 5/8/41. Actor, son of Robert. *Thunder Road*.

MOFFAT, DONALD. Plymouth, England, 12/26/30. Actor. *Clear and Present Danger*.

MOL, GRETCHEN. 11/8/72. Actor. *Rounders*.

MOLL, RICHARD. Pasadena, CA, 1/13/43. Actor, stands 6' 8". Bailiff Nostradamus "Bull" Shannon on *Night Court*.

MOLLAND, JOEY. Liverpool, England, 6/21/48. Guitarist, keyboardist, singer. Badfinger.

MONARCH, MICHAEL. Los Angeles, CA, 7/5/50. Guitarist. Steppenwolf.

MONDALE, WALTER "FRITZ." Ceylon, MN, 1/5/28. Politician, former Vice President of the United States, former presidential candidate. Father of Eleanor.

MONEY, EDDIE (Eddie Mahoney). Brooklyn, NY, 3/21/49. Singer.

MONTALBAN, RICARDO. Mexico City, Mexico, 11/25/20. Actor. *Fantasy Island*.

MONTANA, JOE. New Eagle, PA, 6/11/56. Football great.

MONTGOMERY, GEORGE (George Letz). Brady, MT, 8/29/16. Actor. *The Texas Rangers*.

MONTGOMERY, JOHN MICHAEL. Lexington, KY, 1/20/65. Country singer.

MOODY, MICKY. 8/30/50. Guitarist. Whitesnake.

MOONEY, KEVIN. England, 5/5/62. Bassist. Adam & The Ants.

MOORE, DUDLEY. Dagenham, England, 4/19/35. Actor. *Arthur*.

MOORE, MARY TYLER.

Brooklyn, NY, 12/29/36. Actor. *The Mary Tyler Moore Show*.

MOORE, MELBA (Beatrice Hill). New York, NY, 10/29/45. R&B singer, actor. *Purlie*.

MOORE, ROGER. London, England, 10/14/27. Actor, replaced Sean Connery as James Bond. *Live and Let Die*.

MOORE, SAM. Miami, FL, 10/12/35. Singer. Sam & Dave.

MORAN, ERIN. Burbank, CA, 10/18/61. Actor. Joanie Cunningham on *Happy Days*.

MORANIS, RICK. Toronto, Canada, 4/18/54. Actor, writer. *Honey, I Shrunk the Kids*.

MOREAU, JEANNE. Paris, France, 1/23/28. Actor. *Jules et Jim*.

MORENO, RITA (Rosita Dolores Alverio). Humacao, PR, 12/11/31. Actor. *West Side Story*.

MORGAN, LORRIE (Loretta Lynn Morgan). Nashville, TN, 6/27/59. Singer.

MORIARTY, CATHY. The Bronx, NY, 11/29/60. Actor. *Raging Bull*.

MORIARTY, MICHAEL. Detroit, MI, 4/5/41. Actor. *Law and Order*.

MORITA, NORIYUKI "PAT." Isleton, CA, 6/28/32. Actor. *The Karate Kid*.

MORRIS, STEPHEN. Macclesfield, England, 10/28/57. Drummer. New Order.

MORRISSEY (Stephen Morrissey). Manchester, England, 5/22/59. Singer. The Smiths.

MORROW, ROB. New Rochelle, NY, 9/21/62. Actor. *Northern Exposure*.

MORSE, DAVID. Hamilton, MA, 10/11/53. Actor. *St. Elsewhere*.

MORTON, JOE. New York, NY, 10/18/47. Actor. *Terminator*

2: Judgment Day.

MORVAN, FABRICE. Guadeloupe, 5/14/66. "Singer." Milli Vanilli.

MOSLEY, BOB. Paradise Valley, CA, 12/4/42. Bassist. Moby Grape.

MOSS, JON. Wandsworth, England, 9/11/57. Drummer. Culture Club.

MOSS, KATE. London, England, 1/16/74. Supermodel.

MOST, DONNY. New York, NY, 8/8/53. Actor. Ralph Malph on *Happy Days.*

MOSTEL, JOSH. New York, NY, 12/21/46. Actor. *City Slickers.*

MOULDING, COLIN. Swindon, England, 8/17/55. Bassist, singer. XTC.

MOUNT, DAVE. Carshalton, England, 3/3/47. Drummer, singer. Mud.

MOYERS, BILL. Hugo, OK, 6/5/34. Journalist, commentator. *Bill Moyers' Journal.*

MOYET, ALISON (Genevieve Moyet). Basildon, England, 6/18/61. Singer. Yazoo.

MUDD, ROGER. Washington, DC, 2/9/28. Broadcast journalist, newscaster.

MULDAUR, DIANA. New York, NY, 8/19/38. Actor. *L.A. Law; Star Trek: The Next Generation.*

MULGREW, KATE. Dubuque, IA, 4/29/55. Actor. Capt. Kathryn Janeway on *Star Trek: Voyager.*

MULHERN, MATT. Philadelphia, PA, 7/21/60. Actor. 2nd Lt. Gene Holowachuk on *Major Dad.*

MULL, MARTIN. Chicago, IL, 8/18/43. Actor. *Mary Hartman, Mary Hartman.*

MULLEN, LARRY JR. Dublin, Ireland, 10/31/61. Drummer. U2.

MULLIGAN, RICHARD. New York, NY, 11/13/32. Actor. Dr. Harry Weston on *Empty Nest.*

MUMY, BILLY. El Centro, CA, 2/1/54. Actor. *Lost in Space.*

MURPHY, MICHAEL. Los Angeles, CA, 5/5/38. Actor. *Manhattan.*

MURPHY, PETER. 7/11/57. Singer. Bauhaus.

MURRAY, DAVE. London, England, 12/23/58. Lead guitarist. Iron Maiden.

MUSIC, LORENZO. Brooklyn, NY, 5/2/37. Actor, writer. Carlton the Doorman on *Rhoda.*

NABORS, JIM. Sylacauga, GA, 6/12/32. Actor. Gomer Pyle on *The Andy Griffith Show.*

NADER, RALPH. Winsted, CT, 2/27/34. Political activist, author. *Unsafe at Any Speed.*

NAMATH, JOE. Beaver Falls, PA, 5/31/43. Football great, endorser.

NASH, BRIAN. Liverpool, England, 5/20/63. Guitarist. Frankie Goes to Hollywood.

NASH, GRAHAM. Blackpool, England, 2/2/42. Guitarist. The Hollies; Crosby, Stills, Nash & Young.

NAUGHTON, DAVID. West Hartford, CT, 2/13/51. Actor, brother of James. *An American Werewolf in London.*

NAUGHTON, JAMES. Middletown, CT, 7/6/45. Actor, brother of David. *The Good Mother.*

NAVRATILOVA, MARTINA. Prague, Czechoslovakia, 10/18/56. Tennis player.

NEAL, PATRICIA. Packard, KY, 1/20/26. Actor. *Hud.*

NEGRON, CHUCK. The Bronx, NY, 6/8/42. Singer. Three Dog Night.

NEIL, VINCE (Vince Wharton). Hollywood, CA, 2/8/61. Singer. Mötley Crüe.

NEILL, SAM. Ireland, 9/14/47. Actor. *Jurassic Park.*

NELLIGAN, KATE. London, Canada, 3/16/51. Actor. *The Prince of Tides.*

NELSON, CRAIG T. Spokane, WA, 4/4/46. Actor, writer. Hayden Fox on *Coach.*

NELSON, DAVID. New York, NY, 10/24/36. Actor, son of Ozzie and Harriet, brother of Ricky. David Nelson on *The Adventures of Ozzie and Harriet.*

NELSON, JUDD. Portland, ME, 11/28/59. Actor. *The Breakfast Club.*

NELSON, SANDY. Santa Monica, CA, 12/1/38. Rock/jazz drummer.

NELSON, TRACY. Santa Monica, CA, 10/25/63. Actor, daughter of Rick Nelson. *Father Dowling Mysteries.*

NEMES, LES. Surrey, England, 12/5/60. Bassist. Haircut 100.

NESMITH, MIKE (Robert Nesmith). Houston, TX, 12/30/42. Singer, guitarist, actor. The Monkees.

NEVILLE, AARON New Orleans, LA, 1/24/41. Singer. The Neville Brothers.

NEVILLE, ART. New Orleans, LA, 12/17/37. Singer, keyboardist. The Neville Brothers.

NEVILLE, CHARLES. New Orleans, LA, 12/28/38. Saxophonist. The Neville Brothers.

NEVILLE, CYRIL. 1/10/48. Singer, percussionist. The Neville Brothers.

NEWHART, BOB (George Newhart). Chicago, IL, 9/5/29. Actor, comedian. *The Bob Newhart Show.*

NEWMAN, RANDY. Los Angeles, CA, 11/28/43. Singer, songwriter.

NEWTON, JUICE. Lakehurst, NJ, 2/18/52. Country singer. "Angel of the Morning."

NEWTON-JOHN, OLIVIA. Cambridge, England, 9/26/48. Singer, actor. *Grease.*

NGUYEN, DUSTIN. Saigon, Vietnam, 1962. Actor. *21 Jump Street.*

NICHOL, AL. Winston-Salem, NC, 3/31/46. Guitarist, keyboardist, singer. The Turtles.

NICKS, STEVIE. Phoenix, AZ, 5/26/48. Singer. Fleetwood Mac.

NIELSEN, RICK. Rockford, IL, 12/22/46. Singer, guitarist. Cheap Trick.

NIELSON, BRIGITTE. Denmark, 7/15/63. Actor, formerly married to Sylvester Stallone. *Red Sonja.*

NIMOY, LEONARD. Boston, MA, 3/26/31. Actor, director. Mr. Spock on *Star Trek.*

NOIRET, PHILIPPE. Lille, France, 10/1/31. Actor. *Cinema Paradiso.*

NOLAN, MIKE. Dublin, Ireland, 12/7/54. Singer. Bucks Fizz.

NOONAN, PEGGY. New York, NY, 9/7/50. Author, presidential speechwriter. Responsible for phrase "a kinder, gentler nation."

NOONE, PETER. Manchester, England, 11/5/47. Singer. Herman's Hermits.

NORRIS, CHUCK (Carlos Ray). Ryan, OK, 3/10/40. Karate champion, actor. *Good Guys Wear Black.*

NORTH, OLIVER. San Antonio, TX, 10/7/43. Presidential aide, senatorial candidate. Iran-Contra.

NORTON, KEN. Jacksonville, IL, 8/9/45. Boxer, actor. *The Gong Show.*

NOURI, MICHAEL. Washington, DC, 12/9/45. Actor. *Flashdance.*

NOVAK, KIM (Marilyn Novak). Chicago, IL, 2/13/33. Actor. *Vertigo.*

NOVELLO, DON. Ashtabula, OH, 1/1/43. Actor. Father Guido Sarducci.

NUGENT, TED. Detroit, MI, 12/13/48. Hard rock guitarist, actor.

NUMAN, GARY (Gary Webb). Hammersmith, England, 3/8/58. Singer. "Cars."

O'CONNOR, CARROLL. New York, NY, 8/2/24. Actor. Archie Bunker on *All in the Family.*

O'CONNOR, DONALD. Chicago, IL, 8/28/25. Actor.

Singin' in the Rain.

O'CONNOR, SANDRA DAY. El Paso, TX, 3/26/30. Supreme Court Justice.

O'CONNOR, SINEAD. Dublin, Ireland, 12/8/66. Singer.

O'HARA, BRIAN. Liverpool, England, 3/12/42. Guitarist, singer. The Fourmost.

O'HARA, CATHERINE. Toronto, Canada, 3/4/54. Actor. Mother in *Home Alone.*

O'HARA, MAUREEN (Maureen FitzSimons). Dublin, Ireland, 8/17/21. Actor. *How Green Was My Valley.*

O'NEAL, ALEXANDER. 11/14/53. Singer, songwriter.

O'NEAL, RYAN (Patrick Ryan O'Neal). Los Angeles, CA, 4/20/41. Actor, father of Tatum O'Neal. *Love Story.*

O'NEAL, TATUM. Los Angeles, CA, 11/5/63. Actor, daughter of Ryan, formerly married to John McEnroe. *Paper Moon.*

O'NEILL, ED. Youngstown, OH, 4/12/46. Actor. Al Bundy on *Married ... with Children.*

O'NEILL, JENNIFER. Rio de Janeiro, Brazil, 2/20/48. Actor, former model. *Summer of '42.*

O'NEILL, JOHN. 8/26/57. Guitarist. The Undertones.

O'SHEA, MILO. Dublin, Ireland, 6/2/26. Actor. *The Verdict.*

O'SULLIVAN, GILBERT (Raymond O'Sullivan). Waterford, Ireland, 12/1/46. Singer, songwriter.

O'TOOLE, ANNETTE (Annette Toole). Houston, TX, 4/1/53. Actor. *Superman III.*

O'TOOLE, MARK. Liverpool, England, 1/6/64. Bassist. Frankie Goes to Hollywood.

O'TOOLE, PETER. Connemara, Ireland, 8/2/32. Actor. *Lawrence of Arabia.*

OAKEY, PHILIP. Sheffield, England, 10/2/55. Singer. The Human League.

OAKLEY, BERRY. Chicago, IL, 4/4/48. Bassist. The Allman Brothers Band.

OATES, JOHN. New York, NY, 4/7/48. Singer, guitarist. Hall & Oates.

OCASEK, RIC (Ric Otcasek). Baltimore, MD, 3/23/49. Singer, guitarist, married to Paulina Porizkova. The Cars.

OCEAN, BILLY (Leslie Charles). Fyzabad, Trinidad, 7/21/50. Rock/R&B singer, songwriter.

OLDFIELD, MIKE. Reading, England, 5/15/53. Bassist, composer. "Tubular Bells."

OLDMAN, GARY. New Cross, England, 3/21/58. Actor, formerly married to Uma Thurman. *Bram Stoker's Dracula.*

OLIN, KEN. Chicago, IL, 7/30/54. Actor, director. Michael Steadman on *thirtysomething.*

OLIN, LENA. Stockholm, Sweden, 3/22/55. Actor. *Havana.*

OLMOS, EDWARD JAMES. East Los Angeles, CA, 2/24/47. Actor. Martin Castillo on *Miami Vice.*

ONO, YOKO. 2/18/33. Singer, wife of John Lennon, mother of Julian Lennon and Sean Lennon.

ONTKEAN, MICHAEL. Vancouver, Canada, 1/24/46. Actor. *Twin Peaks.*

OPPENHEIMER, ALAN. New York, NY, 4/23/30. Actor. Gene Kinsella on *Murphy Brown.*

ORANGE, WALTER. Florida, 12/10/47. Singer, drummer. The Commodores.

ORBACH, JERRY. The Bronx, NY, 10/20/35. Actor. *Law and Order.*

ORLANDO, TONY (Michael Cassivitis). New York, NY, 4/3/44. Singer. Tony Orlando & Dawn.

ORMOND, JULIA. Epsom, England, 1/4/65. Actor. *Legends of the Fall.*

ORR, BENJAMIN (Benjamin

Orzechowski). Cleveland, OH, 8/9/55. Singer, bass guitarist. The Cars.

ORZABAL, ROLAND (Roland Orzabal de la Quintana). Portsmouth, England, 8/22/61. Guitarist, keyboardist. Tears for Fears.

OSBORNE, JEFFREY. Providence, RI, 3/9/48. Singer, songwriter, drummer. L.T.D.

OSGOOD, CHARLES. New York, NY, 1/8/33. Broadcast journalist, author.

OSKAR, LEE (Oskar Hansen). Copenhagen, Denmark, 3/24/46. Harmonicist. War.

OSMOND, ALAN. Ogden, UT, 6/22/49. Singer, member of the Osmond family. The Osmonds.

OSMOND, JAY. Ogden, UT, 3/2/55. Singer, member of the Osmond family. The Osmonds.

OSMOND, MERRILL. Ogden, UT, 4/30/53. Singer, member of the Osmond family. The Osmonds.

OSMOND, WAYNE. Ogden, UT, 8/28/51. Singer, member of the Osmond family. The Osmonds.

OTIS, CARRE. 9/28/68. Model, actor, married to Mickey Rourke.

OTIS, JOHNNY (John Veliotes). Vallejo, CA, 12/28/21. R&B drummer, pianist, and songwriter.

OWEN, RANDY. Fort Payne, AL, 12/13/49. Singer, guitarist. Alabama.

OWENS, SHIRLEY. Passaic, NJ, 6/10/41. Lead singer. The Shirelles.

OVITZ, MICHAEL. Encino, CA, 12/14/46. Studio executive.

OXENBERG, CATHERINE. New York, NY, 9/21/61. Actor. Amanda Carrington on *Dynasty.*

OZ, FRANK. Hereford, England, 5/25/44. Puppeteer, film director. *The Muppet Show.*

PACULA, JOANNA. Tamaszow

Lubelski, Poland, 1/2/57. Actor. *Gorky Park.*

PAGE, JIMMY. Heston, England, 1/9/44. Guitarist. Led Zeppelin.

PAICE, IAN. Nottingham, England, 6/29/48. Drummer. Deep Purple.

PAICH, DAVID. Los Angeles, CA, 6/25/54. Keyboardist, singer. Toto.

PALANCE, JACK (Walter Palanuik). Lattimer, PA, 2/18/20. Actor. *City Slickers.*

PALIN, MICHAEL. Sheffield, England, 5/5/43. Actor, writer. *Monty Python's Flying Circus.*

PALMER, BETSY. East Chicago, IN, 11/1/26. Actor, panelist on *I've Got a Secret.*

PALMER, CARL. Birmingham, England, 3/20/51. Drummer. Emerson, Lake & Palmer; Asia.

PALMER, JOHN. 5/25/43. Keyboardist. Family.

PALMER, ROBERT (Alan Palmer). Batley, England, 1/19/49. Singer, songwriter. "Addicted to Love."

PALMINTERI, CHAZZ (Chalogero Lorenzo Palminteri). Bronx, NY, 5/15/51. Actor, playwright, screenwriter. *A Bronx Tale.*

PANKOW, JAMES. Chicago, IL, 8/20/47. Trombonist. Chicago.

PANOZZO, CHUCK. Chicago, IL, 9/20/47. Bassist. Styx.

PAQUIN, ANNA. Wellington, New Zealand, 7/24/82. Actor. *The Piano.*

PARAZAIDER, WALTER. Chicago, IL, 3/14/45. Saxophonist. Chicago.

PARE, MICHAEL. Brooklyn, NY, 10/9/59. Actor. *Eddie and the Cruisers.*

PARFITT, RICK (Richard Harrison). Redhill, England, 10/25/43. Guitarist, singer. Status Quo.

PARILLAUD, ANNE. France, 1961. Actor. *La Femme Nikita.*

PARKER, FESS. Fort Worth, TX, 8/16/24. Actor. *Daniel Boone.*

PARKER, GRAHAM. Deepcut, England, 11/18/50. Singer. Graham Parker & The Rumour.

PARKER, JAMESON. Baltimore, MD, 11/18/47. Actor. *Simon and Simon.*

PARKER, MARY-LOUISE. Ft. Jackson, SC, 8/2/64. Actor. *Fried Green Tomatoes.*

PARKER, RAY JR. Detroit, MI, 5/1/54. Singer, songwriter. "Ghostbusters."

PARKER, TREY. 10/19/69. Actor, cartoonist. *South Park.*

PARSONS, ESTELLE. Lynn, MA, 11/20/27. Actor. *Roseanne.*

PARTRIDGE, ANDY. Malta, 11/11/53. Guitarist, singer. XTC.

PASTORELLI, ROBERT. 6/21/54. Actor. *Murphy Brown.*

PATERSON, GERRY. Winnepeg, Canada, 5/26/45. Drummer. The Guess Who.

PATINKIN, MANDY (Mandel Patinkin). Chicago, IL, 11/30/52. Actor. *Yentl.*

PATRIC, JASON (Jason Patrick Miller). Queens, NY, 6/17/66. Actor. *Rush.*

PATRICK, ROBERT. Marietta, GA, 1959. Actor. Evil T-1000 in *Terminator 2: Judgment Day.*

PATTEN, EDWARD. Atlanta, GA, 8/2/39. Singer. Gladys Knight & The Pips.

PATTERSON, LORNA. Whittier, CA, 6/1/57. Actor. *Private Benjamin.*

PATTERSON, MELODY. Los Angeles, CA, 1947. Actor. Wrangler Jane on *F Troop.*

PATTINSON, LES. Ormskirk, England, 4/18/58. Bassist. Echo & The Bunnymen.

PATTON, MIKE. Eureka, CA, 1/27/68. Lead singer. Faith No More.

PATTON, WILL. Charleston, SC, 6/14/54. Actor. *No Way*

Out.

PAYCHECK, JOHNNY (Donald Eugene Lytle). Greenfield, OH, 5/31/41. Singer. "Take This Job and Shove It."

PAYNE, BILL. Waco, TX, 3/12/49. Keyboardist. Little Feat.

PAYS, AMANDA. Berkshire, England, 6/6/59. Actor, married to Corbin Bernsen. *The Flash.*

PAYTON, DENIS. Walthamstow, England, 8/11/43. Saxophonist. The Dave Clark Five.

PAYTON, WALTER. Columbia, MS, 6/25/54. Football player.

PEARSON, DELROY. Romford, England, 4/11/70. Singer. Five Star.

PEARSON, DENIECE. Romford, England, 6/13/68. Lead singer. Five Star.

PEARSON, DORIS. Romford, England, 6/8/66. Singer. Five Star.

PEARSON, LORRAINE. Romford, England, 8/10/67. Singer. Five Star.

PEARSON, STEDMAN. Romford, England, 6/29/64. Singer. Five Star.

PEART, NEIL. Hamilton, Canada, 9/12/52. Drummer. Rush.

PECK, GREGORY (Eldred Peck). La Jolla, CA, 4/5/16. Actor, producer. *To Kill a Mockingbird.*

PEEK, DAN. Panama City, FL, 11/1/50. Singer, guitarist. America.

PELE, PEROLA NEGRA (Edson Arantes do Nascimento). Tres Coracoes, Brazil, 10/23/40. Soccer legend.

PELLOW, MARTI (Mark McLoughlin). Clydebank, Scotland, 3/23/66. Singer. Wet Wet Wet.

PENA, ELIZABETH. Elizabeth, NJ, 9/23/61. Actor. *La Bamba.*

PENDER, MIKE (Michael Prendergast). Liverpool,

England, 3/3/42. Singer, lead guitarist. The Searchers.

PENDERGRASS, TEDDY. Philadelphia, PA, 3/26/50. R&B singer, songwriter, drummer.

PENDLETON, AUSTIN. Warren, OH, 3/27/40. Actor. *What's Up Doc?*

PENDLETON, BRIAN. Wolverhampton, England, 4/13/44. Guitarist. The Pretty Things.

PENGILLY, KIRK. 7/4/58. Guitarist, saxophonist, singer. INXS.

PENNY, JOE. London, England, 9/14/56. Actor. Jake Styles on *Jake and the Fatman.*

PEPA (Sanda Denton). Queens, NY, 9/9/64. Rap artist. Salt-N-Pepa.

PEREZ, ROSIE. Brooklyn, NY, 9/4/66. Actor, choreographer. *Do the Right Thing.*

PERKINS, ELIZABETH. Queens, NY, 11/18/61. Actor. *Big.*

PERLMAN, RHEA. Brooklyn, NY, 3/31/48. Actor, married to Danny DeVito. Carla Tortelli LeBec on *Cheers.*

PERLMAN, RON. New York, NY, 4/13/50. Actor. The Beast in *Beauty and the Beast.*

PEROT, HENRY ROSS. Texarkana, TX, 6/27/30. Self-made billionaire businessman, former presidential candidate.

PERRINE, VALERIE. Galveston, TX, 9/3/43. Actor. *Lenny.*

PERRY, JOE. Boston, MA, 9/10/50. Guitarist. Aerosmith.

PERRY, LUKE (Perry Coy III). Fredericktown, OH, 10/11/66. Actor. *Beverly Hills 90210.*

PERRY, STEVE. Hanford, CA, 1/22/53. Singer. Journey.

PERRY, WILLIAM "THE REFRIGERATOR." Aiken, SC, 12/16/62. Very large football player. Chicago Bears.

PESCOW, DONNA. Brooklyn, NY, 3/24/54. Actor. *Saturday Night Fever.*

PETERS, BROCK. New York, NY, 7/2/27. Actor, singer. *To Kill a Mockingbird.*

PETERS, MIKE. Prestatyn, Wales, 2/25/59. Guitarist, singer. The Alarm.

PETERSEN, WILLIAM. Chicago, IL, 1953. Actor. *To Live and Die in L.A.*

PETERSON, DEBBI. Los Angeles, CA, 8/22/61. Drummer, singer. The Bangles.

PETERSON, SYLVIA. New York, NY, 9/30/46. Singer. The Chiffons.

PETERSON, VICKI. Los Angeles, CA, 1/11/58. Guitarist, singer. The Bangles.

PETERSSON, TOM. Rockford, IL, 5/9/50. Singer, bassist. Cheap Trick.

PETTY, LORI. Chattanooga, TN. Actor. *A League of Their Own.*

PFEIFFER, DEDEE. 1/1/64. Actor, sister of Michelle Pfeiffer. *Cybill.*

PFISTERER, ALBAN. Switzerland, 1947. Drummer, keyboardist. Love.

PHANTOM, SLIM JIM (Jim McDonnell). 3/20/61. Drummer. The Stray Cats.

PHAIR, LIZ. New Haven, CT, 4/17/67. Singer, songwriter. *Exile in Guyville.*

PHILIP, PRINCE (Philip Mountbatten). Corfu, Greece, 6/10/21. Husband of Queen Elizabeth II, Duke of Edinburgh.

PHILLIPS, CHYNNA. Los Angeles, CA, 1/12/68. Singer, half-sister of Mackenzie, daughter of John and Michelle, married to Billy Baldwin. Wilson Phillips.

PHILLIPS, JOHN. Parris Island, SC, 8/30/35. Singer, formerly married to Michelle, father of Mackenzie and Chynna. The Mamas & the Papas.

PHILLIPS, LOU DIAMOND (Lou Upchurch). Philippines, 2/17/62. Actor. *La Bamba.*

PHILLIPS, MACKENZIE (Laura Mackenzie Phillips). Alexandria, VA, 11/10/59. Actor, daughter of John Phillips, half-sister of Chynna. Julie Cooper Horvath on *One Day at a Time.*

PHILLIPS, MICHELLE (Holly Gilliam). Santa Ana, CA, 6/4/44. Actor, formerly married to John, mother of Chynna. Anne Matheson on *Knots Landing.*

PHILTHY ANIMAL (Philip Taylor). Chesterfield, England, 9/21/54. Drummer. Motorhead.

PICKETT, WILSON. Prattville, AL, 3/18/41. Singer, songwriter. "In the Midnight Hour."

PIERSON, KATE. Weehawken, NJ, 4/27/48. Organist, singer. The B-52's.

PINCHOT, BRONSON. New York, NY, 5/20/59. Actor. Balki Bartokomous on *Perfect Strangers.*

PINDER, MIKE. Birmingham, England, 12/12/42. Keyboardist. The Moody Blues.

PINKNEY, BILL. Sumter, NC, 8/15/25. Bassist. The Drifters.

PIRNER, DAVE. Green Bay, WI, 4/16/64. Singer, songwriter, guitarist. Soul Asylum.

PIRRONI, MARCO. England, 4/27/59. Guitarist. Adam & The Ants.

PISCOPO, JOE. Passaic, NJ, 6/17/51. Actor. *Saturday Night Live.*

PITNEY, GENE. Hartford, CT, 2/17/41. Singer, songwriter. "Town Without Pity."

PLACE, MARY KAY. Tulsa, OK, 9/23/47. Actor. *The Big Chill.*

PLANT, ROBERT. Bromwich, England, 8/20/48. Singer. Led Zeppelin.

PLATT, OLIVER. 1/12/60. Actor. *Flatliners.*

PLESHETTE, JOHN. New York, NY, 7/27/42. Actor. Richard Avery on *Knots Landing.*

PLESHETTE, SUZANNE. New York, NY, 1/31/37. Actor. Emily Hartley on *The Bob Newhart Show.*

PLOWRIGHT, JOAN. Brigg, England, 10/28/29. Actor, widow of Laurence Olivier. *Enchanted April.*

PLUMB, EVE. Burbank, CA, 4/29/58. Actor. Jan Brady on *The Brady Bunch.*

PLUMMER, AMANDA. New York, NY, 3/23/57. Actor, daughter of Christopher Plummer. *The Fisher King.*

PLUMMER, CHRISTOPHER. Toronto, Canada, 12/13/27. Actor, father of Amanda Plummer. Baron von Trapp in *The Sound of Music.*

POINTER, ANITA. East Oakland, CA, 1/23/48. Singer. Pointer Sisters.

POINTER, BONNIE. East Oakland, CA, 6/11/51. Singer. Pointer Sisters.

POINTER, JUNE. East Oakland, CA, 11/30/54. Singer. Pointer Sisters.

POINTER, RUTH. East Oakland, CA, 3/19/46. Singer. Pointer Sisters.

POITIER, SIDNEY. Miami, FL, 2/20/27. Actor. *Guess Who's Coming to Dinner.*

POLANSKI, ROMAN. Paris, France, 8/18/33. Director, writer. *Rosemary's Baby.*

POLLAK, KEVIN. 10/30/57. Actor.

POLLACK, SYDNEY. South Bend, Indiana, 7/1/34. Director, producer, actor. *The Way We Were.*

POLLAN, TRACY. New York, NY, 6/22/60. Actor, married to Michael J. Fox. *Family Ties.*

POOLE, BRIAN. Barking, England, 11/2/41. Singer. Brian Poole & The Tremeloes.

POP, IGGY (James Osterburg). Ann Arbor, MI, 4/21/47. Singer, songwriter.

POPCORN, FAITH. New York, NY, 5/11/43. Trend analyst, consultant.

PORCARO, STEVE. Los Angeles, CA, 9/2/57. Keyboardist, singer. Toto.

PORTZ, CHUCK. Santa Monica, CA, 3/28/45. Bassist. The Turtles.

POST, MARKIE. Palo Alto, CA, 11/4/50. Actor. Christine Sullivan on *Night Court.*

POTTER, CAROL. Tenafly, NJ, 5/21/48. Actor. *Beverly Hills 90210.*

POTTS, ANNIE. Nashville, TN, 10/28/52. Actor. Mary Jo Shively on *Designing Women.*

POUNDSTONE, PAULA. Alabama, 12/29/60. Comedian, actor.

POVICH, MAURY. Washington, DC, 1/17/39. Talk show host, married to Connie Chung. *A Current Affair.*

POWELL, BILLY. Florida, 6/3/52. Keyboardist. Lynyrd Skynyrd.

POWELL, COLIN. New York, NY, 4/5/37. Military leader.

POWELL, DON. 9/10/50. Drummer. Slade.

POWERS, STEPHANIE (Stefania Federkiewicz). Hollywood, CA, 11/12/42. Actor. Jennifer on *Hart to Hart.*

POWTER, SUSAN. Sydney, Australia, 1957. Weightloss expert. *Stop the Insanity!*

PRENTISS, PAULA (Paula Ragusa). San Antonio, TX, 3/4/38. Actor. *What's New Pussycat?*

PRESLEY, PRISCILLA. Brooklyn, NY, 5/24/45. Actor, producer, married and divorced Elvis Presley.

PRESLEY, REG (Reginald Ball). Andover, England, 6/12/43. Singer. The Troggs.

PRESTON, KELLY. Honolulu, HI, 10/13/62. Actor, married to John Travolta. *52 Pick-*

Up.

PRICE, ALAN. Fairfield, Durham, 4/19/41. Keyboardist. The Animals.

PRICE, LLOYD. Kenner, LA, 5/9/33. Singer, songwriter.

PRICE, RICK. 6/10/44. Bassist. Wizzard.

PRIDE, CHARLEY. Sledge, MS, 3/18/38. Country singer, songwriter.

PRIEST, STEVE. London, England, 2/23/50. Bassist. Sweet.

PRIESTLEY, JASON. Vancouver, Canada, 8/28/69. Actor. Brandon Walsh on *Beverly Hills 90210.*

PRIESTMAN, HENRY. 7/21/58. Singer. The Christians.

PRIME, JAMES. Kilmarnock, Scotland, 11/3/60. Keyboardist. Deacon Blue.

PRINCE MARK D. 2/19/60. Rap artist. Fat Boys.

PRINCIPAL, VICTORIA. Fukuoka, Japan, 1/3/50. Actor. Pam Ewing on *Dallas.*

PRITCHARD, BARRY. Birmingham, England, 4/3/44. Guitarist, singer. The Fortunes.

PROBY, P. J. (James Smith). Houston, TX, 11/6/38. Singer, actor.

PRYCE, JONATHAN. North Wales, 6/1/47. Actor. *Miss Saigon.*

PRYOR, NICHOLAS. Baltimore, MD, 1/28/35. Actor. *Risky Business.*

PRYOR, RICHARD. Peoria, IL, 12/1/40. Actor. *Stir Crazy.*

PUERTA, JOE. 7/2/51. Bassist, singer. Bruce Hornsby & The Range.

PULLMAN, BILL. Hornell, NY, 12/17/53. Actor. *While You Were Sleeping.*

PURCELL, SARAH. Richmond, IN, 10/8/48. TV personality. Cohost on *Real People.*

QADDAFI, MUAMMAR. Sirta, Libya, 1942. Political leader. Libyan head of state.

QUAID, RANDY. Houston, TX, 10/1/50. Actor, brother of Dennis. *The Last Picture Show.*

QUAIFE, PETE. Tavistock, England, 12/31/43. Bassist. The Kinks.

QUATRO, SUZI (Suzi Quatrocchia). Detroit, MI, 6/3/50. Singer, songwriter, actor.

QUAYLE, DAN. Indianapolis, IN, 2/4/47. Vice president under George Bush.

QUAYLE, MARILYN. Indianapolis, IN, 7/29/49. Lawyer, author, married to Dan. *Embrace the Serpent.*

QUEEN LATIFAH. 3/18/70. Singer, actor. *Living Single.*

QUINLAN, KATHLEEN. Mill Valley, CA, 11/19/54. Actor. *Apollo 13.*

QUINN, AIDAN. Chicago, IL, 3/8/59. Actor. *The Playboys.* Married to Elizabeth Bracco.

QUINN, ANTHONY. Chihuahua, Mexico, 4/21/15. Actor. *Zorba the Greek.*

QUINN, DEREK. Manchester, England, 5/24/42. Lead guitarist. Freddie & The Dreamers.

QUIVERS, ROBIN. 8/8/52. Radio personality, author. *The Howard Stern Show.*

RAFFERTY, GERRY. Paisley, Scotland, 4/16/47. Singer, songwriter. "Baker Street."

RAFFI. Cairo, Egypt, 7/8/48. Singer, songwriter, children's performer. *Everything Grows.*

RAFFIN, DEBORAH. Los Angeles, CA, 3/13/53. Actor. *Once Is Not Enough.*

RALPH, SHERYL LEE. Waterbury, CT, 12/30/56. Actor. *The Distinguished Gentleman.*

RALPHS, MICK. Hereford, England, 3/31/44. Guitarist. Mott The Hoople; Bad Company.

RAMIS, HAROLD. Chicago, IL, 11/21/44. Writer, director, actor. Egon Spengler in *Ghostbusters.*

RAMONE, DEE DEE (Douglas Colvin). Fort Lee, VA, 9/18/52. Bassist. The Ramones.

RAMONE, JOEY (Jeffrey Hyman). Forest Hills, NY, 5/19/52. Singer. The Ramones.

RAMONE, JOHNNY (John Cummings). Long Island, NY, 10/8/48. Guitarist. The Ramones.

RAMONE, TOMMY (Thomas Erdelyi). Budapest, Hungary, 1/29/49. Drummer. The Ramones.

RAMOS, LARRY JR. (Hilario Ramos Jr.). Kauai, HI, 4/19/42. Singer, guitarist. The Association.

RAMPLING, CHARLOTTE. Surmer, England, 2/5/46. Actor. *The Verdict.*

RAMSEY, AL. New Jersey, 7/27/43. Guitarist. Gary Lewis & The Playboys.

RANDALL, TONY (Leonard Rosenberg). Tulsa, OK, 2/26/20. Actor. Felix Unger on *The Odd Couple.*

RAPHAEL, SALLY JESSY. Easton, PA, 2/25/43. talk show hostess. *Sally Jessy Raphäel.*

RAPP, DANNY. Philadelphia, PA, 5/10/41. Lead singer. Danny & The Juniors.

RAREBELL, HERMAN. 11/18/49. Drummer. Scorpions.

RASCHE, DAVID. St. Louis, MO, 8/7/44. Actor. *Sledge Hammer.*

RASHAD, AHMAD. Portland, OR, 11/19/49. Football player, sportscaster, husband of Phylicia.

RASHAD, PHYLICIA. Houston, TX, 6/19/48. Actor, sister of Debbie Allen, wife of Ahmad. Clair Huxtable on *The Cosby Show.*

RATZENBERGER, JOHN. Bridgeport, CT, 4/6/47. Actor. Cliff Claven on *Cheers.*

RAWLS, LOU. Chicago, IL, 12/1/36. R&B singer. "You'll Never Find Another Love Like Mine."

RAY, JAMES EARL. Alton, IL, 3/10/28. Assassin. Killed Martin Luther King Jr.

REA, CHRIS. Middlesbrough, England, 3/4/51. Singer, songwriter, guitarist. "Fool (If You Think It's Over)."

REAGAN, NANCY. New York, NY, 7/6/21. Former First Lady, married to president Ronald Reagan.

REAGAN, RONALD. Tampico, IL, 2/6/11. Politician, actor, father of Ron Jr., husband of Nancy. Fortieth U.S. president. *Bedtime for Bonzo.*

REAGAN, RONALD JR. Los Angeles, CA, 5/20/58. Performer, son of former president Ronald Reagan.

REASON, REX. Berlin, Germany, 11/30/28. Actor. *This Island Earth.*

RECORD, EUGENE. 12/23/40. Lead singer. The Chi-Lites.

REDDING, NOEL. Folkestone, England, 12/25/45. Bassist, The Jimi Hendrix Experience.

REDDY, HELEN. Melbourne, Australia, 10/25/41. Pop singer. *The Helen Reddy Show.*

REDGRAVE, CORIN. London, England, 6/16/39. Actor, brother of Lynn and Vanessa. *A Man for All Seasons.*

REDGRAVE, LYNN. London, England, 3/8/43. Actor, sister of Corin and Vanessa. *House Calls.*

REDGRAVE, VANESSA. London, England, 1/30/37. Actor, sister of Corin and Lynn. *Playing for Time.*

REED, LOU (Louis Firbank). Long Island, NY, 3/2/43. Singer, songwriter. The Velvet Underground.

REED, PAMELA. Tacoma, WA, 4/2/53. Actor. *The Right Stuff.*

REEMS, HARRY (Herbert Streicher). The Bronx, NY, 8/27/47. Actor. *Deep Throat.*

REESE, DELLA. 7/6/32. Actor. *Touched By An Angel.*

REEVES, STEVE. Glasgow, MT, 1/21/26. Actor. *Hercules.*

REGALBUTO, JOE. Brooklyn, NY. Actor. Frank Fontana on *Murphy Brown.*

REID, DON. Staunton, VA, 6/5/45. Musician, brother of Harold. Statler Brothers.

REID, HAROLD. Staunton, VA, 8/21/39. Musician, brother of Don. Statler Brothers.

REID, JIM. East Kilbride, Scotland, 1961. Guitarist, singer. The Jesus & Mary Chain.

REID, TIM. Norfolk, VA, 12/19/44. Actor, producer. Gordon "Venus Flytrap" Sims on *WKRP in Cincinnati.*

REID, WILLIAM. East Kilbride, Scotland, 1958. Guitarist, singer. The Jesus & Mary Chain.

REINER, CARL. New York, NY, 3/20/22. Actor, writer, and director. *The Dick Van Dyke Show.*

REINER, ROB. New York, NY, 3/6/45. Actor, writer, producer, director, son of Carl, formerly married to Penny Marshall. Mike Stivic on *All in the Family.*

REINHOLD, JUDGE (Edward Ernest Reinhold Jr.). Wilmington, DE, 5/21/57. Actor. Rosewood in *Beverly Hills Cop.*

REINKING, ANN. Seattle, WA, 11/10/49. Actor, dancer. *Annie.*

REITMAN, IVAN. Komarno, Czechoslovakia, 10/26/46. Director, producer. *Ghostbusters.*

REVERE, PAUL. Harvard, NE, 1/7/38. Keyboardist. Paul Revere & The Raiders.

REYNOLDS, DEBBIE (Mary Frances Reynolds). El Paso, TX, 4/1/32. Actor, formerly married to Eddie Fisher, mother of Carrie Fisher. *Sin-*

gin' in the Rain.

RHAMES, VING. 5/12/59. Actor. *Only in America: The Don King Story.*

RHODES, NICK (Nicholas Bates). Mosely, England, 6/8/62. Keyboardist. Duran Duran.

RIBEIRO, ALFONSO. New York, NY, 9/21/71. Actor, dancer. *Fresh Prince of Bel Air.*

RICH, ADAM. New York, NY, 10/12/68. Actor. Nicholas Bradford on *Eight Is Enough.*

RICHARD, CLIFF (Harry Webb). Lucknow, India, 10/14/40. Singer, drummer. The Shadows.

RICHARDS, KEITH. Dartford, England, 12/18/43. Guitarist. The Rolling Stones.

RICHARDSON, MIRANDA. Lancashire, England, 3/3/58. Actor. *The Crying Game.*

RICHARDSON, SUSAN. Coatesville, PA, 3/11/52. Actor. Susan Bradford on *Eight Is Enough.*

RICHIE, LIONEL. Tuskegee, AL, 6/20/49. Singer, songwriter. The Commodores.

RICHRATH, GARY. Peoria, IL, 10/18/49. Guitarist. REO Speedwagon.

RICKLES, DON. New York, NY, 5/8/26. Actor. *The Don Rickles Show.*

RICKMAN, ALAN. Hammersmith, England, 1946. Actor. *Die Hard.*

RIDGELEY, ANDREW. Windlesham, England, 1/26/63. Guitarist. Wham!

RIEGERT, PETER. New York, NY, 4/11/47. Actor. *Crossing Delancey.*

RIGBY, CATHY. Long Beach, CA, 12/12/52. Gymnast, actor.

RIGG, DIANA. Doncaster, England, 7/20/38. Actor. Emma Peel on *The Avengers.*

RIGGS, BOBBY. Los Angeles, CA, 2/25/18. Tennis player,

defeated by Billie Jean King.

RILEY, PAT. Rome, NY, 3/20/45. Basketball coach. Former New York Knicks coach.

RINGWALD, MOLLY. Sacramento, CA, 2/18/68. Actor. *Sixteen Candles.*

RITTER, JOHN. Burbank, CA, 9/17/48. Actor, producer. Jack Tripper on *Three's Company.*

RIVERA, CHITA. Washington, DC, 1/23/33. Singer.

RIVERS, JOHNNY (John Ramistella). New York, NY, 11/7/42. Soul/rock singer, songwriter.

RIZZUTO, PHIL. New York, NY, 9/25/18. Baseball great, sports announcer.

ROBARDS, JASON. Chicago, IL, 7/26/22. Actor, formerly married to Lauren Bacall. *Inherit the Wind.*

ROBERTS, ERIC. Biloxi, MS, 4/18/56. Actor, brother of Julia. *The Pope of Greenwich Village.*

ROBERTS, ORAL. Ada, OK, 1/24/18. Evangelist. Oral Roberts University.

ROBERTS, TANYA (Tanya Leigh). The Bronx, NY, 10/15/55. Actor. *Charlie's Angels.*

ROBERTS, TONY. New York, NY, 10/22/39. Actor. *Play It Again, Sam.*

ROBERTS, XAVIER. Cleveland, GA, 10/31/55. Businessman. Creator of Cabbage Patch Kids.

ROBERTSON, BRIAN. Glasgow, Scotland, 9/12/56. Guitarist. Thin Lizzy.

ROBERTSON, CLIFF. La Jolla, CA, 9/9/23. Actor. *Charly.*

ROBERTSON, PAT (Marion Gordon Robertson). Lexington, VA, 3/22/30. Evangelist, TV personality. Founder of Christian Broadcasting Network.

ROBERTSON, ROBBIE (Jaime Robertson). Toronto, Canada, 7/5/44. Guitarist,

singer. The Band.

ROBINSON, CHRIS. Atlanta, GA, 12/20/66. Singer. The Black Crowes.

ROBINSON, CYNTHIA. Sacramento, CA, 1/12/46. Trumpeter. Sly & The Family Stone.

ROBINSON, JAY. New York, NY, 4/14/30. Actor. *The Robe.*

ROBINSON, RICH. Atlanta, GA, 5/24/69. Guitarist. The Black Crowes.

ROBINSON, SMOKEY (William Robinson). Detroit, MI, 2/19/40. Motown singer, songwriter. Smokey Robinson & The Miracles.

ROCKER, LEE (Leon Drucher). 1961. Double bassist. The Stray Cats.

ROCKWELL (Kenneth Gordy). Detroit, MI, 3/15/64. Singer, son of Berry Gordy. "Somebody's Watching Me."

RODGERS, NILE. New York, NY, 9/19/52. Guitarist. Chic.

RODGERS, PAUL. Middlesbrough, England, 12/17/49. Singer. Free; Bad Company.

RODMAN, DENNIS. Trenton, NJ, 5/13/61. Basketball player. Married to Carmen Electra.

ROE, TOMMY. Atlanta, GA, 5/9/42. Singer, songwriter.

ROGERS, KENNY. Houston, TX, 8/21/38. Country singer, actor. "The Gambler."

ROGERS, MIMI. Coral Gables, FL, 1/27/55. Actor. Formerly married to Tom Cruise. *Someone To Watch Over Me.*

ROGERS, FRED. Latrobe, PA, 3/20/28. Children's host, producer. *Mr. Rogers' Neighborhood.*

ROGERS, ROY (Leonard Slye). Cincinnati, OH, 11/5/12. TV cowboy, singer. *Happy Trails with Roy and Dale.*

ROGERS, WAYNE. Birmingham, AL, 4/7/33. Actor. Trapper John on *M*A*S*H.*

ROGERS, WILL JR. New York, NY, 10/20/12. Actor, lec-

turer. *The Story of Will Rogers.*

ROLLE, ESTHER. Pompano Beach, FL, 11/8/22. Actor. *Driving Miss Daisy.*

RONSTADT, LINDA. Tucson, AZ, 7/15/46. Singer, actor. *The Pirates of Penzance.*

ROONEY, ANDY. Albany, NY, 1/14/19. News commentator. *60 Minutes.*

ROONEY, MICKEY (Joe Yule Jr.). Brooklyn, NY, 9/23/20. Actor. *National Velvet.*

ROSE, AXL (William Bailey). Lafayette, IN, 1962. Singer. Guns N' Roses.

ROSE, PETE. Cincinnati, OH, 4/14/41. Baseball player and manager. Cincinnati Reds.

ROSS, KATHARINE. Hollywood, CA, 1/29/43. Actor. *The Graduate.*

ROSS, MARION. Albert Lea, MN, 10/25/28. Actor. Marion Cunningham on *Happy Days.*

ROSS, RICKY. Dundee, Scotland, 12/22/57. Singer. Deacon Blue.

ROSSELLINI, ISABELLA. Rome, Italy, 6/18/52. Actor, formerly married to Martin Scorsese. *Blue Velvet.*

ROSSI, FRANCIS. Forest Hill, England, 4/29/49. Guitarist, singer. Status Quo.

ROSSINGTON, GARY. Jacksonville, FL, 12/4/51. Guitarist. Lynyrd Skynyrd.

ROTH, DAVID LEE. Bloomingtom, IN, 10/10/54. Singer. Van Halen.

ROTH, TIM. London, England, 1961. Actor. *Reservoir Dogs.*

ROTHERY, STEVE. Brampton, England, 11/25/59. Guitarist. Marillion.

ROTHWELL, RIC. Stockport, England, 3/11/44. Drummer. Wayne Fontana & The Mindbenders.

ROUNDTREE, RICHARD. New Rochelle, NY, 9/7/42. Actor. *Shaft.*

ROURKE, MICKEY. Schenectady, NY, 9/16/56. Actor, married to Carre Otis. *9 1/2 Weeks.*

ROWLAND, KEVIN. Wolverhampton, England, 8/17/53. Singer, guitarist. Dexy's Midnight Runners.

ROWLANDS, GENA. Cambria, WI, 6/19/30. Actor. *Gloria.*

RUCKER, DARIUS. Charleston, SC, 5/13/66. Singer, songwriter, guitarist. Hootie & The Blowfish.

RUDD, PHILIP. Australia, 5/19/46. Drummer. AC/DC.

RUDNER, RITA. Miami, FL, 9/11/55. Actor, comedian.

RUEHL, MERCEDES. Queens, NY, 2/28/52. Actor. *Lost in Yonkers.*

RUFFIN, DAVID. Meridian, MS, 1/18/41. Singer. The Temptations.

RUNDGREN, TODD. Philadelphia, PA, 6/22/48. Singer, songwriter.

RUSHDIE, SALMAN. Bombay, India, 6/19/47. Author. *The Satanic Verses.*

RUSSELL, GRAHAM. Nottingham, England, 6/1/50. Singer. Air Supply.

RUSSELL, JACK. 12/5/60. Singer. Great White.

RUSSELL, JANE. Bemidji, MN, 6/21/21. Actor, pinup girl. *The Outlaw.*

RUSSELL, LEON (Hank Wilson). Lawton, OK, 4/2/41. Country/blues singer, songwriter.

RUSSELL, NIPSEY. Atlanta, GA, 10/13/24. Actor. *Car 54, Where Are You?*

RUSSELL, THERESA (Theresa Paup). San Diego, CA, 3/20/57. Actor. *Black Widow.*

RUTHERFORD, MIKE. Guildford, England, 10/2/50. Guitarist. Genesis; Mike & The Mechanics.

RUTHERFORD, PAUL. Liverpool, England, 12/8/59. Singer. Frankie Goes to Hollywood.

RUTTAN, SUSAN. Oregon

City, OR, 9/16/48. Actor. Roxanne on *L.A. Law.*

RYAN, TOM. Anderson, IN, 6/6/26. Cartoonist. *Tumbleweeds.*

RYDER, MITCH (William Levise Jr.). Detroit, MI, 2/26/45. Singer. Mitch Ryder & The Detroit Wheels.

RYDER, PAUL. Manchester, England, 4/24/64. Bassist. Happy Mondays.

RYDER, SHAUN. Little Hulton, England, 8/23/62. Singer. Happy Mondays.

SABATINI, GABRIELA. Buenos Aires, Argentina, 5/16/70. Tennis player.

SADE (Helen Folasade Adu). Ibadan, Nigeria, 1/16/59. Singer.

SAGAL, KATEY. Los Angeles, CA, 1/19/54. Actor. Peg on *Married ... with Children.*

SAGET, BOB. Philadelphia, PA, 5/17/56. Actor. *Full House.*

SAHM, DOUG. San Antonio, TX, 11/6/41. Singer, guitarist. Sir Douglas Quintet.

SAINT, EVA MARIE. Newark, NJ, 7/4/24. Actor. *On the Waterfront.*

SAINT JAMES, SUSAN (Susan Miller). Los Angeles, CA, 8/14/46. Actor. Kate on *Kate & Allie.*

SAJAK, PAT. Chicago, IL, 10/26/46. Game show host. *Wheel of Fortune.*

SALAZAR, ALBERTO. Havana, Cuba, 8/7/58. Track athlete, won New York City Marathon.

SALES, SOUPY (Milton Supman). Franklinton, NC, 1/8/26. TV personality. *The Soupy Sales Show.*

SALINGER, J. D. (Jerome David Salinger). New York, NY, 1/1/19. Author. *The Catcher in the Rye.*

SALT (Cheryl James). Brooklyn, NY, 3/8/64. Rap artist. Salt-N-Pepa.

SALT, JENNIFER. Los Angeles, CA, 9/4/44. Actor. *Midnight Cowboy.*

SAMBORA, RICHIE. 7/11/59. Guitarist, married to Heather Locklear. Bon Jovi.

SAMMS, EMMA. London, England, 8/28/60. Actor. Fallon Carrington Colby on *Dynasty* and *The Colbys.*

SAMPRAS, PETE. Washington, DC, 8/12/71. Tennis player.

SAMWELL-SMITH, PAUL. Richmond, England, 5/8/43. Bassist. The Yardbirds.

SAN GIACOMO, LAURA. Denville, NJ, 11/14/61. Actor. *Just Shoot Me.*

SANDERS, RICHARD. Harrisburg, PA, 8/23/40. Actor. Les Nessman on *WKRP in Cincinnati.*

SANDS, JULIAN. Yorkshire, England, 1/15/58. Actor. *A Room with a View.*

SANDY, GARY. Dayton, OH, 11/3/46. Actor. Andy Travis on *WKRP in Cincinnati.*

SANFORD, ISABEL. New York, NY, 8/29/17. Actor. Louise on *The Jeffersons.*

SANTANA, CARLOS. Autlan de Navarro, Mexico, 7/20/47. Guitarist, singer. Santana.

SANTIAGO, HERMAN. New York, NY 2/18/41. Singer. Frankie Lymon & The Teenagers.

SARANDON, CHRIS. Beckley, WV, 7/24/42. Actor, former husband of Susan. Leon in *Dog Day Afternoon.*

SASSOON, VIDAL. London, England, 1/17/28. Hairstylist.

SAVAGE, FRED. Highland Park, IL, 7/9/76. Actor, brother of Ben. Kevin Arnold on *The Wonder Years.*

SAVAGE, JOHN (John Youngs). Long Island, NY, 8/25/49. Actor. *The Deer Hunter.*

SAVAGE, RICK. Sheffield, England, 12/2/60. Bassist. Def Leppard.

SAVANT, DOUG. 6/21/64. Actor. *Melrose Place.*

SAWYER, RAY. Chickasaw,

AL, 2/1/37. Lead singer. Dr. Hook.

SAYER, LEO (Gerard Sayer). Shoreham-by-Sea, England, 5/21/48. Singer, songwriter. "You Make Me Feel Like Dancing."

SAYLES, JOHN. 9/28/50. Director.

SCABIES, RAT (Chris Miller). Kingston-upon-Thames, England, 7/30/57. Drummer. The Damned.

SCACCHI, GRETA. Milan, Italy, 2/18/60. Actor. *Presumed Innocent.*

SCAGGS, BOZ (William Scaggs). Ohio, 6/8/44. Guitarist, singer, songwriter. "Lowdown."

SCALIA, JACK. Brooklyn, NY, 11/10/51. Actor. *Dallas.*

SCARPELLI, GLENN. Staten Island, NY, 7/6/68. Actor. Alex Handris on *One Day at a Time.*

SCAVULLO, FRANCESCO. 1/16/29. Photographer.

SCHACHER, MEL. Flint, MI, 4/3/51. Bassist. Grand Funk Railroad.

SCHEIDER, ROY. Orange, NJ, 11/10/32. Actor. Chief Brody in *Jaws.*

SCHELL, MAXIMILIAN. Vienna, Austria, 12/8/30. Actor. *Judgment at Nuremberg.*

SCHENKER, RUDOLPH. 8/31/48. Guitarist. Scorpions.

SCHERMIE, JOE. Madison, WI, 2/12/45. Bassist. Three Dog Night.

SCHNEIDER, FRED. Newark, GA, 7/1/51. Keyboardist, singer. The B-52's.

SCHNEIDER, MARIA. Paris, France, 3/27/52. Actor. *Last Tango in Paris.*

SCHNEIDER-ESLEBEN, FLORIAN. Dusseldorf, Germany, 1947. Keyboardist, drummer, singer, woodwindist. Kraftwerk.

SCHOLZ, TOM. Toledo, OH, 3/10/47. Guitarist, keyboardist. Boston.

SCHON, NEAL. San Mateo, CA, 2/27/54. Guitarist. Journey.

SCHORR, DANIEL. New York, NY, 8/31/16. Broadcast journalist. NPR.

SCHULTZ, DWIGHT. Baltimore, MD, 11/24/47. Actor. H. M. "Howling Mad" Murdock on *The A-Team*.

SCHWARZKOPF, NORMAN. Trenton, NJ, 8/22/34. Retired army general, Gulf War hero.

SCHYGULLA, HANNA. Katlowitz, Germany, 12/25/43. Actor. *Dead Again*.

SCIORRA, ANNABELLA. New York, NY, 3/24/64. Actor. *The Hand That Rocks the Cradle*.

SCOLARI, PETER. New Rochelle, NY, 9/12/54. Actor. *Bosom Buddies*.

SCOTT, ANDY. Wrexham, Wales, 6/30/51. Guitarist. Sweet.

SCOTT, BON (Ronald Scott). Kirriemuir, Scotland, 7/9/46. Singer. AC/DC.

SCOTT, GORDON (Gordon Werschkul). Portland, OR, 8/3/27. Actor. *Tarzan's Hidden Jungle*.

SCOTT, HOWARD. San Pedro, CA, 3/15/46. Guitarist, singer. War.

SCOTT, MIKE. Edinburgh, Scotland, 12/14/58. Singer, guitarist. The Waterboys.

SCOTT, RIDLEY. South Shields, England, 11/30/37. Director, brother of director Tony. *Thelma and Louise*.

SCOTT, WILLARD. Alexandria, VA, 3/7/34. Weatherman. *Today*.

SEAL, ELIZABETH. Genoa, Italy, 8/28/33. Actor. *Irma La Douce*.

SEALE, BOBBY. Dallas, TX, 10/20/36. Political activist, author. Cofounder of the Black Panthers.

SEALS, JIM. Sidney, TX, 10/17/41. Singer, guitarist, saxophonist, violinist. Seals & Crofts.

SEAVER, TOM. Fresno, CA, 11/17/44. Baseball pitcher.

SEBASTIAN, JOHN. New York, NY, 3/17/44. Singer, guitarist, harmonicist, autoharpist. "The Lovin' Spoonful."

SEDAKA, NEIL. Brooklyn, NY, 3/13/39. Pop singer, songwriter. "Laughter in the Rain."

SEDGWICK, KYRA. New York, NY, 8/19/65. Actor, married to Kevin Bacon. *Phenomenon*.

SEEGER, PETE. New York, NY, 5/3/19. Folk singer, songwriter, guitarist, social activist. Founded The Weavers.

SEGAL, ERICH. 6/16/37. Author. *Love Story*.

SEGAL, GEORGE. New York, NY, 2/13/34. Actor. *Look Who's Talking*.

SEGER, BOB. Dearborn, MI, 5/6/45. Singer, songwriter. The Silver Bullet Band.

SELLECCA, CONNIE (Concetta Sellecchia). The Bronx, NY, 5/25/55. Actor, married to John Tesh. *Hotel*.

SELLECK, TOM. Detroit, MI, 1/29/45. Actor. *Magnum, P.I.*

SENDAK, MAURICE. New York, NY, 1/10/28. Author, illustrator. *Where the Wild Things Are*.

SENSIBLE, CAPTAIN (Ray Burns). England, 4/23/55. Bassist. The Damned.

SERAPHINE, DANNY. Chicago, IL, 8/28/48. Drummer. Chicago.

SERGEANT, WILL. Liverpool, England, 4/12/58. Guitarist. Echo & The Bunnymen.

SETZER, BRIAN. 4/10/60. Guitarist, singer. The Stray Cats.

SEVERIN, STEVE. 9/25/55. Bassist. Siouxsie & The Banshees.

SEYMOUR, STEPHANIE. San Diego, CA, 7/23/68. Supermodel.

SHAFFER, PAUL. Toronto, Canada, 11/28/49. Musician, bandleader. *Late Show with David Letterman*.

SHALIT, GENE. New York, NY, 1932. Critic. *Today*.

SHAPIRO, HELEN. Bethnal Green, England, 9/28/46. Singer, actor, cabaret performer.

SHARIF, OMAR (Michel Shalhoub). Alexandria, Egypt, 4/10/32. Actor. *Dr. Zhivago*.

SHARKEY, FEARGAL. Londonderry, Northern Ireland, 8/13/58. Singer. The Undertones.

SHARP, DAVE. Salford, England, 1/28/59. Guitarist. The Alarm.

SHARPTON, AL. Brooklyn, NY, 1954. Politician, activist, clergyman.

SHAVER, HELEN. St. Thomas, Canada, 2/24/51. Actor. *The Amityville Horror*.

SHAW, SANDIE (Sandra Goodrich). Dagenham, England, 2/26/47. Pop singer.

SHAW, TOMMY. Montgomery, AL, 9/11/52. Lead guitarist. Styx.

SHAWN, WALLACE. New York, NY, 11/12/43. Playwright, actor. *My Dinner with Andre*.

SHEA, JOHN. North Conway, NH, 4/14/49. Actor. *Lois & Clark*.

SHEARER, HARRY. Los Angeles, CA, 12/23/43. Actor. *This Is Spinal Tap*.

SHEEDY, ALLY. New York, NY, 6/13/62. Actor. *WarGames*.

SHEEHAN, FRAN. Boston, MA, 3/26/49. Bassist. Boston.

SHEEN, CHARLIE Los Angeles, CA, 9/3/65. Actor. *Platoon*.

SHEILA E. (Sheila Escovedo). Oakland, CA, 12/12/57. Drummer, singer.

SHELDON, SIDNEY. Chicago, IL, 2/11/17. Novelist, producer. *The Other Side of Midnight*.

SHELLEY, CAROLE. London, England, 8/16/39. Actor. *The Elephant Man*.

SHELLEY, PETE (Peter McNeish). Lancashire, England, 4/17/55. Guitarist, singer. The Buzzcocks.

SHEPARD, SAM (Sam Rogers). Ft. Sheridan, IL, 11/5/43. Playwright, actor. *True West*; *The Right Stuff*.

SHEPHERD, CYBILL Memphis, TN, 2/18/50. Actor. *Cybill*.

SHERIDAN, JIM. Dublin, Ireland, 1949. Director, writer. *My Left Foot*.

SHERIDAN, NICOLLETTE. Worthington, England, 11/21/63. Actor, model. *The Sure Thing*.

SHIRE, TALIA (Talia Rose Coppola). Lake Success, NY, 4/25/45. Actor, sister of Francis Ford Coppola. *Rocky I–V*.

SHORE, PAULY. 2/1/68. Actor. "The Weez."

SHORROCK, GLENN. Rochester, England, 6/30/44. Singer. The Little River Band.

SHOW, GRANT. Detroit, MI, 2/27/62. Actor. *Melrose Place*.

SHRIVER, MARIA. Chicago, IL, 11/6/55. Broadcast journalist, married to Arnold Schwarzenegger. *First Person with Maria Shriver*.

SHUE, ANDREW. South Orange, NJ, 2/20/67. Actor, brother of Elizabeth Shue. *Melrose Place*.

SIEGEL, JAY. Brooklyn, NY, 10/20/39. Baritone singer. The Tokens.

SIKKING, JAMES B. Los Angeles, CA, 3/5/34. Actor. Lt. Howard Hunter on *Hill Street Blues*.

SILLS, BEVERLY. New York, NY, 5/25/29. Opera singer.

SILVER, RON. New York, NY, 7/2/46. Actor, director. *Reversal of Fortune*.

SILVERMAN, JONATHAN. Los Angeles, CA, 8/5/66. Actor. *The Single Guy*.

SIMMONS, GENE (Chaim Witz). Haifa, Israel, 8/25/49. Long-tongued bassist, singer. Kiss.

SIMMONS, JEAN. London, England, 1/31/29. Actor. *The Thorn Birds*.

SIMMONS, JOSEPH. Queens, NY, 1964. Rap artist. Run-D.M.C.

SIMMONS, PATRICK. Aberdeen, WA, 1/23/50. Guitarist, singer. The Doobie Brothers.

SIMMONS, RICHARD. New Orleans, LA, 7/12/48. Health guru. *Sweatin' to the Oldies*.

SIMON, CARLY. New York, NY, 6/25/45. Singer, songwriter, childrens' book author.

SIMONE, NINA. Tryon, NC, 2/21/33. Singer. Soundtrack for *The Crying Game*.

SIMONON, PAUL. Brixton, England, 12/15/55. Bassist. The Clash.

SIMPSON, O.J. San Francisco, CA, 7/9/47. Football player, actor, indicted for murder of ex-wife, guilty in a civil trial but not the criminal one.

SINGER, LORI. Corpus Christi, TX, 5/6/62. Actor. *Fame*.

SINGLETON, JOHN. Los Angeles, CA, 1/6/68. Director, writer. *Boyz N the Hood*.

SINGLETON, STEPHEN. Sheffield, England, 4/17/59. Saxophonist. ABC.

SIOUX, SIOUXSIE (Susan Dallon). Chiselhurst, England, 5/27/57. Singer. Siouxsie & The Banshees.

SIXX, NIKKI (Frank Ferrano). Seattle, WA, 12/11/58. Bassist. Mötley Crüe.

SKERRITT, TOM. Detroit, MI, 8/25/33. Actor. *Picket Fences*.

SKYE, IONE (Ione Leitch). London, England, 9/4/71. Actor, daughter of folk singer Donovan, sister of Donovan Leitch. *Say Anything*.

SLASH (Saul Hudson). Stoke-on-Trent, England, 1965. Guitarist. Guns N' Roses.

SLATER, HELEN. New York, NY, 12/15/65. Actor. *Supergirl*.

SLATER, RODNEY. Lincolnshire, England, 11/8/44. Saxophonist, trumpeter. The Bonzo Dog Doo-Dah Band.

SLEDGE, DEBBIE. Philadelphia, PA, 7/9/54. Singer. Sister Sledge.

SLEDGE, JONI. Philadelphia, PA, 9/13/56. Singer. Sister Sledge.

SLEDGE, KATHY. Philadelphia, PA, 1/6/59. Singer. Sister Sledge.

SLEDGE, KIM. Philadelphia, PA, 8/21/57. Singer. Sister Sledge.

SLEDGE, PERCY. Leighton, AL, 11/25/41. Singer. "When a Man Loves a Woman."

SLICK, GRACE (Grace Wing). Chicago, IL, 10/30/39. Singer. Jefferson Airplane/Starship.

SLIWA, CURTIS. New York, NY, 3/26/54. Founder of the Guardian Angels.

SMIRNOFF, YAKOV (Yakov Pokhis). Odessa, Russia, 1/24/51. Actor. *What a Country!*

SMITH, ADRIAN. Huckney, England, 2/27/57. Guitarist. Iron Maiden.

SMITH, BOBBIE. 4/10/36. Singer. The (Detroit) Spinners.

SMITH, CHARLES MARTIN. Los Angeles, CA, 10/30/53. Actor. *American Graffiti*.

SMITH, CLAYDES (Charles Smith). Jersey City, NJ, 9/6/48. Guitarist. Kool & The Gang.

SMITH, CURT. Bath, England, 6/24/61. Singer, bassist. Tears for Fears.

SMITH, JACLYN. Houston, TX, 10/26/45. Actor. Kelly Garrett on *Charlie's Angels*.

SMITH, JEFF. Seattle, WA,

1/22/39. TV personality, chef, author. *The Frugal Gourmet*.

SMITH, LARRY. Oxford, England, 1/18/44. Drummer. The Bonzo Dog Doo-Dah Band.

SMITH, LIZ. Fort Worth, TX, 2/2/23. Gossip columnist.

SMITH, MAGGIE. Ilford, England, 12/28/34. Actor. *Sister Act*.

SMITH, MIKE. Neath, Wales, 11/4/47. Tenor saxophonist. Amen Corner.

SMITH, MIKE. Edmonton, England, 12/12/43. Singer, keyboardist. The Dave Clark Five.

SMITH, PATTI. Chicago, IL, 12/30/46. Singer, songwriter.

SMITH, PHIL. 5/1/59. Saxophonist. Haircut 100.

SMITH, ROBERT. Crawley, England, 4/21/59. Guitarist, singer. The Cure.

SMOTHERS, DICK. New York, NY, 11/20/38. Actor, singer, brother of Tom. *The Smothers Brothers Comedy Hour*.

SMOTHERS, TOM. New York, NY, 2/2/37. Actor, singer, brother of Dick. *The Smothers Brothers Comedy Hour*.

SMYTH, PATTY. New York, NY, 6/26/57. Singer, relationship with John McEnroe. "The Warrior."

SNEED, FLOYD. Calgary, Canada, 11/22/43. Drummer. Three Dog Night.

SNODGRESS, CARRIE. Chicago, IL, 10/27/46. Actor. *Diary of a Mad Housewife*.

SOMERS, SUZANNE (Suzanne Mahoney). San Bruno, CA, 10/16/46. Actor. *Three's Company*.

SOMERVILLE, JIMMY. Glasgow, Scotland, 6/22/61. Dance/rock singer, keyboardist.

SOMMER, ELKE (Elke Schletz). Berlin, Germany, 11/5/40. Actor. *A Shot in the Dark*.

SORVINO, PAUL. New York, NY, 4/13/39. Actor, father of Mira. *GoodFellas*.

SOTHERN, ANN (Harriet Lake). Valley City, ND, 1/22/09. Actor. *The Ann Sothern Show*.

SOUL, DAVID (David Solberg). Chicago, IL, 8/28/43. Actor. Kevin "Hutch" Hutchinson on *Starsky and Hutch*.

SOUTH, JOE. Atlanta, GA, 2/28/40. Rock/country guitarist, singer, songwriter.

SOUTHSIDE JOHNNY (Johnny Lyon). Neptune Park, NJ, 12/4/48. Singer. Southside Johnny & The Asbury Jukes.

SPACEK, SISSY (Mary Elizabeth Spacek). Quitman, TX, 12/25/49. Actor. *Coal Miner's Daughter*.

SPADER, JAMES. Boston, MA, 2/7/60. Actor. *sex, lies, and videotape*.

SPANO, JOE. San Francisco, CA, 7/7/46. Actor. Henry Goldblume on *Hill Street Blues*.

SPANO, VINCENT. New York, NY, 10/18/62. Actor. *Rumble Fish*.

SPEAR, ROGER. London, England, 6/29/43. Saxophonist, kazooist. The Bonzo Dog Doo-Dah Band.

SPECTOR, PHIL. New York, NY, 12/26/39. Music producer. Wall of sound.

SPECTOR, RONNIE (Veronica Bennett). New York, NY, 8/10/43. Lead singer. The Ronettes.

SPELLING, TORI. Los Angeles, CA, 5/16/73. Actor, daughter of Aaron Spelling. Donna on *Beverly Hills, 90210*.

SPENCE, ALEXANDER. Windsor, Canada, 4/18/46. Guitarist, lead singer. Moby Grape.

SPENCER, JEREMY. West Hartlepoole, England, 7/4/48. Guitarist. Fleetwood Mac.

SPILLANE, MICKEY (Frank

Morrison). New York, NY, 3/9/18. Author. Mike Hammer detective stories.

SPINKS, LEON. St. Louis, MO, 7/11/53. Boxer, former heavyweight champion, brother of Michael.

SPINKS, MICHAEL. St. Louis, MO, 7/29/56. Boxer. Olympic gold medalist, brother of Leon.

SPOONER, BILL. Phoenix, AZ, 4/16/49. Guitarist. The Tubes.

SPRINGFIELD, DUSTY (Mary O'Brien). Hampstead, England, 4/16/39. Folk/pop singer.

SPRINGFIELD, RICK (Richard Spring Thorpe). Sydney, Australia, 8/23/49. Singer, actor. *General Hospital.*

SQUIER, BILLY. Wellesley, MA, 5/12/50. Singer. "Everybody Wants You."

SQUIRE, CHRIS. London, England, 3/4/48. Bassist. Yes.

SQUIRE, JOHN. Sale, England, 11/24/62. Lead guitarist. The Stone Roses.

ST. JOHN, JILL (Jill Oppenheim). Los Angeles, CA, 8/19/40. Actor, married to Robert Wagner. *Diamonds Are Forever.*

STACK, ROBERT. Los Angeles, CA, 1/13/19. Actor. Eliot Ness on *The Untouchables.*

STAFFORD, JIM. Eloise, FL, 1/16/44. Singer, songwriter. "Spiders and Snakes."

STAMOS, JOHN. Cypress, CA, 8/19/63. Actor. *Full House.*

STAMP, TERENCE. London, England, 7/23/38. Actor. *Superman II.*

STANLEY, PAUL (Paul Eisen). Queens, NY, 1/20/50. Guitarist, singer. Kiss.

STANSFIELD, LISA. Rochdale, England, 4/11/66. Singer, songwriter. "All Around the World."

STANTON, HARRY DEAN. West Irvine, KY, 7/14/26.

Actor. *Paris, Texas.*

STAPLES, NEVILLE. 4/11/56. Singer, percussionist. The Specials.

STAPLES, PETE. Andover, England, 5/3/44. Bassist. The Troggs.

STAPLETON, JEAN (Jeanne Murray). New York, NY, 1/19/23. Actor. Edith Bunker on *All in the Family.*

STAPLETON, MAUREEN. Troy, NY, 6/21/25. Actor. *Airport.*

STARR, RINGO (Richard Starkey). Liverpool, England, 7/7/40. Drummer, singer, actor, married to Barbara Bach. The Beatles.

STAUBACH, ROGER. Cincinnati, OH, 2/5/42. NFL football player. Dallas Cowboys.

STAX, JOHN (John Fullegar). London, England, 4/6/44. Bassist. The Pretty Things.

STEEL, JOHN. Gateshead, England, 2/4/41. Drummer. The Animals.

STEELE, DAVID. Birmingham, England, 9/8/60. Keyboardist, bassist. Fine Young Cannibals.

STEELE, MICHAEL. 6/2/54. Bassist, singer. The Bangles; The Runaways.

STEELE, TOMMY (Thomas Hicks). Bermondsey, England, 12/17/36. Guitarist, singer, actor.

STEENBURGEN, MARY. Newport, AR, 2/8/53. Actor, married to Ted Danson. *Parenthood.*

STEIGER, ROD. Westhampton, NY, 4/14/25. Actor. *In the Heat of the Night.*

STEIN, CHRIS. Brooklyn, NY, 1/5/50. Guitarist. Blondie.

STEIN, MARK. Bayonne, NJ, 3/11/47. Singer, organist. Vanilla Fudge.

STEINBERG, DAVID. Winnipeg, Canada, 8/9/42. Actor, director. *Paternity.*

STEINEM, GLORIA. Toledo, OH, 3/25/34. Women's rights activist.

STERBAN, RICHARD. Camden, NJ, 4/24/43. Singer,

bassist. The Oak Ridge Boys.

STERN, DANIEL. Bethesda, MD, 8/28/57. Actor, narrator of *The Wonder Years. City Slickers.*

STERN, ISAAC. Kreminiecz, Russia, 7/21/20. Violinist.

STERNHAGEN, FRANCES. Washington, DC, 1/13/30. Actor. *Driving Miss Daisy.*

STEVENS, ANDREW. Memphis, TN, 6/10/55. Actor, son of Stella. *Dallas.*

STEVENS, CAT (Steven Georgiou). Soho, England, 7/21/47. Folk singer, songwriter—left recording upon conversion to Islam.

STEVENS, CONNIE (Concetta Ann Ingolia). Brooklyn, NY, 8/8/38. Actor. *Hawaiian Eye.*

STEVENS, FISHER. Chicago, IL, 11/27/63. Actor. *Short Circuit.*

STEVENS, RAY (Ray Ragsdale). Clarksdale, GA, 1/24/39. Singer. *Andy Williams Presents Ray Stevens.*

STEVENS, SHAKIN' (Michael Barratt). Ely, Wales, 3/4/48. Singer, actor.

STEVENS, STELLA (Estelle Eggleston). Hot Coffee, MS, 10/1/36. Actor, mother of Andrew. *Santa Barbara.*

STEVENSON, DON. Seattle, WA, 10/15/42. Drummer. Moby Grape.

STEVENSON, PARKER. Philadelphia, PA, 6/4/52. Actor. Formerly married to Kirstie Alley. *Falcon Crest.*

STEWART, AL. Glasgow, Scotland, 9/5/45. Guitarist, singer, songwriter.

STEWART, DAVE. Sunderland, England, 9/9/52. Keyboardist, guitarist. Eurythmics.

STEWART, ERIC. Manchester, England, 1/20/45. Singer, guitarist. 10cc.

STEWART, MARTHA (Martha Haworth). Bardwell, KY, 10/7/22. Actor. *Holocaust.*

STEWART, ROD. Highgate,

England, 1/10/45. Singer, songwriter.

STIERS, DAVID OGDEN. Peoria, IL, 10/31/42. Actor. Dr. Charles Emerson Winchester on *M*A*S*H.*

STILES, RAY. Carshalton, England, 11/20/46. Bassist, singer. Mud.

STILLER, JERRY. New York, NY, 6/8/27. Actor, partner/married to Anne Meara, father of Ben. *Seinfeld.*

STILLS, STEPHEN. Dallas, TX, 1/3/45. Singer, guitarist. Buffalo Springfield; Crosby, Stills, Nash & Young.

STOCKDALE, JAMES. Abington, IL, 12/23/23. Vietnam POW, running mate of presidential candidate Ross Perot.

STOCKWELL, DEAN. Hollywood, CA, 3/5/36. Actor. Al Calavicci on *Quantum Leap.*

STOCKWELL, JOHN (John Samuels). Galveston, TX, 3/25/61. Actor. *My Science Project.*

STOLTZ, ERIC. American Samoa, 9/30/61. Actor. *Mask.*

STONE, DEE WALLACE (Deanna Bowers). Kansas City, MO, 12/14/48. Actor. Mother in *E.T., the Extra-Terrestrial.*

STONE, FREDDIE. Dallas, TX, 6/5/46. Guitarist. Sly & The Family Stone.

STONE, MATT. 5/26/71. Actor, cartoonist. *South Park.*

STONE, ROSIE. Vallejo, CA, 3/21/45. Singer, keyboardist. Sly & The Family Stone.

STONE, SLY (Sylvester Stewart). Dallas, TX, 3/15/44. Singer, keyboardist, guitarist. Sly & The Family Stone.

STORCH, LARRY. New York, NY, 1/8/23. Actor. *F Troop.*

STORM, GALE (Josephine Cottle). Bloomington, TX, 4/5/22. Actor. *My Little Margie.*

STOWE, MADELEINE. Los Angeles, CA, 8/18/58. Actor. *The Last of the Mohicans.*

STRASSMAN, MARCIA. New York, NY, 4/28/48. Actor. Julie Kotter on *Welcome Back Kotter.*

STRATHAIRN, DAVID. San Francisco, CA, 1949. Actor. *Matewan.*

STRATTON, DENNIS. London, England, 11/9/54. Guitarist. Iron Maiden.

STRAUSS, PETER. Croton-on-Hudson, NY, 2/20/47. Actor. *The Jericho Mile.*

STRINGFIELD, SHERRY. Colorado Springs, CO, 6/24/67. Actor. *ER.*

STRICKLAND, KEITH. Athens, GA, 10/26/53. Drummer. The B-52's.

STRITCH, ELAINE. Detroit, MI, 2/2/25. Actor. *September.*

STRUMMER, JOE (John Mellors). Ankara, Turkey, 8/21/52. Singer, guitarist. The Clash.

STRUTHERS, SALLY. Portland, OR, 7/28/47. Actor. Gloria Bunker Stivic on *All in the Family.*

STRYKERT, RON. Australia, 8/18/57. Guitarist. Men at Work.

STUART, CHAD. England, 12/10/43. Singer, guitarist. Chad & Jeremy.

STUART, HAMISH. Glasgow, Scotland, 10/8/49. Singer, guitarist. Average White Band.

STUBBS, LEVI (Levi Stubbles). Detroit, MI, 6/6/36. Lead singer. The Four Tops.

SUCH, ALEC. 11/14/56. Bassist. Bon Jovi.

SULLIVAN, SUSAN. New York, NY, 11/18/44. Actor. Maggie Gioberti Channing on *Falcon Crest.*

SULLIVAN, TOM. Boston, MA, 3/27/47. Singer, actor, composer. "If You Could See What I Hear."

SUMMER, DONNA (LaDonna Gaines). Boston, MA,

12/31/48. Disco/pop singer. "Love To Love You Baby."

SUMMERS, ANDY (Andrew Somers). Poulton le Fylde, France, 12/31/42. Guitarist, singer. The Police.

SUMNER, BARNEY (Bernard Dicken). Salford, England, 1/4/56. Guitarist, singer. New Order.

SUTHERLAND, DONALD. St. John, Canada, 7/17/35. Actor, father of Kiefer. *Ordinary People.*

SUTHERLAND, KIEFER. Los Angeles, CA, 12/21/66. Actor, son of Donald. *Flatliners.*

SUZMAN, JANET. Johannesburg, South Africa, 2/9/39. Actor. *Nicholas and Alexandra.*

SVENSON, BO. Goreborg, Sweden, 2/13/41. Actor. *North Dallas Forty.*

SWAGGART, JIMMY. Ferriday, LA, 3/15/35. Evangelist.

SWAIN, DOMINIQUE. 8/12/80. Actor. *Lolita.*

SWANN, LYNN. Alcoa, TN, 3/7/52. NFL football player.

SWAYZE, PATRICK. Houston, TX, 8/18/52. Actor, dancer. *Dirty Dancing.*

SWEENEY, D. B. (Daniel Bernard Sweeney). Shoreham, NY, 11/14/61. Actor. *The Cutting Edge.*

SWEET, DERRELL. 5/16/47. Drummer, percussionist, singer. Nazareth.

SWEET, MATTHEW. Lincoln, NE, 10/6/64. Singer, songwriter, guitarist. "Girlfriend."

SWENSON, INGA. Omaha, NE, 12/29/32. Actor. Gretchen Kraus on *Benson.*

SWIT, LORETTA. Passaic, NJ, 11/4/37. Actor. Margaret "Hot Lips" Houlihan on *M*A*S*H.*

SYLVIAN, DAVID (David Batt). Lewisham, England, 2/23/58. Singer, guitarist. Japan.

T, MR. (Lawrence Tero). Chicago, IL, 5/21/52. Actor

and wrestler. Bosco "B.A." Baracus on *The A-Team.*

TAJ MAHAL. New York, NY, 5/17/42. Singer, songwriter, composer. "Sounder."

TAKEI, GEORGE. Los Angeles, CA, 4/20/39. Mr. Sulu on *Star Trek.*

TALBOT, MICK. London, England, 9/11/58. Keyboardist. The Style Council.

TALLEY, GARY. Memphis, TN, 8/17/47. Guitarist. The Box Tops/Big Star.

TALLEY, NEDRA. New York, NY, 1/27/46. Singer. The Ronettes.

TAMBLYN, RUSS. Los Angeles, CA, 12/30/34. Actor. *West Side Story.*

TAMBOR, JEFFREY. San Francisco, CA, 7/8/44. Actor. *The Larry Sanders Show.*

TANDY, RICHARD. Birmingham, England, 3/26/48. Bassist. Electric Light Orchestra (ELO).

TARKENTON, FRAN. Richmond, VA, 2/3/40. Football player, sportscaster. *Monday Night Football.*

TAUPIN, BERNIE. Sleaford, England, 5/22/50. Lyricist. Wrote for Elton John.

TAYLOR, ANDY. Tynemouth, England, 2/16/61. Guitarist. Duran Duran.

TAYLOR, CLIVE. Cardiff, Wales, 4/27/49. Bassist. Amen Corner.

TAYLOR, DICK. Dartford, England, 1/28/43. Lead guitarist. The Pretty Things.

TAYLOR, JAMES. South Carolina, 8/16/53. Lead singer. Kool & The Gang.

TAYLOR, JAMES. Boston, MA, 3/12/48. Folk-oriented singer, songwriter.

TAYLOR, JOHN. Birmingham, England, 6/20/60. Bassist. Duran Duran.

TAYLOR, LARRY. Brooklyn, NY, 6/26/42. Bassist. Canned Heat.

TAYLOR, LILI. Chicago, IL, 1967. Actor. *Mystic Pizza.*

TAYLOR, ROD. Sydney, Aus-

tralia, 1/11/30. Actor. *The Time Machine.*

TAYLOR, ROGER. King's Lynn, England, 7/26/49. Drummer. Queen.

TENCH, BENMONT. Gainesville, FL, 9/7/54. Keyboardist. Tom Petty & The Heartbreakers.

TENNANT, NEIL. Gosforth, England, 7/10/54. Singer. Pet Shop Boys.

TENNANT, VICTORIA. London, England, 9/30/50. Actor, formerly married to Steve Martin. *L.A. Story.*

TENNILLE, TONI. Montgomery, AL, 5/8/43. Singer. The Captain & Tennille.

TERRANOVA, JOE. 1/30/41. Baritone. Danny & The Juniors.

THICKE, ALAN. Ontario, Canada, 3/1/47. Actor. *Growing Pains.*

THISTLETHWAITE, ANTHONY. Leicester, England, 8/31/55. Saxophonist. The Waterboys.

THOMAS, B. J. (Billy Joe Thomas). Hugo, OK, 8/7/42. Pop singer. "Raindrops Keep Fallin' on My Head."

THOMAS, BETTY. Saint Louis, MO, 7/27/47. Actor, director. Lucy Bates on *Hill Street Blues.*

THOMAS, DAVE. Saint Catharines, Canada, 6/20/49. Actor. Doug MacKenzie on *SCTV.*

THOMAS, HENRY. San Antonio, TX, 9/8/72. Actor. Elliot in *E.T., the Extra-Terrestrial.*

THOMAS, JAY. New Orleans, LA, 7/12/48. Actor, radio personality. *Murphy Brown.*

THOMAS, MARLO (Margaret Thomas). Detroit, MI, 11/21/37. Actor, married to Phil Donahue, daughter of Danny Thomas. *That Girl.*

THOMAS, MARY. Brooklyn, NY, 1946. Singer. The Crystals.

THOMAS, PHILIP MICHAEL. Columbus, OH, 5/26/49. Actor. Ricardo Tubbs on *Miami Vice.*

THOMAS, RAY. Stourport-on-Severn, England, 12/29/42. Flautist, harmonicist, singer. The Moody Blues.

THOMAS, RICHARD. New York, NY, 6/13/51. Actor. John Boy on *The Waltons*.

THOMPKINS, RUSSELL JR. Philadelphia, PA, 3/21/51. Lead singer. The Stylistics.

THOMPSON, LEA. Rochester, MN, 5/31/61. Actor. *Caroline in the City*.

THOMPSON, PAUL. Jarrow, England, 5/13/51. Drummer. Roxy Music.

THOMPSON, SADA. Des Moines, IA, 9/27/29. Actor. *Family*.

THOMSON, DOUGIE. Glasgow, Scotland, 3/24/51. Bassist. Supertramp.

THORN, TRACEY. Hartfordshire, England, 9/26/62. Singer. Everything but the Girl.

THORNTON, BLAIR. Vancouver, Canada, 7/23/50. Guitarist. Bachman-Turner Overdrive.

THOROGOOD, GEORGE. Wilmington, DE, 1951. Singer, guitarist. George Thorogood and the Delaware Destroyers.

TICH (Ian Amey). Salisbury, England, 5/15/44. Lead guitarist. Dave Dee, Dozy, Beaky, Mick and Tich.

TIEGS, CHERYL. Alhambra, CA, 9/25/47. Model, author. *The Way to Natural Beauty*.

TIFFANY (Tiffany Renee Darwish). Norwalk, CA, 10/2/71. Singer.

TILBROOK, GLENN. London, England, 8/31/57. Singer, lead guitarist. Squeeze.

TILLIS, MEL. Pahokee, FL, 8/8/32. Singer, songwriter, father of Pam Tillis.

TILLIS, PAM. Plant City, FL, 7/24/57. Singer, daughter of Mel Tillis.

TILLY, MEG. Texada, Canada, 2/14/60. Actor, sister of Jennifer. *The Big Chill*.

TILTON, CHARLENE. San Diego, CA, 12/1/58. Actor. Lucy Ewing Cooper on *Dallas*.

TIPTON, GLENN. Birmingham, England, 10/25/48. Guitarist. Judas Priest.

TOLHURST, LOL (Laurence Tolhurst). 2/3/59. Keyboardist. The Cure.

TOLKAN, JAMES. Calumet, MI, 6/20/31. Actor. Principal in *Back to the Future*.

TOMEI, MARISA. Brooklyn, NY, 12/4/64. Actor. *My Cousin Vinny*.

TOMLIN, LILY (Mary Jean Tomlin). Detroit, MI, 9/1/39. Actor. *Rowan & Martin's Laugh-In*.

TONE-LOC. Los Angeles, CA, 3/3/66. Rap artist. "Wild Thing."

TOPHAM, ANTHONY "TOP." England, 1947. Guitarist. The Yardbirds.

TORK, PETER (Peter Halsten Thorkelson). Washington, DC, 2/13/44. Keyboardist, bassist, actor. The Monkees.

TORN, RIP. (Elmore Rual Torn Jr). Temple, TX, 2/6/31. Actor. *Blind Ambition*.

TORRENCE, DEAN. Los Angeles, CA, 3/10/40. Singer. Jan & Dean.

TOWNSEND, ROBERT. Chicago, IL, 2/6/57. Actor. *Hollywood Shuffle*.

TOWNSHEND, PETE. Chiswick, England, 5/19/45. Guitarist. The Who.

TOWNSON, RON. St. Louis, MO, 1/20/33. Singer. The 5th Dimension.

TRAVANTI, DANIEL J. Kenosha, WI, 3/7/40. Actor. Captain Frank Furillo on *Hill Street Blues*.

TRAVERS, BILL. Newcastle-upon-Tyne, England, 1/3/22. Actor, producer, director. *Born Free*.

TRAVERS, BRIAN. Birmingham, England, 2/7/59. Saxophonist. UB40.

TRAVIS, NANCY. 9/21/61. Actor. *Three Men and a Baby*.

TRAVIS, RANDY (Randy Traywick). Marshville, NC, 5/4/59. Country singer, songwriter.

TREBEK, ALEX. Sudbury, Canada, 7/22/40. Game show host. *Jeopardy!*

TRESVANT, RALPH. Boston, MA, 5/16/68. Singer. New Edition.

TREWAVAS, PETER. Middlesborough, England, 1/15/59. Keyboardist. Marillion.

TRIPPLEHORN, JEANNE. Tulsa, Oklahoma, 1963. Actor. *The Firm*.

TRITT, TRAVIS. Marietta, GA, 2/9/63. Country singer, songwriter.

TROWER, ROBIN. Southend, England, 3/9/45. Guitarist. Procol Harum.

TRUDEAU, GARRY (Garretson Beckman Trudeau). New York, NY, 1948. Cartoonist, married to Jane Pauley. *Doonesbury*.

TRUGOY THE DOVE (David Jolicoeur). 9/21/68. Musician. De La Soul.

TRUMP, DONALD. New York, NY, 6/14/46. Real estate developer, author. Married to Marla Maples, formerly married to Ivana Winkelmayr Trump.

TRUMP, MARLA MAPLES. 10/27/63. Actor. Married to Donald Trump. *The Will Rogers Follies*.

TUCKER, JIM. Los Angeles, CA, 10/17/46. Guitarist. The Turtles.

TUCKER, MICHAEL. Baltimore, MD, 2/6/45. Actor, married to Jill Eikenberry. *L.A. Law*.

TUCKER, MICK. Harlesden, England, 7/17/49. Drummer. Sweet.

TUFANO, DENNIS. Chicago, IL, 9/11/46. Guitarist, lead singer. The Buckinghams.

TUNE, TOMMY. Wichita Falls, TX, 2/28/39. Actor, director, choreographer, dancer.

TURBO B. (Durron Maurice Butler). Pittsburgh, PA, 4/30/67. Rap artist. Snap.

TURNER, C. F. Winnipeg, Canada, 10/16/43. Bassist, singer. Bachman-Turner Overdrive.

TURNER, IKE. Clarksdale, MS, 11/5/31. Singer, songwriter, formerly married to Tina Turner. Ike & Tina Turner.

TURNER, JANINE (Janine Gauntt). Lincoln, NE, 12/6/63. Actor. *Northern Exposure*.

TURNER, KATHLEEN Springfield, MO, 6/19/54. Actor. *Romancing the Stone*.

TURNER, LONNIE. Berkeley, CA, 2/24/47. Bassist, singer. The Steve Miller Band.

TUROW, SCOTT. Chicago, IL, 4/12/49. Author. *The Burden of Proof*.

TURTURRO, JOHN. Brooklyn, NY, 2/28/57. Actor. *Barton Fink*.

TWIGGY (Lesley Hornby). London, England, 9/19/49. Model, actor. *The Boy Friend*.

TWIST, NIGEL. Manchester, England, 7/18/58. Drummer. The Alarm.

TYLER, BONNIE (Gaynor Hopkins). Swansea, Wales, 6/8/53. Singer. "Total Eclipse of the Heart."

TYLER, RICHARD. Sunshine, Australia, 1948. Designer.

TYSON, CICELY. New York, NY, 12/19/24. Actor. *The Autobiography of Miss Jane Pittman*.

TYSON, MIKE New York, NY, 6/30/66. Boxer, convicted of rape.

UECKER, BOB. Milwaukee, WI, 1/26/35. Actor. *Mr. Belvedere*.

UGGAMS, LESLIE. New York, NY, 5/25/43. Singer, actor. Kizzy in *Roots*.

ULLMAN, TRACEY. Hackbridge, England, 12/30/59. Actor. *The Tracey Ullman Show*.

ULLMANN, LIV. Tokyo, Japan, 12/16/39. Actor. *Persona*.

ULVAEUS, BJORN. Gothenburg, Sweden, 4/25/45. Guitarist, singer. Abba.

UNDERWOOD, BLAIR. Tacoma, WA, 8/25/64. Actor. *L.A. Law*.

URICH, ROBERT. Toronto, Canada, 12/19/46. Actor. *Spenser: For Hire*.

VACCARO, BRENDA. Brooklyn, NY, 11/18/39. Actor. *Midnight Cowboy*.

VALE, JERRY. New York, NY, 7/8/32. Pop singer. "Innamorata."

VALE, MIKE. 7/17/49. Bassist. Tommy James & The Shondells.

VALENTINE, HILTON. North Shields, England, 5/21/43. Guitarist. The Animals.

VALENTINE, SCOTT. Saratoga Springs, NY, 6/3/58. Actor. Nick Moore on *Family Ties*.

VALLI, FRANKIE (Frank Castelluccio). Newark, NJ, 5/3/37. Lead singer. The Four Seasons.

VALLONE, RAF (Raffaele Vallone). Tropea, Italy, 2/17/18. Actor. *Obsession*.

VALORY, ROSS. San Francisco, CA, 2/2/49. Bassist. Journey.

VAN ARK, JOAN. New York, NY, 6/16/43. Actor. Val Ewing *Knots Landing*.

VAN DAMME, JEAN-CLAUDE. Brussels, Belgium, 10/18/60. Actor, martial arts expert. *Kickboxer*.

VAN DEVERE, TRISH (Patricia Dressel). Englewood Cliffs, NJ, 3/9/45. Actor, married to George C. Scott. *The Day of the Dolphin*.

VAN DOREN, MAMIE (Joan Lucile Olander). Rowena, SD, 2/6/31. Actor. *High School Confidential!*

VAN DYKE, DICK. West Plains, MO, 12/13/25. Actor and performer, brother of Jerry. *The Dick Van Dyke Show*.

VAN DYKE, JERRY. Danville, IL, 7/27/31. Actor, brother of Dick. *Coach*.

VAN HALEN, ALEX. Nijmegen, Holland, 5/8/55. Drummer. Van Halen.

VAN HALEN, EDDIE. Nijmegen, Holland, 1/26/55. Singer, guitarist. Van Halen.

VAN PATTEN, DICK. New York, NY, 12/9/28. Actor. *Eight Is Enough*.

VAN PEEBLES, MARIO. New York, NY, 1/15/57. Actor, director, writer, son of Melvin. *Posse*.

VAN PEEBLES, MELVIN. Chicago, IL, 8/21/32. Actor, writer, composer, father of Mario. *Sweet Sweetback's Badasssss Song*.

VAN ZANDT, DONNIE. Florida, 6/11/52. Singer, guitarist. .38 Special.

VAN ZANDT, STEVIE. Boston, MA, 11/22/50. Bassist. E Street Band.

VANDA, HARRY (Harry Vandenberg). The Hague, The Netherlands, 3/22/47. Guitarist. The Easybeats.

VANDERBILT, GLORIA. New York, NY, 2/20/24. Fashion designer. Gloria Vanderbilt Jeans.

VANIAN, DAVE (David Letts). 10/12/56. Singer. The Damned.

VANNELLI, GINO. Montreal, Canada, 6/16/52. Singer, songwriter. "Living Inside Myself."

VAUGHN, ROBERT. New York, NY, 11/22/32. Actor. *The Man from U.N.C.L.E.*

VEDDER, EDDIE Chicago, IL, 12/23/64. Pearl Jam.

VEE, BOBBY (Robert Velline). Fargo, ND, 4/30/43. Singer, songwriter.

VEGA, SUZANNE. New York, NY, 8/12/59. Folk-oriented guitarist, singer, songwriter. "Luka."

VELEZ, EDDIE (Edwin Velez). New York, NY, 6/4/58. Actor. *Extremities*.

VELJOHNSON, REGINALD.

Queens, NY, 8/16/52. Actor. *Family Matters*.

VENDELA (Vendela Kirsebom). Sweden, 1/12/67. Supermodel.

VERDON, GWEN. Culver City, CA, 1/13/25. Actor, dancer, choreographer. *The Cotton Club*.

VEREEN, BEN. Miami, FL, 10/10/46. Actor, performer. Chicken George Moore on *Roots*.

VERLAINE, TOM (Thomas Miller). Mt. Morris, NJ, 12/13/49. Singer, lead guitarist. Television.

VERUSCHKA. 1943. Model, actor. *Blow Up*.

VESTINE, HENRY. Washington, DC, 12/25/44. Guitarist. Canned Heat.

VICKERS, MIKE. Southampton, England, 4/18/41. Guitarist. Manfred Mann.

VIDAL, GORE (Eugene Luther Vidal). West Point, NY, 10/3/25. Author, dramatist. *Lincoln: A Novel*.

VINCENT, JAN-MICHAEL. Denver, CO, 7/15/45. Actor. *The Mechanic*.

VINTON, BOBBY. Canonsburg, PA, 4/16/35. Singer, songwriter.

VIRTUE, MICKEY. Birmingham, England, 1/19/57. Keyboardist. UB40.

VOIGHT, JON. Yonkers, NY, 12/29/38. Actor. *Midnight Cowboy*.

VOLMAN, MARK. Los Angeles, CA, 4/19/47. Singer, saxophonist. The Turtles.

VON BULOW, CLAUS. Copenhagen, Denmark, 8/11/26. Businessman. Subject of the motion picture *Reversal of Fortune*.

VON SYDOW, MAX. Lund, Sweden, 7/10/29. Actor. *The Greatest Story Ever Told*.

VONNEGUT, KURT JR. Indianapolis, IN, 11/11/22. Author. *Slaughterhouse Five*.

WAAKTAAR, PAUL. Oslo, Norway, 9/6/61. Guitarist,

singer. a-ha.

WAGGONER, LYLE. Kansas City, KS, 4/13/35. Actor. *Wonder Woman*.

WAGNER, JACK. Washington, MO, 10/3/59. Actor, singer. Frisco Jones on *General Hospital*.

WAGNER, LINDSAY. Los Angeles, CA, 6/22/49. Actor. *The Bionic Woman*.

WAGNER, ROBERT. Detroit, MI, 2/10/30. Actor, widower of Natalie Wood, married to Jill St. John. Jonathan Hart on *Hart to Hart*.

WAHL, KEN. Chicago, IL, 2/14/57. Actor. Vinnie Terranova on *Wiseguy*.

WAHLBERG, DONNIE. Dorchester, MA, 8/17/69. Singer, brother of Mark. New Kids on the Block.

WAILER, BUNNY (Neville O'Riley Livingston). Kingston, Jamaica, 4/10/47. Singer, percussionist. Bob Marley & The Wailers.

WAITE, JOHN. Lancaster, England, 7/4/54. Singer, songwriter.

WAITS, TOM. Pomona, CA, 12/7/49. Singer, actor, composer. *Short Cuts*.

WALKER, ALICE. Eatonton, GA, 2/9/44. Author. *The Color Purple*.

WALKER, CLINT. Hartford, IL, 5/30/27. Actor. *Cheyenne*.

WALKER, DAVID. Montgomeryville, AL, 5/12/43. Keyboardist. Gary Lewis & The Playboys.

WALKER, JIMMIE. New York, NY, 6/25/48. Actor. J. J. Evans on *Good Times*.

WALKER, JUNIOR (Autry DeWalt II). Blytheville, AR, 1942. Saxophonist, singer. Junior Walker & The All-Stars.

WALKER, MORT. El Dorado, KS, 9/3/23. Cartoonist. *Beetle Bailey*.

WALLACE, MIKE (Myron Leon Wallace). Brookline, MA, 5/9/18. News reporter and interviewer, anchor. *60 Minutes*.

WALLACH, ELI. Brooklyn, NY, 12/7/15. Actor. *The Good, the Bad and the Ugly*.

WALLER, GORDON. Braemar, Scotland, 6/4/45. Singer. Peter and Gordon.

WALLER, ROBERT JAMES. Rockford, IA, 8/1/39. Author. *The Bridges of Madison County*.

WALLINGER, KARL. Prestatyn, Wales, 10/19/57. Keyboardist, guitarist. World Party.

WALSH, JOE. Cleveland, OH, 11/20/47. Guitarist, singer. The Eagles; The James Gang.

WALSH, M. EMMET. Ogdensburg, NY, 3/22/35. Actor. *Blood Simple*.

WALSTON, RAY. New Orleans, LA, 11/2/14. Actor. Uncle Martin on *My Favorite Martian*.

WALTER, JESSICA. Brooklyn, NY, 1/31/41. Actor. *Play Misty for Me*.

WALTER, TRACEY. Jersey City, NJ. Actor. Bob the Goon in *Batman*.

WARD, BILL. Birmingham, England, 5/5/48. Drummer. Black Sabbath.

WARD, BURT. Los Angeles, CA, 7/6/46. Actor. *Batman*.

WARD, FRED. San Diego, CA, 12/30/42. Actor. *Henry and June*.

WARD, RACHEL. London, England, 1957. Actor. *Against All Odds*.

WARDEN, JACK (Jack Warden Lebzelter). Newark, NJ, 9/18/20. Actor. Harry Fox on *Crazy Like a Fox*.

WARE, MARTYN. Sheffield, England, 5/19/56. Synthesizer player. The Human League; Heaven 17.

WARFIELD, MARSHA. Chicago, IL, 3/5/55. Actor. Roz Russell on *Night Court*.

WARNER, DAVID. Manchester, England, 7/29/41. Actor. *The Omen*.

WARNER, JULIE. New York, NY, 1965. Actor. *Doc Hollywood*.

WARNER, MALCOLM-JAMAL. Jersey City, NJ, 8/18/70. Actor. Theo Huxtable on *The Cosby Show*.

WARNES, JENNIFER. Orange County, CA, 1947. Pop singer.

WARREN, LESLEY ANN. New York, NY, 8/16/46. Actor. *Mission: Impossible*.

WARRICK, RUTH. St. Joseph, MO, 6/29/15. Actor. Phoebe Wallingford on *All My Children*.

WARWICK, CLINT (Clinton Eccles). Birmingham, England, 6/25/40. Bassist. The Moody Blues.

WARWICK, DIONNE (Marie Warrick). East Orange, NJ, 12/12/40. Gospel/pop singer.

WATERS, JOHN. Baltimore, MD, 4/22/46. Director, writer, actor. *Hairspray; Pink Flamingos; Serial Mom*.

WATERS, ROGER. Great Bookham, England, 9/9/44. Singer, bassist. Pink Floyd.

WATERSTON, SAM. Cambridge, MA, 11/15/40. Actor. *The Killing Fields*.

WATLEY, JODY. Chicago, IL, 1/30/59. Singer. Shalamar.

WATSON, BRUCE. Ontario, Canada, 3/11/61. Guitarist. Big Country.

WATT, BEN. 12/6/62. Guitarist, keyboardist, singer. Everything but the Girl.

WATTS, CHARLIE. Islington, England, 6/2/41. Drummer. The Rolling Stones.

WATTS, OVEREND (Peter Watts). Birmingham, England, 5/13/49. Bassist. Mott The Hoople.

WAXMAN, AL. Toronto, Canada, 3/2/34. Actor. Bert Samuels on *Cagney and Lacey*.

WAYANS, KEENEN IVORY. New York, NY, 6/8/58. Actor, director, writer. *In Living Color*.

WAYBILL, FEE (John Waldo). Omaha, NE, 9/17/50. Singer. The Tubes.

WAYNE, CARL. Mosely, England, 8/18/44. Singer. The Move.

WAYNE, PATRICK. Los Angeles, CA, 7/15/39. Actor, son of John. *McClintock!*

WEATHERS, CARL. New Orleans, LA, 1/14/48. Actor. Apollo Creed in *Rocky*.

WEAVER, BLUE (Derek Weaver). Cardiff, Wales, 3/3/49. Organist. Amen Corner.

WEAVER, DENNIS. Joplin, MO, 6/4/24. Actor. *McCloud*.

WEAVER, FRITZ. Pittsburgh, PA, 1/19/26. Actor. *Marathon Man*.

WEBB, PAUL. 1/16/62. Bassist. Talk Talk.

WEIDER, JOHN. England, 4/21/47. Bassist. Family.

WEIR, BOB. San Francisco, CA, 10/6/47. Guitarist. Grateful Dead.

WEITZ, BRUCE. Norwalk, CT, 5/27/43. Actor. Mick Belker on *Hill Street Blues*.

WELCH, BRUCE (Bruce Cripps). Bognor Regis, England, 11/2/41. Guitarist. The Shadows.

WELCH, RAQUEL (Raquel Tejada). Chicago, IL, 9/5/40. Actor. *One Million Years B.C.*

WELD, TUESDAY (Susan Weld). New York, NY, 8/27/43. Actor. *Looking for Mr. Goodbar*.

WELLER, PAUL. 5/25/58. Singer, bassist. The Jam.

WELLER, PAUL. Woking, England, 5/25/58. Singer, guitarist. The Style Council.

WELLER, PETER. Stevens Point, WI, 6/24/47. Actor. *Robocop*.

WELLS, CORY. Buffalo, NY, 2/5/42. Singer. Three Dog Night.

WELLS, KITTY (Muriel Deason). Nashville, TN, 8/30/19. Country singer.

WELNICK, VINCE. Phoenix, AZ, 2/21/51. Keyboardist.

The Tubes.

WENDT, GEORGE. Chicago, IL, 10/17/48. Actor. Norm Peterson on *Cheers*.

WEST, ADAM (William Anderson). Walla Walla, WA, 9/19/28. Actor. *Batman*.

WEST, JOHN. Uhrichsville, OH, 7/31/39. Guitarist. Gary Lewis & The Playboys.

WEST, RICK. Dagenham, England, 5/7/43. Lead guitarist. Brian Poole & The Tremeloes.

WESTHEIMER, RUTH (Karola Ruth Siegel). Frankfurt, Germany, 6/4/28. Sex therapist. *Ask Dr. Ruth*.

WETTON, JOHN. Derbyshire, England, 7/12/49. Lead singer, bassist. Asia.

WEYMOUTH, TINA. Coronado, CA, 11/22/50. Bassist. Talking Heads.

WHALEY, FRANK. Syracuse, NY, 1963. Actor. *The Doors*.

WHALLEY, JOANNE. Manchester, England, 8/25/64. Actor, formerly married to Val Kilmer. *Willow*.

WHELCHEL, LISA. Fort Worth, TX, 5/29/63. Actor. Blair Warner on *The Facts of Life*.

WHITAKER, JOHNNY. Van Nuys, CA, 12/13/59. Actor. Jody on *Family Affair*.

WHITE, BETTY. Oak Park, IL, 1/17/22. Actor. Rose Nylund on *The Golden Girls*.

WHITE, CHRIS. Barnet, England, 3/7/43. Bassist. The Zombies.

WHITE, DAVE (David Tricker). Philadelphia, PA, 9/1/40. Singer. Danny & The Juniors.

WHITE, JALEEL. Los Angeles, CA, 11/27/76. Actor. Steve Urkel on *Family Matters*.

WHITE, MARK. Sheffield, England, 4/1/61. Guitarist. ABC.

WHITE, MAURICE. Memphis, TN, 12/19/41. Singer, drummer, kalimba player. Earth, Wind & Fire.

WHITE, VANNA (Vanna

Rosich). North Myrtle Beach, SC, 2/18/57. Letter turner extraordinaire. *Wheel of Fortune.*

WHITE, VERDINE. Illinois, 7/25/51. Singer, bassist. Earth, Wind & Fire.

WHITELAW, BILLIE. Coventry, England, 6/6/32. Actor. *Charlie Bubbles.*

WHITFORD, BRAD. Winchester, MA, 2/23/52. Guitarist. Aerosmith.

WHITMORE, JAMES. White Plains, NY, 10/1/21. Actor. *Will Rogers, USA.*

WHITNEY, CHARLIE. Leicester, England, 6/4/44. Guitarist. Family.

WIEST, DIANNE. Kansas City, MO, 3/28/46. Actor. *Hannah and Her Sisters.*

WILCOX, LARRY. San Diego, CA, 8/8/47. Actor. Officer Jon Baker on *CHiPS.*

WILDE, KIM (Kim Smith). London, England, 11/18/60. Singer, songwriter.

WILDER, ALAN. 6/1/59. Singer, synthesizer player. Depeche Mode.

WILDER, GENE (Jerome Silberman). Milwaukee, WI, 6/11/33. Actor, director, writer, widower of Gilda Radner. *Young Frankenstein.*

WILLIAM, PRINCE. London, England, 6/21/82. British royalty, son of Prince Charles and Princess Diana.

WILLIAMS, ANDY. Wall Lake, IA, 12/3/27. Pop singer. "Where Do I Begin?"

WILLIAMS, BARRY. Santa Monica, CA, 9/30/54. Actor. Greg on *The Brady Bunch.*

WILLIAMS, BILLY DEE. New York, NY, 4/6/37. Actor. *Lady Sings the Blues.*

WILLIAMS, CINDY. Van Nuys, CA, 8/22/47. Actor. Shirley Feeney on *Laverne & Shirley.*

WILLIAMS, CLARENCE III. New York, NY, 8/21/39. Actor. Lincoln Hayes on *The Mod Squad.*

WILLIAMS, CLIFF. Rumford, England, 12/14/29. Bass guitarist. AC/DC.

WILLIAMS, DENIECE (Deniece Chandler). Gary, IN, 6/3/51. Gospel/pop singer.

WILLIAMS, ESTHER. Los Angeles, CA, 8/8/21. Actor, swimmer, widow of Fernando Lamas. *Bathing Beauty.*

WILLIAMS, HANK JR (Randall Hank). Shreveport, LA, 5/26/49. Country singer, songwriter. "Texas Women."

WILLIAMS, JOBETH. Houston, TX, 12/6/48. Actor. *The Big Chill.*

WILLIAMS, JOHN TOWNER. Queens, NY, 2/8/32. Composer, conductor. *Jaws; Star Wars.*

WILLIAMS, MAISIE. Montserrat, West Indies, 3/25/51. Singer. Boney M.

WILLIAMS, MILAN. Mississippi, 3/28/48. Keyboardist, trombonist, guitarist, drummer. The Commodores.

WILLIAMS, MONTEL. Baltimore, MD, 7/3/56. Talk show host. *The Montel Williams Show.*

WILLIAMS, OTIS (Otis Miles). Texarkana, TX, 10/30/49. Singer. The Temptations.

WILLIAMS, PAUL. Birmingham, AL, 7/2/39. Singer. The Temptations.

WILLIAMS, TREAT (Richard Williams). Rowayton, CT, 12/1/51. Actor. *Prince of the City.*

WILLIAMS, WALTER. 8/25/42. Singer. The O'Jays.

WILLIAMS, WENDY O. (Wendy Orlean Williams). Rochester, NY, 1946. Entertainer, singer.

WILLIAMSON, NICOL. Hamilton, Scotland, 9/14/38. Actor. *Excalibur.*

WILLIG, GEORGE. New York, NY, 6/11/49. Actor, stuntman. Climbed World Trade Center.

WILSON, AL "BLIND OWL." Boston, MA, 7/4/43. Guitarist, singer, harmonicist. Canned Heat.

WILSON, ANN. San Diego, CA, 6/19/51. Lead singer. Heart.

WILSON, BARRY J. London, England, 3/18/47. Drummer. Procol Harum.

WILSON, BRIAN. Inglewood, CA, 6/20/42. Bassist, keyboardist, singer, father of Wendy and Carnie. The Beach Boys.

WILSON, CARNIE. Los Angeles, CA, 4/29/68. Singer, daughter of Brian, sister of Wendy. Wilson Phillips.

WILSON, CINDY. Athens, GA, 2/28/57. Guitarist, singer. The B-52's.

WILSON, DEMOND. Valdosta, GA, 10/13/46. Actor. *Sanford and Son.*

WILSON, DON. Tacoma, WA, 2/10/37. Guitarist. The Ventures.

WILSON, JOYCE. Detroit, MI, 12/14/46. Singer. Tony Orlando & Dawn.

WILSON, MARY. Greenville, MS, 3/6/44. Singer. The Supremes.

WILSON, NANCY. Chillicothe, OH, 2/20/37. R&B singer.

WILSON, NANCY. San Francisco, CA, 3/16/54. Guitarist, singer. Heart.

WILSON, TOM. Grant Town, WV, 8/1/31. Cartoonist. *Ziggy.*

WILSON, TONY. Trinidad, 10/8/47. Bassist, singer. Hot Chocolate.

WILSON, WENDY. Los Angeles, CA, 10/16/69. Singer, sister of Carnie, daughter of Brian. Wilson Phillips.

WINCHELL, PAUL. New York, NY, 12/21/22. Ventriloquist, actor. *The Paul Winchell-Jerry Mahoney Show.*

WINDOM, WILLIAM. New York, NY, 9/28/23. Actor. *Murder She Wrote.*

WINFIELD, DAVE. Saint Paul, MN, 10/3/51. Baseball player.

WINFIELD, PAUL. Los Angeles, CA, 5/22/41. Actor. *Sounder.*

WINGER, DEBRA (Mary Debra Winger). Cleveland, OH, 5/16/55. Actor. *Terms of Endearment.*

WINKLER, HENRY. New York, NY, 10/30/45. Actor, producer, director. Arthur "The Fonz" Fonzarelli on *Happy Days.*

WINNINGHAM, MARE. Phoenix, AZ, 5/6/59. Actor. *St. Elmo's Fire.*

WINSTON, JIMMY (James Langwith). London, England, 4/20/45. Organist. The Small Faces.

WINTER, EDGAR. Beaumont, TX, 12/28/46. Blues/rock keyboardist, brother of Johnny.

WINTER, JOHNNY. Beaumont, TX, 2/23/44. Blues/rock guitarist, brother of Edgar.

WINTERS, JONATHAN. Dayton, OH, 11/11/25. Actor. *The Jonathan Winters Show.*

WINTERS, SHELLEY (Shirley Schrift). St. Louis, MO, 8/18/20. Actor. *The Poseidon Adventure.*

WINWOOD, MUFF (Mervyn Winwood). Birmingham, England, 6/14/43. Singer, songwriter, bassist. The Spencer Davis Group.

WINWOOD, STEVE. Birmingham, England, 5/12/48. Singer, songwriter. The Spencer Davis Group; Traffic; Blind Faith.

WITHERS, BILL. Slab Fork, WV, 7/4/38. Pop singer, songwriter, guitarist.

WITHERS, JANE. Atlanta, GA, 4/12/26. Actor. Josephine the Plumber on TV commercials.

WOLF, PETER (Peter Blankfield). New York, NY, 3/7/46. Singer. The J. Geils Band.

WOLTERS, JOHN. 4/28/45. Drummer, singer. Dr. Hook.

WOMACK, BOBBY. Cleveland, OH, 3/4/44. Gospel/R&B singer, songwriter, guitarist.

WONDER, STEVIE (Steveland Morris). Saginaw, MI, 5/13/50. Singer, songwriter, formerly married to Syreeta Wright.

WONG, B. D. San Francisco, CA, 10/24/62. Actor. *M. Butterfly.*

WOOD, DANNY. Boston, MA, 5/14/71. Singer. New Kids on the Block.

WOOD, RON. London, England, 6/1/47. Guitarist. The Rolling Stones.

WOOD, ROY (Ulysses Adrian Wood). Birmingham, England, 11/8/46. Singer, guitarist, cellist. Electric Light Orchestra (ELO); Wizzard; The Move.

WOOD, STUART. Edinburgh, Scotland, 2/25/57. Guitarist. The Bay City Rollers.

WOODARD, ALFRE. Tulsa, OK, 11/8/53. Actor. *Cross Creek.*

WOODWARD, EDWARD. Croydon, England, 6/1/30. Actor. *The Equalizer.*

WOODWARD, JOANNE. Thomasville, GA, 2/27/30. Actor, married to Paul Newman. *The Three Faces of Eve.*

WOODWARD, KEREN. Bristol, England, 4/2/61. Singer. Bananarama.

WORLEY, JO ANNE. Lowell, IN, 9/6/39. Actor, singer. *Laugh-In.*

WRAY, FAY. Alberta, Canada, 9/10/07. Actor. *King Kong.*

WRIGHT, ADRIAN. Sheffield, England, 6/30/56. Projector operator for on-stage slides and films. The Human League.

WRIGHT, LITTLE STEVIE. Leeds, England, 12/20/48. Singer. The Easybeats.

WRIGHT, MAX. Detroit, MI, 8/2/43. Actor. Willie Tanner on *ALF.*

WRIGHT, PAT. Brooklyn, NY,

1945. Singer. The Crystals.

WRIGHT, RICK. London, England, 7/28/45. Keyboardist. Pink Floyd.

WRIGHT, STEVEN. Burlington, MA, 12/6/55. Comedian.

WRIGHT, SYREETA. Pittsburgh, PA, 1946. Singer, songwriter, formerly married to Stevie Wonder.

WUHL, ROBERT. Union City, NJ, 10/9/51. Actor, writer. *Bull Durham.*

WYATT, JANE. Campgaw, NJ, 8/13/12. Actor. *Father Knows Best.*

WYMAN, BILL (William Perks). London, England, 10/24/36. Bassist. The Rolling Stones.

WYMAN, JANE (Sarah Jane Fulks). St. Joseph, MO, 1/4/14. Actor, formerly married to Ronald Reagan. Angela Channing on *Falcon Crest.*

YAMAGUCHI, KRISTI. Hayward, CA, 7/12/71. Skater. Olympic gold medalist.

YANKOVIC, WEIRD AL (Alfred Matthew Yankovic). Los Angeles, CA, 10/23/59. Singer, spoof artist. "Like a Surgeon."

YANOVSKY, ZAL. Toronto, Canada, 12/19/44. Guitarist, singer. The Lovin' Spoonful.

YARROW, PETER. New York, NY, 5/31/38. Composer, author, singer. Peter, Paul and Mary.

YEARWOOD, TRISHA. Monticello, GA, 9/19/64. Singer.

YELTSIN, BORIS. Burka, Russia, 2/1/31. Russian political leader.

YESTER, JIM. Birmingham, AL, 11/24/39. Singer, guitarist. The Association.

YOAKAM, DWIGHT. Pikesville, KY, 10/23/56. Country singer. "Honky Tonk Man."

YORK, MICHAEL. Fulmer, England, 3/27/42. Actor. *Logan's Run.*

YORK, PETE. Redcar, England, 8/15/42. Drummer. The Spencer Davis Group.

YOUNG, ANGUS. Glasgow, Scotland, 3/31/59. Guitarist. AC/DC.

YOUNG, GEORGE. Glasgow, Scotland, 11/6/47. Guitarist. The Easybeats.

YOUNG, JAMES. Chicago, IL, 11/14/48. Guitarist. Styx.

YOUNG, JESSE COLIN (Perry Miller). New York, NY, 11/11/41. Guitarist, bassist, singer. The Youngbloods.

YOUNG, MALCOLM. Glasgow, Scotland, 1/6/53. Guitarist. AC/DC.

YOUNG, NEIL. Toronto, Canada, 11/12/45. Singer, songwriter, guitarist. Buffalo Springfield; Crosby, Stills, Nash & Young.

YOUNG, RUSTY. Long Beach, CA, 2/23/46. Pedal steel guitarist. Poco.

YOUNG, SEAN. Louisville, KY, 11/20/59. Actor. *No Way Out.*

YOUNG MC (Marvin Young). London, England, 1968. Rap artist.

ZADORA, PIA. New York, NY, 5/4/56. Actor. *Naked Gun 33 1/3.*

ZAHN, PAULA. Naperville, IL, 2/24/56. Broadcast journalist. *CBS This Morning.*

ZAL, ROXANA. Los Angeles, CA, 11/8/69. Actor. *Something About Amelia.*

ZANDER, ROBIN. Rockford, IL, 1/23/53. Singer, guitarist. Cheap Trick.

ZAPPA, DWEEZIL. Los Angeles, CA, 9/5/69. Guitarist, son of Frank, brother of Moon Unit.

ZAPPA, MOON UNIT. Hollywood, CA, 9/28/67. Singer, daughter of Frank, sister of Dweezil. "Valley Girl."

ZEMECKIS, ROBERT Chicago, IL, 5/14/51. Director, producer, screenwriter. *Forrest Gump.*

ZEVON, WARREN. Chicago,

IL, 1/24/47. Singer, songwriter. "Werewolves of London."

ZIERING, IAN. 3/30/64. Actor. *Beverly Hills 90210.*

ZIMBALIST, STEPHANIE. Encino, CA, 10/8/56. Actor, daughter of Efrem. Laura Holt on *Remington Steele.*

ZMED, ADRIAN. Chicago, IL, 3/4/54. Actor. Vince Romano on *T. J. Hooker.*

ZUNIGA, DAPHNE. Berkeley, CA, 10/28/62. Actor. *Melrose Place.*

HAPPY BIRTHDAY! THE GREATS' NATAL DATES

JANUARY 1
Frank Langella
Don Novello
Dedee Pfeiffer
J.D. Salinger

JANUARY 2
Jim Bakker
Gabrielle Carteris
Chick Churchill
Taye Diggs
Cuba Gooding Jr.
Joanna Pacula

JANUARY 3
Melody Anderson
Dabney Coleman
Mel Gibson
Robert Loggia
Danica McKellar
Victoria Principal
Stephen Stills
Bill Travers

JANUARY 4
Bernie Albrecht
Dyan Cannon
Matt Frewer
Ann Magnuson
Julia Ormond
Michael Stipe
Barney Sumner
Jane Wyman

JANUARY 5
Suzy Amis
George Brown
Robert Duvall
Diane Keaton
Ted Lange
Marilyn Manson
Walter Mondale
Chris Stein

JANUARY 6
Rowan Atkinson
Syd Barrett
Bonnie Franklin
Mark O'Toole
John Singleton
Kathy Sledge
Malcolm Young

JANUARY 7
Nicolas Cage
Katie Couric
Sammo Hung
Kenny Loggins
Paul Revere

JANUARY 8
David Bowie
Stephen Hawking
Robbie Krieger
Yvette Mimieux
Charles Osgood
Soupy Sales
Larry Storch

JANUARY 9
Joan Baez
Bill Cowsill
Bob Denver
Scott Engel
Crystal Gayle
David Johansen
Judith Krantz
Herbert Lom
AJ McLean
Jimmy Page

JANUARY 10
Trini Alvarado
Pat Benatar
Shawn Colvin
Donald Fagen
George Foreman
Bob Lang
Cyril Neville
Maurice Sendak
Rod Stewart

JANUARY 11
Mary J. Blige
Naomi Judd
Vicki Peterson
Rod Taylor

JANUARY 12
Kirstie Alley
Anthony Andrews
Melanie Chisholm
Per Gessle
William Lee
 Golden
Rush Limbaugh
Oliver Platt
Chynna Phillips
Cynthia Robinson
Vendela

JANUARY 13
Kevin Anderson
Nick Clooney
Patrick Dempsey
Robert "Squirrel"
 Lester
Julia Louis-Drey-
 fus
Graham McPher-
 son

Penelope Ann
 Miller
Richard Moll
Robert Stack
Frances
 Sternhagen
Gwen Verdon

JANUARY 14
Jason Bateman
Faye Dunaway
L.L. Cool J
Andy Rooney
Emily Watson
Carl Weathers

JANUARY 15
Captain Beefheart
Charo
Martha Davis
Chad Lowe
Andrea Martin
Pamela Sue Mar-
 tin
Julian Sands
Peter Trewavas
Mario Van Peebles

JANUARY 16
Debbie Allen
Bob Bogle
John Carpenter
Bill Francis
Kate Moss
Sade
Laura Sch-
 lessinger
Jim Stafford
Paul Webb

JANUARY 17
Muhammad Ali
Jim Carrey
David Caruso
John Crawford
Steve Earle
Joe Frazier
Susanna Hoffs
James Earl Jones
Eartha Kitt
Maury Povich
Vidal Sassoon
Betty White

JANUARY 18
Kevin Costner
David Ruffin
Larry Smith

JANUARY 19
Desi Arnaz Jr.
Dewey Bunnell

Michael Crawford
Phil Everly
Shelley Fabares
Tippi Hedren
Harvey Hinsley
Robert MacNeil
Robert Palmer
Dolly Parton
Katey Sagal
Jean Stapleton
Mickey Virtue
Fritz Weaver

JANUARY 20
Buzz Aldrin
Arte Johnson
Lorenzo Lamas
David Lynch
Bill Maher
John Michael
 Montgomery
Patricia Neal
Paul Stanley
Eric Stewart
Ron Townson

JANUARY 21
Robby Benson
Emma Bunton
Geena Davis
Mac Davis
Jill Eikenberry
Richie Havens

JANUARY 22
Linda Blair
Olivia D'Abo
Balthazar Getty
John Hurt
Diane Lane
Piper Laurie
Chris Lemmon
Steve Perry
Jeff Smith
Ann Sothern

JANUARY 23
Richard Dean
 Anderson
Princess Caroline
Bill Cunningham
Earl Falconer
Gil Gerard
Rutger Hauer
Jeanne Moreau
Anita Pointer
Chita Rivera
Patrick Simmons
Robin Zande

JANUARY 24
Ernest Borgnine
Neil Diamond
Jools Holland
Nastassja Kinski
Michael Ontkean
Oral Roberts
Yakov Smirnoff
Ray Stevens
Warren Zevon

JANUARY 25
Corazon Aquino
Andy Cox
Richard Finch
Etta James
Dean Jones
Dinah Manoff

JANUARY 26
Jazzie B
David Briggs
Ellen DeGeneres
Scott Glenn
Wayne Gretsky
Paul Newman
Andrew Ridgeley
Bob Uecker
Eddie Van Halen

JANUARY 27
Bobby Bland
Troy Donahue
Brian Downey
Bridget Fonda
Gillian Gilbert
Seth Justman
Nick Mason
Mike Patton
Mimi Rogers
Nedra Talley

JANUARY 28
Alan Alda
Mikhail
 Baryshnikov
John Beck
Nick Carter
Joey Fatone
Brian Keenan
Marthe Keller
Sarah McLachlan
Nicholas Pryor
Dave Sharp
Dick Taylor
Elijah Wood

JANUARY 29
David Byron
Ed Burns
John Forsythe

Roddy Frame
Sara Gilbert
Heather Graham
Noel Harrison
Eddie Jackson
Anne Jillian
Greg Louganis
Tommy Ramone
Katharine Ross
Tom Selleck
Oprah Winfrey

JANUARY 30
Christian Bale
Marty Balin
Phil Collins
Charles Dutton
Gene Hackman
William King
Dorothy Malone
Steve Marriott
Dick Martin
Vanessa Redgrave
Joe Terranova
Jody Watley

JANUARY 31
John Agar
Harry Wayne
 Casey
Carol Channing
Lloyd Cole
Portia De Rossi
Minnie Driver
John Paul Jones
Terry Kath
John Lydon
Phil Manzanera
Suzanne Pleshette
Jean Simmons
Justin Timberlake

FEBRUARY 1
Mike Campbell
Don Everly
Dennis Farina
Sherilynn Fenn
Sherman Hemsley
Rick James
Terry Jones
Billy Mumy
Lisa Marie Pres-
 ley-Jackson
Ray Sawyer
Pauly Shore
Boris Yeltsin

FEBRUARY 2
Christie Brinkley
Garth Brooks
Alan Caddy
Farrah Fawcett

Gale Gordon
Peter Lucia
Graham Nash
Liz Smith
Tom Smothers
Elaine Stritch
Ross Valory

FEBRUARY 3
Joey Bishop
Thomas Calabro
Angelo D'Aleo
Blythe Danner
Dave Davies
Morgan Fairchild
Eric Haydock
Nathan Lane
Fran Tarkenton
Lol Tolhurst

FEBRUARY 4
Gabrielle Anwar
Michael Beck
Clint Black
David Brenner
Alice Cooper
Natalie Imbruglia
Florence LaRue
Dan Quayle
John Steel

FEBRUARY 5
Bobby Brown
Christopher Guest
Barbara Hershey
Jennifer Jason
 Leigh
Laura Linney
Charlotte Ram-
 pling
Roger Staubach
Cory Wells

FEBRUARY 6
Rick Astley
Tom Brokaw
Natalie Cole
Fabian
Mike Farrell
Zsa Zsa Gabor
Alan Jones
Patrick Macnee
Ronald Reagan
Rip Torn
Robert Townsend
Michael Tucker
Mamie Van Doren

FEBRUARY 7
David Bryan
Miguel Ferrer
Jimmy Greenspoon
Alan Lancaster
Chris Rock
James Spader
Brian Travers

FEBRUARY 8
Brooke Adams
Brian Bennett
Creed Bratton
Gary Coleman
John Grisham
Robert Klein
Ted Koppel
Vince Neil
Nick Nolte
Mary Steenburgen
John Williams

FEBRUARY 9
Mia Farrow
Carole King
Judith Light
Master P
Roger Mudd
Joe Pesci
Janet Suzman
Travis Tritt
Alice Walker

FEBRUARY 10
Laura Dern
Donovan
Roberta Flack
Jimmy Merchant
Mark Spitz
Robert Wagner
Don Wilson

FEBRUARY 11
Jennifer Aniston
Brandy
Sheryl Crow
Conrad Janis
Tina Louise
Leslie Nielsen
Burt Reynolds
Sidney Sheldon

FEBRUARY 12
Maud Adams
Joe Don Baker
Judy Blume
Cliff DeYoung
Arsenio Hall
Joanna Kerns
Simon
 MacCorkindale
Ray Manzarek
Christina Ricci
Joe Schermie

FEBRUARY 13
Tony Butler
Stockard Chan-
 ning
Roger Christian
Peter Gabriel
Peter Hook
David Naughton
Kim Novak
George Segal

Jerry Springer
Mena Suvari
Bo Svenson
Peter Tork

FEBRUARY 14
Hugh Downs
Roger Fisher
Florence Hender-
 son
Gregory Hines
Meg Tilly
Paul Tsongas
Ken Wahl

FEBRUARY 15
Mick Avory
Marisa Berenson
Claire Bloom
David Brown
Ali Campbell
Mikey Craig
Matt Groening
John Helliwell
Harvey Korman
Kevin McCarthy
Jane Seymour

FEBRUARY 16
LeVar Burton
James Ingram
William Katt
John McEnroe Jr.
Andy Taylor

FEBRUARY 17
Billie Joe Arm-
 strong
Alan Bates
Jim Brown
Brenda Fricker
Hal Holbrook
Michael Jordan
Lou Diamond
 Phillips
Gene Pitney
Denise Richards
Rene Russo
Raf Vallone

FEBRUARY 18
Robbie Bachman
Randy Crawford
Sinead Cusack
Dennis DeYoung
Matt Dillon
George Kennedy
Toni Morrison
Juice Newton
Yoko Ono
Jack Palance
Molly Ringwald
Herman Santiago
Greta Scacchi
Cybill Shepherd
John Travolta

Vanna White

FEBRUARY 19
Mark Andes
Justine Bateman
Francis Buchholz

Lou Christie
Jeff Daniels
Tony Iommi
Holly Johnson
Smokey Robinson
Seal

FEBRUARY 20
Edward Albert
Robert Altman
Charles Barkley
Walter Becker
Ian Brown
Randy California
Cindy Crawford
Sandy Duncan
J. Geils
Kelsey Grammer
Brian Littrell
Jennifer O'Neill
Sidney Poitier
Andrew Shue
Peter Strauss
Gloria Vanderbilt
Nancy Wilson

FEBRUARY 21
Christopher Atkins
William Baldwin
Jean-Jacques
 Burnel
Mary Chapin Car-
 penter
Tyne Daly
David Geffen
Kelsey Grammer
Jerry Harrison
Jennifer Love
 Hewitt
Gary Lockwood
Rue McClanahan
Nina Simone
Vince Welnick

FEBRUARY 22
Drew Barrymore
Jonathan Demme
Julius Erving
Ted Kennedy
Kyle MacLachlan
John Mills
Miou-Miou

FEBRUARY 23
Kristen Davis
Peter Fonda
Howard Jones
Mike Maxfield
Steve Priest

David Sylvian
Brad Whitford
Johnny Winter
Rusty Young

FEBRUARY 24
Barry Bostwick
James Farentino
Steven Hill
Paul Jones
Edward James
 Olmos
Helen Shaver
Lonnie Turner
Paula Zahn

FEBRUARY 25
Sean Astin
George Harrison
Téa Leoni
Mike Peters
Sally Jessy
 Raphael
Bobby Riggs
Veronica Webb
Stuart Wood

FEBRUARY 26
Erykah Badu
Michael Bolton
Jonathan Cain
Johnny Cash
Fats Domino
John Jon
Tony Randall
Mitch Ryder
Sandie Shaw

FEBRUARY 27
Adam Baldwin
Garry Christian
Chelsea Clinton
Eddie Gray
Steve Harley
Howard Hesseman
Paul Humphreys
Ralph Nader
Neal Schon
Grant Show
Adrian Smith
Elizabeth Taylor
Rozonda Thomas
Joanne Woodward

FEBRUARY 28
Mario Andretti
Stephanie
 Beacham
Frank Bonner
Charles Durning
Phil Gould
Robert Sean
 Leonard
Gavin MacLeod
Bernadette Peters
Mercedes Ruehl

Bubba Smith
Joe South
Tommy Tune
John Turturro
Cindy Wilson

MARCH 1
Harry Belafonte
Dirk Benedict
Roger Daltrey
Timothy Daly
Jimmy Fortune
Ron Howard
Alan Thicke

MARCH 2
Jon Bon Jovi
John Cowsill
John Cullum
Mark Evans
Mikhail Gorbachev
John Irving
Jennifer Jones
Jay Osmond
Lou Reed
Al Waxman

MARCH 3
Jessica Biel
Willie Chambers
Jance Garfat
Jackie Joyner-
 Kersee
Tim Kazurinsky
Dave Mount
Mike Pender
Miranda
 Richardson
Tone-Loc
Blue Weaver

MARCH 4
Chastity Bono
Evan Dando
Patsy Kensit
Catherine O'Hara
Paula Prentiss
Chris Rea
Chris Squire
Shakin' Stevens
Bobby Womack
Adrian Zmed

MARCH 5
Alan Clark
Samantha Eggar
Eddy Grant
James B. Sikking
Dean Stockwell
Marsha Warfield

MARCH 6
Tom Arnold
Marion Barry
Kiki Dee
David Gilmour

Hugh Grundy
D.L. Hughley
Ed McMahon
Shaquille O'Neal
Rob Reiner
Mary Wilson

MARCH 7
Tammy Faye
  Messner
Paul Davis
Matthew Fisher
John Heard
Willard Scott
Lynn Swann
Daniel J. Travanti
Chris White
Peter Wolf

MARCH 8
Mike Allsup
Cheryl Baker
Clive Burr
Cyd Charisse
Mickey Dolenz
Ralph Ellis
Peter Gill
Camryn Manheim
Randy Meisner
Gary Numan
Aidan Quinn
Lynn Redgrave
James Van Der
  Beek

MARCH 9
Juliette Binoche
Trevor Burton
John Cale
Jim Cregan
Linda Fiorentino
Martin Fry
Marty Ingels
Emmanuel Lewis
Mark Lindsey
Jeffrey Osborne
Mickey Spillane
Robin Trower
Trish Van Devere

MARCH 10
Neneh Cherry
Prince Edward
Jasmine Guy
Chuck Norris
James Earl Ray
Tom Scholz
Sharon Stone
Dean Torrence

MARCH 11
Douglas Adams
Sam Donaldson
Lisa Loeb
Bobby McFerrin
Susan Richardson

Ric Rothwell
Mark Stein
Bruce Watson

MARCH 12
Barbara Feldon
Mike Gibbins
Marlon Jackson
Al Jarreau
Paul Kantner
Liza Minnelli
Brian O'Hara
Bill Payne
James Taylor

MARCH 13
Adam Clayton
Dana Delany
Glenne Headly
William H. Macy
Deborah Raffin
Neil Sedaka

MARCH 14
Michael Caine
Billy Crystal
Megan Follows
Boon Gould
Taylor Hanson
Quincy Jones
Walter Parazaider
Kevin Williamson

MARCH 15
Ry Cooder
David Costell
Terence Trent
  D'Arby
Fabio
Renny Harlin
Judd Hirsch
Phil Lesh
Mike Love
Bret Michaels
Rockwell
Howard Scott
Sly Stone
Jimmy Lee Swag-
  gart

MARCH 16
Michael Bruce
Erik Estrada
Isabelle Huppert
Jerry Lewis
Kate Nelligan
Nancy Wilson

MARCH 17
Harold Brown
Lesley-Anne Down
Patrick Duffy
Scott Gorham
Mike Lindup
Rob Lowe
Patrick McCauley

Kurt Russell
John Sebastian
Gary Sinise

MARCH 18
Bonnie Blair
Irene Cara
Kevin Dobson
Peter Graves
John Hartman
Wilson Pickett
Charley Pride
Queen Latifah
John Updike
Vanessa Williams
Barry J. Wilson

MARCH 19
Ursula Andress
Paul Atkinson
Glenn Close
Terry Hall
Clarence Henry
Derek Longmuir
Ruth Pointer
Bruce Willis

MARCH 20
John Clark Gable
Holly Hunter
William Hurt
Kathy Ireland
Spike Lee
Hal Linden
Carl Palmer
Slim Jim Phantom
Carl Reiner
Mr. Rogers
Theresa Russell

MARCH 21
Matthew Broderick
Timothy Dalton
Cynthia Geary
Roger Hodgson
Eddie Money
Rosie O'Donnell
Gary Oldman
Rosie Stone
Russell
  Thompkins Jr.

MARCH 22
George Benson
Jeremy Clyde
Randy Hobbs
Werner Klemperer
Kelly LeBrock
Andrew
  Lloyd Webber
Karl Malden
Marcel Marceau
Stephanie Mills
Matthew Modine
Lena Olin
Pat Robertson

William Shatner
Harry Vanda
M. Emmet Walsh
Reese Wither-
  spoon

MARCH 23
Princess Eugenie
Chaka Khan
Ric Ocasek
Marti Pellow
Amanda Plummer
Keri Russell

MARCH 24
Lara Flynn Boyle
Robert Carradine
Tommy Hilfiger
Star Jones
Lee Oskar
Donna Pescow
Annabella Sciorra
Dougie Thomson

MARCH 25
Bonnie Bedelia
Aretha Franklin
Paul Michael
  Glaser
Mary Gross
Jeff Healey
Elton John
Neil Jones
Sarah Jessica
  Parker
Gloria Steinem
John Stockwell
Maisie Williams

MARCH 26
Alan Arkin
James Caan
Kenny Chesney
Leeza Gibbons
Jennifer Grey
Vicki Lawrence
Leonard Nimoy
Teddy Pendergrass
Diana Ross
Fran Sheehan
Martin Short
Curtis Sliwa
Richard Tandy
Steven Tyler

MARCH 27
Tony Banks
Mariah Carey
Judy Carne
Andrew Farriss
Austin Pendleton
Maria Schneider
Tom Sullivan
Quentin Tarantino
Michael York

MARCH 28
Dirk Bogarde
Ken Howard
Lucy Lawless
Reba McEntire
Chuck Portz
Salt
Dianne Wiest
Milan Williams

MARCH 29
Jennifer Capriati
Bud Cort
Eric Idle
Bobby Kimball
Christopher Lam-
  bert
Elle Macpherson

MARCH 30
John Astin
Warren Beatty
Tracy Chapman
Eric Clapton
Richard Dysart
Graeme Edge
Hammer
Peter Marshall
Paul Reiser
Ian Ziering

MARCH 31
Rod Allen
Herb Alpert
Richard
  Chamberlain
Liz Claiborne
William Daniels
Albert Gore
Sean Hopper
Shirley Jones
Ewen McGregor
Ed Marinaro
Al Nichol
Rhea Perlman
Mick Ralphs
Christopher
  Walken
Angus Young

APRIL 1
John Barbata
Alan Blakley
Billy Currie
Rudolph Isley
Gordon Jump
Ali MacGraw
Phil Margo
Annette O'Toole
Bijou Phillips
Debbie Reynolds
Mark White

APRIL 2
Dana Carvey
Glen Dale

Buddy Ebsen
Emmylou Harris
Linda Hunt
Pamela Reed
Leon Russell
Keren Woodward

APRIL 3
Alec Baldwin
Jan Berry
Marlon Brando
Doris Day
Jennie Garth
Jane Goodall
Marsha Mason
Eddie Murphy
Wayne Newton
Tony Orlando
Barry Pritchard
Mel Schacher

APRIL 4
Maya Angelou
Robert Downey Jr.
Steve Gatlin
Dave Hill
David E. Kelley
Kitty Kelley
Graeme Kelling
Christine Lahti
Mick Mars
Nancy McKeon
Craig T. Nelson
Berry Oakley

APRIL 5
Allan Clarke
Paula Cole
Agnetha Faltskog
Maxwell Gail
Frank Gorshin
Peter Greenaway
Mike McCready
Michael Moriarty
Gregory Peck
Colin Powell
Gale Storm

APRIL 6
Stan Cullimore
Marilu Henner
Jason Hervey
Ari Meyers
John Ratzenberger
John Stax
Billy Dee Williams

APRIL 7
Mick Abrahams
Patricia Bennett
Jackie Chan
Francis Ford Cop-
  pola
Russell Crowe
Buster Douglas
Spencer Dryden

James Garner
Bruce Gary
Janis Ian
Elaine Miles
John Oates
Wayne Rogers

APRIL 8
Patricia Arquette
Roger Chapman
Steve Howe
Julian Lennon
Robin Wright Penn

APRIL 9
Jean-Paul
  Belmondo
Les Gray
Hugh Hefner
Mark Kelly
Michael Learned
Cynthia Nixon
Dennis Quaid

APRIL 10
Kenneth "Baby-
  face" Edmonds
Peter MacNicol
John Madden
Mandy Moore
Steven Seagal
Brian Setzer
Omar Sharif
Bobbie Smith
Bunny Wailer

APRIL 11
Stuart Adamson
Joel Grey
Bill Irwin
Louise Lasser
Delroy Pearson
Peter Riegert
Richie Sambora
Lisa Stansfield
Neville Staples

APRIL 12
Alex Briley
David Cassidy
Tom Clancy
Claire Danes
Shannen Doherty
Andy Garcia
Vince Gill
Herbie Hancock
John Kay
David Letterman
Ann Miller
Ed O'Neill
Will Sergeant
Scott Turow
Jane Withers

APRIL 13

Peabo Bryson
Jack Casady
Lester Chambers
Jimmy Destri
Tony Dow
Al Green
Garry Kasparov
Howard Keel
Brian Pendleton
Ron Perlman
Rick Schroder
Paul Sorvino
Lyle Waggoner

APRIL 14
Ritchie Blackmore
Dennis Bryon
Julie Christie
Larry Ferguson
Sarah Michelle
  Gellar
Anthony Michael
  Hall
Suge Knight
Buddy Knox
Jay Robinson
Pete Rose
John Shea
Rod Steiger

APRIL 15
Claudia Cardinale
Lois Chiles
Graeme Clark
Roy Clark
Samantha Fox
Emma Thompson

APRIL 16
Edie Adams
Ellen Barkin
Jon Cryer
Lukas Haas
Diana Krall
Gerry Rafferty
Bill Spooner
Dusty Springfield
Bobby Vinton

APRIL 17
Victoria Beckham
Boomer Esiason
Liz Phair
Pete Shelley
Stephen Singleton

APRIL 18
Barbara Hale
Melissa Joan Hart
Jane Leeves
Hayley Mills
Rick Moranis
Conan O'Brien
Les Pattinson
Eric Roberts
Alexander Spence

Mike Vickers
James Woods

APRIL 19
Don Adams
Tim Curry
Kate Hudson
Ashley Judd
Dudley Moore
Alan Price
Larry Ramos Jr.
Mark Volman

APRIL 20
Carmen Electra
Craig Frost
Jessica Lange
Joey Lawrence
Ryan O'Neal
George Takei
Luther Vandross
Jimmy Winston

APRIL 21
Paul Carrack
Tony Danza
Queen Elizabeth II
Charles Grodin
Patti LuPone
Andie MacDowell
Elaine May
Iggy Pop
Anthony Quinn
Robert Smith
John Weider

APRIL 22
Eddie Albert
Joseph Bottoms
Glen Campbell
Peter Kenneth
  Frampton
Ace Frehley
Chris Makepeace
Jack Nicholson
Aaron Spelling
John Waters

APRIL 23
Valerie Bertinelli
David Birney
Steve Clark
Sandra Dee
Jan Hooks
Melinda Kanakare-
  des
Lee Majors
Alan Oppenheimer
Captain Sensible

APRIL 24
Eric Bogosian
Doug Clifford
Glenn Cornick
Billy Gould
Shirley MacLaine

Paul Ryder
Richard Sterban
Barbra Streisand

APRIL 25
Hank Azaria
Andy Bell
Michael Brown
Stu Cook
Meadowlark Lemon
Paul Mazursky
Al Pacino
Talia Shire
Bjorn Ulvaeus
Renee Zellwegger

APRIL 26
Carol Burnett
Duane Eddy
Giancarlo Esposito
Jet Li
Tionne Watkins

APRIL 27
Anouk Aimee
Sheena Easton
Pete Ham
Jack Klugman
Kate Pierson
Marco Pirroni
Clive Taylor

APRIL 28
Ann-Margret
Penelope Cruz
Saddam Hussein
Bruno Kirby
Jay Leno
Marcia Strassman
John Wolters

APRIL 29
Andre Agassi
Duane Allen
Stephen Arenholz
Keith Baxter
Daniel Day-Lewis
Lonnie Donegan
Carl Gardner
Celeste Holm
Tommy James
Coretta Scott King
Rod McKuen
Zubin Mehta
Kate Mulgrew
Michelle Pfeiffer
Eve Plumb
Francis Rossi
Jerry Seinfeld
Uma Thurman
Carnie Wilson

APRIL 30
Turbo B
Jill Clayburgh
Gary Collins

Kirsten Dunst
Perry King
Cloris Leachman
Al Lewis
Willie Nelson
Merrill Osmond
Bobby Vee

MAY 1
Judy Collins
Johnny Colt
Steve Farris
Nick Fortune
Tim McGraw
Ray Parker Jr.
Phil Smith

MAY 2
Christine Baranski
Lesley Gore
Lou Gramm
Engelbert
  Humperdinck
Bianca Jagger
Goldy McJohn
Lorenzo Music
Donatella Versace

MAY 3
David Ball
James Brown
Christopher Cross
Bruce Hall
Mary Hopkin
Pete Seeger
Pete Staples
Frankie Valli
Wynonna

MAY 4
Nickolas Ashford
Jay Aston
Lance Bass
Ronnie Bond
Ed Cassidy
Jackie Jackson
Randy Travis
Pia Zadora

MAY 5
Sarah Ban
  Breathnach
Gary Daly
Lance Henriksen
Ian McCulloch
Kevin Mooney
Cathy Moriarty
Michael Murphy
Michael Palin
Bill Ward

MAY 6
George Clooney
Roma Downey
Willie Mays
Bob Seger

Lori Singer
Mare Winningham

MAY 7
Michael Knight
Bill Kreutzmann Jr.
Traci Lords
Darren McGavin
Rick West

MAY 8
Philip Bailey
Rick Derringer
Chris Frantz
Melissa Gilbert
Gary Glitter
Enrique Iglesias
David Keith
Janet McTeer
James Mitchum
Don Rickles
Paul Samwell-
  Smith
Toni Tennille
Alex Van Halen

MAY 9
Candice Bergen
Pete Birrell
James L. Brooks
Sonny Curtis
Nokie Edwards
Albert Finney
Richie Furay
Dave Gahan
Paul Heaton
Glenda Jackson
Billy Joel
Steve Katz
Mike Millward
Tom Petersson
Dave Prater
Lloyd Price
Tommy Roe
Mike Wallace

MAY 10
Jim Abrahams
Bono
Linda Evangelista
Henry Fambrough
Jay Ferguson
Graham
  Gouldman
Dave Mason
Danny Rapp

MAY 11
Eric Burdon
Les Chadwick
Louis Farrakhan
Faith Popcorn
Natasha
  Richardson

MAY 12

Burt Bacharach
Stephen Baldwin
Bruce Boxleitner
Gabriel Byrne
George Carlin
Lindsay Crouse
Billy Duffy
Emilio Estevez
Kim Fields
Susan Hampshire
Katharine Hepburn
Ian McLagan
Ving Rhames
Tom Snyder
Billy Squier
David Walker
Steve Winwood

MAY 13

Beatrice Arthur
Harvey Keitel
Danny Klein
Lorraine McIntosh
Dennis Rodman
Darius Rucker
Paul Thompson
Overend Watts
Stevie Wonder

MAY 14

Ian Astbury
Cate Blanchett
Jack Bruce
David Byrne
Tom Cochrane
Gene Cornish
Meg Foster
George Lucas
Fabrice Morvan
Danny Wood
Robert Zemeckis

MAY 15

Brian Eno
Graham Goble
Mike Oldfield

MAY 16

Pierce Brosnan
Tracey Gold
Glenn Gregory
Janet Jackson
Barbara Lee
Gabriela Sabatini
Derrell Sweet
Debra Winger
Ralph Tresvant

MAY 17

Bill Bruford
Dennis Hopper
Pervis Jackson
Jordan Knight

Sugar Ray
  Leonard
Bill Paxton
Trent Reznor
Bob Saget
Taj Mahal

MAY 18

Joe Bonsall
Pope John Paul II
George Strait

MAY 19

Nora Ephron
James Fox
David Hartman
Dusty Hill
Grace Jones
Nancy Kwan
Joey Ramone
Philip Rudd
Pete Townshend
Martyn Ware

MAY 20

Warren Cann
Cher
Joe Cocker
Sue Cowsill
Tony Goldwyn
Nick Heyward
Brian Nash
Bronson Pinchot
Ronald Reagan Jr.

MAY 21

Mike Barson
Peggy Cass
Al Franken
Ronald Isley
Stan Lynch
Carol Potter
Judge Reinhold
Leo Sayer
Mr. T
Hilton Valentine

MAY 22

Charles Aznavour
Richard Benjamin
Naomi Campbell
Michael Constantine
Jerry Dammers
Iva Davies
Morrissey
Bernie Taupin
Paul Winfield

MAY 23

Drew Carey
Rosemary Clooney
Joan Collins
Betty Garrett
Bill Hunt
Jewel

Anatoly Karpov

MAY 24

Gary Burghoff
Roseanne Cash
Thomas Chong
Bob Dylan
Lenny Kravitz
Priscilla Presley
Derek Quinn
Rich Robinson
Kristin Scott
  Thomas

MAY 25

Dixie Carter
Patti D'Arbanville
Anne Heche
Justin Henry
Lauryn Hill
Robert Ludlum
Mitch Margo
Ian McKellen
Klaus Meine
Mike Myers
Frank Oz
John Palmer
Connie Sellecca
Beverly Sills
Leslie Uggams
Paul Weller

MAY 26

Verden Allen
James Arness
Helena Bonham-
  Carter
Ray Ennis
Genie Francis
Bobcat Goldthwait
Pam Grier
Levon Helm
Wayne Hussey
Peggy Lee
Stevie Nicks
Gerry Paterson
Matt Stone
Philip Michael
  Thomas
Hank Williams Jr.

MAY 27

Cilla Black
Todd Bridges
Joseph Fiennes
Peri Gilpin
Louis Gossett Jr.
Tony Hillerman
Henry Kissinger
Lisa Lopes
Cynthia McFadden
Siouxsie Sioux
Bruce Weitz

MAY 28

Carroll Baker

John Fogerty
Roland Gift
Gladys Knight
Sondra Locke
Kylie Minogue

MAY 29

Annette Bening
Larry Blackmon
Gary Brooker
Melanie Brown
Kevin Conway
Roy Crewsdon
Melissa Etheridge
Rupert Everett
Anthony Geary
Bob Hope
Clifton James
Lisa Whelchel

MAY 30

Lenny Davidson
Keir Dullea
Marie Fredriksson
Nicky Headon
Ted McGinley
Clint Walker

MAY 31

Tom Berenger
Clint Eastwood
Sharon Gless
Gregory Harrison
Augie Meyers
Joe Namath
Johnny Paycheck
Brooke Shields
Lea Thompson
Peter Yarrow

JUNE 1

Rene Auberjonois
David Berkowitz
Lisa Hartman
  Black
Pat Boone
Powers Boothe
Pat Corley
Jason Donovan
Morgan Freeman
Andy Griffith
Mike Joyce
Peter Masterson
Alanis Morissette
Lorna Patterson
Jonathan Pryce
Graham Russell
Alan Wilder
Ron Wood
Edward Woodward

JUNE 2

Joanna Gleason
William Guest
Tony Hadley
Charles Haid

Marvin Hamlisch
Stacy Keach
Sally Kellerman
Jerry Mathers
Charles Miller
Milo O'Shea
Michael Steele
Charlie Watts

JUNE 3

Michael Clarke
Tony Curtis
Ian Hunter
Billy Powell
Suzi Quatro
Scott Valentine
Deniece Williams

JUNE 4

Roger Ball
John Drew
  Barrymore
El DeBarge
Bruce Dern
Angelina Jolie
Michelle Phillips
Parker Stevenson
Eddie Velez
Gordon Waller
Dennis Weaver
Ruth Westheimer
Charlie Whitney
Scott Wolf
Noah Wyle

JUNE 5

Laurie Anderson
Richard Butler
Spalding Gray
Kenny G
Robert Lansing
Marky Mark
Bill Moyers
Don Reid
Freddie Stone
Mark Wahlberg

JUNE 6

Sandra Bernhard
Gary Bonds
David Dukes
Robert Englund
Harvey Fierstein
Roy Innis
Amanda Pays
Tom Ryan
Levi Stubbs
Billie Whitelaw

JUNE 7

James Ivory
Tom Jones
Anna Kournikova
Liam Neeson
Prince

JUNE 8

Kathy Baker
Mick Box
Barbara Bush
Russell Christian
Griffin Dunne
Mick "Red"
  Hucknall
Julianna Margulies
Neil Mitchell
Chuck Negron
Doris Pearson
Nick Rhodes
Joan Rivers
Boz Scaggs
Jerry Stiller
Bonnie Tyler
Keenen Ivory
  Wayans

JUNE 9

Trevor Bolder
Patricia Cornwell
Johnny Depp
Michael J. Fox
Billy Hatton
Jon Lord
Jackie Mason
Natalie Portman

JUNE 10

Shirley Alston
Human Beatbox
Lionel Jeffries
Tara Lipinski
Grace Mirabella
Shirley Owens
Prince Philip
Rick Price
Leelee Sobieski
Andrew Stevens

JUNE 11

Adrienne Barbeau
Joey Dee
Chad Everett
Joshua Jackson
John Lawton
Joe Montana
Bonnie Pointer
Donnie Van Zandt
Gene Wilder
George Willig

JUNE 12

Marv Albert
Timothy Busfield
George Bush
Bun Carlos
Vic Damone
Brad Delp
Jenilee Harrison
Jim Nabors
Reg Presley

JUNE 13
Tim Allen
Christo
Bobby Freeman
Howard Leese
Dennis Locorriere
Mark Mendoza
Deniece Pearson
Ally Sheedy
Richard Thomas

JUNE 14
Rod Argent
Jasmine Bleeth
Boy George
Marla Gibbs
Steffi Graf
Jimmy Lea
Will Patton
Donald Trump
Muff Winwood

JUNE 15
Jim Belushi
Simon Callow
Courteney Cox
Mario Cuomo
Julie Hagerty
Russell Hitchcock
Noddy Holder
Helen Hunt
Waylon Jennings

JUNE 16
Eddie Levert
Ian Matthews
Laurie Metcalf
Corin Redgrave
Erich Segal
Joan Van Ark
Gino Vannelli

JUNE 17
Greg Kinnear
Norman Kuhlke
Mark Linn-Baker
Peter Lupus
Barry Manilow
Jason Patric
Joe Piscopo

JUNE 18
Tom Bailey
Roger Ebert
Carol Kane
Paul McCartney
Alison Moyet
Isabella Rossellini

JUNE 19
Paula Abdul
Tommy DeVito
Larry Dunn
Louis Jourdan
Malcolm McDowell

Phylicia Rashad
Gena Rowlands
Salman Rushdie
Kathleen Turner
Ann Wilson

JUNE 20
Danny Aiello
Michael Anthony
Chet Atkins
Olympia Dukakis
John Goodman
Billy Guy
Martin Landau
Alan Longmuir
John Mahoney
Lionel Richie
John Taylor
Dave Thomas
James Tolkan
Brian Wilson

JUNE 21
Meredith Baxter
Berke Breathed
Chris Britton
Mark Brzezicki
Ray Davies
Michael Gross
Mariette Hartley
Bernie Kopell
Joey Kramer
Juliette Lewis
Nils Lofgren
Joey Molland
Robert Pastorelli
Jane Russell
Doug Savant
Maureen Stapleton
Prince William

JUNE 22
Peter Asher
Gary Beers
Bill Blass
Klaus Maria
  Brandauer
Amy Brenneman
Bruce Campbell
Tom Cunningham
Carson Daly
Green Gartside
Howard Kaylan
Kris Kristofferson
Cyndi Lauper
Michael Lerner
Alan Osmond
Tracy Pollan
Todd Rundgren
Jimmy Somerville
Meryl Streep
Lindsay Wagner

JUNE 23
Bryan Brown
Adam Faith
Karin Gustafson
Frances McDormand

JUNE 24
Nancy Allen
Jeff Beck
Colin Blunstone
Georg Stanford
  Brown
Jeff Cease
Mick Fleetwood
John Illsley
Michele Lee
Andy McCluskey
Curt Smith
Sherry Stringfield
Peter Weller

JUNE 25
Tim Finn
Eddie Floyd
Allen Lanier
June Lockhart
Ian McDonald
George Michael
David Paich
Walter Payton
Carly Simon
Pearly Sweets
Jimmie Walker
Clint Warwick

JUNE 26
Billy Davis Jr.
Chris Isaak
Mick Jones
Chris O'Donnell
Larry Taylor

JUNE 27
Isabelle Adjani
Julia Duffy
Bob Keeshan
Toby Maguire
Lorrie Morgan
Henry Ross Perot
Vera Wang

JUNE 28
Kathy Bates
Gil Bellows
Mel Brooks
John Cusack
Dave Knights
Alice Krige
Mary Stuart
  Masterson
Noriyuki "Pat"
  Morita

JUNE 29
Maria Conchita
  Alonso
Gary Busey
Fred Grandy
Colin Hay
Richard Lewis
Little Eva
Ian Paice
Stedman Pearson
Roger Spear
Ruth Warrick

JUNE 30
Vincent D'Onofrio
David Alan Grier
Lena Horne
Hal Lindes
Andy Scott
Glenn Shorrock
Mike Tyson
Adrian Wright

JULY 1
Wally Amos Jr.
Pamela Anderson
Dan Aykroyd
Claude Berri
Karen Black
Roddy Bottum
Delaney Bramlett
Genevieve Bujold
Leslie Caron
Olivia De Havilland
Princess Diana
Jamie Farr
Farley Granger
Deborah Harry
Estee Lauder
Carl Lewis
Alanis Morissette
Sydney Pollack
Fred Schneider
John Tesh
Liv Tyler

JULY 2
Pete Briquette
Johnny Colla
Jerry Hall
Imelda Marcos
Brock Peters
Joe Puerta
Ron Silver
Paul Williams

JULY 3
Paul Barrere
Dave Barry
Betty Buckley
Neil Clark
Vince Clarke
Tom Cruise
Johnny Lee
Montel Williams

JULY 4
Leona Helmsley
Gina Lollobrigida
Kirk Pengilly
Geraldo Rivera
Eva Marie Saint
Neil Simon
Jeremy Spencer
John Waite
Al "Blind Owl"
  Wilson
Bill Withers

JULY 5
Edie Falco
Shirley Knight
Huey Lewis
Michael Monarch
Robbie Robertson

JULY 6
Allyce Beasley
Ned Beatty
Gene Chandler
Rik Elswit
Nanci Griffith
Shelley Hack
Bill Haley
Jon Keeble
Janet Leigh
James Naughton
Nancy Reagan
Della Reese
Geoffrey Rush
Glenn Scarpelli
Sylvester Stallone
Burt Ward

JULY 7
Billy Campbell
Pierre Cardin
Shelley Duvall
Warren Entner
Jessica Hahn
David Hodo
Joe Spano
Ringo Starr

JULY 8
Kevin Bacon
Beck
Andy Fletcher
Anjelica Huston
Graham Jones
Raffi
Jeffrey Tambor
Jerry Valy

JULY 9
Marc Almond
Frank Bello
Brian Dennehy
Tom Hanks
Jim Kerr
Kelly McGillis
Mitch Mitchell

Fred Savage
Bon Scott
O.J. Simpson
Debbie Sledge
Jimmy Smits
John Tesh

JULY 10
David Brinkley
Ronnie James Dio
Ron Glass
Arlo Guthrie
Jerry Miller
Neil Tennant
Max Von Sydow

JULY 11
Giorgio Armani
Tab Hunter
Peter Murphy
Leon Spinks
Sela Ward

JULY 12
Milton Berle
Bill Cosby
Mel Harris
Cheryl Ladd
Christine McVie
Liz Mitchell
Richard Simmons
Jay Thomas
John Wetton
Kristi Yamaguchi

JULY 13
Stephen Jo Bladd
Lawrence Donegan
Harrison Ford
Robert Forster
Cheech Marin
Roger "Jim"
  McGuinn
Patrick Stewart
Spud Webb

JULY 14
Polly Bergen
Ingmar Bergman
Chris Cross
Matthew Fox
Rosey Grier
Harry Dean Stanton

JULY 15
Willie Aames
Brian Austin
  Green
Alex Karras
Peter Lewis
Brigitte Nielsen
Linda Ronstadt
Jan-Michael
  Vincent

Patrick Wayne
Forest Whitaker

JULY 16
Ruben Blades
Phoebe Cates
Stewart Copeland
Desmond Dekker
Corey Feldman
Michael Flatley
Tony Jackson

JULY 17
Lucie Arnaz
Geezer Butler
Diahann Carroll
Spencer Davis
Phyllis Diller
David Hasselhoff
Art Linkletter
Donald Sutherland
Mick Tucker
Mike Vale

JULY 18
Papa Dee Allen
James Brolin
Terry Chambers
Hume Cronyn
Vin Diesel
Dion DiMucci
Glenn Hughes
Audrey Landers
Robin MacDonald
Nelson Mandela
Elizabeth
  McGovern
Martha Reeves
Nigel Twist

JULY 19
Allen Collins
Alan Gorrie
Anthony Edwards
Pat Hingle
Bernie Leadon
Brian May

JULY 20
Paul Cook
Chris Cornell
Donna Dixon
John Lodge
Mike McNeil
Diana Rigg
Carlos Santana

JULY 21
Lance Guest
Edward Herrmann
Don Knotts
Leigh Lawson
Jon Lovitz
Jim Martin
Matt Mulhern
Billy Ocean

Henry Priestman
Isaac Stern
Cat Stevens
Robin Williams

JULY 22
Estelle Bennett
Albert Brooks
George Clinton
Willem Dafoe
Richard Davies
Louise Fletcher
Danny Glover
Don Henley
John Leguizamo
David Spade
Alex Trebek

JULY 23
Dino Danelli
David Essex
Martin Gore
Woody Harrelson
Eriq LaSalle
Andy Mackay
Don Imus
Larry Manetti
Edie McClurg
Stephanie Sey-
  mour
Terence Stamp
Blair Thornton

JULY 24
Heinz Burt
Ruth Buzzi
Lynda Carter
Lynval Golding
Kadeem Hardison
Robert Hays
Laura Leighton
Jennifer Lopez
Anna Paquin
Michael Richards
Chris Sarandon

JULY 25
Ray Billingsley
Manuel Charlton
Illeana Douglas
Estelle Getty
Barbara Harris
Iman
Matt LeBlanc
Jim McCarty
Verdine White

JULY 26
Sandra Bullock
Blake Edwards
Dorothy Hamill
Mick Jagger
Duncan Mackay
Jason Robards
Kevin Spacey
Roger Taylor

JULY 27
Peggy Fleming
Norman Lear
Carol Leifer
Maureen McGov-
  ern
Helen Mirren
John Pleshette
Al Ramsey
Betty Thomas
Jerry Van Dyke

JULY 28
Elizabeth Berkley
George Cummings
Jim Davis
Terry Fox
Simon Kirke
Sally Struthers
Rick Wright

JULY 29
Neal Doughty
Peter Jennings
Geddy Lee
Martina McBride
Marilyn Quayle
Michael Spinks
David Warner

JULY 30
Paul Anka
Delta Burke
Kate Bush
Larry Fishburne
Vivica A. Fox
Buddy Guy
Anita Hill
Lisa Kudrow
Ken Olin
Rat Scabies
Arnold Schwarz-
  enegger
Hilary Swank

JULY 31
Daniel Ash
Alan Autry
Bill Berry
Michael Biehn
Dean Cain
Geraldine Chaplin
Norman Cook
Karl Green
Gary Lewis
J.K. Rowling
Wesley Snipes
John West

AUGUST 1
Rick Anderson
Tempestt Bledsoe
Coolio
Ricky Coonce
Robert Cray
Dom DeLuise

Joe Elliott
Giancarlo Giannini
Arthur Hill
Robert James
  Waller
Tom Wilson

AUGUST 2
Joanna Cassidy
Doris Coley
Wes Craven
Garth Hudson
Victoria Jackson
Carroll O'Connor
Peter O'Toole
Mary-Louise
  Parker
Edward Patten
Max Wright

AUGUST 3
Tony Bennett
B.B. Dickerson
James Hetfield
John Landis
Beverly Lee
Gordon Scott
Martin Sheen
Martha Stewart

AUGUST 4
David Carr
Frankie Ford
Jeff Gordon
Billy Bob Thornton

AUGUST 5
Loni Anderson
Neil Armstrong
Rick Derringer
Rick Huxley
Jonathan Silver-
  man

AUGUST 6
Paul Bartel
Geri Halliwell
Dorian Harewood
Catherine Hicks
Abbey Lincoln
Pat McDonald

AUGUST 7
Bruce Dickinson
Andy Fraser
John Glover
Garrison Keillor
David Rasche
Alberto Salazar
B. J. Thomas

AUGUST 8
Richard Anderson
Philip Balsley
Princess Beatrice
Keith Carradine

JC Chasez
Harry Crosby
Dino De Laurentiis
The Edge
Andy Fairweather-
  Low
Chris Foreman
Dustin Hoffman
Donny Most
Robin Quivers
Connie Stevens
Mel Tillis
Larry Dee Wilcox
Esther Williams

AUGUST 9
Gillian Anderson
Kurtis Blow
Sam Elliott
Melanie Griffith
Billy Henderson
Whitney Houston
Aimee Mann
Ken Norton
Benjamin Orr
David Steinberg

AUGUST 10
Ian Anderson
Rosanna Arquette
Antonio Banderas
Veronica Bennett
Michael Bivins
Riddick Bowe
Jimmy Dean
Jon Farriss
Eddie Fisher
Angie Harmon
Bobby Hatfield
Lorraine Pearson

AUGUST 11
Erik Braunn
Eric Carmen
Hulk Hogan
Mike Hugg
Joe Jackson
Jim Kale
Denis Payton
Claus Von Bulow

AUGUST 12
George Hamilton
Roy Hay
Sam J. Jones
Mark Knopfler
Pat Metheny
Pete Sampras
Dominique Swain
Suzanne Vega
Jane Wyatt

AUGUST 13
Kathleen Battle
Danny Bonaduce
Fidel Castro

Dan Fogelberg
Pat Harrington
Don Ho
Feargal Sharkey

AUGUST 14
Halle Berry
Dash Crofts
David Crosby
Alice Ghostley
Larry Graham
Jackee
Magic Johnson
Steve Martin
Susan Saint
  James
Danielle Steel

AUGUST 15
Princess Anne
Ben Affleck
Julia Child
Mike Connors
Linda Ellerbee
Tess Harper
Natasha Hen-
  stridge
Matt Johnson
MCA
Debra Messing
Bill Pinkney
Rose-Marie
Pete York

AUGUST 16
Bob Balaban
Angela Bassett
James Cameron
Robert Culp
Frank Gifford
Kathie Lee Gifford
Eydie Gorme
Timothy Hutton
Madonna
Fess Parker
Carole Shelley
James Taylor
Reginald
  Veljohnson
Lesley Ann Warren

AUGUST 17
Belinda Carlisle
Robert De Niro
Steve Gorman
Colin Moulding
Maureen O'Hara
Sean Penn
Kevin Rowland
Gary Talley
Donnie Wahlberg

AUGUST 18
Carol Alt
Dennis Elliott
Dennis Leary

Martin Mull
Edward Norton
Roman Polanski
Robert Redford
Christian Slater
Madeleine Stowe
Ron Strykert
Patrick Swayze
Malcolm-Jamal
  Warner
Carl Wayne
Shelley Winters

AUGUST 19
Ginger Baker
Bill Clinton
John Deacon
Kevin Dillon
Jonathan Frakes
Peter Gallagher
Ian Gillan
Billy J. Kramer
M.C. Eric
Diana Muldaur
Matthew Perry
Jill St. John
John Stamos

AUGUST 20
Joan Allen
Connie Chung
Doug Fieger
Rudy Gatlin
Isaac Hayes
Don King
Phil Lynott
James Pankow
Robert Plant
Al Roker

AUGUST 21
Kim Cattrall
Carl Giammarese
Kenny Rogers
Kim Sledge
Joe Strummer
Melvin Van
  Peebles
Clarence
  Williams III

AUGUST 22
Ray Bradbury
Howie Dorough
Valerie Harper
John Lee Hooker
Roland Orzabal
Debbi Peterson
Norman
  Schwarzkopf
Cindy Williams

AUGUST 23
Kobe Bryant
Ronny Cox
Barbara Eden

Bobby G.
Shelley Long
Vera Miles
Shaun Ryder
Richard Sanders
Rick Springfield

AUGUST 24
Yasir Arafat
Mark Bedford
Jim Capaldi
Joe Chambers
John Cipollina
Jeffrey Daniel
David Freiberg
Steve Guttenberg
Ken Hensley
Craig Kilborn
Marlee Matlin
Claudia Schiffer

AUGUST 25
Anne Archer
Sean Connery
Elvis Costello
Billy Ray Cyrus
Mel Ferrer
Rob Halford
Monty Hall
Van Johnson
Regis Philbin
John Savage
Gene Simmons
Tom Skerritt
Blair Underwood
Joanne Whalley
Walter Williams

AUGUST 26
Jet Black
Bob Cowsill
Macaulay Culkin
Chris Curtis
Geraldine Ferraro
Michael Jeter
Shirley Manson
Branford Marsalis
Fred Milano
John O'Neill

AUGUST 27
Barbara Bach
Tim Bogert
Jeff Cook
Daryl Dragon
Pee-Wee Herman
Alex Lifeson
Glenn Matlock
Harry Reems
Tuesday Weld

AUGUST 28
Clem Cattini
Hugh Cornwell
Ben Gazzara
Scott Hamilton

Donald O'Connor
Wayne Osmond
Jason Priestley
LeAnn Rimes
Emma Samms
Elizabeth Seal
Danny Seraphine
David Soul
Daniel Stern

AUGUST 29
Richard
  Attenborough
Tim Burton
Rebecca DeMor-
  nay
Elliott Gould
Michael Jackson
Robin Leach
George Mont-
  gomery
Isabel Sanford

AUGUST 30
Elizabeth Ashley
Timothy Bottoms
Cameron Diaz
John McNally
Micky Moody
John Phillips
Kitty Wells

AUGUST 31
Jerry Allison
James Coburn
Richard Gere
Debbie Gibson
Buddy Hackett
Van Morrison
Harold Reid
Rudolph Schenker
Daniel Schorr
Anthony
  Thistlethwaite
Glenn Tilbrook
Chris Tucker

SEPTEMBER 1
Billy Blanks
Greg Errico
Gloria Estefan
Bruce Foxton
Barry Gibb
Lily Tomlin
Dave White

SEPTEMBER 2
Rosalind Ashford
Jimmy Connors
Sam Gooden
Marty Grebb
Mark Harmon
Salma Hayek
Fritz McIntyre
Steve Porcaro

Keanu Reeves

SEPTEMBER 3
Eileen Brennan
Donald Brewer
Al Jardine
Steve Jones
Gary Leeds
Valerie Perrine
Charles Sheen
Mort Walker

SEPTEMBER 4
Martin Chambers
Gary Duncan
Greg Elmore
Mitzi Gaynor
Fawn Hall
Judith Ivey
Merald Knight
Ronald LaPread
Rosie Perez
Jennifer Salt
Ione Skye
Damon Wayans

SEPTEMBER 5
William Devane
Cathy Guisewhite
Carol Lawrence
Bob Newhart
Al Stewart
Raquel Welch
Dweezil Zappa

SEPTEMBER 6
Dave Bargeron
Jane Curtin
Jeff Foxworthy
Macy Gray
Swoosie Kurtz
Claydes Smith
Paul Waaktaar
Jo Anne Worley

SEPTEMBER 7
Alfa Anderson
Corbin Bernsen
Susan Blakely
Chrissie Hynde
Julie Kavner
Peggy Noonan
Richard Roundtree
Benmont Tench

SEPTEMBER 8
Sid Caesar
Brian Cole
Michael Lardie
David Steele
Henry Thomas
Jonathan Taylor
  Thomas

SEPTEMBER 9
Doug Ingle
Michael Keaton
Sylvia Miles
Cliff Robertson
Adam Sandler
Dave Stewart
Goran Visnjic
Roger Waters
Michelle Williams

SEPTEMBER 10
Chris Columbus
Siobhan Fahey
Jose Feliciano
Johnnie Fingers
Colin Firth
Danny Hutton
Amy Irving
Big Daddy Kane
Pat Mastelotto
Joe Perry
Ryan Phillippe
Don Powell
Fay Wray

SEPTEMBER 11
Maria Bartiromo
Harry Connick Jr.
Lola Falana
Mickey Hart
Earl Holliman
Jane Krakowski
Amy Madigan
Virginia Madsen
Kristy McNichol
Jon Moss
Tommy Shaw
Mick Talbot
Dennis Tufano

SEPTEMBER 12
Barry Andrews
Gerry Beckley
Tony Bellamy
Darren E. Burrows
Linda Gray
Neil Peart
Brian Robertson
Peter Scolari
Barry White

SEPTEMBER 13
Fiona Apple
Barbara Bain
Jacqueline Bisset
Nell Carter
Peter Cetera
David Clayton-
  Thomas
Randy Jones
Richard Kiel
Joni Sledge

SEPTEMBER 14
Pete Agnew
Barry Cowsill
Faith Ford
Morten Harket
Walter Koenig
Paul Kossoff
Sam Neill
Joe Penny
Nicol Williamson

SEPTEMBER 15
Les Braid
Jackie Cooper
Prince Henry
Tommy Lee Jones
Oliver Stone

SEPTEMBER 16
Marc Antony
Lauren Bacall
Ed Begley Jr.
Joe Butler
Bernie Calvert
David Copperfield
Peter Falk
Anne Francis
Kenny Jones
B.B. King
Richard Marx
Mickey Rourke
Susan Ruttan

SEPTEMBER 17
Anne Bancroft
Elvira
Jeff MacNelly
Lamonte
  McLemore
John Ritter
Fee Waybill

SEPTEMBER 18
Frankie Avalon
Ricky Bell
Robert Blake
Joanne Catherall
James Gandolfini
Kerry Livgren
Dee Dee Ramone
Jada Pinkett
  Smith
Jack Warden

SEPTEMBER 19
Jim Abbott
John Coghlan
Lol Creme
Lee Dorman
Jeremy Irons
Joan Lunden
Nick Massi
David McCallum
Bill Medley
Nile Rodgers
Twiggy

Adam West

SEPTEMBER 20
Alannah Currie
Crispin Glover
Sophia Loren
Anne Meara
Chuck Panozzo

SEPTEMBER 21
Leonard Cohen
Henry Gibson
Liam Gallagher
Larry Hagman
Faith Hill
Stephen King
Ricki Lake
Rob Morrow
Bill Murray
Catherine
 Oxenberg
Philthy Animal
Alfonso Ribeiro
Nancy Travis
Trugoy the Dove

SEPTEMBER 22
Scott Baio
Shari Belafonte
Andrea Bocelli
David Coverdale
Thomas Harris
Joan Jett
Paul LeMat

SEPTEMBER 23
Jason Alexander
Steve Boone
Ronald Bushy
Ray Charles
Lita Ford
Julio Iglesias
Ben E. King
Elizabeth Pena
Mary Kay Place
Mickey Rooney
Bruce Springsteen

SEPTEMBER 24
Gerry Marsden
Kevin Sorbo

SEPTEMBER 25
Gary Alexander
Michael Douglas
Mark Hamill
John Locke
Heather Locklear
Onnie McIntyre
Christopher Reeve
Phil Rizzuto
Steve Severin
Will Smith
Cheryl Tiegs
Barbara Walters

SEPTEMBER 26
Melissa Sue
 Anderson
Joe Bauer
George Chambers
Craig Chaquico
Donna Douglas
Georgie Fame
Bryan Ferry
Linda Hamilton
Mary Beth Hurt
Winnie Mandela
Olivia Newton-
 John
Tracey Thorn

SEPTEMBER 27
Randy Bachman
Wilford Brimley
Greg Ham
Jayne Meadows
Gwyneth Paltrow
Meat Loaf
Sada Thompson

SEPTEMBER 28
Brigitte Bardot
Jeffrey Jones
Carre Otis
Se Ri Pak
John Sayles
Helen Shapiro
Mira Sorvino
William Windom
Moon Unit Zappa

SEPTEMBER 29
Anita Ekberg
Mark Farner
Bryant Gumbel
Patricia Hodge
Jerry Lee Lewis
Emily Lloyd

SEPTEMBER 30
Angie Dickinson
Lacey Chabert
Fran Drescher
Jenna Elfman
Deborah Kerr
Dewey Martin
Johnny Mathis
Marilyn McCoo
Sylvia Peterson
Victoria Tennant
Barry Williams

OCTOBER 1
Julie Andrews
Jean-Jacques
 Annaud
Jimmy Carter
Stephen Collins
Rob Davis
Richard Harris
Howard Hewett

Jerry Martini
Walter Matthau
Mark McGwire
Philippe Noiret
Randy Quaid
Stella Stevens
James Whitmore

OCTOBER 2
Lorraine Bracco
Richard Hell
Freddie Jackson
Donna Karan
Don McLean
Philip Oakey
Mike Rutherford
Sting
Tiffany

OCTOBER 3
Lindsey Bucking-
 ham
Neve Campbell
Chubby Checker
Barbara Ferris
Pamela Hensley
Tommy Lee
Kevin Richardson
Gwen Stefani
Gore Vidal
Jack Wagner
Dave Winfield

OCTOBER 4
Armand Assante
Jackie Collins
Clifton Davis
Jim Fielder
Charlton Heston
Patti LaBelle
Chris Lowe
Norm MacDonald
Anne Rice
Susan Sarandon
Alicia Silverstone

OCTOBER 5
Karen Allen
Daniel Baldwin
Clive Barker
Leo Barnes
Josie Bissett
Eddie Clarke
Jeff Conaway
Brian Connolly
Bob Geldof
Glynis Johns
Bil Keane
Mario Lemieux
Carlo Mastrangelo
Steve Miller
Kate Winslet

OCTOBER 6
Kevin Cronin
Britt Ekland

Bobby Farrell
Thomas McClary
Elizabeth Shue
Matthew Sweet
Bob Weir

OCTOBER 7
June Allyson
Toni Braxton
Kevin Godley
Dave Hope
Yo-Yo Ma
John Mellencamp
Oliver North

OCTOBER 8
Rona Barrett
Robert Bell
George Bellamy
Chevy Chase
Matt Damon
Michael Dudikoff
Paul Hogan
Jesse Jackson
Sarah Purcell
Johnny Ramone
R.L. Stine
Hamish Stuart
Sigourney Weaver
Tony Wilson
Stephanie
 Zimbalist

OCTOBER 9
Scott Bakula
Jackson Browne
John Entwistle
Sean Lennon
Michael Pare
Robert Wuhl

OCTOBER 10
Charles Dance
Jessica Harper
Martin Kemp
Alan Rachins
David Lee Roth
Tanya Tucker
Ben Vereen

OCTOBER 11
Joan Cusack
Daryl Hall
Ron Leibman
David Morse
Luke Perry
Grant Shaud

OCTOBER 12
Susan Anton
Kirk Cameron
Sam Moore
Luciano Pavarotti
Adam Rich
Dave Vanian

OCTOBER 13
Karen Akers
Tisha Campbell
Sammy Hagar
Beverly Johnson
Nancy Kerrigan
Robert Lamm
Marie Osmond
Kelly Preston
Nipsey Russell
Demond Wilson

OCTOBER 14
Harry Anderson
Marcia Barrett
Greg Evigan
Billy Harrison
Justin Hayward
Ralph Lauren
Roger Moore
Cliff Richard
Usher

OCTOBER 15
Mickey Baker
Richard Carpenter
Chris De Burgh
Sarah Ferguson
Lee Iacocca
Tito Jackson
Emeril Lagasse
Linda Lavin
Penny Marshall
Tanya Roberts
Don Stevenson

OCTOBER 16
Tony Carey
Barry Corbin
Gary Kemp
Angela Lansbury
Dave Lovelady
Tim Robbins
Suzanne Somers
C.F. Turner
Wendy Wilson

OCTOBER 17
Sam Bottoms
Eminem
Beverly Garland
Alan Howard
Wyclef Jean
Mike Judge
Margot Kidder
Chris Kirkpatrick
Ziggy Marley
Michael McKean
Howard Rollins Jr.
Jim Seals
Jim Tucker
George Wendt

OCTOBER 18
Chuck Berry
Peter Boyle

Pam Dawber
Mike Ditka
Russ Giguere
Keith Knudsen
Melina Mercouri
Erin Moran
Joe Morton
Martina
 Navratilova
Gary Richrath
Vincent Spano

OCTOBER 19
Richard Dreyfuss
Jon Favreau
Patricia Ireland
John Lithgow
Trey Parker
Karl Wallinger

OCTOBER 20
Joyce Brothers
William Christo-
 pher
Snoop Dogg
Alan Greenwood
Steve Harvey
Mark King
Ric Lee
Jerry Orbach
Tom Petty
Will Rogers Jr.
Bobby Seale
Jay Siegel

OCTOBER 21
Charlotte Caffey
Julian Cops
Steve Cropper
Eric Faulkner
Lee Loughnane
Steve Lukather
Manfred Mann
Judith Sheindlin

OCTOBER 22
Eddie Brigati
Catherine
 Deneuve
Joan Fontaine
Annette Funicello
Jeff Goldblum
Valeria Golino
Zac Hanson
Derek Jacobi
Ray Jones
Jonathan Lipnicki
Christopher Lloyd
Shelby Lynne
Tony Roberts

OCTOBER 23
Johnny Carson
Michael Crichton
Freddie Marsden

Perola Negra Pele
Weird Al Yankovic
Dwight Yoakam

OCTOBER 24
F. Murray Abraham
Joy Browne
Jerry Edmonton
Kevin Kline
David Nelson
B.D. Wong
Bill Wyman

OCTOBER 25
Jon Anderson
Anthony Franciosa
Matthias Jabs
Midori
Tracy Nelson
Rick Parfitt
Helen Reddy
Marion Ross
Glenn Tipton

OCTOBER 26
Hillary Rodham
  Clinton
Pat Conroy
Cary Elwes
Keith Hopwood
Bob Hoskins
Dylan McDermott
Ivan Reitman
Pat Sajak
Jaclyn Smith
Keith Strickland

OCTOBER 27
Terry Anderson
Roberto Benigni
John Cleese
Ruby Dee
Matt Drudge
Nanette Fabray
John Gotti
Simon LeBon
Marla Maples
Carrie Snodgress

OCTOBER 28
Jane Alexander
Steve Baumgart-
  ner
Wayne Fontana
Dennis Franz
Bill Gates
Jami Gertz
Lauren Holly
Telma Hopkins
Bruce Jenner
Hank Marvin
Stephen Morris
Joan Plowright
Annie Potts
Julia Roberts
Daphne Zuniga

OCTOBER 29
Ralph Bakshi
Kevin Dubrow
Joely Fisher
Kate Jackson
Denny Laine
Melba Moore
Winona Ryder

OCTOBER 30
Harry Hamlin
Kevin Pollak
Gavin Rossdale
Grace Slick
Charles Martin
  Smith
Otis Williams
Henry Winkler

OCTOBER 31
King Ad-Rock
Barbara
  Bel Geddes
Tony Bowers
Bernard Edwards
Dale Evans
Lee Grant
Deidre Hall
Sally Kirkland
Annabella Lwin
Johnny Marr
Larry Mullen Jr.
Jane Pauley
Dan Rather
Xavier Roberts
David Ogden
  Stiers
Chris Tucker

NOVEMBER 1
Rick Allen
Ronald Bell
Barbara Bosson
Keith Emerson
Robert Foxworth
Mags Furuholmen
James Kilpatrick
  Jr.
Lyle Lovett
Eddie MacDonald
Jenny McCarthy
Betsy Palmer
Dan Peek

NOVEMBER 2
k.d. lang
Brian Poole
David Schwimmer
Ray Walston
Bruce Welch
Alfre Woodard

NOVEMBER 3
Adam Ant
Roseanne Arnold
Charles Bronson

Kate Capshaw
Mike Evans
Larry Holmes
Steve Landesberg
Lulu
Dolph Lundgren
Dennis Miller
James Prime
Gary Sandy

NOVEMBER 4
Art Carney
Sean "Puffy"
  Combs
Walter Cronkite
Chris Difford
Ralph Macchio
Delbert McClinton
Matthew
  McConaughey
Markie Post
Kool Rock
Mike Smith
Loretta Swit

NOVEMBER 5
Bryan Adams
Art Garfunkel
Peter Noone
Tatum O'Neal
Roy Rogers
Sam Shepard
Paul Simon
Elke Sommer
Ike Turner

NOVEMBER 6
Sally Field
Glenn Frey
Ethan Hawke
P.J. Proby
Rebecca Romijn
Doug Sahm
Maria Shriver
George Young

NOVEMBER 7
Billy Graham
Joni Mitchell
Johnny Rivers

NOVEMBER 8
Alan Berger
Bonnie Bramlett
Alain Delon
Mary Hart
Rickie Lee Jones
Terry Lee Miall
Gretchen Mol
Parker Posey
Bonnie Raitt
Esther Rolle
Rodney Slater
Courtney Thorne-
  Smith
Roy Wood

Roxana Zal

NOVEMBER 9
Joe Bouchard
Lou Ferrigno
Alan Gratzer
Phil May
Pepa
Sisqó
Dennis Stratton

NOVEMBER 10
Glen Buxton
Greg Lake
MacKenzie Phillips
Ann Reinking
Jack Scalia
Roy Scheider
Sammy Sosa

NOVEMBER 11
Bibi Andersson
Paul Cowsill
Chris Dreja
Calista Flockhart
Roger Lavern
Ian Marsh
Vince Martell
Demi Moore
Andy Partridge
Kurt Vonnegut Jr.
Jonathan Winters
Jesse Colin Young

NOVEMBER 12
Errol Brown
Tonya Harding
Charles Manson
John Maus
Leslie McKeown
Stephanie Powers
Wallace Shawn
Neil Young

NOVEMBER 13
Whoopi Goldberg
Joe Mantegna
Richard Mulligan

NOVEMBER 14
Frankie Banali
Prince Charles
Freddie Garrity
Robert Ginty
Alexander O'Neal
Laura San
  Giacomo
Alec Such
D. B. Sweeney
Yanni
James Young

NOVEMBER 15
Edward Asner
Petula Clark
Beverly D'Angelo

Yaphet Kotto
Frida Lyngstad
Sam Waterston

NOVEMBER 16
Oksana Baiul
Lisa Bonet
Dwight Gooden
Clu Gulager

NOVEMBER 17
Martin Barre
Danny DeVito
Ronald DeVoe
Bob Gaudio
Isaac Hanson
Lauren Hutton
Gordon Lightfoot
Mary Elizabeth
  Mastrantonio
Lorne Michaels
Martin Scorsese
Tom Seaver

NOVEMBER 18
Margaret Atwood
Hank Ballard
Imogene Coca
Linda Evans
Kirk Hammett
Andrea Marcovicci
Graham Parker
Jameson Parker
Elizabeth Perkins
Herman Rarebell
Chloë Sevigny
Susan Sullivan
Brenda Vaccaro
Kim Wilde

NOVEMBER 19
Dick Cavett
Jodie Foster
Savion Glover
Larry King
Jeane Kirkpatrick
Calvin Klein
Hank Medress
Kathleen Quinlan
Ahmad Rashad
Meg Ryan
Ted Turner

NOVEMBER 20
Kaye Ballard
Jimmy Brown
Mike D
Bo Derek
George Grantham
Veronica Hamel
Richard Masur
Estelle Parsons
Dick Smothers
Ray Stiles
Joe Walsh
Sean Young

NOVEMBER 21
Ken Griffey Jr.
Goldie Hawn
Dr. John
Lonnie Jordan
Laurence Luckin-
  bill
Lorna Luft
Juliet Mills
Harold Ramis
Nicollette Sheri-
  dan
Marlo Thomas

NOVEMBER 22
Aston Barrett
Boris Becker
Tom Conti
Jamie Lee Curtis
Rodney Danger-
  field
Terry Gilliam
Mariel Hemingway
Billie Jean King
Floyd Sneed
Stevie "Little
  Steven" Van
  Zandt
Robert Vaughn
Tina Weymouth

NOVEMBER 23
Susan Anspach
Bruce Hornsby

NOVEMBER 24
Donald Dunn
Geraldine
  Fitzgerald
Chris Hayes
Dwight Schultz
John Squire
Jim Yester

NOVEMBER 25
Christina Apple-
  gate
Joe DiMaggio
Amy Grant
John Larroquette
Ricardo Montal-
  ban
Steve Rothery
Percy Sledge

NOVEMBER 26
Cyril Cusack
Robert Goulet
Norman Hassan
Alan Henderson
John McVie
Tina Turner

NOVEMBER 27
Charlie Burchill
Dozy

Robin Givens
Fisher Stevens
Jaleel White

NOVEMBER 28
Beeb Birtles
Ed Harris
Hope Lange
Judd Nelson
Randy Newman
Jon Stewart

NOVEMBER 29
Felix Cavaliere
Don Cheadle
Kim Delaney
Denny Doherty
Barry Goudreau
Jonathan Knight
Diane Ladd
Howie Mandel
John Mayall
Andrew McCarthy
Garry Shandling

NOVEMBER 30
John Aston
Richard Barbieri
Dick Clark
Kevin Conroy
Richard Crenna
Roger Glover
Rob Grill
Robert Guillaume
Billy Idol
Bo Jackson
G. Gordon Liddy
Leo Lyons
Mandy Patinkin
June Pointer
Rex Reason
Ridley Scott
Ben Stiller

DECEMBER 1
Woody Allen
Eric Bloom
John Densmore
Bette Midler
Sandy Nelson
Gilbert O'Sullivan
Richard Pryor
Lou Rawls
Charlene Tilton
Treat Williams

DECEMBER 2
Steven Bauer
Ted Bluechel Jr.
Cathy Lee Crosby
Julie Harris
Lucy Liu
Michael McDonald
Tom McGuinness
Rick Savage
Howard Stern

DECEMBER 3
Brian Bonsall
Brendan Fraser
Julianne Moore
Ozzy Osbourne
Andy Williams

DECEMBER 4
Tyra Banks
Jeff Bridges
Deanna Durbin
Chris Hillman
Jay-Z
Wink Martindale
Bob Mosley
Gary Rossington
Southside Johnny
Marisa Tomei

DECEMBER 5
John Berendt
Morgan Brittany
Gabriel Byrne
Jeroen Krabbe
Charles Lane
Little Richard
Jim Messina
Les Nemes
Jack Russell

DECEMBER 6
Peter Buck
Rick Buckler
Tom Hulce
Janine Turner
Ben Watt
JoBeth Williams
Steven Wright

DECEMBER 7
Larry Bird
Ellen Burstyn
Mike Nolan
Tom Waits
Eli Wallach

DECEMBER 8
Gregg Allman
Kim Basinger
Jerry Butler
David Carradine
Phil Collen
Bobby Elliott
Teri Hatcher
James MacArthur
Sinead O'Connor
Paul Rutherford
Maximilian Schell

DECEMBER 9
Joan Armatrading
Beau Bridges
Dick Butkus
Judi Dench
Kirk Douglas
Morton Downey Jr.

Dennis Dunaway
Buck Henry
Neil Innes
John Malkovich
Michael Nouri
Donny Osmond
Dick Van Patten

DECEMBER 10
Frank Beard
Kenneth Branagh
Susan Dey
Ace Kefford
Mako
Walter Orange
Chad Stuart

DECEMBER 11
Bess Armstrong
Teri Garr
David Gates
Jermaine Jackson
Booker T. Jones
Brenda Lee
Rita Moreno
Nikki Sixx

DECEMBER 12
Bob Barker
Dickey Betts
Mayim Bialik
Clive Bunker
Jennifer Connelly
Sheila E.
Connie Francis
Terry Kirkman
Ed Koch
Rush Limbaugh
Mike Pinder
Cathy Rigby
Mike Smith
Dionne Warwick

DECEMBER 13
Jeff "Skunk" Baxter
Steve Buscemi
John Davidson
Jamie Foxx
Ted Nugent
Randy Owen
Christopher Plummer
Dick Van Dyke
Tom Verlaine
Johnny Whitaker

DECEMBER 14
Patty Duke
Cynthia Gibb
Bridget Hall
Abbe Lane
Jackie McCauley
Mike Scott
Dee Wallace Stone
Cliff Williams

Joyce Wilson

DECEMBER 15
Carmine Appice
Dave Clark
Tim Conway
Reginald Hudlin
Don Johnson
Paul Simonon
Helen Slater

DECEMBER 16
Benny Andersson
Benjamin Bratt
Steven Bochco
Ben Cross
Billy Gibbons
Tony Hicks
William Perry
Liv Ullmann

DECEMBER 17
Sarah Dallin
Dave Dee
Bob Guccione
Milla Jovovich
Eddie Kendricks
Eugene Levy
Mike Mills
Art Neville
Bill Pullman
Paul Rodgers
Tommy Steele

DECEMBER 18
Christina Aguilera
Steve Austin
Ossie Davis
Elliot Easton
Katie Holmes
Ray Liotta
Leonard Maltin
Brad Pitt
Keith Richards
Steven Spielberg

DECEMBER 19
Jennifer Beals
Alvin Lee
Robert Mac-Naughton
Alyssa Milano
Tim Reid
Cicely Tyson
Robert Urich
Maurice White
Zal Yanovsky

DECEMBER 20
Jenny Agutter
Anita Baker
Billy Bragg
Bobby Colomby
John Hillerman
Chris Robinson

Little Stevie Wright

DECEMBER 21
Phil Donahue
Chris Evert
Jane Fonda
Samuel L. Jackson
Jeffrey Katzenberg
Josh Mostel
Ray Romano
Kiefer Sutherland
Kurt Waldheim
Paul Winchell

DECEMBER 22
Barbara Billings-ley
Hector Elizondo
Maurice Gibb
Robin Gibb
Lady Bird Johnson
Rick Nielsen
Ricky Ross
Diane Sawyer

DECEMBER 23
Corey Haim
Jorma Kaukonen
Johnny Kidd
Susan Lucci
Dave Murray
Eugene Record
Ruth Roman
Harry Shearer
James Stockdale
Eddie Vedder

DECEMBER 24
Ian Burden
Lemmy

DECEMBER 25
Jimmy Buffett
Robin Campbell
O'Kelly Isley
Annie Lennox
Shane MacGowan
Barbara Mandrell
Noel Redding
Hanna Schygulla
Sissy Spacek
Henry Vestine

DECEMBER 26
Steve Allen
Abdul Fakir
Alan KingDonald Moffat
Phil Spector

DECEMBER 27
John Amos
Chyna
Goldberg

Peter Criss
Gerard Depardieu
Tovah Feldshuh
Mick Jones
David Knopfler
Les Maguire

DECEMBER 28
Willow Bay
Alex Chilton
Dick Diamonde
Lou Jacobi
Stan Lee
Charles Neville
Johnny Otis
Maggie Smith
Denzel Washing-ton
Edgar Winter

DECEMBER 29
Ted Danson
Mark Day
Marianne Faithfull
Jude Law
Mary Tyler Moore
Paula Poundstone
Inga Swenson
Ray Thomas
Jon Voight

DECEMBER 30
Joseph Bologna
Bo Diddley
Davy Jones
Matt Lauer
Jeff Lynne
Mike Nesmith
Sheryl Lee Ralph
Russ Tamblyn
Tracey Ullman
Fred Ward
Tiger Woods

DECEMBER 31
Barbara Carrera
Rosalind Cash
Burton Cummings
Tom Hamilton
Anthony Hopkins
Val Kilmer
Ben Kingsley
Tim Matheson
Joe McIntyre
Sarah Miles
Pete Quaife
Patti Smith
Donna Summer
Andy Summers

2001'S WATERSHED BIRTHDAYS

The following folks will have reason to celebrate (or toast themselves) a little harder this year as they reach birthday milestones.

TURNING 90
Ronald Reagan

TURNING 80
John Agar
Steve Allen
Charles Bronson
Carol Channing
Rodney
  Dangerfield
Hugh Downs
Deanna Durbin
Monty Hall
Deborah Kerr
Maureen O'Hara
Johnny Otis
Prince Philip
Nancy Reagan
Jane Russell
James Whitmore
Esther Williams

TURNING 75
Don Adams
Richard Anderson
Beatrice Arthur
Kaye Ballard
Tony Bennett
Chuck Berry
Mel Brooks
Fidel Castro
Beverly Garland
Alice Ghostley
Peter Graves
Andy Griffith
Hugh Hefner
Lionel Jeffries
Jeane Kirkpatrick
Cloris Leachman
Jerry Lewis
Patricia Neal
Leslie Nielsen
Milo O'Shea
Betsy Palmer
Don Rickles
Tom Ryan
Soupy Sales
Harry Dean Stan-
  ton
Claus Von Bulow
Fritz Weaver
Jane Withers

TURNING 70
Papa Dee Allen
Barbara Bain
Carroll Baker
Anne Bancroft
Claire Bloom
Leslie Caron
Ed Cassidy
George Chambers
Lonnie Donegan
Olympia Dukakis
Robert Duvall
Anita Ekberg
Mitzi Gaynor
Marla Gibbs
Mikhail Gorbachev
Larry Hagman
Tab Hunter
Dean Jones
James Earl Jones
Don King
Hope Lange
Hal Linden
Gavin MacLeod
Robert MacNeil
Imelda Marcos
Willie Mays
Rita Moreno
Toni Morrison
Leonard Nimoy
Philippe Noiret
Regis Philbin
Dan Rather
William Shatner
James Tolkan
Rip Torn
Ike Turner
Mamie Van Doren
Jerry Van Dyke
Barbara Walters
Tom Wilson
Boris Yeltsin

TURNING 65
Alan Alda
Wally Amos, Jr.
Ursula Andress
Joe Don Baker
Hank Ballard
Rona Barrett
Marion Barry
Jim Brown
Ruth Buzzi
Glen Campbell
David Carradine
Dick Cavett
Bruce Dern

Tommy DeVito
Troy Donahue
Keir Dullea
Hector Elizondo
Chad Everett
Albert Finney
Billy Guy
Buddy Guy
Dennis Hopper
Engelbert
  Humperdinck
Marty Ingels
Glenda Jackson
Shirley Knight
Walter Koenig
Kris Kristofferson
John Madden
Zubin Mehta
Mary Tyler Moore
David Nelson
Lou Rawls
Robert Redford
Burt Reynolds
Bobby Seale
Bobbie Smith
Tom Snyder
Tommie Steele
Stella Stevens
Dean Stockwell
Levi Stubbs
Bill Wyman

TURNING 60
Marv Albert
Shirley Alston
John Amos
Paul Anka
Ann-Margret
Joan Baez
Joe Bauer
Captain Beefheart
George Bellamy
Jan Berry
Pete Birrell
Les Braid
Beau Bridges
Eric Burdon
Manuel Charlton
Charo
Chubby Checker
Julie Christie
David Clayton-
  Thomas
George Clinton
Doris Coley
Tom Conti
Roy Crewsdon

Steve Cropper
David Crosby
Chris Curtis
Angelo D'Aleo
John Davidson
Neil Diamond
Lenny Doherty
Faye Dunaway
Bob Dylan
Donald Dunn
Nora Ephron
Barbara Feldon
Robert Forster
Robert Foxworth
Art Garfunkel
John Gotti
Spalding Gray
William Guest
Susan Hampshire
Billy Hatton
Richie Havens
Alan Howard
Ronald Isley
Jesse Jackson
Dr. John
Stacy Keach
Sally Kirkland
Terry Kirkman
Robin Leach
Beverly Lee
Michael Lerner
Jon Lord
Mike Love
Les Maguire
Hank Marvin
Tom McGuinness
John McNally
Sarah Miles
Juliet Mills
James Mitchum
Michael Moriarty
Aaron Neville
Nick Nolte
Ryan O'Neal
Shirley Owens
Johnny Paycheck
Wilson Pickett
Gene Pitney
Brian Poole
Alan Price
Danny Rapp
Helen Reddy
Martha Reeves
Anne Rice
Pete Rose
David Ruffin
Leon Russell

Doug Sahm
Herman Santiago
Jim Seals
Paul Simon
Percy Sledge
John Steel
Martha Stewart
Bo Svenson
Joe Terranova
Mike Vickers
Jessica Walter
David Warner
Charlie Watts
Bruce Welch
Maurice White
Paul Winfield
Jesse Young

TURNING 50
Edward Albert
Karen Allen
Kirstie Alley
Lucie Arnaz
Philip Bailey
Tony Banks
Ronald Bell
Timothy Bottoms
David Briggs
Morgan Brittany
Dewey Bunnell
Randy California
Bun Carlos
Paul Carrack
Lynda Carter
Harry Wayne
  Casey
Martin Chambers
Phil Collins
Kevin Cronin
Christopher Cross
Beverly D'Angelo
Patti D'Arbanville
Tony Danza
Martha Davis
John Deacon
Brad Delp
Brian Downey
Julia Duffy
Charles Dutton
Elvira
Dan Fogelberg
Al Franken
Chris Frantz
Ace Frehley
Steve Gatlin
Crystal Gayle
Lynval Golding

Scott Gorham
Barry Goudreau
Alan Greenwood
Rob Halford
Mark Hamill
Tom Hamilton
Harry Hamlin
Steve Harley
Mark Harmon
Mary Hart
Catherine Hicks
Tommy Hilfiger
Anjelica Huston
Chrissie Hynde
Janis Ian
Judith Ivey
Jackie Jackson
Ann Jillian
Seth Justman
Anatoly Karpov
Michael Keaton
Cheryl Ladd
Howard Leese
Rush Limbaugh
Nils Lofgren
Phil Lynott
Amy Madigan
Phil Manzanera
Meat Loaf
John Mellencamp
David Naughton
Kate Nelligan
Suze Orman
Wayne Osmond
Carl Palmer
Chazz Palminteri
Joe Piscopo
Bonnie Pointer
Joe Puerta
Chris Rea
Gary Rossington
Geoffrey Rush
Kurt Russell
Jack Scalia
Mel Schacher
Fred Schneider
Andy Scott
Jane Seymour
Helen Shaver
Yakov Smirnoff
Sting
Richard Thomas
Russell Thomp-
  kins, Jr.
Paul Thompson
Dougie Thompson
Luther Vandross

Vince Welnick
Verdine White
Deniece Williams
Maisie Williams
Robin Williams
Treat Williams
Ann Wilson
Dave Winfield
Robert Wuhl
Robert Zemeckis

TURNING 40

Suzy Amis
Jay Aston
Christopher Atkins
Scott Baio
Mark Bedford
Boy George
Gabrielle Carteris
Vince Clarke
George Clooney
Lloyd Cole
Billy Ray Cyrus
Sarah Dallin
Lolita Davidovich
Mark Day
El DeBarge
Kim Delaney

Lawrence
 Donegan
Billy Duffy
Karen Duffy
The Edge
Boomer Esiason
Giancarlo Esposito
Melissa Etheridge
Fabio
Jon Farriss
Laurence
 Fishburne
Michael J. Fox
John Clark Gable
James Gandolfini
Gillian Gilbert
Peri Gilpin
Martin Gore
Wayne Gretzky
Woody Harrelson
Roy Hay
Mariel Hemingway
Nick Heyward
Reginald Hudlin
Eddie Jackson
Matt Johnson
John Jon
Graham Jones
Mark Kelly

Martin Kemp
Nastassja Kinski
k.d. lang
Jane Leeves
Carl Lewis
Heather Locklear
Julia Louis-
 Dreyfuss
Virginia Madsen
Camryn Manheim
Wynton Marsalis
Jim Martin
Dylan McDermott
Elizabeth
 McGovern
Graham
 McPherson
Janet McTeer
Erin Moran
Alison Moyet
Larry Mullen, Jr.
Eddie Murphy
Vince Neil
Roland Orzabal
Catherine
 Oxenberg
Elizabeth Pena
Elizabeth Perkins
Debbi Peterson

Slim Jim Phantom
Dennis Rodman
Meg Ryan
Laura San
 Giacomo
Curt Smith
Jimmy Somerville
John Stockwell
Eric Stoltz
D. B. Sweeney
Andy Taylor
Lea Thompson
Nancy Travis
Paul Waaktaar
Bruce Watson
Forest Whitaker
Mark White
Keren Woodward

TURNING 30

Christina
 Applegate
Sean Astin
Erykah Badu
Mary J. Blige
David Boreanaz
Taye Diggs
Shannen Doherty
Jenna Elfman

Corey Feldman
Jeff Gordon
Tom Green
Corey Haim
Justin Henry
Chris Kirkpatrick
Jordan Knight
Emmanuel Lewis
Lisa Lopes
Ricky Martin
Stella McCartney
Ewan McGregor
Midori
Jay Mohr
Alfonso Ribeiro
Denise Richards
Winona Ryder
Pete Sampras
Ione Skye
Jada Pinkett
 Smith
Snoop Dogg
Matt Stone
Tiffany
Rozonda Thomas
Chris Tucker
Mark Wahlberg
Danny Wood
Noah Wyle

Kristi Yamaguchi

TURNING 21

Christina Aguilera
Nick Carter
Chelsea Clinton
Macaulay Culkin
Isaac Hanson
Monica
Bijou Phillips
Christina Ricci
Dominique Swain
Michelle Williams

TURNING 20

Zlata Filipovic
Anna Kournikova
Natalie Portman
Britney Spears
Jonathan Taylor
 Thomas
Justin Timberlake
Elijah Wood